PRINCIPLES
OF ACCOUNTING
INTERMEDIATE

PRENTICE-HALL ACCOUNTING SERIES

H. A. Finney, Editor

H. A. FINNEY, Ph.B., C.P.A.

HERBERT E. MILLER, Ph.D., C.P.A.
Professor of Accounting, University af Michigan

PRINCIPLES
OF ACCOUNTING
INTERMEDIATE

Fifth Edition

PRENTICE-HALL, INC.
Englewood Cliffs, New Jersey

LIBRARY OF CONGRESS
CATALOG CARD NO.: 58-8792

FIFTH EDITION

First printing...............April, 1958
Second printing..........January, 1959
Third printing..............May, 1960
Fourth printing.............May, 1961
Fifth printing.............March, 1962

PRINTED IN THE UNITED STATES OF AMERICA

70299—C

PREFACE

As in the past, in the preparation of this revision the advice of teachers was sought; they were asked what portions of the preceding edition pleased them, what portions they would like to see revised or perhaps deleted, and what additional subject matter should be included. Helpful responses were received from the people whose names appear after this preface, and to whom we wish to express our gratitude.

Although the revision can be described as thorough-going, the general approach, the level of presentation, and the objectives that characterized the preceding edition have, it is hoped, been maintained.

The authors have continued the practice of quoting liberally from publications of the American Accounting Association and the American Institute of Certified Public Accountants, weaving these quotations into the text discussions to acquaint the student with the pronouncements of these organizations.

A few changes have been made in chapter sequence. The chapters on statement analysis have been moved to a later position in the text to provide a more comprehensive background for them and to bring the chapter on the analysis of working capital into closer proximity with the related chapter on the statement of application of funds. Incidentally, new working papers have been developed to aid the student in the understanding and preparation of this statement.

Conformably with the development of accounting thought, the chapter on Reserves that appeared in the preceding edition has been eliminated and its elements have been assigned to other chapters to which they are germane.

In the preceding edition, theory was discussed throughout the text (it still is) and the next-to-the-last chapter presented a summary and synthesis of accounting theory, with particular attention to the determination of net income. In the new edition, the broad, general principles of accounting theory are discussed in Chapter 8, to provide, early in the text, a compendium of standards to make the subsequent discussion of details throughout the chapters more meaningful.

Several new chapters have been added. They are mentioned below.

Chapter 25, "Cash-Flow Statement." Business managements have shown an increasing interest in the sources and uses of cash, and problems requiring the preparation of cash-flow statements have appeared in recent C. P. A. examinations.

Chapter 26, "Statements from Incomplete Records." In the Fourth Edition this topic was given a brief treatment. Many students have difficulty with problems in this area, and such problems appear frequently in the C. P. A. examinations. A more complete treatment seemed desirable.

Chapter 27, "Quasi-Reorganizations. Business Combinations. Divisive Reorganizations." The material on quasi-reorganizations has been expanded and new material has been added dealing with business combinations, whether by purchase or by pooling of interests. Divisive reorganizations, such as spin-offs, split-offs, and split-ups, are also discussed. In the last several years there have been many business consolidations and mergers, and some divisive reorganizations. This development has had an impact on accounting, and some new theoretical concepts have emerged. They are sufficiently established to warrant inclusion in a text for students being trained for careers in business and accounting.

Chapter 28, "Income Tax Allocation." The practice of allocating income taxes is perhaps the most significant development affecting the basic theoretical structure of accounting, particularly the concept of net income, in the last fifteen years. It is time that this subject was included in accounting textbooks.

Chapter 29, "Price-Level Impact on Financial Statements." In the last decade this broad question has received more controversial attention than any other accounting topic. While the accounting profession has not crystallized a position on this matter, no college student should complete his school training without an exposure to the problems that business management and the accountant face as the result of significant changes in the purchasing power of the dollar, the proposals offered for dealing with these problems, and the arguments in favor of and against these proposals.

Notwithstanding the addition of new material, the size of the text has been slightly reduced. This has been achieved in the following ways:

The first four chapters of the Fourth Edition, written to provide a review of basic material and to reduce the difficulty of the transition from the introductory to the intermediate level, have been condensed to two chapters by eliminating some rudimentary material. It is believed that they still accomplish the desired objective.

Some seldom used accounting techniques and some material covered in courses in corporation finance have been eliminated from the chapters on corporations.

Some of the historical references in the fixed assets chapters have been removed.

As in the Fourth Edition, the assignment material has been tailor-made to be specifically applicable to, and to thoroughly cover, the related text material. There is a wide assortment of short and long, easy and difficult problems. The workbook accompanying the text provides an additional source of problem material, in objective form, for use as class exercises or as homework.

We are indebted to the companies which permitted us to use statements that appeared in their annual reports and that are reproduced in Chapter 3. They are illustrative of modern trends in corporate reports.

Accounting research bulletins of the American Institute of Certified Public Accountants are copyrighted by the Institute. Quotation in this text is by their permission.

Acknowledgments

We are grateful to the following teachers who made valuable suggestions for improvements in this new edition: Wilmer Baer, State College of Washington; Frank N. Beard, University of Toronto; Laurence J. Benninger, University of Florida; Peter C. Briant, University of Michigan; T. A. Budd, University of Pennsylvania; John E. Champion, Florida State University; Robert G.

Cox, University of Pennsylvania; Howard M. Daniels, University of Houston; Raymond C. Dein, University of Nebraska; Tom M. Dickerson, Western Reserve University; Merrill B. Dilley, Drake University; Donald J. Emblen, Montana State University; Theodore E. Fitzgerald, Temple University; Dennis Gordon, University of Akron; W. Rogers Hammond, Georgia State College of Business Administration; Robert D. Haun, University of Kentucky; Harold M. Heckman, University of Georgia; Hugh Jackson, Jr., U. S. Naval Postgraduate School; Hazen W. Kendrick, University of Colorado; Jerome J. Kesselman, University of Denver; R. D. Koppenhaver, University of North Dakota; T. W. Leland, Agricultural & Mechanical College of Texas; W. G. Leonard, Queen's University; William C. McGrew, University of Oklahoma; Louis W. Matusiak, Touche, Niven, Bailey & Smart; Perry T. Mori, University of New Mexico; Frank H. Mulling, University of Georgia; Andrew Nelson, St. John's University; Carl L. Nelson, University of Minnesota; Earl A. Russell, Bryant-Stratton Business Institute; Alton G. Sadler, University of North Carolina; George C. Selzer, Xavier University, Ohio; Victor E. Storli, Fresno State College; Daniel L. Sweeney, State University of Iowa; Vern H. Vincent, West Virginia University; Harry H. Wade, University of Miami; Leland Carling Whetten, Georgia State College of Business Administration; Cecil W. Wilson, Long Beach City College; John A. White, University of Texas; Stephen Zeff, University of Michigan.

H. A. FINNEY
HERBERT E. MILLER

CONTENTS

each statement; Separate working papers with sub-classification columns. REVERSING ENTRIES: Bad debts and depreciation; Cost apportionments—Prepaid expenses; Revenue apportionments; Accrued income; Accrued expense; Adjusting and reversing entries for The Ingram Manufacturing Company.

✓ THREE) $^{5+}$

Financial Statements, 44

Bases of balance sheet valuations; Balance sheet classifications; Current assets and current liabilities; The operating cycle concept; What assets are current? What liabilities are current? ALTERNATIVE STATEMENT FORMS: Statement of cost of goods sold; Condensed statements; Combined statement of income and retained earnings. ALTERNATIVE TREATMENT OF CERTAIN STATEMENT ITEMS: Purchase discounts; Cash discounts on sales; Transportation charges on purchases; Transportation charges on sales; Bad debts; Importance of disclosure; Matters applicable to the statements; Subsequent events and prospects. RECENT TRENDS IN PUBLISHED STATEMENTS: Importance of clarity in published statements; Single-step income statements; Combined single-step income and retained earnings statement; Showing the working capital; Simplified statements; Emphasizing the accountability; Graphic presentations; Conclusion.

✓ FOUR | $^{5+}$

Net Income Concepts and Corrections of Prior Years' Earnings, 73

NET INCOME CONCEPTS: A basic problem; The current operating concept of net income and the all-inclusive (clean surplus) theory; The Institute opinion; Appending extraneous items and corrections to the income statement; Combined income and retained earnings statement; Concluding note. CORRECTIONS OF PRIOR YEARS' EARNINGS: Description of errors; Errors affecting net income; Alternative procedures for dealing with errors; Basis of illustrations; Closing entries; Summary.

✓ FIVE | $^{5+}$

Capital Stock, 99

Objectives in accounting for stockholders' investments; Par and no-par stock; Rights inherent in stock; Common stock and preferred stock; Stock preferred as to dividends; Stock preferred as to assets; Special features of preferred stock; Founders' stock; Common stock; Stock designated by letters; Stated capital; Accounts used to show stockholders' investments; Stock issued for less than par value; Interval between receipt and collection of subscriptions; Balance sheet presentation; Forfeited subscriptions; Stock issued for property; Stock issued for services; Units of preferred and common; Bonus stock; Stock rights or warrants; Nontransferable stock option contracts; Assessments on stockholders; Change from par to no par; Convertible stocks and bonds.

SIX] $\underline{S+}$

Surplus and Dividends, 123

Terminology; Paid-in surplus; Earned surplus (retained earnings); Appraisal increments; Surplus restrictions and appropriations; Reserves for self-insurance; Liquidating value of stock; Surplus availability for dividends; Dividends; Stock split-up; Legality of dividends; Preferred dividends in arrears; Declared dividends a liability; Stock dividends; Fractional shares; Restoration of retained earnings after a stock dividend.

SEVEN | $\underline{S+}$

Miscellaneous Topics Relating to Stockholders' Equity, 145

Treasury stock; Treasury stock is not an asset; Treasury stock and stated capital; Treasury stock transactions: Terminology; Balance sheet presentation of treasury stock; Recording treasury stock transactions—cost basis; Recommended departure from the cost basis; Book value per share of stock; Significance of book value per share; Watered stock; Secret reserves; Comprehensive illustration of a Stockholders' Equity section; Voting trusts and stock pools.

EIGHT / $\underline{S+}$

Generally Accepted Accounting Principles, 165

Introduction; The nature of prevailing accounting rules; Some underlying assumptions; Some basic accounting concepts; Objectivity; The cost principle; Conservatism; Consistency; Income determination; When is revenue realized? The point of sale; Recognizing revenue as earned before the point of sale; Recognition of revenue after the date of sale; Unrealized appreciation; Revenue from services; The dollar amount of realized revenue; Cost outlays; Classification of cost outlays; Cost apportionments; Cost transformations and allocations; Cost expirations; Cost expirations and cost residues; "Anticipate no profit and provide for all possible losses"; Savings versus income; Matching revenues and related expenses; A concluding note.

NINE 2nd

Cash, 186

What is cash? Bank overdrafts; Distorted cash balances; Internal control; Cash over and short account; Imprest cash; Lapping; Noncash credits to customers; Reconciliation of the bank account; Estimating the cash position.

TEN 2*nd*

Receivables, 205

ACCOUNTS RECEIVABLE: Classification; Valuation; Allowance for doubtful accounts; Aging accounts; Percentage of open accounts; Percentage
of sales; Recoveries; Freight; Returns and allowances; Reserve for discounts; Discounts on returned sales; Credit balances; Accounts receivable financing. NOTES AND ACCEPTANCES RECEIVABLE: Definitions;
Terminology; Advantages of trade acceptances; Dishonored notes;
Credit limit on notes and accounts; Valuation of, and losses on, notes;
Bank discount; Notes receivable discounted; Contingent liability in the
balance sheet; Payment by maker; Payment by endorser; Endorsement
without recourse.

ELEVEN 2*nd*

Inventories, 223

Introductory note; Classes of inventories; Inventory all goods owned;
Inventory pricing; Incidental costs; Manufacturing costs; Standard
costs; Relation of purchase discounts to cost; Apportioned costs; Lost
costs. COST SELECTION FOR INVENTORY PRICING: Specific identification;
Last invoice price; Simple-average method; Weighted-average method;
Moving-average method; First-in, first-out (*fifo*) method; Last-in,
first-out (*lifo*) method; Gross profit method; Uses of gross profit method;
Long-term construction contracts.

TWELVE 2*nd*

Inventories (Continued), 244

What is "market"? Limits on usable market prices; Normal profit;
Application of cost or market; Accounting procedures; General discussion of cost or market; Obsolete and depreciated merchandise; Scrap;
Goods in foreign countries; Inventory valuation based on selling price;
Unrealized profits in inventories; Variations in inventory pricings and
the principle of consistency; Reserves for possible future market declines; Retail method; Terminology; Why mark-downs are ignored in
the computation of cost ratio; Retail method is based on averages;
Departmental rates; Special-sale merchandise; Sales of marked-up
and marked-down goods; Period covered by computation; Extended
illustration; Freight, discounts, returns.

THIRTEEN 2*nd*

Inventories (Concluded), 267

Last-in, first-out (*lifo*) method; Unsettled *lifo* problems; Adopting *lifo*;
Lifo layers; How to price *lifo* layers; Dollar-value *lifo*; Inventory reductions; Effect of *lifo* on the gross profit method; *Lifo* and the retail

method; Changing from conventional to *lifo* retail; Subsequent inventories—no changes in the price level; Subsequent inventories—changes in the level of selling prices; Extended illustration; "*Nifo*"; Base-stock method.

FOURTEEN 2nd

Investments, 289

Types of securities; Mortgage bonds; Collateral trust bonds; Guaranteed bonds; Debenture bonds; Income bonds; Participating bonds; Convertible bonds; Registered and coupon bonds. GENERAL MATTERS RELATIVE TO INVESTMENTS: Costs of investments; Exchanges: costs, gains, and losses; Sales: costs, gains, and losses; Valuation of securities; Temporary investments; Long-term investments; Subsequent adjustments of valuation accounts. MATTERS RELATIVE TO INVESTMENTS IN STOCKS: Adjustments of cost; Dividends on stock investments; Stock received as a dividend; Stock rights, or warrants. MATTERS RELATIVE TO INVESTMENTS IN BONDS: Accrued interest at date of purchase; Amortization of bond premium and discount; Amortization of premium—straight-line method; Amortization of discount—straight-line method; Amortization at interim dates; Purchases between interest dates; Sales between interest dates; Redemption before maturity; Carrying bond investments at cost; Bonds purchased with interest in default; Investments in mortgages; Government obligations.

FIFTEEN 2nd

Investments (Concluded), 309

INVESTMENTS IN SUBSIDIARIES: Accounting methods; Legal-basis method; Economic-basis method; Subsidiary acquired by purchase; Minority interest. FUNDS: Funds and reserves distinguished; Classes of funds; Funds in the balance sheet; Accounting for funds; Funds for the payment of existing liabilities; Sinking fund contributions; Theoretical accumulation; Actual accumulation; Sinking fund entries; Purchases between interest dates; Amortization of premium or discount; Cash and accrual basis; Fund with trustee; Own bonds alive in fund; Bond retirement fund; Sinking funds for principal and interest; Sinking fund reserves; Funds for payment of contingent liabilities; Funds for payment for an asset or a service; Stock redemption funds; Fund arrearages and deposit requirements; Related funds and reserves.

SIXTEEN 2nd

Tangible Fixed Assets, 328

PRINCIPLES OF VALUATION: Fixed assets; Tangible and intangible fixed assets; Classification of fixed assets; Valuation of fixed assets; Capital and revenue expenditures; Additions; Improvements and betterments; Replacements; Repairs; Arbitrary classification by dollar amount; Repairs and maintenance; Payment in cash; Discount on fixed assets; Purchases on credit terms; Payments in securities; Mixed acquisitions

of data; Computation of sales; Computation of purchases; Inventories; Completed illustration; Accrued revenue and expense; Revenue and cost apportionments; Depreciation; Allowance for doubtful accounts; Statement of proprietor's capital or retained earnings.

TWENTY-SEVEN

Quasi-Reorganizations. Business Combinations. Divisive Reorganizations, 586

QUASI-REORGANIZATIONS: The situation when the price level has declined; Quasi-reorganization described; Status of upward quasi-reorganizations. BUSINESS COMBINATIONS: Recent history; Purchase versus pooling of interests; Retained earnings; Tests for pooling of interests; Income statement; Preliminary accounting problems; Settlement plans. DIVISIVE REORGANIZATIONS: Nature of divisive reorganizations; Position of accounting theory regarding divisive reorganizations.

TWENTY-EIGHT

Income Tax Allocation, 602

Background; Purpose and nature of the chapter. MATTERS DEALING WITH THE LOCATION OF THE INCOME TAX CHARGE IN THE FINANCIAL STATEMENTS: Material charges to retained earnings that reduce the amount of the income tax liability; Material credits to retained earnings that increase the amount of the income tax liability; Evaluation of preceding illustrations; Income tax allocation within the income statement. MATTERS DEALING WITH THE ALLOCATION OF INCOME TAX THROUGH TIME: Nature of problem; Deferred income tax liability; Deferred income tax expense; Nature of accounts; Continuing divergence; Assumptions and practical difficulties; Other tax allocation applications; Loss provisions and corrections; The influence of distortion; Present status.

TWENTY-NINE

Price-Level Impact on Financial Statements, 623

A basic assumption of accounting; Fundamental questions; Comments supporting conventional accounting; Comments critical of conventional accounting; Reason for criticism; Comparative statements; Current financial statements; Position of the American Accounting Association; Concluding note.

Assignment Material, 641

Index, 935

CHAPTER ONE

Accounting Procedures Reviewed

Accounting defined.   An often-quoted definition of accounting is the one formulated by the Committee on Terminology of the American Institute of Certified Public Accountants.

"Accounting is the art of recording, classifying, and summarizing in a significant manner and in terms of money, transactions and events which are, in part at least, of a financial character, and interpreting the results thereof."

The accounting cycle.   The principal procedural activities of the accounting process, other than the preparation and checking of business papers, are:

Recording transactions in books of original entry.

Posting to ledger accounts.

Taking a trial balance of the general ledger and seeing that the subsidiary ledgers or registers are in agreement with their controlling accounts.

Making adjustments for such matters as bad debts, depreciation, accruals, and revenue and cost apportionments.

Preparing working papers.

Preparing statements showing the results of business operations and the financial position of the business.

Closing the books.

Possibly reversing some of the adjusting entries.

Taking an after-closing trial balance.

1

Debit-credit process. The record-keeping part of accounting is based on a fundamental relationship or equation, namely:

$$\text{Assets} = \text{Liabilities} + \text{Owners' Equity}$$

The elements in the above equation represent broad categories. A business may have anywhere from a few to dozens of different assets, and records must be maintained to show the increases, decreases, and present status of each asset. The same applies to liabilities. And there are numerous causes of increases and decreases in the owners' equity. To record all of the increases and decreases in assets, liabilities, and owners' equity, accounts are maintained.

Increases and decreases are recorded in accounts in the manner shown below.

Asset Accounts		Liability Accounts		Owners' Equity Accounts	
Increases	Decreases	Decreases	Increases	Decreases	Increases

Many business transactions result in revenue or expense. Such transactions affect the amount of the owners' equity. It is customary to use revenue and expense accounts to accumulate the results of such transactions. Since revenues increase the owners' equity and expenses reduce the owners' equity, the revenues and expenses are recorded according to the following plan.

Expense Accounts		Revenue Accounts	
(Debited for expenses)			(Credited for revenues)

Kinds of accounting records. In general, business records consist of the following:

Documents, or business papers, such as invoices, credit memorandums, bank checks, insurance policies, freight bills, and promissory notes. These furnish detailed information about business transactions, state the terms of contracts, and serve as evidence of the propriety of accounting entries.

Books of original entry, such as the general journal, sales books, purchases books, voucher registers, and cash receipts and disbursements books. These books contain chronological records of business transactions and show, among other facts, the names of accounts to be debited and credited to record the transactions.

Ledgers—both general and subsidiary. These show in detail or in summarized form the debits and credits to each account.

Registers and other supplementary records, such as the notes receivable register, the notes payable register, the insurance register, and the voucher register. These furnish more detailed information than can conveniently be recorded in the accounts. They may also serve as books of original entry, and may take the place of subsidiary ledgers.

Working papers in which information for the periodical statements is assembled.

Periodical statements, which show the results of operations and the financial position of the business.

Books of original entry.   A book of original entry contains a record of transactions in their chronological order, names the accounts to be debited and credited to record each transaction, and states the debit and credit amounts. The recording function is completed by posting the debits and credits shown by the journal entries to the various accounts.

Ledgers and controlling accounts.   A *ledger* is a group of accounts. If a ledger contains accounts (some of which may be controlling accounts rather than detailed accounts) for all of the assets, liabilities, ownership claims, revenues, and expenses of a business, it is called a *general ledger*.

In a large business there usually are several groups of similar accounts. There may be many accounts receivable and accounts payable; if deposits are kept in several banks, an account must be kept for each bank account; it may be desirable to maintain a separate account for each parcel of land, for each building, and for each security investment; there will be numerous selling expense accounts, and numerous general expense accounts; and there may be other groups of kindred accounts.

If all of these accounts are kept in one ledger, the posting work may be too much for one bookkeeper. To provide for a division of labor, the following procedure may be applied:

Keep the several accounts of the group in a subsidiary ledger.

Keep a controlling account in the general ledger. It is debited with totals of the charges to the accounts in the subsidiary ledger; it is credited with totals of the credits to the accounts in the subsidiary ledger; and its balance should be equal to the sum of the balances of the accounts in the subsidiary ledger.

The controlling account and subsidiary ledger device also has the advantage of helping to locate errors by isolating them. If the trial balance of the general ledger shows that the general ledger is in balance, but the sum of the balances in a subsidiary ledger does not agree with the balance in its controlling account, it may be presumed (but not definitely known) that the error is in the subsidiary ledger. If the general ledger is not in balance and the subsidiary ledger is in agreement with its control, it may be presumed (but, again, not definitely known) that the error is in the general ledger—some place other than in the controlling account.

Auxiliary accounts. An auxiliary account is one which is closely related to another (major, or principal) account. Auxiliary accounts are sometimes called *offset*, or *contra*, accounts if the principal account has a debit balance and the auxiliary account has a credit balance, or vice versa. They are sometimes called *adjunct* accounts if the balances of the principal and auxiliary accounts are both debits or both credits.

The Sales Returns and Allowances account is an offset to the Sales account. The Purchase Returns and Allowances account is an offset to, and the Freight In account is an adjunct to, the Purchases account. The Allowance for Doubtful Accounts and accumulated depreciation accounts are offsets to asset accounts.

The general journal. It is theoretically possible, although not often practicable, to use a general journal as the only book of original entry. Entries in a general journal are illustrated below.

Journal

19—					
July	1	Cash...	10,000 00		
		Capital stock.............................		10,000 00	
		Issuance of 100 shares of stock.			
	2	Purchases..................................	2,500 00		
		Cash....................................		2,500 00	
		Purchase of merchandise for cash.			

Accountants have given a great deal of thought to the development of books of original entry that effect a division and saving of labor. Two principal devices have been employed: special-purpose books and special columns. Some illustrations follow.

Special-purpose books of original entry. The following sales book is a special-purpose book of original entry.

Sales Book   (Page 1)

Date	√	Name	Invoice No.	Amount
19—				
May 2	√	R. E. West.................................	1	300 00
7	√	G. O. Davis...............................	2	450 00
12	√	S. E. Bates...............................	3	600 00
18	√	R. E. West.................................	4	850 00
23	√	G. O. Davis...............................	5	280 00
30	√	R. E. West.................................	6	300 00
				3,280 00
				(10) (40)

The check marks show that the individual entries have been posted to the customers' accounts in the subsidiary ledger. The number (10) at the foot of the Amount column shows that the total has been posted to the debit of the Accounts Receivable controlling account. The number (40) shows that the total has been posted as a credit to the Sales account.

Such a book facilitates a division of labor because one bookkeeper can be assigned to recording sales on account. It saves posting work because the column total, instead of the individual entries, is posted to the Sales account.

Some of the other special-purpose books of original entry that may be kept are:

Sales returns and allowances book.
Purchases book.
Purchase returns and allowances book.
Cash receipts book.
Cash disbursements book.

Special columns. Special columns may be introduced in books of original entry for the following purposes:

For classification of data.
To facilitate recording transactions.
To save labor in posting.

Special columns for these purposes are shown in the cash receipts book on page 6.

Columns for classification of data are illustrated by the two Sales columns.

The Sales Discounts debit and Interest Earned credit columns are examples of columns to facilitate recording transactions when the entry includes more than one debit or credit. If no special column is provided, entries may be made in the Sundry sections.

Posting labor is saved when there is more than one entry in a column, because the column total, rather than the individual entries, can be posted to the general ledger. For this reason, a special Accounts Receivable controlling account credit column should usually be provided in the cash receipts book. Postings of totals of special columns are indicated by writing the account numbers below the totals.

Combined books of original entry and subsidiary records. The voucher register is one of the most frequently used records combining the features of a book of original entry and the features of a subsidiary record. Many other such dual-purpose books are used in the accounting systems of large enterprises.

Cash Receipts Book

(Left side)

DEBITS

Line No.	Date	Explanation	Cash	Sales Discounts	Sundry Accounts — Name	L.F.	Amount
1	19— May 1	Sale	480 00				
2	2	Invoice April 24, less 2%	980 00	20 00			
3	3	Fred White's note	505 00				
4	4	Note discounted at bank	990 00		Interest expense	51	10 00
5							
28	29	Invoice May 21, less 2%	1,470 00	30 00			
29	30	Sales	490 00				
30			29,578 00 (1)	298 00 (47)			80 00
31							

(Right side)

CREDITS

Line No.	Account Credited	Accounts Receivable ✓	Accounts Receivable Amount	Sales Dept. A	Sales Dept. B	Interest Earned	Sundry Accounts L.F.	Sundry Accounts Amount
1				280 00	200 00			
2	Frank Brown	✓	1,000 00					
3	Notes receivable						13	500 00
4	Notes payable					5 00	28	1,000 00
5								
28	George White	✓	1,500 00					
29				315 00	175 00			
30			15,875 00 (10)	4,860 00 (45)	5,645 00 (46)	60 00 (50)		3,516 00
31								

When a voucher system is in use, a formal voucher must be prepared and approved before a cash disbursement can be made. Each voucher is recorded in a voucher register; the proper asset, expense, or other account is debited, and the Vouchers Payable account is credited. When the cash disbursement is made (either immediately or at a later date), an entry is made in the cash disbursements book (sometimes called a *check register*) debiting Vouchers Payable and crediting Cash, and also crediting Purchase Discounts if a discount is taken.

The form of the voucher register is indicated by the very abridged illustration below.

Voucher Register

Voucher No.	Date	Payee	Explanation	Terms	Date Paid	Check No.	Credit Vouchers Payable	DEBITS Purchases	Freight In	Name of Account	L.F.	Amount
	19—											
6-93	July 6	The Osborne Company.....	Invoice, July 3	1/10; n/30			270 00	270 00				

The entry in the voucher register on page 7 records a debit to Purchases and a credit to Vouchers Payable, which is another name for Accounts Payable. Voucher registers usually contain many debit columns for accounts which are frequently debited. Only three debit columns are shown in the illustration—one for purchases, one for freight in, and one for accounts for which no special column is provided.

The cash disbursements entry for the payment of The Osborne Company voucher is shown below.

Check Register

Check No.	Date	Payee	Debit Vouchers Payable	CREDITS Purchase Discounts	CREDITS Cash
1668	19— July 12	The Osborne Company	270 00	2 70	267 30

When a voucher is paid, notations are made in the Date Paid and Check Number columns of the voucher register, in the manner illustrated below.

Voucher Register

Voucher No.	Date	Payee	Explanation	Terms	Date Paid	Check No.	Credit Vouchers Payable	DEBITS Purchases	DEBITS Freight In	Sundry Accounts Name of Account	L.F.	Amount
6-93	19— July 6	The Osborne Company	Invoice, July 3	1/10; n/30	July 12	1668	270 00	270 00				

Entries in the voucher register with no notations in the Date Paid and Check Number columns are "open," or unpaid, items. Their total should agree with the balance in the Vouchers Payable controlling account in the general ledger. The voucher register thus serves as a subsidiary record which takes the place of the accounts payable subsidiary ledger.

Posting from documents.   One illustration should suffice to show how labor can be saved by posting directly from documents. Instead of recording sales in a sales book and posting therefrom, carbon copies of all sales invoices can be kept in a binder, which thus serves as a sales book. The amount of each charge sale can be posted directly from the carbon copy of the invoice to the customer's account in the subsidiary accounts receivable ledger, and the total, shown by an adding-machine tape (retained in the binder), can be posted as a debit to the Accounts Receivable controlling account and as a credit to the Sales account.

Trial balance and subsidiary ledger schedules.   The general ledger trial balance taken periodically serves as a test of the mechanical accuracy of the bookkeeping procedures (to the extent of establishing the equality of debits and credits) and provides a list of account balances to be used in the preparation of statements. If the general ledger is well organized, the account balances will appear in the trial balance in a sequence similar to that in which they will appear in the statements. However, amounts may appear in the statements although they do not appear in the general ledger trial balance—for instance, the credit balances in accounts in the subsidiary accounts receivable ledger.

The schedules of the subsidiary ledgers are also a test of mechanical accuracy; they establish the agreement of the subsidiary ledgers with their related controlling accounts.

Cut-off.   There must be a correct cut-off at the end of any period for which statements are prepared. That is, the accounts should include entries for all transactions which occurred before the end of the period, and should not include entries for any transactions which occurred after the end of the period. Complete information regarding some transactions may not be available on the last day of the period in which they occurred; for this reason, it often is necessary to wait a few days after the end of the period before completing the recording and posting and taking a trial balance.

Mistakes in the accounts.   An accountant not infrequently discovers that mistakes have been made in the accounts. This becomes apparent if the trial balance does not balance, or if the balance in a controlling account is out of agreement with the sum of the account balances in its subsidiary ledger.

If the general ledger trial balance does not balance, the accountant should perform the following operations, in the order indicated:

(1) Refoot the general ledger trial balance.
(2) Compare the balances shown by the trial balance with those shown by the accounts in the general ledger.

    (3) Recompute the balances of the general ledger accounts.

    (4) Trace the postings to the general ledger.

    (5) Refoot the books of original entry.

    (6) See whether the sum of the totals of the debit columns is equal to the sum of the totals of the credit columns of each columnar book of original entry; if they are not in balance, refoot each column. If this does not disclose the error, see whether the debits and credits in each entry are equal.

When the general ledger is in balance but a subsidiary ledger is out of agreement with its control, the presumption is that the error or errors causing the disagreement are within the subsidiary ledger. In this case the accountant should:

    (1) Refoot the schedule of the subsidiary ledger.

    (2) See that the balances were carried correctly from the subsidiary ledger to the schedule.

    (3) Recompute the balance of each subsidiary ledger account.

    (4) Trace the postings to the subsidiary ledger.

Adjusting Entries

Cash and accrual bases of accounting. Because statements of operations and financial position are prepared periodically, it is necessary to determine the accounting period to which revenues, expenses, and losses are applicable. There are two principal bases for assigning revenues and expenses to accounting periods: the cash basis and the accrual basis.

Cash basis. On a pure cash basis, no income is taken from sales on account until collections are received; purchases are regarded as costs chargeable against revenue in the period in which payment is made; and no consideration is given to inventories.

Revenue from other sources is regarded as earned in the period in which the cash collection is received. No revenue is regarded as having been earned for services performed unless the cash has been collected; and any cash collections for services to be rendered in the future are regarded as revenue of the period in which the collections are received, even though nothing has been done to earn it.

Expenses are regarded as applicable to the period in which the cash payment is made. No charge for bad debts appears in the operating statement because no earning is taken until the receivable is collected; and there is no charge for depreciation because the entire cost of a fixed asset is regarded as an expense of the period in which the purchase disbursement is made.

It is obvious that such an accounting basis is wholly unsatisfactory for a business with material amounts of expenses accrued or prepaid, revenue accrued or collected in advance, fixed assets, inventories, accounts receivable, or accounts payable.

The so-called cash basis of reporting income for federal income tax purposes, as governed by the law and the regulations, is really a mixed cash-accrual basis. If sales of purchased or manufactured goods are a major source of revenue, recognition must be given to sales on account, purchases on account, and inventories. An expenditure for fixed assets cannot be taken as a deduction wholly in the period in which the purchase disbursement is made; deductions can be taken only for periodical depreciation and amortization. But consideration need not be given to bad debt provisions (since the taxpayer may elect the charge-off basis), nor to accrued or deferred revenue or expense.

Accrual basis. On the accrual basis of accounting, revenue is regarded as earned in the period in which sales were made or the services rendered (regardless of when collected), and expenses are regarded as applicable to the period in which they are incurred (regardless of when paid).

The "matching" of revenues and expenses for the purpose of determining net income on an accrual basis often requires the exercise of trained judgment, and not infrequently involves estimates. But it is fundamental that, if the books are to reflect the results of operations and the financial position on an accrual basis, adjusting entries must be made for bad debts, accruals, and cost and revenue apportionments.

Illustrative adjusting entries. Adjusting entries dealing with matters such as those mentioned in the preceding section are illustrated below. Instead of showing the adjusting journal entries, their effect on the accounts is shown.

Provision for doubtful accounts. The adjusting entry to provide for doubtful accounts debits an expense account and credits an allowance account, which is contra to the accounts receivable.

	Bad Debts		Allowance for Doubtful Accounts	
1959				
Dec. 31 Adjusting entry.....	1,000			1,000

The debit balance in the Bad Debts account will be shown as an expense in the income statement.

The credit balance in the allowance account will be shown in the balance sheet as a deduction from the accounts receivable.

Cost apportionments—Depreciation and amortization.
The cost of a fixed asset should be written off as an expense gradually over the life of the asset. The periodical adjusting entry includes a debit to a depreciation (expense) account and a credit to an accumulated depreciation account.

	Depreciation of Building	Accumulated Depreciation —Building
1959		
Dec. 31 Balance from prior periods...........		6,000
31 Adjusting entry.....	1,500	1,500

The $1,500 debit balance in the Depreciation of Building account will be shown as an expense in the income statement.

The $7,500 credit balance in the Accumulated Depreciation—Building account will be shown in the balance sheet as a deduction from the balance in the Building account.

Cost apportionments—Prepaid expenses. The kind of adjusting entry to be made for the apportionment of an expense prepayment that will benefit more than one period depends on the nature of the account that was charged with the expenditure.

To illustrate, assume that a company paid $300 at the beginning of the year for a three-year insurance policy. The adjusting entry at the end of the year, to show that the insurance expense for the year amounts to $100, will depend on whether the $300 expenditure was charged to an unexpired insurance (asset) account or to an insurance expense account. The two conditions are illustrated below.

Original charge to an asset account: The adjusting entry should transfer the *expired* portion from the asset account to an expense account.

	Unexpired Insurance	Insurance Expense
1959		
Jan. 2 Original expenditure............	300	
Dec. 31 Adjusting entry................	100	100

Original charge to an expense account: The adjusting entry should transfer the *unexpired* portion from the expense account to an asset account.

	Unexpired Insurance	Insurance Expense
1959		
Jan. 2 Original expenditure............		300
Dec. 31 Adjusting entry................	200	200

In either case:

The $200 debit balance in the Unexpired Insurance account
should appear as an asset in the balance sheet.
The $100 debit balance in the Insurance Expense account
should appear in the income statement.

Revenue apportionments. The kind of adjusting entry to
be made for the apportionment of revenue booked in advance and
to be earned during more than one period depends on the nature
of the account that was originally credited.

To illustrate, assume that a magazine publisher made collections
of $100,000 during the year for one-, two-, and three-year sub-
scriptions, and that at the end of the year only $40,000 had been
earned by the issuance of magazines. The adjusting entry at the
end of the year, to show that $40,000 had been earned, will depend
on whether the $100,000 was credited to Subscriptions Collected
in Advance (an unearned revenue account) or to Subscriptions
Earned. The two conditions are illustrated below.

Original credit to an unearned revenue account: The adjusting
entry should transfer the *earned* portion from the unearned
revenue account to an earned revenue account.

		Subscriptions Collected in Advance		Subscriptions Earned	
1959					
Various					
dates	Advance collections		100,000		
Dec. 31	Adjusting entry...........	40,000			40,000

Original credit to a revenue account: The adjusting entry should
transfer the *unearned* portion from the revenue account to an
unearned revenue account.

		Subscriptions Collected in Advance		Subscriptions Earned	
1959					
Various					
dates	Advance collections........				100,000
Dec. 31	Adjusting entry...........		60,000	60,000	

In either case:

The $40,000 credit balance in the Subscriptions Earned ac-
count should appear in the income statement.
The $60,000 credit balance in the Subscriptions Collected in
Advance account should appear on the liability side of the
balance sheet.

Accrued income. Assume that, in addition to $100 of interest collected on notes receivable during the year, uncollected accrued interest at the end of the year amounts to $50. The adjusting entry consists of a debit to an asset account and a credit to an income account.

		Accrued Interest on Notes Receivable		Interest Earned
1959				
Various				
dates	Collected..................			100
Dec. 31	Adjusting entry...........	50		50

The $50 debit balance in the Accrued Interest on Notes Receivable account should appear in the balance sheet as an asset.
The $150 credit balance in the Interest Earned account should appear in the income statement.

Accrued expenses. Assume that, in addition to $10,000 of wages and salaries paid during the year, accrued and unpaid wages at the end of the year amount to $500. The adjusting entry consists of a debit to an expense account and a credit to an accrued liability account.

		Wages and Salaries		Accrued Wages and Salaries
1959				
Various				
dates	Paid.....................	10,000		
Dec. 31	Adjusting entry...........	500		500

The $10,500 debit balance in the Wages and Salaries account should appear in the income statement.
The $500 credit balance in the Accrued Wages and Salaries account should appear as a liability in the balance sheet.

CHAPTER TWO

Working Papers
Closing Procedures

Purpose of working papers. Working papers facilitate the preparation of financial statements by classifying the account balances according to the statements in which they will appear, and the preparation of entries involved in the procedure of closing the books. The form in which working papers are prepared depends to some extent on the preference of the accountant. Several illustrations are presented.

Mercantile Business

First illustration—Working papers prepared from adjusted trial balance. Some accountants prepare and post the adjusting entries before beginning the working papers. If this is done, the Trial Balance columns of the working papers show the account balances after adjustments, as illustrated on pages 16 and 17. These working papers were prepared as follows:

Step 1. The general heading and column headings were entered.

Step 2. The trial balance was entered in the first pair of columns.

Step 3. Each account balance was extended to the appropriate debit or credit column for the statement in which the balance should appear.

(*Continued on page 18.*)

15

THE A COMPANY
Working Papers
For the Year Ended December 31, 1959

	Trial Balance (After Adjustments)		Income Statement		Retained Earnings		Balance Sheet	
Cash	9,800						9,800	
Accounts receivable	14,000						14,000	
Allowance for doubtful accounts		1,650						1,650
Inventory—December 31, 1958	30,000		30,000					
Unexpired insurance	130						130	
Delivery equipment	3,000						3,000	
Accumulated depreciation—Delivery equipment		1,800						1,800
Accounts payable		9,350						9,350
Accrued salaries payable		150						150
Capital stock		25,000						25,000
Retained earnings—December 31, 1958		6,610				6,610		
Dividends	2,500				2,500			
Sales		150,000		150,000				
Sales returns and allowances	1,800		1,800					
Purchases	110,100		110,100					
Purchase returns and allowances		1,300		1,300				
Salesmen's salaries	11,000		11,000					
Rent expense	1,750		1,750					
Delivery expense	3,900		3,900					
Depreciation—Delivery equipment	600		600					

	Income Statement			Balance Sheet	
Miscellaneous selling expenses	1,500		1,500		
Office salaries	3,400		3,400		
Office expense	1,200		1,200		
Property taxes	250		250		
Insurance expense	180		180		
Bad debts	750		750		
	195,860	195,860			
Inventory—December 31, 1959		32,000	32,000		32,000
Net income before income tax—down	166,430	183,300			
	16,870		183,300		
Net income before income tax—brought down	183,300	183,300		16,870	
Federal income tax	5,060			5,060	
Net income	11,810	16,870		11,810	18,420
				2,500	
				15,920	
				18,420	18,420
Retained earnings—December 31, 1959				15,920	15,920
				58,930	58,930

Step 4. The ending inventory, $32,000, was entered in the Income Statement credit column and the Balance Sheet debit column.

Step 5. The Income Statement columns were footed; the net income before income tax was entered as a balancing figure and brought down after again footing the columns.

Step 6. The income tax was computed and entered in the Income Statement debit column, and in the Balance Sheet credit column as a liability. If the federal income tax is not recorded until the net income before tax is computed in the working papers, an additional adjusting entry therefor is required.

If the income tax was recorded in the accounts before the working papers were prepared, Step 5 would consist merely of footing the Income Statement columns, and Step 6 would be omitted.

Step 7. The net income was entered as a balancing figure in the Income Statement debit column and in the Retained Earnings credit column.

Step 8. The Retained Earnings columns were footed; the amount of the retained earnings at the end of the year was entered as a balancing figure in the Retained Earnings debit column and in the Balance Sheet credit column. The Retained Earnings and Balance Sheet columns were footed.

Second illustration—Working papers prepared from trial balance before adjustments. In the working papers on pages 20 and 21, the trial balance shows the account balances before adjustments. A pair of columns for adjustments is therefore required. They contain adjustments for the following matters:

(A) The allowance for doubtful accounts is increased $600.

```
Bad debts.............................................. 600
    Allowance for doubtful accounts......................      600
```

(B) Depreciation of the delivery equipment is computed at 20% of the $4,000 balance in the asset account.

```
Depreciation—Delivery equipment......................... 800
    Accumulated depreciation—Delivery equipment..........      800
```

(C) Interest on the bank loan to maturity, in the amount of $120, was paid and debited to Interest Paid in Advance. The portion applicable to 1959 is $80.

```
Interest expense........................................ 80
    Interest paid in advance.............................      80
```

(D) Insurance premiums were debited to Unexpired Insurance. The expired portion, $160, is transferred to an expense account.

```
Insurance expense........................................ 160
    Unexpired insurance..................................      160
```

(E) On November 1, the company collected $300 for services to be rendered in making deliveries for another store during November, December, and January. The credit was made to Delivery Fees Collected in Advance. By the end of the year, $200 was earned; it is transferred to a revenue account.

```
Delivery fees collected in advance......................... 200
    Delivery earnings....................................      200
```

(F) Accrued salesmen's salaries amount to $500, and accrued office salaries amount to $130.

```
Salesmen's salaries....................................... 500
Office salaries............................................ 130
    Accrued salaries payable.............................      630
```

(G) Accrued interest on notes receivable is $25.

```
Accrued interest receivable............................... 25
    Interest earned......................................       25
```

Some accountants make the adjusting entries in the journal and then apply them to the unadjusted balances in the working papers. Other accountants first enter the adjustments in the working papers and do not make the adjusting entries in the journal until later, when they make the entries to close the books.

If statements are prepared monthly but the books are closed only annually, the monthly adjustments may be applied to the working papers only, without making adjusting entries in the books.

The amount shown as accounts receivable in the Trial Balance debit column of the working papers is the balance of the controlling account. The subsidiary ledger contains accounts with debit balances totalling $20,000 and accounts with credit balances totalling $500. These amounts were entered in the Balance Sheet columns.

THE B COMPANY
Working Papers
For the Year Ended December 31, 1959

	Trial Balance (Before Adjustments)		Adjustments		Income Statement		Retained Earnings		Balance Sheet	
Cash	9,730								9,730	
Accounts receivable	19,500								20,000	
Allowance for doubtful accounts		700		500 A						500
										1,300
Notes receivable	5,000								5,000	
Inventory—December 31, 1958	30,000				30,000					
Unexpired insurance	375			160 D					215	
Interest paid in advance	120			80 C					40	
Delivery equipment	4,000								4,000	
Accumulated depreciation—Del. equip.		1,600		800 B						2,400
Bank loans		8,000								8,000
Accounts payable		10,300								10,300
Delivery fees collected in advance		300	200 E							100
Capital stock		25,000								25,000
Retained earnings—December 31, 1958		6,470						6,470		
Dividends	5,000						5,000			
Sales		206,000				206,000				
Sales returns and allowances	980				980					
Sales discounts	1,670				1,670					
Purchases	150,000				150,000					
Purchase returns and allowances		1,300				1,300				
Purchase discounts		1,210				1,210				
Salesmen's salaries	12,650		500 F		13,150					
Rent expense	3,000				3,000					
Advertising	10,200				10,200					
Delivery expense	3,275				3,275					

Account	Trial Balance Dr	Trial Balance Cr	Adjustments Dr	Adjustments Cr	Income Statement Dr	Income Statement Cr	Retained Earnings / Balance Sheet Dr	Retained Earnings / Balance Sheet Cr
Miscellaneous selling expenses	860				860			
Office salaries	3,260		130 F		3,390			
Office expense	930				930			
Property taxes	190				190			
Interest earned		60		25 G		85		
Interest expense	200		80 C		280			
	260,940	260,940						
Bad debts			600 A		600			
Depreciation—Delivery equipment			800 B		800			
Insurance expense			160 D		160			
Delivery earnings				200 E / 630 F		200		630
Accrued salaries payable				25 C				25
Accrued interest receivable			25 C				25	
			2,495	2,495				
Inventory—December 31, 1959						28,650	28,650	
					219,485	237,445		
Net income before income tax—down					17,960			
					237,445	237,445		
Net income before income tax—brought down						17,960		
Federal income tax					5,388			5,388
Net income					12,572			12,572
					17,960	17,960		
Retained earnings—December 31, 1959							14,042	14,042
							5,000	
							19,042	19,042
							67,660	67,660

Closing entries. After the statements for a year have been prepared, it is customary to close the books. This is accomplished by making and posting closing entries. Several illustrations of closing entries are presented; they are based on data in the preceding working papers.

First Procedure

The first of the following entries closes all of the accounts whose balances were extended to the Income Statement credit column of the working papers, and also records the end-of-period inventory (the amount of which also appears in the Income Statement credit column of the working papers).

The second entry closes all of the accounts whose balances were extended to the Income Statement debit column of the working papers, and also the income tax expense.

The third entry closes the Revenue and Expense account.

The last entry closes the Dividends account.

Sales..	206,000	
Purchase returns and allowances......................	1,300	
Purchase discounts..................................	1,210	
Delivery earnings...................................	200	
Interest earned.....................................	85	
Inventory—December 31, 1959......................	28,650	
Revenue and expense............................		237,445
To close accounts with credit balances and also record the end-of-year inventory.		
Revenue and expense................................	224,873	
Inventory—December 31, 1958....................		30,000
Sales returns and allowances.......................		980
Sales discounts...............................		1,670
Purchases.....................................		150,000
Salesmen's salaries........		13,150
Rent expense......................................		3,000
Advertising.......................................		10,200
Delivery expense..................................		3,275
Depreciation—Delivery equipment................		800
Miscellaneous selling expenses....................		860
Office salaries....................................		3,390
Office expense....................................		930
Property taxes....................................		190
Insurance expense................................		160
Bad debts..		600
Interest expense..................................		280
Federal income tax...............................		5,388
To close accounts with debit balances.		
Revenue and expense...............................	12,572	
Retained earnings...............................		12,572
To close the Revenue and Expense account.		
Retained earnings..................................	5,000	
Dividends......................................		5,000
To close the latter account.		

It was formerly the custom to show complete details in the Revenue and Expense account by using the following posting procedure: Instead of crediting Revenue and Expense with the $237,-445 total of the first entry, it was credited with all of the amounts debited to other accounts in the entry; and, instead of debiting Revenue and Expense with the $224,873 total of the second entry, it was debited with all of the amounts credited to the other accounts in the entry. The Revenue and Expense account, after it was closed by the third entry, appeared as follows:

Revenue and Expense

1959			1959		
Dec. 31	Inventory—12/31/58..	30,000	Dec. 31	Sales...............	206,000
31	Sales returns and allow-		31	Purchase returns and	
	ances	980		allowances.........	1,300
31	Sales discounts.......	1,670	31	Purchase discounts....	1,210
31	Purchases............	150,000	31	Delivery earnings.....	200
31	Salesmen's salaries....	13,150	31	Interest earned.......	85
31	Rent expense.........	3,000	31	Inventory—12/31/59..	28,650
31	Advertising..........	10,200			
31	Delivery expense.....	3,275			
31	Depreciation—Del.				
	equip..............	800			
31	Misc. selling expenses.	860			
31	Office salaries........	3,390			
31	Office expense........	930			
31	Property taxes.......	190			
31	Insurance expense....	160			
31	Bad debts...........	600			
31	Interest expense......	280			
31	Federal income tax....	5,388			
31	To Retained Earnings.	12,572			
		237,445			237,445

Many accountants feel that it is unnecessary to show all the details in the Revenue and Expense account when they already are shown in the income statement. They therefore post only the totals of the first two entries. The Revenue and Expense account after closing then appears as follows:

Revenue and Expense

1959			1959	
Dec. 31		224,873	Dec. 31	237,445
31	To Retained Earnings	12,572		
		237,445		237,445

Second Procedure

Some accountants combine the first two entries, and credit Revenue and Expense with the net income for the period, as illustrated on the following page.

Sales... 206,000
Purchase returns and allowances..................... 1,300
Purchase discounts................................. 1,210
Delivery earnings.................................. 200
Interest earned.................................... 85
Inventory—December 31, 1959...................... 28,650
    Inventory—December 31, 1958................... 30,000
    Sales returns and allowances...................... 980
    Sales discounts................................... 1,670
    Purchases.. 150,000
    Salesmen's salaries.............................. 13,150
    Rent expense..................................... 3,000
    Advertising...................................... 10,200
    Delivery expense................................. 3,275
    Depreciation—Delivery equipment................ 800
    Miscellaneous selling expenses.................... 860
    Office salaries................................... 3,390
    Office expense.................................... 930
    Property taxes.................................... 190
    Insurance expense................................ 160
    Bad debts.. 600
    Interest expense................................. 280
    Federal income tax............................... 5,388
    Revenue and expense............................. 12,572

To close the revenue and expense accounts and record the end-of-year inventory.

Third Procedure

Some accountants do not use a Revenue and Expense account, but credit the net income shown by the combined entry directly to the Retained Earnings account.

Proprietorship and partnership working papers. Instead of a pair of Retained Earnings columns, the working papers for a proprietorship have a pair of columns headed, for example, John Smith, Capital. The balances of the proprietor's capital and drawing accounts and the net income or net loss for the period are extended to these columns, and the balance of the columns is extended to the Balance Sheet credit column.

Working papers for a partnership contain a pair of similar columns for each partner, showing the balances of the capital and drawing accounts and the division of the net income or net loss.

Manufacturing Business

Three types of working papers are illustrated in this chapter.

Pages 26–28. Single set of working papers.
Pages 31–34. Separate working papers for each statement.
Page 36.   Separate working papers for each statement, with sub-classification columns.

All of the illustrations are based on the same trial balance and adjustments. The adjusting entries appear below:

(A) Bad debts.. 300
       Allowance for doubtful accounts..................   300
       To add $300 to the allowance account.

(B) Factory supplies expense............................ 2,070
       Factory supplies................................   2,070
       Supplies used.

(C) Insurance expense.................................. 975
       Unexpired insurance.............................   975
       Premium expiration for the year. (Manufacturing, $910; General, $65.)

(D) Depreciation—Factory buildings...................... 2,600
       Accumulated depreciation—Factory buildings.......   2,600
       Depreciation for the year.

(E) Depreciation—Machinery and equipment.............. 4,788
       Accumulated depreciation—Machinery and equipment...................................   4,788
       Depreciation for the year.

(F) Depreciation—Office equipment...................... 314
       Accumulated depreciation—Office equipment.......   314
       Depreciation for the year.

(G) Interest expense—Bonds............................ 250
       Discount on bonds..............................   250
       Amortization of discount for the year.

(H) Rent collected in advance........................... 50
       Rent earned....................................   50
       Earned portion of rent collected in advance.

(I) Accrued interest on notes receivable.................. 45
       Interest earned—Notes receivable.................   45
       Interest accrued on notes.

(J) Interest expense—Notes payable..................... 20
       Accrued interest on notes payable................   20
       Interest accrued on notes.

The end-of-year inventories were: Finished goods, $10,991; goods in process, $13,212; materials, $9,923.

Some expenses cannot be regarded as entirely manufacturing, selling, or general, but should be apportioned to two or more of these groups on some appropriate basis. In this illustration, property taxes and insurance are apportioned $14/_{15}$ to manufacturing and $1/_{15}$ to general expense, as indicated by the amounts in the Manufacturing and the Income Statement columns. Stationery and printing expense is apportioned 20 per cent to selling expense and 80 per cent to general expense; the apportionment is indicated by the letters S and G beside the related amounts in the Income Statement debit column.

Single set of working papers. A single set of working papers for a manufacturing business is illustrated on pages 26, 27, and 28.

Single set of working papers.

THE INGRAM MANUFACTURING COMPANY
Working Papers
For the Year Ended December 31, 1959

	Trial Balance Dr.	Trial Balance Cr.	Adjustments Dr.	Adjustments Cr.	Manufacturing Dr.	Manufacturing Cr.	Income Statement Dr.	Income Statement Cr.	Retained Earnings Dr.	Retained Earnings Cr.	Balance Sheet Dr.	Balance Sheet Cr.
Cash	27,600										27,600	
Marketable securities	10,000										10,000	
Accounts receivable	35,365										35,365	
Allowance for doubtful accounts		650		300 A								950
Notes receivable	8,000										8,000	
Notes receivable discounted		2,000										2,000
Inventories—December 31, 1958:												
Finished goods	12,400						12,400					
Goods in process	8,120				8,120							
Materials	6,325				6,325							
Factory supplies	2,420			2,070 B							350	
Unexpired insurance	1,375			975 C							400	
Stock of Murdock Sales Company	5,000										5,000	
Land	23,000										23,000	
Factory buildings	65,000										65,000	
Accumulated depreciation—Factory buildings		14,500		2,600 D								17,100
Machinery and equipment	53,900										53,900	
Accumulated depreciation—Machinery and equip.		13,600		4,788 E								18,388
Office equipment	3,140										3,140	
Accumulated depreciation—Office equipment		750		314 F								1,064
Discount on bonds	2,500			250 G							2,250	
Accounts payable		4,000										4,000
Notes payable		5,000										5,000
Rent collected in advance		150	50 H									100
Bonds payable		50,000										50,000
Capital stock—Preferred		40,000										40,000
Capital stock—Common		75,000										75,000
Premium on common stock		7,500										7,500
Retained earnings—December 31, 1958		18,714								18,714		
Dividends—Common	6,000								6,000			
Dividends—Preferred	2,400								2,400			
Sales		228,625						228,625				
Sales returns and allowances	1,315						1,315					
Sales discounts	1,617						1,617					
Totals forward	275,477	460,489	50	11,297	14,445	—	15,332	228,625	8,400	18,714	234,005	221,102

THE INGRAM MANUFACTURING COMPANY
Working Papers (Continued)
For the Year Ended December 31, 1959

	Trial Balance		Adjustments		Manufacturing		Income Statement		Retained Earnings		Balance Sheet	
Totals brought forward	275,477	460,489	50	11,297	14,445	—	15,332	228,625	8,400	18,714	234,005	221,102
Purchases—Materials	54,630				54,630							
Purchase returns and allowances		425				425						
Purchase discounts		675				675						
Freight in	1,200				1,200							
Direct labor	65,805				65,805							
Indirect labor	14,260				14,260							
Heat, light, and power—Factory	8,920				8,920							
Repairs to buildings and machinery	635				635							
Property taxes	960				896		64					
Miscellaneous factory expenses	3,700				3,700							
Advertising	7,320						7,320					
Salesmen's salaries	8,000						8,000					
Salesmen's traveling expenses	4,100						4,100					
Freight out	850						850					
Miscellaneous selling expenses	875						875					
Officers' salaries	6,500						6,500					
Office salaries	4,200						4,200					
Office supplies expense	312						312					
Stationery and printing expense	415						{ 83 S 332 G					
Miscellaneous general expenses	561						561					
Interest earned—Notes receivable		141		45 I				186				
Dividends on Murdock stock		400						400				
Interest expense—Bonds	3,000		250 G				3,250					
Interest expense—Notes payable	410		20 J				430					
	462,130	462,130										
Bad debts			300 A				300					
Factory supplies expense			2,070 B		2,070							
Insurance expense			975 C		910		65					
Depreciation:												
Factory buildings			2,600 D		2,600							
Machinery and equipment			4,788 E		4,788							
Office equipment			314 F				314					
Rent earned				50 H				50				
Totals forward			11,367	11,392	174,859	1,100	52,888	229,261	8,400	18,714	234,005	221,102

THE INGRAM MANUFACTURING COMPANY
Working Papers (Concluded)
For the Year Ended December 31, 1959

	Trial Balance	Adjustments		Manufacturing		Income Statement		Retained Earnings		Balance Sheet	
Totals brought forward............		11,367	11,392	174,859	1,100	52,888	229,261	8,400	18,714	234,005	221,102
Accrued interest on notes receivable...		45 I								45	
Accrued interest on notes payable......			20 J								20
Inventories—December 31, 1959:											
Finished goods................							10,991			10,991	
Goods in process..............					13,212					13,212	
Materials.....................		11,412	11,412		9,923					9,923	
					24,235						
Cost of goods manufactured.........				174,859	150,624	150,624					
				174,859	174,859						
Net income before income tax—down...						203,512					
						36,740					
						240,252	240,252				
Net income before income tax—brought down....							240,252				
Federal income tax................						13,600					13,600
Net income........................						23,140			23,140		
						36,740	36,740				
Retained earnings—December 31, 1959.....								8,400	41,854		33,454
								33,454			
								41,854	41,854	268,176	268,176

Separate working papers for each statement. If the general ledger trial balance is very long, some accountants prefer to make a separate work sheet for each statement. This practice has the advantage of classifying the data so that each statement can be prepared from its own working papers.

The forms are illustrated on pages 31 through 34. Observe that accounts that have no balances but that are affected by adjusting entries are entered in the working papers in their proper sequence, with no amounts in the Trial Balance columns. This can be easily accomplished by listing the account titles shown by a chart of accounts and then entering the account balances. The same procedure could have been followed in the preceding illustration.

Separate working papers are prepared for the following statements: statement of cost of goods manufactured; income statement; statement of retained earnings; balance sheet. Observe the following matters with respect to these working papers:

The working papers for each statement contain the trial balance items and all of the adjustments applicable to that statement.

Totals of the Trial Balance and Adjustments columns are forwarded:

From the cost of goods manufactured papers to the income statement papers.

From the income statement papers to the retained earnings papers.

From the retained earnings papers to the balance sheet papers.

Balancing figures are forwarded as follows:

The cost of goods manufactured is forwarded from the cost of goods manufactured papers to the income statement papers.

The net income is forwarded from the income statement papers to the retained earnings papers.

The amount of the retained earnings at the end of the year is forwarded from the retained earnings papers to the balance sheet papers.

End-of-year inventories and balances brought forward from preceding papers are entered in the positions in which they will appear in the statements.

The income tax expense for 1959 and the related liability are entered in the income statement papers and the balance sheet papers by adjusting entry K.

It will be remembered that, in the preceding illustration, insurance and property taxes were apportioned between manufacturing and general expenses, and stationery and printing was apportioned between selling and general expenses. In the preceding working papers, the apportionments were made as follows:

A portion of the insurance expense was extended to the Manufacturing debit column and the remainder was extended to the Income Statement debit column.

The apportionment of the property taxes was accomplished in the same manner.

The apportionment of the stationery and printing expense was indicated by extending the two portions of the balance of the account to the Income Statement debit column, with identifying letters S and G.

In the working papers in this illustration, no new problem is presented with respect to showing the apportionment of stationery and printing, because the selling and general expenses appear in the same working papers. The apportionment is indicated in the same manner as in the preceding illustration.

The apportionments of insurance and property taxes are dealt with as follows:

Insurance:

Insurance premiums had been charged to Unexpired Insurance and an adjusting entry (C) was made as follows:

```
Insurance expense.......................................  975
     Unexpired insurance.................................        975
     Premium expiration for the year.  (Manufacturing, $910;
     General, $65.)
```

The $910 is entered in the debit Adjustments column of the cost of goods manufactured papers, and the $65 is entered in the debit Adjustments column of the income statement papers.

Property taxes:

There is no adjusting entry for property taxes. Since the major portion of the tax is classified as manufacturing expense, the balance of the property tax account is shown in the Trial Balance debit column of the cost of goods manufactured working papers, and a transfer of the $64 portion to be included in general expenses is made by a credit in the Adjustments columns of the cost of goods manufactured papers and a debit in the Adjustments columns of the income statement papers. The transfer is identified by a lower-case letter (*a*) to distinguish it from ordinary adjusting entries, which are identified by capital letters.

Separate working papers for each statement.

THE INGRAM MANUFACTURING COMPANY
Statement of Cost of Goods Manufactured Working Papers
For the Year Ended December 31, 1959

	Trial Balance		Adjustments		Cost of Goods Manufactured	
Goods in process inventory—December 31, 1958	8,120				8,120	
Materials inventory—December 31, 1958	6,325				6,325	
Purchases—Materials	54,630				54,630	
Purchase returns and allowances		425				425
Purchase discounts		675				675
Freight in	1,200				1,200	
Direct labor	65,805				65,805	
Indirect labor	14,260				14,260	
Heat, light, and power—Factory	8,920				8,920	
Repairs to buildings and machinery	635				635	
Factory supplies expense			2,070 B		2,070	
Insurance expense			910 C		910	
Property taxes	960			64a	896	
Depreciation—Factory buildings			2,600 D		2,600	
Depreciation—Machinery and equipment			4,788 E		4,788	
Miscellaneous factory expenses	3,700				3,700	
Goods in process inventory—December 31, 1959						13,212
Materials inventory—December 31, 1959						9,923
Totals forward	164,555	1,100	10,368	64	174,859	24,235
						150,624
Cost of goods manufactured—forward					174,859	174,859

THE INGRAM MANUFACTURING COMPANY
Income Statement Working Papers
For the Year Ended December 31, 1959

	Trial Balance		Adjustments		Income Statement	
	Dr.	Cr.	Dr.	Cr.	Dr.	Cr.
Totals brought forward	164,555	1,100	10,368	64		
Sales		228,625				228,625
Sales returns and allowances	1,315				1,315	
Sales discounts	1,617				1,617	
Finished goods inventory—December 31, 1958	12,400				12,400	
Cost of goods manufactured—brought forward					150,624	
Finished goods inventory—December 31, 1959						10,991
Advertising	7,320				7,320	
Salesmen's salaries	8,000				8,000	
Salesmen's traveling expenses	4,100				4,100	
Freight out	850				850	
Miscellaneous selling expenses	875				875	
Officers' salaries	6,500				6,500	
Office salaries	4,200				4,200	
Office supplies expense	312				312	
Stationery and printing expense	415				83 S / 332 G	
Bad debts			300 A		300	
Insurance expense			65 C		65	
Depreciation—Office equipment			314 F		314	
Property taxes			64 a		64	
Miscellaneous general expenses	561				561	
Dividends on Murdock stock	400					400
Interest earned—Notes receivable	141			45 I		186
Rent earned				50 H		50
Interest expense—Bonds	3,000		250 G		3,250	
Interest expense—Notes payable	410		20 J		430	
					203,512	240,252

Net income before income tax—down..........		36,740	240,252	240,252
Net income before income tax—brought down....		240,252		36,740
Federal income tax.........	13,600 K		13,600	
Totals forward........	216,430	230,266	24,981	159
Net income—forward......			23,140	23,140
			36,740	36,740

THE INGRAM MANUFACTURING COMPANY
Statement of Retained Earnings Working Papers
For the Year Ended December 31, 1959

	Trial Balance		Adjustments		Retained Earnings	
Totals brought forward...........	216,430	230,266		159		
Balance—December 31, 1958........			24,981			18,714
Net income—brought forward.......	18,714					23,140
Dividends—Common...........	6,000				6,000	
Dividends—Preferred..........	2,400				2,400	
Totals forward............	224,830	248,980	24,981	159	8,400	33,454
Balance—December 31, 1959—forward........					41,854	41,854

THE INGRAM MANUFACTURING COMPANY
Balance Sheet Working Papers
December 31, 1959

	Trial Balance		Adjustments		Balance Sheet	
Assets						
Totals brought forward	224,830	248,980	24,981	159		
Cash	27,600				27,600	
Marketable securities	10,000				10,000	
Accounts receivable	35,365				35,365	
Allowance for doubtful accounts		650		300 A		950
Notes receivable	8,000				8,000	
Notes receivable discounted		2,000				2,000
Accrued interest on notes receivable			45 I		45	
Inventories—December 31, 1959:						
Finished goods					10,991	
Goods in process					13,212	
Materials					9,923	
Factory supplies	2,420			2,070 B	350	
Unexpired insurance	1,375			975 C	400	
Stock of Murdock Sales Company	5,000				5,000	
Land	23,000				23,000	
Factory buildings	65,000				65,000	
Accumulated depreciation—Factory buildings		14,500		2,600 D		17,100
Machinery and equipment	53,900				53,900	
Accumulated depreciation—Machinery and equipment		13,600		4,788 E		18,388
Office equipment	3,140				3,140	
Accumulated depreciation—Office equipment		750		314 F		1,064
Discount on bonds	2,500			250 G	2,250	
Liabilities and Stockholders' Equity						
Accounts payable		4,000				4,000
Notes payable		5,000				5,000
Federal income tax payable				13,600 K		13,600
Accrued interest on notes payable				20 J		20
Rent collected in advance		150	50 H			100
Bonds payable		50,000				50,000
Capital stock—Preferred		40,000				40,000
Capital stock—Common		75,000				75,000
Premium on common stock		7,500				7,500
Retained earnings—brought forward						33,454
	462,130	462,130	25,076	25,076	268,176	268,176

Separate papers with sub-classification columns. Separate working papers for the various statements make it possible to provide columns in which to show groups of related items. An illustration appears on page 36.

Closing the books. The closing of the books of a manufacturing business involves closing the accounts used in the preparation of the statement of cost of goods manufactured and recording the end-of-period inventories of materials and goods in process; closing the accounts used in the preparation of the income statement and recording the end-of-period inventory of finished goods; and closing any other accounts affecting retained earnings. Entries are shown below. The numbers at the left are for comment reference purposes only.

(1) Manufacturing...................................	174,859	
Goods in process.............................		8,120
Materials................................		6,325
Purchases—Materials........................		54,630
Freight in.................................		1,200
Direct labor................................		65,805
Indirect labor..............................		14,260
Heat, light, and power—Factory..............		8,920
Repairs to buildings and machinery...........		635
Factory supplies expense....................		2,070
Insurance expense..........................		910
Property taxes..............................		896
Depreciation—Factory buildings..............		2,600
Depreciation—Machinery and equipment......		4,788
Miscellaneous factory expenses...............		3,700
To close accounts with debit balances.		
(2) Purchase returns and allowances.................	425	
Purchase discounts............................	675	
Goods in process.............................	13,212	
Materials.....................................	9,923	
Manufacturing............................		24,235
To close accounts with credit balances and record end-of-year inventories.		

(Postings to the Manufacturing account may be totals only or details.—See page 23.)

(3) Revenue and expense...........................	150,624	
Manufacturing.............................		150,624
To transfer the cost of goods manufactured to the Revenue and Expense account.		

Entries 1 and 2 may be combined, with a net debit of $150,624 to Manufacturing.

Entries 1, 2, and 3 may be combined, with a net debit of $150,624 to Revenue and Expense, thus eliminating the Manufacturing account.

(*Continued on page 37.*)

Separate working papers with sub-classification columns.

THE INGRAM MANUFACTURING COMPANY
Income Statement Working Papers
For the Year Ended December 31, 1959

	Trial Balance Dr	Trial Balance Cr	Adjustments Dr	Adjustments Cr	Selling Expenses	General Expenses	Sundry Charges	Sundry Credits	Summary Dr	Summary Cr
Totals brought forward	164,555	1,100	10,368	64						
Sales		228,625								228,625
Sales returns and allowances	1,315								1,315	
Sales discounts	1,617								1,617	
Finished goods inventory—December 31, 1958	12,400								12,400	
Cost of goods manufactured—brought forward									150,624	
Finished goods inventory—December 31, 1959										10,991
Advertising	7,320				7,320					
Salesmen's salaries	8,000				8,000					
Salesmen's traveling expenses	4,100				4,100					
Freight out	850				850					
Miscellaneous selling expenses	875				875					
Officers' salaries	6,500					6,500				
Office salaries	4,200					4,200				
Office supplies expense	312					312				
Stationery and printing expense	415				83	332				
Bad debts			300 A			300				
Insurance expense			65 C			65				
Depreciation—Office equipment			314 F			314				
Property taxes			64 a			64				
Miscellaneous general expenses	561					561				
Dividends on Murdock stock		400						400		
Interest earned—Notes receivable		141		45 I				186		
Rent earned				50 H				50		
Interest expense—Bonds	3,000		250 G				3,250			
Interest expense—Notes payable	410		20 J				430			
Total selling expenses					21,228				21,228	
Total general expenses						12,648			12,648	
Total sundry charges							3,680		3,680	
Total sundry credits								636		636
Net income before income tax—down	216,430	230,266	24,981	24,981					203,512	240,252
				159					36,740	
									240,252	240,252
Net income before income tax—brought down										36,740
Federal income tax			13,600 K						13,600	
Totals forward									13,600	36,740
Net income—forward									23,140	
									36,740	36,740

(4) Sales... 228,625
    Interest earned—Notes receivable................. 186
    Dividends on Murdock stock.................. 400
    Rent earned.................................. 50
    Finished goods............................... 10,991
        Revenue and expense..................... 240,252
        To close accounts with credit balances and record
        end-of-year inventory of finished goods.

(5) Revenue and expense........................... 66,488
    Finished goods............................... 12,400
    Sales returns and allowances.................. 1,315
    Sales discounts.............................. 1,617
    Advertising.................................. 7,320
    Salesmen's salaries.......................... 8,000
    Salesmen's traveling expenses................ 4,100
    Freight out.................................. 850
    Miscellaneous selling expenses............... 875
    Officers' salaries........................... 6,500
    Office salaries.............................. 4,200
    Office supplies expense...................... 312
    Stationery and printing expense.............. 415
    Bad debts................................... 300
    Insurance expense........................... 65
    Depreciation—Office equipment.............. 314
    Property taxes............................... 64
    Miscellaneous general expenses............... 561
    Interest expense—Bonds.................... 3,250
    Interest expense—Notes payable............. 430
    Federal income tax.......................... 13,600
    To close accounts with debit balances.

(Postings to the Revenue and Expense account may be totals or details.)

(6) Revenue and expense........................... 23,140
    Retained earnings............................ 23,140
    To transfer the net income to Retained Earnings.

Entries 4 and 5 may be combined, with a net credit of $173,764 to Revenue and Expense.

Entry 3 may be omitted and the $150,624 credit to Manufacturing may be included in entry 5. If that is done, the net credit to Revenue and Expense in an entry combining 4 and 5 will be $23,140, the amount of the net income. The Revenue and Expense account can be eliminated by crediting Retained Earnings with the $23,140 net income.

Entries 1, 2, 4, and 5 may be combined, eliminating all debits and credits to Manufacturing and Revenue and Expense in those entries, and having one net credit of $23,140 to Revenue and Expense or to Retained Earnings.

(7) Retained earnings.............................. 8,400
    Dividends—Common....................... 6,000
    Dividends—Preferred..................... 2,400
    To close the dividends accounts.

Reversing Entries

Adjusting entries made at the end of a period are sometimes reversed at the beginning of the next period. This matter is discussed in the remainder of this chapter.

Bad debts and depreciation. Adjusting entries for bad debts and depreciation are not reversed. The Allowance for Doubtful Accounts and accumulated depreciation accounts are contra to the related asset accounts. Together they show the net book values of the assets.

Cost apportionments—Prepaid expenses. Page 12, Chapter 1, shows how accounts are adjusted for the apportionment of a prepaid expense. The accounts are repeated below, with the addition of the closing entry.

Original charge to an asset account:

			Unexpired Insurance	Insurance Expense	
1959					
Jan.	2	Original expenditure............	300		
Dec. 31		Adjusting entry...............	100	100	
31		Closing entry................			100

A reversing entry debiting Unexpired Insurance and crediting Insurance Expense would be improper. The $200 balance of the Unexpired Insurance account is the correct amount of the remaining asset.

Original charge to an expense account:

			Unexpired Insurance	Insurance Expense	
1959					
Jan.	2	Original expenditure............		300	
Dec. 31		Adjusting entry...............	200		200
31		Closing entry................			100

In this case, a reversing entry is desirable.

			Unexpired Insurance	Insurance Expense	
1959					
Jan.	2	Original expenditure............		300	
Dec. 31		Adjusting entry...............	200		200
31		Closing entry................			100
1960					
Jan.	1	Reversing entry...............		200	200

The desirability of the reversing entry becomes apparent if we assume that no reversing entry is made, and that an additional premium of $175 is paid and charged (in accordance with the company's previous procedure) to Insurance Expense.

		Unexpired Insurance	Insurance Expense
1959			
Jan. 2	Original expenditure............		300
Dec. 31	Adjusting entry...............	200	200
31	Closing entry.................		100
1960			
Feb. 1	Additional premium...........		175

An undesirable situation is produced. At the end of 1960, when it came time to make the annual adjusting entry, part of the apportionable costs would be in the Unexpired Insurance account and part would be in the Insurance Expense account. This would be a confusing situation, which the reversing entry avoids.

If an expense prepayment will benefit more than one period, it is advisable to charge the expenditure to an asset account because a reversal of the adjusting entry will thus be avoided.

Revenue apportionments.   As shown by the Subscriptions Collected in Advance illustration on page 13 of Chapter 1, prospective revenue booked in advance may be credited to:

An unearned revenue account:

The adjusting entry will transfer the earned portion to a revenue account and no reversing entry need be made.

A revenue account:

The adjusting entry will transfer the unearned portion to an unearned revenue account and a reversing entry will be desirable.

If prospective revenue booked in advance will be earned during more than one period, it is advisable to credit an unearned revenue account because a reversing entry will thus be avoided.

Accrued income.   Page 14 of Chapter 1 shows how accounts are adjusted for accrued income. The accounts are repeated below, with the addition of the closing entry. It was assumed that, in addition to the $100 collected on notes receivable during the year, uncollected accrued interest at the end of the year amounted to $50.

		Accrued Interest on Notes Receivable	Interest Earned
1959			
Various			
dates	Collected on matured notes....		100
Dec. 31	Adjusting entry............ ..	50	50
31	Closing entry................	150	

If the adjusting entry is reversed and interest in the amount of $75 is collected at maturity, the accounts will appear as follows:

		Accrued Interest on Notes Receivable		Interest Earned	
1959					
Various					
dates	Collected on matured notes....				100
Dec. 31	Adjusting entry.............	50			50
31	Closing entry................			150	—
1960					
Jan. 1	Reversing entry.............	—	50	50	
?	Collected...................				75

The $25 credit balance in the Interest Earned account is the amount earned in 1960.

If the $50 accrued at the end of 1959 was all applicable to one note, there would be little advantage in the reversing entry. The collection of the note and interest could be recorded as follows:

```
Cash.................................................. 5,075
    Notes receivable..............................        5,000
    Accrued interest on notes receivable..........           50
    Interest earned...............................           25
```

But if the $50 was applicable to several notes and no reversing entry was made, it would be necessary, each time an interest collection was received, to determine what portion thereof should be credited to Accrued Interest on Notes Receivable and what portion should be credited to Interest Earned. To illustrate, assume the following facts with respect to interest on notes receivable:

	Accrued December 31, 1959	Collected During 1960	Earned During 1960
Note A.................	$20	$30	$10
Note B.................	30	45	15
	$50	$75	$25

The reversing entry simplifies the recording of interest collections, as shown below:

		Accrued Interest on Notes Receivable		Interest Earned	
1959					
Various					
dates	Collected on matured notes.....				100
Dec. 31	Adjusting entry...............	50			50
31	Closing entry.................			150	—
1960					
Jan. 1	Reversing entry...............	—	50	50	
?	Collection of interest on Note A.				30
?	Collection of interest on Note B.				45

The $25 credit balance in the Interest Earned account is the amount earned in 1960.

As indicated by this illustration, a reversing entry, although not necessary, is desirable since it simplifies the subsequent recording of collections.

Because reversing entries for accrued income are desirable in many instances, and because it is advisable to establish a uniform policy, many accountants reverse all adjusting entries for accrued income.

Accrued expense.   Page 14 of Chapter 1 shows how accounts are adjusted for accrued expenses. The illustration is repeated below, with the addition of the closing entry.

		Wages and Salaries	Accrued Wages and Salaries
1959			
Various			
dates	Paid........................	10,000	
Dec. 31	Adjusting entry................	500	
31	Closing entry..................	10,500	500

If wages and salaries are payable on the same future date, a reversing entry is not important. But if they are payable on different dates, it may be advisable to reverse the adjusting entry, so that, when payments are made, it will not be necessary to determine how much of the $500 accrual was for wages and how much was for salaries. The illustration is continued by showing the reversing entry and the payments.

		Wages and Salaries		Accrued Wages and Salaries
1959				
Various				
dates	Paid........................	10,000		
Dec. 31	Adjusting entry................	500		
31	Closing entry..................		10,500	500
1960				
Jan. 1	Reversing entry................		500	500
8	Wages paid....................	1,200		
10	Salaries paid..................	1,800		

The $2,500 debit balance in the wages and salaries expense account is the portion of the January payments that is a January expense.

For the reasons stated at the end of the discussion of accrued income, it may be desirable to establish a policy of reversing all adjusting entries for accrued expenses.

Adjusting and reversing entries for The Ingram Manufacturing Company.   The adjusting entries of The Ingram

Manufacturing Company, shown on page 25 of this chapter, are restated below. Related reversing entries are indicated in a parallel column. It is customary to date reversing entries as of the first business day of the new accounting period.

Adjusting Entries			Reversing Entries	
Bad debts..............	300			
Allowance for doubtful accounts......		300		
Factory supplies expense.	2,070			
Factory supplies....		2,070		
Insurance expense.......	975			
Unexpired insurance		975		
Depreciation—Factory buildings.............	2,600			
Accumulated depreciation—Factory buildings........		2,600		
Depreciation—Machinery and equipment.......	4,788			
Accumulated depreciation—Machinery and equipment		4,788		
Depreciation—Office equipment...........	314			
Accumulated depreciation—Office equipment.......		314		
Interest expense—Bonds.	250			
Discount on bonds..		250		
Rent collected in advance	50			
Rent earned........		50		
Accrued interest on notes receivable...........	45		Interest earned—Notes receivable	45
Interest earned—Notes receivable..		45	Accrued interest on notes receivable................	45
Interest expense—Notes payable.............	20		Accrued interest on notes payable.	20
Accrued interest on notes payable.....		20	Interest expense—Notes payable....................	20
Federal income tax......	13,600			
Federal income tax payable..........		13,600		

The reasons why some of the adjusting entries are not reversed are:

Bad debts and depreciation:
  Since the Allowance for Doubtful Accounts and the accumulated depreciation accounts are contras to the related asset accounts, the adjusting entries for bad debts and depreciation are not reversed.

Other cost apportionments—Factory supplies used, expired insurance, and bond discount amortized:
>Since the original charges were made to asset or deferred
charge accounts, the adjusting entries are not reversed.

Revenue apportionment—Rent collected in advance:
>Since the original credit was made to an unearned revenue
account, the adjusting entry is not reversed.

Accrued federal income tax:
>Since the liability account is customarily debited when the
tax is paid, the adjusting entry is not reversed.

CHAPTER THREE

Financial Statements

The statements in this chapter are based on the working papers of The Ingram Manufacturing Company in Chapter 2.

THE INGRAM MANUFACTURING COMPANY   Exhibit D
Statement of Cost of Goods Manufactured
For the Year Ended December 31, 1959

Materials:

Inventory—December 31, 1958.......................... $ 6,325

Cost of purchases:

    Purchases.................................. $54,630

    Deduct:

        Purchase returns and allowances.......... $425

        Purchase discounts..................... 675   1,100

      Net.................................... $53,530

    Freight in.................................. 1,200   54,730

Total inventory and purchases............................ $ 61,055

Deduct inventory—December 31, 1959..................... 9,923

    Materials used.. $ 51,132

Direct labor... 65,805

Manufacturing overhead:

    Indirect labor.................................... $14,260

    Heat, light, and power—Factory................... 8,920

    Repairs to buildings and machinery................ 635

    Factory supplies expense.......................... 2,070

    Insurance expense................................ 910

    Property taxes.................................... 896

    Depreciation—Factory buildings................... 2,600

    Depreciation—Machinery and equipment........... 4,788

    Miscellaneous factory expenses.................... 3,700   38,779

Total manufacturing cost................................... $155,716

Add goods in process—December 31, 1958..................... 8,120

Total.. $163,836

Deduct goods in process—December 31, 1959................. 13,212

Cost of goods manufactured................................ $150,624

THE INGRAM MANUFACTURING COMPANY   Exhibit C
Income Statement
For the Year Ended December 31, 1959

Gross sales...			$228,625
Deduct:			
Sales returns and allowances.............................	$ 1,315		
Sales discounts..	1,617	2,932	
Net sales..			$225,693
Deduct cost of goods sold:			
Finished goods inventory—December 31, 1958..............	$ 12,400		
Add cost of goods manufactured—Exhibit D...............	150,624		
Total..	$163,024		
Deduct finished goods inventory—December 31, 1959........	10,991	152,033	
Gross profit on sales..			$ 73,660
Deduct operating expenses:			
Selling expenses:			
Advertising......................................	$7,320		
Salesmen's salaries..............................	8,000		
Salesmen's traveling expenses....................	4,100		
Freight out......................................	850		
Stationery and printing expense..................	83		
Miscellaneous selling expenses..................	875	$ 21,228	
General expenses:			
Officers' salaries...............................	$6,500		
Office salaries..................................	4,200		
Office supplies expense..........................	312		
Stationery and printing expense..................	332		
Bad debts..	300		
Insurance expense................................	65		
Depreciation—Office equipment...................	314		
Property taxes...................................	64		
Miscellaneous general expenses..................	561	12,648	33,876
Net operating income...			$ 39,784
Other expenses:			
Interest expense—Bonds..........................	$3,250		
Interest expense—Notes payable..................	430	$ 3,680	
Other revenue:			
Dividends on Murdock stock......................	$ 400		
Interest earned—Notes receivable.................	186		
Rent earned.....................................	50	636	3,044
Net income before income tax......................................			$ 36,740
Federal income tax..			13,600
Net income..			$ 23,140

THE INGRAM MANUFACTURING COMPANY   Exhibit B
Statement of Retained Earnings
For the Year Ended December 31, 1959

Retained earnings—December 31, 1958........................		$18,714
Add net income for the year—Exhibit C......................		23,140
Total..		$41,854
Deduct dividends:		
Common...	$6,000	
Preferred..	2,400	8,400
Retained earnings—December 31, 1959........................		$33,454

THE INGRAM MANUFACTURING COMPANY   Exhibit A
Balance Sheet
December 31, 1959
Assets

Current assets:

Cash		$ 27,600
Marketable securities—at the lower of cost or market		10,000
Accounts receivable	$35,365	
Less allowance for doubtful accounts	950	34,415
Notes receivable		6,000
Accrued interest on notes receivable		45
Inventories—at the lower of cost or market:		
Finished goods	$10,991	
Goods in process	13,212	
Materials	9,923	34,126
Factory supplies		350
Unexpired insurance		400
Total current assets		$112,936
Stock of Murdock Sales Company—at cost		5,000
Fixed assets:		
Land—at cost		$ 23,000
Factory buildings—at cost	$65,000	
Less accumulated depreciation	17,100	47,900
Machinery and equipment—at cost	$53,900	
Less accumulated depreciation	18,388	35,512
Office equipment—at cost	$ 3,140	
Less accumulated depreciation	1,064	2,076
Total fixed assets		108,488
Deferred charges:		
Discount on bonds		2,250
		$228,674

Liabilities and Stockholders' Equity

Current liabilities:

Accounts payable		$ 4,000
Notes payable		5,000
Federal income tax payable		13,600
Accrued interest on notes payable		20
Rent collected in advance		100
Total current liabilities		$ 22,720
Long-term liabilities:		
Real estate mortgage bonds payable—6%—due		
December 31, 1968		50,000
Total liabilities		$ 72,720
Stockholders' equity:		
Capital stock—$100 par value:		
Preferred—6% cumulative; authorized, 500 shares;		
issued, 400 shares	$40,000	
Common—authorized and issued, 750 shares	75,000	$115,000
Premium on common stock		7,500
Retained earnings—Exhibit B		33,454
Total stockholders' equity		155,954
		$228,674

Note: At the balance sheet date the company was contingently liable on notes receivable discounted in the amount of $2,000.

Bases of balance sheet valuations.   Many people who have little knowledge of accounting probably think that the amounts shown in a balance sheet are determined with the precision of pure mathematics, on the basis of immediately realizable market values of assets and definitely ascertainable liabilities. Accountants know that such ideas are incorrect; that realizable market value is not, in general, the conventional basis of accounting for assets; and that asset valuations and liability amounts are very often based on estimates.

A few assets are stated in the balance sheet at actual present realizable values. This presumably is the case with cash on hand and in domestic banks, and presumably should be (but not always is) the case with short-term marketable investments when the market value is less than cost.

In a few other cases, assets may be stated at estimated realizable values; for instance, the creation of an allowance for doubtful accounts is presumed to produce such a net valuation in the case of receivables.

Inventories are not valued at actual, or even estimated, realizable values, even when the "cost or market" rule is applied. The cost or market rule does give some recognition to market values, but only to decreases therein. Moreover, "market" refers to replacement price and not to selling price. The realizable value of an inventory to a going concern presumably would be more than cost or market, and its realizable value to a concern in liquidation might be less than cost or market, since losses probably could be expected.

Fixed assets, current expense prepayments, and long-term deferred charges usually are carried in the accounts in accordance with accounting principles or conventions which are not concerned with currently realizable values but are concerned with the equitable absorption of costs by charges to operations over the periods of utilization.

Since the assets are not all valued at actual, or even estimated, realizable values, and since estimates have so much effect on asset and liability accounts, the amount shown in the balance sheet as the proprietorship equity cannot be regarded as representing "net worth" in the sense of an amount which would be distributable to the owners upon immediate disposal of the assets and payment of the liabilities.

Balance sheet classifications.   The classifications used in a balance sheet depend upon the nature of the business and the nature of the items appearing in the balance sheet. The classifications mentioned on the following page are typical, but others are sometimes used.

ASSET SIDE

Current assets:

The rules determining the classification of assets as current are stated later in the chapter.

Sundry assets:

Stocks, bonds, and other securities not representing temporary investments properly classified as current assets.

Any assets, such as sinking funds, land held for plant expansion, and abandoned plant held for disposal, which do not fall into the other classifications.

Fixed assets:

Property of a relatively permanent nature, used in the operation of the business and not intended for sale. Tangible and intangible fixed assets may be separately classified.

Deferred charges:

Charges to be included in the determination of net income of subsequent periods covering a time span in excess of an operating cycle—a concept, discussed on page 50, that serves as a major criterion for the classification of assets as current.

LIABILITY AND OWNERS' EQUITY SIDE

Current liabilities:

The rules determining the classification of liabilities as current are stated later in the chapter.

Long-term liabilities:

Bonds, mortgages, and other debts not maturing in the near future.

Deferred credits:

Credits to be included in the determination of net income of subsequent periods covering a time span in excess of an operating cycle.

Owners' equity:

The proprietorship interest.

Current assets and current liabilities. In its Bulletin No. 30, issued in 1947, and slightly revised in Bulletin No. 43, issued in

1953, the Institute's Committee on Accounting Procedure made some important recommendations with respect to definitions of current assets and current liabilities.* There were three principal reasons why such a bulletin was needed.

First, confusion existed because accountants had been unable to make a unanimous choice between the two following conflicting definitions:

> Current assets consist of cash and other assets which presumably *will be* converted into cash in the near future (generally regarded as a year) *as a result of* regular operations.
>
> Current assets consist of cash and other assets which presumably *can be* converted into cash in the near future (generally regarded as a year) *without interference with* the regular operations.

The second definition was considerably more inclusive than the first. For instance, the cash surrender value of life insurance, although immediately available, was not a current asset under the first definition, because life insurance is not purchased for the purpose of being converted into cash. But the cash surrender value was a current asset under the second definition, since it could be converted into cash without interference with the regular operations.

Second, both of the old definitions were often challenged because current expense prepayments, such as unexpired insurance, were excluded. From the standpoint of a going concern, what essential difference in current position exists on December 31st between a company which used cash in December to buy insurance and another company which will use cash in January for the same purpose? From a liquidating standpoint, to be sure, there is a difference. In the past, when bankers were primarily concerned with the "pounce" possibilities, and were therefore primarily interested in knowing how quickly their loans could be collected from the proceeds of forced liquidation, the liquidating concept strongly influenced accountants in their definition of current assets. But creditors are coming to give more consideration to a debtor's ability to pay as a going concern.

Third, the old one-year rule or convention was somewhat arbitrary and was not consistently applied. It was arbitrary because it gave no consideration to the fact that one concern might convert its merchandise to cash several times a year, whereas

---

* Such bulletins are often referred to as *A.R.B. 30* or *A.R.B. 43*, the initials standing for *Accounting Research Bulletin*.

another concern might require considerably more than a year to make one such conversion. It was not consistently applied because assets were sometimes included in the current classification although they would not be converted into cash within twelve months. For instance, under the one-year rule, materials should not have been included in current assets unless within a year the materials would be converted into finished goods, the finished goods would be sold, and the resulting receivables would be collected. But accountants sometimes took the inconsistent position of excluding from current assets those receivables which would not mature within a year, while including the total of all inventories in the current assets.

The one-year rule was also arbitrary when applied to liabilities. Just why should a debt which matures in eleven and a half months be included in current liabilities, and a debt which matures in twelve and a half months be excluded?

The operating cycle concept. The Institute bulletin recommends that the "operating cycle" be recognized as a concept of major importance in the determination of working capital. Operations consist of a round of conversions—cash to inventories and prepaid expenses, to receivables, to cash. The average time required to complete this round is referred to in the bulletin as the "operating cycle."

Bulletin No. 43 states that: "A one-year time period is to be used as a basis for the segregation of current assets in cases where there are several operating cycles occurring within a year. However, where the period of the operating cycle is more than twelve months, as in, for instance, the tobacco, distillery, and lumber businesses, the longer period should be used. Where a particular business has no clearly defined operating cycle, the one-year rule should govern."

What assets are current? The bulletin says that the following assets are properly regarded as current:

Cash available for current operations.

Inventories, including supplies.

Trade receivables.

Receivables from officers, employees, affiliates, and others, if collectible in the ordinary course of business within a year from the balance sheet date.

Installment and deferred receivables, if due in accordance with terms prevailing throughout the industry.

Temporary investments.

Prepaid current expenses.

The bulletin mentions the following as items that should not be regarded as current assets:

Cash not available for current operations because segregated or required for the acquisition of noncurrent assets or the payment of noncurrent debts.

Long-term investments or advances.

Receivables arising from nonoperating transactions and not expected to be collected within twelve months.

Cash surrender value of life insurance.

Fixed assets.

Long-term deferred charges, such as bond discount.

What liabilities are current?   The bulletin states:

"The term *current liabilities* is used principally to designate obligations whose liquidation is reasonably expected to require the use of existing resources properly classifiable as current assets, or the creation of other current liabilities. As a balance-sheet category, the classification is intended to include obligations for items which have entered into the operating cycle, such as payables incurred in the acquisition of materials and supplies to be used in the production of goods or in providing services to be offered for sale; collections received in advance of the delivery of goods or performance of services; and debts which arise from operations directly related to the operating cycle, such as accruals for wages, salaries, commissions, rentals, royalties, and income and other taxes. Other liabilities whose regular and ordinary liquidation is expected to occur within a relatively short period of time, usually twelve months, are also intended for inclusion, such as short-term debts arising from the acquisition of capital assets, serial maturities of long-term obligations, amounts required to be expended within one year under sinking fund provisions, and agency obligations arising from the collection or acceptance of cash or other assets for the account of third persons.

"This concept of current, liabilities would include estimated or accrued amounts which are expected to be required to cover expenditures within the year for known obligations (a) the amount of which can be determined only approximately (as in the case of provisions for accruing bonus payments) or (b) where the specific person or persons to whom payment will be made cannot as yet be designated (as in the case of estimated costs to be incurred in connection with guaranteed servicing or repair of products already sold). The current liability classification, however, is not intended to include a contractual obligation falling due at an early date which is expected to be refunded, or debts to be liquidated by funds which have been accumulated in accounts of a type not properly classified as current assets, or long-term obligations incurred to provide increased amounts of working capital for long periods . . . "

Alternative Statement Forms

Statement of cost of goods sold. The statement of cost of goods manufactured may be extended, by including the finished goods inventories, to show the cost of goods sold. This figure (instead of the cost of goods manufactured) is then carried to the income statement.

THE INGRAM MANUFACTURING COMPANY   Exhibit D

Statement of Cost of Goods Sold

For the Year Ended December 31, 1959

Cost of goods manufactured:			
Materials:			
Cost of purchases:			
Purchases			$ 54,630
Deduct:			
Purchase returns and allowances	$	425	
Purchase discounts		675	1,100
Net			$ 53,530
Freight in			1,200
Total			$ 54,730
Deduct increase in materials inventory:			
December 31, 1959	$ 9,923		
December 31, 1958	6,325		3,598
Materials used			$ 51,132
Direct labor			65,805
Manufacturing overhead:			
Indirect labor		$14,260	
Heat, light, and power—Factory		8,920	
Repairs to buildings and machinery		635	
Factory supplies expense		2,070	
Insurance expense		910	
Property taxes		896	
Depreciation—Factory buildings		2,600	
Depreciation—Machinery and equipment		4,788	
Miscellaneous factory expenses		3,700	
Total manufacturing overhead			38,779
Total manufacturing cost			$155,716
Deduct increase in goods in process inventory:			
December 31, 1959		$13,212	
December 31, 1958		8,120	5,092
Cost of goods manufactured			$150,624
Add decrease in finished goods inventory:			
December 31, 1958		$12,400	
December 31, 1959		10,991	1,409
Cost of goods sold			$152,033

Slight modifications are necessary in the working papers. Referring to pages 26–28, the heading of the third pair of columns would be Cost of Goods Sold; the finished goods inventories at the beginning and end of the period would be entered in these columns; and the balance transferred to the Income Statement columns would be the cost of goods sold. On page 31, the heading would be Cost of Goods Sold Working Papers; the caption of the last pair of columns would be Cost of Goods Sold; the finished goods inventories would be entered in the working papers; and the balance carried forward would be the cost of goods sold.

The statement on page 52 also illustrates the procedure of dealing with inventories by the "variation" method.

Condensed statements. Condensed statements can be prepared showing totals of related items, supported by schedules, as illustrated below.

THE INGRAM MANUFACTURING COMPANY   Exhibit C

Income Statement

For the Year Ended December 31, 1959

Gross sales..		$228,625
Deduct:		
Sales returns and allowances........................	$ 1,315	
Sales discounts......................................	1,617	2,932
Net sales..		$225,693
Deduct cost of goods sold—Exhibit D (Page 52)...............		152,033
Gross profit on sales..		$ 73,660
Deduct operating expenses—Schedule 1:		
Selling...	$21,228	
General...	12,648	33,876
Net operating income...		$ 39,784
Deduct other expense and revenue—net—Schedule 2..........		3,044
Net income before income tax................................		$ 36,740
Deduct federal income tax....................................		13,600
Net income..		$ 23,140

THE INGRAM MANUFACTURING COMPANY   Exhibit C

Schedule of Selling and General Expenses   Schedule 1

For the Year Ended December 31, 1959

Selling expenses:	
Advertising...	$ 7,320
Salesmen's salaries...................................	8,000
Salesmen's traveling expenses.........................	4,100
Freight out...	850
Stationery and printing expense.......................	83
Miscellaneous selling expenses........................	875
Total..	$21,228
General expenses:	
Officers' salaries....................................	$ 6,500
Office salaries.......................................	4,200
Office supplies expense...............................	312
Stationery and printing expense.......................	332
Bad debts...	300
Insurance expense.....................................	65
Property taxes..	64
Depreciation—Office equipment.........................	314
Miscellaneous general expenses........................	561
Total..	$12,648

THE INGRAM MANUFACTURING COMPANY   Exhibit C
Schedule of Other Revenue and Expense   Schedule 2
For the Year Ended December 31, 1959

Expense:
Bond interest, including amortization of discount........ $3,250
Interest on notes payable............................ ..   430
  Total... $3,680
Revenue:
Dividends on Murdock stock......................... $ 400
Interest earned—Notes receivable.....................   186
Rent earned...   50
  Total..   636
Net expense... $3,044

Combined statement of income and retained earnings.

To show all of the causes of the change in retained earnings during
the period in one statement, a combined statement of income and
retained earnings may be prepared. The income statement items
may be shown in detail, as on page 45, or condensed, as below.

THE INGRAM MANUFACTURING COMPANY
Statement of Income and Retained Earnings
For the Year Ended December 31, 1959

Gross sales... $228,625
Deduct:
Sales returns and allowances...................... $ 1,315
Sales discounts................................   1,617   2,932
Net sales... $225,693
Deduct cost of goods sold—Exhibit D (Page 52)..............   152,033
Gross profit on sales....................................... $ 73,660
Deduct operating expenses—Schedule 1:
Selling... $21,228
General..   12,648   33,876
Net operating income....................................... $ 39,784
Deduct other expense and revenue—net—Schedule 2...........   3,044
Net income before income tax.............................. $ 36,740
Deduct federal income tax.................................   13,600
Net income... $ 23,140
Add retained earnings—December 31, 1958...................   18,714
Total... $ 41,854
Deduct dividends:
Common...................................... $ 6,000
Preferred.......................................   2,400   8,400
Retained earnings—December 31, 1959...................... $ 33,454

Alternative Treatment of Certain Statement Items

There have been some differences of opinion about the proper
location of certain items in the operating statements. These are
discussed on the three following pages.

Purchase discounts. Traditionally, cash discounts on purchases were shown in the income statement as an item of other income. Current practice generally recognizes that, from the standpoint of accounting theory, cash discounts on purchases should be deducted from purchases to arrive at cost. It is a basic principle of accounting that profits are not made on purchases. A company cannot earn income merely by making purchases and taking the discounts, without making a sale.

The nature of purchase discounts as related to cost rather than as an earning would be more obvious if it were customary to invoice goods at the net price, with an addition representing a supplementary charge or penalty for late payment. A purchase would then be recorded by a debit to Purchases and a credit to an account payable at the net price; if payment was made within the non-penalty period, the payment would be recorded by a debit to the account payable and a credit to Cash. If payment was made after the non-penalty period, it would be recorded by a debit to the account payable, a debit to some account such as Discounts Lost, or Late Payment Penalties, and a credit to Cash. Accounts are sometimes kept in this way, even with the present system of billing. If they are kept in the customary manner, it is still possible to show the balance of the Purchase Discounts account as a deduction from purchases in the operating statement.

However, there is a matter of consistency to consider. If purchase discounts are shown in the operating statement as a deduction from purchases, complete consistency would require that perpetual or physical inventories be priced at the net amounts after deduction of discounts. This immediately raises a question of accounting expediency. Assume that 1,000 articles are purchased at $.69 each, or a total of $690, subject to a cash discount of 1½%; this would make the net price of the invoice $679.65, and the unit price $.67965. But the use of such net prices for all inventory items would add materially to the work of the accounting department. It would be necessary to compute the net price of every item on every invoice subject to a cash discount, and perpetual or physical inventory computations would have to be made at prices carried to extended decimal fractions of a cent.

The pricing of inventories at gross unit prices, in order to avoid this work, must be recognized as a departure from accounting principles because income is anticipated to the extent of the discounts on goods in the inventory; but the violation of principle can probably be considered of minor consequence. So far as the operating statement is concerned, the anticipations of income at the beginning and end of the period tend to offset each other, and the net income for the period is misstated to only a minor degree. The departure from principle has a greater effect on the balance sheet; but, considering the low rates of cash discount usually offered, the overstatement of the inventory can perhaps be regarded as of insufficient consequence to justify insistence upon the accounting principle at the expense of inconvenience and added work.

Cash discounts on sales. Cash discounts on sales are sometimes shown in the operating statement as miscellaneous expense, and sometimes as direct deductions from sales. The effect on income is the same, and the only accounting principle involved is the principle of consistency. If discounts on purchases are shown as a deduction from purchases, discounts on sales should be shown as deductions from sales. If discounts on purchases are shown as miscellaneous income, discounts on sales should be shown as miscellaneous expense.

Transportation charges on purchases. Transportation charges on purchases are undoubtedly an addition to the cost of purchases, and should be so shown in statements. To be consistent it would be necessary to include the transportation cost in the inventory valuation. But, since it often is difficult to apportion transportation costs to various items in the inventory, the transportation costs frequently are excluded from the inventory valuation although they are added to the purchases in the operating statements. However, if freight charges are a substantial portion of the cost incurred in acquiring inventoriable goods, such as coal and steel, the accountant presumably will insist on the inclusion of freight charges in the determination of cost for inventory purposes.

Transportation charges on sales. Different opinions are held regarding this item, as follows:

(1) Such charges are a selling expense because they are an expense incident to the disposal of goods.

(2) Transportation charges on sales, like sales returns and allowances, should be deducted from gross sales in the determination of net sales. Those who hold this view maintain that, if it is a regular practice of the seller to pay the transportation charges, the price is raised sufficiently to include them; hence they should be deducted from the sales to determine the price received for the merchandise. On the other hand, if it is not the custom of the seller to pay the transportation charges, any concessions on this point to a few customers or in a few instances are virtually a reduction of the sales price.

It seems to the authors that the first opinion is the better, and that transportation out should be considered a selling expense. The fact that the price should be high enough to include such charges does not seem a conclusive argument for deducting them from the sales, since the selling price should be high enough to cover all expenses. If occasional concessions are given, transportation out seems to be all the more clearly a selling expense. Of course, if the price quoted on shipments f.o.b. destination is higher than that on shipments f.o.b. shipping point, transportation out is a logical deduction from sales.

Bad debts.　The following opinions are held with respect to the classification of bad debts:

(1) Bad debts are a selling expense because they result from sales.
(2) Bad debts are a general or administrative expense because the granting of credit is usually a function of the administrative department of the business.
(3) Bad debts are a direct deduction from sales.

It has long been the custom to show bad debts in the income statement as an expense rather than as a direct deduction from sales. If they are to be so treated, it seems to the authors that they should be charged to the department which supervises the granting of credit. If the sales department passes on credit, bad debt losses should be considered a selling expense. If the general administrative department supervises credit, the loss should be classified as a general expense.

Some accountants have advocated showing bad debts as a direct deduction from sales, on the theory that such losses represent revenues which did not materialize rather than expense outlays.

Importance of disclosure.　Increasing emphasis is being placed on the importance of full disclosure of significant information. This is a logical development, in view of the increasing use being made of financial statements for investment, regulatory, and other business purposes.

The capital of corporations is now provided, in large measure, by stockholders who take no active part in the management of the business and are not intimately acquainted with its affairs. Therefore, published financial statements should provide the stockholders with the information they need in order to arrive at an informed opinion about the conduct of the business by the management to which they have delegated authority and entrusted their investments. A stockholder should be able to rely on such reports in reaching a decision as to whether he will keep his stock or sell it; and a person who is considering purchasing the stock of a company should be able to rely on its reports in making his decision. For these reasons, it is important that accountants make clear and complete disclosure of significant information.

Article (5) of the Rules of Professional Conduct of The American Institute of Certified Public Accountants has the following to say with respect to disclosure:

> "In expressing an opinion on representations in financial statements which he has examined, a member may be held guilty of an act discreditable to the profession if
>
> "(a) he fails to disclose a material fact known to him which is not disclosed in the financial statements but disclosure of which is necessary to make the financial statements not misleading; or
>
> "(b) he fails to report any material misstatement known to him to appear in the financial statement; or
>
> . . . .
>
> "(e) he fails to direct attention to any material departure from generally accepted accounting principles or to disclose any material omission of generally accepted auditing procedure applicable in the circumstances."

The Securities and Exchange Commission also is insistent upon adequate disclosure of material and significant information, and numerous deficiencies have been cited by the Commission because of failure to make disclosure or because disclosure was inadequate.

The matters which may require disclosure can be classified into two general groups:

(1) Facts applicable to the statements showing the results of operations during a period and the financial position at the end of a period.

(2) Information relative to subsequent events or prospective events.

Some of these matters are mentioned in the following paragraphs. It is not always practicable to make disclosure in the body of a statement; in such cases, disclosure may be made in footnotes appended to the statements or in comments accompanying the statements in an audit report.

Matters applicable to the statements. Bare-bone statements consisting merely of account titles and balances will rarely give a clear and complete picture of the results of operations during a period and the financial position at the end thereof. Some matters which may require disclosure, either in the body of the statement or in the accompanying opinion, footnotes, or comments, are mentioned below:

If there has been any departure from consistency in the accounting principles applied, the nature of the inconsistency should be clearly stated, as well as the dollar effect thereof on the statements, if the effect is material and determinable.

If changes in classifications may result in misleading comparisons of current and preceding statements, the changes should be disclosed if the effect is consequential. If comparative statements are prepared, reclassifications should be made in the prior statements to conform with the current classifications, or the inconsistency should be disclosed.

There should be disclosure of mortgaged, or otherwise pledged, assets and the liabilities secured thereby.

Any cash not subject to unrestricted withdrawal should be separately stated.

Receivables from stockholders, directors, officers, and employees should be separately stated, unless they arose from ordinary trade transactions and are collectible in accordance with the customary trade terms; even in that case, it is preferable to distinguish them from accounts with ordinary trade debtors, if they are of material amount.

Receivables from subsidiaries or other affiliated companies should be shown separately even though they arose from trade transactions.

Deposits as security or guarantees, and advances to suppliers for future delivery of merchandise, should be separately shown.

Notes and accounts receivable maturing later than one year from the balance sheet date, including installment receivables, should be segregated unless such a treatment is impracticable or contrary to trade practice.

Inventories should be detailed, and the bases of valuation (such as *at the lower of cost or market,* or *cost on a first-in, first-out basis*) should be stated.

The valuation basis of securities owned should be disclosed. If the securities represent temporary investments of funds and are therefore classified as current assets, they should be shown in the balance sheet at market value if market is lower than cost. If they represent long-term investments, they may be carried in the accounts and shown in the balance sheet at cost, regardless of minor decreases in market value; but if the market value is materially less than cost, the investment should be written down or the market value should be shown parenthetically, the choice depending on such factors as (a) the seriousness of the market decline and (b) the reason for holding the investment—for instance, if the investment consists of stock acquired for the purpose of maintaining a desirable material purchase or finished goods sale relationship, there seems to be no necessity for anticipating a loss that there is no prospect of incurring.

Fixed assets should be detailed. The basis of valuation (cost, cost less depreciation, appraisal value, or other) should be indicated. If the fixed assets are shown at appraised values, the basis of the appraisal (such as replacement cost new less depreciation thereon) and the date thereof should be stated. It is also desirable to tell who made the appraisal, as an indication of the independence and reliability of the appraisers.

Intangible fixed assets, such as patents, franchises, and goodwill, should be detailed.

Prepayments of current expenses should be distinguished from long-term deferred charges, and amortization procedures applicable to deferred charges should be described unless they are obvious.

Current liabilities payable to affiliated companies, as well as those payable to stockholders, directors, officers, and employees, should be set out separately if material in amount.

If estimates of liabilities are subject to considerable uncertainty, the amount stated should be indicated to be an estimate. If the amount of a tax or other liability is in dispute, adequate provision should be made or the facts should be stated in a footnote.

Currently maturing installments of long-term liabilities should be included in current liabilities. If the entire amount of a long-term liability is due within a year, it should be included in current liabilities unless a program of refunding is in prospect; in that case, the reason for excluding the debt from current liabilities should be stated.

It is not sufficient to show merely the amounts of long-term debts. There should also be disclosure of any bonds or other evidences of indebtedness authorized but not issued, the interest rate, the maturity, whether in installments or otherwise, and any sinking fund or other requirements for debt retirement. There should be disclosure of any defaults in interest, principal, or sinking fund payments.

Each class of capital stock should be shown separately. There should be disclosure of the par value per share, or, in the case of no-par stock, the stated or assigned value, if any. There should also be disclosure of the numbers of shares authorized, issued, in treasury, and outstanding. The preferred dividend rate, cumulative and participating rights, and redemption and liquidating prices should be shown. If there are any outstanding purchase options or warrants, or if one class of stock is convertible into another class, or if any class of stock is callable, these facts should be disclosed.

Treasury stock should be shown in the Stockholders' Equity section of the balance sheet as a deduction from capital stock, from retained earnings, or from the total thereof, as the laws of the state of incorporation or other considerations may indicate to be proper.

The balance sheet should state separately any (a) retained earnings, (b) paid-in surplus, and (c) unrealized increments in asset values shown by recorded appraisals. The changes in the various elements of stockholders' equity during the period should be accounted for. If any stock dividends have been distributed during the period, this fact should be clearly stated. There should be a disclosure of any restrictions on retained earnings, such as those in state laws which limit dividend payments to the amount of retained earnings in excess of the cost of treasury stock, or those which arise from agreements made in connection with the incurring of liabilities.

There should be an adequate description of any significant contingent liabilities not covered by insurance or provided for in the accounts, such as judgments and pending law suits, notes receivable discounted, and claims for damages. There should be disclosure of any preferred dividends in arrears; any commitments for purchases if the amounts thereof are significant or if there is a prospect that the market price may decline, after the balance sheet date, below the commitment price; any contracts for the construction or acquisition of fixed assets; and any commitments on long-term leases. There should be a statement of the date to which federal income tax returns have been examined.

The income statement should show the gross, or at least the net, sales; it should not begin with gross profit unless the disclosure of sales volume would be detrimental from the standpoint of competition. The statement should indicate whether profits on installment sales are taken into income in the period of sale, or proportionately to collections. It is desirable to show the amounts of depreciation, depletion, and amortization for the period, and any extraordinary expenses of material amount charged to operations.

Subsequent events and prospects.   The primary function of accounting statements is to report the results of operations during a period and the financial position at the end of a period. The accountant is not a prophet, and he should never assume the position of forecasting the future. But, at the same time, he must recognize that the statements he renders are likely to be used as indications of probable future earnings and probable future financial position. He is under certain obligation, therefore, to disclose matters occurring after the balance sheet date but before the year-end statements are completed and released which materially affect the operating results or financial position portrayed by the financial statements. Such matters might include:

The purchase, sale, or destruction of a plant, or the destruction of inventories.

A material decline in the market value of inventories or investments.

The expiration of a patent which had given the company a virtual monopoly in the sale of one of its principal products.

The settlement of income tax liabilities of prior periods.

The settlement of a law suit, adversely or favorably, which was pending at the balance sheet date.

The institution of important legal proceedings by or against the company.

A material change in the capital structure resulting from an issuance, retirement, or conversion of stock, a stock split-up, or a stock dividend.

The accountant may also be under obligation to disclose contemplated actions which might have a material effect on the financial position or the profitability of operations, such as a proposed reorganization, refinancing, or change in plant, product, or management. But in this realm of the possible, the accountant should tread cautiously. The mere fact that an action is under consideration is rarely sufficient reason for disclosure; contemplation must usually have reached the point of decision.

Recent Trends in Published Statements

Importance of clarity in published statements.   Financial statements are receiving increasing attention from management, credit grantors, stockholders, governmental agencies, and the general public. They provide a basis for the formulation of many business decisions. Financial statements also serve as a device by which management reports on its accountability for, or stewardship of, the properties placed under its control.

With regard to published statements—those released to stockholders and the general public—the accountant is naturally interested in designing statements which will minimize misunderstandings by persons or groups of persons who are entitled to receive the statements and who make a sincere effort to understand them. This concern on the part of the accountant has caused him to consider whether the use of technical accounting terminology may cause misunderstanding, particularly in those cases where accounting has adopted terms found in our general vocabulary and has attached special meanings to them. The words *reserve* and *surplus* are cases in point.

Similarly, accountants recognize the possibility that conventional statement forms, while logical to a trained accountant, may not be as effective as less conventional forms in giving the nonaccountant information about the financial position of a business and the results of its operations.

These considerations have led many corporations to experiment with alternative statements and alternative terminology. Some of these alternatives are illustrated in the remainder of this chapter.

Notes accompanying the published statements shown in this chapter have been omitted because the objective is merely to illustrate statement forms.

Single-step income statements. The income statements previously shown are multiple-step statements—so-called because costs and expenses are deducted, and certain income items are added, in such a manner as to show remainders such as gross profit on sales, net operating income, and net income. The single-step statement presents all items of revenue and income at the top, with a total thereof; all costs and expenses are then shown, and their total is deducted to determine the net income. No intermediate balances, such as gross profit, are shown. An illustration of a single-step statement, from the annual report of Corning Glass Works, appears on the following page.

CONSOLIDATED STATEMENT OF INCOME

	Year Ending	
	December 30 1956	January 1 1956
SALES, less discounts, returns and allowances	$163,053,554	$157,663,837
DIVIDENDS AND OTHER INCOME	3,832,717	3,574,689
	166,886,271	161,238,526
COSTS AND EXPENSES (Note 8):		
Cost of goods sold	109,015,676	102,830,612
Selling, general and administrative expenses	14,638,269	13,409,574
Research and development expenses	4,792,272	5,319,275
Interest and other charges	707,301	782,394
Federal taxes on income	18,900,000	19,900,000
State income taxes	400,000	370,000
	148,453,518	142,611,855
NET INCOME FOR PERIOD	$ 18,432,753	$ 18,626,671

The advocates of the single-step statement present the following arguments in its favor:

The multiple-step statement implies that some costs and expenses take precedence over others as deductions from revenues, and that "profits" remain after each deduction. This implication, they maintain, is fallacious; all costs and expenses rank alike as deductions from income, and there is no "profit" until all costs and expenses have been deducted.

By listing miscellaneous income after the deduction of selling and general expenses, the statement carries the erroneous implication that such income is earned without the incurring of any expense.

The subtotals and titles in the multiple-step statement have no universally recognized meaning.

The single-step statement is simple and easy to understand.

Combined single-step income and retained earnings statement. The following statement of Caterpillar Tractor Co. is an illustration of a combined single-step income statement and statement of retained earnings.

————————Consolidated Results of Operations Year 1956————————

Sales..$685,939,782

Costs:

Inventories brought forward from previous year......................	$140,842,794	
Materials, supplies, services purchased, etc........................	381,330,023	
Wages, salaries and contributions for employee benefits..............	205,420,430	
Portion of original cost of buildings, machinery and equipment allocated to operations (depreciation and amortization)........................	22,329,174	
Interest on borrowed funds..	1,409,609	
United States and foreign taxes based on income.....................	59,677,274	
	$811,009,304	
Deduct: Inventories carried forward to following year...............	180,473,900	
Costs allocated to year...		630,535,404
Profit for year...		$ 55,404,378

Add:

Profit employed in the business at beginning of year................		96,020,286
		$151,424,664

Deduct:

Dividends paid in cash during year:

Preferred stock—$4.20 per share.....................................	$ 939,750	
Common stock—$1.95 per share..	16,927,742	
		17,867,492
Profit employed in the business at end of year......................		$133,557,172

Showing the working capital. The statement of financial position of Blaw-Knox Company illustrates the increasingly popular procedure of deducting the current liabilities from the current assets to emphasize the working capital.

BLAW-KNOX COMPANY

STATEMENT OF FINANCIAL POSITION
DECEMBER 31, 1956

	1956	1955
CURRENT ASSETS:		
Cash	$12,767,739	$12,604,823
Receivables, less estimated doubtful accounts....	25,900,124	18,147,246
Inventories	69,272,570	34,529,239
Prepaid insurance, taxes, etc.	579,590	661,691
Billings on contracts in progress (deduct).......	(37,196,924)	(9,897,434)
Total current assets	$71,323,099	$56,045,565
CURRENT LIABILITIES:		
Bank loan	$ 6,000,000	$ 7,000,000
Accounts payable—trade	12,797,152	7,661,902
Salaries, wages and other employee compensation	4,812,549	4,282,089
Federal taxes on income and renegotiation......	7,728,402	4,704,620
Long-term debt payable within one year........	425,000	
Other current liabilities	3,991,005	2,633,350
Total current liabilities	$35,754,108	$26,281,961
Working capital	$35,568,991	$29,763,604
LONG-TERM RECEIVABLES, FOREIGN INVESTMENTS AND OTHER ASSETS	1,451,599	1,100,928
PROPERTY, PLANT AND EQUIPMENT	31,795,991	32,725,026
Total assets less current liabilities......	$68,816,581	$63,589,558
LONG-TERM DEBT	20,575,000	21,000,000
Excess of assets over liabilities— Stockholders' equity	$48,241,581	$42,589,558
STOCKHOLDERS' EQUITY		
Capital stock—authorized 3,000,000 shares, $10 par value—Issued, 1,676,114 and 1,569,449 shares	$16,761,140	$15,694,490
Other capital	4,473,493	2,009,713
Undistributed earnings, excluding amounts capitalized ....:	27,006,948	24,885,355
	$48,241,581	$42,589,558

Simplified statements. Some companies present simplified or informal versions of their financial statements in addition, or as supplements, to the conventional variety. The following examples are typical of this practice. The first statement was included in the 1956 report of Chain Belt Company; the second was taken from the report of Parke, Davis & Company for the same year.

Simplified Statements for 1956

RESULTS OF OPERATIONS

THE COMPANY RECEIVED	Amount	Per Dollar of Sales
from customers	$56,772,795	$1.00

THIS MONEY WAS USED FOR:

	Amount	Per Dollar of Sales
Wages, salaries and employee benefits	$22,544,863	$ .40
Materials, supplies and services, and depreciation	26,422,481	.47
	48,967,344	.87
Less increase in inventory during the year	2,737,920	.05
Costs applicable to operations for the year	46,229,424	.82
Income taxes owing to state and federal governments	5,870,000	.10
Dividends paid to stockholders	2,169,510	.04
Retained for use in the business	2,503,861	.04
	$56,772,795	$1.00

FINANCIAL CONDITION

	Amount	Per Share
As a result of these operations, the financial statements at October 31, 1956 showed the Company: Owned cash and U.S. Government Securities of	$ 6,003,700	$ 8.65
Was owed by customers	7,110,751	10.24
Had raw materials, products being manufactured and products ready for sale of	15,084,204	21.72
Had paid in advance for insurance and other expenses	828,284	1.19
Amounting to total current assets of	29,026,939	41.80
Against this the Company owed: To employees for wages and salaries, to suppliers for materials, to stockholders for dividends, etc. ..	4,095,965	5.90
To state governments for income taxes (federal tax liability is covered by U.S. securities)	602,247	.87
Leaving working capital of	24,328,727	35.03
To this add the buildings, machinery, tools and land of	13,623,724	19.62
And other assets of	562,321	.81
Making a total of	38,514,772	55.46
From this deduct the long term debt of	3,637,470	5.24
This is the stockholders' investment in the Company	$34,877,302	$50.22

HOW WE STAND AT THE END OF 1956

		Investment Per Employee	
		1956	1955
WHAT WE OWN			
Cash and marketable securities needed for prompt payment of current obligations and to provide for expansion programs................	$ 42,144,046	$ 4,279	$ 2,911
Due from customers for merchandise delivered and from others for various charges........	20,187,268	2,050	1,823
Recoverable excise taxes..................	511,187	52	59
Invested in inventories and supplies for servicing customer needs................	34,480,458	3,501	3,508
Taxes, insurance, and other expenses paid in advance........................	1,675,161	170	153
Land, buildings, and equipment which originally cost $63,892,484 and against which depreciation in the amount of $24,489,790 has been charged to operations........	39,402,694	4,001	3,957
Sundry other assets.....................	861,591	87	88
	$139,262,405	$14,140	$12,499
WHAT WE OWE			
To employees for wages, salaries, and commissions; to manufacturers for materials purchased; to various governments for taxes other than taxes on income; and to stockholders for dividends.........	$ 15,967,646	$ 1,621	$ 1,445
To United States and foreign governments for taxes on income.............	18,555,024	1,884	1,504
Money borrowed to provide for current requirements in foreign countries.........	1,831,038	186	116
	$ 36,353,708	$ 3,691	$ 3,065
STOCKHOLDERS' INVESTMENT AND SAVINGS			
Balance of total owned less amounts owed, representing the value of the original investment made by stockholders plus accumulated savings...........	$102,908,697	$10,449	$ 9,434

Emphasizing the accountability. The statement of financial condition of Burroughs Corporation is distinctive in that it emphasizes the accountability of management to the stockholders. It states the amount of the stockholders' equity and the sources thereof, as well as the disposition of the investment entrusted to the management. Incidentally, it shows a detailed computation of working capital.

Statement of Financial Condition

	December 31	
	1956	**1955**
STOCKHOLDERS' INVESTMENT		
$5 PAR VALUE COMMON STOCK—7,500,000 shares authorized— issued 6,035,861 shares in 1956; 5,558,366 shares in 1955	$ 30,179,305	$ 27,791,830
ADDITIONAL CAPITAL	9,115,768	3,754,611
INCOME INVESTED IN THE BUSINESS	62,985,968	61,779,145
COST OF SHARES HELD BY THE COMPANY—4,910 shares in 1956; 9,510 shares in 1955	(79,270)	(153,535)
	$102,201,771	$ 93,172,051
USED IN THE BUSINESS AS FOLLOWS		
WORKING CAPITAL:		
Assets required to carry on daily transactions—		
Cash	$ 13,727,808	$ 8,575,276
U.S. and foreign government bonds	1,819,997	1,387,053
Amounts receivable from customers and others, less estimated doubtful accounts	61,916,818	47,937,495
Inventories of purchased materials and finished and partly finished products, less progress billings on uncompleted military contracts	89,071,204	73,784,797
Expenses paid in advance	1,254,981	984,799
CURRENT ASSETS	$167,790,808	$132,669,421
Amounts owing by the companies to meet current obligations—		
Owing on loans to be repaid in one year	$ 10,688,873	$ 2,356,326
Unpaid bills for materials and services	11,574,373	8,702,104
Wages and commissions owing to employees	10,190,410	8,282,346
Estimated income taxes owing to the U.S. and foreign governments	13,349,256	14,122,567
Owing for social security, property and other taxes	4,649,526	3,800,046
Payments by customers for products and services to be delivered in the future	18,749,900	18,015,613
Estimated cost of guaranteed maintenance on machines sold	743,377	554,857
Dividends payable to stockholders in January of following year	1,507,730	1,387,214
CURRENT LIABILITIES	$ 71,453,445	$ 57,221,573
WORKING CAPITAL	$ 96,337,363	$ 75,447,848
COST OF LAND, BUILDINGS, EQUIPMENT AND PATENTS used in connection with the production, sale and lease of products, reduced by the estimated cost of wear and exhaustion (depreciation and amortization)	64,276,761	48,572,252
OTHER ASSETS	1,311,147	351,951
	$161,925,271	$124,372,051
OWING ON LONG-TERM LOANS	59,723,500	31,200,000
	$102,201,771	$ 93,172,051

Graphic presentations. Many companies, in their annual reports, make good use of graphic material as part of their public relations programs.

From the Annual Report of Bates Manufacturing Company

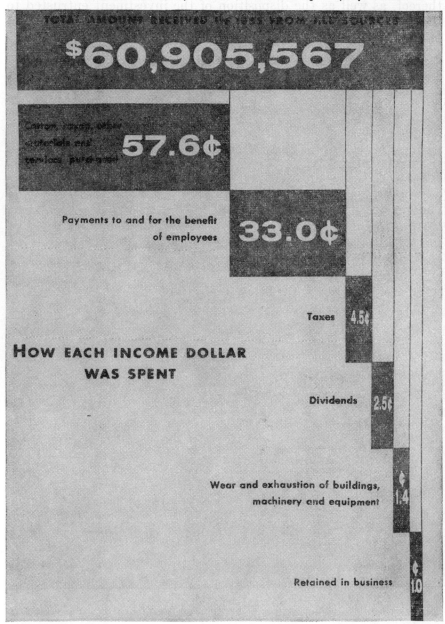

TOTAL AMOUNT RECEIVED IN 1955 FROM ALL SOURCES

$60,905,567

Cotton, rayon, other materials and services purchased 57.6¢

Payments to and for the benefit of employees 33.0¢

Taxes 4.5¢

HOW EACH INCOME DOLLAR WAS SPENT

Dividends 2.5¢

Wear and exhaustion of buildings, machinery and equipment 1.4¢

Retained in business 1.0¢

From the Annual Report of Celanese Corporation of America

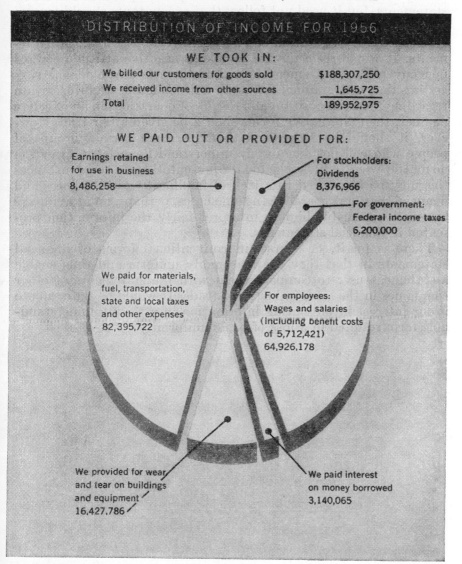

DISTRIBUTION OF INCOME FOR 1956

WE TOOK IN:

We billed our customers for goods sold	$188,307,250
We received income from other sources	1,645,725
Total	189,952,975

WE PAID OUT OR PROVIDED FOR:

Earnings retained
for use in business
8,486,258

For stockholders:
Dividends
8,376,966

For government:
Federal income taxes
6,200,000

We paid for materials,
fuel, transportation,
state and local taxes
and other expenses
82,395,722

For employees:
Wages and salaries
(including benefit costs
of 5,712,421)
64,926,178

We provided for wear
and tear on buildings
and equipment
16,427,786

We paid interest
on money borrowed
3,140,065

Conclusion. If there is any likelihood that the end product of the accounting process is subject to misunderstanding, accountants should be encouraged to explore all possible avenues to avoid such an undesirable condition. However, it may be relevant to note that the desirable policy of avoiding, in published financial statements, terms subject to misunderstanding by members of the general public should not necessarily require that those terms be discarded from the accountant's vocabulary. For instance, it may be sensible to avoid the term *surplus* in published financial statements, but it need not follow that accountants should forever strike *surplus* from their technical terminology.

Much the same position can be taken regarding financial statements. It would seem unwise to take a negative attitude toward nonconventional statement forms. If there is any evidence suggesting that conventional forms do not communicate information regarding financial position and results of operations in an effective manner, then alternative forms should be given a fair trial. However, it should be recognized that there are certain groups of people who will not adequately understand financial information no matter what form is selected for presentation. In some instances this may be attributed to a lack of familiarity with business and financial matters generally. In some cases, perhaps, an individual's bias will not enable him to interpret fairly the information presented in financial statements.

There is merit, of course, in conventional forms of financial statements in that they are reasonably uniform and thus enable a statement user to compare them with the statements of other companies in the same industry or trade. It would be unfortunate if our interest in presenting information in a readily understandable form resulted in a loss of basic uniformity.

CHAPTER FOUR

Net Income Concepts and Corrections of Prior Years' Earnings

Net Income Concepts

A basic problem. In the preparation of financial statements, the accountant may encounter unusual, and presumably nonrecurring, gains and losses and may have to do something about errors made during prior periods which caused the net income of such prior periods to be incorrectly reported. How should these items be dealt with in the financial statements, keeping in mind that the objective of the accountant is always to present meaningful and useful financial statements?

The problem narrows down to the basic question of *what* is properly includible in the computation of net income *for the period?* For instance, is the net income for the period affected by unusual, extraneous, and nonrecurring gains and losses, such as an uninsured flood loss? Is the net income for the current period affected by corrections of income-computation errors of prior periods?

The current operating concept of net income and the all-inclusive (clean surplus) theory. For many years accountants adhered to the current operating concept of net income, believing that corrections of the net income of prior years and unusual, extraneous, and nonrecurring items of income and expense (such as gains and losses resulting from disposals of fixed assets) should be shown in the earned surplus statement. The procedure of showing all such items in the statement of earned surplus was considered desirable because the income statement then showed the results of *regular operations* for the *current period*, unaffected by unusual, extraordinary, or extraneous transactions or by corrections of the income statements of prior years.

During the last two decades, the procedure described in the preceding paragraph has been challenged. A considerable number of accountants question the propriety, or at least the advisability, of showing extraneous gains and losses and corrections of prior years' earnings in the earned surplus statement. They adhere to the clean surplus theory. They believe that, as a matter of pure theory, such items are related to income determination, and that net income for the period would be misstated if they were excluded.

The clean surplus theory. The advocates of this concept maintain that all items of revenue, expense, gain, or loss are necessary factors in determining net income. They believe, and in fact urge, that extraordinary and correction items should be included (properly described and segregated) in the income statement. They contend that mere size, unusualness, or timing does not convert what would otherwise be an item of revenue, expense, gain, or loss into something else. Some of the additional arguments presented by the advocates of this school of thought are stated below.

The total of the amounts shown as net income in the statements for a series of years should be the aggregate net income for those years. This will not be the case if corrections of net income of prior years are shown in the retained earnings statement rather than the income statement. Incidentally, including corrections of prior years' net income in the income statement calls attention to the tentative and estimated nature of the income statement.

When an accountant charges retained earnings with a loss because he considers it extraordinary or extraneous, he implies that it is nonrecurring. But a study of business history indicates that, over a period of years, such losses do recur, and that the retained earnings charges tend to exceed the retained earnings credits, with the result that the income statements for a series of years give an exaggerated impression of a company's earning power.

The line of demarcation between operating items and extraordinary or extraneous items is not clear cut and is often a matter of opinion. There are many borderline cases. For instance, assume that a department was closed during the year, and that severe losses were incurred in the disposal of the inventories. Does the fact that this department's operations were a part of the regular operations in the past require that the liquidation loss be charged to operations? Or do the department's activities become extraneous to operations when the decision to discontinue its operations is reached?

The Securities and Exchange Commission has cited numerous deficiencies because, in its opinion, retained earnings have been charged with losses which should have been charged to income.

Studies of annual reports have shown many inconsistencies in classifications between the income statement and the statement of retained earnings made by different companies, and by the same company in different years. Wide variations in net income and in earnings per share can be caused by such inconsistencies.

Many so-called extraordinary or extraneous charges and credits are closely related to operations—not to the operations of a single year, but to those of a series of years.

They may be regarded as corrections of the stated net income of a number of past years. For instance, a gain or loss on the disposal of a fixed asset may be regarded as a correction of prior years' income charges for depreciation, which were misstated because of an error in estimating the effect of use or obsolescence on the useful life of the asset, or because of an inability to foresee the effect of changing price levels on the residual value of the property.

Or extraordinary charges may relieve future operations of charges which would otherwise be made against them. This is the case when fixed assets are written off or written down, and future years are thereby relieved of depreciation and amortization charges.

Permitting charges and credits to retained earnings thus creates an opportunity for manipulation in the determination of stated net income, since charges and credits to retained earnings may be made to take the place of income charges and credits properly applicable to the operations of past or future periods.

Many people who are not trained accountants but have occasion to rely on accountants' statements do not realize that the income statement does not always tell the complete story about the year's activities, and that the statement of retained earnings should also be scrutinized. They are probably somewhat influenced by the practice of financial reporting services in reporting earnings per share based on the net income shown by the income statement.

The following statement was prepared in accordance with the clean surplus theory.

THE JONES CORPORATION
Income Statement
For the Year Ended December 31, 1959

Net sales...		$1,204,960
Deduct cost of goods sold...............................		826,940
Gross profit on sales...................................		$ 378,020
Deduct expenses (including income tax)...................		261,290
Net income before corrections and extraneous items.........		$ 116,730
Add—deduct*:		
Correction of net income of 1958 for undervaluation of inventory on December 31, 1958.......	$19,600	
Adjustment of prior years' depreciation..........	15,325*	4,275
Net income...		$ 121,005

The current operating concept of net income. The opposing school of thought holds that the income statement should be concerned only with items of revenue and expense that are applicable to the *regular operations* of the *current period*. The proponents of the current operating concept of net income support their position by the following arguments:

Investors and prospective investors are more interested in the net income of a business than in any other one figure shown by the annual statements. And the net income in which they are interested is that produced by the normal operating activities of the business during the year. Although the net income of one or more years is only one of numerous factors which should be considered in the formation of opinions about prospective earning power, the stated net income should reflect, as nearly as possible, what happened during the year as the result of normal operating transactions. Otherwise, it is difficult to determine the trend of a company's operations and to compare the results of operations of one company with those of other companies.

If the stated net income of one year is affected by a material correction of the net income of a prior year, there is a distortion. The error is compounded, because the current year's net income is overstated or understated to the extent that the net income of the past was understated or overstated. Indicated trends are therefore misleading. When an accountant renders an opinion with respect to the net income *for a year,* he indulges in an obvious contradiction if the amount of net income he shows in the statement includes a correction of the net income of some other year.

If the stated net income includes extraordinary and extraneous items not likely to recur, the reader of the statement is left to make his own decisions regarding the items which should be excluded to determine the results of normal operations. Although it is often difficult to draw a clear and definite line of demarcation between operating and extraordinary items, management and the trained accountant, familiar with the facts, are in a better position to do so than outsiders can possibly be.

While there should be full disclosure of all material extraneous and extraordinary items and corrections of earnings of prior years, such disclosure should be made in a way which will avoid any possible distortion and any confusion in the mind of the reader of the statements regarding the results of the regular operations of the business during the year.

If the income statement of The Jones Corporation were prepared in accordance with the current operating concept, the amount shown as net income would be $116,730. (See page 76.)

The Institute opinion. It is apparent that accountants differ on a very fundamental and important issue: What classes of items should be included in the computation of net income? The shift in emphasis in recent years from the balance sheet to the income statement has increased the importance of the issue.

The position of the Committee on Accounting Procedure of the American Institute of Certified Public Accountants, as expressed in Bulletin 43, is set forth below:

" . . . it is the opinion of the committee that there should be a general presumption that all items of profit and loss recognized during the period are to be used in determining the figure reported as net income. The only possible exception to this presumption relates to items which in the aggregate are material in relation to the company's net income and are clearly not identifiable with or do not result from the usual or typical business operations of the period. Thus, only extraordinary items such as the following may be excluded from the determination of net income for the year, and they should be excluded when their inclusion would impair the significance of net income so that misleading inferences might be drawn therefrom:

"(a) Material charges or credits (other than ordinary adjustments of a recurring nature) specifically related to operations of prior years, such as the elimination of unused reserves provided in prior years and adjustments of income taxes of prior years;

"(b) Material charges or credits resulting from unusual sales of assets not acquired for resale and not of the type in which the company generally deals;

"(c) Material losses of a type not usually insured against, such as those resulting from wars, riots, earthquakes, and similar calamities or catastrophes except where such losses are a recurrent hazard of the business;

"(d) The write-off of a material amount of intangibles;

"(e) The write-off of material amounts of unamortized bond discount or premium and bond issue expenses at the time of the retirement or refunding of the debt before maturity."

Appending extraneous items and corrections to the income statement.   Some accountants, while believing that certain classes of items should be excluded from the determination of net income for the period, oppose showing them in the statement of retained earnings. They fear that readers of accounting reports are likely to assume that the income statement tells all that is to be told about revenues, expenses, gains, and losses, and will not be aware of the significance of matters disclosed in the statement of retained earnings. These accountants advocate protecting (helping) such readers by showing corrections and extraordinary items in the income statement, but below the amount described as net income for the period. The final balance of the income statement (carried to the statement of retained earnings) would be given some title such as "Net income plus (or minus) corrections applicable to prior periods," or "Net income plus (or minus) extraneous gains and losses."

Combined income and retained earnings statement. The combined statement of income and retained earnings is sometimes described as a compromise between the current operating and clean surplus concepts of net income. It is not such a compromise. The net income may be computed in accordance with either concept. The purpose is to combine in one statement all elements affecting the retained earnings during the period, so that none will be overlooked.

Concluding note.   The proper concept of net income remains unsettled. It is an important issue, and an accounting student should be thoroughly familiar with the points of view discussed and be able to follow alternative approaches, as directed. Until the issue is more clearly resolved, an instructor is justified in suggesting the adoption of a single point of view, if for no other reason than to achieve class uniformity.

Corrections of Prior Years' Earnings

Description of errors.   The accounting problems created by the necessary correction of errors that affected prior financial statements are not limited to matters of statement location and disclosure; the accounting techniques involved warrant explanation and illustration.

Many mistakes affecting financial statements are merely classification errors; loans to officers recorded or classified as trade accounts receivable, or salesmen's salaries charged to Office Salaries, are examples. Mistakes of a more significant nature result in incorrect net income amounts. Of course, such mistakes also affect the balance sheet. If the net income is overstated as a result of accounting errors, the retained earnings are overstated on the companion balance sheet. If retained earnings are overstated, the net assets are overstated—by overstatement of assets, understatement of liabilities, or a combination thereof. An understatement of net income and retained earnings is accompanied by a balance sheet understatement of net assets.

Errors affecting net income.   Errors that affect the income statement for a period and the balance sheet at the end of the period are of two kinds:

(1) Errors that overstate (or understate) the net income of one period and correspondingly understate (or overstate) the net income of the following period. These are *counterbalancing* errors; although the net income for each period and the balance sheet at the end of the first period are incorrect, the net income for the two periods combined is correct, and the balance sheet at the end of the second period is correct.

For example, assume that an accountant overlooks the accrual of $1,000 of interest expense as of December 31, 1958. In 1959 the interest is paid and charged to Interest Expense. The net income for 1958 is overstated $1,000 and the net income for 1959 is understated $1,000. By the end of 1959, the error has been counterbalanced; the total net income for the two years is correct, and the balance sheet at the end of 1959 is correct.

(2) Errors that overstate or understate the net income of one period and are not counterbalanced by a corresponding understatement or overstatement of the net income of the succeeding period. Such errors leave the retained earnings and one or more asset or liability accounts inaccurate until an entry is made to correct the errors, or, in the case of fixed assets, until they are disposed of or become fully depreciated—either of which removes the effects of the error from the account balances.

For example, assume that the depreciation charged to operations and credited to an accumulated depreciation account in 1958 was too small. As a result, the net income for 1958 was overstated; this error will not be automatically counterbalanced by any corresponding understatement of net income in 1959. Therefore, retained earnings will remain overstated and the accumulated depreciation will remain understated until a correcting entry is made or until the asset involved is disposed of or becomes fully depreciated.

Alternative procedures for dealing with errors. The accountant, concerned with the importance of presenting meaningful and useful financial statements, must decide on the best statement procedure for dealing with errors that have caused misstatements of the net income of prior periods.

He has the following choices:

If the errors are not material in amount, they may be absorbed in the income statement of the year of discovery without disclosure. This procedure is permissible if the current income statement will not thereby be appreciably distorted. However, it should be noted that several immaterial errors may produce material consequences.

If the errors are material in amount, the accountant has three alternatives:

The errors may be disclosed in the income statement for the year of discovery.

—The errors may be disclosed in the statement of retained earnings for the year of discovery.

Revised statements for prior years may be prepared.

The choice of procedure is important, since an unwise selection of a method of dealing with the corrections may have the unfortunate effect of causing the statement user to misunderstand or overlook the correction.

Illustrations of the four methods mentioned above are shown in the remainder of this chapter.

Basis of illustrations. Assume that The A. B. Company found it necessary to replace its accountant at the end of 1960, before the financial statements had been prepared. The new accountant is informed that the company follows the accrual basis of accounting, and he determines that adjusting entries are required to give recognition to depreciation ($2,200), accrued wages ($250), and office supplies on hand ($400). After recording the above adjustments, the new accountant prepares the following adjusted trial balance.

THE A. B. COMPANY
Adjusted Trial Balance
December 31, 1960

Cash..	17,615	
Inventory—beginning of year..........................	16,100	
Office supplies on hand................................	400	
Furniture and fixtures.................................	28,300	
Accumulated depreciation.............................		12,305
Accounts payable......................................		11,390
Accrued wages payable................................		250
Capital stock..		30,000
Retained earnings.....................................		6,650
Dividends...	6,000	
Sales...		124,000
Purchases...	90,650	
Wages...	15,280	
Office supplies expense...............................	1,375	
Depreciation..	2,200	
Other expense..	6,675	
	184,595	184,595

At this point the accountant discovers that his predecessor had committed several errors in the preparation of financial statements for previous years. He had (1) failed to make adjusting entries for accrued wages and office supplies on hand; (2) miscomputed depreciation for 1957 and 1958; and (3) made clerical errors in computing the inventories as of December 31, 1958 and 1959.

In order to determine the effects of these mistakes, the accountant develops the following information.

Accrued wages of prior periods:

No entries for accrued wages were made at the end of 1957, 1958, or 1959; such wages were charged to the wages expense account in the following year, when they were paid. The accruals amounted to:

December 31:
1957... $175
1958...   215
1959...   230

The counterbalancing effects on net income as a result of failing to adjust for accrued wages are shown by the following schedule:

	December 31, 1957 Retained Earnings Were Overstated	Net Income Was Overstated- Understated* 1958	1959	1960 Net Income Will Be Understated*
Failure to adjust for accrued wages:				
December 31, 1957.......	+ 175	− 175*		
December 31, 1958.......		+ 215	− 215*	
December 31, 1959.......			+ 230	− 230*
Net overstatement.....		+ 40	+ 15	

The foregoing schedule reveals that, as a result of the failure to make adjusting entries for accrued wages, the December 31, 1957 retained earnings were overstated $175, the 1958 reported net income was overstated $40, the 1959 reported net income was overstated $15, and (unless a correction is made) the current year's net income will be understated $230 as a result of the accrued wages as of December 31, 1959, being charged to the 1960 wages expense account.

Office supplies on hand:

No recognition was given to the amount of office supplies on hand at the end of 1957, 1958, or 1959. As a result, all purchases of office supplies were treated as an expense in the year of purchase, whether or not they were used in that period. The amounts on hand were:

December 31:
1957.. $365
1958.. 415
1959.. 505

The counterbalancing effects are shown below.

	December 31, 1957 Retained Earnings Were Understated*	Net Income Was Overstated-Understated*		1960 Net Income Will Be Overstated
		1958	1959	
Failure to inventory office supplies:				
December 31, 1957........	365*	365		
December 31, 1958........		415*	415	
December 31, 1959........			505*	505
Net understatement*....		50*	90*	

Merchandise inventories:

Year-end inventories were understated and overstated as follows:

December 31:
1958—understated............................. $1,390
1959—overstated.............................. 615

The counterbalancing effects are shown below.

	Net Income Was Overstated-Understated*		1960 Net Income Will Be Understated*
	1958	1959	
Error in computing merchandise inventory:			
December 31, 1958—understated	1,390*	1,390	
December 31, 1959—overstated..........		615	615*
Net overstatement-understatement*....	1,390*	2,005	

As the above schedule reveals, an understated ending inventory will understate earnings for the current period and overstate earnings for the following period, and vice versa.

Depreciation:

> Depreciation for 1957 was overstated $160.
> Depreciation for 1958 was understated $200.
> Depreciation for 1959 was correct.

The effects of depreciation errors on net income work themselves out only when the depreciating asset is disposed of or becomes fully depreciated. In the case of The A. B. Company, no assets subject to depreciation have been disposed of or become fully depreciated during the 1957–1960 period. As a result, the depreciation errors have had the following effects:

	December 31, 1957 Retained Earnings Were Understated*	Net Income Was Overstated-Understated* 1958	Net Income Was Overstated-Understated* 1959	December 31, 1960 Accumulated Depreciation Will Be Understated*
Error in computing depreciation:				
1957—depreciation overstated...............	160*			
1958—depreciation understated..........		200		40*

In order to determine the net effect of all of the errors on the financial statements, a work sheet similar to the example on page 84 may be prepared.

Such a work sheet is useful for two purposes: It shows whether the net effect of the errors is sufficiently material to require disclosure; and it assembles the information required for statement-correction purposes. In this instance, the work sheet shows that:

(1) By the end of 1959, all errors except the following were counterbalanced:

> December 31, 1959 wage accrual ignored—$230.
> December 31, 1959 office supplies on hand omitted—$505.
> December 31, 1959 inventory overstated—$615.
> 1957 depreciation overstated—$160.
> 1958 depreciation understated—$200.

(2) By the end of 1960, all errors except the depreciation misstatements will have been counterbalanced. However, the net income for 1960 will be understated by $340 as a result of the 1959 errors relating to wages, office supplies, and the merchandise inventory.

The small letters appearing in the work sheet are key references used later in the chapter in illustrative working papers.

THE A. B. COMPANY
Work Sheet to Determine Effect of Errors
On Prior and Current Years' Financial Statements
Overstatement-Understatement*

	References	Prior Years' Financial Statements — Retained Earnings December 31, 1957	Net Income 1958	Net Income 1959	1960 Financial Statements If No Corrections Are Made — Income Statement Net Income	Balance Sheet Accumulated Depreciation	Balance Sheet Retained Earnings
Failure to adjust for accrued wages:							
December 31, 1957	a	175					
December 31, 1958	b		175*	215*			
December 31, 1959	c		215	230	230*		
Failure to inventory office supplies:							
December 31, 1957	d	365*					
December 31, 1958	e		365	415*			
December 31, 1959	f		415*	505*	505		
Errors in computing merchandise inventory:							
December 31, 1958—understated	g		1,390*	1,390			
December 31, 1959—overstated	h			615	615*		
Errors in computing depreciation:							
1957—depreciation overstated	i	160*					
1958—depreciation understated	j		200			40*	40
Net overstatement—understatement*		350*	1,200*	1,930	340*	40*	40

Procedure If Corrections Are to Be Absorbed
in the Current Year's Income Statement Without Disclosure

Assume that the errors of prior years are not considered sufficiently material to require disclosure, and that those not already counterbalanced will be allowed to affect the 1960 income statement, without listing or otherwise disclosing them. Therefore, only the depreciation errors will need correcting; the other errors have been counterbalanced or will be counterbalanced in 1960 by the operation of normal accounting procedures.

The following correcting entry will be required:

Depreciation		40
Accumulated depreciation		40
To correct for:		
Underdepreciation in 1958	$200	
Overdepreciation in 1957	160	
Net	$ 40	

The working papers for the preparation of the 1960 statements are on page 86.

The income statement and retained earnings statement for 1960 shown below are based on these working papers. The balance sheet is not presented in the examples used in this chapter because there are no special features to illustrate.

THE A. B. COMPANY
Income Statement
For the Year Ended December 31, 1960

Sales			$124,000
Cost of goods sold:			
Inventory—beginning of year		$ 16,100	
Purchases		90,650	
Total		$106,750	
Inventory—end of year		16,200	90,550
Gross profit on sales			$ 33,450
Expenses:			
Wages		$ 15,280	
Office supplies expense		1,375	
Depreciation		2,240	
Other expense		6,675	25,570
Net income			$ 7,880

THE A. B. COMPANY
Statement of Retained Earnings
For the Year Ended December 31, 1960

Retained earnings—December 31, 1959	$ 6,650
Net income—per income statement	7,880
Total	$14,530
Dividends	6,000
Retained earnings—December 31, 1960	$ 8,530

THE A. B. COMPANY
Working Papers
For the Year Ended December 31, 1960

	Adjusted Trial Balance		Corrections		Income Statement		Statement of Retained Earnings		Balance Sheet	
Cash	17,615								17,615	
Inventory—beginning of year	16,100				16,100					
Office supplies on hand	400								400	
Furniture and fixtures	28,300								28,300	
Accumulated depreciation		12,305		40 i-j						12,345
Accounts payable		11,390								11,390
Accrued wages payable		250								250
Capital stock		30,000								30,000
Retained earnings		6,650						6,650		
Dividends	6,000						6,000			
Sales		124,000				124,000				
Purchases	90,650				90,650					
Wages	15,280				15,280					
Office supplies expense	1,375				1,375					
Depreciation	2,200		40 i-j		2,240					
Other expense	6,675				6,675					
	184,595	184,595	40	40	132,320	140,200				
Inventory—end of year						16,200			16,200	
Net income					7,880			7,880		
					140,200	140,200				
Retained earnings—December 31, 1960							8,530			8,530
							14,530	14,530	62,515	62,515

Procedure If Errors Are to Be Disclosed
in the Current Income Statement

If the accountant prefers to *disclose* the correction of prior years' earnings in the income statement, he will make correcting entries for *all* of the errors not counterbalanced at the beginning of 1960.

Correction of prior years' earnings—1959 wage accrual...........	230	
Wages...		230
To remove wages applicable to 1959.		

Office supplies expense.......................................	505	
Correction of prior years' earnings—Office supplies improperly expensed in 1959.....................................		505
Supplies on hand at beginning of year.		

Correction of prior years' earnings—Inventory overstatement—December 31, 1959..	615	
Inventory...		615
To correct the 1960 beginning inventory.		

Correction of prior years' earnings—Depreciation errors..........	40	
Accumulated depreciation................................		40
To correct Accumulated Depreciation account for errors made in computing depreciation for 1957 and 1958.		

Working papers showing such corrections appear on page 88. The income statement prepared from these working papers is presented below. The statement of retained earnings for 1960 would be the same as the one presented on page 85.

THE A. B. COMPANY
Income Statement
For the Year Ended December 31, 1960

Sales..			$124,000
Cost of goods sold:			
Inventory—beginning of year.....................	$ 15,485		
Purchases.......................................	90,650		
Total...	$106,135		
Inventory—end of year...........................	16,200	89,935	
Gross profit on sales.......................................			$ 34,065
Expenses:			
Wages...	$ 15,050		
Office supplies expense...........................	1,880		
Depreciation.....................................	2,200		
Other expense...................................	6,675	25,805	
Net income before correction of prior years' earnings...........			$ 8,260
Correction of prior years' earnings:			
Add office supplies improperly expensed in 1959..............			505
Total..			$ 8,765
Deduct:			
1959 wage accrual.............................	$ 230		
Inventory overstatement........................	615		
Depreciation:			
Insufficient provision in 1958.............	$200		
Excess provision in 1957.................	160	40	885
Net income...			$ 7,880

THE A. B. COMPANY
Working Papers
For the Year Ended December 31, 1960

	Adjusted Trial Balance		Corrections		Income Statement		Statement of Retained Earnings		Balance Sheet	
Cash	17,615								17,615	
Inventory—beginning of year	16,100			615 h	15,485					
Office supplies on hand	400								400	
Furniture and fixtures	28,300								28,300	
Accumulated depreciation		12,305		40 i-j						12,345
Accounts payable		11,390								11,390
Accrued wages payable		250								250
Capital stock		30,000								30,000
Retained earnings		6,650						6,650		
Dividends	6,000						6,000			
Sales		124,000				124,000				
Purchases	90,650				90,650					
Wages	15,280			230 c	15,050					
Office supplies expense	1,375		505 f		1,880					
Depreciation	2,200				2,200					
Other expense	6,675				6,675					
	184,595	184,595								
Correction of prior years' earnings:										
1959 wage accrual			230 c		230					
Office supplies improperly expensed in 1959				505 f		505				
Inventory overstatement—December 31, 1959			615 h		615					
Depreciation errors			40 i-j		40					
			1,390	1,390						
Inventory—end of year						16,200			16,200	
					132,825	140,705				
Net income					7,880			7,880		
					140,705	140,705				
							6,000	6,650		
							8,530	7,880		
Retained earnings—December 31, 1960							14,530	14,530		8,530
									62,515	62,515

Procedure If Errors Are Disclosed in the
Retained Earnings Statement

If the accountant prefers to show the correction of errors affecting prior years' earnings in the statement of retained earnings, the working papers (which appear on page 90) would be the same as those in the immediately preceding illustration, except that the correction entries at the bottom of the working papers would be extended to the Retained Earnings columns instead of to the Income Statement columns, and the net income amounts would be different because of the difference in the treatment of the correction items.

Under the procedure being illustrated, there would be nothing unusual in either the form or the content of the income statement. The statement of retained earnings, however, would appear as follows:

THE A. B. COMPANY
Statement of Retained Earnings
For the Year Ended December 31, 1960

Retained earnings—December 31, 1959:			
Per books...			$ 6,650
Corrections of prior years' earnings:			
Add:			
Office supplies improperly expensed in 1959..............			505
Total...			$ 7,155
Deduct:			
1959 wage accrual.................................		$230	
Inventory overstatement—12/31/59................		615	
Depreciation:			
Insufficient provision in 1958..............	$200		
Excess provision in 1957...................	160	40	885
As adjusted...			$ 6,270
Net income—per income statement..........................			8,260
Total..			$14,530
Dividends...			6,000
Retained earnings—December 31, 1960......................			$ 8,530

Closing entries.   When the correction items are shown in the statement of retained earnings, the inventory, revenue, and expense accounts and the Revenue and Expense account will be closed in the usual manner. The correction accounts will be closed to Retained Earnings, as follows:

Retained earnings...	380	
Correction of prior years' earnings—Office supplies improperly expensed..	505	
Correction of prior years' earnings—1959 wage accrual.......		230
Correction of prior years' earnings—Inventory overstatement, December 31, 1959..		615
Correction of prior years' earnings—Depreciation errors.....		40
To close correction-of-prior-years'-earnings accounts.		

THE A. B. COMPANY
Working Papers
For the Year Ended December 31, 1960

	Adjusted Trial Balance		Corrections		Income Statement		Statement of Retained Earnings		Balance Sheet	
Cash	17,615								17,615	
Inventory—beginning of year	16,100			615 h	15,485					
Office supplies on hand	400								400	
Furniture and fixtures	28,300								28,300	
Accumulated depreciation		12,305		40 i-j						12,345
Accounts payable		11,390								11,390
Accrued wages payable		250								250
Capital stock		30,000								30,000
Retained earnings		6,650						6,650		
Dividends	6,000						6,000			
Sales		124,000				124,000				
Purchases	90,650				90,650					
Wages	15,280			230 c	15,050					
Office supplies expense	1,375		505 f		1,880					
Depreciation	2,200				2,200					
Other expense	6,675				6,675					
	184,595	184,595								
Correction of prior years' earnings:										
1959 wage accrual			230 c				230			
Office supplies improperly expensed in 1959				505 f				505		
Inventory overstatement—December 31, 1959			615 h				615			
Depreciation errors			40 i-j				40			
			1,390	1,390						
Inventory—end of year						16,200			16,200	
					131,940	140,200	6,885	15,415		
Net income					8,260			8,260		
					140,200	140,200				
Retained earnings—December 31, 1960							8,530			8,530
							15,415	15,415	62,515	62,515

For 1960, the Retained Earnings account would show the following amounts:

Retained Earnings

1960			1960		
12/31	Correction accounts.......	380	1/ 2	Balance..................	6,650
12/31	Dividends..............	6,000	12/31	From Revenue and Expense	8,260

The year-end account balance is $8,530, which agrees with the statement of retained earnings.

Procedure If Statements for Prior Years Are to Be Revised

When errors are discovered that caused prior years' financial statements to be incorrect, revised financial statements for such prior periods may be prepared. As a practical matter, this is done only if the earlier statements are materially in error and therefore possibly misleading, or if the company is faced with the task of submitting current and prior years' financial statements to prospective investors in connection with an issuance of bonds or stocks. Waiving the question whether the errors illustrated are significant, The A. B. Company case will be used to show how revised statements may be prepared. Although some of the errors affected the 1957 statements, we shall assume (in order to shorten the illustration somewhat) that 1958 is the first year for which revised statements are to be presented. The working papers used in the preparation of revised statements for 1958 are presented on page 92. Note the following about the working papers.

(1) The amounts shown in the first two money columns were copied from the financial statements prepared before the discovery of the errors in the statements of prior years.

(2) The corrections were taken from the work sheet prepared by the new accountant to determine the effects of the errors he discovered. (See page 84.) The key references refer to that work sheet. The necessary corrections are repeated here to make it easier to follow the working papers.

a) Corrections required because of failure to adjust for
b)   accrued wages.
d) Corrections required because of failure to give recognition
e)   tion to office supplies on hand.
g Correction required because of clerical error in computing merchandise inventory.
i) Correction required because of errors in computing
j)   depreciation provisions.

THE A. B. COMPANY
Working Papers to Revise Financial Statements
For the Year Ended December 31, 1958

	Per Statements		Corrections		Revised Statements	
Income Statement						
Sales..........................		114,500				114,500
Cost of goods sold:						
Inventory—beginning of year....	15,000				15,000	
Purchases....................	84,800				84,800	
Inventory—end of year........		15,700		1,390 g		17,090
Expenses:						
Wages......................	13,200		215 b	175 a	13,240	
Office supplies expense.......	1,620		365 d	415 e	1,570	
Depreciation.................	1,745		200 j		1,945	
Other expense...............	7,035				7,035	
	123,400	130,200			123,590	131,590
Net income—down.............	6,800				8,000	
	130,200	130,200			131,590	131,590
Statement of Retained Earnings						
Retained earnings—beginning of year..		5,000	175 a	365 d, 160 i		5,350
Net income—brought down.....		6,800				8,000
Dividends....................	6,000				6,000	
Retained earnings—end of year—down...	5,800				7,350	
	11,800	11,800			13,350	13,350
Balance Sheet						
Cash........................	12,545				12,545	
Inventory...................	15,700		1,390 g		17,090	
Office supplies on hand.......			415 e		415	
Furniture and fixtures........	27,000				27,000	
Accumulated depreciation.....		7,945	160 i	200 j		7,985
Accounts payable.............		11,500				11,500
Accrued wages payable........				215 b		215
Capital stock................		30,000				30,000
Retained earnings—brought down...		5,800				7,350
	55,245	55,245	2,920	2,920	57,050	57,050

(3) The three errors affecting the December 31, 1957 retained earnings are applied to the December 31, 1957 retained earnings figure of $5,000 (corrections a, d, and i). All other errors affect 1958 income statement or balance sheet accounts.

Working papers to revise the 1959 financial statements are presented on page 94. In connection with these working papers, note that when the beginning-of-year retained earnings has been properly corrected, the revised amount, $7,350, agrees with the end-of-year revised retained earnings figure shown in the working papers to revise the financial statements for the year ended December 31, 1958 (page 92).

If revised statements are prepared for 1958 and 1959, the prior years' errors need not appear in the 1960 financial statements. The four correction amounts shown in the Corrections columns in the working papers on page 90, under the side caption "Corrections of prior years' earnings," are applied to the retained earnings balance of $6,650, thus producing a corrected balance of $6,270. Working papers following the above suggestion appear on page 95. They agree with the working papers on page 90, except for the location of the prior years' corrections which affected the December 31, 1959 balance of retained earnings. As adjusted, the December 31, 1959 balance of retained earnings is $6,270, which agrees with the amount that would be reported in the revised statements for 1959. (See the working papers on page 94.)

The correction entries would be made directly to Retained Earnings. The 1960 statement of retained earnings will show a beginning-of-year balance of $6,270, as in the following statement.

THE A. B. COMPANY
Statement of Retained Earnings
For the Year Ended December 31, 1960

Retained earnings—December 31, 1959—per revised statements..	$ 6,270
Net income—per income statement	8,260
Total	$14,530
Dividends	6,000
Retained earnings—December 31, 1960	$ 8,530

It is also acceptable to include the correction items in the above statement. If this is done, the statement will be the same as the statement of retained earnings illustrated on page 89.

THE A. B. COMPANY
Working Papers to Revise Financial Statements
For the Year Ended December 31, 1959

	Per Statements	Corrections (Dr.)	Corrections (Cr.)	Revised Statements
Income Statement				
Sales	116,000			116,000
Cost of goods sold:				
Inventory—beginning of year	15,700	1,390 g		17,090
Purchases	85,450			85,450
Inventory—end of year	16,100		615 h	15,485
Expenses:				
Wages	14,100	230 c	215 b	14,115
Office supplies expense	1,715	415 e	505 f	1,625
Depreciation	2,160			2,160
Other expense	6,125			6,125
	125,250 132,100			126,565
Net income—down	6,850			4,920
	132,100 132,100			131,485 131,485
Statement of Retained Earnings				
Retained earnings—beginning of year	5,800	40 i-j 215 b	415 e } 1,390 g }	7,350
Net income—brought down	6,850			4,920
Dividends	6,000			6,000
Retained earnings—end of year—down	6,650			6,270
	12,650 12,650			12,270 12,270
Balance Sheet				
Cash	15,455			15,455
Inventory	16,100		615 h	15,485
Office supplies on hand		505 f		505
Furniture and fixtures	28,000			28,000
Accumulated depreciation	10,105		40 i-j	10,145
Accounts payable	12,800			12,800
Accrued wages payable			230 c	230
Capital stock	30,000			30,000
Retained earnings—brought down	6,650			6,270
	59,555 59,555	3,410	3,410	59,445 59,445

THE A. B. COMPANY
Working Papers
For the Year Ended December 31, 1960

	Adjusted Trial Balance		Corrections		Income Statement		Statement of Retained Earnings		Balance Sheet	
Cash	17,615								17,615	
Inventory—beginning of year	16,100			615 h						
Office supplies on hand	400								400	
Furniture and fixtures	28,300								28,300	
Accumulated depreciation		12,305		40 i-j						12,345
Accounts payable		11,390								11,390
Accrued wages payable		250								250
Capital stock		30,000								30,000
Retained earnings		6,650	230 c 615 h 40 i-j	505 f				6,270		
Dividends	6,000						6,000			
Sales		124,000				124,000				
Purchases	90,650				90,650					
Wages	15,280			230 c	15,050					
Office supplies expense	1,375		505 f		1,880					
Depreciation	2,200				2,200					
Other expense	6,675				6,675					
	184,595	184,595	1,390	1,390						
Inventory—end of year						16,200			16,200	
					131,940	140,200	6,000	14,530		
Net income					8,260			8,260		
Retained earnings—December 31, 1960							8,530			8,530
					140,200	140,200	14,530	14,530	62,515	62,515

Corrections

c—Correction for 1959 wage accrual.
f—Correction for office supplies improperly expensed.
h—Correction for inventory overstatement.
i-j—Correction for depreciation errors.

Summary. To indicate clearly how the four methods of dealing with corrections of errors affecting prior years' earnings differ, the income statements and statements of retained earnings of The A. B. Company for 1960, prepared by the four methods, are compared below and on page 97. Balance sheets are not shown; they would all be alike.

THE A. B. COMPANY

Comparison of Results of the Four Methods of Dealing With Errors in Statements of Prior Years

INCOME STATEMENT	1960 Errors Absorbed in Current Income Statement Without Disclosure	Errors Disclosed in Current Income Statement	Errors Disclosed in Current Statement of Retained Earnings	Statements for Prior Years Revised
Sales	$124,000	$124,000	$124,000	$124,000
Cost of goods sold:				
Inventory—beginning of year	$ 16,100	$ 15,485	$ 15,485	$ 15,485
Purchases	90,650	90,650	90,650	90,650
Total	$106,750	$106,135	$106,135	$106,135
Inventory—end of year	16,200	16,200	16,200	16,200
Cost of goods sold	$ 90,550	$ 89,935	$ 89,935	$ 89,935
Gross profit on sales	$ 33,450	$ 34,065	$ 34,065	$ 34,065
Expenses:				
Wages	$ 15,280	$ 15,050	$ 15,050	$ 15,050
Office supplies expense	1,375	1,880	1,880	1,880
Depreciation	2,240	2,200	2,200	2,200
Other expense	6,675	6,675	6,675	6,675
Total expenses	$ 25,570	$ 25,805	$ 25,805	$ 25,805
Net income before corrections of prior years' earnings		$ 8,260		
Add (Deduct*) corrections of prior years' earnings:				
Office supplies improperly expensed in 1959		$ 505		
1959 wage accrual		230*		
Inventory overstated—December 31, 1959		615*		

Underdepreciation—1958		200*	
Overdepreciation—1957		160	
Total corrections		$ 380*	$ 8,260
Net income		$ 7,880	$ 8,260

STATEMENT OF RETAINED EARNINGS

Retained earnings—December 31, 1959:			
Per books		$ 6,650	$ 6,650
Add (Deduct*) corrections of prior years' earnings:			
Office supplies improperly expensed in 1959			$ 505
1959 wage accrual			230*
Inventory overstatement—December 31, 1959			615*
Underdepreciation—1958			200*
Overdepreciation—1957			160
Total corrections			$ 380*
As adjusted			$ 6,270
Net income—per above		7,880	8,260
Total		$ 14,530	$ 14,530
Dividends		6,000	6,000
Retained earnings—December 31, 1960		$ 8,530	$ 8,530

The first method (absorbing the corrections in the current income statement without disclosure) should be used only if the errors are not material in amount. What is material is a matter of judgment. It is probably desirable for the accounting student to treat all errors as material.

The second method (disclosing the errors in the current income statement) and the third method (disclosing the errors in the current statement of retained earnings) are the methods most commonly used. As noted earlier in this chapter, accountants differ as to which is the preferable practice.

The fourth method (preparing revised statements) is not often used, for several reasons: errors may apply to a number of prior periods, and numerous prior statements would have to be revised; the counterbalancing effects of certain types of accounting errors tend to make the net result thereof in any one year insignificant; it is not always possible to determine the year to which the correction should apply—for instance, the allowance for doubtful accounts at the end of some year might be discovered to be too great or too small, but there might be great difficulty in apportioning the correction over prior years; the revised statements give corrected figures, but do not show the amounts of the corrections— they can be determined only by comparisons with the original statements; furthermore, it is probably true that most statement users are not greatly interested in historical information—their interest is primarily in current and prospective earnings.

....

CHAPTER FIVE

Capital Stock

Objectives in accounting for stockholders' investments.
Corporate accounts need not differ from the accounts of other
types of business organization except in the manner of reflecting
the elements of the owners' equity. In accounting for the elements
of owners' equity in a corporation, the emphasis is placed on
source. How much of the owners' equity was produced by stockholders' capital contributions? How much consists of retained
earnings? How much, if any, was produced in other ways?

Proper accounting for the elements of stockholders' equity
according to their source requires a knowledge of the nature of
capital stock and of the various classes of surplus. These matters
are discussed in this and subsequent chapters.

Par and no-par stock. Prior to 1912, it was required that the
capital stocks of all corporations in the United States have a par
value. In that year, the first American law permitting the issuance
of stock without par value was enacted in New York. Other states
have since passed similar laws, but, unfortunately, the laws of the
several states are not uniform.

Generally, the organizers of a corporation, if they choose to use
par value stock, may select the amount for par. Thus, par value
may be $100, $25, $7.50, $1, or any other dollar amount.

Rights inherent in stock. The capital stock of a corporation
is divided into shares which entitle their holders to certain basic
rights, the most important of which are mentioned on page 100.

(1) The right to vote at stockholders' meetings, and thus to participate in the management.

(2) The right to share in the earnings; that is, to receive dividends when they are declared by the directors.

(3) The right to participate in any additional issues of stock of the class owned, ratably to their holdings at the date of the additional issue (known as the "pre-emptive right"). This right is often abridged or withheld.

(4) The right to share in the distribution of the assets of the corporation upon dissolution.

If there is only one class of stock, these rights are enjoyed proportionately, share and share alike, by all stockholders. If there are two or more classes of stock, one class may enjoy more or less than its proportionate share of certain rights.

Common stock and preferred stock. The two principal classes of stock are common and preferred. Holders of preferred shares have one or more "preferences" over the common stockholders. Thus, preferred stockholders may enjoy special privileges in the sharing of earnings or in the distribution of assets in liquidation. On the other hand, preferred stockholders may have no rights, or only limited rights, to vote.

Stock preferred as to dividends. Stock that is preferred as to dividends entitles its holders to a dividend at a specified rate on par (or of a specified amount per share, in the case of no-par stock) before dividends are paid on the common stock.

A preference as to dividends is not an assurance that dividends will be paid. No stockholder, whether holding preferred or common shares, has an unconditional right to receive a dividend, for two reasons. First, the payment of dividends on stock of any class depends upon whether the corporation has a legal right to pay a dividend. Second, even though the corporation has a legal right to pay a dividend, the directors, after giving due consideration to matters of corporate policy and cash requirements, may decide that it would be inexpedient to distribute funds to the stockholders. In general, the stockholders' only remedy is to bring an action in a court of equity, and undertake to present evidence to prove that dividends have been unjustifiably withheld. This has not proved to be much of a remedy, because courts have shown a reluctance to order dividend payments. For this reason, preferred dividends should not be regarded as accruing.

A company cannot *guarantee* the payment of dividends on its preferred stock. However, dividends on the stocks of one company are sometimes guaranteed by another company; for instance, Company *A*, in connection with a lease of facilities of Company *B*, may guarantee the payment of dividends on Company *B*'s stock.

Cumulative and noncumulative stock. If preferred stock is cumulative, any preferred dividends in arrears must be paid in the future before any dividends can be paid on the common stock. If a partial dividend is paid, the unpaid portion accumulates. If preferred stock is noncumulative, a dividend lost in one year is lost forever.

Participating and nonparticipating stock. Preferred stock may be participating or nonparticipating. Participating preferred stock shares with the common stock in any dividends paid after the common has received a dividend at the preference rate. That is, if the preferred is entitled to dividends of 6% on par, and if both preferred and common have received 6% dividends, an additional payment on the common stock would require an additional payment on the preferred stock. Preferred stock may be fully participating (that is, entitled to dividends at a rate, or in an amount per share, equal to that paid on the common stock); its right of participation may be limited (that is, a maximum may be placed on the total dividends which may be paid annually on the preferred stock); or it may be nonparticipating. If preferred stock is nonparticipating, its holders are entitled to dividends at the preferred rate and no more, regardless of the rate at which dividends are paid on the common stock.

Cumulative or participating rights not stated. If preferred stock is issued without a specific statement as to its cumulative or participating rights, what is its status with respect to such rights? This is a question to which no general answer can be given, as there is no uniformity of law in the various states.

Stock preferred as to assets. Stock that is preferred as to assets entitles its holders to payment in liquidation before any payments are made to the common stockholders. The fact that stock is preferred as to dividends does not make it also preferred as to assets; this preference must be specifically stated.

Most (but not all) stock which is preferred as to assets in liquidation is so preferred not only to the extent of par, or a stated liquidation value in the case of no-par stock, but also with respect to cumulative dividends in arrears. Therefore, in the event of liquidation, the holders of such preferred stock are entitled to a distribution equal to such dividends even though the company has no surplus.

Special features of preferred stock. Various classes of preferred stock may be issued. If there are first and second preferred stocks, the rights of the second preferred are subject to the rights of the first preferred, although the rights of all preferred stockholders are superior, in certain particulars, to the rights of common stockholders.

Corporations sometimes obtain an authorization of a certain number of shares of preferred stock with the right to issue portions thereof from time to time with different features—for instance, with different dividend rates. Thus, a company may obtain an authorization for the issuance of 10,000 shares of $100 par value preferred stock; it may immediately issue 4,000 shares designated as 5% series; later it may issue 4,000 shares designated as 6% series; and still later it may issue the remaining 2,000 shares designated as 5½% series.

As the right to vote is one of the basic rights of stockholders, preferred stock carries this right unless it is specifically withheld. In some states the right to vote cannot be withheld.

Preferred stock sometimes carries the right of conversion into bonds or common stock. This right is intended to make the investment an attractive one. For instance, if the stock is cumulative and participating, the holder has the chance of sharing in the earnings of a successful business, but his dividend income is dependent upon earnings, and he has no security for his principal; if earnings prove to be small, the privilege of conversion into bonds allows him to obtain a security that makes his income independent of earnings and safeguards the principal. Or, if the preferred stock is nonparticipating, and earnings prove to be good, the right to convert into common stock allows the holder to switch to a type of investment having full participation in the larger earnings.

Preferred stock may be subject to gradual retirement through the operation of a redemption fund (frequently called a *sinking fund*) or otherwise. Or it may be redeemable at the option of the corporation; in other words, the stock may be made callable after a certain date and at a stipulated or determinable price. If called, all dividends in arrears must usually be paid if the stock is cumulative, and the right to redeem cannot be exercised if creditors' rights would thereby be jeopardized. Charter clauses that provide for redemption of stock should be made permissive and not obligatory, because a corporation cannot enter into an unconditional contract to pay off its stockholders.

The terms of issuance of preferred stocks frequently contain provisions intended to safeguard the interests of the preferred stockholders. For instance, the consent of the preferred stockholders may be required before the management can participate in a merger or change the nature of the company's operations. The most customary restrictive provisions have to do with the payment of cash dividends on common stock or the retirement of common shares or their acquisition as treasury stock. The restrictions take various forms. For instance, the payment of common dividends or reductions of outstanding common shares may not be permissible if contributions to preferred stock retirement funds are in arrears; or if the working capital is less than a stated amount or less than a certain number of times the preferred dividend requirements; or if the net tangible assets are less than a certain number of times the liquidating value of the preferred stock; or if the surplus available for dividends is less than a stipulated amount. This last restriction often takes the form of "freezing" the surplus at the date of issuance of the preferred stock, by providing that dividend payments on, and retirements of, common shares or their acquisition as treasury stock can be made only to the extent of the increase in earned surplus since that date.

Founders' stock. The peculiar feature of founders' stock is the right that it confers upon its holders to receive dividends which are equal in amount to, or a stated percentage of, those paid on the common stock, regardless of the amounts of founders' stock and common stock outstanding.

To illustrate, assume that $10,000 par of founders' stock and $100,000 par of common stock are outstanding, and that the founders' stock is entitled to dividends equal in amount to those paid on the common stock. If a 6% dividend is paid on the common stock, $6,000 will be distributed to the common stockholders. A dividend of $6,000 must also be paid to the holders of the founders' stock; this amount represents a 60% dividend.

Only a few states permit the issuance of founders' stock.

Common stock. The term *common stock* is applicable to corporate shares which have no preferences. If all of the stock is of one class, there obviously are no preferences, and all of the shares are common.

Stock designated by letters. Companies issuing more than one class of stock frequently use letters to designate the various classes, as Class A, Class B, and Class C stock. One of these classes must necessarily be common stock; the others enjoy some special privilege (and perhaps are subject to some curtailment) with respect to one or more of the basic rights—to share in the management, in the profits, in additional stock issues, and in the distribution of assets in liquidation.

For example, Class A stock may be preferred as to dividends, with cumulative and participating rights; it may have no power to vote; and it may have no preference with respect to the distribution of assets in liquidation. Or it may be preferred as to dividends, with cumulative but no participating rights; it may have full or limited voting rights; and it may be preferred as to assets in liquidation.

The point to be understood clearly is that designation by letter necessitates the determination of the rights appertaining to the stock by reference to the charter, to the stock certificates, or to other sources of information.

Some corporations issue two classes of "common" stock distinguished by letter: for instance, Class A common and Class B common. In many cases, one of the classes of so-called common stock would be more properly designated as preferred.

Stated capital.   In addition to the emphasis on source, which, as noted earlier, is a primary consideration in the accounting for stockholders' equity, there is the matter of stated capital to consider.

Among the advantages of the corporate form of business organization is that of limited liability, which means that the stockholders normally cannot be held personally liable for the debts of the corporation. Since the law gives stockholders this immunity, it is only fair that creditors should be given some assurance that the corporation will not be permitted to make payments or distributions to its stockholders which will reduce the stockholders' equity below a stipulated amount known as *stated capital.* In the absence of any restriction on the amount of assets that can be returned to shareholders, the directors of a corporation in financial difficulty could strip the corporation of most of its assets by declaring dividends or by using company funds to purchase or retire the corporation's capital stock, to the benefit of shareholders and to the detriment of creditors. In general, there is less risk associated with a creditor's claim if there is a prescribed amount of stockholders' equity that cannot be reduced by payments or distributions to the shareholders.

The amount of the stated capital is determined by the law of the state in which the corporation is organized. Since there is considerable variation in the state laws on this matter, only the more common definitions are mentioned below:

In the case of par value shares, stated capital is usually defined as an amount equal to the aggregate par value of the shares issued.

In the case of no-par shares, stated capital is the aggregate credited to the capital stock accounts. The amounts thus credited may equal

(1) the total received for the shares issued, or

(2) an amount based on a stated value per share.

Generally the board of directors has the right to designate a stated value per share; in some states the amount which the directors elect to establish as stated value per share cannot be less than a minimum set forth in the law, for example, $5 per share. Thus, all corporations have a stated capital but some may not have a stated value per share.

As a general rule, accountants will credit amounts received in excess of stated capital to a paid-in surplus account. Thus, if $25 par value shares are issued for $28 per share, $3 per share will be treated as paid-in surplus; similarly, if no-par shares having a stated value of $10 per share are issued for $12 per share, $2 per share will be treated as paid-in surplus.

Stated capital can be reduced (provided that the action complies with the provisions of the state corporation act) by a reduction in the number of issued shares or in their par or stated value, by changing par value shares to no-par shares with a lower stated value than the former par, or by changing no-par shares to par shares with a par less than the former stated value.

Perhaps it should be noted that the existence of legal provisions regarding stated capital reduces, but does not eliminate, the risk of loss by creditors. Stated capital can be impaired by unprofitable operations. Also, some of the assets may not be available to satisfy the claims of general creditors, since the directors of the corporation may have mortgaged or pledged them as security for specific obligations.

Since stated capital is a legal concept, and since there is considerable variation in the state laws, it is impracticable to deal exhaustively with the subject in an accounting text; it must suffice to call attention to the fact that the treatment of matters related to stated capital is governed by the law of the state in which the company is incorporated.

Accounts used to show stockholders' investments. The following types of accounts are used in connection with investments by stockholders.

Capital stock accounts. A separate account is set up in the ledger for each class of stock authorized. The account title should be broadly descriptive of the stock. The number of shares authorized and pertinent details regarding the stock are indicated by a memorandum notation in the account. Thus, if a corporation is authorized to issue 10,000 shares of $25 par value, 5% cumulative preferred stock and 50,000 shares of common stock with a stated value of $10 per share, the ledger accounts would be set up as shown on page 106.

Preferred Stock
_____
(Authorized issue, 10,000 shares, $25 par, 5% cumulative)

Common Stock
_____
(Authorized issue, 50,000 | shares, $10 stated value)

Capital stock accounts are credited when the stock certificates are issued to the stockholders; the accounts are credited with the par or stated value of the shares issued or, in the case of no-par stock without stated value, the aggregate price paid for the shares issued.

Paid-in surplus accounts. Amounts received in excess of the par or stated value of shares are credited to paid-in surplus accounts, the titles of such accounts indicating the source of the credits. Thus, if par value preferred shares are issued at a premium, Premium on Preferred Stock would be a suitable account title. If no-par common shares are issued at a price in excess of their stated value, the account credited for the excess could be described as Paid-in Surplus—No-par Common.

Illustrative journal entries are shown below.

(a) One hundred shares of $25 par value preferred stock are issued at $28 per share.

```
Cash...................................................  2,800
    Preferred stock....................................          2,500
    Premium on preferred stock.........................            300
    Issuance of 100 authorized shares at a premium of $3 per
    share.
```

(b) Two hundred shares of no-par common stock with a stated value of $10 per share are issued at $12 per share.

```
Cash...................................................  2,400
    Common stock.......................................          2,000
    Paid-in surplus—No-par common......................            400
    Issuance of 200 authorized shares at $12 per share.
```

(c) Three hundred shares of no-par common stock (having no stated value) are issued at $6 per share.

```
Cash...................................................  1,800
    Common stock.......................................          1,800
    Issuance of 300 authorized shares at $6 per share.
```

Stock issued for less than par value. Stock is rarely issued for less than its par value for two reasons:

(1) In many states it is illegal to do so.
(2) In states where it is legal, the original holders of stock issued at a discount generally face a contingent liability; should

the corporation become insolvent, they may be held personally liable to the corporation's creditors for amounts equal to such deficiency. As a general rule, the contingent liability does not pass to a subsequent holder unless he had notice of the discount or should have known about it.

If capital stock is issued for less than par value, the discount should be debited to a separate account (the word "discount" and the class of stock involved should appear in the account title) and shown as a deduction in the Stockholders' Equity section of the balance sheet.

Interval between receipt and collection of subscriptions.
Time may elapse between the date when subscriptions for stock are received and the date when they are collected and the stock is issued. Under such circumstances, there is need for accounts to show the amount receivable from the subscribers and the shares that have been subscribed for but as yet are unissued. The accounts to be used under such circumstances are described below.

Subscriptions Receivable:
>   When subscriptions are received, this account is debited with the aggregate price of shares subscribed.
>   As collections are received from subscribers, the account is credited.

Common (or Preferred) Stock Subscribed:
>   When subscriptions are received, this account is credited with the par or stated value or, in the case of no-par stock without stated value, the subscription price of the shares subscribed.
>   When stock certificates are issued, this account is debited and Common (or Preferred) Stock is credited.
>   The credit balance in this account shows the par or stated value or subscription price, as the case may be, of the shares subscribed for but not issued.
>   The account is shown in the Stockholders' Equity section below the presentation for the stock issued.

Common (or Preferred) Stock:
>   When certificates are issued, this account is credited with the par or stated value or aggregate subscription price of the shares represented by the certificates. In other words, whatever amount was credited to the stock subscribed account when the shares were subscribed for is credited to the Common (or Preferred) Stock account when the shares are issued.

Illustration. Subscriptions are received for 200 shares of no-par common stock with a stated value of $10 per share. The subscription price is $12 per share.

```
Subscriptions receivable.................................  2,400
    Common stock subscribed...........................          2,000
    Paid-in surplus—No-par common....................           400
    Subscriptions for 200 shares at $12 per share.
```

Each subscriber pays one-third of the subscription price.

```
Cash..................................................    800
    Subscriptions receivable............................          800
    Partial collection of subscriptions receivable.
```

Each subscriber pays the balance of the subscription price.

```
Cash..................................................  1,600
    Subscriptions receivable............................        1,600
    Collection of balance of subscriptions receivable.

Common stock subscribed..............................  2,000
    Common stock........................................        2,000
    Issuance of 200 shares after collection of subscriptions in
    full.
```

A corporation may issue stock before the subscriber has paid in full for the subscribed shares. A variety of terms or conditions may be set forth in subscription agreements concerning the requirements that must be satisfied before the shares are issued. For instance, the subscription agreement may provide that shares are to be issued when the subscriber has paid 90 per cent of the subscription price. Whatever the conditions, whenever they are satisfied and the shares are issued, the stock subscribed account is debited and the capital stock account is credited.

The subscription agreement might provide that the shares are to be issued when subscriptions are received. If so, the entry for the subscription and issuance would be as follows:

```
Subscriptions receivable.................................  4,000
    Common stock........................................          2,500
    Paid-in surplus—No-par common....................           1,500
    Issuance of 500 shares of no-par common at $8 per share;
    stated value, $5 per share.
```

Balance sheet presentation. The balance sheet should show, with respect to each class of stock:

(1) The par value, if any, or the fact that the stock is without par value.
(2) The special rights appertaining to any class of stock.
(3) The number of shares authorized; the number unissued; the number issued and outstanding; and the number, if any, subscribed for but not issued.

(4) The paid-in surplus, if any, applicable to each class of stock.

(5) The balances of any subscriptions receivable.

Where should the uncollected subscriptions receivable be shown? If it is expected that the subscriptions will be collected, they can be shown on the asset side of the balance sheet. If collection is expected in the relatively near future, it is customary to show the subscriptions receivable as a current asset, but they should be clearly shown as subscriptions to capital stock, and not as ordinary accounts receivable. If there is no immediate intention to call upon the subscribers for the uncollected balances of their subscriptions, the subscriptions may still be shown on the asset side of the balance sheet, but not as a current asset.

However, if there is some question whether the uncollected balances will ever be called, or whether they are collectible, it is preferable to exclude them from the assets and show them as a deduction in the Stockholders' Equity section, in some manner similar to the following:

```
Stockholders' equity:
  Capital stock:
    Preferred—6% cumulative, participating; par value,
      $100; authorized, 1,000 shares; unissued, 250
      shares; issued and outstanding, 750 shares......  $75,000
      Less uncollected subscriptions.................   15,000  $ 60,000
                                                        --------
    Common—No par value; authorized, 5,000 shares;
      unissued, 1,900 shares; issued and outstanding,
      3,100 shares, at stated value of $50.....................  155,000
      Total.............................................  $215,000
    Paid-in surplus—Common stock..........................   31,000
                                                             --------
      Total...............................................  $246,000
```

Forfeited subscriptions. A subscriber may fail to pay his subscription in full. The accounting procedure depends upon the law of the state of incorporation. To illustrate, assume that the following transactions occur:

A. B. Jones subscribes at par for 5 common shares with an aggregate par value of $500.

He pays $200 and defaults.

The shares are issued to another for $480.

The expenses incurred as a result of the default are $30.

In some states the subscriber is allowed a specified time to complete his payments; if he remains delinquent at the close of that period, he is entitled to no refund, whether or not the shares are issued to another. Under these conditions the entries would be:

```
Subscriptions receivable.......................................  500
    Common stock subscribed................................       500
  Subscription of A. B. Jones.
```

```
Cash.............................................................. 200
      Subscriptions receivable...............................         200
   Collection from Jones.

Common stock subscribed................................... 500
      Subscriptions receivable...............................         300
      Paid-in surplus—Common—Forfeited subscriptions..........   200
   Forfeiture of subscription.

Cash.............................................................. 480
Paid-in surplus—Common—Forfeited subscriptions.............  20
      Common stock............................................         500
   Issuance of stock to another.

Paid-in surplus—Common—Forfeited subscriptions.............  30
   Cash..........................................................           30
   Expense incurred as a result of default by subscriber.
```

In other states, an effort must be made to find another subscriber for the forfeited shares. If the corporation is successful, the amount received from the original subscriber, minus any discount and expense incurred as a result of the default, must be refunded to him.

```
Subscriptions receivable...................................... 500
      Common stock subscribed................................         500
   Subscription from A. B. Jones.

Cash.............................................................. 200
      Subscriptions receivable...............................         200
   Collection from Jones.

Common stock subscribed................................... 500
      Subscriptions receivable...............................         300
      Liability to defaulted subscriber.......................         200
   Default by stock subscriber.

Cash.............................................................. 480
Liability to defaulted subscriber..............................  20
      Common stock............................................         500
   Stock issued to another.

Liability to defaulted subscriber..............................  30
      Cash......................................................           30
   Expense incurred as a result of default by subscriber.

Liability to defaulted subscriber.............................. 150
      Cash......................................................          150
   Refund to Jones.
```

There is also the possibility that the defaulting subscriber may be entitled to receive the number of shares which his partial payments will pay for in full. Referring to the preceding illustration, the subscriber would receive shares with a par value of $200 and the following entry would be made:

```
Common stock subscribed................................... 500
      Subscriptions receivable...............................         300
      Common stock............................................         200
   Issuance of shares and cancellation of balance of defaulted
      subscription.
```

But assume that Jones had paid $230 on his subscription. The immediately preceding entry would become:

Common stock subscribed......................................	500	
Subscriptions receivable.......................................		270
Common stock...		200
?..		30

If the law required that Jones be reimbursed for the $30, a liability account (or Cash) would be credited with the $30. If the $30 was forfeited by Jones, a paid-in surplus account would be credited.

Stock issued for property.   When stock is issued for noncash assets, a valuation problem may arise. If a valuation is placed on the property in an arm's-length transaction, and if related facts do not make the valuation questionable, it may be accepted for purposes of determining the entry to be made to record the transaction. In other cases the valuation may be based on the fair market value of the property or the fair market value of the stock, whichever is more readily determinable. The price at which other shares were issued for cash at about the time when stock was issued for property may be a good evidence of fair value. Such evidence is not conclusive, however; instances have been known in which a few shares have been issued for cash at a price in excess of fair value, in a transaction not at arm's length, for the very purpose of attempting to establish an inflated stock value to support an inflated asset value.

The existence of a par value for stock and the accounting necessity for balancing the books have been responsible for much inflation in the recorded valuations of assets acquired by issuance of stock. If the property acquired is not worth the par of the stock, a discount on stock account should appear on the books; such an account is not likely to appear, however, because directors are disposed to value the property at the par of the stock. The law allows directors great latitude in exercising their discretion as to the value of property taken for stock. The general rule of law has been that courts will not overrule the directors' valuation even when creditors are trying to prove that par value stock was in reality issued at a discount, unless valuations have been grossly excessive and unless fraud is apparent. There is, however, a growing tendency for courts to scrutinize the valuations of assets taken for stock when creditors are attempting to prove that stock was issued for property at a discount.

The Securities and Exchange Commission has taken a more positive attitude and has frequently found that statements were misleading when property taken for stock was set up at arbitrary and inflated values. This attitude has strengthened the position of the accountant, even in cases outside the jurisdiction of the Commission. Although it may still be impossible for an accountant to insist on the recording of noncash assets at a fair cash value lower than the directors' valuation thereof, an independent public accountant should give serious consideration to the advisability of mentioning the facts in his report, particularly in view of the increasing degree of responsibility which governmental agencies and the public are expecting him to assume.

Stock issued for services. What should be the basis of valuation for stock given to an employee for services? Should it be the par or stated value, the market value, the book value, the cost to the company (if treasury stock is used), or the fair value of the services?

The fair value of the services is the most logical basis, but the market value of the stock is presumptive evidence of the value of the services, because the corporation foregoes the opportunity to sell the stock at the market price. In other words, the issuance of stock to the employee seems tantamount to issuing the stock for cash and giving the cash to the employee.

For income tax purposes, the fair value of the stock at the date of receipt is income to the recipient. Consistency would presumably require that this be recognized by the corporation as the cost of the services. However, the market value at the date when the contract was made is a more logical basis; cost to a subscriber paying in installments would be the cost at the date of the subscription, and there seems to be no difference between a cost payable in installments of cash and a cost payable in installments of services.

Income (or perhaps Retained Earnings, if the stock was issued for services in prior periods) should be charged with the determined value of the services or stock; a capital stock account should be credited with the par or stated value of the stock; and a paid-in surplus account should be credited with any excess of the total charge for the services over the amount credited to capital stock. A paid-in surplus account should be credited just as it would be with any excess of cash received for stock over its par or stated value.

The cost of treasury stock issued for services is not a proper basis for a charge to income unless this cost happens to represent the fair value of the services.

Units of preferred and common. A peculiar difficulty arises when preferred and common shares are sold in units, with no separate prices for the two classes, or when preferred and common stocks are issued together in the acquisition of a business. Under such circumstances the accountant may have difficulty in showing separate valuations for the common and preferred stocks in the balance sheet unless the directors establish stated values for the two classes of stock which will account for the entire issuance price.

To illustrate, assume that 1,000 shares of preferred stock and 1,000 shares of common stock, both without par value, are issued in the acquisition of a business. The charter provides a liquidating value of $50 per share for the preferred. The business acquired is valued at $90,000.

Let us assume, first, that the directors declare a stated value of $50 for the preferred, and a stated value of $40 for the common. The accountant can then record the acquisition of the business and the issuance of the shares as follows:

```
Net assets...........................................  90,000
    Preferred stock..................................           50,000
    Common stock.....................................           40,000
    To record stated values of 1,000 shares of preferred stock
    and 1,000 shares of common stock issued for business net
    assets.
```

The aggregate stated value of the two classes of stock may be less than the valuation placed on the net assets acquired, so that there is paid-in surplus to consider. How should the paid-in surplus be apportioned to the two classes of stock? If sales of either class of stock were made for cash, shortly before or after the issuance of the two classes in units, the cash price for the shares sold could be regarded as a fair measure of the value of the shares of that class issued with other shares, and the remainder of the issuance price could be assigned to the other class of stock. Having thus determined the aggregate amount apportionable to each class of stock, the paid-in surplus applicable to each class could be determined by subtracting the total stated value of the shares of that class issued from the aggregate amount assigned to that class.

Bonus stock.　To make a preferred stock issue or a bond issue more attractive to an investor, common stock is sometimes offered as a bonus. When par value stock is issued as a bonus, the entire par value of the bonus stock may be charged to a bonus account. For instance, if one share of common stock, par value $100, is given as a bonus with ten shares of preferred stock of the same par value per share, the entry may be:

```
Cash.................................................  1,000
Bonus to preferred stockholders.....................    100
    Preferred stock..................................           1,000
    Common stock.....................................             100
```

The objection to such an entry is that it does not face squarely the fact that there is an element of discount, on the preferred stock or the common stock or both, which should be recognized. If it is possible to determine the price at which either the preferred stock or the common stock could be sold alone, recognition can be given to the discount. For instance, referring to the foregoing illustration, assume that it is known that the preferred stock could be sold at 95 without the bonus; the transaction could be recorded as follows:

Cash	1,000	
Discount on preferred stock	50	
Discount on common stock	50	
Preferred stock		1,000
Common stock		100

The same theory applies to transactions in which stock is given as a bonus to the purchasers of bonds. Theoretically, the discount should be apportioned between the bonds and the stock on the basis of the market prices of the two securities if issued separately. However, if the corporation issuing the bonus stock was organized in a state where stock discount is illegal, the management probably would want the records to indicate that the stock was issued at par and that the bonds were issued at a discount.

As a practical matter, bonus transactions usually are managed in some manner that will avoid any debit to either a bonus account or a discount account. Corporations naturally seek to avoid having such accounts on their books, and investors who are aware of the law do not care to risk a stock discount liability. To avoid bonus and discount accounts, corporations sometimes obtain donations of stock from their stockholders; since such treasury shares are acquired at no cost, no debit to Treasury Stock is required when they are received by the corporation; therefore, no credit to Treasury Stock is required when they are reissued as a bonus; and, since no credit to Treasury Stock is required, no debit to a bonus or discount account is required.

Stock rights or warrants. Stock warrants, or rights to acquire stock, may be issued by a corporation:

(1) After a decision to issue additional shares. The holders of shares of the same class may have a pre-emptive right to subscribe to the new shares, and the warrants may be issued to them as evidence of this right.

(2) Concurrently with the issuance of securities of a class other than those obtainable by exercise of the rights. For instance, bonds may be issued with rights to purchase stock;

or stock of one class may be issued with rights to acquire stock of another class.

(3) To personnel in connection with employment contracts.

If a corporation has outstanding stock rights, its balance sheet should indicate the number of shares of stock reserved to meet the issuance requirements to which it is committed by the rights.

Some accounting problems incident to the issuance and redemption of stock warrants are discussed below.

(1) *Pre-emptive rights.* No entry need be made upon the issuance of warrants evidencing the pre-emptive right of stockholders to acquire additional shares, of the same class held by them, about to be issued. Nor are any special entries required upon the issuance of the shares if par value shares are paid for by the stockholders at par, or if no-par shares are paid for at the amount to be set up as stated value. But, assume that the rights entitle the stockholders to acquire, at $25 per share, no-par stock to be set up at a stated value of $30; upon issuance of the shares, a transfer from retained earnings to capital stock of $5 per share would be required, regardless of the market price of the stock at the time of issuance.

(2) *Stock rights issued with other securities.* To illustrate transactions of this type, let us assume that a corporation sells 1,000 shares of preferred stock at $100 per share, with warrants entitling the holders to purchase 1,000 shares of common stock of no par value at $25 per share. The customary method of recording such a transaction is to debit Cash and credit the Preferred Stock account at par; no entries are made with respect to the rights. If 1,000 shares of common stock are subsequently issued, the entry is simply:

Cash...	25,000	
Common stock—No par value....................		25,000

An alternative and perhaps a better method would give cognizance to the market value of the rights at the time of their issuance. To illustrate the procedure, let us assume that the purchase rights are detachable and that the market value of the common stock at the date of the issuance of the rights is $27 per share. Since the rights entitle the holder or a transferee to purchase common shares at $25 each, the rights apparently have a value of $2 each. Entries for the sale of the preferred stock and the issuance of the rights, giving recognition to the $2 valuation of the rights, could be made as follows:

Cash...	100,000	
Discount on preferred stock.........................	2,000	
Preferred stock...................................		100,000
Common stock warrants outstanding..............		2,000

Such an entry gives recognition to the economic fact of inferential discount logically assignable to the preferred stock. If entries are made in this manner, the subsequent issuance of 1,000 shares of common stock at $25 would be recorded as follows:

```
Cash.................................................. 25,000
Common stock warrants outstanding....................  2,000
    Common stock—No par value........................        27,000
```

(3) *Warrants issued to officers and employees.* Warrants may be issued to members of a corporation's personnel entitling them to purchase stock during some specified time period at stated prices. Sometimes such a plan is used as a means of raising additional capital, but it is used more often as a device to obtain a more widespread ownership of the corporation's stock by its employees with a consequent increased employee interest in the corporation's activities. If the value of the corporation's stock should increase above the price stated in the warrants, those holding the warrants would be in the attractive position of being able to invest in the corporation's stock at less than the currently prevailing market price for the stock.

Disclosure should be made of the number of shares reserved to meet the possible requirements of the warrants.

If the warrants are transferable, or if they can be exercised immediately upon issuance, the warrants provide little if any inducement for the officers and employees to remain in the company's employ. For this reason, a currently common procedure is to offer the personnel nontransferable stock option contracts.

Nontransferable stock option contracts. Consider the following hypothetical facts:

July 1, 1959—The board of directors of a corporation adopts a plan whereby stock options may be granted to all or some of the personnel entitling them to purchase stated numbers of shares of $10 par value common stock at an established price. The options are nontransferable and they cannot be exercised (1) until two years after the date of grant, and (2) unless the holder continues in the employment of the corporation. Options not exercised within one year after becoming exercisable lapse.

Aug. 1, 1959—Options for 12,000 shares are granted. The options establish the purchase price of the shares at $20 per share. Today's market price is $22 per share.

Aug. 1, 1961—The options may be exercised by holders still in the company's employ because the conditions stated above have been satisfied.

June 1, 1962—The options are exercised and 12,000 shares of stock are acquired by the option holders for $20 per share. Today's market price is $30.

It is presumable that the efforts of the officers and employees holding the stock options contributed to the rise in per-share values; the stock option plan rewards them for the consequences of their efforts and thus results in additional compensation. The accountant faces the problems (1) of measuring the amount of such compensation—to ignore it would result in understating the cost of services received from the officers and employees and overstating net income—and (2) of determining the period or periods which should be charged for the cost of the services.

The latest position taken by the Committee on Accounting Procedure on this question is indicated by the following quotation from A.R.B. 43.

"When compensation is paid in a form other than cash the *amount* of compensation is ordinarily determined by the fair value of the property which was agreed to be given in exchange for the services to be rendered. The time at which such fair value is to be determined may be subject to some difference of opinion but it appears that the date on which an option is granted to a specific individual would be the appropriate point at which to evaluate the cost to the employer. . . . It follows that it is the value of the option at that time, rather than the grantee's ultimate gain or loss on the transaction, which for accounting purposes constitutes whatever compensation the grantor intends to pay. . . .

"The date of grant also represents the date on which the corporation foregoes the principal alternative use of the shares which it places subject to option, i.e., the sale of such shares at the then prevailing market price. Viewed in this light, the *cost* of utilizing the shares for purposes of the option plan can best be measured in relation to what could then have been obtained through sale of such shares in the open market. However, the fact that the grantor might, as events turned out, have obtained at some later date either more or less for the shares in question than at the date of the grant does not bear upon the measurement of the compensation which can be said to have been in contemplation of the parties at the date the option was granted."

Following the committee's position, $24,000 is an acceptable measure of the additional compensation under the conditions set forth in the preceding case. It is computed in the manner shown on the following page.

Market value per share on date options were granted............ $	22
Exercise price..	20
Excess of market price over exercise price..................... $	2
Multiply by number of shares issued...........................	12,000
Total additional compensation................................	$24,000

Which period or periods should be charged with the additional compensation? Since the employee must work for two years after the date of issuance of the stock options to obtain the additional compensation, that period seems to be an appropriate one over which to charge the additional compensation to operations.

The following entries spread the $24,000 of additional compensation over the two-year period; it is assumed that the company is on a calendar-year accounting basis.

Dec. 31, 1959	Additional compensation.......................	5,000	
	Accumulated credit under stock option plan..		5,000
	Portion of additional compensation under stock option plan applicable to 1959.		
Dec. 31, 1960	Additional compensation.......................	12,000	
	Accumulated credit under stock option plan..		12,000
	Portion of additional compensation under stock option plan applicable to 1960.		
Aug. 1, 1961	Additional compensation.......................	7,000	
	Accumulated credit under stock option plan..		7,000
	Final apportionment of additional compensation under stock option plan.		

The following entry is made when the stock is issued:

June 1, 1962	Cash..	240,000	
	Accumulated credit under stock option plan......	24,000	
	Common stock—$10 par value..............		120,000
	Premium on common stock................		144,000
	Issuance of 12,000 shares at $20 per share pursuant to option agreement.		

The $144,000 credit to Premium on Common Stock is the excess of the consideration received (cash and services) over the par value of the stock issued.

The credit balance, at any time, in the Accumulated Credit Under Stock Option Plan account is a part of stockholders' equity and is somewhat analogous to a stock subscribed account.

Should the employees fail to exercise their options and permit them to lapse, the accountant should remove the credit balance in the accumulated credit account, but there is some question whether the resulting credit should be considered

(1) as a correction of prior years' net income;

As it turned out, no additional compensation was distributed to the employees, and hence the prior years' charges for additional compensation were unnecessary and resulted in understating the net income figures.

(2) or as additional paid-in surplus (Donated Surplus would be a suitable account title).
The services were performed and, if the estimated value of the services was reasonable and determined in good faith, in effect additional capital was contributed to the company.

The authors are inclined to favor the latter alternative.

Assessments on stockholders. Under certain circumstances a corporation may make an assessment against its stockholders. The method of recording the collection of assessments paid by stockholders depends upon whether the stock was originally issued at a discount. If it was not issued at a discount, the amount received should be credited to a paid-in surplus account with some title such as "Paid-in Surplus—Common—Stockholders' Assessments." If the stock was originally issued at a discount, a portion of the assessment equal to the discount should be credited to the discount account, and only the remainder, if any, should be credited to paid-in surplus.

Change from par to no par. Most state laws permit corporations with par value stock outstanding to change to a no-par basis, or vice versa.

If a change from a par to a no-par basis consists merely of calling in shares which had been issued at par and issuing an equal number of no-par shares with a stated value equal to the par value of the old shares, the only entry required is one closing out the par value stock account and opening a new account with the same balance. For instance, assume that a company's authorized issue consists of 1,000 shares of common stock of $100 par value, and that 600 shares were issued at par and are outstanding; assume also that the charter is amended to cancel the old par value shares and authorize the issuance of 1,000 shares of no par value; assume further that the directors assign a stated value of $100 per share to the no-par stock. The only entry required is:

Common stock	60,000	
Common stock		60,000

The old and new Common Stock accounts appear as follows:

Common Stock

(Authorized issue, 1,000 shares, $100 par value)				
Date 600 shares converted to shares of no par value	60,000	Date 600 shares issued		60,000

Common Stock

(Authorized issue, 1,000 shares,	$100 stated value)	
	Date 600 shares issued	60,000

Assume that 2,000 no-par shares were authorized and that they were given a stated value of $50 per share. The journal entry to record the conversion would be the same as that shown above. The 2,000 shares of no-par stock authorized and the 1,200 shares issued would be shown in the new Common Stock account.

If a company changing from a par to a no-par basis has any surplus accounts resulting either from operations or from transactions in the stock which is being converted to a no-par basis, the balances of these accounts should not be transferred, in whole or in part, to capital stock unless the directors authorize such a transfer entry or take some formal action which is equivalent to authorizing such an entry. Any such transfers usually would be made first from any premium on stock or other paid-in surplus accounts resulting from transactions in the par value shares which are being converted to a no-par basis; the remainder should be transferred from Retained Earnings. To illustrate a formal board action equivalent to the authorization of a transfer from surplus to capital stock and the related entries, assume that a company has 1,000 shares of common outstanding with a par value of $100,000 and surplus accounts as follows:

Premium on common stock................................. $25,000
Retained earnings... 40,000

Assume, also, that the par value shares are called in and that 3,000 shares of no-par common stock are issued with a stated value of $50 per share. This would mean a declaration of $150,000 as stated capital. The entry for the conversion would be:

Common stock..................................... 100,000
Premium on common stock......................... 25,000
Retained earnings................................ 25,000
   Common stock................................. 150,000

After a change from a par basis to a no-par basis has been recorded, any balance remaining in a premium on stock account or any other paid-in surplus account related to the par value shares converted should be transferred to new paid-in surplus accounts; the titles of the old accounts would be inappropriate in relation to the new no-par shares.

If a company with par value stock and an accumulated deficit from operations changes its capital structure to no-par stock with a stated value less than the par value of the stock previously outstanding, thus creating a paid-in surplus, the law may permit the elimination of the deficit by charge to such paid-in surplus.

If the par value stock was issued at a discount, the permission to change to a no-par basis might carry an implied permission to eliminate the discount account; this is a matter of law.

Convertible stocks and bonds. Some stocks and bonds are convertible into other securities of the issuing corporation at the option of the holder. The specified conversion ratios will affect the accounting for the conversion. For instance, a $1,000 bond may provide that it can be converted into common stock at a conversion price of $20 per share. In effect, such a bond can be used to buy 50 shares of common stock. At the time of the bond issuance, the market price of the common stock will presumably be below $20 per share. Should the issuing company prosper and the market value of its shares increase, a bondholder may find it attractive to convert his investment into common stock.

The following generalizations suggest the framework within which the accountant approaches the recording of conversions.

Conversions should not result in an increase in retained earnings. All amounts related to the securities being converted must be transferred to accounts associated with the new securities issued at conversion.

The examples below indicate the application of the above requirements.

Example—Convertible bonds.

Facts: Each $1,000 bond may be exchanged at any interest date for 30 shares of the company's no-par, $20 stated value, common stock.

Ten bonds are presented for conversion when the company's accounts show the following information relating to the bonds:

Bonds payable	$500,000
Discount on bonds	5,000

Entries for conversion:

Bonds payable......................................	10,000	
Discount on bonds............................		100
Common stock.................................		6,000
Paid-in surplus—No-par common...................		3,900

Issuance of 300 shares of no-par common in exchange for ten bonds, per conversion terms.

Example—Convertible preferred stock.

Facts: Each share of $50 par value preferred stock may be exchanged for four shares of no-par (no stated value) common stock.

Four hundred shares are presented for conversion when the company's accounts show the following information relating to the outstanding preferred stock:

Preferred stock....................	$200,000
Premium on preferred stock	10,000

Entries for conversion:

Preferred stock......................................	20,000	
Premium on preferred stock..........................	1,000	
Common stock...................................		21,000
Issuance of 1,600 shares of no-par common in exchange for 400 shares of preferred (one-tenth of the outstanding shares), per conversion terms.		

If one class of a company's stock is convertible at the holder's option into shares of another class, the balance sheet (or a footnote appended thereto) should state the number of authorized but unissued shares of stock which have been reserved to meet the conversion requirements.

CHAPTER SIX

Surplus and Dividends

Terminology. Formerly it was the custom to use only one Surplus account, and it was credited with such diverse elements as earnings, portions of contributed capital, and unrealized increases in the valuation of assets shown by appraisals or market values.

During the quarter-century following World War I, much thought was given to the desirability of classifying the elements of surplus according to their *source,* and the adoption of appropriate distinguishing terminology. As a consequence, the terms *earned surplus, capital surplus, paid-in surplus,* and *appraisal surplus* came into use.

In more recent years accountants have become concerned about the term "surplus" as a potential source of misunderstanding by users of financial statements. In 1948 the American Accounting Association dropped the term "surplus" from its statement of accounting concepts and standards. In 1949 the Institute's Committee on Accounting Procedure authorized the publication, as Bulletin 39, of a report of its Subcommittee on Terminology, in which the discontinuance of the use of the term "surplus" was recommended. The subcommittee noted the misleading connotations associated with the term "surplus," such as excess, overplus, residue, or "that which remains when use or need is satisfied"—meanings which are not intended in its accounting usage. Words

123

indicating source, such as "retained income," "retained earnings," or "accumulated earnings," were suggested as suitable replacements for "earned surplus." In place of paid-in surplus, the somewhat lengthy phrase "capital contributed for shares in excess of par (or stated value)" was proposed. Similarly, "excess of appraised or fair value of fixed assets over cost" or "appreciation of fixed assets" was recommended in place of "appraisal surplus."

The positions noted above were reiterated in Accounting Terminology Bulletin No. 1, issued in 1953, and in the 1957 revision of accounting concepts and standards, prepared by a committee of the American Accounting Association. With regard to the term "earned surplus," these recommendations have had a significant impact on the terminology of financial statements. There has been a marked decline in the use of earned surplus for financial statement purposes, although the term "earned surplus" is still used by accountants in discussions and writings as a technical term of accounting.

In this text, the term "surplus" has not been discarded completely. In illustrations of financial statements, the more modern terminology has been favored. But in discussions, terms are used interchangeably—as they are in practice. However, the term "capital surplus" will not be used because it does not have a definite and generally recognized meaning. It has not been authoritatively defined, nor has it been uniformly used by accountants. There is some unanimity of opinion that it should not be used as the title of an account, but should be regarded merely as a generic term to be applied to a class of accounts. However, accountants are not in agreement as to the accounts which should be regarded as belonging to the capital surplus class.

Accountants are in general agreement that the term "capital surplus" is properly applied to accounts credited with surplus arising from:

(a) Transactions in the company's own stock.
(b) Donations by stockholders.
(c) Donations by outsiders.

But accountants are not in agreement as to whether the term should be applied to an account credited with an unrealized increment in the valuation of an asset. Many accountants believe that the word *surplus*, however modified or qualified, should not be applied to unrealized increments in asset values. The word "surplus" will not be used in this text in connection with unrealized increments in asset values.

Paid-in surplus.   Paid-in surplus includes the following:

(A) Surplus resulting from transactions in the company's own
      stock:
   (1) Premiums on par value stock.
   (2) Excess of amounts received for no-par stock over
        amounts set up as stated values thereof.
   (3) Forfeited part payments on stock subscriptions.
   (4) Surplus resulting from miscellaneous stock transac-
        tions and changes:
      (a) Sale of treasury stock at more than cost.
      (b) Retirement of stock at a cost less than the
           amount set up as stated capital.
      (c) Conversion of stock of one kind into a smaller
           amount of stock of another kind.
      (d) Reduction of stated capital.
(B) Surplus resulting from stockholders' contributions:
   (1) Donations by stockholders, including gifts and for-
        giveness of indebtedness.
   (2) Assessments on stockholders.
(C) Surplus resulting from contributions by outsiders, including
      gifts of assets (such as a plant given to induce a company
      to locate in the donor city) and forgiveness of indebted-
      ness.

Although all of these elements may be regarded as paid-in
surplus, the reader is aware that they should not all be recorded
in a single paid-in surplus account. To so record them would result
in an inadequate classification of paid-in surplus according to
source and a failure to maintain the detailed record necessary for
proper accounting and statement-preparation purposes.

The term *paid-in surplus* is sometimes used as a generic term to
apply to all accounts of that category; it is sometimes included
in specific account titles. One reason for keeping separate accounts
with the various elements of paid-in surplus is that certain elements of paid-in surplus may be available for dividends whereas
other elements are not.

Writers have frequently expressed the opinion that dividends
should not be charged to paid-in surplus. Such statements are
likely to be misleading, since they may create the impression that
paid-in surplus is not legally available for dividends. Paid-in
surplus may or may not be available for dividends, depending
upon how the paid-in surplus arose and upon the law of the state
in which the company was incorporated. In many states there
seems to be little or no restriction against the payment of dividends

from paid-in surplus. It probably would be better to state that stockholders should have the right to assume that dividends come from earnings unless they are informed to the contrary, and that, if dividends are charged against paid-in surplus, disclosure of that fact will be made to them.

What, if any, charges can with propriety be made against paid-in surplus accounts? Paid-in surplus accounts can properly be reduced by certain direct opposites of proper credits thereto. For instance, a paid-in surplus resulting from the issuance of stock at a premium can properly be charged with a premium paid on the retirement of stock *of the same class.* But if preferred stock is issued at par and common stock is issued at a premium of, say, $40,000, and if the preferred stock is subsequently retired at a premium of $15,000, the Securities and Exchange Commission refuses to sanction charging the premium on retirement of the preferred stock against the paid-in surplus resulting from the issuance of the common stock at a premium. And most accountants appear to recognize the propriety of the refusal.

If stock was issued for property and the debit to the property account was offset in part by a credit to a paid-in surplus account, and if the property is subsequently found to be overvalued, can the book value of the property be reduced by a debit to the paid-in surplus account which was credited when the property was acquired? To do so does not seem to be a defensible procedure unless the property was overvalued when it was received. But even in such a case it may be argued that a charge to the paid-in surplus account is improper because, after a company has once made an avowal as to the valuation of the property and established its depreciation accounting on the basis thereof, it is bound to abide thereafter by that avowal. It is not bound to retain the overvaluation in the asset account, but it is restrained from recording a reduction in the valuation in any way which would relieve retained earnings of proper direct charges thereto or of indirect charges which would result from periodical depreciation provisions.

As to asset write-downs and losses generally, the basic principle was stated in A. R. B. No. 1, issued in 1939, which contained the following statement: "Capital surplus, however created, should not be used to relieve the income account of the current or future years of charges which would otherwise fall to be made there-against." This is in conformity with the following statement contained in the Securities and Exchange Commission's Accounting Series Release No. 1, issued in 1937: "It is my conviction that capital surplus should under no circumstances be used to write off losses which, if currently recognized, would have been chargeable against income." A similar position was taken as early as 1936 by the American Accounting Association.

The basic principle is somewhat modified to permit a company to utilize paid-in surplus to absorb a debit balance in the Earned Surplus account which may have been caused in whole or in part by a write-down or write-off of assets, if this is done in connection with a quasi-reorganization. This matter is discussed later.

Earned surplus (retained earnings). Earned surplus represents the retained portion of current and prior years' net income, plus or minus the cumulative effect of unusual and nonrecurring gains or losses or other credits and charges assigned directly to earned surplus.

Under certain circumstances earned surplus may be transferred to other accounts within the stockholders' equity group. Some such transfers reduce the earned surplus legally; this can be achieved by suitable action on the part of the board of directors, with the result that some designated amount of earned surplus is changed into stated capital. As an example, suppose that a corporation's capital stock consists of $10 par value stock which was issued at par, that there was no paid-in surplus, and that the board of directors, after complying with the applicable legal requirements, changed the par value stock to no par with a stated value of $15 per share. Thus, for each share of outstanding stock, $5 of earned surplus would be capitalized.

It is possible for earned surplus to be a negative quantity, in which case it is customarily described as a deficit.

Appraisal increments. Accounting Research Bulletin No. 5, issued in 1940, contained the following statement: "Accounting for fixed assets should normally be based on cost, and any attempt to make property accounts in general reflect current values is both impracticable and inexpedient." Nevertheless, the accounts of some businesses have been adjusted to reflect fixed asset valuations based upon appraisals; and, when such asset revaluations have been upward, credits have not infrequently been made to accounts with titles such as "Appraisal Surplus" and "Appreciation Surplus." As previously stated, it seems undesirable to use the word "surplus" in the title of an account unless its balance represents an increment which has been realized. Therefore, a title such as "Unrealized Increment in Valuation of Fixed Assets" seems preferable.

If an unrealized increment in value is recorded in the accounts, what disposition should be made of the resulting credit-balance account when the written-up assets have been fully depreciated or sold? The answer is not settled, but there is support for treating the credit item as part of permanent capital. The board of directors could formalize the treatment by issuing additional shares of stock to the stockholders, debiting the unrealized increment account for the amount thereby capitalized and considered to be a part of permanent capital. An alternative approach is to transfer the unrealized increment to retained earnings when the asset is disposed of or written off as fully depreciated. This matter and other accounting problems incident to appraisals are discussed at some length in Chapter 18.

Surplus restrictions and appropriations. Some portion of a corporation's surplus may be restricted, either as a result of the operation of certain provisions of the state's corporation act, or as a consequence of clauses in contracts with creditors or stockholders, or by voluntary action of the board of directors. The primary purpose of such restrictions is to indicate that designated amounts of surplus are not available for dividends, or that the directors intend to refrain from using them for that purpose.

The accountant faces the responsibility of reporting to users of financial statements the existence of any surplus restrictions. One common method of communicating to statement users is by transfer of the restricted surplus to a separate account whose title discloses the nature of the restriction. Such accounts are known as *surplus reserves* or *surplus appropriations*. To illustrate, suppose that a corporation is planning a large expansion of its manufacturing facilities and that the expansion will be financed "from retained earnings." In other words, no additional securities will be issued, as no new funds are needed to finance the new facilities. In effect this means that a portion of the assets acquired through profitable operations and not distributed to stockholders as dividends is being invested in fixed assets. A probable consequence of this is that dividends may be limited—at least for the near future. To indicate the expectation that dividends will be limited, the directors may order the establishment of a Reserve for Plant Expansion out of retained earnings in the amount of, say, $500,000. The accounting entry would be:

```
Retained earnings...................................  500,000
    Reserve for plant expansion......................          500,000
    Surplus restriction ordered by the board of directors
    because of plant expansion plans.
```

Of course, the directors can limit the payment of dividends and retain the funds for other purposes without making any book entries, but they often feel that it is desirable to reduce the balance in the Retained Earnings account and thus avoid, at least partially, the dividend clamor which might otherwise come from the stockholders.

A similar disclosure requirement exists when a corporation faces a type of contingency in which there is only a remote probability that the outcome may materially affect the financial position or the results of operations. Suppose that a corporation is sued for patent infringement. If the corporation loses the case, the amount of the loss will be known and can be reported as such in the financial statements. Prior to such definite determination, all that can and need be disclosed is the fact that the corporation faces a possible loss with an estimate of the number of dollars involved. Disclosure of this information can be achieved by establishing a surplus reserve with some such title as Reserve for Contingencies.

It should be understood that neither the retained earnings nor the stockholders' equity is reduced as a result of entries made to show surplus restrictions. Also, when the conditions that caused the appropriation of surplus are no longer present, the reserve account is closed by a reversing entry, which returns the amount involved to retained earnings. In fact, the only proper debit to a surplus reserve account is for its return to retained earnings. Surplus reserves are not set up to take debits that are properly made to expense or loss accounts or directly to retained earnings.

To show how surplus reserves, often referred to as "surplus appropriations," are set forth in the balance sheet, it is assumed that a corporation has four surplus reserve accounts.

```
Retained earnings:
  Appropriated:
    Sinking fund reserve........................... $ 60,000
    Reserve for retirement of preferred stock........    50,000
    Reserve for plant expansion....................    75,000
    Reserve for contingencies......................    10,000
      Total......................................  $195,000
  Free...........................................   115,000
      Total retained earnings........................   $310,000
```

It is probably true that many nonaccountants misunderstand the nature of surplus reserve accounts. Since the primary purpose of surplus reserves is to inform the statement user of contingencies or that certain amounts of surplus are restricted and not available as a basis for dividends, there is merit in the alternative of using one or more footnotes to communicate such information. It seems reasonable to believe that footnotes to financial statements are less likely to confuse the reader. An example follows:

```
Retained earnings (See Note A)........................... $700,000
```

Note A:
　　In view of the extensive addition to the company's manufacturing facilities now being planned, the directors have earmarked $300,000 of the retained earnings as not available for dividend purposes.

A serious problem associated with setting up such surplus reserves is the difficulty of getting rid of them. If a reserve for plant expansion is established, it cannot be charged with the cost of any additional plant acquired; the new plant must be charged to the asset accounts. A reserve for advertising, created as an appropriation of retained earnings to disclose an advertising program, cannot be charged with advertising expenditures; these must be charged to the expense accounts. Therefore, setting up surplus reserves to reduce retained earnings to the amount which the directors feel may be distributed in dividends has its disadvantages. Setting up such reserves merely temporizes with the situation, because there is no way of getting rid of the reserves except by returning them to retained earnings. Furthermore, the appropriation of retained earnings for purposes other than dividend payments, if carried to its logical conclusion, could result in the complete disappearance of the retained earnings account from the balance sheet. All earnings retained in the business are presumably retained for one purpose or another; if one purpose is to be indicated by an appropriation of retained earnings, why should not all purposes be similarly indicated? For instance, if funds are retained for additional working capital, why not have a reserve for working capital?

When a significant portion of the funds provided by past earnings has been permanently committed to the business by being invested in fixed assets or required inventories, management sometimes declares a stock dividend. In effect, such action transfers a portion of retained earnings to capital stock and possibly paid-in surplus, and thereby gives explicit recognition to the fact that a portion of past earnings is not subject to distribution as dividends.

Reserves for self-insurance. If a company has tangible assets distributed in relatively small amounts in a large number of locations, it may decide upon a policy of self-insurance; no insurance is carried, and the company must stand all losses suffered. Under these circumstances, businesses sometimes establish a reserve for self-insurance by charges to expense, the reserve account being charged with the losses if and when they occur. In this way, losses may be spread more evenly over successive fiscal periods. Accountants are not in agreement whether this type of reserve procedure is acceptable.

Some accountants maintain that such a reserve should not be established by charges to operations. They argue that no expense is incurred unless and until a loss is sustained; until this occurs, the assets are still in existence, no loss or expense has been incurred, the stockholders' equity has not been diminished, and the reserve is actually a part of retained earnings, set aside as a provision for a contingency. Sir A. Lowes Dickinson took this position when he wrote that "provisions for insurance against future possible losses from fire and other insurable risks [are] mere allocations of surplus." Following this line of reasoning, if reserves for self-insurance are established, they should be created by charges to Retained Earnings; they should not be used to absorb charges for expenses or losses arising from the failure to carry insurance; and they should eventually be returned by credits to Retained Earnings.

On the other hand, it is sometimes argued that, if a company practices so-called self-insurance, it should charge operations and credit a reserve with an amount which it would otherwise pay for insurance premiums, in order to put its accounts on a basis comparable with that of other companies and to avoid the distorting effects of unusual or nonrecurring losses attributable to the self-insurance program. The answer to this argument seems to be that a company on a self-insurance program is different from companies carrying insurance; why should accounting attempt to cover up this difference by hypothetical entries for insurance expense? A company which pays insurance premiums incurs an operating expense; a company which does not pay such premiums does not incur a premium expense, and no loss is incurred unless a fire or accident occurs.

The following statements summarize the prevailing alternative methods of dealing with reserves for self-insurance:

Alternative 1. Reserves for self-insurance may be created by charges to Retained Earnings as a method of disclosing the contingency that losses may arise from an election to self-insure.

Such reserves, being surplus reserves, should not be used to absorb any expenses or losses.

Expenses or losses arising from an election to self-insure should be recorded and reported as though no reserve for self-insurance existed.

Alternative 2. Reserves for self-insurance may be created by periodic charges to operating expense.

Reserves of this origin may absorb expenses and losses arising from an election to self-insure.

Reserves of this origin, not having been created by charges to Retained Earnings, should not be classified in the Stockholders' Equity category.

From the preceding discussion it may be readily seen why it is often difficult to decide whether a reserve intended to even out expenses and losses by years should be condemned as a device to equalize reported earnings or accepted as a sensible procedure to determine more accurately the periodic net income. It is generally agreed that, whenever reserves of this type develop relatively large balances, they probably are, in fact, profit-equalization reserves.

Liquidating value of stock. In the event of liquidation, the preferred stockholders may be entitled to receive, in addition to cumulative dividends in arrears, an amount in excess of the valuation at which the stock is shown in the balance sheet. For instance, the stock may have a par value of $100 per share, but carry a preference right to $110 per share in liquidation; or no-par stock carried in the balance sheet at $50 per share may have a liquidating value of $60 per share.

When preferred stock has a liquidating value greater than the amount at which it is shown in the balance sheet, a clear disclosure of that fact should be made in the balance sheet, or in a footnote appended thereto. Disclosure (parenthetically in the balance sheet or by footnote) may be made by stating the total dollar amount of the liquidating value; or by stating the excess of the total liquidating value over the total par or other amount at which it is shown in the balance sheet; or by stating the number of shares outstanding and the liquidating value per share.

If the aggregate liquidating value of the preferred stock, plus any preferred dividends in arrears, equals or exceeds total stockholders' equity with the result that the holders of stocks junior to the preferred stock have no liquidating equity in the company, this fact should be clearly disclosed.

There may be a dividend restriction on surplus in an amount equal to the excess of the liquidating value of the preferred stock over its par or stated value. For instance, assume that the preferred stock has a par value of $100,000 and a liquidating value of $110,000, and that the company has retained earnings of $25,000. There may be a $10,000 restriction on the retained earnings, so that dividends of only $15,000 can be paid. The balance sheet or an appended footnote should so state if such a restriction exists. If the company has a paid-in surplus which was created by transactions in the preferred stock, such paid-in surplus may reduce the restriction on retained earnings.

If there are more than two classes of stock, two of the classes may have liquidating values in excess of the amounts at which they are shown in the balance sheet. Disclosures such as those mentioned

above should then be made with respect to both such classes of
stock.

Surplus availability for dividends. Although it is sometimes necessary for the accountant to disclose surplus restrictions
or appropriations, it should be emphasized that the objective is
to make the financial statements more useful and informative.
It is not the accountant's responsibility to determine amounts
legally available for dividends; this is a matter of law, and availability differs in various states.

Accountants are primarily interested in a classification of surplus according to *source*. Source is determined by the facts and
not by the law, and therefore is not affected by jurisdictional differences; moreover, the determination of source is properly within
the province of the accountant. Although the determination of the
amount of surplus available for dividends is not the function of the
accountant, the classification of surplus according to source provides information which may be essential to a legal determination
of the amount available for dividends.

Dividends. Dividends distributed by corporations to their
stockholders may be classified as follows:

(A) Dividends which reduce retained earnings or paid-in surplus
   legally available for dividends:
   (1) Decreasing stockholders' equity:
      (a) Cash dividends.
      (b) Dividends paid in noncash assets. For exam-
         ple, a company holding securities may dis-
         tribute these securities among its stock-
         holders as a dividend.
         Although dividends received in property
         other than cash generally are taxable to the
         recipients at the fair market value thereof,
         the corporation paying the dividend should
         ordinarily give no recognition to such market
         value, but should record the distribution at
         the book value of the assets distributed.
         A peculiar problem may arise if a company
         has participating preferred stock and com-
         mon stock and pays a property dividend on
         one class of shares and a cash dividend on
         the other class. For instance, assume that
         a company has outstanding $100,000 par
         value of common stock and participating
         preferred stock of an equal par value; that
         it distributes as a dividend to the common

stockholders certain investment securities carried at $6,000 but having a fair market value of $10,000; and that a matching cash dividend is to be paid to the preferred stockholders. Since equity would require that the preferred stockholders receive a cash dividend of $10,000, and since the accounts should show that the two classes of stock participated equally in the dividends, it probably would be desirable to write up the securities to their market value before distributing them as a dividend to the common stockholders.

(c) Liability dividends. Dividends may be distributed in the form of bonds, notes, or scrip. Bonds or notes so issued usually have a definite maturity and bear interest; scrip dividends may or may not have a definite maturity, and may or may not bear interest. When scrip or some other evidence of short-term indebtedness is issued as a dividend, it is usually done for the purpose of maintaining the appearance of a regular dividend when cash is temporarily not available for payment. The issuance of long-term securities as a dividend is not common; such securities occasionally are issued to convert surplus available for dividends into funded debt. The issuance of evidences of indebtedness as a dividend may require the authorization of the stockholders.

(2) Not decreasing stockholders' equity:

This classification covers stock dividends. A stock dividend does not change the amount of the stockholders' equity of a corporation; it merely changes the portions of stockholders' equity represented by surplus and by capital stock. If all of a corporation's stock is of one class, a stock dividend does not change the individual stockholder's interest in the stockholders' equity; it merely increases the number of shares by which his interest is represented. If a company has more than one class of stock, the issuance of a stock dividend to shareholders of one class may

alter the stockholders' interests, particularly if
the dividend is paid in shares of another class.
(B) Dividends out of capital. Such dividends return to the
stockholders a portion or all of the capital. They may be
classified as follows:
   (1) Intentional liquidating dividends, intended to return
all of the capital to the stockholders because the
company is discontinuing operations, or to return
a portion thereof to the stockholders because the
scope of the business is being reduced and the total
capital is no longer required. If a liquidating dividend is paid, stockholders should be informed of
its nature. It is desirable to set up a special account
to show the amount of capital returned by liquidating dividends. In the balance sheet it can be shown
in the Stockholders' Equity section contra to the
accounts credited with the capital invested by the
stockholders.
   (2) Unintentional returns of capital resulting from the
payment of dividends that, although intended to
be dividends out of surplus, are in reality partly
out of capital. The payment of such dividends may
result from accounting errors which have overstated earnings.

Dividends on par value stock are usually stated as a per cent
of par. Dividends on no-par stock must be stated in terms of dollars or cents per share, since the stock does not have a par value
on which a per cent can be based.

Stock split-up. A split-up should be distinguished from a
stock dividend; a stock split-up is a transaction in which the outstanding shares are called in and replaced by a larger number, the
larger number being a multiple of the number of previously outstanding shares. To be properly classified as a split-up, the transaction should not be accompanied by any change in the dollar
amount representing the stockholders' equity or, as a general rule,
in the subtotals of the paid-in capital and retained earnings elements thereof. A split-up may involve a reduction in the par or
stated value of the shares, or a change from par to no-par stock or
vice versa, but, as just noted, as a general rule this will not result
in any change in the aggregate amount shown in the accounts as
paid-in capital.

Split-ups frequently occur when a corporation's stock has so
high a market value as to interfere with trading. If, for example,

a corporation's stock has a market value of $500 per share, the market at such a price may be limited. To increase the market, the corporation may call in its outstanding shares and issue new shares at the rate of five for one. As a consequence, the market price will probably be reduced to approximately $100 per share, and public trading may be facilitated.

Legality of dividends. In general it may be said that:

> The laws seek to prohibit the impairment of stated capital by the payment of dividends.
>
> The legality of a dividend declaration may depend upon current earnings, retained earnings, or the satisfaction of certain conditions relating to aggregate stockholders' equity, or it may be determined by other statutory provisions, such as that the fair value of the assets must exceed the liabilities of the corporation. The legality of a dividend is not dependent upon the amount of the corporation's cash. The adequacy of the cash balance has a bearing on the financial expediency of paying a dividend, but not upon the legal right to declare one.
>
> Gains from extraneous transactions are generally included with earnings from regular operations for purposes of determining availability for dividends.

Aside from the foregoing, few rules applicable to the country as a whole can be stated.

Current net income is the normal source of dividends. Retained earnings are generally acceptable as a basis for dividends, subject, however, to certain limitations and modifications, among which may be mentioned the following:

> (1) In some states, dividends may be paid if there are sufficient earnings, before a discount on the issuance of stock has been written off; in other states, dividends can be paid only to the extent that surplus has been accumulated in excess of the discount.
>
> (2) In most states, dividends can be paid in an amount equal to the sum of the surplus and the depletion provisions; in some states, this is prohibited if the rights of creditors are jeopardized; and, in a few states, the rights of preferred stockholders are similarly safeguarded.
>
> (3) If losses have impaired the stated capital, most states prohibit the payment of dividends. The impairment of stated capital may be remedied by profitable operations and abstaining from the payment of dividends, or by taking the proper legal action to reduce the stated capital. A few

states permit the payment of dividends equal to current earnings, regardless of the existence of an accumulated deficit. Dividends can ordinarily be paid if surplus has been accumulated in the past, even though a loss has been incurred during the current period.

(4) Some states make the legality of a dividend dependent upon the solvency of the corporation; that is, no dividend can be paid if the corporation is insolvent or if the payment of the dividend would render it insolvent. This seems clearly to mean that the value of the assets must be in excess of the liabilities; however, there seems to be an uncertainty as to whether, under such statutes, the assets should be valued on a cost basis or on a current market basis. In one state, no dividends may be paid if the liabilities exceed two-thirds of the assets.

(5) Surplus which normally would be available for dividends may become temporarily or permanently not so available. Such restrictions may be imposed by law or may result from contracts. A legal restriction results in many states from the acquisition of treasury stock; this matter will be discussed later in connection with treasury stock. A sinking fund reserve is an illustration of surplus temporarily not available for dividends because of a contract with creditors.

We now turn to the question of the availability of paid-in surplus as a source of dividends, and here we face a great diversity of laws. Some states prohibit charging any dividends to paid-in surplus; in other states, preferred dividends can be charged to it. Most states appear to permit charging dividends against premiums on par value stock. Some states require that the entire amount received for no-par shares shall be regarded as stated capital; however, many states permit a portion of the amount received to be credited to paid-in surplus and make such surplus available for dividends.

In some states, a reduction of capital stock or stated capital does not produce a surplus available for dividends; in other states, a dividend may be charged to surplus thus produced; and, in at least one state, a reduction in the common stock may create a surplus available for dividend payments on the preferred stock.

Although appreciation "surplus" is unrealized and is therefore regarded by accountants as a dubious, if not improper, source of dividends, the laws of the various states do not uniformly prohibit its use for that purpose. Some states prohibit the payment of any dividends from unrealized appreciation of assets; others permit the distribution of stock dividends from unrealized appreciation; and some permit the distribution of either cash or stock dividends from such a source. The trend of recent legislation seems to be in the direction of explicitly prohibiting the payment of cash dividends (but not always stock dividends) by charge to unrealized appreciation; such a provision is incorporated in the Uniform Business Corporation Act which was recommended to state legislatures in 1928. Although the act has not been widely adopted, the trend of legislation seems to indicate that its provisions with respect to unrealized appreciation have had considerable influence on the state legislatures.

A good many writers on accounting have said that dividends should be paid from earned surplus only. If they mean that dividends from other sources are illegal, the statement is subject to contradiction; if an action is permitted by law, accountants can interpose no effective "should not" deterrent. However, since it is quite possible that stockholders may be uninformed as to the law and may assume that all dividends received represent distributions of retained earnings, the ethics of business management may properly require that, if a dividend is paid from any source other than retained earnings, the stockholders be informed of the source.

Because of the diversities in corporation laws, accountants can scarcely hope, without making an intensive study of the laws, to master more than the general principles underlying the legality of dividends. The determination of the legality of a dividend should be understood to lie within the province of the attorney. An accountant should not state in a balance sheet the amount which is legally available for dividends, unless his statement is based on an attorney's opinion. Even so, such a statement is not customary.

Preferred dividends in arrears. If dividends on cumulative preferred stock are in arrears, the balance sheet should disclose the fact, because common stockholders are entitled to know the prior claims of preferred stockholders against the surplus. Disclosure is usually made by a footnote, with some wording similar to the following: "On (the balance sheet date) dividends on the preferred stock were in arrears since (date)"; or, "No dividends have been paid on the preferred stock since (date)"; or, "On (the balance sheet date) dividends on the preferred stock were in arrears in the amount of $_____." If the company has retained earnings which exceed the preferred dividend arrearage, disclosure may be made as follows:

Retained earnings:
Equal to dividends in arrears on preferred stock...... $12,000
Remainder....................................... 35,000 $47,000

In this connection it may be noted that partial dividends may be paid on preferred stock.

Declared dividends a liability. The notice of the declaration of a dividend should state the date of the declaration, the date on which the stock records will be closed to determine the stockholders of record, and the date on which the dividend will be paid.

After a cash dividend has been legally declared and notice of the declaration has been given to the stockholders, the unpaid dividend ranks as a liability and should be shown as such in the balance sheet. A declared but unpaid dividend is a current liability if it is payable in cash, in short-term scrip or notes, or in property classified as a current asset.

The declaration of a dividend can be rescinded by the directors if no one but the directors has knowledge of the declaration. It can be rescinded by the stockholders at any time before the date of payment.

The fact that cash has been deposited with a trustee or fiscal agent for the payment of a dividend does not justify the omission of the liability from the balance sheet. The depositary is the agent of the company, not of the stockholders; a deposit with the company's agent does not constitute payment to the stockholders. This rule applies to the total dividend prior to the payment date, and to unclaimed dividends thereafter.

If a corporation becomes insolvent before the payment of a legally declared dividend of which the stockholders had notice, the stockholders will be entitled to share pro rata with unsecured creditors in the payment of declared dividends and debts. For instance, if there are unpaid dividends of $5,000, other liabilities of $45,000, and assets of $40,000, distribution should be made as follows:

> To stockholders: $4/5$ of $ 5,000, or $ 4,000
> To creditors: $4/5$ of $45,000, or $36,000

But this rule will not hold if the corporation was insolvent when the dividend was declared, or if the dividend was illegal, or if notice of the declaration was not given to the stockholders until after the company became insolvent.

If, when the corporation is solvent, a fund is set aside for the payment of a declared dividend, and if the company becomes insolvent before the fund is used for the designated purpose, the fund will be considered a trust fund for the stockholders, and will not be available for payments to general creditors.

Stock dividends. The principal question which accountants face in connection with stock dividends is the determination of the

amount or amounts which should be transferred from certain stockholders' equity accounts to other stockholders' equity accounts.
The laws differ in their requirements. In some cases, stock dividends are intended merely to convert paid-in surplus into capital
stock; such dividends have no effect on retained earnings, and no
accounting problems arise in recording them.

We are here concerned with the important problems which arise
in connection with the issuance of stock dividends which are presumed to constitute a capitalization of retained earnings. In such
cases the laws usually specify a minimum amount which must be
transferred from retained earnings to stated capital. With respect
to par value stock, the legal minimum usually is par. With respect
to no-par stock, the legal minimum may be the minimum amount
for which the stock could be sold, or the stated value per share of
the stock of the same class previously outstanding. In the case of
preferred stock, it is often the liquidating value.

But the minimum transfers required by law are not always regarded by accountants as sufficient to meet the requirements of
proper accounting. Corporate practice has varied as to the amount
of retained earnings capitalized in connection with such stock
dividends, and accountants have held different opinions as to the
amount which should be capitalized. Following are some of the
bases which accountants have advocated for determining the
amount per share of dividend stock to be transferred from retained
earnings:

> The amount credited to the capital stock account for shares
> previously outstanding, divided by the number of shares
> outstanding.
> The total amount received for shares previously outstanding
> (whether credited to capital stock or paid-in surplus accounts)
> divided by the number of shares outstanding.
> The total amount received for shares previously issued plus any
> other paid-in surplus applicable to the shares, divided by the
> number of shares previously issued.
> The per-share fair value of the additional shares issued. This is
> the procedure advocated in A. R. B. 43, which is discussed
> below.

In its treatment of this matter, the Committee on Accounting
Procedure concerned itself only with the most frequently encountered type of stock dividend, namely, common shares issued as a
dividend to common shareholders. The committee placed considerable weight on a belief that "many recipients of stock dividends

look upon them as distributions of corporate earnings and usually in an amount equivalent to the fair value of the additional shares received. Furthermore, it is to be presumed that such views of recipients are materially strengthened in those instances, which are by far the most numerous, where the issuances are so small in comparison with the shares previously outstanding that they do not have any apparent effect upon the share market price and, consequently, the market value of the shares previously held remains substantially unchanged." In other words, the recipients do not view stock dividends as mere capitalizations of retained earnings, but consider them as a distribution of earnings much like ordinary dividends except that shares of stock are received in place of cash.

The committee therefore recommended that "where these circumstances exist the corporation should in the public interest account for the transaction by transferring from earned surplus to the category of permanent capitalization (represented by the capital stock and capital surplus accounts) an amount equal to the fair value of the additional shares issued."

In reaching the above position, considerable weight was attached to the expectation that the additional shares issued as a stock dividend have no influence on the market value of the stock. This expectation was believed to be likely if the additional shares issued were "less than, say, 20% or 25% of the number previously outstanding . . . "

In a following paragraph the committee commented that "where the number of additional shares issued as a stock dividend is so great that it has, or may reasonably be expected to have, the effect of materially reducing the share market value, . . . the transaction clearly partakes of the nature of a stock split-up [and] under such circumstances there is no need to capitalize earned surplus, other than to the extent occasioned by legal requirements."

To illustrate the accounting entries under the above approach, assume that a company has 10,000 authorized shares of common stock of $10 par value, of which 6,000 shares are outstanding; also assume that a 10% stock dividend (600 shares) is declared and immediately issued. Assuming that the shares issued in this illustration have a fair value of $12 each, the entry to record the distribution of the stock dividend is:

```
Stock dividends (to be closed to Retained Earnings).........  7,200
        Common stock......................................         6,000
        Paid-in surplus—From stock dividends...............         1,200
    Issuance of a 10% dividend: 600 shares of $10 par value stock
    having a fair value of $12 each.
```

Assume that the stock was without par value and that it had been given a stated value of $7.50 per share; the entry would be:

```
Stock dividends.......................................  7,200
     Common stock...................................          4,500
     Paid-in surplus—From stock dividends..............          2,700
     Issuance of a 10% dividend: 600 shares of no-par stock
     (stated value, $7.50 per share) having a fair value of $12
     each.
```

If time intervenes between the declaration and issuance of the stock dividend, the entries (for the dividend on par value stock, for instance) should be:

At date of declaration:

```
Stock dividends.......................................  7,200
     Stock dividend payable...........................          6,000
     Paid-in surplus—From stock dividends..............          1,200
     Declaration of 10% stock dividend to stockholders of record
     on December 31, 1959; shares to be issued February 1, 1960.
```

At date of issuance:

```
Stock dividend payable................................  6,000
     Common stock...................................          6,000
     Issuance of 600 shares as a stock dividend.
```

If a balance sheet is prepared between the date of declaration and the date of distribution of a stock dividend, the Stockholders' Equity section should appear as illustrated below:

```
Stockholders' equity:
  Common stock—$10 par value; authorized,
    10,000 shares.
       Issued, 6,000 shares....................  $60,000.00
       To be issued February 1, 1960, as a stock
          dividend—600 shares.................    6,000.00  $66,000.00
  Surplus:
     Paid-in—Retained earnings capitalized in con-
       nection with a stock dividend..............  $ 1,200.00
     Retained earnings...........................   11,000.00   12,200.00
```

There is merit to one of the suggestions made in an earlier bulletin (Number 11) on this topic to the effect that: "In the case of any stock dividend, the issuing corporation should inform its stockholders, by notice at the time of issuance, as to the amount capitalized per share and the aggregate amount thereof, as well as to the account or accounts to which such aggregate has been charged and credited, whether or not such notification is required by statute or regulation."

The committee made no reference to the date, period of time, or sources of information that should be used in determining the fair value per share. Presumably this is a matter requiring the exercise of professional judgment. Certainly, recent market prices and trends would be important factors to consider. However, it would seem desirable to eliminate the influence of temporary conditions that may have distorted the current values of corporate shares.

Fractional shares. When stock dividends are issued, it usually is impossible to issue full shares to all of the stockholders. For instance, if a stock dividend of one share for each ten shares outstanding is to be issued, the holder of three shares could not receive a full share, and the holder of 25 shares would be entitled to receive two full shares and a fractional (1/2) share. Sometimes corporations will pay cash to the stockholders in lieu of fractional shares. Or they may issue special certificates for the fractional shares. Such special certificates customarily provide that no voting or dividend rights attach to the fractional shares. Often corporations sponsor an arrangement which will enable the recipients of fractional shares to sell them, or to buy the needed additional fractional interest to obtain full shares.

Returning to the last preceding illustration, assume that, although the dividend declaration contemplated the issuance of 600 dividend shares, it was necessary to issue special fractional share certificates equivalent to 60 shares. The entry for the distribution of the full shares and the special certificates for fractional shares should be:

Stock dividend payable.............................. 6,000		
Common stock....................................	5,400	
Fractional share certificates—Common..............	600	
Issuance, as a stock dividend, of 540 full shares and special certificates for fractional shares equivalent to 60 shares.		

When any of the stockholders have acquired special certificates aggregating full shares, they can be presented to the corporation in exchange for regular stock certificates. Entries similar to the following should be made for such exchanges.

Fractional share certificates—Common................... 100		
Common stock..	100	
Issuance of 10 shares in exchange for special certificates covering that number of full shares.		

The right to exchange the special certificates for full shares may expire at a specified date. Returning to the foregoing illustration, assume that special certificates amounting to 5 shares, issued with the dividend shares, expire. A $50 balance remains in the Fractional Share Certificates—Common account. What disposition should be made of it? Since the declaration of a cash dividend creates a liability, it would seem that the declaration of a stock dividend similarly capitalizes a portion of the retained earnings. If, under the law of the state of incorporation, the declaration of the dividend cannot be in part rescinded, the aggregate amount of retained earnings to be capitalized (in part by credit to Common Stock and in part by credit to Paid-in Surplus—From Stock Dividends) is irrevocably determined. If the amount credited to common stock is reduced because of the expiration of fractional share certificates, the amount credited to paid-in surplus should be correspondingly increased. The entry to clear the Fractional Share Certificates—Common account would then be:

```
Fractional share certificates—Common.........................  50
    Paid-in surplus—From stock dividends......................       50
    Lapse of fractional share certificates covering 5 full shares of
    common stock.
```

If it is legally possible for the directors to rescind the dividend to the extent of the full shares not issued, and this is done, the following entry would be in order:

```
Fractional share certificates—Common.........................  50
Paid-in surplus—From stock dividends..........................  10
    Retained earnings.........................................       60
    Return to Retained Earnings of amount of stock dividend related
    to lapsed fractional share certificates.
```

Restoration of retained earnings after a stock dividend. Assume that a company has issued shares as a stock dividend; that it has subsequently incurred losses which have created a deficit in its Retained Earnings account; and that it proposes to reduce its stated capital by reducing the number of shares outstanding, or the par or stated value of the shares. Can retained earnings be restored to the extent of the amount debited to Retained Earnings when the dividend shares were issued? Accountants generally agree that this would be improper.

■■

CHAPTER SEVEN

Miscellaneous Topics
Relating to Stockholders'
Equity

Treasury stock. Treasury stock is a corporation's own stock, once issued and later reacquired but not cancelled. Technically it is still classed as issued stock, although no longer outstanding. It will be noted that there are three important elements in this definition:

(1) Treasury stock must be the company's own stock; holdings of stock of other companies should not be called "treasury stock."

(2) The stock must have been issued; unissued stock should not be called "treasury stock." There are several reasons why a distinction should be maintained between unissued stock and treasury stock: Stockholders' pre-emptive rights do not apply to treasury stock; treasury stock may be sold without stockholders' authorization; treasury stock and unissued stock have wholly different relations to stated capital (as discussed hereafter); and, if treasury stock was fully paid when originally issued, it can be sold at a discount without imposing any discount liability on the purchaser.

(3) The stock must not have been cancelled. Cancellation is effected by procedures specified by the law. In some cases cancellation may result in reducing the authorized issue of stock; in other cases the shares remain authorized, the

145

only reduction being in the issued shares, which constitute the stated capital of the corporation.

Treasury stock may be acquired by donation, by purchase, or in settlement of a debt. Stockholders may donate stock to the corporation which it may sell to obtain working capital, or they may donate stock to be given as a bonus to the purchasers of other securities or for other reasons. It may be purchased to buy out a stockholder, to reduce the total capital, or to create a market demand for the stock and thus retard a downward trend in the market price.

Treasury stock is not an asset. Although treasury stock is occasionally shown in balance sheets as an asset (sometimes even combined with securities which are assets, under such a conglomerate title as "Government bonds and other securities"), it is generally recognized that the purchase of treasury stock does not result in the acquisition of an asset, but causes a reduction in the stockholders' equity. Treasury shares may have a ready marketability and may be sold, but so may unissued shares be sold; and it seems obvious that treasury stock, like unissued stock, is not an asset but is merely a possible source of additional funds. A corporation which acquires its own stock obviously cannot acquire the basic rights inherent in stock ownership: The right to vote, the right to participate in dividend distributions, the pre-emptive right, and the right to receive a proportionate share of the corporation's assets in the event of liquidation.

As a general rule, it is clear that treasury stock is not an asset. There are cases, however, where the merits of the general rule seem less obvious to some. For example, companies may purchase treasury shares for the purpose of reselling them to employees. This is done to encourage employee interest and support in the affairs of the company; the price of the shares to the employees may be slightly below current market price, and the company may help the employees by using some sort of installment plan to spread the cost of the shares over a period of time. The accounts of the company may show a long history with such a plan and that there is a steady turnover of the treasury shares. Under these circumstances, are the treasury shares assets? The answer is still no.

However, there are occasional circumstances that *may* warrant some modification of the above position. Suppose that a corporation has a bonus agreement with its officers and employees which provides that the bonus liability, after being determined, must be satisfied by distributing shares of the company's stock to those who have earned a bonus. Under these circumstances, assuming that the corporation had no unissued shares or that it preferred not to increase the number of shares outstanding, the bonus liability would be satisfied in two steps: cash would be used to acquire treasury shares; then treasury shares would be transferred to those entitled to a bonus, thus satisfying the liability. As a practical matter, there would probably be a time interval between the acquisition and disposition of the treasury shares. Under the circumstances described above, the treasury shares have the capacity to satisfy or remove, directly, a liability—which is a characteristic associated with certain kinds of assets, for instance, cash. Perhaps it would be reasonable to permit a company to show as an asset treasury shares (at cost) equal to the amount of liability that will be settled in the near future by transfer of treasury shares to officers and employees.

Although such cases are rare and do not significantly detract from the generalization that treasury stock is not an asset, it may be this sort of situation that influenced the Committee on Accounting Procedure, in its Bulletin No. 43, to state: "While it is perhaps in some circumstances permissible to show stock of a corporation held in its own treasury as an asset, if adequately disclosed, the dividends on stock so held should not be treated as a credit to the income account of the company."

Treasury stock and stated capital. As mentioned in Chapter 5, stated capital is a measure of creditor protection; it is intended to give the creditors assurance that a minimum capital will be maintained as a safeguard for the payment of liabilities, subject, of course, to the risk that unprofitable operations could impair the minimum capital as well as cause a weakening of financial position that could make it difficult for the company to meet its obligations. If the intended protection for creditors is to be effective, it is necessary to limit the amount which can be paid out or returned to stockholders. Therefore, the laws which establish and define stated capital have usually placed a limitation on the combined disbursements for dividends and purchases of treasury shares. In a large majority of the states, the limitation is related to surplus —a restriction which is often referred to as the "surplus rule." In some states, purchases of treasury stock can be made only to the extent of the earned surplus; in other states, purchases can be made to the extent of the total surplus which is available for dividends.

The differing effects of a dividend and a treasury stock purchase on the surplus of a corporation chartered in a state which has the surplus rule regarding treasury stock should be noted. Assume that a company has retained earnings of $25,000 and pays a $12,000 dividend; the retained earnings are reduced to $13,000. If, on the other hand, it pays $12,000 for treasury stock, the retained earnings are still $25,000, but $12,000 thereof is restricted and cannot be used for dividends or additional treasury stock purchases. It is possible to remove the restriction by either disposing of the treasury shares or cancelling them (restoring them to the status of unissued shares) and thereby reducing the stated capital; a corporation may effect a reduction of stated capital by filing with the proper state authorities a certificate of reduction or otherwise complying with the statutory requirements.

Treasury stock transactions: Terminology. It has long been customary to speak of *purchases* and *sales* of treasury stock. However, there is a certain inappropriateness in the use of these words in connection with treasury stock. Some effort has been made to substitute other terminology, such as *contraction of capital* for *purchase*, and *reissue* for *sale*. If a disposal of treasury stock is called a "reissue" instead of a "sale," the words *gain* and *loss* seem equally inappropriate as labels for the difference between "cost" and "selling price" of treasury shares. Efforts to introduce substitute terminology have not been very successful. Custom and habit are powerful forces; the authors do not choose in this case to attempt to combat them.

Balance sheet presentation of treasury stock. The history of the development of procedures for recording treasury stock transactions and showing treasury stock in the balance sheet is an interesting one. It has been affected by the enactment of laws permitting the issuance of no-par stock, by the split-up of the old general surplus account into retained earnings and paid-in surplus accounts, and by the enactment of laws relative to stated capital.

The old par value procedure. In the old days when all stock had a par value, it was customary, in the balance sheet, to deduct the par value of the treasury stock from the par value of the issued stock to show the par value of the stock outstanding. To facilitate this procedure, it was customary to debit the Treasury Stock account with the par value of stock acquired, and to record any difference between the par value and the acquisition price in the general surplus account.

Early no-par procedure. When laws were passed permitting the issuance of stock without par value, it was natural to attempt to apply the methods which had been found suitable for use with par value stock. No difficulty was encountered if, at the time of the issuance of the shares, the Capital Stock account was credited with the same amount per share for all shares issued.

This was the case if all shares were issued at one price and the Capital Stock account was credited with the issuance price. The

Treasury Stock account could be debited with this issuance price, as it had formerly been debited with par. In the balance sheet, the debit balance in the Treasury Stock account could be deducted from the credit balance in the Capital Stock account so that the issuance price of the shares outstanding would be shown.

It was also the case if, regardless of different issuance prices, the Capital Stock account was credited with a uniform amount per share and excesses of issuance prices over this uniform amount were credited to Paid-in Surplus. The Treasury Stock account could be debited with the uniform amount previously credited to Capital Stock. The debit balance in the Treasury Stock account could be deducted in the balance sheet from the credit balance in the Capital Stock account to show the amount credited to Capital Stock when the remaining outstanding shares were issued.

Difficulties were encountered, however, if the Capital Stock account had been credited with differing amounts per share of stock issued. These difficulties were met in two ways:

> Some accountants advocated debiting the Treasury Stock account with the amount credited to Capital Stock when the specific shares being acquired were issued.

> Because of the difficulty frequently encountered in attempting to determine the original issuance price of the specific shares being acquired, most accountants considered it satisfactory to debit the Treasury Stock account with the *average* amount which had been credited to Capital Stock for all shares of the class issued.

Effect of laws relative to stated capital. All of the foregoing procedures were based on the assumption that the balance in a Treasury Stock account should be deducted in the balance sheet from the balance in the related Capital Stock account, so that a net balance would be shown representing, in the case of par value stock, the par value of the shares outstanding, and, in the case of no-par stock, the original (actual or average) credit to Capital Stock for the shares still remaining outstanding.

The enactment of laws relative to stated capital, and the restriction of surplus as a result of treasury stock purchases, made the balance sheet presentations of treasury stock described above inappropriate or inadequate in certain cases.

> They would be *inappropriate* for corporations organized in states in which the stated capital is based on the shares issued, because the treasury shares are still issued shares, and the acquisition of treasury stock does not reduce the stated capital. To deduct the treasury stock from the capital stock issued

would therefore leave a balance sheet remainder which would be less than the stated capital.

The described balance sheet procedures would be *inadequate* if the law placed a restriction on surplus as a result of the treasury stock acquisition, because the surplus restriction would not be disclosed.

There has been some difference of opinion among accountants regarding the most desirable balance sheet presentation when the acquisition of treasury stock does not reduce the stated capital and when it places a restriction on surplus. All agree, however, that in such cases the balance sheet presentation of treasury stock should be such as to indicate that the stated capital has not been reduced, but that the surplus has become restricted.

To illustrate some of the procedures which have been used, assume that a company's accounts contain the following balances:

Common stock (representing 1,000 shares of $100 par value)....	$100,000
Paid-in surplus—Common.................................	15,000
Retained earnings.....................................	25,000

and that the company purchases 100 shares for $12,000.

Most accountants believe that the cost of the treasury stock should be deducted from the total issued stock, paid-in surplus, and retained earnings. They differ as to the method of disclosing the surplus restriction. Three acceptable procedures are illustrated.

(1) The surplus restriction is disclosed parenthetically:

Stockholders' equity:	
Common stock—authorized and issued, 1,000 shares of $100 par value, of which 100 shares are in the treasury.............	$100,000
Paid-in surplus—Common.................................	15,000
Retained earnings (of which $12,000, the cost of treasury stock, is restricted).......................................	25,000
Total...	$140,000
Less cost of treasury stock..............................	12,000
Stockholders' equity..................................	$128,000

(2) The surplus restriction is indicated by dividing the retained earnings into two parts:

Stockholders' equity:		
Common stock—authorized and issued, 1,000 shares of $100 par, of which 100 shares are in the treasury..........		$100,000
Paid-in surplus—Common..............................		15,000
Retained earnings:		
Restricted—equal to cost of treasury stock........	$12,000	
Free...	13,000	25,000
Total...		$140,000
Less cost of treasury stock..............................		12,000
Stockholders' equity..................................		$128,000

(3) The surplus restriction may be indicated by a footnote—a method increasing in popularity:

Stockholders' equity:

Common stock—authorized and issued, 1,000 shares of $100 par value, of which 100 shares are in the treasury	$100,000
Paid-in surplus—Common	15,000
Retained earnings (See note)	25,000
Total	$140,000
Less cost of treasury stock	12,000
Stockholders' equity	$128,000

Note. Dividends and treasury stock acquisitions are restricted to the amount of the retained earnings less the cost of treasury stock held.

A few accountants have advocated deducting the cost of the treasury stock from the retained earnings, thus:

Stockholders' equity:

Common stock—authorized and issued, 1,000 shares of $100 par, of which 100 shares are in the treasury		$100,000
Paid-in surplus—Common		15,000
Retained earnings	$25,000	
Less portion applied to purchase of treasury stock	12,000	13,000
Stockholders' equity		$128,000

This procedure has met with objection on the ground that it suggests an actual reduction in the retained earnings instead of merely a restriction. The company still has retained earnings of $25,000, but $12,000 of it is restricted.

Recording treasury stock transactions—cost basis. In all of the foregoing balance sheet presentations, there was a deduction of treasury stock *at cost*. Although the procedures illustrated are particularly applicable to companies subject to laws relative to stated capital and surplus restrictions resulting from treasury stock purchases, most accountants seem to believe that companies not subject to such laws can also show treasury stock properly as a deduction at cost in the Stockholders' Equity section of the balance sheet. For this reason it has become a rather general custom to carry treasury stock in the accounts at cost.

Entries for purchases. The accounting for treasury stock purchases on the cost basis is, of course, very simple. Assume that 100 shares of treasury stock were purchased at $85 per share. Regardless of whether the stock has or has not a par value, and regardless of the amount received for the stock when it was issued and the amount credited to the capital stock account at that time, the entry for the purchase is merely:

Treasury stock	8,500	
Cash		8,500
Purchase of 100 treasury shares.		

Of course, the treasury stock account title should indicate the class of stock if more than one class has been issued. Thus, the account title might be: "Treasury Stock—Preferred," or "Treasury Stock—Common," or "Treasury Stock—Common—No Par Value."

Entries for sales. The entries for sales of treasury stock will depend upon whether the stock is sold at the price at which it was purchased, at a price above cost, or at a price less than cost.

Sale at cost. Assume that the shares mentioned above were sold at $85 per share. The entry is:

```
Cash.................................................  8,500
    Treasury stock...................................          8,500
    Sale of 100 treasury shares, at cost.
```

Sale at a price in excess of cost. There is a general agreement among accountants that any gain on the sale of treasury stock should be recorded in a paid-in surplus account clearly described as to source. Assume that the shares mentioned above were sold at $90 per share. The sale might be recorded as follows:

```
Cash.................................................  9,000
    Treasury stock...................................          8,500
    Paid-in surplus—From treasury stock transactions......          500
    Sale of 100 treasury shares at $90 per share.
```

Sale at a price less than cost. In practice, the accounts charged with losses on sales of treasury shares depend on the law of the state of incorporation and the kinds of surplus accounts on the company's books. While a logical case can be made in favor of charging losses from treasury stock transactions first to any paid-in surplus resulting from previous treasury stock transactions and next to retained earnings, it is well established that such losses may be charged to any other paid-in surplus related to the same class of stock as the treasury shares, provided that such paid-in surplus is available for dividends and therefore is not a part of legal capital. The latter condition is pertinent because the amount of legal capital is governed by statute and not necessarily by the results of treasury stock transactions.

If paid-in surplus is not a part of legal capital under the law of the state of incorporation, and if a company has paid-in surplus resulting from the issuance of shares of the same class or resulting from other transactions in shares of that class, it is customary to assign treasury stock losses in the sequence shown on the following page.

1 If there is paid-in surplus resulting from previous treasury stock transactions, losses are first charged thereto until it is exhausted.

2 If there is other paid-in surplus applicable to the same class of shares, and not a part of legal capital, losses may be charged thereto until it is exhausted.

3 In the absence or inadequacy of suitable paid-in surplus, losses are chargeable to retained earnings.

Three cases are presented to illustrate the accounting for losses from treasury stock transactions.

	Case		
	1	2	3
Stockholder-equity accounts:			
Common stock, 10,000 shares issued, $10 stated value..........................	$100,000	$100,000	$100,000
Paid-in surplus—Common..............	10,000	60,000	1,000
Paid-in surplus—From treasury stock transactions.........................	2,000	None	None
Retained earnings......................	38,000	10,000	49,000
Treasury stock, 100 shares, at cost.......	2,500	1,500	2,400

CASE 1—Treasury shares are sold at $23 per share.

Cash..	2,300	
Paid-in surplus—From treasury stock transactions..........	200	
Treasury stock....................................		2,500
Sale of 100 shares of treasury stock at $23 per share.		

CASE 2—Treasury shares are sold at $12 per share.

Cash..	1,200	
Paid-in surplus—Common.............................	300	
Treasury stock....................................		1,500
Sale of 100 shares of treasury stock at $12 per share.		

CASE 3—Treasury shares are sold at $10 per share.

Cash..	1,000	
Paid-in surplus—Common.............................	1,000	
Retained earnings.......................................	400	
Treasury stock....................................		2,400
Sale of 100 shares of treasury stock at $10 per share.		

The basic objectives that govern the accounting for treasury stock transactions may be summarized as follows:

Retained earnings are not to be increased as a result of treasury stock transactions.

Retained earnings are to be decreased as a result of treasury stock transactions only in the absence of available paid-in surplus applicable to the same class of shares.

Retirement of treasury shares. If a corporation complies with the required legal formalities and cancels any reacquired shares, the capital stock account should be debited for the amount credited thereto when such shares were issued, except that, in the case of no-par stock without a stated value, an average issuance price is acceptable unless the shares being cancelled can be traced to a specific issuance, in which case the issuance price should be used to record the cancellation.

It is also necessary to debit any related paid-in surplus accounts for any amount specifically traceable to the shares being cancelled; or, in those cases where it is impossible or impracticable to make such an identification, it is acceptable to debit the related paid-in surplus accounts for the pro-rata portions thereof applicable to the shares being cancelled. To balance the entry, the Retained Earnings account is charged, or, if a credit is needed to balance the entry, a special paid-in surplus account is used. In any event, it is unacceptable to handle the cancellation of shares in a fashion that would increase retained earnings.

The following entries record the cancellation of the treasury shares shown under each of the three assumed fact situations presented on page 153.

CASE 1.

Common stock	1,000	
Paid-in surplus—From treasury stock transactions	20	
Paid-in surplus—Common	100	
Retained earnings	1,380	
Treasury stock		2,500

Cancellation of 100 shares of treasury stock reacquired at $25 per share.

CASE 2.

Common stock	1,000	
Paid-in surplus—Common	600	
Treasury stock		1,500
Paid-in surplus—From retirement of common stock		100

Cancellation of 100 shares of treasury stock reacquired at $15 per share.

CASE 3.

Common stock	1,000	
Paid-in surplus—Common	10	
Retained earnings	1,390	
Treasury stock		2,400

Cancellation of 100 shares of treasury stock reacquired at $24 per share.

Donated stock. If treasury stock is recorded at cost, it is obvious that no debit to a treasury stock account can be made for donated stock. However, a memorandum notation of the number of shares acquired should be made in that account.

The *usual* methods of recording sales are stated below:

1. If the treasury shares consist wholly of donated stock, the entire proceeds of reissue are credited to a paid-in surplus account.

2. If purchased and donated shares are held and the shares sold are specifically identified as donated shares, the entire proceeds are credited to paid-in surplus. If the shares sold are not specifically identified as donated shares, paid-in surplus can be credited with the excess of the sale price over a cost computed on the first-in, first-out basis or on an average basis.

The word *usual* was included in the above statement to provide for a possible exception. Stock is sometimes issued to the organizers of a corporation for noncash assets, and a portion of the stock is then donated to the company to be resold to provide working capital. This procedure was often used by mining and other speculative companies before the introduction of no-par stock made the expedient unnecessary. If such a company undertook to sell par value stock to the public, the stock usually had to be offered at a discount to make it attractive. But if unissued stock were sold at a discount, the purchasers might be liable for the discount, and this contingency might detract from the salability of the stock. Such companies therefore resorted to the "treasury stock subterfuge." By issuing all of the stock for the mine or other property and reacquiring part of it as treasury stock, the reacquired stock became, theoretically at least, fully paid treasury stock which could be resold at a discount. To credit paid-in surplus with the proceeds of the sale of such donated stock is of doubtful propriety. The financial position of the business would doubtless be more truly reflected if the proceeds of the sale were credited to the account with the property which was received when the stock was originally issued, since the property was obviously overvalued.

Recommended departure from the cost basis. The American Accounting Association has not favored the cost basis for treasury stock transactions. The 1957 revision, "Accounting and Reporting Standards for Corporate Financial Statements," covered the matter as follows:

"The acquisition of its own shares by a corporation represents a contraction of its capital structure. However, statutory requirements are particularly restrictive in this area of corporate activity and, to an important degree, are controlling in the reporting of such transactions. Preferably, the outlay by a corporation for its own shares is reflected as a reduction of the aggregate of contributed capital, and any excess of outlay over the pro-rata portion of contributed capital as a distribution of retained earnings. The issuance of reacquired shares should be accounted for in the same way as the issuance of previously unissued shares, that is, the entire proceeds should be credited to contributed capital."

To illustrate the procedure recommended by the above revision, assume that a company's stock was originally issued at $80 per share, of which $75, the stated value per share, was credited to Common Stock and $5 was credited to Paid-in Surplus—Common. If 100 shares were purchased at $85 per share, the entry, according to the method described above, would be:

Treasury stock...	7,500	
Paid-in surplus—Common ($5 × 100)......	500	
Retained earnings.......................................	500	
Cash....................................		8,500
Acquisition of 100 treasury shares.		

The recommendation that the issuance of treasury shares should be accounted for in the same way as the issuance of previously unissued shares is not as definite as might be desired.

If the treasury stock mentioned above is reissued for $9,000, the entry undoubtedly would be:

Cash...	9,000	
Treasury stock................................ .. .		7,500
Paid-in surplus—Reissue of treasury stock........... .		1,500

But if the treasury stock is reissued at $7,000, we face a problem which does not arise in connection with an original issue: What should be done with the excess of the carrying value of the treasury stock over the reissue price? Presumably it would be debited to an account with some clearly descriptive title, such as "Excess of Par (or Stated) Value of Treasury Stock over Proceeds of Reissue."

Book value per share of stock. The following describes the approach ordinarily used by accountants in computing book value per share: What would the stockholders receive on a per-share basis if the company were liquidated without gains, losses, or expenses; in other words, if the cash available for distribution, after the payment of all liabilities, were exactly equal to the stockholders' equity shown by the balance sheet?

It seems relevant to emphasize that book figures are based on a "going concern" assumption, which is in conflict with the "liquidation" approach used in book value computations. It may also be observed that stockholders' equity amounts are generally classified by source, and not according to what each class of stockholders is entitled to receive if the corporation should discontinue operations —a fact which affects the computation of book values per share of various classes of stock.

Computations of book value per share must give consideration to the rights of various classes of stockholders. It is impracticable to give more than a few typical illustrations—enough to indicate the nature of the problems involved.

If there is only one class of stock, the book value per share is computed by dividing the total stockholders' equity (or book value of all of the stock) by the number of shares outstanding, or by the total number of shares outstanding and subscribed for but not issued. The total book value of all the shares should include any reserves which are mere appropriations of surplus.

Assume that the stockholders' equity of a corporation includes the following:

Common stock—2,000 shares outstanding	$200,000
Paid-in surplus	50,000
Sinking fund reserve	60,000
Reserve for contingencies	25,000
Retained earnings	65,000
Total	$400,000

The book value per share is $400,000 ÷ 2,000, or $200.

The computation is not so simple if there are common and preferred shares outstanding. It is then necessary to determine the portion of the stockholders' equity, or aggregate book value, applicable to the preferred stock, divide this amount by the number of shares of preferred stock outstanding to determine the book value per share of the preferred, and divide the remainder of the stockholders' equity by the number of common shares outstanding to determine the book value per share of the common.

The determination of the portion of stockholders' equity applicable to the preferred stock consists of a computation of the amount which the preferred stockholders would be entitled to receive if the company were liquidated without gain or loss. This involves consideration of the following questions:

What preference rights do the preferred stockholders have with respect to dividends? Is the preferred stock cumulative or noncumulative? If it is cumulative, are there any dividends in arrears? If there are dividends in arrears, is there any surplus from which they can be paid? Is the preferred stock participating or nonparticipating?

What preference rights do the preferred stockholders have with respect to assets in liquidation?

There are so many combinations of conditions, and consequently so many answers to these questions, that it is impracticable to illustrate them all. The following illustrations may suffice.

First illustration. The stockholders' equity of a company on June 30, 1960, consisted of the following:

Preferred stock—6% cumulative, nonparticipating; $100 par value; 1,000 shares outstanding	$100,000
Common stock—$100 par value; 1,000 shares outstanding	100,000
Retained earnings	50,000
Total	$250,000

Preferred dividends have been paid to December 31, 1959.

Under the terms of issuance of the preferred stock, it can be called at 105; but in the event of liquidation it is entitled only to par and unpaid cumulative dividends. Some accountants believe that the book value per share of preferred should be based on the call price plus the unpaid dividends. If this procedure is adopted, the book values per share will be computed as follows:

Total stockholders' equity		$250,000
Portion applicable to preferred stock:		
Call price	$105,000	
Unpaid dividends for six months	3,000	
Total		108,000
(Book value per share = $108,000 ÷ 1,000 = $108)		
Remainder applicable to common stock		$142,000
(Book value per share = $142,000 ÷ 1,000 = $142)		

But a call price does not seem appropriate. A call price for preferred stock is applicable when the preferred stock is to be retired but the common stock is to remain outstanding. As previously stated, the computation of book values per share is based on an assumption of liquidation. Therefore, it seems preferable to ignore call prices, and make the computations as follows:

Total stockholders' equity		$250,000
Portion applicable to preferred stock:		
Par value	$100,000	
Unpaid dividends for six months	3,000	
Total		103,000
(Book value per share = $103,000 ÷ 1,000 = $103)		
Remainder applicable to common stock		$147,000
(Book value per share = $147,000 ÷ 1,000 = $147)		

A call price should be distinguished from a liquidating value. If the preferred stockholders in the foregoing illustration were entitled to receive $105 per share in the event of liquidation, this valuation should be used in the computation.

Second illustration. The stockholders' equity of a company on December 31, 1960, consisted of the items listed on page 159.

Preferred stock—6% cumulative, participating; $100 par value; 1,000 shares outstanding....................................	$100,000
Common—No par value; stated value, $50 per share; 3,000 shares outstanding...	150,000
Retained earnings..............................	50,000
Total..	$300,000

After 6% dividends are paid on the preferred stock, the common stockholders are entitled to receive $3 per share; thereafter, the two classes of stock are entitled to participate in dividends in the ratio of $2 per preferred share to $1 per common share; since there are 1,000 shares of preferred and 3,000 shares of common outstanding, the participation ratio is $2,000 to $3,000, or ⅖ to the preferred and ⅗ to the common. Dividends for the first six months of 1960 have been paid on the preferred stock; no dividends have been paid for 1960 on the common stock. The computations are made as follows:

		Preferred	Common
Par or stated value.............................		$100,000	$150,000
Retained earnings:			
Total.................................	$50,000		
Amount required for preferred dividend for second six months of 1960........	3,000*	3,000	
Portion required for dividends on common stock for year.......................	9,000*		9,000
Remainder—divisible ⅖ and ⅗.........	$38,000	15,200	22,800
Total....................................		$118,200	$181,800
Shares outstanding..............................		1,000	3,000
Book value per share............................		$ 118.20	$ 60.60

* Deduction.

Third illustration. Assume the same facts as in the second illustration except that the retained earnings are only $7,000. The computations would then be made as follows:

		Preferred	Common
Par or stated value................:................		$100,000	$150,000
Retained earnings:			
Total.....................................	$7,000		
Deduct amount required for preferred dividend for second six months of 1960.......	3,000	3,000	
Remainder...............................	$4,000		
Since the common stockholders are entitled to receive dividends of $3 per share before any participating dividends are paid on the preferred stock, and since the remaining $4,000 of retained earnings is not sufficient to pay such a dividend on the common stock, the entire remaining $4,000 is applicable to the common stock...........			4,000
Total...		$103,000	$154,000
Shares outstanding.................................		1,000	3,000
Book value per share..............................		$103.00	$51.33

Fourth illustration. The stockholders' equity of a company on December 31, 1960, consisted of the following:

Preferred stock—6% cumulative, nonparticipating; no par value;
    stated value, $50 per share; 1,000 shares outstanding........ $ 50,000
Common stock—No par value; stated value, $10 per share;
    10,000 shares outstanding.............................. 100,000
Deficit... 20,000*
      Total... $130,000

* Deduction.

Dividends of $25,000 are in arrears on the preferred stock.

Before book values per share can be computed, it is necessary to know whether the preferred stockholders are entitled, in the event of liquidation, to the dividends in arrears notwithstanding the existence of the deficit.

If they are entitled to the dividends in arrears, the book values should be computed as follows:

Total stockholders' equity................................. $130,000
Portion applicable to preferred stock:
    $50 × 1,000.................................... $50,000
    Dividends in arrears........................... 25,000
    Total... 75,000
      (Book value per share = $75,000 ÷ 1,000 = $75)
Remainder applicable to common stock...................... $ 55,000
    (Book value per share = $55,000 ÷ 10,000 = $5.50)

If the preferred stockholders are not entitled to the dividends in arrears, the book values should be computed as follows:

Total stockholders' equity................................. $130,000
Portion applicable to the preferred stock:
    $50 × 1,000.................................... 50,000
      (Book value per share = $50,000 ÷ 1,000 = $50)
Remainder applicable to common stock...................... $ 80,000
    (Book value per share = $80,000 ÷ 10,000 = $8)

Significance of book value per share. Unfortunately, book values per share are more likely to be misunderstood than understood. This condition is attributable, in part at least, to the fact that book-value-per-share computations are made on the basis of a liquidating concept, although the balance sheet amounts used in the computation are based on a going concern concept. Since "value" may be misinterpreted as synonymous with "worth," the term *book equity per share* might be preferable because it is less likely to be misunderstood.

It is obvious that accounting errors or improprieties will affect the book value per share. Recognition of this fact is given in the definition in the Institute's Accounting Terminology Bulletin No. 3, on the following page.

"*Book value* is the amount shown on accounting records or related financial statements at or as of the date when the determination is made, after adjustments necessary to reflect (1) corrections of errors, and (2) the application of accounting practices which have been consistently followed."

Watered stock. Stock is said to be *watered* when the stockholders' equity is overstated in the balance sheet. The overstatement of stockholders' equity may be accompanied by an understatement of liabilities, but is usually accompanied by an overstatement of assets.

The water may be eliminated by any procedure which eliminates the overstatement of stockholders' equity and net assets. It may be eliminated by a scaling down of the outstanding stock (which may be accomplished by reduction of either the number of shares or the par or stated value) and a corresponding reduction of the book values of the overstated assets. If each stockholder suffers a pro-rata reduction, his proportionate interest in the corporation is not affected. Or stock may be donated and resold, thus increasing the assets without increasing the outstanding stock, but the credit for the proceeds of the donated stock should be made in the overvalued asset account rather than in paid-in surplus, or the asset overvaluation and the water in the stock will not be eliminated. The water may be eliminated by writing down the overvalued assets. Or capital expenditures may be charged to expense. This method is not to be recommended, because it corrects one error by committing another, namely, the misstatement of operating income.

Secret reserves. A secret reserve exists whenever the stockholders' equity shown in the balance sheet is understated. It is, in a sense, the exact opposite of water in the stock. A secret reserve may be created by any device which understates assets or overstates liabilities. Capital expenditures may be charged to expense, income may be credited to the asset which produced the income, excessive depreciation or bad debt provisions may be made, liabilities may be deliberately overstated, assets may be written off, and a great variety of other devices may be employed.

The creation of secret reserves is not so common now as it was before the income tax rendered inexpedient the misstatement of income. In the old days, corporations frequently wrote down assets arbitrarily, defending the procedure on the grounds of conservatism, and directors often deliberately created secret reserves because such reserves made it possible to equalize earnings and thus to maintain an appearance of uniformity and stability which was considered advantageous to the corporation.

The theory and operation of the secret reserve were somewhat as follows: In a prosperous year, when income was above normal, it was wise to conceal the company's prosperity, partly to avoid attracting competition and partly to avoid creating in the stockholders' minds an expectation of similarly abnormal earnings in the future. The directors, therefore, charged excessive depreciation or resorted to some other method of overstating the expenses. In a subsequent year, when earnings were subnormal, and when a disclosure of this fact might adversely affect the standing and stability of the corporation, expenses were understated.

Secret reserves may be deliberate or unintentional. Provisions for depletion, depreciation, bad debts, and certain other expenses are necessarily based on estimates. If the estimate is excessive, the expenses are overstated, the earnings and stockholders' equity are understated, and a secret reserve is thereby created. Even when estimates are made in the most careful manner possible, secret reserves may develop. But when discovered, the secret reserve, whether the result of deliberate or inadvertent actions, should be eliminated by a proper correction of the accounts.

Comprehensive illustration of a Stockholders' Equity section. The following illustration shows the balance sheet treatment of various matters affecting the stockholders' equity.

Stockholders' equity:			
Capital stock:			
Preferred stock—6% participating, cumulative; par value, $100; authorized and issued, 1,000 shares................		$100,000.00	
Common stock—No par value; stated value, $10; authorized and issued, 10,000 shares, of which 500 shares are in the treasury..		100,000.00	$200,000.00
Surplus:			
Paid-in:			
Premium on preferred stock............		$ 5,000.00	
Paid-in surplus—Common stock........		27,000.00	
Paid-in surplus—From treasury stock transactions.......................		2,000.00	
Retained earnings capitalized in connection with a stock dividend...........		3,000.00	
Donated surplus.......................		1,000.00	38,000.00
Retained earnings:			
Appropriated:			
Reserve for contingencies............		$ 25,000.00	
Reserve for plant extensions..........		15,000.00	
Not available for dividends—Equal to cost of treasury stock..............		7,500.00	
Total........................		$ 47,500.00	
Free..............................		132,000.00	179,500.00
Total.......................................			$417,500.00
Deduct cost of treasury stock—Common................			7,500.00
Stockholders' equity........................			$410,000.00

In published financial statements it is often necessary to combine or group some of the related stockholders' equity accounts. This is acceptable provided that the subtotals for paid-in surplus and retained earnings are clearly set forth and that any restrictions or appropriations of surplus are disclosed. If there are any accounts showing unrealized increments in asset amounts, they should be clearly labeled and presented below the subtotal for retained earnings and above any treasury shares. Such accounts are rarely found because it is considered unacceptable to write up assets to reflect current values.

Voting trusts and stock pools. Since stockholders are entitled to votes in proportion to the stock they hold, the control of a corporation lies with the majority stockholders. For the protection of the minority holders, the device of pooling a portion of the stock is sometimes used. Assume that A, B, and C, formerly in partnership, form a corporation, the shares being issued as follows: to A, 105 shares; to B, 55 shares; and to C, 40 shares. In order to protect B and C against A, and also to give all stockholders equal shares in the management, A and B may place all of their shares in excess of 40 (the number held by C) in the hands of a trustee, the terms of the trust or pool requiring that the trustee shall vote the stock so held as directed by a majority (or two-thirds, or three-fourths, or unanimous, or any other specified) vote of the unpooled stock. The condition would then be:

Stockholder	Shares Owned	Shares Pooled	Shares Not Pooled
A	105	65	40
B	55	15	40
C	40	0	40
Total	200	80	120

If the pooled stock can be voted at the direction of a two-thirds vote of the unpooled stock, any two stockholders can control the company. If the pooled stock can be voted only at the direction of a three-fourths vote of the unpooled stock, no action can be taken without the consent of all stockholders.

A stock pool or trust may also be used to effect a distribution of profits in a ratio other than the ratio of stockholdings. For instance, assume that A, B, and C, in the preceding illustration, had previously been partners with differing capital interests but sharing profits equally. If it is desired to continue the equal interests in profits notwithstanding the differing capital interests, the numbers of shares shown above as pooled might be placed in trust, under an agreement providing that dividends on the shares in trust should be paid to the trustees and distributed by them in equal amounts to A, B, and C.

Before the merger and the holding company devices attained their present popularity as methods of combining corporations, the stock pool or trust was frequently resorted to. In such cases all of, or a controlling interest in, the stock of each affected company was placed in trust to be voted by trustees. Although each company retained its separate legal entity, the activities of all companies were subjected to a unified control by the trustees.

Since, in the early days of corporate combinations, trusts of this nature were frequently established, large businesses generally came to be known as *trusts*, but this is loose terminology.

CHAPTER EIGHT

Generally Accepted
Accounting Principles

Introduction. It is generally agreed that the primary function of accounting is to accumulate information about the financial activities of a business entity in a manner that will permit its meaningful summarization in the form of financial statements. It is agreed, also, that there can be no widespread understanding of, and reliance on, accounting statements unless they have been prepared in conformity with a body of generally accepted rules or conventions. The necessity of some common agreement on accounting matters becomes apparent when we contemplate the chaotic condition that would prevail if every businessman or every accountant could follow his own notions about the measurement of revenue and expense.

The nature of prevailing accounting rules. It would be incorrect to suggest that the rules which establish whether a given accounting procedure is acceptable or unacceptable are in the nature of principles like those found in physics or chemistry. Accounting principles are more properly associated with such terms as *concepts*, *conventions*, and *standards*. It is important to remember that accounting principles are man-made, in contrast to natural law.

It is also important to remember that accounting principles are not rigid. They are constantly evolving, being influenced by business practices; the needs of statement users; legislative and govern-

165

mental regulation; the opinions and actions of stockholders, creditors, labor unions, and management; and the reasoning and experience of accountants. Such influences affect the definitions, assumptions, and procedures that form the content of generally accepted accounting. In final analysis, accounting must serve the needs of society; it must be reasonably sensitive to changes in the economic system.

Although professional accountants pretty clearly understand the concepts, standards, and conventions (no single word seems quite adequate) to which they should conform, there is no comprehensive *authoritative* compilation or code of accounting principles. Principles cannot be established in accounting, as they are in the realm of natural sciences, by experimentation; nor have they been determined, as in the law, by authoritative pronouncement, although the accounting procedures of railroads, utilities, and certain other lines of business have been standardized by governmental regulation. The Securities and Exchange Commission has issued rules and regulations which touch the realm of accounting principles; these are binding only on those persons who are subject to the authority of the Commission, but they have exercised a profound influence on the practice of accounting generally. The American Institute of Certified Public Accountants, through its Committee on Accounting Procedure, has issued numerous bulletins dealing with matters which may be regarded as accounting principles, but the bulletins themselves state: "Except in cases in which formal adoption by the Institute membership has been asked and secured, the authority of the bulletins rests upon the general acceptability of opinions so reached." The American Accounting Association has also done commendable work in formulating a statement of accounting standards, but the pronouncements of the Association, as well as those of the Institute, have not been greeted with unanimous acceptance.

In the final analysis, the subject matter of accounting represents the cumulative results of years of experience with the intricate problems of providing a record of business transactions and measuring and reporting on the interim position and progress of business enterprises. In recent decades there has been a widespread interest in periodic income results. As a consequence, the income statement has received more attention than the balance sheet. To some extent, the balance sheet is becoming a statement of residuals; that is, the balances shown therein are the result of the application of procedures that are considered proper to account for revenue and expense.

Some underlying assumptions. The accounting process is

based on an assumption that the business involved is going to continue operations indefinitely. This "going concern" assumption makes it unnecessary for the accountant to place any particular emphasis on forced-sale or liquidation values. In fact, the accounting process cannot be characterized as being predominantly a "valuation" process. It is primarily a process of income determination; attention is directed to revenue realization, cost expiration, and those costs that may properly be regarded as residues which will be of benefit to a going concern in the future; it does not require opinions or speculations regarding the realizable values of assets acquired for use in carrying on the operating activities of the business. Besides, some realizable values are not particularly relevant to the going concern. For a going concern that intends to continue using a particular combination of assets for business purposes, the objective is one of spreading the cost of such assets over the periods benefited by the use of such assets in the conduct of business operations.

Another basic assumption for accounting purposes is that the monetary unit (the dollar) is of constant dimensions; in other words, it is assumed that the purchasing power of the dollar remains unchanged. During certain periods this assumption has squared substantially with reality. But it is also true that during other periods the purchasing power of the dollar has changed. In spite of such changes, accounting has continued to treat all dollars as equal, whether the dollar amounts in the accounts represent 1932 dollars or 1949 dollars or current dollars. Such accounting could result in misleading financial statements.

Although the assumption of a stable dollar is an assumption contrary to fact, to date the majority of accountants have felt no compulsion to modify accounting methods or procedures in an attempt to make allowance for such variation in the unit of measurement. Such reluctance is hardly the result of an unawareness on the part of accountants that prices change. It is more likely attributable to a belief that changes in the value of money, during most periods, have been so gradual as not to materially undermine the validity of the assumption. Another reason is that cost is a determinable fact. Financial accounting in terms of cost outlays does provide a meaningful accountability of management's utilization of the resources at its disposal. There is considerable apprehension that procedures directed toward modifying account balances so that they might show current costs or the current price level would result in less objective information.

Some basic accounting concepts. Although the accounting profession has never adopted a comprehensive code of accounting principles, as noted earlier, the following may be considered to have fundamental importance:

(1) The accounts and statements should give expression, as far as possible, to facts evidenced by completed transactions and supportable by objective data.

(2) Cost is the proper basis for the accounting for assets and asset expirations, subject to an occasional modification in those instances where there is convincing evidence that cost cannot be recovered, either through use or sale, whichever is normal for the asset.

(3) Conservatism, while generally desirable, is not a justification for the understatement of the owners' equity or the misstatement of periodic net income.

(4) Consistency should be maintained between the statements prepared at the end of one period, and between the statements of successive periods. However, a proper regard for consistency need not preclude a desirable change in procedure. If a change of material consequence is made, the fact should be mentioned and the effect thereof on the statements should be indicated, if determinable.

(5) The determination of net income requires a proper matching of revenues and expenses.

    (a) Revenues should not be regarded as earned until an increment has been realized, or until its realization is reasonably assured.

    (b) Expenses are expired costs.

(6) Statements should not be misleading, and should make full disclosure of significant information. This was discussed in Chapter 3.

Objectivity. Contrary to a belief held by some nonaccountants, accounting statements are not entirely factual. Judgment, opinion, and estimate enter into the accounting process. This is necessarily so, but it does not follow from the above observation that it would be desirable if accounting were completely discretionary in nature. To the extent practicable, the accounting process is based on bargained transactions where the money amounts represent prices determined in the market place as opposed to amounts based on opinion. The accountant prefers amounts that can be verified by reference to business documents originating outside of the enterprise. Such support lends validity to accounting data.

The criterion of realization is another example of preference for objectivity. Informed opinion or even price increases are not considered to be sufficiently objective to warrant revenue recognition. There must be a transfer or exchange, a business agreement, or some ascertainable change in an asset or liability to remove or minimize what might be described as the "flaw of indefiniteness."

The cost principle.   Accounting literature has had much to say about the "cost principle," which may be stated as follows: Subject to generally recognized exceptions, and excluding cash and receivables, cost is the proper basis of accounting for assets and expenses, and accounting records should reflect acquisition costs and the transformation, flow, and expiration of these costs.

The cost basis for recording and reporting is sometimes criticized by people who believe that reports would be more informative if all assets were stated on the basis of market prices or realizable values at the date of the report. It is questionable whether such bases of valuation would be more significant than the cost basis. Usually there is no intention to convert fixed assets into cash immediately; therefore, information relative to their market or realizable values is not of great importance, except perhaps to certain creditors, and the information can be given parenthetically in the balance sheet or in supplementary schedules without abandoning the cost basis in the records themselves. More definite and objective evidence is available for the determination of cost than for the determination of market or realizable values, which in many instances would be matters of pure conjecture. Less use of cost would certainly make accounting more subjective in character.

Conservatism.   In the past, accountants were primarily concerned with presenting a conservative picture of the financial condition of a business in its balance sheet. They regarded the balance sheet as of primary, and the income statement as of secondary, importance. Moreover, they were inclined to assume that a conservative balance sheet was a good balance sheet for all purposes, and that balance sheet conservatism automatically resulted in a proper and conservative income statement.

The emphasis upon the balance sheet and upon conservative asset valuations and liability and loss provisions doubtless resulted from the fact that, in the early days of the development of accounting, the services of public accountants were required principally for the preparation of reports for bankers and other grantors of short-term credit who were primarily concerned with the question of the margin of security. For many years, bankers and other short-term creditors were much more interested in the balance sheet than in the income statement, and they were naturally disposed to regard balance sheet conservatism as a safeguard and hence a basic virtue. Accountants naturally were influenced by their attitude.

While balance sheet conservatism is still regarded as an accounting virtue, the time-honored emphasis upon the balance sheet and upon conservatism in asset valuations has been subjected to critical reconsideration. One reason for this is the recognition that, with the increase in the number of corporate stockholders who are not active in the management, accounting reports must serve the requirements of investors as well as of short-term creditors. Ultra-conservatism may be prejudicial to the interests of stockholders or other security holders who, having been led to believe that the company in which they have made investments is less prosperous than it really is, may sell their securities for less than they are really worth.

Also, with the income statement now receiving the emphasis formerly accorded the balance sheet, accountants have become increasingly aware that adherence to a doctrine of balance sheet conservatism may result in incorrect, and even unconservative, income statements. If an expenditure or a cost which can be presumed to be essential or beneficial to the operations of more than one period is charged either to surplus or to current income in one period—a procedure which may be conservative from the balance sheet standpoint—the income statements for all periods are distorted, and the income statements for the periods which are relieved of their just portions of the cost are the opposite of conservative.

At the present time, conservatism is a less potent force. However, it continues to be a factor when matters of opinion or estimate are involved, accountants believing that it is commendable, in instances of doubt, to understate net income and owners' equity rather than to overstate them. The consequences of an understatement of assets and net income do not seem as serious as the opposite. However, conservatism can scarcely be regarded as a virtue if, as its consequence, balance sheets and income statements do not fairly present the financial position and the results of operations.

Consistency. The accountant, perhaps more than any other person, is aware of the influence that estimates and policy decisions have on periodic net income determinations and of the fact that such estimates and policy decisions cannot be eliminated from the accounting process. However, it would be most unfortunate if the stated net income of a business could be determined by the whim or fancy, and particularly by the changing whim or fancy, of those directing its affairs.

There are many areas of accounting in which different procedures may be acceptable from the standpoint of approved current practice. The accountant should seek to apply the method best suited to each particular case, but it is important that the method selected be applied consistently year after year. Inconsistency destroys comparability; it has the potential of misleading users of financial statements. For example, by changing depreciation or inventory methods, the net income for the current period could be increased or decreased, perhaps significantly. A statement user might be misled and think that the increase or decrease was the result of a change in business conditions or management effectiveness, whereas in reality it was the result of a change in an accounting method. Changes in net income reported in successive statements should be traceable to things more fundamental than mere changes in accounting methods.

Whenever financial statements are audited by a certified public accountant, it is customary for the auditor to issue an accompanying opinion or certificate so that statement users may know that there has been an audit by an independent professional accountant. Consistency has come to be regarded as of such primary importance that a declaration with respect thereto can be found in the typical auditor's opinion. The last paragraph of the opinion is customarily worded somewhat as follows:

"In our opinion, the accompanying balance sheet and statement(s) of income and surplus present fairly the financial position of X Company on December 31, 19—, and the results of its operations for the year then ended, in conformity with generally accepted accounting principles applied on a basis consistent with that of the preceding year."

A proper regard for consistency need not preclude a desirable change in procedure. But if a change is made, the fact should be mentioned and the dollar effect thereof on the statements should be disclosed, if determinable.

Income determination. Since the majority of accountants probably would agree that the accountant faces his greatest challenge when he undertakes the determination of net income, and since income determination is a factor to be considered in the discussion of most accounting matters, and hence is frequently referred to throughout this text, it may prove helpful to devote the balance of this chapter to a brief digest of the topic.

A preliminary consideration concerns terminology. The terminology of accounting is not crystallized and precise, and it therefore is advisable to indicate the senses in which certain words are used in the following discussion and generally throughout the text.

We shall consider the word *revenue* to mean an inflow of assets,*

---

* Revenues sometimes take the form of a decrease in liabilities—a variation from normal which could be recognized by saying "an inflow of net assets," but which is ignored here for purposes of simplicity of statement.

but it must be recognized that there are inflows of assets which are not revenue. Obviously, an inflow of capital funds from stockholders is not revenue to a corporation, nor should a business regard as revenue an inflow of assets which is offset by an increase in liabilities. Increases in the value of assets resulting from growth, natural increase, or a rise in market prices are not generally regarded as revenue. Revenue consists of an inflow of assets from customers and clients, and is related to sales and the rendering of services. The 1957 revision, "Accounting and Reporting Standards for Corporate Financial Statements," published by the American Accounting Association, states that revenue is "the monetary expression of the aggregate of products or services transferred by an enterprise to its customers during a period of time."

The term *revenue* has sometimes been used by accountants to mean the *gross* proceeds from operating activities such as sales and the rendering of services, and to mean, in the case of incidental transactions consummated at a gain, only the *net* proceeds after deduction of the related costs. For example, if investment securities carried on the books at cost, $10,000, are sold for $12,000, some accountants think that it would be misleading to treat the gross proceeds of $12,000 as revenue because such transactions are incidental to the primary operating activities of the typical business. Such considerations may have influenced an earlier committee of the American Accounting Association, for, in "Accounting Concepts and Standards Underlying Corporate Financial Statements," its definition of *revenue* applies the gross proceeds concept in the case of sales and services and the net concept in the case of incidental transactions. The definition of *revenue* is stated as embracing:

> "(a) the amount of assets received or liabilities liquidated in the sale of the products or services of an enterprise, (b) the gain from sales or exchanges of assets other than stock in trade, and (c) the gain from advantageous settlements of liabilities."

As a general rule, the text will use the term *revenue* in its gross sense.

Revenue may be received before it is earned, as in the case of rent collected in advance. Since there may be a lapse of time between the date when revenue is received and the date when, in accordance with accepted accounting procedures, it is regarded as earned, there may be *unearned revenues* and *earned revenues*.

The word *cost* is related to expenditure. An expenditure is a payment, in cash or otherwise, or the incurring of an obligation to make a future payment, for a benefit received. *Cost* is the measure of the expenditure. But when used without modifying words, *cost* does not always have a sufficiently definite and refined meaning. For precision of expression, we shall use several terms.

The expression *cost outlay* will be used with reference to expenditures and acquisitions, regardless of whether the benefit received is chargeable to an asset or an expense account.

The term *cost transformation* refers to such changes as the conversion of material, labor, and overhead costs into finished goods costs.

Expired costs are those which no longer have any asset status. Expired costs are of two classes: *utilized costs* and *lost costs*. *Utilized costs* include the cost of merchandise sold and the costs of services, utilities, and other benefits used for the purpose of producing revenue. *Lost costs* are costs which have expired without utilization or without contributing to the production of revenue. A *cost residue* is the unexpired portion of a cost outlay; it may properly appear on the asset side of the balance sheet of a going concern.

The income-determination process in accounting is a matter of matching, or associating, revenues with related expenses (and, occasionally, lost costs). Thus, revenue is a gross concept, whereas income is a net or resultant amount. If revenues exceed expenses, the business earns income, the dollar amount thereof being shown in the income statement usually as "net income." If expenses exceed revenues, a loss results. Whether or not all items affecting income given recognition during a period should be included in the determination of periodic net income is a matter on which accountants do not agree, as indicated by the discussion of the all-inclusive and current operating concepts in Chapter 4.

Most businesses can be characterized as being engaged in a continuing "stream" of activity. Not until a business has ceased to function as a going concern and has disposed of its assets is it possible to compute with absolute accuracy the net income earned or the loss sustained. But it obviously would be impractical to make no computations of net income until the business completes its life span. Unless interim computations are made, no adequate basis exists for reporting on the success of a business, because it is the net income figure, more than any other bit of information, that provides a means of comparing the operations of a business during different periods, or of comparing the results of operations of different businesses. But it must be recognized that, in the whole history of the operations of a business, the income statement for a period is merely a chapter—subject to possible revision.

When is revenue realized? Business operations customarily involve a long series of activities: The purchase of materials, the fabrication of product, the sale of the product, the collection of the proceeds of the sale, and sometimes the subsequent rendering of service or fulfilment of guarantees. All of these activities are conducted for the purpose of earning revenue. At what point in the series should the revenue be regarded as earned?

The point of sale.   The sale is the step in the series of activities at which revenue generally is regarded as realized. Realization of revenue does not necessarily require a collection in cash, since a valid receivable from a solvent debtor is an asset in as good standing as cash.

The point of sale is generally regarded as the point of revenue realization because (1) it is the point at which a conversion takes place—an exchange of one asset for another—and conversion is regarded as evidence of realization; and (2) it is the point at which the amount of the revenue is, in the normal case, objectively determinable from a sale price acceptable to both parties.

The legal rules governing the passing of title determine when a sale is made, but these rules are complex and full of technicalities. Delivery to the vendee or his agent is a general test of the passing of title, and for general accounting purposes throughout the period it is advisable, for convenience, to regard a sale as having been made when the goods are invoiced and delivery or shipment is made to a purchaser. (Delivery alone is not a sufficient test because delivery may be made on consignment.) At the close of the accounting period it may be necessary to consider the legal aspects of title-passing more closely and to exclude from realized revenue the billed price of goods which have been delivered without passing of title, and to include in realized revenue the billable price of goods which have not been delivered but the title to which has passed. Even such end-of-period adjustments are usually ignored if the amounts are small.

It must be recognized that even after the date of sale, events may occur which will modify the amounts of revenue and income on the sale transaction. Merchandise may be returned, allowances may be given to customers, service expenses may be incurred, and losses may arise from bad debts. However, these possibilities are usually not regarded as of sufficient importance to serve as a deterrent to the adoption of the sales basis for recognizing revenue realization; business experience may indicate that the revenue deductions and costs arising from these sources are so inconsequential in amount that they can be ignored, or that they can be forecast with reasonable accuracy and provided for by allowances created during the period of sale.

Recognizing revenue as earned before the point of sale. Adopting the point of sale as the point of recognition of revenue realization, although appropriate and recommended for most revenue transactions, is not followed in all cases. Under certain conditions it is considered both acceptable and advisable to recognize revenues as earned before all the requirements of a completed sale have been met. Some of these special situations are mentioned below.

If goods are being manufactured under a cost-plus contract and the amounts of revenue applicable to completed portions of the contract are determinable and the collection of revenue is reasonably assured, there is little to recommend postponing the recognition of revenue until delivery and transfer of title. There is some reluctance on the part of the accountant to recognize revenue on fixed-price contracts in process, not because the revenue is less definite, but because the ultimate outcome (whether the contract will prove to be profitable or unprofitable) is much less predictable. However, when the execution of a contract extends into two or more accounting periods, there may be a question as to whether the income statements fairly reflect the results of operations during these periods if the entire revenue is reported in the period of completion, particularly if the major portion of the work was done prior to the period of completion. If a portion of the contract price on contracts in process is recognized as earned, it should be evident that the reported income may be based to a greater degree on estimate and opinion than the accountant would prefer. However, this disadvantage should be weighed against the alternative of the less informative and less equitable income statement which might result from deferring the matching of revenue and expense on fixed-price contracts until their completion.

The mining industry provides another case where more equitable and informative accounting may result if revenue recognition is not delayed until the point of sale. In the case of certain metals, a mining company can dispose of all it can mine at an established price with no selling effort. Delivery and transfer of title is a mere formality and under the circumstances would not provide as meaningful a basis for revenue recognition as production. Agricultural products provide an analogous case. With government-supported prices for farm products, delaying revenue recognition until delivery and transfer of title would seem somewhat artificial.

Recognition of revenue after the date of sale. The practice of postponing the recognition of revenue as earned until some time after delivery and transfer of title is considered appropriate in the case of installment sales. The unusual collection hazards and the considerable collection expenses incurred in periods subsequent to the period of sale justify delaying recognition of revenue realization.

Whenever the collection of the receivable is not reasonably assured, the accountant prefers to take a cautious position and not treat the revenue as realized until collection is made or until it is reasonably apparent that collection will be made in the due course of business.

Unrealized appreciation.   Is unrealized appreciation revenue? Let us consider this question first with respect to marketable securities, where it is possible to make the strongest case for an affirmative answer. If marketable securities were purchased for $50,000, were worth $60,000 at the end of the year of purchase, and were sold for $70,000 during the following year, was there a $20,000 gain in the second year or a $10,000 gain in each year? Although a $10,000 gain could have been realized the first year, realization did not occur until the second year. The requirements of realization were not met during the first year, because the management elected not to sell but preferred to take the hazards of market fluctuation, and thus there was no realization nor any reasonable assurance that any revenue would ever be realized.

If readily marketable securities cannot properly be valued above cost, although a gain could be immediately realized by a sale at the prevailing market price, the valuation of inventories at market prices in excess of cost is, under ordinary conditions, even less proper. For one thing, a rise in market selling prices usually is not immediately realizable, for it is rarely possible, and it presumably would be inexpedient even if it were possible, to sell the total inventory at the end of the period, as could be done with marketable securities. If it is considered improper as a general rule to regard any revenue as being earned by manufacturing or by any other operating activities prior to sale, it certainly is much less proper to take up as realized revenue mere increases in value resulting from rises in market prices.

Turning to the field of fixed assets, if it is improper to take up as realized revenue an increase in the market value of current assets which presumably will soon be realized through sales, there is even less reason for considering that any revenue has resulted from an increase in the disposal value of fixed assets which the business, as a going concern, presumably must retain.

Very plausible arguments have been advanced for taking increments in asset values into the accounts prior to sale if the production process consists of a natural increase during two or more accounting periods. Such conditions exist in the case of growing crops, timber, and live stock, and in the case of some inventories, such as wines and liquors, which increase in value as a result of aging. Although such increments in value are in certain instances recognized as income for tax purposes, the accountant is disinclined to report such increments as revenue because there is no certainty that the items will ever be sold or that market prices will remain at prevailing levels.

Revenue from services. When should revenue from services, as distinguished from sales of merchandise, be regarded as earned? The logical answer probably is: When the service is rendered. However, the taking up of revenue from services frequently is postponed until the service is completed and billed, because of uncertainty as to the amount to be charged; or until the cash is received, because of uncertainty regarding collection. If expenses are incurred in performing the service in a period prior to that in which the revenue is recognized, consistency requires that such expenses be deferred until the period in which the revenue is taken up, unless, of course, it appears that the revenue being postponed will not be collected, in which case it may never be recognized. The related expenses under these circumstances should be regarded as lost costs and be written off.

The dollar amount of realized revenue. Having considered the question of *when* revenue should be regarded as realized, we turn to the question of the *dollar valuation* that should be placed on the revenue.

Most revenues arise from bargained transactions, and the price agreed upon by the parties to the transaction is an appropriate measure of the resulting revenue. Thus, if goods costing $100 are sold at a cash price of $150, the selling price is the measure of the revenue resulting from the sale. The same measure is appropriate for sales on account, since there is an expectation that cash will be received in due course.

More difficult problems may arise when noncash assets are traded, no transaction price being established in terms of money. Bases for the determination of the revenue, if any, to be recognized in trades are discussed below.

If a business trades articles it normally sells, accepting in exchange assets other than cash, the accountant would be justified in most cases in using the selling price of the product normally sold as the measure of revenue. But if there were any unusual features surrounding the trade transaction (for instance, if an unusually large quantity of the product was involved), due allowance for such features should be made in measuring the resulting revenue. In some circumstances where stock in trade is exchanged for other property, the accountant would be justified in using the market value of the assets received as the measure of revenue. This would be an appropriate procedure where the articles received had a more well-established market price than the articles disposed of. For example, suppose a real estate dealer sold a plot of land for 10,000 bushels of wheat. Since the value of wheat is readily determinable by reference to market quotations on any organized grain exchange, the prevailing price of wheat might be the more objective measure of revenue.

If the trade involves assets not held for sale, the accountant would be justified in using the market value of the asset being traded or the market value of the asset being acquired, whichever value could be determined with the greater assurance. In the rare instances when neither the asset traded nor the asset received has a reasonably determinable market value, the accountant is justified in bringing the acquired asset onto the books at the carrying value of the asset traded off. In this case, although there is an inflow of assets, the valuation problem is so subjective as to justify no recognition of revenue.

Cost outlays.   Since business management does not ordinarily toss dollars to the wind, accounting is based on the assumption that all cost outlays result in the acquisition of something of value to the business—something tangible like merchandise or fixed assets, or something intangible like insurance protection or the right to occupy and use certain premises. It may therefore be said that, in a broad sense, all cost outlays result in the acquisition of assets. It does not follow, however, that all cost outlays must necessarily be charged to asset accounts when the outlays are made.

Classification of cost outlays.   If it is known at the time of making a cost outlay that the benefit derived will not extend beyond the current accounting period (as when a month's rent is paid at the beginning of the month), it is customary and expedient to charge the cost immediately to an expense account. Although the cost may not have expired at the time of the outlay, the accounting entries are reduced by making an immediate charge to an expense account rather than charging an asset account and subsequently making a transfer from the asset account to an expense account.

If a cost outlay will presumably benefit more than one period, but only a few periods (as in the case of insurance costs), accounting procedures differ; sometimes the outlay is charged to an asset account (such as Unexpired Insurance) and the expired portions of cost are transferred periodically to an expense account (such as Insurance Expense). Sometimes the cost outlay is charged to an expense account and cost residues are transferred periodically to an asset account.

If a cost outlay results in the acquisition of an asset which presumably will benefit a considerable number of periods (as in the case of the acquisition of a fixed asset), the cost should be charged to an asset account and the periodical cost expirations should be charged to expense.

Some of the most difficult problems of classification of cost outlays at the time when the outlays are made arise in connection with fixed assets. These problems are discussed in Chapter 16, which comprehensively differentiates capital and revenue expenditures.

Cost apportionments. When assets of several classes are acquired at a lump-sum cost, an apportionment of the cost outlay should be made, so that there will be a basis for subsequent entries recording cost transformations, cost expirations, and cost residues applicable to the various assets. Such apportionments may be made on the basis of appraisals, market quotations, or proposed selling prices.

Cost transformations and allocations. Between the time when a cost outlay is made and the time when the cost expires, many transformations may take place. In manufacturing operations cost outlays are made for materials, labor, and factory overhead; by the transformations of the manufacturing process, these costs become merged into costs of goods in process and finished goods. It therefore becomes essential to trace the initial costs through the processes of transformation and to allocate them, as accurately as possible, to the products. This is the function of cost accounting, which cannot be discussed at length here. However, two matters of fundamental importance require mention.

First, a distinction must be maintained between transformed costs and expired costs. Use does not necessarily mean expiration of cost. If gasoline is used in a truck with which merchandise deliveries are made, its cost expires with use. But if gasoline is used in an engine which furnishes power for manufacturing purposes, its cost becomes transformed into the cost of the product.

Second, in the allocation of costs to various products, including fixed assets constructed, no special favors or cost exemptions should be granted.

Cost expirations. Expired costs are of two kinds: utilized costs and lost costs. Although it is important to distinguish between transformed costs and expired costs, it is not usually considered important to distinguish in the income statement between expired costs which have been utilized and expired costs which have been merely lost. Some accountants do undertake to make such a distinction in the income statement, and classify as losses those cost expirations which have no traceable association with the production of revenue. Thus, rent for a building used in current operations would be classified in the income statement as an expense, whereas rent for premises not in use and hence not contributing to the generation of revenue would be classified in the statement as a loss. Similarly, the undepreciated cost of plant being discarded would be classified as a loss.

Although the above distinction is commonly found in accounting literature, income statements which reflect such a distinction may be misunderstood unless it is recognized that lost costs are a type of expense, peculiar only in that there is no traceable association between them and the production of revenue. And, even if the distinction were important, it often would be difficult to make, because the decision as to whether there is a traceable relationship between the cost expiration and the production of revenue is frequently a matter of opinion.

The American Accounting Association's "Accounting Concepts and Standards Underlying Corporate Financial Statements" mentions three categories of expired costs. It states that costs should be regarded as expiring in the period in which there is:

"(a) a direct identification or association with the revenue of the period, as in the case of merchandise delivered to customers;

(b) an indirect association with the revenue of the period, as in the case of office salaries or rent; or

(c) a measurable expiration of asset costs even though not associated with the production of revenue for the current period, as in the case of losses from flood or fire."

Cost expirations and cost residues. The end-of-period determination of cost expirations for income statement purposes is, of course, directly associated with the determination of asset valuations for balance sheet purposes. In a sense, an expense calculation is at the same time an asset valuation procedure, and vice versa.

In some situations the accountant approaches the problem of measuring expenses by determining the portion of the cost outlay that may fairly be assignable to future periods. Under this general approach, the expense figure is derived incidentally as a consequence of an asset calculation. Such asset computations may be made by taking an inventory of the items on hand and unused, or by relying on their estimated use-life as a basis, or by estimating the recoverable value of the particular asset.

In other situations, the accountant approaches the problem of expense measurement by computing the amount of cost outlay that has expired during the current period and that will have no usefulness or benefit to future periods, the amount carried forward being the residue to be assigned to future periods. The accountant will follow the approach most likely to produce a reasonably conclusive answer.

An illustration of each approach follows:

(*1*) *Expense measurement approached from the point of view of asset valuation.*

> An example would be the acceptable accounting practice of taking an inventory of tools on hand and reducing the fixed asset account balance to reflect the inventory; the amount written off is the expense for the period.

(*2*) *Expense measurement approached from the point of view of expense computation.*

> Accounting for the purchase and use of coal by a public utility or large industrial plant provides an example of this approach. As coal is acquired and dumped on the coal pile, an asset account is charged. As the coal is consumed, its quantity is determined and the cost is assigned to expense; the asset balance is the cost residue assignable to future periods.

Irrespective of the measurement approach, the accountant will disapprove carrying forward cost residues if there is no reasonable likelihood that they can be recovered, either through use or by sale. To illustrate, if significant in amount, the undepreciated cost of idle, excess plant should be written down to a figure reflecting an amount fairly assignable to future periods. Or the valuation of temporary investments should be reduced below cost if there is evidence that the amount invested cannot be recovered. Such considerations are always being weighed by the accountant.

In some cases it is practically impossible to arrive at a conclusive figure for the current period's cost expiration or for the residue to be carried forward for assignment to expense in future periods. Depreciation of fixed assets is an excellent example. There often is no way to be certain that the current charge for depreciation or the asset amount carried forward will prove to be even a reasonably correct approximation. The amortization of many intangibles is similarly subject to approximations that may prove to be substantially inaccurate.

"Anticipate no profit and provide for all possible losses." The accounting student of two decades ago was taught to apply to all questions involving income determination and asset valuation the precept, "Anticipate no profit and provide for all possible losses." It was the expression of the doctrine of conservatism—a doctrine which was given the position of greatest importance. In the matter of income recognition, the accountant took the position that, no matter how sure the businessman might be of capturing the bird in the bush, he, the accountant, must see it in the hand. And in the matter of loss recognition, the accountant again resisted optimism; loss recognition must not be postponed to the point of certainty. Moreover, he refused to accept actual realization of a loss as a necessary prerequisite to loss recognition, because this would have enabled management to postpone loss recognition by postponing asset disposals.

As noted earlier, conservatism is now regarded as a matter of lesser importance. Accountants no longer feel that they can merely say: It is conservative to provide for *all possible* losses; therefore, we will provide for them. They are coming more and more to apply certain criteria to the determination of the propriety of a loss provision. Among these criteria are the following:

(1) The loss should relate to presently owned assets or assets on order.
(2) The actual realization of the loss must be reasonably certain to occur within the foreseeable future.
(3) The prospect of loss should be such that a reasonable approximation of the amount can be made.

Savings versus income.   A saving, but not income, results from manufacturing a thing at a price less than that at which it could be purchased.

Companies sometimes construct their own fixed assets, and when this is done at a cost lower than the price at which they could be purchased, there is often an inclination to value the fixed assets at a theoretical purchase price and to take up a "profit." There is a subtle semblance of fairness in such a procedure. Why should a company utilize its manufacturing facilities to make fixed assets for its own use and thus forego the opportunity of manufacturing merchandise that could be sold at a profit? The answer is that, even if the manufacture of fixed assets curtailed the manufacture of merchandise (which would be unlikely), the income statement should show what really happened instead of what might have happened. The manufacture of fixed assets may increase future net income by reducing depreciation charges, but a present saving with a prospect of increased future net income must not be confused with a present, realized gain.

Manufacturing merchandise at a cost lower than the price at which it could be purchased, or purchasing merchandise at a cost which is less than the normal market price, should not be regarded as producing income. Such an action may ultimately increase net income, but such an increase should be recognized as resulting from a reduction in the cost of goods sold rather than an increase in revenue; moreover, whether or not the gross profit will be increased is a problematical matter not determinable at the time of making the cost outlay.

The accounting procedure, sometimes adopted, of passing inventories from one stage of production to another at a valuation in excess of cost (for the purpose of reflecting a "profit" resulting from manufacturing instead of buying) is merely another way of anticipating income by confusing it with savings and is indefensible, for the reasons stated above.

Matching revenues and related expenses. In the determination of periodic net income, it is imperative that revenues and related expenses be reported in the same period. Thus, if revenue is deferred because it is regarded as not yet earned, all elements of expense related to such deferred revenue must be deferred also, in order to achieve the matching of revenue and expense which is essential to a proper determination of net income.

As a simple illustration, assume that commissions are paid to salesmen when orders are received for future delivery; to obtain a proper matching, the commissions should not be reported as an expense until the period in which the sales are reported as revenue.

In cases where a "future" expense is associated with current revenue, provisions for such future outlays should be made by charges to expense in the period when the related revenue is earned. Companies sometimes sell equipment or other merchandise with agreements to provide service for a period of time without cost to the purchaser; goods are sold with guarantees; a lessee may agree to return the leased property to the lessor at the end of the lease period in the condition in which it existed at the beginning of the lease; cemetery companies sell lots with agreements to provide perpetual care; pension systems are in operation; premium coupons redeemable in merchandise are issued. As a result of these and similar transactions and contracts, revenue may be earned in one period and expense payments applicable thereto may be made in subsequent periods. Such conditions may properly be, and frequently are, dealt with by taking revenues into income in the period in which they are earned and providing for the estimated future expense payments in the same period, by charges to operations. Any estimates so recorded should usually be shown with the liabilities because they generally are established to reflect obligations.

Another peculiar problem sometimes arises when some of the cost expenditures are applicable to future production. To illustrate, assume that the estimated cost of a logging railroad, adequate to meet the requirements of an entire timber tract, is $18,000; this cost should be spread equitably over all of the timber cut from the tract. A railroad from the waterfront one-half the distance to the back of the tract has been completed.

Assume that it is considered equitable to allocate half of the $18,000 total estimated cost to each half of the tract. If the first half of the road cost $12,000, only $9,000 of this cost should be charged against the product of the front half of the tract and $3,000 should be deferred. This deferred cost, plus the $6,000 completion cost, will produce a charge of $9,000 against the back half.

A concluding note.   The area of acceptable accounting alternatives is so extensive that one should not attribute too much precision to the income-determination process. An income figure is an approximation, partly the product of facts objectively determined, partly the product of accounting policy decisions, and partly the product of judgment and estimate.

The lack of unanimity that exists regarding the inclusion or exclusion of certain items in the process of income determination is a serious matter. If the current operating concept of income determination has been applied, the reported income figures may be construed as those that may normally be expected in the future, provided that the currently prevailing business conditions and volume levels continue, because extraneous, extraordinary, and nonrecurring items do not affect the reported income. Obviously, income figures thus determined are more affected by judgment decisions than are those arrived at by following the all-inclusive concept of income determination. However, it may be relevant to observe that the actual position and earnings of a business are not altered by the income concept adopted; only the "appearance" is affected.

If the all-inclusive approach is used, the interpretation to place on income figures should be modified accordingly. Under this approach, the income statement becomes more of a report of accountability and less of an attempt at measuring normal earning power. Less judgment is required of the accountant because he does not have to decide whether some element of revenue or cost expiration is normal or is extraneous, extraordinary, or nonrecurring.

There can be no doubt that income figures are misunderstood and misinterpreted by many persons who have an interest in business earnings. Accountants cannot entirely escape responsibility for some of this lack of understanding. The variety of acceptable alternatives and the changes that occur within the area of acceptable practices are bound to be confusing to the nonaccountant. But it would be unrealistic to expect accounting to be static. Change is an inevitable feature of accounting in a relatively free economy. This characteristic was nicely described by Marquis G. Eaton when he was president of the American Institute of Certified Public Accountants in the following words:

"What is happening, in fact, is a never-ending search for better and more refined methods of reporting the truth about the financial affairs of corporations. But these affairs grow more and more complex, the truth is not clear and simple, and as a matter of fact there is no ultimate truth in the practical affairs of man. As George O. May once said, 'Accounting can rise no higher in the scale of certainty than the events which it reflects.'

"In this search for improved methods there are bound to be differences of opinion, at any given moment of time, as to which method among two or more alternatives, all supportable in theory and in logic, would yield the result most useful to all concerned. Experience alone reveals which one is superior, and that method eventually becomes generally adopted. Meanwhile, however, there are variations in practice."

....

CHAPTER NINE

Cash

What is cash? Cash consists of legal tender, checks, bank drafts, money orders, and demand deposits in banks. In general, nothing should be considered unrestricted cash unless it is available to the management for disbursements of any nature.

Monies advanced to salesmen or other representatives for traveling and other expense disbursements have ceased to be under the control of the management for immediate disbursement for other purposes, and are therefore properly shown in the balance sheet as prepaid expense or receivables from employees.

Some concerns make a practice of allowing customers ordering goods by mail to make payment in postage stamps; such remittances should not be recorded as cash, but should be recorded as postage inventory.

The practice of carrying due bills or I.O.U.'s in the cash in place of money advanced to individuals should be discouraged. If they are found in the cash, they should be shown in the balance sheet as amounts receivable from officers, employees, and so forth, and not as cash.

Although checks payable to a company are usually included in its cash, there are some exceptions. If a check credited to a customer's account and sent to the bank for deposit is returned by the bank because of insufficient funds, the entry crediting the customer should be reversed. (A reversing entry is not necessary if the check is returned for lack of endorsement.) Post-dated checks

186

should not be recorded until the date when they can be deposited. Company officials and others in a position to do so sometimes "pay" the debit balances in their accounts by checks which it is understood will not be deposited; obviously, if there is any restriction upon the deposit or cashing of a check, the check is not an available source of current funds; any statement prepared while such a check is held should show the amount thereof as a receivable.

Deposits in savings accounts are usually classified in the balance sheet as cash, notwithstanding the legal right of the bank to demand a certain notice before withdrawal; the classification of such balances as cash appears to be justified, because the bank's right to demand notice is rarely exercised. Demand certificates of deposit may be classified as cash, but time certificates should not be so classified. A portion of the balance on deposit in an ordinary commercial checking account may not be subject to immediate withdrawal because, under the terms of a bank loan, the depositor is obligated to maintain a minimum or compensating balance; notwithstanding such restrictions, it is customary to include the entire bank balance as current cash.

Deposits in closed banks should not be regarded as current cash, nor should balances in foreign banks be so considered if they are subject to any restrictions. If the deposits in foreign banks are available for unrestricted withdrawal, they may be classified as current cash at an amount determined by conversion at the current exchange rate.

Cash deposits made in connection with contract or other bids, or deposits made in connection with purchase contracts, should be shown as deposits on contract bids or as advances against purchases, rather than as cash, even though the deposits are returnable in cash under certain circumstances.

A distinction should be made in the balance sheet between cash available for general operating purposes and cash tied up in special-purpose funds. If a fund is to be used for the payment of a current liability, as is the case with money deposited with a trustee for the payment of mortgage interest and taxes on mortgaged property, it should not be merged with the general cash. However, since the debt is a current liability, the special fund can properly be classified under the Current Assets caption, with a statement of the purpose for which it is available. Special funds not available for current purposes, such as a sinking fund for the payment of the principal of a long-term debt, a fund for the retirement of capital stock, or the proceeds of a construction mortgage which are impounded and available for disbursement only for construction work, should not be shown under the Current Assets caption.

Whether notes and acceptances endorsed to a bank should be shown in the balance sheet as cash or as receivables depends on whether the bank took the paper as deposits or merely for collection. If the bank credited the depositor's account with the paper, the item may properly be included in the cash; otherwise not.

Bank overdrafts.   There is some difference of opinion among accountants as to the proper balance sheet treatment of overdrafts.

If there is only one bank account and this account is overdrawn, the amount of the overdraft must be shown as a liability.

If there are several bank accounts, one or more with overdrafts and one or more with available balances, and if the available balances are in excess of the overdrafts, it has until recently been regarded as permissible to show on the asset side of the balance sheet the excess of the available bank balances over the overdrafts, particularly if it is the company's practice to transfer funds from bank to bank as required. However, this opinion is no longer generally held, and it is now considered better practice to show the bank balances on the asset side and the overdrafts on the liability side. Some accountants still consider it permissible merely to show on the asset side the net available bank funds, provided that reference is made to the overdrafts by the use of some clearly descriptive balance sheet title, such as "Cash in Banks—Net of Overdrafts." If assets are controlled by a bank as protection against an overdraft, the virtual pledge of the assets should be disclosed.

Some accountants have taken the position that, if the company's books show an overdraft, whereas the bank statement shows an available balance (the difference being represented by outstanding checks), such an overdraft may be offset against balances in other banks without disclosure in the balance sheet, disclosure being necessary only if the bank statement shows an overdraft. Such a distinction scarcely seems logical. If the checks are outstanding, the issuing company has no control over them and, so far as available funds are concerned, an overdraft in fact exists. Of course, if the checks have been merely drawn and recorded but have not been issued, and are therefore under the company's control, adjusting entries should be made to restore the amounts thereof to the bank balance and to the accounts payable.

Distorted cash balances.   To make a better showing in its balance sheet, a company may resort to the practice of holding its cash book open for a few days after the close of the period and recording as of the last day of the period remittances received after the close of the period. Such a procedure has the effect of overstating the most current asset, cash, by correspondingly understating the less current asset of accounts receivable.

The company may then go one step further by drawing checks after the close of the period for payment of current liabilities, and recording such payments as of the last day of the period.

To illustrate the effect of this practice upon the current position shown by the balance sheet, let us assume that a company holds its cash book open for collections of receivables amounting to $25,000, and for payments totaling $20,000 on current liabilities. The true current position and the distorted position are shown below:

| | CORRECT | | INCORRECT | |
	Amount	Per Cent of Total Current Assets	Amount	Per Cent of Total Current Assets
Current assets:				
Cash...................	$ 5,000	5.88%	$10,000	15.38%
Accounts receivable.....	50,000	58.82	25,000	38.46
Inventories............	30,000	35.30	30,000	46.16
Total current assets...	$85,000	100.00%	$65,000	100.00%
Current liabilities:				
Accounts payable.......	50,000	58.82	30,000	46.16
Net current assets........	$35,000	41.18%	$35,000	53.84%
Dollars of current assets per dollar of current liabilities...................	$1.70		$2.17	

By this artifice, the company shows a working capital ratio of 2.17 to 1 instead of 1.70 to 1, and considerably overstates its cash balance and the ratio of cash to total current assets, thus overstating the liquidity of its position.

Internal control. A system of internal control consists of a division and integration of procedures to such an extent that the activities of various members of an organization are so interrelated that accounting errors and omissions presumably will be detected automatically and the perpetration and concealment of fraud will require collusion.

An adequate system of internal control to safeguard the cash requires a control over both receipts and disbursements. The methods of effecting this control vary greatly; the system described below should be understood to be indicative of the objectives to be attained rather than a procedure to be invariably followed.

The danger of misappropriation of cash is reduced if collusion is made necessary to conceal an abstraction of cash receipts; it is therefore desirable to divide the work of handling cash receipts among several people, whose records must agree. One method of providing such an internal control is indicated below.

(1) All mail receipts and the totals of cash register tapes should be listed and totaled by a trusted employee who is neither

the cashier nor a bookkeeper; the letter or other evidence of remittance accompanying each mail receipt should be marked by this employee with the amount of the remittance, initialed by him, and turned over to the accounts receivable bookkeeper, who should also be given duplicates of prenumbered receipts issued to customers for any cash received on account and rung up on the cash register. The cash should be turned in to the cashier, and a copy of the list mentioned above should be given to the general ledger bookkeeper.

(2) All cash received should be deposited daily. The cashier, after making up the deposit, should submit the deposit slip to the employee mentioned in (1), who should compare the amount of the deposit with the amount of cash received, as shown by his list; if the deposit slip and the list of receipts are in agreement, this employee should initial the deposit slip. When the bank's monthly statement is received, it should be checked by the general ledger bookkeeper, and the deposits shown by it should be compared by the employee mentioned in (1) with the daily lists prepared by him.

(3) The cashier, the general ledger bookkeeper, and the accounts receivable bookkeeper should be different persons.

(4) An added safeguard may be introduced by having a fifth individual reconcile the bank account.

With such a system of internal control, fraud with respect to collections from debtors cannot be practiced and concealed even for a day without collusion. The first employee has no access to the books and cannot falsify the records to conceal a misappropriation; he cannot expect to withhold funds received from debtors without detection because the debtors will receive statements or letters from the credit department and will report their remittances. If the cashier withholds any cash, his daily deposit will not agree with the first employee's list or with the general ledger bookkeeper's cash receipts record made from the list of receipts. The general ledger and accounts receivable ledger bookkeepers, having no access to the cash, have no opportunity to misappropriate any of it, and, therefore, have no incentive to falsify their records unless they are parties to collusion.

The bank should be instructed to cash no checks of outsiders payable to the company but should accept them only for deposit. Checks drawn by the company itself for petty cash or other requirements may be cashed.

Since all receipts are deposited daily in the bank, all disbursements (except from petty cash) must be made by check. Disbursements from petty cash should be approved by someone in authority, and periodical totals thereof should be represented by replenishing checks. The person authorized to sign checks should have no authority to make entries in any of the books; thus, a fraudulent disbursement by check could not be concealed without the collusion of two persons. A file of approved invoices, expense bills, and other documents evidencing the propriety of the disbursements should be maintained.

The collusion of a third person in the falsification of disbursements can be made necessary

(1) Either by requiring that all checks shall be signed by one person and countersigned by another, or

(2) By allowing checks to be signed by one person, but only upon authorization by another person, evidenced by approved invoices, expense bills, and so forth, or by a formal voucher used in connection with a voucher system. The documents presented to the authorizing person as evidence of the propriety of the disbursement should be initialed or otherwise marked by him to prevent their use a second time.

All checks should be prenumbered. All spoiled, mutilated, or voided checks should be preserved. Some companies even go so far as to require that such checks be recorded in their proper sequence in the cash disbursements record, without entry in the money column but with a notation to the effect that the check is void.

It is advisable to review the system of internal control from time to time to see whether any revisions are desirable as a result of changed operating conditions, and also to determine whether the system of internal control is actually being operated as planned or whether deviations or omissions have been allowed to impair the system.

Cash over and short account. As a part of the system of internal control, frequent and unannounced cash counts should be made by the internal auditing department. Any unlocated differences between the balance per books and the cash on hand and in bank, whether discovered by the accounting staff or by the internal auditing staff, may be set up in a Cash Over and Short account. If all reasonable efforts fail to disclose the cause of the shortage or overage, the account may be closed to Revenue and Expense.

Cash Over and Short should not be charged with an ascertained defalcation; the amount of a defalcation should be charged to a special account, which should be written off only in the event of failure to collect from the party responsible therefor or from a bonding company.

Imprest cash. In the discussion of internal control it was stated that all disbursements should be made by check. Petty expenditures not made by checks can nevertheless be represented by checks through the operation of an imprest cash, or petty cash, fund. A check is drawn for an amount which will provide for petty expenditures for a reasonable time, and cashed. The cash is held in the office. The drawing of the check is recorded by a debit to Petty Cash and a credit to the general Cash account. As expenditures are made from the petty cash fund, receipts and other memoranda are retained to evidence the nature and propriety of the disbursements. A petty cash book may be kept with a number of columns in which to classify the disbursements, or the classification may be made from the memoranda when the fund is replenished. When the fund is nearly exhausted, another check is cashed for the amount of the expenditures, thus restoring the fund to its original amount; this check is recorded by a credit to the general Cash account and debits to various expense or other accounts properly chargeable with the disbursements.

The petty cash fund should be replenished or increased only by check, and never from undeposited cash receipts. The fund should be replenished at the end of each accounting period, even though it is not depleted to the customary replenishing point, so that the disbursements will be recorded in the proper period. If the issuance of a replenishing check is overlooked at the end of the period, an adjusting journal entry may be made debiting the proper expense or other accounts and crediting Petty Cash; when a replenishing check is issued in a subsequent period, the Petty Cash account should be debited with the amount with which it was credited in the adjusting entry, and other accounts should be debited with the remainder of the replenishing check. Except for such possible credits and debits, no entries should be made in the Petty Cash account other than the original debit unless the established amount is increased or decreased.

When the petty cashier requests a replenishing check, he should submit a report of his disbursements, accompanied by receipts or other evidences of the authenticity of the disbursements. This report should be audited, and all of the supporting documents should be initialed, or otherwise marked, by the person who audits the report, so that the petty cashier cannot subsequently use the supporting receipts or other vouchers to obtain a check to which he is not entitled. The internal control over the petty cash fund is also improved by unexpected counts thereof made by the internal auditing staff.

The imprest system can be applied to the control of funds of small or large amounts required at factories, branches, or offices located at a distance from the main office.

Lapping. Lapping is a device for concealing a shortage; it consists of a series of postponements of entries for collections of receivables. Lapping would be difficult if not impossible without collusion in an office where the previously described system of internal control is in operation, but it would be possible if the cashier were also the bookkeeper.

To illustrate, assume that $100 in currency is received from A on account. The cashier pockets the money and makes no entry. But it is dangerous to leave A's account uncredited for any length of time, since A may receive a statement and make a protest, which will bring the facts to light. Therefore, within a day or two, when $110 is collected from B, the cashier turns in $100 of the cash, debits Cash and credits A with $100, and pockets the extra $10. This process may be carried on indefinitely, the cashier being short all the time, but the credit to each customer's account being delayed only a few days.

If customers remit only by check, and no currency is received from other sources, a lapping of receipts will require the forging of endorsements, unless lax procedures enable the cashier to obtain funds on checks payable to the company. But if currency is received from cash sales or other sources, lapping can be carried on even though all remittances from debtors are received in the form of checks. For instance, assume the following chain of events:

Monday—A check for $100 is received from X, and $150 is received for cash sales. The cashier takes $100 of currency, deposits the remaining $50 of currency and X's check, and makes the following entry:

Cash	150	
Sales		150

The shortage is $100, the amount of the unrecorded credit to X.

Tuesday—A check for $125 is received from Y, and $165 is received for cash sales. The cashier takes $25 of currency, deposits the remaining $140 of currency and Y's check, and makes the following entry:

Cash	265	
X		100
Sales		165

The shortage is now $125, the amount of the unrecorded credit to Y.

Wednesday—A check for $115 is received from Z, and $130 is received for cash sales. The cashier deposits the $115 check, the $130 of currency, and $10 from his pocket, and makes the following entry:

Cash..	255	
Y......................................		125
Sales..................................		130

The shortage is now $115, the amount of the unrecorded credit to Z.

Noncash credits to customers. Another method of covering a shortage consists of taking money received from a customer and passing a noncash credit through the books, usually for some item such as returns and allowances. The system of safeguarding receipts already discussed will make this practice difficult; but, in addition, it is desirable to have all noncash credits supported by duplicate credit memorandums, which should be initialed by someone in authority other than the cashier.

Reconciliation of the bank account. The balance at the end of the month shown by the bank statement rarely agrees with the balance shown by the depositor's books.

Very frequently there are items on the depositor's books which do not appear on the bank statement. For instance, there may be outstanding checks, and deposits mailed toward the end of the month may not reach the bank and be recorded on its books until the next month.

Less frequently there are items on the bank statement which do not appear on the depositor's books. For instance, the bank may have made collection or other charges which the depositor may not know about and record until the bank statement is received; or the bank may have credited the depositor with the proceeds of paper left with it for collection and the notice of collection may not have been received by the depositor before the end of the month.

First illustration. If outstanding checks and deposits in transit are the only reconciling items, the reconciliation is very simple and may be made as follows:

FIRST NATIONAL BANK
Reconciliation—December 31, 1959

Balance per bank statement...............................		$ 862.57
Add deposit in transit—December 31......................		216.31
Total..		$1,078.88
Deduct outstanding checks:		
No. 965..	$31.53	
971..	15.31	46.84
Balance per books.......................................		$1,032.04

Second illustration. In this illustration, there are items on the books which do not appear on the bank statement (as in the first illustration), and also items on the bank statement which do not appear on the books. The following facts are assumed:

The books of Chicago Wholesale Grocery Company show a balance of $9,215.33 on deposit with The City National Bank on December 31, 1959.

The bank statement shows a balance of $10,361.51 on that date.

On December 31, 1959, the company mailed a deposit of $9,849.83 to the bank; this deposit does not appear on the bank statement.

The following checks were outstanding at the end of the year:

No. 1264	$1,000.00
1329	52.80
1499	84.70
1510	108.07
1511	2,500.00
1512	3,281.70
1513	3,370.91
1514	100.80

The bank has credited the company with the proceeds of a $500 sight draft on J. C. White which the company had left with the bank for collection.

The bank has made the following charges which have not been recorded on the company's books:

Telegram	$1.80
Collection charges	1.17

The bank reconciliation appears below:

THE CITY NATIONAL BANK
Reconciliation—December 31, 1959

Balance per bank statement			$10,361.51
Add:			
Deposit in transit—mailed December 31			9,849.83
Bank's charges:			
Telegram	$	1.80	
Collection charges		1.17	2.97
Total			$20,214.31
Deduct:			
Outstanding checks:			
No. 1264	$1,000.00		
1329	52.80		
1499	84.70		
1510	108.07		
1511	2,500.00		
1512	3,281.70		
1513	3,370.91		
1514	100.80	$10,498.98	
Proceeds of draft on J. C. White		500.00	10,998.98
Balance per books			$ 9,215.33

The company should make entries (equivalent to the one on page 196) to record the items on the bank statement but not on the books.

```
Cash................................................... 497.03
Telephone and telegraph............................    1.80
Collection and exchange............................    1.17
        Accounts receivable (J. C. White).................         500.00
```

Third illustration. This illustration is based on the same assumed facts as the second illustration; it differs from that illustration only in the manner of assembling and presenting the information. If there are many reconciling items, they may be assembled in a work sheet in the manner illustrated below.

A four-column work sheet in this form is also a convenient device to be used in the reconciliation of any accounts that are supposed to be reciprocal, such as the accounts of a debtor and a creditor, or the current accounts of a branch and a home office.

THE CITY NATIONAL BANK
Reconciliation Work Sheet
December 31, 1959

	ON COMPANY BOOKS ONLY		ON BANK STATEMENT ONLY	
	Debits	Credits	Debits	Credits
Deposit in transit—mailed Dec. 31...............	9,849.83			
Outstanding checks:				
No. 1264..........		1,000.00		
1329..........		52.80		
1499..........		84.70		
1510..........		108.07		
1511..........		2,500.00		
1512..........		3,281.70		
1513..........		3,370.91		
1514..........		100.80		
Telegram..............			1.80	
Collection charges.......			1.17	
Proceeds of draft on J. C. White..............				500.00
	9,849.83	10,498.98	2.97	500.00

After the work sheet has been completed, the bank reconciliation can be prepared in summary form, as shown below:

THE CITY NATIONAL BANK
Reconciliation—December 31, 1959

```
Balance per bank statement............................ ... $10,361.51
Add:
    Company's debits.......................................   9,849.83
    Bank's debits..........................................       2.97
Total....................................................  $20,214.31
Deduct:
    Company's credits.......................... $10,498.98
    Bank's credits..............................    500.00   10,998.98
Balance per books........................................  $ 9,215.33
```

Again, the company should make entries for the items which are on the bank statement but not on the books.

Fourth illustration. This illustration is based on the assumed facts of the second and third illustrations, with some additional information, stated below.

Reconciliation—November 30, 1959—before the recording of items which were on the bank statement but not on the books:

Balance per bank statement	$11,216.22
Add: Deposit in transit	7,216.85
Bank's charges	3.15
Total	$18,436.22
Deduct outstanding checks	6,215.30
Balance per books	$12,220.92

Reconciliation—November 30, 1959—after recording items on the bank statement but not on the books:

Balance per bank statement	$11,216.22
Add deposit in transit	7,216.85
Total	$18,433.07
Deduct outstanding checks	6,215.30
Balance per books	$12,217.77

Summary of the books for December:

Balance in bank, November 30, 1959	$12,217.77
Add cash receipts—all deposited	47,763.78
Total	$59,981.55
Deduct disbursements—all by check	50,766.22
Balance in bank, December 31, 1959	$ 9,215.33

Summary of the bank statement for December:

Balance, November 30, 1959	$11,216.22
Credits for deposits	45,630.80
Total	$56,847.02
Charges for checks, et cetera	46,485.51
Balance, December 31, 1959	$10,361.51

The $45,630.80 total of deposits was determined by running an adding-machine tape of the deposits shown on the bank statement.

The $46,485.51 total of checks paid and other charges was determined by running an adding-machine tape of them, or by the following computation:

Balance, November 30, 1959, per bank statement	$11,216.22
Credits for deposits	45,630.80
Total	$56,847.02
Balance, December 31, 1959, per bank statement	10,361.51
Checks and other charges	$46,485.51

The reconciling items on December 31, 1959, as in the preceding illustrations, were:

Deposit in transit...................................... $ 9,849.83
Outstanding checks..................................... 10,498.98
Bank charges...   2.97
Bank credit for collection of sight draft on J. C. White.......   500.00

The reconciliation procedure described below is more than a bank reconciliation. It consists of three reconciliations:

(1) It is assumed that, in accordance with good internal control procedure, all cash receipts are deposited in the bank. The receipts by the bank, as shown by its statement, are reconciled with the receipts shown by the books.
(2) It is also assumed that all disbursements are made by check. The bank's disbursements and other charges are reconciled with the disbursements shown by the books.
(3) The balance shown by the bank statement is reconciled with the balance shown by the books.

The reconciliation statement is started as follows:

THE CITY NATIONAL BANK
Reconciliation of Receipts, Disbursements, and Bank Account
For the Month of December, 1959

	Balance, Nov. 30, 1959	Add Receipts	Deduct Disburse- ments	Balance, Dec. 31, 1959
Per bank.............	$11,216.22	$45,630.80	$46,485.51	$10,361.51
Deposits in transit:				
November 30........	7,216.85			
Outstanding checks:				
November 30........	6,215.30*			
Per books.............	$12,217.77	$47,763.78	$50,766.22	$ 9,215.33

* Deduction.

Observe that the first line consists of a summary of the bank statement for December. The first column shows the bank reconciliation on November 30, 1959, after the company recorded the items which were on the bank statement for November but which had not been recorded before the bank statement was received. The last line is a summary of the cash records for December. The complete reconciliation statement is on page 199. The three reconciliations are made as follows:

(1) Reconciliation of receipts per bank statement ($45,630.80) with receipts per books ($47,763.78):

The $7,216.85 deposit in transit on November 30 was included in the receipts per books in November; therefore, it is deducted from the receipts per bank for December to reconcile with the receipts per books.

The $9,849.83 deposit in transit on December 31 is added to the receipts per bank to reconcile with the receipts per books.

The $500 collected on the sight draft appeared on the bank statement but was not recorded on the books; therefore, it is deducted from the receipts per bank to reconcile with the receipts per books.

(2) Reconciliation of the disbursements per bank statement ($46,485.51) with the disbursements per books ($50,-766.22):

The $6,215.30 of checks outstanding on November 30 were recorded on the books as disbursements prior to December; therefore, they are deducted from the December disbursements per bank to reconcile with the December disbursements per books.

The $10,498.98 of checks outstanding on December 31 are added to the disbursements per bank to reconcile with the disbursements per books.

The $2.97 of bank charges are not included in the disbursements per books; therefore, they are deducted from the disbursements per bank.

(3) The items in the bank reconciliation (last column) are the same as those in the reconciliations in the second and third illustrations.

The completed reconciliation appears below:

THE CITY NATIONAL BANK
Reconciliation of Receipts, Disbursements, and Bank Account
For the Month of December, 1959

	Balance, Nov. 30, 1959	Add Receipts	Deduct Disbursements	Balance, Dec. 31, 1959
Per bank..........	$11,216.22	$45,630.80	$46,485.51	$10,361.51
Deposits in transit:				
November 30...	7,216.85	7,216.85*		
December 31...		9,849.83		9,849.83
Outstanding checks:				
November 30...	6,215.30*		6,215.30*	
December 31...			10,498.98	10,498.98*
Bank's charges.....			2.97*	2.97
Proceeds of draft on				
J. C. White......		500.00*		500.00*
Per books..........	$12,217.77	$47,763.78	$50,766.22	$ 9,215.33

* Deduction.

The treatment of the checks outstanding at the beginning and end of December does not mean that all of the checks which were outstanding on November 30 had cleared the bank in December, and that all of the checks which were outstanding on December 31 had been issued in December. Let us assume that, of the checks outstanding on December 31, check No. 1264 for $1,000.00 was issued in November. The outstanding checks *could have been shown* in the reconciliation statement as follows:

	Balance, Nov. 30, 1959	Add Receipts	Deduct Disburse- ments	Balance, Dec. 31, 1959
Outstanding checks:				
Issued prior to December....	6,215.30*		5,215.30*	1,000.00*
Issued in December.........			9,498.98	9,498.98*

Using the standard procedure shown in the reconciliation statement, there is a net addition of $4,283.68 (the difference between $6,215.30 and $10,498.98) in the Disbursements column; in the alternative procedure, there is also a net addition of $4,283.68 (the difference between $5,215.30 and $9,498.98). And, by both procedures, the outstanding checks shown in the last column total $10,498.98.

In addition to reconciling the recorded receipts with the bank's credits, and reconciling the disbursements per books with the bank's charges, this procedure has the advantage of localizing errors. If there is an error in the cash receipts records (and there are no errors elsewhere), the Receipts column and the Balance (bank reconciliation) column will be "out" the same amount. The error is thus localized, and only the amounts in the Receipts column need be checked.

Fifth illustration. In all of the preceding illustrations, we have reconciled the balance per bank to the balance per books. But if there are items on the books which do not appear on the bank statement *and also* items on the bank statement which do not appear on the books, neither the balance per bank nor the balance per books is the true balance. In such cases it is advisable to reconcile the balance per bank and the balance per books to the correct balance. To illustrate, using the data in the preceding illustration, the reconciliation statement may be prepared as follows:

THE CITY NATIONAL BANK
Bank Reconciliation—December 31, 1959

Balance per bank statement...............................	$10,361.51
Add deposit in transit....................................	9,849.83
Total...	$20,211.34
Deduct outstanding checks................................	10,498.98
Correct balance..	$ 9,712.36

Balance per books......................................	$ 9,215.33
Add proceeds of draft on J. C. White.....................	500.00
Total..	$ 9,715.33
Deduct bank charges....................................	2.97
Correct balance..	$ 9,712.36

Prior to the preparation of a reconciliation statement in this form, the reconciling data may, if desired, be assembled in a work sheet similar to the one shown in the third illustration or in a reconciliation statement like the one shown in the fourth illustration.

Sixth illustration. The following reconciliation of the bank account of Bailey Transformer Company includes several reconciling items not previously mentioned.

THE FIRST NATIONAL BANK
Bank Reconciliation—September 30, 1959

Balance per bank statement...............................		$5,215.60
Add: Deposit in transit....................................		723.90
Check of Bailey Transit Company charged to our account..		350.00
Check of Henry Bigley returned for endorsement........		216.50
Total...		$6,506.00
Deduct outstanding checks:		
No. 2345....................................	$115.21	
2347.......................................	579.99	
2362—Certified—$300.00..................		695.20
Correct balance...		$5,810.80
Balance per books.......................................		$5,900.05
Add error in recording check No. 2357 as $297.20 instead of as $279.20, the amount for which it was drawn...........		18.00
Total..		$5,918.05
Deduct: N.S.F. check—H. E. Gates..................	$ 75.50	
Check No. 132 issued in 1956, written off in May, 1959, but now cleared..............	25.00	
Monthly service charge....................	6.75	107.25
Correct balance...		$5,810.80

The items included in this reconciliation are stated below.

The books of Bailey Transformer Company showed a balance of $5,900.05 in The First National Bank on September 30, 1959. There was a deposit of $723.90 in transit. The following checks had not cleared:

No. 2345...	$115.21
2347..	579.99
2362..	300.00

Although check No. 2362 had not cleared, a memo accompanying the bank statement reported that the check had been certified, and consequently charged to the company's account. A check for $350.00 drawn by Bailey Transit Company was improperly charged to Bailey Transformer Company. Check No. 132 for $25.00 was issued in 1956; it was restored to the bank balance in May, 1959, as it was believed at that time that, having been outstanding so long, it would not be presented; the entry made in May was a debit to Cash and a credit to Miscellaneous Income. This check was paid by the bank in September. Two checks deposited on September 29 were returned: One was a check for $75.50 received from H. E. Gates to apply on account, and returned because there were insufficient funds in the drawer's account to provide for payment of the check; the other was a check for $216.50 received from Henry Bigley, which was returned because it had not been endorsed by Bailey Transformer Company. The latter check was endorsed and redeposited on October 1. Check No. 2357 for $279.20 was improperly recorded as $297.20; the offsetting debit was to Purchases. The bank's service charge for September was $6.75.

Although check No. 2362 has not cleared the bank, it was certified and charged by the bank to the company's account; therefore, it is not shown as a reconciling item.

The check returned by the bank because of insufficient funds is shown as a deduction from the balance per books, because the check is not good and should be charged back to the maker.

The check returned for endorsement is added to the balance per bank because the check was immediately endorsed and redeposited.

The following entries should be made.

Cash..	18.00	
Purchases...		18.00
To correct error in recording Check No. 2357 as $297.20 instead of $279.20.		
Accounts receivable (H. E. Gates).......................	75.50	
Cash...		75.50
To charge Gates with check returned N.S.F.		
Bank service charges...................................	6.75	
Cash...		6.75
Charges for September.		
Miscellaneous income..................................	25.00	
Cash...		25.00
To reverse entry made in May, 1959, eliminating Check No. 132 from outstanding checks; it has now cleared.		

Estimating the cash position. For various reasons it may be desired to estimate the probable cash position during some future period. For instance, assume that a company wishes to obtain a loan at the bank, and the bank requests a statement showing the probable date when the loan can be repaid. On June 30, 1959, the company had the current assets and liabilities shown on page 204.

Forecast of Cash and Current Position
For the Six Months Ending December 31, 1959

	Cash	Accounts Receivable	Merchandise	Accounts Payable and Accruals	Bank Loan
June 30:					
Balances.......	$ 3,000	$8,000	$10,000	$ 7,000	
July:					
Collections.....	8,000	8,000*			
Payments......	7,000*			7,000*	
Sales..........		8,000	6,000*		
Purchases......			10,000	10,000	
Expenses......				600	
Balances.......	$ 4,000	$8,000	$14,000	$10,600	
August:					
Bank loan.....	5,000				$5,000
Collections.....	8,000	8,000*			
Payments......	10,600*			10,600*	
Sales..........		8,000	6,000*		
Purchases......			9,000	9,000	
Expenses......				600	
Balances.......	$ 6,400	$8,000	$17,000	$ 9,600	$5,000
September:					
Collections.....	8,000	8,000*			
Payments......	9,600*			9,600*	
Sales..........		8,000	6,000*		
Purchases......			8,000	8,000	
Expenses......				600	
Balances.......	$ 4,800	$8,000	$19,000	$ 8,600	$5,000
October:					
Collections.....	8,000	8,000*			
Payments......	8,600*			8,600*	
Sales..........		8,000	6,000*		
Purchases......			6,000	6,000	
Expenses......				600	
Balances.......	$ 4,200	$8,000	$19,000	$ 6,600	$5,000
November:					
Collections.....	8,000	8,000*			
Payments......	6,600*			6,600*	
Sales..........		8,000	6,000*		
Purchases......			5,000	5,000	
Expenses......				600	
Balances.......	$ 5,600	$8,000	$18,000	$ 5,600	$5,000
December:					
Collections.....	8,000	8,000*			
Payments......	5,600*			5,600*	
Sales..........		8,000	6,000*		
Purchases......			4,000	4,000	
Expenses.......				600	
Bank loan paid.	5,000*				5,000*
Balances.......	$ 3,000	$8,000	$16,000	$ 4,600	$ —

* Deduction.

```
Cash.....................................................................  $ 3,000
Accounts receivable.....................................................    8,000
Merchandise.............................................................   10,000
Accounts payable and accruals...........................................    7,000
```

Some of the merchandise in which the company deals is obtainable only in the summer months, and purchases are therefore high from June to September. The prospective purchases for the next six months are:

```
July....................................................................  $10,000
August..................................................................    9,000
September...............................................................    8,000
October.................................................................    6,000
November................................................................    5,000
December................................................................    4,000
```

The company wishes to borrow $5,000 on August 1, and assures the bank that the loan can be repaid at the end of December. The bank asks for a cash forecast, which appears on page 203. The forecast is based on the following facts and assumptions: The company's sales are fairly uniform through the year, averaging about $8,000 a month; they are made at an average gross profit of 25%. Expenses average about $600 per month. It is assumed that liabilities for purchases and expenses will be paid in the month following that in which they are incurred, and that accounts receivable will be collected in the month following the month of sale.

CHAPTER TEN

Receivables

Accounts Receivable

Classification. Since accounts receivable are classed as current assets in the balance sheet, no balances (with a few exceptions mentioned later) should appear as accounts receivable unless they presumably will be converted into cash during the operating cycle.

Amounts receivable from officers, directors, and stockholders, except in instances where goods have been sold to them on account for collection in accordance with the regular credit terms, are not likely to be collected with any promptness and should be shown under some noncurrent caption.

Accounts for advances to stockholders, officers, and directors are often found on the books of close corporations, particularly if the business was previously conducted as a partnership. The former partners, having become accustomed to taking drawings, continue to do so, not realizing that, whereas partners are allowed to take drawings in any free and easy manner they desire, the profits of a corporation can be legally divided only by the formal declaration of a dividend. Until a dividend is declared, these advances are in the nature of loans, recoverable by creditors in case the corporation is unable to pay its debts.

Although advances to subsidiary companies are, in a sense, accounts receivable, they should not be included with customers' accounts in the balance sheet. Advances are usually of a more permanent nature and are not current. To show them in the balance sheet as accounts receivable is likely to be misleading: The casual reader of the balance sheet will probably obtain too favorable an impression of the financial position because of the overstatement of current assets and working capital. On the other hand, a more penetrating reader may compute the ratio of receivables to sales and may gain the unwarranted and unfavorable impression that too great a percentage of the period's sales remains uncollected, and that the receivables are therefore of dubious value.

Receivables resulting from sales to subsidiaries, collectible currently, can be included in accounts receivable under the Current Assets caption.

It has often been said that the term *accounts receivable* is too inclusive and that it should therefore be abandoned. The term *customers' accounts* has been suggested to take its place. *Trade debtors* has also been suggested as an even better term, since it corresponds with the similar term *trade creditors*.

A distinction should be made between the words *receivable* and *due*. An account receivable is a claim against a debtor. A receivable which is due is a claim which the creditor has a right to collect at the present time. Accounts receivable may be due, or not yet due. Hence, it is undesirable to speak of the total accounts receivable as "receivables due from customers" or by any other expression in which "due" is used improperly.

In most businesses, the terms of sale require payment within 30, 60, or 90 days, but in some types of business the accounts receivable are due in installments over a long period of time. It was formerly considered improper to include among current assets any receivables due beyond one year from the balance sheet date; Institute Bulletin No. 43 sanctions including in the current assets any "installment or deferred accounts and notes receivable if they conform generally to normal trade practices and terms within the business."

If special deposits made in connection with contract bids or for other purposes are likely to remain outstanding for considerable periods of time, they should not be classed as current assets.

Some receivables which can properly be classified as current assets should nevertheless be segregated from the receivables from customers. Some of these are: debit balances in suppliers' accounts; claims against railroads and other common carriers for damages to goods in transit; uncollected stock subscriptions; currently recoverable deposits made against contract bids; claims for cash refunds; declared dividends receivable on stock investments; insurance claims receivable; and advances on purchases. If the circumstances of a particular case indicate that collection will not be received currently, the item should not be classified under the current caption.

If contingent receivables such as claims under guarantees and amounts thought to be recoverable in litigation are placed on the books as a matter of record, proper consideration should be given to both the question of valuation and the question of classification in the balance sheet. The degree of probability of collection will determine the advisability of establishing an allowance account; the date of probable collection will determine the current or non-current classification.

Memorandum charges to consignees for goods shipped on consignment should not be included in accounts receivable because title to the merchandise has not passed to the consignee and there is no valid claim against him. Receivables from consignees arise only upon the sale of the consigned goods.

Valuation. In the valuation of the total of customers' accounts, consideration should be given to certain possible deductions. These deductions are for:

Uncollectible accounts.
Freight.
Returns and allowances.
Discounts.

The deduction for uncollectible accounts is almost invariably applicable; the deductions for freight, returns and allowances, and discounts are applicable only under special circumstances.

Allowance for doubtful accounts. The creation of an allowance for doubtful accounts is intended to accomplish two results, namely:

To charge the loss against the period that caused the loss by the sale of goods to customers whose accounts prove to be uncollectible.
To show the estimated realizable value of the customers' accounts.

It is not always possible, however, to accomplish both of these results, as will be shown in the following discussion of methods of estimating the amounts to be credited to the allowance account.

The three customary procedures for computing the periodical credits to the allowance account are indicated below:

(1) Adjusting the allowance account to the amount of loss estimated by aging the accounts receivable and considering supplementary data.

(2) Adjusting the allowance account to a percentage of the accounts open at the end of the period.

(3) Increasing the allowance account by a percentage of the sales for the period.

The per cents used in the second and third methods are usually determined from the loss experience of prior periods. However, full consideration should be given to changes in economic conditions or in the credit policy of the company, because such changes may cause the losses to differ materially from those of the past.

Aging accounts.   When this method is used, a list of all accounts may be made on working papers, with columns with various headings such as "Not due," "1 to 30 days past due," "31 to 60 days past due," and so forth. All accounts in the subsidiary ledger are then listed, and the component elements of the balances are classified in the proper columns.

An accounts receivable aging schedule, summarizing the data assembled in the working papers, is illustrated below:

Age of Accounts Receivable
December 31, 1959 and 1958

	DECEMBER 31, 1959		DECEMBER 31, 1958	
	Amount	Per Cent of Total	Amount	Per Cent of Total
Not due......................	$15,000	30.93%	$20,000	41.67%
1 to 30 days past due...........	12,000	24.74	16,000	33.33
31 to 60 days past due..........	8,000	16.50	5,000	10.42
61 to 90 days past due..........	6,000	12.37	4,500	9.38
91 to 120 days past due.........	4,000	8.25	1,000	2.08
More than 120 days past due....	2,000	4.12	1,000	2.08
Bankrupt or with attorneys.....	1,500	3.09	500	1.04
Total......................	$48,500	100.00%	$48,000	100.00%

The amount of the allowance account is then determined on the basis of the age of the past-due accounts. Supplementary information must also be considered, since it may be known that some accounts not past due are doubtful, whereas others long past due may be collectible. In this connection, the credit terms must, of course, be taken into consideration, for the terms will determine when an account is past due.

This method has the advantage of accomplishing the second of the two objectives stated above, since it results in a fairly accurate valuation of the accounts on the books. However, it may easily result in a failure to distribute losses to the periods during which they were caused. Bad debt losses are caused by making sales to customers who do not pay their accounts. Theoretically, therefore, provision for the loss should be made in the period in which the sales were made. But, if the aging method is used, accounts may not appear to be uncollectible until a date subsequent to the period of sale; in that case the loss, or the provision therefor, will not be charged to income until a period subsequent to that of the sale. Thus, one period will get the credit for the income and a later period will get the charge for the loss.

Percentage of open accounts. If a company's experience indicates that a certain per cent of the accounts open at any date will ultimately prove uncollectible, the total allowance requirement at any date can be estimated by multiplying the open account balances by the loss experience per cent. The allowance account is then credited with an amount sufficient to increase the existing balance to the estimated required balance. The theory of this method is the same as the theory of the preceding method; the difference lies in the procedure of estimating the total allowance requirement. It is not a method to be recommended; it is subject to the disadvantage pointed out in connection with the aging method, and it is difficult to obtain experience data from which to make a reliable estimate of the per cent to be applied.

Percentage of sales. The most equitable distribution of bad debt losses among periods is usually made by crediting the allowance account at the end of the period with a percentage of the sales of the period. The rate is computed on the basis of the statistics of sales and bad debt losses of the past periods. Theoretically, the rate should be computed by dividing the losses of past periods by the charge sales of past periods, not by the total sales. The rate thus ascertained should be applied to the charge sales for the current period. But, practically, it makes very little difference whether or not this distinction is made. By using the total sales to compute the rate, a per cent is obtained lower than that which results from dividing losses by credit sales. This lower rate is then applied to the total sales for the period instead of to the credit sales.

If statements are prepared monthly, it is important that allowance provisions be made monthly rather than annually; otherwise, the monthly balance sheets may show very inaccurate net valuations of the receivables. Assume that balance sheets are prepared monthly, but no provision for losses on the year's sales is made until the end of the year. Obviously, in all balance sheets prepared before the close of the year, the receivables will be shown without provision for losses on receivables which arose from sales during the year—presumably the major portion of the receivables. On the other hand, if an adequate allowance account exists throughout the year by reason of provisions in prior years, the year-end provision based on the total sales for the year will produce an excessive allowance account.

When the credit to the allowance account is computed as a percentage of sales, there is some danger that the account balance may become excessive or may prove to be inadequate, regardless of whether provisions are made monthly or annually. For this reason, the accounts receivable should be reviewed from time to time for the purpose of estimating probable losses, the amount of which can be compared with the existing allowance account balance. If it is excessive or inadequate, the per cent applied to sales should be revised accordingly.

Recoveries. If a collection is made on an account once charged off as uncollectible, the customer's account should be recharged with the amount collected, and possibly with the entire amount previously written off if it is now expected that collection will be received in full. The collection should then be credited to the customer's account. These entries are made in the customer's account so that it will show that the debtor has attempted to re-establish his credit by the payment.

What account should be credited when the customer's account is recharged? From the standpoint of theory, the following may be said:

It is conservative to credit recoveries to the allowance account if the credits to it were determined by multiplying the sales by a per cent representing the relation of net bad debt losses (losses less recoveries) to sales. It is not correct if the per cent used in computing the provision represents the relation of gross write-offs to sales; in this case, recoveries should be credited to an income account.

If the allowance account was created on a valuation basis (by aging the accounts or using a per cent representing the relation of losses to account balances), it makes no difference, from a theoretical standpoint, whether recoveries are credited to the allowance account, to the Bad Debts expense account, or to an income account, as the allowance account balance and likewise the net income will be the same in any case. For, if a recovery is credited to the allowance account, the amount to be charged to expense at the end of the period to raise the allowance account to its required balance will be reduced by the amount of the recovery; if the recovery is credited to the Bad Debts expense account or to an income account, the charge to operations will be correspondingly increased; the net income will be the same by either method.

From a practical standpoint, the choice of methods is usually of no serious consequence, because the loss reserve and the net operating charge for bad debts are usually matters of estimate; the theoretical considerations, therefore, seem to be of no great practical importance unless recoveries are of abnormally large amounts.

Freight. Merchants sometimes sell goods f.o.b. destination, with an understanding that the purchaser will pay the freight and deduct the amount thereof in making his remittance. In such instances, any freight to be deducted in the settlement of accounts which are open at the end of the period should be deducted from the accounts receivable by setting up a reserve. In this connection it is worth noting that the customer is entitled to discount on the full amount of the invoice, and not on the amount of the invoice less the freight. If the shipper paid the freight, the invoice would not be subject to a freight deduction, and discount would probably be taken on the whole amount of the invoice. The purchaser should not suffer a loss of discount merely because he pays the freight for the seller.

Returns and allowances. Should a reserve be set up to provide for the probable allowances to be credited to customers on accounts open at the end of the period, and for losses represented by the difference between probable credits for returns and the valuation which can properly be placed on the goods returned to inventory? Theoretically, yes, because otherwise the realizable value of the accounts receivable, as well as the net sales, would be overstated. In practice the provision is rarely made.

Reserve for discounts. From a theoretical standpoint, a reserve should be set up for the discounts which will probably be taken on the accounts receivable; otherwise, the net realizable value of the receivables presumably will be overstated. However, the creation of such a reserve is not customary, and the charge to income to set up such a reserve is not deductible for federal income tax purposes.

Discounts on returned sales. Assume that a customer buys goods invoiced at $1,000, subject to a 2% discount, and that he pays the invoice within the discount period with a check for $980. Subsequently he returns one-tenth of the goods, which had been billed to him at $100 and which were paid for at the net amount of $98. What credit should he receive? Although this is largely a matter of policy, it would seem that the credit should be $98 if the customer is to be reimbursed in cash, and $100 if the credit is to be traded out. The reason behind this conclusion may be made clearer by assuming that the entire invoice is returned. If a credit of $1,000 were allowed, to be paid in cash, the discount privilege could be abused, for the customer who paid $980 could obtain $1,000 in cash; on the other hand, if a credit of only $980 were allowed, payable in merchandise, the customer would lose the benefit of having paid his bill within the discount period.

Credit balances. If the subsidiary accounts receivable ledger contains accounts with credit balances, the balance of the controlling account will be the difference between the total of the debit balances and the total of the credit balances in the subsidiary ledger. At what figure should the accounts receivable be shown in the balance sheet? The accounts receivable should be shown at the total of the debit balances, and the credit balances should be shown on the liability side of the balance sheet, as a separate item: Credit balances of customers' accounts.

Accounts receivable financing. Some businesses, usually because they are not sufficiently established to obtain an assurance of funds from a bank, finance their current operations to some extent by utilizing their accounts receivable. The procedures are of two kinds: open accounts receivable financing and factoring.

Open accounts receivable financing. Under this procedure an agreement is made with a finance company to advance funds against accounts receivable for a definite period of time, usually a year, with a provision that the contract can be terminated by written notice by either the client or the finance company six months prior to the termination date stated in the contract. The contract states the percentage of the accounts which the finance company will advance. The rate ranges from 75% to 90%, depending on the quality of the accounts and their average size, as well as the financial status of the client. An 80% rate is normal.

The client usually pledges the receivables as collateral to the obligation for the funds advanced, with full recourse to the client if an account is not collected when due.

Such financing usually is done on a nonnotification basis; that is, the client's customer is not informed that his account has been assigned to a finance company. The client makes the collections and agrees to transmit them, in the form in which received, to the finance company, which deposits them. The finance company makes arrangements with its bank to use a code endorsement, so that the checks returned to the customers will bear no evidence that the accounts have been financed.

Since the amount received from the finance company at the time of the financing is less than the amount of the receivables, the client retains an equity in the accounts, which the finance company credits to the client. Any returns, allowances, and discounts reduce the equity. If the equity is exhausted or reduced to an amount which the finance company regards as an inadequate cushion of protection, the client sends the finance company a check in an amount sufficient to create an acceptable equity. When accounts are collected, the related equity may be paid to the client immediately or periodically.

The finance company's charges consist of interest, usually at a daily rate of $\frac{1}{30}$ of 1% applied

Sometimes to the daily uncollected balances of the accounts; for instance, if the uncollected balances on a certain day totalled $75,000, the interest charge for the day would be $\frac{1}{30}$ of 1% of $75,000, or $25.

Sometimes to the cash-advanced element of the daily uncollected balances; for instance, if the amount originally advanced was 80% of the accounts, the interest charge for the day would be $\frac{1}{30}$ of 1% of ($75,000 \times 80\%$), or $20.

Because of the contingent liability which the client assumes in open accounts receivable financing, the transaction is similar in nature to the discounting of notes receivable and may be similarly recorded. To illustrate, assume that $10,000 of accounts receivable were financed and that $8,000 in cash was advanced to the client. The entry to record the financing would be:

```
Cash.........................................   8,000
Equity in assigned accounts.......................   2,000
       Accounts receivable assigned...................          10,000
```

The ledger should indicate the accounts that have been assigned. The balance sheet presentation at this point, assuming that the company has $20,000 of unassigned accounts, would be:

```
Current assets:
  Accounts receivable.............................. $20,000
  Equity in assigned accounts.......................   2,000 $22,000
```

The balance sheet should disclose, preferably by a footnote, the contingent liability on the financed accounts. This is always the total of the uncollected balances of the assigned accounts, minus the equity. The footnote might state:

On December 31, 19—, the company was contingently liable in the amount of $8,000 on accounts receivable financed.

Assume a return or an allowance of $175; the following entries would be required:

```
Sales returns and allowances.............................. 175
     Equity in assigned accounts..........................          175

Accounts receivable assigned.............................. 175
     Accounts receivable....................................          175
```

No cash book entries should be made for collections on assigned accounts; they do not belong to the company but must be forwarded to the finance company. However, they should be recorded in the company's books to show the reduction in the accounts receivable assigned and in the contingent liability. If a $2,000 account is collected, with or without a deduction for discount, the entry should be:

```
Accounts receivable assigned.............................. 2,000
     Accounts receivable..................................         2,000
     (Details should be posted to the accounts receivable ledger.)
```

Assuming that a $40 discount was taken, the following additional entry would be required:

```
Sales discounts.........................................    40
     Equity in assigned accounts..........................         40
```

The contingent liability to be shown in a balance sheet footnote at this point is computed as follows:

```
Uncollected balances of assigned accounts:
  Original amount.................................. $10,000
  Deduct:
    Collections—including cash discounts........ $2,000
    Returns and allowances....................    175    2,175  $7,825
Deduct equity:
  Original amount..................................        $ 2,000
  Deduct:
    Returns and allowances..................... $  175
    Cash discounts...........................      40      215   1,785
Contingent liability..........................................  $6,040
```

The finance company's interest charges are reported to the client monthly and are payable in cash.

The above discussion is descriptive of usual procedures, but there are some variations among finance companies.

Factoring. Factoring is the outright purchase of receivables by a factor. The purchase is made on a notification basis, and the customer makes his remittances direct to the factor, who assumes the responsibility of keeping the receivable records and collecting delinquent accounts.

Before merchandise is shipped to a customer, the client requests the factor's credit approval. If it is obtained, the account is sold to the factor immediately after shipment of the goods. The factor credits the client's account for the amount of the invoice less the amount of the permitted cash discount, and less the factor's commission and a holdback intended primarily to absorb charges for returns and allowances. The per cent of holdback (applied to the face of the account minus cash discount and commission) is a matter of agreement, but is normally about 20%. After there is no further prospect of returns and allowances or anything else that reduces the amount of the receivable, any remaining balance in the holdback is returned to the client. The client assumes no responsibility for loss.

The factor's compensation consists of:

Commission, which is a percentage of the net amount of the invoice—the gross amount minus available cash discount. The commission is a charge for the service of passing on credits, assuming all credit risks, and keeping the accounts. It usually varies from 1%, or somewhat less, to 2% or more, depending upon the amount of work and risk involved. Customary rates are $1\frac{1}{8}\%$ or $1\frac{1}{4}\%$.

Interest, which is computed—usually at 6% per annum or at an equivalent daily rate—on amounts withdrawn by the client before the due date. Withdrawals can be made on the due date interest free. After the due date, interest (also usually at 6%) accrues to the client on any amounts not withdrawn.

The "due date" of a single invoice is ten days after the date on which the discount period expires. Clients frequently sell several invoices to a factor at the same time. It then becomes necessary to compute the average due date. This is done as follows:

(1) Select an arbitrary "focal date"; the most convenient focal date is the last day of the month preceding the earliest due date of any of the invoices.

(2) Determine, for each invoice, the number of days between the focal date and the date on which the discount period expires.

(3) Multiply the net amount (gross amount minus available discount) of each invoice by the number of days between the focal date and the date when the discount period expires, to determine an amount called *dollar-days*.

(4) Add the net invoice amounts.

(5) Add the dollar-days amounts.

(6) Divide the dollar-days total by the net invoice total. The quotient is the number of days between the focal date and the average discount period expiration date.

(7) Add ten days to this quotient to determine the average "due date."

To illustrate, assume that four invoices, all subject to 2% discount if paid within ten days, are sold to a factor on August 28.

The computation (using August 31 as the focal date) of the average due date is shown below.

Invoice Date	Latest Discount Date	Invoice Amount Gross	Net	Days Between Focal Date and Latest Discount Date	Dollar-Days
Aug. 28	Sept. 7	$1,000	$ 980	7	6,860
26	5	1,500	1,470	5	7,350
25	4	2,500	2,450	4	9,800
30	9	3,000	2,940	9	26,460
		$8,000	$7,840		50,470

50,470 ÷ 7,840 = 6.4 (rounded off to 6) Days from focal date to average
discount period expiration date.
September 6 + 10 = September 16, the average "due date."

Assuming that the commission rate is 1¼% and that the hold-back rate is 20%, the client's entry to record the factoring will be:

Sales discounts (2% of $8,000)...................... 160.00
Factoring commission (1¼% of $7,840).............. 98.00
Factor's holdback [20% of ($8,000 − $258)].......... 1,548.40
Factor... 6,193.60
    Accounts receivable........................... 8,000.00

As with accounts receivable financing, it should be observed that factors' procedures are not entirely uniform.

Notes and Acceptances Receivable

Definitions. A *note* is defined by the Uniform Negotiable Instruments Law as follows:

"A negotiable promissory note within the meaning of this act is an unconditional promise in writing made by one person to another, signed by the maker, engaging to pay on demand or at a fixed or determinable future time a sum certain in money to order or to bearer."

A *bill of exchange* is defined by the same law as follows:

"A bill of exchange is an unconditional order in writing addressed by one person to another, signed by the person giving it, requiring the person to whom it is addressed to pay on demand or at a fixed or determinable future time a sum certain in money to order or to bearer."

After a bill of exchange has been accepted by the drawee, it becomes an acceptance.

A *trade acceptance,* as defined by the Federal Reserve Board, is a "bill of exchange, drawn by the seller on the purchaser, of goods sold, and accepted by such purchaser."

Terminology. Because bills of exchange instead of notes have been commonly used in England, the terms *bills receivable* and *bills payable* found their way into American terminology. However,

the terms *notes receivable* and *notes payable* have now come into
general use as more exactly indicative of the form of paper most
in use here. If the bulk of a company's paper is in the form of
notes, there is no serious objection to recording a few acceptances in
the note accounts. But if acceptances are frequently used, it
may be desirable to distinguish between the two classes of paper
in the accounts by the terms *notes receivable* and *acceptances receivable*, and *notes payable* and *acceptances payable*.

Advantages of trade acceptances. Banks usually prefer to
discount a customer's trade acceptance receivable rather than to
discount his own note payable—for two reasons. First, the acceptance is two-name paper, a primary liability of the acceptor and a
secondary liability of the drawer. Second, it is "self-liquidating";
since the acceptance arose out of a purchase of goods, it is assumed
that sales will provide the funds with which to pay the paper.

From the standpoint of the selling merchant, the trade acceptance is preferable to the open account because (1) it is a written
promise to pay a stated amount at an agreed date; (2) it relieves
the seller of the financial burden of tying up a considerable portion
of his capital in customers' accounts, because acceptances can be
discounted at the bank more readily and more cheaply than
accounts receivable can be assigned; and (3) it may reduce losses
from bad debts.

Since trade acceptances are assumed to have a better credit
standing than notes receivable, because the nature of their origin
makes them presumably self-liquidating, it may be advisable to
show them as separate items in the balance sheet if they are of any
considerable amount.

Dishonored notes. When a note has reached its maturity
and been presented to the maker without being collected, it is said
to have been *dishonored*. It should then be taken out of the Notes
Receivable account and transferred to the customer's account by
the following entry:

Accounts receivable (John Doe)............................. 500
   Notes receivable.......................................   500
   To charge Doe's dishonored note back to his account. (The purpose of this entry is to show the dishonor of the note in Doe's
   account for purposes of credit information.)

If the dishonored note bore interest, the Interest Earned account
should be credited and the maker of the note should be debited.
This should be done in order to maintain a record of the interest
earned and the total amount receivable from the debtor. If any
protest fees were paid, they should be charged to the maker. Any
amount regarded as uncollectible should be written off.

It has been suggested that dishonored notes be passed on to a Dishonored Notes Receivable account, thus:

Dishonored notes receivable..	500	
Accounts receivable (John Doe)............................		500
To transfer the note to a dishonored notes account.		

This entry takes the item out of the accounts receivable, which are assumed to be current and collectible, and shows its true nature as a past-due note.

Credit limit on notes and accounts. When the credit department fixes a maximum credit limit for a customer, and when customers settle their accounts by notes, it may be desirable to keep the records in such a way as to show the combined liability of each customer on notes and on account. This purpose can be accomplished by providing customers' accounts with two debit and two credit columns, the inner columns to be used as memorandum note columns. When a customer is credited with a note in the outer credit column, he is also charged in the inner, or memorandum, debit column. When he pays the note, Notes Receivable is credited and a memorandum entry is made in the inner credit column of the customer's personal account. Thus, the balance of the outer columns will show the customer's liability on open account, and the balance of the inner columns will show his liability on notes.

Valuation of, and losses on, notes. Notes receivable, whether interest-bearing or without interest, are stated in the accounts and the balance sheet at their face. Since non-interest-bearing notes are not worth their face until maturity, it would be theoretically correct to reduce their gross valuation by the deduction of discount to maturity. Such an accounting refinement is not, however, recognized in practice.

If ample provision is made in the allowance account (reserve for bad debts) for losses on notes as well as on accounts, note losses should be charged to the allowance account. If the provisions made to the allowance account are not intended to be sufficient to cover losses on both classes of receivables, the note losses should be charged to an expense account.

When estimating the amount required for possible losses on notes, it may be advisable to determine whether the notes were received in the regular course of trade and in accordance with settlement terms made at the time of sale, or were taken from debtors whose accounts had become old and were not immediately collectible. Notes of the latter class are obviously less likely to be collected than those of the former.

Bank discount. The bank discount and the proceeds of a note or acceptance discounted at a bank are computed as follows:

Compute the value of the note at maturity.
> The value of a non-interest-bearing note is its face.
> The value of an interest-bearing note is its face plus interest, at the rate stated by the note, for the full term of the note.
Compute the bank discount; this is equivalent to interest, on the value at maturity and at the discount rate, for the discount period.
Deduct the discount from the value at maturity.

Three illustrations are given below. In each case the principal of the note is $600, its date is June 15, it is due in 60 days, and it is discounted on June 27. The discount period, therefore, is 48 days. The discount rate is 6%. The first column shows the computation if the note does not bear interest; the second column shows the computation if the note bears 4% interest; the third column shows the computation if the note bears 7%.

	No Interest	4% Interest	7% Interest
Value at maturity:			
Face of note....................	$600.00	$600.00	$600.00
Interest on face for term of note:			
None.......................			
At 4% for 60 days...........		4.00	
At 7% for 60 days...........			7.00
Value at maturity............	$600.00	$604.00	$607.00
Bank discount at 6% for 48 days:			
On $600......................	4.80		
On $604......................		4.83	
On $607......................			4.86
Proceeds......................	$595.20	$599.17	$602.14

Notes receivable discounted. When a note or an acceptance receivable is discounted, the credit should be made to Notes Receivable Discounted or Acceptances Receivable Discounted, to show the contingent liability resulting from the endorsement.

The traditional method of recording the discounting of a note or an acceptance receivable involved a debit to Interest Expense or a credit to Interest Earned for the difference between the face of the paper and the proceeds. Entries made in this manner, based on the foregoing illustrations, are shown below:

Cash..	595.20	
Interest expense...	4.80	
Notes receivable discounted........................		600.00
Cash..	599.17	
Interest expense...	.83	
Notes receivable discounted........................		600.00

Cash..	602.14	
Interest earned...............		2.14
Notes receivable discounted................		600.00

Such entries do not appear to give adequate expression to the facts if the paper is interest-bearing. They ignore the interest earned between the date of the note and the date of discounting. They also ignore the fact that we are parting with two assets (the note and the accrued interest) and that there is a loss or gain equal to the difference between the total amount of these assets and the proceeds of the note.

Referring to the 4% note, the facts are:

Assets parted with:		
Face of note...		$600.00
Accrued interest on $600 for 12 days at 4%..................		.80
Total..		$600.80
Proceeds..		599.17
Loss..		$ 1.63

and the following entries would appear desirable:

Accrued interest receivable............................\....	.80	
Interest earned...................................		.80
Cash......................................	599.17	
Loss on discounting notes receivable.....................	1.63	
Accrued interest receivable.........................		.80
Notes receivable discounted.......................		600.00

Referring to the 7% note, the facts are:

Proceeds..		$602.14
Assets parted with:		
Face of note.......................................	$600.00	
Accrued interest at 7% for 12 days..................	1.40	
Total..		601.40
Gain..		$ .74

and the following entries should be made:

Accrued interest receivable............................	1.40	
Interest earned...................................		1.40
Cash..	602.14	
Accrued interest receivable........................		1.40
Notes receivable discounted........................		600.00
Gain on discounting notes receivable.................		.74

If an Accrued Interest Receivable account stands debited with an interest accrual applicable to the note being discounted, recorded by an adjusting entry at the close of a prior period, the amount of the credit to Accrued Interest Receivable in the entry to record the discounting should be the sum of the prior accrual and the interest accrued since the date of the adjusting entry.

Contingent liability in the balance sheet. It was formerly the custom to indicate the contingent liability on discounted paper by a deduction in the balance sheet, thus:

```
Current assets:
  Notes receivable...................................  $5,000
    Less notes receivable discounted.....................   1,000
  Notes receivable on hand................................  $4,000
```

Modern practice appears to favor the method of showing on the asset side only the notes receivable on hand, with a footnote indicating the contingent liability, thus:

```
Current assets:
  Notes receivable.........................................  $4,000
```

Note. The company was contingently liable on December 31, 1959, in the amount of $1,000 on customers' notes discounted.

Payment by maker. If a discounted note is paid by the maker, the contingent liability should disappear from the endorser's books. This is accomplished by debiting Notes Receivable Discounted and crediting Notes Receivable.

Since notice of dishonor must be given to the endorser promptly in order to hold him, the endorser may safely assume that a discounted note has been paid at maturity unless he receives notice to the contrary within a few days after the maturity of the paper.

Payment by endorser. Assume that the $600 note, bearing 7% interest, the proceeds of which were computed on page 219, could not be collected from the maker, and that the bank obtained collection from the endorser. Assume that the total collected included the face, the $7 interest payable on the note, and protest fees of $4.30. The endorser's entries are:

```
Accounts receivable (maker)........................... 611.30
  Cash.............................................            611.30
  Payment of note discounted June 27, and interest and
  protest fees.

Notes receivable discounted........................... 600.00
  Notes receivable..................................            600.00
  To eliminate the note and the contingent liability from
  the accounts.
```

Endorsement without recourse. According to the Uniform Negotiable Instruments Law:

"Every person negotiating an instrument by delivery or by a qualified indorsement, warrants:

(1) That the instrument is genuine and in all respects what it purports to be;

(2) That he has a good title to it;

(3) That all prior parties had capacity to contract;

(4) That he has no knowledge of any fact which would impair the validity of the instrument or render it valueless."

As compared with the contingent liability arising from an unqualified endorsement, these warranties implied by an endorsement without recourse impose so slight a liability that it is usually ignored, and notes transferred by such endorsements are credited to Notes Receivable instead of to Notes Receivable Discounted.

NO CONTINGENT LIABILITY

CHAPTER ELEVEN

Inventories

Introductory note. Inventories are a source of some of the most difficult accounting problems, both theoretical and practical. While there is much settled opinion relating to the subject of inventories, there are many points on which there is a noticeable absence of settled opinion. Accountants, individually and collectively, have given, and continue to give, considerable thought to inventory matters, and fresh areas of theory seem to be constantly opening up. To some extent, this condition will remain as long as businesses continue to expand and become more complex and as long as prices continue to change. A dynamic business economy is not conducive to static accounting theory.

Classes of inventories. The inventory of a concern that buys its goods in condition for sale is usually called a *merchandise inventory*. Merchandise inventories are found in wholesale and retail businesses. These businesses do not alter the form of the goods purchased for sale.

Manufacturing concerns have the following classes of inventories:

Finished goods.
Goods in process.
Materials.
Manufacturing supplies.

Finished goods consist of manufactured articles which are ready for sale.

223

Goods in process consist of partially manufactured goods, and their cost includes the material, labor, and manufacturing overhead applicable to them.

Materials consist of articles purchased for use in manufacture but on which no work has been done by the concern inventorying them. Work may have been done on them by the concern from which they were purchased. Thus, things which are finished goods for one concern may be materials for another. If parts are manufactured before they are required, and are held for future use in manufacturing, they may be classed as finished parts, but they are usually included in the materials inventory.

Manufacturing supplies are distinguished from materials in the manner stated below.

> Materials can be directly associated with, and become a part of, the finished product; and they are used in sufficient amounts to make it practicable to allocate their costs to the product.
>
> Some manufacturing supplies, like lubricants, are used indirectly in the process of manufacture, and do not become part of the finished product. Some other things classified as manufacturing supplies, like paint and nails, do become part of the finished product, but the amounts involved are so insignificant that it is impracticable to attempt to allocate their cost to the product.

The inventories discussed thus far may be listed under the Inventories caption in the current asset group. Since the expenditures for both manufacturing supplies and materials are made for the purpose of producing merchantable goods, there seems to be no theoretical necessity for considering supplies to be less current than materials; both will enter into the cost of manufacture and will be converted into cash by the sale of the product.

Supplies which will be charged to selling and general expense are of a somewhat different nature. Shipping supplies and office supplies are examples. These are more appropriately classified as prepaid expenses but they may be shown under the Current Assets caption.

Some companies classify under the Inventories caption of the balance sheet any advances made to vendors against purchase commitments. This seems to be of doubtful propriety, since the company does not have title to the related merchandise. Such advances should probably appear in the balance sheet after the inventories. Current assets, with the exception of prepaid expenses, are usually marshalled under the current caption in the order of their liquidity—cash, receivables, and inventories. Advances on purchase commitments are less current than goods on hand. Wherever the advances appear, they should be clearly distinguished from debit balances in suppliers' accounts resulting from merchandise returns, overpayments, and other similar causes. Prepaid expenses are shown as the last items under the current caption.

Inventory all goods owned.　What should be included in the inventory, and what should be excluded therefrom? The general rule is that the inventory should include all goods for which the company holds title, wherever they may be.

If goods sold under contract or ordered by customers for future delivery are being held in stock, it is important to determine whether title has passed. The mere fact that the goods have been segregated from other merchandise may or may not mean that title has passed to the vendee. If title has passed, the goods should be excluded from the inventory; if title has not passed, they should be included.

On the other hand, goods which have been ordered but not received at the balance sheet date may properly belong in the inventory. If the goods are in transit, the general rule as to passing of title is as follows: If the goods were shipped f.o.b. shipping point, they belong to the purchaser; if they were shipped f.o.b. destination and have not arrived at the destination, they belong to the seller. If merchandise purchases are in transit and title has passed, it is advisable to postpone the completion of the inventory tabulation until the merchandise has been received and checked into stock; this procedure will avoid inventory errors arising from differences between merchandise merely invoiced to the company and merchandise received in good condition. Since the completion of the inventory-taking normally requires some time, the checking of the receipt of merchandise in transit will not ordinarily cause any delay.

Two types of errors may result from a failure to include all owned goods in the inventory.

First, the purchase may be recorded, and the goods may be omitted from the inventory. This omission, of course, results in an understatement of net income.

Second, no entry may be made for the purchase, and the goods may be omitted from the inventory. This omission does not result in an understatement of net income, since the purchases and the closing inventory are equally understated. The practice is to be condemned, however, because it results in an incorrect showing of purchases and inventory in the income statement, and also because it understates the current assets and current liabilities in the balance sheet. Thus, the current financial position appears more favorable than the facts really warrant, partly because the working capital ratio is overstated, and partly because, in many instances, the accounts payable will have to be paid before the merchandise is sold and converted into cash.

Inventory pricing. There are a number of acceptable bases for pricing inventories. Some are considered acceptable only under special circumstances, while others are widely applicable. In matters relating to inventory pricing, consistency of method is of prime importance. The principal pricing bases may be listed as follows:

(1) Cost.
(2) Cost or market, whichever is lower.
(3) Selling price.

In this chapter we shall deal with matters related to inventory pricing on a cost basis. Pricing on a cost-or-market basis is discussed in Chapter 12.

Incidental costs. Cost includes not only the purchase price but also any additional costs necessary to placing the goods on the shelves. These incidental costs include duties, freight or other transportation costs, storage, insurance while the goods are being transported or stored, and expenses incurred during any aging period. The total of these items is clearly an addition to the total purchase price of all goods; it is not a simple matter, however, to apply the incidental costs to individual purchases and to determine what portion of the total incidental costs is applicable to the goods in the inventory. Some incidental costs may be easily applied to the particular goods on which the costs were incurred. Other costs may be prorated on a percentage basis; such a distribution is not likely to be strictly accurate, because the incidental costs are not usually incurred in amounts exactly proportionate to the cost of the merchandise. Greater accuracy may be obtained by an attempt to apply each expense bill to its corresponding invoice, but this procedure usually involves more labor and expense than are warranted by the slightly greater degree of accuracy.

Theoretically, there is some justification for regarding the cost of operating the purchasing department as a part of the cost of the merchandise acquired and including an element of such cost in the inventory valuations. However, such a procedure is not usually regarded as practicable or advisable. In the first place, it involves the allocation of general overhead to the purchasing department and thus raises questions as to an equitable determination of the cost of operating the department. In the second place, such a procedure necessitates the apportioning of the purchasing department cost to the various purchases during the period and to the various classes of goods in the inventory at the end of the period, and questions arise as to an appropriate basis for the apportionment of such costs.

If the incidental costs are immaterial, the accountant will consent to either their inclusion or their exclusion for inventory-pricing purposes. This does not mean that all incidental costs must be treated alike; for instance, it is acceptable to include freight and exclude storage costs, or vice versa. And it does not follow that, if freight charges are included in computing one section of the inventory, they must be included in computing the other sections of the inventory; but if freight charges are included in pricing an inventory or any section of an inventory, then that practice should be consistently followed over the years.

Manufacturing costs. The purchase price of materials and merchandise bought can, of course, be determined from invoices. But the cost of goods in process and the cost of finished goods can be determined only by keeping accurate cost records showing costs of materials, labor, and overhead assignable to the product.

Some companies have followed the practice of omitting manufacturing overhead from the inventory valuation, on the theory that this is a conservative procedure. There seems to be no more propriety in omitting the overhead element of manufacturing cost than in omitting the material or labor cost.

A similar conclusion seems justified in the case of a recent proposal favoring a procedure known as *direct costing*. Advocates of direct costing contend that manufacturing costs should be divided into two main categories, variable and fixed, and that no portion of the latter should be assigned to inventories or used in computing the inventory valuation. Following this plan, fixed manufacturing costs (those that do not vary with changes in the volume of output) would be treated as expenses of the period, as selling and administrative expenses are treated; only variable costs would be considered when determining cost for inventory purposes. Those arguing in favor of direct costing point out that the plan minimizes the problem of overhead application (which, in practice, is often arbitrary and questionable) because fewer costs are subject to allocation. It is also mentioned that direct costing lends itself to more meaningful cost analyses. For example, changes in the volume of output usually result in considerable fluctuations in unit costs. This effect is primarily attributable to the impact of fixed costs, which are mostly beyond the control of management. As a consequence, the usefulness of unit cost data is impaired because management is not able to determine readily whether a change in unit cost is the result of a change in volume or the result of poor control over those costs that are subject to management's control. On the other hand, variations in unit costs under direct costing would signal cost variations presumably subject to managerial control, since fixed costs would be expensed and not included in unit cost data. But the point remains that under direct costing a portion of the costs of manufacturing would be ignored for inventory-valuation purposes—which is not a commendable result, considering the effects on financial statements.

The allocation of the total production costs during a period to those goods which have been completed and to those which remain in process is admittedly a difficult problem. Elaborate cost records may be used for this purpose. In the absence of such records, it may be necessary to compute unit costs, for purposes of inventory pricing, from general accounting and production data. If there was work in process at the beginning and/or the end of the period, and if there was any change in the quantity or stage of completion of the work in process at the two dates, unit costs of goods completed during the period cannot be computed by dividing the total manufacturing costs for the period by the number of units of product completed during the period. Consideration must be given to the inventories of work in process at the beginning and end of the period, and to the stages of completion thereof. To illustrate, let us assume the following data:

	Work in Process— Stage of Completion	1959 Costs
Work in process—December 31, 1958—400 units:		
Materials...................................	75%	
Direct labor.................................	50	
1959 cost and production data:		
Cost of material placed in production............		$30,000
Direct labor cost.............................		39,600
Overhead (125% of direct labor)................		49,500
Units completed—9,800.		
Work in process—December 31, 1959—500 units:		
Materials...................................	100%	
Direct labor.................................	60	

The amounts shown in the 1959 Costs column cannot be divided by the 9,800 units completed in 1959 to obtain unit costs, for two reasons: (1) some of these costs were incurred to complete the work in process on December 31, 1958, and (2) some of the costs were incurred on the work still in process on December 31, 1959. If we take into consideration the work done on the beginning and ending inventories, we can compute the *equivalent production* for the period. This information will enable us to arrive at unit costs for inventory-pricing purposes. The computation of equivalent production is illustrated on page 229.

Computation of Equivalent Quantities Produced—1959

	Materials	Direct Labor
Units completed in 1959.............................	9,800	9,800
Work in process—December 31, 1958—400 units:		
75% of the material was put into process in 1958; hence, 300 units (75%) must be deducted as applicable to 1958...	300	
50% of the labor was performed in 1958; hence, 200 units (50%) must be deducted as applicable to 1958..		200
Remainder...	9,500	9,600
Work in process—December 31, 1959—500 units:		
100% of the material was put into process; hence, 500 units must be added to production quantity........	500	
60% of the labor was performed; hence, 300 units must be added to production quantity..................		300
Equivalent production—1959.........................	10,000	9,900

We can now compute the unit costs applicable to the 1959 ending inventories of finished goods and work in process, as follows:

```
Unit costs:
  Materials...............$30,000 ÷ 10,000.....................  $ 3
  Direct labor............$39,600 ÷  9,900.....................    4
  Overhead...............125% of direct labor.................    5
     Total...................................................... $12
```

The inventory computations are shown below. Quantity and stage-of-completion data were previously given for the work in process. It is assumed that 1,000 units of finished goods are on hand at the end of 1959.

```
Cost of finished goods on hand, December 31, 1959:
  Finished goods...........1,000 units at $12................. $12,000
Cost of work in process, December 31, 1959:
  Materials...............500 units 100% complete at $3..... $ 1,500
  Direct labor............500 units  60% complete at $4.....   1,200
  Overhead...............125% of direct labor..............   1,500
     Total............................................... $ 4,200
```

The foregoing does not constitute a discussion of cost accounting. Its purpose is merely to indicate some of the difficulties involved in the ascertaining of costs in manufacturing concerns.

Standard costs. It is not uncommon for manufacturing concerns to price their work in process and finished goods inventories by using standard costs. There are several varieties of standard costs; they may be developed by relying on time and motion studies, past costs and manufacturing performance, expected costs and manufacturing performance, theoretical costs, or some combination thereof. They may be described as predetermined costs or estimated costs.

To illustrate, the material requirements for a given product are computed and the quantity required to complete one unit of product is priced, perhaps at current purchase prices or at expected purchase prices. Labor cost per unit of product is similarly developed, perhaps by reference to production studies or past performance. And finally, estimated overhead is allocated on the basis of an expected or average volume of production.

As products are completed, the finished goods are charged to the inventory account on the basis of their standard costs. Actual costs probably will differ from predetermined costs, with the result that cost-variance balances will develop in the accounts. These variances are commonly closed to Cost of Sales. For inventory-pricing purposes, it is desirable to review standard costs periodically to see that they do not deviate significantly from actual costs.

Relation of purchase discounts to cost. From a theoretical standpoint, purchase discounts are unquestionably cost reductions. However, because of the amount of work involved, it does not seem reasonable for accountants to insist that they be so treated in the accounts.

If purchase discounts are considered in the computation of cost for purposes of inventory pricing, they should be classified in the income statement in the cost of sales section. If purchase discounts are ignored for inventory-pricing purposes, it might seem to follow that they should be treated in the income statement as financial income. However, there appears to be no objection to classifying purchase discounts as a deduction from purchases in the cost of sales section of the income statement even though they are ignored in the development of cost figures for inventory purposes.

Apportioned costs. A special problem arises when a whole, acquired at a lump price, is divided into parts which, because of differences in nature or in quality, are to be sold at different prices. To determine a cost for the parts sold and a cost for the parts remaining in the inventory, it is necessary to make an apportionment of the lump-sum price.

To illustrate, assume that land is purchased, developed, and subdivided into cemetery lots. The total cost, assumed to be $60,000, may be apportioned to individual lots in the ratio of selling price, thus:

Selling Price Per Lot	Number of Lots	Product	Per Cent of Total	Apportioned Cost Total	Per Lot
$200	40	$ 8,000	8%	$ 4,800	$120
500	60	30,000	30	18,000	300
600	80	48,000	48	28,800	360
700	20	14,000	14	8,400	420
Total		$100,000	100%	$60,000	

Lost costs. Cost for inventory purposes may be less than the total original cost because, under some circumstances, it may be apparent that the costs invested in the inventory may not be fully recoverable. This condition may be the result of style changes, technological improvements, deterioration, spoilage, or damage attributable to storm or fire. Whatever the cause, the implication is the same: All or a portion of a cost outlay for merchandise or goods on hand has been lost.

A strict cost basis would be unrealistic if it required all items in the inventory to be priced at full cost irrespective of their potential realizable value. To avoid stating a current asset at an amount in excess of its realizable value, it is customary, even though the basis is described as a cost basis, to price inventory items below cost whenever it is apparent that the cost outlay cannot be recovered through sale in the ordinary course of business.

If an item has once been priced in an inventory below cost, the lower amount becomes a "new" cost for accounting purposes. Items once reduced for inventory purposes should not be reinstated to their original cost in a subsequent period.

Cost Selection for Inventory Pricing

Identical goods may be purchased or produced at different costs. Consequently, accountants are faced with the problem of determining which costs apply to the goods that have been sold and which costs apply to the goods that remain in the inventory. The customary way of dealing with this problem is to choose a method for selecting the costs to be regarded as applicable to the goods in the inventory, and regarding all other costs as applicable to the goods sold.

Most of the acceptable methods of selecting the costs to be regarded as applicable to the inventory are based on an assumption regarding either:

The flow of goods—for example, an assumption that goods are sold in the order in which they are purchased or produced; or

The flow of costs—for example, an assumption that the most recent costs are applicable to the goods sold, and that the earlier costs are applicable to the goods on hand.

Several methods of selecting the costs which are to be regarded as applicable to the inventory are discussed in the following sections.

For purposes of illustration, assume that purchases have been made as shown on the following page.

```
First purchase:   100 units at $1.00......................... $100
Second purchase: 200 units at  1.10.........................  220
Third purchase:  250 units at  1.20.........................  300
Fourth purchase: 100 units at  1.25.........................  125
```

There are 150 units in the ending inventory.

Specific identification.   If the goods on hand can be identified as pertaining to specific purchases or specific production orders, they may be inventoried at the costs shown by the invoices or the cost records. Specific identification requires the keeping of records by which goods can be definitely identified and their costs determined.

Although this method appears to have an excellent logical foundation, it is often impossible or impracticable to apply.

Last invoice price.   Under this method, the cost applicable to the last purchase transaction is used to price the entire inventory quantity. In other words, $1.25 would be applied to the 150 units in the inventory. If there is a rapid physical turnover of the inventory in the normal course of the business, and the goods are sold in approximately the same order in which they are acquired, the last invoice price may closely approximate the results produced by the use of the specific identification method, with much less clerical effort.

Simple-average method.   The simple arithmetical average of the unit prices is determined by adding the unit prices of all purchases* and dividing by the number of purchases. Using the foregoing data, the simple average unit cost and the inventory valuation are computed as follows:

$$\text{Unit cost} = \frac{\$1.00 + \$1.10 + \$1.20 + \$1.25}{4} = \$1.1375$$

$$\text{Inventory valuation} = \$1.1375 \times 150 = \$170.63$$

This is a rather illogical method, because the unit prices applicable to large and small purchases are given the same weight in the computation.

Weighted-average method.   The cost of the purchases* is divided by the total units purchased, and a weighted-average unit cost is thus determined. Applied to the foregoing data, this method produces an inventory valuation computed as follows:

```
Total cost of purchases—$745
Total units purchased—650
Unit cost = $745 ÷ 650 = $1.14615
Inventory valuation = $1.14615 × 150 = $171.92
```

---

* If there was an inventory at the beginning of the period, it should be included in the computation.

This method is theoretically illogical because it is based on an assumption that all sales are made proportionately from all acquisitions, and that inventories will forever contain some goods of the earliest acquisitions—assumptions which are contrary to ordinary merchandising procedure.

Since the costs determined by the weighted-average method are affected by purchases early in the period as well as toward the end of the period, there may be a considerable lag between purchase costs and inventory valuations. Thus, on a rising market, the weighted-average costs will be less than current costs, and, on a falling market, the weighted-average costs will be in excess of the current costs.

Moving-average method.   This method may be used when perpetual inventories are kept, new unit average costs being computed after each purchase. Assume that the purchases stated in the preceding illustration and the sales were made in the following order and amounts:

	Units	Unit Cost
First purchase	100	$1.00
Second purchase	200	1.10
First sale	175	
Third purchase	250	1.20
Second sale	275	
Fourth purchase	100	1.25
Third sale	50	

The following tabulation shows how the moving-average unit costs are computed. Each sale is costed out at the latest computed average cost, and the resulting inventory valuation is on the moving-average unit-cost basis.

	Units	Unit Cost	Amount	Moving-Average Cost
First purchase	100	$1.00	$100.00	$1.00
Second purchase	200	1.10	220.00	
Inventory	300		$320.00	1.0666
First sale	175		186.67	
Inventory	125		$133.33	
Third purchase	250	1.20	300.00	
Inventory	375		$433.33	1.1555
Second sale	275		317.78	
Inventory	100		$115.55	
Fourth purchase	100	1.25	125.00	
Inventory	200		$240.55	1.2028
Third sale	50		60.14	
Inventory	150		$180.41	

A perpetual inventory on the moving-average cost basis appears on the following page.

Perpetual Inventory—Moving-Average Cost

	QUANTITY			COST		
Date	Into Stock	Out of Stock	Balance	Into Stock	Out of Stock	Balance
June 1	100		100	$100.00		$100.00
5	200		300	220.00		320.00
8		175	125		$186.67	133.33
13	250		375	300.00		433.33
18		275	100		317.78	115.55
23	100		200	125.00		240.55
29		50	150		60.14	180.41

This method is subject to the same theoretical objection as applied to the weighted-average method. There is implicit in the method an assumption that each sale consists in part of merchandise from each preceding purchase, which is contrary to general merchandising procedure. Moreover, since the cost applied to the inventory is affected to some extent by the cost of all purchases, there is (as in the weighted-average method) a lag between market prices and inventory valuations. However, the lag is less pronounced in the moving-average method than in the weighted-average method.

Widely fluctuating costs. A modification of the moving-average cost computation is peculiarly suited for the determining of monthly inventory valuations when unit costs vary widely from month to month because of differences in the quantity of production. To illustrate, let us assume that a company manufactures a product which sells heavily in warm months and poorly in cold months, and that its production fluctuates with sales. The following are the quantities and the monthly costs of production during two years:

	1958			1959		
	Units Produced	Total Cost	Unit Cost	Units Produced	Total Cost	Unit Cost
January	100	$ 1,660	$16.600	90	$ 1,705	$18.944
February	115	1,738	15.113	75	1,688	22.507
March	220	2,232	10.145	250	2,195	8.780
April	3,200	8,745	2.733	3,720	10,503	2.823
May	4,600	11,935	2.595	4,360	11,700	2.683
June	5,950	13,665	2.297	6,325	15,260	2.413
July	6,300	15,060	2.390	6,720	16,800	2.500
August	6,750	15,855	2.349	7,310	18,215	2.492
September	5,200	13,470	2.590	6,205	16,225	2.615
October	850	4,170	4.906	960	4,515	4.703
November	300	2,475	8.250	412	2,925	7.100
December	140	1,940	13.857	125	2,025	16.200
Totals and averages	33,725	$92,945	2.756	36,552	$103,756	2.839

High unit costs appear in the months of low production because a large fixed overhead is distributed over a small number of units.

The inventories at the close of the year can be valued at the average costs for the year: $2.756 at the end of 1958, and $2.839 at the close of 1959. But what basis can be used for the valuation of monthly inventories, if monthly statements are desired? Obviously, the monthly unit costs would not be appropriate, because of their wide fluctuation. Nor would it be entirely correct to use, in the 1959 monthly statements, the average cost for 1958 ($2.756), since 1959 costs appear to be on a higher level, as evidenced by the higher average for the year ($2.839).

A moving-average cost, computed in the manner illustrated below, appears suitable for such a situation.

	UNITS			COST			
	This Year (Add)	Last Year (Deduct)	Twelve Months	This Year (Add)	Last Year (Deduct)	Twelve Months	Moving Average
Year 1958			33,725			$ 92,945	$2.756
Year 1959:							
January........	90	100	33,715	$ 1,705	$ 1,660	92,990	2.758
February.......	75	115	33,675	1,688	1,738	92,940	2.760
March.........	250	220	33,705	2,195	2,232	92,903	2.756
April.........	3,720	3,200	34,225	10,503	8,745	94,661	2.766
May...........	4,360	4,600	33,985	11,700	11,935	94,426	2.778
June..........	6,325	5,950	34,360	15,260	13,665	96,021	2.795
July..........	6,720	6,300	34,780	16,800	15,060	97,761	2.811
August........	7,310	6,750	35,340	18,215	15,855	100,121	2.833
September.....	6,205	5,200	36,345	16,225	13,470	102,876	2.831
October.......	960	850	36,455	4,515	4,170	103,221	2.831
November.....	412	300	36,567	2,925	2,475	103,671	2.835
December......	125	140	36,552	2,025	1,940	103,756	2.839

The moving-average cost (using January as an example) is computed as follows:

	Units	Cost
Total—Twelve months ended December 31, 1958........	33,725	$92,945
Add amounts for January, 1959..................... ...	90	1,705
Total...	33,815	$94,650
Deduct amounts for January, 1958.................	100	1,660
Total—Twelve months ended January 31, 1959........ ...	33,715	$92,990

　　$92,990 ÷ 33,715 = $2.758.

The use of such a moving-average cost eliminates the irrational fluctuations in inventory values that would result from pricing the monthly inventories at the widely varying unit costs of production during the busy and slack seasons. The moving-average costs are preferable to the average cost of the preceding year, because the moving averages are affected by the factors that increased the average yearly unit costs from $2.756 in 1958 to $2.839 in 1959.

In the application of this moving-average cost theory, the sales each month, as well as the inventory at the end of the month, should be costed on the moving-average basis. This method will result in overabsorptions and underabsorptions of cost in the monthly statements, and will probably require an adjustment at the end of the year for the net overabsorption or underabsorption. For example, the underabsorption for January 1959 (costing the opening inventory at the $2.756 average for 1958, and the sales and the January 31 inventory at the January average of $2.758) would be determined as follows:

Inventory, December 31, 1958....	1,200 units at $2.756.......	$3,307.20
January production..............	90 units at actual cost...	1,705.00
Total........................	1,290 units................	$5,012.20
January sales...................	120 units at $2.758.......	$ 330.96
Inventory, January 31, 1959......	1,170 units at 2.758.......	3,226.86
Total............................		$3,557.82
Underabsorption of costs....................................		$1,454.38

The cumulative underabsorptions and overabsorptions of cost during the year, computed similarly, are shown below.

	Underabsorption Overabsorption*
End of:	
January..	$ 1,454.38
February...	2,933.04
March..	4,443.56
April..	4,651.80
May..	4,231.09
June...	1,799.21
July...	301.50*
August...	2,820.76*
September..	4,159.78*
October..	2,362.54*
November...	611.94*
December...	1,051.46

The cumulative adjustment for the year, $1,051.46, is only slightly more than 1% of the actual costs for the year.

First-in, first-out (*fifo*) method. This method is based on an assumption regarding the flow of goods: The goods on hand are considered to be those most recently purchased. Using the data on page 232, the inventory is assumed to be composed of goods:

From the fourth purchase: 100 units at $1.25....................		$125.00
From the third purchase: 50 units at 1.20....................		60.00
Total...		$185.00

The assumption that the older stock is usually the first to be disposed of is generally in accordance with good merchandising policy. There are, of course, exceptions in practice; for instance, the first coal dumped on a dealer's pile will be the last sold. This method has also been considered desirable because it produces an inventory valuation which is in conformity with price trends; since the inventory is priced at the most recent costs, the pricings follow the trend of the market. A perpetual inventory on the first-in, first-out basis appears below:

PERPETUAL INVENTORY—FIRST-IN, FIRST-OUT BASIS

	Quantity			Cost		
Date	Into Stock	Out of Stock	Balance	Into Stock	Out of Stock	Balance
June 1.............	100		100	$100.00		$100.00
5.............	200		300	220.00		320.00
8.............		175	125		$182.50	137.50
13.............	250		375	300.00		437.50
18.............		275	100		317.50	120.00
23.............	100		200	125.00		245.00
29.............		50	150		60.00	185.00

The first sale consisted of:

100 units at a cost of $1.00 each (first purchase)................	$100.00
75 " " " " " 1.10 " (second purchase)..............	82.50
Total..	$182.50

The inventory after the first sale consisted of 125 units at a cost of $1.10 each.

The second sale consisted of:

125 units at a cost of $1.10 each (second purchase)..............	$137.50
150 " " " " " 1.20 " (third purchase)................	180.00
Total..	$317.50

The inventory after the second sale consisted of 100 units at a cost of $1.20.

The third sale consisted of:

50 units at a cost of $1.20 (third purchase).....................	$ 60.00

The inventory after the third sale consisted of:

50 units at $1.20 (third purchase)............................	$ 60.00
100 " " 1.25 (fourth purchase)...........................	125.00
Total..	$185.00

The first-in, first-out method can be applied without great difficulty even though perpetual inventories are not maintained; it is necessary only to determine prices shown by the most recent invoices for quantities sufficient to equal the number of units in the inventory.

Last-in, first-out (*lifo*) method. This method, based on an assumption regarding a flow of costs, is discussed in Chapter 13.

Gross profit method. The gross profit method of approximating an inventory is based on the assumption that the per cent of gross profit should be approximately the same in successive periods. This does not mean that the amount of gross profit should be the same, since the amount of profit will depend upon the volume of sales; it means only that the rate of gross profit on sales is assumed to be uniform. If, for instance, the rate of gross profit has been uniformly about 25% of the sales for a number of past years, it is assumed that the rate was 25% during the current period. If this assumption is in reasonable conformity with the facts, then it should be possible to approximate, with a fair degree of accuracy, the inventory at the end of the current period.

To illustrate, assume the following data:

Inventory—January 1	$ 10,000
Purchases for the year	94,000
Net sales for the year	124,000
Average rate of gross profit in recent years, 25% of sales.	

What should be the approximate inventory on December 31?

Inventory—January 1		$ 10,000
Purchases		94,000
Total		$104,000
Deduct approximate cost of goods sold:		
Sales—net	$124,000	
Less estimated gross profit:		
25% of $124,000	31,000	93,000
Approximate inventory—December 31		$ 11,000

If the rate of gross profit is a composite produced by selling several types or classes of merchandise at different gross profit rates, sales and purchases data must be classified by gross profit classes. The gross profit method is applied to each inventory class. To illustrate, assume the following:

Article *A* is marked to produce a gross profit of 20%.
Article *B* is marked to produce a gross profit of 40%.
Last year's gross profit on all sales was 25%.

Computation of Inventories—Gross Profit Method
CURRENT YEAR

	A	B	Total
Inventory—January 1	$15,000	$ 25,000	$ 40,000
Purchases for the year	80,000	120,000	200,000
Total	$95,000	$145,000	$240,000
Deduct approximate cost of goods sold:			
Sales—net	$90,000	$210,000	$300,000
Less estimated gross profit:			
20% of $90,000	18,000		18,000
40% of $210,000		84,000	84,000
Approximate cost of goods sold	$72,000	$126,000	$198,000
Approximate inventory—December 31	$23,000	$ 19,000	$ 42,000

If the data had not been classified by commodity, the combined inventory would have been estimated at $15,000, as illustrated below:

		Combined
Inventory—January 1 ($15,000 plus $25,000).................		$ 40,000
Purchases for the year ($80,000 plus $120,000)...............		200,000
Total..		$240,000
Deduct approximate cost of goods sold:		
Sales ($90,000 plus $210,000)—net...............	$300,000	
Less estimated gross profit:		
25% of $300,000............................	75,000	225,000
Approximate inventory—December 31......................		$ 15,000

In the above illustration, the average rate of gross profit of the business as a whole for the preceding year was an unreliable measure to apply in approximating inventories for the current year because of the significant change that occurred in the average rate of gross profit. Last year's gross profit margin on all sales was 25%, whereas the gross profit margin on all sales for the current year is probably in the neighborhood of 34%. This is evident from the following computation.

Sales, current year—net................................	$300,000	100%
Approximate cost of goods sold ($72,000 + $126,000).......	198,000	
Approximate gross profit..............................	$102,000	34%

If there are any conditions present in the current year that would result in a change in the rate of gross profit, the gross profit method, being based on prior gross margin data, will not produce reliable inventory approximations.

Uses of gross profit method. The gross profit method may be used by an auditor as one of the means of verifying an inventory; for instance, referring to the illustration on page 238, if the December 31 inventory submitted to the auditor was $25,000, whereas the gross profit method indicated that the inventory should be approximately $11,000, either a satisfactory explanation of the increase in the rate of gross profit would have to be forthcoming, or the auditor would have reason to believe that the inventory was overstated. An ending inventory of $25,000 would imply that the gross profit margin had increased to 36% in contrast to the 25% rate which had prevailed in past periods. The gross profit method may also be used to approximate the cost of an inventory which has been destroyed by fire.

Merchandise turnovers based on the average of the inventories at the beginning and the end of the year will be inaccurate if the year-end inventories differ materially in amount from those carried during the year. This error will be avoided if the average of monthly inventories is used. If such inventories are not available, they may be estimated by the gross profit method. The use of the gross profit method for this purpose is illustrated by the following problem.

Problem.   On January 1, a concern dealing in a single commodity had an inventory of merchandise that cost $20,000. The goods were marked to sell at 125% of cost (note that this should result in a gross profit rate of 20%), and all subsequent purchases during the six months ending June 30 were marked at the same rate. The selling price of the inventory on June 30 was $24,000. Purchases and sales by months were:

	Purchases (Cost)	Sales (Selling Price)
January	$ 8,000	$ 9,000
February	9,000	9,500
March	14,000	12,000
April	16,000	18,000
May	13,000	22,000
June	10,000	18,000

Compute estimated inventories at cost price at the end of each of the six months.

Compute the rate of turnover for the six-month period, using (1) the January 1 and June 30 inventories; (2) all of the inventories.

This illustration differs from the preceding one in that it is based on the rate of gross profit for the period under consideration instead of on the rate of gross profit for prior periods.

Solution:

	Computation of Inventories	Opening and Closing Inventories	All Inventories
Inventory—January 1	$20,000	$20,000	$ 20,000
Add purchases for January	8,000		
Total	$28,000		
Deduct cost of sales: $9,000 ÷ 125%	7,200		
Inventory—January 31	$20,800		20,800
Add purchases for February	9,000		
Total	$29,800		
Deduct cost of sales: $9,500 ÷ 125%	7,600		
Inventory—February 28	$22,200		22,200
Add purchases for March	14,000		
Total	$36,200		
Deduct cost of sales: $12,000 ÷ 125%	9,600		
Inventory—March 31	$26,600		26,600
Add purchases for April	16,000		
Total	$42,600		
Deduct cost of sales: $18,000 ÷ 125%	14,400		
Inventory—April 30	$28,200		28,200

Add purchases for May..................	13,000		
Total...................................	$41,200		
Deduct cost of sales: $22,000 ÷ 125%.....	17,600		
Inventory—May 31.....................	$23,600		23,600
Add purchases for June..................	10,000		
Total...................................	$33,600		
Deduct cost of sales: $18,000 ÷ 125%.....	14,400		
Inventory—June 30.....................	$19,200	19,200	19,200
Totals.................................		$39,200	$160,600
Average................................		$19,600	$ 22,943

Inventory—January 1.......................................	$20,000	
Add purchases for six months................................	70,000	
Total...	$90,000	
Deduct inventory—June 30.................................	19,200	
Cost of sales..	$70,800	

Rate of turnover, using an average of the opening and closing
inventories:

$$\$70,800 \div \$19,600 = 3.61, \text{ turnovers in six months.}$$

Rate of turnover, using an average of the monthly inventories:

$$\$70,800 \div \$22,943 = 3.09, \text{ turnovers in six months.}$$

The turnover computed by using all inventories is the more accurate because of the larger number of inventories used in determining the average investment in stock. This method can be used
only when there is reason to believe that the rate of gross profit
for the period has been uniform throughout the period.

Long-term construction contracts. A special inventory-
valuation problem arises in the case of long-term construction
contracts if the completion of a contract requires a considerable
amount of time and statements are prepared before the contract
is completed. There are two accounting methods for dealing with
such contracts:

The completed-contract method—no income is taken up until
the contract is completed.
The percentage-of-completion method—income is taken up as
the work progresses.

Completed-contract method. Under this method the balance
sheet will show, usually as a current asset, the costs incurred to
date less progress billings. It may be appropriate to include general and administrative costs in the contract cost, rather than
to regard them as period costs; this procedure may result in a better
matching of income and costs, particularly in a year in which no
contracts were completed.

If progress billings exceed the accumulated contract costs, the excess should be shown as a liability—usually as a current one.

This method has the advantage of eliminating guesswork, which is more or less inherent in the percentage-of-completion method. Its disadvantage lies in the fact that, since income is taken up in the year of completion, the amounts reported as net income for several successive years may vary widely although operations were fairly uniform through the years.

Although income is not taken up under this method before completion, if a loss appears to be in prospect, provision should be made for it.

Percentage-of-completion method. Under this method, the balance sheet will show, usually as a current asset, the sum of the accumulated costs and recorded income minus the progress billings. If the progress billings exceed the accumulated costs and recorded income, the excess should be shown as a liability—usually in the current section.

When the percentage-of-completion method is used, the income to be taken up before completion may be computed in the manner illustrated below:

Contract price		$50,000
Less estimated cost:		
Cost to date	$25,000	
Estimated cost to complete	15,000	40,000
Estimated total income		$10,000
Portion of estimated income earned to date:		
$25/40$ of $10,000		$ 6,250

Observe that progress billings were given no consideration in the preceding computation. The timing and amounts of the progress billings may have little or no relationship to the progress of the work—which, under this method, is the basic test of income earning.

If a loss on the contract is in prospect, provision should be made for the total loss, not for portions thereof computed on a percentage-of-completion basis.

If a contract is on a cost-plus basis, there is no hazard in taking up income on an uncompleted contract; but if a contract is on a flat-price basis, there is usually an element of hazard in doing so because of the possibility that unforeseen costs may turn a prospective profit into a smaller profit or into a loss.

The hazards of taking up income on uncompleted contracts may, of course, be eliminated or minimized if the work to be done, or the product to be delivered, is divisible into identifiable units to which portions of the total contract price are definitely applicable. Thus, if a contract calls for the manufacture and delivery of 1,000 units of a certain commodity, there is no lack of conservatism in taking up the earnings applicable to the completed and accepted units. If the contract calls for the construction and delivery of a single unit, such as a ship, the contract may specify certain completion stages and provide for progress payments thereon, a portion of the contract price applicable to each stage being retained as a guarantee of satisfactory completion of the contract as a whole; in such instances, the hazards of taking up income as the work progresses are somewhat minimized.

Although, from the standpoint of a going concern, it is always conservative to defer the taking of any income until the contract is completed, consideration should be given to the fact that such conservatism may work an injustice on partners or stockholders. If a partner is to retire before the completion of a contract, and is to sell his interest to the remaining partners, he should, in fairness, receive some benefit for the income reasonably to be regarded as applicable to work done up to the date of his retirement. Since stockholders of a corporation may change before the completion of a long contract, there may also be a responsibility on the part of the corporate management to recognize the question of fairness involved. The holders of noncumulative preferred stock may suffer a peculiar hardship if the taking of contract income is deferred until the completion of the contract and if there is no previously accumulated surplus to which preferred dividends can be charged.

Rigid adherence to a policy of taking up no income from contracts until they are completed not only may impose unreasonable hardships on partners or stockholders, but may result in the showing of income from period to period quite at variance with the operating facts. For instance, if we assume that a company is engaged throughout one year on a single contract which was uncompleted at the end of the year, the taking of no income at the end of the year would result in showing a loss if administrative overhead expenses were charged off. The income statement of the succeeding period would also show a distorted picture because it would include income resulting largely from the activities of the prior period. The assumed conditions of this illustration have been made somewhat extreme to emphasize the point; the fact that the distortion may be concealed because other contracts are being carried on concurrently only emphasizes the necessity of recognizing the conditions.

CHAPTER TWELVE

Inventories (Continued)

Chapter 11 dealt principally with matters related to the determination of cost for inventory-pricing purposes. We now turn to matters related to the so-called "cost or market" rule.

What is "market"?   "Market" may be determined on one of the following bases, depending on the type of inventory involved.

Purchase or replacement basis:

This basis applies to purchased merchandise or materials. It has been defined by the Treasury Department for tax purposes as follows: "Upon ordinary circumstances and for normal goods in an inventory, 'market' means the current bid price prevailing at the date of the inventory for the particular merchandise in the volume in which usually purchased by the taxpayer." The restriction concerning quantity is important; if it were omitted, inapplicable market values might be used.

"Replacement" is probably a better word than "purchase," as it is broad enough to include the incidental acquisition costs, such as freight and duties, which are properly included with the purchase price in the inventory computation.

Reproduction basis:

This basis applies to manufactured goods and goods in process. It is determined on the basis of market prices for materials, prevailing labor rates, and current overhead.

Realization basis:

For some items in the inventory, such as obsolete or repossessed merchandise, a purchase or reproduction market value may not be determinable, and it may be necessary to accept, as an estimate of market value, the prospective selling price minus all prospective costs to be incurred in conditioning and selling the goods, and minus a reasonable profit.

Limits on usable market prices. Current accounting practice has sanctioned certain limits on the application of market values for inventory purposes. These limits have been stated by the Committee on Accounting Procedure in Bulletin 43 as follows:

> "As used in the phrase *lower of cost or market* the term *market* means current replacement cost (by purchase or by reproduction, as the case may be) except that:
>
> "(1) Market should not exceed the net realizable value (i.e., estimated selling price in the ordinary course of business less reasonably predictable costs of completion and disposal); and
>
> "(2) Market should not be less than net realizable value reduced by an allowance for an approximately normal profit margin."

To illustrate the application of the above refinement of the "market" concept, the following table shows relevant prices for five different inventory items. The underlined prices are those to be used for inventory purposes if the definition of "market" set forth in Bulletin 43 is followed.

	1	2	3	4	5
(a) Cost	.72	.85	.85	.68	.84
(b) Market—cost to replace at inventory date	.76	.80	.70	.65	.83
(c) Selling price less estimated cost to complete and sell	.82	.82	.82	.82	.82
(d) Selling price less estimated cost to complete and sell and normal profit margin	.73	.73	.73	.73	.73

(The underlined figures used for inventory purposes are: column 1, cost .72; column 2, market .80; column 3, (d) .73; column 4, cost .68; column 5, (c) .82.)

Column notes:

1. Cost is used because it is lower than market.
2. Market is used because it is lower than cost, not greater than (c), and not less than (d).
3. Market is used because it is lower than cost. Price (d) is used because it measures the limit of reduction.
4. Market is less than cost, but it is not used because it is lower than (d). Cost is used.
5. Market is lower than cost; it is not used because it is less than (d). But, since cost is less than (d), cost is used.
6. Market is lower than cost, but it is higher than (c); therefore, (c) is used.

Exception (2) is a specific instance of the growing practice of not reducing cost except to the extent of a clearly apparent loss.

Normal profit. The quotation in the preceding sub-section from Bulletin 43 refers to "an approximately normal profit margin." This expression is used in the statement that, if market is lower than cost, in no event should the figure used for inventory pricing be less than net realizable value (estimated selling price less reasonably predictable costs of completion and disposal) reduced by an allowance for an approximately normal profit margin.

The use of a normal profit concept seems somewhat unfortunate. How is a "normal" profit determined? By whom? What is the normal profit margin for General Motors Corporation? Can an estimate of a normal profit margin be more than a matter of individual opinion?

There is an additional troublesome feature in the use of normal profit. If an inventory is reduced to "net realizable value reduced by an allowance for an approximately normal profit margin," then in the period of sale a normal profit will be reported, if the sales price is correctly forecast. Such results, however, may be somewhat misleading, since they are attributable to a method of inventory pricing. It seems logical to price the inventory at less than cost if it is clearly apparent that the investment in inventory cannot be recovered. But why adopt an accounting procedure which reduces an inventory figure to such an extent that a profit will likely be reported in the subsequent period?

If December 31 was the close of the accounting period and the goods in question had been sold on December 29, a loss would have been reported. If the goods are priced in the inventory to permit a normal profit when sold, and they are sold on January 5, a profit is reported. The close of an accounting period and the application of an accounting convention have thus made a loss transaction appear to be profitable. By understating profits or overstating losses in one year, a larger profit can be reported in a subsequent year.

It may be relevant to note that this result would arise only if market were below net realizable value. If market is above net realizable value, then cost is reduced to net realizable value without further reduction to provide for an approximately normal profit. The goods thus reduced would be sold at no loss in the period of sale. Only when market is below net realizable value will the inventory be reduced to produce a subsequent accounting profit.

Application of cost or market. Three ways of applying the cost or market method are illustrated on page 247.

(1) By comparing the cost and market for each item in the inventory, and using the lower figure.

Determination of Lower of Cost or Market—Item-by-Item Method

		Unit Price		Extended		Lower of Cost or Market
	Quantity	Cost	Market	Cost	Market	
Men's clothing:						
Suits..........	200	$40	$37			$ 7,400
Coats.........	100	35	31			3,100
Jackets........	50	15	17			750
Hats..........	80	5	6			400
Ladies' clothing:						
Dresses........	300	10	12			3,000
Suits..........	100	40	38			3,800
Coats.........	80	30	32			2,400
Robes.........	60	5	5			300
Inventory at lower of cost or market........................						$21,150

(2) By comparing the total cost and market for major inventory categories, and using the lower figure.

Determination of Lower of Cost or Market—Category Method

		Unit Price		Extended		Lower of Cost or Market
	Quantity	Cost	Market	Cost	Market	
Men's clothing:						
Suits..........	200	$40	$37	$ 8,000	$ 7,400	
Coats.........	100	35	31	3,500	3,100	
Jackets........	50	15	17	750	850	
Hats..........	80	5	6	400	480	
Total.......				$12,650	$11,830	$11,830
Ladies' clothing:						
Dresses........	300	10	12	$ 3,000	$ 3,600	
Suits..........	100	40	38	4,000	3,800	
Coats.........	80	30	32	2,400	2,560	
Robes.........	60	5	5	300	300	
Total.......				$ 9,700	$10,260	9,700
Inventory at lower of cost or market........................						$21,530

(3) By comparing the total cost and market for the entire inventory, and using the lower figure.

Determination of Lower of Cost or Market—Total Inventory Method

		Unit Price		Extended		Lower of Cost or Market
	Quantity	Cost	Market	Cost	Market	
Men's clothing:						
Suits..........	200	$40	$37	$ 8,000	$ 7,400	
Coats.........	100	35	31	3,500	3,100	
Jackets........	50	15	17	750	850	
Hats..........	80	5	6	400	480	
Ladies' clothing:						
Dresses........	300	10	12	3,000	3,600	
Suits..........	100	40	38	4,000	3,800	
Coats.........	80	30	32	2,400	2,560	
Robes.........	60	5	5	300	300	
Total				$22,350	$22,090	$22,090

For many years it was considered imperative to use the item-by-item method; the category and total inventory methods are now regarded as acceptable alternatives.

Accounting procedures. The accounting for inventories on the basis of a market valuation lower than cost may be effected by:

A direct inventory reduction procedure.
An inventory reserve procedure.

Since accounting procedures always depend upon whether periodical or perpetual inventories are used, we have the following classification:

Direct inventory reduction procedure:
    With periodical inventories.
    With perpetual inventories.
Inventory reserve procedure:
    With periodical inventories.
    With perpetual inventories.

For purposes of illustrating these procedures, let us assume that, during the first year of the life of a company, its purchases totalled $100,000; that it sold half of the goods for $80,000; that market replacement prices declined; and that the remaining half of the goods (in the inventory) are priced, at the lower of cost or market, at only $40,000.

Direct inventory reduction procedure—Periodical inventories. If the company's accounts are on a periodical inventory basis, the entry to record the inventory will be:

```
Inventory........................................... 40,000
    Revenue and expense............................        40,000
    To place the end-of-year inventory on the books.
```

The income statement will appear as follows:

```
Sales................................................         $80,000
Less cost of sales:
    Purchases....................................  $100,000
    Less inventory—December 31....................    40,000   60,000
Gross profit on sales...............................         $20,000
Less expenses.......................................          12,000
Net income..........................................         $ 8,000
```

It is obvious that this procedure, although perhaps correctly stating the net income, overstates the cost of goods sold and understates the gross profit.

Direct inventory reduction procedure—Perpetual inventories. If the accounts are on a perpetual inventory basis, the Cost of Sales and Inventory accounts will both have debit balances of $50,000. The entry to write down the inventory *may* be:

```
Cost of sales.........................................  10,000
    Inventory.........................................           10,000
    To reduce the inventory to the lower of cost or market.
```

If an entry of this nature is made, the income statement will appear as follows:

```
Sales..................................................  $80,000
Less cost of sales.....................................   60,000
Gross profit on sales..................................  $20,000
Less expenses..........................................   12,000
Net income.............................................  $ 8,000
```

This procedure also misstates the cost of goods sold and the gross profit. These misstatements can be avoided by charging the inventory write-down to a special account, thus:

```
Loss on reduction of inventory to market...............  10,000
    Inventory.........................................           10,000
```

If an entry of this nature is made, the income statement may appear as follows:

```
Sales..................................................  $80,000
Less cost of sales.....................................   50,000
Gross profit on sales..................................  $30,000
Less loss on reduction of inventory to market..........   10,000
Gross profit less inventory loss.......................  $20,000
Less expenses..........................................   12,000
Net income.............................................  $ 8,000
```

It seems hardly necessary to say that, if the inventory controlling account is written down, the subsidiary perpetual inventory records should be adjusted to a comparable basis.

Inventory reserve procedure—Periodical inventories. When a reserve procedure is used, the inventory is shown in the accounts at cost, and the reduction to market is indicated by a reserve.

Assuming that the accounts are on a periodical inventory basis, the journal entries to set up the inventory and the reserve could be:

```
Inventory..............................................  50,000
    Revenue and expense...............................           50,000
    To set up the inventory at cost.

Loss on reduction of inventory to market...............  10,000
    Reserve to reduce inventory to market.............           10,000
    To reduce inventory to market.
```

The income statement could then be prepared in the manner shown on the following page, to report the true gross profit on a cost basis and the inventory loss.

Sales...		$80,000
Less cost of goods sold:		
Purchases.......................................	$100,000	
Less inventory—December 31, at cost..............	50,000	50,000
Gross profit on sales...		$30,000
Less loss on reduction of inventory to market...................		10,000
Gross profit less inventory loss...............................		$20,000
Less expenses...		12,000
Net income................................... :		$ 8,000

In the balance sheet the inventory could be shown at cost, and the reserve could be deducted therefrom.

Continuing the illustration, let us assume that, at the close of the second year, the cost valuation of the inventory is $60,000 and the market value is $52,500. The reserve-method entries under the periodical inventory procedure are:

Inventory...	60,000	
Revenue and expense.............................		60,000
To record the end-of-year inventory at cost.		
Reserve to reduce inventory to market..................	2,500	
Reduction in reserve to reduce inventory from cost to		
market (to be closed to Revenue and Expense).....		2,500
To adjust the reserve by reducing the balance from		
$10,000 to the present requirement of $7,500.		

In the foregoing income statement, the amount of the reduction of inventory to market was deducted from the gross profit. The $2,500 decrease in the reserve may be added to the gross profit.

Inventory reserve procedure—Perpetual inventories. If the accounts are kept on a perpetual inventory basis, the following entry will be made:

Loss on reduction of inventory to market................	10,000	
Reserve to reduce inventory to market..............		10,000

The income statement can be presented in the manner illustrated above.

Again continuing the illustration to the second year, the perpetual inventory records would show the inventory at the $60,000 cost, and only the following entry would be made:

Reserve to reduce inventory to market..................	2,500	
Reduction in reserve to reduce inventory from cost to		
market.......................................		2,500

Advantages and disadvantages of the reserve method. The reserve method has the following advantages:

The cost of sales and the gross profit are stated on a cost basis, both in the period when the market decrease occurred and in the subsequent period (because the inventory is carried over to the subsequent period at cost);

The effect of market changes is shown as a separate item in the
income statement;

If the company maintains perpetual inventories, they can be
kept on a cost basis without adjustment of all of the detailed
records to a market basis.

On the other hand, if the accounts are kept on a periodical
inventory basis, and the inventory is determined on an item-by-
item basis, the reserve method necessitates doing all of the work
involved in extending each inventory item at both cost and market.
If the direct write-down method is used, it is necessary to multiply quantities by only the cost or market price, whichever is
lower, to obtain an inventory valuation on the item-by-item basis.

General discussion of cost or market. The cost-or-market
basis of inventory pricing conforms with an old rule of accounting
conservatism often stated as follows: Anticipate no profit and provide for all possible losses. If market purchase prices decline, it is
assumed that selling prices will decline with them; reducing the
inventory valuation to market purchase price reduces the profit of
the period when the cost price decline took place and transfers
the goods to the next period at a price which will presumably
permit the earning of a normal gross profit on their sale. If the
market purchase price increases, the inventory is valued at cost
so that a profit will not be anticipated.

The cost-or-market basis has been, in the past, one of the most
generally accepted applications of conservative accounting principles. It was developed and widely accepted during the long
period when bankers and other creditors were primarily concerned
with the balance sheet and when relatively little consideration was
given to the income statement. With the emphasis thus placed
on the balance sheet, the primary essential was a conservative
valuation of the assets shown therein. The valuation of the inventory at the lower of cost or market is unquestionably conservative
from the balance sheet standpoint.

To obtain this balance sheet conservatism, all other considerations were ignored or their importance was minimized. It was
recognized that the cost-or-market approach was subject to question on the ground of consistency; to absorb against current gross
profits an unrealized and even problematical loss on unsold merchandise, while ignoring an unrealized potential increase in gross
profit which might result from a rising market, was recognized as
inconsistent; but such an inconsistency was regarded as of no concern when questions of conservatism were at issue. It was recognized that, even from the balance sheet standpoint, the cost-or-

market rule resulted in inconsistencies and in valuations which were not comparable. Different items in an inventory might be priced on different bases—some at cost and some at market; the inventories of the same concern at two dates might be priced on different bases—at cost on a rising market and at market on a falling market—and a comparison of the balance sheet valuations might therefore lead to incorrect interpretations; the inventories of two concerns might be priced on different bases, because acquired at different dates, and therefore not be comparable. But all inconsistencies of this nature were considered unimportant in comparison with considerations of conservatism in the valuation of each inventory.

However, income performance has become increasingly recognized as a significant measure of debt-paying ability and investment desirability. As a consequence, bankers, other creditors, business management, and stockholders are becoming increasingly concerned with the income statement—and not only with the income statement for a single period, but with the trend of earnings as shown by a series of income statements. For this reason the propriety of the cost-or-market approach is becoming a subject of question.

Accountants are now raising the question as to whether, giving consideration to the income statements for a series of periods, the cost-or-market rule is as conservative as it formerly seemed to be. If, at the close of one period, the market value of the inventory is less than its cost, the reduction of the inventory valuation to market undoubtedly produces a conservative balance sheet valuation and a conservative computation of income in the statements for that period. But what is the effect on the income statement of the subsequent period? The effect may be so great a distortion of stated earnings of successive periods as to render a series of income statements definitely misleading.

To illustrate, assume that, at the beginning of January, merchandise was purchased at a cost of $100,000; that half of the goods were sold in January for $75,000; that the remaining half were sold in February for $73,000; and that the inventory at the end of January, which cost $50,000, had a market value (replacement cost) of $40,000. The statement on page 253 shows:

In the first column, the computation of gross profits for the two months under the cost-or-market rule.
In the second column, the computation of gross profits for the two months with the inventory valued at cost.

	With Inventory Valued At	
	Cost or Market	Cost
January:		
Sales..	$75,000	$75,000
Cost of goods sold ($100,000 of purchases, minus the inventory)	60,000	50,000
Gross profit...	$15,000	$25,000
February:		
Sales..	$73,000	$73,000
Cost of goods sold (consisting of the opening inventory).......	40,000	50,000
Gross profit...	$33,000	$23,000

The balance sheet valuation of the inventory at the end of January on the cost-or-market basis instead of on the cost basis ($40,000 instead of $50,000), and the resulting statement of gross profit for January ($15,000 instead of $25,000), may be accepted as conservative. But is the February income statement on the cost-or-market basis (showing $33,000 of gross profit instead of $23,000) conservative? And would not the statements for the two months on the cost-or-market basis give a misleading impression as to the trend of operations to anyone who did not realize that the increase in profit shown by the statements was caused by the write-down of the inventory and the consequent transfer of profits from January to February?

The cost-or-market inventory-pricing basis is founded on the assumption that a decrease in market purchase costs will be accompanied by a similar decrease in selling prices before the disposal of the inventory. This was not the case in the foregoing illustration, and in the actual conduct of business affairs it frequently is not the case. Therefore, there is a trend toward the opinion that it is not necessary or desirable to reduce the inventory valuation to market if there is no probability that sales prices will also decrease; there is also some trend of opinion in favor of the idea that reduction to market is unnecessary if, even though some decline in selling prices has occurred or can be expected, the inventory can probably be disposed of at a selling price which will include the cost and some profit. And there is even some opinion that reduction to market is unnecessary if the inventory can probably be disposed of without loss.

Some accountants, therefore, believe that, instead of assuming that a decrease in selling prices will promptly follow a decrease in cost, consideration should be given to the trend in selling prices, and that the inventory valuation should not be reduced unless selling prices have decreased at the balance sheet date or unless it is expected that they will decrease sufficiently after that date and before the disposal of the inventory to cause a loss.

If a decrease in the realizable value of the inventory is in prospect, balance sheet conservatism undoubtedly requires a reduction in the inventory valuation; however, bearing in mind the importance of the income statement, there still remains the question as to whether the customary procedure of reducing the inventory valuation by an accounting method which also reduces the gross profit of the period in which market costs declined is desirable. The question of distortion of profits between periods still remains. To illustrate, let us return to the foregoing case in which the inventory at the end of January cost $50,000 and had a market cost value of $40,000. In that illustration it was assumed that the selling prices in February did not similarly decline, notwithstanding the decrease in market costs. Let us now assume that the selling prices decreased $10,000—an amount equal to the decrease in inventory valuation. Statements are presented below:

	With Inventory Valued At	
	Cost or Market	Cost
January:		
Sales	$75,000	$75,000
Cost of goods sold	60,000	50,000
Gross profit	$15,000	$25,000
February:		
Sales	$65,000	$65,000
Cost of goods sold	40,000	50,000
Gross profit	$25,000	$15,000

The figures in the "Cost" column seem to reflect the facts more truly: The company made less profit in February than in January because of the decrease in selling prices. The "Cost or Market" column tells a very strange story: The company made more profit in February than in January, notwithstanding the decrease in selling prices.

It seems to the authors that accountants might expect that the shift in emphasis from the balance sheet to the income statement would produce a similar shift in emphasis in the accounting approach to inventory pricing. When the emphasis was on reporting financial position, the approach to the inventory problem was one of valuation for purposes of properly reflecting financial position. Under these conditions cost or market, whichever is lower, seemed well suited. With the emphasis currently on the measurement of net income, the accountant logically gives preeminent consideration to those procedures associated with the assignment or "matching" of costs against related revenues. With the emphasis on a matching of costs and revenues, it would seem that the approach should be shifted to one of determining the portion of the total merchandise cost outlay for a period that should be charged against current revenues and the portion that should be assigned to future periods. The emphasis, thus, would not be one of inventory "valuation," but of cost assignment, the residue being carried forward to apply to future periods.

To some extent, this shift in approach to inventory pricing has occurred. Cost or market, whichever is lower, is receiving less support from accountants and is being refined in a number of ways, all in the direction of not reducing the cost figure unless a loss on the inventory investment is clearly in prospect.

Obsolete and depreciated merchandise. Regardless of the inventory-pricing basis adopted, merchandise which has become obsolete or has depreciated because of shop wear or damage should be excluded entirely from the inventory if it is unsalable or cannot be utilized in production. If it can be sold at a reduced price, a conservative estimate of realizable value may be assigned to it. The loss on goods which have been damaged or have become obsolete should be taken in the period when the loss developed.

The question of the proper treatment of write-downs for losses on obsolete, shopworn, or otherwise damaged goods requires some consideration. If write-downs are required as a result of shop-wear, style changes, or other operating causes, they should be treated as a charge against income, either by a reduction of gross profit or as a special income deduction. However, extraordinary losses, such as those caused by fire or flood, should be set out as extraneous losses.

Goods repossessed in a worn or damaged condition should be priced for inventory purposes at an amount not in excess of the net realizable value (estimated selling price in the ordinary course of business less reasonably predictable costs of reconditioning and disposal). It is also acceptable, and logically justifiable, to reduce the net realizable value by an allowance for an approximately normal profit margin. That procedure would place the repossessed merchandise on a basis comparable with that of new merchandise.

Scrap. The valuation of scrap material presents some special problems. If the scrap cannot be sold or used, it should, of course, be given no inventory value. If it can be sold, it can be priced for inventory purposes on a net realization basis.

If the scrap is used in the manufacture of a by-product, the entire original cost of the material may be charged to the main product; in that case, the cost of the by-product will be computed without the inclusion of any charge for scrap material used, and no valuation should be placed on the scrap for inventory purposes; or the original cost of the material may be charged in part to the main product and in part to the by-product; in that case, the scrap can be given an inventory value. It is important that consistency be maintained, and that the error of charging the main product with the entire cost of the material and also placing a valuation on the scrap in the inventory be not committed; such a procedure obviously would result in an inflation of asset values and profits to the extent of the valuation placed on the scrap.

Goods in foreign countries. If a company operates a branch or factory in a foreign country, the problems of inventory pricing already discussed are applicable, and, in addition, it must meet the problem of converting values stated in a foreign currency to values stated in domestic currency.

In general, it may be said that the conversion should be made by applying to the foreign currency valuation the exchange rate current on the balance sheet date. This general rule requires some modification. Some companies keep the accounts of foreign branches in such a manner as to show the dollar cost of the foreign money used for the payment of manufacturing costs.

Inventory valuation based on selling price. In some lines of industry, such as meat packing, in which material costs cannot be specifically allocated to joint products, practical considerations may make it advisable or even necessary to determine the inventory valuation on the basis of the relative selling prices of the various commodities. Although selling prices in such cases serve as a convenient basis for the determination of inventory valuations, conservatism requires at least the deduction of a sufficient allowance for marketing and transportation charges to be incurred; and, to avoid an anticipation of profits, the deductions from selling prices should include a provision for profits.

Valuation of the inventory at selling prices less a provision for disposal costs is often regarded as acceptable practice if production costs are difficult to determine and the product has a ready marketability. This condition is recognized as prevailing in farming. It is therefore considered acceptable practice to value crops and live stock on the basis of selling prices less estimated selling and other disposal costs. Any other procedure might involve practical impossibilities of inventory valuation, and might result in imposing the burden of production on one period while waiting to take the related income until a succeeding period.

Unrealized profits in inventories. When the process of manufacturing involves the transfer of work in process from one department to another, the transfer value is sometimes based on the price at which products at that stage of completion could be obtained from outside suppliers. This value may be used for the purpose of comparing manufacturing costs with a presumptive acquisition cost to see whether a manufacturing department is an advantageous or "profitable" one to maintain. A system of bonus payments may be in effect, the bonuses being determined by the difference between manufacturing costs and suppliers' prices. Although such a basis for pricing interdepartmental transfers may be desirable for purposes of management, all such unrealized profits should be excluded from the inventory valuation for balance sheet and income statement purposes.

Variations in inventory pricings and the principle of consistency. We have seen that there are various acceptable methods of inventory pricing. Inventories may be priced at cost, at the lower of cost or market, at cost or less, or on a basis of selling prices. The cost figures may be affected by such matters as the treatment of freight, purchase discounts, and incidental expenditures, and by the choice of the method to be used in the selection of costs for inventory purposes. The lower of cost or market may be determined on a basis of individual items, inventory categories, or inventory totals.

Although the amount of permissible variation in inventory pricing by different companies is somewhat disturbing, the matter is not so serious as it might seem, because the principle of consistency requires that the basis and method of inventory pricing adopted by each company be consistently applied by it over the years, or that the effect of any departure from consistency, if material, be disclosed. The principle of consistency thus reduces the troublesome consequences that might otherwise develop from having a variety of acceptable inventory procedures.

Reserves for possible future market declines. The inventory reserves discussed on pages 249–251 gave recognition to market declines which had occurred prior to the balance sheet date. Such reserves are properly set up by charges to current income, so that net income will be computed in accordance with the cost-or-market basis of inventory valuation. They should not be created by direct charges to Retained Earnings. A reserve of this nature should be treated in the balance sheet as a contra account, and should be deducted from the balance in the Inventory account.

Reserves for price declines that have already taken place must be distinguished from reserves reflecting anticipated, prospective, or possible inventory price declines. Regarding the latter type of reserves, the Committee on Accounting Procedure made a comment in Bulletin 43 that is quoted on page 258.

"It has been argued with respect to inventories that losses which will have to be taken in periods of receding price levels have their origins in periods of rising prices, and that therefore reserves to provide for future price declines should be created in periods of rising prices by charges against the operations of those periods. Reserves of this kind involve assumptions as to what future price levels will be, what inventory quantities will be on hand if and when a major price decline takes place, and finally whether loss to the business will be measured by the amount of the decline in prices. The bases for such assumptions are so uncertain that any conclusions drawn from them would generally seem to be speculative guesses rather than informed judgments. When estimates of this character are included in current costs, amounts representing mere conjecture are combined with others representing reasonable approximations."

The same statement would be equally true with respect to estimates of possible price declines made during periods of declining prices. Such estimates are necessarily based on assumptions regarding the extent of the decline, its duration, the inventory quantity affected, and the response of selling prices to the decline.

If a reserve for possible future market declines is set up, it should be created by a debit to Retained Earnings and a credit to an account with some title such as "Reserve for Possible Future Inventory Losses." The reserve is a part of the stockholders' equity and should be shown as such in the balance sheet.

What disposition should be made of the reserve thus created? It should be returned to Retained Earnings whether or not the declines occur. If they do not occur, the reserve is thus proved to have been unnecessary. But if they do occur, the loss should be charged against the operations of the period during which the market decline took place; this is accomplished by charging operations with the recorded beginning inventory unadjusted for prospective price declines (which was also the amount used in closing the books at the end of the prior period).

Thus, if a concern values its inventory at the lower of cost or market, and if, at the end of 1959, the cost of the inventory is $50,000 and the market value is $40,000, the books should be closed and the income for 1959 ascertained on the basis of an inventory valuation of $40,000. If there is a prospect of additional market declines, a reserve may be set up out of Retained Earnings. But this reserve should be returned to Retained Earnings during, or at the end of, 1960, and the Revenue and Expense account for 1960 should be charged with the opening inventory at $40,000.

Retail method. The so-called "retail" method of inventory pricing is frequently used in department and other retail stores; it is suitable for use by wholesalers also. It is not suitable, however, for manufacturing businesses, because the articles purchased are not immediately priced for resale.

With records showing the opening inventory and purchases at both cost and retail, it is possible to determine a ratio of cost to retail, the uses of which are described below:

(1) To estimate the inventory at any time without taking a physical inventory; the procedure is as follows:

	Cost	Retail
Inventory at beginning of period....................	$ 10,000	$ 15,000
Purchases during the period.......................	110,000	185,000
Totals......................................	$120,000	$200,000
(Ratio of cost to retail—60%)		
Sales...		180,000
Inventory at retail...............................		$ 20,000

Inventory computation—60% of $20,000 = $12,000.

> The retail method makes it possible to prepare monthly, weekly, or even daily estimates of the inventory. Such estimates may be useful for purposes of inventory control and formulating purchasing policy.

(2) To permit pricing a physical inventory at marked selling prices and reducing the selling price valuation by applying to it the ratio of cost to retail.

> Using retail prices eliminates the necessity of marking costs on the merchandise, referring to invoices, and dealing with the problem of identical merchandise acquired at different costs.

Physical inventories, priced by the retail method, should be taken from time to time as a check on the accuracy of the estimated inventories determined by the procedure described under (1) above. If the inventory determined by procedure (2) is less than the amount estimated by procedure (1), the difference may be attributable to "shrinkages" resulting from theft, breakage, or other causes. However, the difference may be attributable in part to errors in the retail inventory records or in the physical inventory priced at retail.

Terminology. The foregoing illustration ignores the problem created whenever changes are made in selling prices after the original selling prices have been placed on the goods. The fact that businessmen do revise or modify prices of goods on hand necessitates an understanding of the following terms:

Original retail is the price at which the goods are first offered for sale.

Mark-ups are additions that raise the selling price above the original retail.

Mark-downs are deductions that lower the price below the original retail.

Mark-up cancellations are deductions that do not decrease the selling price below the original retail.

Mark-down cancellations are additions that do not increase the selling price above the original retail.

To illustrate, assume the following:

The goods cost $100.	
The original retail price was..........................	$140
There was a mark-up of.......................................	20
Which advanced the selling price to.........................	$160
There was a mark-up cancellation of...........................	5
Which reduced the selling price to...........................	$155
The selling price was further reduced $30:	
This included a mark-up cancellation of......................	15
Which reduced the selling price to original retail.............. ..	$140
It also included a mark-down of..............................	15
Which reduced the selling price to...........................	$125
There was a mark-down cancellation of.........................	5
Which increased the selling price to..........................	$130

Mark-ups minus mark-up cancellations may be referred to as *net mark-up;* mark-downs minus mark-down cancellations may be referred to as *net mark-down.*

A clear understanding of mark-ups, mark-up cancellations, mark-downs, and mark-down cancellations, and a careful differentiation thereof in the records are necessary because, in determining the ratio of cost to retail, it is customary to include mark-ups and mark-up cancellations, but to ignore mark-downs and mark-down cancellations. To illustrate, assume the following:

	Cost	Retail
Inventory at beginning of period....................	$20,000	$ 30,000
Purchases.......................................	80,000	120,000
Mark-ups.......................................		10,000
Mark-up cancellations............................		2,000*
Mark-downs.....................................		7,000*
Mark-down cancellations.........................		1,000

The per cent to be used in computing the inventory by the retail method (including net mark-ups and excluding net mark-downs) is determined as follows:

	Cost	Retail
Inventory at beginning of period....................	$ 20,000	$ 30,000
Purchases.......................................	80,000	120,000
Mark-ups.......................................		10,000
Mark-up cancellations............................		2,000*
Totals.....................................	$100,000	$158,000
(Ratio of cost to retail: 63.29%)		

---

* Starred items throughout this discussion are deductions from retail prices.

Mark-on is the difference between the cost and the original retail plus net mark-ups. In the above example, the mark-on is $58,000; the per cent of mark-on is 36.71% ($58,000 ÷ $158,000); and the ratio of cost to retail is the complement of this per cent, or 63.29%. This rate is used in the following inventory computation.

	Cost	Retail
Inventory at beginning of period....................	$ 20,000	$ 30,000
Purchases..	80,000	120,000
Mark-ups...		10,000
Mark-up cancellations............................		2,000*
Totals (Cost ratio, 63.29%)....................	$100,000	$158,000
Mark-downs......................................		7,000*
Mark-down cancellations.........................		1,000
Remainder.................................		$152,000
Sales...		120,000
Inventory at retail..............................		$ 32,000

Inventory computation: 63.29% of $32,000, or $20,253.

Why mark-downs are ignored in the computation of cost ratio. The intent of the retail inventory method, as conventionally applied, is so to compute the inventory that its sale at prevailing prices will yield at least the normal or prevailing rate of gross profit. The dollar amounts thus determined are intended to conform generally to the cost or market rule.

Referring to the preceding illustration, let us compute by four different methods the per cents that might be applied to the inventory at selling price, and note which method produces an inventory figure that conforms most nearly to the lower of cost or market.

	Use Mark-Ups and Mark-Downs	Use Mark-Ups but Not Mark-Downs (as above)	Use Mark-Downs but Not Mark-Ups	Use Neither Mark-Ups Nor Mark-Downs
Original retail:				
Inventory...........	$ 30,000	$ 30,000	$ 30,000	$ 30,000
Purchases...........	120,000	120,000	120,000	120,000
Mark-ups—net........	8,000	8,000		
Mark-downs—net......	6,000*		6,000*	
Totals............	$152,000	$158,000	$144,000	$150,000
Cost................	100,000	100,000	100,000	100,000
Cost ratio..........	65.79%	63.29%	69.44%	66.67%
Inventory at retail.....	$ 32,000	$ 32,000	$ 32,000	$ 32,000
Computed inventory...	21,053	20,253	22,221	21,334

It is obvious that the lowest inventory figure is obtained by the second method, in which net mark-ups are used and net mark-downs are ignored in the computation of the cost ratio. But is such a procedure merely conservative without being logical? Two illustrations bearing on this question are presented.

Illustration with mark-ups. Mark-ups in retail prices are presumably related to market increases in wholesale prices; the inventory should, therefore, be priced at cost. In the following illustration it is assumed that half of the merchandise was sold.

	Cost	Retail
Opening inventory and purchases................	$60,000	$ 90,000
(Cost ratio, ignoring mark-ups = 66⅔%)		
Mark-ups—net.........		10,000
Total......................................		$100,000
(Cost ratio, including mark-ups = 60%)		
Sales...................		50,000
Inventory at retail...............................		$ 50,000

Inventory figure:
   At rate ignoring mark-ups: 66⅔% of $50,000 = $33,333.
   At rate including mark-ups: 60% of $50,000 = $30,000.

The $33,333 figure is affected by the rise in market prices and is incorrect; the $30,000 figure is on a cost basis, and is correct because cost is lower than market. Therefore mark-ups should be used in the determination of the cost ratio.

Illustration with mark-downs. Mark-downs may be necessitated by market decreases in wholesale prices; if such a situation exists, the inventory (if it is to conform to cost or market, whichever is lower) should be reduced to market.

	Cost	Retail
Opening inventory and purchases....................	$60,000	$90,000
(Cost ratio, ignoring mark-downs = 66⅔%)		
Mark-downs—net..........		10,000
Remainder.......................................		$80,000
(Cost ratio, including mark-downs = 75%)		
Sales.................................		40,000
Inventory at retail...............................		$40,000

Inventory figure:
   At rate ignoring mark-downs: 66⅔% of $40,000 = $26,667.
   At rate including mark-downs: 75% of $40,000 = $30,000.

The $26,667 figure was affected by the decrease in market value, and is appropriate in view of the fact that the traditional objective of the retail method is to approximate the results produced by the cost or market, whichever is lower, method. It therefore appears that mark-downs should not be used in determining the cost ratio.

Retail method is based on averages. The retail inventory method is based on the assumption that an average cost ratio can appropriately be applied to the selling price of the inventory. Some factors which might tend to make the assumption unwarranted are discussed in the following paragraphs.

Departmental rates. The first point to be considered is the effect of differences in departmental rates of mark-on. The retail inventory method assumes that high-cost-ratio goods and low-cost-ratio goods will be found in the same proportions in the final inventory as in the total of goods offered for sale. But let us assume the following conditions:

| | DEPARTMENT A | | DEPARTMENT B | | TOTAL | |
| | 50%-Cost-Ratio Merchandise | | 80%-Cost-Ratio Merchandise | | 72.5% Average Cost Ratio | |
	Cost	Retail	Cost	Retail	Cost	Retail
Opening inventory and purchases (or total offered for sale)........	$25,000	$50,000	$120,000	$150,000	$145,000	$200,000
Sales.................		45,000		105,000		150,000
Inventory at retail......		$ 5,000		$ 45,000		$ 50,000

It will be noted that the proportions of high-cost-ratio goods and low-cost-ratio goods are not the same in the closing inventory as in the total goods offered for sale. Instead, the proportions are those shown below.

	50% Cost Ratio	80% Cost Ratio
Offered for sale:		
Amounts—at selling price...................	$50,000	$150,000
Per cents................................	25%	75%
Final inventory:		
Amounts—at selling price...................	$ 5,000	$ 45,000
Per cents................................	10%	90%

Under such circumstances it is desirable to keep departmental records, in order that a separate computation can be made for the inventory of each department, thus:

Department A inventory: 50% of $ 5,000 = $ 2,500.
Department B inventory: 80% of $45,000 = $36,000.

Without the necessary departmental records, the inventory figure would be misstated, thus:

72.5% (average cost ratio) of $50,000 = $36,250.

Special-sale merchandise. Special sales of merchandise carrying low rates of mark-on may distort the average. To illustrate, assume the conditions shown below.

| | MERCHANDISE AT NORMAL COST RATIO—50% | | SPECIAL-SALE MERCHANDISE 90% COST RATIO | | TOTAL (58% AVERAGE COST RATIO) | |
	Cost	Retail	Cost	Retail	Cost	Retail
Opening inventory and purchases................	$40,000	$80,000	$18,000	$20,000	$58,000	$100,000
Sales....................		61,000		19,000		80,000
Inventory at retail........		$19,000		$ 1,000		$ 20,000

Again we find that the proportions of high-cost-ratio and low-cost-ratio merchandise in the inventory and in the total of goods offered for sale are not the same, but are as follows:

	50% Cost Ratio	90% Cost Ratio
Offered for sale:		
Amounts—at selling price	$80,000	$20,000
Per cents	80%	20%
Final inventory:		
Amounts—at selling price	$19,000	$ 1,000
Per cents	95%	5%

An attempt to compute the inventory by use of the average cost ratio of 58% would produce erroneous results as shown below:

```
Using average rate:
  58% of $20,000.........................................  $11,600
Using separate rates:
  50% of $19,000.................................  $9,500
  90% of $  1,000.................................     900
     Total...................................................  $10,400
```

Under such circumstances it is usually considered desirable to set up separate records, and to make a separate inventory computation, for special-sale merchandise as if such special merchandise constituted a department by itself.

Sales of marked-up and marked-down goods. Let us assume that, after all of the merchandise of a department is marked at a uniform original retail, half of the merchandise is given an additional mark-up and the other half is marked down; let us also assume that 70% of the sales are made from marked-down merchandise and only 30% from marked-up merchandise. Obviously, under such circumstances, it is fallacious to assume that high-cost-ratio goods and low-cost-ratio goods will be found in the same proportions in the final inventory as in the total of goods offered for sale; and the retail method in such instances would give fallacious results.

Period covered by computation. A year is too long a period to embrace in the inventory computation unless approximately the same rate of mark-on prevails throughout the year. This situation will not exist if, for example, different rates of gross profit are made on spring- and fall-season sales, or if extensive mark-downs are made during one period of the year whereas extensive mark-ups are made during another season.

The illustration on the following page indicates the desirability of making interim inventory computations if the rate of mark-on is not fairly uniform throughout the year.

If the inventory is computed semiannually:

	Cost	Retail
First Six Months:		
Opening inventory	$100,000	$150,000
Purchases	300,000	450,000
Totals	$400,000	$600,000
(Cost ratio: 66⅔%)		
Mark-downs		20,000
Remainder		$580,000
Sales		500,000
Inventory at retail		$ 80,000

Inventory computation, June 30: 66⅔% of $80,000 = $53,333.

	Cost	Retail
Second Six Months:		
Opening inventory	$ 53,333	$ 80,000
Purchases	400,000	500,000
Mark-ups		25,000
Totals	$453,333	$605,000
(Cost ratio: 74.9311%)		
Sales		385,000
Inventory at retail		$220,000

Inventory computation, December 31: 74.9311% of $220,000 = $164,848.

If the inventory is computed annually:

	Cost	Retail
Opening inventory	$100,000	$ 150,000
Purchases	700,000	950,000
Mark-ups		25,000
Totals	$800,000	$1,125,000
(Cost ratio: 71.1111%)		
Mark-downs		20,000
Remainder		$1,105,000
Sales		885,000
Inventory at retail		$ 220,000

Inventory computation, 71.1111% of $220,000 = $156,444.

The inventory figure of $156,444, obtained by the foregoing computations covering the full year, is erroneous. Although the average cost ratio during the whole year was about 71%, the cost ratio for the second half of the year was about 75%.

It is apparent that, in this instance, the use of a cost ratio applicable to only the last half of the year will result in the determination of an inventory valuation more nearly approximating the lower of cost or market at the end of the year. By the application of the average cost ratio, 71%, the December 31 inventory computation is unjustifiably affected by the low cost ratio of the first half-year.

If the rates of mark-on vary during the year, it is obvious that monthly, or even more frequent, inventory computations will produce more correct results than can be obtained by annual computations.

Extended illustration. The following statement shows the treatment of various elements in the computation of inventory by the retail method:

	Cost	Retail
Opening inventory	$ 65,000	$100,000
Purchases	350,000	520,000
Returned purchases	10,000*	14,800*
Freight in	2,500	
Mark-ups		12,500
Mark-up cancellations		3,000*
Totals	$407,500	$614,700
(Cost ratio—66.2925%)		
Deductions:		
Sales	$511,000	
Less returned sales	7,000	$504,000
Mark-downs	$ 5,000	
Less mark-down cancellations	1,500	3,500
Total deductions		$507,500
Inventory at retail		$107,200

Inventory computation: 66.2925% of $107,200 = $71,066.
* Deduction.

Freight, discounts, returns. Freight in and other charges which, in accordance with good accounting theory, are proper additions to merchandise costs, should be added to purchase costs in the retail records. If cash discounts are regarded as deductions from purchases, the purchases should be shown net in the retail records. If such discounts are regarded as financial income, they should not be included in the retail inventory computations.

Purchases should be entered at cost and at retail in the inventory computation; returned purchases should be similarly shown. Returned sales should be deducted from sales to obtain a net sales figure for use in the computation.

CHAPTER THIRTEEN

Inventories (Concluded)

1850
1300

550 = units sold

8000
2250
500
10750

Last-in, first-out (*lifo*) method. This method assumes that the most recent goods received are the first ones sold. Thus, to price an ending inventory, the accountant refers to the cost data applicable to the beginning inventory, and uses cost data applicable to purchases of the current year only in case the ending inventory is larger than the beginning inventory.

Consider the following facts:

end inv

	Quantity	Cost	Total
Beginning inventory............................	1,000	$ 8	$8,000
Purchases during the current period:			
First purchase...............................	250	9	2,250
Second purchase.............................	300	10	3,000
Third purchase..............................	100	13	1,300
Fourth purchase.............................	200	14	2,800

cGS

The following illustrates the approach used under the last-in, first-out method if the ending inventory consists of 1,300 units.

1850

	Quantity	Cost	Total
The beginning inventory.......................	1,000	$ 8	$ 8,000
The first purchase.............................	250	9	2,250
Part of the second purchase....................	50	10	500
Total.......................................			$10,750

An ending inventory of 900 units would be priced at $8 per unit.

In the minds of the advocates of the *lifo* method, the expression "last-in, first-out" does not refer to an assumption regarding the flow of goods, but rather to an assumption regarding the flow of costs. The advocates of the method maintain that during periods of changing costs and prices, more meaningful income statements are produced if "current" costs are applied to current sales, thus achieving a better matching of costs and revenues. To illustrate the point by a simple, and rather arbitrary, example, let us assume that a company sells one unit of a commodity each year. At the beginning of the first year it bought one unit for $1 and marked it to sell for $1.50, as a gross margin of $.50 was considered necessary to cover expenses and leave the desired profit. Before any sale was made, the company purchased another unit for $1.05, and raised the selling price to $1.55. It then sold one unit for $1.55.

By the *fifo* method the gross profit would be computed thus:

Sale..	$1.55
Cost of unit sold..	1.00
Gross profit...	$ .55

And the inventory would be priced at a cost of $1.05.

By the *lifo* method the gross profit would be computed thus:

Sale..	$1.55
Current cost..	1.05
Gross profit...	$ .50

And the inventory would be priced at a cost of $1.00.

The purchase and sale operations for a period of eight years are tabulated below; the period embraces a cycle in which costs went from $1.00 to $1.50 and back to $1. The goods were always sold at a price $.50 above the cost of the most recent purchase. The tabulation also shows the gross profit on the *fifo* and *lifo* bases. (The costs applied against the sales are indicated by letters in the "Purchases" and "Gross Profit" columns.)

				GROSS PROFIT		
Year	Purchases		Sales	*Fifo* Basis		*Lifo* Basis
1	A	$1.00				
	B	1.05	$1.55	A	$0.55	B $0.50
2	C	1.15	1.65	B	0.60	C 0.50
3	D	1.30	1.80	C	0.65	D 0.50
4	E	1.50	2.00	D	0.70	E 0.50
5	F	1.30	1.80	E	0.30	F 0.50
6	G	1.15	1.65	F	0.35	G 0.50
7	H	1.05	1.55	G	0.40	H 0.50
8	I	1.00	1.50	H	0.45	I 0.50
					$4.00	$4.00

The aggregate gross profits for the eight years were the same in this instance because the first and the last purchase costs were the same.

It will be observed that the *fifo* method resulted in the showing of widely fluctuating gross profits although the company continually adjusted its selling prices to keep them closely related to current purchase costs. The advocates of the *lifo* method would say that it is unrealistic, when the quantity of yearly sales is uniform and sales prices are adjusted in conformity with cost changes, to show annual gross profits varying as widely as 70 and 30. The opponents of the *lifo* method would say that it is unrealistic to price a commodity in the inventory, for balance sheet purposes, at a remote cost not representative of current costs.

Another reason advanced in support of the *lifo* method is that, on a rising market, a portion of the net income shown under the *fifo* method is necessarily plowed back into the inventory, and, although such net income amounts are legally available for dividends, it may be inexpedient, from the working capital standpoint, to distribute them. The *lifo* method tends to keep out of the stated net income any amounts which are not realized in the sense of being represented by a net increase in current assets other than merchandise. To make this point clear, let us refer to the foregoing illustration and assume that the company whose purchases and sales are stated there began its life with the balance sheet shown below.

Cash......................	$5.00	Capital stock	$5.00

After the first purchase, its balance sheet appears as follows:

Cash......................	$4.00	Capital stock.............	$5.00
Inventory.................	1.00		
	$5.00		$5.00

By the end of the fourth year, the company has made additional purchases totalling $5 and sales totalling $7. Assume, to simplify the case, that it has incurred no expenses and paid no dividends; therefore, its cash has increased $2, and it has a cash balance of $6. Under the *fifo* method its net income for the four years will amount to $2.50, and its balance sheet will be as follows:

Cash......................	$6.00	Capital stock..............	$5.00
Inventory.................	1.50	Retained earnings..........	2.50
	$7.50		$7.50

If cash in the amount of the entire retained earnings is now distributed as a dividend, the balance sheet will be:

Cash......................	$3.50	Capital stock.............	$5.00
Inventory.................	1.50		
	$5.00		$5.00

After the first purchase, the company had one unit in its inventory and $4 in cash; it now has one unit of inventory and $3.50 in cash. It is not inconceivable that the continuance of such a procedure might result in leaving the company with inadequate cash to carry on successful operations. Of course, the company could limit its dividends to $2, but are not the stockholders perhaps justified in feeling that there is something deficient or peculiar in a situation where reported earnings cannot be distributed without risking the impairment of working funds?

Under the *lifo* method, the earnings for the four years are shown at $2, the inventory is valued at $1, and the balance sheet appears as follows:

Cash	$6.00	Capital stock	$5.00
Inventory	1.00	Retained earnings	2.00
	$7.00		$7.00

The company can now pay out its entire stated earnings and be in the same asset position as it was after the first purchase—with one unit of merchandise and $4 in cash.

Income which is deferred under the *lifo* method during a period of rising merchandise costs is taken into earnings during any subsequent period of declining costs. For instance, observe the data for the fifth year. The gross profit for that year under the *fifo* method is $.30 and the gross profit under the *lifo* method is $.50; the $.20 difference is equal to the decrease from $1.50 to $1.30 in the unit cost of merchandise, or the decrease in the dollar investment in merchandise. Thus, it may be said that, under the *lifo* method, the portion of the sales proceeds which is plowed back into the inventory during a period of rising costs is not taken into income until it is released from the inventory in a period of declining costs.

Unsettled *lifo* problems. The argument between *lifo* and *fifo* seems to boil down to a question of whether current costs should be regarded as applicable to the inventory to be shown in the balance sheet (*fifo* method) or be matched against current revenue in the income statement (*lifo* method).

The *lifo* method places the emphasis on the income statement, but its effect on the balance sheet, and particularly on the working capital shown therein, should not be overlooked.

If a sustained price rise follows an adoption of the *lifo* method, the dollar balance reported for inventories among the current assets will be substantially less than current costs. Although the *lifo* advocates contend that achieving a more appropriate matching of costs against revenues is such an important objective that it offsets the "incorrect" balance sheet results, the fact remains that, conceivably, inventory quantities might eventually be priced at such "old" costs as to produce a misstatement of working capital position that would be seriously misleading. To some extent, this could be remedied by disclosing current costs for the inventory parenthetically or in a footnote to the balance sheet. This proposal is resisted in some quarters because of the clerical burden it would impose in computing the inventory on two bases. It would be possible to avoid this burden by permitting the use of estimates for purposes of parenthetical disclosure of current costs for the inventory.

In discussions of *lifo*, there seems to be a tacit assumption that a company will adopt the *lifo* method when prices are relatively low though rising. But suppose a company adopts *lifo* when the price level is not at a low point. Under these conditions, it is conceivable that subsequent price declines might bring the replacement costs below the cost level prevailing at the time the company adopted the *lifo* method. In this event, should the *lifo* costs be used for inventory pricing, or should those costs be reduced to coincide with the newer and lower replacement costs? A strict application of the *lifo* method would preclude such a reduction because the matching of current costs against current revenues would thereby be disturbed. However, there is reason to expect that, as with all so-called cost bases of inventory pricing, accountants would sanction a reduction in *lifo* costs where it was apparent that the valuation of a current asset would otherwise be overstated.

A disturbing problem arises whenever a company using the *lifo* method fails, for some reason, to maintain its usual inventory position. If the inventory quantity is drawn down after a significant price rise, a strict application of the *lifo* method would result in matching some old, low costs against current revenues produced by selling goods at current prices. To illustrate, let us assume the following conditions:

Inventory, January 1—1,000 units priced on the *lifo* basis at
$100 each. . . . . $ 100,000
Purchases during the year—10,000 units at an average cost
of $150 each.   1,500,000
Sales during the year—10,300 units at an average selling price
of $175 each.   1,802,500
Inventory, December 31—700 units priced on the *lifo* basis
at $100 each.   70,000

We here face a situation in which current revenues may be charged with some current costs and with some old costs, as shown on the following page.

Sales—10,300 units.................................. ...... $1,802,500
Cost of sales:
  10,000 units at current costs—$150 each....... $1,500,000
     300 units at old costs   —$100 each.......   30,000 1,530,000
Gross profit... $ 272,500

This partial matching of old costs against current revenue
would cause some distortion in the net income of the period in
which the inventory reduction occurred, because current revenue
would not be entirely matched with current costs. Moreover, if
the inventory reduction was only temporary and the inventory
was replenished in the near future at current costs, a comparison
of the replenished inventory with the prior inventory might create
a misleading impression, for an equal inventory quantity would be
set forth in the accounts at a higher dollar figure—15% higher in
the illustration being developed here. This is demonstrated by
the following computation, based on the assumption that the
inventory was replenished by the purchase of 300 units at $150
each.

Inventory before temporary reduction:
  1,000 units at $100 each.................................. $100,000
Inventory after replenishment:
  700 units at $100 each..................... .... $70,000
  300 units at $150 each........................... 45,000 115,000

In some instances an inventory reduction, or "liquidation,"
may be involuntary, resulting from such uncontrollable causes as
shortage of supply or delivery delays due to strikes. In other
instances, the quantity reduction may be voluntary, management
expecting more favorable purchase prices in the near future. In
either case, the inventory quantity impairment could very likely
be temporary; and it would seem to be regrettable if income statement and balance sheet distortions were to result from the mere
fact that inventory quantities happened to be temporarily low at
the end of the accounting period.

Adherents of *lifo* accounting, concentrating on the fundamental
objective of matching current costs with current revenues, advocate dealing with such a situation by charging Cost of Sales with
current costs, even though some of the goods sold were carried in
the accounts at old, lower costs. Referring to the preceding illustration, they would make an entry similar to the following:

Cost of goods sold (10,300 units at $150 each)...... 1,545,000
  Inventory (to reduce balance in this account to
    lifo cost of 700 units at $100 each)............   30,000
  Excess of replacement cost over *lifo* cost of basic
    inventory temporarily liquidated ($50 × 300)..   15,000
  Purchases................................... .   1,500,000

When the inventory was replenished by the purchase of 300 units, at the current price of $150 per unit, the entry would be:

```
Inventory (300 units at $100—lifo cost)................... 30,000
Excess of replacement cost over lifo cost of basic inventory
  temporarily liquidated................................... 15,000
  Cash.............................................             45,000
```

The income statement would then show the following:

```
Sales—10,300 units.......................................... $1,802,500
Cost of goods sold—10,300 units at current cost of $150 each..  1,545,000
Gross profit...............................................  $  257,500
```

The consequences of making entries of the nature indicated above can be shown by a comparison of the results produced without making the foregoing entries and the results obtained by making the entries:

	Without Suggested Entries	With Suggested Entries
Sales.......................................	$1,802,500	$1,802,500
Cost of goods sold.........................	1,530,000	1,545,000
Gross profit...............................	$ 272,500	$ 257,500
Inventory before replenishment.............	$ 70,000	$ 70,000
Excess replacement cost reserve............		15,000
Inventory after replenishment..............	115,000	100,000

The account Excess of Replacement Cost Over *Lifo* Cost of Basic Inventory Temporarily Liquidated would be shown in the balance sheet among the current liabilities.

Adopting *lifo*. If a company changes its inventory pricing method, the resulting effect on net income should be computed and disclosed in the financial statements for the year in which the change was made. This requirement makes it necessary to compute the ending inventory by both the old method and the new method. Thus, if a company decides to abandon *fifo* and adopt *lifo* as of December 31, 1959, it will be necessary to calculate the December 31, 1959 inventory by both the *fifo* and *lifo* methods.

Having made the decision to adopt *lifo* as of December 31, 1959, how are *lifo* costs computed? An acceptable method is to refer to the beginning inventory (December 31, 1958) for this information. The cost figures used there are assumed to be the appropriate costs to apply in pricing the ending inventory quantities not in excess of the December 31, 1958 inventory quantity. For reasons of expediency, the December 31, 1958 inventory cost figures are averaged in order to arrive at uniform unit-cost data. For example, assume the facts shown on the following page in connection with an abandonment of first-in, first-out and the adoption of the last-in, first-out inventory method.

December, 31, 1958 inventory (fifo):

Article	Quantity	Inventory Price	Total	Average Unit Costs
A	1,000	$ 9	$ 9,000	
	500	10	5,000	
	500	12	6,000	
Total—A..................	2,000		$20,000	$10
B	800	24	$19,200	
	400	27	10,800	
Total—B.................	1,200		$30,000	25
Total................			$50,000	

1959 purchases:

	Quantity		Cost		
	A	B	A	B	Total
February 1..........................	1,000		$11		$ 11,000
March 1..........................		600		$28	16,800
June 15..............................	4,000		12		48,000
August 20...........................		1,500		29	43,500
November 25..........................	1,500		13		19,500
December 10..........................		1,200		30	36,000
Total purchases....................					$174,800

December 31, 1959 inventory:

Quantity: 2,100 units of A
1,100 units of B

Pricing on Last-In, First-Out Basis

Article	Explanation	Quantity	Inventory Price	Total
A	*Lifo* base quantity at established *lifo* cost..........................	2,000	$10	$20,000
	From February 1 purchase.........	100	11	1,100
	Total—A....................	2,100		$21,100
B	*Lifo* base quantity is not exceeded, so entire December 31, 1959 quantity is priced at established *lifo* cost	1,100	25	27,500
	Total..........................			$48,600

Pricing on First-In, First-Out Basis

Article	Explanation	Quantity	Inventory Price	Total
A	From November 25 purchase.......	1,500	$13	$19,500
	From June 15 purchase............	600	12	7,200
	Total—A....................	2,100		$26,700
B	From December 10 purchase.......	1,100	30	33,000
	Total.......................			$59,700

Computation of effect of change in inventory method on 1959 net income before income taxes:

Inventory, December 31, 1959, first-in, first-out................	$59,700
Inventory, December 31, 1959, last-in, first-out.................	48,600
Net effect—decrease in net income before income taxes........	$11,100

The effect on net income (either before or after income taxes) produced by a change in inventory method is generally disclosed by a footnote to the financial statements.

Lifo layers.　　The technique of inventory valuation on the *lifo* basis can perhaps be best indicated by a graphic presentation of inventory layers at successive dates, as shown on page 276.

We shall assume that the *lifo* method was adopted on December 31, 1955, at which time the inventory consisted of 1,000 units at a *lifo* cost of $10 per unit.

On December 31, 1956, the inventory consisted of 1,800 units: the 1955 base of 1,000 units, and the 1956 incremental layer of 800 units priced at 1956 costs.

On December 31, 1957, there were 2,400 units in the inventory, consisting of the 1955 base, the 1956 layer, and a 600-unit layer priced at 1957 *lifo* cost.

On December 31, 1958, the inventory had decreased. On the last-in, first-out basis, the decrease came out of the 1957 layer, reducing that layer to 300 units.

On December 31, 1959, the inventory had further decreased. The 1957 layer was gone, and only 500 units of the 1956 layer remained.

On December 31, 1960, the inventory had again decreased, and consisted only of 900 units of the 1955 base.

On December 31, 1961, the inventory had increased 2,000 units. This 2,000-unit increment must be regarded as a new layer, to be priced at 1961 *lifo* cost.

How to price lifo layers.　　Three alternatives are acceptable in pricing an incremental layer. The following data are used to illustrate the application of the alternatives.

Current year's purchases:

Date	Quantity	Cost	Total
January 10......	250	$ 9	$2,250
May 15..	300	10	3,000
September 20................................	100	13	1,300
December 27................................	200	14	2,800
Total......................................	850		$9,350

Average cost—$9,350 ÷ 850 = $11.
Current year's inventory increase (layer)—300 units.

Alternatives:

(1) The incremental quantity is assumed to relate to the first acquisitions of the current year.

> Amount to be used in computing new layer of *lifo* inventory:
> 250 × $ 9 = $2,250
> 50 × $10 = 　500
> *Lifo* cost 　$2,750

2,000 units at $15	900 units at $10
1961 Layer	1955 Base

1961

900 units at $10
1955 Base

1960

500 units at $11	1,000 units at $10
1956 Layer	1955 Base

1959

300 units at $12	800 units at $11	1,000 units at $10
1957 Layer	1956 Layer	1955 Base

1958

600 units at $12	800 units at $11	1,000 units at $10
1057 Layer	1956 Layer	1955 Base

1957

800 units at $11	1,000 units at $10
1956 Layer	1955 Base

1956

1,000 units at $10
1955 Base

1955

Inventory Layers and *Lifo* Costs at Ends of Stated Years

(2) Average costs for the current year may be used.

> Amount to be used in computing new layer of *lifo* inventory:
> 300 × $11 = $3,300

(3) The incremental quantity is assumed to relate to the last acquisitions of the current year.

> Amount to be used in computing new layer of *lifo* inventory:
> 200 × $14 = $2,800
> 100 × $13 =   1,300
> *Lifo* cost $4,100

Alternative (1) seems to be the most logical, since it follows the last-in, first-out assumption. However, all three alternatives are acceptable for federal income tax purposes; as a result, all three methods are used in practice.

Once the aggregate dollar amount for any given layer has been determined, it remains unchanged until all or some portion of the layer is sold or utilized.

Dollar-value *lifo*. In the preceding illustration showing how the base inventory and subsequent layers are separated in *lifo* inventory accounting, quantity on hand was the basis used to determine the increments or reductions in the *lifo* inventory. This requires considerable clerical detail, since increments and reductions must be determined for each item in the inventory. Thus, if a business stocks 100 different articles, a record of base and layer quantities must be maintained for each article. To avoid this handicap, dollars may be used as a measure of increments or reductions in a *lifo* inventory.

For example, assuming no change in the price level during the current year, if last year's inventory was $1,000 (at cost) and this year's inventory was $1,100 (at cost), it can be inferred that the inventory has increased 10%. Under *lifo* this would mean that we have an additional layer to deal with. In a sense, this approach views an inventory as a pool or aggregate, in contrast to an item-by-item approach. In practice, the inventory would likely be divided by broad product categories or by departments, with separate *lifo* bases and layers for each grouping.

Of course, the price level changes. So, before we can compare the dollar amount of a current inventory with the dollar amount of a previous inventory to determine whether there has been an increase or decrease, the two inventories being compared must be stated in dollars "of the same size." This could be done by the use of index numbers which measure the extent of changes in the price level. For instance, if it were known that the prices of goods purchased for resale had increased 10% during the current year, an inventory of $11,550, priced by using the current year's costs, could be converted to last year's price level by dividing by 1.10; thus, $11,550 ÷ 1.10 = $10,500.

If last year's inventory amounted to $10,000, the comparison between the $10,500 amount and the $10,000 amount would indicate that the inventory had increased 5%, or by $500 in terms of last year's prices. For purposes of determining the *lifo* inventory, this layer should be stated in terms of the current year's price level, or $550, which is computed by multiplying $500 by 1.10.

Since price index numbers are not available for many industries or lines of business, some alternative device for measuring price change as it affects the inventory of a particular business must be applied. The approach used is to compute an inventory first in terms of current costs and second in terms of the costs prevailing when *lifo* was adopted.

For example, if the current inventory amounts to $110,000 at current costs and to $100,000 in terms of costs prevailing when the *lifo* method was adopted (see below), it can be concluded that as far as this company is concerned, prices of inventory items have gone up 10%.

Inventory

| | | Unit Costs | | Total | |
| | Current Quantity | Current Period | Prevailing When *Lifo* Was Adopted | At Current Costs | At Costs Prevailing When *Lifo* Was Adopted |
Description					
A	80	$3.00	$2.75	$ 240	$ 220
B	100	2.45	2.25	245	225
C	200	5.50	5.00	1,100	1,000
				$110,000	$100,000

In the above paragraph it was stated that each inventory is computed twice—once using current year's costs and again using costs prevailing when the *lifo* method was adopted. It should be pointed out that only a representative sample of the inventory need be thus double-priced, since the purpose of the extra computation is to obtain an index or measure of price change. It should also be mentioned that, as a practical matter, some provision must be made for the effects of discontinued and new products in developing a measure of price change.

The basic techniques of dollar-value *lifo* are illustrated on the following page. Zero is used to designate the year when *lifo* was adopted.

	Inventory of Year			
	0	1	2	3
Priced by using costs of year 0.......	$10,000			
Priced by using costs of year 1.......		$10,710		
Priced by using costs of year 2.......			$11,340	
Priced by using costs of year 3.......				$11,880
Priced by using costs of year 0.......	$10,000	$10,500	$10,800	$10,800

Index of price change since year 0, when
　lifo was adopted:
　　$10,710 ÷ $10,500..............　　　　　102
　　$11,340 ÷ $10,800..............　　　　　　　　　105
　　$11,880 ÷ $10,800..............　　　　　　　　　　　　110

Inventory—*lifo* cost:
　Year 0..................... .... $10,000
　Year 1:
　　By comparing the year 1 inventory with the year 0 inventory, both stated in dollars of the same price level (year 0), it is apparent that there has been an increment to the inventory. This layer amounts to $500 ($10,500 − $10,000) in terms of the price level at year 0. But a new layer must be computed in terms of the current price level, or $500 × 1.02.
　　　Year 1 layer...................................... $ 510
　　　Base... 10,000
　　　Inventory—*lifo* cost............................... $10,510
　Year 2:
　　By comparing year 2 and year 1 inventories, both stated in dollars of the same price level (year 0), it is apparent that there has been a further increment to the *lifo* inventory. The year 2 layer amounts to $300 ($10,800 − $10,500) in terms of the price level when *lifo* was adopted. To convert to the year 2 price level, the $300 is multiplied by 1.05.
　　　Year 2 layer ($300 × 1.05).......................... $ 315
　　　Year 1 layer...................................... 510
　　　Base.. 10,000
　　　Inventory—*lifo* cost............................... $10,825
　Year 3:
　　By comparing year 3 and year 2 inventories, both stated in dollars of the same price level (year 0), it is apparent that there has been no change in the aggregate inventory ($10,800 − $10,800). Therefore, the *lifo* inventory for year 3 is the same as for year 2.
　　　Inventory—*lifo* cost............................... $10,825

Inventory reductions. Reductions in *lifo* inventories are subtracted first from the most recent layer (or layers, depending on the extent of the reduction), and, after all layers have been utilized, then from the base inventory. To show how a reduction is handled under dollar-value *lifo*, continue the illustration for an additional year and assume that the inventory for year 4 is as follows:

　Priced using costs of year 4................................. $11,770
　Priced using costs of year 0................................. $10,700

By comparing year 4 and year 3 inventories, both stated in dollars of the same price level (year 0), it is apparent that there has been a reduction of $100 ($10,800 − $10,700). This reduction is taken from the year 2 layer, as follows:

end inv

↑ *lt*

c/c/s

Year 2 layer stated in terms of year 0 prices..........	$300
Reduction occurring during year 4.......................	100
Remaining layer..	$200
Price index for year 2.................................	1.05
Remainder of year 2 layer in terms of *lifo* cost.............	$210

Inventory—*lifo* cost:
Year 4:

Year 2 layer..	$	210
Year 1 layer..		510
Base...		10,000
Inventory—*lifo* cost...................................		$10,720

Big Trouble if used

Effect of *lifo* on the gross profit method. If a company is using the *lifo* inventory method, the gross profit method for approximating an ending inventory in terms of *lifo* costs can be used only with extreme caution. This situation is attributable to the fact that typically the relation of *lifo* inventory costs to selling prices is considerably at variance with the relation of recent purchase prices to selling prices. Suppose that a company establishes a pricing policy of selling, for $10 each, articles that currently cost $6 to acquire at wholesale. If the company has been on a *lifo* basis for a considerable period of time, the articles might conceivably be carried in the beginning inventory at $3 each. If it should develop in any given year that more items were sold than were purchased, the resulting net reduction in the inventory would produce a distortion in the actual gross profit margin, because some of the goods sold would have been assigned to cost of sales at $3 each, thus inflating the gross profit margin.

For example, assume the following case, where goods are sold for $10 each and the gross profit rate for several preceding periods was 40%:

Sales, at $10 each, 6,000 units...............................		$60,000
Cost of goods sold:		
Inventory, January 1, 2,000 units at $3 each.........	$ 6,000	
Purchases for the year at $6 each, 5,000 units........	30,000	
Total...	$36,000	
Inventory, December 31, 1,000 units at $3 each......	3,000	33,000
Gross profit on sales.......................................		$27,000

The gross profit rate indicated by the above is 45%. If this distorted gross profit per cent were used in the following period to estimate the inventory by the gross profit method, the results would be unreliable. To illustrate, assume that 5,000 units were

sold during the following year, and that sufficient units were purchased to cover the quantity sold. An estimate of the ending inventory by the gross profit method would indicate an inventory of
$5,500, while in fact the inventory would be $3,000, an error
of 83⅓%.

Inventory, January 1, 1,000 units at $3 each....................		$ 3,000
Purchases for the year at $6 each, 5,000 units..................		30,000
Total...		$33,000
Deduct approximate cost of goods sold:		
Sales, at $10 each, 5,000 units......................	$50,000	
Less estimated gross profit of 45%..................	22,500	27,500
Approximate inventory, December 31........................		$ 5,500

Under *lifo* procedures, the ending inventory would be priced as
follows:

Inventory, December 31, 1,000 units (see computation below) at $3 each...	$3,000

Computation of Inventory Quantity

	Units
Inventory, January 1..	1,000
Purchases for the year.......................................	5,000
Total..	6,000
Sales..	5,000
Inventory, December 31......................................	1,000

Incidentally, the accountant should realize that with the *lifo*
method management can intentionally distort gross profit and
net income by deliberately curtailing purchases and thereby
"dipping into" the *lifo* base quantity.

Lifo and the retail method. When an accountant applies
the *lifo* concept to the retail method, he must use procedures which
are somewhat different from those used under the conventional
retail method.

As previously stated, the conventional retail method produces
an inventory valuation which closely approximates the amount
which would be obtained by taking a physical inventory and pricing the goods at the lower of cost or market.

Lifo, on the other hand, is a cost method. It is possible to modify
the retail method to produce results reasonably conforming to a
cost basis by *including mark-downs* as well as mark-ups in the
determination of the cost ratio.

The contrasting procedures under the conventional retail
method (intended to produce an inventory valuation on the basis
of the lower of cost or market) and under the *lifo* method (intended to produce an inventory valuation on a cost basis) are
illustrated on page 282.

	Conventional Retail		*Lifo* Retail	
	Cost	Retail	Cost	Retail
Purchases...........................	$72,000	$ 95,000	$72,000	$ 95,000
Mark-ups............................		5,000		5,000
Total..............................		$100,000		$100,000
Ratio ignoring mark-downs: $72,000 ÷ $100,000..........	(72%)			
Mark-downs.........................		4,000		4,000
Remainder..........................		$ 96,000		$ 96,000
Ratio including mark-downs: $72,000 ÷ $96,000...........			(75%)	
Sales..............................		80,000		80,000
Inventory at retail.................		$ 16,000		$ 16,000
Applicable ratio...................		72%		75%
Inventory valuation................		$ 11,520		$ 12,000

Changing from conventional to *lifo* retail. If a conventional retail procedure has been in operation and it is decided to change to a *lifo* procedure, the inventory as of the date of the change must be restated on the *lifo* basis. This is done by the use of a cost ratio for the immediately preceding period determined by giving recognition to mark-downs as well as to mark-ups. For instance, refer to the above illustration and assume that the company had been operating on the conventional retail basis, that the data given were for the year ended December 31, 1959, that the company used the inventory valuation of $11,520 in closing its books at the end of 1959, and that it decided to change to the *lifo* retail method as of the beginning of 1960; the December 31, 1959 inventory should be recomputed by applying the 75% cost ratio to the $16,000 inventory at retail; the inventory would be restated at $12,000. The adjustment resulting from the change in inventory method may be disclosed in the 1960 income statement or statement of retained earnings.

In the foregoing illustration it was assumed that there was no inventory at the beginning of 1959. Let us now assume that the following data for 1959 are applicable to a company which has been on a conventional retail basis for several years.

	Cost	Retail
Inventory—beginning of 1959.....................	$ 77,040	$120,000
Purchases..	498,960	640,000
Mark-ups...		40,000
Total...	$576,000	$800,000
(Cost ratio: $576 ÷ $800 = 72%)		
Mark-downs......................................		32,000
Remainder.......................................		$768,000
Sales...		650,000
Inventory at retail.............................		$118,000
Multiply by cost ratio..........................		72%
Inventory used in closing the books at the end of 1959..		$ 84,960

The company proposes to change to the *lifo* retail method at the beginning of 1960.

It might seem that the ratio to be used in computing the inventory valuation at *lifo* retail at the end of 1959 should be determined as follows:

$$\$576,000 \div \$768,000 = 75\%,$$

and that the inventory valuation at the beginning of *lifo* retail would be:

$$75\% \text{ of } \$118,000 = \$88,500.$$

But we must remember that, since *lifo* is a cost method, we are trying to determine a ratio representative of cost; and we must also remember that the inventory at the beginning of 1959 was determined by the conventional retail method and presumably is stated at the lower of cost or market. Therefore, if we were to include the opening inventory in the determination of the ratio, the ratio would not be truly indicative of cost because it would be affected by any reduction of the December 31, 1958 inventory from cost to market. Therefore, it is considered preferable to compute the cost ratio by ignoring the opening inventory, as illustrated below.

	Cost	Retail
Purchases	$498,960	$640,000
Mark-ups		40,000
Total		$680,000
Mark-downs		32,000
Remainder		$648,000

Cost ratio: $498,960 ÷ $648,000 = 77%.

Valuation of December 31, 1959 inventory for use as beginning inventory under the *lifo* method if adopted in 1960:
$$77\% \text{ of } \$118,000 = \$90,860.$$

It will be noted that the mark-ups and mark-downs were applied, in the foregoing computation, to the selling price of the goods purchased, although they presumably applied in part to the opening inventory. Obviously, this is not strictly correct; however, the slight theoretical impropriety usually is ignored.

The practice of disregarding the beginning inventory when computing the cost ratio is a feature of the *lifo* retail method and, therefore, is followed in all subsequent years and not confined merely to the computation of the base or beginning *lifo* inventory.

Subsequent inventories—no changes in the price level. The basic operational features of *lifo* are not affected by the retail-method application. Distinctions must be maintained between the base inventory and any subsequent layers or increments to the inventory. The cost ratio of a particular period is used only to convert the layer of that period to cost. If there is no increase in the inventory in a given year, the cost ratio of that year is not used in converting the inventory from retail to cost.

The following schedule, covering a period from year 0 (when *lifo* was adopted) through year 6, illustrates the application of *lifo* procedures to the retail inventory method.

Year	Cost Ratio For Year	Inventory at Retail	Base-Period Inventory at Retail	Increments at Retail (Reference to Year)	Applicable Cost Ratio	Lifo Cost Layers	Lifo Cost Base	Inventory Total
0	66⅔%	$ 6,000	$6,000		66⅔%		$4,000	$4,000
1	70	8,000	6,000	$2,000 (1)	70	$1,400	4,000	5,400
2	75	9,000	6,000	2,000 (1)	70	1,400		
				1,000 (2)	75	750	4,000	6,150
3	80	12,000	6,000	2,000 (1)	70	1,400		
				1,000 (2)	75	750		
				3,000 (3)	80	2,400	4,000	8,550
4	78	10,000	6,000	2,000 (1)	70	1,400		
				1,000 (2)	75	750		
				1,000 (3)	80	800	4,000	6,950
5	73	7,000	6,000	1,000 (1)	70	700	4,000	4,700
6	69	4,800	6,000					
			1,200*					
			4,800		66⅔		3,200	3,200

* Reduction of base.

Since the inventory at retail is now smaller than the inventory at retail when the *lifo* method was established, the 66⅔% cost ratio prevailing at that time is applicable, and the inventory at the end of the sixth period is stated at a *lifo* cost of 66⅔% of $4,800, or $3,200.

Subsequent inventories—changes in the level of selling prices. In the preceding illustration it was assumed that the level of retail selling prices remained unchanged during the entire period. When retail prices are not stable, it is necessary to make use of retail price indices to adjust the inventory to a retail valuation which would have been shown by the retail records if there had been no change in selling prices.

To illustrate, assume that the retail records of a store showed the following:

	Cost	Retail	Cost Ratio
Inventory, December 31, 1959	$ 3,000	$ 6,000	
Purchases	21,000	28,000	75%
Total		$34,000	
Sales		24,100	
Inventory at retail, December 31, 1960		$ 9,900	

Assume, also, that the retail index applicable to this business was 100 for 1959, and 110 for 1960.

We first reduce the December 31, 1960 inventory at retail to the basis of 1959 selling prices:

$9,900 ÷ 1.10...	$9,000
And then deduct the December 31, 1959 inventory at retail.......	6,000
To determine the inventory increment in terms of 1959 selling prices	$3,000
The inventory increment in terms of 1960 selling prices was $3,000 × 1.10, or..	$3,300

The December 31, 1960 inventory priced at $9,900 retail can now be reduced to *lifo* cost as follows:

	Lifo Cost	Retail
Segment equal to preceding inventory:		
On 1959 price basis.................................		$6,000
Old cost..	$3,000	
Price inflation.....................................		600
Incremental segment:		
At retail...		3,300
At *lifo* cost—determined by applying the cost ratio of the period—75% of $3,300........................	2,475	
Total...	$5,475	$9,900

Extended illustration. The *AB* Store adopts the retail inventory method and *lifo* in 1959. Its December 31, 1958 inventory was $80,000 at cost and $130,000 at retail. Inventory computations at three subsequent dates are shown below. Applicable index numbers were as follows: 1958, 100; 1959, 104; 1960, 110; 1961, 105.

	Cost	Retail	Cost Ratio
Data for 1959:			
Inventory—beginning of year..................	$ 80,000	$130,000	
Purchases...................................	240,000	400,000	60%
Total.......................................		$530,000	
Sales.......................................		389,600	
Inventory—end of year......................		$140,400	
Reduction to *lifo* cost:			
1959 inventory in terms of 1958 prices—			
$140,400 ÷ 1.04.........................		$135,000	
1958 inventory (base)......................	$ 80,000	130,000	
Increment in inventory:			
In terms of 1958 prices...................		$ 5,000	
In terms of 1959 prices—$5,000 × 1.04.....		$ 5,200	
At *lifo* cost—60% of $5,200..............	3,120		
1959 inventory at *lifo* cost..................	$ 83,120		
Data for 1960:			
Inventory—beginning of year..................	$ 83,120	$140,400	
Purchases...................................	260,400	420,000	62%
Total.......................................		$560,400	
Sales.......................................		408,600	
Inventory—end of year......................		$151,800	

	Cost	Retail	Cost Ratio
Reduction to *lifo* cost:			
1960 inventory in terms of 1958 prices—			
$151,800 ÷ 1.10...........................		$138,000	
1958 inventory (base)......................	$ 80,000	130,000	
Increment over 1958 inventory..............		$ 8,000	
Portion of increment arising in 1959 (see above)..................................	3,120	5,000	
Portion of increment arising in 1960:			
In terms of 1958 prices..................		$ 3,000	
In terms of 1960 prices—$3,000 × 1.10...		$ 3,300	
At *lifo* cost—62% of $3,300.............	2,046		
1960 inventory at *lifo* cost..................	$ 85,166		
Data for 1961:			
Inventory—beginning of year..................	$ 85,166	$151,800	
Purchases.................................	292,500	450,000	65%
Total.....................................		$601,800	
Sales.....................................		463,200	
Inventory—end of year.......................		$138,600	
Reduction to *lifo* cost:			
1961 inventory in terms of 1958 prices:			
$138,600 ÷ 1.05.........................		$132,000	
1958 inventory (base)......................	$ 80,000	130,000	
Increment over 1958 inventory—regarded under *lifo* theory as acquired in 1959:			
In terms of 1958 prices..................		$ 2,000	
In terms of 1959 prices—computed by using 1959 price index—$2,000 × 1.04..		$ 2,080	
At *lifo* cost—reduced by using 1959 cost ratio—60% of $2,080.................	1,248		
1961 inventory at *lifo* cost..................	$ 81,248		

"*Nifo.*" *Nifo* is an abbreviation for "next-in, first-out." Thus far, *nifo* has not attained a status of acceptability as an inventory-pricing method. As the expression indicates, under this approach cost of sales would be computed by using replacement costs. As a result, income would be measured by matching current revenues and the replacement costs of the goods sold.

The argument for *nifo* is founded on reasoning that can be summarized in the following manner. Assume that a merchant has on hand an article that cost $10. Suppose that it is sold for $15. If the merchant is going to continue in business, he must replace the article sold. Assume that the replacement cost is $12. Under these conditions, a proponent of *nifo* would argue that conventional accounting misstates gross profit by reporting it as $5 (since $2 of the $5 reported gross profit is needed to maintain the inventory), and that gross profit and net income would be more truthfully reported if the article sold were "costed" at the $12 replacement cost. The $3 gross profit thus reported under the *nifo* method would measure the real gain produced by the sale, because of the elimination of the "fictitious" profit element that would have to be used merely to maintain a normal inventory.

Base-stock method.　The base-stock (sometimes called "normal stock") method is founded on a theory which may be indicated as follows: If a company considers that its inventory of a certain commodity should never normally fall below 100 units, the 100 units are the base stock, and no increase in the market replacement cost of this base stock should be regarded as realized income because, like fixed assets, the base stock cannot be disposed of if the business is to continue operations. To avoid the taking of any profit on such "unrealized" market increases, the base-stock quantities should be priced for inventory purposes at not more than the lowest cost experienced. It should be noted that the base quantity is the minimum quantity a given business needs to carry on normal operations, not an average inventory quantity.

Units sold or issued for manufacture are priced out at the most recent acquisition cost; in this regard, the base-stock method is similar to the last-in, first-out method, since current costs are matched against current revenues. For this reason, the base-stock method (which was developed before the last-in, first-out method) is sometimes regarded as the precursor of the *lifo* method.

The operation of the base-stock method may be illustrated as follows:

	Units	Unit Price	Amount
First purchase (and base-stock quantity)........	100	$1.00	$100.00
Second purchase............................	200	1.10	220.00
Total......................................	300		$320.00
First sale..................................	175	1.10	192.50
Inventory..................................	125		$127.50
Third purchase.............................	250	1.20	300.00
Total......................................	375		$427.50
Second sale................................	275	1.20	330.00
Inventory..................................	100		$ 97.50
Fourth purchase............................	100	1.25	125.00
Total......................................	200		$222.50
Third sale.................................	50	1.25	62.50
Inventory..................................	150		$160.00

Perpetual Inv.

Observe that, after the second sale, and as a result of costing out 275 units at the most recent unit cost of $1.20, although only 250 units were purchased at so high a cost, the inventory of 100 units—the base quantity—is priced at less than the original base cost of $100.

The results disclosed above are those which would result from a perpetual inventory record. If valuations are determined by physical inventories, the pricing procedure usually adopted is as follows:

If quantities are in excess of base stock:

Base-stock quantities at base price.
Plus excess quantities at current cost.

For instance, if there are 150 units in the inventory, the valuation would be determined as follows:

100 units at $1.00...	$100.00
50 units at 1.25...	62.50
150...	$162.50

If quantities are less than base stock:

Base-stock quantities at base price.
Less deficient quantities at current cost.

For instance, if there are 95 units in the inventory, the valuation would be determined as follows:

100 units at $1.00...	$100.00
5 units at 1.25...	6.25
95...	$ 93.75

The above computations disclose the primary contrasting feature of the base-stock method and the *lifo* method. Under *lifo* procedures, if the ending-inventory quantity is less than the beginning-inventory quantity, the entire quantity is priced by using the *lifo* unit costs used in the beginning inventory. No use is made of current costs or costs applicable to recent purchases.

Since the base price should be the lowest cost experienced, a reduction of market costs below the originally adopted base price should result in the adoption of the new and lower cost as the base price.

The base-stock method is not in general use and is not acceptable for income tax purposes.

Under the base-stock method, the prices used are ordinarily lower—often substantially lower—than current market costs. As a consequence, the inventory shown in the balance sheet may be misleading. This is also typical of *lifo*. It would seem equally appropriate, as suggested in the case of *lifo*, to disclose by footnote the approximate difference between the amount shown and the valuation on a current-cost basis, or by stating parenthetically the inventory on a current-cost basis. Such disclosure is not required by present reporting standards.

CHAPTER FOURTEEN

Investments

Types of securities. The two principal classes of securities are stocks and bonds. There are so many varieties of each of these two classes that it is impossible to give a complete list of the various types; the following outline includes some of them.

(A) Stocks:
    (1) Common.
    (2) Preferred:
        (a) As to dividends.
            Cumulative or noncumulative.
            Participating or nonparticipating.
        (b) As to assets.

The characteristics of stocks are described in Chapter 5. ✓

(B) Bonds:
    (1) Classification as to nature of business or obligor:
        (a) Governments.
        (b) Municipals: cities and other governmental subdivisions.
        (c) Public utilities: gas and electric companies, city bus lines, and so forth.
        (d) Railroads.
        (e) Industrials: manufacturing and trading concerns.
        (f) Real estate: apartments, hotels, office buildings, and so forth.

(2) Classification as to nature of obligation:
   (a) Mortgage bonds.
   (b) Collateral trust bonds.
   (c) Guaranteed bonds.
   (d) Debenture bonds.
   (e) Income bonds.
   (f) Participating bonds.
   (g) Convertible bonds.
(3) Classification as to evidence of ownership and method of collecting interest:
   (a) Registered bonds.
   (b) Coupon bonds.

Mortgage bonds.   There are so many kinds of bonds, carrying so many different kinds of rights, that a general definition can be stated only in the broadest terms. A bond is a promise to pay the principal of and interest on a loan. It differs from a note in that it is more formal and is under seal. In corporate financing, notes are usually given for short-time loans, and bonds for long-time loans; this is a matter of expediency and is not a necessary characteristic of a note or a bond.

A mortgage is a transfer of title to property, usually made by a borrower to a lender, subject to the condition that, upon due payment of the debt, the title to the property is to revest in the borrower. Formerly, a mortgage was considered an actual, although conditional, conveyance of title to the property; if the debt was not paid, the title to the mortgaged property then vested in the mortgagee absolutely.

The modern theory of a mortgage is that it is primarily a security device. Although the mortgage deed does purport to convey to the mortgagee title to the pledged property, actually it serves only to create a lien on the property.

Mortgages may be used with either notes or bonds. If the borrower is able to find a person who is willing to loan the entire amount desired, the note and mortgage may be used; the note recites the terms of the obligation, and the mortgage serves as the security.

If it is necessary to borrow the money from a number of persons, the bond and trust deed are used. The bond issue creates a number of obligations, all of equal rank and all equally secured. However, since there are a number of lenders, since these lenders are not known when the bond issue is being arranged, and since the lenders will change with each transfer of a bond, a mortgage cannot name the lenders personally as the transferees of the pledged property. Therefore, a trust deed, rather than a mortgage deed, is used. Corporations, when borrowing funds on long-time bond issues, generally use the trust deed. By such a deed the corporation conveys the property to a third person, usually a bank or a trust company, as trustee. Upon final payment of the bonds by the corporation, the trustee executes and delivers to the corporation a release deed, whereby the lien on the corporate property created by the trust deed is removed. In the event of a default in payment of the bonds, the trustee may commence foreclosure proceedings for the benefit of the bondholders. It should be understood, therefore, that the issuance of bonds secured by a trust deed is, for all practical purposes, a mortgage transaction and is so considered by law.

Bonds may be secured by first, second, third, or even more mortgages. If the obligations are not met and foreclosure ensues, the proceeds of the property must go first to the satisfaction of the first-mortgage bondholders, any residue to the satisfaction of the second-mortgage bondholders, and so on. Bonds secured by prior liens are called *underlying bonds;* the others are called *junior bonds*.

The mere fact that a bond is called a *first-mortgage bond* does not necessarily mean that it has a lien prior to all others. To illustrate, assume that each of three companies, *A*, *B*, and *C*, has two mortgages on its property. A consolidation is effected by which the three companies are combined, and a new issue of bonds is marketed, secured by a mortgage on all of the property. This issue might be called *First Consolidated Bonds*, but it is really secured by a third mortgage. On the other hand, assume that first-, second-, and third-mortgage bonds have been issued, and that the first and second have been paid; the third-mortgage bonds really have a first lien on the pledged property.

b **Collateral trust bonds.** Collateral trust bonds are similar to collateral notes in that they are secured by pledged collateral. To illustrate, assume that a corporation holds stocks and bonds of several subsidiaries. The tangible property of the holding company and the subsidiaries may be mortgaged to the point where junior mortgage issues cannot be marketed; therefore, the holding company issues its own bonds and places the stocks and bonds of the subsidiaries in the hands of a trustee as collateral.

c **Guaranteed bonds.** A corporation obligates itself to pay the principal of and interest on its bonds, but it cannot guarantee to do so. If a guarantee is made, it must be made by a third party. Sometimes a holding company will guarantee the principal and interest of the bonds of its subsidiaries, and sometimes a company leasing the property of another company will guarantee the bonds of that company.

2d **Debenture bonds.** A debenture bond, or debenture, is merely an unsecured bond. It is similar to an unsecured note, in that it rests on the general credit of the debtor. It may or may not be a safe investment, depending upon the financial condition of the issuing company.

2e **Income bonds.** The peculiar feature of an income bond is that the payment of interest is conditional upon the earning of income. If the debtor company's income is not sufficient to pay the interest, there is no obligation to pay interest. The bond may be cumulative or noncumulative. If cumulative, any interest not paid in one year becomes a lien against future earnings; if noncumulative, any interest lost in one year is lost forever. The principal may or may not be secured.

Such bonds are sometimes used in reorganizations, in which a scaling down of interests results in security holders taking a less desirable form of security than the one formerly held.

2f **Participating bonds.** These are sometimes called "profit-sharing bonds" because, in addition to assuring the holder a definite rate of return regardless of operating results, they entitle him to participate with the stockholders in the earnings of the company. The participation may be pro rata or limited.

2g **Convertible bonds.** A convertible bond gives its holder the right to exchange the bond for some other security, usually common stock, of the issuing company. The bond stipulates the terms on which the transfer can be made: that is, par for par; or par for the bond, and book value for the stock; or par and accrued interest for the bond, and par and "accrued" dividends for the stock; or any other arrangement.

Such bonds give the holder a more assured income and secured principal during the development period of the issuing company than he might have as a stockholder, with a right to become a stockholder if the company is successful.

3a, b **Registered and coupon bonds.** Bonds may be divided into three general types, on the basis of registry:

(1) Registered both as to principal and as to interest.

The name of the owner of the bond is registered on the books of the issuing company or its fiscal agent, and interest is paid by check, drawn to the order of the bondholder. This method has the advantage of safeguarding the owner against loss or theft, because the transfer of a stolen bond could be accomplished only by a forgery. On the other hand, a sale and transfer can be made only by assignment and registry, instead of by delivery.

(2) Registered as to principal only.

If the bond is registered as to principal only, and coupons for the interest are attached, the owner is safeguarded against loss or theft of principal, while the debtor company is relieved of the burden of issuing interest checks.

(3) No registration.

Such a bond is transferable by delivery, without endorsement; interest is collected by clipping coupons and presenting them to a bank for deposit or collection.

General Matters Relative to Investments

Costs of investments. The cost of an investment includes brokerage, taxes, and other expenditures incident to acquisition. If securities are purchased through a broker on margin account, the books and the balance sheet should reflect as an asset the full cost of the securities and not merely the margin deposit, and the unpaid balance should be shown as a liability. Similarly, if securities are purchased on an installment contract, it is important to set up as an asset the full cost of the securities.

If two or more classes of securities are purchased for a single lump-sum payment, market values may be used for the purpose of apportioning the cost. For example, if 100 shares of common stock and 100 shares of preferred stock of a company are bought at a lump price at a time when the preferred stock has a market value of $105 per share and the common stock has a market value of $140 per share, the total purchase cost may be apportioned in the ratio of 105/245 to the preferred stock and 140/245 to the common stock. If only one of the classes of securities acquired has an ascertainable market value, the lump price may be apportioned by allocating the known market value to the one class of securities, and the remainder of the price to the securities with no ascertainable market value. If neither of the securities has a known market value, it may be necessary to postpone any apportionment of the purchase price until at least one market value can be established.

Exchanges: costs, gains, and losses. If, in accordance with the terms of issuance, securities of one class are convertible at the option of the holder into other securities of the same company, the entries for the conversion will depend upon whether a fair market value at the date of conversion is determinable for either class of securities. If no such market value is ascertainable, the securities received should be recorded at the cost or carrying value of the securities parted with.

If there is an ascertainable market value for one or the other class of securities, this market value should govern the entries to be made and the amount of gain or loss to be recorded. For example, if a company owns 100 shares of preferred stock of X Company which it acquired and is carrying at a cost of $100 per share, or a total of $10,000, and if this stock is exchanged for 100 shares of common stock of the same company with a market value of $125 per share, the entry for the conversion should be made as follows:

Investment in X Co. common stock	12,500	
Investment in X Co. preferred stock		10,000
Gain on conversion of X Co. stock		2,500
Conversion of preferred shares.		

If there is accrued interest on either class of securities at the date of conversion, the entry for the conversion should give recognition to the interest. For instance, assume that the security parted with in the foregoing illustration consisted of bonds of the X Company, that $300 of interest was accrued at the date of conversion, and that $200 of this interest had previously been recorded as accrued and taken into income. The entry for the conversion would be:

Investment in X Co. common stock	12,500	
Investment in X Co. bonds		10,000
Accrued interest receivable		200
Interest earned		100
Gain on conversion of X Co. securities		2,200
Conversion of bonds.		

In reorganizations and mergers in which the exchange of securities is not made at the option of the holder as the exercise of a privilege granted under the terms of issuance of the securities held, the entry for the exchange of the securities will depend primarily upon whether the holder remains in essentially the same position with respect to his equities after the exchange as before. If his status remains practically unchanged, the security received can be put on the books at the cost or carrying value of the security relinquished, and no gain or loss need be recognized. If, however, the holder's status is materially affected, by reason of a change in the number or nature of the securities held before and after the transaction, the newly acquired securities should be put on the books at their fair market value, and the difference between this value and the carrying value of the old securities should be recorded as a gain or loss.

Sales: costs, gains, and losses. If several purchases of the same security are made at different prices, a question may arise concerning the gain or loss on the sale of a portion of the holdings. To illustrate, assume that twenty shares of X Company stock were purchased at $100 per share; another twenty shares were subsequently purchased at $125; and ten shares were later sold at $110. Did the sale produce a gain of $10 per share (the difference between the selling price and the cost of the first shares purchased), or a loss of $15 per share (the difference between the selling price and the cost of the second shares purchased), or a loss of $2.50 per share (the difference between the selling price and the average cost)?

For tax purposes, average costs are not recognized. If the shares sold can be identified as pertaining to the first lot purchased, the transaction can be regarded as producing a gain of $10 per share. If they can be identified as belonging to the second lot purchased, a loss of $15 per share may be reported. If they cannot be identified as pertaining to either lot (which would be the case if the certificates for the two purchases had been converted into a single certificate for all of the shares), the shares sold should be regarded as pertaining to the first lot purchased.

This rule, which is obligatory for tax purposes, appears to be reasonable for general accounting purposes. However, average costs are also recognized from the standpoint of general accounting theory.

Valuation of securities. The rules for the valuation of securities in the accounts and on the balance sheet, and the methods of accounting for investments, depend to some extent on whether the investment is to be held for a short period or for a long period. The following classification reflects this distinction:

(1) Temporary investments:
    (a) Merchandise of a dealer in securities.
    (b) Speculative holdings.
    (c) Investments of surplus funds, forming part of the working capital. Such temporary investments are usually found in industries doing a seasonal business; the excess funds not needed during a slack period are invested temporarily to obtain the income.
    (d) Securities taken on account.

(2) Long-term investments:
    (a) Stock interests in subsidiaries.
    (b) Small holdings maintained for the purpose of establishing business connections.
    (c) Sinking funds and other funds.

Temporary investments. Investments may be classified as current assets if they are of a temporary nature, if it is the owner's intention to convert them into cash to meet cash requirements during the operating cycle, and if there is a ready market for them either on a securities exchange or elsewhere. The mere fact that a security is readily marketable is not sufficient justification for marshalling it among the current assets; the nature of the business of the owning company and the nature and purpose of the investment should be such as to make the current disposal of the security probable. Unless this rule is rigidly adhered to, there is a danger of overstating the working capital by including among current assets securities which, though having a ready market, are really long-term investments.

Since temporary investments in securities are current assets, they should be valued at the lower of cost or market for balance sheet purposes. It is not customary to apply the cost or market rule to investments by taking the lower value for each item; it is considered sufficient to determine the total valuation of the portfolio at cost and at market and to use the lower of these totals.

Investors cannot take losses from market declines as a tax deduction, but can take gains and losses only upon disposal, the gain or loss being the difference between cost and sales price; therefore, a record of the cost of the securities should be maintained, and any write-downs to market values are preferably made by credit to a contra account rather than to the asset account. The offsetting charge should be made against income.

Long-term investments. Minor declines in the market value of long-term investments in stocks or bonds need not be reflected by entries in the accounts; the market may recover before the investments are realized. But serious declines in the market values of long-term investments should be reflected in the accounts; the credit to record the decrease in valuation should be made in a contra account rather than in the asset account, so as to preserve a record of costs for tax purposes. For example, if a company owns securities which cost $100,000 and which have a market value of only $90,000, the journal entry to record the decrease in value should be:

CHG. TO INCOME

Market loss on securities....................................... 10,000
    Allowance to reduce securities to market.............   10,000
    Provision for decline in market value.

The investment may be shown on the asset side of the balance sheet thus:

Stocks owned:
    Cost... $100,000
    Less reduction to market..................................   10,000 $90,000

or merely thus:

Stocks owned—at market, which is lower than cost.............. $90,000

If, for any reason, declines in the market value of long-term or temporary investments in securities are not recorded in the accounts, and the securities are stated in the balance sheet at a value other than market, it is important to state the market value parenthetically.

Subsequent adjustments of valuation accounts. If a contra account has been set up to reflect the decline in the market value of temporary or long-term investments, and the market further declines, the contra account can be increased by an additional charge against income.

If, after a contra account has been set up, the market value increases, it has been generally regarded as acceptable to reduce the valuation account in order to reflect the new market value. If such an adjustment is made, it should be recorded as a correction of prior years' earnings. However, there is an increasing school of thought which maintains that, while the reduction in the carrying value of the investment is justified on the ground of conservatism, a subsequent credit to income or retained earnings prior to sale would be unjustified because of the absence of realization.

Matters Relative to Investments in Stocks

Adjustments of cost. After stock investments are made, any subsequent assessments paid or any contributions made for the purpose of eliminating a deficit or for other reasons should be added to the original cost; and any receipts from the issuing corporation representing a return of capital should be deducted from the original cost.

Dividends on stock investments. Dividends are usually declared on one day, payable on a subsequent day, to stockholders of record at some intermediate date. At which of these dates should the dividends be recorded as income to the stockholder? Income should not be taken up until the date of record because the stock may be sold before that date and the right to receive the dividend be thereby lost. At the date of record an entry can be made debiting Dividends Receivable and crediting Dividend Income. When the dividend is collected, the entry is: debit Cash and credit Dividends Receivable.

Dividends received in property should be recorded at the fair market value of the property received. Dividends received from companies engaged in the exploitation of assets subject to depletion may consist partly of income and partly of a return of capital.

The portion representing a liquidating dividend should be so designated by the corporation and should be recorded by the recipient as a reduction of the cost of the stock investment.

Stock received as a dividend. As a general rule stock dividends are not income from either the general accounting or the income tax standpoint. There is no distribution of assets of the corporation, but merely a change in the component elements of the stockholders' equity; far from being a distribution from surplus, a stock dividend constitutes a notice to stockholders that a portion of the surplus will not thereafter be available for asset distribution.

If a person owns 100 shares out of a total of 1,000 outstanding shares, and if the corporation issues a 25% stock dividend, the stockholder's shares are increased to 125 and the total outstanding shares are increased to 1,250; but, so far as the stockholder is concerned, he still has a 10% interest in the corporation and the only effect of the stock dividend is an increase in the number of shares by which his equity is represented. Therefore, the receipt of a stock dividend should not be recorded by any entry increasing the carrying value of the investment or taking up income. The only necessary record of the dividend received is a notation in the investment account indicating the increase in the number of shares held.

If stock is acquired at various times and at different prices, if some of the shares are sold, and if the shares sold cannot be identified as pertaining to any particular lot, the cost of the shares sold can be determined, for purposes of computing gain or loss, on the first-in, first-out theory. How should stock received as a dividend be dealt with in applying this theory? If 100 shares were purchased in 1957 at $100 each, another 100 shares were purchased in 1958 at $125 each, another 100 shares were acquired in 1959 at a cost of $150 per share, and a 25% stock dividend was received in 1960, the 75 shares received as a dividend should not be regarded as having been acquired in 1960; they should be associated with the shares on which they were received as a dividend. Thus, the three purchases should now be regarded as follows:

Date	Shares Purchased	Cost	Shares Owned	Cost per Share
1957	100	$10,000	125	$ 80
1958	100	12,500	125	100
1959	100	15,000	125	120

If bonds or other similar evidences of indebtedness are received as a dividend, proper accounting and the tax regulations require that they be taken up as assets and income at their fair market value.

Dividends payable in stock or in cash at the option of the stockholder, and taken in stock at his option, are regarded as taxable income.

Likewise, a stock dividend is taxable to the extent distributed in discharge of preference dividends for the distributing corporation's current or preceding tax year.

Stock rights, or warrants. When a corporation is about to issue additional shares, each holder of stock of the class to be issued may receive warrants evidencing his right to subscribe for new shares in the ratio that his holdings bear to the total shares outstanding before the additional issuance. Such a stock right, subscription right, or purchase warrant frequently entitles the stockholder to purchase only a fraction of a share of new stock for each old share held, and the number of rights is expressed in terms of the number of shares owned rather than the number of shares which may be acquired. For instance, assume that the rights entitle the stockholders to acquire one new share for each ten shares owned; if a stockholder owns fifty shares, he is entitled to acquire five new shares; he is said to hold fifty rights—not five.

The announcement of the granting of the rights states the date when the stock records will be closed to determine the stockholders of record to whom the warrants will be issued, and also the later date when subscriptions will be payable. Between the date of the announcement and the date of the issuing of the warrants, the stock and the rights are inseparable, and the stock is dealt in "rights-on." After the warrants are issued, the stock is dealt in "ex-rights," and the rights are dealt in separately. During the period in which the stock is selling rights-on, no special problems arise, since any transactions involve the stock and the rights as a unit. After the warrants are issued and the stock is selling ex-rights, problems arise which require an apportionment of the cost of the originally acquired stock between the stock and the rights; this is done on the basis of the market value of the right and the market value of the stock ex-rights at the time of the issuance of the rights. For instance, assume the following facts:

Cost of share of stock owned	$120
Market values on date of issuance of rights:	
Right	30
Stock	150
Apportionment of $120 cost:	
Right—$30/180$ of $120	20
Stock—$150/180$ of $120	100

When the apportioned cost of the right is ascertained, it is advisable to make an entry setting up a Cost of Stock Rights account, thus:

Cost of stock rights	20	
Investment in stock of X Company		20
Receipt of stock right.		

The Investment in Stock of X Company account and the Cost of Stock Rights account will then appear as follows:

Investment in Stock of X Company

| Cost of 1 share | 120 | Apportioned cost of right | 20 |

Cost of Stock Rights

| Apportioned cost of right | 20 | |

Assume that the right entitled the holder to purchase one share of stock for $120, and that he exercised the right. The cost of the new share should be regarded as including the disbursement made to the issuing corporation therefor and the $20 apportioned cost of the right. The entry for the acquisition of the share is:

Investment in stock of X Company	140	
Cost of stock rights		20
Cash		120
Purchase of stock for cash and right.		

The first share of stock acquired is now regarded as having a cost of $100, and the second share acquired is regarded as having a cost of $140.

Assume that, instead of using the right, the holder sold it at its market value of $30. The entry would be:

Cash	30	
Cost of stock rights		20
Gain on sale of stock rights		10
Sale of stock right.		

If the holder of a right is careless enough to neither use it nor sell it but allows it to lapse, the apportioned cost of the right should be written off as a loss.

As stated above, the right appertaining to each share may entitle the holder to purchase only a fraction of a share; for instance, the warrants may entitle the holder to purchase one-tenth of a share for each share held. The holder of four shares would, in such a case, receive warrants entitling him to purchase four-tenths of one share. The cost to be assigned to each right would be determined in the manner illustrated above. The holder of the rights may:

Buy additional rights to enable him to buy a full share; the cost of the new share will include the apportioned cost of his rights for four-tenths of a share, plus the cost of the rights for six-tenths of a share, plus the subscription price.

Sell his rights for four-tenths of a share, in which case he should compute his gain or loss and make an entry for the sale of the rights in the manner illustrated above.

Matters Relative to Investments in Bonds

Accrued interest at date of purchase. When bonds are acquired between interest dates, the purchase price normally includes the accrued interest. In the entry to record the acquisition of the bonds, the accrued interest should be charged to Accrued Interest Receivable, and only the remainder of the purchase price should be charged to the bond investment account.

Pur. of Bond
A/I Rec ×
Bonds ×
Cash ✓

Amortization of bond premium and discount. If a bond is purchased at a cost (including incidental costs such as brokerage) in excess of par, the purchase is made "at a premium." The value of the bond tends to decrease to par as its maturity approaches; therefore, for balance sheet purposes, it appears proper to amortize the premium over the life of the bond, and thus gradually to reduce its carrying value to par.* Moreover, the net income on a bond purchased at a premium, held to maturity and collected at par, is the total of the interest collections minus the premium lost; therefore, it appears proper to charge a portion of the premium periodically against the income from interest.

Similarly, the value of a bond of a solvent debtor purchased at a discount tends to increase to par as the maturity approaches; hence, for balance sheet purposes, it appears proper to amortize the discount over the life of the bond, thus gradually increasing its carrying value to par. Moreover, the total income earned on a bond purchased at a discount, held to maturity and collected at par, is the total of the interest collections plus the discount; therefore, it appears proper to regard a portion of the discount as earned periodically.

If bonds are purchased at a premium or a discount, the bond investment account is usually charged with the cost; amortizations (sometimes called *accumulations*) of discount are then charged to the account and amortizations of premium are credited to it. Some accountants prefer to charge the bond investment account with par, and to set up a premium or discount account. The former method is preferable. But if bonds are issued at a premium or a discount, it is better to credit the bond account with par and to set up a separate account with the bond premium or the bond discount.

Amortizations of bond premium and discount may be made by straight-line methods or by scientific effective-interest methods.

---

* For tax purposes the regulations should be consulted, as they are complicated and not entirely in conformity with the procedures discussed in this chapter, which are regarded as acceptable from the standpoint of accounting theory.

Straight-line methods are discussed in this chapter; effective-interest-rate methods are discussed in the advanced text.

Amortization of premium—straight-line method. Assume that a $1,000 bond, bearing 6% interest payable semiannually on January 1 and July 1, and due in four years, is purchased on January 1, 1959 for $1,035.85. Although coupons of $30 will be collected each six months, this amount cannot all be considered income; a portion of each coupon must be considered a partial repayment of the premium. Since there are eight interest periods, the premium may be written off by eight semiannual entries of $35.85 ÷ 8, or $4.48 (really seven entries of $4.48 and one of $4.49). Using this straight-line method, the entry to be made at each interest date except the last would be:

N.B. For C.F. add from to int earned

Cash.. ...	30.00	
Interest earned...............................		25.52
Bond account (for premium amortized)......		4.48

The amortization may be scheduled as follows:

Premium

Schedule of Amortization
Four-Year 6% Bond Bought for $1,035.85

Date	Debit Cash	Credit Interest Earned	Credit Bond Account	Carrying Value
Jan. 1, 1959..................... ...				$1,035.85
July 1............................. ...	$ 30.00	$ 25.52	$ 4.48	1,031.37
Jan. 1, 1960....	30.00	25.52	4.48	1,026.89
July 1........................ ...	30.00	25.52	4.48	1,022.41
Jan. 1, 1961..................... ...	30.00	25.52	4.48	1,017.93
July 1........................ ...	30.00	25.52	4.48	1,013.45
Jan. 1, 1962..................... ...	30.00	25.52	4.48	1,008.97
July 1........................ ...	30.00	25.52	4.48	1,004.49
Jan. 1, 1963..................... ...	30.00	25.51	4.49	1,000.00
	$240.00	$204.15	$35.85	

Thus, the amortization of a premium gradually brings the carrying value of the bond down to par, spreading the premium over the life of the bond as a reduction of the bond interest.

Amortization of discount—straight-line method. Assume that a $1,000 bond, bearing 6% interest payable semiannually on January 1 and July 1, and due in four years, is purchased on January 1, 1959 for $965.63. The discount of $34.37 could be spread over the eight periods, in semiannual amounts of $34.37 ÷ 8, or $4.30. (Eight of these amounts would total $34.40 instead of $34.37; hence, three entries must be for $4.29.)

The semiannual entries are indicated by the amortization schedule on the following page.

Discount [handwritten]

Schedule of Amortization
Four-Year 6% Bond Bought for $965.63

Date	Debit Cash	Debit Bond Account	Credit Interest Earned	Carrying Value
Jan. 1, 1959....................				$ 965.63
July 1.........................	$ 30.00	$ 4.30	$ 34.30	969.93
Jan. 1, 1960...................	30.00	4.30	34.30	974.23
July 1.........................	30.00	4.30	34.30	978.53
Jan. 1, 1961...................	30.00	4.30	34.30	982.83
July 1.........................	30.00	4.30	34.30	987.13
Jan. 1, 1962...................	30.00	4.29	34.29	991.42
July 1.........................	30.00	4.29	34.29	995.71
Jan. 1, 1963...................	30.00	4.29	34.29	1,000.00
	$240.00	$34.37	$274.37	

N.B. For cif. deduct disc from int earned [handwritten]

Thus, the amortization of the discount gradually brings the carrying value of the bond up to par, spreading the discount over the life of the bond as an addition to the bond interest.

Amortization at interim dates.   The foregoing illustrations are based on the assumption that an interest date coincides with the close of the fiscal year of the owner of the bonds. Referring to the two schedules above, let us now assume that the investing company closes its books on February 28th.

Entries applicable to the bond purchased at a premium are shown below:

February 28, 1959: — *CLOSING ENTRY* [handwritten]
    Accrued interest receivable............................ 10.00
        Bond account (⅓ of $4.48)..........................   1.49
        Interest earned....................................   8.51

July 1, 1959:
    Cash... 30.00
        Accrued interest receivable........................   10.00
        Bond account ($4.48 − $1.49)......................   2.99
        Interest earned....................................   17.01

January 1, 1960:
    Cash... 30.00
        Bond account......................................   4.48
        Interest earned....................................   25.52

February 28, 1960:
    Accrued interest receivable............................ 10.00
        Bond account......................................   1.49
        Interest earned....................................   8.51

Entries applicable to the bond purchased at a discount are shown below:

February 28, 1959:
    Accrued interest receivable............................ 10.00
    Bond account (⅓ of $4.30).............................   1.43
        Interest earned....................................   11.43

July 1, 1959:
```
Cash.........................................    30.00
Bond account ($4.30 − $1.43)...................     2.87
    Accrued interest receivable..................              10.00
    Interest earned...........................               22.87
```

January 1, 1960:
```
Cash.........................................    30.00
Bond account.................................     4.30
    Interest earned...........................               34.30
```

February 28, 1960:
```
Accrued interest receivable......................    10.00
Bond account.................................     1.43
    Interest earned...........................               11.43
```

Purchases between interest dates.   Assume that a 6% bond due on December 31, 1966 is purchased for $1,051.80 and accrued interest on October 31, 1960, or six years and two months before maturity. Then the premium to be amortized per year on the straight-line basis is $51.80 ÷ 6⅙, or $8.40; the premium to be amortized each six months is $4.20; and the premium to be amortized for the two-months period between the date of purchase and the first interest date, December 31, 1960, is ⅓ of $4.20, or $1.40.

The entry for the purchase is:

October 31, 1960:
```
Bond account.....................................  1,051.80
Accrued interest receivable.......................     20.00
    Cash........................................            1,071.80
```

The entry for the first interest collection is:

December 31, 1960:
```
Cash.........................................    30.00
    Bond account..............................               1.40
    Accrued interest receivable..................              20.00
    Interest earned...........................                8.60
```

Assume that the bond was bought at a discount of $51.80 instead of at a premium of that amount.

The entry for the purchase is:

October 31, 1960:
```
Bond account.................................   948.20
Accrued interest receivable.......................    20.00
    Cash........................................             968.20
```

The entry for the first interest collection is:

December 31, 1960:
```
Cash.........................................    30.00
Bond account.................................     1.40
    Accrued interest receivable..................              20.00
    Interest earned...........................               11.40
```

Sales between interest dates.   Refer to the schedule on page 302 showing the amortization of bond premium; observe that the carrying value of the bond on January 1, 1962 was $1,008.97. Assume that the bond was sold on March 1, 1962 for $1,020. A proper accounting for the sale should give recognition to the income from January 1 to March 1, and to the gain or loss. These elements are computed as follows:

Selling price...		$1,020.00
Amount received for accrued interest at 6% for two months....		10.00
Price received for the bond...............................		$1,010.00
Amortized value of bond at date of sale:		
Carrying value, January 1, 1962.................	$1,008.97	
Less amortization of premium for two months—		
⅓ of $4.48 (see amortization schedule).........	1.49	1,007.48
Gain on sale...		$ 2.52

The entry to record the sale would be:

Cash...	1,020.00	
Bond account................................		1,008.97
Interest earned ($10.00 − $1.49)...............		8.51
Gain on sale of bond.........................		2.52

Refer to the schedule on page 303 showing the amortization of bond discount; observe that the carrying value on January 1, 1962 was $991.42. Assume that the bond was sold on March 1, 1962 for $1,000. The computation of the loss on the sale follows:

Selling price...		$1,000.00
Amount received for accrued interest at 6% for two months....		10.00
Price received for the bond...............................		$ 990.00
Amortized value of bond at date of sale:		
Carrying value, January 1, 1962.................	$991.42	
Plus amortization of discount for two months—⅓ of		
$4.29 (see amortization schedule)...............	1.43	992.85
Loss on sale of bond......................................		$ 2.85

The entry to record the sale would be:

Cash...	1,000.00	
Loss on sale of bond...............................	2.85	
Bond account................................		991.42
Interest earned ($10.00 + $1.43)...............		11.43

Redemption before maturity. Bonds frequently carry the right of redemption before maturity, usually at a premium. For instance, a bond issued on January 1, 1960 and maturing on January 1, 1980 might be redeemable at the option of the issuing company at premiums as follows:

From January 1, 1970 to January 1, 1976	—at 105
During 1976	—at 104
During 1977	—at 103
During 1978	—at 102
During 1979	—at 101

If such a bond is acquired at a premium greater than the premium at which it can be retired at the next optional retirement date, the premium amortization should be such that the bond will not be carried at any date at an amount greater than the amount at which it can be retired on that date.

If the bond is acquired at a discount, the discount should be amortized in such a manner as to raise the carrying value to par at maturity, without regard for retirement premiums. The retirement privilege may never be exercised, and no redemption premium may be received.

Carrying bond investments at cost.   Bond investments may properly be carried at cost if the investments are temporary ones, or if an investment is so small that an amortization procedure is not worth the trouble.

If bonds are purchased at a considerable discount because the issuing company is in a weak financial condition, the collection of par at maturity may be doubtful and the accumulation of the discount may therefore be unjustified.

Bonds purchased with interest in default.   In *Accounting Series Release No. 36*, the Chief Accountant of the Securities and Exchange Commission expressed the opinion that, if an investment company acquires bonds with defaulted interest coupons attached, "collections on account of the defaulted interest coupons should be treated not as interest on the sum invested, but rather as repayments thereof. Moreover, in view of the uncertainty of eventually receiving payments in excess of the purchase price, . . . ordinarily no part of any payment, whether on account of principal or the defaulted interest, should be considered as profit until the full purchase price has been recovered."

Although the opinion is specifically applicable to investment companies, the accounting procedure described seems to be appropriate for use by any investor.

Investments in mortgages.   The accounting for investments in individual mortgages does not differ in essence from the accounting for bond investments. Mortgages should be recorded at their cost, and the principles of discount and premium amortization apply to them as well as to bonds.

A special situation arises when property is sold and a mortgage is taken for a portion of the sale price. If the sum of the cash and the mortgage received is in excess of the fair cash value of the property sold, the excess is, in effect, discount on the mortgage. Conservative accounting would require that the mortgage be recorded at a discounted value, determined on the basis of the fair cash value of the property.

Government obligations. No peculiar accounting problems arise in connection with short-term government securities such as the treasury bills, treasury notes, and certificates of indebtedness. Some special problems do arise in connection with the Series E long-term savings bonds.

The Series E bonds are issued at a discount; they yield income at stated annual rates, compounded semiannually, if held to maturity; they are redeemable at the holder's option before maturity at prices stated in a schedule in the bond; but the redemption prices are below par, and therefore the yield rate if the bond is redeemed is less than the rate earned if the bond is held to maturity. Some of the principal characteristics of the Series E bonds are indicated in the following table.

Life......................................	8 years, 11 months
Issuance price per $100 of maturity value	$75
Denominations (maturity value)........	$25 $50 $100 $200 $500 $1,000 $10,000 $100,000
Periodic interest payments.............	None
Yield rate per annum, compounded semi-annually, if held to maturity.........	3.25%
The bonds may be registered...........	In the names of natural persons. In the names and titles of the legal representatives of natural persons and of the trustees of a limited class of trusts.

Three methods are used for taking up income on such bonds:

(1) No income is taken until the maturity of the bond. This is probably the method most in use by individual holders of small amounts of such bonds.
(2) Income is taken up over the life of the bond:
    (a) By debiting the investment account and crediting income in amounts sufficient to increase the carrying value of the investment to the increasing redemption prices shown in the schedule.
    (b) By debiting the investment account and crediting income with amounts computed by applying the yield rate of 3.25% to the increasing carrying value of the investment. This method is probably not widely used, partly because it is more convenient to use method (a), and partly because income may be overstated if the bond is redeemed before maturity.

There is another series of long-term savings bonds (Series H), but they have a number of distinguishing features. The Series H bonds are issued at par in denominations of $500, $1,000, $5,000, and $10,000. The H bonds mature in ten years, but are redeemable at the owner's option at par any time after the first six months. Holders receive semiannual interest payments based on a graduated scale of amounts which have been fixed to result in an investment yield of approximately 3.25% over the ten-year life of the bonds.

CHAPTER FIFTEEN

Investments (Concluded)

Investments in Subsidiaries

Accounting methods. If a corporation holds more than a fifty per cent interest in the voting stock of another company, the relation of parent and subsidiary exists. The parent may adopt either the legal-basis or the economic-basis method of accounting for its investment in the subsidiary, and for the income or loss thereon.

Legal-basis method. From a legal standpoint, a parent and its subsidiary are separate entities; the net income or loss of the subsidiary is not a part of the net income or loss of the parent; dividends received from the subsidiary are income to the parent. If the parent company adopts the legal basis of accounting for its investment in the subsidiary and its income thereon, it will carry the investment at cost and will record dividends as income. To illustrate:

Company P organizes a subsidiary, Company S, and acquires its entire stock issue by an investment of $100,000.

Investment in stock of Company S.................... 100,000
   Cash... 100,000
   Acquisition of stock of subsidiary.

During the first year of its operations, the subsidiary earns a net income of $30,000 (for which the parent makes no entry) and pays a dividend of $5,000.

Cash.. 5,000
   Dividend income................................ 5,000
   Dividend from subsidiary.

The Dividend Income account is closed to Revenue and Expense, and thence to Retained Earnings.

During the second year, the subsidiary loses $15,000 (the parent makes no entry) and pays a dividend of $5,000 from retained earnings produced by the earnings of the preceding year.

Cash.. 5,000
    Dividend income........................ 5,000
    Dividend from subsidiary.

During the third year, the subsidiary loses $12,000. The parent company makes no entry.

The foregoing entries under the legal-basis method are summarized below; starred items are credits.

	Investment	Cash	Dividend Income	Retained Earnings
First year:				
Investment.........................	$100,000	$100,000*		
Subsidiary net income—no entry.				
Subsidiary dividend................		5,000	$5,000*	
Closing entry......................			5,000	$5,000*
Second year:				
Subsidiary net loss—no entry.				
Subsidiary dividend................		5,000	$5,000*	
Closing entry.....................			5,000	5,000*
Third year:				
Subsidiary net loss—no entry.				

This accounting procedure conforms strictly to the legal realities of separate corporate entities. However, when this method is used, the balance in the investment account will not reflect the underlying book value of the subsidiary's net assets. The changing amounts of subsidiary net assets and the unchanging balance of the parent's investment account are compared below:

	Net Assets of Subsidiary	Parent's Investment Account
First year:		
Investment by parent........................	$100,000	$100,000
Increase in subsidiary's net assets resulting from net income...............................	30,000	
Decrease in subsidiary's net assets resulting from payment of dividend......................	5,000*	
Balance at end of year......................	$125,000	$100,000
Second year:		
Decrease in subsidiary's net assets resulting from loss.....................................	15,000*	
Decrease in subsidiary's net assets resulting from payment of dividend......................	5,000*	
Balance at end of year......................	$105,000	$100,000
Third year:		
Decrease in subsidiary's net assets resulting from loss.....................................	12,000*	
Balance at end of year......................	$ 93,000	$100,000
* Deduction.		

Of even more consequence is the fact that the dividends taken up by the parent company as income bear no relation to the results of the subsidiary's operations. The parent company is in a position to dictate the dividend policy of the subsidiary; therefore, so long as the subsidiary has a surplus available for dividends, the parent company, by determining the dividends to be paid to it, can take into income any amounts which it may desire, instead of taking up the net income or loss resulting from the subsidiary's operations.

Suppose that the dividends paid by a subsidiary after the acquisition of its stock by the parent company exceed its earnings since that date. How should the parent company record the portion of the dividend which was paid from surplus created prior to acquisition? Although a dividend from surplus created prior to acquisition appears to have a legal status of income to the parent company, accountants are in general agreement that such a dividend should not be recorded as income, but should be regarded as a partial recovery of cost and credited to the investment account.

Economic-basis method. The economic-basis method gives recognition to the fact that subsidiary earnings increase the subsidiary net assets which underlie the investment, and subsidiary losses and dividends decrease these net assets. The parent's entries on the economic basis increase and decrease the balance in the investment account in accordance with increases and decreases in the underlying subsidiary net assets. Also, on the economic basis, the amounts shown as income or loss on the investment each year correspond with the amounts shown as income and loss by the subsidiary. To illustrate, assume the same facts as those in the illustration on the legal basis; the entries on the economic basis are indicated below:

	Investment	Cash	Subsidiary Income	Retained Earnings
First year:				
Investment..............	$100,000	$100,000*		
Subsidiary net income....	30,000		$30,000*	
Subsidiary dividend......	5,000*	5,000		
Closing entry............			30,000	$30,000*
Balance at end of year....	$125,000			
Second year:				
Subsidiary net loss........	15,000*		$15,000	
Subsidiary dividend......	5,000*	5,000		
Closing entry............			15,000*	15.000
Balance at end of year....	$105,000			
Third year:				
Subsidiary net loss.......	12,000*		$12,000	
Closing entry............			12,000*	12,000
Balance at end of year....	$ 93,000			
* Credit.				

When entries are made by the parent company in this manner, the changes in the balance of the investment account keep pace with the changes in the net assets of the subsidiary, and the amounts recorded by the parent as income or loss on the investment are in accordance with the income or loss of the subsidiary instead of arbitrary amounts transferred from the subsidiary to the parent as dividends. This accounting procedure undoubtedly reflects the economic realities. The only objection to it is that it violates the legal realities, because the parent's Retained Earnings account is affected by subsidiary earnings and losses although it can legally be affected only by subsidiary dividends.

Subsidiary acquired by purchase.   In the preceding illustrations, it was assumed that the subsidiary was organized by the parent; consequently, the stockholders' equity of the subsidiary at the date of organization was equal to the parent's investment; also, if the parent adopted the economic-basis method of accounting, the balance in the parent's investment account was always equal to the book value of the subsidiary's net assets.

But let us modify the preceding illustrations by assuming that the subsidiary had been in existence for some time, and that the parent company bought its stock. We shall assume, also, that the subsidiary had $75,000 of capital stock and $25,000 of retained earnings at the date of acquisition, and that the parent company paid $110,000 for the stock. The parent's entries during the subsequent three years, by each method, would be the same as those shown above. Moreover, the parent company's statements would be affected in only one way: If the economic-basis method was used, it would not be appropriate to describe the basis of valuation of the investment in the balance sheet as "At underlying book value," because the balance in the investment account would always be $10,000 greater than the book value of the subsidiary's net assets. The following wording would be appropriate: "Investment in stock of Company S—at cost, adjusted for increase (or decrease) in subsidiary's retained earnings since acquisition."

Minority interest.   Assume the following facts: Company P acquired 90% of the stock of Company S at a time when Company S had $75,000 of capital stock and $25,000 of retained earnings; Company P paid $90,000 for the stock. The net income, loss, and dividend amounts of the subsidiary during the three years subsequent to acquisition were the same as in the preceding illustration:

	Net Income Loss*	Dividends
First year	$30,000	$5,000
Second year	15,000*	5,000
Third year	12,000*	—

The legal-basis entries are:

	Investment	Cash	Dividend Income	Retained Earnings
First year:				
Investment.......................	$ 90,000	$90,000*		
Net income—$30,000—no entry.				
Dividend—$5,000.................		4,500	$ 4,500*	
Closing entry..........			4,500	$ 4,500*
Second year:				
Loss—$15,000—no entry.				
Dividend—$5,000.................		4,500	$ 4,500*	
Closing entry....			4,500	4,500*
Third year:				
Loss—$12,000—no entry.				
* Credit.				

The economic-basis entries are:

	Investment	Cash	Subsidiary Income	Retained Earnings
First year:				
Investment.......................	$ 90,000	$90,000*		
Subsidiary net income—$30,000.....	27,000		$27,000*	
Dividend—$5,000.................	4,500*	4,500		
Closing entry.....................			27,000	$27,000*
Balance at end of year............	$112,500			
Second year:				
Loss—$15,000.....	13,500*		$13,500	
Dividend—$5,000	4,500*	4,500		
Closing entry....			13,500*	13,500
Balance at end of year.	$ 94,500			
Third year:				
Loss—$12,000.....	10,800*		$10,800	
Closing entry.........			10,800*	10,800
Balance at end of year............	$ 83,700			
* Credit.				

Funds

Funds and reserves distinguished. Although funds and reserves are wholly different in nature, there seems to be an inclination to confuse them.

Funds are assets, usually set aside for particular purposes. Fund accounts, therefore, always* have debit balances, always represent assets, and always appear on the asset side of the balance sheet.

Reserves, on the other hand, normally have credit balances and, therefore, never represent assets. At present, it is desired merely to emphasize one fact: Namely, fund accounts always represent assets, and reserves never do.

---

* This is true so far as general industrial accounting is concerned; terminology is different in municipal and institutional accounting.

The term *reserve fund* has no well-defined meaning, and its use is not to be recommended.

Classes of funds. Funds may be classified as follows:

(A) As to the use to be made of the assets in the fund:

    (1) Payment of an existing liability.
    (2) Payment of a contingent liability.
    (3) Payment for an asset or a service.
    (4) Retirement of capital stock.

(B) As to obligatory or voluntary creation:

    (1) Obligatory—required by contract.
    (2) Voluntary—created by action of the management.

The classification of funds as obligatory and optional is important because of the bearing it has on the question of the relation existing between the amount of a fund and the amount of a related reserve.

Funds in the balance sheet. Funds should be classified in the balance sheet as current assets if they are created for the payment of current liabilities or for current expenditures. Thus, periodical deposits for the payment of bond interest or for the payment of taxes on property mortgaged as security to a short-term or a long-term liability should properly be shown as current assets.

Funds for the payment of long-term indebtedness should be shown in the balance sheet as a noncurrent account.

It has been suggested that a fund established for plant expansion should be shown under the Fixed Assets caption. This seems unsound because the fund is not being used as a plant asset, and its inclusion under that caption would distort any ratios involving fixed assets. Moreover, funds set aside by the management for plant expansion can be diverted by the management to other purposes. The case is somewhat different with respect to the impounded proceeds of a mortgage issued for construction purposes, but even in such cases the fund should be shown under a special caption rather than under the Fixed Assets caption.

Companies are sometimes required to deposit funds for the payment of current interest on long-term indebtedness and taxes on the mortgaged property, as well as for the repayment of the principal of the indebtedness. In such instances, it seems advisable to divide the fund into two parts for balance sheet presentation, the funds available for current purposes being shown under the Current Assets caption, and the remainder being shown under a special caption.

Accounting for funds. The bookkeeping entries required in the operation of funds are usually not complicated. Typical fund transactions may include the following:

(1) The transfer of assets to the fund.
(2) The investment of fund cash in fund securities.
(3) The collection of income on the fund. The entries for this transaction may include the amortization of premium or discount on fund securities.
(4) The payment of expenses incurred in the operation of the fund.
(5) The application of the fund to its intended purpose.

Entries for these transactions are illustrated in the subsequent section devoted to sinking funds.

The discussion in Chapter 14 with respect to the valuation of stocks and bonds held as investments applies equally to securities held in special funds. If a fund is established for the payment of a current liability or for other current expenditures, the principles governing the valuation of temporary investments apply. If securities in a fund are to be held for a considerable period of time, the principles applicable to long-term investments should govern their valuation in the accounts.

Funds for the payment of existing liabilities. Funds may be created for the payment of current liabilities. For example, such funds may be accumulated to meet bond interest requirements or social security tax obligations, or for the purchase of savings bonds with monies deducted from employees' pay.

Funds for the payment of long-term liabilities are more common. Funds for the retirement of long-term liabilities may be classified as follows:

(1) Sinking funds.
A sinking fund, strictly defined, consists of assets set aside, together with the accumulated earnings thereon, for the payment of an existing liability at its maturity.
(2) Redemption funds.
A redemption fund consists of assets set aside for the piecemeal retirement of obligations. The resources of the fund may be applied to meet serially maturing obligations or to purchase outstanding obligations of the company.

The distinction between sinking funds and redemption funds is interesting as a matter of precision in terminology. However, usage modifies meanings, and business usage seems to have sanctioned the extension of the term *sinking fund* to include funds used in the periodical retirement of bonds and other obligations and funds for the retirement of capital stock.

Sinking funds are usually administered by a trustee. Sometimes the company itself retains custody and control of the fund, but this plan usually is not entirely satisfactory to the creditors for whose protection the fund is being accumulated.

Sinking fund contributions. The amount of the periodical contribution to the sinking fund is usually stipulated in the trust indenture. The following requirements are typical:

(1) A certain number of cents per unit of output. This method of computing the periodical contributions is often required by the trust indenture when the bonds are secured by a mortgage on wasting assets such as mines and timber lands; the contributions are based on the number of tons mined or thousand feet of timber cut. Thus, the sinking fund increases as the physical security back of the mortgage decreases. But since operations may not be carried on with sufficient rapidity to provide an adequate fund at the maturity of the bonds, a minimum annual contribution may be required.

(2) A percentage of the annual earnings. This method is frequently used in connection with so-called sinking funds for the retirement of preferred stock. From the standpoint of bondholders, it is not satisfactory to make the provision for the repayment of the bonds conditional upon the uncertain earnings of the business, although in the long run it might be advisable to allow the debtor corporation to make small contributions in poor years with offsetting large contributions in good years; otherwise, the drain upon the working capital when uniform contributions are required even in poor years may handicap the company in its operations and make it impossible for the company to meet its future contribution requirements.

(3) An equal annual amount computed by dividing the total required fund by the number of years of the life of the bonds. For instance, if a fund of $20,000 is to be provided in ten years, the annual addition to the fund will be $2,000. The first year, the contribution out of general cash will be $2,000, but the interest earned on the fund will reduce the subsequent contributions from the general cash.

(4) An equal annual contribution computed on an actuarial

basis. The method of computing the periodical contributions required to produce a fund of a given amount
is explained in the authors' *Principles of Accounting,
Advanced.*

Theoretical accumulation. Often a company will prepare a
schedule showing a theoretical accumulation of its sinking fund.
Such a schedule is presented below for a sinking fund to be created
by deposits computed on an actuarial basis and intended to accumulate to $20,000 in a ten-year period. It is assumed that all
deposits in the fund can be invested in securities on the dates of the
deposits, that 5% interest will be earned on all investments from
the dates of their acquisition to the date of their disposal at the
end of the fund period, and that no gains or losses will be realized
when the securities are converted into cash.

Schedule of Accumulation

End of Year	Debit Fund	Credit Cash	Credit Income	Total Fund
1	$ 1,590.09	$ 1,590.09		$ 1,590.09
2	1,669.59	1,590.09	$ 79.50	3,259.68
3	1,753.07	1,590.09	162.98	5,012.75
4	1,840.73	1,590.09	250.64	6,853.48
5	1,932.76	1,590.09	342.67	8,786.24
6	2,029.40	1,590.09	439.31	10,815.64
7	2,130.87	1,590.09	540.78	12,946.51
8	2,237.42	1,590.09	647.33	15,183.93
9	2,349.29	1,590.09	759.20	17,533.22
10	2,466.75	1,590.09	876.66	19,999.97
	$19,999.97	$15,900.90	$4,099.07	

Actual accumulation. Actually, a sinking fund planned as
above will not accumulate with any such mathematical exactness.
Conditions in the securities markets may delay the prompt investment of sinking fund cash. The fund assets may earn more or less
than the expected interest rate. Gains may be realized or losses
incurred when the securities in the fund are converted into cash at
the end of the fund period. For all these reasons, the actual accumulation of the fund cannot be expected to conform with the
theoretical accumulation.

If the sinking fund is required by contract, the contract may
call for supplemental contributions whenever the fund is below its
scheduled level. If the sinking fund is a voluntary one, the management of the company may make supplemental contributions
at its discretion.

Sinking fund entries. The operations of a sinking fund consist of making contributions to the fund, investing in securities,
collecting income, paying expenses, disposing of fund securities,

and using the cash fund for its intended purpose, such as the
retirement of bonded indebtedness. Entries for these transactions,
assuming that the fund is being accumulated to pay off bonded
indebtedness, are illustrated below:

Contributions of cash:
    Sinking fund cash............................ xx,xxx.xx
        Cash....................................   xx,xxx.xx

Purchase of securities:
    Sinking fund securities—A B bonds........... xx,xxx.xx
        Sinking fund cash.......................   xx,xxx.xx
        (Entry if securities are purchased at par and
        without accrued interest. Purchases at a pre-
        mium or discount and purchases with accrued
        interest are considered later.)

Collection of income:
    Sinking fund cash............................   xxx.xx
        Sinking fund income.....................   xxx.xx
        (Entry for income on securities purchased at
        par.)

Payment of expenses:
    Sinking fund expense.....................   xxx.xx
      — Sinking fund cash.......................   xxx.xx
        (Entry if expenses are paid from fund cash.)

    Sinking fund expense..................   xxx.xx
      — Cash...................................   xxx.xx
        (Entry if expenses are paid from general cash.)

Disposal of sinking fund securities:
    Sinking fund cash......................... xx,xxx.xx
        Sinking fund securities.................   xx,xxx.xx
        (Entry if securities are sold at carrying value.)

    Sinking fund cash......................... xx,xxx.xx
    Loss on sinking fund securities...............   xxx.xx
        Sinking fund securities.................   xx,xxx.xx
        (Entry if securities are sold at a loss.)

    Sinking fund cash......................... xx,xxx.xx
        Gain on sinking fund securities...........   xxx.xx
        Sinking fund securities.................   xx,xxx.xx
        (Entry if securities are sold at a gain.)

Cancellation of bonds at maturity:
    Sinking fund cash......................... x,xxx.xx
        Cash...................................   x,xxx.xx
        (Entry if sinking fund cash after disposal of
        securities is inadequate for retirement of
        bonds.)

    Bonds payable............................. xxx,xxx.xx
        Sinking fund cash.......................   xxx,xxx.xx
        (Entry for retirement of bonds.)

    Cash..................................... x,xxx.xx
        Sinking fund cash.......................   x,xxx.xx
        (Entry if any residue remains in the fund and
        is returned to general cash.)

The Sinking Fund Income and Sinking Fund Expense accounts should be closed at the end of each period to Revenue and Expense. Losses or gains on disposals of sinking fund securities should be handled in the same manner as any other extraneous item.

Purchases between interest dates. If securities are purchased for the sinking fund at par plus accrued interest, the following entry is required:

```
Sinking fund securities.................................  xx,xxx.xx
Accrued interest on sinking fund securities.........        xxx.xx
     Sinking fund cash.....  ...........................              xx,xxx.xx
     (Entry for purchase of sinking fund securities be-
     tween interest dates.)
```

At the date of the first collection of interest, the following entry is made:

```
Sinking fund cash.......................................  xxx.xx
     Accrued interest on sinking fund securities...........        xxx.xx
     Sinking fund income..............................         xx.xx
     (Entry for first interest collection when securities were
     purchased between interest dates.)
```

Amortization of premium or discount. If bonds are purchased for the sinking fund at a premium or a discount, the Sinking Fund Securities account should be charged with their cost. Entries for the collection of interest and amortization of premium or discount will be as follows:

```
Sinking fund cash...........................................  x,xxx.xx
     Sinking fund securities. PREMIUM...........              xx.xx
     Sinking fund income.............................         x,xxx.xx
     (Entry for semiannual interest collection on sinking
     fund securities purchased at a premium.)
Sinking fund cash...........................................  x,xxx.xx
Sinking fund securities. DISCOUNT ............              xx.xx
     Sinking fund income.............................                x,xxx.xx
     (Entry for semiannual interest collection on sinking
     fund securities purchased at a discount.)
```

Cash and accrual basis. If the interest dates on securities purchased for the sinking fund do not coincide with the dates of closing the company's books, adjusting entries may be made for accrued interest. For instance, assuming that interest at 5% on $150,000 of bonds in the fund is due on October 31 and April 30, and that the books are closed on December 31, entries could be made as illustrated below.

```
December 31:
     Accrued interest receivable—S. F. securities.............. 1,250
          Sinking fund income...............................          1,250
          (Entry for accrual of interest at closing date.)
```

April 30:
```
Sinking fund cash...................................  3,750
    Accrued interest receivable—S. F. securities.........      1,250
    Sinking fund income...............................      2,500
    (Entry for collection of interest.)
```

Fund with trustee.   If the sinking fund is placed in the hands of a trustee, the company's records generally will not show the individual transactions relating to the purchase and sale of securities and to the earnings and expenses of the fund. The records will show the deposits made with the trustee and summary entries for the earnings and expenses as reported periodically by the trustee.

Own bonds alive in fund.   Investments for the sinking fund may be made in the securities of other companies or in the very bonds which the fund is intended to retire. If the sinking fund trustee or manager can obtain the company's own bonds at favorable prices, it is advisable to do so if the company is in a strong financial condition, because the risk associated with an investment in outside securities is thereby eliminated. If the company is not in good financial condition, there is some question regarding the propriety of acquiring the company's own bonds for the fund, because such a transaction may be regarded as giving preference to the bondholders whose bonds are acquired.

If the company's own bonds are purchased, the question arises whether these bonds should be canceled or be "held alive" in the fund.

If the bonds are canceled when purchased, both the fund and the outstanding liability will be reduced, and the entry will be as follows:

```
Bonds payable...............................  xxx,xxx.xx
    Sinking fund cash.........................          xxx,xxx.xx
    (If the bonds are purchased at par.)
```

Whenever bonds are purchased and canceled, any unamortized discount or premium on the issuance of these retired bonds should also be written off.

As already pointed out, if the company's own bonds are purchased year by year and immediately canceled, the fund is a redemption fund rather than a true sinking fund. Although questions of terminology are interesting and important, the essential thing is, of course, the fulfillment of the purpose of the fund. If the entire bond issue can be retired by periodical purchases and immediate cancellations, there is no reason why the fund should not be operated on the redemption-fund basis instead of on the sinking-fund basis. But it is necessary to realize that, when the contributions to the fund are computed on the assumption that interest will be earned thereon for the remaining life of the fund, the cancellation of the bonds when purchased will result in a reduction of the interest earned on the fund assets and will make the fund inadequate for the retirement of all of the bonds. This point can be clearly illustrated by referring to the schedule of accumulation on page 317. The contributions out of general cash amount to $15,900.90, and interest is depended upon to make up the remaining $4,099.10. But if the company's own bonds are purchased each year with the contributions out of cash, and if these bonds are canceled, the $4,099.10 interest will not be earned by the fund, the fund will provide for the payment of only $15,900 of bonds, and no provision may be made for the retiring of the remaining $4,100 of bonds.

This condition may not be disadvantageous to the company, or even to the remaining bondholders, because future interest requirements are reduced each time an outstanding bond is acquired and canceled. Even if supplemental contributions to the fund were made necessary because of periodic redemptions of outstanding bonds, the aggregate cash outlay to finance and repay the bond obligation need not be greater, because the cash requirements for bond interest are reduced.

A possible inadequacy in the fund is avoided if the annual contributions are determined on the basis of the third method discussed on page 316. By this method, $2,000 would be provided each year, partly from interest and the balance from general cash. If the securities were canceled and no interest was earned, the entire contribution would have to be made from the general cash, and ten contributions of $2,000 each would provide for the retirement of the entire $20,000 bond issue.

When the company's own bonds are held alive in the sinking fund, they usually have been regarded, for statement purposes, as though they were the bonds of some other company. That is, the balance sheet liability of bonds payable includes those in the sinking fund as well as those in the hands of the public, and the bonds held alive are included in the fund assets. Although this is contrary to the usual rule that a company's own securities should not appear in its balance sheet as an asset, the argument has been presented that the reduction of the sinking fund and the bond liability, by the amount of the bonds held alive, would distort the ratio between the original amount of the bond issue and the funds set aside to date for the retirement of the bonds. The fact that generally a sinking fund is controlled by a trustee rather than by the company itself gives added justification for showing the bonds as assets. Some accountants advocate showing the fund in two parts in the balance sheet: the bonds held alive as a deduction from the liability, and the remainder of the fund as an asset; such a treatment is definitely not customary; if adopted, a cross reference should be made between the two fund amounts in the balance sheet. If bonds held alive are shown as assets, the balance sheet should disclose the fact in some manner, either in the description of the fund or in a footnote.

If the company's own bonds are purchased above or below par and held alive in the sinking fund, the question arises concerning the disposition of the premium or discount on the purchase. This question may be further complicated if there is unamortized discount or premium on the issuance of the bonds. Some accountants prefer to write off immediately the premium or discount on the purchase of such bonds, and also any unamortized issuance premium or discount applicable to these purchased bonds. Although no serious objection can be raised to this procedure, it seems to the authors that if the bonds are still being carried as outstanding liabilities, the discount or premium on issuance should remain on the books; and that, since the securities are being recorded in the fund in the same manner that securities of other companies would be handled, they should be charged to Sinking Fund Securities at cost and the premium or discount on purchase amortized over the period between the date of purchase and the date of maturity.

Following the same line of reasoning, it would be acceptable to continue interest payments on bonds held alive. If the bonds held alive are in the hands of a trustee, it may be legally necessary to continue the interest payments on these bonds. To illustrate the entries to be made if interest payments are continued on bonds held alive, assume that there are $20,000 of 5% bonds in the issue, and that $5,000 of the bonds are being held alive in the sinking fund. The entries for the interest would be:

```
Bond interest.......................................... 1,000
     Cash.............................................         1,000
     For payment of interest on bond issue.

Sinking fund cash......................................   250
     Sinking fund income (or Bond interest)..............        250
     For collection of interest on securities in fund.
```

Bond retirement fund.   If a company acquires its own bonds by expenditure of fund cash and retires them instead of holding them as live securities in the fund, the accounting will be somewhat different from that described in the foregoing pages.

Upon purchase and retirement of the bonds, an entry will be made debiting Bonds Payable and crediting Sinking Fund Cash.

Any unamortized premium or discount on issuance applicable to the bonds thus retired should be written off when the bonds are canceled.

If the company's own bonds are purchased and canceled, an extraneous loss or gain probably will develop from the transaction. The amount of the loss or gain is the difference between the outlay made to reacquire the bonds and their carrying value on the company's books. The carrying value of bonds outstanding equals their par value plus or minus any unamortized premium or discount.

Sinking funds for principal and interest. Companies are sometimes required to place with a sinking fund trustee monthly deposits for the payment of the semiannual interest as well as the principal of the bonds. In such instances, it should be remembered that making a deposit with a trustee does not constitute payment of the interest any more than it constitutes payment of the principal; the total funds on deposit with the trustee should be shown on the asset side of the balance sheet, and the liability on accrued unpaid interest as well as on principal should be shown on the liability side of the balance sheet. The liability on principal and interest cannot be eliminated from the balance sheet until the trustee has applied the funds to the payment of the liability.

Sinking fund reserves. Indentures executed in connection with long-term debt obligations frequently place a restriction on the payment of dividends. For many years this restriction commonly took the form of a requirement for the creation of a sinking fund reserve in conjunction with a sinking fund; the borrowing company, in addition to being required to deposit cash in the sinking fund, was required to make periodical transfers from Retained Earnings to a reserve. The object was to avoid or minimize the possibility of a working capital impairment which might result from the combined drain upon cash which would be caused by depositing cash in the fund and also paying dividends to the full amount of the current earnings—an impairment which might reduce earnings and thus lead to a default by the borrowing corporation in its payments to the fund.

If such a sinking fund reserve is required, what should be the amount of the periodical credits to the reserve? The answer to this question is usually found in the indenture. Generally, the prescribed periodical credits are set at a level sufficient to produce in the reserve an increasing balance equal to the amount which would be in the fund if all contributions were made as required and if the actual income accretions to the fund were exactly equal to the anticipated accretions. The balance in the reserve would then show the amount which should be in the fund.

This is true, of course, only with respect to funds and reserves provided for the retirement of obligations at maturity; if bonds are purchased at intervals and canceled, the balance in the fund account will rise and fall, but the balance in the reserve account should continually increase until the last bonds have been retired, because the holder of the last bond to be retired is entitled to all of the protection afforded by the limitation upon dividends measured by the required transfers from Retained Earnings to the restricted surplus reserve.

A sinking fund reserve, being a surplus reserve, is created by charges to Retained Earnings. The reserve should not be charged with expenses incident to the operation of the sinking fund, nor credited with income on the fund assets. After the liability has been paid, the sinking fund reserve may be closed by returning its credit balance to Retained Earnings, thus indicating that the portion of the Retained Earnings once tied up and not available as a basis of dividends has again become free and available for that purpose. Whether or not the company will have the funds with which to pay a dividend is another matter.

Sinking fund reserves have also been required in connection with the periodical retirement of preferred stock.

Sinking fund reserves seem to be going out of use. They are not an entirely satisfactory safeguard against impairment of working capital. If a company is required to deposit $10,000 in a sinking fund, it may not be sufficient merely to require that $10,000 also be transferred from Retained Earnings to a reserve; this requirement may be met, but the borrowing company may still deplete its working capital by paying dividends and charging them to the surplus accumulated before the long-term debt was incurred. For this reason it is becoming increasingly customary for indentures to provide that the surplus at the date of the issuance of the obligations (or a stated portion thereof) shall be "frozen" and shall not be available for charges for dividend payments until the obligations are retired. Such restrictions usually are disclosed parenthetically in the balance sheet or by a balance sheet footnote.

Funds for payment of contingent liabilities.   Funds for the payment of contingent liabilities are rarely encountered. A deposit by a contractor to guarantee the performance of work in accordance with specifications is an illustration of an obligatory fund for the payment of a contingent liability. A fund for the payment of damages which may result from an adverse decision of a pending patent infringement suit is an illustration of a voluntary fund which may be created for the payment of a contingent liability.

Funds for payment for an asset or a service. Sometimes the directors of a corporation adopt the policy of establishing a fund for the acquisition of plant assets. A Building Fund, Machinery Fund, or similar fund account may then be put on the books.

Funds for the payment of services may be compulsory or voluntary. They are compulsory if the establishment of the fund is based on a contract with outsiders. For example, leases frequently contain clauses requiring the immediate deposit of cash to be applied in payment of rent for subsequent (often the last) years of the lease. Cemeteries frequently sell lots under agreements that a certain portion of the sale price shall be deposited with a trustee as a fund to provide perpetual care.

Funds for future expenditures chargeable to expense accounts may be created voluntarily, by authorization of the management. A fund for advertising is an example.

It is important that the operation of a fund of the type mentioned here not be confused with the proper measurement of revenue and expense. To illustrate, assume that a company leases property for a period of five years at a rental of $3,000 payable annually, with a further agreement to pay the owners $5,000 at the termination of the lease, to be used in restoring the property to its original condition. Assume also that the contract requires that this $5,000 be provided by the creation of a fund by contributions of $2,000 at the end of the first and second years of the life of the lease and $1,000 at the end of the third year. The amount which should be in the fund at any date is determined by the contract; but the expense element relating to the termination payment accrues at the rate of $1,000 per year, and a liability should be credited (and Rent Expense should be debited) with $1,000 each year, to spread the $5,000 item over the life of the lease.

If this distinction is not clearly recognized, there is danger of assuming that the requirements concerning the fund determine also the charges to expense. But if expense were charged with $2,000 at the end of the first and second years, and with $1,000 at the end of the third year, the operations of the first two years would be burdened with an undue proportion of the expense, and the fourth and fifth years would be relieved of their proper share of the expense.

As another illustration, assume that a cemetery sells lots under an agreement that $50 shall be set aside from the proceeds of the sale of each lot until a fund of $90,000 is accumulated; and that, when all of the lots are sold, the fund shall be turned over to a trustee and the income used to provide perpetual care of the cemetery. Assume that the cemetery contains 3,000 lots having a uniform selling price. The fund should be provided from the sale of the first 1,800 lots, since $50 × 1,800 = $90,000. But each of the 3,000 lots should bear its share of the cost of perpetual care; therefore, the charge to expense should be made at the rate of $90,000 ÷ 3,000, or $30 per lot. As each of the first 1,800 lots is sold, entries should be made as follows:

```
Perpetual care fund...................................  ...........  50
   Cash................................................  ...........      50
      To record the required contribution to the fund.

Perpetual care expense.......................................  30
   Perpetual care liability.......................................      30
      To charge operations with the pro rata cost of perpetual care of
lot sold.
```

After 1,800 lots have been sold, the fund should be $90,000 and the liability should be $54,000. No further contributions to the fund need be made, but the $30 expense entry will have to be made when each of the remaining 1,200 lots is sold. When all of the lots have been sold, there will be a $90,000 fund and a $90,000 liability; the fund will have been accumulated in accordance with the contract, and the liability will have been credited in accordance with the expense accrual.

Stock redemption funds. The redemption-fund method has long been used for the retirement of bonds, and is also used for retiring preferred stock. The provisions of the stock issue may require that a definite amount of stock shall be retired annually, but it is doubtful whether this requirement could be enforced against the corporation if earnings were inadequate and creditors' rights were jeopardized. More frequently, the amount of stock to be retired annually is based upon the amount of the net income of the preceding year; it may be a fixed percentage of the net income, or it may be determined by a sliding scale of rates.

Fund arrearages and deposit requirements. If fund deposits required by contract are in arrears, the balance sheet should disclose this fact. It should also disclose the amount, if material, of any deposits required to be made soon after the balance sheet date and which therefore constitute a demand upon the current assets. Footnotes are probably the best device for making such disclosures. Such footnotes might be somewhat as follows: "On (the balance sheet date) the company was in arrears as to sinking fund deposits in the amount of $10,000"; or, "The company is obligated to make a deposit of $15,000 on (a date subsequent to the balance sheet date) in a fund for the retirement of its preferred stock."

Related funds and reserves. In the preceding pages there were occasional references to related funds and reserves, for example, sinking fund and reserve for sinking fund. What relation should exist between the amount of a fund and the amount of an accompanying reserve? Obviously, if either the fund or the reserve is voluntary, no necessary relationship exists, since the voluntary fund or reserve can be created in any desired amount.

If the reserve is required by contract or is used to show a surplus restriction required by law, those considerations govern the dollar amounts. But, as a general rule, the mere fact that a reserve is related to a fund is no basis for assuming that the fund account and reserve account balances must be maintained at identical amounts.

CHAPTER SIXTEEN

Tangible Fixed Assets

Fixed Assets:
1) Permanent Nature
2) Used in Operations
3) Not Intended For Sale

Principles of Valuation

Fixed assets.   Fixed assets are assets of a relatively permanent nature used in the operation of the business and not intended for sale.

A building used as a factory is a fixed asset. It is relatively permanent property; it is used in the operation of the business; and it is not intended for sale.

Land held as a prospective site for a future plant is not a fixed asset. It is permanent property and it is not intended for sale, but it is not used in the operation of the business.

A factory building no longer used in operations is not a fixed asset because it is not used in the operation of the business.

Tangible and intangible fixed assets.   The term *tangible* means having bodily substance. An asset is *intangible* if it has no bodily substance and its value resides only in the rights which its possession confers upon its owner.

egs. Tangible fixed assets include land, buildings, machinery, tools, patterns, delivery equipment, furniture and fixtures, and other similar property having physical substance. Intangible fixed assets include goodwill, patents, copyrights, trademarks, franchises, and other similar assets having no bodily substance but having value because of the rights inherent in them.

328

Classification of fixed assets.   Fixed assets may be classified as follows:

(A) Tangible:
- (1) Plant property.
  - (a) Not subject to depreciation.
    Example: Land.
  - (b) Subject to depreciation.
    Examples: Buildings, machinery, tools and equipment, delivery equipment, furniture and fixtures.
- (2) Natural resources, subject to depletion.
  Examples: Timber tracts, mines, oil wells.

(B) Intangible:
- (1) Normally subject to amortization.
  Examples: Patents, copyrights, franchises, leasehold improvements.
- (2) Not normally subject to amortization.
  Examples: Trademarks, goodwill.

Valuation of fixed assets.   Fixed assets usually are carried in the accounts on one of the following bases of valuation:

— Cost.
— Cost less depreciation, depletion, or amortization.
— Appraised value—usually replacement cost new less depreciation thereon.

In this chapter we shall be concerned primarily with matters related to the determination of the cost of tangible fixed assets, which are discussed in the following sequence:

(I) Matters applicable to fixed assets in general:
- (A) Capital and revenue expenditures.
- (B) Additions, improvements and betterments, replacements, and repairs.
- (C) The cost of fixed assets:
  - (1) Purchased:
    - (a) For cash.
    - (b) Subject to a cash discount.
    - (c) On credit terms.
    - (d) For securities.
    - (e) In a mixed acquisition at a lump cost.
  - (2) Constructed for own use.
- (D) Interest during construction.
- (E) Valuation of fixed assets received as a gift.

(II) Matters applicable to specific assets.

A **Capital and revenue expenditures.** An expenditure is a payment, or the incurring of an obligation to make a future payment, for a benefit received. Expenditures applicable to fixed assets are of two classes: capital and revenue. Capital expenditures are chargeable to asset accounts or to accumulated depreciation accounts; revenue expenditures are chargeable to operations.

It is not always easy to determine whether an expenditure should be classified as a capital expenditure or as a revenue expenditure. Attempts have been made to state principles or to lay down rules, but the principles and rules are not always susceptible of exact interpretation or application.

1 - Capital expenditures have been defined as those which result in additions or improvements of a permanent character and a substantial amount, and which add value to the property. This is not a wholly satisfactory definition. No fixed asset, with the possible exception of land, is permanent in the sense of having an endless life; permanency is relative. Some expenditures may properly be capitalized even though they are not of substantial amount. And all expenditures, even those for ordinary repairs, are presumed to add some value to the property; otherwise, they would not be made.

2 - Capital expenditures have also been defined as those which should increase net income, either by increasing revenue or by reducing expense. This, also, is not a wholly satisfactory definition. Expenditures which merely keep net income from declining are sometimes properly capitalizable. If this were not so, business management would find itself in the absurd position of being required to make expenditures to keep earnings from decreasing, and at the same time being required to charge the expenditures to operations, thereby reducing the net income.

It has also been said that an expenditure should be charged to expense if it is not expected to benefit any period beyond the one in which it is made, and that an expenditure should be capitalized if it is expected to benefit at least one future period. As George O. May stated clearly and succinctly,* "The distinction . . . between capital and revenue expenditures . . . rests . . . upon the relation of the useful life of the property acquired and the length of the accounting period for which income is being determined. A capital expenditure is one, the usefulness of which is expected to extend over several accounting periods. If the accounting period were increased from the customary year to a decade, most of what is now treated as capital expenditure would become chargeable

---

* *The Journal of Accountancy*, Vol. LXIII, page 335.

to income; while if the period were reduced to a day, much of what is now treated as current maintenance would become capital expenditure." This is a helpful criterion but it is not a wholly adequate one; the usefulness of an expenditure for an ordinary repair may extend over more than one period, but the expenditure is not properly capitalizable.

Expenditures for extraordinary repairs which extend the estimated useful life of fixed assets are capital expenditures.

General principles and rules need to be supplemented by a consideration of expenditures of various kinds, such as those for additions, improvements and betterments, replacements, and extraordinary and ordinary repairs. These are discussed in the following sections.

Additions.   An addition is something which does not merely replace a thing previously owned. Additions include entirely new units and extensions, expansions, and enlargements of old units. Thus, an entirely new building is an addition; so, also, is an enlargement of an existing building.

An expenditure for an addition consisting of an entirely new unit presents no accounting problems other than those relative to the determination of cost, which are discussed later. It is a capital expenditure, and the cost of the addition is chargeable to an asset account.

If an addition is an extension, expansion, or enlargement of an old unit, some special problems may arise; for instance, it may be necessary to tear out walls between the old and new portions of the building, or change roof structures, or increase the capacity of water pipes in the old building in order to provide plumbing facilities in the addition. Should the asset accounts be relieved of any of the old costs? The answer is generally in the negative. A negative answer may have some theoretical justification; it may be contended that it is correct to regard all costs, old and new, less salvage from demolished or reconstructed portions of the old structure, as costs of the enlarged building. But it is probable that practical considerations are the usual reason for the negative answer; in most cases it is not feasible to break down the cost of an entire building to determine the cost applicable to some relatively minor portion thereof.

Improvements and betterments.   The essential difference between an addition and an improvement or a betterment is that in an addition there is an increase in quantity, whereas in an improvement or a betterment there is a substitution with an increase only in quality. The new thing is better than the old one was when it was acquired. There is an improvement or betterment when a tile roof is substituted for wooden shingles, or shatter-proof glass is substituted for ordinary glass, or high-wattage electric light bulbs are substituted for bulbs of low wattage.

The proper accounting treatment of improvements and betterments depends upon whether they are of a major or a minor nature. Major expenditures, such as those for a better roof or better glass should be capitalized; minor expenditures, such as those for better light bulbs, should be charged to expense.

In the recording of major improvements, the cost of the thing replaced should be eliminated from the asset account, and the cost of the new property should be charged to it. If the accumulated depreciation on the replaced asset can be determined, it should be eliminated from the accounts. There should be no duplication of capitalized installation costs.

If plant assets are acquired in a run-down condition and rehabilitation expenditures are made, these expenditures result in improvements and are a proper charge to the asset accounts. Even if the expenditures are made over a considerable period of time, it still is proper to capitalize them so long as they result in an improved condition of the property or improved operating effectiveness as compared with the status at the time of acquisition. However, if the rehabilitation program extends over a long period, it is important to distinguish carefully between true rehabilitation costs and repairs. The charges to the property accounts for rehabilitation expenditures should be net of any amount recovered from salvage.

Replacements. A replacement also involves a substitution; but, unlike an improvement or a betterment, the new thing is no better than the old one was when it was acquired. Replacements are of three kinds:

(1) Replacements of whole units.

       Amounts related to the asset are removed from the accounts.

(2) Replacements of parts which may be regarded as ordinary repairs.

       These are discussed in the next section.

(3) Extensive replacements of parts which constitute extraordinary repairs.

       These also are discussed in the next section.

Repairs. Repairs usually involve replacements of parts, but repairs may be made without replacements. Repairs are of two classes: ordinary and extraordinary.

Ordinary repairs are those frequently encountered or involving relatively small sums of money. They require charges to operations. They may be accounted for in either of two ways.

(1) The expenditures may be charged to expense when made. This procedure requires no explanation.

(2) A reserve procedure may be used.

　　Since repair costs vary from year to year, normally increasing with the life of the asset, and also vary from month to month (because repair work may be done during slack operating periods), it may be desirable to equalize the expense over the life of the asset or during a year by the creation of an allowance account. The periodical charge to operations and credit to the allowance account should be determined by estimating the total of such repair expenditures to be made during the entire life of the asset, or during a year, and apportioning the provisions in equal periodical amounts. Although such an apportionment procedure may be desirable for the purpose of equalizing the expense, the charges to operations for the creation of the allowance account are not deductible for income tax purposes. The tax deduction must be based on the actual expenditures charged to the allowance account.

The theoretically ideal method of recording extraordinary repairs is to eliminate the cost of the replaced parts from the asset account, relieve the accumulated depreciation account of the depreciation provided thereon, and charge the asset account with the entire cost of the repairs, including the cost of the new parts. This can be done if the subsidiary records give the necessary information regarding the cost of, and the depreciation provided on, individual parts. In cases in which the necessary information is not available, it has been regarded as acceptable accounting to charge the expenditures to the accumulated depreciation account on the theory that the extraordinary repairs extend the life of the asset beyond the originally estimated period; in other words, the extraordinary repairs make good a portion of the depreciation for which provision has been made in the accumulated depreciation account. When this treatment is accorded to extraordinary repairs, it must be recognized that the procedure is a departure from strict theoretical correctness, since it ignores the difference between the cost of the original asset and the cost of the replacement, does not give consideration to the question of the adequacy of the remaining balance in the accumulated depreciation account as a provision for depreciation to date, and does not squarely face the question of the probable length of the period of extended usefulness and the related question of any necessary revision in the depreciation rate.

Arbitrary classification by dollar amount. Many companies establish a somewhat arbitrary policy of charging expense with all disbursements (except for additions) which are less than a fixed amount, say, $10, $50, or $100. The entries for an expenditure in excess of the fixed amount are determined by the nature of the expenditure.

Repairs and maintenance. A theoretical distinction between repairs and maintenance is sometimes made, maintenance being directed to keeping the assets in good condition and repairs being directed to putting them back into good condition. Maintenance is preventive; repairs are curative. The theoretical distinction usually is difficult to maintain in the accounts.

The term *deferred maintenance* is sometimes encountered, particularly in utility accounting. It means neglected maintenance requirements.

Payment in cash. If fixed assets are purchased for cash, the problem of determining the cost is relatively simple, since no question arises concerning the value of the thing parted with in exchange for the fixed asset. Cost includes the purchase price and all incidental payments such as freight, installation charges, and other items discussed in detail in the sections devoted to specific assets.

Discount on fixed assets. If cash discounts are taken on purchases of fixed assets, should the discount be recorded as financial income or as a reduction of the cost of the property? This is a question on which a considerable difference of opinion has existed. Accountants generally hold to the opinion that purchase discounts of all kinds are theoretically deductions in the determination of cost; that their treatment as financial income is a departure from good accounting principles and is acceptable only for reasons of expediency; but that reasons of expediency generally do not exist with respect to discounts on purchases of fixed assets, and that such discounts should be recorded as cost deductions regardless of the treatment accorded discounts on merchandise purchases.

Purchases on credit terms. If fixed assets are offered at a cash price and at a higher credit price, and are purchased at the credit price, accounting principles dictate that the asset be recorded at the cash price, and that the difference be recorded as interest.

If fixed assets are purchased on the installment plan, and stated amounts of interest are included in the payment, the interest element should be recorded as a financial expense.

In some instances carrying charges may be implicit in the purchase price without being explicitly stated as such. For instance, if an asset is purchased for $2,400 payable in 24 monthly installments of $100 each, no interest is mentioned, but a conservative accounting procedure would require a recognition of the economic reality that the cash cost of the fixed asset is the present value of all of the installments. Although it would be theoretically correct to record the acquisition of the fixed asset at a cost of $2,400 minus some amount charged as interest, this is rarely done—partly because of the necessity of arbitrarily deciding on an interest rate.

Payments in securities.　When a corporation acquires fixed assets by issuing its own bonds or stock, there may be some question as to whether or not the securities so issued are worth their par, and whether the cost of the fixed assets is equal to the par value of the securities or is something other than that amount.

If some of the stock or bonds is sold to third parties for cash at approximately the same time that similar securities are issued for other property, the cash price of the securities is indicative of their value, and fixed assets acquired by issuance of securities may be placed on the books at the value thus established.

The words "to third parties" are significant, for, if the same party takes a portion of the stock for cash at par and a very considerable portion of the remaining stock for fixed assets, the two transactions are so closely related as to make the cash sale price a doubtful measure of the real value of the stock. One must consider not only the arm's-length nature of the transaction in which stock is issued for cash, but also the amount of stock sold; otherwise, a small block of stock might be sold to outsiders for cash at par, or even at a premium, but such a transaction might not serve to establish the fair cash value of the stock.

If all of the stock or all of the bonds of a company are issued in payment for fixed assets, there will be no cash sales of the securities to serve as a measure of their cash value. If there is also no appraisal, it may be necessary to value the fixed assets at the par or stated value of the securities issued for them.

The law allows the directors of a corporation a large measure of discretion in valuing property taken in payment for stock. Creditors may, at some later date, attack the values in court in an attempt to show that the stock was really issued at a discount, and that the stockholders are liable for the discount. However, this is a contingency which the company's accountant cannot anticipate by insisting upon a valuation less than that approved by the directors and upon setting up an account with discount on stock.

The public accountant's position is somewhat different. He probably would be considered guilty of misrepresentation if he gave an unqualified opinion regarding financial statements containing gross inflations of asset values. He cannot be expected to assume the responsibility of placing an acceptable valuation on the assets, but he can be expected to qualify his report.

Mixed acquisitions at a lump cost. If several assets are acquired in one purchase at a lump price, it is necessary to apportion the cost to the various assets in order to show costs not subject to depreciation, or subject to depreciation at various rates. The apportionment of cost can be made on the basis of an appraisal by outside appraisers or by company officials. For instance, if land, buildings, and machinery are acquired at a cost of $120,000 and if they are appraised at $15,000, $60,000, and $75,000, respectively, the cost can be apportioned in the ratio of the appraised value of each class of assets to the total appraised value. The computation is shown below:

Assets	APPRAISAL Amount	Per Cent	Apportioned Cost
Land	$ 15,000	10%	$ 12,000
Buildings	60,000	40	48,000
Machinery	75,000	50	60,000
Total	$150,000	100%	$120,000

Assets constructed. Two matters require consideration with respect to the costs of fixed assets constructed:

(1) The propriety of including manufacturing overhead in the cost.

(2) The construction-period theory.

Overhead as an element of cost. The inclusion of material and labor costs in the cost of fixed assets manufactured by a company for its own use has never been, and should not be, questioned. Over the years, there has been a change in accounting thought relative to the propriety of including factory overhead in the cost of fixed assets manufactured.

It was originally believed that *no overhead should be charged to fixed assets.* This opinion was defended by the following reasoning:

The production of fixed assets presumably will not be allowed to interfere with the manufacture of goods which can be sold, since otherwise any saving on the production of fixed assets would be offset by the loss of profits on finished goods which might have been manufactured and sold.

Therefore, the production of fixed assets will normally occur during periods when the plant facilities will not be required for the manufacture of the salable product; consequently, there will be no increase, or at least no appreciable increase, in the overhead as the result of the production of fixed assets.

To charge fixed assets with part of the normal overhead would result in a corresponding reduction in the overhead charged to the cost of goods manufactured, and a corresponding increase in the profits on merchandise sales.

Since this additional profit would be the result of a charge to the fixed assets for the overhead capitalized, the company would be taking a profit on the manufacture of its fixed assets.

To illustrate the point, let us assume the following facts concerning the costs of manufacturing finished goods during two years and the cost of constructing fixed assets during the second year:

	1958 Finished Goods Only	1959 Total	1959 Finished Goods	1959 Fixed Assets
Materials	$ 50,000	$ 75,000	$50,000	$25,000
Direct labor	50,000	75,000	50,000	25,000
Factory expense	50,000	50,000	?	?
Total	$150,000	$200,000		
Selling price	200,000			
Gross profit	$ 50,000			

Assume that the same quantity of finished goods was manufactured in 1959 as in 1958 and sold at the same price. If we charge part of the factory overhead in 1959 to finished goods and part to fixed assets (on the basis of the direct labor, for instance), we produce the following results:

	1959 Total	1959 Finished Goods	1959 Fixed Assets
Materials	$ 75,000	$ 50,000	$25,000
Direct labor	75,000	50,000	25,000
Factory overhead (apportioned on basis of direct labor)	50,000	33,333	16,667
Total	$200,000	$133,333	$66,667
Selling price of finished goods		200,000	
Gross profit		$ 66,667	

The gross profit in 1959 is shown to be $16,667 more than it was in 1958, although the same quantity of merchandise was manufactured, and sales were made at the same price. This $16,667 is the amount of overhead charged to fixed assets. Therefore it was argued that the overhead charged to the fixed assets resulted in an increase in reported net income, and that the company, in effect, was taking a profit on work done for itself.

This illustration is, of course, a simple one because the labor and material costs and the selling prices of finished goods were assumed to be identical during the two years, and because the construction of fixed assets was assumed to cause no increase in overhead. Nonessential variations were purposely eliminated in order to stress the theoretical point.

The next step in the development of thought relative to the inclusion of overhead in the cost of fixed assets manufactured may be stated as follows: *Fixed assets should be charged with overhead specifically incurred in their manufacture.* Those who proposed this procedure maintained, and probably rightly so, that the manufacture of fixed assets cannot be carried on without incurring some overhead costs which would not otherwise be incurred. Although there are many fixed charges which would not be increased, there are variable costs which are more or less proportionate to the utilization of the factory facilities. The cost of power is one illustration. It would be improper to load the cost of finished goods with expenses which were not incurred in their manufacture and which would not have been incurred if fixed assets had not been produced. The now well-established emphasis on the cost principle has resulted in an increasing belief that, in the allocation of costs, no special favors or cost exemptions should be granted, and, therefore, that *overhead should be charged to fixed assets manufactured on the same basis and at the same rate that it is charged to goods manufactured.* This point of view does encounter some resistance from those accountants still influenced by the fetish of conservatism. The increasing recognition of the importance of cost as the basis of accounting has been accompanied by an increasing tendency to sanction the inclusion of overhead in the cost of fixed assets at the same rate as that applied to finished goods, so that there may be no special favors or exemptions resulting in the undercosting of fixed assets and a consequent overcosting of finished goods.

The construction-period theory. The accounting principle which sanctions the capitalization of all expenditures during the construction period applies particularly to buildings. It was at first regarded as applying to a building constructed before the company commenced operations, and it was defended on two grounds: First, if a company was engaged only in the construction of a plant, all of its expenditures (even those which, during operations, would be regarded as administrative expenses) were incurred for the purpose of construction and hence were properly capitalizable; second, a company should not be required to begin operations under the embarrassment of a deficit. The theory is now regarded as also applying to plant additions made while operations are in progress; however, it is not intended that this should result in any favoritism to regular operations.

A period sometimes elapses between the completion of a plant and its occupancy or other utilization as an income-producing factor of the business, and management sometimes desires to capitalize expenses during that period. If operations are being conducted elsewhere, there seems little justification for such a capitalization. If operations have not been commenced, the situation may be somewhat different, and it is sometimes regarded as permissible to capitalize, after completion of construction, some expenditures which normally would be charged to income. For instance, if occupancy of a factory building is necessarily postponed for some time after its completion, capitalizing the carrying charges until the date of occupancy may be sanctioned. However, the construction-period theory should not be abused by capitalizing carrying charges over a long interim period; a long waiting period should probably be recognized as an indication that executive planning was poor, that the building has proved to be a losing venture, and that losses should be taken into the accounts. Even if interim-period expenses appear to be properly capitalizable, it is probably preferable to record them as deferred charges instead of including them in fixed asset costs.

Although a building or other fixed asset may deteriorate to some extent during the construction period, it is customary to ignore such depreciation in the accounts, and to spread the depreciation charges over the period of utilization. There certainly would be no object in making a charge for depreciation during the construction period and recapitalizing such charges by adding them back to the cost of the asset as a construction-period cost.

Interest during construction. Utility commissions permit utility companies to charge the fixed asset accounts with interest costs incurred during the construction period, regardless of whether the construction is done by the company itself or by a contractor. Such a capitalization of interest is permitted because no income is earned by the asset during construction to cover the interest. Since the interest cannot be recovered before the asset is put to use, the utility is permitted to recover it by including it in the investment on which it is permitted to earn a rate of return.

Although no similar reason exists for allowing industrials to capitalize interest during the construction period, the sanction of utility commissions has been carried over into the field of accounting for industrials without a consideration of the difference in conditions. Interest paid, by either a utility or an industrial, is not a necessary cost of construction; the interest could be avoided by the use of the proceeds of stock. Utilities are permitted to capitalize interest in order that rate-fixing bodies will give it proper consideration in determining future rates and earnings; industrials do not need to capitalize interest for any such reason, because they are permitted to earn what they can.

Charging to construction the interest on securities issued by an industrial company to obtain funds for construction has little justification in theory. Some attempt has been made to justify it under the general theory that all costs during the construction period can be capitalized; but interest is a money cost, not a construction cost, and it can be avoided by an additional investment of proprietorship capital. However, the practice is now so well established that it is no longer challenged.

Donated assets. Corporations sometimes receive gifts of fixed assets, either from their stockholders or from cities which attract industries by providing them with plants or with sites for plants. It has long been established practice to record such assets at their fair value. It has recently been argued that such accounting is a departure from the cost basis. However, since the purpose of accounting is to reflect accountability, it would seem proper for management to report some value for all assets for which it is accountable. If an asset is acquired by gift, the amount of the accountability seems to be properly measured by the fair value of the property.

Gifts of assets may be unconditional or conditional. If they are unconditional, the recipient obtains immediate title to them, and custom sanctions making entries debiting the asset accounts at appropriate valuations and crediting an account with some title such as Paid-in Surplus—Plant Donation.

Gifts of fixed assets from a city are frequently subject to some condition, such as continued operations over a stated period of time, or the employment of a certain minimum number of men for a specified number of years. To illustrate, assume that a business is given factory land and buildings on condition that it employ at least one hundred men each year for five years. Any entries made to record the contingent gift should clearly indicate that title has not been obtained and that no addition to paid-in surplus has been assuredly realized. An entry may be made debiting such accounts as Contingent Asset—Land, and Contingent Asset—Buildings, and crediting an account with some title such as Contingent Paid-in Surplus—Plant Donation.

If title is obtained at the end of the five-year period, the balances in the contingent asset accounts should be transferred to the Land and Buildings accounts, and the contingent paid-in surplus should be transferred to Paid-in Surplus—Plant Donation. It would be improper to transfer one-fifth of the contingent surplus to paid-in surplus annually, since the stipulated conditions must be met during all of the years. Failure to comply with the requirements during any one year will cause a forfeiture.

Fixed assets acquired by gift should be depreciated on the basis of the appraisal values recorded in the accounts. But if the gift is conditional, should depreciation be provided on the assets before the date on which title is obtained? It might be contended that such depreciation should be ignored, because production costs should not be charged with depreciation of assets not owned. On the other hand, if no depreciation is provided during this period, high depreciation charges, sufficient to compensate for the lack of such charges during the period before title was acquired, will be necessary during the period of use following the acquisition of title. These high charges will introduce an element of variation in income charges during two periods of similar operating conditions and will load the total depreciation on the period of ownership rather than on the entire period of use. The authors are, therefore, of the opinion that operations during the period prior to the acquisition of title should be charged with depreciation.

Special Points on Specific Assets

Real estate.   Rights in real estate may be classified as follows:

(1) Freehold estates:
  (a) Estates in fee simple, or estates of inheritance, which descend to one's heirs.
  (b) Estates for life.
(2) Estates less than freeholds:
  These are otherwise known as *leaseholds*.

Only freeholds can properly and legally be considered real property, to be recorded under the heading of "land." Leaseholds are personal property, and are considered later under the classification of intangible assets. Persons holding leaseholds for long periods of time, such as 63, 84, and 99 years, are likely to consider them as freeholds, but the legal distinction should not be lost sight of in the accounts.

Accounts.   Land and buildings should not be carried in a single account called "Real Estate." Separate accounts should be opened for the land and the buildings, because land does not depreciate and does not have to be insured, whereas buildings do depreciate and should be insured.

Although land does not decrease in value as a result of use and the passing of years, losses may be incurred as a result of obsolescence or a sort of supersession. Neighborhoods change, and there are consequent declines in income productivity. Although it probably would be improper for a business to make regular provisions for such obsolescence, it might be advisable for management to observe neighborhood changes and give consideration to the possibility that obsolescence is in prospect and make provisions therefor. Any such occurrence would presumably affect the value of the buildings as well as the value of the land.

Land. If any land is held for speculative purposes, or with the intention of using it for future plant extensions, such land should be distinguished in the accounts from land in use as a plant site. The distinction can be made by using such account titles as "Plant Land" and "Nonplant Land." Plant-site land should be shown in the balance sheet under the Fixed Assets caption; land held for speculation or possible plant expansion should be shown under some other caption.

Not only should plant-site and speculative land be separated in the accounts, but various premises should be recorded in separate accounts if there are a considerable number of them. While one general ledger account for plant land and one for nonplant land may be sufficient, subsidiary records of some kind should be kept, particularly if some of the parcels of land are mortgaged and others are not.

If wasting assets are acquired and the land will have a residual value after the wasting asset is exhausted, the portion of the cost applicable to the land itself should be set up in a separate account.

Cost is the generally accepted basis of accounting for land. Cost includes the purchase price, broker's commission, fees for examining and recording title, surveying, draining, clearing (less salvage), and landscaping.

Expenditures for land improvements may be charged to the Land account if the expenditures result in the addition of costs which are not subject to depreciation. If depreciation must be considered in relation to such expenditures, an account with Land Improvements should be opened. Such an account would be charged with expenditures for fences, water systems, and sidewalks, and with paving costs.

Assessments for such local benefits as paving and street lighting are often spread so wide geographically that property owners who benefit little, if any, from an improvement are required to contribute to the cost. It would seem that a proper valuation of the land would exclude the cost of such assessments, and that they should be treated as expenses, although for federal income tax purposes special assessments are not recognized as allowable deductions.

Land costs should include any interest, accrued at the date of purchase, on mortgages or other encumbrances on the land, and apportioned to the purchaser.

In the case of land being held for speculation or for future plant-site use, the question arises concerning the treatment of taxes and other carrying charges. It is certainly a conservative procedure to charge off such carrying expenses immediately. On the other hand, it may be reasonably contended that, as the purpose of buying such land is either to take advantage of a rising market or to obtain the property when it is available, the carrying charges are proper additions to the cost, particularly since the land produces no income against which the expenses can be charged.

It is often stated that such charges should not be added to the Land account unless the market value is increasing sufficiently to cover both the original cost and the subsequent carrying charges. However, if the land is being held for plant purposes, market values have no bearing on the proper valuation for accounting purposes, since the land may properly be carried at the total of all costs up to the time a plant is constructed on it and occupied. In other words, it is not the liquidating basis of market which governs, but the going-concern basis of cost. If the land is being held for speculation, the eventual gain or loss is the difference between selling price and cost plus carrying charges. If the carrying costs are charged against income from other sources, and if the books show a gain or loss on the sale equal to the difference between purchase and sale prices, both the gain or loss from the speculation and the income from other sources are distorted.

For federal income tax purposes, the taxpayer has the option of capitalizing the carrying charges on vacant land which produces no revenue or treating them as deductible expenses.

Although the accounts with land should reflect cost, the market value of land held for speculation or plant expansion, if substantially below cost, should be shown parenthetically in the balance sheet or be otherwise disclosed. This need not be done in the case of plant land, because, from the going-concern standpoint, market values of fixed assets need not be given recognition.

Buildings. If a building is purchased, cost includes the purchase price plus all repair charges incurred in making good depreciation which occurred before the building was purchased, as well as all costs of alterations and improvements.

If a building is constructed instead of purchased, the cost includes the material, labor and supervision, and other expenses, or the contract price, and a great variety of incidentals, some of which are mentioned below:

(1) If land and an old building which is to be razed are purchased at a flat price, the total cost may be charged to the land. The cost of wrecking, minus any proceeds from the sale of salvage, should be charged to the Land account.

If an old building, formerly occupied by the business, is replaced, the loss on the retirement of the old building should not be capitalized and included in the cost of the new building.

(2) If property is purchased subject to an existing lease, and the building is to be razed to make room for a new structure, any payments made to tenants to induce them to vacate before the expiration of the lease may be included in the cost of the new building.

(3) Costs of excavation should be charged to the building, rather than to the land.

(4) Costs of building permits and licenses may be capitalized.

(5) Costs of temporary buildings used for construction offices or as tool and material sheds may be capitalized, but the cost of temporary buildings used for operations during the construction of the permanent buildings should be absorbed in operations.

(6) Architect's fees and superintendents' salaries are a part of the cost.

(7) The cost of construction of a building can properly include all insurance premiums applicable to the construction period, including premiums on insurance against claims for damages or accidents. If no insurance is carried, any disbursements made in settlement of such claims can be capitalized unless their amount is so excessive as to inflate grossly the valuation of the building.

(8) As indicated on page 338, certain expenditures which ordinarily would be charged to expense may be capitalized if made during the construction period.

(9) Interest accrued during the construction period on bonds or other obligations assumed or issued to obtain funds for construction purposes may be capitalized; the proportion of bond discount applicable to the construction period may be similarly treated.

Building occupancy account. In Chapter 2 all accounts reflecting costs of building occupancy were closed directly to the Manufacturing account or to the Revenue and Expense account. It may be desirable, under certain circumstances, to close them to intermediate clearing, or assembly, accounts. The purposes for which such procedures are used are discussed below.

To simplify proratings. If building occupancy costs are to be apportioned to several departments (and possibly to functions within departments), it may be desirable to close all accounts reflecting such costs to a Building Occupancy clearing account so that apportionment can be made of the aggregate amount instead of making apportionments of all of the individual accounts. The clearing account would be closed to Building Occupancy—Manufacturing, Building Occupancy—Selling, and Building Occupancy —General, or to sub-function accounts within the three main classifications.

To compare occupancy costs on ownership or rental bases. If it is desired to assemble, in the accounts, information indicating whether it is more "profitable" to own or to rent, the individual accounts may be closed to two clearing accounts:

Costs Incurred in Lieu of Rent.
  This account would be debited with the balances (or portions of the balances) of accounts reflecting costs (such as insurance, taxes, and depreciation) which would not be incurred if the building were rented. After comparing the resulting balance of this account with an amount regarded as a fair rental for the premises, the account is closed to
Building Occupancy.
  In addition to the debit mentioned above, this account is charged with transfers to complete the closing of the individual accounts related to occupancy of the building. Its balance will then be the same as that resulting from the procedure described above in the paragraph "To simplify proratings," and the proratings may be made in the same manner.

To determine income from rentals to tenants. If portions of the premises (whether owned or rented) are leased to tenants, the following accounts may be kept:

Rental Activities.
  The portions of the individual expense accounts regarded as applicable to space leased to tenants are transferred to this account. It is credited with the rental income and its resulting balance is closed to Revenue and Expense and is shown in the income statement as miscellaneous income or expense.
Building Occupancy.
  The remaining expenses, regarded as applicable to the space occupied by the company itself, are transferred from the individual expense accounts to this account. The balance of the account can then be apportioned to departments or subfunctions.

Building expense and income. Concerns owning their own buildings sometimes set up a Building Expense and Income account, charging it with all occupancy costs and crediting it with income, if any, from rents for leased space; the account is also credited, by charge to operations, with an estimated amount representing the cost that would be incurred for space occupied by the company if the premises were leased instead of owned. The balance of the account is then presumed to indicate whether ownership is desirable, and is closed to Revenue and Expense.

It should be noted that, if the theoretical rent for company-occupied space is greater than the actual occupancy cost, the portion of the excess charged to manufacturing overstates the cost of goods manufactured, with an offsetting credit to income. Such offsetting misstatements are undesirable. The situation is made worse if some of the manufactured goods are unsold at the end of the period; in that case, part of the overstated manufacturing cost is lodged in the end-of-period inventory, with a consequent overstatement of net income.

Machinery. The cost of machinery includes the purchase price, freight, duty, and installation costs. If machinery has to be operated for a time for the purpose of breaking it in and testing it, the costs of such necessary preliminary operation may be capitalized.

The records for machinery should be kept in considerable detail, to provide information concerning location, price, and condition for insurance purposes, and to supply information concerning life and repairs for depreciation purposes. Depreciation rates are at best only estimates, which should be revised as the history of the business furnishes statistics on which more accurate estimates may be based. Hence, adequate statistical records should be kept. A subsidiary plant ledger should be maintained, with a page or card for each machine. Punched cards used in connection with tabulating procedures have been found serviceable as subsidiary property records. Each unit of equipment should be tagged or otherwise marked with a number which will definitely identify it, and the same identifying code number should appear in the subsidiary ledger. The subsidiary plant ledger should contain the following information, part of which will be posted from books of original entry and part of which will be recorded merely as memoranda:

Name of machine
Number (to identify the machine)
Location
Manufacturer
Manufacturer's guarantee period
From whom purchased

Date of installation

Purchase price
Cost of installation
Other elements of original cost ⎱ (The total of these elements in all subsidiary accounts is controlled by the asset accounts in the general ledger.)

Types of machine tools used with the equipment
Service and depreciation data:
  Estimated life
  Actual life
  Estimated residual value
  Actual residual value
Depreciation rate
Periodical depreciation provision, and accumulated amount provided to date (The total in all subsidiary accounts is controlled by accumulated depreciation accounts in the general ledger.)
Ordinary and extraordinary repairs, with information regarding date, cost, and nature
Information concerning abnormal operating conditions, such as overtime work, affecting depreciation and the operating life of the asset

Such records provide data desirable for insurance purposes and are extremely helpful in proving a claim for loss. The service information is valuable as a guide to future purchases, and the information concerning actual life and actual residual value realized upon the disposal of the asset is helpful in making future estimates of depreciation rates to be applied to similar equipment.

The data concerning total depreciation provided up to any given date are valuable for two reasons:

(1) To avoid overdepreciating any asset. For instance, the general ledger may contain a Machinery account with a debit balance of $50,000, and an Accumulated Depreciation—Machinery account with a credit balance of $20,000. On the average, the machinery is 40% depreciated. But this is an average of old and new machinery. Some of the old machinery may have been fully depreciated; for example, one machine costing $1,000 may have been depreciated at 10% per annum for ten years. Reference to the subsidiary record for this machine will disclose this fact, and no further depreciation will be taken on the machine.

(2) To show the depreciated book value of each unit of machinery, in order that the gain or loss on disposals can be accurately determined.

The subsidiary records should, in some cases, be carried to greater detail than a single unit of equipment. If the unit of equipment consists of various parts subject to different depreciation rates, and if the costs of the various elements can be ascertained, it is advisable to keep the records in such a way as to show the portions of cost subject to the various depreciation rates. A delivery truck is a good illustration of a fixed asset for which subdivided subsidiary records can be kept; the tires will require replacement before the remainder of the truck.

If entries are made in the general ledger to give effect to an appraisal, the subsidiary plant ledger should thereafter be kept on both a cost and an appraisal basis. The cost basis should be retained for income tax purposes, and the appraisal-basis data will be required for purposes of maintaining an agreement between the general ledger controlling accounts and the subsidiary records.

Reinstallation costs. If machinery is rearranged in the factory for the purpose of improving the "routing," and thus reducing the time and cost of production, a question arises with respect to the proper treatment of the reinstallation expense. Presumably the cost of one installation will already have been charged to the Machinery account. Theoretically, therefore, the cost, or the undepreciated remainder of the cost, of the first installation should be removed from the accounts, and the reinstallation cost should be capitalized by charge to the Machinery account.

Tools. Tools may be divided into two classes: machine tools and hand tools. Machine tools are really a part of the machine and may, therefore, be charged to the Machinery account. However, since they usually wear out much more rapidly than the machine, are likely to be lost or stolen, and hence have to be replaced, and since they are similar to hand tools in these respects, it is usually better to carry both classes of tools in the Tools account.

As the element of loss and theft plays a large part in determining the cost of tool replacements, it is usually advisable to abandon the idea of applying a depreciation rate to the tools, and to substitute the physical inventory method. The tools on hand at the close of the period are listed and valued at cost, with an allowance for wear and tear, and the Tools account is written down to the value thus ascertained.

Patterns. Some patterns are used for regular stock work, and thus have a long-term value which can be charged to the asset account and reduced by depreciation charges. Other patterns are made for special jobs and should be charged to the cost of the jobs and not to the Patterns account. Although it may be possible, and even perhaps probable, that orders will be repeated for the special jobs, conservatism requires charging the pattern cost to the first order.

Furniture and fixtures.   This account should be charged with the cost of relatively permanent property such as showcases and counters, shelving, display fixtures, safes, and office equipment. It is preferable to have a Store Fixtures account and an Office Fixtures account, in order that the depreciation charges may be properly allocated as selling and administrative expenses. Unless carefully watched, these accounts may become inflated with charges for trivial items and with rearrangement and replacement costs which add no value.

Delivery equipment.   What was said with regard to sub-sidiary records for machinery applies equally to records for delivery equipment. Service records are particularly important in furnishing data on which a per-mile depreciation rate may be based. Parts, such as tires, requiring frequent replacement may be charged off as expenses rather than capitalized and subjected to depreciation.

Containers.   Concerns that deliver goods in containers, such as milk bottles, vinegar and oil barrels, cement sacks, steel tanks, drums, carboys, and bakers' baskets, face the problem of accounting for such property.

The record of returnable containers in customers' hands may be kept in a purely memorandum manner without making any charges to the customers' accounts. If, as in the retail milk business, there are no billings to customers and there is a high percentage of loss, the containers may be regarded as operating supplies rather than fixed assets, and the loss thereon should be determined by periodical inventories. If containers not billed to customers are carried in the accounts as fixed assets, a liberal allowance should be set up for the loss incurred from the customers' failure to make returns.

It is not uncommon to bill customers for containers shipped to them, with the understanding that full credit will be granted upon return of the container. The entries below, for a sale and for a return of containers, illustrate such an arrangement.

Accounts receivable	1,075	
Sales		1,000
Allowance for returnable containers		75
To record a sale.		
Allowance for returnable containers	75	
Accounts receivable		75
To record a return of containers.		

The Allowance for Returnable Containers should be deducted in the balance sheet from the receivables for containers.

Customers sometimes pay for and retain the containers billed to them. The entries for such a collection will depend upon whether the billings were at cost or above cost. Referring to the preceding illustration and assuming that the billing was at cost, the entry for a collection for the containers would be:

```
Cash................................................... 75
    Accounts receivable................................        75
    To record the collection.

Allowance for returnable containers.................. 75
    Containers.........................................        75
    To relieve the asset account of the cost of containers sold.
```

If the billing was above cost (say, $25 above cost), the second entry would be as indicated below:

```
Allowance for returnable containers.................. 75
    Containers.........................................        50
    Income from containers sold.......................        25
```

It will be noted that there are no debits to an accumulated depreciation account in the foregoing entries relieving the asset account for the containers sold. This is so because containers are usually carried in the fixed asset accounts on an inventory basis; in other words, no accumulated depreciation account is provided, and the asset account is adjusted periodically to a valuation determined by preparing a physical inventory of the containers on hand and those with customers and making an estimate of their condition.

If customers are billed for the containers, their accounts may be kept in such a manner as to distinguish between balances receivable from customers in cash and balances to be settled by the return of containers. It may be convenient also to provide a separate column in the sales book for charges to customers for containers.

If cash deposits for returnable containers are collected from customers when sales are made, the amount collected should be credited to a liability account, such as Customers' Container Deposits. When the deposit is refunded upon the return of the containers, the Customers' Container Deposits account is debited and Cash is credited.

It may be the company's experience that some containers are never returned, perhaps because of breakage or disappearance while in the customer's possession. Under such circumstances, periodic adjusting entries are required to reduce the liability account and the Containers account. If the required deposit exceeds cost, the difference will be credited to Income from Containers

Sold in the adjusting entry. To illustrate such an adjusting entry, assume the following facts:

Cost of containers......................................	$10 per unit
Cash deposit required of customers......................	$15 per unit
Estimated number of containers that will not be returned..	100

Customers' container deposits...........................	1,500	
Containers...		1,000
Income from containers sold...........................		500
Adjusting entry for estimated nonreturns.		

CHAPTER SEVENTEEN

Tangible Fixed Assets
(Continued)

Depreciation

Similarity of fixed assets and prepaid expenses.   The cost of a machine which will last twenty years and the cost of a three-year insurance policy on the machine both represent outlays to be charged to expense and recovered, if possible, out of revenue—one during a period of twenty years, the other during a period of three years. The fact that the twenty-year life of the machine is estimated, whereas the three-year life of the insurance policy is definite, should not result in any failure to recognize that the cost exhaustions in both cases represent expenses. The portion of the insurance cost to be absorbed in expense annually is definitely determinable, whereas the portion of the machine cost to be absorbed in expense annually must be estimated; but there is no more justification for preparing a statement of operations in which some amount is shown as net income before depreciation than there would be in preparing an operating statement showing some amount as net income before insurance. Net income is not known until charges have been made for all expirations of costs.

Causes of expiration of plant property costs.   The following words are used to denote the causes of the exhaustion or expiration of investments in tangible fixed assets used as plant property:

Depreciation.	Supersession.	Accidents.
Obsolescence.	Inadequacy.	

Obsolescence, supersession, inadequacy, and accidents. Little comment is required with respect to accidents, as the meaning of the word is obvious. In some businesses, accidents, although not occurring with regularity, do occur with sufficient frequency to make them virtually a normal element of operations. In such businesses, it is acceptable accounting to equalize the cost of accidents by establishing a reserve by periodical charges to operations sufficient to absorb the losses which the experience of the business indicates will occur. For federal income tax purposes, accident losses are deductible only in the year in which they are incurred; reserve provisions are not deductible.

Supersession and inadequacy may be regarded as causes of obsolescence. A fixed asset may become obsolete because it is superseded by another fixed asset which operates so much more cheaply or efficiently than the old one that it is profitable to discard the old while it is still usable and install the new. A fixed asset may also become obsolete because its product is superseded by some other article. Thus, if a fixed asset is used in the manufacture or distribution of an article whose sale is dependent on a fad or a fashion, and the fixed asset is capable of use only in connection with this article, the fixed asset will become obsolete if the article is superseded in public favor by some other article. Fixed assets used in the manufacture of player piano rolls suffered obsolescence with the advent of the radio.

Inadequacy usually results from expansion in operations. For instance, a company may begin operations cautiously with equipment capable of small production and find that the sale of the product justifies an increase in production and the utilization of equipment of larger capacity.

Supersession and inadequacy are not the only causes of obsolescence. Any event or condition which renders the continued use of a fixed asset (which is still physically capable of use) inexpedient, impracticable, or impossible is a cause of obsolescence.

Obsolescence may be classified as ordinary or extraordinary. Ordinary obsolescence results from improvements in the arts and from other normal occurrences incident to operations. Extraordinary obsolescence results from causes not normally incident to operations. During World War II automobile and other factories were converted to war production; at the conclusion of the war, changes in models and in consumer demands caused an extraordinary obsolescence in many fixed assets in use before the war. For tax purposes, ordinary obsolescence may be included in the depreciation provision; extraordinary obsolescence is deductible only when determined.

The necessity of providing for physical deterioration was recognized long before recognition was given to the desirability of making provisions for obsolescence. The increasing inclination of management to include provisions for obsolescence with the provisions for physical deterioration in the periodical charges to income is perhaps due less to considerations of business prudence and sound accounting than to their deductibility for tax purposes.

There is some difference of opinion among accountants regarding the proper accounting procedure to be applied when a fixed asset becomes obsolete. Some maintain that the cost of the asset, minus any accumulated depreciation and obsolescence and minus the proceeds of disposal, should immediately be written off to Retained Earnings; others agree to the advisability of an immediate write-off but say that the charge should be made to current income; a few consider it permissible to treat the loss as a deferred charge. If the obsolete asset is not disposed of, accountants are in general agreement that it should not be classified in the balance sheet as a fixed asset; some accountants advocate a reduction in carrying value to a realizable basis; others, while recognizing the theoretical desirability of such a reduction, are influenced by the practical difficulty of estimating a realizable value, and are disposed to adhere to the tax procedure of taking no loss until the period when disposal occurs or the loss is otherwise determined.

Depreciation. Depreciation was formerly rather generally regarded by accountants as the physical deterioration of a tangible asset caused by wear and tear and the action of the elements. The concept of depreciation expressed by the foregoing definition is now regarded by most accountants as unsatisfactory, for two reasons:

First, depreciation, as defined above, has reference to only a physical phenomenon: decay or deterioration. The more modern accounting concept is that depreciation is related to all forces, economic as well as physical, which ultimately terminate the economic usefulness of a fixed asset. There certainly can be no quarrel with those who advocate absorbing the cost of a fixed asset by charges against income during the useful life of the asset, whether its life be terminated by physical or by economic forces; however, with words such as *obsolescence, inadequacy*, and *supersession* available to denote the economic causes of the demise of fixed assets, it might be preferable to limit the use of the word *depreciation* to signify the expiration of cost or value which is the consequence of the physical changes which we recognize as incident to growing old.

Second, the advocates of the more modern definition believe that, from the accounting standpoint, depreciation should apply to the *investment* in the asset, rather than to the asset itself. Placing the emphasis on exhaustion of the investment rather than on exhaustion of the asset might not satisfy an engineer, who is concerned with depreciation as a physical function, but it is a useful emphasis from the standpoint of the accountant, who is concerned with the erosion of fixed asset costs and their absorption as expenses into the stream of operations. Placing the accounting emphasis on the assignment of cost rather than on physical deterioration gives recognition to the fact that depreciation charges are not intended to parallel physical decline. Depreciation charges are intended to spread the cost of the asset over the years of its usefulness in an equitable manner; this result would not be accomplished if the accumulated depreciation charges followed the curve of physical depreciation. For one reason, physical depreciation usually is less during the early years than during the later years of an asset's life; if the accounting charges followed this curve, the early years would be charged less for the use of the machine than the later years, although a new asset presumably is of more benefit to the business than an old one. For another reason, management often considers it desirable to replace fixed assets before physical depreciation is complete; therefore, if income is to be properly measured, depreciation charged should equal cost less scrap value during the period of useful life.

The more modern concept of depreciation is expressed by the following definition proposed by the Committee on Terminology of the American Institute of Certified Public Accountants: "*Depreciation accounting* is a system of accounting which aims to distribute the cost or other basic value of tangible capital assets, less salvage (if any), over the estimated useful life of the unit (which may be a group of assets) in a systematic and rational manner. It is a process of allocation, not of valuation. *Depreciation for the year* is the portion of the total charge under such a system that is allocated to the year. Although the allocation may properly take into account occurrences during the year, it is not intended to be a measurement of the effect of all such occurrences."

The committee suggested in an earlier bulletin that the annual charge should be described as " 'depreciation allocated to the year' in order to emphasize the fact that depreciation accounting is a process of allocation"—a suggestion not widely adopted.

Depreciation is an expense.　Early accountants were confronted with the task of convincing businessmen that depreciation is an expense which must be provided for regardless of the level of earnings; their clients preferred to write off little or no depreciation in years of poor earnings or of losses, and to make large provisions for depreciation in prosperous years. Profits were stated before depreciation was deducted, and the directors then decided how much to credit to the depreciation reserve and how much to pay in dividends.

As accountants began to drive home the argument that depreciation is an expense which must be provided for in bad years as well as in good, they were met by several arguments. One was that depreciation had been offset by an increase in the market value of the property, and that the assets, even after a number of years of use, were worth as much as they cost. Such an argument was unsound because it failed to recognize the fact that, regardless of changes in market values, fixed assets wear out and the resulting cost expiration is an operating expense.

Another argument was that depreciation provisions were unnecessary because repairs kept the asset as good as new. It is difficult to find a better answer to this argument than Professor Hatfield's much-quoted and now almost classic sentence: "All machinery is on an irresistible march to the junk heap, and its progress, while it may be delayed, cannot be prevented by repairs."

The federal income tax law changed the attitude of many businessmen with respect to depreciation. Before the passage of the law, the attitude frequently was: How little depreciation can I take to make as good a profit showing as possible? Since the passage of the law, the attitude in many cases has become: How much depreciation can I take to reduce my taxable income?

Relation of depreciation to dividends. American courts were somewhat slow in recognizing depreciation as an expense to be provided for before the earned surplus available for dividends was determined. There is now, however, a sufficient body of court decisions to establish the fact that the law requires a provision for depreciation, and that the payment of dividends to the full amount of the surplus, without a provision for depreciation, would constitute an impairment of capital.

Factors of depreciation. The factors theoretically to be taken into consideration in estimating the amounts to be charged to expense periodically for fixed asset expirations are:

(1) The depreciation base.
(2) Residual or scrap value.
(3) Estimated life.

These factors determine the total depreciation to be provided and the period over which the total depreciation is to be spread.

The amount charged to each period depends upon the apportionment method adopted.

The depreciation base. The base generally used for the computation of depreciation is cost, which includes installation and other capitalized incidental expenditures. The base may also include an allowance for removal costs at the expiration of the life of the asset, although it is more customary to apply such costs as a reduction of the realization from salvage.

Replacement or other appraisal values are sometimes used as the depreciation base. The propriety of the use of such bases is discussed in the next chapter.

In the interest of a more exact computation of depreciation provisions, there has been some tendency in recent years to subdivide the plant records so that they show, not merely the total cost or other depreciation base of all fixed assets of a certain class, but also the cost or other base of various units having different expected service lives. With such information, various rates can be applied to depreciate different structural elements or other units.

Residual or scrap value. The residual or scrap value of an asset is the amount which can be recovered by its disposal when it is taken out of service. The estimated residual value to be used in the computation of depreciation should be net after estimated costs of dismantling and removal are deducted.

Although residual value should theoretically be taken into consideration in determining the total amount of cost expiration to be charged to operations during the life of an asset, it frequently is ignored. This may be justified if the residual value is small, or not subject to reliable estimate, or if the dismantling and removal costs cannot be accurately estimated.

Estimated life. The life of a fixed asset will be affected by repairs, and the repair policy should be taken into consideration when the life is being estimated. Estimated life may be stated in any one of the following ways:

(a) Time periods, as years or months.
(b) Operating periods, or working hours.
(c) Units of output.

Estimating the life of a fixed asset requires consideration of both physical depreciation and obsolescence. In essence, it is the period of expected economic usefulness that governs. Plates used in the printing of a book may be in usable condition long after the sale of the book has ceased, but their cost should be charged to operations during the period when sales are made. Patterns and molds, although physically usable for years, may have a life for production purposes only during the manufacture of one annual model.

Depreciation methods. The following methods of apportioning depreciation by periods are discussed in this chapter:

Straight line.   Appraisal.
Working hours.   Income basis.
Production.   Retirement basis.
Reducing charge. (Accelerated depreciation)

The annuity and sinking fund methods are not discussed in this chapter, as they involve compound interest computations. They are described in *Principles of Accounting, Advanced*.

Symbols. The following symbols are used in the formulas discussed in this chapter:

C = Cost.
S = Scrap or residual value.
n = Estimated life (periods, working hours, or units of product).
r = Rate of depreciation (per period, per working hour, or per unit of product).
D = Depreciation per period.

Basis of illustrations. For purposes of illustration it will be assumed that:

The cost of an asset is $6,000,
The estimated residual value is $400, and
The estimated life is eight years (except in two illustrations in which the life is stated in terms of working hours and units of product).

In the illustrations of methods in which the life is expressed in operating hours or units of product, the necessary additional information is furnished.

Straight-line method. This is the simplest and most commonly used method. It results in spreading the total depreciation equally over all periods of life, unless the periodical charge is adjusted because of abnormal operating activities. The formula for computing the periodical depreciation charge is:

$$D = \frac{C - S}{n}$$

Using the assumed facts,

$$D = \frac{\$6,000 - \$400}{8}$$
$$= \$5,600 \div 8$$
$$= \$700$$

The table on page 359 shows the accumulation of depreciation.

Table of Depreciation—Straight-Line Method

End of Year	Debit Depreciation Expense	Credit Accumulated Depreciation	Total Accumulated Depreciation	Carrying Value
				$6,000
1	$ 700	$ 700	$ 700	5,300
2	700	700	1,400	4,600
3	700	700	2,100	3,900
4	700	700	2,800	3,200
5	700	700	3,500	2,500
6	700	700	4,200	1,800
7	700	700	4,900	1,100
8	700	700	5,600	400
	$5,600	$5,600		

In practical applications of the straight-line method, the residual value usually is ignored and a rate determined from the estimated life of the asset is applied to cost. Thus, in the foregoing illustration, the rate would be 12½% and the annual depreciation would be 12½% of $6,000, or $750.

The straight-line method has the advantage of simplicity. Moreover, because it has been widely used, a considerable body of experience data is available for the determination of straight-line depreciation rates applicable to various classes of tangible fixed assets.

Working-hours method. This method recognizes the fact that property, particularly machinery, depreciates more rapidly if it is used full time or overtime than if it is used part time. Not only is the wear and tear greater, but there is less opportunity for making repairs. Moreover, the full-time and overtime years get more benefit from the asset than do the part-time years. In the application of this method, the total number of working hours of which the machine is capable of operating is estimated, and a charge per hour is determined by the following formula:

$$r = \frac{C - S}{n}$$

If it is assumed that the asset used for illustrative purposes is expected to have an operating life of 22,400 working hours, the depreciation rate per hour of use is computed in the manner illustrated below:

$$r = \frac{\$6,000 - \$400}{22,400}$$
$$= \$.25$$

The table on the following page shows the number of hours the asset was used during each of eight years, and the depreciation provided on the basis of working hours.

Table of Depreciation—Working-Hours Method

Year	Hours Worked	Debit Depreciation Expense	Credit Accumulated Depreciation	Total Accumulated Depreciation	Carrying Value
					$6,000
1	2,600	$ 650	$ 650	$ 650	5,350
2	2,900	725	725	1,375	4,625
3	3,400	850	850	2,225	3,775
4	2,400	600	600	2,825	3,175
5	1,800	450	450	3,275	2,725
6	2,700	675	675	3,950	2,050
7	3,000	750	750	4,700	1,300
8	3,600	900	900	5,600	400
	22,400	$5,600	$5,600		

Production method. This method is similar to the working-hours method in that it distributes the depreciation among the periods in proportion to the use made of the asset during each period. The estimated life is stated in units of product or service, and the rate of depreciation is a rate per unit. The figures in the illustration of the working-hours method can serve as an illustration of this method also, if we assume that the estimated life is stated as 22,400 units of product (instead of working hours), and that the figures in the Hours Worked column represent units of finished goods produced. The depreciation rate is then $.25 per unit, and the depreciation each year is computed by multiplying the number of units produced by the rate per unit.

The production method is peculiarly suitable to the depreciation of assets for which the total service units can be rather definitely estimated and when the service is not uniform by periods. The method might, for instance, be appropriately applied in depreciating automobile tires on a mileage basis.

If a fixed asset is subject to obsolescence, the production method appears to be an illogical procedure for establishing a reserve intended to provide for both physical deterioration and obsolescence, because obsolescence presumably develops on a time basis rather than on the basis of units of output. During a period of small production, the depreciation charges might be less than the amount which should be provided for obsolescence on the basis of the lapse of time, and this inadequacy might not be compensated for in periods of larger production.

Reducing-charge methods (accelerated depreciation). A depreciation procedure by which larger charges are made during the early years of the life of a fixed asset than during the later years of its life was originally supported by the following reasoning: The cost of the use of a fixed asset includes depreciation and repairs; the sum of these charges should be a fairly uniform amount year by year; since repairs tend to increase with the age of the asset, the depreciation charge should decrease, so that the increasing repair charges and the decreasing depreciation charges will tend to equalize each other and produce a uniform total charge. This may be good theory, but the plan of making decreasing depreciation charges assumes that repairs will increase in the same amount that the depreciation charges decrease; perhaps they will, but it is likely to be a matter of luck. If it is desirable to equalize the total repair and depreciation charges, it would seem better to create two reserves: one for depreciation and another for repairs. Such a plan is subject to the objection that it may be difficult to estimate accurately the total future repair cost, but with statistics showing past experience it should be no more difficult to do this than to estimate depreciation. Such a repair reserve would not be deductible for federal income tax purposes.

Diminishing-charge methods were also sometimes advocated on the ground that the large charge in the early part of an asset's life was desirable to correspond with the large initial reduction in value from cost to second-hand market value. This argument seems to be in conflict with the general accounting principle that market values need not be given consideration in the accounting for fixed assets.

A new theory in support of diminishing-charge procedures developed after World War II. It perhaps had its origin in the fact that some companies made large expenditures for fixed assets at postwar prices that were relatively high, with the hope of making large immediate profits by supplying goods to meet the accumulated postwar demand. It was contended that such expenditures would not have been made except for the prospect of such quick profits, and that a proper matching of revenue and costs required making relatively large depreciation charges during this profitable postwar period.

This theory was then expanded until the argument was stated somewhat as follows: Since management cannot foresee the conditions which will exist during the entire physical life of a fixed asset, its decisions regarding the advisability of making large capital expenditures are often determined by the prospects of economic usefulness during a much shorter period; immediate prospects of profits may warrant taking a chance with respect to later periods; larger depreciation charges should be made in the earlier periods than in the later ones, because the expenditures were made with these early periods primarily in mind. George D. Bailey, in an article* quoted in part on the following page, mentions some instances:

---

* *The Journal of Accountancy*, Vol. 88, page 376.

"For instance, an entire plant, built in a hurry to take care of the immediate postwar demand for the product, might properly have been amortized in substantial part during the period of immediate heavy and perhaps noncompetitive demand. Another company may have built a store in a high risk location with the belief that the immediate profits would be so good as to offset a loss in value after a short time. Another may have built outlets in highly competitive locations where the future economic risk was high but short-term prospects good. Another may have made a substantial expansion in current facilities merely to get the immediate market, or to keep a competitive position. Others may be influenced by the normal business prudence which can look ahead a few years with confidence but more than that only with some doubt as to type, location, processes, etc."

In depreciation discussions there is increasing emphasis on the theory that since new assets are generally capable of producing more revenue than old assets, a better matching of revenue and expense is achieved by larger depreciation charges in the early periods when assets have their greatest economic usefulness. Such a depreciation procedure is often referred to as accelerated depreciation, meaning essentially that depreciation charges follow a constantly decreasing pattern although initially greater than those under the straight-line method.

Three methods of providing a diminishing depreciation charge are illustrated in the following sections. These methods are:

(1) Declining balance.
(2) Sum of years' digits or life periods.
(3) Diminishing rates on cost.

Declining balance method. Under this method a fixed or uniform rate is applied to the carrying value of the asset. Theoretically, the depreciation rate to be used in this method is computed by the following formula:

$$
\begin{aligned}
r &= 1 - \sqrt[n]{S \div C} \\
&= 1 - \sqrt[8]{\$400 \div \$6,000} \\
&= 1 - \sqrt[8]{.0666\tfrac{2}{3}}
\end{aligned}
$$

In extracting the eighth root of $.0666\tfrac{2}{3}$, a table of logarithms must be used.

Log $.0666\tfrac{2}{3}$	$8.8239088 - 10$
Add	$\underline{70 \qquad\qquad -70}$
Divide by 8:	$8)\overline{78.8239088 - 80}$
	$9.8529886 - 10$, which is log $.712834$

Then $r = 1 - .712834$
  $= .287166$
  $= 28.7166\%$

This rate is applied at the end of the first period to cost, and thereafter to the carrying value at the beginning of each successive period, as shown by the following table. Thus, the depreciation charge the first year is $28.71\frac{2}{3}\%$ of \$6,000; the second year, it is $28.71\frac{2}{3}\%$ of \$4,277.

Depreciation Table—Uniform Rate on Diminishing Value

Rate: $28.71\frac{2}{3}\%$

Year	Debit Depreciation Expense	Credit Accumulated Depreciation	Total Accumulated Depreciation	Carrying Value
				$6,000.00
1	$1,723.00	$1,723.00	$1,723.00	4,277.00
2	1,228.21	1,228.21	2,951.21	3.048.79
3	875.51	875.51	3,826.72	2,173.28
4	624.09	624.09	4,450.81	1,549.19
5	444.87	444.87	4,895.68	1,104.32
6	317.12	317.12	5,212.80	787.20
7	226.06	226.06	5,438.86	561.14
8	161.14	161.14	5,600.00	400.00
	$5,600.00	$5,600.00		

The formula requires the use of a residual value. If an asset is assumed to have no residual value, a nominal residual value of \$1 can be used.

As a practical matter, the rate used is likely to be based on what is permissible for income tax purposes. The law and regulations in effect at the time of this writing permit, for the declining balance method, the use of a depreciation rate not exceeding twice that acceptable as a straight-line rate. The regulations also provide that scrap value is to be ignored. Thus, if it is acceptable for income tax purposes to use $12\frac{1}{2}\%$ as a straight-line rate (this would agree with the eight-year use life being used in the illustrations), a rate up to 25% is acceptable for the declining balance method. Assuming that an asset cost \$6,000 and that the taxpayer adopted the 25% rate, the depreciation would be

$1,500.00 for the first year—$6,000 × 25%;
$1,125.00 for the second year—$4,500 × 25%;
$ 843.75 for the third year—$3,375 × 25%;

and so on.

Sum of years' digits or life-periods method. This method is difficult to reduce to a brief formula; it will be more readily understood if it is stated as follows:

Add the numbers representing the periods of life:
  Thus, $1 + 2 + 3 + 4 + 5 + 6 + 7 + 8 = 36$
Use the sum thus obtained as a denominator.
Use as numerators the same numbers taken in inverse order:
  Thus, $\frac{8}{36}$, $\frac{7}{36}$, etc.
Multiply the total depreciation $(C - S)$ by the fractions thus produced.

Depreciation Table—Sum of Years' Digits or Life Periods

Year	Fraction of $5,600.00	Debit Depreciation Expense	Credit Accumulated Depreciation	Total Accumulated Depreciation	Carrying Value
					$6,000.00
1	8⁄36	$1,244.45	$1,244.45	$1,244.45	4,755.55
2	7⁄36	1,088.89	1,088.89	2,333.34	3,666.66
3	6⁄36	933.33	933.33	3,266.67	2,733.33
4	5⁄36	777.78	777.78	4,044.45	1,955.55
5	4⁄36	622.22	622.22	4,666.67	1,333.33
6	3⁄36	466.67	466.67	5,133.34	866.66
7	2⁄36	311.11	311.11	5,444.45	555.55
8	1⁄36	155.55	155.55	5,600.00	400.00
	36⁄36	$5,600.00	$5,600.00		

The sum of the years' digits can be computed by using the following formula:

$$S = N \left(\frac{N + 1}{2} \right)$$

N equals the number of periods of estimated useful life. Applying the formula where the use life is 8 years—

$$S = 8 \left(\frac{8 + 1}{2} \right)$$
$$S = 8(4.5)$$
$$S = 36$$

Diminishing rates on cost method. No formula can be given for determining the rates, as they are chosen arbitrarily when the depreciation program is set up. The following table shows how the method operates, the rate arbitrarily chosen for each year being shown in the table.

Depreciation Table—Diminishing Rates on Cost

Year	Rates	Debit Depreciation Expense	Credit Accumulated Depreciation	Total Accumulated Depreciation	Carrying Value
					$6,000
1	15⅔%	$ 940	$ 940	$ 940	5,060
2	14⅔	880	880	1,820	4,180
3	13	780	780	2,600	3,400
4	12	720	720	3,320	2,680
5	11	660	660	3,980	2,020
6	10	600	600	4,580	1,420
7	9	540	540	5,120	880
8	8	480	480	5,600	400
	93⅓%	$5,600	$5,600		

Fractional-period depreciation under accelerated methods. If an asset to be depreciated by an accelerated method is acquired during the year, it is customary to compute the depreciation applicable to the partial period in the manner stated on page 365.

(1) Compute the depreciation for a full year.
(2) Take a fraction thereof, the fraction being representative of the partial year since acquisition.

To illustrate the application of this procedure, assume that the following data relate to a company whose accounting year is the calendar year.

Asset cost... $4,000
Date of acquisition.. April 1, 1960
Declining balance rate..................................... 20%

Depreciation applicable to 1960:
Depreciation applicable to the year ended April 1, 1961:
   20% of $4,000 = $800
Portion applicable to 1960:
   $9/12$ of $800 = $600

Depreciation applicable to 1961:
Depreciation applicable to the year ended April 1, 1962:
   20% of ($4,000 − $800) = $640
Depreciation applicable to 1961:
   $3/12$ of $800 = $200
   $9/12$ of $640 =   480
                    $680

Appraisal method. This method cannot be reduced to a mathematical formula. It consists merely of estimating the value of the asset at the end of each period and writing off as depreciation the difference between the balance of the asset account and the appraised value. This method is likely to result in burdening some periods with heavy charges and relieving other periods, because, if the depreciation charges correspond with physical deterioration, the charges will be light during the early years and heavy during the later ones. On the other hand, the burden may be reversed by charging the early periods with large amounts on the theory that the property loses value rapidly in the early part of its life, because its value is quickly reduced to a second-hand basis. This practice improperly introduces the element of realizable values, when only going-concern values should be considered.

When this method is used, care should be taken to exclude upward or downward fluctuations in market value. If the appraisals are made on the basis of current market values, the method may result in a depreciation charge which is a composite of cost exhaustion and market fluctuations. Giving effect, in the computation of income, to unrealized appreciation resulting from market increases is not to be condoned merely because the appreciation is buried in the depreciation provision; the fact that the market fluctuation is netted in the depreciation and the effect thereby obscured makes the practice even more subject to censure.

Sixty months' amortization. It seems appropriate to mention during the discussion of depreciation that considerable sums invested in fixed assets during the 1940's and 1950's were, or are being, systematically written off for income tax purposes in five years. This situation is traceable to a special tax deduction provision relating to emergency facilities constructed or acquired as a result of war or national defense requirements. Before a taxpayer can write off a fixed asset of the type normally having a use-life expectancy exceeding five years in such a short period, he must secure an approved certificate of necessity from the appropriate governmental agency, which in effect states that the facility is necessary in the interests of national defense and permits the cost thereof to be amortized for income tax purposes over 60 months. The resulting charges are generally referred to as amortization, since, considering the type of property involved, it is unlikely that depreciation rules would require such a rapid write-off.

In some instances the 60 months' period was used in the books of the taxpayer as well as in the income tax return, and, considering the specialized nature of some of the facilities, this may have been a reasonable practice for depreciation purposes. In this connection, the Committee on Accounting Procedure, in Bulletin 43, expressed the opinion "that from an accounting standpoint there is nothing inherent in the nature of emergency facilities which requires the depreciation or amortization of their cost for financial accounting purposes over either a shorter or a longer period than would be proper if no certificate of necessity had been issued." If, in specific cases, the amortization deductible for tax purposes is not materially different from depreciation charges based on estimates of useful life, for practical reasons the amortization amounts may be used in the financial statements. However, the committee believes "that when the amount allowed as amortization for income-tax purposes is materially different from the amount of the estimated depreciation, the latter should be used for financial accounting purposes."

Depreciation based on income. There still persists, in the management of some businesses, an inclination to determine the amount of the depreciation provision after having ascertained the net income for the period before depreciation. This tendency is possibly a survival from the days when the true nature of depreciation as an expense was not as well recognized as it is now; it possibly also arises from the confused assumption that a credit to an accumulated depreciation account in some way constitutes a provision of funds for asset replacements, and that the amount to be thus provided is a matter of managerial policy to be determined on the basis of the amount of earnings available for that and other purposes; the practice may also stem from the desire of management to use the depreciation provisions as a means of stabilizing the reported net income, a practice which should be recognized as conscious or unconscious deception.

There are, of course, instances in which the relating of depreciation charges to income constitutes a procedure closely akin to the production method. This seems to be true with respect to the computation of depreciation provisions by a public utility on the basis of gross revenue, since gross revenue is presumably very directly related to operating activity, and, therefore, to the utilization of the plant assets.

Retirement and replacement systems.   The retirement and replacement systems of dealing with depreciation have numerous advocates in the public utility field. In effect, these procedures give no recognition to depreciation until the end of the life of the asset. They are akin to providing no allowance for bad debts and charging ascertained losses to operations.

Under the retirement system, operations are charged with the cost, less salvage, of plant units retired during the period, and new assets acquired are charged to the property accounts at cost. Under the replacement system, operations are charged with the cost of the new assets acquired as replacements, less the salvage recovery on the old assets. Of the two methods, the retirement system is preferable because it produces property account balances which reflect the cost of assets in use rather than the cost of assets replaced.

Retirement or replacement systems are perhaps peculiarly suited to the public utility field because the fixed assets of utilities include large numbers of units of relatively small value in any location (poles, conduits, and so forth), and the distinction between maintenance and replacements is often confused by borderline cases. Such systems probably are also advocated by utilities because property values have a direct bearing upon the rates sanctioned by controlling commissions, and utility companies are indisposed to admit that accumulated depreciation, which may reflect a percentage of depreciation which is acceptable for general accounting purposes but is in excess of the percentage of accrued physical deterioration, is a justifiable deduction from investment for purposes of rate making.

The two principal objections to these procedures are: First, operations are relieved of any charge for the expiration of asset costs until the period of retirement; as a consequence, the operating results of the early periods are relieved of normal charges, and the asset values are stated in the balance sheet without any recognition of accrued depreciation. Second, instead of charging operations by periods with a uniform cost for the services of the fixed asset, operations become charged with variable amounts determined by the necessity for or the policy of replacements.

Recording depreciation.   The provision for depreciation may be credited to the asset account, thus writing down the asset, or it may be credited to a valuation account, so called since it is necessary to consider both the asset account and the related valuation account in determining the carrying value of the asset. Credits to such a contra account instead of to the asset account are preferable for two reasons. First, the depreciation is an estimate, and this fact is indicated more clearly if a contra account is credited than if the asset account is credited. Second, if a contra account is credited, the balance of the asset account represents the cost of the assets still in service.

Some assets are subject to loss or breakage or other factors which make a theoretical computation of depreciation by the application of an annual rate inexact in practice. In accounting for such assets, some concerns retain a balance in the asset account which is assumed to represent the cost of a normal stock, and all replacements are charged to expense. This is an inexact procedure; it is preferable to charge all replacements to the fixed asset account, and to adjust the fixed asset account periodically by an inventory and appraisal.

Lapsing schedules.   An often-used device for determining the annual amounts of depreciation and keeping track of the accumulated depreciation is known as a lapsing schedule. A common form of lapsing schedule is illustrated on page 369.

The operation of a lapsing schedule is probably self-evident. When an asset is acquired, pertinent facts relating to the asset are entered in the schedule and the depreciation charges for the entire use-life period are extended across the schedule by years. Annual depreciation charges are determined each year by adding the current year's column. If an asset is retired before it has been fully depreciated, the depreciation charges applicable to the remaining estimated useful life are subtracted in the Annual Depreciation columns. This is demonstrated in the illustrative schedule where the Ford truck was traded in on January 3, 1960.

Relating the depreciation charge to use.   Since depreciation accounting is intended to charge fixed asset costs to operations over the periods of use, much can be said in favor of making larger charges for depreciation in periods of more-than-average use and smaller charges in periods of less-than-average use. The working-hours and production methods of computing depreciation accom-

Delivery Equipment
Lapsing Schedule

Date	Description	Use Life	Depreciable Cost	Annual Depreciation							
				1957	1958	1959	1960	1961	1962	1968	1969
7/1/57	Ford truck..........	4 years	2,800	350	700	700	700	350			
1/3/58	Dodge wagon.......	4 years	3,200		800	800	800	800			
7/2/58	Chevrolet truck.....	4 years	2,600		325	650	650	650	325		
4/1/59	Plymouth wagon....	4 years	2,880			540	720	720	720		
1/3/60	Ford truck traded in—below......						700*	350*			
1/3/60	Ford truck..........	4 years	3,000				750	750	750		
	Total depreciation........			350	1,825	2,690	2,920	2,920	1,795		

plish this purpose. The straight-line method will not produce this result unless adjustments are made to increase the charge in large-use periods and reduce it in small-use periods.

Accountants generally recognize the propriety of increasing the depreciation in any period in which unusual operating activities (such as excessive overtime, additional shifts, overload, and use by inexperienced operators) tend to decrease the probable useful life of the asset below the original estimate. Management does not seem equally disposed to reduce the depreciation charge when opposite conditions prevail, since it is concerned with the consequent effect upon income taxes.

Although physical deterioration is undoubtedly affected by use, and although it is proper to adjust depreciation charges to give consideration to varying levels of operations, it does not follow that the depreciation charges should be exactly proportionate to use. The normal periodical depreciation charge may include provisions for (a) deterioration caused by wear and tear, (b) deterioration caused by the action of the elements, and (c) obsolescence. If a machine which normally is operated for one eight-hour shift daily is, for some reason, operated on a twenty-four-hour basis, the proper depreciation may be more or less than three times the normal charge. Physical deterioration may be more than tripled, particularly if it is impossible to take care of maintenance and repairs. On the other hand, deterioration caused by the action of the elements will not be tripled, and the hazard of obsolescence is not increased by use.

Depreciation and replacement. People who are not trained in accounting often have the idea that the purpose of accounting for depreciation is to provide funds for the replacement of fixed assets when they wear out. Accountants are perhaps themselves to blame for this confusion because of their use of the expression "*provision* for depreciation." At any rate, there is a prevalent idea that depreciation is an expense for which a cash disbursement will be made in the future when replacement of the asset becomes necessary, and that the "depreciation provision" somehow provides for the expenditure.

From the accounting standpoint, depreciation is an expense for which the cash expenditure was made in the more or less remote past; any future expenditures which may be made to replace the asset will be capital expenditures which will subject the operations to a new series of depreciation expense charges.

Depreciation provisions are in no sense replacement provisions. Writing off the cost of a fixed asset by charges to expense over a twenty-year period and writing off the cost of an insurance policy over a three-year period may, by including these elements in the cost of the product, increase the probability of recovering them in the selling price and thus obtaining funds which may be utilized for their replacement. But the entries recording the expiration of plant and insurance costs do not either provide or segregate funds for the replacement of the plant or the insurance.

The segregation of funds for replacement purposes is not customary. Very few industrial concerns create such funds, as it is usually considered that the provision for financing replacements can be postponed until the necessity for, and the cost of, the replacements become definite. In the meantime, it is usually regarded as more advisable to retain the available funds in the working capital with the hope of earning a higher return by their use in operations than could be obtained as income on fund investments.

Income taxes and depreciation methods. It would be unrealistic not to concede that income tax considerations are an important factor in the selection of depreciation methods. In view of the high level of income tax rates, the amount and pattern of depreciation deductions have an important effect on the cash position of a business. With an income tax rate of 50% (which approximates present rates), a method which results in $20,000 greater depreciation in any one year will reduce the cash requirements for income taxes for that year by $10,000. It is very likely that this may not be a permanent saving, since during the life of an asset the depreciation deduction cannot exceed its cost. But for new or expanding businesses particularly, and for all businesses to some extent, a postponement or deferment of income taxes is attractive, since it may permit an earlier retirement of debt created to finance the purchase of the assets being depreciated, or may permit the use of such cash for additional equipment.

Although considerations such as these are primarily financial in character, they can have a significant effect on income measurement. The matter is further complicated if the business wishes to adopt one depreciation method for its tax return and another for its records. Many of the accounting problems caused by income taxes are discussed in Chapter 28. For the moment a tentative opinion is offered: Nonaccounting considerations have had a considerable influence on depreciation accounting, with the inevitable result that the income-determination process is perhaps more subject to the effects of policy decisions than was formerly the case.

Composite life. The composite life of a plant as a whole, sometimes called the *average* or *mean* life, may be computed as in the illustration on the following page.

Asset	Cost	Residual Value	Total Depreciation	Estimated Life	Annual Depreciation (Straight-Line)
A	$20,000	$5,000	$15,000	20 years	$ 750
B	12,000	2,000	10,000	10 years	1,000
C	8,000	2,000	6,000	8 years	750
D	2,100	100	2,000	4 years	500
			$33,000		$3,000

$33,000 ÷ $3,000 = 11, the composite, or average, life.

It is possible to compare the lives of different plants by determining the composite life of each; but since depreciation should be provided on each class of fixed assets on the basis of the life of each class and not on the basis of composite life, accountants are rarely called upon to make composite-life computations. The term is used and the computations are made more frequently by engineers than by accountants.

Depletion of Tangible Fixed Assets

The depletion base. Depletion is the exhaustion of the cost or value of a wasting asset, such as a mine, a timber tract, or an oil well, resulting from the conversion of the natural resource into inventories. The depletion base is the total cost or value of the wasting asset to be charged to operations during the period of exploitation of the natural resource. If there is a residual land value, it should be recorded in a separate account.

Development costs, such as those incurred in the removal of surface earth for strip-mining operations, the sinking of shafts, drilling of wells, and timbering of mines, should be set up in the accounts separately from the original cost of the wasting asset. They should be written off in amounts proportionate to the write-offs of the original cost of the wasting asset if the developments will render service throughout the entire life of the wasting asset. They should be written off over a shorter period if their usefulness will expire before the wasting asset is completely depleted.

If development expenditures prove fruitless, as in the case of the drilling of a dry well, they should be written off. It is not acceptable to carry forward any lost costs. However, if a company is engaged more or less continuously in developmental work of the type in which only a fraction of the projects can be expected to be successful, it can be argued that the cost of the unsuccessful projects is a necessary cost to secure the successful projects. Therefore, the cost of fruitless efforts need not be written off immediately but should be assigned to the successful developments.

If the cutting of a tract of timber land is deferred to obtain the benefit of growth, it is permissible to capitalize the costs of protection, insurance, and administrative expenses.

Development costs may be incurred after operations begin. Three procedures are used in dealing with such costs. A reserve may be set up for the estimated aggregate development costs to be incurred during the life of the property, so that this aggregate cost will be spread ratably over each unit of product. Or development costs incurred after operations begin can be capitalized when the expenditures are made, and the depletion charge may be adjusted. Or they may be charged to current income.

After operations begin, a careful distinction must be made between operating expenses and expenditures which may be regarded as development costs to be capitalized.

Depletion methods.　Depletion is usually computed by dividing the cost or appraised value of the wasting asset by the estimated number of tons, barrels, thousand feet, or other units in the asset, thus determining a unit depletion charge. The total depletion charge for each period is then computed by multiplying the unit charge by the number of units converted during the period from a fixed nature into merchandise.

To illustrate, assume that $90,000 is paid for a mine which is estimated to contain 300,000 tons of available deposit. The unit depletion charge is:

$$\$90,000 \div 300,000 = \$.30$$

If 20,000 tons are mined in a given year, the depletion charge for that year will be $.30 × 20,000, or $6,000.

For purposes of correct income determination and inventory valuation, the periodical depletion charge should be computed by applying the unit depletion rate to the number of units extracted during the period. For income tax purposes, however, the depletion deduction must be based on the number of units sold. For general accounting purposes, the *net* charge to income is also based on the units sold because the depletion applicable to the units not sold is included in the cost of the inventory.

The federal income tax regulations with respect to depletion are too extensive and complex to be discussed here, except to state that, in general, the acceptable depletion bases are: with respect to assets acquired prior to March 1, 1913, cost or fair market value at that date, whichever is higher; with respect to wasting assets acquired as such subsequent to that date, cost; and with respect to certain assets discovered in land purchased without knowledge of

the existence of the deposit, discovery value—which means fair
market value on the date of discovery or within thirty days thereafter. However, in some instances, depletion need not be based on
either cost or discovery value, but can be computed as a percentage
of gross income. When this method is used, the depletion charge
cannot exceed fifty per cent of the taxable income of the taxpayer
from the property, computed without allowance for depletion, but
the total depletion charge over the life of the wasting asset may
exceed the total cost.

Wasting-asset write-ups.   Writing up wasting assets because
of increases in market value is subject to the same objections that
apply to writing up other fixed assets for the same reason. However, write-ups to reflect discovery value and accretion are generally regarded as permissible.

Discovery value is a term applicable in situations where property
which was acquired at a mere land cost is found to contain deposits
of natural resources, or when deposits are found to be more extensive than they were believed to be when purchased.

Accretion is a term particularly applicable to timber tracts. For
many years, timber tracts were generally regarded as wasting
assets, because it was the custom to cut tracts without reforesta-
tion, and the recording of accretion was not considered to be in
accordance with good accounting. Now that many companies
which are dependent on a constant supply of forest products have
adopted a policy of maintaining timber tracts from which successive crops are harvested on a partial and selective basis, timber
tracts are no longer always wasting assets. When timber tracts are
operated on a crop basis, accountants consider it acceptable accounting to charge the asset account with amounts representing
growth accretion.

If wasting assets are written up to reflect discovery value or
accretion, the asset write-up should be offset by a credit to an
unrealized increment account. Depletion will thereafter be based
on the appraised value. There is some opinion to the effect that
the credit for the unrealized increment should be considered as
part of the permanent capital of the enterprise. The traditional
conservative accounting requires that no portion of this credit
be taken into income until the depletion charges have accumulated
to an amount equal to the cost of the asset; thereafter, transfers
may be made from unrealized increment to income or retained
earnings in amounts equal to the periodical depletion. It is less
conservative, although usually regarded as permissible, after
charging operations with depletion on the appraised value, to
transfer immediately from the unrealized increment account to

income or retained earnings the portion of the periodical depletion charge representing so-called "realized appreciation." Realized appreciation is determined by applying the following formula:

Depletion rate based on appraisal value, minus depletion rate based on cost, times number of units sold.

If the depletion charge based on appraised value is $.08 per unit of ore, and the depletion charge based on cost is $.05 per unit, and 100,000 units are mined, operations would be charged with $8,000 of depletion. If the 100,000 units are sold, a transfer of $3,000 would be made from unrealized increment to income or retained earnings.

In making the entry for realized appreciation, the accountant should give recognition to inventories. For instance, assume that the above data apply to the first year of a company's operations, and that 10,000 units remain in the inventory; the transfer entry would be:

Unrealized appreciation of ore in mine..................... 3,000		
Allowance for unrealized appreciation in inventory......	300	
Realized appreciation (or Retained earnings)...........	2,700	

If, during the second year of operations, the same quantity is mined but the inventory is reduced to 5,000 units, the transfer entry would be:

Unrealized appreciation of ore in mine.................. ... 3,000		
Allowance for unrealized appreciation in inventory..........	150	
Realized appreciation (or Retained earnings)...........	3,150	

Depletion and dividends. Companies operating wasting assets are permitted to pay dividends in amounts equal to the net income plus depletion charges. Corporations paying such dividends should inform their stockholders that the dividends represent a partial return of capital. The theory of the law is that stockholders and creditors, knowing the nature of the business, should realize that the receipts from sales are in part earnings and in part a return of investment. If the return of investment could not legally be made to the stockholders, the corporation would be obliged to hold the funds until the exhaustion of the property. This might be advisable if the corporation expected to acquire and operate another similar piece of property, but not otherwise. The law, therefore, allows the corporation to follow the financial policy best suited to its plans, basing this permission on the assumption that the creditors, knowing the nature of the business, are in a position to protect their interests.

Depletion must, of course, be provided as an expense before net income can be known. The fact that dividends can be paid in an amount equal to the net income plus the depletion has given rise to the too-prevalent belief that depletion need not be recognized as an expense for accounting purposes. When it is remembered that the cost of a wasting asset is, in effect, the cost of a long-time supply of raw material, it becomes apparent that the omission of a depletion charge is equivalent to the omission, by a manufacturing company, of an operating charge for the cost of the materials used.

The fact that companies operating wasting assets can legally pay dividends to the extent of the net income plus the credit to the accumulated depletion account has given rise to the expression, "dividends paid out of depletion reserves." Such dividends are in no sense paid out of the accumulated depletion account. They may be equal to the depletion charges, but when it is recognized that the accumulated depletion account is a valuation account reflecting a decrease in an asset resulting from operations, it becomes obvious that dividends cannot be paid out of, or charged to, the accumulated depletion account. They should be charged to a special account which will clearly indicate that they represent a distribution of the invested capital.

Ignoring depletion. The sunk cost theory. The estimating of a proper depletion charge is often a very difficult matter. In the first place, it is necessary to have information as to the number of recoverable units. This is not so difficult in the case of surface assets, such as standing timber, or in the case of ores and minerals lying close to the surface. If mining is conducted at low levels, the problem is more difficult and the estimates are frequently a matter of pure conjecture and must be revised as mining proceeds. In the second place, even if the number of units could be determined with absolute accuracy, the proper depletion charge per unit to be extracted could hardly be known without information relative to future selling prices and operating costs. For, if selling prices or costs change to a point where extraction is not profitable, the unextracted units might as well not exist, and the entire cost of the deposit should have been charged to the extracted units. On the other hand, there is the possibility that scientific discoveries or inventions will reduce the cost of extraction to a point where abandoned property can again be profitably operated. In the third place, special hazards, such as floods or other catastrophes, may make a considerable portion of the existing deposit unavailable for extraction. And, in the fourth place, the deposit may be so large that a unit rate based on actual quantity would not provide depletion of the wasting asset during a period to be reasonably contemplated as the operating life of a corporation.

Some mining companies consider that the difficulties of estimating depletion justify them in making no depletion charge in their accounts; they defend this procedure on the ground that their stockholders and the public are on notice as to the nature of their investments and operations, and that no charge is preferable to one based on a sheer guess which they cannot support. Some public accountants who specialize in mining accounts appear to feel that this procedure is sometimes justifiable, and that, if any depletion provision is made, the statements should indicate that it is an estimate.

Other corporations deal with the problem by adopting an ultra-conservative procedure based on the sunk cost theory. They regard all capital expenditures for wasting assets and organization and development expenses as costs to be recovered before any earnings are reported. Such a deferment of reporting any earnings, although admittedly conservative, might be grossly unfair to stockholders, particularly those who hold the stock during only the early portion of the corporation's life.

Depreciation of plant.   Depreciation must, of course, be provided on buildings and machinery located on a wasting asset. If the life of the wasting asset is estimated to be less than the life of the plant, it is customary to accept the life of the wasting asset as the life of the plant for depreciation purposes. This is done on the theory that the plant will have only a scrap value when it is no longer needed for operations in its present location. As the life of the wasting asset is contingent upon the amount of annual operations, the depreciation of the plant may be computed on the same basis that is used for depletion; that is:

$$\text{Annual depreciation} = (\text{Cost} - \text{Scrap}) \times \frac{\text{Units extracted during year}}{\text{Total estimated units}}$$

CHAPTER EIGHTEEN

....

Tangible Fixed Assets
(Concluded)

Disposals

Disposals of fixed assets.   When fixed assets which are subject to depreciation are sold or otherwise disposed of, the property account should be relieved of the cost of the asset. Since most fixed asset disposals occur during, rather than at the end of, the year, we must consider what entries, if any, should be made for depreciation up to the date of disposal, and the amount which should be debited to the accumulated depreciation account to relieve it of the total depreciation provided on the asset. The entries with respect to depreciation at the time of disposal will depend upon the company's depreciation policy with respect to additions and disposals. Four depreciation policies are described below. Entries to be made in each case (by the straight-line method) are based on the following assumed facts:

Asset cost	$4,000
Scrap value	0
Date of acquisition	April 1, 1960
Annual depreciation rate	20%
Date of disposal	November 15, 1964

   (1) Fractional-period depreciation is computed on acquisitions from the date of acquisition to the end of the period.

378

Fractional-period depreciation is computed on disposals from the beginning of the period of disposal to the date of the disposal.

The depreciation provisions to December 31, 1963, would have been:

1960—$\frac{9}{12}$ of 20% of $4,000	$	600
1961		800
1962		800
1963		800

The depreciation to be provided at the date of disposal would be:

1964—$10\frac{1}{2}/12$ of 20% of $4,000	700

And the amount to be charged to the accumulated depreciation account in the entry for the disposal would be............ ... $3,700

(2) Depreciation is computed at the annual rate on the opening balance in the fixed asset account, plus or minus depreciation at one-half the annual rate on the net additions or deductions during the year. *This is equivalent to computing depreciation on acquisitions and disposals for a half-year, regardless of the date of the acquisition or the disposal.*

The depreciation provisions to December 31, 1963, would have been:

1960—$\frac{1}{2}$ of 20% of $4,000	$	400
1961		800
1962		800
1963		800

The depreciation to be provided at the date of disposal would be:

1964—$\frac{1}{2}$ of 20% of $4,000	400

And the amount to be charged to the accumulated depreciation account in the entry for the disposal would be................ $3,200

(3) Depreciation is computed at the annual rate on the opening balance in the asset account. *Thus, no depreciation is taken on acquisitions in the year of acquisition, and a full year's depreciation is taken on disposals.*

The depreciation provisions to December 31, 1963, would have been:

1960	$	0
1961		800
1962		800
1963		800

The depreciation to be provided at the date of disposal would be:

1964	800

And the amount to be charged to the accumulated depreciation account in the entry for the disposal would be................ $3,200

(4) Depreciation is computed at the annual rate on the closing balance in the asset account. *This is equivalent to computing depreciation for a full year on acquisitions, regardless of the date of acquisition, and taking no depreciation on disposals in the year of disposal.*

The depreciation provisions to December 31, 1963, would have been:

1960..$	800
1961..	800
1962..	800
1963..	800

The depreciation to be provided at the date of disposal would be:

1964..	0

And the amount to be charged to the accumulated depreciation account in the entry for the disposal would be................. $3,200

Whichever method is adopted by a company, it must be followed consistently. The accountant must know which method is in use, in order that overdepreciation or underdepreciation may be avoided and the accumulated depreciation account be relieved of the correct amount of depreciation when fixed assets are disposed of.

It is customary to assume that Method No. 1 is in use in the absence of definite information to the contrary.

At one time it was the general custom to record any loss or gain on the disposal of a fixed asset by a debit or credit to Retained Earnings, on the theory that the loss or gain represented a correction of the depreciation charges of prior periods, or an extraneous item resulting from a price change. Present-day practice generally treats such losses and gains as income statement items. To illustrate, assume that a machine cost $5,000, that depreciation of $3,000 has been provided, and that the machine is sold for $1,500. The entry for the disposal would be:

Cash..	1,500	
Accumulated depreciation— Machinery.....................	3,000	
Loss on disposal of machinery............................	500	
Machinery..		5,000
Sale of fixed asset.		

If the asset is sold for $2,300, the entry would be:

Cash..	2,300	
Accumulated depreciation—Machinery.....................	3,000	
Machinery..		5,000
Gain on disposal of machinery........................		300
Sale of fixed asset.		

It is only in those cases in which gains or losses arising from fixed asset disposals are so large that their inclusion in the income statement would distort or otherwise impair the significance of the net income amount that accountants consider assigning them directly to retained earnings. Advocates of the all-inclusive income concept would include these gains or losses in the income statement irrespective of size, though properly described and segregated if material.

Disposals of fixed assets are sometimes erroneously recorded by merely debiting Cash and crediting the asset account with the amount received. Adjustments are then required to relieve the asset account of the balance of the cost, to relieve the accumulated depreciation account of the recorded depreciation, and to take up the gain or loss.

Fixed assets are sometimes retired from service without being sold or even removed from the locations where they were formerly used. If they are retained as standby units, the cost and depreciation provisions applicable to them may be retained in the accounts. If, however, their usefulness as operating assets is at an end, their salvage or recovery value should be estimated and set up in an abandoned property account, with appropriate entries to relieve the asset and accumulated depreciation accounts of the cost and recorded depreciation and to record the estimated loss or gain.

Trade-ins. When recording fixed asset trade-ins, what recognition should the accountant give to any gain or loss on the disposal of the old asset, and at what price should he record the new asset? To illustrate, assume the following conditions:

	Case A	Case B
Old asset:		
Cost	$5,000	$5,000
Accumulated depreciation	3,000	3,000
Net book value	2,000	2,000
Second-hand market value	1,800	2,100
Trade-in allowance	2,300	2,300
List price of new asset	6,000	6,000
Cash payment	3,700	3,700

Probably the most theoretically accurate method is to use the second-hand market value (rather than the trade-in allowance) in the computation of any gain or loss on the disposal of the old asset and also in the determination of the price at which the new asset would be recorded. On this basis, the computations would be made as follows:

	Case A	Case B
Loss or gain on disposal of old asset:		
Net book value	$2,000	$2,000
Second-hand market value	1,800	2,100
Loss	$ 200	
Gain		$ 100
Price at which to record new asset:		
Second-hand value of old asset	$1,800	$2,100
Cash payment	3,700	3,700
Total	$5,500	$5,800

The entries are shown on the following page.

	Case A	Case B
Asset account (new asset)................	5,500	5,800
Accumulated depreciation.................	3,000	3,000
Loss on disposal of old asset............	200	
Gain on disposal of old asset............		100
Asset account (old asset)................		5,000	5,000
Cash.....................................		3,700	3,700

This method of recording the exchange treats the transaction in effect as the sale of the old asset at its market price and the purchase of the new asset at a cost which includes the market value of the old asset and an additional $3,700.

In Case A the trade-in allowance was $500 in excess of the second-hand market value of the old asset, and in Case B it was $200 in excess of the market value. If the trade-in allowances had been as low as the second-hand values, the cash payments and the total cost of the new asset would have been correspondingly increased and the entries would have been:

	Case A	Case B
Asset account (new asset)................	6,000	6,000
Accumulated depreciation.................	3,000	3,000
Loss on disposal of old asset............	200	
Gain on disposal of old asset............		100
Asset account (old asset)................		5,000	5,000
Cash.....................................		4,200	3,900

Second-hand market values are sometimes ignored and the trade-in allowance is accepted as the basis for measuring the gain or loss on the disposal of the old asset. Referring to the preceding cases, a gain of $300 would in each case be regarded as realized on this basis—this being the excess of the $2,300 trade-in allowance over the net book value. The entry to record the exchange in each case would be:

Asset account..	6,000	
Accumulated depreciation.................................	3,000	
Asset account..		5,000
Cash...		3,700
Gain on disposal of fixed asset..........................		300
New asset acquired for cash plus trade-in.		

Objections may be raised to this procedure on the ground that a gain is taken into the accounts without realization other than by addition to the fixed asset account. When it is remembered that dealers frequently make allowances in excess of market values, the validity of such a gain becomes open to serious question.

As a practical matter, it often is necessary to use the trade-in allowance as the basis for determining the gain or loss on trades because there is no other second-hand market value supportable by objective data.

If the offered trade-in allowance is less than the second-hand market value, the old asset normally will be sold instead of turned in as part payment for the new asset; in such cases, the offered allowance will have no bearing on the entries. For reasons of expediency or because a trade-in is demanded (as frequently happened when automobiles were purchased after World War II), a trade-in allowance lower than market value may be accepted. In such cases, it is customary to use the trade-in allowance as the basis of the entries for the exchange.

For income tax purposes, no gain or loss should be taken on an exchange; the cost of the new asset, for purposes of computing depreciation and the gain or loss on subsequent disposal, should be the sum of the book value of the old asset and the additional expenditure made in the acquisition. On this basis, the entry to record the exchange of assets in the foregoing cases A and B would be:

Asset account...	5,700	
Accumulated depreciation................................	3,000	
Asset account.......................................		5,000
Cash..		3,700
New asset acquired for cash plus trade-in.		

Fire and casualty losses. To illustrate the accounting procedure applicable to insured losses, let us assume the following facts: A building which cost $100,000, on which depreciation of $30,000 has been provided, and which thus has a book value of $70,000, is insured for $75,000. It is destroyed by fire. A valuation of $77,000 is agreed upon for insurance-settlement purposes, and a check for $75,000, the full amount of the policy, is received.

The entry to record the settlement will include a credit of $100,000 to the asset account, a debit of $30,000 to the accumulated depreciation account, a credit of $5,000 to a special income statement account (or possibly to Retained Earnings if the amount is so large as to distort the net income for the period) for the excess of the settlement price over the carrying value, and a debit of $75,000 to Cash. The $5,000 credit should not be regarded as a gain on the fire; it may be merely an adjustment of the depreciation provisions of prior periods, or a realization of increased market values, or a combination of both.

In fact, the fire may actually have resulted in a loss. In the illustration, this appears to have been the case. Accepting the $77,000 settlement value as a proper market valuation, the $5,000 credit is the net of two amounts: $7,000 representing increase in market value or excessive depreciation provisions, and a $2,000 loss on the fire.

Income tax regulations give relief to taxpayers who realize a nominal or book gain from such events as fires, other casualties, or condemnation proceedings. No taxable income is regarded as resulting from such "involuntary conversions" if the entire amount received as compensation for the converted property is expended in its replacement. If less than the total proceeds is expended in replacement, the book gain is taxable only to the extent of the unexpended funds. Thus, in the foregoing illustration, if $72,000 was expended to replace the destroyed property, $3,000 of the $5,000 book gain would be taxable.

The cost basis of the new property for income tax purposes is actual cost reduced by the amount of the untaxable gain. Thus, in the foregoing illustration the book gain was $5,000, the taxable gain was $3,000, and the untaxable gain was $2,000. The $72,000 cost of the new property is therefore to be reduced by $2,000 to arrive at the cost basis for income tax purposes.

Assuming that the property was replaced at a cost of $68,000, the entire $5,000 would be taxable gain. Since there would be no untaxable gain, the cost basis of the new property would be the entire $68,000.

A loss is deductible for tax purposes.

Revision of rates. After an asset has been in operation for some time, it may be found that too much or too little depreciation has been provided. Such a condition may be due to an error in estimating the life of the asset or to an incorrect estimate of the residual value.

If an overprovision has been made and is to be corrected in the accounts, the accumulated depreciation account may be charged and a special income statement account (or possibly Retained Earnings) credited; if an underprovision has been made, the correction entry will be just the opposite. The correction should be sufficient to adjust the accumulated depreciation account to the amount which it would have contained if depreciation had originally been based on the estimates which now seem to be correct. After the accumulated depreciation amount has been adjusted, the rate should be revised for subsequent depreciation to prevent a continuation of the overprovision or underprovision.

As an alternative treatment, the undepreciated cost of the asset may be spread over the remaining life of the asset by revised depreciation provisions, without making any adjustment or correction of the current balance in the accumulated depreciation account.

The latter alternative is found more commonly in practice, possibly because it is the procedure permitted for federal income tax purposes.

Fully depreciated assets. If an asset has no salvage value, it is said to be fully depreciated when the credits for accumulated depreciation applicable to it are equal to its cost. If the asset is retired from use, an entry should be made removing the cost and accumulated depreciation from the accounts.

If there is salvage value, an asset is fully depreciated when its related accumulated depreciation plus its realizable salvage value is equal to its cost. In such cases, if the asset is removed from use, the salvage value should be set up in a sundry asset account.

If fully depreciated assets are still in service, it is obvious that their service life was underestimated and the depreciation provisions were excessive. Accountants are not in agreement as to the proper procedure to be applied in such cases.

Some accountants advocate leaving the cost of the property and the accumulated depreciation provisions in the accounts, and merely discontinuing the depreciation provisions. Others believe that the asset account and the accumulated depreciation account should be relieved of the cost and the depreciation provisions, so that the property accounts will contain either scrap values or balances which are applicable only to assets still subject to depreciation charges. Under either of these plans there is merit in disclosing, by a balance sheet footnote, the cost of fully depreciated fixed assets still in service.

Other accountants take an entirely different approach. They believe in making a new estimate of the total life of the asset, re-computing the depreciation which would have been provided to date if the new life estimate had been made originally, correcting the accumulated depreciation account to conform to the new estimate, and continuing depreciation provisions, but at a revised rate. This procedure is defended on the ground that depreciation accounting is intended to spread the cost of fixed assets over their useful lives; that the provision of full depreciation at too early a date was an error; and that future periods should not receive service from an asset without bearing a depreciation charge for its use. The reply, but not a conclusive one, to this argument is that, after operations have once been charged with the full cost of an asset, any accounting procedure which produces additional charges against income results in charging the income for the entire period of the asset's life with depreciation in excess of the cost of the asset, and that this is contrary to sound accounting theories relative to depreciation.* Any additional depreciation charges for

---

* The same objection could be raised (with similar inconclusiveness) against reductions of accumulated depreciation such as those discussed on page 384 under the caption "Revision of rates."

fully depreciated assets are, of course, not allowable for income tax purposes.

The procedure just discussed would merit attention if the remaining life and depreciation charges, if continued, were significant. However, the accountant might justifiably wonder why such a significant mistake was ignored, perhaps deliberately, until the assets became fully depreciated.

Unit and group bases of depreciation accounting. In the discussion thus far it has been assumed that the accountant, in his attempts to compute and account for depreciation, approaches the problem by considering each asset as a separate unit. Thus, the estimated useful life or depreciation rate selected is one believed to be specifically applicable to the unit of property being depreciated. Accumulated depreciation is related to each unit, and if an asset is retired, the accumulated depreciation related to that particular asset is removed from the accounts when the cost of the asset is removed. It is not uncommon for gains and losses on disposals to arise under this general plan of depreciation accounting.

In contrast, the accountant may approach the depreciation matter as one involving groups of assets. This may be characterized as an "averaging" procedure. Suppose that a business owns ten similar machines. The accountant will try to determine the useful life or depreciation rate that on the average best fits the expectancy with respect to such machines when considered as a group. If the machines are depreciated on the basis of a fifteen-year useful life, it is expected that some of the individual machines may in fact have shorter useful lives and that some may in fact have longer useful lives. It is expected only that, considering the group as a whole, fifteen years will work out to be a reasonably close estimate. In fact, prior experience with similar groups of assets, by the company or perhaps by a trade or industry, is generally available to support such an expectation.

Under this plan, accumulated depreciation is not associated with individual assets. When assets are disposed of or retired, the cost less salvage is charged against the accumulated depreciation account, and no loss or gain is recognized. This procedure is based on a presumption, which should be supported by past experience, that any underdepreciation on assets retired early will be offset by overprovisions of depreciation on assets which prove to have a longer life than estimated. If disposals or retirements in significant amounts take place for reasons not contemplated when the group depreciation rate was established, with the result that the presumption mentioned above is invalidated, the accumulated depreciation account may be charged with only the depreciation provided at the group rate during the period of use, and a loss or gain may be recognized and recorded.

Departures from the Cost Basis

Bases of appraisals. Appraisals are sometimes made on the basis of original cost less depreciation. The purpose of such an appraisal is merely to determine whether the asset accounts properly reflect the cost of the plant, and whether the depreciation provisions are justified in the light of events subsequent to acquisition. If the appraiser's estimate of original cost differs from the balance in the asset account, an adjustment of the asset account to conform to the appraisal can be assumed to be an adjustment to a corrected cost basis, and not a departure from the cost basis. If the appraiser's estimate of accrued depreciation differs from the balance in the accumulated depreciation account, it should be remembered that the appraiser's estimate of accrued depreciation may be based on physical deterioration of the plant; that the depreciation provisions in the accounts are intended to absorb the cost of the asset by charges to operations in reasonably equitable periodical amounts; and that the progress of physical deterioration and the accumulation of depreciation in the accounts are not presumed to keep in step. Therefore, a disagreement between the depreciation per books and the depreciation per the appraisal does not necessarily indicate that an adjustment of the accumulated depreciation account should be made. Such an adjustment might be in order if the appraisal indicated that the depreciation provisions had been based on an incorrect estimate of useful life.

Appraisals usually are made for the purpose of determining reproduction cost new and sound value. Reproduction cost new is the computed cost of replacing the asset in its present location at current production costs. Sound value is reproduction cost new less depreciation to date computed by applying the condition per cent to the reproduction cost new. The determination of reproduction cost new and sound value may be desired for tax, insurance, sale, consolidation, credit, and other purposes.

Recent history of accounting thought. Changes in price levels and the purchasing power of the dollar affect the value of plant assets; values tend to increase during periods of inflation and tend to decrease during periods of deflation. Beginning during World War I and continuing until the late nineteen-twenties, there was a period of rising costs, and appraisals showed sound values in excess of depreciated cost. During the depression, the converse was the case. After World War II, there was another period of inflation.

It seems desirable to consider briefly the development of accounting thought, during this span of years, relative to the propriety of recording appraisals and the propriety of making depreciation provisions on any basis other than cost.

Period of inflation during and after World War I.   At the beginning of this period, accountants were generally of the opinion that fixed assets should be carried in the accounts at cost, and that depreciation should be based on cost. But businessmen often thought otherwise. In some cases, business management wanted to write up the fixed assets to appraised values, while continuing to make depreciation charges on the basis of cost. In other cases, they wanted to write up the fixed assets and also base depreciation on replacement value.

Appraised values and the balance sheet.   During this period, particularly during the latter part of the twenties, a great many issues of securities were marketed, and accountants were under pressure, from business management and investment bankers, to show fixed assets in the balance sheet at appraised values. Accountants frequently faced situations such as the following, in which the sound value shown by the appraisal was considerably in excess of the depreciated book value:

	Value Per Appraisal	Value Per Books	Excess Per Appraisal
Cost:			
Reproduction cost new—per appraisal....................	$140,000		
Original cost—per books.......		$100,000	
Excess of reproduction cost new over original cost...........			$40,000
Depreciation:			
On reproduction cost—per appraisal....................	35,000		
On original cost—per books....		25,000	
Excess of depreciation on reproduction cost over depreciation on original cost.............			10,000
Depreciated value:			
Sound value—per appraisal....	$105,000		
Net book value..............		$ 75,000	
Excess of sound value per appraisal over net book value...			$30,000

If a $60,000 mortgage was placed on the property and the accountant insisted upon showing the property in the balance sheet at the net book value of $75,000, without disclosure of the appraised value, a number of statement users probably would have concluded that a liability of $60,000 was secured by property valued at only $75,000. The accountant probably would have been told that his balance sheet was an unfair deterrent to the sale of the securities because it did not indicate the current value of the property serving as security to the mortgage.

To meet such a situation, the accountant might show the facts in the balance sheet thus:

Balance Sheet—December 31, 192—

Asset Side

Machinery (Reproduction cost new, less depreciation, per appraisal by The Blank Appraisal Company, as of December 31, 192—, $105,000):

Cost.	$100,000	
Less depreciation on cost.	25,000	$75,000

Liability Side

Mortgage payable.	$60,000

But such a balance sheet, in which the appraised value of the fixed assets was merely shown parenthetically, was obviously much less satisfactory, from the standpoint of the company and the investment banker offering securities to the public, than one in which appraised values appeared in the money columns, thus:

Balance Sheet—December 31, 192—

Asset Side

Machinery—per appraisal by The Blank Appraisal Company as of December 31, 192—:

Reproduction cost new.	$140,000	
Less depreciation.	35,000	$105,000

Liability Side

Mortgage payable.	$ 60,000

Accountants, therefore, reconsidered their position, and practice for a number of years indicated that many accountants had reached the conclusion that appraisals could be recorded in the accounts and reflected in the balance sheet, provided the increase in valuation was not credited to Earned Surplus but was carried to a special account such as Unrealized Increment per Appraisal. The use of such a special account was desirable for two reasons: First, it clearly segregated the appraisal increment from the stockholders' equity which arose from stockholders' investments and from the retention of earnings; second, the laws of most states make such unrealized credits unavailable for the payment of dividends.

Recording appraisals. Two methods, widely used during the period which we are discussing, for recording appraisals when sound values exceeded net book values are described on page 390. They are based on the assumed data shown on page 388, which are summarized on the next page.

	Value Per Appraisal	Value Per Books	Excess Per Appraisal
Gross:			
Reproduction cost new.........	$140,000		
Cost........................		$100,000	
Excess per appraisal...........			$40,000
Depreciation:			
On reproduction cost new......	35,000		
On cost.....................		25,000	
Excess per appraisal...........			10,000
Net.........................	$105,000	$ 75,000	$30,000

First method. The entry to record an appraisal was sometimes made as follows:

Machinery...	40,000	
Reserve for depreciation—Machinery................		10,000
Unrealized increment per appraisal..................		30,000

Second method. The foregoing entry did not maintain a clear distinction between cost and appraisal write-up. To maintain this distinction,

A separate property account was charged with the excess of reproduction cost new over original cost, and

A separate contra account was credited with the excess of the depreciation on reproduction cost over the depreciation on original cost.

The entry to record the appraisal by this method was:

Machinery—Appraisal increase.........................	40,000	
Reserve for depreciation—Machinery—Appraisal increase.......................................		10,000
Unrealized increment per appraisal..................		30,000

The accounts then contained the following balances:

Machinery (original cost)..........................	$100,000	
Machinery—Appraisal increase......................	40,000	
Reserve for depreciation (on cost)....................		$25,000
Reserve for depreciation—Appraisal increase...........		10,000
Unrealized increment per appraisal..................		30,000

The second method of recording appraisals was preferable because it preserved a record in terms of cost, which was essential information for tax purposes.

In many cases appraisals indicated that the useful life of the asset was different from the one being used for depreciation purposes. If the revised useful life was adopted, the accumulated depreciation was generally adjusted, in the manner described on page 384, before the appraisal was recorded. However, it should be remembered that if the difference between recorded depreciation and the appraiser's estimate of depreciation is attributable to the difference between observable depreciation and accounting depreciation, there is no need generally to adjust the accounts.

Depreciation after recording an appraisal. During the period now under discussion, the recording of increased values disclosed by appraisals usually appealed to management from the balance sheet standpoint only. Management usually desired to continue making depreciation charges to operations on a cost basis even after recording the appraisal. In some cases, however, management desired to base depreciation charges on replacement values, for reasons discussed below.

Depreciation on replacement cost. Some businessmen, and a few accountants, advanced the idea that, when replacement costs of fixed assets were higher than actual costs, depreciation should be based on replacement cost. This practice is, of course, not permitted for income tax purposes, except that replacement values as of March 1, 1913, can be substituted for the cost of fixed assets acquired before that date.

Some of the arguments, pro and con, presented during the period of rising prices following the first World War, with respect to the advisability and propriety of computing depreciation on the basis of appraised values, are stated below.

(1) Basing depreciation on replacement cost in a period of rising prices is desirable to avoid a possible impairment of working capital.

Pro: If a manufacturer is using fixed assets acquired at less than present replacement costs, and if he computes depreciation on cost, his depreciation charges will be lower than those of other manufacturers using fixed assets purchased later at a higher price level; his total manufacturing costs may, therefore, be lower than those of his competitors, and he may be disposed to lower his selling prices accordingly. Such a procedure may give him a temporary advantage in meeting competition, but it may be disastrous in the long run; if the proceeds of his sales are not sufficient to include a provision for fixed asset replacements, the expenditures for replacements may impair his working capital.

Con: To charge operations with depreciation on more than cost overstates the actual expenses. A good businessman knows that his selling prices must be high enough to enable him to buy new equipment when the old is worn out, and he should be able to fix his selling prices at a proper level without misstating his costs. Providing for the replacement of fixed assets in a rising market is analogous to providing for the replacement of merchandise on a rising market. Suppose that a merchant buys an article for $1 and marks it to sell for $1.50. Before it is sold, the market purchase price goes up from $1 to $1.35; the merchant then advances his selling price to $1.85 so that he can buy another article for $1.35 and still have $.50 to cover expenses and dividends. But he does not say that the first article cost $1.35; he does not consider it necessary to misstate the cost of goods sold on the first article.* Similarly, the manufacturer using old, low-cost machinery can establish the selling price of his product in order to provide for the replacement of his fixed assets without overstating depreciation charges and misstating net income.

(2) Basing depreciation on replacement cost tends to compensate for the fluctuating value of the dollar.

Pro: Assume that, in the interval since the acquisition of the plant, the price level has materially changed, and that it now requires two dollars to purchase what one dollar would then have bought; if we charge manufacturing costs with material, labor, and miscellaneous manufacturing expense items at the prevailing dollar cost, and depreciation of plant on the basis of a prior dollar cost, the resulting "cost" stated in dollars is really a sum of two different kinds of dollars, and we are unconsciously doing something comparable to adding corn and beans. Stated in another way, a dollar now has half the purchasing power that a dollar had when the plant was acquired; therefore, the dollar used in the acquisition of the plant was worth two present dollars; consequently, to put all manufacturing-cost dollars on a common basis, the depreciation-cost dollar should be recognized as equivalent to two material- or labor-cost dollars, and the depreciation charge should be doubled; this can be roughly accomplished by basing depreciation on replacement cost.

Con: This argument assumes a major premise that the determination of cost should give recognition to the changing purchasing power of the dollar. Such a premise

---

* In the period which we are now discussing, the *lifo* inventory method had not yet come into use. The analogy of the *lifo* inventory method and the provision of depreciation on replacement cost is mentioned in Chapter 29.

has never been accepted by accountants. Little, if any, attempt has ever been made to base actual accounting procedures on it; and any accountant who undertook, in the determination of all costs, to give recognition to changes in the purchasing power of the dollar would find himself confronted with the herculean task of ascertaining, on the day of use, what everything acquired at some prior date would cost at present prices.

Pro: The fact that a thing has never been done or is difficult to do is not a logical reason for contending that it should not be done. It does not face up to the question: Should accounting give recognition to changes in price levels?

Period of deflation during the depression. During the depression which began in 1929, many concerns adopted the policy of writing down their fixed assets.

In many instances, no doubt, the fixed assets were written down with the idea of more fairly reflecting the financial position of the business. During the depression, the demand for products decreased, production decreased, and prices of products and fixed assets declined. If fixed assets were pledged as security to long-term liabilities, the security behind the liabilities was impaired; moreover, the reduction in asset values affected the proprietorship equity from the standpoint of possible enforced liquidation; information with respect to declines in value was therefore of interest to creditors and stockholders.

But it is probable that most of the asset write-downs during this depression period were made for the purpose of establishing a lower depreciation base, thus reducing the depreciation charges, so that more favorable operating results could be shown in the income statement. Such reductions in depreciation charges may have seemed, at the time, to be justified by a theory which was the converse of that which had previously been used by those who advocated charging operations with depreciation on replacement values which were in excess of cost. If earnings should be reduced by increased depreciation charges to provide for the replacement of fixed assets on a rising market, then earnings might presumably be increased by reducing the depreciation charges if the replacement cost of the fixed assets had decreased.

When fixed assets were written down, the charges were sometimes made to the unrealized increment accounts created by recording former upward appraisals. The write-offs were sometimes made against paid-in surplus, and sometimes against earned surplus.

The favorite procedure was the quasi-reorganization, which is discussed in Chapter 27. The quasi-reorganization has come to be regarded as the only procedure, conformable with accepted accounting principles, by which fixed assets can be written down and the future depreciation charges to operations be correspondingly reduced.

Asset write-ups in the present period of inflation. At the time of this writing we are again in a period of high and rising prices. During the inflation of the twenties, management was primarily concerned with high replacement costs from the balance sheet standpoint; it desired to write up fixed assets in order to reflect a better financial position, and thus increase the marketability of securities. This time, interest centers mainly in the income statement; management would like to be able to increase depreciation charges to a basis approximating the replacement cost of the fixed asset.

The prevailing attitude of most accountants reflects agreement with the position expressed in Institute Bulletin No. 5, issued in 1940, which stated that "accounting for fixed assets should normally be based on cost, and any attempt to make property accounts in general reflect current values is both impracticable and inexpedient. Appreciation normally should not be reflected on the books of account of corporations." However, there has been one significant change in contrast to the twenties. It is now held that when appreciation has been recorded in the accounts, depreciation should be based on the written-up amounts. As the Committee on Accounting Procedure stated in Bulletin 43, "A company should not at the same time claim larger property valuations in its statement of assets and provide for the amortization of only smaller amounts in its statement of income."

A minority of the committee added the further thought that, "as a matter of consistency, where increased property valuations have been entered on the books the credit item should be treated as permanent capital and would therefore not be available for subsequent transfer to earned surplus as *realized* through depreciation or sale." While the authors believe there is some merit in the position of the minority, it is probably true that generally accepted accounting would approve of the procedure shown below covering the matter of depreciation and the consequent piecemeal realization of the write-up credit.

Illustrative entries. There are presented, on the following page, certain account balances after an appraisal was recorded, other assumed facts used in the illustration, and journal entries for depreciation after the appraisal.

Machinery (original cost)................................ $100,000

Accumulated depreciation (on cost).................... $25,000
    When the property was acquired, it was estimated to
    have a life of twenty years and no residual value. A 5%
    depreciation rate was therefore adopted. Five years of
    the estimated life of the asset had expired before the
    appraisal.

Machinery (appraisal increase).......................   40,000

Accumulated depreciation—Appraisal increase.........   10,000

Unrealized increment per appraisal...................   30,000

The periodic entries associated with depreciation are shown below.

Depreciation (chargeable to operations)................... 7,000
    Accumulated depreciation (on cost)....................   5,000
    Accumulated depreciation—Appraisal increase..........   2,000
    To provide depreciation on the written-up amount.

Unrealized increment per appraisal....................... 2,000
    Retained earnings....................................   2,000
    To transfer the realized appreciation to Retained Earnings.

The amount of the last entry above is the difference between depreciation based on recorded value and that based on cost. Such periodic entries will, over the remaining life of the asset, transfer the unrealized increment to retained earnings. In lieu of such periodic transfers, a one-time entry transferring the unrealized increment to retained earnings can be made when the asset is disposed of or written off as fully depreciated.

It has been contended that the theory of the quasi-reorganization, which sanctions fixed asset write-downs as an incident to a "fresh start," with subsequent decreased depreciation charges to income, should be extended to permit fixed asset write-ups with increased depreciation charges. Neither the Institute nor the Securities and Exchange Commission has, up to the present time, looked favorably upon such a procedure.

Depreciation in the present period. It has long been a basic theory of accounting that depreciation is concerned merely with the assignment of the cost of a fixed asset to operations during the periods of its useful life. Accountants maintain that the provision for depreciation is not a provision for replacement, and that changes in the purchasing power of the monetary unit should not be given consideration in the determination of periodic depreciation or in the computation of net income.

Admittedly, business management today faces problems of vital importance resulting from inflation and high income taxes, and some businessmen would like to have accounting theories revised in some way so that, in the determination of operating costs and expenses, recognition could be given to the increased cost of plant replacements. One of the chief arguments advanced in support of the proposition that depreciation charges against income must be sufficient to provide for the replacement of plant assets is based on the economic concept of income as distinguished from the monetary concept. The argument goes somewhat as follows: The difference between real and nominal wages (or economic and monetary wages) has long been recognized; the same distinction should be recognized between the economic income and the monetary income of a business enterprise. The economic capital of a business —its capital, not in dollars, but in things—must be maintained before there is any economic income. Accounting concepts relative to depreciation are based on an assumption of stable money; if this assumption were warranted, economic and monetary income would be the same, and depreciation based on cost could result in the maintenance of economic capital. But the assumption is false, and accountants should not stand adamant upon conclusions that are based on false assumptions. Unless the charges to operations for things used up or otherwise disposed of in the process of operations are sufficient to replace these things, there is no economic income, and the real capital is impaired, no matter what the books may show as monetary income.

Although accountants are conscious of the problems of management, they have, up to the time of this writing, stood firm in the position that depreciation accounting is intended only to charge asset costs against operations; they hold that depreciation is one thing, and that the financing of replacements is another.

Accountants object to departures from the cost basis, not only because they believe that the cost basis is theoretically correct, but also because they fear that, if the door is opened, a miscellany of methods may come in, with resulting confusion and uncertainty as to the significance of reported earnings. They feel that such confusion would arise even if depreciation on replacement cost were the only permitted substitute for depreciation on cost. As the Institute's Committee on Accounting Procedure said in a special statement issued in 1947, "It would not increase the usefulness of reported corporate income figures if some companies charged depreciation on appraised values while others adhered to cost. The committee believes, therefore, that consideration of radical changes in accepted accounting procedure should not be undertaken, at least until a stable price level would make it practicable for business as a whole to make the change at the same time."

This general matter is discussed at some length in Chapter 29.

CHAPTER NINETEEN

Intangible Fixed Assets

Classification and general principles.　Accountants customarily use the categories Type A and Type B to classify intangible assets.

Type A—Those having a limited term of existence, the limitation being a consequence of some law, regulation, or agreement, or the very nature of a given intangible. Examples are patents, copyrights, franchises for limited periods, leaseholds, and leasehold improvements.

Type B—Those having no such limited term of existence. Examples are trademarks, trade names, secret formulas and processes, perpetual franchises, going value, goodwill, and organization costs.

In accordance with the principle that cost is the fundamental basis of accounting, intangible fixed assets should be recorded at their cost. And, in accordance with the generally accepted rule of convenience applicable in such cases, the cost of an intangible fixed asset acquired in some transaction other than a separate purchase for cash can be measured by the fair value of the asset acquired or by the fair value of the consideration given, whichever is the more definitely determinable.

If, in a lump-sum purchase, several intangible assets are acquired, or intangibles are acquired with other assets, a separate cost should be established for each intangible of Type A, so that the separate costs can be amortized over the respective periods of life. An aggregate cost for all intangibles of Type B may be satisfactory unless there is reason to believe that some of them may immediately or ultimately be subject to amortization, in which event their separate costs will need to be known, in order to establish bases for the amortization.

The cost of a Type A intangible should be amortized by systematic charges in the income statement over the period benefited. It should be understood that the period fixed by law, regulation, or contract is the maximum period, and that the usefulness of such assets may cease prior to the expiration of that period; in such instances, the shorter useful life period should be the period of amortization. As noted by the Committee on Accounting Procedure in Bulletin No. 43, "If it becomes evident that the period benefited will be longer or shorter than originally estimated, recognition thereof may take the form of an appropriate decrease or increase in the rate of amortization or, if such increased charges would result in distortion of income, a partial write-down may be made by a charge to earned surplus."

Intangible fixed assets of Type B may be carried indefinitely at cost if there is no reason to believe that their useful lives will ever terminate. However, although assets of this class are not normally subject to amortization, their amortization or complete write-off may be proper under several conditions. First, at the time of acquisition there may be good reason to fear that the useful life of such an asset will terminate, even though there is no conclusive evidence to that effect; in such instances, periodical amortization charges may be made against income. Second, at some time subsequent to acquisition, conditions may have developed which indicate that the life of the asset will terminate; in such instances, the cost of the asset may be amortized over the estimated remaining life; or, if such charges would result in a material distortion in the income statement, a partial write-off may be made against retained earnings and the remainder of the cost may be amortized. Third, an asset may be found to be valueless; under such circumstances it should be written off. The amount of the write-off should be assigned to the income statement, unless the amount is so large that its effect on net income may give rise to misleading inferences. In that case the write-off should be against retained earnings, but never against paid-in surplus.

Many business concerns have written off intangible fixed assets before their useful lives have terminated, or have written them down more rapidly than a normal amortization procedure would require, justifying such action on the grounds of conservatism. There is a growing belief among accountants that conservatism does not justify such eliminations of value from the accounts, since they violate the fundamental principle that accounting should provide as accurate a record as possible of costs and of the expiration of costs.

If management desires to relieve the accounts of the cost of intangibles of Type B merely for reasons of conservatism, and without the justification of any knowledge of conditions which indicate the contingency of an expiration of usefulness, the elimination may be accomplished by a gradual amortization or by an immediate write-off. Since neither of these procedures would be required by generally accepted accounting principles, management would seem to be under an ethical obligation not to adopt either of them without the formal approval of the stockholders or directors, and it would seem that such approval should be disclosed in the financial statements.

A practice of arbitrarily writing off intangibles upon or immediately after acquisition is improper. It runs counter to the basic accounting assumption that all expenditures result initially in the acquisition of short- or long-term benefits.

Intangible Fixed Assets Normally Subject to Amortization

Patents.   Patents may be productive of earnings through the reduction of manufacturing costs, or by the creation of a monopolistic condition which permits the charging of prices very favorable to the patent owner. Income may be earned directly from patents through royalties collected under license agreements; some outstanding present examples of this procedure are found in the radio and television industries.

If a patent is acquired by purchase, its cost is the purchase price. If it is obtained by the inventor, its cost is the total of experimental expense, costs of working models, and expenses of obtaining the patent, including drawings, attorneys' fees, and filing fees.

If a company operates an experimental department for the purpose of developing patentable devices, it is faced with the question of the proper accounting treatment of the expenditures of the department. Three different opinions are held with respect to the proper treatment of such costs:

(1) The entire cost of the department may be capitalized as the cost of the patents obtained.

(2) Cost records should be kept, so that costs applicable to work

which results successfully in a patent can be capitalized and the remaining expenses can be charged to revenue. If this method is used, expenditures can be charged to an account with some title such as "Unallocated Experimental Department Costs," from which transfers can be made to the Patents account or to an expense account when the proper allocation of the costs is ultimately determined.

(3) The entire expense of the department should be charged to operations, because competing concerns presumably are operating similar departments and the expense of the department is essential merely to keep abreast of the industry.

A patent has no proven worth until it has stood the test of an infringement suit. The cost of a successful suit may be charged to the Patents account as representing an additional cost of establishing the patent. If litigation costs incurred or other expenditures made in protecting a patent are charged to the Patents account as additions to the cost, the amortization procedure should be such as to insure writing off these additional costs at the expiration of the life of the patent. While the cost of litigation in successfully defending a patent case seems logically to be a proper addition to the cost of the patent to be set up and amortized over the patent's remaining life, decisions in income tax cases do not so recognize it, but require that it be expensed in the tax year in which it is incurred.

If the suit is unsuccessful and the patent is thereby proved to be worthless, both the cost of the suit and the unamortized cost of the patent should be written off.

Amortizing patents. A patent is issued for seventeen years; hence, the cost of the patent should usually be written off during that period. Of course, if a patent is purchased some time after it was granted, the purchaser will have to write it off in less than seventeen years.

Protection under the patent starts when the patent is applied for, and runs for seventeen years after issuance. Hence, the period of protection may be more than seventeen years; but since it is usually difficult to estimate the period that will expire between the date of application and the date of issuance, this additional time prior to actual issuance is usually ignored.

If an additional patent is obtained that is so closely related to a former patent that it in effect extends the life of the basic patent, any unamortized balance of the cost of the old patent remaining in the account at the date of obtaining the new one may be carried forward and written off over the life of the new one. This procedure can properly be adopted only in case there is a reasonable certainty that the productivity of the original patent will continue through the life of the new patent. In the absence of such certainty, the old patent should be amortized over the remainder of its own life.

Although seventeen years is the theoretical period for writing off a patent, practical considerations often make it desirable to write off the cost in less than that time. If the patent covers an article which will be marketable only during the period of a fad, it is advisable to write off the patent during the probable continuance of the fad.

If the article patented is subject to the danger of being superseded by some other invention, the element of supersession should be taken into consideration as a probable factor in making the effective life of the patent shorter than its legal life.

If the owner of a patent finds that the product manufactured under it is not in demand and cannot be profitably marketed, the patent is evidently valueless even though its legal life has not expired; in such a case it should be written off.

A patent is sometimes purchased for the purpose of controlling the patent and thus preventing the manufacture of a competing article. Such a patent should be written off over its life unless the sole purpose of the purchase of the patent was to provide additional protection during the remaining life of a patent already owned; in that case, the cost of the new patent should be written off over the remaining life of the old patent.

Assume that several patents with differing remaining lives are purchased at a lump price, and that there is no information by which the cost can be apportioned to the several patents on the basis of prospective profitability. An arithmetical procedure for the computation of amortization of such costs, giving consideration only to the different lives of the patents, is indicated by the following illustration. Assume that three patents are purchased; one has a remaining life of 15 years or 180 months; another, a life of 12 years or 144 months; another, a life of 6 years or 72 months; the total of months is 396. The monthly amortization would be determined by multiplying the cost of the patents by a fraction, the numerator of which is the number of unexpired patents and the denominator of which is the aggregate original number of months of remaining life, in this case 396. The monthly amortization during the first six years would be $\frac{3}{396}$ of the total cost. At the end of six years one of the patents will have expired, and the numerator of the fraction will change to 2; the denominator will remain 396.

Copyrights. A copyright gives its owner the exclusive right to produce and sell reading matter and works of art. The fee for obtaining a copyright is only a nominal amount, insufficient to justify an accounting procedure of capitalization and amortization. Costs sufficient in amount to justify such a procedure do arise, however, when copyrights are purchased.

Copyrights are issued for twenty-eight years with a possibility of renewal for an additional twenty-eight years. However, publications rarely have an active market for a period as long as twenty-eight years, and it is usually regarded as advisable to write off the copyright cost against the income from the first printing. The nature of certain publications may justify a less conservative procedure.

Franchises. Franchises should not appear on the books unless a payment, either direct or indirect, was made in obtaining them. Franchises may be perpetual, in which case the cost need not be amortized. They may be granted for a definite period of time, in which case the cost should be systematically written off during that period. They may be revocable at the option of the city or other governmental body that granted them, in which case it is advisable to write them off rapidly, although there is a tendency to look upon such franchises as perpetual and make no provision for amortization of their cost.

Periodical payments made to the governmental unit from which the franchise was obtained are operating expenses.

Leaseholds. A leasehold is an estate for years. It should not be entered on the books as an intangible asset unless payments applicable to a period of time exceeding that covered by an operating cycle have been made under the lease agreement, in which case such payments should be carried forward and assigned to expense during the applicable years. In other words, normal rent prepayments should be shown in the Current Assets section with other prepaid expenses. Only longer-term prepayments are treated as intangible assets.

The possession of a long-term lease to property in a neighborhood in which rents are rapidly advancing may be a very great advantage; this advantage cannot properly be capitalized. There can be no objection to indicating the value of such a leasehold by a balance sheet footnote.

It is unusual for a lessee to make an advance payment of the total rent for the entire period of the lease; frequently, however, leases contain agreements similar to the following: terms of lease, ten years; annual rent, $3,000; advance payment, $10,000; annual payment, $2,000. Under these terms, the Rent Expense account should receive $3,000 of charges during each year of the lease, with offsetting credits of $2,000 to Cash and $1,000 to Leasehold.

Leasehold improvements. Leases frequently provide that the lessee shall pay the costs of any alterations or improvements of the leased real estate, such as new fronts, partitions, and built-in shelving. Such alterations and improvements become a part of the real estate and revert to the owner of the real estate at the expiration of the lease. The lessee obtains only the intangible right to benefit by the improvements during the life of the lease. The lessee should therefore charge such expenditures to a Leasehold Improvements account, which should be amortized over the life of the lease or the useful life of the improvements, whichever is shorter.

Buildings constructed by a lessee on leased land revert to the owner of the fee at the expiration of the lease. The lessee should spread their cost, by proportionate charges, over the life of the lease, unless it is expected that the buildings will become useless before the lease has expired, in which case, the cost should be systematically written off during the estimated life of the buildings.

Although leasehold improvements increase the value of the property of the lessor, it seems advisable for the lessor to postpone making any entries therefor in his accounts until the expiration of the lease. The owner obtains no benefit from the improvements until the expiration of the lease, and may receive no benefit even then because of depreciation, obsolescence, or lack of increase in rent or rentability.

Intangible Fixed Assets Not Normally Subject to Amortization

Trademarks. Trademarks may be registered, but they are valid under the common law without registry if the claimant is able to prove his prior use of the mark. As trademarks do not expire, it is not necessary to write off any cost which may have been incurred in obtaining them.

Trade names, labels, advertised brand names, and secret processes are similar intangibles.

Goodwill. Goodwill exists when the actual or expected earnings of a business are in excess of what is considered to be normal, after making allowance for the type of industry, the risk, the state of business conditions, and other relevant alternative investment opportunities. To illustrate, let us assume the conditions shown on the following page.

	Company A	Company B
Net assets, exclusive of goodwill................	$100,000	$100,000
Rate of net income which, for the particular industry, may be agreed upon by the purchaser and seller of a business as normal, or which a new company entering the field may reasonably be expected to earn—say................	10%	10%
Net income earned...........................	$ 10,000	$ 15,000
Income at "normal" rate on net assets exclusive of goodwill...............................	10,000	10,000
Excess earnings...........................	$ —	$ 5,000

The excess earnings of Company B indicate that it has a goodwill; Company A apparently has none.

The list of sources or causes of goodwill includes everything that could contribute to an attractive earnings result. Some of these sources are: satisfactory customer relations; location; manufacturing efficiency; good employee relations; marketing or production "know-how"; and weak or ineffective competition.

Although businesses customarily spend considerable sums for the purpose of creating goodwill, or at least in the hopes that such expenditures will ultimately result in an advantage to them over their competition, it is generally impossible to establish whether any goodwill was in fact created. Therefore, disbursements made in an attempt to create goodwill are expensed. The only goodwill given recognition in the accounts is that specifically paid for in connection with the purchase of a business, a product line, or some group of assets.

How is the price paid for goodwill determined? To meet the requirements of accounting, the goodwill amount must be the result of a bargained transaction. The figure agreed upon for goodwill may have been selected rather arbitrarily or may have been the result of carefully prepared computations. Some of the factors to be considered in making estimates of goodwill are mentioned in the following paragraphs.

Probable future earnings. When the purchaser of a business pays a price for goodwill, he is not paying for the excess earnings of the past, but for the probable excess earnings of the future. The accomplishments of the past, however, may furnish the best available evidence of the probable accomplishments in the future, and, hence, it is customary to estimate the future earnings on the basis of past net income data. In making a statement of past earnings which is to be used as the basis for computing the goodwill, the following points should be considered:

First: The results of operations for one preceding year are not a sufficient basis for estimating future results of operations, because a statement for one year would not disclose fluctuations in earnings. On the other hand, too many past years should not be included in the base if the earnings of the more remote years were affected by conditions at variance with present conditions or trends.

Second: All extraneous and nonoperating gains and losses should be excluded. If income is earned on investments, such as securities or real estate, the fair market value of the assets should govern their sale price, and the income received from them should be excluded from the net income used in computing the goodwill.

Third: If any known facts point to a possible difference between past and future income results, these facts should be considered.

Have the earnings been derived from sales of articles protected by patents, copyrights, licenses, or royalty agreements? If so, how long will such protection continue in the future? To what extent does the success of the business depend upon its present location, and what tenure of the premises is assured either by ownership or by lease? What is the trend of competition in the field? Are there any prospects of changes in labor conditions?

If management salaries have not been deducted by the vendor, or if the salaries have been merely nominal, deductions should be made for the management salaries to be paid by the purchaser, provided that these salaries are reasonable.

If the success of the business in the past has been due largely to the personality or business ability of the old management, and if those who are responsible for this success are not to go with the business to the new owners, this fact should be considered in estimating future earnings.

If the fixed assets of the business are to be transferred to the purchaser at a higher price than that at which they have been carried on the seller's books, recognition should be given to the fact that higher depreciation charges will be required in the future, and that future net income will be correspondingly diminished.

It is often contended that interest paid on borrowed capital should be ignored, because the purchaser may have sufficient capital to finance his business without borrowing and can thus retain for himself the portion of the gross profits which heretofore has been consumed by interest payments. This theory seems to be incorrect. For, to avoid the payment of interest, the purchaser must make an additional investment equal to the amount of capital formerly borrowed; the additional profit which he will thus retain will compensate him for the additional capital investment. But it does not seem equitable to expect him to pay for this income twice: first as part of the goodwill payment, and second by the investment of additional funds in the business.

Fourth: Consideration should be given to the trend of earnings and perhaps to the trend of some of the important items of revenue and expense. It is unwise to accept the average net income of a number of past years as the basis of a goodwill computation without giving consideration to variations and the trend of earnings. This fact may be shown by the following illustration.

Schedule of Net Income Amounts

	A Co.	B Co.	C Co.	D Co.
1953	$ 25,000	$ 19,100	$ 30,000	$ 10,000
1954	40,000	19,800	25,000	15,000
1955	19,000	20,400	20,000	20,000
1956	2,000*	20,200	15,000	25,000
1957	18,000	20,500	10,000	30,000
Total	$100,000	$100,000	$100,000	$100,000
Average	$ 20,000	$ 20,000	$ 20,000	$ 20,000

* Loss.

Although each of these concerns has made an average net income of $20,000 per year, it is evident that it would be unwise to pay the same amount for the goodwill of each business. Company A's earnings show a wide range of fluctuation, from $40,000 net income in 1954 to a loss of $2,000 in 1956. Such a history furnishes very poor evidence of stable earnings in the future.

Company B's earnings, on the other hand, are very uniform year by year and show a slight tendency to increase. Assuming that a net income of $20,000 represents more than a normal return on the capital invested, it would be reasonable and safe to make a payment for B's goodwill based on an average net income of $20,000.

Company C probably has no goodwill, because its earnings are steadily declining, and if the curve of decline continues at the same rate for two more years, there will be no net income whatever.

Company D, on the other hand, probably has the most goodwill of all (assuming equal capitals), because its earnings are steadily increasing. In fact, just as it would be unwise for a purchaser to pay for goodwill based on the average of the earnings of Company C, which are on the decline, so also would it probably be unfair to the seller to base the goodwill of Company D on the average earnings, since the earnings are steadily increasing. The indication is that future earnings will be considerably more than the average.

If an accountant is called upon to prepare a statement of the average net income of a business for purposes of computing goodwill, he should, as a general rule, submit a statement showing the net income of each year as well as the average net income. A statement of only the average is likely to be misleading, because it fails to furnish information concerning the variation and trend of the earnings.

Methods of computation. The price paid for goodwill is usually determined by sheer bargaining; however, the six methods of computation illustrated below indicate factors and procedures which may be considered by the purchaser and seller during the negotiations. The illustrations of the six methods are based on the following assumed facts: The purchaser and the seller of a business have agreed that the net assets, other than goodwill, shall be valued at $100,000; the net income figures for the five years next preceding the date of sale were $19,000, $19,500, $19,000, $21,500, and $21,000, or an annual average of $20,000.

(1) *Years' purchase of past annual earnings.* Assume that the goodwill is to be valued at an amount equal to the total net income of the last preceding two years; the payment to be made for goodwill is called a "two years' purchase of past earnings." The amount is computed below.

Net income of second preceding year	$21,500
Net income of first preceding year	21,000
Total, and price to be paid for the goodwill	$42,500

This is an illogical method of computing goodwill, because it fails to recognize the fact that the goodwill is not dependent upon total earnings, no matter how large, but upon the relation of the earnings to the net assets other than goodwill, and that no goodwill exists unless the earnings are in excess of a normal income on the net assets other than goodwill.

(2) *Years' purchase of average past earnings.* This method differs from the preceding one in only one particular: Average earnings are used instead of aggregate earnings for a given number of years. Assume that the goodwill is to be valued at two years' purchase of the average earnings of the past five years; the goodwill value will be computed as follows:

Average earnings of last 5 years (as stated above)	$20,000
Multiply by number of years of purchase	2
Goodwill	$40,000

This method is as illogical as the preceding one, since it ignores the fact that goodwill is dependent upon excess earnings and not upon total earnings.

(3) *Years' purchase of excess earnings.* Assume that the goodwill is to be valued at three years' purchase of the past earnings in excess of $12\frac{1}{2}\%$ of the net assets other than goodwill. This may mean net income in excess of $12\frac{1}{2}\%$ of the capital actually invested during each of the three years, or net income in excess of $12\frac{1}{2}\%$ of

the $100,000 price determined as the value of the net assets other than goodwill; the latter is the more logical basis. Assuming that the latter basis is agreed upon, the amount to be paid for the goodwill will be computed as follows:

Year Preceding Sale	Net Income	12½% of Net Assets	Excess
Third........................	$19,000	$12,500	$ 6,500
Second.......................	21,500	12,500	9,000
First.........................	21,000	12,500	8,500
Total payment for goodwill............			$24,000

(4) *Years' purchase of average excess earnings.* Assume that the goodwill is to be valued at three years' purchase of the average earnings of the past five years in excess of 12½% of the $100,000 agreed value of the net assets other than goodwill. This method is similar to the preceding one except that averages are used. The goodwill computation is shown below.

Average earnings of past 5 years.............................	$20,000
Deduct 12½% of $100,000....................................	12,500
Excess..	$ 7,500
Multiply by number of years of purchase......................	3
Goodwill...	$22,500

(5) *Capitalized earnings, minus net assets.* Assume that the purchaser and the seller agree upon 12½% as a normal or basic rate, and that they decide to base the valuation of the business upon a capitalization, at that rate, of the average income for the past five years.

The goodwill will be computed as follows:

Capitalized value of average net income, or total value of business:

$20,000 ÷ 12½%...	$160,000
Deduct agreed value of net assets other than goodwill..........	100,000
Goodwill...	$ 60,000

(6) *Excess earnings capitalized.* A serious theoretical objection can be raised to the preceding method. This objection may be made apparent by dividing the total purchase price into two parts and noting what the purchaser of the business obtains in return for his payment.

	Net Assets	Earnings
For the first $100,000 of the purchase price, the purchaser receives:		
Net assets other than goodwill...................	$100,000	
Prospective income of 12½% thereof.............		$12,500
For the remaining $60,000 of the purchase price, the purchaser receives:		
An intangible asset of goodwill...................	60,000	
Prospective income of 12½% thereof.............		7,500

For the first $100,000, the purchaser acquires assets which presumably will have some realizable value even though the prospective earnings fail to materialize; for the $60,000, the purchaser acquires an asset which presumably will have no value if the prospective earnings fail to materialize. It therefore appears that, if 12½% is a fair rate for the capitalization of the first $12,500 of income, a higher rate should be used for the capitalization of the remaining $7,500. The use of two rates is illustrated by the following computation of goodwill; it is assumed that the purchaser and the seller have agreed that 12½% is a fair rate for the capitalization of earnings accompanied by net assets other than goodwill, and that the remaining earnings should be capitalized at 25%.

Average earnings of past 5 years	$20,000
Deduct earnings regarded as applicable to net assets other than goodwill—12½% of $100,000	12,500
Remaining earnings, regarded as indicative of goodwill	$ 7,500
Goodwill = $7,500 ÷ 25%	$30,000

Excess earnings may be divided into brackets, and graduated rates may be used in capitalizing them: Earnings at the higher levels are capitalized at a higher rate (and thus given a lower capitalized value) than earnings at lower levels because of the greater danger that they will not continue. This procedure is illustrated below:

Excess earnings regarded as indicative of goodwill (as above)	$ 7,500
Goodwill:	
Capitalization of first $5,000 at 25%	$20,000
Capitalization of remaining $2,500 at 50%	5,000
Total goodwill	$25,000

Net assets other than goodwill; normal income rate. If goodwill is to be computed as the capitalized value of earnings in excess of a normal return on the net assets other than goodwill, consideration must be given to the valuation of the other assets and a decision must be reached as to what is a normal income rate.

For general accounting purposes, cost (less depreciation, amortization, and so forth) is, in most instances, regarded as the proper basis for the valuation of assets, but this may not be the proper basis when asset valuations are being determined for purposes of goodwill computation. For that purpose, current appraisal values are more appropriate. If they are not used, the difference between the fair present value of the assets and their book value will find its way into the valuation of the goodwill.

What is the normal or basic rate of income to be earned before a business can be regarded as having a goodwill? This is purely a matter of opinion. The basic or normal income is, fundamentally, the amount which would attract proprietorship capital equal to the agreed valuation of the net assets other than goodwill. It varies with different businesses because of variations in hazards and other conditions peculiar to industries. Moreover, no two investors might hold the same opinion as to the normal rate of income applicable to any one business. The determination of the basic rate applicable to net assets other than goodwill, and of the rate to be used in the capitalization of excess earnings, is, therefore, a matter of bargaining between the purchaser and seller.

Goodwill cost not specifically computed. When a going business has been acquired at a lump-sum price, it too frequently has been the practice to record the assets shown in the accounts of the seller, other than goodwill, at appraised values and to assume that any excess of cost, after making allowance for the liabilities taken over, represented goodwill. This procedure is undesirable, for there may be other intangibles, not shown in the books of the seller, on which valuations should be placed for accounting purposes.

Similarly, in cases where the purchase was made by the issuance of capital stock, there have been too many instances where the par or stated value of the stock has been used as the measure of total cost. As a result, any excess of the aggregate par or stated value of the stock issued over the appraised values of the net assets other than goodwill has been treated as goodwill. The possibility that the difference represented stock discount or something akin thereto and not goodwill has been ignored.

Justifiable Goodwill account. We have seen that a business possesses a goodwill if it has excess earnings; but even under such a condition a business is not always justified in having a Goodwill account on its books. As noted earlier, a Goodwill account may properly appear on the books of a business only if the goodwill has been paid for in connection with the acquisition of a going and profit-making business, or some segment thereof, and the balance in the Goodwill account cannot properly be more than the amount so paid.

It is often contended that when a concern conducts an extensive advertising campaign for the purpose of developing business, and spends a sum greatly in excess of a normal advertising expenditure, the purpose is to create a goodwill, and the amount by which the cost of the campaign exceeds a normal advertising expenditure can be capitalized as goodwill. Even if such a procedure were theoretically acceptable, the practical difficulties involved in its application are so great as to make it a dangerous one. What will be the normal advertising expenditure necessary to retain the business after the conclusion of the campaign? It is easy to be optimistic about this matter, but there is always a danger that future advertising costs may be much greater than expected. The portion of the expenditure capitalized as goodwill will then be found to be excessive, and the net income of the past will have been overstated. Perhaps the most reasonable compromise is to set up a portion of the campaign cost as a deferred charge to be written off over the periods which the advertising may reasonably be expected to benefit.

Patents and goodwill. A patent may give its owner a monopoly that enables him to develop his business to a point at which, after the expiration of the patent, competitors will find it extremely difficult to enter the field and overcome the handicap. The patent value thus merges into a goodwill value, and it is often argued that, under such circumstances, the patent may be written off to a Goodwill account instead of against income. This practice is considered improper because of the uncertainty of maintaining the monopoly and thereby preserving the goodwill after the expiration of the patent.

Unjustifiable Goodwill account. If the Goodwill account always represented the amount actually paid for goodwill, the account would not be in its present state of disrepute. Unfortunately, the account has been used for all sorts of ulterior purposes, until it is itself so discredited that it is looked upon with little more favor than the stock discount and deficit accounts for which it has often been substituted.

The chief misuse of the Goodwill account has been charging it with discount on stock. Since goodwill is based on earnings, it cannot exist apart from a business; therefore, if stock is issued for cash or for other assets which are not a part of a going business, and if the value of the assets received is less than the par of the stock issued, there is no justification whatever for charging the discount on stock to a Goodwill account. Even when stock is issued in payment for a going business, the Goodwill account may be overstated. For instance, partners who incorporate may issue stock to themselves greatly in excess of the value of the goodwill and other assets transferred to the corporation.

Another abuse of the Goodwill account is charging it with expenses and losses incurred during the early life of the business when it is establishing itself on a paying basis. Under such circumstances the Goodwill account is merely a device for effecting an eventual inflation of the Retained Earnings account by in effect relieving it of the results of charges for expenses and losses.

A company, after years of successful and profitable operation, may feel that it has created a goodwill, and may proceed to put it on the books. Although the company may be entirely correct in maintaining that it has created a goodwill, it is not justified in placing the account on its books by a credit to a surplus account or by any other credit.

Sometimes a company, in the process of reorganization, will call in its old stock and issue a larger amount in its place. This procedure is entirely proper if the company has a surplus against which it can charge the additional stock issue. But it is not proper if the stock issue is made possible by writing a Goodwill account on the books. Since the final result of such a procedure is a debit to Goodwill and a credit to Capital Stock, the books leave a record which would be correct only if the corporation had purchased goodwill from its stockholders and paid for it with stock. Such stock issues may be made because new stockholders are to be admitted and because the business has proved so successful that the old stockholders are entitled to some consideration for having developed the business. The proper way to give the old stockholders such consideration is by requiring the new stockholders to pay more than par for their stock.

Writing up or down.   It has already been stated that goodwill should not be placed on the books unless it has been paid for. Having once recorded purchased goodwill at its cost, the balance of the account should not be written up, no matter how much the value of the goodwill may have increased.

Accountants and businessmen sometimes have expressed the belief that, even though excess earnings continue in amounts sufficient to justify the valuation placed on the goodwill at the time of its purchase, it is desirable to write off the Goodwill account by charges to Retained Earnings, because the Goodwill account has been so misused as to make it meaningless and to bring it into disrepute. The write-off is advocated on the ground that it is conservative to "clear the balance sheet of fancy assets." The practice, however, is not wholly commendable. A purchased goodwill represents a part of the investment on which the operations should earn a return. The ratio of earnings to stockholders' equity may appear to be satisfactory only because the stockholders' equity has been reduced by writing off the goodwill element of the investment. Instead of advocating the write-off of a purchased and still-existing goodwill because Goodwill accounts have often been improperly used to absorb stock discount, and otherwise, accountants would render a greater service by bringing the account into good repute by strictly limiting its use to the showing of the cost of goodwill

paid for at the time of acquiring a going business, and by educating
the business public so that it will come to realize that the Goodwill
account shows a purchase cost, but that the value of the goodwill
at any time can be ascertained only by a consideration of the net
assets other than goodwill, the operating results, and the normal or
basic rate of income for businesses of the class under consideration.

In the past it has usually been considered proper to carry permanently as an asset the cost of a purchased goodwill, even though
the earnings may have declined to a point where goodwill no longer
exists. Modern accounting theory, with its emphasis on the recording of costs and cost expirations, seems to be inclining somewhat in
the direction of favoring the writing off of the cost of goodwill
which has lost its potency as a producer of "better-than-average"
earnings. In this connection, the Securities and Exchange Commission appears to incline to the opinion that goodwill is no different from any other asset, and that if its value is permanently
impaired, the loss in value should be recognized in the accounts.
The Commission has also indicated that a write-off of goodwill
against paid-in surplus is improper, except, perhaps, in cases where
the goodwill was grossly overvalued and the entry originally
setting up the Goodwill account carried a credit to a paid-in surplus
account.

Since the value of the goodwill is dependent upon earnings, and
since earnings fluctuate, it follows that the value of the goodwill
fluctuates also. However, accountants have never advocated adjusting the balance of the Goodwill account from time to time to
reflect the fluctuation in its value resulting from changes in the
earnings level. To attempt to do so would require not only consideration of the earnings level at the time of the adjustment, but
also an estimate of the immediate and long-time earning probabilities; the impracticability of such a procedure is obvious.

Goodwill as an asset subject to amortization. All of the
foregoing discussion is based on the prevailing concept of goodwill
as an asset which is not normally subject to amortization. There
are good theoretical reasons for believing that this concept is not
entirely justified by the facts.

Methods 5 and 6 on page 408 for the computation of a goodwill
valuation have inherent in them the assumption that the excess
earnings over a fair return on the tangible net assets will continue
in perpetuity—that they will well up forever from inexhaustible
springs of profit existing at the time of the transfer of ownership.
This assumption is at the bottom of the traditional accounting
attitude that purchased goodwill is a permanent asset, the cost of
which need not be eliminated from the accounts.

There are many reasons why such an assumption may be false. The vicissitudes of business and the history of individual business enterprises furnish much evidence to nullify such an assumption. There is much reason to believe that the attitude of accountants with respect to goodwill should be revised; that, in any equitable computation of the value of goodwill, recognition should be given to the probability that the profit impetus given to a business by one proprietary management will not continue indefinitely; that the reasonable price to be paid for goodwill should be based on the excess earnings and the number of years during which the momentum given to the business by the vendor management will continue to be reflected in the income statement; and that goodwill should be regarded as an asset subject to amortization.

For instance, referring to Method 6, where excess earnings of $7,500 were used for purposes of illustration, it would be more consistent with the probabilities to base the computation on an assumption that the accumulated momentum may continue to produce excess earnings, not forever, but for a period of, say, five years. If this assumption be accepted as a reasonable basis of computation, the purchaser of the business should pay for the excess earnings for five years.

A further refinement of this theory of goodwill would give recognition to the probable gradual reduction in the momentum and the consequent tapering off of earnings attributable to such momentum. That is, unless the new management continued to supply the factors which produced the excess earnings, the $7,500 annual excess might be reduced year by year.

If businessmen, when computing the valuation of goodwill existing in a business to be transferred, would recognize that excess earnings in perpetuity cannot be acquired by the purchase of goodwill, accountants might more generally question the propriety of accounting procedures applicable to goodwill which are now regarded as acceptable. Instead of regarding the cost of goodwill as something which can be carried indefinitely in the accounts, it would seem necessary to regard goodwill as an intangible subject to amortization—something like bond premiums paid for the right to receive excess interest income during a period. If the purchaser, when buying goodwill, is paying for excess earnings for a specific number of years, it seems reasonable that the payment made for the right to receive these excess earnings should be charged to income, as a cost of the excess earnings purchased, during the period for which the earnings were purchased.

The attitude of the Securities and Exchange Commission on this matter is indicated by the following quotation from Chapter 38 of

Contemporary Accounting, * of which the then Chief Accountant of the Commission was a co-author:

"The Commission has adopted no general rule as to the amortization of goodwill. However, in those cases in which a registrant has retained 'goodwill' indefinitely in its accounts, the staff has inquired into the propriety of this accounting treatment. As a result of an analysis of the nature of the account a number of registrants have undertaken programs of amortization which will result in charging the goodwill to income or, in some cases, earned surplus, over a reasonable number of years."

Rights of purchaser and seller. The rights of a purchaser and a seller of goodwill are not so clearly defined in this country as in England, where goodwill has more frequently been the subject of litigation. In general, it may be said that the purchaser has the right to advertise himself as the successor of the seller, but has no right to use the name of the old business unless that right was expressly granted.

The seller, on the other hand, has the right to go into business again as a competitor unless he has expressly waived that right. The sale of the goodwill of a business entitles the purchaser to the income from that business, but it does not keep the seller from attempting to develop another business. However, the seller must not attempt to utilize the goodwill that he sold, by advertising himself as formerly connected with the business that he sold.

Goodwill in the balance sheet. Goodwill is, in a sense, the most fixed of all assets, since it cannot be sold without selling the business. However, the balance sheet should show the total tangible fixed assets, and the goodwill and other intangibles should be set out separately. The separation may be made as follows:

```
Fixed assets:
  Land and buildings......................  $40,000
  Machinery..............................    55,000  $95,000
  Goodwill.......................................    15,000  $110,000
```

The following balance sheet presentation is probably preferable:

```
Tangible fixed assets:
  Land and buildings...............................  $40,000
  Machinery.......................................    55,000  $95,000
  Goodwill................................................    15,000
```

The separation is desirable because tangible and intangible fixed assets are fundamentally different; the bases of valuation

---

* Thomas W. Leland, editor. Published by the American Institute of Certified Public Accountants, New York, 1945.

applicable to them are different; and ratios of total fixed assets to other amounts shown in the balance sheet or income statement are usually intended to show the relation of only the tangible fixed assets to the other amounts used in the computation.

Organization expenses.   The traditional attitude of accountants toward organization expenses is that they are a sheer loss, and that there is no theoretical justification for any treatment other than writing them off as soon as possible. However, since such a treatment would create a deficit before the company began operations, accountants have sanctioned carrying organization expenses as a deferred charge to be written off to Retained Earnings during the early years of the company's life.

There seems to be much theoretical justification for regarding organization expenses as the cost of an intangible asset not requiring amortization. An immediate write-off to Retained Earnings can be theoretically justified only on the assumption that the business obtained no benefit whatever from the expenditures, which is obviously contrary to fact, because without such expenditures the business could not have been organized and operations could not have been conducted. Writing them off during the early years of a corporation's life can be theoretically justified only on the assumption that the early years are the only ones benefited. Presumably, the benefits will continue through the whole life of the business; for this reason there is theoretical justification for regarding organization expenditures as producing an intangible asset which, while having no disposal value, is a continuing part of the value inherent in the business.

Because accountants are so strongly influenced by considerations of conservatism in balance sheet valuations, it is doubtful whether the profession will accept the theory that organization expenses are an intangible asset. However, there seems to be more theoretical justification for regarding organization costs as a continuing asset entitled to a place in the balance sheet than for indefinitely carrying a purchased goodwill which may long since have lost its potency.

CHAPTER TWENTY

Liabilities and Reserves

Nature of accounting problems.   One of the chief problems in dealing with liabilities arises from the danger of omissions from the books and the balance sheet at the end of the period. This matter is dealt with at some length in a subsequent section of this chapter.

Problems of valuation of assets arise more frequently than problems of determining the amounts of liabilities. However, not all amounts of liabilities are definitely determinable. It often is necessary to make estimates—particularly in the case of operating reserves set up to obtain a proper matching of revenue and expense.

Security for liabilities.   The balance sheet should clearly indicate the nature and amount of the security supporting the liabilities. Some accountants are satisfied to indicate the security on the liability side of the balance sheet, in the description of the liability itself. Other accountants also indicate on the asset side of the balance sheet the amounts of any pledged assets; this procedure seems desirable, since it enables the reader of the balance sheet to identify easily the assets which are pledged and which, therefore, are not available for the payment of unsecured liabilities.

Offsetting liabilities against assets.   A relationship frequently exists between an asset and a liability; in such cases, the balance sheet should show the gross amount of the asset and the gross amount of the liability, rather than merely the difference between them. Showing gross amounts is sometimes described as showing the facts "broad"; showing only differences is called stating the facts "net." One of the situations most frequently met is that in which the subsidiary accounts receivable ledger contains accounts with credit balances; it is important that the balance sheet show the gross amount of the debit balances and the total amount of the credit balances, rather than merely the balance of the controlling account. A comparable situation may be found in the accounts payable subsidiary ledger, and a similar treatment should be given it.

Unpaid installments on contracts for the purchase of assets are sometimes omitted from the liabilities, either because they have not been set up on the books or because a deduction on the asset side may be regarded as desirable in order to show the company's equity in the property. Showing the liabilities on the right side of the balance sheet is preferable to showing only net amounts; the relation of the unpaid installments to the carrying value of the assets can be indicated by cross references in the balance sheet.

When securities are purchased from a broker on margin account, the total cost of the securities should be shown as an asset, and the liability to the broker should appear in the balance sheet.

One exception to the rule against offsetting related assets and liabilities is sanctioned in A. R. B. 43, which states that the deduction of United States Government securities from tax liabilities, "although a deviation from the general rule against offsets, is not so significant a deviation as to call for an exception in an accountant's report on the financial statements."

Long-Term Liabilities

Nature of long-term liabilities. Long-term liabilities (sometimes called "fixed liabilities") are usually represented by bonds or mortgages. Some of the principal classes of bonds are mentioned in Chapter 14, where they are discussed as investments. Although obligations secured by mortgages are often called *mortgages payable*, the expression is not strictly correct. The obligation is represented by a note, and the mortgage serves as security; a more precise title would therefore be *long-term mortgage notes*. Advances received by one affiliated company from another may be, in effect, long-term liabilities, although represented merely by open accounts.

Recording the bond issue. Bonds may be sold direct by the corporation, or they may be underwritten by an investment banker or a syndicate. Underwriting usually consists of the actual purchase and resale of the bonds by the banker or the syndicate, but it may consist of an agreement by the banker or the syndicate to take over at a certain future time all bonds not sold by the corporation at that time. The method of marketing, however, does not determine the entries; these depend upon whether all or a portion of the authorized bonds are sold, and upon whether they are sold at par, at a premium, or at a discount.

Very frequently an amount of bonds will be authorized larger than that intended for immediate issuance. To illustrate, assume that the fixed property of the corporation is ample in value to secure an issue of $500,000 of first-mortgage bonds. Only $300,000 of funds are now required, but there may be future requirements of $200,000. If the first issue were made for only $300,000, a subsequent issue could be secured by a second mortgage only, which would perhaps necessitate a higher interest rate and might make the marketing of the bonds difficult. By authorizing $500,000 of bonds and issuing $300,000, the corporation is in a position to market the remaining $200,000 at any future date without incurring the disadvantages incident to a second-mortgage bond issue.

The $200,000 of unissued bonds may be held for use as collateral on short-term note issues. Since these bonds are secured by a first mortgage, they are as good collateral as the bonds of another company would be (assuming equal security behind the bonds), except that the creditor would be able to hold only one debtor instead of two.

A distinction should be made between unissued and treasury stock, but no such distinction is necessary with respect to bonds. Unissued bonds may, therefore, be carried in the accounts and shown in the balance sheet either as unissued bonds or as treasury bonds.

If the entire authorized issue is sold at par on the date of issue, the entry is: debit Cash, credit Bonds Payable at par.

If some of the bonds are held unissued, the authorized issue may be shown by a memorandum notation in the Bonds Payable account, which is then credited with the par of the bonds issued. The balance sheet should show, not merely the amount of bonds issued, but also the amount of bonds authorized to be issued under the mortgage. If $500,000 of bonds are authorized under a mortgage on property carried in the balance sheet at $1,000,000, but only $300,000 of the bonds are immediately issued, the holders of the $300,000 of issued bonds should be, and presumably would be, interested in knowing that $200,000 more bonds could be issued under the same mortgage.

If bonds are issued at a price below or above par, the difference between par and selling price should be charged to Discount on Bonds or credited to Premium on Bonds.

If the bonds are issued in payment for property, it is customary to charge the property accounts with the par of the bonds. In reality the bonds may have been issued at a discount, because the vendor may have demanded a larger price payable in bonds than he would have demanded payable in cash. This fact is, of course, difficult to establish unless both a cash price and a bond price were quoted, or unless other bonds of the same issue were marketed for cash at about the same time. If information of this nature is available to indicate that the bonds were really issued at a discount or premium, the discount or premium should be set up.

If the bonds are registered as to principal or interest or both, subsidiary records similar to a stockholders' ledger should be kept. If the bonds are not registered, no subsidiary records are necessary.

Bonds in the balance sheet. The reasons for showing unissued bonds have already been discussed. The question remains concerning where such bonds should be shown in the balance sheet. The best practice is to deduct them from the authorized issue on the liability side, carrying out the net amount of bonds outstanding. If any of the unissued bonds have been pledged as collateral, this fact should be shown in the following manner:

```
Long-term liabilities:
  First-mortgage, 6% bonds payable—due 1980:
    Bonds authorized...........................  $500,000
    Less unissued bonds:
    Pledged as collateral to notes payable.  $ 25,000
    In treasury.......................  175,000  200,000  $300,000
```

Or the same facts may be shown thus:

```
Long-term liabilities:
  First-mortgage, 6% bonds payable—due 1980; authorized,
    $500,000; unissued, $200,000, of which $25,000 are pledged
    as collateral to notes payable; outstanding................  $300,000
```

Payment of interest. If the bonds are registered as to interest, checks will be mailed to the holders, and interest payments will be recorded by debiting Bond Interest and crediting Cash.

If the bonds are coupon bonds, the interest may be payable by the fiscal agent of the corporation or direct by the corporation. If the interest is payable by a fiscal agent, the corporation will send the agent a check for the full amount of the interest; when recording this deposit with the agent, the accountant should remember that a deposit of cash with the agent does not constitute payment of the liability; if the agent fails to make payment, the company is still liable. To record the facts fully, entries should be made as follows: debit Bond Interest, and credit Bond Interest Payable; debit Deposits for Payment of Bond Interest, and credit Cash. When the agent reports payment of the interest, debit Bond

Interest Payable and credit Deposits for Payment of Bond Interest. Since fiscal agents are usually institutions of unquestioned financial integrity, the possibility of nonpayment by the fiscal agent sometimes is ignored, and no entries are made other than a debit to Bond Interest and a credit to Cash.

If interest on coupon bonds is payable direct, an entry should be made debiting Bond Interest and crediting Bond Interest Payable. As coupons are received and paid, Bond Interest Payable should be debited and Cash credited. Any interest unpaid at a balance sheet date should appear on the balance sheet as a current liability.

There remains for consideration the question of the disposition of the paid coupons. These coupons may be turned over to the trustee under the mortgage, who will destroy them and issue a cremation certificate stating the amount paid and destroyed. Or the paid coupons may be pasted in a register. The register may have a page for each interest date, with spaces numbered to conform with the numbers of the bonds issued. Paid coupons are then pasted in their respective spaces; vacant spaces indicate the numbers of the bonds on which interest due has not been paid. Or the register may have a page for each bond, with a space for the bond itself and a space for each coupon. Paid coupons, and eventually the paid bond, are pasted in their respective spaces.

Amortization of premium and discount. The relation of bond premium and discount to bond interest was discussed in Chapter 14, where bonds were considered from the investment standpoint. The same relation exists with respect to bonds issued. The premium and discount on bonds issued may be amortized by the straight-line, or equal-installment, method, as illustrated in the following schedules; or they may be amortized by the effective-interest method, which is described in the Advanced text.

Straight-Line Amortization Schedule
Five-Year 6% $100,000 Bond Issue at a Premium

Period	Debit Bond Interest	Debit Bond Premium	Credit Cash	Unamortized Premium
				$4,376.03
1	$ 2,562.40	$ 437.60	$ 3,000	3,938.43
2	2,562.40	437.60	3,000	3,500.83
3	2,562.40	437.60	3,000	3,063.23
4	2,562.40	437.60	3,000	2,625.63
5	2,562.40	437.60	3,000	2,188.03
6	2,562.40	437.60	3,000	1,750.43
7	2,562.40	437.60	3,000	1,312.83
8	2,562.39	437.61	3,000	875.22
9	2,562.39	437.61	3,000	437.61
10	2,562.39	437.61	3,000	—
	$25,623.97	$4,376.03	$30,000	

Straight-Line Amortization Schedule
Five-Year 4% $100,000 Bond Issue at a Discount

Period	Debit Bond Interest	Credit Cash	Credit Bond Discount	Unamortized Discount
				$4,376.03
1	$ 2,437.60	$ 2,000	$ 437.60	3,938.43
2	2,437.60	2,000	437.60	3,500.83
3	2,437.60	2,000	437.60	3,063.23
4	2,437.60	2,000	437.60	2,625.63
5	2,437.60	2,000	437.60	2,188.03
6	2,437.60	2,000	437.60	1,750.43
7	2,437.60	2,000	437.60	1,312.83
8	2,437.61	2,000	437.61	875.22
9	2,437.61	2,000	437.61	437.61
10	2,437.61	2,000	437.61	—
	$24,376.03	$20,000	$4,376.03	

Some companies have been known to write off bond discount by charge to Retained Earnings at the date of issuance, or shortly thereafter, and have defended this procedure on the ground of conservatism, claiming that it is commendable to eliminate from the balance sheet an element of such intangible value as bond discount. The procedure is not to be commended, partly because the balance sheets thereafter fail to state the true facts relative to the obligation, but primarily because the income statements of subsequent periods are relieved of proper charges for bond interest expense.

A corresponding procedure by which bond premium is immediately credited to Retained Earnings does not even have the justification of conservatism, since it takes up as an immediate credit to Retained Earnings an amount which should be applied gradually over the life of the bonds as a deduction from interest expense.

Premium or discount on convertible or redeemable bonds should be amortized on the basis of the full life of the bonds without consideration of the possible retirement before maturity. Any balance of premium or discount remaining unamortized when the bonds are retired before maturity should be taken into consideration in determining the gain or loss on retirement.

Amortization at interim dates.   The foregoing illustrations of the amortization of bond premium and discount are based on the assumption that an interest date coincides with the close of the issuing company's fiscal year. We shall now assume that the bonds were issued on October 31, and that the fiscal year ends on December 31.

Refer to the foregoing schedule of amortization of premium. The semiannual amortization is $437.60, so the amortization for two months would be one-third of $437.60, or $145.87. The bond interest entries are indicated below:

First fiscal year:
December 31:

Bond premium	145.87	
Bond interest	854.13	
Accrued bond interest payable		1,000.00

Second fiscal year:
April 30:

Bond premium	291.73	
Bond interest	1,708.27	
Accrued bond interest payable	1,000.00	
Cash		3,000.00

October 31:

Bond premium	437.60	
Bond interest	2,562.40	
Cash		3,000.00

December 31:

Bond premium	145.87	
Bond interest	854.13	
Accrued bond interest payable		1,000.00

Similar procedures would apply to bonds issued at a discount. Refer to the foregoing schedule of amortization of discount. The semiannual amortization is $437.60, so the amortization for two months would be one-third of $437.60, or $145.87.

First fiscal year:
December 31:

Bond interest	812.54	
Bond discount		145.87
Accrued bond interest payable		666.67

Second fiscal year:
April 30:

Bond interest	1,625.06	
Accrued bond interest payable	666.67	
Bond discount		291.73
Cash		2,000.00

October 31:

Bond interest	2,437.60	
Bond discount		437.60
Cash		2,000.00

December 31:

Bond interest	812.54	
Bond discount		145.87
Accrued bond interest payable		666.67

Issuances between interest dates. When bonds are issued between interest dates, an Accrued Bond Interest Payable account (or the Bond Interest expense account) should be credited with the accrued interest to the date of issuance. Assume that $100,000 of 6% bonds due in ten years, dated January 1, 1959, are issued on March 1, 1959 for $108,962.87. The accrued interest for two months is $1,000; the entry to record the issuance may be:

Cash..	108,962.87	
Bonds payable.............................		100,000.00
Accrued bond interest payable..............		1,000.00
Premium on bonds........................		7,962.87

When the bond interest is paid on July 1, 1959, the entry (exclusive of the premium amortization) will be:

Accrued bond interest payable..................	1,000.00	
Bond interest.................................	2,000.00	
Cash.....................................		3,000.00

Or the entries may be:

At time of issuance:

Cash.....................................	108,962.87	
Bonds payable..........................		100,000.00
Bond interest...........................		1,000.00
Premium on bonds......................		7,962.87

At time of payment of interest:

Bond interest.............................	3,000.00	
Cash..................................		3,000.00

The discount or premium on bonds issued subsequent to their date should be amortized over the period between the date of issuance and the date of maturity. In the foregoing illustration, for instance, the $7,962.87 premium should be amortized, not over ten years, but over nine years and ten months.

Bond discount and premium in the balance sheet. It has long been recognized practice to show discount on bonds issued under the Deferred Charges caption of the balance sheet, and premium on bonds issued under the Deferred Credits caption. It has been advocated that discount should be deducted from and premium should be added to the face amount of the bonds on the liability side of the balance sheet. Some of the arguments presented by the proponents of this procedure are discussed below.

With respect to bond discount, one argument runs as follows: Deferred charges are expenses paid in advance; bond discount, although ultimately chargeable to interest expense, is not interest paid in advance at the time of issuance of the bonds, but is unpaid interest; therefore, bond discount is not a deferred charge. This argument seems to depend wholly on an arbitrary definition of deferred charges. If no debit in an account can be regarded as a deferred charge unless the debit was offset by a credit to Cash, bond discount is not a deferred charge. If, however, deferred charges include debits, ultimately chargeable to operations, which were recorded by offsetting credits to liability accounts, bond discount appears to qualify as a true deferred charge. In the past, debits ultimately chargeable to operations have been regarded as deferred charges regardless of whether the offsetting credit was to Cash or to a liability account; to adopt a limited definition of deferred charges in order to defend a method of showing bond discount in the balance sheet does not impress the authors.

With respect to bond premium, the advocates of the proposed balance sheet presentation find themselves unable to advance an argument analogous to that discussed above relative to bond discount. If bonds are issued for cash at a premium, the premium *is* collected in advance. A slightly different argument is therefore advanced, which goes as follows: A deferred credit is an item of income collected in advance; bond premium is not income but is an offset against an expense; therefore, bond premium is not a deferred credit. But must all deferred credits be ultimately applied as credits to income accounts? Credits to expense accounts have an equivalent effect on net income, and it therefore appears that unamortized premium on bonds can properly be regarded as a deferred credit.

A more logical argument, and one which can be applied consistently to both discount and premium, derives by analogy from the long-established practice of carrying bond investments on the asset side of the balance sheet at an amortized valuation. It is advocated that the liability on bonds should be shown in the balance sheet similarly on an amortized basis. This argument is not without merit, although practicing accountants have generally shown no inclination to accept the proposition that amortization methods recognized as applicable to the determination of asset valuations are similarly applicable to the balance sheet presentation of liabilities.

Although the proposed method of showing bond discount and premium on the balance sheet has gained no wide acceptance, it should be recognized that it strikes at an inconsistency which indicates some loose thinking with respect to both current and long-term liability presentation in the balance sheet. For instance, if a $1,000 6% interest-bearing note is issued to mature in one year, the liability will be shown in the balance sheet at the end of three months as follows:

Note payable.. $1,000
Accrued interest......................................   15 $1,015

But if interest for a year is included in the face, the liability will be shown at $1,060 and a prepaid expense of $45 will appear in the balance sheet. Perhaps we should be more concerned with consistency than with arbitrary face values, and show the liability as follows:

```
Note payable..........................................  $1,060
Less unamortized interest included in face................    45  $1,015
```

The issuance of a note with interest included in the face is, of course, a method of issuing a note at a discount; the immediately preceding case therefore does not differ essentially from the issuance of a $1,000 non-interest note at a $60 discount. Consistency would suggest, therefore, a balance sheet presentation as follows:

```
Note payable..........................................  $1,000
Less unamortized discount..............................    45  $ 955
```

And for the same reason of consistency it might be desirable to adopt a similar procedure with respect to unamortized discount on bonds. Perhaps the accounting profession will ultimately change to such a procedure.

The advocates of this procedure make a distinction between bond discount and the expenses of issuance, such as attorneys' fees, printing costs, and marketing expenses. Although they believe that bond discount should be deducted in the balance sheet from the par of the bonds, they consider it proper to classify the issuance expenses as a deferred charge. The expenses, as well as the discount, should, of course, be amortized. When bonds are sold through underwriters who share issuance expenses, and a net amount is received from the underwriters, a difficulty may arise in determining how much of the difference between par and net proceeds to the issuing company should be regarded as discount and how much should be regarded as expense. In such cases it probably would be necessary to regard the entire difference as discount.

Serial bonds. Bonds may be repayable in a series instead of at a single maturity. No special problems are involved in accounting for serial bonds unless they are issued at a premium or a discount. A simple procedure for amortizing premiums and discounts on serial bonds is described below. Amortization procedures using an effective interest rate are described in *Principles of Accounting, Advanced.*

To simplify the illustration by using small numbers, it is assumed that five bonds of $100 par value are issued on January 1, 1959, at a discount of $31.20, or for $468.80. One bond matures on December 31st of each of the years 1964, 1965, 1966, 1967, and 1968.

The amount of discount to be amortized each year is computed in the manner shown on the opposite page.

Year	Number of Bonds Outstanding	Fraction	Discount Amortization
1959	5	$5/40$	$ 3.90
1960	5	$5/40$	3.90
1961	5	$5/40$	3.90
1962	5	$5/40$	3.90
1963	5	$5/40$	3.90
1964	5	$5/40$	3.90
1965	4	$4/40$	3.12
1966	3	$3/40$	2.34
1967	2	$2/40$	1.56
1968	1	$1/40$	.78
	40	$40/40$	$31.20

If a bond is retired before its maturity, the amount of un-amortized discount applicable to the bond (to be written off in the entry recording the retirement) may be computed by determining the amount of discount per bond per year, thus:

$$\$31.20 \div 40 = \$.78$$

Now, assume that at the end of 1961 the bond maturing at the end of 1965 is retired—four years before maturity. The unamortized discount is $.78 \times 4$, or $3.12.

Since a bond has been retired, the amounts of discount amortization shown in the foregoing table will have to be revised by deducting $.78 from the amounts shown for the years 1962 to 1965, inclusive.

Sinking funds and redemption funds. For many years it was common practice to require a company borrowing on bonds to establish a sinking fund which accumulated, as the result of deposits and interest accumulations, until the maturity of the bonds and was used at that time for their payment. Bonds to be retired in full at their maturity from such a fund were called sinking fund bonds.

More recently it has become rather general practice to require the borrowing company to make periodical deposits with a trustee to be used for the purpose of making periodical bond retirements. The term "sinking fund" is frequently applied to such funds and the related bonds. Such usage of the term is of somewhat doubtful propriety because, strictly defined, a sinking fund is a fund accumulating at compound interest for the payment of a debt at its maturity. A fund to be used for periodical bond retirements would be more properly called a bond redemption fund.

Conversion of bonds to other securities. Bonds sometimes contain a provision entitling their holders to convert them into other securities of the issuing company, such as stock. When such a conversion is made, consideration must be given to the terms of the conversion, any unamortized premium or discount on the bonds, and any accrued interest.

Assume that $10,000 of bonds are converted into 200 shares of no-par common stock; that there is unamortized discount of $300 applicable to the bonds converted; that $15 of this discount should be amortized by charge to operations for the period between the last preceding interest date and the date of conversion; that the accrued interest on the bonds at the date of conversion is $100; and that the stock is to be set up in the accounts at a stated value of $40 per share, in accordance with a resolution of the directors. The entry for the conversion is:

Bonds payable...		10,000
Bond interest..		115
Bond discount.......................................	300	
Common stock.......................................	8,000	
Paid-in surplus—Common stock.....................	1,815	

The credit to paid-in surplus is based on the theory that, since the cancellation of the liability on the bonds and accrued interest constitutes the payment for the stock, the amount at which the liability is carried in the accounts (par of bonds minus unamortized discount plus accrued interest) is the amount received for the stock. The excess of the amount received over the stated value of the stock is a proper credit to paid-in surplus.

If the par or stated value of the stock issued was in excess of the net liability canceled, the account to be charged with the excess would be the same as in the case of the issuance of stock for cash at less than par or stated value. Such a transaction is unlikely.

Redemption of bonds before maturity. Bonds may be retired before maturity either by exercise of a call privilege or by purchase in the market. Assume that bonds of $100,000 par value are outstanding, and that discount of $2,000 remains unamortized at a date when $10,000 of bonds are retired for $10,100. If the bonds are retired by call, the call presumably will be made at an interest date, and it can be assumed that the payment of the interest on the entire $100,000 of bonds and the amortization of the discount applicable to the entire issue will have been recorded. The entry to record the call and retirement of the bonds at 101 will be:

Bonds payable..	10,000	
Loss on bond retirement..............................	300	
Bond discount ($\frac{1}{10}$ of $2,000).....................		200
Cash...		10,100

Assume the same facts as above except that the bonds are purchased in the market two months after an interest date, for $9,500 plus accrued interest at 6%. The accrued interest on the bonds to be retired is, therefore, $100; the price, including interest, is $9,600. The $2,000 of unamortized discount is the balance as of the last interest date, which we shall assume was five years before maturity; the unamortized discount applicable to the bonds purchased is one-tenth of $2,000, or $200; the discount per year is one-fifth of $200, or $40; and the discount applicable to the two months since the last preceding interest date is one-sixth of $40, or $6.67. The entries to record the retirement are:

Bond interest expense............................	106.67	
Accrued bond interest payable.................		100.00
Bond discount...............................		6.67
Bonds payable....................................	10,000.00	
Accrued bond interest payable....................	100.00	
Bond discount ($200.00 − $6.67)..............		193.33
Cash.......................................		9,600.00
Gain on bond retirement.....................		306.67

The gain or loss on retirement may be shown as a nonoperating item in the income statement or, if the amount is so material as to distort net income, it may be shown in the retained earnings statement.

Retirements by exercise of call privileges usually must be made at interest dates; any interest paid in connection with a bond retirement should, of course, be charged to Bond Interest Expense.

Refunding. Matured bonds may be paid from general cash, from a sinking fund, or from funds obtained by a refunding issue of new securities. No peculiar accounting problems arise in connection with such a refunding transaction; entries of the nature previously discussed are made to record the issuance of the new securities and the payment of the old.

Bonds frequently contain a provision giving the issuer an option to retire the bonds before maturity; if interest rates have declined, it may be advantageous to float a new bond issue at the lower rate to obtain funds to pay off the old bonds. Optional retirement provisions usually require the borrower to pay a premium to retire the bonds before maturity, and the proper accounting treatment of such a premium requires consideration. There may also be unamortized discount and expense or unamortized premium on the old bonds.

To illustrate, let us assume that bonds of a par value of $1,000,-000 were issued for $950,000, maturing in twenty years, and bearing an interest rate of 5%; after these bonds were outstanding ten years, it was decided to call them at 106, using for their payment the proceeds of a new issue of $1,000,000 of 4% bonds due in fifteen years and sold at par. Of the $50,000 discount on the original issue, $25,000 remains unamortized; what disposition should be made in the accounts of this $25,000 of unamortized discount and of the $60,000 premium paid on the retirement of the old bonds? Three procedures have been advocated:

(1) Charge the $85,000 to income or retained earnings at the time of the refunding. (This is acceptable procedure from the tax standpoint, since these costs are deductible expenses in the year in which the refunding transaction occurred.)

(2) Amortize the $85,000 by charges to interest expense during the life of the new issue.

(3) Amortize the $85,000 by charges to interest expense during what would have been the remaining life of the old issue.

The first two of these methods were those in most common use prior to 1939, when the Committee on Accounting Procedure of the American Institute issued a pronouncement expressing disapproval of the second method (except for companies subject to regulatory bodies which approve it), giving a somewhat modified sanction to the first method, and stating a definite preference for the third method.

Advocates of the immediate charge to Retained Earnings maintained that the unamortized discount and the retirement premium are costs related solely to the old issue, and that there is no more justification for carrying such costs forward as deferred charges than there would be for capitalizing as part of the cost of a new fixed asset the undepreciated cost of a retired asset and the removal costs. The Institute committee stated that the immediate write-off was sanctioned because it resulted in a conservative balance sheet from which the intangible of bond discount and retirement premium had been eliminated, but the committee further stated that the write-off was subject to criticism because it relieved future income statements of charges for costs of borrowed money.

Those who advocated writing off the unamortized discount and call premium on the old issue over the life of the new issue defended the procedure by reasoning which may be summarized somewhat as follows: Assume that A gives B a 5% note for $1,000 due in ten years and receives $940 in cash; at the end of the first five years $30 of the discount has been amortized; at that date B (in consideration of $10 received from A) consents to extend the note to mature ten years thereafter; the money cost per year during the first five years (on the basis of the facts known during that period) was $50 interest plus $6 (one-tenth of $60) discount; the money cost during each of the last ten years was $50 interest plus

$3 (one-tenth of $30) discount, plus $1 (one-tenth of the $10 cost incurred to convert a liability maturing in five years into one maturing in ten years). The reasoning then proceeded as follows: The issuance of bonds and their refunding is essentially analogous to the above-described transaction; in both instances, funds of a certain amount are received, the original borrowing period is extended, the money costs for the entire period include the original discount, the periodical interest, and a cost incurred in postponing the maturity of the obligation; the change in parties, the change in documents, and the change in interest rate incident to a refunding of bonds are immaterial and do not destroy the analogy.

The Institute committee, in advocating the write-off of the unamortized discount and the call premium over the life of the old issue, reasoned as follows: Charges should not be deferred unless they will benefit future periods, and they should be deferred over only those periods which they can reasonably be assumed to benefit. Referring to our original illustration in which 5% bonds due in ten years were refunded by the issuance of 4% bonds due in fifteen years, the committee would say that the refunding would obviously be of benefit during the next ten years (the unexpired life of the old bond issue) by reducing the interest rate from 5% to 4%, but whether or not the refunding transaction would be beneficial during the last five years of the new issue is a matter which cannot be determined at the time of the refunding, since it depends upon the interest rate at which money could be borrowed at the beginning of that five-year period.

The committee's opinion has not been unanimously accepted. Advocates of the immediate charge to Retained Earnings remain unconvinced by the committee's reasoning. And the advocates of amortization during the life of the new issue still have spokesmen who reply to the committee's argument as follows: Refunding is presumably effected with the expectation of benefiting the borrower through the full life of the new issue; otherwise, the refunding would cover only the unexpired period of the old bonds, because a shorter-term financing could presumably be done at a lower rate; the longer period is adopted in order to give the borrower assurance of a satisfactory money cost for the longer period. To say that the unamortized discount and retirement premium "benefit" only the life of the old bonds because it is only that period which can be assured of a saving in money costs distorts the meaning of "benefit" as used in determining the propriety of deferring costs; a cost "benefits" a future period if it gives that period the use of a good or of a service; the unamortized discount and retirement premium are costs incurred for the use of money and should be spread over

the full period of use; they benefit the full period of the life of the
new bonds because they are part of the cost of giving the borrower
the use of funds during that period.

Although the proposal to charge off unamortized discount and retirement premium over the remaining life of the old issue runs
counter to tax regulations and is not acceptable to all accountants,
there appears to have been some swing in the direction of acceptance of the pronouncement of the committee of the Institute.

The foregoing comments are applicable to situations in which
bonds were refunded by the issuance of other bonds. The generally accepted idea of the proper treatment of any unamortized
discount on bonds retired from the proceeds of the issuance of
capital stock was well expressed by the Chief Accountant of the
Securities and Exchange Commission in *Accounting Series Release
No. 10,* from which the following is quoted:

> "While it may be permissible to retain on the books and amortize
> any balance of discount and expense applicable to bonds refunded by
> other evidences of indebtedness, similar treatment is not ordinarily
> acceptable, in my opinion, when funds used to retire the existing bonds
> are derived from the sale of capital stock. In such cases it is my opinion
> that, as a general rule, sound and generally accepted accounting
> principles and practice require that the unamortized balance of the debt
> discount and expense applicable to the retired bonds should be written
> off by a charge to earnings or earned surplus, as appropriate, in the
> accounting period within which the bonds were retired."

Installment contracts. Fixed assets are sometimes purchased on contracts payable in installments over a considerable
term of years. The error is sometimes made of charging the fixed
asset account with only the installments as paid; and the error is
sometimes compounded by charging the fixed asset accounts with
the interest payments as well as the payments on principal.

The proper treatment is to set up the total purchase price by a
charge to the fixed asset account at the time of acquisition, with an
offsetting liability. As periodical payments are made, the amount
applicable to principal is charged to the liability account, and the
amount applicable to interest is charged as an expense. In the
balance sheet, the current installments should be shown as current
liabilities, and the noncurrent installments as long-term liabilities.

Long-term liabilities in the balance sheet. The balance
sheet should show, with respect to long-term liabilities, the maturity, the interest rate, the nature of the obligation (such as
mortgage bond, or collateral trust bond), and the nature of the
underlying security. If there are too many long-term liabilities to
permit a detailed description in the balance sheet, the details may
be furnished in a supplementary statement.

With one possible exception, unissued or reacquired bonds should not be shown in the balance sheet as an asset, but should be deducted from the total authorized issue to show the par value of the bonds outstanding.

The one possible exception consists of a company's own bonds, acquired for, and held in, a special-purpose fund, such as a sinking fund. If a company's own bonds are purchased and held by a sinking fund trustee, such purchased bonds are customarily regarded as fund assets to be shown on the asset side of the balance sheet, and as outstanding liabilities to be shown on the liability side. This treatment is, of course, theoretically illogical, but the procedure has long been regarded as acceptable from a practical standpoint, because of the necessity of holding the bonds alive for the purpose of collecting interest in order to safeguard the bondholders who are relying on the fund, and also to indicate the extent of accumulation in the fund on the balance sheet date. If contributions have been made to the fund in accordance with requirements, and if investments of fund cash have been made in the company's own bonds, the elimination of the purchased bonds from the fund and from the liability would distort the ratio between the fund and the liability and would make the balance sheet subject to the possible misinterpretation that the company had not complied with its sinking fund deposit requirements. However, it would still be possible to conform to good theory by eliminating the treasury bonds from the fund and from the liability, and mentioning the elimination in a footnote.

Current Liabilities

Inclusion of all liabilities. Some of the liabilities not infrequently omitted from balance sheets are:

(1) Accounts payable for goods purchased before the close of the accounting period.

In most concerns it is the custom to record liabilities for purchases when the goods are received. But there is always some delay in getting the record on the books, and goods received during the last few days of the accounting period may not be recorded until the early days of the succeeding period. If the goods are not included in the inventory, the net income is not misstated, because the purchases and the inventory are equally understated. But the assets and liabilities are both understated in the balance sheet, and the ratio of current assets to current liabilities is thus distorted. Moreover, it is a question

whether the customary business policy of recording purchases only after the receipt of the goods is sound. A
liability exists as soon as title to the goods passes to the
purchaser, and, according to the legal rules governing
sales, title may pass to the purchaser before he receives
the goods. It would seem, therefore, that if the books
are to show the facts, entries for purchases should be
made when the title passes according to law, which may be
before the goods are received.

(2) Miscellaneous liabilities for services rendered the business
prior to the close of the accounting period but not billed
until the succeeding period.

(3) Accrued liabilities for wages, interest, taxes, employees'
bonuses, and so forth.

(4) Liabilities to be liquidated in merchandise, arising from the
issuing of due bills, merchandise coupon books, and gift
certificates.

(5) Dividends which have been declared and therefore represent a liability, but which have not been recorded.

Classification. Two general problems of classification may be
mentioned:

(1) What rule should be followed in differentiating between
current and fixed liabilities?

(2) To what extent and in what way should the current liabilities be detailed in the balance sheet?

Concerning the first problem, reference is made to page 51
in Chapter 3, where the portion of Institute Bulletin No. 43 dealing with current liabilities is discussed. In general, it may be said
here that, although the bulletin does not entirely abandon the old
one-year dividing line between current and fixed liabilities, the
basic criterion established by the bulletin is this: Current liabilities
are those debts which will be paid from current assets during the
operating cycle.

A special problem arises when long-term liabilities approach
their maturity and are due within, say, a year. Should they be
included among the current liabilities although, in preceding balance sheets, they have been included among the long-term liabilities? The proximity of the maturity date probably should not
be the sole determining factor. If bonds maturing in, say, nine
months are to be paid by a refinancing program which will involve
the issuance of new bonds, the inclusion of the old bonds among the
current liabilities would convey the impression that the bonds were

to be paid out of current assets, and would so distort the ratio of current assets to current liabilities as to give an entirely erroneous idea of the concern's working capital. It seems, therefore, that all necessary facts would be shown by leaving the bonds among the long-term liabilities, with a statement of the maturity date and a footnote mentioning the contemplated refinancing program.

The situation is different, however, when an installment is shortly to become due on a serial bond issue. The natural assumption is that the installment will be paid out of working capital, and it would seem proper to show the condition as follows:

Balance Sheet—December 31, 1959

Current liabilities:
   Serial bonds payable, due February 10, 1960.................. $10,000

Long-term liabilities:
   Serial bonds payable............................. $90,000
     Less bonds due February 10, 1960....... .... 10,000 80,000

Current installments need not be classified as current liabilities if they are payable from a fund not classified as a current asset.

With respect to the second problem, that is, the extent to which the current liabilities should be detailed in the balance sheet, it may be said that the answer will properly depend to some extent on the purpose for which the statement is to be used. If a balance sheet is prepared specifically for credit purposes, much more extensive detailing will be required than is expected in an ordinary published balance sheet.

It may be contended that an accountant rendering a balance sheet for publication cannot control its use; but the present attitude is that banks and other creditors or prospective creditors are entitled to much more information than need be given general publicity in the published balance sheet, and that requirements for general balance sheet purposes are satisfied if the current liabilities are detailed as follows:

Accounts payable.
Trade notes payable.
Other notes payable.
Accounts owed to officers, stockholders, and employees.
Notes given to officers, stockholders, and employees.
Accrued liabilities.
Income taxes payable.
Other current liabilities.

The fact that salaries, wages, taxes, or other liabilities may have priority in case of liquidation is given no consideration in the classification of the current liabilities on the balance sheet because the balance sheet is prepared from the standpoint of a going concern.

Theoretically, it is desirable to list the current liabilities in the order of their maturity, but from a practical standpoint this is usually impossible because each class of liability includes debts maturing at different dates. However, since a bank overdraft represents an immediate cash requirement, it is desirable to show it as the first of the current liabilities.

Operating Reserves, Contingencies, and Commitments

Operating reserves classified as current liabilities. Operating reserves are those which are set up by charges to income to reflect provisions for prospective cash disbursements, the costs of which should be matched against revenues that have been taken into income. If goods are sold with guarantees of performance or with agreements to give free service for a stated period, a proper matching of revenue and expense requires the creation of an operating reserve for the prospective disbursements. Although there may be no present liability to any specific person, and although the amount of the reserve may be an estimate, such reserves are properly shown among the liabilities. The reserve represents a current liability if there is an obligation to make a cash disbursement in the near future.

The word "reserve" has been used above because, although its use in such connections is eschewed for purposes of financial statements, it still is a part of the accountants' working vocabulary.

Liability reserves. It was formerly the custom to use the term *reserve* in a liability account title when the amount of the liability was estimated. Used in this fashion, the word did not imply that the existence of the liability was in any way contingent or unsettled; it merely indicated that the dollar amount of the liability could only be estimated under the existing circumstances.

The account Reserve for Income Tax was an example. There might have been no question about the fact that a given business had an obligation to pay an income tax, but the exact amount of the tax liability might not have been determinable at the time the financial statements were prepared.

As used in this connection, *reserve* was synonymous with *estimate*. It is becoming increasingly common to use the word *estimate* or *estimated* in place of the term *reserve* in all cases where the dollar figure for any liability is an approximation; thus, "Estimated Liability for Federal Income Tax" has been generally substituted for "Reserve for Income Tax."

The term *reserve* was also used when there was an element of uncertainty regarding the existence of a liability. For example, assume that a decision of a lower court resulted in an adverse judgment of a stated amount, thus creating a liability which had to be recognized in the accounts. However, if the case was under appeal at the time the financial statements were prepared, and if there was some prospect that the decision might be reversed or the controversy settled outside of court for a different amount, the term *reserve* was considered appropriate terminology to convey such uncertainty regarding the status of the liability. However, to comply with the recommendations of the Committee on Accounting Procedure, some title such as "Judgment Under Appeal" might be used.

Contingent liabilities. A contingent liability exists when there is no present debt but when conditions are such that a liability may develop, usually as the result of an action or default by an outsider. For instance, if a note receivable is discounted, no immediate liability is created, but a contingent liability exists because the maker of the note may default and the endorser may be required to make payment.

The method to be used in reflecting contingent liabilities in the balance sheet depends upon the conditions in each case.

If there is a strong probability that a liability and loss will develop (as might be the case, for instance, if funds are on deposit in a bank in a blocked-exchange country), a loss provision usually would be created by charge to income; accountants who are not advocates of the clean surplus theory might, under some circumstances, consider that a charge to Retained Earnings would be in order. The account thus created might be deducted from the related asset or shown as a liability— usually in the current section.

If the probability of loss is remote but disclosure is nevertheless desirable, the disclosure may be made by the creation of a contingency reserve (appropriation of retained earnings) or by a footnote. The use of footnotes is increasing because the nature and purpose of appropriated surplus reserves are not widely understood and footnotes can be made much more informative.

Some of the more common contingent liabilities, or sources thereof, are mentioned below:

(1) Notes receivable discounted.
   The proper procedure for recording the discounting of notes receivable was discussed in Chapter 10. Any esti-

mated liability for prospective payments would be shown under the current classification.

(2) Accounts receivable assigned.

The procedure for recording the assignment of accounts receivable was also discussed in Chapter 10.

(3) Accommodation paper.

A person may become an accommodation party on a promissory note either as a maker or as an endorser. If he signs the note as a maker, he should debit an account with the accommodated party and credit Accommodation Notes Payable. If he signs as an endorser, he should debit an account with the accommodated party and credit Endorser's Liability. These pairs of offsetting accounts should be regarded as memorandum accounts so long as there is no prospect that the accommodating party will have to make payment. If it develops that the accommodating party probably will have to make payment, the credit-balance account should be transferred to a liability account, presumably to be classified as current. If recovery from the accommodated party is a possibility, the debit balance in his account can be shown in the balance sheet as an asset, with an allowance deduction if provision for possible loss should be made.

(4) Lawsuits.

(5) Additional taxes.

No comments in addition to the general introductory remarks in this section seem required in connection with these contingent liabilities.

(6) Guarantees of liabilities of other companies.

One company may guarantee the interest on, or both the principal of and interest on, the bonds of another company, which may or may not be a subsidiary. Any estimated liability set up to reflect prospective payments under the guarantee might be offset by a loss charge, or by a charge to the company whose obligations were assumed.

(7) Mutual insurance.

Although the holders of policies issued by mutual insurance companies are usually subject to assessments, the history of such companies indicates that policyholders are rarely required to pay such assessments; therefore, the contingency is generally regarded by accountants as too remote to require any recognition.

Cumulative preferred dividends in arrears. Arrearages of cumulative preferred dividends are often referred to as contingent liabilities. Strictly speaking, this is a misnomer. Usually, contingent liabilities become real liabilities as the result of an action or default of an outsider; dividend liabilities are created by action of the board of directors. Methods of disclosing preferred dividends in arrears are described in Chapter 6.

Purchase commitments. Losses arising from purchase commitments cannot be ignored in the financial statements. Losses may be forthcoming if prices are declining, although not necessarily, since a business may be protected by hedging operations and contracts to sell products in the future at an established price.

If a loss is clearly in prospect, the amount of the loss should be estimated and deducted in the income statement in arriving at net income. If the amount is significant, it should be separately disclosed in the income statement. The credit offsetting the charge to a loss account is listed among the liabilities under some account title such as "Provision for Losses on Purchase Commitments."

A distinction must be made between losses on purchase commitments which have actually developed and can be measured and mere contingent losses on purchase commitments. The latter may be disclosed, if significant, by mention in a footnote or by setting up a surplus reserve. The surplus thus appropriated should be returned to the Retained Earnings account and may not be used to absorb charges for losses, should they develop.

Contracts for fixed asset acquisitions. If, at the balance sheet date, a company is committed in a material amount on contracts for plant construction or for other fixed asset acquisitions, disclosure should be made in a balance sheet footnote. Although such commitments do not involve prospective losses for which a provision is required, disclosure is important because the use of funds for additions to fixed assets may significantly affect the working capital.

Long-term leases. Institute Bulletin No. 38 expressed the opinion that, if rentals on long-term leases are material in amount, disclosure of the amounts of the annual rentals and the term of the lease should be made, presumably in a balance sheet footnote.

Special consideration is given to a comparatively new type of transaction in which a company, instead of raising funds by mortgaging its real estate (in which case an asset and a liability appear in its balance sheet), sells the property and retains occupancy under a long-term lease, often with a right of repurchase (thus converting fixed assets into cash and avoiding the appearance of a liability in the balance sheet). The bulletin indicates that the foot-

note disclosure applicable to an ordinary long-term lease is sufficient in such cases *unless* the lease arrangement is in essence an
installment repurchase of the property. There may be a presumption to that effect if there is an option to repurchase at a price
obviously much less than the price at which the property would
presumably be sold in an arm's-length transaction, or if the agreement provides that part of the so-called rental payments can be
applied against the purchase price, or if the rentals are so high that
it seems obvious that portions of the rentals are in reality installment payments on the purchase price. The bulletin says that "all
such leases should be carefully considered, and that, where it is
clearly evident that the transaction involved is in substance a
purchase, the 'leased' property should be included among the assets of the lessee with suitable accounting for the corresponding liabilities and for the related charges in the income statement."

Profit-sharing and pension agreements. The employee
profit-sharing and pension plans adopted by business enterprises
are too diversified in nature to permit any detailed description of
them here. However, two matters require brief consideration.

In order to qualify the plan under the Internal Revenue Code,
funds provided by the company and its employees usually are
deposited with trustees or paid to insurance companies. The
amount of any obligation at the balance sheet date for such
deposits or payments should appear in the balance sheet as a
liability.

If a pension plan is funded with an insurance company, premiums will be payable to the insurance company annually (or at
shorter intervals) in amounts based on the number of employees,
their ages, and the amounts of the annuities to be paid to them
after retirement. These premiums are chargeable against income
in the period in which they accrue, and any premiums accrued at
the end of the period should be included in the balance sheet as a
liability.

But, in addition, it may be necessary to pay the insurance company the amount of the annuity cost applicable to past services—in
other words, an amount in lieu of the premiums which would have
been paid to the insurance company from the beginning of each
employee's service if the pension plan had been in operation during
that period. This past-service annuity cost usually is payable in
installments, rather than as a lump sum. In the past, many companies set up a liability account for the full amount of the past-
service cost, by charge to Retained Earnings. It was argued that
the charge to Retained Earnings was justified as a correction of
the earnings of prior periods, on the theory that the past-service
annuity cost was an additional cost of services in prior periods. In

its Bulletin No. 43, the Institute's Committee on Accounting Procedure said:

> "The committee believes that, even though the calculation is based on past service, costs of annuities based on such service are incurred in contemplation of present and future services. . . . The element of past service is one of the important considerations in establishing pension plans, and annuity costs measured by such past service contribute to the benefits gained by the adoption of a plan. . . .
> "The committee, accordingly, is of the opinion that:
>> "(a) Costs of annuities based on past service should be allocated to current and future periods; however, if they are not sufficiently material in amount to distort the results of operations in a single period, they may be absorbed in the current year;
>> "(b) Costs of annuities based on past service should not be charged to surplus."

The bulletin is silent regarding the number of periods to which the past-service costs should be allocated. In this connection, it is of interest to note that they are deductible for federal income tax purposes over a period of ten years.

The bulletin is also silent as to whether, when the pension plan is started, an entry should be made debiting a deferred expense account with the full amount of the past-service costs, with an offsetting credit to Cash (if payment is made in full at once) or to a liability account (if payment is to be made in installments). If payment is made in full immediately, such a deferred expense account would seem necessary. If payment is made in installments (the customary procedure), and if each installment is charged to income when payment is made, it might be permissible to omit the deferred expense and liability accounts from the books and the balance sheet, but it would seem essential to make some disclosure of the facts.

General contingency reserves.   Reserves for contingencies which are vague, remote, and not susceptible of measurement with respect to the degree of probability that they will ever be required, or with respect to the amount which might ultimately be required, should ordinarily be created, if at all, by appropriations of earned surplus, and not be shown as liabilities.

The Institute's Committee on Accounting Procedure has taken the following position concerning general-purpose contingency reserves:

General contingency reserves, such as those created:

(a) for general undetermined contingencies, or
(b) for a wide variety of indefinite possible future losses, or

(c) without any specific purpose reasonably related to the operations for the current period, or

(d) in amounts not determined on the basis of any reasonable estimates of costs or losses,

are of such a nature that charges or credits relating to such reserves should not enter into the determination of net income. Hence,

(1) Provisions for such reserves should not be included as charges in determining net income.

(2) When such a reserve is set up, it should be created preferably by a segregation or appropriation of surplus.

(3) Costs or losses should not be treated as charges to such reserves, and no part of such a reserve should be transferred to income or in any way used to affect the determination of net income for any year.

(4) When such a reserve or any part thereof is no longer considered necessary, it should be restored to surplus.

Profit equalization and "budgetary" reserves. Management is sometimes disposed to establish reserves for the purpose of arbitrarily equalizing earnings over a series of years because of a belief that stable earnings add to the attractiveness of a business. Any procedure for arbitrarily and artificially influencing or leveling reported earnings is not acceptable accounting.

The preceding comment relates to annual earnings figures. An accounting procedure adopted to spread an annual expense evenly throughout the year is acceptable without question. Such a procedure is particularly appropriate if monthly or quarterly financial statements are prepared; otherwise, interim income figures would be misleading because certain expenses are not incurred evenly throughout the year. Spreading an annual expense evenly throughout the year may require the use of a "budgetary reserve," the operation of which can be summarized as follows:

(1) An estimate for the year would be made for the particular expense involved in the budgetary reserve procedure.

(2) Each month, one-twelfth of the estimated annual expense would be charged to the appropriate expense account and credited to a budgetary reserve account.

(3) As disbursements were made for the expense involved, they would be charged to the reserve account.

(4) At the end of the year, if the actual expense for the year differed from the estimate, the budgetary reserve account would be adjusted in order that the balance in the expense account would equal the actual expense for the year.

The above procedure can be illustrated by using an example involving vacation pay. Suppose that a company closes its plant for two weeks each August in order that its production employees may take their vacations (with pay) at that time. If the full amount for vacation pay were charged to expense in the month of August, the income statement for that month would be considerably distorted, because payments were made for which services were not received during the month. This distortion can be avoided by making monthly provisions for vacation pay. Assume that the company estimates that the vacation pay will amount to $120,000 for the two-week vacation period. Under these circumstances, the monthly provision would equal $10,000, and the following entry would be appropriate:

```
Vacation pay expense...  ........................... 10,000
    Allowance for vacation pay......................         10,000
    To set up monthly provision for vacation pay.
```

This entry would be repeated each month during the year. Assume further that the disbursement for vacation pay equalled $118,500. This would be recorded as follows:

```
Allowance for vacation pay.......................... 118,500
    Cash.........................................         118,500
    To record payment of vacation pay allowance.
```

At the year-end, since the actual expense was $1,500 less than the estimate, the following adjusting entry would be appropriate:

```
Allowance for vacation pay..........................  1,500
    Vacation pay expense...........................          1,500
    To adjust the budgetary reserve to actual expense.
```

On the income statement for the year, Vacation Pay Expense would be reported at $118,500.

The entries for the entire year for the above case are illustrated in the following T-accounts:

Vacation Pay Expense

Jan. Monthly provision........	10,000	Dec. Adjustment to bring total	
Feb.	10,000	of monthly provisions	
Mar.	10,000	into agreement with ac-	
Apr.	10,000	tual annual cost for va-	
May	10,000	cation pay............	1,500
June	10,000	Dec. Close to Revenue and Ex-	
July	10,000	pense........	118,500
Aug.	10,000		
Sept.	10,000		
Oct.	10,000		
Nov.	10,000		
Dec.	10,000		
	120,000		120,000

Allowance for Vacation Pay

Aug. Disbursement	118,500	Jan. Monthly provision........	10,000
Dec. Adjustment to bring total		Feb.	10,000
of monthly provisions		Mar.	10,000
into agreement with ac-		Apr.	10,000
tual annual cost for va-		May	10,000
cation pay	1,500	June	10,000
		July	10,000
		Aug.	10,000
		Sept.	10,000
		Oct.	10,000
		Nov.	10,000
		Dec.	10,000
	120,000		120,000

Cash

	Aug. Disbursement for vacation	
	pay.................	118,500

In the above example, notice that during some of the months the Allowance for Vacation Pay account had a debit balance. This is not uncommon. On interim balance sheets, budgetary reserves are presented among the current liabilities if they have credit balances. If they have debit balances, they are presented among the prepaid expenses.

In the preceding example, the objective of the accounting procedure adopted was merely to spread an annual expense evenly throughout the year. A similar procedure is sometimes used in an attempt to achieve more equitable annual charges for certain operating expenses. For example, it may be contended that, if the expense of machinery repairs were spread equally over the years of use, net income would be more precisely measured than if repairs are charged as expense in the years when the repair work is actually performed. This becomes more evident when it is recognized that, typically, repairs are made only when necessary or when the level of operations makes a repair program convenient. Use of a budgetary reserve would avoid the fluctuations that might appear if repair costs were recorded only when repair work was actually undertaken. The use of a budgetary reserve for repairs was discussed on page 333.

Budgetary reserves are acceptable without question when their objective is to spread an annual expense evenly throughout the year. Their use is permitted when the objective, as in the case of a reserve for repairs, is to assign *operating expense charges* to years on a basis that permits more precise income determination than would be achieved under the alternative of recording expense at the time a cash disbursement is made or an obligation is incurred. Their acceptability is questioned by accountants when such reserve techniques are proposed with the intention of equalizing *operating or extraneous losses* by years over a long term. The reason is that reserves of this type are susceptible of becoming, in fact, profit-equalization reserves. The latter are not acceptable, as noted above. But often it is difficult to draw a dividing line between a budgetary reserve and a profit-equalization reserve.

A "Reserves" caption in the balance sheet.   The matters discussed in this chapter reveal the difficulties encountered at times in determining the amounts of certain liabilities and in selecting a suitable balance sheet location for some contingent liabilities. A review of published financial statements will show the occasional use of a "Reserves" category located between liabilities and stockholders' equity, and usually comprising contingent loss provisions. The use of such a category is evidence of the practical difficulty often encountered in determining with reasonable certainty whether some credit-balance accounts represent asset deductions, liabilities, or a part of the stockholders' equity. Practicing accountants not infrequently encounter situations where the probability of a loss is so strong that a stockholders' equity classification of an account provided therefor seems too optimistic; but, on the other hand, no actual impairment of asset values has occurred (so that a deduction from an asset does not seem justified), and no liability exists at the balance sheet date (so that the liability classification does not seem warranted). Under such circumstances, an "in-between" location is sometimes used.

One of the weaknesses associated with the use of a "Reserves" category is that the origin of the reserves located therein is not always clear to the statement user. Furthermore, there is usually no information regarding the nature of the charges that may be made against the reserve accounts thus classified.

Ordinarily the source of a reserve has a direct bearing on its proper location in the balance sheet, as indicated by the following generalizations:

A credit-balance account created by a charge to an expense account should not be classified under stockholders' equity.

Valuation and operating reserves, once having been properly classified, may not be reclassified in subsequent financial statements as part of stockholders' equity. If their credit balances need revision or correction, the necessary adjustment should appear in either the income statement or the statement of retained earnings.

Surplus reserves, once properly classified under stockholders' equity, may not be used to absorb charges for expenses or losses.

CHAPTER TWENTY-ONE

Interpretation of Financial

Statements

Underlying premise. As stated in "Accounting and Reporting Standards for Corporate Financial Statements," issued in 1957 by a committee of the American Accounting Association, "Accounting procedures and reports are based on the premise that quantitative data provide an effective means of description and are basic to the communication of qualitative information about the enterprise." Money amounts, like words, are means of communication. And if the agencies of communication used in reporting accounting data are understood by the reader, considerable information can be conveyed by financial statements.

To continue the analogy between words and money amounts, words may communicate effectively or ineffectively, depending on the skill of the writer, his choice of words, the number of words used, and other variables. Likewise, the communicative value of accounting data depends on a number of variables, such as the amount of information supplied, the excellence of its presentation, the stability of the value of the monetary unit, and the consistency of the accounting procedures in use. And, just as two readers may attach different meanings to the same written material, users of financial statements often attach different meanings to the same accounting data.

It is probably obvious that the interpretation of financial statements will be affected by the experience, judgment, and temperament of the analyst. No single accounting text can make a student

446

an expert, but a presentation and discussion of commonly used analytical devices should be of considerable help in acquiring an ability to analyze and interpret financial statements.

Comparative Statements

Institute committee's recommendations.   Bulletin 43 of the Institute's Committee on Accounting Procedure contains the following remarks on the subject of comparative statements:

"1. The presentation of comparative financial statements in annual and other reports enhances the usefulness of such reports and brings out more clearly the nature and trends of current changes affecting the enterprise. Such presentation emphasizes the fact that statements for a series of periods are far more significant than those for a single period and that the accounts for one period are but an instalment of what is essentially a continuous history.

"2. In any one year it is ordinarily desirable that the balance sheet, the income statement, and the surplus statement be given for one or more preceding years as well as for the current year. Footnotes, explanations, and accountants' qualifications which appeared on the statements for the preceding years should be repeated, or at least referred to, in the comparative statements to the extent that they continue to be of significance. If, because of reclassifications or for other reasons, changes have occurred in the manner of or basis for presenting corresponding items for two or more periods, information should be furnished which will explain the change. This procedure is in conformity with the well recognized principle that any change in practice which affects comparability should be disclosed."

Illustrative statements.   A comparative balance sheet, a comparative statement of income and retained earnings, and a comparative statement of cost of goods manufactured and sold, with some supporting schedules, are presented on pages 448 to 453. These statements are the basis of discussions of procedures of statement analysis in this and succeeding chapters.

The illustrative statements also show the use of analytical and comparative per cents and ratios.

Analytical per cents.   Analysis is the process of resolving a thing into its elements, or an examination of the component parts in relation to a whole.

In the balance sheet on pages 448 and 449, there are two columns for analytical per cents:

Per cent of each balance sheet item to the balance sheet total.
Per cent of each item of a balance sheet group to the group total.

In the income statement on page 450, the analytical per cents are based on the net sales. (*Continued on page 453.*)

Exhibit A

THE OSBORNE COMPANY
Balance Sheets
December 31, 1959, 1958, and 1957

Assets	1959			1958			Increase-Decrease* 1959-1958		1957
	Amount	Per Cent of Total	Per Cent of Group	Amount	Per Cent of Total	Per Cent of Group	Amount	Per Cent	
Current assets:									
Cash	$ 22,360	2.85%	5.76%	$ 21,085	2.81%	6.36%	$ 1,275	6.05%	$ 10,740
Accounts receivable	$215,420			$168,845			$ 46,575		$239,240
Less allowance for doubtful accounts	11,065			15,430			4,365*		30,095
Net	$204,355	26.11	52.61	$153,415	20.46	46.27	$ 50,940	33.20	$209,145
Notes receivable	$ 34,050	4.35	8.77	$ 41,600	5.55	12.55	$ 7,550*	18.15*	$ 50,095
Inventories:									
Finished goods	$ 50,710	6.48	13.05	$ 42,300	5.64	12.76	$ 8,410	19.88	$ 37,150
Goods in process	30,260	3.86	7.79	24,860	3.32	7.50	5,400	21.72	17,650
Materials	33,430	4.27	8.61	37,050	4.94	11.17	3,620*	9.77*	25,260
Total	$114,400			$104,210			$ 10,190	9.78	$ 80,060
Supplies	$ 5,995	.77	1.54	$ 4,710	.63	1.42	$ 1,285	27.28	$ 4,280
Unexpired insurance	$ 7,270	.93	1.87	$ 6,540	.87	1.97	$ 730	11.16	$ 6,280
Total current assets	$388,430	49.62%	100.00%	$331,560	44.22%	100.00%	$ 56,870	17.15	$360,600

	Amount	%	%	Amount	%	%	Amount	%	Amount
Fixed assets:									
Land	$ 30,500	3.90%	7.79%	$ 30,500	4.07%	7.36%	$ —	—	$ 30,500
Buildings	$193,000			$193,000			$ —		$193,000
Less accumulated depreciation	65,110			59,320			5,790	9.76	53,530
Net	$127,890	16.34	32.68	$133,680	17.83	32.25	5,790*	4.33*	$139,470
Machinery and equipment	$349,680			$349,515			165	.05	$334,790
Less accumulated depreciation	116,700			99,215			17,485	17.62	81,740
Net	$232,980	29.76	59.53	$250,300	33.38	60.39	17,320*	6.92*	$253,050
Total fixed assets	$391,370	50.00%	100.00%	$414,480	55.28%	100.00%	23,110*	5.58*	$423,020
Deferred charges:									
Unamortized bond discount	$ 3,000	.38%		$ 3,750	.50%		750*	20.00*	$ 5,400
	$782,800	100.00%		$749,790	100.00%		$ 33,010	4.40	$789,020
Liabilities and Stockholders' Equity									
Current liabilities:									
Bank loans	$ 30,000	3.83%	24.26%	$ 80,000	10.67%	47.33%	$ 50,000*	62.50%*	$ 85,000
Accounts payable	58,215	7.44	47.08	53,350	7.11	31.56	4,865	9.12	64,210
Accrued taxes and expenses	35,435	4.53	28.66	35,680	4.76	21.11	245*	.69*	20,490
Total current liabilities	$123,650	15.80%	100.00%	$169,030	22.54%	100.00%	$ 45,380*	26.85*	$169,700
First mortgage, 4% bonds	150,000	19.16		150,000	20.01		—		180,000
Total liabilities	$273,650	34.96%		$319,030	42.55%		$ 45,380*	14.22*	$349,700
Stockholders' equity:									
Preferred stock—7%	$ 75,000	9.58%	14.73%	$120,000	16.01%	27.86%	$ 45,000*	37.50*	$140,000
Common stock	375,000	47.90	73.65	200,000	26.67	46.43	175,000	87.50	200,000
Retained earnings	59,150	7.56	11.62	110,760	14.77	25.71	51,610*	46.60*	99,320
Total stockholders' equity	$509,150	65.04%	100.00%	$430,760	57.45%	100.00%	$ 78,390	18.20	$439,320
	$782,800	100.00%		$749,790	100.00%		$ 33,010	4.40	$789,020
Net sales	$969,065			$834,880			$134,185	16.07	

THE OSBORNE COMPANY
Statement of Income and Retained Earnings
For the Years Ended December 31, 1959, 1958, and 1957

	Year Ended December 31,				1959–1958		Year Ended December 31, 1957
	1959		1958				
	Amount	Per Cent of Net Sales	Amount	Per Cent of Net Sales	Increase Decrease*	Ratio	
Gross sales	$992,580	102.43%	$853,795	102.27%	$138,785	1.16	$938,055
Deduct:							
Sales returns and allowances	$ 3,280	.34%	$ 3,175	.38%	$ 105	1.03	$ 4,690
Sales discounts	20,235	2.09	15,740	1.89	4,495	1.29	22,360
Total	$ 23,515	2.43%	$ 18,915	2.27%	$ 4,600	1.24	$ 27,050
Net sales	$969,065	100.00%	$834,880	100.00%	$134,185	1.16	$911,005
Deduct cost of goods sold—Exhibit C	667,940	68.93	553,845	66.34	114,095	1.21	612,455
Gross profit on sales	$301,125	31.07%	$281,035	33.66%	$ 20,090	1.07	$298,550
Deduct operating expenses:							
Selling expenses—Schedule 1	$160,825	16.59%	$143,060	17.14%	$ 17,765	1.12	$179,765
General expenses—Schedule 2	70,710	7.30	53,215	6.37	17,495	1.33	65,680
Total	$231,535	23.89%	$196,275	23.51%	$ 35,260	1.18	$245,445
Net operating income	$ 69,590	7.18%	$ 84,760	10.15%	$ 15,170*	.82	$ 53,105
Deduct net financial expense—Schedule 3	4,400	.45	10,320	1.24	5,920*	.43	9,440
Net income before federal income tax	$ 65,190	6.73%	$ 74,440	8.91%	$ 9,250*	.88	$ 43,665
Deduct federal income tax	28,400	2.93	33,200	3.97	4,800*	.86	17,200
Net income	$ 36,790	3.80%	$ 41,240	4.94%	$ 4,450*	.89	$ 26,465
Add retained earnings—January 1	110,760		99,320				118,255
Total	$147,550		$140,560				$144,720
Deduct dividends:							
Preferred	$ 8,400		$ 9,800				$ 15,400
Common	80,000		20,000				30,000
Total	$ 88,400		$ 29,800				$ 45,400
Retained earnings—December 31	$ 59,150		$110,760				$ 99,320

Exhibit C

THE OSBORNE COMPANY
Statement of Cost of Goods Manufactured and Sold
For the Years Ended December 31, 1959, 1958, and 1957

| | Year Ended December 31, | | | | |
| | 1959 | | 1958 | | 1957 |
	Amount	Per Cent of Cost of Manufacturing	Amount	Per Cent of Cost of Manufacturing	
Materials:					
Inventory—beginning of year..........	$ 37,050		$ 25,260		$ 42,750
Purchases...........................	$286,380		$204,960		$184,750
Deduct:					
Purchase returns and allowances.....	$ 2,960		$ 3,280		$ 2,470
Purchase discounts..................	7,420		4,400		5,980
Total...........................	$ 10,380		$ 7,680		$ 8,450
Net purchases.......................	$276,000		$197,280		$176,300
Total inventory and purchases.......	$313,050		$222,540		$219,050
Deduct inventory—end of year........	33,430		37,050		25,260
Cost of materials used..........	$279,620	41.01%	$185,490	32.76%	$193,790
Direct labor..........................	252,170	36.99	254,905	45.02	259,195
Manufacturing overhead—Schedule 1....	149,960	22.00	125,810	22.22	136,280
Total cost of manufacturing......	$681,750	100.00%	$566,205	100.00%	$589,265
Goods in process—beginning of year...	24,860		17,650		28,600
Total................................	$706,610		$583,855		$617,865
Goods in process—end of year.........	30,260		24,860		17,650
Cost of goods manufactured...........	$676,350		$558,995		$600,215
Finished goods—beginning of year.....	42,300		37,150		49,390
Total................................	$718,650		$596,145		$649,605
Finished goods—end of year...........	50,710		42,300		37,150
Cost of goods sold...................	$667,940		$553,845		$612,455

THE OSBORNE COMPANY   Exhibit B
Schedule of Selling Expenses   Schedule 1
For the Years Ended December 31, 1959, 1958, and 1957

	Year Ended December 31,		
	1959	1958	1957
Salesmen's salaries	$ 32,465	$ 31,830	$ 39,120
Traveling expense	20,310	14,615	27,095
Advertising	31,375	25,600	34,780
Branch office expense	23,050	21,645	32,610
Dealer service	25,700	24,810	17,065
Freight out	20,080	15,700	20,810
Miscellaneous	7,845	8,860	8,285
Total	$160,825	$143,060	$179,765

THE OSBORNE COMPANY   Exhibit B
Schedule of General Expenses   Schedule 2
For the Years Ended December 31, 1959, 1958, and 1957

	Year Ended December 31,		
	1959	1958	1957
Officers' salaries	$ 25,000	$ 20,000	$ 20,000
Office salaries	13,750	9,840	12,810
Rent	4,000	4,000	5,000
Stationery and supplies	3,600	2,465	2,800
Telephone and telegraph	4,680	2,910	2,870
Bad debts	8,625	8,295	13,650
Legal and auditing	6,410	3,330	3,650
Miscellaneous	4,645	2,375	4,900
Total	$ 70,710	$ 53,215	$ 65,680

THE OSBORNE COMPANY   Exhibit B
Schedule of Net Financial Expense   Schedule 3
For the Years Ended December 31, 1959, 1958, and 1957

	Year Ended December 31,		
	1959	1958	1957
Financial expense:			
Bond interest	$ 6,000	$ 7,200	$ 8,000
Amortizaton of bond discount	750	900	1,000
Other interest	3,075	5,150	5,940
Total	$ 9,825	$ 13,250	$ 14,940
Financial income:			
Interest earned	$ 4,030	$ 2,810	$ 4,160
Miscellaneous	1,395	120	1,340
Total	$ 5,425	$ 2,930	$ 5,500
Net financial expense	$ 4,400	$ 10,320	$ 9,440

THE OSBORNE COMPANY   Exhibit C
Schedule of Manufacturing Overhead   Schedule 1
For the Years Ended December 31, 1959, 1958, and 1957

	Year Ended December 31,		
	1959	1958	1957
Indirect labor	$ 31,950	$ 23,600	$ 29,310
Superintendence	12,900	7,250	10,840
Heat, light, and power	25,100	15,650	17,150
Repairs and maintenance	21,575	24,700	23,040
Depreciation:			
Buildings	5,790	5,790	5,790
Machinery and equipment	17,485	17,475	16,740
Insurance	4,860	4,255	4,110
Taxes	7,350	6,400	6,500
Supplies	19,260	16,810	16,710
Miscellaneous	3,690	3,880	6,090
Total	$149,960	$125,810	$136,280

In the statement of cost of goods manufactured and sold on page 451, the analytical per cents are based on the total cost of manufacturing.

Analytical per cents might have been included in the supporting schedules. The per cents for each schedule usually are computed on the same base used in the statement it supports.

The analytical percentage analysis of a statement for a single date or period is of limited usefulness unless there is some standard with which the per cents can be compared.

A comparison of the analytical per cents in a series of statements for a business may be helpful in disclosing trends. However, a word of caution is in order. A change in the per cent of one item to another may be caused by a change in either item or by changes in both items. Therefore, before a change in an analytical per cent can be judged to be good or bad, the cause or causes of the change must be known. For instance, refer to the statement of income and retained earnings on page 450. Selling expenses decreased from 17.14% of net sales in 1958 to 16.59% in 1959—not a very significant change, but in the right direction. But before the change is interpreted too favorably, it should be observed that the selling expenses increased from $143,060 to $160,825, and the slight decrease in the analytical per cent was caused by the fact that the increase in sales more than offset the increase in expenses.

The analysis of a statement by the computation of analytical per cents is sometimes called *vertical analysis* because the per cents apply to related amounts usually shown in a column.

Increases and decreases: Amounts, per cents, and ratios. The balance sheet on pages 448 and 449 and the income statement on page 450 show increases and decreases in 1959 amounts compared with 1958 amounts.

The balance sheet shows per cents of increase and decrease; the income statement shows ratios of 1959 amounts to 1958 amounts. The difference in procedure is indicated below, using figures not taken from the statements.

Amounts		Increase	Per Cent Increase	Ratio 1959 to
1959	1958	Decrease*	Decrease*	1958
$ —	$100	$ 100*	100%*	0
125	100	25	25	1.25
60	100	40*	40*	.60
1,500	100	1,400	1,400	15.00

Ratios are less commonly used than per cents of increase and decrease; however, ratios have certain advantages. The Per Cent of Increase-Decrease column requires the use of red ink for decreases, or the indicating of decreases in some manner such as 100* or (100), and the distinction must be constantly recognized. The figures in a Ratio column are all on a common basis, expressing the ratio of later amounts to earlier amounts. Perhaps most important of all, it is difficult for many people to grasp quickly the significance of large per cents, such as a 1,400% increase; it is much easier to understand that one item is 15 times as large as the other item.

The computation of increases and decreases and related per cents or ratios is sometimes called *horizontal analysis* because the dollar amounts involved usually appear on the same line.

Negative amounts—Computing increases and decreases. A negative amount is one which, when appearing in a column of figures, is deducted from the positive items. When negative items appear in a statement, care must be exercised in determining the amount to be shown in the Increase-Decrease column, and in determining whether this amount should be shown as an increase or a decrease. Some typical cases are illustrated below. Negative amounts are indicated by #.

Item	This Year	Last Year	Increase Decrease*
A	$3,000	$2,800	$ 200
B	500	800	300*
C	200#	1,000	1,200*
D	200	300#	500
E	1,000#	800#	200*
F	500#	800#	300
Total	$2,000	$2,700	$ 700*

Items shown as increases tend to cause the total of the This Year column to be greater than the total of the Last Year column. Items shown as decreases tend to cause the total of the This Year column to be less than the total of the Last Year column.

Computation of increases, decreases, per cents, and ratios. Following are illustrations of some problems that arise in the determination of increases and decreases, and the computation of related per cents and ratios.

	This Year	Last Year	Increase-Decrease* Amount	Increase-Decrease* Per Cent	Ratio This Year to Last Year
Positive amounts last year:					
A.............................	$1,500	$1,000	$ 500	50%	1.50
B.............................	500	1,000	500*	50*	.50
C.............................	—	1,000	1,000*	100*	0.00
D.............................	500#	1,000	1,500*	150*	—
No amounts last year:					
E.............................	1,500	—	1,500	—	—
F.............................	500#	—	500*	—	—
Negative amounts last year:					
G.............................	1,500#	1,000#	500*	—	—
H.............................	500	1,000#	1,500	—	—
I.............................	—	1,000#	1,000	—	—

The computation of the per cents in A, B, C, and D and the ratios in A, B, and C are obvious; no ratio can be computed for D because there is no ratio relationship between a negative and a positive number. No per cents or ratios can be computed in the second group because no amounts are shown in the Last Year column. And none can be computed for the third group because the Last Year amounts were negative quantities.

Horizontal analysis of more than two statements.   If comparative statements show data for more than two periods or at more than two dates, there are two bases for computing increases and decreases.

(1) Comparisons may be made with data for the immediately preceding period or date, thus:

THE A COMPANY
Comparative Income Statement
For the Years Ended December 31, 1959, 1958, and 1957

	Year Ended December 31, 1959	1958	1957	Increase-Decrease* 1959–1958	1958–1957
Gross sales..........	$780,000	$600,000	$800,000	$180,000	$200,000*

(2) Comparisons may be made with data for the earliest date or period, thus:

THE A COMPANY
Comparative Income Statement
For the Years Ended December 31, 1959, 1958, and 1957

	Year Ended December 31, 1959	1958	1957	Increase-Decrease* 1959–1957	1958–1957
Gross sales..........	$780,000	$600,000	$800,000	$20,000*	$200,000*

If price levels have changed materially, the choice of a base date or period too far in the past may distort the comparisons, because changes in amounts may have been caused principally by changes in the purchasing power of the dollar.

If a statement shows dollar increases and decreases based on the data for the immediately preceding date or period, considerations of consistency only would suggest that per cents of increase and decrease or ratios be based on the data for the immediately preceding date or period, thus:

THE A COMPANY
Comparative Income Statement
For the Years Ended December 31, 1959, 1958, and 1957

	Year Ended December 31,			Increase-Decrease*			
				1959–1958		1958–1957	
	1959	1958	1957	Amount	Per Cent	Amount	Per Cent
Gross sales.......	$780,000	$600,000	$800,000	$180,000	30%	$200,000*	25%*

But the danger of confusion outweighs the considerations of consistency. The above statement indicates a 25% decrease in sales in 1958 and a 30% increase in 1959. Consideration of these per cents alone would result in an incorrect conclusion that the increase in 1959 had more than offset the decrease in 1958. The confusion arises, of course, from the fact that the per cents are computed on two different bases: the per cent of decrease in 1958 is computed on a base of $800,000, whereas the per cent of increase in 1959 is computed on a base of $600,000.

Therefore, in cases similar to this, it seems desirable to compute the per cents of increase and decrease or the ratios on the basis of data for the earliest date or period, thus:

THE A COMPANY
Comparative Income Statement
For the Years Ended December 31, 1959, 1958, and 1957

	Year Ended December 31,			Increase-Decrease*			
				1959–1957		1958–1957	
	1959	1958	1957	Amount	Per Cent	Amount	Per Cent
Gross sales....	$780,000	$600,000	$800,000	$20,000*	2.5%*	$200,000*	25.0%*

Significance of horizontal analysis. It has been pointed out that vertical-analysis per cents may result in misleading conclusions because the percentage change in an item may be caused by a change in the amount of the item, or a change in the amount of the base, or changes in both. Horizontal-analysis per cents and ratios are not subject to this objection because they are affected by changes in the item only.

Horizontal analysis is useful in disclosing balance sheet trends and relationships. For instance, refer to the balance sheet on pages 448 and 449, and observe the per cents of increase, particularly in receivables, inventories, and accounts payable. But also observe the relationship between these per cents and the per cent of increase in net sales shown at the bottom of the balance sheet. The following question immediately arises: With a 16.07% increase in net sales, are a 33.20% increase in accounts receivable, a 19.88% increase in finished goods, and a 9.12% increase in accounts payable indicative of an unfavorable condition and trend?

Horizontal analysis of the income statement is also useful. Refer to the income statement on page 450 and observe that, with a 1.16 ratio of 1959 to 1958 sales, the cost of goods sold ratio is 1.21, with the result that the gross profit ratio is only 1.07. Furthermore, the total selling and general expense ratio is 1.18, with the result that the net operating income ratio is .82.

An increase or decrease cannot be interpreted as desirable or undesirable until its cause is known. An increase in inventories may be advantageous if stocks have previously been inadequate, or if heavy purchases have been made against a rising market or in anticipation of a period when goods will not be available. On the other hand, an increase in inventories may have resulted from unwise purchasing policies or from a decline in sales. An increase in receivables may have resulted from an increase in sales or from an increase in delinquent accounts.

The reliability of horizontal-analysis per cents and ratios may be affected by changes in price levels. For instance, a 19.88% increase in the finished goods inventory does not necessarily mean a 19.88% quantity increase. It may be due wholly to cost increases; in fact, cost increases may more than offset a quantity decrease.

Monthly comparative and cumulative statements.   Statements are sometimes prepared for management purposes showing:

> The results of operations for the current month, and for the same month of the preceding year;
> The results of operations for the year to date, and for the corresponding period of the preceding year.

Such comparisons of operations by months may not be wholly satisfactory because of variations in the calendar; the two months in different years may not be strictly comparable because of differences in the number of Sundays, or because holidays may fall on Sundays in one month and on business days in another, with a consequent difference in the number of business days.

If comparisons are made of the operations of different months in the same year, there is the additional disturbing factor of differences in the number of days in a month.

Statement of Change in Stockholders' Equity and Net Assets

The following statements co-ordinate information shown by the income and retained earnings statements with information shown by the comparative balance sheet.

First illustration—Increase in stockholders' equity and net assets. The statement on page 459 and its supporting schedules on pages 459 and 460 show an increase in stockholders' equity and net assets.

Second illustration—Decrease in stockholders' equity and net assets. The statement on page 460 shows a decrease in stockholders' equity and net assets. Supporting schedules would be similar in form to those previously illustrated.

Third illustration—Statement covering two years. In a statement covering a series of years, it is not convenient to detail the elements of stockholders' equity in columns at the head of the statement; observe the alternative procedure in the statement on page 461.

Statements for first illustration:

THE OSBORNE COMPANY
Statement Accounting for Increase in Stockholders' Equity
and Resulting Increase in Net Assets
Year Ended December 31, 1959

Increase (decrease*) in stockholders' equity:

| | CAPITAL STOCK | | Retained | |
	Preferred	Common	Earnings	Total
Changes in capital stock:				
Preferred stock retired.....	$45,000*			$ 45,000*
Common stock issued				
for cash		$175,000		175,000
Net income.................			36,790	36,790
Cash dividends paid:				
Preferred.................			8,400*	8,400*
Common.................			80,000*	80,000*
Net increase (decrease*).....	$45,000*	$175,000	$ 51,610*	$ 78,390

Resulting increase in net assets:

| | December 31, | | Increase |
	1959	1958	Decrease*
Assets:			
Current assets—Schedule 1..........	$388,430	$331,560	$ 56,870
Fixed assets—Schedule 2............	391,370	414,480	23,110*
Deferred charges...................	3,000	3,750	750*
Total assets...................	$782,800	$749,790	$ 33,010
Liabilities:			
Current liabilities—Schedule 1.......	$123,650	$169,030	$ 45,380*
First mortgage, 4% bonds...........	150,000	150,000	—
Total liabilities................	$273,650	$319,030	$ 45,380*
Net assets.........................	$509,150	$430,760	$ 78,390

THE OSBORNE COMPANY
Comparative Schedule of Working Capital   Schedule 1
December 31, 1959 and 1958

| | December 31, | | Increase |
	1959	1958	Decrease*
Current assets:			
Cash.................................	$ 22,360	$ 21,085	$ 1,275
Receivables—less allowance............	238,405	195,015	43,390
Inventories:			
Finished goods......................	50,710	42,300	8,410
Goods in process....................	30,260	24,860	5,400
Materials...........................	33,430	37,050	3,620*
Supplies.............................	5,995	4,710	1,285
Unexpired insurance..................	7,270	6,540	730
Total current assets...............	$388,430	$331,560	$ 56,870
Current liabilities:			
Bank loans...........................	$ 30,000	$ 80,000	$ 50,000*
Accounts payable.....................	58,215	53,350	4,865
Accrued taxes and expenses............	35,435	35,680	245*
Total current liabilities............	$123,650	$169,030	$ 45,380*
Working capital........................	$264,780	$162,530	$102,250

THE OSBORNE COMPANY   Schedule 2
Comparative Schedule of Fixed Assets
December 31, 1959 and 1958

	December 31, 1959	December 31, 1958	Increase Decrease*
Cost:			
Land..............................	$ 30,500	$ 30,500	$ —
Buildings...........................	193,000	193,000	—
Machinery and equipment..............	349,680	349,515	165
Total..........................	$573,180	$573,015	$ 165
Depreciation to date:			
Buildings...........................	$ 65,110	$ 59,320	$ 5,790
Machinery and equipment..............	116,700	99,215	17,485
Total..........................	$181,810	$158,535	$ 23,275
Cost less depreciation....................	$391,370	$414,480	$ 23,110*

Statement for second illustration:

THE OSBORNE COMPANY
Statement Accounting for Decrease in Stockholders' Equity
and Resulting Decrease in Net Assets
For the Year Ended December 31, 1958

Increase (decrease*) in stockholders' equity:

	CAPITAL STOCK Preferred	CAPITAL STOCK Common	Retained Earnings	Total
Changes in capital stock:				
Preferred stock retired.......	$20,000*			$20,000*
Net income...................			$41,240	41,240
Dividends paid:				
Preferred...................			9,800*	9,800*
Common...................			20,000*	20,000*
Net increase (decrease*).......	$20,000*	$ —	$11,440	$ 8,560*

Resulting decrease in net assets:

	December 31, 1958	December 31, 1957	Increase Decrease*
Assets:			
Current assets—Schedule 1...........	$331,560	$360,600	$29,040*
Fixed assets—Schedule 2.............	414,480	423,020	8,540*
Deferred charges....................	3,750	5,400	1,650*
Total assets.....................	$749,790	$789,020	$39,230*
Liabilities:			
Current liabilities—Schedule 1........	$169,030	$169,700	$ 670*
First mortgage, 4% bonds............	150,000	180,000	30,000*
Total liabilities..................	$319,030	$349,700	$30,670*
Net assets...........................	$430,760	$439,320	$ 8,560*

Statement for third illustration:

THE OSBORNE COMPANY
Statement Accounting for Changes in Stockholders' Equity and Resulting Changes in Net Assets
Years Ended December 31, 1959 and 1958

	December 31, 1959	Increase Decrease*	December 31, 1958	Increase Decrease*	December 31, 1957
Increase (decrease*) in stockholders' equity:					
Capital stock:					
Preferred stock:					
Retired................		$ 45,000*		$20,000*	
Common stock:					
Issued for cash........		$175,000		$ —	
Retained earnings:					
Net income............		$ 36,790		$41,240	
Dividends:					
On preferred..........		8,400*		9,800*	
On common............		80,000*		20,000*	
Total..............		$ 51,610*		$11,440	
Increase (decrease*) in stockholders' equity.....		$ 78,390		$ 8,560*	
Increase (decrease*) in net assets:					
Assets:					
Current assets—Schedule 1...	$388,430	$ 56,870	$331,560	$29,040*	$360,600
Fixed assets—Schedule 2....	391,370	23,110*	414,480	8,540*	423,020
Deferred charges.......	3,000	750*	3,750	1,650*	5,400
Total assets........	$782,800	$ 33,010	$749,790	$39,230*	$789,020
Liabilities:					
Current liabilities—Schedule 1....	$123,650	$ 45,380*	$169,030	$ 670*	$169,700
First mortgage, 4% bonds....	150,000		150,000	30,000*	180,000
Total liabilities......	$273,650	$45,380*	$319,030	$30,670*	$349,700
Net assets..........	$509,150	$ 78,390	$430,760	$ 8,560*	$439,320
Capital structure:					
Capital stock:					
Preferred............	$ 75,000	$ 45,000*	$120,000	$20,000*	$140,000
Common.............	375,000	175,000	200,000		200,000
Retained earnings......	59,150	51,610*	110,760	11,440	99,320
Total..............	$509,150	$ 78,390	$430,760	$ 8,560*	$439,320

Miscellaneous Ratios

Equity ratios. Three equity ratios, based on data of The Osborne Company, are computed below:

		December 31,		
		1959	1958	1957
Total assets	(a)	$782,800	$749,790	$789,020
Total liabilities	(b)	273,650	319,030	349,700
Stockholders' equity	(c)	$509,150	$430,760	$439,320
Ratio of total liabilities to total assets (b ÷ a)		.35	.43	.44
Ratio of stockholders' equity to total assets (c ÷ a)		.65	.57	.56
Ratio of stockholders' equity to total liabilities (c ÷ b)		1.86	1.35	1.26

These ratios serve as an indication of long-term solvency; the working capital ratio is a measure of short-term solvency.

A low ratio of liabilities to assets, a high ratio of stockholders' equity to assets, and a high ratio of stockholders' equity to total liabilities all express the same condition, namely, a relatively large cushion of security to the creditors, and therefore they are regarded favorably by creditors. From the creditors' standpoint, the changes in the ratios from 1957 to 1959 indicate an improvement.

From the stockholders' standpoint, the changes in the ratios may not be wholly desirable. From the stockholders' standpoint, it is desirable to maintain a sufficient equity to safeguard the company's credit; beyond that point, an increase in the ratio of equity to assets or equity to liabilities may be disadvantageous. Within limits of safety, it is advantageous to the stockholders for a company to "trade on the equity"; in other words, it is advantageous, to the greatest extent practicable, to use interest-free creditors' funds or funds obtained by borrowing at a rate lower than the rate of income which can be earned by the use of the funds. To illustrate: Assume that a company needs $100,000 worth of assets; if the stockholders invest the entire amount and the company earns a net income of $8,000, the income will be 8% of the investment; but if the stockholders invest only $60,000 and the company borrows $40,000 at 5%, the interest will be $2,000, the net income will be $6,000, and the rate of income on the $60,000 of stockholders' equity will be 10%.

If the working capital ratio has improved between two dates, it may be desirable to compare the equity ratios at the two dates. An increase in the working capital ratio may have been caused by profitable operations, which presumably would also cause an improvement in the equity ratios; improvements caused by operations might be expected to continue. But the working capital position might have been improved by converting a portion of the current liabilities into funded debt, which would not cause any improvement in the equity ratios; the question would then naturally arise whether the improved working capital position could be maintained or whether the working capital might again become impaired.

Ratio of security to long-term liabilities. The long-term liabilities are usually secured by mortgages on fixed assets, and the mortgage holders are interested in the ratio of the security to the liability. If obtainable, market values of the mortgaged properties should be used in the computation; if these values are not available, depreciated book values may be used, as in the following computation, which is based on the assumption that the bonds of The Osborne Company are secured by a mortgage on *all of the fixed assets.*

		December 31,		
		1959	1958	1957
Land..................................		$ 30,500	$ 30,500	$ 30,500
Buildings—cost less accumulated depreciation............................		127,890	133,680	139,470
Machinery and equipment—cost less accumulated depreciation............		232,980	250,300	253,050
Total.........................	(a)	$391,370	$414,480	$423,020
Long-term liabilities.................	(b)	$150,000	$150,000	$180,000
Ratio of security to long-term liabilities (a ÷ b)...........................		2.61	2.76	2.35

The ratio of security to long-term liabilities is significant not only from the standpoint of measuring the protection against the presently outstanding debt, but also because it is indicative of the available sources of additional funds. If the mortgage obligations are low in relation to fixed assets, additional funds may be obtainable on the same security; on the other hand, if the properties are already mortgaged to their limit, any additional funds required will have to be obtained from other sources.

If a sinking fund is being maintained for the redemption of a long-term liability, the method of computing the ratio of security to debt will depend upon the nature of the sinking fund. To illustrate, assume that a company has a long-term liability of $500,000, a sinking fund of $100,000, and mortgaged fixed assets of $700,000.

If the sinking fund is invested in the company's own bonds, which are being held alive until their maturity, the ratio should be computed as follows:

Fixed assets...	(a)	$700,000
Bonds outstanding ($500,000 minus $100,000 in the fund)...	(b)	400,000
Ratio of security to bonds outstanding (a ÷ b).............		1.75

But if the sinking fund is invested in other securities, the ratio should be computed as follows:

Fixed assets		$700,000
Sinking fund		100,000
Total	(a)	$800,000
Bonds outstanding	(b)	500,000
Ratio of security to bonds outstanding (a ÷ b)		1.60

Income available for bond interest. Bondholders are interested in the debtor company's earnings as well as in the mortgaged security, because current income is the normal source of the funds required for the payment of bond interest. Since the bond interest is a claim against revenue which takes precedence over income taxes, and since the earnings available for bond interest are, of course, the earnings before bond interest, the bond interest and income taxes are added to the net income in the following computation.

		Year Ended December 31,		
		1959	1958	1957
Net income		$36,790	$41,240	$26,465
Add: Bond interest	(a)	6,000	7,200	8,000
Federal income tax		28,400	33,200	17,200
Net income before bond interest and income tax	(b)	$71,190	$81,640	$51,665
Number of times bond interest earned (b ÷ a)		11.87	11.34	6.46

Since all charges against income, including bond interest and income taxes, take precedence over dividends on any class of stock, the relation of earnings to preferred dividend requirements is computed by dividing the net income by the amount required to pay dividends on the preferred stock at the preference rate.

Ratio of stockholders' equity to fixed assets. Is there a tendency toward overinvestment in fixed assets? To obtain a partial answer, we may compute the ratio of stockholders' equity to fixed assets.

		December 31,		
		1959	1958	1957
Stockholders' equity	(a)	$509,150	$430,760	$439,320
Fixed assets less accumulated depreciation	(b)	391,370	414,480	423,020
Ratio of stockholders' equity to fixed assets less accumulated depreciation (a ÷ b)		1.30	1.04	1.04

Ratio of sales to fixed assets. Additional light can be thrown on the question of possible overinvestment in fixed assets by computing the ratio of sales to fixed assets, as illustrated on the opposite page.

		1959	1958	1957
Net sales for the year.................	(a)	$969,065	$834,880	$911,005
Fixed assets less accumulated depreciation—end of year	(b)	391,370	414,480	423,020
Ratio of net sales to fixed assets less accumulated depreciation (a ÷ b)........		2.48	2.01	2.15

Ratio of sales to stockholders' equity.

Other things being equal, the higher the ratio of sales to stockholders' equity, the greater the rate of income earned on the stockholders' equity. If, for instance, two concerns have sales of $100,000 and net income of $5,000, while one has a stockholders' equity of $50,000 and the other has a stockholders' equity of $100,000, the ratios are as follows:

		Company *A*	Company *B*
Sales...	(a)	$100,000	$100,000
Net income....................................	(b)	5,000	5,000
Stockholders' equity............................	(c)	100,000	50,000
Ratio of sales to stockholders' equity (a ÷ c)........		1 to 1	2 to 1
Ratio of net income to stockholders' equity (b ÷ c)...		5%	10%

This illustration makes apparent the fact that high ratios of sales to stockholders' equity tend to increase the rate of income. However, exceptionally high ratios may be undesirable, since they may merely indicate that the company is in an overextended position, doing a larger volume of business than it has the capital to carry safely.

The Osborne Company's ratios are computed below:

		1959	1958	1957
Sales..	(a)	$992,580	$853,795	$938,055
Stockholders' equity—end of year..............	(b)	509,150	430,760	439,320
Ratio of sales to stockholders' equity (a ÷ b)....		1.95	1.98	2.14

Ratio of cost of goods manufactured to fixed assets.

Ratios of sales to fixed assets are affected by the profit on the sales, an element which should be eliminated in a determination of the relative use made of the fixed assets in production. For this reason, it is preferable to use the cost of goods manufactured instead of the sales. Ratios based on the cost of manufacture will still include the disturbing element of variation in manufacturing costs due to changes in the price level.

		1959	1958	1957
Cost of goods manufactured...........	(a)	$676,350	$558,995	$600,215
Fixed assets less accumulated depreciation—end of year..................	(b)	391,370	414,480	423,020
Ratio of cost of goods manufactured to fixed assets less accumulated depreciation (a ÷ b)......................		1.73	1.35	1.42

The operating ratio.   Usually this ratio is computed by dividing the total operating expenses by the net sales. Operating expenses include the cost of goods sold and selling and administrative expenses; excluded are financial expense, unusual and nonrecurring items, and income taxes.

		1959	1958	1957
Operating expenses..................	(a)	$899,475	$750,120	$857,900
Net sales for the year.................	(b)	969,065	834,880	911,005
Operating ratio (a ÷ b)...............		.928	.898	.942

The operating ratio is considered a measure of efficiency: the smaller the ratio, the better; but of most significance is its trend.

Book value per share of stock.   An increase in the total capital stock and retained earnings of a company indicates that the aggregate stockholders' equity has increased, but this does not necessarily mean an increase in the book value of the individual stockholdings; the increase in the stockholders' equity may have been caused by the issuance of additional stock. It is therefore desirable to determine the book value of each share of stock.

If there is only one class of stock, the book value per share is computed by dividing the total stockholders' equity (capital stock and retained earnings, including all appropriated surplus reserves) by the number of shares of stock outstanding. If common and preferred stocks are outstanding, the question arises concerning the apportionment of the retained earnings between the two classes of stock. This matter is discussed at length in Chapter 7.

On the assumption that the preferred stock of The Osborne Company is nonparticipating and that no dividends were in arrears, its book value is par, and the book value per share of the common stock is computed as follows:

		December 31,		
		1959	1958	1957
Common stock.......................		$375,000	$200,000	$200,000
Retained earnings....................		59,150	110,760	99,320
Total............................	(a)	$434,150	$310,760	$299,320
Number of shares outstanding.........	(b)	3,750	2,000	2,000
Book value per share (a ÷ b)..........		$ 115.77	$ 155.38	$ 149.66

It will be noted that, although the total of the common stock and retained earnings increased during 1959, the book value per share of common stock decreased because of the issuance of 1,750 additional shares.

Ratio of net income to stockholders' equity.   The computation of the ratio of net income to stockholders' equity is illustrated on the following page.

		1959	1958	1957
Stockholders' equity—end of year:				
Capital stock:				
Preferred—7%..................		$ 75,000	$120,000	$140,000
Common......................		375,000	200,000	200,000
Retained earnings................		59,150	110,760	99,320
Total stockholders' equity........	(a)	$509,150	$430,760	$439,320
Net income for the year..............	(b)	$ 36,790	$ 41,240	$ 26,465
Ratio of net income to stockholders' equity (b ÷ a)....................		7.23%	9.57%	6.02%

Depending upon the date of issuance of the additional shares, it may be more accurate to determine the ratio of income by using the average stockholders' equity for the year, thus:

		1959	1958	1957
Stockholders' equity:				
Beginning of year..................		$430,760	$439,320	$488,255
End of year.......................		509,150	430,760	439,320
Average.......................	(a)	$469,955	$435,040	$463,788
Net income........................	(b)	$ 36,790	$ 41,240	$ 26,465
Ratio of net income to average stockholders' equity (b ÷ a).............		7.83%	9.48%	5.71%

If a considerable portion of the capital is invested in securities or other properties not closely associated with operations, it may be desirable to compute two income ratios: First, an over-all ratio of net income to stockholders' equity; second, an operating income ratio computed by dividing net income exclusive of income on nonoperating assets by the stockholders' equity minus investments in nonoperating assets.

Ratio of net income to total assets.   Another earnings ratio is computed by dividing the net income by the total assets.

		1959	1958	1957
Net income for the year..............	(a)	$ 36,790	$ 41,240	$ 26,465
Total assets—end of year.............	(b)	782,800	749,790	789,020
Ratio of net income to total assets (a ÷ b)		4.70%	5.50%	3.35%

This ratio is useful in comparing businesses with different capital (stock and bond) structures. Also, this ratio may prove informative in preparing historical analyses in those cases where a business has had one or more significant changes in its capital structure, such as bonds converted to stock.

Earnings per share.   Earnings-per-share data are frequently included in annual reports to stockholders and are widely circulated through publications dealing with business conditions and the stock market. Ordinarily the data relate to the common shares. Although extensively quoted with reference to market prices of shares of stock, it is a statistic of questionable value.

In computing earnings per share, the amount reported as net income is used, except in cases where deductions therefrom must be made for dividends, paid or cumulative, on preferred shares. As a general rule, the number of common shares outstanding at year end is used; however, if the number of outstanding shares has increased significantly during the year as a result of the raising of additional capital, it is considered preferable to base the computation on a weighted average of the shares outstanding during the period. To illustrate, assume that the 1,750 additional shares of common stock of The Osborne Company were issued for cash on November 1, 1959. The weighted average of outstanding common shares would be computed as follows:

$$
\begin{array}{rl}
2{,}000 \text{ shares outstanding for } 10 \text{ months} = & 20{,}000 \\
3{,}750 \text{ shares outstanding for } \ 2 \text{ months} = & \underline{\ 7{,}500} \\
\text{Total} \dots\dots\dots\dots\dots\dots\dots\dots\dots\dots\dots & \underline{27{,}500}
\end{array}
$$

$27{,}500 \div 12 = 2{,}292$ weighted-average number of shares.

The earnings-per-share data for The Osborne Company are shown below:

		1959	1958	1957
Net income for the year..................		$36,790	$41,240	$26,465
Deduct dividend paid at the 7% preference rate on preferred stock................		8,400	9,800	15,400
Net income applicable to common stock....	(a)	$28,390	$31,440	$11,065
Shares of common stock outstanding at end of year..............................	(b)		2,000	2,000
Weighted average of shares outstanding during year..............................	(b)	2,292		
Earnings per share (a ÷ b)..............		$ 12.39	$ 15.72	$ 5.53

When the change in the number of shares outstanding is the result of a stock dividend or a stock split during the year, the computation should be based on the number of shares outstanding at the end of the period.

Distortions in ratios. Comparisons of the ratios of one company with those of another or with composites of numerous companies should be made with great caution. Differences in accounting methods applied by different businesses may cause differences in ratios, and these variations may be more apparent than real. Different classifications of charges to expense accounts, different procedures of providing for depreciation, different bases of inventory and fixed asset valuations, differences in financing methods, arbitrary decisions as to whether distributions to the proprietorship group shall be made in the form of salaries, bonuses, or dividends, and innumerable other possibilities of diverse treatment of similar matters can affect the ratios to an extent that may make any conclusions based upon them very misleading.

To a less extent the same caution is in order with respect to comparing the ratios of the same business for several years. Changes in accounting or administrative policies may affect the ratios, and the basic financial condition or operating results may not be affected to the extent indicated. Moreover, changes in price levels and the purchasing power of the dollar may cause misleading conclusions to be drawn from a comparison of ratios for a series of years.

Income taxes and income ratios.   In the computation of the ratios of net income to sales or any other base, should the net income used be the amount after or before the deduction of federal income taxes? Looking at the results of operations for one year only, it seems preferable to use an income figure after the deduction of income taxes, because the remainder is the amount which accrues to the benefit of the stockholders. But because of the wide fluctuation in tax rates over a period of time, it may be preferable in statements showing comparative data for several years to use an income figure computed before the deduction of income taxes; this procedure eliminates the fluctuation in ratios due to tax requirements over which the management has no control, and thus tends to bring out more clearly the fluctuation in ratios resulting from conditions which the management presumably has power to regulate.

CHAPTER TWENTY-TWO

The Analysis of
Working Capital

Working capital schedule. The working capital of The
Osborne Company at various dates is shown below:

THE OSBORNE COMPANY
Schedule of Working Capital
December 31, 1959, 1958, and 1957

	December 31,		
	1959	1958	1957
Current assets:			
Cash................................	$ 22,360	$ 21,085	$ 10,740
Receivables:			
Accounts............................	$215,420	$168,845	$239,240
Notes..............................	34,050	41,600	50,095
Total receivables...................	$249,470	$210,445	$289,335
Less allowance for doubtful accounts...	11,065	15,430	30,095
Net receivables.....................	$238,405	$195,015	$259,240
Inventories:			
Finished goods.......................	$ 50,710	$ 42,300	$ 37,150
Goods in process....................	30,260	24,860	17,650
Materials...........................	33,430	37,050	25,260
Total inventories..................	$114,400	$104,210	$ 80,060
Supplies..............................	$ 5,995	$ 4,710	$ 4,280
Unexpired insurance....................	7,270	6,540	6,280
Total current assets..............	$388,430	$331,560	$360,600
Current liabilities:			
Bank loans...........................	$ 30,000	$ 80,000	$ 85,000
Accounts payable........	58,215	53,350	64,210
Accrued taxes and expenses.............	35,435	35,680	20,490
Total current liabilities..........	$123,650	$169,030	$169,700
Net current assets—working capital........	$264,780	$162,530	$190,900

Changes indicated by ratios. The changes in the current assets and current liabilities, over a period of time, may be indicated by a statement similar to that below.

THE OSBORNE COMPANY
Comparative Statement of Working Capital
December 31, 1959, 1958, and 1957

				Ratios	
	Amounts—December 31,			1959 to	1958 to
	1959	1958	1957	1957	1957
Current assets:					
Cash........................	$ 22,360	$ 21,085	$ 10,740	2.08	1.96
Receivables—net..............	238,405	195,015	259,240	.92	.75
Inventories:					
Finished goods.............	50,710	42,300	37,150	1.37	1.14
Goods in process...........	30,260	24,860	17,650	1.71	1.41
Materials..................	33,430	37,050	25,260	1.32	1.47
Supplies.....................	5,995	4,710	4,280	1.40	1.10
Unexpired insurance..........	7,270	6,540	6,280	1.16	1.04
Total current assets......	$388,430	$331,560	$360,600	1.08	.92
Current liabilities:					
Bank loans...................	$ 30,000	$ 80,000	$ 85,000	.35	.94
Accounts payable............	58,215	53,350	64,210	.91	.83
Accrued taxes and expenses...	35,435	35,680	20,490	1.73	1.74
Total current liabilities...	$123,650	$169,030	$169,700	.73	1.00
Working capital...............	$264,780	$162,530	$190,900	1.39	.85
Net sales for the year..........	$969,065	$834,880	$911,005	1.06	.92

In such a statement it is desirable to show the changes in net sales, as these changes should have a bearing on the changes in current assets and current liabilities. For instance, we find that the sales of 1958 were only .92 of those for 1957; the receivables at the end of 1958 were .75 of those at the end of 1957. These conditions indicate the possibility that the receivables were relatively not so old at the end of 1958 as at the end of 1957. On the other hand, with a decrease in net sales, all of the inventories have increased. Looking at the ratios for 1959, we find that the sales were slightly in excess of those for 1957, as shown by the sales ratio of 1.06; the investments in inventories have increased more rapidly than the sales have increased, thus suggesting a possible over-investment in inventories.

Working capital ratio. The working capital ratio expresses the relation of the amount of current assets to the amount of current liabilities. For instance, if the current assets are twice the amount of the current liabilities, the working capital ratio is 2 to 1.

Both the amount of working capital and the working capital ratio should be given consideration by anyone who contemplates granting short-term credit to a business. The amount of working capital has a bearing on the *amount* of such credit which may be extended; the working capital ratio is indicative of the *degree of safety* with which short-term credit may be extended, since this ratio reflects the relation of current assets to current debts, and, thus, the per cent of shrinkage in current assets which will not too greatly jeopardize the interests of the current creditors. To illustrate, assume that two companies have the following current assets and current liabilities:

	Company A	Company B
Total current assets	$200,000	$1,000,000
Total current liabilities	100,000	900,000
Net current assets	$100,000	$ 100,000

Each company has a working capital of $100,000, but Company A's working capital position is relatively more favorable than that of Company B, because Company A has $2 of current assets per dollar of current liabilities, whereas Company B has only $1.11 of current assets per dollar of current liabilities.

The working capital ratios of The Osborne Company are shown below. They were computed by dividing the current assets by the current liabilities.

THE OSBORNE COMPANY
Working Capital Ratios
December 31, 1959, 1958, and 1957

	December 31,		
	1959	1958	1957
Total current assets	$388,430	$331,560	$360,600
Total current liabilities	123,650	169,030	169,700
Working capital	$264,780	$162,530	$190,900
Working capital ratio, or dollars of current assets per dollar of current liabilities	3.14	1.96	2.12

A working capital ratio (sometimes called "current ratio") of at least 2 to 1 was for many years regarded as a standard of satisfactory current position. For reasons discussed in this chapter, analysts are now coming rather generally to recognize that no such arbitrary current-ratio standard can be applied indiscriminately to all types of business (perhaps not even to the same business at different dates during the year), and that the current ratio alone is by no means an adequate measure of the short-term credit position of a business.

The acid-test ratio. The inventories are relatively much less current than the cash and receivables. The inventories must be sold before their proceeds can be used for the payment of current liabilities; selling them involves the uncertain factor of the marketability of the inventories, as well as the element of time required for the conversion of raw materials and goods in process into finished goods and for the sale of the finished product.

For these reasons many analysts supplement the working capital ratio by the so-called acid-test ratio, sometimes called the "quick current ratio." The acid-test ratio is sometimes defined as the ratio of cash and receivables (quick current assets) to current liabilities. However, most analysts advocate including among the quick current assets, for purposes of computing the acid-test ratio, not only the cash and current accounts and notes receivable, but also any marketable investments which it is expected will be converted into cash as an incident to the regular operations. This seems to be a justifiable procedure in view of the purpose of the acid-test ratio. However, investments should not be regarded as quick current assets unless (a) they can be disposed of without hampering the operations of the business, (b) there is a ready market for them, and (c) trading is in sufficient volume to reflect a price applicable to the quantity of securities held.

The acid-test ratios of The Osborne Company at various dates are shown below.

THE OSBORNE COMPANY
Acid-Test Ratios
December 31, 1959, 1958, and 1957

	December 31,		
	1959	1958	1957
Quick current assets:			
Cash..............................	$ 22,360	$ 21,085	$ 10,740
Accounts and notes receivable, less allowance for doubtful accounts...........	238,405	195,015	259,240
Total quick assets...............	$260,765	$216,100	$269,980
Total current liabilities..................	123,650	169,030	169,700
Excess of quick current assets over current liabilities..........................	$137,115	$ 47,070	$100,280
Acid-test ratio—dollars of quick current assets per dollar of current liabilities..........	2.11	1.28	1.59

An acid-test ratio of at least 1 to 1 usually has been regarded as desirable. However, the fact that a company has a 1-to-1 acid-test ratio is no positive evidence that it will be able to pay its current liabilities as they mature. Cash may be required for the payment of operating expenses or for other purposes, and the receivables may not become due before payments of current liabilities must be made.

Distribution of current assets. It is obvious from the foregoing discussion of the acid-test ratio that the current position of a company is not entirely dependent upon the ratio of total current assets to total current liabilities, but is affected by the kinds of current assets owned. This fact may be further emphasized by the following comparison of a company's current position at two dates:

	December 31,	
	1959	1958
Current assets:		
Cash...	$10,000	$30,000
Receivables....................................	20,000	20,000
Inventories....................................	30,000	10,000
Total current assets......................	$60,000	$60,000
Current liabilities..............................	30,000	30,000
Working capital................................	$30,000	$30,000

The company had the same working capital ($30,000) and the same working capital ratio (2 to 1) at the two dates. However, its working capital position at the two dates was not the same. From one standpoint its position was much weaker at the end of 1959 than at the end of 1958 because of the shift from the very current asset of cash to the much less current asset of inventories. On the other hand, the amount ultimately to be realized from the current assets may have been increased because there are larger inventories to be converted at a profit.

Notwithstanding the fact that the current assets at the end of 1959 may have had a greater ultimate realizable value because of the element of prospective profit in the larger inventories, a shift from the more current assets of cash and receivables to the less current asset of inventories is usually regarded as undesirable. To determine whether any such shift is taking place, a statement similar to the following may be prepared.

THE OSBORNE COMPANY
Percentage Distribution of Current Assets
December 31, 1959, 1958, and 1957

	December 31,		
	1959	1958	1957
Cash....................................	5.76%	6.36%	2.98%
Receivables—less allowance...............	61.38%	58.82%	71.89%
Inventories:			
Finished goods.........................	13.05%	12.76%	10.30%
Goods in process.......................	7.79	7.50	4.89
Materials..............................	8.61	11.17	7.01
Total inventories......................	29.45%	31.43%	22.20%
Supplies.................................	1.54%	1.42%	1.19%
Unexpired insurance......................	1.87	1.97	1.74
Total current assets..................	100.00%	100.00%	100.00%

Breakdown of working capital ratio.　Since any considerable shifts from the relatively more current assets to the relatively less current assets, or vice versa, will materially affect a company's ability to pay its current debts promptly, it may be desirable to break down the working capital ratio in a manner which will show whether the current liabilities can be paid from the cash on hand, or whether their payment will require all of the cash and part of the proceeds of the receivables, all of the cash and receivables and part of the proceeds of the finished goods, and so on. The following rather extreme case is used for purposes of an emphatic illustration:

	December 31,		
	1959	1958	1957
Cash	$30,000	$15,000	$ 5,000
Receivables	20,000	10,000	10,000
Finished goods	15,000	20,000	15,000
Goods in process	10,000	30,000	20,000
Materials	5,000	5,000	30,000
Total	$80,000	$80,000	$80,000

The current liabilities at each date were $40,000, and the working capital ratio at each date was, therefore, 2 to 1. However, the company's current position changed materially, as shown by the following summary. The ratios are stated cumulatively; for instance, at the end of 1959, the cash was equal to .75 of the current liabilities; the total cash and receivables were equal to 1.25 times the current liabilities; and so on.

Table Showing Accumulation of Working Capital Ratio

	December 31,		
	1959	1958	1957
Cash	.750	.375	.125
Receivables	1.250	.625	.375
Finished goods	1.625	1.125	.750
Goods in process	1.875	1.875	1.250
Materials	2.000	2.000	2.000

Following is a similar tabulation for The Osborne Company.

THE OSBORNE COMPANY
Table Showing Accumulation of Working Capital Ratio
December 31, 1959, 1958, and 1957

	December 31,		
	1959	1958	1957
Cash	.18	.12	.06
Receivables—less allowance	2.11	1.28	1.59
Finished goods	2.52	1.53	1.81
Goods in process	2.76	1.68	1.91
Materials	3.03	1.89	2.06
Supplies	3.08	1.92	2.09
Unexpired insurance	3.14	1.96	2.12

Working capital turnover. The adequacy of the working capital is also dependent upon the frequency with which the current assets are converted. To determine how rapidly the working capital moves, some analysts compute a so-called "working capital turnover," by dividing the sales for the period by the average working capital used during the period.

THE OSBORNE COMPANY
Statement of Working Capital Turnover
Years Ended December 31, 1959, 1958, and 1957

	1959	1958	1957
Net current assets:			
End of year........................	$264,780	$162,530	$190,900
Beginning of year....................	162,530	190,900	197,395
Average.............................	213,655	176,715	194,148
Net sales for the year...................	969,065	834,880	911,005
Working capital turnovers................	4.54	4.72	4.69

Criticism of working capital turnover. In the authors' opinion, the working capital turnover is of practically no significance.

A turnover is supposed to be a measure of movement. It should indicate *how many times* something happened during a period. And an increase in the turnover should indicate an improvement. But an increase in the turnover may be caused by an increase in the current liabilities, which is not an improvement. To illustrate, let us assume the following:

		1959	1958
Sales.......................................	(a)	$500,000	$500,000
Working capital:			
Current assets..............................	(b)	$100,000	$100,000
Current liabilities..........................	(c)	60,000	50,000
Working capital............................	(d)	$ 40,000	$ 50,000
Working capital ratio (b ÷ c)...................		1.67	2
Working capital turnover (a ÷ d)..............		12.5	10

If the increase in the turnover from 10 to 12.5 is considered an indication of improvement, the conclusion is false. The increase in turnover was caused wholly by an increase in current liabilities, which was not an improvement. A much more meaningful analysis can be made by computing two ratios:

(a) The *number* of turnovers based on cost of sales and expenses, which is a measure of the use of the total current assets.

(b) The *rate of income* per turnover of total current assets, which is a measure of the profitability with which the current assets were used.

Let us assume the following facts relative to the cost of sales and expenses and the net income:

	1959	1958
Sales.......................................	$500,000	$500,000
Cost of sales and expenses......................	480,000	450,000
Net income.................................	$ 20,000	$ 50,000

Frequency of Current Asset Turnover

		1959	1958
Cost of sales and expenses....................	(a)	$480,000	$450,000
Total current assets.........................	(b)	100,000	100,000
Number of current asset turnovers (a ÷ b).......	(c)	4.8	4.5

Rate of Net Income Per Current Asset Turnover

		1959	1958
Net income.................................	(d)	$ 20,000	$ 50,000
Ratio of net income to total current assets (d ÷ b).	(e)	20.00%	50.00%
Rate of net income per turnover of total current assets (e ÷ c)...............................		4.17%	11.11%

We now have some really significant information. Instead of assuming that the increase in the working capital turnover from 10 to 12.5 (see page 476) represented an improvement, which was a false conclusion, we now know that the working capital ratio decreased from 2 to 1.67; the current assets were turned somewhat more frequently—4.8 times instead of 4.5 times; and the turnovers were less profitable—a drop from 11.11% to 4.17%.

Number and profitability of current asset turnovers. The desirability of using the procedures recommended in the preceding section instead of computing a working capital turnover is further indicated by the following illustration, based on data of The Osborne Company presented below:

		Year Ended December 31,		
		1959	1958	1957
Net sales...........................	(a)	$969,065	$834,880	$911,005
Cost of sales and expenses............	(b)	932,275	793,640	884,540
Net income.........................	(c)	$ 36,790	$ 41,240	$ 26,465
Current assets:				
Beginning of year...................	(d)	$331,560	$360,600	$383,705
End of year........................	(e)	388,430	331,560	360,600
Average............................	(f)	$359,995	$346,080	$372,153
Current liabilities:				
Beginning of year...................	(g)	$169,030	$169,700	$186,310
End of year........................	(h)	123,650	169,030	169,700
Average............................	(i)	$146,340	$169,365	$178,005
Working capital:				
Beginning of year (d − g)...........	(j)	$162,530	$190,900	$197,395
End of year (e − h)................	(k)	264,780	162,530	190,900
Average............................	(l)	$213,655	$176,715	$194,148

The following computations make use of yearly averages of current assets, current liabilities, and working capital.

If we were to compute the working capital turnover by using sales and average working capital, thus:

	1959	1958	1957
Working capital turnover (a ÷ l)...............	4.54	4.72	4.69

it would look as though things were worse, because the turnover decreased in 1959. But if we make the following computations:

		1959	1958	1957
Turnover of average total current assets (using cost of sales and expenses instead of sales, and using average total current assets instead of average working capital) (b ÷ f)	(m)	2.59	2.29	2.38
Ratio of net income to average total current assets (c ÷ f)	(n)	10.22%	11.92%	7.11%
Rate of net income per turnover of average total current assets (n ÷ m)		3.95%	5.21%	2.99%

we see a different picture. The turnover decreased in 1958, but this decrease was more than offset in 1959. The ratios indicating profitability increased in 1958; although they dropped off in 1959, they were still much higher than in 1957.

A slight theoretical objection can be made to the foregoing computation of current asset turnover. When we divide the cost of sales and expenses by the average current assets, we are attempting to obtain a ratio which will be indicative of the number of times the average current assets were used in the payment of costs and expenses. But the costs and expenses included depreciation charges, which did not involve the use of current assets. This theoretical objection usually is of such slight practical importance that it can be ignored.

Turnovers of various current assets. The foregoing computations determine the frequency with which the total current assets are turned during a period. Further information can be obtained by determining the turnovers of materials, finished goods, and receivables.

Although the time required for these various operations cannot be determined with absolute accuracy from data furnished by the periodical statements (the statement of cost of goods manufactured and sold, the income statement, and the balance sheet), the methods indicated by the following illustrations are frequently used. The data are those of The Osborne Company.

Material turnovers. The material turnovers are computed as follows:

		1959	1958	1957
Cost of materials used (per statement of cost of goods manufactured and sold)	(a)	$279,620	$185,490	$193,790
Material inventories:				
Beginning of year		$ 37,050	$ 25,260	$ 42,750
End of year		33,430	37,050	25,260
Average	(b)	$ 35,240	$ 31,155	$ 34,005
Number of material turnovers (a ÷ b)	(c)	7.93	5.95	5.70
Days per turnover (365 ÷ c)		46	61	64

This computation assumes a steady flow of production through the year and no great fluctuations in the inventories during the year. If these conditions do not exist, the turnovers and turnover periods are misstated.

Finished goods turnovers. The following computations also are based on assumptions of uniformity; it is assumed that the cost of sales and the inventories did not fluctuate greatly during the year.

		1959	1958	1957
Cost of goods sold (per income statement)	(a)	$667,940	$553,845	$612,455
Finished goods inventories:				
Beginning of year....................		$ 42,300	$ 37,150	$ 49,390
End of year........................		50,710	42,300	37,150
Average..........................	(b)	$ 46,505	$ 39,725	$ 43,270
Finished goods turnovers (a ÷ b).......	(c)	14.36	13.94	14.15
Days per turnover (365 ÷ c)...........		25	26	26

Trade receivables conversion periods. Assuming an even flow of sales and a uniformity of collectibility during the year, the approximate time required for the collection of receivables may be computed as follows:

		1959	1958	1957
Net sales..........................	(a)	$969,065	$834,880	$911,005
Trade receivables at end of year........	(b)	249,470	210,445	289,335
Per cent of year's sales uncollected at end of year (b ÷ a).....................	(c)	25.74%	25.21%	31.76%
Average number of days' sales uncollected (365 × c)...................		94	92	116

Even though sales and collections may be uniform throughout the year, the average number of days' charge sales uncollected will be misstated if there are large amounts of cash sales, or if a considerable number of the customers pay their accounts within a short discount period.

The foregoing computation should not be understood to mean that at the end of 1959 all of the sales for the last 94 days were uncollected. The probabilities are that some sales during that period have been collected, and that some receivables remain on the books which arose from sales made more than 94 days before the end of the year.

It will be observed that the receivables at the end of the year, not the average receivables at the beginning and end of the year, are used in this computation. The receivables at the beginning of the year have no bearing on the per cent of the year's sales uncollected at the end of the year. For a similar reason, the payables at the end of the year, not the average payables, are used in the computation on the following page.

Ratio of accounts payable to purchases. It is desirable, if possible, to determine whether the current liabilities are being paid more promptly or less promptly than in the past. Assuming an even flow of purchases and a uniformity of payment policy during the year, some light may be thrown on this question by computing the ratio of accounts payable to purchases; an increase in the ratio indicates that a larger percentage of the accounts payable remains unpaid than in the past, and a decrease in the ratio indicates that a smaller percentage remains unpaid.

	1959	1958	1957
Accounts payable—end of year............	$ 58,215	$ 53,350	$ 64,210
Net purchases—Materials.................	276,000	197,280	176,300
Ratio of accounts payable to purchases.....	.21	.27	.36

If notes payable and bank loans appear in the balance sheet, the ratio of accounts payable to purchases is not very significant because decreases in the accounts payable may be offset by increases in notes payable and bank loans, and vice versa. Nor is it of great value to determine the ratio of the total accounts payable, notes, and bank loans to purchases, since the notes and loans may have been incurred for the payment of other costs.

The annual cycle. When turnovers, ratios, and per cents are computed by use of the data shown by annual statements, the results obtained can be relied upon only if production, sales, and collections are carried on uniformly through the year.

But in many businesses the sales fluctuate greatly from month to month; production may also vary from month to month, either because of the fluctuations in sales or because raw materials are available at only certain periods of the year.

In all businesses subject to considerable fluctuations in seasonal sales or production, the working capital will vary from month to month. For instance, if we looked at a company's balance sheet a few months after the close of its heavy selling season and before the beginning of a heavy production season, we would probably find the inventories small, the receivables well realized, and the accounts payable and bank loans reduced to a minimum; the working capital ratio would be higher than the average because of the small amount of current liabilities. A few months later, after a heavy production season and before the next heavy selling season, we might find the inventories large in anticipation of the coming business, the receivables small because recent sales have been small, and the accounts payable and bank loans large as the result of large recent production; the working capital ratio would then be relatively low because of the abnormally large current liabilities.

Obviously, no adequate conception of the working capital position of a business can be obtained from an inspection of its balance sheet unless we know whether or not seasonal fluctuations in business cause its working capital position to vary during the year. If such variations are to be expected in the business under consideration, one should know what condition in the cycle the balance sheet depicts.

Illustration.   To illustrate the importance of using monthly statements in arriving at conclusions with respect to a company's working capital position, let us compare the results shown by an analysis of annual statements with those shown by an analysis of monthly statements. To simplify the illustration somewhat, data for a trading company will be used instead of data for a manufacturing company.

Working capital ratio.   The statement on page 482 shows the working capital of a company at the close of each of thirteen successive months. It will be noted that the working capital ratio ranges from 1.60 (December 31, 1958) to 2.81 (April 30, 1959), with variations throughout the year, and, therefore, that the 2.08 ratio at the end of the year is not indicative of conditions throughout the year.

Acid-test ratio.   The variation in the acid-test ratio is shown in the following statement.

	Cash and Receivables	Current Liabilities	Ratio
1958—December 31	$78,000	$80,000	.98
1959—January 31	68,000	68,000	1.00
February 28	59,500	53,000	1.12
March 31	51,500	38,000	1.36
April 30	44,000	26,500	1.66
May 31	45,000	27,500	1.64
June 30	55,000	35,500	1.55
July 31	56,000	40,500	1.38
August 31	66,500	61,500	1.08
September 30	61,000	58,500	1.04
October 31	82,000	77,500	1.06
November 30	99,000	80,500	1.23
December 31	89,000	67,000	1.33

Frequency of current asset conversion.   The variations in working capital ratios show the changes in the working capital position during the year. The table at the top of page 483 shows the variations in the rapidity with which the current assets are converted at different times during the year. The turnovers are computed by dividing the cost of sales and expenses for the month by the current assets at the beginning of the month; slightly more accurate results might be obtained by using the average current assets for the month.

	Current Assets				Current Liabilities			Working Capital	Working Capital Ratio
	Cash	Accounts Receivable	Inventories	Total	Accounts Payable	Bank Loans	Total		
	$13,000	$65,000	$50,000	$128,000	$60,000	$20,000	$80,000	$48,000	
1958—December 31	13,000	65,000	50,000	128,000	60,000	20,000	80,000	48,000	1.60
1959—									
January 31	15,000	53,000	52,000	120,000	48,000	20,000	68,000	52,000	1.76
February 28	18,500	41,000	46,000	105,500	33,000	20,000	53,000	52,500	1.99
March 31	18,500	33,000	38,500	90,000	28,000	10,000	38,000	52,000	2.37
April 30	18,000	26,000	30,500	74,500	26,500	—	26,500	48,000	2.81
May 31	24,000	21,000	27,000	72,000	27,500	—	27,500	44,500	2.62
June 30	22,000	33,000	24,500	79,500	35,500	—	35,500	44,000	2.24
July 31	24,000	32,000	27,000	83,000	40,500	—	40,500	42,500	2.05
August 31	19,500	47,000	40,000	106,500	61,500	—	61,500	45,000	1.73
September 30	7,000	54,000	46,500	107,500	58,500	—	58,500	49,000	1.84
October 31	11,000	71,000	51,500	133,500	67,500	10,000	77,500	56,000	1.72
November 30	9,000	90,000	49,000	148,000	70,500	10,000	80,500	67,500	1.84
December 31	21,000	68,000	50,500	139,500	57,000	10,000	67,000	72,500	2.08

	Cost of Sales and Expenses	Current Assets Beginning of Month	Turnover for Month	Working Capital Ratio Beginning of Month
January.................	$37,000	$128,000	.29	1.60
February................	29,500	120,000	.25	1.76
March..................	25,500	105,500	.24	1.99
April...................	21,500	90,000	.24	2.37
May....................	18,500	74,500	.25	2.81
June...................	25,500	72,000	.35	2.62
July....................	26,500	79,500	.33	2.24
August.................	37,500	83,000	.45	2.05
September..............	41,000	106,500	.38	1.73
October................	53,000	107,500	.49	1.84
November..............	63,500	133,500	.48	1.72
December..............	45,000	148,000	.30	1.84

Merchandise turnover. If the merchandise turnover is computed by using the average of the two December 31 inventories, the computation will be as follows:

Inventory, December 31, 1958................................ $50,000

Inventory, December 31, 1959............................. 50,500

Average inventory... $50,250

$315,000 (cost of goods sold) ÷ $50,250 = 6.3 turnovers, which is at the average rate of approximately one-half of one turnover per month.

The turnover obtained by this computation is misleading because the December 31 inventories are larger than the average inventories carried during the year. The average of the thirteen inventories shown on page 482 is $41,000. On the basis of this average inventory, the turnover is computed thus:

$315,000 ÷ $41,000 = 7.68, which is at the average rate of .64 of one turnover per month.

But the rate of turnover varies radically during the year; interesting information with respect to this variation is obtained from the following statement:

	Inventory at Beginning	Cost of Sales	Fraction Sold
January....................................	$50,000	$28,000	.56
February...................................	52,000	21,000	.40
March......................................	46,000	17,500	.38
April.......................................	38,500	14,000	.36
May..	30,500	10,500	.34
June..	27,000	17,500	.65
July..	24,500	17,500	.71
August.....................................	27,000	28,000	1.04
September..................................	40,000	31,500	.79
October....................................	46,500	42,000	.90
November..................................	51,500	52,500	1.02
December..................................	49,000	35,000	.71

An analysis of this kind may raise such pertinent questions as the following: If an inventory of $27,000 at the beginning of August was adequate to provide for sales, during that month, of goods which cost $28,000, was an inventory of $50,000 at the beginning of January necessary to provide for sales, during that month, of goods which cost the same amount ($28,000)?

Age of accounts receivable. If we estimate the average age of the receivables by a computation involving the sales for the year and the receivables at the end of the year, thus:

$68,000 (accounts receivable) ÷ $450,000 (sales) = 15.1% (per cent of year's sales uncollected)
365 × 15.1% = 55 (number of days' sales uncollected)

we obtain a misleading result, because the $68,000 balance of accounts receivable at the end of the year is larger than the average balance carried during the year. More meaningful data can be obtained by a computation similar to the following:

	Sales for Month	Receivables at End of Month	Ratio of Receivables to Month's Sales	Days' Sales Un-collected
January	$40,000	$53,000	133%	40
February	30,000	41,000	137	41
March	25,000	33,000	132	40
April	20,000	26,000	130	39
May	15,000	21,000	140	42
June	25,000	33,000	132	40
July	25,000	32,000	128	38
August	40,000	47,000	118	35
September	45,000	54,000	120	36
October	60,000	71,000	118	35
November	75,000	90,000	120	36
December	50,000	68,000	136	41

The figures in the Days' Sales Uncollected column are still slightly misleading, owing to the wide variation in monthly sales. For instance, note the drop in sales from November to December. The large November sales affect the $68,000 balance of receivables at the end of December; as this balance is divided by the December sales only, the decrease in December sales probably accounts to a great extent for the increase in the ratio from 120% to 136% and the increase in the days from 36 to 41. Nevertheless, the figures in the Days' Sales Uncollected column are far more meaningful than the 55 days shown by the computation using the year's sales and the receivables at the end of the year.

The natural business year. Companies whose operations and current position are subject to major fluctuations through the year may advantageously adopt a fiscal year ending on a date immediately subsequent to the low operating period, when the inventories, the receivables, and the payables are reduced to their minimum and the working capital ratio is therefore high.

The presentation in the natural-year-end balance sheet of a favorable working capital position is not the only advantage. The inventory can be more easily taken, partly because of the reduced quantity and partly because in a slack operating period there is less interference with operating activities and more employees are available for the work. Also, the valuation of the inventories and the receivables, which are important assets from a current credit standpoint, necessarily involves the making of estimates, and it is desirable that such estimates apply to the smallest amounts carried at any time during the year.

Questionnaire Grouping of Ratios

We may facilitate the interpretation of ratios by assembling them as answers to a questionnaire. When this is done, all ratios should be computed in such a manner that increases in the ratios will be indicative of improvements. The accomplishment of this result may require some modification of the procedures already explained; such a modification is discussed in a note following the tabulation. The ratios are those of The Osborne Company; the numbers in parentheses indicate the pages on which the computations of the ratios are shown.

	1959	1958	1957	(Page)
Is the working capital position improving?				
Working capital ratio—end of year...	3.14	1.96	2.12	472
Acid-test ratio.....................	2.11	1.28	1.59	473
Current asset turnovers.............	2.59	2.29	2.38	478
Material turnovers.................	7.93	5.95	5.70	478
Finished goods turnovers...........	14.36	13.94	14.15	479
Ratio of net sales to gross receivables (See note on following page.)	3.88	3.97	3.15	
Is the stockholders' equity increasing?				
Ratio of stockholders' equity to total debt............................	1.86	1.35	1.26	462
Book value per share of common stock	$115.77	$155.38	$149.66	466
Is the security for the long-term liabilities increasing?				
Ratio of security to long-term liabilities	2.61	2.76	2.35	463
Is there any tendency toward overinvestment in fixed assets?				
Ratio of stockholders' equity to fixed assets less depreciation...........	1.30	1.04	1.04	464
Ratio of net sales to fixed assets less depreciation....................	2.48	2.01	2.15	465
Are the earnings increasing?				
Per cent of net income to stockholders' equity.........................	7.23%	9.57%	6.02%	467
Net income per share of common stock	$ 12.39	$ 15.72	$ 5.53	468
Per cent of net income to sales.......	3.80%	4.94%	2.91%	450
Per cent of gross profit to sales......	31.07%	33.66%	32.77%	450

Note. On page 479 the relative condition of the receivables was determined by computing the following per cents and turnover periods:

	1959	1958	1957
Per cent of year's sales uncollected—at end of year......	25.74%	25.21%	31.76%
Average number of days' sales uncollected..............	94	92	116

Improvements are indicated immediately above by decreases, as it is better to have only 25.21% of the year's sales uncollected than to have 31.76% uncollected. These per cents were obtained by dividing the receivables by the sales. The ratios (3.88, 3.97, and 3.15) shown in the tabulation on page 485 were obtained by dividing the sales by the receivables, in order that increases in the ratios would indicate improved conditions.

··

CHAPTER TWENTY-THREE

Analysis of Operations

Statement Accounting for Variation in Net Income

Causes of variation in net income. The causes of the variation in net income from one period to another may be summarized as follows:

(1) Change in gross profit on sales, due to:
  (a) Change in sales.
  (b) Change in cost of goods sold.
(2) Changes in expenses.
(3) Changes in any other credits and charges to income, such as miscellaneous income, expenses, gains, and losses.

The statement accounting for the variation in net income shows how the net income was affected by these various changes. The statement may be prepared in a very simple manner by the mere assembling of the data shown by a condensed income statement in such a manner as to group the elements which tended to increase the net income and those which tended to decrease the net income; or it may be amplified by inclusion of analytical per cents and comparative per cents or ratios.

Basis of illustrations. The condensed comparative income statement of Company *A* on the following page is used for purposes of illustration.

COMPANY A
Condensed Comparative Income Statement
For the Years Ended December 31, 1959 and 1958

	Year Ended December 31,		Increase Decrease*
	1959	1958	
Net sales..............................	$253,000	$200,000	$53,000
Cost of goods sold......................	181,125	150,000	31,125
Gross profit on sales....................	$ 71,875	$ 50,000	$21,875
Operating expenses:			
Selling expenses......................	$ 25,000	$ 20,000	$ 5,000
General expenses.....................	12,000	10,000	2,000
Total operating expenses............	$ 37,000	$ 30,000	$ 7,000
Operating income......................	$ 34,875	$ 20,000	$14,875
Net financial expense..................	4,000	5,000	1,000*
Net income...........................	$ 30,875	$ 15,000	$15,875

First illustration. The following statement rearranges the income statement figures into two groups: One showing the items tending to increase the net income, and another showing the items tending to decrease the net income.

As there are no per cents or ratios in the statement, it is difficult to see whether the increase in the cost of goods sold and the increases in selling and general expenses were proportionate to the increase in sales.

COMPANY A
Statement Accounting for Increase in Net Income
Years 1959 and 1958

Elements tending to increase net income:
  (1) Increase in gross profit on sales, caused by:
      (a) Increase in net sales:

1959................................	$253,000		
1958................................	200,000	$53,000	

      (b) Less increase in cost of goods sold:

1959................................	$181,125		
1958................................	150,000	31,125	
Resulting increase in gross profit........................		$21,875	

  (2) Decrease in net financial expense:

1958....................................	$ 5,000		
1959....................................	4,000	1,000	
Total elements tending to increase net income....................			$22,875

Elements tending to decrease net income:
  (1) Increase in selling expenses:

1959....................................	$ 25,000		
1958....................................	20,000	$ 5,000	

  (2) Increase in general expenses:

1959....................................	$ 12,000		
1958....................................	10,000	2,000	
Total elements tending to decrease net income....................			7,000

Resulting increase in net income:

1959....................................	$ 30,875		
1958....................................	15,000		$15,875

Second illustration.   The statement can be made more informative by the addition of a column showing per cents of various items to net sales, and a column showing the ratio of each 1959 amount to the corresponding 1958 amount. Such a statement is illustrated below:

COMPANY A

Statement Accounting for Increase in Net Income

Years 1959 and 1958

	Per Cent of Net Sales	Amounts	Ratio 1959 to 1958
Elements tending to increase net income:			
(1) Increase in gross profit on sales, caused by:			
(a) Increase in net sales:			
1959........................		$253,000	1.27
1958........................		200,000	
Increase....................		$53,000	
(b) Less increase in cost of goods sold:			
1959........................	71.59%	$181,125	1.21
1958........................	75.00	150,000	
Increase in amount............		31,125	
Decrease in per cent of sales....	3.41%		
Resulting increase in gross profit:			
1959........................	28.41%	$ 71,875	1.44
1958........................	25.00	50,000	
Increase....................	3.41%	$21,875	
(2) Decrease in net financial expense:			
1958.............................	2.50%	$ 5,000	
1959.............................	1.58	4,000	.80
Decrease.........................	.92%	1,000	
Total elements tending to increase net income............................		$22,875	
Elements tending to decrease net income:			
(1) Increase in selling expenses:			
1959.............................	9.88%	$ 25,000	1.25
1958.............................	10.00	20,000	
Increase in amount...............		$ 5,000	
Decrease in per cent of sales.........	.12%		
(2) Increase in general expenses:			
1959.............................	4.74%	$ 12,000	1.20
1958.............................	5.00	10,000	
Increase in amount...............		2,000	
Decrease in per cent of sales..........	.26%		
Total elements tending to decrease net income............................		$ 7,000	
Resulting increase in net income:			
1959.......................................	12.20%	$ 30,875	2.06
1958.......................................	7.50	15,000	
Increase...................................	4.70%	$15,875	

Illustration of decrease in net income. The following statement accounts for a decrease in net income.

THE Z COMPANY
Statement Accounting for Decrease in Net Income
Years 1959 and 1958

	Per Cent of Net Sales	Amounts	Ratio 1959 to 1958
Elements tending to decrease net income:			
(1) Decrease in gross profit on sales:			
(a) Decrease in net sales:			
1958............................		$600,000	
1959............................		513,000	.86
Decrease......................		$87,000	
(b) Decrease in cost of goods sold:			
1958...........................	75.00%	$450,000	
1959...........................	77.37	396,900	.88
Decrease in amount............		53,100	
Increase in per cent of sales.....	2.37%		
Resulting decrease in gross profit:			
1958...........................	25.00%	$150,000	
1959...........................	22.63	116,100	.77
Decrease......................	2.37%	$33,900	
Elements tending to increase net income:			
(1) Decrease in selling expenses:			
1958.............................	8.71%	$ 52,280	
1959.............................	9.11	46,735	.89
Decrease in amount................		$ 5,545	
Increase in per cent of sales...........	.40%		
(2) Decrease in general expenses:			
1958.............................	8.99%	$ 53,915	
1959.............................	8.72	44,720	.83
Decrease.........................	.27%	9,195	
(3) Decrease in net financial expense:			
1958.............................	.92%	$ 5,540	
1959.............................	.83	4,235	.76
Decrease.........................	.09%	1,305	
Total elements tending to increase net income...........................		$16,045	
Resulting decrease in net income:			
1958...............................	6.38%	$ 38,265	
1959...............................	3.98	20,410	.53
Decrease...........................	2.40%	$17,855	

This statement shows that the net sales decreased (as shown by the Ratio column) 14% and the cost of goods sold decreased only 12%; since the rate of decrease in the cost of goods sold was less than the rate of decrease in sales, the gross profit rate decreased—from 25.00% to 22.63%.

All of the expenses decreased. The selling expenses decreased only 11% as compared with the 14% decrease in sales; consequently, the ratio of selling expenses to sales increased from 8.71% to 9.11%. The general expenses decreased 17% as compared with the 14% decrease in sales; therefore, the ratio of general expenses to sales decreased from 8.99% to 8.72%.

Accounting for Variation in Gross Profit

The foregoing statements are interesting as far as they go, but they do not go very far in showing the causes of the change in gross profit. The statement on page 489, for instance, shows that the $21,875 increase in gross profit was caused by a $53,000 increase in sales which was partially offset by a $31,125 increase in the cost of goods sold. But this does not get to the root of the matter. It does not answer the following questions:

What caused the increase in sales?
    How much was caused by a change in the quantity volume of goods sold?
    How much was caused by a change in selling prices?
What caused the increase in the cost of goods sold?
    How much was caused by a change in the quantity volume of goods sold?
    How much was caused by a change in unit costs?

Analytical procedures for determining the effects of changes in quantity volume, in selling prices, and in unit costs are discussed in the following sections.

Procedures using detailed statistics—First illustration. The comparative income statement of Company *A* on page 488 shows the following information:

	1959	1958	Increase
Net sales	$253,000	$200,000	$53,000
Cost of goods sold	181,125	150,000	31,125
Gross profit on sales	$ 71,875	$ 50,000	$21,875

Assume that we have the following additional information:

	1959	1958	Increase
Units sold	1,150	1,000	150
Selling price per unit	$220.00	$200.00	$20.00
Unit cost	157.50	150.00	7.50

Causes of the $53,000 increase in sales. With the statistics presented above, we can show the causes of the increase in sales in the manner illustrated on the following page.

Quantity factor:
  Amount by which sales would have been increased by the
  increase in volume if there had been no increase in sales
  price:

    1958 unit selling price............................ $200
    Multiply by increase in quantity.................. 150 $30,000

Price factor:
  Amount by which sales would have been increased by the
  increase in sale price if there had been no increase in
  volume:

    Increase in sale price............................ $ 20
    Multiply by 1958 quantity volume................. 1,000   20,000

Quantity-price factor:
  Increase in selling price applied to increase in volume:

    $20 × 150..   3,000

Total increase in sales....................................... $53,000

The $30,000 was the result of volume change only, but it was
not the total effect of the volume change; the $20,000 was the
result of price change only, but it was not the total effect of the
price change; the $3,000 increase was caused partly by the increase
in volume and partly by the increase in selling price.

This analysis can perhaps be better explained by use of the
following graph, which consists basically of a horizontal axis along

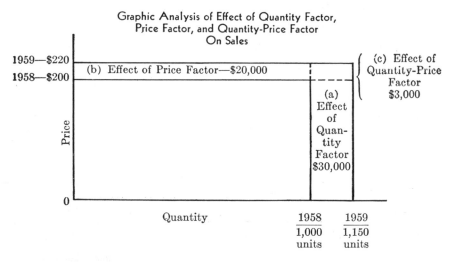

Graphic Analysis of Effect of Quantity Factor,
Price Factor, and Quantity-Price Factor
On Sales

which quantities are measured, and a vertical axis along which
prices are measured. The 1959 price was greater than the 1958
price, so the 1959 point on the vertical axis is higher than the 1958
point; the 1959 quantity was greater than the 1958 quantity, so the
1959 point on the horizontal axis is to the right of (further away
from zero than) the 1958 point.

By erecting lines perpendicular to both the horizontal and vertical axes at these points, we can construct two rectangles, one superimposed on the other. The larger rectangle represents the 1959 sales (price times quantity); the smaller rectangle represents the 1958 sales; and the L-shaped margin represents the difference between the two years' sales.

Further analysis discloses that the L-shaped margin (which, as stated above, represents the $53,000 increase in sales) consists of three rectangles. Rectangle (a) obviously represents the effect which the quantity increase would have had on sales *had there been no change in the price;* rectangle (b) represents the effect which the price increase would have had on sales *had there been no change in the quantity;* and the small rectangle (c) in the corner of the L represents the additional effect on sales caused by the simultaneous increase in both price and quantity.

Causes of the $31,125 increase in cost of goods sold. The causes of this increase are determined as follows:

Quantity factor:
    Amount by which the cost of goods sold would have been
      increased by the increase in volume if there had been no
      increase in unit costs:

1958 unit cost..................................	$ 150	
Multiply by increase in quantity..................	150	$22,500

Cost factor:
    Amount by which the cost of goods sold would have been
      increased by the increase in unit cost if there had been
      no increase in volume:

Increase in unit cost.............................	$7.50	
Multiply by 1958 quantity volume................	1,000	7,500

Quantity-cost factor:
    Increase in unit cost applied to increase in volume:

$7.50 × 150..	1,125

Total increase in cost of goods sold............................	$31,125

The $22,500 was the result of volume change only, but it was not the total effect of the volume change; the $7,500 was the result of cost change only, but it was not the total effect of the cost change; the $1,125 increase was due partly to the increase in volume and partly to the increase in unit cost.

The analyses of the $53,000 increase in sales (page 492) and the $31,125 increase in cost of goods sold (above) may be combined in the manner shown on the following page.

COMPANY A
Statement Accounting for Changes in Sales, Cost of Goods Sold, and Gross Profit
For the Years Ended December 31, 1959 and 1958

	Sales	Cost of Sales	Gross Profit
Amounts:			
1959	$253,000	$181,125	$71,875
1958	200,000	150,000	50,000
Increases	$ 53,000	$ 31,125	$21,875
Increases (decreases*) due to:			
Quantity factor—Amounts by which increased volume would have affected sales and cost of sales if there had been no changes in unit price and cost:			
150 (increase in units sold) multiplied by:			
$200 (1958 sale price)	$ 30,000		$30,000
$150 (1958 unit cost)		$ 22,500	22,500*
Price factor—Amount by which change in unit price would have affected sales if there had been no change in quantity:			
$20 (increase in sale price) multiplied by 1,000 (units sold in 1958)	20,000		20,000
Cost factor—Amount by which change in unit cost would have affected cost of sales if there had been no change in quantity:			
$7.50 (increase in unit cost) multiplied by 1,000 (units sold in 1958)		7,500	7,500*
Quantity-price factor:			
$20 (increase in sale price) multiplied by 150 (increase in units sold)	3,000		3,000
Quantity-cost factor:			
$7.50 (increase in unit cost) multiplied by 150 (increase in units sold)		1,125	1,125*
Totals	$ 53,000	$ 31,125	$21,875

Since it may be presumed that the statement would be prepared for the use of management personnel who would know the nature of the various factors, the statement may be condensed as follows:

COMPANY A
Statement Accounting for Changes in Sales, Cost of Goods Sold, and Gross Profit
For the Years Ended December 31, 1959 and 1958

	Sales	Cost of Sales	Gross Profit
Amounts:			
1959	$253,000	$181,125	$71,875
1958	200,000	150,000	50,000
Increases	$ 53,000	$ 31,125	$21,875
Increases (decreases*) caused by:			
Quantity factor	$ 30,000	$ 22,500	$ 7,500
Price factor	20,000		20,000
Cost factor		7,500	7,500*
Quantity-price factor	3,000		3,000
Quantity-cost factor		1,125	1,125*
Totals	$ 53,000	$ 31,125	$21,875

Procedure using detailed statistics—Second illustration. In the preceding illustration, there was an increase in volume, in selling prices, and in unit costs. In this illustration there is a decrease in volume, with increases in selling prices and costs. The illustration shows the opposing effects of increases and decreases. Assume the following facts:

	1959	1958	Increase Decrease*
Net sales.........................	$183,600	$200,000	$16,400*
Cost of goods sold..................	140,400	150,000	9,600*
Gross profit on sales...............	$ 43,200	$ 50,000	$ 6,800*
Units sold.........................	900	1,000	100*
Selling price per unit.............	$ 204	$ 200	$ 4
Cost per unit.....................	156	150	6

Using the foregoing data, we can show the causes of the decreases in sales, cost of goods sold, and gross profit as follows:

COMPANY B
Statement Accounting for Changes in Sales,
Cost of Goods Sold, and Gross Profit
For the Years Ended December 31, 1959 and 1958

	Sales	Cost of Sales	Gross Profit
Amounts:			
1959...	$183,600	$140,400	$43,200
1958...	200,000	150,000	50,000
Decreases*...............................	$ 16,400*	$ 9,600*	$ 6,800*
Increases (decreases*) due to:			
Quantity factor—Amounts by which decreased volume would have affected sales and cost of sales if there had been no change in unit sale price or cost:			
100* (decrease in units sold) multiplied by:			
$200 (1958 sale price)....................	$ 20,000*		$20,000*
$150 (1958 unit cost)....................		$ 15,000*	15,000
Price factor—Amount by which change in unit price would have affected sales if there had been no change in quantity:			
$4 (increase in unit sale price) multiplied by 1,000 (units sold in 1958)................	4,000		4,000
Cost factor—Amount by which change in unit cost would have affected cost of sales if there had been no change in quantity:			
$6 (increase in unit cost) multiplied by 1,000 (units sold in 1958).....................		6,000	6,000*
Quantity-price factor:			
$4 (increase in sale price) multiplied by 100* (decrease in units sold)...................	400*		400*
Quantity-cost factor:			
$6 (increase in unit cost) multiplied by 100* (decrease in units sold)....................		600*	600
Totals.......................................	$ 16,400*	$ 9,600*	$ 6,800*

A condensed statement may be prepared as follows:

COMPANY B
Statement Accounting for Changes in Sales,
Cost of Goods Sold, and Gross Profit
For the Years Ended December 31, 1959 and 1958

	Sales	Cost of Sales	Gross Profit
Amounts:			
1959............................	$183,600	$140,400	$43,200
1958............................	200,000	150,000	50,000
Decreases*......................	$ 16,400*	$ 9,600*	$ 6,800*
Increases (decreases*) caused by:			
Quantity factor....................	$ 20,000*	$ 15,000*	$ 5,000*
Price factor.......................	4,000		4,000
Cost factor........................		6,000	6,000*
Quantity-price factor...............	400*		400*
Quantity-cost factor................		600*	600
Totals.............................	$ 16,400*	$ 9,600*	$ 6,800*

Procedure using quantity records. The preceding illustrations made use of detailed statistics relative to quantity volume of sales, unit selling prices, and unit costs. Such data can be developed if there are good inventory and purchase or production records stated in quantities. To illustrate, in the preceding Company *A* illustration, it was assumed that we had the following information:

		1959	1958
Sales..................................	(a)	$253,000.00	$200,000.00
Cost of goods sold......................	(b)	181,125.00	150,000.00
Unit selling price.......................	(c)	220.00	200.00
Unit cost..............................	(d)	157.50	150.00
Units sold.............................	(e)	1,150	1,000

Let us now assume that we are given only items (a) and (b), but that (using records of inventories and of purchases or production) we can determine the quantities sold, thus:

		Units 1959	1958
Inventory at beginning of year........................		750	675
Purchased or produced.........................		1,300	1,075
Total..		2,050	1,750
Inventory at end of year.............................		900	750
Sold..	(u)	1,150	1,000

We can then determine average unit selling prices and costs.

		1959	1958
Sales:			
Total.................................	(a)	$253,000.00	$200,000.00
Price per unit (a ÷ u)..................		220.00	200.00
Cost of goods sold:			
Total.................................	(b)	181,125.00	150,000.00
Cost per unit (b ÷ u)..................		157.50	150.00

The analysis to disclose the effects of changes in quantities, selling prices, and unit costs can then proceed in the manner illustrated on pages 491 to 494.

Procedures using per cents. If, in addition to the dollar amounts of sales and cost of goods sold, we know the per cent of change in any one of the three factors—quantity, selling price, and unit cost of goods sold—we can compute the per cent of change in each of the other two factors. To illustrate, we shall use the following data, which appeared in the preceding Company *A* illustration:

	1959	1958	Increase
Sales	$253,000	$200,000	$53,000
Cost of goods sold	181,125	150,000	31,125
Gross profit	$ 71,875	$ 50,000	$21,875

In each of the following three cases it is assumed that we know *one* of the three ratios of change, and we shall compute the other two ratios.

		Sales		Cost of Goods Sold
1958	(a)	$200,000	(A)	$150,000
1959	(b)	253,000	(B)	181,125

CASE 1—Volume increase known—15%:
　Price ratio:
　　1959 volume on 1958 sales price basis (a × 1.15).. (c) $230,000
　　Price ratio (b ÷ c)............................ 1.10
　Cost ratio:
　　1959 volume on 1958 cost basis (A × 1.15)....... (C) $172,500
　　Cost ratio (B ÷ C)............................ 1.05

CASE 2—Price increase known—10%:
　Volume ratio:
　　1959 volume on 1958 sales price basis (b ÷ 1.10).. (c) $230,000
　　Volume ratio (c ÷ a)........................... 1.15
　Cost ratio:
　　1959 volume on 1958 cost basis (A × 1.15)....... (C) $172,500
　　Cost ratio (B ÷ C)............................ 1.05

CASE 3—Cost increase known—5%:
　Volume ratio:
　　1959 volume on 1958 cost basis (B ÷ 1.05)....... (C) $172,500
　　Volume ratio (C ÷ A)........................... 1.15
　Price ratio:
　　1959 volume on 1958 price basis (a × 1.15)....... (c) $230,000
　　Price ratio (b ÷ c)............................ 1.10

Statements. When the per cents of change in volume, price, and cost are known, we can determine the effects of the changes in quantity volume, sales price, and unit cost in the manner shown on the following page.

COMPANY A
Statement Accounting for Changes in Sales, Cost of Goods Sold, and Gross Profit
For the Years Ended December 31, 1959 and 1958

	Sales	Cost of Sales	Gross Profit
Amounts:			
1959..	$253,000	$181,125	$71,875
1958..	200,000	150,000	50,000
Increases..................................	$ 53,000	$ 31,125	$21,875
Increases (decreases*) due to:			
Quantity factor—Amounts by which increased volume would have affected sales and cost of sales if there had been no change in unit price or cost:			
15% of $200,000 (1958 sales)...............	$ 30,000		$30,000
15% of $150,000 (1958 cost of sales).........		$ 22,500	22,500*
Price factor—Amount by which change in unit price would have affected sales if there had been no change in quantity:			
10% of $200,000 (1958 sales)...............	20,000		20,000
Cost factor—Amount by which change in unit cost would have affected cost of sales if there had been no change in quantity:			
5% of $150,000 (1958 cost of sales)...........		7,500	7,500*
Quantity-price factor:			
15% (quantity increase) × 10% (price increase) of $200,000 (1958 sales)....................	3,000		3,000
Quantity-cost factor:			
15% (quantity increase) × 5% (cost increase) of $150,000 (1958 cost of sales)...............		1,125	1,125*
Totals....................................	$ 53,000	$ 31,125	$21,875

The condensed statement would be the same as the one on page 494.

Analysis by commodities. In the Company *A* illustration on page 494 and the Company *B* illustration on page 495, it was assumed that each company dealt in one commodity. To show how information relative to changes in sales, cost of goods sold, and gross profit can be assembled if a company deals in more than one commodity, let us assume that the data relative to Company *A* apply to Commodity A, and that the data relative to Company *B* apply to Commodity B, both sold by one company. The combined data are shown below.

Data for A B Company

	Sales	Cost of Goods Sold	Gross Profit
1959:			
Commodity A......................	$253,000	$181,125	$ 71,875
Commodity B......................	183,600	140,400	43,200
Total..........................	$436,600	$321,525	$115,075

Data for A B Company (Continued)

	Sales	Cost of Goods Sold	Gross Profit
1958:			
Commodity A...	$200,000	$150,000	$ 50,000
Commodity B......................	200,000	150,000	50,000
Total...........................	$400,000	$300,000	$100,000
Increase-decrease*:			
Commodity A.....................	$ 53,000	$ 31,125	$ 21,875
Commodity B.....................	16,400*	9,600*	6,800*
Total...........................	$ 36,600	$ 21,525	$ 15,075

Using the analyses previously made for Company *A* and Company *B*, and regarding them as now applicable to Commodities A and B, respectively, we can account for the changes in sales, cost of goods sold, and gross profit by commodities and in total as follows:

A B COMPANY

Statement Accounting for Changes in Sales, Cost of Goods Sold, and Gross Profit—By Commodities and in Total

For the Years Ended December 31, 1959 and 1958

	Commodities		
	A	B	Total
Increase-decrease*:			
In sales:			
Quantity factor........................	$30,000	$20,000*	$10,000
Price factor...........................	20,000	4,000	24,000
Quantity-price factor..................	3,000	400*	2,600
Total...............................	$53,000	$16,400*	$36,600
In cost of goods sold:			
Quantity factor........................	$22,500	$15,000*	$ 7,500
Cost factor...........................	7,500	6,000	13,500
Quantity-cost factor...................	1,125	600*	525
Total...............................	$31,125	$ 9,600*	$21,525
In gross profit.........................	$21,875	$ 6,800*	$15,075

Unit Cost and Profit Statements

Statement of cost of goods manufactured and sold. If the goods in process inventories can be analyzed into their components of material, labor, and overhead, a statement can be prepared similar to the one on page 500, showing the total and the per-unit costs of goods manufactured and sold during two years.

If a company manufactures and sells only one commodity, such a statement may be prepared for the business as a whole. If several commodities are dealt in, a separate statement may be prepared for each commodity.

THE A B C COMPANY
Comparative Statement of Cost of Goods Manufactured and Sold in Total and Per Unit
For the Years Ended December 31, 1959 and 1958

	YEAR ENDED DECEMBER 31, 1959					YEAR ENDED DECEMBER 31, 1958				
	Units	Material	Direct Labor	Manufacturing Overhead	Total	Units	Material	Direct Labor	Manufacturing Overhead	Total
In process, January 1............	40	$ 800	$ 740	$ 310	$ 1,850	50	$ 1,050	$ 940	$ 360	$ 2,350
Put into process during year.	4,000					5,000				
Manufacturing costs during the year.............		108,975	149,500	61,525	320,000		140,900	176,750	67,620	385,270
Total...........	4,040	$109,775	$150,240	$61,835	$321,850	5,050	$141,950	$177,690	$67,980	$387,620
In process, December 31....	45	920	780	550	2,250	40	800	740	310	1,850
Manufactured during year..	3,995	$108,855	$149,460	$61,285	$319,600	5,010	$141,150	$176,950	$67,670	$385,770
Manufacturing cost per unit.		$ 27.25	$ 37.41	$15.34	($ 80.00)		$ 28.17	$ 35.32	$13.51	($ 77.00)
Finished goods inventory, January 1...............	900 at	$ 77.00			69,300	850 at	$ 75.00 (1957 cost)			63,750
Total...........	4,895				$388,900	5,860				$449,520
Finished goods inventory, December 31............	825 at	$ 80.00			66,000	900 at	$ 77.00			69,300
Sold...............	4,070 at	$ 79.34			$322,900	4,960 at	$ 76.66			$380,220

Note: It is assumed that the work in process inventories at the beginning and end of the year were in the same stage of completion.

To determine the unit cost of goods sold, we must take into consideration the opening and closing inventories of finished goods. For instance, in 1959,

The 3,995 units manufactured cost....	$319,600	or $80 per unit
The 900 units in the opening inventory cost.................	69,300	or $77 per unit
The 4,895 units available for sale cost..	$388,900	
The 825 units on hand at the end of the year are assumed to be part of those manufactured during the year for.......	66,000	or $80 per unit
Hence, the 4,070 units sold cost.............	$322,900	or $79.34 per unit

Income statements.   The following statements illustrate a total and per-unit income statement and expense schedule.

THE A B C COMPANY
Comparative Income Statement in Total and Per Unit Sold
For the Years Ended December 31, 1959 and 1958

	1959 Total	1959 Per Unit	1958 Total	1958 Per Unit	Increase Decrease* Per Unit
Number of units sold....		4,070		4,960	
Gross sales............	$468,050	$115.00	$620,000	$125.00	$10.00*
Less sales allowances....	5,700	1.40	6,800	1.37	.03
Net sales..............	$462,350	$113.60	$613,200	$123.63	$10.03*
Cost of goods sold.......	322,900	79.34	380,220	76.66	2.68
Gross profit on sales.....	$139,450	$ 34.26	$232,980	$ 46.97	$12.71*
Less:					
Selling expense........	$ 62,635	$ 15.39	$ 76,200	$ 15.36	$ .03
General expense......	49,785	12.23	68,750	13.86	1.63*
Total.............	$112,420	$ 27.62	$144,950	$ 29.22	$ 1.60*
Net income............	$ 27,030	$ 6.64	$ 88,030	$ 17.75	$11.11*

THE A B C COMPANY
Comparative Statement of Selling Expenses in Total and Per Unit Sold
For the Years Ended December 31, 1959 and 1958

	1959 Total	1959 Per Unit	1958 Total	1958 Per Unit	Increase Decrease* Per Unit
Number of units sold........		4,070		4,960	
Advertising................	$20,000	$ 4.92	$30,000	$ 6.05	$1.13*
Salesmen's salaries..........	25,000	6.14	25,000	5.04	1.10
Salesmen's expenses.........	9,130	2.24	10,300	2.08	.16
Freight and cartage out.	5,670	1.39	6,400	1.29	.10
Miscellaneous selling expense.	2,835	.70	4,500	.90	.20*
Total.................	$62,635	$15.39	$76,200	$15.36	$ .03

Departmental Operations

Income statement by departments. An attempt is sometimes made to prepare a statement showing the net income by departments, in the manner illustrated below.

THE TWO DEPARTMENT STORE
Income Statement
For the Year Ended December 31, 1959

	Department A	Department B	Total
Net sales.........................	$300,000	$500,000	$800,000
Cost of goods sold..................	256,500	352,800	609,300
Gross profit on sales...............	$ 43,500	$147,200	$190,700
Operating expenses:			
Selling expenses:			
Store rent......................	$ 9,600	$ 14,400	$ 24,000
Advertising.....................	6,400	9,600	16,000
Salesmen's salaries.............	24,000	28,000	52,000
Delivery expense................	6,000	10,000	16,000
Total selling expenses.........	$ 46,000	$ 62,000	$108,000
General expenses:			
Office salaries..................	$ 3,600	$ 6,000	$ 9,600
Officers' salaries...............	15,000	25,000	40,000
Insurance.......................	800	1,600	2,400
Bad debts.......................	400	1,200	1,600
Miscellaneous...................	1,800	3,000	4,800
Total general expenses.........	$ 21,600	$ 36,800	$ 58,400
Total operating expenses....	$ 67,600	$ 98,800	$166,400
Net operating income (loss*)........	$ 24,100*	$ 48,400	$ 24,300
Interest earned....................	1,950	3,250	5,200
Total..............................	$ 22,150*	$ 51,650	$ 29,500
Interest expense...................	2,400	4,000	6,400
Net income (loss*) before income tax.	$ 24,550*	$ 47,650	$ 23,100

While such a statement may have the superficial appearance of great accuracy, it usually is based on so many assumptions, estimates, and approximations that the results it shows are not worthy of absolute credence. It may be possible to determine, for each department, the sales, cost of goods sold, and certain expenses, such as salesmen's salaries if each salesman works in only one department. Also, some joint expenses may be apportioned with a reasonable degree of accuracy. For instance, store rent may be apportioned on the basis of floor space occupied, with adjustments in recognition of the relative desirability of the space; advertising may be apportioned on the basis of space, with adjustments for differences in costs of planning, layout, and artwork; and other costs may be apportionable on similarly logical bases, with reasonably accurate results. But many apportionments are arbitrarily made on the basis of sales for want of a better basis.

Significance of the departmental statement. Because the apportionments of expenses in the above statement were largely estimates, many of which were arbitrarily based on sales, complete reliance should not be placed on the amounts shown as net loss for Department A and net income for Department B.

Moreover, even if no estimates had been necessary in the apportionment of overhead expenses, the fact that Department A shows a loss should not be accepted as a conclusive reason for discontinuing it. The discontinuance of Department A would result in eliminating all of the gross profit resulting from its operations, but it would not result in eliminating all of the expenses which were charged to it. Before reaching any decision with respect to the advisability of discontinuing Department A, the management should make a study of the expenses and items of miscellaneous income for the purpose of determining the probable reductions which would result from such a discontinuance. The following statement is assumed to be the result of such a study:

Probable Reduction in Expenses and Miscellaneous Income Which Would
Result from Discontinuance of Department A

	Amounts Allocated to Department A	EFFECT OF DISCONTINUANCE OF DEPARTMENT A	
		Eliminated	Not Eliminated
Selling expenses:			
Store rent....................	$ 9,600		$ 9,600
Advertising................ ...	6,400	$ 6,400	
Salesmen's salaries............	24,000	24,000	
Delivery expense.............	6,000		6,000
Total....................	$46,000	$30,400	$15,600
General expenses:			
Office salaries................	$ 3,600		$ 3,600
Officers' salaries..............	15,000		15,000
Insurance....................	800	$ 800	
Bad debts....................	400	400	
Miscellaneous.................	1,800	600	1,200
Total....................	$21,600	$ 1,800	$19,800
Interest earned (customers' notes)	$ 1,950	$ 1,950	$ —
Interest expense................	$ 2,400	$ 2,400	$ —

The store rent charged to Department A would not be eliminated, because the entire space would have to be retained under the lease and there is no possibility of subleasing it. The advertising and salesmen's salary charges could be eliminated. The delivery equipment and driver would have to be retained to make deliveries for Department B. The office employees would be retained. The officers' salaries would not be reduced. The cost of insurance on Department A inventories would be eliminated. With the elimination of sales by Department A, its bad debt losses would disappear. It is estimated that one-third of the miscellaneous general expenses apportioned to Department A could be eliminated. The interest income was earned on notes received from customers, and the interest expense was incurred to carry inventories.

The consequences of discontinuing Department A can now be estimated, as follows:

Net income before income tax of Departments A and B..			$23,100
Net income which would be lost by discontinuing Department A:			
Income lost:			
Gross profit on sales...........................		$43,500	
Interest earned...............................		1,950	
Total income lost...........................		$45,450	
Expense reductions:			
Selling expenses.......................	$30,400		
General expenses......................	1,800		
Interest expense.......................	2,400		
Total expense reduction......................		34,600	
Net income lost..			10,850
Resulting net income before income tax.......................			$12,250

Surprising as it may at first seem, this statement shows that, although the departmental statement on page 502 shows that Department A's operations resulted in a net loss of $24,550, the elimination of that department would not cause a $24,550 increase in the net income of the business as a whole, but probably would reduce it by $10,850.

Statement showing contribution to overhead. Some accountants now prepare a statement similar to the following:

THE TWO DEPARTMENT STORE
Statement of Income and Expense
For the Year Ended December 31, 1959

	Department A	Department B	Total
Departmental income:			
Net sales..............................	$300,000	$500,000	$800,000
Cost of goods sold.........................	256,500	352,800	609,300
Gross profit on sales.......................	$ 43,500	$147,200	$190,700
Interest earned..........................	1,950	3,250	5,200
Total................................	$ 45,450	$150,450	$195,900
Direct departmental overhead—per schedule on page 505...............................	34,600	45,400	80,000
Contribution to nondepartmental overhead.....	$ 10,850	$105,050	$115,900
Deduct nondepartmental overhead—per schedule on page 505.............................			92,800
Net income before income tax...............			$ 23,100

Schedule of Expenses

	Total	DIRECT DEPARTMENTAL OVERHEAD		Non-departmental Overhead
		Department A	Department B	
Selling expenses:				
Store rent..................	$ 24,000			$24,000
Advertising...............	16,000	$ 6,400	$ 9,600	
Salesmen's salaries........	52,000	24,000	28,000	
Delivery expense..........	16,000			16,000
Total selling expenses..	$108,000	$30,400	$37,600	$40,000
General expenses:				
Office salaries.............	$ 9,600			$ 9,600
Officers' salaries...........	40,000			40,000
Insurance.................	2,400	$ 800	$ 1,600	
Bad debts.................	1,600	400	1,200	
Miscellaneous.............	4,800	600	1,000	3,200
Total general expenses.	$ 58,400	$ 1,800	$ 3,800	$52,800
Interest expense.............	$ 6,400	$ 2,400	$ 4,000	$ —
Total expenses........	$172,800	$34,600	$45,400	$92,800

It will be observed that no attempt is made to show the net income by departments. Instead, the statement shows, for each department, the income and expenses which, in the opinion of the management, would disappear if the department were discontinued. The excess represents the contribution of the department to what may be called the nondepartmental overhead, or the expenses not specifically allocable to any department.

The amounts of "direct departmental overhead" are those which the management believes would disappear following the discontinuance of either department.

Analysis of departmental gross profit. When a business consists of several departments with different gross profit rates, the gross profit of the business as a whole will depend on:

The total sales,
The distribution of sales among the departments, and
The gross profit rates of the departments;

and changes in the amount and rate of gross profit of the business as a whole will depend upon changes in these factors. Therefore, an analysis of the causes of the change in the amount and rate of gross profit of a business as a whole requires consideration of the three factors mentioned above.

Basis of illustration. Assume that the statements of a business for three years showed the facts presented on the following page.

	1959	1958	1957
Net sales...............................	$412,250	$380,600	$390,550
Cost of goods sold......................	207,662	223,166	212,675
Gross profit on sales.....................	$204,588	$157,434	$177,875
Increase (decrease*) in sales from preceding year:			
Amount.............................	$ 31,650	$ 9,950*	
Per cent............................	8.32%	2.55%*	
Increase (decrease*) in gross profit:			
Amount.............................	$ 47,154	$ 20,441*	
Per cent............................	29.95%	11.49%*	
Rate of gross profit......................	49.63%	41.36%	45.55%

How could a decrease of only $9,950 (2.55%) in sales in 1958 have caused a decrease of $20,441 (11.49%) in the gross profit? The answer is obvious: The average rate of gross profit decreased—from 45.55% in 1957 to 41.36% in 1958.

Again, how could an increase of $31,650 (8.32%) in sales in 1959 have caused an increase of $47,154 (29.95%) in gross profit? The answer is of the same nature: The average rate of gross profit increased from 41.36% in 1958 to 49.63% in 1959.

A change in the average ra e of gross profit of a business with departments depends upon:

(1) The rate of gross profit of each department.
   (a) Its relation to the rates of other departments.
   (b) Its change since the preceding period.
(2) Any change in the distribution of sales among departments with different gross profit rates.

Departmental gross profit rates. The relation of the gross profit rate of each department to the gross profit rates of the other departments, and the changes in the departmental rates, are shown in the following summary.

	1959	1958	1957
Department A:			
Sales.................................	$285,600	$119,375	$204,370
Cost of goods sold.....................	121,740	53,370	94,725
Gross profit..........................	$163,860	$ 66,005	$109,645
Rate of gross profit...................	57.37%	55.29%	53.65%
Department B:			
Sales.................................	$ 76,350	$185,325	$125,900
Cost of goods sold.....................	51,190	117,460	76,132
Gross profit..........................	$ 25,160	$ 67,865	$ 49,768
Rate of gross profit...................	32.95%	36.62%	39.53%
Department C:			
Sales.................................	$ 50,300	$ 75,900	$ 60,280
Cost of goods sold.....................	34,732	52,336	41,818
Gross profit..........................	$ 15,568	$ 23,564	$ 18,462
Rate of gross profit...................	30.95%	31.05%	30.63%

This summary shows that the gross profit rate in Department A is relatively high, and increasing; the rates in Departments B and C are relatively low; the rate for Department B is decreasing; and the rate for Department C has remained fairly constant throughout the three years.

Distribution of sales among departments. From the foregoing summary of departmental gross profit rates, it is obvious that the average gross profit rate of the business as a whole will increase if the sales of Department A become an increasing percentage of the total sales, and the average rate will decrease if the sales of Department A become a decreasing percentage of the total sales. Therefore, it is of interest to note the per cent of sales in each department each year, as shown below:

Department	Amount of Sales			Per Cent of Total		
	1959	1958	1957	1959	1958	1957
A..............	$285,600	$119,375	$204,370	69.28%	31.36%	52.33%
B..............	76,350	185,325	125,900	18.52	48.69	32.24
C..............	50,300	75,900	60,280	12.20	19.95	15.43
Total..............	$412,250	$380,600	$390,550	100.00%	100.00%	100.00%

It is obvious that the decrease in the average rate of gross profit from 45.55% in 1957 to 41.36% in 1958 was largely due to the decrease in the percentage of business done by Department A, the high gross-profit-rate department. And the increase in the average rate from 41.36% in 1958 to 49.63% in 1959 was largely due to the fact that the sales in Department A increased from 31% to 69% of the total.

Departmental rates and sales distribution. The combined effect on the average gross profit rate of the business as a whole of changes in the departmental rates and changes in the distribution of sales among departments operating at different gross profit levels may be shown by a computation in the following form:

	Per Cent of Total Sales	Departmental Rate of Gross Profit	Components of the Average Rate of Gross Profit		
			1959	1958	1957
Department A..............	69.28%	× 57.37% =	39.75%		
	31.36%	× 55.29% =		17.34%	
	52.33%	× 53.65% =			28.08%
Department B..............	18.52%	× 32.95% =	6.10%		
	48.69%	× 36.62% =		17.83%	
	32.24%	× 39.53% =			12.74%
Department C..............	12.20%	× 30.95% =	3.78%		
	19.95%	× 31.05% =		6.19%	
	15.43%	× 30.63% =			4.73%
Average gross profit rate of the business..			49.63%	41.36%	45.55%

A similar analysis could be made by commodities—a fact which becomes obvious if we merely assume that the data, instead of applying to Departments A, B, and C, apply to Commodities A, B, and C.

Departmental merchandise turnovers.   The foregoing statements show that the gross profit rate of the business as a whole was very adversely affected in 1958 by the large decrease in sales in Department A, where the highest rate of gross profit is earned. The following statement shows that the turnover in Department A also suffered in 1958.

The foregoing statements also show that Departments B and C are relatively less valuable than Department A from the standpoint of volume of sales and rate of gross profit. The following statement shows that Departments B and C are losing ground in the matter of inventory turnovers.

Departmental Finished Goods Inventory Turnovers

		Department A	Department B	Department C	Total
Finished goods inventories— December 31:					
1959		$ 37,570	$ 15,655	$ 9,395	$ 62,620
1958		36,850	17,210	4,490	58,550
1957		29,360	14,450	2,885	46,695
1956		34,975	20,300	3,355	58,630
Average inventories:					
1959	(a)	$ 37,210	$ 16,433	$ 6,942	$ 60,585
1958	(b)	33,105	15,830	3,688	52,623
1957	(c)	32,168	17,375	3,120	52,663
Cost of sales:					
1959	(d)	$121,740	$ 51,190	$34,732	$207,662
1958	(e)	53,370	117,460	52,336	223,166
1957	(f)	94,725	76,132	41,818	212,675
Turnovers:					
1959 (d ÷ a)		3.27	3.12	5.00	3.43
1958 (e ÷ b)		1.61	7.42	14.19	4.24
1957 (f ÷ c)		2.94	4.38	13.40	4.04

Fixed and Variable Expenses

The break-even point.   Assume that a company's income statement may be summarized as follows:

Sales	$500,000
Less cost of sales and expenses	475,000
Net profit	$ 25,000

To what extent can the sales decrease before the company begins to lose money? The costs and expenses, amounting to $475,000, are 95% of the sales. If the costs and expenses remained in that proportion to sales, regardless of increases or decreases in sales, the company would always make some profit, no matter how small the sales might be.

But some of the expenses are fixed in amount, regardless of the amount of sales, whereas others vary more or less directly in proportion to sales. The so-called "break-even point" computations are based on the assumption that the expenses can be divided into two classes:

(1) Fixed expenses, which are not affected by changes in the amount of sales.
(2) Variable expenses, which vary in direct proportion to the sales.

If we assume that the $475,000 of costs and expenses are divisible as follows:

Fixed expenses... $200,000
Variable expenses... 275,000

the break-even point can be computed as follows:

Let S = the sales at the break-even point.
The variable expenses incurred in making $500,000 of sales are $275,000, or 55% of the sales. Since the variable expenses, by definition, always vary in proportion to sales, they will be 55% of any sales volume.
Since the sales at the break-even point will exactly equal the fixed and variable expenses,

S = $200,000 (fixed expenses) + .55S (variable expenses)
S − .55S = $200,000
.45S = $200,000
S = $444,444.44, the break-even point; if the sales fall below this amount, the company will incur losses.

Relation of fixed expenses to break-even point. It is obvious that, if any portion of the fixed expense can be converted to variable expense, the break-even point will be lowered. To illustrate, assume the following division of the $475,000 total of costs and expenses:

Fixed expenses.. $100,000
Variable expenses—75% of net sales........................ 375,000
Let S = the sales at the break-even point.
Then S = $100,000 (fixed expenses) + .75S (variable expenses).
S − .75S = $100,000
.25S = $100,000
S = $400,000, the break-even point.

Use of break-even computations in management. Guidance in the solution of management problems may often be obtained by the use of the break-even computation. One problem will be presented as an illustration. A company's income statement is summarized at the top of the next page.

Net sales..	$1,000,000
Costs and expenses:	
Fixed..	$ 300,000
Variable (64% of sales).................................	640,000
Total..	$ 940,000
Net income...	$ 60,000

The company is considering increasing its investment in fixed assets; if it does so, the fixed expenses will be increased from $300,000 to $400,000 per year; the variable expenses will continue to be 64% of sales. Is the increase in fixed assets expedient?

In the first place, let us determine what will happen to the break-even point.

Under present conditions:

$$S = \$300,000 \text{ (fixed)} + .64S \text{ (variable)}$$
$$.36S = \$300,000$$
$$S = \$833,333.33$$

Under the proposed conditions:

$$S = \$400,000 \text{ (fixed)} + .64S \text{ (variable)}$$
$$.36S = \$400,000$$
$$S = \$1,111,111.11$$

It thus becomes apparent that the sales must be increased $111,111.11 from their present level of $1,000,000 before the company will have any net income.

In the second place, let us determine what sales must be made to produce the same net income, $60,000, as at the present time. Since the sales must provide for the fixed expenses, the variable expenses, and the $60,000 net income,

$$S = \$400,000 \text{ (fixed)} + .64S \text{ (variable)} + \$60,000$$
$$.36S = \$460,000$$
$$S = \$1,277,777.77$$

In the third place, let us consider the probable limits of net income under the two conditions. With the present plant facilities, the maximum production is estimated at an amount which would enable the company to make sales of $1,200,000. The increased production with the additional facilities would permit the company to make sales of $1,600,000. The probable limits of net income may therefore be estimated as follows:

	Without Plant Additions	With Plant Additions
Sales.......................................	$1,200,000	$1,600,000
Fixed expenses.............................	$ 300,000	$ 400,000
Variable expenses—64% of sales...........	768,000	1,024,000
Total expenses..........................	$1,068,000	$1,424,000
Limits of net income.....................	$ 132,000	$ 176,000

These findings may be summarized as follows:

	Present	Prospective	Difference
Break-even point............	$ 833,333.33	$1,111,111.11	$277,777.77
Sales to make the same net income as at present.......	1,000,000.00	1,277,777.77	277,777.77
Limits of net income.........	132,000.00	176,000.00	44,000.00
Sales for limits of net income.	1,200,000.00	1,600,000.00	400,000.00

The management should now estimate the sales possibilities to determine the wisdom of the proposed expenditures. If the company makes the expenditures, but the sales remain at the present level of $1,000,000, it will lose $40,000 instead of making $60,000, because it will have increased its fixed expenses $100,000 without changing its variable expenses. With the additional plant, the break-even point will be advanced $277,777.77, and the sales must be increased the same amount to make the $60,000 net income now earned. Against these disadvantages may be set off the possibility of making $44,000 more net income than is possible under present conditions, but the earning of this additional net income will depend upon the company's ability to obtain sales of $1,600,000.

Classification of expenses. Break-even computations are predicated on the assumption that all expenses can be grouped into two classes: Those which are absolutely fixed in amount, regardless of sales; and those which vary in direct proportion to the sales.

Such an assumption is not always justified. Some expenses may be fixed to the extent that they will not vary up to a certain sales limit; if the sales are increased above that limit, these expenses will increase, but may remain fixed at the higher amount up to a new sales limit. Moreover, although some expenses may vary in exact proportion to sales, the increases and decreases in other expenses will not be in exact proportion to the increases and decreases in sales.

The rudiments of the break-even computation have been discussed because the computation is becoming of increasing interest to accountants and executives. The practical application of the theory requires a recognition of the fact that expenses cannot be rigidly classified as *fixed* and *variable*.

CHAPTER TWENTY-FOUR

Statement of Application of Funds

Change in working capital.   Bankers and other grantors of short-term credit are interested in the working capital position of their debtors or prospective debtors and in the change therein between two dates. Such information is furnished by a statement in the following form:

THE A COMPANY
Schedule of Working Capital
December 31, 1959 and 1958

	December 31,		Changes in Working Capital	
	1959	1958	Increase	Decrease
Current assets:				
Cash..........................	$ 20,000	$17,000	$ 3,000	
Accounts receivable............	35,000	37,500		$ 2,500
Inventory....................	50,000	45,000	5,000	
Total current assets..........	$105,000	$99,500		
Current liabilities:				
Notes payable.................	$ 10,000	$15,000	5,000	
Accounts payable..............	30,000	38,000	8,000	
Total current liabilities.......	$ 40,000	$53,000		
Working capital.................	$ 65,000	$46,500		
Working capital ratio............	2.63	1.88		
Increase in working capital........				18,500
			$21,000	$21,000

Causes of increase in working capital.   The foregoing schedule of working capital would create a favorable impression: the working capital has increased $18,500; the working capital ratio has increased from 1.88 to 2.63.

But the prospective grantor of short-term credit should not rely wholly on this statement. He should find out what caused the increase.

Suppose that The *A* Company told him that the increase was caused as follows:

```
Funds provided (increasing working capital):
  By operations.................................................  $24,500
Funds applied (decreasing working capital):
  Dividends paid................................................    6,000
Increase in working capital.....................................  $18,500
```

This information would increase the favorable impression created by the schedule of working capital.

But suppose that The *A* Company furnished the following information:

```
Funds provided:
  By operations...............................................  $10,000
  By sale of long-term investments............................   14,500
    Total.....................................................  $24,500
Funds applied:
  Dividends paid..............................................    6,000
Increase in working capital...................................  $18,500
```

A much less favorable impression would be created. The change from the rather unsatisfactory working capital position at the end of 1958 was caused more by the sale of investments than by operations; the sale of the investments increased the working capital at the cost of depriving the company of the income thereon.

Or assume that The *A* Company furnished the following information:

```
Funds provided:
  By operations..............................................  $ 4,500
  By issuance of three-year notes............................   20,000
    Total....................................................  $24,500
Funds applied:
  Dividends paid.............................................    6,000
Increase in working capital..................................  $18,500
```

A very unfavorable impression would be created. Paying dividends in excess of current net income and at the same time borrowing money would probably be regarded as questionable financial management; and, if the funds provided by operations remain at their 1959 level, a continuance of the dividend policy and the payment of the notes at their maturity will leave the company in a seriously depleted working capital position unless long-term funds can be obtained from other sources.

Statement of application of funds.   The *causes* of a change in working capital are shown by a statement of application of funds, but before the statement is illustrated it will be helpful to look at the comparative balance sheet on page 515 in which the changes in account balances are classified in two pairs of columns:

A pair of columns showing changes in the balances of current asset and current liability (working capital) accounts. The $55,000 net debit in this pair of columns is the amount of the increase in working capital.

A pair of columns showing changes in the balances of other (noncurrent) accounts. The $55,000 net credit in this pair of columns is also the amount of the increase in working capital.

The net debits in the working capital accounts are equal to the net credits in the noncurrent accounts. By referring to the noncurrent accounts and determining what caused the changes in them, we shall at the same time ascertain the causes of the change in the amount of working capital.

The causes of the changes in the noncurrent accounts and the related effects on working capital are shown below:

	Changes in Noncurrent Account Balances		Effect on Working Capital	
	Debit	Credit	Increase	Decrease
Long-term investments:				
Cause of change—Investments sold.......		$ 5,000		
Effect on working capital—Increase......			$ 5,000	
Land:				
Cause of change—Land purchased........	$10,000			
Effect on working capital—Decrease......				$10,000
Three-year notes payable:				
Cause of change—Notes issued..........		20,000		
Effect on working capital—Increase......			20,000	
Capital stock:				
Cause of change—Stock issued..........		25,000		
Effect on working capital—Increase......			25,000	
Retained earnings:				
Cause of change—Net income..........		15,000		
Effect on working capital—Increase......			15,000	
Net credits to noncurrent accounts and increase in working capital................	55,000			55,000
	$65,000	$65,000	$65,000	$65,000

THE B COMPANY
Comparative Balance Sheet
With Classification of Changes in Account Balances
December 31, 1959 and 1958

| | Account Balances December 31, | | Changes in Account Balances | | | |
| | | | In Working Capital Accounts | | In Other (Non-current) Accounts | |
	1959	1958	Debits	Credits	Debits	Credits
Assets						
Cash	$ 75,000	$ 35,000	$40,000			
Accounts receivable	90,000	98,000		$ 8,000		
Merchandise inventory	120,000	87,000	33,000			
Long-term investments	10,000	15,000				$ 5,000
Land	30,000	20,000			$10,000	
	$325,000	$255,000				
Liabilities and Stockholders' Equity						
Accounts payable	$ 45,000	$ 50,000	5,000			
Notes payable (short-term)	35,000	20,000		15,000		
Notes payable (due November 30, 1962)	20,000					20,000
Capital stock	150,000	125,000				25,000
Retained earnings	75,000	60,000				15,000
	$325,000	$255,000				
Net debits in working capital accounts				55,000	55,000	
Net credits in noncurrent accounts			$78,000	$78,000	$65,000	$65,000

Statements. The information shown by the comparative balance sheet on page 515 and the statement on page 514 showing the causes of the changes in the noncurrent accounts can be used to prepare the following statements.

THE B COMPANY
Schedule of Working Capital
December 31, 1959 and 1958

	December 31,		Changes in Working Capital	
	1959	1958	Increase	Decrease
Current assets:				
Cash	$ 75,000	$ 35,000	$40,000	
Accounts receivable	90,000	98,000		$ 8,000
Merchandise inventory	120,000	87,000	33,000	
Total current assets	$285,000	$220,000		
Current liabilities:				
Accounts payable	$ 45,000	$ 50,000	5,000	
Notes payable	35,000	20,000		15,000
Total current liabilities	$ 80,000	$ 70,000		
Working capital	$205,000	$150,000		
Increase in working capital				55,000
			$78,000	$78,000

THE B COMPANY
Statement of Application of Funds
For the Year Ended December 31, 1959

Funds provided by:
Sale of long-term investments	$ 5,000	
Issuance of three-year notes payable	20,000	
Issuance of capital stock	25,000	
Operations	15,000	
Total		$65,000
Funds applied to:		
Purchase of land		10,000
Increase in working capital—per schedule		$55,000

As used in this statement, "funds" means working capital. Items under "Funds provided by" are causes of increases in working capital; items under "Funds applied to" are causes of decreases in working capital.

Working papers. The working papers on page 517 show a convenient device for assembling the information required for the preparation of a statement of application of funds.

Since the working capital schedule is prepared before the statement of application of funds, details of current assets and current liabilities may be omitted from the working papers and only the net change in working capital need be shown.

The statement of application of funds does not show the noncurrent account balances at the beginning and end of the year, but only the changes therein. Therefore, only the changes in the balances need be shown in the working papers. The working papers were prepared in the following manner:

The change in working capital and the changes in the balances of the noncurrent accounts were entered in the first pair of columns. These columns were totalled to be sure that everything that should be included was included.

The changes in the noncurrent account balances were extended to the Funds Applied and Funds Provided columns, with an explanation of the cause of the change in each balance.

The Funds Provided column was footed; the Funds Applied column was footed and its total was extended to the Funds Provided column.

The total of the funds applied was subtracted from the total of the funds provided to determine the increase in working capital; the amount should agree with the increase shown by the schedule of working capital and with the first item entered in the working papers.

THE B COMPANY
Statement of Application of Funds Working Papers
For the Year Ended December 31, 1959

	YEAR'S CHANGES—NET		FUNDS APPLIED		FUNDS PROVIDED	
	Debit	Credit	Amount	Explanation	Amount	Explanation
Working capital................	55,000					
Noncurrent accounts:						
Long-term investments.......		5,000			5,000	Sale
Land......................	10,000		10,000	Purchase		
Three-year notes payable.....		20,000			20,000	Issuance of 3-year notes
Capital stock...............		25,000			25,000	Issued
Retained earnings...........		15,000			15,000	Operations
	65,000	65,000				
Total funds provided........					65,000	
Total funds applied.........			10,000		10,000	
Increase in working capital..					55,000	

Detailing changes in retained earnings. Observe, in the working papers below, the detailing of the changes in retained earnings, which has two advantages: (1) It gives assurance that all of the causes of the net change in retained earnings have been determined; (2) it allots a separate line to each cause of change in retained earnings, thus facilitating the extension of the various items to the appropriate columns at the right. **More than one cause of change in other noncurrent account balances.** The working papers below show that the $8,000 increase in long-term investments was the net effect of: (1) A $10,000 purchase— this amount is shown in the Funds Applied column; (2) a $2,000 sale—this amount is shown in the Funds Provided column. As a general rule, if the change in a noncurrent account balance had two or more causes, the several causes of the change should be shown in the statement of application of funds, and therefore in the working papers.

THE C COMPANY
Statement of Application of Funds Working Papers
For the Year Ended December 31, 1959

	Year's Changes—Net		Funds Applied		Funds Provided	
	Debit	Credit	Amount	Explanation	Amount	Explanation
Working capital	26,000					
Noncurrent accounts:						
Long-term investments	8,000		10,000	Purchase	2,000	Sale
Land	5,000		5,000	Purchase		
Long-term notes payable		15,000			15,000	Issuance
Capital stock		10,000			10,000	Issuance
Retained earnings		14,000				
	39,000	39,000				
Details of changes in retained earnings:						
Net income		20,000			20,000	Operations
Dividends	6,000		6,000	Paid		
Increase in retained earnings	14,000					
	20,000	20,000				
Funds provided					47,000	
Funds applied			21,000		21,000	
Increase in working capital					26,000	

Noncurrent account changes not affecting funds. If a debit to one noncurrent account is offset by a credit to another noncurrent account, the working capital is not affected, and the changes should not appear in the funds statement. Observe, in the working papers below, the reversal entries for: (1) Writing off the $10,000 Goodwill account; (2) the conversion of $20,000 of preferred stock into common stock. ($30,000 of common stock was also issued for cash.)

THE D COMPANY
Statement of Application of Funds Working Papers
For the Year Ended December 31, 1959

	YEAR'S CHANGES		REVERSAL OF ENTRIES NOT AFFECTING FUNDS		FUNDS APPLIED		FUNDS PROVIDED	
	Debit	Credit	Debit	Credit	Amount	Explanation	Amount	Explanation
Working capital............	58,200							
Noncurrent accounts:								
Investments...............		4,000					4,000	Sale
Goodwill..................		10,000	10,000 A					
Capital stock:								
Preferred.................	20,000			20,000 B				
Common...................		50,000	20,000 B				30,000	Issued for cash
Retained earnings.........		14,200						
	78,200	78,200						
Details of changes in retained earnings:								
Goodwill written off......	10,000			10,000 A				
Dividends paid:								
Preferred.................	1,800				1,800	Preferred dividends		
Common...................	9,000				9,000	Common dividends		
Net income...............		35,000					35,000	Net income
Increase in retained earnings......	14,200							
	35,000	35,000	30,000	30,000				
Funds provided...........							69,000	
Funds applied............					10,800		10,800	
Increase in working capital....							58,200	

Income and expense items not affecting working capital.
The income statement may contain items which affected the net income without affecting the working capital. For instance, consider the following:

Depreciation and amortization of fixed assets, and amortization of long-term deferred charges. These reduce the net income without reducing the working capital. Therefore, they must be added to the net income to determine the increase in working capital attributable to operations.

Amortization of long-term deferred credits. These amortizations increase the net income without increasing the working capital. Therefore, they must be deducted from the net income to determine the increase in working capital attributable to operations.

To deal with such items in the working papers, it is advisable to have a separate Funds Provided—By Operations section in which to assemble the items used in the computation of the funds provided by operations. Working papers containing such a section appear on page 521. The illustration is based on the following condensed comparative balance sheet.

THE E COMPANY
Condensed Comparative Balance Sheet
December 31, 1959 and 1958

	December 31, 1959	December 31, 1958	Net Change Debit	Net Change Credit
Assets				
Working capital....................	$33,550	$29,300	$4,250	
Furniture.......................	8,750	8,000	750	
Less accumulated depreciation......	2,400*	1,600*		$ 800
Leasehold improvements............	4,500	5,000		500
	$44,400	$40,700		
Liabilities and Stockholders' Equity				
Bonds payable....................	$20,000	$20,000		
Premium on bonds payable..........	900	1,000	100	
Capital stock....................	17,000	15,000		2,000
Retained earnings.................	6,500	4,700		1,800
	$44,400	$40,700	$5,100	$5,100

   * Deduction.

The net income for the year was $2,800; dividends in the amount of $1,000 were paid.

The items affecting net income but not affecting working capital were:

Depreciation of furniture, $800.
Amortization of leasehold improvements, $500.
Amortization of premium on bonds payable, $100.

THE E COMPANY
Statement of Application of Funds Working Papers
For the Year Ended December 31, 1959

	Year's Changes Affecting Funds		Reversal of Entries Not Affecting Funds		Funds Applied		Funds Provided — By Operations		Funds Provided — Other Sources	
	Debit	Credit	Debit	Credit	Amount	Explanation	Amount	Explanation	Amount	Explanation
Working capital.................	4,250									
Noncurrent accounts:										
Furniture.....................	750				750	Purchase				
Accumulated depreciation—Furniture.		800					800	Depreciation		
Leasehold improvements........		500					500	Amortization		
Premium on bonds payable......	100						100*	Amortization		
Capital stock.................		2,000							2,000	Issued
Retained earnings.............		1,800								
	5,100	5,100								
Details of changes in retained earnings:										
Dividends paid................	1,000				1,000	Dividends				
Net income...................		2,800					2,800			
Increase in retained earnings......	1,800									
	2,800	2,800								

Funds provided:
By operations..................... 4,000
Total............................. 6,000
Funds applied..................... 1,750
Increase in working capital....... 4,250

* Deduction.

Observe how the total of the Funds Provided—By Operations column is extended to the Funds Provided—Other Sources column so that the total funds provided may be determined.

Following is the statement of application of funds.

THE E COMPANY
Statement of Application of Funds
For the Year Ended December 31, 1959

Funds provided by:			
Operations:			
Net income for the year..........................	$2,800		
Add charges (deduct credits*) to operations not affecting working capital:			
Depreciation of furniture.......................	800		
Amortization of leasehold improvements.........	500		
Amortization of premium on bonds payable......	100*	$4,000	
Issuance of capital stock.....................................		2,000	
Total funds provided.....................................			$6,000
Funds applied to:			
Purchase of furniture...		$ 750	
Payment of a dividend..		1,000	1,750
Increase in working capital......................................			$4,250

Fund changes affecting more than one noncurrent account. Some transactions affecting working capital cause changes in two or more noncurrent accounts. In such cases, the changes in all of the noncurrent accounts affected must be taken into consideration in the determination of the total or net effect on working capital. Several such instances are shown in this illustration.

Illustrative working papers and the related statement of application of funds are shown on pages 523 and 525. The illustration is based on the following condensed comparative balance sheet.

THE F COMPANY
Condensed Comparative Balance Sheet
December 31, 1959 and 1958

	December 31, 1959	December 31, 1958	Net Change Debit	Net Change Credit
Assets				
Working capital...........................	$63,600	$23,000	$40,600	
Investments..............................		10,000		$10,000
Land....................................	9,000	15,000		6,000
Machinery...............................	10,000	12,000		2,000
Accumulated depreciation—Machinery......	5,300*	4,000*		1,300
	$77,300	$56,000		
Liabilities and Stockholders' Equity				
Capital stock............................	$35,000	$25,000		10,000
Premium on stock........................	1,000			1,000
Retained earnings........................	41,300	31,000		10,300
	$77,300	$56,000	$40,600	$40,600

* Deduction.

THE F COMPANY
Statement of Application of Funds Working Papers
For the Year Ended December 31, 1959

	Year's Changes		Reversal of Entries Not Affecting Funds		Transfers for Grouping Purposes		Funds Applied		Funds Provided — By Operations		Funds Provided — Other Sources	
	Debit	Credit	Debit	Credit	Debit	Credit	Amount	Explanation	Amount	Explanation	Amount	Explanation
Working capital	40,600											
Noncurrent accounts:												
Investments		10,000			10,000 A							
Land		6,000			6,000 B							
Machinery		2,000			2,000 C							
Accumulated depreciation—Machinery		1,300				700 C			2,000	Depreciation		
Capital stock		10,000			10,000 D							
Premium on stock		1,000			1,000 D							
Retained earnings		10,300										
	40,600	40,600										
Details of changes in retained earnings:												
Dividends	2,100						2,100					
Gain on sale of land		5,000			5,000 B							
Net income of $7,400 consisting of:												
Gain on sale of investments		500			500 A							
Loss on sale of machinery	300					300 C						
From operations		7,200							7,200			
Increase in retained earnings	10,300											
	12,700	12,700			34,500	34,500						
Funds provided by sale of investments						10,500 A					10,500	
Funds provided by sale of land						11,000 B					11,000	
Funds provided by sale of machinery						1,000 C					1,000	
Funds provided by issuance of stock at a premium						11,000 D					11,000	
					34,500	34,500						
Funds provided:												
By operations									9,200		9,200	
Total											42,700	
Funds applied								2,100				2,100	
Increase in working capital											40,600	

The $10,300 net change in Retained Earnings was caused by:

	Debits	Credits
Dividends..	$2,100	
Gain on sale of land.................................		$5,000
Net income of $7,400, consisting of:		
Gain on sale of investments.......................		500
Loss on sale of machinery..........................	300	
From operations..................................		7,200

The net income details shown above are listed in the working papers so that:

The gain on the sale of investments can be grouped with the change in the balance of the Investments account to show the total funds provided by the sale.

The gain on the sale of land can be grouped with the change in the balance of the Land account to show the total funds provided by the sale.

The loss on the sale of machinery can be grouped with the change in the balances of the Machinery and Accumulated Depreciation—Machinery accounts to show the net funds provided by the sale.

The $7,200 can be extended to the Funds Provided—By Operations column.

When a transaction affecting working capital causes changes in two or more noncurrent accounts, the effect on working capital is the sum or net amount of the changes in the noncurrent accounts affected by the transaction. A pair of columns may be provided in the working papers in which to group the several changes in the noncurrent accounts and to show their total or net amount as a single item—the amount of funds provided or funds applied—which can be extended to the appropriate column of the working papers. Observe the working paper treatment of the following matters.

Sale of investments. The amount of funds provided by the sale of investments is the sum of:

The credit to Investments account............................	$10,000
The gain—included in net income.............................	500
Total...	$10,500

Entry (A) transfers these credits to the line "Funds provided by sale of investments—$10,500."

Sale of land. The amount of funds provided by the sale of land is the sum of:

The credit to Land account..................................	$ 6,000
The credit to Gain on Sale of Land...........................	5,000
Total...	$11,000

Entry (B) transfers these credits to the line "Funds provided by sale of land—$11,000."

— *Sale of machinery.*   The amount of funds provided by the sale of machinery is the net amount of:

The credit to Machinery—for cost........................		$2,000
Debits:		
Accumulated Depreciation—Machinery—for accumulated depreciation to date of sale..........................	$700	
Loss on Sale of Machinery............................	300	1,000
Net...		$1,000

Entry (C) combines the three changes in the noncurrent accounts into one net amount, shown in the working papers as "Funds provided by sale of machinery—$1,000."

— *Issuance of capital stock.*   The amount of funds provided by the issuance of capital stock is the sum of:

The credit to Capital Stock for the par......................	$10,000	
The credit to Premium on Stock...........................	1,000	
Total..	$11,000	

Entry (D) combines the two credits, and shows the total as "Funds provided by the issuance of stock at a premium—$11,000."

Balances in the Year's Changes columns showing changes in noncurrent accounts, modified by application of the debits and credits in the Reversal and Transfers columns, are extended to the appropriate Funds columns. So, also, are the total or net amounts produced by the transfer entries and shown at the bottom of the working papers.

Observe that no notation is made in the "Explanation" space if the nature of the amount is clearly indicated at the left of the working papers.

THE F COMPANY
Statement of Application of Funds
For the Year Ended December 31, 1959

Funds provided by:			
Operations:			
Net operating income.................................		$ 7,200	
Add charge to operations not affecting working capital:			
Depreciation of machinery...........................		2,000	$ 9,200
Sale of investments....................................			10,500
Sale of machinery.....................................			1,000
Sale of land..			11,000
Issuance of capital stock:			
Par..		$10,000	
Premium...		1,000	11,000
Total funds provided..............................			$42,700
Funds applied to:			
Payment of dividends..................................			2,100
Increase in working capital.............................			$40,600

Let us assume that the $500 gain on the sale of investments and the $300 loss on the sale of machinery are not shown as separate items under the "Details of changes in retained earnings" caption, and that $7,400 is shown as net income. The gain and loss would be treated in the working papers in the manner shown in the partial working papers shown below. Columns and amounts not required for purposes of the illustration are omitted.

THE F COMPANY
Partial Statement of Application of Funds Working Papers
For the Year Ended December 31, 1959

| | YEAR'S CHANGES | | TRANSFERS FOR GROUPING PURPOSES | | FUNDS PROVIDED | |
	Debit	Credit	Debit	Credit	By Operations	Other Sources
Noncurrent accounts:						
Investments........	10,000		10,000 A			
Machinery.........	2,000		2,000 C			
Accumulated depreciation—Machinery		1,300		700 C		
Details of changes in retained earnings:						
Net income.......		7,400	500 A	300 C	7,200	
Funds provided by sale of investments......				10,500 A		10,500
Funds provided by sale of machinery.......				1,000 C		1,000

Net loss—funds provided. Funds may be provided by operations even though a loss is incurred, because the operating charges, such as depreciation, not affecting the working capital may be greater than the net loss. A statement illustrating such a case appears below. The working papers are on page 527.

THE G COMPANY
Statement of Application of Funds
For the Year Ended December 31, 1959

Funds provided by:
Operations:
Net loss for the year.............................. $ 600*
Charges to operations not affecting working capital:
Depreciation—Buildings........................ 1,000 $ 400
Issuance of capital stock................................... 7,500

Total funds provided....................................... $7,900
Funds applied to:
Purchase of securities..................................... $2,000
Payment of dividends....................................... 500

Total funds applied....................................... 2,500
Increase in working capital.................................. $5,400
    * Red.

THE G COMPANY
Statement of Application of Funds Working Papers
For the Year Ended December 31, 1959

	Year's Changes		Reversal of Entries Not Affecting Funds		Transfers for Grouping Purposes		Funds Applied		Funds Provided — By Operations		Funds Provided — Other Sources	
	Debit	Credit	Debit	Credit	Debit	Credit	Amount	Explanation	Amount	Explanation	Amount	Explanation
Increase in working capital....	5,400											
Noncurrent accounts:												
Investment securities....	2,000						2,000	Purchase				
Land....												
Buildings....												
Accumulated depreciation—Buildings....		1,000							1,000	Depreciation		
Capital stock....		7,500									7,500	Issuance
Retained earnings....	1,100											
	8,500	8,500										
Details of changes in retained earnings:												
Net loss....	600								600*			
Dividends....	500						500					
Decrease in retained earnings....		1,100										
	1,100	1,100										
Funds provided:												
By operations....									400		400	
Total....											7,900	
Funds applied....								2,500			2,500	
Increase in working capital....											5,400	
* Deduction.												

Net loss—funds not provided. If the income charges not affecting working capital were less than the net loss, funds were lost in operations. The funds so lost are sometimes shown in the statement of application of funds under the Funds Applied caption; it seems preferable, when possible, to show the amount as a deduction from funds provided from other sources. This procedure is shown in The H Company statement on page 529.

THE H COMPANY

Statement of Application of Funds Working Papers

For the Year Ended December 31, 1959

	Year's Changes		Reversal of Entries Not Affecting Funds		Transfers for Grouping Purposes		Funds Applied		Funds Provided — By Operations		Funds Provided — Other Sources	
	Debit	Credit	Debit	Credit	Debit	Credit	Amount	Explanation	Amount	Explanation	Amount	Explanation
Increase in working capital	2,700											
Noncurrent accounts:												
Investment securities	2,000						2,000	Purchase				
Land												
Buildings												
Accumulated depreciation—Buildings		600							600	Depreciation		
Capital stock		6,000									6,000	Issued
Retained earnings	1,900											
	6,600	6,600										
Details of changes in retained earnings:												
Dividends	1,000						1,000					
Net loss	900								900*			
Decrease in retained earnings		1,900										
	1,900	1,900										
Funds provided—Other sources											6,000	
Funds lost in operations									300*		300*	
Net funds provided									300*		5,700	
Funds applied							3,000					
Increase in working capital							2,700					

* Red.

THE H COMPANY
Statement of Application of Funds
For the Year Ended December 31, 1959

Funds provided by:		
Issuance of capital stock....................................		$6,000
Deduct funds lost in operations:		
Net loss for the year.............................. $ 900*		
Charges to operations not affecting working capital:		
Depreciation—Buildings......................... 600		300
Net funds provided...................................		$5,700
Funds applied to:		
Purchase of investment securities..................... $2,000		
Payment of dividends............................. 1,000		
Total funds applied.................................		3,000
Increase in working capital..................................		$2,700

* Red.

Decrease in working capital.   A decrease in working capital is best shown in the statement of application of funds by reversing the usual sequence of the statement, as illustrated in the following statement of The *I* Company.

THE I COMPANY
Statement of Application of Funds
For the Year Ended December 31, 1959

Funds applied to:		
Purchase of office furniture.....................................		$7,500
Payment of dividends..		500
Total funds applied..		$8,000
Funds provided by:		
Operations:		
Net income for the year............................. $1,500		
Charges to operations not affecting working capital:		
Depreciation—Furniture......................... 1,300	$2,800	
Issuance of capital stock....................................	2,500	
Total funds provided.......................................		5,300
Decrease in working capital...		$2,700

In the working papers the total funds provided would be deducted from the total funds applied to determine the decrease in working capital.

Steps in preparation of working papers.   The steps in the preparation of the statement of application of funds working papers are:

Prepare the schedule of working capital, to determine the change in working capital to be shown on the first line of the working papers.

Enter the change in working capital and the changes in noncurrent balance sheet accounts in the first two columns of the working papers; foot these columns as a test of accuracy.

Enter the details of changes in retained earnings in the first two columns of the working papers; to determine that everything has been included, see that the balance of these items agrees with the net change in retained earnings shown above the column totals.

If the net income was affected by extraneous transactions, detail the elements affecting net income to facilitate groupings and extensions.

Make appropriate entries in the Reversal and Transfers columns; see that the totals of each pair of columns are in agreement.

Extend the balances in the Year's Changes columns, modified by the debits and credits in the Reversal and Transfers columns, to the appropriate Funds Applied and Funds Provided columns.

Foot the Funds Provided—By Operations column and extend the total to the Funds Provided—Other Sources column.

If the working capital has increased:

Foot the Funds Provided—Other Sources column;

Foot the Funds Applied column and extend the total to the Funds Provided—Other Sources column.

Deduct the total funds applied from the total funds provided to show the increase in working capital.

If the working capital has decreased:

Foot the Funds Applied column;

Foot the Funds Provided—Other Sources column and carry the total to the Funds Applied column.

Deduct the total funds provided from the total funds applied to show the decrease in working capital.

Extended illustration.   The next illustration is based on the comparative statement on page 531.

The first step in the solution is the preparation of the schedule of working capital, which appears on page 536.

Preceding working papers have contained a pair of columns headed Reversal of Entries Not Affecting Funds and another pair of columns headed Transfers for Grouping Purposes. These two pairs of columns were used to help the reader understand the nature of the two classes of adjustments. For practical purposes it is not necessary to have two pairs of columns; all adjustments can be shown in one pair of columns. This is done in the working papers for The J Company.

Information relative to the changes in the noncurrent accounts is given on the following pages.

THE J COMPANY
Comparative Balance Sheet
December 31, 1959 and 1958

	December 31, 1959	December 31, 1958	Net Change Debit	Net Change Credit
Assets				
Cash..............................	$ 3,500	$ 2,000	$ 1,500	
Accounts receivable..................	14,500	14,000	500	
Allowance for doubtful accounts........	1,200*	1,350*	150	
Notes receivable....................	10,000	5,000	5,000	
Accrued interest on notes receivable.....	160	100	60	
Finished goods.......................	19,000	13,500	5,500	
Goods in process....................	8,500	8,200	300	
Materials...........................	21,900	22,600		$ 700
Unexpired insurance..................	470	420	50	
Manufacturing supplies...............	580	675		95
Investment in stock of X Company.....		15,000		15,000
Sinking fund........................	2,000		2,000	
Land...............................	17,000	10,000	7,000	
Buildings...........................	60,000	60,000		
Accumulated depreciation—Buildings...	6,300*	8,000*	1,700	
Machinery..........................	43,000	32,000	11,000	
Accumulated depreciation—Machinery..	9,000*	7,500*		1,500
Delivery equipment..................	9,500	9,500		
Patents............................	16,000	17,000		1,000
Goodwill............................		10,000		10,000
Organization expense.................	3,000	4,500		1,500
Discount on 5% bonds payable........		50		50
	$212,610	$207,695		
Liabilities and Stockholders' Equity				
Accounts payable....................	$ 4,500	$ 3,200		1,300
Notes payable—Trade................	6,000	5,000		1,000
Accrued wages......................	210	170		40
Bonds payable—5%..................		50,000	50,000	
Sinking fund bonds payable—4½%.....	40,000			40,000
Premium on 4½% bonds payable.......	900			900
Long-term, unsecured notes payable:				
Current installment.................	5,000			5,000
Noncurrent portion..................	20,000	25,000	5,000	
Capital stock—Preferred..............	10,000	25,000	15,000	
Capital stock—Common...............	85,000	60,000		25,000
Paid-in surplus......................	600			600
Sinking fund reserve..................	2,000			2,000
Retained earnings....................	38,400	39,325	925	
	$212,610	$207,695	$105,685	$105,685

* Deduction.

The $15,000 investment in X Company stock was sold at a gain of $750, which was included in the net income for the year.

Land was purchased at a cost of $10,000. Land carried at $3,000 was sold for $4,500; the gain was included in the net income for the year.

Extraordinary building repairs costing $3,700 were charged to the Accumulated Depreciation—Buildings account.

(*Continued on page 534.*)

THE J COMPANY
Statement of Application of Funds Working Papers
For the Year Ended December 31, 1959

	Year's Changes—Net		Adjustments		Funds Applied	Funds Provided	
	Debit	Credit	Debit	Credit		By Operations	Other Sources
Increase in working capital	4,925						
Noncurrent accounts:							
Investment in stock of X Company		15,000	15,000 A				
Sinking fund	2,000				2,000 Deposit		
Land	7,000		3,000 B		10,000 Purchase		
Buildings	1,700				3,700 Extraordinary repairs		
Accumulated depreciation—Buildings	11,000					2,000 Depreciation	
Machinery		1,500	2,000 C		13,000 Purchase		
Accumulated depreciation—Machinery				375 C		1,875 Depreciation	
Delivery equipment		1,000			2,000 Purchase	2,000 Depreciation	
Patents		1,000				1,000 Amortization	
Goodwill		10,000	10,000 D				
Organization expense		1,500	1,500 E				
Discount on 5% bonds payable		50				50 Amortization	
Bonds payable—5%	50,000				50,000 Retired		
Sinking fund bonds payable—4½%		40,000	40,000 F				
Premium on 4½% bonds payable		900	1,000 F			100* Amortization	
Noncurrent portion of long-term notes	5,000				5,000 Became current		
Capital stock—Preferred	15,000			{ 10,000 G / 5,000 H			
Capital stock—Common		25,000	{ 10,000 G / 5,000 I / 10,000 J				
Paid-in surplus		600	600 J				
Sinking fund reserve		2,000	2,000 K				
Retained earnings	925						
	97,550	97,550					

Details of changes in retained earnings:					
Write-off of goodwill..........	10,000			10,000 D	
Write-down of organization expense....	1,500			1,500 E	
Premium on preferred stock retired....	350			350 H	
Common stock issued as a dividend....	5,000			5,000 I	
Cash dividend on preferred stock.....	1,500				1,500
Cash dividend on common stock......	3,000				3,000
Transfer to sinking fund reserve.......	2,000			2,000 K	
Net income:					
Gain on sale of investments........	750	750 A			1,500
Gain on sale of land.............	1,500	1,500 B		625 C	
Loss on sale of machinery..........	625				
From operations................	20,800		20,800		
Decrease in retained earnings.......	925				
	23,975	23,975			
Funds provided by sale of stock of X Company........		15,750 A			15,750
Funds provided by sale of land.......		4,500 B			4,500
Funds provided by sale of machinery.....		1,000 C			1,000
Funds provided by issuance of 4½% bonds at a premium of $1,000......		41,000 F			41,000
Funds applied to retire preferred stock at a premium of $350.........		5,350 H		5,350	
Funds provided by issuance of common stock at a premium of $600..........		10,600 J			10,600
Funds provided by operations.........			27,625		27,625
Total funds provided.............		107,700			100,475
Funds applied.................			95,550		95,550
Increase in working capital					4,925

* Deduction.

Building depreciation for the year was $2,000.

Machinery carried at its $2,000 cost, less $375 depreciation, was sold for $1,000. The $625 loss was reported in the income statement.

New machinery was purchased at a cost of $13,000.

Machinery depreciation for the year was $1,875.

Delivery equipment was purchased at a cost of $2,000.

Depreciation of delivery equipment, $2,000, was credited to the asset account.

Operations were charged $1,000 for amortization of patents.

Goodwill was written off by debit to Retained Earnings.

The Organization Expense account was written down $1,500 by debit to Retained Earnings.

The $50 of discount on the 5% bonds was amortized by charge to income.

The 5% bonds were retired at par.

New sinking fund 4½% bonds of $40,000 par were issued at a premium of $1,000.

Bond premium in the amount of $100 was amortized.

A portion, $5,000, of the long-term unsecured notes payable became current during the year.

Preferred stock of $10,000 par value was converted into common stock of an equal par value.

Preferred stock of $5,000 par value was retired at a premium of $350, which was charged to Retained Earnings.

Common stock of $5,000 par value was issued as a dividend.

Common stock of $10,000 par value was issued for cash at 106. The premium was credited to Paid-in Surplus.

Cash dividends of $1,500 were paid on the preferred stock.

Cash dividends of $3,000 were paid on the common stock.

The net income, including items mentioned above, amounted to $22,425.

Problems frequently do not give information about all of the changes in the noncurrent accounts, leaving students to form their own conclusions. There is one such instance in this illustration: The cause of the $2,000 increase in the sinking fund is not stated; presumably the increase was caused by a deposit in the sinking fund.

Observe that a line is devoted in the working papers to each noncurrent account, even though there was no change in the balance. There may have been offsetting debit and credit entries during the year. This was the case with the Delivery Equipment account.

In a statement of application of funds containing numerous items, it may be desirable to classify the items under side captions, such as the following:

Funds provided:	Funds applied:
Operations	Payments to stockholders:
Capital sources:	Retirement of stock
Issuances of stock	Payment of dividends
Issuance of long-term obligations:	Retirement of long-term debt:
Bonds	Payment of mortgage
Disposal of assets:	Deposits in sinking fund for bonds
Sales of investments	Expenditures for fixed assets
Sales of fixed assets	Other
Other	Increase in working capital

The statement of application of funds below, which is based on the working papers on pages 532 and 533, illustrates such classifications.

THE J COMPANY

Statement of Application of Funds

For the Year Ended December 31, 1959

Funds provided by:
Operations:

Net income from operations		$20,800	
Add net depreciation and amortization, which reduced net income without affecting working capital		6,825	$ 27,625
Issuance of $10,000 par value of common stock at a premium			10,600
Issuance of $40,000 par value of bonds at a premium			41,000
Sale of assets:			
Stock of X Company		$15,750	
Land		4,500	
Machinery		1,000	21,250
Total funds provided			$100,475

Funds applied to:
Payments to stockholders:

Retirement of $5,000 par value of preferred stock at a premium			$ 5,350
Dividends:			
On preferred stock		$ 1,500	
On common stock		3,000	4,500
Reduction of long-term debt or provision therefor:			
Retirement of 5% bonds		$50,000	
Sinking fund deposit for 4½% bonds		2,000	
Installment of long-term unsecured notes payable which became a current liability during the year		5,000	57,000
Expenditures for fixed assets:			
Purchase of land		$10,000	
Purchase of machinery		13,000	
Purchase of delivery equipment		2,000	
Extraordinary building repairs		3,700	28,700
Total funds applied			95,550
Increase in working capital			$ 4,925

THE J COMPANY
Schedule of Working Capital
December 31, 1959 and 1958

	December 31, 1959	December 31, 1958	Changes in Working Capital Increase	Changes in Working Capital Decrease
Current assets:				
Cash.................................	$ 3,500	$ 2,000	$ 1,500	
Accounts receivable....................	14,500	14,000	500	
Allowance for doubtful accounts........	1,200*	1,350*	150	
Notes receivable.......................	10,000	5,000	5,000	
Accrued interest receivable.............	160	100	60	
Finished goods........................	19,000	13,500	5,500	
Goods in process......................	8,500	8,200	300	
Materials.............................	21,900	22,600		$ 700
Unexpired insurance...................	470	420	50	
Manufacturing supplies.................	580	675		95
Total current assets.................	$77,410	$65,145		
Current liabilities:				
Accounts payable.....................	$ 4,500	$ 3,200		1,300
Notes payable—Trade.................	6,000	5,000		1,000
Accrued wages........................	210	170		40
Current installment of long-term note...	5,000			5,000
Total current liabilities..............	$15,710	$ 8,370		
Working capital........................	$61,700	$56,775		
Increase in working capital......				4,925
			$13,060	$13,060

* Deduction.

Conflicting opinions about statement content. The primary purpose of the statement of application of funds is to account for the change in working capital. Accountants hold two opinions about whether any other changes in financial condition should be shown. These opinions are stated below.

Opinion 1: The only changes in noncurrent accounts which need be shown in the statement are those which were offset by changes in working capital. Therefore, the statement should show:

Under the Funds Provided caption:
Only those credits to noncurrent accounts which were offset by debits to working capital accounts.

Under the Funds Applied caption:
Only those debits to noncurrent accounts which were offset by credits to working capital accounts.

Opinion 2: In addition to accounting for the change in working capital, the statement should give a comprehensive picture of the other changes in financial condition by including the items mentioned on the following page.

Under the Funds Provided caption:

All credits to noncurrent accounts resulting from transactions (but not mere book entries), regardless of whether the offsetting debit was to a working capital account or to some other noncurrent account.

Under the Funds Applied caption:

All debits to noncurrent accounts resulting from transactions (but not mere book entries), regardless of whether the offsetting credit was to a working capital account or to some other noncurrent account.

The illustrations on the preceding pages of this chapter are in conformity with the first opinion. Illustrative statements prepared in accordance with both opinions are presented below.

Basis of illustrations. The illustrative statements prepared in accordance with the two conflicting opinions are based on the following condensed comparative balance sheet.

THE K COMPANY
Condensed Comparative Balance Sheet
December 31, 1959 and 1958

	December 31,		Net Change	
	1959	1958	Debit	Credit
Assets				
Working capital..........................	$24,000	$20,000	$ 4,000	
Investment securities.....................		5,000		$ 5,000
Land....................................	8,000	5,000	3,000	
Buildings................................	50,000	30,000	20,000	
Accumulated depreciation—Buildings........	4,000*	3,000*		1,000
Equipment...............................	22,000	15,000	7,000	
Accumulated depreciation—Equipment......	3,000*	2,250*		750
Goodwill................................		5,000		5,000
	$97,000	$74,750		
Liabilities and Stockholders' Equity				
Long-term unsecured notes payable..........		$10,000	10,000	
Mortgage payable.........................	$15,000			15,000
Capital stock............................	65,000	50,000		15,000
Retained earnings.......	17,000	14,750		2,250
	$97,000	$74,750	$44,000	$44,000

* Deduction.

The causes of the changes in the noncurrent accounts are stated below:

Depreciation of buildings during the year was $1,000; depreciation of equipment was $750.

The $5,000 Goodwill account was written off. This was a mere book entry which will not be reflected in either statement of application of funds.

(*Continued on page 539.*)

Working papers—Opinion 1.

THE K COMPANY
Statement of Application of Funds Working Papers
For the Year Ended December 31, 1959

	Year's Changes—Net		Adjustments		Funds Applied	Funds Provided	
	Debit	Credit	Debit	Credit		By Operations	Other Sources
Increase in working capital	4,000						
Noncurrent accounts:							
Investment securities		5,000	5,000 C				
Land	3,000			3,000 C			
Buildings	20,000			20,000 C			
Accumulated depreciation—Buildings		1,000				1,000 Depreciation	
Equipment	7,000			7,000 C			
Accumulated depreciation—Equipment		750				750 Depreciation	
Goodwill		5,000	5,000 A				
Long-term unsecured notes payable	10,000			10,000 B			
Mortgage payable		15,000	15,000 C				5,000 Issuance
Capital stock		15,000	10,000 B				
Retained earnings		2,250		5,000 A			
	44,000	44,000					
Details of changes in retained earnings:							
Goodwill write-off	5,000						
Dividends	3,500				3,500		
Net income		10,750				10,750	
Increase in retained earnings	2,250						
	10,750	10,750					
Funds applied to acquisition of fixed assets			10,000 C		10,000		
			45,000	45,000			
					13,500	12,500	

Funds provided:

By operations	12,500
Total	17,500
Funds applied	13,500
Increase in working capital	4,000

Capital stock of $10,000 par value was issued to retire the long-term notes payable.

Capital stock of $5,000 par value was issued for cash.

A dividend of $3,500 was paid.

The net income for the year was $10,750.

A purchase of fixed assets was made as follows:

Acquired from seller:

Land...	$ 3,000
Buildings...	20,000
Equipment..	7,000
Total...	$30,000

Given to seller:

Investment securities.............................	$ 5,000
Mortgage payable.................................	15,000
Cash...	10,000
Total...	$30,000

THE K COMPANY

Statement of Application of Funds

(*Opinion 1 Form*)

For the Year Ended December 31, 1959

Funds provided by:

Operations:

Net income for the year..............................	$10,750	
Add charges to operations not affecting working capital:		
Depreciation of buildings..........................	1,000	
Depreciation of equipment.........................	750	$12,500
Issuance of capital stock.............................		5,000
Total funds provided.............................		$17,500

Funds applied to:

Acquisition of fixed assets...........................	$10,000	
Payment of dividends...............................	3,500	
Total funds applied.............................		13,500
Increase in working capital............................		$ 4,000

Observe that this statement does not show the issuance of capital stock to retire the long-term notes payable, because working capital was not affected; and the only fact shown about the acquisition of fixed assets is the $10,000 decrease in working capital resulting from the cash payment.

Working papers—Opinion 2.

THE K COMPANY
Statement of Application of Funds Working Papers
For the Year Ended December 31, 1959

	Year's Changes—Net		Adjustments		Funds Applied	Funds Provided	
	Debit	Credit	Debit	Credit		By Operations	Other Sources
Increase in working capital..........	4,000						
Noncurrent accounts:							
Investment securities..........		5,000					5,000
Land..........	3,000				3,000 Acquired		
Buildings..........	20,000				20,000 Acquired		
Accumulated depreciation—Buildings.....		1,000				1,000 Depreciation	
Equipment..........	7,000				7,000 Acquired		
Accumulated depreciation—Equipment...		750				750 Depreciation	
Goodwill..........		5,000	5,000 A				
Long-term unsecured notes payable.......	10,000				10,000 Retired		
Mortgage payable..........		15,000					15,000
Capital stock..........		15,000					15,000
Retained earnings..........		2,250					
	44,000	44,000					
Details of changes in retained earnings:							
Goodwill write-off..........	5,000			5,000 A			
Dividends..........	3,500				3,500		
Net income..........		10,750				10,750	
Increase in retained earnings..........	2,250						
	10,750	10,750	5,000	5,000			
Funds provided:							
By operations..........						12,500	12,500
Total..........							47,500
Funds applied..........					43,500		43,500
Increase in working capital..........							4,000

THE K COMPANY
Statement of Application of Funds
(*Opinion 2 Form*)
For the Year Ended December 31, 1959

Funds provided by:
  Operations:
    Net income for the year................................. $10,750
    Add charges to operations not affecting working capital:
      Depreciation of buildings.............................. 1,000
      Depreciation of equipment............................. 750 $12,500
  Issuance of capital stock... 15,000
  Issuance of mortgage.. 15,000
  Disposal of investment securities................................ 5,000
    Total funds provided... $47,500
Funds applied to:
  Acquisitions of fixed assets:
    Land... $ 3,000
    Buildings...................................... 20,000
    Equipment..................................... 7,000 $30,000
  Retirement of long-term unsecured notes payable........... 10,000
  Payment of dividends...................................... 3,500
    Total funds applied... 43,500
Increase in working capital...................................... $ 4,000

The differences between the statements are shown below:

	Opinion 1	Opinion 2
Funds provided by:		
Operations....................................	$12,500	$12,500
Issuance of capital stock........................	5,000	15,000
Issuance of mortgage............................		15,000
Disposal of investment securities................		5,000
Total funds provided.......................	$17,500	$47,500
Funds applied to:		
Acquisition of fixed assets......................	$10,000	$30,000
Payment of dividends...........................	3,500	3,500
Retirement of long-term debt...................		10,000
Total funds applied........................	$13,500	$43,500
Increase in working capital......................	$ 4,000	$ 4,000

The authors favor Opinion 1. They believe that:

The statement should account for the change in working capital;

It is not intended to account for all of the changes in the balances of noncurrent accounts;

Even if that were the purpose, it would not be accomplished by preparing the statement in accordance with Opinion 2, because the effects of mere book entries are excluded;

Since the statement cannot properly account for all of the changes in noncurrent accounts, there is no good reason for including any of the changes in noncurrent accounts which were not accompanied by changes in working capital;

On the contrary, there is an excellent reason for excluding them. For instance, if capital stock was issued to retire a long-term debt, it seems improper to prepare the statement of application of funds in such a way as to create the false impression that the stock was issued for cash and the debt was paid in cash.

The authors recognize that, in a case such as the acquisition of fixed assets, which was recorded by the entry:

Land..	3,000	
Buildings..	20,000	
Equipment...	7,000	
Investment securities.............................		5,000
Mortgage payable...................................		15,000
Cash...		10,000

the statement of application of funds can properly give more information than was furnished by the statement on page 539, which showed merely:

Funds applied to:
Acquisition of fixed assets................................. $10,000

The statement could be expanded to give detailed information, thus:

Funds applied to:
Acquisition of fixed assets:

Land...	$ 3,000		
Buildings.......................................	20,000		
Equipment......................................	7,000		
Total..	$30,000		
Deduct:			
Investment securities transferred........	$ 5,000		
Mortgage given.......................	15,000	20,000	$10,000

The information required for this presentation of facts can be obtained from the working papers on page 538, prepared in conformity with Opinion 1.

Terminology. A great deal of effort has been expended in the past in rather fruitless attempts to define the word *funds*, as used in the statement of application of funds.

Obviously, it does not mean *cash*. The statement is not a statement of cash receipts and disbursements.

To avoid the implication that *funds* means *cash*, it has been suggested that the word *resources* be used instead of *funds*. In fact, the statement is sometimes called a "statement of resources received and applied."

The objection to the word *resources* is that it is synonymous with *assets*, but a transaction can increase the working capital without having any effect on the assets; for instance, a current liability can be converted into a long-term debt. Similarly, there can be a decrease in working capital without any effect on assets; for instance, the first installment of a serial bond issue may become current during the period.

Another title, somewhat crude and rather indefinite, and not often used, but avoiding the implication of a close relationship to cash, is *Where got, Where gone*. It retains the implication of a close relationship to assets.

Actually, all of these terms are inappropriate because they imply that the statement reflects only the flow of assets into and out of the business, without consideration of changes in the amounts or nature of liabilities.

Some accountants, desiring to avoid the use of terminology which is inappropriate and perhaps confusing, and wishing to emphasize the fact that the primary purpose of the statement is to show the causes of the change in working capital, have abandoned the use of such terms as *funds* and *resources* and have used terminology such as that illustrated in the statement below.

THE L COMPANY
Statement Accounting for the Increase in Working Capital
During the Year Ended December 31, 1959

Working capital was increased by:		
Operations...		$ 6,000
Issuance of capital stock..................................		5,000
Conversion of short-term notes payable into long-term		
debt..		10,000
Total...		$21,000
Working capital was decreased by:		
Purchase of land...	$2,000	
Payment of dividends....................................	5,000	
Total...		7,000
Increase in working capital..............................		$14,000

But this terminology becomes inappropriate if the statement of application of funds is prepared in accordance with Opinion 2, described above, and shows, as funds provided and applied, changes in noncurrent accounts which did not affect working capital.

In this book the traditional *funds* terminology is employed; it is subject to criticism, but it is in common use.

Alternative form. There has been some tendency to depart from the traditional form of statement of application of funds. Such departures usually consist of changes in the manner of showing the results of operations and their effect upon working capital. An illustration of an alternative form appears on page 545.

The traditional form shows the net income or loss, with adjustments thereof for depreciation and other charges and credits which affected the net income for the period but did not affect the working capital.

The alternative form does not show the net income or loss and the income debits and credits which did not affect working capital; instead, it shows, as sources of working capital, the sales, items of income, and other causes of increases in working capital; and it shows, as deductions therefrom, the costs, expenses, and other charges which tended to decrease the working capital. Depreciation provisions and amortization charges and credits, therefore, do not appear in statements in this form.

The illustration is based on the following trial balances of The *M* Company.

THE M COMPANY
Trial Balances
December 31, 1959 and 1958

	December 31,			
	1959 Before Closing		1958 After Closing	
	Debit	Credit	Debit	Credit
Cash...	16,250		11,250	
Accounts receivable.........................	39,925		33,960	
Allowance for doubtful accounts..............		3,000		2,800
Notes receivable............................	20,000		22,500	
Merchandise inventory—end of year...........	48,000		44,625	
Unexpired insurance.........................	250		275	
Prepaid expense.............................	390		270	
Land..	5,000		5,000	
Buildings...................................	50,000		50,000	
Accumulated depreciation—Buildings..........		13,750		12,500
Office equipment............................	13,000		10,000	
Accumulated depreciation—Office equipment...		4,650		4,000
Delivery equipment..........................	7,500		7,000	
Accumulated depreciation—Delivery equipment		3,600		2,800
Accounts payable............................		7,900		9,250
Notes payable...............................		10,000		12,000
Federal income tax payable..................		7,750		5,000
Capital stock...............................		100,000		75,000
Retained earnings...........................		31,530		61,530
Sales.......................................		250,000		
Cost of goods sold..........................	198,950			
Depreciation:				
Buildings................................	1,250			
Office equipment.........................	650			
Delivery equipment.......................	1,500			
Other selling and general expenses..........	21,600			
Interest earned.............................		55		
Interest expense............................	20			
Loss on sale of delivery equipment..........	200			
Federal income tax..........................	7,750			
	432,235	432,235	184,880	184,880

The following additional information is furnished:

Office equipment was purchased at a cost of $3,000.

Delivery equipment (cost, $1,000; accumulated depreciation, $700) was sold for $100.

Delivery equipment was purchased at a cost of $1,500.

Capital stock of a par value of $15,000 was issued as a dividend.

Capital stock of $10,000 par value was issued for cash at par.

A cash dividend of $15,000 was paid.

THE M COMPANY
Schedule of Working Capital
December 31, 1959 and 1958

	December 31, 1959	December 31, 1958	Changes in Working Capital Increase	Changes in Working Capital Decrease
Current assets:				
Cash.............................	$ 16,250	$ 11,250	$ 5,000	
Accounts receivable.................	39,925	33,960	5,965	
Allowance for doubtful accounts......	3,000*	2,800*		$ 200
Notes receivable....................	20,000	22,500		2,500
Merchandise inventory...............	48,000	44,625	3,375	
Unexpired insurance.................	250	275		25
Prepaid expense.....................	390	270	120	
Total current assets...............	$121,815	$110,080		
Current liabilities:				
Accounts payable...................	$ 7,900	$ 9,250	1,350	
Notes payable......................	10,000	12,000	2,000	
Federal income tax payable..........	7,750	5,000		2,750
Total current liabilities...........	$ 25,650	$ 26,250		
Working capital.......................	$ 96,165	$ 83,830		
Increase in working capital............				12,335
			$17,810	$17,810

* Deduction.

THE M COMPANY
Statement of Application of Funds
For the Year Ended December 31, 1959

Funds provided:

Sales...		$250,000
Interest earned..		55
Issuance of capital stock.................................		10,000
Sale of delivery equipment.		100
Total funds provided.................................		$260,155

Funds applied:

Cost of goods sold...............................	$198,950	
Selling and general expenses, excluding depreciation and amortization.............................	21,600	
Interest expense.................................	20	
Federal income tax...............................	7,750	
Cash dividends..................................	15,000	
Purchase of delivery equipment....................	1,500	
Purchase of office equipment......................	3,000	
Total funds applied.....................................		247,820
Increase in working capital..................................		$ 12,335

THE M COMPANY
Statement of Application of Funds Working Papers
For the Year Ended December 31, 1959

	Year's Changes—Net		Adjustments		Funds Applied	Funds Provided
	Debit	Credit	Debit	Credit		
Increase in working capital..........	12,335					
Noncurrent balance sheet accounts:						
Land..........						
Buildings..........						
Accumulated depreciation—Buildings..........		1,250	1,250 A			
Office equipment..........	3,000				3,000 Purchase	
Accumulated depreciation—Office equipment....		650	650 B			
Delivery equipment..........	500		1,000 D		1,500 Purchase	
Accumulated depreciation—Delivery equipment.		800	1,500 C	700 D		
Capital stock..........		25,000	15,000 E			10,000 Issued for cash
Retained earnings:						
Stock dividend..........	15,000			15,000 E		
Cash dividend..........	15,000				15,000	
Revenues and expenses:						
Sales..........		250,000				250,000
Cost of goods sold..........	198,950				198,950	
Depreciation:						
Buildings..........	1,250			1,250 A		
Office equipment..........	650			650 B		
Delivery equipment..........	1,500			1,500 C		
Other selling and general expenses..........	21,600				21,600	
Interest earned..........		55				55
Interest expense..........	20				20	
Loss on sale of delivery equipment..........	200			200 D		
Federal income tax..........	7,750				7,750	
	277,755	277,755				
Funds provided by sale of delivery equipment.				100 D		100
			19,400	19,400		
Funds provided..........						260,155
Funds applied..........					247,820	247,820
Increase in working capital..........						12,335

CHAPTER TWENTY-FIVE

Cash-Flow Statement

Nature and purpose of the statement. The cash-flow statement answers such questions, prevalent in the minds of nonaccountants, as: If the net income for the year was $50,000, why was not the cash increased an equal amount?

Causes of difference between net income or loss and cash change. There are two reasons why the net income or loss for a period may differ from the cash increase or decrease during the period.

(1) Unless the accounting is on an absolute cash basis, the revenues reported as earned during a period will not be the same as the cash receipts related to operations, and the costs and expenses reported will not be the same as the cash disbursements related to operations.

(2) Cash may be received from sources other than operations and disbursed for purposes other than operations.

Working papers. Following are several illustrations showing how data for a cash-flow statement are assembled in working papers. The first illustrations deal only with cash flows related to operations; they are intended to show various causes for the difference between the cash change and the net income or net loss. Later working papers show other causes of the change in cash. Illustrations of cash-flow statements are postponed until the working papers have dealt with enough matters to make the cash-flow statements fairly comprehensive.

The working papers show the changes in all balance sheet accounts except Retained Earnings. The change in retained earnings is accounted for by detailing the items in the income statement (and the statement of retained earnings, if it contains any items other than net income or net loss).

Cash flows related to operations. The first four illustrations deal only with cash flows related to operations, there being no cash receipts from other sources and no cash disbursements for other purposes. The working papers show how various matters are dealt with in the working papers.

Sales and merchandise costs. The cash receipts during a year arising from sales may not be the amount of the sales for the year. The cash receipts may be computed as follows:

Sales − Increase in accounts receivable = Cash receipts arising from past- or current-period sales.

Or

Sales + Decrease in accounts receivable = Cash receipts arising from past- or current-period sales.

Similarly, the cash disbursements during a year resulting from purchases may not be the amount of the purchases for the year. The cash disbursements may be computed as follows:

Purchases − Increase in accounts payable = Cash disbursements arising from past- or current-period purchases.

Or

Purchases + Decrease in accounts payable = Cash disbursements arising from past- or current-period purchases.

This illustrative case is based on the following data:

THE A COMPANY
Comparative Balance Sheet
December 31, 1959 and 1958

	December 31, 1959	December 31, 1958	Net Changes Debit	Net Changes Credit
Assets				
Cash..........................	$ 31,000	$28,000	$ 3,000	
Accounts receivable..............	41,000	45,000		$ 4,000
Inventory.......................	35,000	26,000	9,000	
	$107,000	$99,000		
Liabilities and Stockholders' Equity				
Accounts payable—Trade..........	$ 30,000	$25,000		5,000
Capital stock....................	50,000	50,000		
Retained earnings................	27,000	24,000		3,000
	$107,000	$99,000	$12,000	$12,000

THE A COMPANY
Income Statement
For the Year Ended December 31, 1959

Sales..		$180,000
Deduct cost of goods sold:		
Inventory—December 31, 1958...................	$ 26,000	
Purchases.....................................	131,000	
Total...	$157,000	
Inventory—December 31, 1959...................	35,000	
Cost of goods sold.....................................		122,000
Gross profit on sales..		$ 58,000
Deduct expenses...		55,000
Net income..		$ 3,000

THE A COMPANY
Cash-Flow Statement Working Papers
For the Year Ended December 31, 1959

	Year's Changes—Net		Adjustments		Cash	
	Debit	Credit	Debit	Credit	Applied	Provided
Balance sheet accounts:						
Cash..............	3,000					
Accounts receivable.		4,000	4,000 A			
Inventory..........	9,000			9,000 B		
Accounts payable—						
Trade..........		5,000	5,000 C			
Capital stock.......						
Retained earnings...		3,000				
	12,000	12,000				
Details of changes in retained earnings:						
Sales..............		180,000		4,000 A		184,000
Inventory—December 31, 1958......	26,000			26,000 B		
Purchases..........	131,000			5,000 C	126,000	
Inventory—December 31, 1959......		35,000	35,000 B			
Expenses...........	55,000				55,000	
Increase in retained earnings.......	3,000					
	215,000	215,000	44,000	44,000	181,000	184,000
Net cash provided......					3,000	
					184,000	184,000

Adjustments (A) and (C) have been explained.

Adjustment (B) is made because the $9,000 debit in the asset account is offset by the $9,000 net credit ($35,000 credit minus $26,000 debit) in the income statement, the cash not being affected.

Returns and allowances; cash discounts. If the income statement shows sales returns and allowances and sales discounts, only the net sales need be shown in the working papers; or, the returns and allowances and the discounts may be shown in the working papers and offset, by adjustment, against the gross sales. The same two alternative procedures may be applied in dealing with purchase returns and allowances and purchase discounts.

Bad debts and depreciation. Allowances for bad debts and depreciation contribute to the difference between the net income and the change in cash. Therefore, adjustments are made as shown in the working papers on page 551, which are based on the following data:

THE B COMPANY
Comparative Balance Sheet
December 31, 1959 and 1958

	December 31, 1959	December 31, 1958	Net Changes Debit	Net Changes Credit
Assets				
Cash...................................	$ 25,000	$ 20,000	$5,000	
Accounts receivable......................	20,000	20,000		
Allowance for doubtful accounts..........	1,500*	1,000*		$ 500
Inventory...............................	52,000	50,000	2,000	
Store equipment........................	20,000	20,000		
Accumulated depreciation—Store equipment	6,000*	5,000*		1,000
	$109,500	$104,000		
Liabilities and Stockholders' Equity				
Accounts payable.......................	$ 15,000	$ 15,000		
Capital stock..........................	75,000	75,000		
Retained earnings......................	19,500	14,000		5,500
	$109,500	$104,000	$7,000	$7,000

    * Deduction.

THE B COMPANY
Income Statement
For the Year Ended December 31, 1959

Sales...			$165,000
Deduct cost of goods sold:			
Inventory—December 31, 1958..................		$ 50,000	
Purchases....................................		137,000	
Total..		$187,000	
Inventory—December 31, 1959..................		52,000	135,000
Gross profit on sales.......................................			$ 30,000
Deduct expenses:			
Bad debts....................................	$ 500		
Depreciation—Store equipment.................	1,000		
Other expenses...............................	23,000	24,500	
Net income...			$ 5,500

THE B COMPANY
Cash-Flow Statement Working Papers
For the Year Ended December 31, 1959

	Year's Changes—Net		Adjustments		Cash	
	Debit	Credit	Debit	Credit	Applied	Provided
Balance sheet accounts:						
Cash..............	5,000					
Accounts receivable.						
Allowance for doubt-						
ful accounts......		500	500 A			
Inventory..........	2,000			2,000 C		
Store equipment....						
Accumulated depre-						
ciation—Store						
equipment........		1,000	1,000 B			
Accounts payable...						
Retained earnings...		5,500				
	7,000	7,000				
Details of changes in re-						
tained earnings:						
Sales..............		165,000				165,000
Inventory—Decem-						
ber 31, 1958......	50,000			50,000 C		
Purchases..........	137,000				137,000	
Inventory—Decem-						
ber 31, 1959......		52,000	52,000 C			
Bad debts..........	500			500 A		
Depreciation—Store						
equipment........	1,000			1,000 B		
Other expenses.....	23,000				23,000	
Net increase in re-						
tained earnings.	5,500					
	217,000	217,000	53,500	53,500	160,000	165,000
Net cash provided......					5,000	
					165,000	165,000

Accruals and tax liability. This illustration is based on the following data:

THE C COMPANY
Comparative Balance Sheet
December 31, 1959 and 1958

	December 31, 1959	December 31, 1958	Net Changes Debit	Net Changes Credit
Assets				
Cash..............................	$10,650	$ 3,400	$7,250	
Accounts receivable..................	25,000	25,000		
Notes receivable.....................	10,000	10,000		
Accrued interest receivable...........	100		100	
Inventory............................	35,000	35,000		
	$80,750	$73,400		
Liabilities and Stockholders' Equity				
Accounts payable.....................	$10,000	$10,000		
Accrued salaries payable..............	750	1,000	250	
Income tax payable..................	3,000	2,400		$ 600
Capital stock........................	50,000	50,000		
Retained earnings....................	17,000	10,000		7,000
	$80,750	$73,400	$7,600	$7,600

THE C COMPANY
Income Statement
For the Year Ended December 31, 1959

Sales..			$150,000
Deduct cost of goods sold:			
Inventory—December 31, 1958...................		$ 35,000	
Purchases.....................................		101,500	
Total......................................		$136,500	
Inventory—December 31, 1959...................		35,000	101,500
Gross profit on sales.......................................			$ 48,500
Deduct expenses:			
Salaries......................................		$ 15,000	
Other expenses................................		24,000	39,000
Net income from operations................................			$ 9,500
Interest earned...			500
Net income before income tax.............................			$ 10,000
Income tax..			3,000
Net income...			$ 7,000

Adjustments are made for the following matters which caused the net income and the net cash provided to differ.

(A) Although the income statement shows $500 of interest earned, $100 thereof was accrued and uncollected at the end of the year; consequently, the cash received was only $400.

(B) The salaries expense was $15,000; however, the cash payments related to salaries were in the amount computed on the following page.

Expense for 1959..		$15,000
Decrease in accrued salaries:		
December 31, 1958...............................	$1,000	
December 31, 1959...............................	750	250
Total...		$15,250

The $250 adjustment changes the expense amount to the cash payment amount.

(C) The income tax expense for 1959 was $3,000; the tax paid in 1959 was $2,400, the 1958 tax. Entry C in the working papers makes the adjustment from the tax expense to the tax payment.

(D) This adjustment disposes of the inventories; since the inventories at the beginning and end of the year were the same, there is no balance sheet adjustment.

THE C COMPANY
Cash-Flow Statement Working Papers
For the Year Ended December 31, 1959

	Year's Changes—Net		Adjustments		Cash	
	Debit	Credit	Debit	Credit	Applied	Provided
Balance sheet accounts:						
Cash..............	7,250					
Accounts receivable.						
Notes receivable....						
Accrued interest receivable.........	100			100 A		
Inventory.........						
Accounts payable...						
Accrued salaries payable............	250			250 B		
Income tax payable.		600	600 C			
Capital stock.......						
Retained earnings...		7,000				
	7,600	7,600				
Details of changes in retained earnings:						
Sales..............		150,000				150,000
Inventory—December 31, 1958......	35,000			35,000 D		
Purchases.........	101,500				101,500	
Inventory—December 31, 1959......		35,000	35,000 D			
Salaries...........	15,000		250 B		15,250	
Other expenses.....	24,000				24,000	
Interest earned.....		500	100 A			400
Income tax.........	3,000			600 C	2,400	
Net increase in retained earnings.	7,000					
	185,500	185,500	35,950	35,950	143,150	150,400
Net cash provided......					7,250	
					150,400	150,400

Cost and revenue apportionments. This illustration is based on the following data:

THE D COMPANY
Comparative Balance Sheet
December 31, 1959 and 1958

	December 31, 1959	December 31, 1958	Net Changes Debit	Net Changes Credit
Assets				
Cash..............................	$ 12,075	$ 5,950	$6,125	
Accounts receivable..................	30,000	30,000		
Inventory...........................	60,000	60,000		
Interest paid in advance on bank loans..	50		50	
Unexpired insurance.................	200	300		$ 100
	$102,325	$96,250		
Liabilities and Stockholders' Equity				
Accounts payable....................	$ 5,000	$ 5,000		
Bank loans.........................	10,000	10,000		
Service fees collected in advance.......	200			200
Debentures payable..................	25,000	25,000		
Premium on debentures..............	1,125	1,250	125	
Capital stock.......................	50,000	50,000		
Retained earnings...................	11,000	5,000		6,000
	$102,325	$96,250	$6,300	$6,300

THE D COMPANY
Income Statement
For the Year Ended December 31, 1959

Sales..		$200,000
Service fees earned.......................................		700
Total..		$200,700
Deduct:		
Cost of sales....................................	$167,725	
Insurance.......................................	100	
Other operating expenses........................	25,000	
Interest on bank loans...........................	500	
Interest on debentures...........................	1,375	194,700
Net income..		$ 6,000

Adjustments are made for the following matters:

(A) Interest expense on bank loans is shown in the income statement as $500, but at the end of the year the balance sheet shows $50 as interest paid in advance on bank loans, making a total cash disbursement during the year of $550.

(B) The insurance expense for the year was $100, but this is the amount of the decrease in the Unexpired Insurance account, which indicates that there was no cash expenditure for insurance during the year.

(C) The income statement shows $700 of service fees earned, and the comparative balance sheet shows $200 of service fees collected in advance. Since no such advance collections were shown in the 1958 balance sheet, the $200 must have been collected during 1959, making the total cash collection $900.

(D) The income statement shows interest on debentures in the amount of $1,375. The comparative balance sheet shows that $125 of the premium on debentures (a cost offset) was amortized during the year. Therefore, the cash interest payment must have been $1,500.

THE D COMPANY
Cash-Flow Statement Working Papers
For the Year Ended December 31, 1959

	Year's Changes—Net		Adjustments		Cash	
	Debit	Credit	Debit	Credit	Applied	Provided
Balance sheet accounts:						
Cash....................	6,125					
Accounts receivable......						
Inventory...............						
Interest paid in advance on bank loans............	50			50 A		
Unexpired insurance......			100	100 B		
Accounts payable........						
Bank loans..............						
Service fees collected in advance...............			200	200 C		
Debentures payable......						
Premium on debentures...	125			125 D		
Capital stock............						
Retained earnings.......		6,000				
	6,300	6,300				
Details of changes in retained earnings:						
Sales...................		200,000				200,000
Service fees earned......		700		200 C		900
Cost of sales.............	167,725				167,725	
Insurance...............	100			100 B		
Other operating expenses..	25,000				25,000	
Interest on bank loans....	500		50 A		550	
Interest on debentures....	1,375		125 D		1,500	
Net increase in retained earnings.............	6,000					
	200,700	200,700	475	475	194,775	200,900
Net cash provided...........					6,125	
					200,900	200,900

Procedure if income statement shows only cost of sales. Assume that the income statement of The *A* Company for the year ended December 31, 1959, was:

THE A COMPANY
Income Statement
For the Year Ended December 31, 1959

Sales.........		$180,000
Deduct:		
Cost of sales....................................	$122,000	
Expenses......................................	55,000	177,000
Net income...		$ 3,000

Since the income statement does not show the amount of the purchases, it must be computed by applying, to the cost of sales, adjustments for the change in the inventory and the change in the accounts payable.

THE A COMPANY
Cash-Flow Statement Working Papers
For the Year Ended December 31, 1959

	Year's Changes—Net Debit	Year's Changes—Net Credit	Adjustments Debit	Adjustments Credit	Cash Applied	Cash Provided
Balance sheet accounts:						
Cash..............	3,000					
Accounts receivable.		4,000	4,000 A			
Inventory.........	9,000			9,000 B		
Accounts payable—						
Trade...........		5,000	5,000 C			
Capital stock.......						
Retained earnings...		3,000				
	12,000	12,000				
Details of changes in retained earnings:						
Sales.............		180,000		4,000 A		184,000
Cost of sales........	122,000		9,000 B	5,000 C	126,000	
Expenses..........	55,000				55,000	
Increase in retained earnings.......	3,000					
	180,000	180,000	18,000	18,000	181,000	184,000
Net cash provided.......					3,000	
					184,000	184,000

Review. Each of the preceding illustrations was relatively simple, since each dealt with only a certain type of adjustment. This illustration is more complex, although no essentially new adjustments are introduced.

The adjustments can be traced by the cross-reference letters, and the purpose of each thereby determined.

The illustration is based on the statements presented on the following page.

THE REVIEW COMPANY
Comparative Balance Sheet
December 31, 1959 and 1958

	December 31, 1959	December 31, 1958	Net Changes Debit	Net Changes Credit
Assets				
Cash..................................	$ 13,875	$ 5,000	$ 8,875	
Accounts receivable.....................	41,000	45,000		$ 4,000
Allowance for doubtful accounts..........	1,500*	1,000*		500
Notes receivable........................	10,000	10,000		
Accrued interest receivable..............	100		100	
Inventory..............................	35,000	26,000	9,000	
Interest paid in advance on bank loans....	50		50	
Unexpired insurance.....................	200	300		100
Store equipment........................	20,000	20,000		
Accumulated depreciation—Store equipment	6,000*	5,000*		1,000
	$112,725	$100,300		
Liabilities and Stockholders' Equity				
Accounts payable.......................	$ 30,000	$ 25,000		5,000
Bank loans.............................	10,000	10,000		
Accrued salaries payable.................	750	1,000	250	
Income tax payable.....................	3,000	2,400		600
Service fees collected in advance..........	200			200
Debentures payable.....................	25,000	25,000		
Premium on debentures..................	1,125	1,250	125	
Capital stock...........................	25,000	25,000		
Retained earnings.......................	17,650	10,650		7,000
	$112,725	$100,300	$18,400	$18,400

* Deduction.

THE REVIEW COMPANY
Income Statement
For the Year Ended December 31, 1959

Sales...			$180,000
Deduct cost of goods sold:			
Inventory—December 31, 1958...................		$ 26,000	
Purchases............................		109,000	
Total.......................................		$135,000	
Inventory—December 31, 1959................		35,000	100,000
Gross profit on sales.......................................			$ 80,000
Service fees earned......................................			700
Total..			$ 80,700
Deduct operating expenses:			
Salaries.......................................		$ 15,000	
Bad debts.......................................		500	
Depreciation—Store equipment...................		1,000	
Insurance.......................................		100	
Other operating expenses.......................		52,725	69,325
Net income from operations...............................			$ 11,375
Deduct net interest expense:			
Interest on debentures...........................		$ 1,375	
Interest on bank loans...........................		500	
Total..		$ 1,875	
Less interest earned...........................		500	1,375
Net income before income tax..............................			$ 10,000
Federal income tax..			3,000
Net income...			$ 7,000

THE REVIEW COMPANY
Cash-Flow Statement Working Papers
For the Year Ended December 31, 1959

	Year's Changes—Net		Adjustments		Cash	
	Debit	Credit	Debit	Credit	Applied	Provided
Balance sheet accounts:						
Cash	8,875					
Accounts receivable		4,000	4,000 A			
Allowance for doubtful accounts		500	500 B			
Notes receivable						
Accrued interest receivable	100			100 C		
Inventory	9,000			9,000 D		
Interest paid in advance on bank loans	50			50 E		
Unexpired insurance						
Store equipment		100	100 F			
Accumulated depreciation—Store equipment		1,000	1,000 G			
Accounts payable		5,000	5,000 H			
Bank loans						
Accrued salaries payable	250			250 I		
Income tax payable		600	600 J			
Service fees collected in advance		200	200 K			
Debentures payable						
Premium on debentures	125			125 L		
Capital stock						
Retained earnings		7,000				
	18,400	18,400				

Details of changes in retained earnings:

Sales		180,000		4,000 A		184,000
Inventory—December 31, 1958	26,000			26,000 D		
Purchases	109,000			5,000 H	104,000	
Inventory—December 31, 1959		35,000	35,000 D			
Service fees earned		700		200 K		900
Salaries	15,000		250 I		15,250	
Bad debts	500			500 B		
Depreciation—Store equipment	1,000			1,000 G		
Insurance	100			100 F		
Other operating expenses	52,725				52,725	
Interest on debentures	1,375		125 L		1,500	
Interest on bank loans	500		50 E		550	
Interest earned		500	100 C			400
Federal income tax	3,000		600 J		2,400	
Net increase in retained earnings	7,000					
	216,200	216,200	46,925	46,925	176,425	185,300
Net cash provided					8,875	
					185,300	185,300

Other sources and applications of cash. In the following illustration, cash is provided by operations, as in the preceding illustrations. In addition, cash is provided by the issuance of capital stock, and is applied to the purchase of investment securities, the payment of a dividend, and the payment of long-term notes payable.

Observe that, in the working papers, separate columns are used for cash provided by operations and cash provided from other sources.

The illustration is based on the following data:

THE E COMPANY
Comparative Balance Sheet
December 31, 1959 and 1958

	December 31, 1959	December 31, 1958	Net Changes Debit	Net Changes Credit
Assets				
Cash....................................	$ 4,000	$ 6,000		$ 2,000
Accounts receivable.....................	30,000	20,000	$10,000	
Allowance for doubtful accounts..........	1,500*	1,000*		500
Inventory..............................	60,000	45,000	15,000	
Investment securities...................	10,000	4,000	6,000	
Store equipment........................	25,000	20,000	5,000	
Accumulated depreciation—Store equipment	6,000*	5,000*		1,000
	$121,500	$89,000		
Liabilities and Stockholders' Equity				
Accounts payable.......................	$ 12,500	$15,000	2,500	
Long-term notes payable.................		10,000	10,000	
Capital stock..........................	90,000	50,000		40,000
Retained earnings......................	19,000	14,000		5,000
	$121,500	$89,000	$48,500	$48,500

* Deduction.

THE E COMPANY
Statement of Retained Earnings
For the Year Ended December 31, 1959

Balance, December 31, 1958..................................		$14,000
Net income..		27,000
Total...		$41,000
Deduct:		
Stock dividend....................................	$10,000	
Cash dividend.....................................	12,000	22,000
Balance, December 31, 1959.................................		$19,000

THE E COMPANY
Income Statement
For the Year Ended December 31, 1959

Sales...		$250,000
Deduct:		
Cost of sales....................................	$150,000	
Bad debts.......................................	500	
Depreciation—Store equipment...................	1,000	
Other expenses..................................	71,500	223,000
Net income..		$ 27,000

THE E COMPANY
Cash-Flow Statement Working Papers
For the Year Ended December 31, 1959

	Year's Changes—Net Debit	Year's Changes—Net Credit	Adjustments Debit	Adjustments Credit	Cash Applied Amount	Cash Applied Explanation	Cash Provided By Operations	Cash Provided Other Sources Amount	Cash Provided Other Sources Explanation
Balance sheet accounts:									
Cash		2,000							
Accounts receivable	10,000			10,000 A					
Allowance for doubtful accounts		500	500 B						
Inventory	15,000			15,000 C					
Investment securities	6,000				6,000	Purchase			
Store equipment	5,000				5,000	Purchase			
Accumulated depreciation—Store equipment		1,000	1,000 D						
Accounts payable	2,500			2,500 E					
Long-term notes payable	10,000				10,000	Paid			
Capital stock		40,000						30,000	Issued
Retained earnings		5,000	10,000 F						
	48,500	48,500							
Details of changes in retained earnings:									
Stock dividend	10,000			10,000 F					
Cash dividend	12,000				12,000				
Operations:									
Sales		250,000					240,000		
Cost of sales	150,000		10,000 C; 15,000 C; 2,500 E				167,500*		
Bad debts	500			500 B					
Depreciation—Store equipment	1,000			1,000 D					
Other expenses	71,500						71,500*		
Net increase in retained earnings	5,000								
	250,000	250,000	39,000	39,000					
Cash applied					33,000				
Cash provided:									
By operations							1,000	1,000	
Total								31,000	
Decrease in cash					2,000				

* Deduction.

The cash-flow statement. A simple cash-flow statement based on the preceding working papers is presented below:

THE E COMPANY
Cash-Flow Statement
For the Year Ended December 31, 1959

Cash applied to:		
Purchase of investment securities....................	$ 6,000	
Purchase of store equipment........................	5,000	
Payment of long-term notes payable................	10,000	
Payment of a cash dividend........................	12,000	
Total cash applied.......................................		$33,000
Cash provided by:		
Issuance of capital stock...........................	$30,000	
Operations.......................................	1,000	
Total cash provided.....................................		31,000
Decrease in cash..		$ 2,000

Reconciling the net income and the cash change. If it is desired to show in detail the causes of the difference between the net income or loss and the cash change from operations during the period, the cash-flow statement may be supported by a schedule similar to the following:

THE E COMPANY
Reconciliation of Net Income and Cash Increase from Operations
For the Year Ended December 31, 1959

	Income Statement Debit	Income Statement Credit	Add Deduct*	Cash Receipts	Cash Payments
Sales.....................		$250,000		$240,000	
Increase in accounts receivable...................			$10,000*		
Merchandise cost...........	$150,000				$167,500
Decrease in accounts payable			2,500		
Increase in inventory......			15,000		
Bad debts.................	500		Noncash		
Depreciation..............	1,000		Noncash		
Other expenses.............	71,500				71,500
Net income................	27,000				
Cash increase from operations					1,000
	$250,000	$250,000		$240,000	$240,000

Extended illustration. This illustration, which is intended to show the working-paper treatment of a considerable variety of items, is based on the data on the following pages.

THE F COMPANY
Comparative Balance Sheet
December 31, 1959 and 1958

	December 31, 1959	December 31, 1958	Net Changes Debit	Net Changes Credit
Assets				
Cash..................................	$ 65,985	$ 48,625	$ 17,360	
Accounts receivable...................	20,000	18,000	2,000	
Allowance for doubtful accounts........	1,200*	1,050*		$ 150
Merchandise inventory.................	50,000	47,000	3,000	
Unexpired insurance...................	585	175	410	
Investment securities.................	45,000	30,000	15,000	
Sinking fund..........................	5,000		5,000	
Land..................................	30,000	30,000		
Building..............................	60,000	60,000		
Accumulated depreciation—Building....	18,500*	18,000*		500
Store fixtures........................	18,000	20,000		2,000
Accumulated depreciation—Store fixtures	7,100*	6,000*		1,100
Delivery equipment...................	4,900	4,500	400	
Accumulated depreciation—Delivery equipment.........................	980*	3,600*	2,620	
Office equipment......................	4,800	4,000	800	
Accumulated depreciation—Office equipment............................	2,040*	1,600*		440
Goodwill.............................		10,000		10,000
Discount on 5% sinking fund bonds.....	1,800		1,800	
	$276,250	$242,050		
Liabilities and Stockholders' Equity				
Accounts payable.....................	$ 10,000	$ 11,500	1,500	
Federal income tax payable...........	25,700	22,800		2,900
Accrued interest on long-term notes.....	750	750		
Bonds payable—5% sinking fund.......	50,000			50,000
Long-term unsecured notes payable:				
Current installment.................	5,000			5,000
Noncurrent installment..............	20,000	25,000	5,000	
Capital stock—Preferred..............		50,000	50,000	
Capital stock—Common...............	125,000	100,000		25,000
Sinking fund reserve..................	5,000			5,000
Reserve for contingencies.............		10,000	10,000	
Retained earnings....................	34,800	22,000		12,800
	$276,250	$242,050	$114,890	$114,890

* Deduction.

THE F COMPANY
Statement of Retained Earnings
For the Year Ended December 31, 1959

Balance—December 31, 1958.................................		$22,000
Add:		
Net income...		34,300
Transfer from Reserve for Contingencies....................		10,000
Total...		$66,300
Deduct:		
Damage suit...	$ 8,000	
Goodwill write-off...................................	10,000	
Premium on preferred stock retired.............	1,000	
Transfer to Sinking Fund Reserve....................	5,000	
Dividends on common stock.........................	7,500	31,500
Balance—December 31, 1959.............................		$34,800

THE F COMPANY
Income Statement

For the Year Ended December 31, 1959

Sales			$304,000
Deduct cost of goods sold:			
Inventory—December 31, 1958		$ 47,000	
Purchases		200,000	
Total		$247,000	
Inventory—December 31, 1959		50,000	197,000
Gross profit on sales			$107,000
Deduct operating expenses:			
Selling expenses:			
Salesmen's salaries	$ 8,000		
Advertising	3,500		
Depreciation:			
Building	3,000		
Store fixtures	1,950		
Delivery equipment	980		
Other selling expenses	3,225		
Total selling expenses		$ 20,655	
General expenses:			
Officers' salaries	$15,000		
Office salaries	4,500		
Insurance	175		
Depreciation—Office equipment	440		
Bad debts	900		
Other general expenses	1,530		
Total general expenses		22,545	43,200
Net income from operations			$ 63,800
Add gain on sale of investment securities			400
Total operating and other income			$ 64,200
Deduct other expenses:			
Interest on bonds payable		$ 2,700	
Interest on long-term notes payable		1,500	4,200
Net income before income tax			$ 60,000
Federal income tax			25,700
Net income			$ 34,300

Additional Information

Adjust-
ment

(A) Provision for doubtful accounts, in the amount of $900, was charged to operations.

(B) Uncollectible accounts in the amount of $750 were written off to Allowance for Doubtful Accounts.

  A working-paper adjustment reversing this write-off is required. The amount to be shown in the cash-flow statement as the cash proceeds from sales is the amount of the sales ($304,000) minus the increase in uncollected accounts receivable. The increase in uncollected accounts is the $2,000 increase shown by the comparative balance sheet plus the $750 of uncollected accounts written off.

(C)   The $2,750 increase in uncollected accounts is deducted from Sales.

(D)   The $3,000 increase in inventory shown in the balance sheet section of the working papers is offset against the opening and closing inventories shown in the operating section of the working papers.

(E)   Transfer the $410 debit change in the Unexpired Insurance account to the Insurance account.

—   After this adjustment is made, the Insurance line has a gross debit of $585. This was the cost of a policy purchased during 1959. Extend the $585 as other operating debit items are extended.

(F)   Investment securities which cost $5,000 were sold for $5,400; the gain is shown in the operations section of the working papers. To show in one amount the total cash provided by the transaction, make the following adjusting entry:

```
Investment securities...........................  5,000
Gain on sale of investments.....................    400
    Cash provided by sale of investments (at bottom
    of working papers)........................             5,400
```

—   Investment securities were purchased at a cost of $20,000; extend this amount to the Cash Applied column on the Investment Securities line.

—   A $5,000 deposit was made in the sinking fund; extend this amount to the Cash Applied column.

(G)   Reverse the book entry debiting Depreciation—Building (in the operations section) and crediting Accumulated Depreciation—Building (in the balance sheet section) $3,000, the amount of the depreciation for the year.

—   The Accumulated Depreciation—Building line now shows a net debit of $2,500. This was the amount of an extraordinary repair made during the year. Extend the $2,500 to the Cash Applied column.

(H)   Store fixtures were sold during the year at their book value. Their cost was $2,000 and the accumulated depreciation at the date of sale was $850, leaving a book value of $1,150. To show in one amount the cash provided by the sale, make the following adjusting entry:

```
Store fixtures...................................  2,000
    Accumulated depreciation—Store fixtures......          850
    Cash provided by sale of store fixtures.........      1,150
```

(I)   Reverse the book entry debiting Depreciation—Store Fixtures and crediting Accumulated Depreciation—Store Fixtures $1,950, the depreciation for the year.

(J)   Old delivery equipment was traded at the beginning of the year for new equipment. The old equipment cost $4,500 and the accumulated depreciation thereon at the date of its sale was $3,600. A cash payment of $4,000 was made.

If, at the time of the sale, the Delivery Equipment account had been relieved of the $4,500 cost of the equipment traded, the Delivery Equipment account (after having been debited with the $4,000 cash payment) would have shown a $500 decrease. Instead, it shows a $400 increase. Apparently $900 of the cost of the old equipment was left in the asset account at the time of the trade. This was the undepreciated cost of the old equipment; presumably it was left in the asset account so that the balance of that account, immediately after the trade, would be the tax-acceptable basis for depreciation of an asset acquired in a trade: undepreciated cost of the old equipment plus the additional payment.

Since, at the time of the trade, Accumulated Depreciation—Delivery Equipment was debited and Delivery Equipment was credited $3,600, a reversing adjusting entry should be made.

—   The Delivery Equipment line now shows a gross debit of $4,000, the amount of the cash disbursement. Extend this amount to the Cash Applied column.

(K)   Reverse the book entry debiting Depreciation—Delivery Equipment and crediting Accumulated Depreciation—Delivery Equipment $980.

—   The $800 debit on the Office Equipment line is the cost of equipment purchased during the year.

(L)   Reverse the entry debiting Depreciation—Office Equipment and crediting Accumulated Depreciation—Office Equipment $440.

(M)   The $10,000 balance in the Goodwill account was written off by debit to Retained Earnings. Since the entry did not affect cash, it is reversed.

(N)   Ten-year 5% sinking fund bonds, face value $50,000, were issued at the beginning of 1959 at 96. The $2,000 discount was charged to Discount on 5% Sinking Fund Bonds. To show the net amount of cash provided, make the adjusting entry on the following page.

```
Bonds payable—5% sinking fund ................. 50,000
  Discount on 5% sinking fund bonds .........            2,000
  Cash provided by issuance of 5% sinking fund
    bonds ................................            48,000
```

(O)   One-tenth of the bond discount was charged to Interest on Bonds Payable. Since this entry did not involve cash, it is reversed.

(P)   Transfer the $1,500 debit from the Accounts Payable line (balance sheet section) to the Purchases line (operations section). Extend the $201,500 gross debit.

(Q)   Transfer the $2,900 credit from the Federal Income Tax Payable line (balance sheet section) to the Federal Income Tax line (operations section). The Federal Income Tax line now has a net debit of $22,800, the amount of the 1958 tax—which was paid in 1959. Extend this balance.

(R)   The fact that $5,000 of the long-term unsecured notes payable became current during the year did not affect cash. Therefore, a working-paper adjustment should be made offsetting the $5,000 current installment increase against the $5,000 decrease in the noncurrent installments.

(S)   The preferred stock, $50,000 par value, was retired at a premium. To show the total amount of cash applied, make the following adjusting entry:

```
Funds applied to retirement of preferred stock.... 51,000
  Capital stock—Preferred ..................            50,000
  Retained earnings ........................             1,000
```

—   The $25,000 increase in the Capital Stock—Common account was caused by the issuance of stock for cash at par.

(T)   The Sinking Fund Reserve account was credited $5,000 by transfer from Retained Earnings. Cash was not affected; therefore, the entry is reversed in the working papers.

—   Because of a pending damage suit, a reserve for contingencies in the amount of $10,000 was created in 1958 by transfer from Retained Earnings. The suit was settled in 1959 for $8,000, which was debited to Retained Earnings. Extend this amount to the Cash Applied column.

(U)   The $10,000 balance in the reserve was returned to Retained Earnings. Since the entry did not involve cash, it is reversed in the working papers.

Complete the extensions to the Cash Applied and Cash Provided columns.

THE F COMPANY
Cash-Flow Statement Working Papers
For the Year Ended December 31, 1959

	Year's Changes—Net		Adjustments		Cash Applied		Cash Provided		
	Debit	Credit	Debit	Credit	Amount	Explanation	By Operations	Other Sources Amount	Explanation
Balance sheet accounts:									
Cash	17,360								
Accounts receivable	2,000		750 B	2,750 C					
Allowance for doubtful accounts		150	900 A	750 B					
Merchandise inventory	3,000			3,000 D					
Unexpired insurance	410			410 E					
Investment securities	15,000				20,000	Purchase			
Sinking fund	5,000		5,000 F		5,000	Deposit			
Land									
Building		500	3,000 G		2,500	Extraordinary repair			
Accumulated depreciation—Building									
Store fixtures		2,000	2,000 H						
Accumulated depreciation—Store fixtures		1,100	1,950 I	850 H					
Delivery equipment	400		3,600 J		4,000	Payment on trade			
Accumulated depreciation—Delivery equip.	2,620		980 K	3,600 J					
Office equipment	800				800	Purchase			
Accumulated depreciation—Office equipment		440	440 L						
Goodwill		10,000	10,000 M						
Discount on 5% sinking fund bonds	1,800			2,000 N					
Accounts payable	1,500		200 O	1,500 P					
Federal income tax payable		2,900	2,900 Q						
Accrued interest on long-term debt		440							
Bonds payable—5% sinking fund		50,000	50,000 N						
Long-term unsecured notes payable:									
Current installment	5,000		5,000 R						
Noncurrent installment	5,000			5,000 R					
Capital stock—Preferred	50,000			50,000 S					
Capital stock—Common		25,000						25,000	Issued at par
Sinking fund reserve		5,000	5,000 T						
Reserve for contingencies	10,000			10,000 U					
Retained earnings		12,800							
	114,890	114,890							
Details of changes in retained earnings:									
Damage suit	8,000				8,000	Claim paid			

Transfer from Reserve for Contingencies....	10,000	10,000	10,000 U			
Goodwill write-off....				10,000 M		
Premium on preferred stock retired....	1,000		1,000 S			
Transfer to Sinking Fund Reserve....	5,000		5,000 T			
Dividends on common stock....	7,500		7,500			
Operations:						
Sales....	304,000		2,750 C			301,250
Inventory—December 31, 1958....	47,000			47,000 D		
Purchases....	200,000		1,500 P			201,500*
Inventory—December 31, 1959....		50,000		50,000 D		
Salesmen's salaries....	8,000					8,000*
Advertising....	3,500					3,500*
Depreciation—Building....	3,000			3,000 G		
Depreciation—Store fixtures....	1,950			1,950 I		
Depreciation—Delivery equipment....	980			980 K		
Other selling expenses....	3,225					3,225*
Officers' salaries....	15,000					15,000*
Office salaries....	4,500					4,500*
Insurance....	175		410 E			585*
Depreciation—Office equipment....	440			440 L		
Bad debts....	900			900 A		
Other general expenses....	1,530					1,530*
Gain on sale of investments....		400		400 F		
Interest on bonds payable....	2,700		200 O			2,500*
Interest on long-term notes payable....	1,500					1,500*
Federal income tax....	25,700		2,900 Q			22,800*
Increase in retained earnings....	12,800					
	364,400	364,400				36,610
Cash provided by sale of investment securities....				5,400 F	5,400	
Cash provided by sale of store fixtures....				1,150 H	1,150	
Cash provided by issuance of 5% sinking fund bonds at a $2,000 discount....				48,000 N	48,000	
Cash applied to retirement of preferred stock at a $1,000 premium....			51,000	51,000 S		
			51,000 S / 207,780	207,780	51,000	

Cash provided:

By operations....			36,610
Total....	36,610		116,160
Cash applied....		98,800	98,800
Increase in cash....			17,360

* Deduction.

THE F COMPANY
Cash-Flow Statement
For the Year Ended December 31, 1959

Cash provided by:

Operations...	$ 36,610
Issuance of $50,000 of bonds at a discount....................	48,000
Issuance of common stock at par...........................	25,000
Sale of investment securities..............................	5,400
Sale of store fixtures.....................................	1,150
Total..	$116,160

Cash applied to:

Retirement of $50,000 of preferred stock at a premium	$51,000	
Purchase of investment securities....................	20,000	
Payment of damage claim...........................	8,000	
Payment of dividends on common stock.............	7,500	
Sinking fund deposit..............................	5,000	
Purchase of delivery equipment....................	4,000	
Extraordinary repairs to building...................	2,500	
Purchase of office equipment.......................	800	
Total...		98,800
Increase in cash...		$ 17,360

Manufacturing. The cash-flow working papers of a manufacturing business do not necessarily differ from those of a trading business except that there are three inventories instead of one.

Assume that the following data are presented relative to the cost of goods sold:

THE MANUFACTURING COMPANY
Statement of Cost of Goods Sold
For the Year Ended December 31, 1959

Materials:		
· Inventory—December 31, 1958.................	$ 50,000	
Purchases...................................	300,000	
Total.......................................	$350,000	
Inventory—December 31, 1959.................	56,000	
Materials used......................................	$	294,000
Direct labor...		500,000
Manufacturing overhead................................		375,000
Total manufacturing cost............................		$1,169,000
Goods in process inventory—December 31, 1958.............		25,000
Total...		$1,194,000
Goods in process inventory—December 31, 1959.............		30,000
Cost of goods manufactured.............................		$1,164,000
Finished goods inventory—December 31, 1958...............		75,000
Total...		$1,239,000
Finished goods inventory—December 31, 1959...............		68,000
Cost of goods sold....................................		$1,171,000

It is further assumed that the accounts payable for material purchases increased $10,000 during the year.

Partial working papers are on the following page.

THE MANUFACTURING COMPANY
Cash-Flow Statement Partial Working Papers
For the Year Ended December 31, 1959

	Year's Changes—Net		Adjustments	
	Debit	Credit	Debit	Credit
Selected balance sheet accounts:				
Materials inventory..............	6,000			6,000 A
Goods in process inventory.......	5,000			5,000 B
Finished goods inventory.........		7,000	7,000 C	
Accounts payable...............		10,000	10,000 D	
Selected operating accounts:				
Materials:				
Inventory—December 31, 1958.	50,000			50,000 A
Purchases....................	300,000			10,000 D
Inventory—December 31, 1959.		56,000	56,000 A	
Goods in process inventory:				
December 31, 1958............	25,000			25,000 B
December 31, 1959............		30,000	30,000 B	
Finished goods inventory:				
December 31, 1958............	75,000			75,000 C
December 31, 1959............		68,000	68,000 C	

Assume that the data submitted show the cost of goods sold but no details of the items used in the computations. The adjustments shown above would all be applied to the cost of goods sold, as illustrated in the partial working papers below.

THE MANUFACTURING COMPANY
Cash-Flow Statement Partial Working Papers
For the Year Ended December 31, 1959

	Year's Changes—Net		Adjustments	
	Debit	Credit	Debit	Credit
Selected balance sheet accounts:				
Materials inventory...........	6,000			6,000 A
Goods in process inventory.....	5,000			5,000 B
Finished goods inventory.......		7,000	7,000 C	
Accounts payable.............		10,000	10,000 D	
Selected operating account:				
Cost of goods sold.............	1,171,000		{ 6,000 A 5,000 B	7,000 C 10,000 D }

CHAPTER TWENTY-SIX

Statements from Incomplete Records

In this chapter we shall deal with the preparation of statements for businesses which do not keep complete double-entry books. We shall deal first with the so-called single-entry method of computing net income, and then with procedures for developing an income statement in the form that would be used if complete double-entry records were maintained.

Single-Entry Income Statement

Single-entry bookkeeping. The minimum essentials of a single-entry bookkeeping system consist of accounts with debtors and creditors and a record of cash receipts and disbursements. Other accounts, records, and memoranda may be maintained, but a bookkeeping system short of a complete set of double-entry accounts is still regarded as a single-entry system.

Single-entry income statement. The single-entry method of determining the net income for a period is as follows:

(1) Prepare a statement of assets and liabilities as of the beginning of the period, and a similar statement as of the end of the period. From these statements, the owner's equity at the beginning and end of the period can be determined.

Information regarding accounts receivable, accounts payable, and cash, required for these statements, can be obtained from the ledger and cash records. Information concerning other assets and liabilities must be obtained from any available information.

(2) Add the owner's equity at the beginning of the period and the additional investments during the period; the total

572

represents the proprietor's gross contribution to the business for the period.

(3) Add the owner's equity at the end of the period and the owner's withdrawals during the period; the total represents the amount made available to the owner as the result of contributions and business operations.

(4) Compute the difference between the totals determined in (2) and (3); this difference is accepted as the net income or loss for the period.

First illustration:

Owner's equity—end of period		$12,000
Add drawings		1,000
Total		$13,000
Deduct:		
Owner's equity—beginning of period	$10,000	
Additional investments	500	10,500
Net income		$ 2,500

Second illustration:

Owner's equity—beginning of period		$10,000
Additional investments		1,800
Total		$11,800
Deduct:		
Owner's equity—end of period	$11,000	
Drawings	300	11,300
Net loss		$ 500

Statements in Double-Entry Form

Sources of data.   If there is a record of cash receipts and disbursements,

An analysis of the cash receipts will show:
    Cash sales
    Collections from customers
    Receipts from other sources

An analysis of the cash disbursements will show:
    Cash purchases
    Payments to creditors
    Payments for expenses
    Other disbursements

With this information and with information concerning accounts receivable, accounts payable, inventories, and such other matters as accrued and deferred items at the beginning and end of the period, data for the preparation of an income statement in double-entry form can be assembled.

Computation of sales. Several illustrations are presented below showing the computation of sales by the use of data shown by the cash and receivable records.

Basic illustration. This first illustration shows the basic procedure.

Cash sales...		$ 75,000
Sales on account:		
Collections from customers.......................	$80,000	
Less accounts receivable—beginning of period........	8,100	
Collections from sales for the period................	$71,900	
Add accounts receivable—end of period.............	8,000	79,900
Total sales...		$154,900

The computation can be somewhat simplified as follows:

Cash sales...	$ 75,000
Add collections from customers.............................	80,000
Total...	$155,000
Less decrease in accounts receivable........................	100
Sales..	$154,900

This chapter will show how a systematic set of working papers can be prepared to assemble all of the data required for an income statement in double-entry form. Such working papers consist of three sections:

Comparative balance sheet data.
Cash receipts and disbursements data.
Income statement data.

The balance sheet and cash data are first entered in the working papers in the manner shown below.

Income Statement Working Papers
For the Year Ended December 31, 1959

	Comparative Balance Sheet			
	December 31,		Year's Changes—Net	
	1959	1958	Debit	Credit
BALANCE SHEETS:				
Assets:				
Accounts receivable.............	8,000	8,100		100

	Cash	
	Debit	Credit
CASH:		
Cash sales.....................................	75,000	
Collections on accounts receivable........	80,000	

	Income Statement	
	Debit	Credit
INCOME STATEMENT:		

The $154,900 credit offsetting the amounts shown in the last two columns of the working papers is then entered in the Income Statement section of the papers, in the manner shown below. Observe that the amounts are given a cross-reference letter (A) so that the items entering into the computation of the $154,900 can be traced.

Income Statement Working Papers
For the Year Ended December 31, 1959

	Comparative Balance Sheet			
	December 31,		Year's Changes—Net	
	1959	1958	Debit	Credit
BALANCE SHEETS:				
Assets:				
Accounts receivable.............	8,000	8,100		100 A

	Cash	
	Debit	Credit
CASH:		
Cash sales..................................	75,000 A	
Collections on accounts receivable............. ...	80,000 A	

	Income Statement	
	Debit	Credit
INCOME STATEMENT:		
Sales..................................		154,900 A

Notes received from customers. If notes are taken from customers, the difference between the notes receivable at the beginning and end of the period, as well as the change in the accounts receivable, must be taken into the computation of sales.

Income Statement Working Papers
For the Year Ended December 31, 1959

	Comparative Balance Sheet			
	December 31,		Year's Changes—Net	
	1959	1958	Debit	Credit
BALANCE SHEETS:				
Assets:				
Accounts receivable.............	5,000	5,600		600 A
Notes receivable................	3,000	2,500	500 A	

	Cash	
	Debit	Credit
CASH:		
Cash sales..................................	75,000 A	
Collections on accounts receivable............ . .	60,000 A	
Collections on notes receivable.................	20,000 A	

	Income Statement	
	Debit	Credit
INCOME STATEMENT:		
Sales..................................		154,900 A

Returns and allowances. Assume the same facts as in the preceding illustration except that an analysis of the accounts receivable showed credits of $350 for returns and allowances.

Income Statement Working Papers
For the Year Ended December 31, 1959

	Comparative Balance Sheet			
	December 31,		Year's Changes—Net	
	1959	1958	Debit	Credit
BALANCE SHEETS:				
Assets:				
Accounts receivable.............	5,000	5,600		600 A
Notes receivable................	3,000	2,500	500 A	

	Cash	
	Debit	Credit
CASH:		
Cash sales....................................	75,000 A	
Collections on accounts receivable...............	60,000 A	
Collections on notes receivable..................	20,000 A	

	Income Statement	
	Debit	Credit
INCOME STATEMENT:		
Sales returns and allowances....................	350 A	
Sales..		155,250 A

The $350 debit was entered in the Income Statement debit column, and the $155,250 entered in the credit column was the amount necessary to balance the debits and credits.

Cash discounts on sales. Assume the same facts as in the immediately preceding illustration; in addition, there were cash discounts on sales amounting to $450.

Income Statement Working Papers
For the Year Ended December 31, 1959

	Comparative Balance Sheet			
	December 31,		Year's Changes—Net	
	1959	1958	Debit	Credit
BALANCE SHEETS:				
Assets:				
Accounts receivable.............	5,000	5,600		600 A
Notes receivable................	3,000	2,500	500 A	

	Cash	
	Debit	Credit
CASH:		
Cash sales....................................	75,000 A	
Collections on accounts receivable...............	60,000 A	
Collections on notes receivable..................	20,000 A	

	Income Statement	
	Debit	Credit
INCOME STATEMENT:		
Sales returns and allowances....................	350 A	
Sales discounts..............................	450 A	
Sales..		155,700 A

Bad debts. Assume the same facts as in the preceding illustration; also assume that $1,200 of accounts had been removed from the ledger as uncollectible. This removal, of course, affected the change in the accounts receivable during the year. If no consideration is given to this matter, the sales will be understated and the loss from bad debts will be ignored.

Income Statement Working Papers
For the Year Ended December 31, 1959

	Comparative Balance Sheet			
	December 31,		Year's Changes—Net	
	1959	1958	Debit	Credit
BALANCE SHEETS:				
Assets:				
Accounts receivable.............	5,000	5,600		600 A
Notes receivable...............	3,000	2,500	500 A	

	Cash	
	Debit	Credit
CASH:		
Cash sales.....................................	75,000 A	
Collections on accounts receivable...............	60,000 A	
Collections on notes receivable..................	20,000 A	

	Income Statement	
	Debit	Credit
INCOME STATEMENT:		
Sales returns and allowances....................	350 A	
Sales discounts...............................	450 A	
Bad debts....................................	1,200 A	
Sales..		156,900 A

Computation of purchases. Two illustrations are presented below showing the computation of purchases.

Basic illustration. The first illustration shows the basic procedure.

Cash purchases...		$ 3,600
Purchases on account:		
Payments to trade creditors.........................	$92,700	
Less accounts payable—beginning of period...........	5,900	
Payments for purchases during the period............	$86,800	
Add accounts payable—end of period................	5,500	92,300
Total purchases...		$95,900

The computation can, of course, be simplified by merely deducting the decrease in accounts payable during the year, thus:

Cash purchases.......................................	$ 3,600
Add payments to trade creditors..............................	92,700
Total..	$96,300
Less decrease in accounts payable............................	400
Purchases..	$95,900

The working-paper treatment is shown below.

Income Statement Working Papers
For the Year Ended December 31, 1959

	Comparative Balance Sheet			
	December 31,		Year's Changes—Net	
	1959	1958	Debit	Credit
BALANCE SHEETS:				
Liabilities:				
Accounts payable—Trade.......	5,500	5,900	400 B	

	Cash	
	Debit	Credit
CASH:		
Cash purchases................................		3,600 B
Payments to trade creditors.....................		92,700 B

	Income Statement	
	Debit	Credit
INCOME STATEMENT:		
Purchases....................................	95,900 B	

Notes, returns and allowances, and cash discounts. This illustration is based on the same facts as the preceding one, with the following additions:

Notes were given to trade creditors.
Purchase returns and allowances amounted to $1,400.
Purchase discounts amounted to $1,675.

Income Statement Working Papers
For the Year Ended December 31, 1959

	Comparative Balance Sheet			
	December 31,		Year's Changes—Net	
	1959	1958	Debit	Credit
BALANCE SHEETS:				
Liabilities:				
Accounts payable—Trade.......	3,000	3,900	900 B	
Notes payable—Trade..........	2,500	2,000		500 B

	Cash	
	Debit	Credit
CASH:		
Cash purchases................................		3,600 B
Payments on accounts payable—Trade...........		79,800 B
Payments on notes payable—Trade..............		12,900 B

	Income Statement	
	Debit	Credit
INCOME STATEMENT:		
Purchase returns and allowances................		1,400 B
Purchase discounts............................		1,675 B
Purchases....................................	98,975 B	

Inventories.   The working-paper treatment of the inventories at the beginning and end of the period is illustrated below.

Income Statement Working Papers
For the Year Ended December 31, 1959

	Comparative Balance Sheet			
	December 31,		Year's Changes—Net	
	1959	1958	Debit	Credit
BALANCE SHEETS:				
Assets:				
Merchandise inventory........	16,000	15,460		540 C

	Cash	
	Debit	Credit
CASH:		

	Income Statement	
	Debit	Credit
INCOME STATEMENT:		
Inventory—December 31, 1958..................	15,460 C	
Inventory—December 31, 1959.................		16,000 C

Completed illustration.   The working papers on the following page combine those in the last illustrations of the computation of sales and purchases and the illustration of the treatment of inventories. It is now also assumed that the expenses for the year were $50,000—all paid in cash.

H. W. BROWN
Income Statement Working Papers
For the Year Ended December 31, 1959

| | Comparative Balance Sheet | | | |
| | December 31, | | Year's Changes—Net | |
	1959	1958	Debit	Credit
BALANCE SHEETS:				
Assets:				
Cash......................	12,740	4,040	8,700	
Accounts receivable...........	5,000	5,600		600 A
Notes receivable—Trade.......	3,000	2,500	500 A	
Inventory..................	16,000	15,460	540 C	
	36,740	27,600		
Liabilities and owner's equity:				
Accounts payable.............	3,000	3,900	900 B	
Notes payable—Trade.........	2,500	2,000		500 B
Owner's equity...............	31,240	21,700		9,540
	36,740	27,600	10,640	10,640

| | Cash | |
	Debit	Credit
CASH:		
Cash sales.....................................	75,000 A	
Collections on accounts receivable..............	60,000 A	
Collections on notes receivable—Trade...........	20,000 A	
Cash purchases................................		3,600 B
Payments on accounts payable.............		79,800 B
Payments on notes payable—Trade...... ...		12,900 B
Expenses.....................................		50,000 D
Increase in cash......................		8,700
	155,000	155,000

| | Income Statement | |
	Debit	Credit
INCOME STATEMENT:		
Sales returns and allowances...........	350 A	
Sales discounts.......................	450 A	
Bad debts....................................	1,200 A	
Sales..........................		156,900 A
Purchase returns and allowances...............		1,400 B
Purchase discounts...........................		1,675 B
Purchases...................................	98,975 B	
Inventory—December 31, 1958.................	15,460 C	
Inventory—December 31, 1959.................		16,000 C
Expenses.....................................	50,000 D	
Net income..................................	9,540	
	175,975	175,975

Accrued revenue and expense. The illustration on the following page shows the working-paper treatment of accruals.

Income Statement Working Papers
For the Year Ended December 31, 1959

	Comparative Balance Sheet			
	December 31,		Year's Changes—Net	
	1959	1958	Debit	Credit
BALANCE SHEETS:				
Assets:				
Accrued interest receivable.......	85	60	25 E	
Liabilities:				
Accrued wages payable..........	700	625		75 F
Accrued interest payable.........	45	58	13 G	

	Cash	
	Debit	Credit
CASH:		
Interest on notes receivable.....................	330 E	
Wages.............................		9,500 F
Interest on notes payable.......................		625 G

	Income Statement	
	Debit	Credit
INCOME STATEMENT:		
Interest earned............................. ...		355 E
Wages.......................................	9,575 F	
Interest on notes payable......................	612 G	

Revenue and cost apportionments.   The following illustration shows the treatment of revenues collected in advance and expenses paid in advance.

Income Statement Working Papers
For the Year Ended December 31, 1959

	Comparative Balance Sheet			
	December 31,		Year's Changes—Net	
	1959	1958	Debit	Credit
BALANCE SHEETS:				
Assets:				
Unexpired insurance.............	650	435	215 H	
Liabilities:				
Rent collected in advance........	300	400	100 I	

	Cash	
	Debit	Credit
CASH:		
Insurance policy purchased.....................		400 H

	Income Statement	
	Debit	Credit
INCOME STATEMENT:		
Insurance expense.............................	185 H	
Rent earned....		100 I

Depreciation. The best procedure for dealing with depreciation expense is to include in the Comparative Balance Sheet columns the accumulated depreciation at the beginning and end of the year.

Income Statement Working Papers
For the Year Ended December 31, 1959

	Comparative Balance Sheet			
	December 31,		Year's Changes—Net	
	1959	1958	Debit	Credit
BALANCE SHEETS:				
Assets:				
Store equipment............	35,000	30,000	5,000	
Accumulated depreciation—				
Store equipment..........	6,300*	4,800*		1,500 J
* Deduction.				

	Cash	
	Debit	Credit
CASH:		

	Income Statement	
	Debit	Credit
INCOME STATEMENT:		
Depreciation—Store equipment.................	1,500 J	

Allowance for doubtful accounts. A preceding illustration (page 577) showed the treatment of bad debts when no Allowance for Doubtful Accounts was included in the Comparative Balance Sheet columns, and accounts determined to be uncollectible were simply removed from the ledger. The following illustration shows the procedure if the Comparative Balance Sheet columns contain an allowance account. The illustration assumes that:

Accounts receivable in the amount of $1,000 were removed from the ledger as uncollectible.

It was believed that the allowance required for the remaining accounts should be $1,500. This is $300 more than was believed necessary a year ago.

The $1,000 must be included in the computation of the sales, as explained on page 577. The bad debts expense is the sum of the $1,000 of accounts found to be worthless and the $300 increase in the allowance account.

Income Statement Working Papers
For the Year Ended December 31, 1959

	Comparative Balance Sheet			
	December 31,		Year's Changes—Net	
	1959	1958	Debit	Credit
BALANCE SHEETS:				
Assets:				
Accounts receivable................	30,000	25,000	5,000 K	
Allowance for doubtful accounts......	1,500*	1,200*		300 L
* Deduction.				

	Cash	
	Debit	Credit
CASH:		
Collections on accounts receivable......................	95,000 K	

	Income Statement	
	Debit	Credit
INCOME STATEMENT:		
Bad debts... $\begin{cases} \end{cases}$	300 L	
	1,000 K	
Sales...		101,000 K

Statement of proprietor's capital or retained earnings.
If it is desired to prepare a statement of the proprietor's capital,
the working papers may be expanded in the manner illustrated
below.

HENRY BARTON
Income and Proprietor's Capital Statements Working Papers
For the Year Ended December 31, 1959

	Comparative Balance Sheet			
	December 31,		Year's Changes—Net	
	1959	1958	Debit	Credit
BALANCE SHEETS:				
Assets:				
Cash......................	7,600	3,600	4,000	
Accounts receivable...........	25,000	21,000	4,000 A	
Inventory....................	40,000	38,000	2,000 C	
	72,600	62,600		
Liabilities and proprietor's equity:				
Accounts payable.............	15,000	20,000	5,000 B	
Henry Barton, capital.........	57,600	42,600		15,000
	72,600	62,600	15,000	15,000

	Cash	
	Debit	Credit
CASH:		
Collections on accounts receivable..............	125,000 A	
Payments on accounts payable.................		70,000 B
Expenses......................................		45,000 D
Drawings.....................................		6,000 E
Increase in cash..............................		4,000
	125,000	125,000

	Income Statement	
	Debit	Credit
INCOME STATEMENT:		
Sales..		129,000 A
Purchases....................................	65,000 B	
Inventory—December 31, 1958.................	38,000 C	
Inventory—December 31, 1959.................		40,000 C
Expenses.....................................	45,000 D	
Net income—down..........................	21,000	
	169,000	169,000

	Statement of Proprietor's Capital	
	Debit	Credit
STATEMENT OF PROPRIETOR'S CAPITAL:		
Balance—December 31, 1958—Per balance sheet..		42,600
Net income.........		21,000
Drawings..........................	6,000 E	
Balance—December 31, 1959..................	57,600	
	63,600	63,600

If the business is a corporation and it is desired to prepare a statement of retained earnings, the working papers may be prepared in the manner shown below.

THE BARTON COMPANY
Income and Retained Earnings Statements Working Papers
For the Year Ended December 31, 1959

| | Comparative Balance Sheet | | | |
| | December 31, | | Year's Changes—Net | |
	1959	1958	Debit	Credit
BALANCE SHEETS:				
Assets:				
Cash........................	7,600	3,600	4,000	
Accounts receivable...........	25,000	21,000	4,000 A	
Inventory..................	40,000	38,000	2,000 C	
	72,600	62,600		
Liabilities and stockholders' equity:				
Accounts payable.............	15,000	20,000	5,000 B	
Capital stock................	30,000	30,000		
Retained earnings............	27,600	12,600		15,000
	72,600	62,600	15,000	15,000

| | Cash | |
	Debit	Credit
CASH:		
Collections on accounts receivable...............	125,000 A	
Payments on accounts payable.....		70,000 B
Expenses......................................		45,000 D
Dividends.....................................		6,000 E
Increase in cash..............................		4,000
	125,000	125,000

| | Income Statement | |
	Debit	Credit
INCOME STATEMENT:		
Sales...		129,000 A
Purchases....................................	65,000 B	
Inventory—December 31, 1958.................	38,000 C	
Inventory—December 31, 1959.................		40,000 C
Expenses.....................................	45,000 D	
Net income—down...........................	21,000	
	169,000	169,000

| | Retained Earnings | |
	Debit	Credit
RETAINED EARNINGS STATEMENT:		
Balance—December 31, 1958—Per balance sheet..		12,600
Net income....................................		21,000
Dividends.....................................	6,000 E	
Balance—December 31, 1959..................	27,600	
	33,600	33,600

···

Quasi-Reorganizations

Business Combinations

Divisive Reorganizations

The preceding chapters supply ample evidence of the importance of the cost basis and the going-concern assumption within the structure of generally accepted accounting. These contribute to a continuity of accountability in the accounts and financial statements. Thus, fixed assets are recorded at cost, and the cost basis is carried forward year after year, generally without regard to current values because current values are not of particular interest in accounting for a going concern. Without detracting from the importance or usefulness of these two features of present-day accounting theory, it would be misleading to create an impression that the application of these concepts creates no difficulties. For example, consider the following questions:

Must a business entity always remain on the cost basis, or are there conditions or circumstances that justify or require a departure from the cost basis?

Is it ever desirable to permit a company to make a fresh start, as far as its basis of accounting is concerned?

Is an accounting basis something that is identified with a particular asset or with a business entity? For example, if assets are transferred from the ownership of Company A to the ownership of Company B, should the accounting basis ever be carried forward or transferred with the asset?

These are important and complex questions. Essentially they deal with the broad question of when, if ever, and under what circumstances, if any, there may be a break in the historical continuity of account balances. The first two questions are particularly relevant during and after periods of significant change in the level of prices. There is the possibility that financial statements may cease being meaningful. This could be the case when the amounts shown in accounts were stated in dollars not reasonably comparable with present-day dollars. Thus, an account balance showing a cost of $100,000 incurred in 1937 certainly carries different connotations than an account balance showing a cost of $100,000 incurred in 1957. Yet the accounting process does not distinguish between two such amounts. In the preparation of financial statements, the fact that the two $100,000 amounts consist of dollars of unequal size is ignored.

The third question is particularly relevant in those cases where properties are transferred from one company to another and the transaction *in substance* results in no new conditions, either as to the control over, or the underlying stockholder interest in, the properties. This sort of situation arises in mergers and similar devices, often induced by income tax considerations, through which new corporate entities may be created and old ones discarded, and through which assets may be shifted about without altering, in any significant degree, the underlying proprietary interests.

The accounting matters associated with the questions raised here will be discussed under the headings of Quasi-Reorganizations, Business Combinations, and Divisive Reorganizations. All involve, fundamentally, the matter of continuity of an accounting basis.

Quasi-Reorganizations

The situation when the price level has declined.   If there has been a significant decline in the level of prices, it is very likely that business, in general, will be depressed, with net losses being the typical result of operations. A number of the assets acquired prior to the fall of prices may no longer be worth their cost or carrying value. Reasonable men may believe that there is only a remote chance for a business to recover, through operations, the outlays made for fixed assets.

Under such conditions, the question arises as to whether financial statements prepared following generally accepted principles of accounting result in meaningful reports. What is the merit of continuing to charge depreciation on cost, when it is likely that a share of such cost outlays has in fact become a "lost" cost? If this is the case, should not the loss be taken now, instead of being taken gradually by continuing the depreciation charges on the basis of the old costs? Are not operating results misstated by continuing to record depreciation on a cost basis associated with a former price level? Also, if the company has a significant deficit, why should it not be permitted to make a fresh start? Instead of carrying forward in the accounts the handicaps associated with the past, why not permit a corporation a fresh start in its accounts?

To bring some of the above questions into sharper focus, assume that a corporation's books show the condition summarized below:

Fixed assets...	$1,000,000
Other assets, net......................................	700,000
Net assets...	$1,700,000
Capital stock...	$1,500,000
Paid-in surplus.......................................	500,000
Less debit balance in Retained Earnings account............	300,000*
Stockholders' equity..................................	$1,700,000
* Deduction.	

It is also assumed that prices have declined materially.

Consider first the matter of the deficit. To eliminate the deficit, the company might transfer its net assets to a newly organized corporation in exchange for the capital stock of the new company, which might begin its corporate existence with the following account balances:

Fixed assets...	$1,000,000
Other assets, net......................................	700,000
Net assets...	$1,700,000
Capital stock...	$1,500,000
Paid-in surplus.......................................	200,000
Stockholders' equity..................................	$1,700,000

It would also be possible to reduce the carrying value of some of the assets by such a device.

Should accounting rules insist upon the creation of a new corporate entity before the historical continuity of any of the account balances can be interrupted?

Quasi-reorganization described. In general, the answer to the above question is no. Within the framework of generally accepted accounting there is a procedure known as a *quasi-reorganization,* by which a fresh start in an accounting sense may be obtained without the expense and other disadvantages incident to the creation of a new corporate entity. It has the following characteristics:

(1) The existing corporate entity is not disturbed.
(2) Recorded asset values may be readjusted (downward) to conform to present conditions.

(3) Typically, a deficit is eliminated.
(4) A quasi-reorganization is accompanied by complete disclosure of the effects it has had on the accounts.

What formalities, if any, are required to effect a quasi-reorganization? Accounting Series Release No. 25 of the Securities and Exchange Commission states that "It has been the Commission's view for some time that a quasi-reorganization may not be considered to have been effected unless . . . the entire procedure is made known to all persons entitled to vote on matters of general corporate policy and the appropriate consents to the particular transactions are obtained in advance in accordance with the applicable law and charter provisions." However, a Commission ruling must be distinguished from a law of general applicability.

A quasi-reorganization is often effected without legal formalities of any kind. If the company has paid-in surplus which is legally available for dividends, the offsetting of the operating deficit against such paid-in surplus does not affect the net amount legally available for dividends. On the other hand, the change in the capital structure may be such as to necessitate obtaining an amendment of the corporate charter.

As indicated above, a quasi-reorganization enables a company to eliminate a deficit. The deficit may be attributable to operating losses or to the recognition of other losses. A deficit need not exist in the accounts before a quasi-reorganization is effected; it may develop as a result of asset write-downs recorded as part of the quasi-reorganization entries. In other words, if fixed assets are overvalued in the accounts, a write-down of such assets to current values should be a part of the quasi-reorganization. It is a part of the fresh start. The write-down establishes a new and current measure of management's accountability; it gives recognition to a loss which occurred prior to the quasi-reorganization; it enables the company to compute its operating charges for depreciation on the basis of values as of the date of the fresh start; and such a write-down may produce a debit balance in the Retained Earnings account.

To illustrate asset write-downs in connection with a quasi-reorganization, let us return to the preceding illustration and assume that the fixed assets carried at $1,000,000 would be more properly valued at $600,000, considering the new conditions. To create a paid-in surplus sufficient to provide for writing down the fixed assets to current values and for eliminating the operating deficit, assume that the capital stock is reduced from $1,500,000 to $1,000,000. If the stock has a par value, the reduction can be accomplished by reducing the number or the par value of the shares outstanding, or by changing from a par to a no-par basis and assigning to the no-par shares an aggregate stated value less than the aggregate par value of the shares formerly outstanding. If the stock is without par value, the number of outstanding shares or the stated value per share may be reduced.

Entries to record the quasi-reorganization are shown below:

Capital stock...	500,000	
Paid-in surplus.....................................		500,000
To record the capital stock reduction from $1,500,000 to $1,000,000.		
Retained earnings......................................	400,000	
Fixed assets......................................		400,000
To record the reduction in the book value of the fixed assets from $1,000,000 to $600,000.		
Paid-in surplus..	700,000	
Retained earnings........................		700,000
To write off the debit balance in Retained Earnings against the paid-in surplus.		

These entries produce the following account balances:

Fixed assets...	$	600,000
Other assets, net......................................		700,000
Net assets...		$1,300,000
Capital stock..		$1,000,000
Paid-in surplus..		300,000
Stockholders' equity...................................		$1,300,000

Any reduction in the book valuation of fixed or other assets which is made in connection with a quasi-reorganization should represent a real loss incurred prior thereto; any write-down in excess of such an incurred loss would have the unjustifiable result of relieving subsequent operations of proper charges for depreciation or other costs, and thus would result in an overstatement of earnings subsequent to the reorganization. In other words, the ultimate result would be an unjustifiable debit to Paid-in Surplus and credit to Retained Earnings. However, it is considered proper to create reserves for losses and expenses which can reasonably be assumed to have been incurred in the past although the amounts thereof may not be definitely determinable at the date of the quasi-reorganization. Unrequired balances in such reserves should ultimately be transferred to the Paid-in Surplus account.

If, subsequent to a quasi-reorganization, it is desired to make additional write-downs in the valuation of assets owned at the time of the reorganization, is it permissible to make such write-downs against Paid-in Surplus? The general opinion seems to be that the results of operations may be misstated unless caution is exercised, and that such subsequent write-downs should be charged to Paid-in Surplus only in case they can be definitely established as representing decreases in value which occurred prior to the quasi-reorganization but were not recognized at that time.

If a corporation receives, after a quasi-reorganization, a dividend paid by a subsidiary from surplus accumulated by it between the date of the acquisition of the stock by the parent company and the date of the reorganization, the dividend should be credited by the parent company to Paid-in Surplus. It should not be taken into retained earnings, because this would be contrary to the general assumption that earned surplus should be exhausted as of the date of the reorganization. The credit to Paid-in Surplus produces the effect which would have been created if the dividend had been paid prior to the reorganization.

In the statements rendered at the close of the period in which a quasi-reorganization was effected, there should be disclosure of all facts relative to the quasi—particularly the amount of the operating deficit eliminated. In the statements for that period and subsequent periods, the earned surplus should be "dated": the statements should show that the retained earnings have been accumulated since the date as of which a quasi-reorganization took place and the operating deficit was eliminated from the accounts. The disclosure may be made as follows:

> Retained earnings—Accumulated since December 31, 1957, the date
> of a quasi-reorganization...................................... $xxxx

How long such dating should be continued has not been determined, but a maximum period of ten years has been mentioned. It has also been suggested that the dating should be continued until the company has established a new earnings record.

As noted earlier, a quasi-reorganization is comparable to a new start. If a deficit in the Retained Earnings account is eliminated at that time, the historical distinction maintained in the accounts between paid-in capital and stockholders' equity resulting from earnings is disrupted. The date of the quasi-reorganization is the starting point for a new record of earned surplus. Should it also be the date of a fresh start in the paid-in surplus accounts? Prior to a quasi, there might have been several paid-in surplus accounts which classified the paid-in surplus according to source; it appears to be acceptable to show all paid-in surplus remaining after the quasi in a single account, indicating in the title of this account that its balance is the aggregate paid-in surplus remaining at the date of the fresh start. Paid-in surplus arising after the quasi should be classified by source in new accounts.

What about charges to paid-in surplus subsequent to the quasi-reorganization? Assume that, before the quasi, the corporation had $100,000 of paid-in surplus arising from transactions in preferred stock and $50,000 of paid-in surplus arising from transactions in common stock, and that it had an aggregate paid-in surplus of $75,000 after the quasi. Subsequent to the quasi, the corporation retires preferred stock at a premium of $60,000. If there had been no quasi, the $60,000 premium could have been charged to the paid-in surplus arising from preferred stock transactions, if such paid-in surplus was legally available for such purposes. After the quasi, can the premium be charged to the $75,000 paid-in surplus remaining immediately after the quasi? There are three theories:

(1) The scale-down of the paid-in surplus from a total of $150,000 to $75,000 should be applied first to the common stock and then to the preferred stock. This would eliminate the $50,000 of paid-in surplus applicable to the common stock and would eliminate $25,000 from the paid-in surplus applicable to the preferred stock; the entire paid-in surplus of $75,000 immediately following the quasi would then be applicable to the preferred stock; the $60,000 premium could be charged to it.

(2) The scale-down should be applied ratably to all classes of stock, with the following results:

	Paid-in Surplus—Preferred	Paid-in Surplus—Common
Balances before quasi.............	$100,000	$50,000
Scale-down.................	50,000	25,000
Balances after quasi.............	$ 50,000	$25,000

Under this theory, $50,000 of the premium on the retirement of the preferred stock could be charged to the paid-in surplus remaining after the quasi, and the remaining $10,000 would have to be charged to Retained Earnings.

(3) When charges are made against paid-in surplus as part of a quasi-reorganization, the choice of the paid-in surplus account to be charged is made arbitrarily. The significance of the classification according to source is thereby destroyed. Under this theory, no portion of the premium paid on the retirement of the preferred stock could be charged to the paid-in surplus left over after the quasi.

Neither the Institute nor the Securities and Exchange Commission appears to have expressed an opinion on this matter. The authors believe that the third theory stated above is the one most compatible with the fresh-start concept, but accountants should recognize the desirability of being guided by legal opinion.

Since the stockholders' authorization of the quasi-reorganization may not occur at a year-end (or other date when the books are closed), it is regarded as permissible for the management to choose some other date as the one at which the quasi becomes effective and from which the earned surplus should be dated. The Securities and Exchange Commission appears to have declined to sanction the adoption, for this purpose, of a date prior to the last closing preceding the authorization of the quasi. The adoption of such an earlier date is not sanctioned, because that would give the management the opportunity arbitrarily to select a date when losses stopped and earnings began.

Quasi-reorganizations are sometimes effected when a company has an earned surplus. If, in such cases, the asset write-downs do not exhaust the earned surplus, subsequent balance sheets should indicate that such remaining surplus arose prior to the date of the quasi-reorganization, and it should be clearly distinguished from earned surplus accumulated after that date.

Status of upward quasi-reorganizations.   Can assets be written up in connection with a quasi-reorganization? Accounting sanction of quasi-reorganizations has been based on a recognition of the desirability of allowing corporations to make a fresh start if they have incurred substantial losses or if their assets are materially overstated. Although there seems to be some tendency to sanction write-ups of some assets so long as the adjustments as a whole result in a net write-down, no approval, up to the time of this writing, has been given to a net write-up.

However, financial statements based on historical cost can become just as misleading from the impact of a significant general price increase as from the opposite, which currently is the only situation that may justify a quasi-reorganization. Therefore, it seems reasonable to expect that, in time, the accounting profession may approve upward quasi-reorganizations, provided, of course, that such procedures are surrounded by strict tests and requirements to eliminate the chance of the procedure being abused by the management of companies in a weak position or with a poor showing who might want to use the device as a "smoke screen."

Business Combinations

Recent history.   Conditions during the period following World War II have been conducive to the combining of businesses. The

desire to diversify, income tax considerations, and the prospect of
economies of larger-scale operations are typical of the incentives
leading to the bringing together of two or more businesses. Such
combining has been achieved through the use of a variety of legal
arrangements. These arrangements have included the formation of
new corporations, the exchange of corporate shares, and the
merger of several corporations with an established corporation, to
mention only a few of the procedures used.

For accounting purposes, the legal formalities are incidentals;
the substantive matter deals with the problem of the accounting
basis that is appropriate for the assets, liabilities, and equities
being combined. If, in fact, there is a continuity, to a significant
degree, of the former ownership, then probably there should be a
continuity of the accounting basis as well.

Purchase versus pooling of interests.   Many business combinations result in no substantive change. Although assets may
be transferred, corporations dissolved, and new corporations
organized in a plan leading to a combination of two or more
businesses, there may, in fact, be a continuance of ownership or
control of the properties involved. In other words, a business combination may be more a matter of *form* than of *substance;* it may
be nothing more than what may be characterized as a pooling of
interests.

In contrast, a combining of two or more businesses may result in
a new ownership arrangement with part or all of the ownership
group of the acquired and now combined businesses being eliminated. Also, the new combination may be accompanied by a change
in the management. Under these circumstances, the combining is
not a mere pooling of interests; the arrangement can be described
as essentially a purchase of one or more businesses with new owners
replacing the former owners.

The situations contrasted above are called a pooling of interests
and a purchase. If a given combination can be characterized as a
purchase rather than a pooling of interests, accountants agree that
the assets purchased should be recorded on the books of the acquiring corporation at cost to the acquiring corporation. In all probability, this will result in a change in the recorded valuation of the
assets being transferred, for there is no reason why the carrying
values of the assets on the books of the seller should coincide with
transfer prices. But if the combination is a mere pooling of interests,
with no substantive change in ownership or control, is there any
reason, assuming that the assets in question have been accounted
for in accordance with generally accepted procedures, for changing

the accounting basis of the assets merely because a change has occurred in the *form* of the business organization?

The Committee on Accounting Procedure has taken a position on this matter, the latest release being in Bulletin No. 48. The following quotation states the committee's position: "When a combination is deemed to be a pooling of interests, a new basis of accountability does not arise. The carrying amounts of the assets of the constituent corporations, if stated in conformity with generally accepted accounting principles and appropriately adjusted when deemed necessary to place them on a uniform accounting basis, should be carried forward . . . " The authors concur in this position, believing that it would be a mistake to base the accounting for combinations on considerations of form rather than substance.

Retained earnings. The same type of question arises in connection with retained earnings. If a combination represents a mere pooling of interests, and asset and liability account balances can be transferred to the new or surviving corporation at existing carrying values, why is it not equally acceptable to transfer undistributed earnings? Bulletin No. 48, mentioned above, approves of such transfers.

However, permitting such transfers means that a new corporation can start with some retained earnings, or that an existing corporation can increase its retained earnings as a result of asset acquisitions. Traditionally, such results did not have the support of generally accepted accounting principles. A corporation's earned surplus represented *its* undistributed earnings, exclusively. In spite of the sensible distinction between a purchase and a pooling of interests, some accountants find it a little difficult to endorse the transfer of retained earnings in connection with a combining of businesses. It appears easier to accept the distinction between a purchase and a pooling of interests in the matter of asset transfers than in the matter of retained earnings transfers. But such transferability seems well established in present-day practice.

With the transfer of retained earnings being permitted in connection with a pooling of interests, it should be recognized that the retained earnings of the new or surviving corporation may be less, but never more, than the sum of the retained earnings amounts of the combined corporations. The combined retained earnings will be less if the stated capital of the new or surviving corporation is larger than the aggregate capital stock and paid-in surplus of the combined corporations. For example, assume the facts stated on the following page.

| | Corporations | | | |
	R	S	T	Total
Common stock..................	$100,000	$125,000	$150,000	$375,000
Paid-in surplus.................	20,000		30,000	50,000
Retained earnings..............	80,000	100,000	70,000	250,000
				$675,000

Assume further that the stockholders of Corporations R, S, and T decide to pool their interests by combining the three corporations into one new corporation having a stated capital of $500,000. After the necessary transfers, the stockholders' equity of the new corporation would appear as follows:

Common stock...	$500,000
Retained earnings...	175,000
	$675,000

If the stated capital of the new corporation is established at an amount less than $375,000, the aggregate stated capital of the old corporations, such reduction is added to paid-in surplus. For example, assume that the stated capital of the new corporation is $300,000. The stockholders' equity will appear as follows:

Common stock...	$300,000
Paid-in surplus..	125,000
Retained earnings...	250,000
	$675,000

Tests for pooling of interests. The distinction between a pooling of interests and a purchase represents a fairly recent development in accounting theory. Since we are dealing with a matter that requires distinguishing between form and substance, there can be no precise list of characteristics of a pooling of interests that will eliminate the necessity for using judgment in evaluating the net results of the provisions of any given combination plan. The following conditions, or some combination of them, have been suggested as necessary in order to justify accounting for a business combination as a pooling of interests:

Continuance of the former ownership.
Continuity of voting rights and consequent control over management.
Continuity of management.
Businesses being combined are engaged in activities that are either similar or complementary.
Businesses being combined are of about the same relative size.

As experience is acquired in this area, no doubt additional criteria will be developed.

Income statement.   When a combination is being treated as a pooling of interests, the income statement issued by the surviving corporation for the year during which the combination occurred should normally include the combined operating results of the several entities for the entire year. As noted in Bulletin 48, "if combined statements are not furnished, statements for the constituent corporations prior to the date of combination should be furnished separately or in appropriate groups."

Preliminary accounting problems.   Whenever negotiations exploring the possibility of combining several companies are in process, one of the foremost problems confronting the several parties to the proposed plan is the determination of the transfer price of the assets of the several companies if it is a purchase arrangement, or of the settlement plan if it is a pooling of interests. It is reasonably certain that some of the businesses being combined will be worth more than others, and some equitable solution must be reached in fairness to the owners of the individual companies, irrespective of whether a purchase or a pooling is being contemplated. Frequently, the books of account provide the starting basis for negotiations, since book values of assets and past earnings may suggest approximate values. It is at this point that the services of an accountant are oftentimes required, because the several books of account may not have been maintained on a reasonably uniform basis and in conformity with generally accepted accounting principles.

It is the accountant's primary function in investigations in anticipation of a combination of businesses to prepare accounting data for the several companies on a reasonably uniform basis. For this purpose, various adjustments of recorded results may be necessary. Errors may have been made. The necessity for some adjustments may arise because of differences in accounting policies. Other adjustments may be needed in order to avoid the possibility that misleading impressions may be produced by unusual transactions.

For these reasons, certain accounts should be analyzed in considerable detail. For example, the accountant should analyze the depreciation accounts of the several companies to determine whether the depreciation policies are acceptable and comparable. If differences are revealed, the effect of these differences on book values and reported earnings must be computed in order to place the accounting data on a reasonably comparable basis. Similarly, the surplus accounts should be analyzed for unusual or nonrecurring items and for evidence of any entries reflecting appraisals or write-downs.

The following list suggests some of the areas where differences are most likely to be discovered:

(1) Depreciation and maintenance policies.
(2) Provision for uncollectible accounts.
(3) Inventory-pricing policy.
(4) Accounting for intangibles.
(5) Valuation of investments.
(6) Provisions for contingencies or losses.
(7) Officers' salaries.
(8) Capitalization policy—division between expense and asset classifications.
(9) Fixed asset valuations in the accounts—cost or appraisal.
(10) Accrual and prepayment policies.
(11) Surplus entries.

It should be recognized that differences in the above areas may not be an indication of incorrect or improper accounting. There are many areas where generally accepted accounting principles permit alternative accounting procedures. In other words, books of account may lack comparability because of clerical mistakes, incorrect accounting, or the application of equally acceptable alternatives. In any event, comparability of accounting data is the objective when a combination is being developed.

After reasonable comparability of accounting data has been achieved, as a general rule the interested parties endeavor to use the data in an intelligent fashion as an aid in arriving at transfer prices or at a settlement plan. Accountants generally recognize that book values, even when comparable, are not always acceptable as a basis for indicating values. Technological changes and the decline in purchasing power of money, to mention only two considerations, may substantially impair the significance of recorded amounts. Furthermore, transfer prices or the settlement plan will be affected not only by the separate values of the assets appearing in the accounts, but by the earning power of the business which owns them. The earning power of a business which has integrated and arranged certain assets as a unit for production or distribution purposes may warrant a total valuation for the business in excess of the combined value of its recorded assets valued separately. In most cases, it is impossible to determine the contribution that an individual asset makes toward earnings. As a practical matter, the value of an individual asset, considered separately, is estimated by considering such matters as its condition, its remaining use-life, its replacement cost, and its resale value. But considering the business as a whole, an estimate of earning power is particularly relevant in determining value, and, in most cases, such estimates are feasible.

If the accountant is asked to review estimates of earning power, the following list is illustrative of the possible pertinent considerations:

(1) Will any items of expense be higher or lower after the combination is effected?
(2) Will key personnel continue with the new or continuing company?
(3) Will any products or productive capacity be discontinued? If so, what will be the effect on overhead?
(4) What is the trend of earnings? Of sales? Of selling prices? Of unit costs?

Settlement plans. Having established values for the several businesses being combined, the plan of settlement must be negotiated. The settlement plan has a definite bearing on the question of whether the arrangement is a purchase or a pooling. A plan whereby the former owners of the voting shares of one or more of the now combined companies receive bonds or cash would indicate a purchase rather than a pooling of interests.

Bulletin 48 makes the following specific references with regard to settlement plans:

"When the shares of stock that are received by the several owners of one of the predecessor corporations are not substantially in proportion to their respective interests in such predecessor, a new ownership or purchase of the predecessor is presumed to result.

"Similarly, if relative voting rights, as between the constituents, are materially altered through the issuance of senior equity or debt securities having limited or no voting rights, a purchase may be indicated.

"Likewise, a plan or firm intention and understanding to retire a substantial part of the capital stock issued to the owners of one or more of the constituent corporations, or substantial changes in ownership occurring shortly before or planned to occur shortly after the combination, tends to indicate that the combination is a purchase."

Divisive Reorganizations

Nature of divisive reorganizations. In the preceding paragraphs, the question of continuity of accounting basis was explored in those cases where two or more businesses are combined under an arrangement called a *pooling of interests*. Similar accounting questions arise in the opposite kind of case; namely, where one business is divided into two or more business entities. Under such an arrangement it is possible to find a continuity of ownership and control, and, accordingly, questions arise as to whether the transfer of assets should be achieved without disturbing their carrying values, and whether some portion of the retained earnings of the original corporation may be transferred to one or more of the new corporations.

Divisive reorganizations may be classified as follows:

"Spin-offs"

A spin-off involves the transfer of a portion of the assets of an existing corporation to a new corporation in exchange for stock of the new corporation, and the subsequent distribution of the stock in the new corporation to the stockholders of the old corporation without surrender by them of any of their stock in the old company.

"Split-offs"

A split-off is like a spin-off except that the stock of the new corporation is distributed to the stockholders of the old corporation in exchange for part of their stock in the old corporation; thus, there is a reduction in the outstanding shares of the old corporation.

"Split-ups"

A split-up involves a transfer of all of the assets of the old corporation to two or more new corporations in exchange for stock in the new corporations. The stock in the new corporations is distributed to the stockholders of the old corporation in exchange for their stock in the old corporation, and the old corporation goes out of existence.

There are detailed and complex income tax regulations applicable to these divisive reorganizations, which influence such plans considerably because, if they comply with the tax rules, the consequences are tax-free.

Position of accounting theory regarding divisive reorganizations. The traditional view is that a new corporation starts its affairs showing assets at the cost in money to the new corporation, or, if other consideration is given, at the fair value of such other consideration, or at the fair value of the property acquired, whichever is more clearly evident. Also, the new corporation commences with no retained earnings. If two or more businesses are combined with no real break in the continuity of ownership and control, the recent emphasis has been on making distinctions between form and substance. In cases of no substantive change, the combined business entity is permitted to carry forward the accounting basis and retained earnings of the predecessor entities.

This raises the question of whether matters of form and substance should not be applied in divisive or break-up cases in a fashion paralleling that applied to the combining case. There would seem to be as much justification.

However, the problem of transferring retained earnings is more difficult in the divisive case. In the combining case, all surpluses and deficits of the constituent corporations are combined. But how does the accountant determine how much or what share of the retained earnings goes to the new corporation where the old corporation continues in existence, or how to divide the retained earnings of the old corporation between or among the new corporations when the old corporation is to be discontinued? Any method or basis used would seem to be arbitrary. This complication may make it difficult to apply, to the divisive situation, the retained earnings carry-over concepts developed for combining situations.

The same difficulty does not exist in connection with the transfers of assets and liabilities; therefore, it is likely that, to an increasing extent, prior carrying values will be used for the assets and liabilities transferred in divisive reorganizations. However, there is not a well-established body of doctrine on this general matter, and it will take further experience with it to develop criteria and customs.

CHAPTER TWENTY-EIGHT

Income Tax Allocation

Background. This chapter is not concerned with the preparation of income tax returns or with the computation of the amount to be shown *in the balance sheet as the liability* for taxes currently payable under federal and state income tax laws. Rather, it considers the question of the amount to be shown *in the income statement as expense.*

It has long been considered proper to show the same amount in both statements, but in recent years the acceptability of this procedure has been seriously and increasingly questioned. The questioning arises from the fact that net income before taxes reported in the income statement may be radically different from taxable net income, with the result that the tax liability may bear no normal relationship to the reported net income before taxes. The fact that tax rates are high augments the distortion.

Differences between net income per books before taxes and taxable net income arise from many causes, among which may be mentioned the following:

Items affecting taxes may be shown in the statement of retained earnings instead of in the income statement.

For example, an extraneous gain of a material amount may be shown in the statement of retained earnings instead of in the income statement.

Accounting rules regarding revenue and expense do not agree in all instances with income tax rules.

For example, provisions for losses under product guaranty agreements are not deductible for income tax purposes; only payments arising from such obligations are deductible. However, it is considered acceptable accounting to make an expense provision for such losses in the year that the product is sold.

A corporation may adopt one accounting method for income tax purposes and another method in its books and financial statements.

For example, a corporation may adopt the completed-contract method for income tax purposes and use the percentage-of-completion method for accounting purposes.

Income tax allocation consists of procedures (discussed at some length in this chapter) intended to cause the tax expense shown in the income statement (but not the tax liability shown in the balance sheet) to bear a more normal relation to the net income before tax reported in the income statement. Tax allocation is intended to reduce or eliminate distortion when:

(a) Material amounts entering into the computation of the income tax liability are not shown in the income statement, or
(b) Material amounts included in the income statement do not enter into the computation of the income tax liability.

An important event in the historical development of this matter occurred in 1944, when the Committee on Accounting Procedure issued A.R.B. No. 23, which stated that: "Income taxes are an expense which should be allocated, when necessary and practicable, to income and other accounts, as other expenses are allocated." In other words, the amount shown in the income statement for income taxes should be the income tax expense properly allocable to the income included in the income statement for the year and not necessarily the amount currently payable for income taxes.

This bulletin stirred up considerable interest and controversy (which has not subsided noticeably in the intervening years). A significant contrary view was expressed in 1945 by the Securities and Exchange Commission. In its Accounting Series Release No. 53 it held that: "The amount shown as provision for taxes should reflect only actual taxes believed to be payable under the applicable tax laws." Since that time, the Committee on Accounting Procedure has issued additional releases on this matter, generally expanding the applicability of the thesis set forth in its Bulletin No. 23; the effectiveness of these releases can be judged by the fact that there have been instances where firms of certified public accountants have qualified their opinion because the client did not use the income tax allocation procedures.

Purpose and nature of the chapter.　The interest in income tax allocation has now become so extensive that the inclusion of a somewhat comprehensive discussion of the subject in a text of this nature seems warranted. The subject raises a number of basic points regarding the accountant's definition of net income.

Although income tax allocation, if generally adopted, would have a bearing on some matters discussed in preceding chapters, it seems desirable to isolate the topic in a separate chapter. For one reason, it is complex. For another, tax allocation, as yet, has not attained the status of a generally accepted accounting principle. To discuss the subject at various places throughout the text, in connection with subjects to which its applicability may ultimately come to be generally recognized, might give the impression that tax allocation was required.

For purposes of this chapter, it is useful to divide the broad issue as follows:

(A) Matters dealing with the location of the income tax charge in the financial statements.
(B) Matters dealing with the allocation of income taxes through time—or, determining the proper income tax expense for the period, which may differ from the current income tax liability.

At the time of this writing, the federal income tax rates applicable to corporate income are:

30% on the first $25,000 of taxable income.
52% on amounts above $25,000 of taxable income.

For convenience, a 50% rate will be used in the following illustrations.

Matters Dealing with the Location of the Income Tax Charge in the Financial Statements

Material charges to retained earnings that reduce the amount of the income tax liability.　Assume that the summary on page 605 was prepared by *A* Company in connection with the computation of its income tax.

Sales...		$800,000
Cost of goods sold.................................	$500,000	
Selling and administrative expenses...................	200,000	
Unusual loss (which is deductible for income tax).....	60,000	760,000
Amount subject to income tax.............................		$ 40,000
Income tax—50%...		$ 20,000

Also assume that the accountant, properly, decided that the unusual loss should not be included in the income statement, because it might cause some statement users to draw misleading inferences, and that it should be charged directly to retained earnings. This leads to the question of the proper statement presentation of the income tax. Consider the following financial statements, where the income tax actually payable is shown in the income statement and the unusual loss is shown in the statement of retained earnings.

A COMPANY
Income Statement
For the Year ___

Sales...		$800,000
Deduct:		
Cost of goods sold.............................	$500,000	
Selling and administrative expenses...............	200,000	700,000
Net income before income tax..........................		$100,000
Income tax...		20,000
Net income...		$ 80,000

A COMPANY
Statement of Retained Earnings
For the Year ___

Retained earnings—beginning of year........................	$480,000
Net income...	80,000
Total..	$560,000
Deduct unusual loss..	60,000
Retained earnings—end of year.............................	$500,000

A statement user might wonder why the income tax on $100,000 of net income before income tax is only $20,000, in view of the common knowledge that income tax rates are near the 50% level. The apparent discrepancy is attributable to the fact that the $60,000 unusual loss, not shown in the income statement, is deductible and has reduced the income tax by $30,000.

Actually, the unusual transaction in this case resulted in a loss of $30,000 to the company, after considering the tax reduction attributable to the loss. Accountants and businessmen often describe the consequences of isolated transactions in terms of their net-of-tax result. Thus, the unusual loss of A Company might be referred to as amounting to $30,000, net of tax.

It was the suggestion of the Committee on Accounting Procedure in its initial release on this topic that, where an item resulting in a material reduction in income taxes is charged to surplus, the tax consequences should also be assigned to surplus, thus in effect reducing the charge to surplus and showing the loss on a net-of-tax basis. In journal form, the entry for the income tax and its allocation would be as follows:

Income tax expense	50,000	
Income tax payable		20,000
Retained earnings		30,000

The income statement and statement of retained earnings of *A* Company, prepared in conformance with tax allocation procedures, are presented below. Note that the effects of income tax allocation procedures are disclosed in the financial statements. Disclosure should always be made when tax allocation procedures are used.

A COMPANY
Income Statement
For the Year ___

Sales		$800,000
Deduct:		
Cost of goods sold	$500,000	
Selling and administrative expenses	200,000	700,000
Net income before income tax		$100,000
Income tax expense		50,000

(The estimated tax liability is $20,000 by reason of a reduction of $30,000 in taxes resulting from an unusual loss. This loss has been charged to retained earnings and the related tax reduction has been treated as an offset thereto.)

Net income	$ 50,000

A COMPANY
Statement of Retained Earnings
For the Year ___

Retained earnings—beginning of year		$480,000
Net income		50,000
Total		$530,000
Deduct:		
Unusual loss	$60,000	
Less tax effect thereof	30,000	30,000
Retained earnings—end of year		$500,000

Under either approach, the balance sheet shows the income tax liability as $20,000.

Material credits to retained earnings that increase the amount of the income tax liability. Assume that *A* Company, instead of suffering a $60,000 unusual loss, had experienced an unusual, taxable gain of $100,000 in addition to the net operating income of $100,000. Under these circumstances, the income tax liability would amount to $100,000, again assuming a 50% tax rate. The income statement and statement of retained earnings, prepared without allocating the income tax, are shown below. The accountant has treated the unusual gain as a direct credit to retained earnings.

A COMPANY
Income Statement
For the Year ___

Sales...		$800,000
Deduct:		
Cost of goods sold..............................	$500,000	
Selling and administrative expenses................	200,000	700,000
Net income before income tax.............................		$100,000
Income tax...		100,000
Net income...		$ -0-

A COMPANY
Statement of Retained Earnings
For the Year ___

Retained earnings—beginning of year.........................	$480,000
Unusual gain..	100,000
Retained earnings—end of year............................	$580,000

If the income tax is allocated, the statements will be:

A COMPANY
Income Statement
For the Year ___

Sales...		$800,000
Deduct:		
Cost of goods sold..............................	$500,000	
Selling and administrative expenses................	200,000	700,000
Net income before income tax.............................		$100,000
Income tax expense...............................	$100,000	
Less portion thereof allocated to taxable gain shown in statement of retained earnings................	50,000	50,000
Net income...		$ 50,000

A COMPANY
Statement of Retained Earnings
For the Year ___

Retained earnings—beginning of year.........................		$480,000
Net income..		50,000
Add unusual gain..................................	$100,000	
Less income tax thereon..........................	50,000	50,000
Retained earnings—end of year............................		$580,000

Evaluation of preceding illustrations. The two preceding illustrations demonstrate the distortion that develops when

A company charges or credits Retained Earnings with losses or gains of material amount;

Such gains or losses are includible in the determination of the income tax liability;

The income statement shows as the tax expense the amount payable; in other words, when income taxes are not allocated.

In the first illustration, where the unusual transaction was adverse in character, nonallocation resulted in increasing the stated net income, as shown below:

Reported net income without tax allocation (See page 605)....... $80,000
Reported net income with tax allocation (See page 606).......... 50,000

In the second illustration, where the unusual transaction was favorable, nonallocation resulted in decreasing the stated net income.

Reported net income without tax allocation (See page 607)....... $ 0
Reported net income with tax allocation (See page 607).......... 50,000

Considering consequences like those shown above, the Committee on Accounting Procedure commented as follows: "Such results ordinarily detract from the significance or usefulness of the financial statements." The authors concur and believe that if the accountant encounters extraordinary items that in his judgment should be excluded from the determination of net income because including them would impair the significance of net income so that misleading inferences might be drawn, then the tax consequences, if any, should also be removed from the income statement. In other words, the tax should follow the extraordinary item.

Income tax allocation within the income statement. If extraordinary items are shown in the income statement, and they have tax consequences, there may be merit in allocating the income tax expense within the income statement. The objective would be to associate the tax effect with the unusual items causing the tax change. Such an allocation procedure can be illustrated by returning to the unusual-gain situation of *A* Company.

A COMPANY
Income Statement
For the Year ___

Sales..		$800,000
Deduct:		
Cost of goods sold...............................	$500,000	
Selling and administrative expenses.................	200,000	700,000
Net operating income before income tax.......................		$100,000
Income tax expense thereon................................		50,000
Net operating income after income tax.......................		$ 50,000
Add unusual gain.................................	$100,000	
Less income tax thereon..........................	50,000	50,000
Net income...		$100,000

Matters Dealing with the Allocation of Income Tax Through Time

Nature of problem. In the preceding section, the problem was merely one of statement location. This section deals with the more difficult problem that arises when the year for tax recognition differs from the year of accounting recognition. The problem will occur under either of the following conditions:

(1) The income per books exceeds the income per tax return.
(2) The income per tax return exceeds the income per books.

Deferred income tax liability. To illustrate the consequences of a situation where the income per books exceeds the income per tax return, assume that *B* Company, engaged in the construction business, uses the percentage-of-completion method of accounting in its financial statements and the completed-contract method for its income tax return. Assume, also, the following facts.

B COMPANY

Construction contracts:	Contract	Year Started	Year Completed	Estimated (and Actual) Total Profit
	A	1960	1961	$ 80,000
	B	1961	1963	200,000
	C	1962	1963	120,000

	1960	1961	1962	1963
Per cent of completion during year:				
A............................	50%	50%		
B............................		30	40%	30%
C............................			75	25
Net income before income tax, reported in the financial statements. (Total estimated profit multiplied by per cent of completion during year.)				
A............................	$40,000	$ 40,000		
B............................		60,000	$ 80,000	$ 60,000
C............................			90,000	30,000
	$40,000	$100,000	$170,000	$ 90,000
Income reported in income tax returns. (Total profit on contracts completed during the year.)				
A............................		$ 80,000		
B............................				$200,000
C............................				120,000
	—	$ 80,000	—	$320,000
Income tax actually payable—50% rate	—	$ 40,000	—	$160,000

A review of the above data will reveal the potential distortion of some of the amounts shown in the financial statements if *B* Company should follow the practice of reporting as tax expense only the tax actually payable currently. For example, no income tax expense or liability would be shown in the 1960 financial statements. By the end of 1962, the company would have reported accumulated earnings before income taxes of $310,000 ($40,000 + $100,000 + $170,000) on the three contracts, but only $40,000 of income tax thereon would have been charged. Furthermore, the 1962 balance sheet would show no income tax liability, although the company is subject to future tax on $230,000 of income already reported in its income statements. The $230,000 amount is the difference between the aggregate net income before income taxes for the years 1960, 1961, and 1962 ($310,000) and the income reported in the 1961 income tax return ($80,000).

Accountants in favor of income tax allocation believe that, on the accrual basis of accounting, a proper matching of revenue and expense requires that the income tax should follow the income. Income that ultimately will be taxable should not be reported in the financial statements as though it were tax-free. The inevitable (or, at least, the reasonably expected) tax liability should be included in the financial statements. They would allocate the income tax on an accrual basis as follows:

	1960	1961	1962	1963
Income statement:				
Net income before income tax...	$40,000	$100,000	$170,000	$ 90,000
Income tax expense............	20,000	50,000	85,000	45,000
Net income....................	$20,000	$ 50,000	$ 85,000	$ 45,000
Balance sheet:				
Income tax payable............		$ 40,000		$160,000
Deferred income tax liability....	$20,000	30,000	$115,000	
	$20,000	$ 70,000	$115,000	$160,000

To acquire an impression of the potential distortion involved in this matter, compare the net figures shown above with the amounts that would be reported without the application of income tax allocation procedures:

	1960	1961	1962	1963
Income statement:				
Net income before income tax..	$40,000	$100,000	$170,000	$ 90,000
Income tax actually payable....	-0-	40,000	-0-	160,000
Net income (loss*)............	$40,000	$ 60,000	$170,000	$ 70,000*
Balance sheet:				
Income tax payable...........	-0-	$ 40,000	-0-	$160,000

If B Company uses income tax allocation procedures, the journal entries for the income tax charges and payments would appear as shown on the following page.

1960 tax expense:

Income tax expense...................................	20,000	
Deferred income tax liability.....................		20,000

1961 tax expense:

Income tax expense...................................	50,000	
Income tax payable.............................		40,000
Deferred income tax liability.....................		10,000

Income tax for 1961 paid:

Income tax payable................................	40,000	
Cash..		40,000

1962 tax expense:

Income tax expense...................................	85,000	
Deferred income tax liability.....................		85,000

1963 tax expense:

Income tax expense...................................	45,000	
Deferred income tax liability........................	115,000	
Income tax payable.............................		160,000

Income tax for 1963 paid:

Income tax payable................................	160,000	
Cash..		160,000

Observe the following with respect to the income tax allocation procedures just described:

In each year, the tax expense to be shown in the income statement is the amount that would be payable if the accounting procedures used in the books were also applied in the tax return.

In each year in which the tax expense shown in the income statement exceeds the tax liability for the year, the excess is credited to a Deferred Income Tax Liability account.

In each year in which the tax liability exceeds the tax expense shown in the income statement, the excess is debited to the Deferred Income Tax Liability account.

Deferred income tax expense.   In the *B* Company case, the net income before tax per books exceeded initially the taxable net income. We now turn to the opposite case, where the taxable income initially exceeds the net income before tax per books.

In such a case, the tax payable in the initial years will be greater than it would have been if it had been computed on the per-books basis; in later years, the reverse can be expected. The tax allocation procedure to be applied is stated on the following page.

In each year, the tax expense to be shown in the income statement is the amount that would be payable if the accounting procedures used in the books were applied in the tax return.

In each year in which the tax liability exceeds the tax expense shown in the income statement, the excess is debited to a Deferred Income Tax Expense account.

In each year in which the tax expense shown in the income statement exceeds the tax liability, the excess is credited to the Deferred Income Tax Expense account.

To illustrate, assume that C Company purchases a fixed asset for $1,500,000. The asset has an estimated use-life of five years, and the company adopts the sum of years' digits depreciation method for its books and the straight-line method for income tax purposes. Data regarding depreciation are presented below:

Year	Books Amount	Books Over-Under* Amount for Taxes	Tax Return Amount
1	$ 500,000	$200,000	$ 300,000
2	400,000	100,000	300,000
3	300,000	-0-	300,000
4	200,000	100,000*	300,000
5	100,000	200,000*	300,000
Total	$1,500,000	-0-	$1,500,000

The tax allocation entries for the five years are indicated below:

	Year 1	Year 2	Year 3	Year 4	Year 5
Assume that the amounts of net income per books before income tax were	$700,000	$600,000	$800,000	$700,000	$900,000
Then the income amounts for tax purposes would be	900,000	700,000	800,000	600,000	700,000
The entries would be:					
Credit Income Tax Payable—for amounts actually payable	$450,000	$350,000	$400,000	$300,000	$350,000
Debit Income Tax Expense—for tax that would be payable on income per books	350,000	300,000	400,000	350,000	450,000
Debit (Credit*) Deferred Income Tax Expense—for difference	$100,000	$ 50,000	-0-	$ 50,000*	$100,000*

Nature of accounts. When income taxes are allocated through time, it is likely that the balance sheet will include either a Deferred Income Tax Liability account or a Deferred Income Tax Expense account. It seems relevant to inquire about the nature of such balance sheet accounts.

It is difficult to fit these accounts into the standard definitions of assets and liabilities. The deferred liability account arises because the income tax amount charged in the income statement exceeds the tax currently payable. There is no existing tax obligation to the government for this excess amount. The deferred liability account is the result of a concept of net income which in effect holds that accrual accounting, in its most complete sense, requires in any given period an income tax charge that would exist if there were no timing differences between the tax return and the books. In short, the objective is to show in the income statement the tax applicable to the income reported in the statement. This theory is in contrast to a concept of net income that holds that the proper measure of tax expense for a period is the amount of the current legal liability arising as a result of current operations.

A similar analysis fits the case of the Deferred Income Tax Expense account. This account arises where the tax actually payable exceeds the amount of the tax charge in the income statement. In no sense is the tax prepaid from the point of view of the government. It is the result of a procedure of net income measurement.

Thus, these balance sheet accounts are justified, so to speak, through a net income concept. For example, the credit balance account arises because of a charge in the income statement believed necessary to properly measure net income. To generalize, a debit or credit balance account resulting from placing in the income statement a necessary amount for revenue or expense is a suitable balance sheet asset or liability. Although these amounts do not represent assets or liabilities in the conventional sense of being things of value owned or legal obligations, it is well established that they should not be included under the Stockholders' Equity caption.

In many cases the deferred tax accounts are properly included under the Current Assets or Current Liabilities captions. In those instances in which the deferment is expected to extend beyond a period approximating the operating cycle, a current classification would be unacceptable.

Continuing divergence.   In the cases presented thus far, the situations were of the type where it was reasonable to expect that accounting income and taxable income would, in time, accumulate to an identical sum. In other words, the divergence between accounting income and taxable income was a temporary phenomenon, the result of a matter of timing and not the result of any items of revenue and expense being permanently excludible for one or the other income-determination purpose.

However, there are some items of revenue that are nontaxable (interest on tax-exempt bonds) and of expense that are not deductible for tax purposes (life insurance premiums). Thus, the divergence will not cancel out but will continue indefinitely and regularly. The reasons favoring the allocation of income taxes do not apply in such cases.

Assumptions and practical difficulties. There are several assumptions and practical difficulties that deserve attention.

Future tax rates. The most obvious practical difficulty concerns the matter of income tax rates. If an item is properly included currently in the determination of net income and will at some later date be includible in the determination of taxable income, what rate should be used for the computation of the deferred income tax liability? Should it be the rate currently prevailing or the rate that may be expected to prevail when the item will be taken for tax purposes? The following quotation from A.R.B. No. 43 is relevant: "The estimated rate should be based upon normal and surtax rates in effect during the period covered by the income statement with such changes therein as can be reasonably anticipated at the time the estimate is made." The problem of rate estimation is particularly vexatious in cases where current earnings are running near the $25,000-per-year level. This fact is attributable to the prevailing rate structure which taxes corporate income above $25,000 at substantially higher rates.

Balancing-out assumption. For tax allocation situations where the timing differs for accounting and tax purposes, there is an assumption that there will ultimately be a balancing-out of the dollar difference. To illustrate the most common instance where such an assumption is cited, consider the case where depreciation charges taken for tax purposes initially exceed the depreciation charges per books. This situation could exist where a company was amortizing emergency facilities over a sixty-month period for income tax purposes and was depreciating them for book purposes over a ten-year life. Another common case is the use of accelerated depreciation for tax purposes and straight-line depreciation per books. Since the aggregate depreciation taken on any asset cannot exceed cost for either tax or book purposes, it can be expected that the periodic differences will cancel out in time. Thus, any tax deferment is temporary; there is no tax saving, unless there is a change of rates in the future.

The above reasoning may be questioned in cases where a business more or less continuously replaces the older assets of a given type or class. Where there is asset turnover, tax and accounting differences, although existing for individual assets, tend to cancel out for the group. Thus, while there is no tax saving from depreciating a single asset on one basis for tax purposes and on another basis for book purposes but only tax postponement (see Table A below), it may work out for a group of assets that a postponed tax is in fact a tax saving from the point of view of the going concern (see Table B).

To illustrate, assume that a company buys one asset each year until it owns five assets. Thereafter it replaces one asset each year, presumably forever. Each asset costs $150,000. Depreciation for accounting purposes is on the straight-line method and for tax purposes is on the sum of years' digits method. For both purposes, a five-year use-life is used.

Table A. Depreciation Schedule for One Asset

| | Depreciation Per | | | | |
| | Tax Return | Books | | | |
Year	Years' Digits Method	Straight-Line Method	Difference	Tax Effect—50% Rate	Cumulative Tax Saving
1	$50,000	$30,000	$20,000	$10,000	$10,000
2	40,000	30,000	10,000	5,000	15,000
3	30,000	30,000	-0-	-0-	15,000
4	20,000	30,000	10,000*	5,000*	10,000
5	10,000	30,000	20,000*	10,000*	-0-

Table B. Depreciation Schedule for the Group of Assets

| | | Depreciation Per | | | | |
Number of Assets Owned	Year	Tax Return Years' Digits Method	Books Straight-Line Method	Difference	Tax Effect—50% Rate	Cumulative Tax Saving
1	1	$ 50,000	$ 30,000	$20,000	$10,000	$10,000
2	2	90,000	60,000	30,000	15,000	25,000
3	3	120,000	90,000	30,000	15,000	40,000
4	4	140,000	120,000	20,000	10,000	50,000
5	5	150,000	150,000	-0-	-0-	50,000
5	6	150,000	150,000	-0-	-0-	50,000
5	7	150,000	150,000	-0-	-0-	50,000
						etc.

The advocates of tax allocation contend that the question of whether a tax deferment is temporary or more or less permanent is not the controlling point. Tax allocation is favored in either case to avoid the distortion of net income that is likely to occur initially whenever a difference in timing develops between the books and the tax return.

Since it is unlikely that amounts treated as tax deferments will be precisely balanced off by opposite differences in the future between the books and the tax return, there is a strong probability that the balance sheet will include, more or less permanently, residuals from the effects of tax allocation procedures. In time, such deferred tax amounts will become meaningless and the accountant will probably consider some plan of correction to remove these amounts from the balance sheet.

This particular problem apparently does not greatly concern the Committee on Accounting Procedure, for in Bulletin 43 it makes the following comment: "The difficulties encountered in allocation of the tax are not greater than those met with in many other allocations of expenses."

Future earnings assumption. There is also an assumption when taxes are deferred as a result of differences in methods per books and per tax return that there will be future earnings. There is some question about how income tax allocation procedures would work out if there were a series of unprofitable years. In the tax rules prevailing at the time of this writing, there is a provision permitting losses to be carried back two years and carried forward five years. Such carry back-carry forward provisions, assuming that they continue to be features of the tax law, minimize this worry considerably. It seems reasonable to expect that businesses generally will not lose the benefit of deductions deferred for income tax purposes or the tax paid on revenues taxed before they are given accounting recognition even though subsequent losses develop.

Other tax allocation applications.   The question of income tax allocation also arises in connection with asset write-offs where the book and tax return treatment differ. Two cases are illustrated below.

Asset write-off for tax purposes only.   Assume that a company determines that there is an advantage in refunding a bond issue five years before maturity. The unamortized discount on the bonds refunded is deductible, for tax purposes, only in the year of refunding. But suppose that, in its books and financial statements, the company decides to continue amortizing the discount over the remaining original life of the bonds refunded. As a result, the income reported in the tax return for the year of refunding will be less than the income per books. During the succeeding five years (remaining original life of refunded bonds), the reverse will prevail, because the books will show a charge for the amortization of bond discount that will not appear in the tax return.

To illustrate this particular matter, assume that the data on the following page show in summary form information from the books and tax return for the year during which the refunding occurred. (For convenience it is assumed that the refunding occurred at the end of the year.)

	Corporate Books	Income Tax Return
Sales.	$600,000	$600,000
Cost of sales and expenses, except regular annual amortization of bond discount.	390,000*	390,000*
Regular annual amortization of bond discount. . . .	10,000*	10,000*
Net income before income tax.	$200,000	
Write-off of unamortized bond discount.		50,000*
Income subject to tax.		$150,000
Income tax actually payable—50%.		$ 75,000
* Deduction.		

If income taxes are not allocated and the tax expense shown in the income statement is the amount of tax currently payable, the net income reported in the financial statements for the year of refunding will be distorted (overstated) by $25,000. This amount equals the immediate tax reduction resulting from the refunding.

Under income tax allocation procedures, the income tax entry for the year during which the refunding occurred is as follows:

Income tax expense.	100,000	
Income tax payable.		75,000
Deferred income tax liability.		25,000

As noted above, during the next five years the taxable income will exceed the book income because the company will have used, for tax purposes, its periodic deduction of the discount on the refunded bond issue. In the books the company will continue to take the regular annual amortization of $10,000 per year. Thus, the tax expense on an allocation basis will differ from the tax actually payable by $5,000 for each of the next five years. This difference is charged each year to the Deferred Income Tax Liability account. For example, assume that, in the year following the bond refunding, the net income before income tax per books was $100,000. The income per tax return would be $110,000. The entry for the income tax would be as follows:

Income tax expense.	50,000	
Deferred income tax liability.	5,000	
Income tax payable.		55,000

Asset write-off for book purposes only. In the above case the tax recognition preceded the accounting recognition. To illustrate an opposite case, that is, where the accounting recognition precedes the tax recognition, assume that the accountant for *D* Company concludes, justifiably, that an intangible asset, with a book value of $100,000 after the current year's amortization of $20,000 has been recorded, is worthless and writes it off the books. However, it is known that such a write-off will not be permitted for income tax purposes, although continued annual amortization charges of $20,000 will be accepted for tax purposes. This means that the income per books and per tax return will differ as follows:

Year of write-off of asset: Tax-return income will be larger by $100,000.

Succeeding five years: Each year the tax-return income will be smaller by $20,000.

Two comparative income statements of *D* Company are presented below. The first statement shows the results of operations without income tax allocation. The second shows the results of operations with income tax allocation.

D COMPANY
Condensed Comparative Income Statement
(Without Income Tax Allocation)
For Two Years

	Year of Write-off	Succeeding Year
Sales....................................	$500,000	$500,000
Cost of sales and expenses, except amortization...	$380,000*	$380,000*
Regular annual amortization of intangible........	20,000*	-0-
Total....................................	$400,000*	$380,000*
Net income before income tax.................	$100,000	$120,000
Income tax (actually payable).................	50,000*	50,000*
Net income (before unusual item in one year)....	$ 50,000	$ 70,000
Write-off of intangible asset...................	100,000*	
Net loss....................................	($ 50,000)	

    * Deduction.

In the preceding comparative income statement, note that the income tax actually payable is the same for both years, since for income tax purposes the regular amortization program is continued.

D COMPANY
Condensed Comparative Income Statement
(With Income Tax Allocation)
For Two Years

	Year of Write-off	Succeeding Year
Sales....................................	$500,000	$500,000
Cost of sales and expenses, except amortization....	$380,000*	$380,000*
Regular annual amortization of intangible.........	20,000*	-0-
Total....................................	$400,000*	$380,000*
Net income before income tax...................		$120,000
Net income before write-off.....................	$100,000	
Write-off of intangible asset....................	100,000*	
Income tax expense............................		60,000*
Net income....................................	$ -0-	$ 60,000

    * Deduction.

Income tax entries following income tax allocation procedures are set forth below:

Year of write-off of asset:

Deferred income tax expense............................	50,000	
Income tax payable...............................		50,000

Succeeding year:

Income tax expense....................................	60,000	
Deferred income tax expense........................		10,000
Income tax payable...............................		50,000

Over the years, the aggregate net income will be the same under either approach. If tax allocation procedures are used, the write-off produces significantly less distortion of the net income in the year of write-off. In effect, the write-off is handled on a net-of-tax basis by the use of tax allocation procedures. Since the $100,000 balance in the intangible asset account is deductible for future tax purposes, and will afford a potential tax reduction of $50,000, those accountants favoring allocation procedures argue that $50,000 is the correct measure of the loss when it is determined that the intangible is worthless.

Loss provisions and corrections.   As noted earlier, income tax allocation procedures in effect treat the results of unusual transactions on a net-of-tax basis. One such case was the $100,000 write-off of the intangible asset, which, under tax allocation procedures, resulted in a $50,000 reduction in the net income for the current year. The question arises as to how far the net-of-tax concept should be extended. Specifically, should net-of-tax reasoning apply in the case of loss provisions and asset reinstatements?

For instance, assume that, shortly before year end, a company receives a number of claims for refund from customers asserting that merchandise recently received was not of standard quality. Investigation shows such claims to be valid and that one batch of the company's product shipped during the year was defective, although it was not known to be defective until the customers' claims initiated the investigation. The company's accountant estimates that a loss of $200,000 will result from the defective batch, although only a small portion of refund claims have been received by the company by year end. Such losses are not deductible for tax purposes until the claims are settled. However, generally accepted accounting holds that provision should be made for all known losses, provided, of course, that the amount can be determined with reasonable precision. Under these circumstances, should the accountant report the loss as $200,000, or, since it will be deductible for tax purposes in some future period, on a net-of-tax basis of $100,000, assuming an income tax rate of 50%?

Although no authoritative answer can be given to this question, there is increasing evidence that accountants are taking the net-of-tax approach into consideration when determining the adequacy of loss provisions not yet deductible for income tax purposes. In other words, when a provision is made in the income statement for an estimated liability which is deductible for income tax purposes in future periods, and such amount is material, the future tax reduction is being anticipated more often than was formerly the case. This is particularly true where the earnings record and prospects indicate that the chances are reasonably good for the prospective deduction to result in a future tax reduction. And, as noted earlier, the present carry back-carry forward provisions in the tax law help in providing such an assurance of ultimate tax benefit.

To illustrate the application of net-of-tax reasoning to loss provisions, let us return to the assumed facts relating to the $200,000 of prospective claims for refund for defective merchandise.

Year of loss provision:

```
Estimated loss from defective merchandise.............  100,000
    Estimated liability for damage claims..............           100,000
    Provision for $200,000 of damage claims on a net of tax
    basis.
```

Year claims are settled:

(Assume that the net income before income tax equals $300,000, exclusive of claims paid; since the claims paid are deductible for tax purposes, the tax return would show income of $100,000.)

```
Claims paid.......................................  200,000
    Cash..........................................           200,000
    Summary entry for claims paid.

Income tax expense................................  150,000
    Income tax payable............................           150,000
    Income tax expense for year.

Estimated liability for damage claims.................  100,000
Income tax payable................................  100,000
    Claims paid...................................           200,000
    To close Claims Paid and Estimated Liability for
    Damage Claims accounts and adjust the Income Tax
    Payable account to amount payable.
```

Another problem in this general area that may be mentioned concerns the reinstatement of asset amounts that have no further tax deductibility. For instance, assume that a company has fully depreciated certain of its fixed assets. It now discovers that the facilities are of further use and proposes to reinstate some portion of their cost in the accounts (in effect, correct prior depreciation).

Since such costs have been deducted for tax purposes in earlier years and will offer no further deduction benefit, there are those who urge that the lack-of-deductibility feature be one of the elements considered in determining the amount to be reinstated. The reasoning is that an asset with a limited-term existence that cannot be depreciated or amortized in the future for income tax purposes is not as "valuable" as an identical asset whose depreciation or amortization is deductible for income tax purposes. In other words, tax deductibility, in and of itself, has value to a profitable enterprise; where such deductibility privilege can be transferred, it has market value.

The following hypothetical facts and journal entries may be helpful in pointing up some of the aspects of this question.

```
Data: Asset cost......................... $600,000
      Original use-life................... 10 years
      Present book value.................    -0-     (fully depreciated)
      Present evidence indicates that the asset will last another five years.
      Depreciation correction, $200,000—but after taxes are considered,
         the prior years' earnings are understated by only $100,000.
```

Correction entry:

```
Accumulated depreciation........................... 100,000
   Correction of prior years' earnings...............          100,000
```

Annual depreciation entry—next five years:

```
Depreciation expense............................... 40,000
   Income tax payable.............................          20,000
   Accumulated depreciation.......................          20,000
```

Entry for income tax expense:

(Assuming that the books show net income before income tax of $100,000, then the tax return would show income of $140,000, because the $40,000 of depreciation charges shown above are not deductible for income tax purposes.)

```
Income tax expense.................................... 50,000
   Income tax payable...............................          50,000
```

Note.   The income tax expense per income statement is $20,000 less than the tax liability. In the above case, the tax liability is $70,000.

The influence of distortion.   A review of the releases by the Committee on Accounting Procedure and a study of some of the applications in published financial statements have led the authors to conclude that an important factor in the development of support for income tax allocation is the accountant's concern with net income distortion. The accountant does not like to see net income made different by a procedure adopted only for tax purposes. The fairly common case arises when a company makes a substantial investment in new equipment and depreciates it on an accelerated plan for tax purposes only. This reduces significantly the current income tax payments. If the tax expense is reported for accounting purposes without tax allocation, the stated net income has been made higher merely by the adoption of a procedure for tax purposes. Such distorted net income figures are often widely publicized, generally in the form of earnings per share or per cent of return on investment. That the apparently favorable showing is really the result of a tax device is not disclosed. To repeat, it is believed that potential distortion is a strong motive in this area of accounting.

Present status. The matter of tax allocation is far from settled. The record to date has been one of continued expansion of the applicability of allocation procedures. However, it is clear that not all accountants favor tax allocation. This is evident from the position taken by the 1957 revision committee of the American Accounting Association, as follows:

"In any given period, some differences may be attributable to the inclusion or exclusion for tax computation of revenue or expired cost recognized under accounting principles as net income determinants in earlier or later periods. Since such differences are often significant, and since they may give rise to expectations of wholly or partially offsetting differences in later periods, they should be disclosed.

"Disclosure is sometimes accomplished by recording the differences as prepayments (given an expectation of future tax savings) or accruals (given the opposing prospect). However, these items do not present the usual characteristics of assets or liabilities; the possible future offsets are often subject to unusual uncertainties; and treatment on an accrual basis is in many cases unduly complicated. Consequently, disclosure by accrual may be more confusing than enlightening and is therefore undesirable."

The accounting student sooner or later will encounter this matter in its practical setting and find it necessary to weigh the merits of tax allocation procedures. The problem has numerous ramifications, is extremely important in its effect on net income measurement, and probably will not be completely settled for years. Of course, any requirement, whether the result of legislation or of voluntary action by accountants, that would minimize or eliminate the differences between the books and tax return would likewise minimize or eliminate the problem that has led to the development of tax allocation procedures.

CHAPTER TWENTY-NINE

Price-Level Impact on Financial Statements

A basic assumption of accounting. The two paragraphs below appear in Chapter 8.

"Another basic assumption for accounting purposes is that the monetary unit (the dollar) is of constant dimensions; in other words, it is assumed that the purchasing power of the dollar remains unchanged. During certain periods this assumption has squared substantially with reality. But it is also true that, during other periods, the purchasing power of the dollar has changed. In spite of such changes, accounting has continued to treat all dollars as equal, whether the dollar amounts in the accounts represent 1932 dollars or 1949 dollars or current dollars. Such accounting could result in misleading financial statements.

"Although the assumption of a stable dollar is an assumption contrary to fact, to date the majority of accountants have felt no compulsion to modify accounting methods or procedures in an attempt to make allowance for such variation in the unit of measurement. Such reluctance is hardly the result of an unawareness on the part of accountants that prices change. It is more likely attributable to a belief that changes in the value of money, during most periods, have been so gradual as not to materially undermine the validity of the assumption. . . ."

In the eight-year period 1940–1948, the price level of consumers' goods increased 71%. Between 1940 and 1957, the price level of consumers' goods doubled. (See the chart on page 624.) As the general level of prices rises, the purchasing power of the dollar declines. Thus, the purchasing power of the dollar declined 50% between 1940 and 1957. This may not be a "typical" period—a period can be described as typical only in retrospect. Nevertheless, the movement of prices has been so significant that a careful evaluation of the basic assumption noted above is probably warranted.

CONSUMERS' PRICE INDEX — U. S. BUREAU OF LABOR STATISTICS

Adjusted to 1940═100

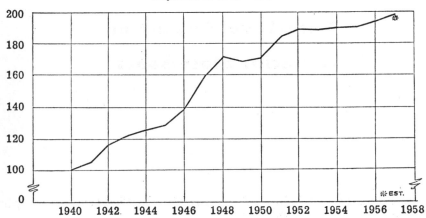

Fundamental questions. Before proceeding with a re-examination of the assumption regarding the stability of the unit of measurement used in accounting, it seems fundamental to inquire about some of the implications arising from the known fact that the purchasing power of the dollar varies. For instance, we know that the dimensions of the unit of measurement vary through time, but what effect, if any, does this have on the data shown in the financial statements?

As a means of clarifying the point just raised, consider the following case:

> In 1940 X purchases some land for $10,000.
> In 1957 X sells the land for $20,000.

First, assume that the purchasing power of the dollar did not change during the period of time that the land was owned by X. Did X make a gain? The answer, clearly, is yes. Since the dollars spent and received had the same purchasing power, X now has twice as much purchasing power.

Second, analyze the transaction in terms of the conditions that actually prevailed—namely, that the purchasing power of the dollar declined 50% between 1940 and 1957. Did X make a gain?

Under such circumstances, it is apparent that X has not increased his purchasing power. But it is a fact that X has 10,000 more dollars after the sale of the land than he invested in the land in 1940. In a "monetary" sense, there has been a gain of $10,000; in an "economic" sense, there has been no gain. (Of course, with a stable price level, monetary and economic results coincide.)

Under prevailing accounting practices, a gain of $10,000 would be reported as a result of the purchase and sale of the land; no consideration would be given to the change in the dimensions of the unit of measurement. The following question seems to be pertinent: Which definition of "gain" should be used in accounting?

As a further case, assume that a service business is organized to operate on a "cash basis," that is, no credit is extended to customers, and the business needs only one fixed asset in its business operations. The fixed asset is purchased for $16,000 and is depreciated over its eight-year useful life. Condensed income statements and dividends data covering the eight-year period since organization are presented below. For convenience, the results of each year are identical.

		Year							Aggregate for
	1	2	3	4	5	6	7	8	8-Year Period
Revenue from services......	$42,000							$42,000	$336,000
Salaries and wages.........	$30,000							$30,000	$240,000
Depreciation..............	2,000			Each year is				2,000	16,000
All other expenses.........	8,000			identical.				8,000	64,000
Net operating income.......	$ 2,000							$ 2,000	$ 16,000
Income tax................	600							600	4,800
Net income................	$ 1,400							$ 1,400	$ 11,200
Dividends.................	$ 1,400							$ 1,400	$ 11,200

A condensed statement of application of funds for the company for the eight-year period would appear as follows:

```
Funds provided by:
   Operations:
      Net income.....................................  $11,200
      Add depreciation charges.......................   16,000 $27,200
Funds applied to:
   Dividends.........................................           11,200
   Increase in working capital (in this case, cash)..          $16,000
```

The income statements report that the company earned $11,200 in the eight-year period. An identical amount was distributed to the owners as dividends. But suppose that during the eight-year period the price level increased 70%, as it did during the 1940–1948 period, and that the company found that $27,200 was needed to replace the fully depreciated and worn-out fixed asset. This price represents a 70% increase in the number of dollars needed to replace the fixed asset. Thus, in order to replace the fully depreciated asset, the company would have to borrow $11,200 or raise additional capital from stockholders in that amount. Management and stockholders might justifiably inquire whether the eight-year period had, in reality, been profitable. Was the aggregate net income $11,200, or $-0-? (Could it be rightfully contended that the "income" tax would in reality be a tax on capital?)

Here, also, it is apparent that accounting rules are based on a "monetary" concept of income. Such accounting is sometimes described as "dollar" accounting. This appears to satisfy some accountants (and some nonaccountants) and to disturb some accountants (and some nonaccountants). Some of the considerations advanced by both groups are submitted in the following paragraphs. In the final analysis, the issue involves the unit of measurement and the way it is used in the accounting process.

Comments supporting conventional accounting. The point is made that the prevailing concepts and practices have worked well over the years. As a consequence, conventional financial statements are widely used and respected. During most periods, the change in the value of money has been so gradual as to have had no discernible effect on financial statements. It is conceded that a period following a world war can hardly be expected to be normal or typical. A conversion from a wartime economy to a peacetime economy inevitably generates some movement in prices. It does not necessarily follow, however, just because prices have been rising rather steadily since World War II, that this condition will continue to prevail. During the four years ending with 1955, the purchasing power of the dollar varied by less than 1%. And in the decade prior to World War II, the purchasing power of the dollar increased approximately 20%—and such a decrease in the price level could occur again.

It is also noted that many legal rules and agreements have been established within the framework of generally accepted accounting. There is some question whether significant revisions could be made in the way the dollar is used in accounting without the revision of numerous statutes and a multitude of contracts.

Some accountants make a point of the fact that, relatively speaking, there are not many "old" dollars in the account balances shown in a current year's financial statements. Therefore, the fact that the dimensions of the dollar have changed does not necessarily lead to a conclusion that financial statements are significantly affected. Old dollars are most likely to be found in the account balances related to the fixed asset group. But, even in this group, the tendency of business management to adopt conservative estimates of useful life removes a considerable portion of the outlays from account balances within ten years. Amounts invested in fixed assets not subject to depreciation or amortization are of slight concern in this matter because they do not enter into the determination of periodic net income.

The point is made by some accountants that price-level changes make it necessary to interpret the results of operations and financial position with greater discrimination, but that users of accounting reports must assume the responsibility for interpreting accounting data. They believe it is the function of accounting to record expenditures and their assignment to expense in cost dollars, which amounts can be adjusted and modified by statement users if desired to serve their objectives and needs.

In this connection it seems relevant to restate the definition of accounting offered in Chapter 1:

"Accounting is the art of recording, classifying, and summarizing in a significant manner and in terms of money, transactions and events which are, in part at least, of a financial character, and interpreting the results thereof."

This definition by the Committee on Terminology is widely quoted and apparently is quite specific in including the responsibility for interpreting the results of the accounting process. But it does not state that the accounting process should include any built-in "interpretive" techniques to give recognition to purchasing-power changes.

There is the accountability function to consider. An important share of the nation's business is conducted by corporations. Decisions covering most aspects of business, including the purchase of additional fixed assets, the revision of product prices, and the curtailment of output, are made by the management group, acting for and in the interests of the owners. In a sense, the relationship between the managers of a corporate enterprise and the owners is one of stewardship. The management group has been entrusted with certain assets, and it is management's responsibility to use the assets in a way advantageous to the stockholders. One of the basic reasons for accounting to exist is to provide a mechanism through which the results of the stewardship may be reported. The consequences of management's decisions must be revealed by the accounting process and discernible in the financial statements; otherwise, an evaluation of managerial effectiveness would be difficult to obtain. If the accounting process prescribed periodic revisions of account balances based on price levels or current values, then the results of decisions, price-level fluctuations, and value judgments could become so commingled as to blur the consequences of management's decisions. It might not be clear whether management was effective or ineffective.

An example typical of those used to stress the importance of the accountability function may be cited as follows: Suppose that the management of Company A reached a decision that it would be good business to expand capacity, and therefore built a new factory costing $500,000, having a daily capacity of 1,000 units. Suppose also that the management of Company B, a competing corporation, reached the same decision three years later and built a plant of identical capacity. However, assume that prices had risen in the intervening period, with the result that Company B's new factory cost $600,000. If accounting procedures prescribed that Company A's accounts and financial statements should show its three-year-old plant at the current cost of $600,000 (before accumulated depreciation) and that depreciation should be computed on the $600,000 amount, thus making the plants identical for accounting purposes, it would be more difficult for the statement users to discern the relative effectiveness of the two managements. There is a basic notion that, if all else were identical, Company A would be more profitable, and that such a condition should be revealed by the accounting process.

Another reason listed in favor of the conventional approach is that cost is a determinable fact, whereas if the accounting process attempted to give recognition to current values or price-level changes, financial statements would become more subjective in character. No attempt is made to deny the generally held opinion that changes in value are important considerations in measuring economic progress. In fact, a common definition of income is stated in terms of the difference between the value of the owners' equity at the beginning and end of the period, after making allowances for withdrawals and additional capital investments. Of course, the value referred to is not book value, but real value. However, there appear to be no suitable tools to facilitate this approach. How is value determined for specialized plant and equipment? Would the use of index numbers solve the problem? Which index is pertinent? Is an index of wholesale prices more relevant than an index of construction costs? Some accountants assert that "there is no basis in economic theory for believing price level adjustments applied to accounting data would result in an adjusted accounting income which would closely approximate economic income."*

---

* Raymond C. Dein, "Price-Level Adjustments: Fetish in Accounting," *The Accounting Review*, January, 1955, page 5.

If the objective of income determination is to provide a "guide for prudent conduct," is it necessary to encumber the accounting process with the chore of estimating changes in wealth from one period to the next? Of more basic interest is an approach that attempts to report the amount that may be distributed to owners and yet leave the business in as favorable an operating position at the end of the year as at the beginning. In other words, the practical emphasis should be on realization, rather than current values, as a test for income.

Comments critical of conventional accounting. The assumption that the unit of measurement is stable is false. The purchasing power or size of the dollar varies through time. This necessarily undermines the accounting process, since it is primarily concerned with numbers of dollars and treats all dollars as idencial. When dollars of differing dimensions are added and subtracted without regard to such dissimilarity, the resulting net income amounts and account balances are subject to misunderstanding. It is obvious that it would be improper to add dollars and francs, yards and meters, or 2,000-pound tons (short tons) and 2,240-pound tons (long tons). Yet this, in effect, is precisely what is done in accounting. The balance of the following account is considered to be $500,000 for all accounting purposes. But each $100,000 debit therein represents a different amount of purchasing power invested in land.

Land	
1929	100,000
1936	100,000
1943	100,000
1949	100,000
1955	100,000

If the amounts were converted to the equivalent of 1955 dollars, the account would appear as follows:

Land	
1929	156,207
1936	193,086
1943	154,730
1949	112,475
1955	100,000

Thus, it is made clear that management did not spend the same amount of purchasing power for each parcel of land.

Although financial statements show dollars of "mixed or varying dimensions," it is doubtful whether statement users so interpret the dollars. It is natural to regard all dollars as present or current dollars. Thus, the $500,000 balance in the first Land account presented above would be thought of in terms of present-day dollars.

The same interpretation would probably apply to the fixed asset category generally. Similarly, dollar amounts shown in income statements most likely are interpreted by statement users as dollars of uniform size, although the depreciation charge, as a general rule, is based on dollars expended in earlier years—often under a price structure not typical of the present period.

The following quotation from a monograph by Sidney S. Alexander points to another possible weakness of conventional accounting.

"The accountant . . . has tried to eliminate the element of subjective judgment from the determination of income. He has tried to establish as nearly as possible hard and fast rules of calculation in order to eliminate the guesswork and to introduce precise measurements. But in a dynamic world subject to unforeseen changes of prices and business conditions, it is not possible to avoid guesswork in the determination of income. To the extent that the accountant can eliminate guesses, he is substituting something else for income. That something else will be a good approximation to income in a fairly static situation when prices and business prospects do not change very much; the approximation will be very poor in a highly dynamic situation when prices and business prospects are fluctuating violently."*

It is probably true that potential income recipients as a group are more interested in knowing how much spending power has been produced by business operations than in an estimate of the current value of the owners' equity. This condition was noted earlier in the chapter and cited as an example against any attempt to make the accounting process solely one of valuation. The comment was made that the emphasis should be on disposability as a test for income and that the income for a period is that which a business entity can distribute to owners and still remain in the same position it was in at the beginning of the period. Those critical of conventional accounting assert that during the years following World War II the amounts reported as income did not meet the disposable test, and that spendable income was significantly below reported income. If price-level changes make it necessary for a business to reinvest a significant portion of reported income to replace fixed assets and maintain productive capacity, the question is raised whether such reported amounts are, in fact, income. Conventional accounting can report as income amounts that must be reinvested in the business in order to maintain capacity.

To most accountants, the matching of revenue and expense is the most important part of the entire accounting process. They

---

* Study Group on Business Income, *Five Monographs on Business Income.* (New York: American Institute of Certified Public Accountants, 1950, pp. 6–7.)

point out that revenue is automatically stated in current dollars and that logic requires that expense matched against such revenue should be stated in current costs. Under conventional procedures, some expenses, like wages and rent, are stated in current costs, while other expenses, like depreciation, and, to a lesser extent, cost of sales, are stated in old (or less current) costs. It is pointed out that one of the principal justifications for *lifo* is that it improves the matching process as a result of its assumption that the "last costs in" are the "first costs out." Thus, under *lifo*, the cost of sales is stated in more recent costs than is the case with *fifo* inventory procedures. There are some critics of conventional accounting who advocate extending the essence of the *lifo* method to other cost elements as a means of curing the flaw of matching dissimilar dollars. This objective could be achieved by basing depreciation charges on current prices for fixed assets and by applying the *lifo* method to supplies and similar expense items.

Reason for criticism. It is apparent that there is a lack of unanimity about the objectives to be achieved by the accounting process. There is criticism because:

Depreciation does not provide for the replacement of assets.
Income taxes are paid on "fictitious" incomes.
Historical dollars are not comparable to present-day dollars.
The balance sheet does not reveal current values.
In the matching of revenue and expense, some of the expenses are stated in old costs.

Although such criticism implies that there are fundamental defects in some of accounting's basic concepts, there appears to be an increasingly vocal group of accountants who contend that the fault is not with accounting's definitions of such concepts as cost, revenue, and expense, but with the imbedded belief that no major consequences result from ignoring fluctuations in the value of money. According to these accountants, the weakness of accounting is its treatment of all dollars in the accounts as identical dollars. The cure is to restate all "old" dollars in terms of their present-day dimensions, but this restatement should be effected by the use of index numbers, which are applicable to dollars, rather than replacement costs, which are applicable to assets. These accountants recognize that this procedure would not result in account balances expressive of present-day *asset values*, but they maintain that such a result would not be a feasible objective of the accounting process.

To pinpoint this basic difference, consider the data on the following page.

A business purchases a given quantity of shipping supplies for
$1,000 when the index of the general price level is stated at 100.
The supplies are used by the business when the index of the
general price level is stated at 105 and when their replacement
cost is $1,100. (In other words, the price of shipping supplies
has risen more than the general level of prices.)

Generally accepted accounting prescribes that expenses should
be measured in terms of costs incurred, thus ruling out the $1,100
amount, which is a "could have been" amount. But does it follow
that cost should be stated in measurement units (dollars) of the
size prevailing at the time goods or services are purchased as
opposed to the size prevailing when the goods or services are used?
Given unstable dollars, can cost measurements have meaning
unless either the date of cost incurrence is known or present-day
dollars are used to convey such financial information?

Those advocating the use of index numbers to adjust recorded
dollars to a "common dollar" basis assert that they are not seeking
to destroy the cost basis of accounting or the well-established
definitions of revenue and expense, but are merely seeking to
eliminate the misleading consequences from commingling dollars
of several sizes. They argue that cost, as a concept, represents an
amount of purchasing power that was committed, but if the unit
of measure has changed in size, then the purchasing power committed should be stated in terms of currently prevailing dimensions
of the dollar. When the accounting process reports that something
consumed (an expense) cost $1,000, that fact will be taken to mean
1,000 present-day dollars. If the $1,000 reported is not stated in
terms of present-day dollars, then the user of financial data will
likely misinterpret such information. The seriousness of such
potential misinterpretation depends upon the extent of the fluctuation in the purchasing power of the dollar and the extent to which
"old" dollars are used in the preparation of accounting reports.

The aim of this group is to adjust dollar amounts so that amounts
compared and interpreted by the statement user will be stated in
dollars of uniform size.

Comparative statements. Many of the dollar amounts
shown in comparative financial statements are "old" dollars.
Thus, comparative statements provide an example of accounting
data which are relatively more susceptible to misunderstanding
as a consequence of variations in the dollar's purchasing power.

An increasing number of businesses regularly present partial or
complete comparative financial statements covering a considerable
number of years. Comparative financial statements for a ten-year
period are fairly common. Some companies regularly report selected

accounting data for a period exceeding thirty years. There are instances where selected yearly data, such as sales, are shown in each annual report for the entire life of the corporation.

When there have been significant movements in the price level, it is obvious that annual data covering several years lose much of their comparability. Consider the following hypothetical data:

	19—	19+1	19+2	19+3	19+4	19+5
Sales........	$100,000	$120,000	$140,000	$160,000	$180,000	$200,000

They imply that sales have doubled in five years. But if the size of the dollar has changed significantly during the period, the data are misleading.

This suggests that during periods of change in the price level, consideration might properly be given to

(1) Discontinuing the presentation of noncomparable data—in effect, abandoning the practice of publishing comparative statements for such long periods as five or ten years, or

(2) Adjusting the data of earlier years by the use of index numbers in such a way as to present dollars of "equal dimensions." Thus, if the index representing the general price level has increased 50% in five years, the sales figure for five years ago would be converted as follows: $100,000 \times 150\% = \$150,000$.

Note the different impression that is gained by using adjusted amounts in the following schedule.

	19+5 (Current Year)	19— (Five Years Ago)
Unadjusted Data		
Sales..............................	$200,000	$100,000
Adjusted Data		
Sales..............................	$200,000	$150,000

In a study undertaken by Professor Ralph C. Jones published by the American Accounting Association, the historical dollars shown in comparative financial statements of four companies were adjusted to a uniform dollar basis.* The effects of such a procedure on the comparative statements can be seen by referring to the following comparative earnings statements of Armstrong Cork Company, one of the four companies studied. In Exhibit A, the dollars have been adjusted and are equivalent to December, 1951, dollars. Exhibit D shows the same comparative data in conventional form.

---

* Ralph Coughenour Jones, *Price Level Changes and Financial Statements—Case Studies of Four Companies,* American Accounting Association, 1955, pp. 86–87 and 92–93.

EXHIBIT A
ARMSTRONG CORK COMPANY
STATEMENTS OF EARNINGS
1941–1951
(Uniform Dollars in Millions—December 1951 Dollar = $1.00)

	1941	1942	1943
Net sales..	$141.4	$134.1	$170.7
Costs and expenses:			
Cost of goods sold (excluding depreciation and amortization)................................	$101.7	$109.2	$141.8
Selling, general and administrative expenses........	19.5	16.2	15.9
Depreciation and amortization....................	4.4	3.9	4.0
	$125.6	$129.3	$161.7
Earnings from operations....................	$ 15.8	$ 4.8	$ 9.0
Other income.....................................	.7	.7	.3
	$ 16.5	$ 5.5	$ 9.3
Interest and nonoperating charges*.................	4.5	.3	.5
Earnings before taxes on income..............	$ 12.0	$ 5.2	$ 8.8
Provision for taxes on income.....................	6.6	3.3	5.9
Net earnings...............................	$ 5.4	$ 1.9	$ 2.9

* Includes purchasing power losses on dispositions of fixed assets and investments.

EXHIBIT D
ARMSTRONG CORK COMPANY
STATEMENTS OF EARNINGS
1941–1951
(Historical Dollars in Millions)

	1941	1942	1943
Net sales..	$ 78.6	$ 82.7	$111.7
Costs and expenses:			
Cost of goods sold (excluding depreciation and amortization)................................	$ 55.6	$ 66.0	$ 91.7
Selling, general and administrative expenses........	10.8	10.0	10.4
Depreciation and amortization....................	2.2	2.0	2.1
	$ 68.6	$ 78.0	$104.2
Earnings from operations....................	$ 10.0	$ 4.7	$ 7.5
Other income.....................................	.4	.4	.2
	$ 10.4	$ 5.1	$ 7.7
Income deductions—interest and miscellaneous nonoperating charges............................	2.5	.1	.1
Earnings before taxes on income..............	$ 7.9	$ 5.0	$ 7.6
Provision for taxes on income.....................	3.7	2.0	3.9
Net earnings...............................	$ 4.2	$ 3.0	$ 3.7

At the time of this writing, there is no evidence to suggest that showing comparative statements in uniform dollars will become the practice of even a small minority of companies. There is no rule of accounting that requires such adjustments. However, it is true that comparative statements showing historical dollars can

EXHIBIT A—(Continued)

ARMSTRONG CORK COMPANY

STATEMENTS OF EARNINGS

1941–1951

(Uniform Dollars in Millions—December 1951 Dollar = $1.00)

1944	1945	1946	1947	1948	1949	1950	1951
$187.4	$160.0	$142.0	$170.6	$190.4	$181.5	$205.5	$204.9
$149.1	$129.3	$114.3	$129.9	$146.4	$134.6	$152.2	$157.3
17.3	17.7	19.1	19.8	21.5	23.0	23.9	24.8
4.4	5.7	4.9	5.4	6.4	7.1	7.5	7.9
$170.8	$152.7	$138.3	$155.1	$174.3	$164.7	$183.6	$190.0
$ 16.6	$ 7.3	$ 3.7	$ 15.5	$ 16.1	$ 16.8	$ 21.9	$ 14.9
.5	.4	.9	.4	1.2	.2	.8	.3
$ 17.1	$ 7.7	$ 4.6	$ 15.9	$ 17.3	$ 17.0	$ 22.7	$ 15.2
.3	1.3	.2	.2	.2	.1	.6	.3
$ 16.8	$ 6.4	$ 4.4	$ 15.7	$ 17.1	$ 16.9	$ 22.1	$ 14.9
11.8	4.2	3.1	7.6	8.2	7.3	12.2	10.7
$ 5.0	$ 2.2	$ 1.3	$ 8.1	$ 8.9	$ 9.6	$ 9.9	$ 4.2

EXHIBIT D—(Continued)

ARMSTRONG CORK COMPANY

STATEMENTS OF EARNINGS

1941–1951

(Historical Dollars in Millions)

1944	1945	1946	1947	1948	1949	1950	1951
$124.5	$108.8	$104.8	$144.0	$173.1	$163.3	$186.8	$201.1
$ 98.8	$ 87.3	$ 82.0	$108.4	$131.6	$121.4	$137.2	$152.7
11.5	12.0	14.1	16.7	19.6	20.7	21.7	24.3
2.3	3.0	2.7	3.0	3.9	4.6	5.0	5.4
$112.6	$102.3	$ 98.8	$128.1	$155.1	$146.7	$163.9	$182.4
$ 11.9	$ 6.5	$ 6.0	$ 15.9	$ 18.0	$ 16.6	$ 22.9	$ 18.7
.3	.3	.6	.3	1.1	.2	.7	.3
$ 12.2	$ 6.8	$ 6.6	$ 16.2	$ 19.1	$ 16.8	$ 23.6	$ 19.0
.2	.8	.1	.1	—	—	.1	—
$ 12.0	$ 6.0	$ 6.5	$ 16.1	$ 19.1	$ 16.8	$ 23.5	$ 19.0
7.8	2.9	2.3	6.5	7.5	6.6	11.1	10.5
$ 4.2	$ 3.1	$ 4.2	$ 9.6	$ 11.6	$ 10.2	$ 12.4	$ 8.5

be misleading, and further fluctuations in the purchasing power of the dollar may stimulate further consideration of uniform-dollar comparative statements.

Current financial statements. Depreciation charges and fixed assets are the amounts most likely to be stated in "old" dollars in the current financial statements. The consequences of this seem less serious for the balance sheet than for the income statement. It is generally agreed that balance sheet usefulness is primarily centered in the reporting of the current position of a business. Under the going-concern assumption, fixed asset balances are residuals and it is not expected that they will be stated in terms of current values or current dollars. Furthermore, the balance sheet is regarded as a statement of secondary importance.

On the other hand, considering the importance attached to net income results, the fact that depreciation is stated in the income statement as a hodgepodge of historical dollars poses a question of considerable significance. As a general rule, the revenues of a business are collectible in reasonably current dollars. And most expenses, other than depreciation, require the disbursement of reasonably current dollars. Such income-statement amounts, although not stated in precisely uniform dollars, are reasonably uniform and reasonably current. This is not the case with depreciation charges; they are based on historical dollars. Thus, if several assets acquired at different dates are being depreciated, the depreciation charge will be a conglomerate of various-size dollars, perhaps bearing only slight semblance to current dollars.

Here is a prime example of accounting's practice of adding non-additive amounts; depreciation is combined (added) with other expense amounts stated in different kinds of dollars, the extent of the difference being determined by the instability of the dollar. Those accountants who believe that the basic cause of misleading income data is related to the failure to adjust dollar amounts to a uniform basis see merit in applying index numbers in the determination of the depreciation charge. Such a conversion procedure would, in their opinion, eliminate most of the source of potential misunderstanding of the net income data.

To illustrate a procedure of converting depreciation charges to current dollars, assume that assets of a certain class have an estimated life of twenty years, and that they have no salvage value. The asset account has a balance of $50,000. A schedule is prepared breaking down the balance of the asset account by year of acquisition and showing the index number applicable to the year, thus:

Elements of Account Balance by Year of Acquisition	Index Number Applicable to the Year of Acquisition
$20,000	100
8,000	120
9,000	125
6,000	130
7,000	145

We shall assume that depreciation is being computed for a year in which the index number is 150. The depreciation on cost would be $2,500, but the depreciation charges adjusted by the index numbers would be $3,248.22, as computed below:

Cost	Depreciation at 5% on Cost	Index Number Ratio	Depreciation Adjusted by Index Number
$20,000	$1,000	150/100	$1,500.00
8,000	400	150/120	500.00
9,000	450	150/125	540.00
6,000	300	150/130	346.15
7,000	350	150/145	362.07
$50,000	$2,500		$3,248.22

The advocates of the use of index numbers do not seem to be in agreement on the question of whether the fixed asset accounts should be written up annually to show valuations adjusted by application of the index numbers. There seems to be little interest in this matter, since the primary concern is to revise the depreciation charged to operations. It would seem that, if index numbers are used for income statement purposes, consistency would require that they be used also for balance sheet purposes. Otherwise, the data used in computing such ratios as those of net income to fixed assets, and net income to stockholders' equity, would not be homogeneous.

If the asset accounts are adjusted, the total depreciation allowance presumably would be credited to the accumulated depreciation account. It has been suggested that, if the asset accounts are not adjusted, only the depreciation on cost ($2,500 in the above illustration) should be credited to the accumulated depreciation account, and the remainder ($748.22 in the illustration) should be credited to a special surplus account.

At the time of this writing, there is considerable interest on the part of accountants in the 1956 annual report of Indiana Telephone Corporation. In that report the corporation, for the first time, presented the 1956 statement amounts in two columns. In Column A the balances were those found in the accounts maintained by conventional accounting procedures for public utilities. In Column B, fixed assets and the depreciation charge were converted to current dollars. Thus, as reported in a note to the stockholders' letter, "the dissimilar units of historical cost are converted to a common present denominator. . . . "

The effect of such procedures is shown by the data on the following page taken from the financial statements presented in the annual report mentioned above.

| | Year 1956 | |
	Column A	Column B
Income statement:		
Property cost consumed in current year's operations (See Note 1).............	$ 301,514.56	$ 410,790.94
Net income (loss)....................	103,557.97	(5,718.41)
Balance sheet:		
Telephone plant.....................	$8,082,910.31	$10,602,381.32
Less—Accumulated allowance for property cost consumed in operations....	1,889,860.74	2,532,026.39
Net telephone plant.............	$6,193,049.57	$ 8,070,354.93
(The following account was shown with the stockholders' equity accounts) Adjustment of stockholders' equity resulting from conversion of recorded plant costs to the common denominator of the current dollar..........	—	$ 1,877,305.36

Note 1 to the financial statements is reproduced below:

"This represents the cost of plant capacity consumed during period indicated and received by telephone users in the form of service for which they pay rates presumably sufficient to cover such cost, including a fair return on the property itself.

"And since the dollars of revenue received from customers in each period are current dollars, this item of cost, representing property currently consumed, should also be expressed in present-day dollars.

"This is not done in Column A, showing data drawn directly from the prescribed 'Uniform System of Accounts,' but these data have been converted into current dollars, with reasonable accuracy, and the result is shown in Column B.

"Under a condition of substantially stable prices, and hence a stable dollar, the recorded costs taken directly from the 'Uniform System of Accounts,' without conversion, could be used, but in view of the marked change that has taken place in the purchasing power of the dollar the recorded data as they stand no longer provide a statement of business and economic truth.

"Therefore, in Column B the cost of property in use and the cost of property consumed are expressed in current dollars, determined by application of appropriate factors, which means that these costs are stated in the same kind of dollars as are being received from customers to compensate for service rendered."

It is too soon to venture an opinion whether such reporting practices may be adopted by other corporations.

Position of the American Accounting Association. In the matter of price-level changes and financial statements, the 1951 supplementary statement prepared by the Committee on Concepts and Standards Underlying Corporate Financial Statements of the American Accounting Association is of interest. In the introductory paragraphs the committee gives recognition to the fact that "under the impact of the price level changes of recent years, challenges have arisen as to the adequacy, for many purposes, of the conventional method of measuring net income." After brief references to some of the arguments pro and con, the committee observes that "ultimately, the desirability of change will be determined by the usefulness of any projected corrective procedures; this in turn will depend largely upon the significance of the problem, a matter not yet fully established by objective measurement."

In order to clarify the problem and to suggest a course of action, the committee addresses its attention to the following questions:

"(1) Is modification of the conventional accounting approach to net income determination to give explicit recognition to changes in the value of the dollar a desirable development?

"(2) If so, what methods are most appropriate for measuring variations in the value of the dollar and for giving effect to such variations in financial reports?

"(3) If such modification is desirable, how is disclosure best to be accomplished?"

The committee's conclusions are set forth below:

"(1) In periodic reports to stockholders, the primary financial statements, prepared by management and verified by an independent accountant, should, at the present stage of accounting development, continue to reflect historical dollar costs.

"(2) There is reason for believing that knowledge of the effects of the changing value of the dollar upon financial position and operating results may be useful information, if a practical and substantially uniform method of measurement and disclosure can be developed.

"(3) The accounting effects of the changing value of the dollar should be made the subject of intensive research and experimentation; the specific significance of the basic problem should be determined with as much accuracy as possible; the means of its solution, if its significance warrants, should be thoroughly investigated.

"(4) The effects of price fluctuations upon financial reports should be measured in terms of the over-all purchasing power of the dollar— that is, changes in the general price level as measured by a GENERAL price index. For this purpose, adjustments should not be based on either the current value or the replacement costs of specific types of capital consumed.

"(5) The measurement of price level changes should be all-inclusive; all statement items affected should be adjusted in a consistent manner.

"(6) Management may properly include in periodic reports to stockholders comprehensive supplementary statements which present the effects of the fluctuation in the value of the dollar upon net income and upon financial position.

"(a) Such supplementary statements should be internally consistent; the income statement and the balance sheet should both be adjusted by the same procedures, so that figures in such complementary statements are coordinate and have the same relative significance.

"(b) Such supplementary statements should be reconciled in detail with the primary statements reflecting unadjusted original dollar costs, and should be regarded as an extension or elaboration of the primary statements, rather than as a departure therefrom.

"(c) Such supplementary statements should be accompanied by comments and explanations clearly setting forth the implications, uses, and limitations of the adjusted data."

Concluding note. Traditionally, accountants have objected to departures from the cost basis, not only because they believed that the cost basis was theoretically correct, but also because they feared that, if the door was opened, a miscellany of methods might come in, with resulting confusion and uncertainty as to the significance of reported earnings. They felt that such confusion would arise even if depreciation charges were the only item revised or adjusted. As the Institute's Committee on Accounting Procedure said in a special statement issued in 1947, and reaffirmed in 1953, "It would not increase the usefulness of reported corporate income figures if some companies charged depreciation on appraised values while others adhered to cost. The committee believes, therefore, that consideration of radical changes in accepted accounting procedure should not be undertaken, at least until a stable price level would make it practicable for business as a whole to make the change at the same time."

As noted above, some of the advocates of index-number accounting do not view their proposal as a departure from the cost basis, but merely as a method to put all recorded dollars on a common footing. Fundamentally, this represents a denial of the conventional assumption regarding the stability of the unit of measurement. To date this distinction has not been recognized by accountants generally and the proposal has been identified as one advocating a departure from the cost basis.

It is clear that generally accepted accounting principles do not include procedures aimed at making allowance for changes in the price level. However, the interest in this matter persists. The authors believe that it is not their function to be that of an advocate, but merely one of stimulating the student to think about this important, unresolved problem.

Assignment Material for Chapter 1

Questions

Question 1-1.   Define accounting.

Question 1-2.   Give the sequence of procedures for the accounting cycle.

Question 1-3.   Give general rules for debiting and crediting:

Asset accounts.   Revenue accounts.
Liability accounts.   Expense accounts.
Owners' equity accounts.

Question 1-4.   What is the function of books of original entry?

Question 1-5.   Describe the relationship between a controlling account and a subsidiary ledger.

Question 1-6.   What objectives are achieved by the use of special columns in books of original entry?

Question 1-7.   Give a brief description of the operation of the voucher system.

Question 1-8.   Give a general description of the posting procedure from special journals.

Question 1-9.

(a) What is the function of the trial balance?
(b) Does a trial balance furnish conclusive evidence of the absence of errors?

Question 1-10.   List the six steps that should be followed to discover errors which have caused the trial balance to be out of balance, and after each operation indicate the general type of error which will be discovered by that operation.

Question 1-11.   For what reason are schedules of subsidiary ledgers prepared at the end of an accounting period?

Question 1-12.   Mention several factors which would influence your decision as to whether you should or should not have a column in the voucher register for travel expense.

Question 1-13.   As the chief accountant of a medium-sized business, why would you choose to use several specialized journals rather than one general journal for recording the company's transactions?

Question 1-14.   Contrast the cash and accrual bases of accounting.

Question 1-15.   Explain why you agree or disagree with the following statement: In any set of books, the adjusting entry to give recognition to office supplies on hand will always involve a debit to an asset account.

Question 1-16.   Give examples of some typical adjusting entries that might be found in the accounts of a business on a pure cash basis of accounting.

Problems

Problem 1-1.   Prepare general journal entries for the transactions of McKee Enterprises on the following page.

19—
June 1—5,000 additional shares of common stock, with a par value of $100, were issued for $505,000 cash.
  3—Delivery equipment, costing $2,500, was purchased from Milton Truck Company; terms, 2/10; n/30.
  4—Merchandise was purchased from Elton Supply Company for $815. A check was issued at this time for $500. The unpaid amount was recorded as a liability.
  7—Merchandise was sold on account to Expansive Corporation for $600.
  9—A 30-day, non-interest-bearing note for $600 was received from Expansive Corporation.
  10—500 shares of McKee Enterprises' own common stock was purchased from shareholders for $45,000.
  11—A check for $2,450 was mailed to Milton Truck Company.
  15—Merchandise was sold on account to Forbes Manufacturing Company for $925.
  17—A $300 premium was paid to Surety Insurance Company for a two-year policy on the office equipment.
  18—The Expansive Corporation note was discounted at the bank. Proceeds amounted to $590.
  21—$100 was collected from Forbes Manufacturing Company to apply on account. Because of the bankruptcy of this customer, the balance of its account was determined to be uncollectible.
  23—A dividend of $1.50 per share was declared, payable July 31 to shareholders of record July 15, on the 9,500 shares of common stock outstanding.
  24—Merchandise with a cost of $50 was returned to Elton Supply Company. Credit memorandum No. 315 was received.
  30—Depreciation on the delivery equipment for the month was $30.
  30—The interest accrued on notes receivable for the month was $10.

Problem 1-2. Dewey Corporation has authorized common stock of 40,000 shares with a par value of $50. On June 15, 19—, 8,000 of these shares are outstanding. The chart of accounts used by the corporation is presented below.

Cash	Premium on Capital Stock
Petty Cash	Retained Earnings
Accounts Receivable	Sales
Allowance for Doubtful Accounts	Sales Returns and Allowances
Notes Receivable	Sales Discounts
Merchandise Inventory	Purchases
Sinking Fund Cash	Transportation In
Land	Purchase Returns and Allowances
Buildings	Purchase Discounts
Accumulated Depreciation—	Depreciation Expense—Buildings
Buildings	Depreciation Expense—Furniture
Furniture	Selling Expense
Accumulated Depreciation—	Transportation Out
Furniture	Office Expense
Vouchers Payable	Miscellaneous General Expense
Notes Payable	Interest Earned
Accrued Interest Payable	Bond Interest Expense
Mortgage Payable	
Bonds Payable	
Capital Stock	

For each of the following transactions, state:

(1) The book of original entry in which the transaction would be recorded if the following journals were used:

Sales	Voucher register
Sales returns and allowances	Check register
Cash receipts	General journal

(2) The general ledger accounts which would be debited and credited.

19—

June 16—Merchandise was sold on account to M. M. White for $380.

17—A petty cash fund of $100 was set up by drawing a check for this amount.

18—Merchandise was purchased from Stoney Corporation for $800; terms, 2/10; n/30.

19—A check for $10,000 was issued to the sinking fund trustee to set up a sinking fund for the retirement of the 20-year, 5% bonds, issued one year ago for $200,000.

20—A 60-day, 4% note was received from M. M. White in settlement of his account.

22—Merchandise was sold to Rapid Grow Company for $730; terms, 2/10; n/30.

23—The corporation issued 1,200 additional shares of capital stock for $62,000 cash.

25—The freight bill for the merchandise sold to Rapid Grow Company was paid, $60.

25—Rapid Grow Company returned merchandise with an invoice value of $200.

26—Furniture was purchased on account for $5,500.

27—Furniture purchased on June 26, with an invoice price of $1,200, was returned to the seller.

30—1,500 shares of capital stock were issued for the following assets and liabilities of a going business:

Merchandise inventory	$35,400
Land	11,600
Buildings	50,000
Mortgage payable	22,000

July 1—Rapid Grow Company settled its account in full.

9—The following expenses were paid: repairs, $123; advertising, $160; bond interest expense, $10,000.

14—The petty cash fund was reimbursed after payment of the following expenses:

Office expense	$35
Transportation in	48

16—The account with Stoney Corporation was settled in full.

Problem 1-3. Following are the voucher register, check register, and general journal of Knobs Supplies Company for the month of November.

(1) Post from these records to the general ledger.
(2) Take a trial balance.

Voucher Register

Voucher No.	Date	Payee	Explanation	Terms	Date Paid	Check No.	Credit Vouchers Payable	Purchases	Transportation In	Sundry Accounts Name of Account	L.F.	Amount
	19—				19—							
11-1	Nov. 2	Emory & Company	Invoice 312	2/10; n/30	Nov. 9	3	1,400 00	1,400 00				
11-2	3	R. & P. Railroad		Cash	3	1	38 00		38 00			
11-3	6	Hoot Advertising		Cash	6	2	350 00			Advertising		350 00
11-4	10	Esther Equipment Co.	Invoice Nov. 10	n/30			680 00	680 00				
11-5	12	Edson Electric Co.		Cash	12	4	35 00			Electricity		35 00
11-6	16	Arbor Sales	Invoice 491	2/10; n/30	25	7	1,060 00	1,060 00				
11-7	20	H. E. Lanson	Rent for Nov.	Cash	20	5	150 00			Rent		150 00
11-8	23	J. B. Benson	Note dated Aug. 15		23	6	1,200 00			Notes payable		1,200 00
11-9	27	Decker & Decker	Invoice 184	n/30			970 00	970 00				
11-10	30	Payroll	For month		30	8	800 00			Accrued payroll		800 00

Check Register

Check No.	Date	Payee	Voucher No.	Debit Vouchers Payable	CREDITS	
					Purchase Discounts	Cash
	19—					
1	Nov. 3	R. & P. Railroad	11-2	38 00		38 00
2	6	Hoot Advertising	11-3	350 00		350 00
3	9	Emory & Company	11-1	1,400 00	28 00	1,372 00
4	12	Edson Electric Co.	11-5	35 00		35 00
5	20	H. E. Lanson	11-7	150 00		150 00
6	23	J. B. Benson	11-8	1,200 00		1,200 00
7	25	Arbor Sales	11-6	1,060 00	21 20	1,038 80
8	30	Payroll	11-10	800 00		800 00

Journal

	DEBITS		Date	L.F.			CREDITS	
Accounts Receivable	Vouchers Payable	General Ledger			Description	General Ledger	Vouchers Payable	Accounts Receivable

		5,000 00	19— Nov. 6		Cash ....
					  Capital stock ....
					    Sale of stock.
						5,000 00		

	100 00		13		Esther Equipment Co. ....
					  Purchase returns and allowances ..
					    Merchandise returned today.
						100 00		

	1,200 00		14		Vouchers payable ....
					  Notes payable ....
					    10-day, non-interest-bearing note given to J. B. Benson.
						1,200 00		

		940 00	19		Notes receivable ....
					  Morrison Works Company ......
					    30-day, 4% note received.
								940 00

		800 00	30		Wages expense ....
					  Accrued payroll ....
					    To record wages expense for month.
						800 00		

Problem 1-4. The monthly column totals of the special journals and the complete general journal of Staples, Incorporated, for the month of May are given below. By using T-accounts, show how the entries would appear in the general ledger after the monthly posting had been completed.

Journal

	Debits						Credits	
Accounts Receivable	Accounts Payable	Sundry	Date	L.F.		Sundry	Accounts Payable	Accounts Receivable
		2,500 00	19— May 6		Notes receivable A Company.... 60-day, 4% note received to apply on account.			2,500 00
		1,800 00	11		Notes receivable discounted Notes receivable.... To eliminate note and contingent liability from the accounts.	1,800 00		
	650 00		15		X Co. X Co.... To correct improper debit to Accounts Receivable.			650 00
330 00			23		E. A. Dale Allowance for doubtful accounts.... To charge back account previously written off but now determined to be collectible.	330 00		
170 00			28		M Corporation Sales returns and allowances.... Merchandise sent to customer to replace goods returned.	170 00		

Sales Book:

  Column total... $48,355.00

Purchases Book:

  Column total... $36,400.00

Cash Receipts Book:

  Column totals:
  Cash... $19,230.00
  Sales Discounts.......................................   68.00
  Accounts Receivable................................... 14,600.00
  Sales...   4,698.00

Cash Disbursements Book:

  Column totals:
  Cash... $26,715.00
  Purchase Discounts....................................   480.00
  Accounts Payable...................................... 22,043.00
  Purchases...   5,152.00

Problem 1-5. Below is information from the accounts of West & Son Company as of December 31, 1959, the close of its accounting year.

(1) The Machinery account has a balance of $75,000. Part of this amount consists of machinery acquired on October 1 of the past year at a cost of $26,000. Machinery has been depreciated at a rate of 8% per year, and the new machinery is to be depreciated at one-fourth the annual rate.

(2) Rent of $6,600 for one year in advance was paid on October 31, 1959, the charge at that time being made to the expense account.

(3) The balance in the Supplies on Hand account on December 31, 1958, after adjustment, was $7,200. Additional supplies costing $3,500 were purchased during 1959 and charged to Supplies Expense. An inventory of supplies, taken on December 31, 1959, showed the amount on hand to be $4,500.

(4) The Allowance for Doubtful Accounts has a balance of $300. It is estimated that 3% of the $19,700 of accounts receivable outstanding on December 31, 1959, will be uncollectible.

(5) A twenty-year, 5% bond issue in the amount of $200,000 was sold on August 1, 1959, for $202,000, interest being payable on February 1 and August 1.

(6) A five-year insurance policy was purchased on May 31, 1958. A prepaid expense account of $900 was established at that time.

Prepare the December 31, 1959 adjusting entries.

Problem 1-6. The following trial balance was taken from the accounts of Reddy and Ready on June 30, 1959. After an examination of these accounts and the additional information which follows, prepare the June 30, 1959 adjusting journal entries.

REDDY AND READY
Trial Balance
June 30, 1959

Cash	18,685.57	
Securities	30,000.00	
Accounts receivable	8,300.10	
Allowance for doubtful accounts		330.00
Notes receivable	1,700.00	
Inventory—June 30, 1958	7,150.08	
Prepaid rent	1,000.00	
Land	5,000.00	
Buildings	40,000.00	
Accumulated depreciation—Buildings		20,000.00
Machinery	75,000.00	
Accumulated depreciation—Machinery		15,000.00
Vouchers payable		19,600.55
Long-term notes payable		4,500.00
Bonds payable		50,000.00
Capital stock		100,000.00
Retained earnings		12,725.60
Sales		89,070.00
Purchases	86,624.00	
Purchase returns and allowances		1,619.20
Transportation in	480.00	
Sales salaries	19,909.20	
Advertising expense	6,500.00	
Office salaries	11,988.40	
Insurance expense	580.00	
Interest expense	120.00	
Interest earned		192.00
	313,037.35	313,037.35

Additional information:

(1) It is estimated that 6% of the outstanding accounts receivable will be uncollectible.

(2) Buildings and machinery are to be depreciated at 8% and 10% per annum, respectively.

(3) The rent is paid on January 1 each year for one year in advance.

(4) The securities held pay interest at 3% per annum on March 1 and September 1.

(5) Of the balance in the insurance account, $430 is the amount of the premium for a two-year policy purchased on April 1, 1959.

(6) Salaries accrued on June 30, 1959, are as follows:

Sales salaries	$925.00
Office salaries	480.45

(7) The accrued interest on notes receivable amounts to $42.50.

(8) The balance in the advertising account represents the cost of advertisements which will appear in the October, November, and December issues of a monthly magazine during 1959.

(9) The interest on the long-term notes payable, amounting to $240 per annum, is payable June 30 and December 31.

(10) The company's bank reconciliation prepared on June 30, 1959, is presented below.

Balance per books...............................		$18,685.57
Deduct:		
N.S.F. check (Arthur Blake).............	$500.00	
Deposit not taken up by bank...........	375.00	875.00
Balance per bank statement...............		$17,810.57

(11) The bonds payable were issued on May 1, 1959, and bear interest at 4% per annum, payable May 1 and November 1.

Problem 1-7. Following are data from the accounts of Royale, Incorporated.

Sales on account..	$29,100
Notes received to settle accounts.............................	3,500
Purchases on account......................................	39,900
Accounts receivable determined to be worthless.................	1,200
Payments to creditors......................................	34,000
Discounts allowed by creditors..............................	1,600
Merchandise returned by customers...........................	810
Collections received to settle accounts.......................	22,700
Notes given to creditors in settlement of accounts...............	1,500
Provision for doubtful accounts.............................	1,900
Interest paid on notes payable..............................	130
Merchandise returned to suppliers...........................	450
Payments made on notes....................................	1,000
Contingent liability eliminated on a customer's note discounted at the bank..	2,000
Discounts permitted to be taken by customers..................	240
Collections received in settlement of notes....................	3,000

Set up controlling accounts for accounts receivable and accounts payable and enter therein the proper amounts as selected from the above information.

Problem 1-8. Selected transactions taken from the accounts of Queen Corporation during 1959 are presented below. Prepare entries for these transactions in general journal form.

(1) A building with a cost of $24,000, and accumulated depreciation of $17,900, was sold on account for $8,500 to Jems Corporation.

(2) The Goodwill account had a balance of $10,000. During the year the account was written off.

(3) Two years ago a $410 account with James Frisby was regarded as worthless and was written off. During the current year the customer informed the company that he would be able to pay $300 on the bill, and sent an accompanying payment of $200.

(4) A fence was placed around a vacant plot of land. The total cost of this improvement was $550.

(5) Semiannual bond interest in the amount of $1,500 was paid. $75 of bond discount was applicable to this period.

(6) Income of $350 was earned on the sinking fund securities.

(7) 3,000 shares of treasury stock, carried at a cost of $29,000, were sold for $28,500. There was no paid-in surplus or premium applicable to these shares.

(8) It was discovered that a previous payment of $175 on account to Richey Brothers had been charged to accounts receivable.

(9) Frank Alders dishonored his non-interest-bearing note for $1,600 which had been discounted by the company at the bank. The bank charged the face of the note plus the $3 protest fee to the company's checking account.

(10) The authorized issue of common stock was increased from 10,000 shares to 15,000 shares. This stock has a $10 par value.

(11) Subscriptions were received for 100 shares of $10 par value common stock at par.

(12) The petty cash fund was increased from $100 to $150.

(13) 1,500 shares of $10 par value common stock were issued for land which had a value of $14,000.

(14) Merchandise costing $320 was received to replace goods of an equal cost returned to the supplier last month.

(15) $7,500 was received from the bank as a result of a mortgage placed on the machinery.

(16) A dividend of $9,000 was paid to satisfy the dividend declaration made one month earlier.

(17) A check for $1,960 was issued in payment for equipment purchased twenty-six days ago with terms of 2/30; n/60.

(18) A $245 collection was made on account from T. Tobb. The customer had incorrectly taken a 2% discount after the expiration of the discount period.

(19) $10 was paid out of the petty cash fund for postage stamps.

(20) Proceeds received from discounting a $500 non-interest-bearing note receivable at the bank were $485.

(21) Freight charge of $12 was paid on a shipment to Richard Elston. The sale had been made f.o.b. shipping point.

(22) A check for $260 was sent to Emory Peters to cover the cost of damaged merchandise sold to him.

(23) A cash sale of $150 was made and the $3 sales tax was collected from the customer.

(24) A collection of $490 was made on Howard Hoag's account. The $500 sale had been made to him f.o.b. destination and the customer paid the $10 shipping charges.

(25) Fully depreciated machinery costing $1,150 was scrapped.

Problem 1-9. Spotless Laundry Company has two major operations. One is dry cleaning, which is done on a credit basis only; the second is the furnishing of twenty-five washing machines and five automatic dryers for self-service use by customers. This function is entirely on a cash basis. All purchases are made for cash. Wages are paid semimonthly and rent is paid monthly. Laundry supplies are purchased frequently.

(1) Suggest a practical set of journals, naming the columnar headings and the arrangement thereof, that can be employed by Spotless Laundry Company.

(2) State the method for posting from these journals.

Problem 1-10. Haughton Company was organized on April 1, 1959. On April 30, 1959, the trial balance and schedules of accounts receivable and accounts payable appearing on the following page were prepared. The trial balance is out of balance and the subsidiary schedules do not agree with their controlling accounts. Also given are the books of original entry, the general ledger accounts, and the accounts receivable and accounts payable ledgers.

(1) Examine these records and prepare a schedule of the errors. (See suggested form at end of problem.)

(2) Prepare a corrected trial balance and schedules of accounts receivable and accounts payable.

HAUGHTON COMPANY
Trial Balance
April 30, 1959

Cash	2,678	
Accounts receivable	1,870	
Notes receivable	250	
Accounts payable		2,280
Mortgage payable		1,000
Capital stock		5,000
Sales		5,230
Sales returns and allowances	50	
Purchases	8,780	
Advertising	100	
Rent	200	
Salaries	4,000	
Purchase discounts		21
Sales discounts	41	
	16,969	13,531

Schedule of Accounts Receivable
April 30, 1959

P. S. Scrip	300
J. E. James	260
Fred Jobe	720*
Roy Abram	600
T. D. Walls	700
Total	1,140

* Credit.

Schedule of Accounts Payable
April 30, 1959

Linden Company	700
Laurel Supply Co.	480
Park Corporation	1,100
Total	2,380

Sales Book (Page 1)

Date	√	Name	Invoice No.	Amount
1959				
April 3	√	Al Bent	1	600
6	√	G. B. Lane	2	400
7	√	Pete Parr	3	140
10	√	P. S. Scrip	4	300
12	√	J. E. James	5	260
16	√	Fred Jobe	6	800
18	√	Roy Abram	7	660
24	√	T. D. Walls	8	700
				3,860

(2) (7)

Purchases Book   (Page 1)

Date	√	Name	Invoice Date	Amount
1959				
April 2	√	Host and Best...............................	April 1	1,300
7	√	Linden Company...........................	7	1,600
12	√	Powell and Son.............................	11	900
22	√	Laurel Supply Co...........................	21	480
27	√	Park Corporation...........................	25	1,100
				5,380
				(9) (4)

Cash Receipts Book   (Page 1)

			DEBITS		CREDITS			
Date	Account Credited	Explanation	Cash	Sales Dis-counts	Accounts Receivable	Sales	Sundry	
					√	Amount		Sales	L.F.	Amount
1959								
April 1	Capital stock.....	Investment	5,000				6	5,000
4	Sales............	Cash sale	500			500		
7	Sales............	Cash sale	330			330		
9	Al Bent..........	Invoice No. 1	594	6	√	600		
10	G. B. Lane.......	Invoice No. 2	150		√	150		
13	Mortgage payable	On machinery	1,000				5	1,000
15	Sales............	Cash sale	450			450		
18	Pete Parr........	Invoice No. 3	140		√	140		
23	Fred Jobe........	Invoice No. 6	792	8	√	800		
28	Sales............	Cash sale	100			100		
			9,056	14		1,690	1,380	6,000
			(1)	(14)		(2)	(7)	

Cash Disbursements Book   (Page 1)

			CREDITS		DEBITS			
Date	Account Debited	Explanation	Cash	Pur-chase Dis-counts	Accounts Payable	Pur-chases	Sundry	
					√	Amount		L.F.	Amount
1959								
April 1	Purchases........	Cash purchase	2,000				2,000	
1	Rent............	For April	200				11	200
5	Advertising......	Pamphlets	100				10	100
8	Host and Best....	Invoice Apr. 1	1,287	13	√	1,300		
12	Linden Company.	Invoice Apr. 7	900		√	900		
16	Purchases........	Cash purchase	500				500	
20	Powell and Son...	Invoice Apr. 11	891	9	√	900		
30	Salaries..........	For April	400				12	400
			6,278	21		3,100	2,500	700
			(1)	(13)		(4)	(9)	

General Journal   (Page 1)

Date			L.F.	Debit	Credit
1959					
April	12	Notes receivable.................................	3	250	
		Accounts receivable (G. B. Lane).............	2/✓		250
		Received 30-day note to settle account.			
	26	Sales returns and allowances.....................	8	50	
		Accounts receivable (T. D. Walls)............	2/✓		50
		Merchandise returned by customer.			

GENERAL LEDGER

Cash   (1)

1959					1959					
April	30	2,678	CR 1	9,056	April	30			CD 1	6,278

Accounts Receivable   (2)

1959					1959					
April	30	1,870	S 1	3,860	April	12			J 1	250
						26			J 1	50
						30			CR 1	1,690

Notes Receivable   (3)

1959										
April	30		J 1	250						

Accounts Payable   (4)

1959					1959					
April	30		CD 1	3,100	April	30	2,280		P 1	5,380

Mortgage Payable   (5)

					1959					
					April	13			CR 1	1,000

Capital Stock   (6)

					1959					
					April	1			CR 1	5,000

Sales   (7)

					1959					
					April	30			S 1	3,860
						30	5,230		CR 1	1,380

Sales Returns and Allowances   (8)

1959										
April	26		J 1	50						

Purchases   (9)

1959							
April	30		P 1	5,380			
	30	7,880	CD 1	2,500			

Advertising   (10)

1959					
April	5		CD 1	100	

Rent   (11)

1959					
April	1		CD 1	200	

Salaries   (12)

1959					
April	30		CD 1	4,000	

Purchase Discounts   (13)

				1959			
				April	30	CD 1	21

Sales Discounts   (14)

1959					
April	30		CR 1	14	

ACCOUNTS RECEIVABLE LEDGER

Al Bent

1959					1959			
April	3		S 1	600	April	9	CR 1	600

G. B. Lane

1959					1959			
April	6		S 1	400	April	10	CR 1	150
						12	J 1	250

Pete Parr

1959					1959			
April	7		S 1	140	April	18	CR 1	140

P. S. Scrip

1959					
April	10		S 1	300	

J. E. James

1959					
April	12		S 1	260	

Fred Jobe

1959			S 1	80	1959		720	CR 1	800
April	16				April	23			

Roy Abram

1959			S 1	660					
April	18								

T. D. Walls

1959		700	S 1	700	1959			J 1	50
April	24				April	26			

ACCOUNTS PAYABLE LEDGER

Host and Best

1959			CD 1	1,300	1959			P 1	1,300
April	8				April	2			

Linden Company

1959			CD 1	900	1959			P 1	1,600
April	12				April	7			

Powell and Son

1959			CD 1	900	1959			P 1	900
April	20				April	12			

Laurel Supply Co.

					1959			P 1	480
					April	22			

Park Corporation

					1959			P 1	1,100
					April	27			

Schedule of Errors

	General Ledger Trial Balance		Accounts Receivable		Accounts Payable	
	Debit	Credit	Control	Schedule	Control	Schedule
General ledger trial balance totals............	16,969	13,531				
Controlling account balances................			1,870		2,280	
Totals of subsidiary ledger schedules..............				1,140		2,380
I. Refoot trial balance: (a) Debit column is underfooted by..	+1,000					
	17,969	13,531				

Problem 1-11.   The trial balance and adjusted trial balance of Howard Steel Company on December 31, 1959, are presented below. Analyze these accounts and present the December 31, 1959 adjusting entries in general journal form.

	Trial Balance December 31, 1959		Adjusted Trial Balance December 31, 1959	
Cash...............................	142,285		142,285	
Accounts receivable.....................	19,900		19,900	
Allowance for doubtful accounts...........		1,230		1,400
Unexpired insurance.....................	500		375	
Accrued interest receivable...............			25	
Truck rental paid in advance..............			155	
Tools................................	1,150		890	
Land................................	5,000		5,000	
Buildings.............................	129,000		129,000	
Accumulated depreciation—Buildings.......		32,200		34,700
Accounts payable.......................		15,400		15,400
Accrued salaries and wages payable........				800
Accrued interest payable.................				20
Dividends payable......................				6,000
Office space rental collected in advance.....				2,000
Purchases............................	132,225		132,225	
Purchase returns and allowances...........		880		880
Truck rental..........................	900		745	
Salaries and wages.....................	82,000		82,800	
Interest expense.......................	110		130	
Bad debts............................			170	
Depreciation—Buildings.................			2,500	
Insurance............................			125	
Tools expense.........................			260	
Dividends............................			6,000	
Capital stock.........................		200,000		200,000
Retained earnings......................		95,000		95,000
Sales................................		158,000		158,000
Office space rental earned................		10,000		8,000
Interest earned........................		360		385
	513,070	513,070	522,585	522,585

Problem 1-12.   Following is the December 31, 1959 trial balance of Sloane Company, prepared at the end of its first year of operations. By analyzing the account balances and assuming typical interrelationships among the accounts, prepare entries in general journal form summarizing the transactions for the year. For example, the $4,000 balance in the Notes Receivable account can be related to a $4,000 credit to Accounts Receivable. After this process is completed, post to T-accounts in order to compare your account balances with those in the trial balance.

SLOANE COMPANY
Trial Balance
December 31, 1959

Cash...	105,000
Sinking fund cash.....................................	5,000
Accounts receivable...................................	4,800
Notes receivable......................................	4,000
Fixed assets...	60,000
U. S. Government bonds...............................	25,000

Accounts payable.....................................		2,300
Bonds payable..		100,000
Capital stock..		100,000
Sales (all on account)................................		40,000
Sales returns and allowances.........................	1,200	
Purchases (all on account)...........................	32,000	
Purchase returns and allowances.....................		1,700
Purchase discounts..................................		1,000
Expenses..	8,000	
	245,000	245,000

Problem 1-13.   J. C. Jiggs Company was formed in 1954 to operate a repair service business. The company has always reported its income on the cash basis. For the year ended December 31, 1959, it showed a net income of $16,400. The management of the company is considering converting from the cash to the accrual basis of accounting at the beginning of 1960, and you are asked to assist in making this change.

The following information is made available:

(1) A delivery truck is rented at the rate of seven cents per mile and the rent is paid once a year on September 1 covering the prior year's mileage. The mileage driven from September 1, 1958, to September 1, 1959, was 36,000 miles. From September 1, 1959, to December 31, 1959, 11,600 miles were driven. It may be assumed that the mileage for each month is the same during any given rental year.

(2) Salaries are paid monthly on the fifteenth of the month. For several years the salary expense has been $450 each month.

(3) On April 1, 1955, the company purchased $50,000 of bonds. They bear interest at the rate of 2½%, payable April 1 and October 1. On October 1, 1959, the company purchased an additional $6,000 of bonds. The interest dates are the same, but the rate on the new bonds is 4%.

(4) Furniture and fixtures were purchased on May 15, 1956, for $5,550. At that time the scrap value was estimated at $300 after a useful life of fifteen years.

Recompute the net income for 1959 on the accrual basis.

Assignment Material for Chapter 2

Questions

Question 2-1. What is the purpose of working papers?

Question 2-2. Under what circumstances, if any, is it acceptable not to enter the adjusting entries in the books of account?

Question 2-3. What is accomplished by closing entries?

Question 2-4. Describe the three different closing procedures illustrated in the text for a mercantile business.

Question 2-5. What is the difference between adjusting entries and closing entries?

Question 2-6. What is the basic difference between the closing procedures of a merchandising organization and those of a manufacturing organization?

Question 2-7. State the important advantages arising from the use of separate working papers for each accounting statement.

Question 2-8. Describe in detail two methods of handling an expense account in separate working papers when 80% of the amount is assignable to manufacturing, 15% to selling expense, and 5% to administrative expense.

Question 2-9. When is it appropriate to use reversing entries, and why do you consider it desirable to use them?

Question 2-10. "Working papers require an unnecessary duplication of effort at year-end." Give the reasons why you agree or disagree with this statement.

Question 2-11. Explain why in some circumstances an adjusting journal entry could be made one way at one year-end and another way at the next year-end.

Question 2-12. The accounts shown below do not appear in the trial balance of *ZYX* Company.

Bad debts expense	Interest expense
Unexpired insurance	Rent received in advance
Accrued rent receivable	

For each of the following adjusting entries, state whether you would or would not make a reversing entry, and give your reason why:

(a) To provide for doubtful accounts.
(b) To record accrued rent receivable.
(c) To record the portion of the prepaid interest on a short-term note payable applicable to the current year.
(d) To record the amount of unexpired insurance premiums at year-end.
(e) To record the portion of rent received in advance which has not been earned.

Problems

Problem 2-1. From the following list of account balances and supplementary data of The Bowman Corporation as of June 30, 1959, prepare working papers. (Ignore federal income taxes.)

Accounts receivable....................................	$ 2,905.20
Accumulated depreciation—Equipment.....................	1,960.00
Allowance for doubtful accounts..........................	230.10
Bond discount.......................................	800.00
Bond interest expense..................................	333.33
Bonds payable.......................................	10,000.00
Cash...	5,498.60
Common stock......................................	17,000.00
Dividends..	500.00
Equipment..	19,600.00
Interest earned.....................................	40.00
Inventory—June 30, 1958.............................	1,640.00
Notes receivable.....................................	1,460.20
Property taxes.......................................	200.00
Purchases..	7,950.00
Purchase returns and allowances.........................	280.25
Rent...	1,200.00
Repairs..	330.00
Retained earnings—June 30, 1958........................	2,543.48
Salaries..	4,200.00
Sales..	14,760.00
Sales discounts......................................	172.65
Sales returns and allowances............................	134.60
Shipping supplies.....................................	1,183.15
Transportation in....................................	106.90
Vouchers payable.....................................	1,400.80

Supplementary data:

(A) The bonds payable were issued at a discount of $1,000 on May 1, 1957, and mature on May 1, 1967. They bear interest at 3%, payable May 1 and November 1.

(B) The allowance for doubtful accounts is to be increased to $400.

(C) The equipment is being depreciated at the rate of 5% per year.

(D) On June 30, 1959, the shipping supplies inventory is determined to be $950.

(E) The inventory on June 30, 1959, is $1,810.

Problem 2-2. The December 31, 1959 adjusted trial balance of Keystone Sales Company is presented on the following page. An inventory taken on December 31, 1959, amounted to $21,500. The company incurred a liability for federal income tax of 50% of its net income for 1959 before income tax.

Required:

(a) Working papers as of December 31, 1959.

(b) Closing entries as of December 31, 1959, using the closing procedure you prefer.

KEYSTONE SALES COMPANY
Adjusted Trial Balance
December 31, 1959

Cash	6,840	
Petty cash	200	
Accounts receivable	10,700	
Allowance for doubtful accounts		1,400
Inventory—December 31, 1958	19,000	
Prepaid insurance	300	
Land	4,400	
Buildings	30,000	
Accumulated depreciation—Buildings		12,500
Delivery equipment	14,000	
Accumulated depreciation—Delivery equipment		5,600
Accounts payable		8,150
Notes payable		2,900
Accrued interest payable		140
Capital stock		50,000
Retained earnings—December 31, 1958		4,230
Dividends	1,500	
Sales		136,000
Sales returns and allowances	1,810	
Purchases	109,300	
Purchase returns and allowances		1,300
Salesmen's salaries	8,000	
Advertising	1,200	
Delivery expense	2,500	
Depreciation—Delivery equipment	1,000	
Rent	2,200	
Office salaries	6,100	
Depreciation—Buildings	2,000	
Insurance expense	150	
Bad debts	800	
Interest expense	220	
	222,220	222,220

Problem 2-3.   Using the financial statements of The Brooks Company, prepare the closing entries as of December 31, 1959, by the closing procedure you prefer.

THE BROOKS COMPANY
Income Statement
For the Year Ended December 31, 1959

Gross sales....			$56,100
Sales returns and allowances	$ 1,200		
Sales discounts	1,630	2,830	
Net sales			$53,270
Cost of goods sold:			
Inventory—December 31, 1958	$19,200		
Purchases	$38,000		
Purchase returns and allowances... $ 900			
Purchase discounts	1,180	2,080	
Net purchases	$35,920		
Transportation in	740	36,660	
Cost of goods available for sale	$55,860		
Inventory—December 31, 1959	21,600	34,260	
Gross profit on sales			$19,010
Selling expenses:			
Store rent	$ 3,000		
Advertising	2,200		
Depreciation—Delivery equipment	1,800	$ 7,000	
General expenses:			
Office expenses	$ 3,800		
Salaries	4,150		
Bad debts expense	340	8,290	15,290
Net operating income			$ 3,720
Other revenue:			
Interest earned	$ 580		
Other expense:			
Interest expense	370	210	
Net income before income tax			$ 3,930
Income tax			1,000
Net income			$ 2,930

THE BROOKS COMPANY
Statement of Retained Earnings
For the Year Ended December 31, 1959

Retained earnings—December 31, 1958	$ 8,990
Net income for the year	2,930
Total	$11,920
Deduct dividends	2,500
Retained earnings—December 31, 1959	$ 9,420

THE BROOKS COMPANY
Balance Sheet
December 31, 1959

Assets

Current assets:			
Cash		$30,500	
Temporary investments		8,000	
Accounts receivable	$14,320		
Less allowance for doubtful accounts	580	13,740	
Accrued interest receivable		200	
Inventory		21,600	$ 74,040

Fixed assets:
Delivery equipment.............................. $39,600
   Less accumulated depreciation.................. 10,800   28,800
                              $102,840

Liabilities and Stockholders' Equity

Current liabilities:
Accounts payable............................... $ 5,905
Notes payable.................................. 6,300
Accrued salaries............................... 215
Accrued income tax payable..................... 1,000 $ 13,420

Stockholders' equity:
Capital stock.................................. $80,000
Retained earnings.............................. 9,420   89,420
                              $102,840

Problem 2-4. Presented below is a summary of the account balances of O'Malley Supply Company on December 31, 1959. By using this information and that which follows:

(a) Prepare separate working papers for each statement.
(b) Prepare two sets of closing entries, using the first two procedures illustrated in the chapter.

Accounts payable...	$ 14,300
Accounts receivable.......................................	22,600
Accumulated depreciation—Buildings........................	12,600
Advertising..	2,500
Allowance for doubtful accounts............................	1,208
Buildings..	28,000
Capital stock..	150,000
Cash..	55,488
Dividends..	6,000
Freight out..	4,520
Interest earned..	310
Interest expense...	370
Inventory—December 31, 1958......................	17,770
Land..	5,000
Long-term investments....................................	75,000
Mortgage payable..	5,000
Office expense...	3,200
Purchases...	62,000
Purchase returns and allowances...........................	2,000
Retained earnings—December 31, 1958....................	26,800
Salaries and wages.......................................	19,900
Sales..	96,110
Sales returns and allowances..............................	1,980
Supplies expense...	4,000

Additional information:

(A) It is estimated that 8% of the outstanding accounts receivable will be uncollectible.
(B) When the buildings were purchased nine years ago, it was estimated that they would have a life of twenty years.
(C) $350 of salaries and wages have accrued on December 31, 1959.
(D) Interest accrued on the long-term investments is $500.
(E) The company is obligated to pay a federal income tax amounting to 50% of its net income before the income tax.
(F) The inventory on December 31, 1959, is $28,300.

Problem 2-5. The trial balance presented below was taken from the ledger of The Uptown Manufacturing Corporation on December 31, 1959, before adjusting entries were posted.

THE UPTOWN MANUFACTURING CORPORATION
Trial Balance
December 31, 1959

Cash	57,744	
Accounts receivable	19,110	
Allowance for doubtful accounts		816
Inventories—December 31, 1958:		
Finished goods	2,090	
Goods in process	12,663	
Materials	18,901	
Unexpired insurance	420	
Land	20,000	
Buildings	94,600	
Accumulated depreciation—Buildings		12,510
Machinery and equipment	106,640	
Accumulated depreciation—Machinery and equipment		29,810
Office equipment	4,600	
Accumulated depreciation—Office equipment		1,030
Accounts payable		9,610
Bonds payable		50,000
Capital stock		200,000
Retained earnings		25,824
Dividends	5,000	
Sales		407,371
Purchases—Materials	128,126	
Purchase discounts		2,410
Transportation in	4,090	
Direct labor	183,200	
Indirect labor	12,640	
Factory supplies	2,100	
Heat, light, and power	16,900	
Tools expense	10,500	
Repairs—Machinery	1,060	
Taxes—Property	3,640	
Sales salaries and expense	14,641	
Advertising	3,938	
Miscellaneous selling expense	1,014	
Office salaries	9,525	
Office supplies	1,816	
Bank charges	75	
Telephone and telegraph	948	
Postage	400	
Interest expense	3,000	
	739,381	739,381

Additional information:

(1) Inventories on December 31, 1959:

Finished goods	$ 3,115
Goods in process	11,981
Materials	19,110

(2) Data for adjusting entries:

    (a) It was estimated that $1,956 of the accounts receivable outstanding on December 31, 1959, would be uncollectible.

    (b) Depreciation for 1959:

Buildings	$ 2,400
Machinery and equipment	4,600
Office equipment	850

    (c) Insurance premiums expired during the year amounted to $200.

    (d) Office salaries of $650 were accrued on December 31, 1959.

    (e) The corporation was liable for $200 of interest expense on December 31, 1959.

(3) The following costs are to be allocated as indicated:

	Manufacturing	Selling Expense	General Expense
Heat, light, and power	80%	5%	15%
Taxes—Property	80	10	10
Insurance	75	10	15
Depreciation—Buildings	80	5	15

(4) The corporation was liable for federal income tax in the amount of 50% of its net income before income tax.

Prepare: (a) Separate working papers for each statement; (b) closing entries, using a Manufacturing and a Revenue and Expense account.

Problem 2-6. Using the trial balance and supplementary data below, prepare separate working papers for each statement with subclassification columns in the income statement working papers.

LAKESIDE SUPPLIES, INCORPORATED
Trial Balance
December 31, 1959

Cash	6,645	
Petty cash	100	
Accounts receivable	17,675	
Allowance for doubtful accounts		400
Notes receivable	3,000	
Inventory—December 31, 1958	25,500	
Advertising supplies	1,200	
Prepaid interest	125	
Furniture and fixtures	8,500	
Accumulated depreciation—Furniture and fixtures		2,150
Delivery equipment	8,200	
Accumulated depreciation—Delivery equipment		3,500
Accounts payable		7,855
Bank loans		10,000
Capital stock		15,000
Retained earnings		5,000
Dividends	7,200	
Sales		151,440
Sales discounts	1,290	
Sales returns and allowances	735	

Purchases...................................	95,300	
Purchase discounts............................		715
Purchase returns and allowances................		995
Advertising..................................	10,700	
Delivery expense.............................	3,125	
Miscellaneous selling expense.................	960	
Rent expense................................	4,800	
Taxes......................................	210	
Office salaries..............................	3,150	
Office expense...............................	660	
Delivery income.............................		220
Commissions earned..........................		1,950
Interest income..............................		300
Interest expense.............................	450	
	199,525	199,525

Supplementary data:

(A) $120 of delivery income applies to 1960.

(B) Depreciation to be provided for 1959:

> 10% of furniture and fixtures
> 20% of delivery equipment

(C) It is estimated that $775 of the accounts receivable will probably prove uncollectible.

(D) Advertising supplies of $800 remain unused.

(E) Office expense includes $120 for a two-year insurance policy to May 1, 1961.

(F) No interest for 1960 has been prepaid.

(G) The following expenses are to be apportioned as indicated:

	Selling	General
Rent..	95%	5%
Taxes.......................................	70	30

(H) Federal income tax liability—$15,255.

(I) Inventory, December 31, 1959—$25,200.

Problem 2-7. The adjusted and unadjusted trial balances of The Renova Supplies Company on March 31, 1959, follow. The inventory on this date was $48,650.15.

Required:

(a) Closing entries on March 31, 1959, using the procedure you prefer.
(b) Reversing entries on April 1, 1959.

THE RENOVA SUPPLIES COMPANY

	March 31, 1959			
	Adjusted Trial Balance		Unadjusted Trial Balance	
Cash.........................	92,189.15		92,189.15	
Accounts receivable.............	61,480.00		61,480.00	
Allowance for doubtful accounts..		5,891.10		3,303.40
Notes receivable................	8,700.00		8,700.00	
Accrued interest receivable.......	200.00			
Inventory—March 31, 1958......	44,400.25		44,400.25	
Unexpired insurance.............	600.00		900.00	

Land...........................	9,200.00		9,200.00	
Buildings.......................	100,000.00		100,000.00	
Accumulated depreciation—Buildings........................		10,000.00		7,500.00
Accounts payable...............		39,605.35		39,605.35
Accrued salaries and wages.......		1,200.00		
Rentals collected in advance......		425.00		
Capital stock...................		200,000.00		200,000.00
Retained earnings...............		53,566.45		53,566.45
Dividends.....................	10,000.00		10,000.00	
Sales...........................		180,142.75		180,142.75
Sales returns and allowances......	2,450.60		2,450.60	
Sales discounts..................	3,770.45		3,770.45	
Purchases......................	129,310.05		129,310.05	
Purchase discounts..............		2,140.00		2,140.00
Transportation in...............	3,605.20		3,605.20	
Insurance......................	300.00			
Salaries and wages..............	19,800.00		18,600.00	
Depreciation—Buildings.........	2,500.00			
Office expenses..................	4,900.80		4,900.80	
Repairs........................	1,745.50		1,745.50	
Postage........................	960.95		960.95	
Freight out.....................	1,455.00		1,455.00	
Bad debts......................	2,587.70			
Rentals earned..................		6,375.00		6,800.00
Interest earned.................		810.00		610.00
	500,155.65	500,155.65	493,667.95	493,667.95

Problem 2-8. The following account balances were selected from the unadjusted June 30, 1959 trial balance of Ames Manufacturing Company:

Inventories—June 30, 1958:
    Finished product... $18,910
    Goods in process... 12,356
    Materials.. 8,612
Purchases—Materials....................................... 62,850
Purchase returns and allowances.............................. 918
Purchase discounts... 614
Freight in... 5,420
Direct labor... 82,309
Indirect labor... 16,350
Heat, light, and power....................................... 9,800
Maintenance and repairs—Factory............................ 2,056
Property taxes... 4,500
Factory supplies expense...................................... 2,800
Miscellaneous factory expense................................. 6,290
Freight out.. 4,012
Bad debts... 1,080
Insurance expense.. 1,400

Adjustments are to be made as follows:

Accrued wages:
    Direct labor... $ 2,100
    Indirect labor... 640
Depreciation:
    Buildings.. $ 4,200
    Machinery... 9,650
    Tools.. 1,800

Expense allocations are to be made as follows:

	Manufacturing	Selling	Administration
Heat, light, and power............	90%	5%	5%
Property taxes....................	90	2	8
Depreciation—Buildings..........	80	10	10
Insurance.......................	90	2	8

Inventories on June 30, 1959 were:

Finished goods...	$25,610
Goods in process...	8,400
Materials..	10,250

Required:

(a) Statement of cost of goods manufactured working papers.
(b) Journal entries to set up and close the Manufacturing account.

Problem 2-9.   Cool Baking Company closes its books quarterly on April 30, July 31, October 31, and January 31. On March 1, 1959, the company borrowed $6,000 at the bank, giving a six-months 6% note. The note was paid at maturity and the interest payment thereon was charged to Interest Expense. The company had no other interest-bearing indebtedness during 1959. On July 1, 1959, the company rented some additional storage space, paying the $900 annual rental in advance. The company's accountant charged the rent to a prepaid account. On July 16, 1959, a premium of $192 was paid for a two-year fire insurance policy effective that date. This was a renewal of an identical policy and is the only insurance carried. A debit of $192 was made to Insurance Expense, which was consistent with the entry made two years earlier for the insurance premium.

Considering this information, you are requested to prepare adjusting and reversing entries related to interest, rent, and insurance as indicated below.

(1) Adjusting entries on April 30, 1959.
(2) Reversing entries on May 1, 1959.
(3) Adjusting entries on July 31, 1959.
(4) Reversing entries on August 1, 1959.

Problem 2-10.   The trial balance and necessary facts for the adjustments on December 31, 1959, of The Empire Manufacturing Corporation appear below.

Required:

(a) Working papers on December 31, 1959.
(b) Closing entries on December 31, 1959, using neither a Manufacturing nor a Revenue and Expense account.

THE EMPIRE MANUFACTURING CORPORATION
Trial Balance
December 31, 1959

Cash...	36,180	
Accounts receivable.............................	35,840	
Allowance for doubtful accounts....................		2,900
Inventories—December 31, 1958:		
Finished goods..................................	10,400	
Goods in process................................	7,310	
Materials.......................................	5,220	

Machinery and equipment............................	70,000	
Accumulated depreciation—Machinery and equipment...		12,500
Office fixtures......................................	4,400	
Accumulated depreciation—Office fixtures..............		1,360
Accounts payable...................................		24,470
Capital stock......................................		100,000
Retained earnings..................................		14,880
Dividends...	2,000	
Sales...		192,200
Purchases—Materials...............................	83,410	
Direct labor......................................	51,600	
Indirect labor.....................................	8,200	
Rent (90% factory; 10% general)....................	8,000	
Factory overhead..................................	11,980	
Selling expenses...................................	9,500	
General expenses..................................	4,270	
	348,310	348,310

Inventories—December 31, 1959:

Finished goods...	$12,300
Goods in process......................................	8,110
Materials...	7,700

50% of the corporation's net income before income tax must be paid to the government as federal income tax.

Facts for adjustments:

(a) $800 is to be added to the allowance for doubtful accounts.
(b) Depreciation on the machinery and equipment for 1959 is $3,000.
(c) Depreciation on the office fixtures for 1959 is $510.

Problem 2-11. The following trial balance was taken from the books of Smith-Perry Company on December 31, 1959:

SMITH-PERRY COMPANY
Trial Balance
December 31, 1959

Cash..	11,460	
Accounts receivable................................	13,755	
Allowance for doubtful accounts......................		1,140
Notes receivable...................................	11,000	
Accrued interest receivable..........................	165	
Inventory—December 31, 1958.......................	41,650	
Store fixtures.....................................	40,750	
Accumulated depreciation—Store fixtures..............		8,150
Accounts payable..................................		16,120
Bank loans..		5,000
D. H. Smith, capital................................		44,180
D. H. Smith, drawings..............................	3,000	
K. B. Perry, capital................................		40,100
K. B. Perry, drawings..............................	2,400	
Sales...		196,550
Sales returns and allowances........................	1,940	
Sales discounts....................................	585	
Purchases...	145,830	
Purchase returns and allowances.....................		2,020
Advertising..	6,500	

Salesmen's salaries	22,800	
Miscellaneous selling expenses	1,315	
Rent expense	6,000	
Taxes	360	
Office salaries	3,000	
Office expense	890	
Interest expense	210	
Interest earned		350
	313,610	313,610

Supplementary data:

Of the interest expense, $25 is prepaid interest for 1960 on the bank loans.

Office expense includes $150 for a one-year insurance policy purchased November 1, 1959.

Of the accounts receivable, $100 should be written off and the balance should have a $1,400 allowance for bad debts.

Depreciation is computed at 10%.

There are 3,000 advertising brochures on hand that relate to 1960-model products that will be handled by Smith-Perry Company. The cost of the brochures, $800, was charged to Advertising.

The accrued interest receivable shown in the trial balance is the amount for December 31, 1958. The amount accrued as of December 31, 1959, is $150.

Inventory—December 31, 1959—$46,110.

The partners share profits and losses equally.

Prepare working papers for 1959, adjusting entries, closing entries (using the procedure you prefer), and reversing entries.

Problem 2-12. From the following adjusted trial balance and list of reversing entries:

(a) Prepare working papers, starting with the unadjusted trial balance.
(b) Prepare closing entries, using two procedures. In one of the procedures do not use a Revenue and Expense account.

S. E. COOK AND COMPANY
Adjusted Trial Balance
December 31, 1959

Cash	27,700	
Accounts receivable	42,260	
Allowance for doubtful accounts		2,200
Accrued interest receivable	110	
Inventory—December 31, 1958	21,600	
Unexpired insurance	400	
Long-term investments	5,000	
Delivery equipment	25,000	
Accumulated depreciation—Delivery equipment		10,000
Accounts payable		18,390
Notes payable		4,500
Commissions collected in advance		1,400
Accrued rent payable		800
Capital stock		75,000
Retained earnings		7,860
Dividends	3,000	
Sales		111,700
Sales returns and allowances	4,810	

Sales discounts....................................	5,600	
Purchases...	78,000	
Purchase returns and allowances......................		2,800
Purchase discounts.................................		4,050
Transportation in..................................	1,400	
Salesmen's salaries.................................	19,370	
Depreciation—Delivery equipment...................	2,500	
Insurance...	200	
Rent..	3,200	
Office supplies expense.............................	2,940	
Bad debts...	1,200	
Interest earned....................................		450
Commissions earned................................		5,400
Interest expense...................................	260	
	244,550	244,550

The inventory on December 31, 1959, was $23,460.
The company's liability for federal income tax for 1959 was $2,500.
Reversing entries as of January 1, 1960:

(1) Interest earned.....................................	110	
Accrued interest receivable.......................		110
(2) Commissions collected in advance......................	1,400	
Commissions earned............................		1,400
(3) Accrued rent payable..............................	800	
Rent..		800

Problem 2-13.   Below are given the total debits and the total credits for the year in certain accounts of Stateside Manufacturing Company, after closing as of December 31, 1959.

(1) Compute the materials and goods in process inventories as of December 31, 1958 and December 31, 1959.
(2) Reconstruct the closing entries in general journal form, using a Manufacturing and a Revenue and Expense account.

	Debits	Credits
Finished goods....................................	$ 17,857	$ 8,764
Goods in process..................................	28,531	13,335
Materials...	42,391	17,683
Material purchases................................	202,303	202,303
Transportation in.................................	3,892	3,892
Direct labor......................................	244,414	244,414
Manufacturing overhead...........................	224,202	224,202
Selling expenses...................................	122,500	122,500
Administrative expenses............................	111,140	111,140
Sales.........	990,900	990,900
Manufacturing....................................	705,829	705,829
Revenue and expense..............................	999,993	999,993
Dividends..	30,000	30,000
Dividends payable.................................	15,000	30,000
Retained earnings.................................	555,000	723,123

Problem 2-14.   The trial balance on the following pages is that of Riffon Corporation taken from its accounting records as of December 31, 1959.

RIFFON CORPORATION
Trial Balance
December 31, 1959

Cash...	17,700	
Accounts receivable................................	82,260	
Allowance for doubtful accounts.......................		3,003
Notes receivable...................................	17,000	
Inventories—December 31, 1958:		
Finished goods....................................	31,218	
Goods in process.................................	23,314	
Materials..	14,602	
Long-term securities (held as investment)..............	20,808	
Land..	23,000	
Factory buildings..................................	54,000	
Accumulated depreciation—Factory buildings...........		13,000
Machinery...	32,600	
Accumulated depreciation—Machinery.................		12,010
Factory tools......................................	4,215	
Salesroom equipment...............................	8,240	
Accumulated depreciation—Salesroom equipment.......		710
Office furniture....................................	11,300	
Accumulated depreciation—Office furniture.............		2,700
Patents...	10,200	
Goodwill..	10,000	
Bond discount.....................................	13,500	
Accounts payable..................................		18,306
Notes payable.....................................		15,000
First mortgage bonds...............................		75,000
Capital stock—Preferred ($100,000 authorized)........		75,000
Capital stock—Common ($200,000 authorized)..........		100,000
Retained earnings..................................		13,615
Dividends—Preferred...............................	3,000	
Dividends—Common...............................	5,000	
Sales...		465,184
Sales returns and allowances........................	30,310	
Sales discounts....................................	13,821	
Purchase—Materials...............................	270,810	
Purchase returns and allowances....................		28,400
Purchase discounts................................		5,020
Transportation in..................................	4,200	
Direct labor.......................................	14,209	
Indirect labor.....................................	6,370	
Superintendence...................................	6,000	
Heat, light, and power.............................	2,400	
Factory supplies expense.	3,703	
Repairs...	1,410	
Taxes...	500	
Insurance...	2,000	
Advertising.......................................	16,000	
Salesmen's traveling expense........................	1,500	
Salesmen's salaries................................	18,000	
Commissions—Salesmen............................	7,240	
Freight out..	10,210	
Delivery expense..................................	5,800	
Miscellaneous selling expenses......................	2,301	
Office salaries.....................................	4,217	
Officers' salaries..................................	21,000	
Telephone and telegraph............................	1,830	

Office supplies expense................................	1,500	
Charity..	200	
Miscellaneous general expenses.........................	810	
Rent earned..		5,600
Interest expense.....................................	4,250	
	832,548	832,548

Additional information:

(a) Inventories—December 31, 1959:

Finished goods..	$ 900
Goods in process......................................	31,214
Materials...	11,200
Tools...	2,700

(b) Depreciation for 1959:

Factory buildings.....................................	$ 1,620
Office furniture......................................	1,130
Salesroom equipment..................................	660
Machinery..	3,912

(c) An allowance for doubtful accounts equal to 5% of the accounts receivable is considered adequate.

(d) Apportionments:

	Manufacturing	Selling	General
Repairs.........................	70%	20%	10%
Taxes...........................	20	75	5
Insurance.......................	60	30	10

(e) Assume that the federal income tax rate for 1959 is 50%.

Required:

(a) Adjusting journal entries as of December 31, 1959.
(b) Single set of working papers.
(c) Closing journal entries as of December 31, 1959, using a Manufacturing and a Revenue and Expense account.
(d) Reversing journal entries as of January 2, 1960.

Problem 2-15.   The unadjusted trial balance of Langtom Corporation is presented below.

LANGTOM CORPORATION
Unadjusted Trial Balance
December 31, 1959

Cash...	2,170	
Investments—6% bonds...............................	6,000	
Accrued interest receivable...........................	30	
Merchandise inventory................................	10,000	
Unexpired insurance..................................	100	
Store fixtures..	3,000	
Accumulated depreciation.............................		600
Accounts payable.....................................		1,740
Accrued salaries payable..............................		500
Accrued office machines rental........................	1,200	

Common stock...		10,000
Retained earnings....................................		4,400
Sales..		80,000
Purchases...	60,000	
Store rent expense...................................	3,000	
Salaries expense.....................................	12,000	
Advertising..	150	
Office machines rent expense..........................		1,000
Insurance expense....................................	300	
Miscellaneous general expense.........................	650	
Interest earned......................................		360
	98,600	98,600

The corporation makes salary payments on the first and sixteenth day of each month.

On March 1, 1958, the corporation signed a five-year lease agreement covering the rental of certain office machines. The $1,200 yearly rental is payable annually, with the first annual payment due on March 1, 1959. The corporation's bookkeeper charged Accrued Office Machines Rental when the first annual payment was made on March 1, 1959.

On the first business day of 1959, the bookkeeper made one reversing entry. After analyzing the unadjusted trial balance, prepare a list of the reversing entries that could have been made as of the beginning of 1959, and also show the one reversing entry that was made.

Assignment Material for Chapter 3

Questions

Question 3-1. In the typical balance sheet, are all of the asset accounts stated on the same valuation basis?

Question 3-2. What elements make up the difference between cost of goods manufactured and cost of goods sold in the case of a manufacturing business?

Question 3-3. Discuss the matter of financial-statement location of purchase discounts.

Question 3-4. Mention several matters which require disclosure in the financial statements.

Question 3-5. In what position on the balance sheet should the following items be placed?

(a) Bonds held as a long-term investment which are due two years hence and which have a ready market.
(b) Accrued interest receivable on bonds which is collectible semiannually.
(c) Mortgage notes receivable due in six months pledged for notes payable which will not be due for 18 months.
(d) Notes receivable discounted with banks.
(e) Prepaid interest expense.
(f) Federal income tax on current year's income.
(g) Mortgage notes payable due in 6, 12, 18, 24, 30, and 36 months.
(h) Accrued interest on mortgage notes, payable semiannually.

Question 3-6. What is the purpose of the income statement? Do you consider that the conventional form of the income statement is satisfactory to meet this purpose? Give reasons for your answer.

Question 3-7. Give several arguments against showing bad debts as a deduction from the Sales account in the income statement.

Question 3-8. The X Corporation makes sales in B City and Z Town. B City is 25 miles and Z Town 450 miles from X Corporation's place of business. The price obtained in B City is $2.50; the price in Z Town is $3.00. The corporate officers explain that the differential is not due to the degree of competition in the two cities. How would you recommend that the X Corporation present freight on sales on its income statement?

Question 3-9. Is the accountant under any obligation to disclose matters occurring after the balance sheet date but before the year-end statements are completed and released? Why?

Question 3-10. Prepare a list of accounts that normally should be included among current assets and current liabilities.

Question 3-11. Criticize the following definition: Current assets consist of cash and other assets which presumably can be converted into cash within one year without interference with the regular operations.

Question 3-12. State and explain fully the theory under which certain prepaid expenses may be classified as current assets and others as noncurrent assets.

Question 3-13. The price received for a business as an entity often differs from the amount shown on the records for the owners' equity. Explain fully why the sale price of a going business may differ from the book value even where acceptable accounting conventions have been followed in keeping the business records.

Question 3-14. In the preparation of a balance sheet of a dealer in office furniture, to be used for credit purposes, you ascertain that for the past twenty years his stock in trade has had an average turnover of once every three years. Would you include the said stock in trade among the current assets? Would it make any difference in your method of handling the inventory if you were told that the balance sheet was not to be used for credit purposes?

Problems

Problem 3-1. Using the data given for Problem 2-2, prepare the financial statements for Keystone Sales Company. The company carries its fixed assets at cost and its inventory at the lower of cost or market. There are 5,000 shares of $10 par value stock outstanding.

Problem 3-2. Prepare the financial statements for Lakeside Supplies, Incorporated, as of December 31, 1959, by using the information given in Problem 2-6, and the additional information given below:

(a) The inventory was valued at cost and the *lifo* method was employed.
(b) All of the fixed assets were recorded at cost.
(c) Of the 500, $50 par value, shares authorized, only 300 had been issued.

Problem 3-3. Use the data given in Problem 2-14 to prepare the December 31, 1959 financial statements of Riffon Corporation. Cost is the basis of valuation of the inventory, long-term securities, and all of the fixed assets. The method of inventory pricing is first-in, first-out. The bonds are secured by real estate, and bear interest at 6% until they are retired on December 31, 1965. The $100 par value preferred capital stock is noncumulative, and 750 of the 1,000 shares authorized are issued. The no-par value common stock has a stated value of $50 and all of the authorized shares have been issued.

Problem 3-4. The account balances appearing below were selected from the ledger of Janette Manufacturing Company on September 30, 1959, the end of the company's accounting year, after adjusting entries were posted. Prepare the statement of cost of goods sold.

Sales...	$212,650
Purchases—Materials.......................................	74,300
Inventories—September 30, 1958:	
Finished goods...	1,150
Goods in process..	18,905
Materials..	6,800
Sales discounts...	4,614
Freight out...	3,470
Direct labor..	22,440
Factory tools expense.....................................	1,232

Depreciation—Store equipment	650
Freight in	1,898
Depreciation—Machinery	2,560
Advertising	7,170
Insurance—Factory	135
Bad debts	1,200
Indirect labor	4,044
Accumulated depreciation—Factory fixtures	9,400
Miscellaneous factory expense	2,140
Purchase discounts	980
Superintendence	1,130
Repairs—Machinery	875
Collection and exchange	68
Purchase returns and allowances. ♪	917
Factory supplies	760
Postage and express	1,005
Depreciation—Factory fixtures	1,500
Machine fuel	250
Inventories—September 30, 1959:	
Finished goods	995
Goods in process	21,717
Materials	8,300

Problem 3-5. The December 31, 1959 adjusted trial balance of The Ypsi Sales Company is presented below. As the account sequence reveals, the company uses some of the alternative treatments mentioned in Chapter 3.

Prepare the financial statements, continuing the company's practice with regard to alternative treatments.

THE YPSI SALES COMPANY
Adjusted Trial Balance
December 31, 1959

Cash	83,100	
Accounts receivable	36,400	
Allowance for doubtful accounts		1,945
Inventory—December 31, 1958	19,800	
Prepaid rent	400	
Long-term investments	52,000	
Delivery equipment (at cost)	20,000	
Accumulated depreciation—Delivery equipment		8,000
Accounts payable		14,620
Notes payable		4,050
Accrued salaries payable		1,000
Withholding and F.I.C.A. tax liabilities		5,687
Federal unemployment tax liability		38
State unemployment tax liability		85
Capital stock—Common		150,000
Retained earnings		16,630
Dividends	11,000	
Sales		119,140
Sales returns and allowances	965	
Bad debts	675	
Freight out	1,330	
Purchases	68,980	
Purchase returns and allowances		660
Advertising	1,400	
Salesmen's salaries	12,530	
Payroll taxes expense—Selling	405	

Depreciation—Delivery equipment.....................	4,000	
Miscellaneous selling expense.........................	800	
Office salaries..	5,750	
Payroll taxes expense—General........................	175	
Office expense..	610	
Rent...	1,000	
Miscellaneous general expense........................	340	
Interest income.......................................		290
Purchase discounts...................................		770
Interest expense......................................	110	
Sales discounts.......................................	1,145	
	322,915	322,915

Supplementary data:

(1) Since the company's organization, the inventories have consistently been valued at cost. In January, 1959, it was decided to convert the inventory valuations to a basis of cost or current market, whichever is lower. The first inventory to be valued in this manner was the one taken on December 31, 1959, which amounted to $25,700. If this inventory had been valued at cost, it would have amounted to $28,350.

(2) Cash in the amount of $5,000 has been placed in escrow as a guaranty on a contract bid.

(3) The outstanding accounts receivable include $4,000 from directors.

(4) The company is presently involved in litigation arising from a negligence claim of $10,000 for injuries which a customer received from use of an article sold by The Ypsi Sales Company.

(5) The stock is common and has a par value of $200; 750 of the 1,000 shares authorized are outstanding.

(6) On December 31, 1959, the company had purchase commitments outstanding in the amount of $14,000.

(7) On the balance sheet date, the market value of the long-term investments was $48,000.

(8) Federal income tax for 1959 is estimated at $10,000.

Problem 3-6. The management of The Ingram Manufacturing Company is concerned with the apparent lack of understanding of its financial statements on the part of the stockholders and employees. To date the statements have been presented in the form shown in the illustrations at the beginning of Chapter 3.

Revise the presentation of the financial statements of The Ingram Manufacturing Company for the year ended December 31, 1959, in a way you believe would make them most effective for use in the 1959 annual report to stockholders and employees.

Problem 3-7. Using the following data taken from the accounts of Connell Producers, Incorporated, prepare a combined single-step income and retained earnings statement for the year ended April 30, 1959.

Materials and services used................................	$393,150
Dividends—Preferred......................................	18,000
Net sales...	784,760
Interest expense..	830
Selling expenses..	69,100
Interest earned..	540
Retained earnings—April 30, 1959.........................	39,990
General expenses...	28,670
Dividends—Common..	8,500

Commissions earned...	3,210
Depreciation expense..	27,910
Federal income tax..	20,000
Wages and salaries...	216,790

Problem 3-8. The Efficiency Corporation has prepared a report of the results of its operations for 1959 in the following manner.

THE EFFICIENCY CORPORATION
Statement of Income and Retained Earnings
For the Year Ended December 31, 1959

Gross sales..			$452,300
Deduct:			
Sales returns and allowances.....................	$	3,500	
Sales discounts..................................		4,270	7,770
Net sales...			$444,530
Deduct cost of goods manufactured:			
Materials·			
Cost of purchases:			
Purchases...................................		$ 99,130	
Deduct:			
Purchase returns and allowances....	$ 1,780		
Purchase discounts................	2,010	3,790	
Net......................................		$ 95,340	
Inventory—December 31, 1958..................		13,450	
Total inventory and purchases................		$108,790	
Freight in......................................		1,960	
Total..		$110,750	
Deduct inventory—December 31, 1959..........		15,690	
Materials used...............................		$ 95,060	
Direct labor...................................		120,350	
Manufacturing overhead.........................		54,720	
Decrease in goods in process inventory to $14,570...		2,710	
Cost of goods manufactured............................			272,840
Net sales less cost of goods manufactured......................			$171,690
Add increase in finished goods inventory to $9,020..............			3,940
Gross profit..			$175,630
Deduct operating expenses:			
Selling expenses:			
Salesmen's salaries......................	$24,900		
Delivery expense.........................	4,640		
Freight out..............................	3,800		
Depreciation—Selling equipment........	2,380		
Miscellaneous selling expenses..........	5,750	$ 41,470	
General expenses:			
Office expenses.........................	$ 5,290		
Office rent.............................	3,500		
Bad debts...............................	1,600		
Miscellaneous general expenses..........	3,200	13,590	55,060
Net operating income.......................................			$120,570
Other expenses:			
Interest expense...........................	$ 4,610		
Bond interest expense.....................	6,000	$ 10,610	
Other revenue:			
Commissions earned.....................	$ 2,140		
Interest earned.........................	1,300	3,440	7,170
Net income before income tax—forward......................			$113,400

Net income before income tax—brought forward $113,400
Federal income tax....................................... 55,000
Net income.. $ 58,400
Add retained earnings—December 31, 1958................... 162,300
Total... $220,700
Deduct dividends.. 60,000
Retained earnings—December 31, 1959..................... $160,700

Prepare an alternative presentation of the above data, relocating as many items as possible to an alternative position, without violating acceptable statement conventions. Do not prepare combined statements.

Problem 3-9. The trial balance presented below was taken from the books as of December 31, 1959, after the recording of adjusting and closing entries.

AMERICAN CORPORATION
Trial Balance (After Closing)
December 31, 1959

Cash in bank.......................................	21,316	
Office cash funds...................................	1,000	
Marketable securities...............................	21,000	
Advances and deposits..............................	16,000	
Trade accounts receivable...........................	133,400	
Allowance for doubtful accounts.....................		14,500
Notes receivable...................................	15,000	
Accrued interest receivable..........................	240	
Receivable from officers and employees................	4,189	
Inventories:		
Finished product.................................	96,210	
Product in process...............................	48,012	
Materials.......................................	68,311	
Manufacturing supplies............................	14,016	
Office supplies...................................	4,220	
Sinking fund for bond retirements.....................	25,000	
Land..	20,000	
Building...	121,900	
Accumulated depreciation—Building...................		28,320
Machinery...	211,418	
Accumulated depreciation—Machinery.................		129,040
Office furniture and fixtures..........................	41,315	
Accumulated depreciation—Office furniture and fixtures..		18,490
Patents...	43,015	
Prepaid expenses and deferred charges.................	26,248	
Trade accounts payable..............................		39,316
Notes payable......................................		40,000
Accrued interest payable.............................		2,860
Withholding and F.I.C.A. taxes payable................		2,115
Income tax payable.................................		38,400
Advances from customers............................		6,000
4% bonds payable..................................		100,000
Capital stock......................................		300,000
Retained earnings..................................		162,769
Reserve for general contingencies.....................		50,000
	931,810	931,810

Using the preceding trial balance and the additional information presented, prepare a schedule showing the details of the working capital of American Corporation on December 31, 1959.

The average period of time elapsing from the purchase of raw materials until the accounts arising from the sale of product manufactured from such materials are collected is approximately eight months.

The corporation owns the following marketable securities on December 31, 1959:

United States Treasury Notes acquired for investment of seasonally idle cash.	$ 8,000
Capital stock of Gem Sales Company, owned as a participant in a co-operative marketing program	13,000

The corporation has advanced $15,000 to A-Z Machine Company to cover the cost of design drawings on machinery for a new product.

The corporation has a $1,000 deposit with the state Workmen's Compensation Fund. (This deposit must be maintained as long as the corporation remains in business.)

Of the notes receivable, $6,000 represents three notes of equal face value arising from the sale of excess production equipment. These notes mature on June 30th of each of the succeeding three years.

The amount shown as being receivable from officers and employees includes $2,189 receivable from employees for merchandise sold on regular credit terms. The balance represents an advance (without interest) to the president, without definite maturity. You are informed that no expectation of current collection exists.

The corporation's inventory of finished product includes $5,000 representing the undepreciated cost of manufacturing machinery no longer needed by the company and being offered for sale.

The corporation has received a cash offer of $15,000 for one of its patents with a book value of $9,000. The management has indicated it will probably accept the offer.

The Prepaid Expenses and Deferred Charges account includes:

Cash surrender value of life insurance	$12,018
Unexpired insurance premiums	12,040
Unamortized bond discount	2,190
	$26.248

Included in the Notes Payable account are:

Bank loan—due June 30, 1960	$30,000
Loan from the insurance company with which insurance on the lives of corporation executives is carried	10,000
(There is no intention to repay this loan in the near future.)	

The amount received from a customer for product to be delivered in April, 1960, is shown in the Advances from Customers account.

The bond issue will be retired from sinking fund assets in ten annual installments beginning September 1, 1960.

Problem 3-10. A schedule showing the cost of materials used by Smooth Company during 1958 and 1959 is presented on the following page. The company has been following a policy of computing the year-end materials inventory at gross invoice cost. In 1959 the company changed its inventory pricing policy and used actual cost in computing the December 31, 1959 materials inventory. All of the company's suppliers offer terms of 2/10; n/30; the company has not missed taking all available purchase discounts since 1956.

	1958		1959	
Materials:				
Inventory—beginning of year...		$ 20,000		$ 25,000
Purchases.....................	$200,000		$180,000	
Add freight in................	25,000		22,500	
Total........................	$225,000		$202,500	
Deduct purchase discounts.....	4,000	221,000	3,600	198,900
Total........................		$241,000		$223,900
Inventory—end of year........		25,000		33,150
Materials used..............		$216,000		$190,750

(a) Prepare a schedule of the cost of materials used in 1959 in which the beginning inventory is priced on the same basis as the end-of-year inventory.

(b) Prepare a second schedule of the cost of materials used in 1959 on a basis consistent with the method used in 1958.

Problem 3-11.

SMITH SUPER COMPANY
Balance Sheet
December 31, 1959
Assets

Current assets:		
Cash...	$ 49,400	
Accounts receivable............................	120,300	
Inventories...................................	218,600	$388,300
Property, plant, and equipment............................		491,100
Deferred charges..		42,500
		$921,900

Liabilities and Stockholders' Equity

Current liabilities:		
Accounts payable..............................	$ 78,800	
Note and interest payable thereon.................	50,500	
Income tax payable...........................	35,000	$164,300
Reserves...		196,200
Stockholders' equity:		
Capital stock.................................	$500,000	
Retained earnings.............................	61,400	561,400
		$921,900

Recast the balance sheet, using a form that shows the working capital, in the light of the information presented below:

(1) Accounts receivable include $50,000 advanced to Automation Corporation on a contract with that company to construct special manufacturing equipment for Smith Super Company.

(2) The details of the items included in inventories are as follows (stated at cost):

Finished goods.......................................	$ 74,800
Goods in process.....................................	21,200
Materials...	96,200
Machinery under construction by company for its use....	26,400
	$218,600

Finished goods costing $50,000 are held in a bonded warehouse as security for the note payable to the bank.

(3) Included in property, plant, and equipment are the following:

Land...	$ 50,000
Building..	110,200
Machinery......................................	290,400
Office fixtures.................................	40,500
	$491,100

(4) Deferred charges include:

Cash surrender value of life insurance...................	$ 18,000
Unamortized cost of patents..........................	20,000
Unexpired insurance.................................	2,200
Other current expense prepayments....................	2,300
	$ 42,500

(5) Accounts payable include advances by customers on unfilled current orders in the amount of $12,400.

(6) The note payable is a six-month note payable to Third National Bank and is due on March 1, 1960, in the amount of $50,000; interest thereon is payable at maturity at 6%.

(7) Included in reserves are:

Accumulated depreciation:		
Building.................................	$ 51,700	
Machinery...............................	108,300	
Office fixtures...........................	31,200	$191,200
Allowance for doubtful accounts.......................		5,000
		$196,200

(8) The company has 75,000 shares of authorized common stock with a par value of $10, of which 50,000 shares were issued at par.

Problem 3-12. Starting with the December 31, 1959 inventories, Waynes Manufacturing Company revised its inventory costing method to include, on a proportional basis, the cost of freight in on all raw materials. The freight in applicable to the raw materials purchased in 1959 amounted to $42,500.

Inventory records reveal that 90% of the raw material purchased during 1959 was placed in production, and that on December 31, 1959, 6% of such material was still in process and 4% was completed but unsold.

As of December 15, 1959, the stockholders of Waynes Manufacturing Company approved an agreement with Research, Incorporated, for the purchase of a patent. The purchase price was $500,000, payment to consist of 3,000 shares of authorized but unissued common stock of the company and $200,000 in cash which the company expects to obtain from a seven-year loan from an insurance company. The settlement date is January 15, 1960.

Illustrate the disclosures you believe would be appropriate in connection with the 1959 financial statements. You may assume that the company is subject to an income tax rate of 40%, and that the change in inventory method has been approved for income tax purposes.

Problem 3-13. A newly hired, inexperienced bookkeeper prepared the following income statement for Victory Corporation for the year ended December 31, 1959.

VICTORY CORPORATION
Income Statement
December 31, 1959

Sales..	$285,822	
Purchase returns and allowances.......	460	
Purchase discounts..............................	998	
Royalties from patents...........................	3,600	
Interest earned.................................	200	
Increase in inventories of finished goods, materials, and factory supplies................................	1,234	$292,314
Sundry manufacturing costs	$209,720	
Depreciation—Factory.........................	6,900	
Freight in......	1,415	
Sales returns....................................	2,112	
Sales discounts..................................	3,113	
Selling expenses.................................	19,876	
Administrative expenses..........................	14,364	257,500
Net income before income tax..............................		$ 34,814
Income tax...		11,500
Net income...		$ 23,314

The management of the corporation gives you the following additional information and requests that you prepare an income statement and a cost of goods manufactured statement in a more conventional form.

Inventories—December 31, 1959:	
Finished goods..	$ 9,788
Materials...	8,440
Factory supplies..	2,170
Materials used during 1959, including freight but after deducting purchase discounts and returns and allowances................	73,580
Factory supplies used during 1959............................	1,205
Direct labor..	57,675
Indirect labor..	9,135
Other manufacturing overhead not specifically set forth above....	69,845
Purchases during 1959:	
Materials...	71,140
Factory supplies...	1,925

There was no work in process either at the beginning or at the end of 1959.

Problem 3-14. From the data below, which summarize in part the results of the first year of operations of True Company, prepare the 1959 statement of cost of goods sold.

√ Of the total manufacturing cost for the year, 40% was for materials, 30% for direct labor, and 30% for manufacturing overhead. Depreciation of factory buildings and equipment amounted to 20% of the manufacturing overhead.

√ The cost of the materials used was 80% of the amount purchased, and 90% of the amount purchased was paid for during the year.

The inventory of finished goods on December 31 was 5% of the cost of units finished during the year, and work in process at that date was twice the finished goods inventory.

The manufacturing overhead, except for depreciation of factory buildings and equipment, is detailed below:

Indirect labor	$36,555
Heat, light, and power	6,733
Repairs	26,612
Insurance—Plant	910
Property taxes	4,600
Miscellaneous factory expense	11,710
Total	$87,120

The accounts payable for materials, as of December 31, amounted to $18,150.

Problem 3-15. The financial statements appearing below have been incorrectly prepared. Review these statements and present revised financial statements in correct form.

THE COMPLEX CORPORATION   Exhibit D
Statement of Cost of Goods Sold
For the Year Ended June 30, 1959

Cost of goods manufactured:			
Materials:			
Cost of purchases:			
Purchases			$ 620,133.17
Deduct:			
Purchase returns and allowances	$ 4,000.00		
Purchase discounts	10,718.43		14,718.43
Net			$ 605,414.74
Freight out			6,850.09
Total			$ 612,264.83
Deduct decrease in materials inventory:			
June 30, 1958	$ 88,998.63		
June 30, 1959	66,840.10		22,158.53
Materials used			$ 590,106.30
Direct labor			220,918.00
Manufacturing overhead:			
Indirect labor	$ 94,828.27		
Insurance—Factory	10,000.50		
Heat, light, and power	57,642.50		
Factory supplies	16,931.17		
Depreciation—Factory building	4,830.00		
Depreciation—Machinery	8,000.10		
Bad debts	4,608.48		
Repairs—Machinery	9,140.00		
Total manufacturing overhead			205,981.02
Total manufacturing cost			$1,017,005.32
Deduct decrease in goods in process inventory:			
June 30, 1958	$ 61,022.95		
June 30, 1959	58,202.00		2,820.95
Cost of goods manufactured			$1,014,184.37
Add increase in finished goods inventory:			
June 30, 1959	$188,913.20		
June 30, 1958	173,933.72		14,979.48
Cost of goods sold			$1,029,163.85

THE COMPLEX CORPORATION
Income Statement
For the Year Ended June 30, 1959

Exhibit C

Gross sales...			$1,599,761.40
Deduct sales returns and allowances.....................			22,314.62
Net sales..			$1,577,446.78
Deduct cost of goods sold—Exhibit D...................			1,029,163.85
Gross profit on sales..................................			$ 548,282.93
Deduct operating expenses:			
Selling expenses:			
Advertising.................	$62,806.50		
Commissions—Salesmen....	19,601.83		
Freight in..................	10,980.10		
Traveling—Salesmen.......	43,220.81		
Rent—Sales office..........	7,000.00		
Salesmen's salaries.........	80,010.21		
Sales discounts.............	15,431.20		
Miscellaneous selling expense	26,900.65	$265,951.30	
General expenses:			
Officers' salaries............	$90,000.00		
Office salaries..............	26,930.14		
Office expense..............	8,800.33		
Telephone and telegraph....	8,900.20		
Printing and stationery.....	6,482.26	141,112.93	407,064.23
Net operating income.................................			$ 141,218.70
Other expenses:			
Interest expense.........................		$ 7,500.00	
Dividends.............................		20,000.00	27,500.00
Net income before income tax..........................			$ 113,718.70
Federal income tax (50%)..............................			56,859.35
Net income..			$ 56,859.35

THE COMPLEX CORPORATION
Statement of Retained Earnings
For the Year Ended June 30, 1959

Exhibit B

Retained earnings—June 30, 1958........................	$134,720.08
Add net income for the year—Exhibit C...................	56,859.35
Retained earnings—June 30, 1959........................	$191,579.43

THE COMPLEX CORPORATION   Exhibit A
Balance Sheet
June 30, 1959

Assets

Current assets:
Cash.. $ 62,212.31
Petty cash....................................   2,000.00
Accounts receivable........................... 169,213.00
Inventories—at lower of cost or market:
  Finished goods.................... $188,913.20
  Goods in process.................   58,202.00
  Materials........................   66,840.10   313,955.30
Current installment of serial bonds pay-
  able in 1960..............................   10,000.00
   Total current assets................................... $ 557,380.61
Fixed assets:
Land—at cost............................... $ 69,998.63
Factory building—at cost............ $155,666.15
  Less accumulated depreciation......   59,865.90   95,800.25
Machinery—at cost................. $490,900.00
  Less accumulated depreciation...... 113,215.13   377,684.87
   Total fixed assets.......................................   543,483.75
    $1,100,864.36

Liabilities and Stockholders' Equity

Current liabilities:
Accounts payable.............................. $ 45,003.41
Notes payable................................. 150,000.00
Federal income tax payable.......................   56,859.35
   Total current liabilities................................. $ 251,862.76
Long-term liabilities:
Serial bonds—6%—$10,000 maturing annually..................   140,000.00
Stockholders' equity:
Capital stock—Common; authorized and issued,
  5,000 shares................................. $500,000.00
Allowance for doubtful accounts..................   17,422.17
Retained earnings—Exhibit B.................... 191,579.43
   Total stockholders' equity...............................   709,001.60
    $1,100,864.36

Assignment Material for Chapter 4

Questions

Question 4-1. State briefly what is meant by:

(a) The current operating concept of net income.
(b) The all-inclusive or clean surplus theory.

Question 4-2. Name five items that would be dealt with differently in the statements, depending on which concept of net income governed.

Question 4-3. Mention some arguments in favor of the current operating concept.

Question 4-4. Mention some arguments in favor of the clean surplus theory.

Question 4-5. On which concept of net income is the combined statement of income and retained earnings based?

Question 4-6. Give an illustration of an error in computing the net income of one year that will be offset by a counterbalancing error in the following year, thus correcting the retained earnings, but leaving the net income incorrectly stated by years.

Question 4-7. What effect has the overstatement of an inventory at the end of 1958 on the statements prepared:

(a) At the end of 1958?
(b) At the end of 1959?

Question 4-8. What will be the effect upon the income statement of the present and future periods if:

Prepaid expenses are ignored?   Accrued expenses are ignored?
Income collected in advance is   Accrued income is ignored?
ignored?

Question 4-9. For three years Evasion Company has charged items to machinery repairs that should have been charged to machinery. It is agreed that 5% is the correct rate of depreciation and that assets are to be depreciated for one-half year in the year of acquisition.

Items incorrectly charged to machinery repairs are as follows:

$$1956............ \$6,000$$
$$1957............ 7,500$$
$$1958............ 8,000$$

Submit journal entries to correct the records as of December 31, 1958, assuming that 1958 depreciation on the unadjusted balance of the Machinery account has been recorded but that the books have not yet been closed.

Question 4-10. State four ways of dealing with errors affecting the net income of prior years.

Problems

Problem 4-1. The following account balances were taken from the ledger of Cedar Company at the close of its fiscal year on June 30, 1959:

Loss on sale of idle plant facilities	$ 31,200
Sales	348,400
Merchandise inventory, June 30, 1959	38,530
Selling expenses	42,600
Dividends received	2,000
Administrative and general expenses	32,400
Cost of goods sold	242,620
Sales discounts	4,835
Correction of overstatement of prior year's depreciation—Equipment	2,900
Dividends—Preferred stock	14,000
Dividends—Common stock	6,000
Assessment of income taxes—prior years	9,130
Retained earnings—June 30, 1958	120,800

Inventory of merchandise—June 30, 1958—$41,200.

Applying the clean surplus approach, prepare a combined income and retained earnings statement.

Problem 4-2. The following information was taken from the books of Turnpike Company; it relates to the year ended December 31, 1959.

Retained earnings—December 31, 1958	$281,705
Gain on sale of machinery on July 15, 1959	28,500
Correction of December 31, 1957 inventory, charged to Retained Earnings and credited to Purchases as of June 30, 1959	15,000
Net loss for the year before corrections and extraneous items	45,678
Payment on January 15, 1959, of dividends declared on December 15, 1958	18,000
Refund of one-half of deposit with State Highway Commission, the balance being forfeited for defective work on a contract completed in 1956	12,500

The board of directors met on December 15, 1959 and declared a regular dividend of $20,000, payable on January 15, 1960.

Show how the statement of retained earnings for 1959 would appear if the company followed the all-inclusive theory.

Problem 4-3. An audit of the records of Maynard Company disclosed the following:

(1) Inventory overstated (understated):

December 31, 1957	$11,600
December 31, 1958	(22,200)

(2) Accrued wages ignored at year end:

December 31, 1957	$ 1,230
December 31, 1958	2,330
December 31, 1959	850

(3) Depreciation overstated (understated):

Year ended December 31, 1958	$ 3,500
Year ended December 31, 1959	(8,900)

(4) Prepaid interest expense overstated (understated):

December 31, 1957	$ (700)
December 31, 1958	1,400

Prepare a work sheet to determine the effect of the above errors on the income statements for the years 1957, 1958, and 1959 and the December 31, 1959 balance sheet.

Problem 4-4. From the following data taken from the books of Capital Corporation, prepare a work sheet showing the corrected net income before income taxes for the years 1957, 1958, and 1959.

	Year Ended December 31,		
	1957	1958	1959
Net income before income taxes, per books.....	$18,720	$24,190	$21,400
Payment of liabilities existing but not recorded at close of preceding year:			
Heat and light..........................	830	720	680
Merchandise (goods on hand and included in inventory)........................	1,200	1,050	810
Unrecorded liabilities as of December 31, 1959:			
Heat and light.............................			600
Merchandise (goods on hand but not included in inventory)...........................			760
Uncollectible accounts charged to expense, arising from sales of preceding year, for which no provision for bad debts was made..............		2,000	
Purchase of delivery equipment good for four years charged to Delivery Expense on July 1, 1958.....................................		4,000	

Problem 4-5. As the result of an examination of the accounts of Doom Corporation by an internal revenue agent, it is discovered that, from time to time, certain items of new equipment have been debited to the Repairs and Maintenance expense account.

Information related to this matter is presented below:

Account Balances, December 31

	Equipment	Accumulated Depreciation	New Equipment Charged to Expense	Net Income Reported
1955.....................	$102,560	$31,810	$12,000	$80,500
1956.....................	116,980	48,360	8,800	72,111
1957.....................	120,100	54,200	-0-	65,432
1958.....................	124,320	59,600	10,000	78,900
1959.....................	126,400	62,240	6,440	75,115

It is the company's practice, which is approved by the internal revenue agent, to compute depreciation by applying the rate of 25% to the balance of the Equipment account at the end of each year.

The accounts have not been closed for the year 1959.

Required:

(a) A schedule showing the necessary adjustments to net income, and the corrected net income for each of the above years.

(b) The adjusting entry necessary to record the corrections in the books as of December 31, 1959, assuming that it is desired to disclose the corrections in the 1959 statement of retained earnings. Ignore income tax considerations.

Problem 4-6. Assume that the following adjusted trial balance is that of Randolph Company on September 30, 1959, the close of its fiscal year:

Adjusted Trial Balance
September 30, 1959

Cash...	4,618	
Accounts receivable.................................	4,110	
Allowance for doubtful accounts.......................		420
Merchandise inventory—September 30, 1958............	12,130	
Unexpired insurance.................................	320	
Prepaid rent..	100	
Furniture and equipment.............................	3,600	
Accumulated depreciation—Furniture and equipment......		900
Accounts payable....................................		3,030
Notes payable......................................		1,000
Accrued interest payable.............................		30
Accrued property taxes payable.......................		80
Capital stock.......................................		10,000
Retained earnings (September 30, 1958)....		4,157
Dividends...	1,000	
Sales...		61,300
Purchases..	42,469	
Wages...	9,100	
Rent expense.......................................	1,200	
Repairs and maintenance.............................	818	
Insurance expense...................................	112	
Depreciation expense................................	290	
Taxes—Property....................................	318	
Bad debts..	150	
Utilities..	508	
Interest expense....................................	74	
	80,917	80,917

Inventory of merchandise, September 30, 1959—$13,100.

An audit of the accounts of Randolph Company on September 30, 1959, and for the year ended that date disclosed that adjustments for accruals and prepayments as of September 30, 1959, had been properly computed and recorded and that the September 30, 1959 inventory of merchandise was correct. However, the following errors had been made in preceding fiscal periods:

(1) The merchandise inventory on September 30, 1958, was overstated $840 owing to an error in adding the inventory count sheets.

(2) Unexpired insurance and prepaid rent were not recorded at the close of preceding fiscal periods. An examination of insurance policies disclosed that the amount of unexpired insurance on September 30, 1958, was $335, and that rent prepaid on that date amounted to $100.

(3) On June 30, 1958, an item of equipment costing $400 had been debited to Repairs and Maintenance. This item was of a type which would be depreciated at a 10% rate.

(4) A sales invoice for $118 covering merchandise sold and shipped on September 20, 1958, was not recorded until October 8, 1958.

Required:

(a) Necessary adjusting journal entries as of September 30, 1959, assuming that the results of any errors relating to prior periods will be absorbed in the current income statement without disclosure.

(b) The income statement for the year ended September 30, 1959, prepared on the basis described in (a).

(c) A computation showing the net income for the year ended September 30, 1959, that would be reported if the consequences of any errors relating to prior periods were disclosed in the statement of retained earnings.

Problem 4-7.   Assume that the adjusted trial balance used in Problem 4-6 is that of Dolphin Corporation. As the corporation's new chief accountant, you discover the following errors:

(a) The inventory of merchandise on September 30, 1957, was overstated $850. The difference was caused by clerical errors in the physical inventory count sheets.

(b) The inventory of merchandise on September 30, 1958, was understated $703, owing to the erroneous exclusion of merchandise out on consignment.

(c) An inventory of repair supplies in the amount of $218, on hand on September 30, 1959, was ignored.

(d) Unexpired insurance was ignored when adjusting entries were made on September 30, 1958. The amount of insurance premiums unexpired on that date was $410.

(e) There were accrued wages on September 30, 1958, in the amount of $345, which were not booked by the adjusting entries made on that date. (There were no accrued wages on September 30, 1959.)

Required:

(1) Working papers for the year ended September 30, 1959, assuming that errors affecting prior years' earnings are to be disclosed in the current income statement.

(2) Closing entries.

Problem 4-8.   The trial balance presented below was taken from the ledger of Local Sales Company after regular adjusting journal entries had been recorded on June 30, 1959.

LOCAL SALES COMPANY
Adjusted Trial Balance
June 30, 1959

Cash	16,615	
Inventory—end of year	15,200	
Office supplies on hand	300	
Automotive equipment	27,300	
Accumulated depreciation		11,305
Accounts payable		10,390
Accrued wages payable		350
Common stock		30,000
Retained earnings		5,450
Dividends	3,000	
Sales		123,000
Cost of goods sold	88,935	
Wages	14,280	
Office supplies expense	1,475	
Depreciation	5,100	
Other expense	8,290	
	180,495	180,495

An examination of the accounts indicates that certain errors were made during prior periods and that these errors were never corrected. These errors are described below:

(a) The June 30, 1958 inventory was understated by $1,200.

(b) A small car trailer acquired on September 30, 1957, at a cost of $800, was charged to Other Expense. Such trailers have a use-life expectancy of five years. Since acquisition, the company has charged the Depreciation account $280 for depreciation on the trailer.

(c) On July 10, 1958, a delivery truck was wrecked in an accident. The truck was a total loss and its cost was removed from the accounts by the following entry:

Accumulated depreciation........................... 3,600
    Automotive equipment........................   3,600
    Cost of truck purchased on July 1, 1953, removed
    from accounts.

In each of the five years preceding the accident the company had recorded $900 depreciation on the truck.

(d) During the three-year period ending June 30, 1958, the company had understated accrued wages by an amount aggregating $1,000. The details are as follows:

	Amount	
	Booked	Ignored
Accrued wages, June 30, 1956....................	$100	$ 350
Accrued wages, June 30, 1957....................	150	500
Accrued wages, June 30, 1958....................	50	150
		$1,000

Required:

(1) Working papers for the year ended June 30, 1959, assuming that errors affecting prior years' earnings are to be disclosed in the current income statement.

(2) Income statement for the year ended June 30, 1959.

Problem 4-9. Assume that the income statements of Davenport Company showed the following:

Net income—Year ended December 31:
1958.. $6,800
1959.. 6,850
1960.. 7,770

The above net income amounts are incorrect because of the following errors and omissions:

X Accrued wages:
No adjusting entries for accrued wages were made at the end of 1958, 1959, and 1960.
The accruals were:

December 31, 1958.. $175
December 31, 1959.. 215
December 31, 1960.. 230

Bad debts:

No provisions for doubtful accounts were made. Instead, the Bad Debts account was charged when accounts were written off, as follows:

1958	$365
1959	415
1960	505

If an Allowance for Doubtful Accounts had been used, the following year-end balances for that account would have been acceptable:

December 31, 1957	$370
December 31, 1958	425
December 31, 1959	525
December 31, 1960	600

⅄ Depreciation:

In computing depreciation for 1958, one asset was overlooked; as a consequence the depreciation for 1958 was understated $160. This asset was sold during 1959, and a loss of $300 was shown as resulting from the sale.

✱ Inventories:

Year-end inventories were overstated and understated as follows:

December 31, 1957—overstated	$500
December 31, 1958—understated	390
December 31, 1959—overstated	610

The 1960 ending inventory was correctly stated.

Prepare a work sheet showing the corrected net income, ignoring any income tax matters, for the years 1958, 1959, and 1960.

Problem 4-10.   The present bookkeeper of Lowden Company started to work for the company at the beginning of 1957. He has never made an adjusting entry. Except for this failing, his work has been satisfactory. By making use of the current trial balance and the additional information, prepare working papers for the year ended December 31, 1959, assuming that any errors affecting prior years' earnings are to be disclosed in the statement of retained earnings. Also prepare the 1959 statement of retained earnings.

LOWDEN COMPANY

Trial Balance—December 31, 1959

Cash	7,650	
Bond investments, at par, 4%	10,000	
Inventory	14,220	
Equipment	36,000	
Accumulated depreciation		11,700
Accounts payable		6,120
Common stock		40,000
Retained earnings		5,560
Dividends	2,000	
Sales		94,300
Purchases	69,780	
Wages	16,140	
Insurance expense	180	
Other expense	2,110	
Interest income		400
	158,080	158,080

Inventory, December 31, 1959—$13,170.

There has been no change in the bond investments since 1955. The bonds pay interest semiannually on April 1 and October 1.

A record of the insurance premiums paid during the last six years is presented below.

Insurance Policies

Date	Coverage	Premium	Term
July 1, 1954.....................	Inventory	$156	2 years
July 1, 1956.....................	Inventory	156	2 years
October 1, 1956..................	Equipment	180	3 years
July 1, 1958.....................	Inventory	156	2 years
October 1, 1959.................	Equipment	180	3 years

The equipment was purchased on October 1, 1953; its use life is ten years, and no scrap value is expected.

Accrued wages at year end:

1955..	$300
1956..	-0-
1957..	200
1958..	275
1959..	225

Problem 4-11. The following financial statements have been prepared by Kansas Company as a part of an application for a bank loan.

KANSAS COMPANY
Income Statement
For the Year Ended October 31, 1959

Net sales..		$81,315
Cost of goods sold:		
Inventory—beginning of year......................	$12,014	
Purchases...	62,012	
Total...	$74,026	
Inventory—end of year...........................	13,100	
Cost of goods sold...........................		60,926
Gross profit...		$20,389
Expenses:		
Wages and salaries................................	$ 8,838	
Insurance...	312	
Taxes...	605	
Repairs...	753	
Rent of building..................................	1,200	
Depreciation......................................	830	
Other expenses....................................	610	
Total expenses.................................		13,148
Net income..		$ 7,241

KANSAS COMPANY
Statement of Retained Earnings
For the Year Ended October 31, 1959

Balance at beginning of year.................................	$ 9,233
Net income for the year......................................	7,241
Total...	$16,474
Dividends...	2,000
Balance at end of year.......................................	$14,474

KANSAS COMPANY
Balance Sheet
October 31, 1959

Assets

Cash		$ 4,230
Accounts receivable		11,930
Merchandise inventory		13,100
Unexpired insurance		710
Furniture and equipment	$ 8,040	
Accumulated depreciation	2,910	5,130
		$35,100

Liabilities and Stockholders' Equity

Accounts payable	$10,190
Taxes payable	436
Capital stock	10,000
Retained earnings	14,474
	$35,100

The bank has requested that the company have its financial statements audited, and you have been retained by Kansas Company for this purpose. In the course of your audit you discover the following:

(a) The beginning inventory was understated $2,000.

(b) Unexpired insurance was overstated $200 on October 31, 1958, and also on October 31, 1959.

(c) Accrued wages and salaries were overstated by $100 on October 31, 1958. The Accrued Wages and Salaries Payable account was closed by the following entry for the first payroll in the current fiscal year:

Wages and salaries	600	
Accrued wages and salaries payable	150	
Cash		750

There were no accrued wages or salaries as of October 31, 1959.

(d) Repair supplies of $115 were included with the October 31, 1959 merchandise inventory. No supplies were included in the merchandise inventory on October 31, 1958.

Required:

(1) Working papers to revise the current financial statements, assuming that any errors affecting prior years' earnings are to be disclosed in the statement of retained earnings.

(2) Closing entries, as of October 31, 1959.

Problem 4-12. At the end of 1959, City Department Store issued the following comparative statements.

CITY DEPARTMENT STORE
Comparative Statement of Retained Earnings
Years Ended December 31, 1958 and 1959

	Year Ended December 31,	
	1959	1958
Retained earnings—beginning of year	$ 94,225	$ 83,763
Net income for the year	17,702	15,462
Total	$111,927	$ 99,225
Dividends	10,000	5,000
Retained earnings—end of year	$101,927	$ 94,225

CITY DEPARTMENT STORE
Comparative Income Statement
Years Ended December 31, 1958 and 1959

	Year Ended December 31,	
	1959	1958
Net sales	$521,000	$555,250
Cost of goods sold	353,169	394,392
Gross profit	$167,831	$160,858
Expenses:		
Selling and delivery	$ 58,016	$ 60,646
Buying	20,311	20,003
Building occupancy	25,902	22,908
General and administrative	38,806	37,311
Total	$143,035	$140,868
Net income from operations	$ 24,796	$ 19,990
Other income (expense) net	1,806	2,312
Net income before income tax	$ 26,602	$ 22,302
Income tax	8,900	6,840
Net income	$ 17,702	$ 15,462

CITY DEPARTMENT STORE
Comparative Balance Sheet
December 31, 1958 and 1959

	December 31,	
	1959	1958
Assets		
Cash	$ 25,534	$ 27,862
Accounts receivable	36,811	44,906
Allowance for bad debts	3,200*	3,000*
Merchandise inventory	94,302	101,311
Prepaid expenses	9,964	8,043
Fixtures	395,585	411,543
Delivery equipment	43,012	41,906
Accumulated depreciation	172,788*	195,042*
	$429,220	$437,529
Liabilities and Stockholders' Equity		
Accounts payable	$ 12,016	$ 32,480
Accrued expenses	6,377	3,984
Income tax payable	8,900	6,840
Capital stock—$100 par	300,000	300,000
Retained earnings	101,927	94,225
	$429,220	$437,529

* Deduction.

During 1960 the following information comes to your attention:

(a) During 1958 certain fixtures were purchased for $1,200 and improperly charged to merchandise purchases. During 1959 the bookkeeper undertook to correct the error by charging the Fixtures account and crediting Purchases with the cost. The company computes depreciation by applying the rate of 5% to the year-end balance in the Fixtures account.

(b) Unexpired insurance on the company's public liability policy in the amount of $385 was ignored when adjusting entries were prepared as of December 31, 1958.

(c) An invoice in the amount of $985 for the purchase of a special lot of merchandise which was received and sold in December, 1958, was not recorded until January 19, 1959.

(d) $1,330 of regular merchandise was inadvertently included in the December 31, 1958 inventory of selling and delivery supplies.

(e) The accrued expenses should have included $600 of accrued personal property taxes as of the end of both 1958 and 1959. In fact, the accrual of such expenses has been disregarded for many years. The bookkeeper charges all property tax payments to the Building Occupancy account.

Prepare working papers for revised comparative financial statements for 1958 and 1959. No change need be made in the provisions for income tax.

Problem 4-13. The adjusted trial balance of Alder Company is presented below.

ALDER COMPANY
Adjusted Trial Balance
December 31, 1960

Cash	11,000	
Inventory	30,000	
Prepaid expenses	1,200	
Equipment	50,000	
Accumulated depreciation		12,250
Accounts payable		8,000
Accrued expenses		710
Common stock		50,000
Retained earnings		16,790
Dividends	2,000	
Sales		180,000
Purchases	143,000	
Selling commissions	18,000	
Depreciation expense	2,500	
Other selling expense	3,710	
Administrative expense	6,340	
	267,750	267,750

Inventory—end of year—$26,000.

A new state law requires the company to file financial statements for the years 1958, 1959, and 1960, with the State Securities Commission. The 1958 and 1959 financial statements are presented below.

ALDER COMPANY
Income Statements—1958 and 1959

	1958		1959	
Sales		$165,000		$174,000
Cost of goods sold:				
Inventory—beginning of year	$ 24,000		$ 27,000	
Purchases	133,000		137,000	
Total	$157,000		$164,000	
Inventory—end of year	27,000	130,000	30,000	134,000
Gross profit		$ 35,000		$ 40,000
Expenses:				
Selling commissions	$ 15,500		$ 18,000	
Depreciation expense	2,100		2,250	
Other selling expense	3,600		3,710	
Administrative expense	7,200	28,400	6,850	30,810
Net income		$ 6,600		$ 9,190

ALDER COMPANY
Statements of Retained Earnings
1958 and 1959

	1958	1959
Retained earnings—beginning of year	$ 5,000	$ 9,600
Net income	6,600	9,190
Total	$11,600	$18,790
Dividends	2,000	2,000
Retained earnings—end of year	$ 9,600	$16,790

ALDER COMPANY
Balance Sheets
December 31, 1958 and 1959

	1958	1959
Assets		
Cash	$ 8,000	$ 8,710
Inventory	27,000	30,000
Prepaid expenses	700	850
Equipment	40,000	44,000
Accumulated depreciation	7,500*	9,750*
	$68,200	$73,810
Liabilities and Stockholders' Equity		
Accounts payable	$ 8,260	$ 6,610
Accrued expenses	340	410
Common stock	50,000	50,000
Retained earnings	9,600	16,790
	$68,200	$73,810

* Deduction.

Additional information:

(a) The company computes depreciation by applying the rate of 5% to the year-end balance in the Equipment account.

(b) Under an agreement effective January 1, 1958, the company is obligated to pay its salesmen a commission of 10% on sales.

(c) Invoices from merchandise suppliers are not recorded until the goods have been inspected and marked, although merchandise in the receiving and marking departments is included in the inventory at the end of each year. The amounts of merchandise (at cost) in this category are set forth below:

December 31, 1957	$2,312	December 31, 1959	$1,916
December 31, 1958	3,018	December 31, 1960	1,820

(d) For years, including the current year, the company has consistently overlooked at year end an item of accrued administrative expense in the amount of $600.

(e) Through an oversight, $300 of shipping supplies were included in the December 31, 1958 merchandise inventory.

Required:

Working papers to revise the prior years' financial statements and working papers for the 1960 financial statements.

Assignment Material for Chapter 5

Questions

Question 5-1. What are the four basic rights inherent in capital stock? In what two general ways may stock be preferred?

Question 5-2. If a company has $100,000 common stock and $100,000 preferred, the preferred to have 6% dividends, and if the company has a net income of $4,000 the first year, $13,000 the second year, and $16,000 the third year, what annual dividends will be paid to each class if the preferred stock is:

    (a) Noncumulative and nonparticipating?
    (b) Cumulative and nonparticipating?
    (c) Cumulative and fully participating?

It must be understood that the directors declare dividends equal to the net income each year.

Question 5-3. In the absence of a specific statement on the subject, is stock that is preferred as to dividends participating or nonparticipating? Cumulative or noncumulative?

Question 5-4. Is stock that is preferred as to assets in liquidation entitled to receive dividends in arrears if the company has no retained earnings at the date of liquidation?

Question 5-5. Under what circumstances might a corporation have a stated capital but no stated value per share?

Question 5-6. How should unissued shares be shown in the ledger? How should such unissued shares be shown in the balance sheet?

Question 5-7. Should premiums and discounts on stock subscriptions be recorded when the subscriptions are received or when they are collected? Give a reason for your answer.

Question 5-8. A stockholder subscribed for his stock at a discount. Is he liable to the corporation for the discount? Has he any liability?

Suppose that he subscribed at par but paid only 80% of his subscription; is there any difference in his liability?

Question 5-9. If preferred stock was issued at a premium of $20,000 and common stock was issued at a discount of $8,000, do you think it would be acceptable to show in the balance sheet merely: Premium on capital stock—net $12,000?

Question 5-10. X subscribed for 10 shares of the common stock of New Corporation at par of $100. He paid $200 at the time of the subscription; subsequent efforts to collect on the subscription proved futile. X demands the return of the $200. New Corporation points out that the state law provides for the payment of losses on resale and expenses incident thereto from the amount paid by the defaulting subscriber, the remainder to be returned. The stock was sold for

$920 and expenses amounting to $20 were paid by the corporation. Give journal entries reflecting the proper procedure and payment.

Question 5-11. State in a single sentence the acceptable basis for the valuation of property acquired by the issuance of stock.

Question 5-12. Why may a bonus of common stock with an issue of preferred stock or bonds be undesirable from the investor's standpoint?

Question 5-13. On December 26, 1958, *L* Company issued, to the holders of its 5,000 shares of common stock, rights permitting them to acquire, for each 10 shares held, one share of 7% cumulative preferred stock ($100 par) at 90. The rights were to expire on May 1, 1959, and payment was to accompany the subscription. Prior to the close of 1958, 55 shares had been issued in accordance with the terms of the rights; prior to the completion of your audit field work (March 31, 1959), 322 additional shares had been issued.

Should any of these facts be shown in the December 31, 1958 balance sheet?

Question 5-14. The *X* Corporation entered into an agreement with certain of its officers whereby nontransferable options to purchase the company's common stock at a fixed price, substantially below current market, will be granted to them at the completion of certain periods of service. The agreement specified the date on which the options will be granted, the periods of service to be performed, the period during which the options are valid, as well as the price and amount of stock to be covered by each officer's option.

As of what date should the compensation represented by these options be determined? Give a reason for your answer.

How should the amount of compensation be computed?

Problems

Problem 5-1. Exodus Corporation is authorized to issue two classes of capital stock:

> 5,000 shares of $10 par value, 6% cumulative preferred.
> 10,000 shares of no-par common.

The business corporation act of the state in which the company is incorporated requires that a minimum of $5 per share shall be paid to a corporation for each share of no-par stock issued, and that at least this amount must be credited to the capital stock account. The directors of Exodus Corporation have taken no action relative to a stated value per share.

On July 20, 1959, 6,000 shares of common stock were issued for $39,000 in cash.

On August 11, 1959, 3,000 shares of preferred stock were issued for $33,000 in cash.

On December 15, 1959, subscriptions were received for 1,000 shares of common stock at $7 per share.

The corporation has selected the calendar year as its accounting year. For the fractional-year ending December 31, 1959, the corporation incurred a deficit of $14,300.

Required:

(1) Journal entries to record the transactions involving the capital stock of the corporation.

(2) The Preferred Stock account, as it would appear in the general ledger as of December 31, 1959.

(3) The Stockholders' Equity section of the December 31, 1959 balance sheet.

Problem 5-2. The following selected account balances appeared in the April 30, 1960 balance sheet of Martin Corporation:

Current assets:
Subscriptions receivable—Common stock..................... $11,000
Subscriptions receivable—Preferred stock................... 7,000

Capital stock:
Preferred—5% cumulative, $40 par; authorized, 4,000
   shares; issued and outstanding, 1,300 shares........ $52,000
Subscribed, but not issued, 300 shares............. 12,000 64,000
Common—No par value; authorized, 9,000 shares;
   issued and outstanding, 800 shares—no stated value. $ 2,000
Subscribed, but not issued, 5,000 shares............ 15,000 17,000

Surplus:
Paid-in:
Premium on preferred stock.............................. 5,000

Martin Corporation issues stock certificates only upon full payment of subscriptions. Subscriptions were received for the preferred shares as follows:

1,100 shares at par.
500 shares at $50 per share.

The common shares outstanding were issued for cash.

Prepare summary entries for the transactions which are indicated by the foregoing data.

Problem 5-3. Construct the Stockholders' Equity section of the June 30, 1960 balance sheet to show correctly the information presented in each of the following unrelated situations:

(1) Alpha Corporation is authorized to issue 12,000 shares of $100 par value, 4% cumulative Class A stock and 25,000 shares of no-par Class B stock. The Class B stock, which is not cumulative, has not been given a stated value.

On July 1, 1952, 4,000 Class A shares were issued for cash at $103 per share. The remaining authorized Class A shares have not been issued.

12,000 Class B shares were issued for $30 per share, cash, on January 2, 1952. An issuance of 6,000 shares, at $35 per share, was completed on August 1, 1953. The remaining authorized Class B shares were issued at $50 per share on May 16, 1955.

From the date of organization to June 30, 1960, the company had total net income of $293,000, and had declared and paid dividends as follows:

Preferred... $128,000
Common... 70,000

(2) Beta Corporation is authorized to issue 9,000 shares of 6% cumulative preferred stock, par value $50, and 18,000 shares of no-par common stock, which has been given a stated value of $10 per share by the board of directors.

The preferred stock is also preferred as to assets in the event of liquidation in an amount equal to par value plus dividends in arrears.

7,000 shares of preferred stock were issued on August 10, 1953, at $54 per share. All of the authorized common shares were issued at $12 per share on March 1, 1952.

As of June 30, 1960, Beta Corporation had a deficit of $80,000, and stock rights to 1,000 preferred shares were outstanding.

Problem 5-4. Speake Steel, Inc., has an issue of convertible bonds outstanding. According to the bond agreement, bondholders are entitled to receive fifteen shares of the company's $60 par common stock in exchange for each $1,000 bond. This privilege became effective on September 1, 1959.

On October 15, 1959, holders of $500,000 of bonds elected to convert their holdings into common stock.

Another conversion was effected on April 1, 1960, when $200,000 of bonds were exchanged for common stock.

On each of the exchange dates the following balances were taken from the ledger:

	October 15	April 1
Bonds payable	$2,500,000	$2,000,000
Premium on bonds	120,000	80,000

Prepare journal entries on October 15, 1959, and April 1, 1960, to record the conversions.

Problem 5-5. Vertical Company is seeking a bank loan. A portion of the company's balance sheet is reproduced below:

VERTICAL COMPANY
Partial Balance Sheet
December 31, 1959

Net worth:
  Capital stock:

6% nonparticipating preferred—$100 par value; 5,000 shares authorized; 2,000 shares issued and outstanding	$200,000
Common—$20 stated value; 50,000 shares authorized; 38,000 shares issued and outstanding	760,000

  Surplus:

Premium on common stock	12,000
Net worth	$972,000

The company's accountant has come to you for advice concerning the desirability of releasing the balance sheet in its present form to the bank. During his visit he discloses the following information:

The preferred stock was issued twenty years ago, when the corporation was organized, for $95 per share. The company has continued to show $4,000 of uncollected subscriptions receivable on the preferred stock as a current asset.

The common stock was issued at an average price of $23 per share.

The company has been losing money.

Required:

The Stockholders' Equity section of the company's balance sheet as you believe it should be presented.

Problem 5-6. River Corporation had the following stockholders' equity on December 31, 1959:

Stockholders' equity:
Capital stock:

Preferred—6% cumulative, nonparticipating, convertible; par value, $50; authorized and issued, 10,000 shares......................	$500,000	
Class A common—$20 stated value, with a cumulative dividend of $1 and an equal per-share participation above this with Class B common; authorized, 50,000 shares; issued and outstanding, 25,000 shares.....................	500,000	
Class B common—No par value; authorized, 50,000 shares; issued and outstanding, 30,000 shares.................................	425,000	$1,425,000
Surplus:		
Premium on preferred stock..................	$ 10,000	
Paid-in surplus—Class A common.............	50,000	
Retained earnings...........................	185,000	245,000
Stockholders' equity..............................		$1,670,000

5,000 shares of Class A common stock were issued on January 2, 1958. All other shares indicated above were outstanding on December 31, 1956, and there were no dividends in arrears as of that date.

The corporation has paid the following dividends:

$$
\begin{array}{ll}
1957\ldots\ldots\ldots\ldots & \$\ 45,000 \\
1958\ldots\ldots\ldots\ldots & 87,000 \\
1959\ldots\ldots\ldots\ldots & 129,000 \\
\end{array}
$$

On January 2, 1960, 1,000 shares of preferred stock were converted into Class A common, the conversion basis being two shares of Class A for each share of preferred converted.

(a) Compute the amount of dividends paid on each class of stock for each of the three years. Present working papers to support your answers.

(b) Submit the entry for the conversion of shares on January 2, 1960.

Problem 5-7. On June 1, 1959, Clinton Distillers Corporation received authorization to issue the following:

20,000 shares of nonvoting 6% cumulative, fully participating Class A stock, par value, $100;
10,000 shares of 6% cumulative, nonparticipating Class B stock, par value, $80; and
50,000 shares of no-par common stock.

The directors assigned a stated value of $40 per share to the common stock.

Class A stock and common stock were to be offered to subscribers in units of one share of Class A and two shares of common.

On August 23, 1959, 3,000 units were subscribed for; in addition, 7,000 units were issued for cash. Both transactions were completed at $200 per unit. Later the same day, Class A shares were traded on a stock exchange at $107 per share.

On November 18, 1959, 6,000 shares of Class B stock were subscribed for at $85 per share.

First installments of $150,000 (one-fourth) on the units and $170,000 (one-third) on Class B shares were collected on January 31, 1960.

The final three-quarters of the subscriptions for all but 100 units were received on April 1, 1960, and the certificates for fully-paid shares were issued.

On April 15, 1960, O. S. Hested notified the company that he would be unable to fulfill his subscription contract for 50 units. In accordance with state law, the company, on April 20, 1960, sold the 50 units for $9,000, cash. The company paid selling expenses on this transaction in the amount of $60. The company then refunded the balance of Hested's installment payment after deducting therefrom the deficiency resulting from the default and the selling expenses.

Prepare journal entries for the preceding transactions.

Problem 5-8.   The Stockholders' Equity section of the December 31, 1958 balance sheet for Nicholson, Inc., was as follows:

```
Stockholders' equity:
    Capital stock—Par value, $75; authorized, 30,000
        shares; issued and outstanding, 10,000 shares..... $750,000
    Surplus:
        Paid-in:
            Premium on capital stock...................    10,000
            Retained earnings...........................   190,000 $950,000
```

On January 1, 1959, company executives were made eligible for a stock option plan. The options were to be nontransferable; they could be exercised no sooner than eighteen months after they were granted. Executives were required to remain in the company's employ in order to exercise the options.

On May 1, 1959, options for 6,000 shares were granted. Purchase price was set at $80 per share. Market price on this date was $83 per share.

Options for 5,000 shares were exercised in accordance with the stock option plan, on November 1, 1960. Market price on this date was $91.

By December 31, 1960, the remaining stock purchase options had not been exercised.

The company uses a calendar-year accounting period.

Required:

(1) The journal entries necessary during 1959 and 1960 as a result of the foregoing transactions.

(2) The Stockholders' Equity section of the December 31, 1960 balance sheet. Assume that 1959 and 1960 net income was used entirely for cash dividends, and that no other transactions affecting the Stockholders' Equity section took place.

Problem 5-9.   Prepare the necessary journal entries to record the change in authorized (and outstanding) common stock of Zeff Corporation from 1,000 shares with $25 par value to 2,000 shares of no par value, in each of the following cases:

(a) The corporation issued the 1,000 shares of $25 par value stock at par. The directors have assigned a stated value of $10 per share to the no-par stock.

(b) The $25 par value stock was issued at a premium of $10 per share. The directors have assigned a stated value of $15 per share to the no-par stock.

(c) The $25 par value stock was issued at a premium of $15 per share. The directors have not assigned a stated value to the no-par stock.

(d) The $25 par value stock was issued at par. The directors have assigned a stated value of $15 per share to the no-par stock. On the date of the change to no-par stock, the corporation had retained earnings of $43,410.

(e) The $25 par value stock was issued for $23 per share. The directors have not assigned a stated value to the no-par stock.

Problem 5-10. Smith operated a small manufacturing concern as a single proprietor. The business needed additional cash in order to be in a position to accept larger orders. Smith interested Ulrich and Norris in becoming stockholders and directors in a new corporation, called The Sun Corporation. The new corporation was authorized to issue 400,000 shares of $5 par value common stock.

On July 1, 1959, The Sun Corporation received the following stock subscriptions:

Subscriber	Shares	Terms
Ulrich	50,000 shares	$260,000 cash.
Norris	50,000 shares	$200,000 in cash and $60,000 in sixty days.
Smith	100,000 shares	Transfer of the following assets used by Smith in his manufacturing business:

Accounts receivable, guaranteed by Smith to be collectible..........................	$100,000
Inventory, at cost or market, whichever is lower...............................	200,000
Machinery, original cost.................	300,000

Stock certificates were issued immediately to Ulrich and Smith.

On September 15, 1959, the corporation made an assessment on its stockholders in the amount of $.25 per share. The assessments were collected on that date.

As of December 31, 1959, the corporation changed its stock from $5 par value to no par value with a stated value of $4 per share. The stockholders exchanged their shares as of this date.

Give the journal entries that would be made in the records of The Sun Corporation as a result of the facts stated above. You may assume that Norris honored his stock subscription agreement on August 30, 1959.

Problem 5-11. On September 30, 1959, the Stockholders' Equity section of Wallace Cement, Inc., appeared as follows:

Stockholders' equity:
Capital stock:

Preferred stock—5% cumulative; par value, $50; authorized, 18,000 shares; issued and outstanding, 7,000 shares...........................	$350,000	
Subscribed, but not issued, 4,000 shares........	200,000	$550,000
Common stock—Par value, $10; authorized, 20,000 shares; issued and outstanding, 10,250 shares...	$102,500	
Subscribed, but not issued, 750 shares.........	7,500	
Total..................................	$110,000	
Less uncollected subscriptions.................	5,000	105,000
Total.......................................		$655,000

Surplus:
Paid-in:

Premium on preferred stock..................	$ 55,000	
Paid-in surplus—Preferred—Forfeited subscriptions.......................................	250	55,250
Stockholders' equity...............................		$710,250

Stock certificates are not issued until full payment has been received.

The accountant, when preparing the balance sheet, discovered that the $5,000 of receivables arising from subscriptions to 750 common shares may not be collectible.

All of the preferred shares were subscribed for at the same price; payment was delayed. R. Jensen, a subscriber to 100 preferred shares, breached his subscription contract. He had paid one installment of $600. The shares were subsequently issued for $5,200, cash, less $50 selling expenses. State law provides that any payments made by a defaulting subscriber may be retained by the issuing corporation.

As of September 30, 1959, $90,000 of the preferred subscriptions have not been collected; they are considered to be fully collectible.

Only 1,800 common shares were subscribed for on a delayed-payment basis.

Required:

(1) The journal entries for the transactions indicated above.
(2) A list of other accounts, not shown above, which would appear in the September 30, 1959 balance sheet as a result of these transactions.

Problem 5-12. Swan Corporation was organized on January 2, 1959, with an authorized capital consisting of 15,000 shares of preferred stock of $100 par value and 60,000 shares of no-par common stock without stated value.

Transactions during 1959 and 1960, relative to capital stock, were:

1959
(1) 20,000 shares of common stock were issued for cash at $10 per share.
(2) 4,000 shares of preferred were subscribed at par under the following conditions:

(a) Subscriptions to preferred shares were accepted only for round lots in multiples of 100-share units.
(b) One share of common stock was to be given as a bonus with each five shares of fully paid preferred stock.
(c) Payment was to be made at the subscriber's convenience, but final settlement was to be made within six months of the subscription date. Shares were to be issued only when subscriptions had been collected in full.
(d) Any amounts paid in on subscriptions not fully paid were to be returned, after deducting any expenses or deficiency incurred in the re-subscription of the shares.

(3) Collections on the subscriptions described in (2) are summarized below:

(a) Subscriptions to 3,800 shares were collected in full within six months and the shares were issued.
(b) Subscribers to 200 shares paid in only $12,700 within the six-month period. Expenses of $2,100 were incurred in securing subscribers for the shares of the defaulted subscribers. The new subscribers paid immediately a total of $18,000 for the preferred and common shares covered in the defaulted subscription agreements.

(4) Late in 1959, 10,000 shares of common stock were issued for cash at $15 per share.
(5) Shortly thereafter, 3,000 additional shares of preferred stock were subscribed at $105 on the same terms set forth under (2).

(6) When the year ended, collections in full had been received on 1,800 of the shares described in (5). $62,800 had been received on 900 of the remaining shares, and the corporation had reason to believe that subscribers to the other 300 shares, from whom no collections had been received, would default.

1960

(7) Early in 1960 the balance owing on the 900 shares was collected. No amounts were received from the subscribers to the 300 shares mentioned in (6).

(8) In September, the corporation secured the necessary approval to double the authorized number of preferred shares and change such shares to no-par preferred with a stated value of $40 per share. The state law permits the corporation to eliminate from its records any discount on par value shares superseded by no-par shares. On September 30, 1960, the preferred stockholders exchanged their shares, receiving two shares of the no-par preferred for each par value share held.

Required:

(a) Journal entries to record all transactions related to capital stock during 1959 and 1960.

(b) The Stockholders' Equity section of the corporation's balance sheet as of December 31, 1959. A deficit of $21,600 was incurred in 1959.

Problem 5-13.   The following account balances were taken from the November 30, 1960 trial balance of Columbus Iron Works, Inc.:

Common stock subscribed...................................	$1,000,000
Subscriptions receivable—Preferred.........................	200,000
Retained earnings (as of December 31, 1959)................	600,000
Paid-in surplus—Common—Forfeited subscriptions...........	1,000
Preferred stock (par value, $100)..........................	3,000,000
Subscriptions receivable—Common.........................	530,000
Paid-in surplus—Common stock...........................	75,000
Common stock (no-par; stated value, $50)..................	500,000
Premium on preferred stock...............................	100,000
Preferred stock subscribed.................................	400,000
Accumulated credit under common stock option plan.........	3,000

During December, 1960, the following stock transactions occurred:

December   3—Received final installment on 10,000 common shares subscribed for at $51 per share; also issued certificates. These subscriptions were paid in three equal installments.

11—Issued 2,000 shares of preferred stock at $106 per share, cash.

11—Acquired a tract of unimproved land in exchange for 2,500 preferred shares. The directors have not assigned a value to the property.

The $3,000 balance in Accumulated Credit Under Common Stock Option Plan arose from an adjusting entry on December 31, 1959. It relates to options granted on October 1, 1959, which allow employees to purchase common stock, on or after October 1, 1961, at $104 per share. This price was $3 per share lower than the market price on October 1, 1959.

The controller reported that net income for 1960 was $250,000. Dividends of $190,000 were declared and paid during the year.

In late December, 1960, it was discovered that $20,000 of subscription installments to common stock may not be collected.

75,000 shares of preferred stock, which is 5% cumulative, have been authorized. 50,000 shares of common stock have been authorized.

Required:

(1) All necessary journal entries during December, 1960, based on the above information.
(2) Stockholders' Equity section of Columbus Iron Works, Inc., balance sheet as of December 31, 1960.

Problem 5-14. A partial balance sheet of Block D Company appears below.

BLOCK D COMPANY
Partial Balance Sheet
June 30, 1959

Stockholders' equity:
  Common stock—$20 stated value; authorized, 100,000
    shares; issued and outstanding, 25,000 shares.............. $500,000
  Surplus:
    Paid-in surplus—Common..................... $ 50,000
    Retained earnings........................... 125,000 175,000
      Total... $675,000

The common stock of Block D Company is currently selling on the regional stock exchange for $27 per share.

On July 1, 1959, the company receives authorization to issue 10,000 shares of $25 par value, 6%, cumulative preferred stock. The preferred shares are offered to the common stockholders at $28 per share, with each preferred share including a detachable warrant good until June 30, 1960, entitling the holder to purchase one share of common stock for $25 per share.

Subscriptions receivable are due in thirty days and the shares are to be issued when the subscription has been collected.

Subscriptions, all dated July 15, 1959, are received from the common stockholders for all of the authorized preferred stock. Cash therefor is collected on August 14, 1959, and the shares are issued.

On September 1, 1959, the board of directors grants nontransferable stock options for 1,000 common shares to the junior officers of the company under the following conditions:

Common shares may be purchased for $25 per share during the six months ended December 31, 1960. Unexercised options lapse at that time.

The market price of the company's common shares on September 1, 1959, is $27 per share.

On December 1, 1959, when the market price of the common stock is $28 per share, the preferred stockholders present cash and warrants for 8,000 common shares, and the stock is issued to them.

During the six months ended June 30, 1960, the company's common stock sells in the range of $21 to $23 per share, and the preferred stockholders allow the remaining detachable warrants to lapse.

On August 15, 1960, when the market price of the common stock is $26 per share, junior officers present cash and options for 200 shares; the stock is issued to them.

On November 1, 1960, when the market price of the common stock is $30 per share, other junior officers present cash and options for 500 shares; the stock is issued to them.

During November and December the market value of the common stock declines significantly and no options are exercised.

Required:

Journal entries for the above, including any entries required as of June 30, 1960, the close of the company's fiscal year, and as of December 31, 1960.

Problem 5-15. Boulder Construction Company has outstanding 50,000 shares of 4% cumulative, convertible preferred stock, par $100; 80,000 shares of $10 par common stock; and $2,000,000 of 5% bonds. The preferred stock was issued at $105 per share; the common stock was issued at $8 per share. The company is authorized to issue 1,000,000 shares of each class of stock. The company has a credit balance of $900,000 in its Retained Earnings account.

The following securities transactions took place during 1960:

February 2—Collected an assessment of $3 per share from common stockholders.

March 11—Holders of 20,000 preferred shares elected to convert their holdings to common shares. Pursuant to the terms of the conversion agreement, nine shares of common were given in exchange for each share of preferred.

May 8—The directors voted to change the $10 par value stock to no par with a stated value of $10 per share and to issue 300,000 shares in exchange for the present number of outstanding shares.

July 26—Holders of $400,000 of bonds chose to exercise stock rights which had been issued to all bondholders in 1957. No entry was made for the issuance of the rights. Each bondholder received one right for each $1,000 bond which he owned. One right could be used to purchase 25 common shares, at $12 per share, cash. In exchange for the rights which were exercised, the aforementioned bondholders were issued 10,000 common shares.

September 14—Warrants representing pre-emptive rights of preferred stockholders were mailed. The rights entitle each preferred stockholder to buy, at $96, one new share of preferred stock for each ten he now owns.

The controller reported 1960 net income of $300,000; dividends of $250,000 were declared and paid during the year.

Required:

(1) All necessary journal entries for the transactions which occurred during 1960, excluding entries for earnings and dividends.
(2) The Stockholders' Equity section of the December 31, 1960 Boulder Construction Company balance sheet.

Assignment Material for Chapter 6

Questions

Question 6-1. Why would it be undesirable to record all kinds of paid-in surplus in a single Paid-in Surplus account?

Question 6-2. Do the classifications of surplus made by accountants indicate which portions of surplus are available for dividends?

Question 6-3. Can any amount received upon the issuance of no-par stock be returned to the stockholders in the form of dividends?

Question 6-4. What, if any, charges can with propriety be made against paid-in surplus?

Question 6-5. What should earned surplus or retained earnings represent?

Question 6-6. Can you mention any distinction between dividends declared out of net income from operations and dividends declared out of profits realized from the increment of invested values?

Question 6-7. Is a surplus reserve always the best means of disclosing a restriction on, or an appropriation of, retained earnings?

Question 6-8. A corporation has a capital stock of $100,000 and net assets amounting to $160,000. To reduce the number of its enterprises, it sells two of its stores for $85,000, which is the valuation at which they are carried in the accounts. It now proposes to distribute this $85,000 among its stockholders. What procedure would you recommend to safeguard all parties to the distribution?

Question 6-9. Distinguish between a split-up and a stock dividend.

Question 6-10. How would you treat the following in the balance sheet of a corporation?

(a) Cumulative dividends in arrears on preferred stock when sufficient income has been earned to pay such dividends, but, owing to rapid growth of the business, the funds produced by these earnings have been used for development and other purposes rather than for the payment of dividends.

(b) Cumulative dividends in arrears on preferred stock of a company that had been operating at a loss and had no accumulated surplus from which to pay the dividends.

Question 6-11. What are the rights of stockholders when a corporation:

(a) Declares a dividend before insolvency and sets aside a fund for its payment?

(b) Same as above, but no fund is set aside for the payment of the dividend?

711

Problems

Problem 6-1. The Cart-rite Corporation has the following three classes of capital stock outstanding on December 31, 1960:

4% cumulative, fully participating preferred; par value, $100...	$ 600,000
6% cumulative, nonparticipating preferred; par value, $100...	500,000
Common, no par value; stated value, $100..................	900,000
Total...	$2,000,000

During recent years, The Cart-rite Corporation has reinvested most of its earnings in more modern plant facilities and additional sales branches. Consequently, dividends have not been paid on the preferred stocks since December 31, 1957, and on the common stock since December 31, 1955. The company having completed its expansion program, the board of directors, on December 31, 1960, declared dividends in the amount of $250,000 and voted to eliminate the $250,000 reserve for expansion from the accounts.

Journalize the dividend declaration, with a computation showing the amount to be paid to each class of stockholders, and the entry required to eliminate the expansion reserve.

Problem 6-2. The Stockholders' Equity section of the December 31, 1960 balance sheet for Thompson Company was as follows:

Stockholders' equity:		
Capital stock—Par value, $100; authorized, 40,000		
shares; issued and outstanding, 10,000 shares............		$1,000,000
Surplus:		
Paid-in—Premium on capital stock............	$ 80,000	
Retained earnings.........................	300,000	380,000
Total..		$1,380,000

On January 2, 1961, the board of directors declared an 8% stock dividend; fair value this date was $103 per share. The stock was to be issued on January 15, 1961. The controller chose the procedure recommended in A.R.B. 43.

(1) Prepare an entry for the declaration and issuance of the stock dividend.

(2) If the stock dividend was not to be issued until February 10, 1961, state how it would be disclosed in the January 31, 1961 balance sheet.

Problem 6-3. (A) From the following list of account balances as of December 31, 1960, compute the total stockholders' equity of Manning Corporation.

Common stock, par $10.....................................	$800,000
Retained earnings..	500,000
Dividends payable..	100,000
Preferred stock subscribed................................	650,000
Paid-in surplus—From stock dividends......................	200,000
Subscriptions receivable—Preferred (fully collectible)...........	80,000
Preferred stock dividend payable..........................	300,000
Preferred stock, par $50..................................	700,000
Donated surplus...	30,000
Premium on common stock.................................	150,000
Fractional share certificates—Preferred.....................	20,000
Reserve for contingencies.................................	90,000
Bonds payable...	350,000

(B) The following summarized transactions involving the stockholders' equity of Manning Corporation occurred during January, 1961. Beginning with your answer for part A, above, compute the stockholders' equity on January 31, 1961.

January 8—The directors declared that the Land account should be increased $200,000 to reflect rising market values.

14—The directors declared a 10% stock dividend on outstanding common shares. Today's market price is $12 per share, and the controller customarily follows A.R.B. recommendations.

20—The company acquired 10,000 shares of its preferred stock at its liquidation price of $65 per share. The shares were cancelled.

31—The controller reported January net income of $100,000.

Problem 6-4. On January 2, 1960, the date of organization, The Bigelow Company issued 15,000 shares of $100 par, 5% cumulative preferred stock (authorized, 30,000 shares) at $104 per share and 10,000 shares of no-par common stock (authorized, 25,000 shares) at $23 per share. Stated value of the common stock is $20 per share; the preferred stock has a liquidation value of $115 per share.

On November 1, 1960, The Bigelow Company issued $5,000,000 of 4% bonds, requiring that $40,000 be set aside in a sinking fund and in a surplus reserve each year, beginning in 1961.

A reserve for retirement of preferred stock was established at $30,000 on May 1, 1961; it is to be increased by $30,000 on each December 31, beginning on December 31, 1961.

On July 1, 1961, 10,000 additional preferred shares were issued at $106 per share.

Net income and cash dividends, which are customarily declared yearly in December, were as follows:

	Net Income	Cash Dividends
1960	$140,000	$ 60,000
1961	145,000	100,000

Present the Stockholders' Equity section of the December 31, 1961 balance sheet.

Problem 6-5. In order to reduce fluctuations in reported net income, Steel Alloy Company, on January 1, 1957, adopted the following policies:

(1) Expense is debited $10,000 annually, in lieu of insurance premiums, and a self-insurance reserve is credited. Fire losses are charged to the reserve. Fire losses for the years 1957–1960, inclusive, are shown below.

(2) A debit or credit is made to Revenue and Expense equal to 66⅔% of the difference between the unadjusted net income and $200,000. The entry in the Revenue and Expense account is offset by an addition to or deduction from a general contingencies reserve account. The balance in the general contingencies reserve account as of January 1, 1961, amounted to $42,000. The net income amounts reported by the company were:

Year	Net Income	Fire Losses
1957	$209,000	$ 7,000
1958	220,000	6,000
1959	197,000	8,000
1960	195,000	15,000

Compute the net income for the years 1957–1960, inclusive, assuming that the above policies had not been adopted.

Problem 6-6. The following accounts appear in the December 31, 1959 trial balance of Petty Company.

Common stock..	$300,000
Fractional share certificates.........................	6,500
Paid-in surplus—From stock dividends.................	15,000
Paid-in surplus—Common.............................	35,000
Retained earnings.....................................	135,400
Reserve for retirement of preferred stock.............	50,000
Unrealized increment in fixed assets..................	90,000

Submit whatever journal entries you believe necessary in view of the following information:

The common stock has no par value, and no stated value has been set.

During 1959, the Paid-in Surplus—Common account was charged $50,000 for the write-off of obsolete parts being carried in the inventory.

The fractional share certificates, issued in connection with a stock dividend, have expired. The directors cannot rescind, in part, a stock dividend.

The $35,000 of paid-in surplus is the excess of the issuance price over the amount credited to Common Stock.

The preferred stock was retired as of July 1, 1959.

As of December 31, 1959, the board of directors declared a stock dividend of 2,000 shares, issuable as of January 10, 1960, for the purpose of transferring the unrealized increment to permanent capital. The fixed assets previously written up have become fully depreciated.

Problem 6-7. On January 1, 1961, the stockholders' equity in Golden Foundries, Inc., was as follows:

(1) 30,000 shares of 5% cumulative, nonparticipating prior preferred stock, with a par value of $10; authorization was 70,000 shares.

(2) 40,000 shares of 3% cumulative, fully participating preferred stock, with a par value of $10; 50,000 shares were authorized.

(3) 80,000 shares of no-par common stock, with a stated value of $10; authorization was 180,000 shares.

(4) Paid-in surplus consisting of:

Excess of issue price over par value of 3% preferred stock....	$50,000
Contributions to company as a result of expired employee stock options.......................................	40,000

(5) Retained earnings of $110,000, $15,000 of which was in a Reserve for Contingencies.

Since the company's organization, dividends have been paid as follows:

Year	5% Preferred	3% Preferred	Common
1953...........................	5%	3%	$10,000
1954...........................	5%	4%	32,000
1955...........................	5%	2%	none
1956...........................	5%	3%	none
1957...........................	5%	1%	none
1958...........................	none	none	none
1959...........................	none	none	none
1960...........................	none	none	none

All shares were issued on the date of organization.

On January 2, 1961, the board of directors reached agreement with representatives of each class of stock to the effect that the dividend arrearages on the preferred stocks would be satisfied by the issuance of common stock as a dividend. Preferred stockholders were to receive one share of common stock for each $12 of dividends in arrears. The necessary common shares were issued on January 13, 1961.

On January 29, 1961, the directors declared a 6% stock dividend on outstanding common shares, to be distributed on February 11, 1961. The directors ordered that the retained earnings to be capitalized should be determined on a basis consistent with the amount of the capitalization in connection with the common stock issuance on January 13, 1961.

Net income for January, 1961, was $90,000.

Required:

(1) Journal entries necessary during January, 1961, for the foregoing stock dividends.
(2) The Stockholders' Equity section of the January 31, 1961 balance sheet.

Problem 6-8. As of October 31, 1959, the Stockholders' Equity section of Dudley Instrument Corporation was as follows:

Stockholders' equity:
  Capital stock:
    Preferred stock—4% cumulative; par value, $100; liquidating value, $110; authorized and issued, 20,000 shares.... $2,000,000
    Common stock—Par value, $80; authorized, 60,000 shares; issued and outstanding, 30,000 shares............... 2,400,000 $4,400,000
  Surplus:
    Paid-in:
      Premium on preferred stock........... $ 20,000
      Retained earnings..................... 400,000 420,000 $4,820,000

The following transactions, given in summary form, occurred between November 1, 1959 and October 31, 1960:

(1) The company acquired, at the liquidation price, all outstanding preferred shares; it thereupon cancelled the shares. No dividends were in arrears.
(2) A 5% stock dividend was declared on the common shares. On the date of declaration, the fair value per share was $84. The controller elected to follow the accounting procedure recommended in A.R.B. 43. By October 31, 1960, the dividend had not been issued.
(3) The company's counsel reported that unfavorable adjudication of pending litigation brought against the company could result in damages of $60,000. Accordingly, the board of directors authorized the creation of a surplus reserve for that amount.
(4) The reported net income for the fiscal year ended October 31, 1960, was $200,000.

Required:

(1) A statement of retained earnings for the year ended October 31, 1960.
(2) The Stockholders' Equity section of the October 31, 1960 balance sheet.

Problem 6-9. Valentine, Incorporated, presented the Stockholders' Equity section of its May 31, 1960 balance sheet in the following form:

Stockholders' equity:
Capital stock—Par value, $100; authorized, 35,000 shares; issued and outstanding, 24,900 shares $2,490,000
Surplus 770,000 $3,260,000

An analysis of the company's records disclosed that the surplus resulted from the transactions summarized below:

—Nonoperating losses .... $ 50,000 ᴄʜᴇ
—Recognition of increased market value of buildings 220,000
Excess of fair value ($105) over par in connection with a stock dividend .... 50,000 ✗
—Net operating income .... 1,700,000——
—Cash dividends declared and paid 180,000
—Cash dividends declared but not yet paid 30,000
—Premium on sale of capital stock 100,000
—Par value of fractional certificates which were not exercised prior to expiration (in connection with stock dividend) 10,000

In addition to the above, the board of directors authorized the establishment of a reserve of $100,000 for the expansion of plant facilities. The action was taken on May 17, 1960.

15,000 shares of capital stock were issued prior to December 1, 1959, date of the stock dividend declaration.

Restate the Stockholders' Equity section of the balance sheet in more acceptable form.

Problem 6-10. Middle River Corporation has outstanding on January 1, 1959, 15,000 of its 20,000 authorized shares of common stock, par value $10 per share.

Retained earnings, unappropriated, on the above date amounted to $63,900, premium on common stock was $30,000, other paid-in surplus was $25,000, and reserve for self-insurance was $10,000.

During the year 1959 the corporation declared, December 1, and paid, December 8, an 8% dividend, the net income was $34,800, and $5,000 was added to the self-insurance reserve.

On January 2, 1960, the corporation took title to a tract of unimproved real estate worth $20,000, received as a gift from the City of Y.   DONATED SUR.

In order to conserve cash for building needs, a 10% stock dividend was declared as of December 1, 1960, and issued on December 15, 1960. It was necessary to issue fractional share certificates for 120 shares. During the latter part of November and the early part of December the corporation's stock was worth $16 per share. Issued   1380 shares

The net income for 1960 was $29,900. The self-insurance reserve was increased by $5,000 and a plant expansion reserve was set up for $30,000.

By December 31, 1960, fractional share certificates had been presented and full share certificates issued for 90 shares. On June 15, 1961, the remaining fractional share certificates expired and the board of directors took appropriate action (in conformity with state law) to give recognition to this fact in the accounts of the corporation. By law, the board of directors is not empowered to rescind any part of a stock dividend.

Required:

(1) Journal entries to record all activity affecting the stockholders' equity accounts of the corporation from January 1, 1959, through June 15, 1961. (Debit Other Assets when recording net income.)
(2) The Stockholders' Equity section of the corporation's balance sheet on December 31, 1960.

Problem 6-11. Prepare journal entries to record the transactions for 1959 indicated by the following information:

(A) Bevis Bottle Company had the following account balances on June 30, 1959:

6% preferred stock—$50 par value; 20,000 shares authorized, issued, and outstanding	$1,000,000
Premium on preferred stock	20,000
Common stock—No par value; no stated value; 100,000 shares authorized; 80,000 shares issued and outstanding	845,500
Paid-in surplus—Common—Stockholders' assessments	80,000
Accumulated credit under stock option plan	6,000
Common stock warrants outstanding (10,000 shares)	5,000
Retained earnings	378,900
Reserve for self-insurance	24,500

On July 10, 1959, when the company's common stock was selling for $11 per share, the board of directors declared a common stock dividend of 4%, stock to be issued to holders of common stock on August 1, 1959. The board also voted to increase the self-insurance reserve to a balance of $30,000.

On August 1, 1959, stock certificates representing the stock dividend were distributed.

On August 10, 1959, the board of directors declared a 3% scrip dividend on the preferred stock. The scrip, bearing 5% interest, is to be issued to stockholders of record on September 1.

On September 1, 1959, the scrip was distributed to the preferred stockholders.

(B) Martin Manufacturing Corporation had authorized capital of $500,000, representing 20,000 shares of $25 par value common stock, 16,000 shares of which were outstanding, having been issued for $28 per share on October 1, 1954, when the corporation was organized.

On July 1, 1959, when the common stock was selling for $30 per share and the corporation had retained earnings of $214,300, the board of directors declared a 10% stock dividend on the 16,000 shares outstanding on that date. The distribution of the outstanding shares indicated that certificates for 1,300 full shares would be issued and that fractional share certificates for the remaining shares would be necessary.

On August 1, 1959, the dividend shares and fractional share certificates were issued.

As of August 10, 1959, fractional share certificates equivalent to 260 shares were presented and certificates were issued. No additional fractional share certificates were presented.

The fractional share certificates expired on December 1, 1959, and the board of directors voted to rescind this portion of the stock dividend.

Problem 6-12. The board of directors of Campus Bike Company, which owns a manufacturing plant and leases sixty retail outlets, decided on January 1, 1957, to cancel the existing fire insurance coverage on its buildings and equipment and to adopt the following policy:

Establish a reserve, offset by a charge to expense, equal to the amount of insurance premiums which would have been paid.

In 1956, during which the number of retail outlets operated had not changed, the insurance expense was as follows:

Manufacturing plant... $2,200
Stores (Locations are leased for ten years and only the equipment
    therein is owned by Campus Bike Company. Each store con-
    tains identical type and quantity of equipment.)............... 4,800

On July 1, 1958, five new stores were opened; on January 2, 1959, ten additional stores were opened.

On January 1, 1959, all fire insurance rates increased 5%.

On December 30, 1959, a fire completely destroyed the equipment in one store. This equipment was purchased on January 2, 1955, the date when the store was leased, and as of December 31, 1958, when it was 40% depreciated, its carrying value was $5,760. On February 1, 1960, the company spent $10,500 to replace all of the equipment destroyed by the fire.

The accounting year for the company is the calendar year.

Prepare journal entries, with supporting computations where necessary, required as a result of the self-insurance program, the fire loss, and the equipment replacement.

Problem 6-13. The condensed balance sheet of Dexter File Company on December 31, 1959, was as follows:

DEXTER FILE COMPANY
Balance Sheet
December 31, 1959

Assets

Cash..		$261,400
Accounts receivable.......................................		88,600
Inventories...		118,300
Unexpired insurance.......................................		12,000
Stock of *XY* Company.....................................		100,000
Property, plant, and equipment.....................	$324,300	
Less accumulated depreciation....................	173,300	151,000
		$731,300

Liabilities and Stockholders' Equity

Accounts payable...		$ 78,400
Accrued expenses...		9,100
4% preferred stock—$100 par value.................	$200,000	
Common stock—No par value—Stated value, $10 per
share..	220,000	
Premium on preferred stock........................	13,600	
Paid-in surplus—Common stock....................	44,000	
Retained earnings...............................	166,200	643,800
		$731,300

Details of the capital stock of the corporation are shown on the opposite page.

	Authorized	Issued
4% cumulative preferred with a liquidating value of $110 per share..................	2,000 shares	2,000 shares
Common...............................	25,000 shares	22,000 shares

The following transactions affecting the company's stockholders' equity accounts occurred during 1960:

January   15—Necessary authorization was obtained to change the authorized common stock to 50,000 shares with a $5 stated value. The change was effective on this date and two new shares were issued for each share of outstanding common.

March   15—The regular quarterly dividend on the preferred stock was declared.

25—The quarterly preferred dividend was paid.

May   15—The board of directors took the necessary action to retire, as of this date, all of the preferred stock at its liquidating value plus cumulative dividend of ½ of 1%.

June   20—Subscriptions were received for 500 shares of common stock at $7 per share. Cash of $4 per share was received with the subscriptions. The shares are to be issued when the subscription price is received in full.

21—A 5% stock dividend was declared, to be issued June 30 on the basis of the number of shares outstanding as of June 26.

25—Subscribers to 200 shares of common paid the balance of their subscriptions and common shares were issued to them.

30—The common stock dividend was issued.

August   15—The directors authorized the establishment of a reserve for general contingencies of $20,000.

December 21—The directors voted to distribute, as of December 31, the stock of XY Company as a dividend to the common stockholders.

31—The stock of XY Company was distributed.

31—Pursuant to an action taken by the board of directors, the Plant account was written up $100,000 to give recognition to current appraisal data. As of December 31, 1960, the plant was 40% depreciated. The resulting unrealized increment amounted to $60,000.

(1) Prepare journal entries to record all transactions indicated by the foregoing information.

(2) Prepare a statement of retained earnings for 1960, assuming that the net income for the year amounted to $85,000.

(3) Show how the Stockholders' Equity section of the December 31, 1960 balance sheet would appear, assuming that half of the subscriptions receivable are uncollectible.

Assignment Material for Chapter 7

Questions

Question 7-1. State the three elements of the definition of treasury stock.

Question 7-2. The *A* Company, whose stock is listed on an exchange, has purchased about 5% of its outstanding stock at current market prices (which are nearly three times the original issuance price) for distribution to employees under a bonus plan. It is estimated that not more than 20% of the present holdings will be distributed during the current year. It has been the practice of the company to show the stock as an asset in its balance sheet and, in its income statement, to show dividends applicable to such stock as miscellaneous income. Do you approve? If not, how would you deal with these items?

Question 7-3. What is meant by the "surplus rule" in connection with the purchase of treasury stock?

Question 7-4. (a) The Zenith Process Company is incorporated with a capital stock of 100,000 shares with no par value. It issues 10,000 shares at $50 per share and issues the remaining 90,000 shares to the same stockholders for property consisting for the most part of a quartz gold mine and its equipment, which it records at a valuation of $4,500,000. The declared paid-in capital is $10 per share. After five years' operations, the company's surplus of all classes was $1,000,000, no dividends having been paid. To get rid of a disgruntled stockholder, the company buys his 5,000 shares at $55 per share. The company debits the purchase price of the stock, $275,000, to Treasury Stock. Would you, as auditor, approve this entry? Give reason.

(b) Assume that the company's operations had resulted in a deficit of $100,000, and that the 5,000 shares of treasury stock were acquired at $35 per share. The entry for the purchased stock debited Treasury Stock with $250,000 (the amount entered in the books at the time of issuance) and credited a paid-in surplus account with $75,000, the amount by which the issuance price exceeded the amount paid for the treasury stock. Would you approve this entry?

Question 7-5. It formerly was the custom to record treasury stock purchases at the par of the stock acquired or, in the case of no par stock, at the actual or average issuance price. Why was this procedure regarded as proper, and what has happened to cause it to now be regarded as improper?

Question 7-6. Conger and Green, who are sole surviving stockholders of Holly Wreath Box Company, agree to and consummate the following transaction: Conger agrees to sell his entire holdings of stock to Green for $75,000. Green receives the stock and pays for it with company funds. Green subsequently agrees to resell the stock to Conger for $30,000. Conger accepts and pays for the stock accordingly. The difference between these two amounts, $45,000, is charged to Retained Earnings. If engaged as auditor for Holly Wreath Box Company, would you approve of such a transaction and the method of handling the $45,000 item? Give reasons for your answer.

Question 7-7.   When a corporation issues stock for land, a valuation problem may arise. If the corporation pays for the land with treasury stock, which has a definitely ascertainable cost, is the valuation problem altered?

Question 7-8.   When capital stock is donated to a corporation, how should the donation be recorded, and how should the proceeds of a subsequent sale be recorded?

Question 7-9.   *A* owns 10,000 shares of stock in Hammond Manufacturing Company and donates 5,000 shares of said stock to the corporation. Would this donation affect the book value of the capital stock? If so, explain.

Question 7-10.   A company whose stock is widely distributed and much dealt in increases its capital stock of $400,000 by a 100% stock dividend. Some years later an original stockholder brings suit for elimination of what he claims to be water in the stock resulting from the stock dividend.

Do you believe that the stock dividend necessarily watered the stock? If it did, how can the water be eliminated?

Problems

Problem 7-1.   On its organization date, January 2, 1959, Kendrick Karton Corporation sold 8,000 shares of $20 par capital stock at $22 per share. 20,000 shares were authorized. The following stock transactions occurred during 1959:

February   21—Acquired 200 shares of capital stock at $23 per share.
March   15—Sold 200 shares at $25 per share.
May   28—Acquired 200 shares of capital stock at $25 per share.
June   4—Sold 200 shares at $24 per share.
September 12—Acquired 200 shares of capital stock at $27 per share.

The controller, on December 31, 1959, reported earnings for the year of $50,000. State law imposes a restriction on retained earnings equal in amount to the cost of treasury shares.

Required:

(1) Journal entries for the treasury stock transactions; use the cost basis.
(2) Stockholders' Equity section of the December 31, 1959 balance sheet.

Problem 7-2.   For each of the following companies, present journal entries for the stock transactions and prepare a Stockholders' Equity section of each company's balance sheet, giving effect to the transactions. Assume that retained earnings restrictions are necessary in both cases.

(A) The Folsom Corporation, empowered to issue 10,000 shares of $30 par capital stock, issued 7,000 shares at $32 per share. 800 shares were acquired at $35 per share; 500 of these were sold at $31 per share. Earnings of $50,000 were reported for the period. The controller employs the procedures recommended by the American Accounting Association in accounting for treasury stock.

(B) Pioneer, Inc., issued 2,000 of its 8,000 authorized $40 par shares for $65 per share. 300 shares were acquired by the company for $70 per share. 100 of such treasury shares were sold at $68 per share. Earnings for the fiscal period were $15,000; the cost basis is used for treasury stock.

Problem 7-3. Draper Disc Dealers, Inc., issued 20,000 shares of $50 par capital stock at $51 per share on January 2, 1957. 30,000 shares were authorized on that date. During the next three years, the company earned $100,000, and, on December 20 each year, paid a dividend of $1 per share.

On January 2, 1958, the company purchased 1,000 shares of its capital stock at $50 per share. On December 31, 1958, it sold 700 treasury shares at $48 per share. On January 2, 1959, 500 shares were presented as a gift to the company.

State law requires that a restriction equal to the cost of treasury shares be placed on retained earnings.

Prepare the Stockholders' Equity section of the December 31, 1959 balance sheet, observing the cost basis in connection with treasury shares.

Problem 7-4. The Mawson Machine Tool Company was organized on January 2, 1959. Considering the following summarized transactions, which occurred during 1959, compute the book value per share of the capital stock at December 31, 1959.

January   2—Sold 3,000 shares of $100 par capital stock at $103 per share.
March   27—Acquired 400 shares of the company's capital stock at $100 per share, cash.
April   20—Sold 100 treasury shares at $102 per share, cash.
June   30—Controller reported earnings of $50,000 for the first six months.
August   31—Declared and issued a 10% stock dividend.
October   3—Reserved $40,000 of retained earnings for plant expansion.
December 10—Declared a cash dividend of $3 per share, payable January 7, 1960.
          31—Controller reported earnings of $30,000 for preceding six months.

Problem 7-5. Roydon Plastics Corp. was incorporated on January 2, 1959, and was authorized to issue 20,000 shares of $10 par value capital stock.

On February 26, 1959, the company issued 8,000 shares of stock at $11 per share. 1,000 shares were acquired by the company on March 18, 1959, at a cost per share of $9. On April 6, 1959, stockholders donated 700 shares; the market price on this date was $10 per share. The company sold 200 treasury shares, at $10 per share, on April 13, 1959. 1,100 treasury shares were sold on May 31, 1959, at $5 per share.

On September 30, the board of directors declared a quarterly dividend of twenty cents per share, payable October 20. In the state of incorporation dividends can be declared from either retained earnings or paid-in surplus, but retained earnings must be restricted to the extent of the cost of any treasury shares.

Nine months' earnings of $20,000 were reported on September 30, 1959.

Required:

(1) Journal entries for the foregoing transactions (except recognition of earnings). Use the cost basis for treasury stock transactions, and assume the first-in, first-out basis for sales of treasury shares.
(2) Stockholders' Equity section of the September 30, 1959 balance sheet.
(3) Book value per share at September 30, 1959.

Problem 7-6. On June 15, 1957, organization date of Roscoe & Son, Inc., unimproved land valued by the board of directors at $500,000 was deeded to the company by Forrest M. Roscoe, one of the founders, in exchange for 5,000 shares of $100 par common stock. The transaction was recorded at par. Immediately after this transaction, the common stock sold for $60 per share in the over-the-counter market.

Substantial losses were incurred in 1957 and 1958. Early in 1959 a number of stockholders joined together for the purpose of securing sufficient votes to displace the directors. The campaign, which emphasized "mismanagement," won the support of a majority of the votes, and the new directors promptly replaced some of the top management personnel.

The new directors recognized that probably the property acquired on June 15, 1957, had been worth only $300,000. After consulting with the controller and an auditor, the directors, desirous of correcting the misstatement, decided to choose one of three alternatives, as follows:

(1) Charge the $200,000 to Miscellaneous Expense, which would appear in the operating section of the income statement.
(2) Write down the Land account by $200,000 and reduce the par value of the 10,000 outstanding shares an equal amount. This action would require approval by the stockholders.
(3) Reduce the Land account by a direct charge of $200,000 to Retained Earnings.

The directors seemed to favor the third alternative, because it would have no effect on the income statement, nor would it need to be voted upon by the stockholders. The third alternative was not as likely, therefore, to attract public attention.

Prepare the journal entries necessary to implement each alternative, and discuss the merits of each.

Problem 7-7. The December 31, 1959 Hooper Brick and Pipe Co. balance sheet, prepared by company officials, appeared as follows:

HOOPER BRICK AND PIPE CO.
Balance Sheet
December 31, 1959

Assets:
Current assets:

Cash	$ 920,000	
Accounts receivable	240,000	$1,160,000

Investments:

Treasury stock, at cost		105,000

Fixed assets:

Equipment	$ 100,000	
Less allowance for depreciation	5,000	95,000
		$1,360,000

Liabilities:
Current liabilities:

Accounts payable	$ 20,000	
Reserve for plant expansion	80,000	$ 100,000

Stockholders' equity:
Capital stock:

Authorized, 30,000 shares; 2,000 issued shares are in the treasury	$1,040,000	

Surplus:

Retained earnings	220,000	1,260,000
		$1,360,000

The company was organized on January 2, 1959. On examining the books and records of the company at December 31, 1959, the auditor discovered:

(1) All acquisitions of treasury stock were completed at the same price. The only sale of treasury shares, involving 500 shares sold at $60 per share on June 1, was recorded by crediting Treasury Stock for the proceeds.

(2) The 20,000 issued shares of par stock were sold on January 2 at a premium of $2 per share.

(3) Directors declared a dividend of $1 per share on December 29. Date of payment was set at January 18, 1960. The credit was made to Accounts Payable.

(4) Pursuant to action by the board of directors, a surplus reserve was established.

(5) The equipment was presented to the company as a gift by a group of stockholders. The credit, for its fair value, was made to Retained Earnings.

State law requires that retained earnings be withheld from use for dividends to the extent of the cost of treasury stock.

(1) Present journal entries as of December 31, 1959, to correct the ledger accounts.

(2) Prepare the balance sheet as it should have appeared on December 31, 1959.

(3) Compute the 1959 net income.

Problem 7-8. Fine Wines & Liquors, Inc., was incorporated at the beginning of 1959. The controller has recorded treasury stock transactions in harmony with the 1957 revision of "Accounting and Reporting Standards for Corporate Financial Statements." The tentative partial December 31, 1959 balance sheet follows.

FINE WINES & LIQUORS, INC.
Partial Balance Sheet
December 31, 1959

Stockholders' equity:
Capital stock—Par value, $20; authorized,
40,000 shares; issued, 25,000 shares, of
which 3,000 are in the treasury (300 by
donation)............................ $500,000
    Less treasury stock, at par........... 54,000 $446,000

Surplus:
Paid-in:
  Premium on capital stock............ $ 25,200
  Paid-in surplus—Reissue of treasury
    stock........................... 5,300
  Donated surplus.................... 9,000 $39,500

Retained earnings [of which $57,240, representing the issue price ($21.20) of purchased treasury stock, is restricted].......... 66,800   106,300

    Stockholders' equity............................. $552,300

Summary of Transactions Relating to Stockholders' Equity

On January 2, 1959, 25,000 shares were issued at $21.20 per share. 4,000 shares were reacquired —the only purchase of treasury shares—on the following March 3.

A stockholder donated 800 shares on May 7, 1959, some of which were exchanged for office equipment on July 30, 1959.

On September 27, 1959, 600 purchased treasury shares were sold for $23 per share. Additional purchased treasury shares were sold on October 18, 1959.

Earnings for the year amounted to $70,000. No dividends were declared.

State law requires that retained earnings be withheld from use for dividends to the extent of the cost of treasury stock.

After lengthy discussions with the company's auditor, the controller decided to adopt the cost basis of handling treasury stock transactions. The auditor thereupon prepared a journal entry, as of December 31, 1959, in order that the accounts appearing in the published December 31, 1959 balance sheet would reflect the cost basis.

(1) Recreate the journal entries relating to stock transactions in 1959. Assume that entries for donated shares are the same for the par basis as for the cost basis.

(2) Prepare a journal entry as of December 31, 1959, to convert the ledger accounts to the cost basis for treasury stock.

(3) Prepare the Stockholders' Equity section of the December 31, 1959 balance sheet, as it would be published.

(4) Explain why, in the tentative balance sheet shown above, $57,240 is used in the parenthetical comment relating to the restriction of retained earnings.

Problem 7-9. From the following list of account balances as of November 30, 1959, prepare the Stockholders' Equity section of Lummis Construction Company's balance sheet as it should appear on that date. Determine the balance which has been omitted.

Reserve for bond sinking fund............................	$120,000
Treasury stock—Preferred (acquired January, 1959)..........	28,800
Retained earnings.......................................	500,000
Common stock, par $40..................................	800,000
Donated surplus—1959..................................	16,400
Declared but unpaid 1959 dividend on preferred stock (credit balance)...	23,200
Treasury stock—Common—Held for distribution to officers...	30,000
Paid-in surplus—From retirement of shares of preferred stock..	to be found
Paid-in surplus—From preferred treasury stock transactions...	1,500
Preferred stock, par $100................................	580,000
Common stock dividend payable...........................	38,400

Additional information:

One preferred treasury stock purchase, 1,000 shares at $96, has been made; some of these shares were sold at $3 per share above cost; some were retired; the latter shares can be reissued.

The cost basis was used for all treasury stock transactions.

No debits have been made to paid-in surplus accounts.

The stock dividend was to be issued on January 14, 1960; A.R.B. No. 43 was followed.

During 1959, one stockholder presented to the company, as a gift, 900 common shares. Some of the shares were thereupon sold at $41 per share.

40,000 preferred shares and 50,000 common shares have been authorized. The preferred stock is cumulative at a 4% rate.

State law requires that retained earnings must be withheld from dividends to the extent of the cost of treasury shares.

The purchase of common treasury shares, made at $37.50 per share, was consummated in 1957. No liability account relating to officers' stock purchase plan was set up, nor is such an account necessary.

The yearly preferred dividend, as referred to above, has not been announced to stockholders. The full preferred dividend requirement has been satisfied in every year.

Problem 7-10. Winston Mills, Inc., was organized on January 2, 1954; authorized capital consisted of 20,000 5% cumulative preferred shares, par $50, and 30,000 common shares, par $20. The liquidation value of the preferred stock was set at $54 plus dividends in arrears. On that date, the company issued 8,000 preferred shares at $52 per share, and 10,000 common shares at par.

A 10% common stock dividend was declared on December 4, 1957, and issued 30 days later. On the declaration date, the fair value was established at $21 per share; the recommendation contained in A.R.B. No. 43 was followed.

On January 2, 1959, the company purchased 1,000 of its common shares at $24 per share. 400 of these shares were sold at $25 per share on April 7, 1959, and 500 shares were sold at $20 per share on October 19, 1959. The remaining treasury shares were retired on November 3, 1959.

On January 2, 1960, the company received as a gift 2,000 of its common shares. Of these shares, 500 were sold at $25 per share on July 1, 1960.

Accumulated earnings from the date of organization through December 31, 1960, were $300,000. Dividends on preferred shares were not paid in 1958 and 1960; 5% was paid in all other years. Common dividends of $1 per share were paid on outstanding shares on December 31 in all years except those in which there was a preferred arrearage.

The retirement of shares does not reduce the authorization.

Required:

(1) Journal entries for transactions which occurred during 1957, 1958, 1959, and 1960 (except earnings and cash dividends).
(2) Stockholders' Equity section of the December 31, 1960 balance sheet.
(3) Book value per share of each class of stock on December 31, 1960.

Problem 7-11. On December 31, 1960, the adjusted trial balance of Buffalo Breakfast Foods Corporation was as follows:

BUFFALO BREAKFAST FOODS CORPORATION
Adjusted Trial Balance
December 31, 1960

Boulder National Bank	58,000	
Accounts receivable	30,000	
Allowance for bad debts		300
Treasury stock, at cost	19,600	
Inventories	70,000	
Equipment	240,000	
Accumulated depreciation		50,000
Accounts payable		10,000
Capital stock		298,000
Surplus		59,300
	417,600	417,600

Considering the following information, prepare the Stockholders' Equity section of the December 31, 1960 balance sheet, and compute the book value per share for each class of stock on December 31, 1960.

The corporation was organized on January 2, 1958, with authorizations of 10,000 preferred shares and 50,000 no-par common shares. The preferred stock had the following features: 5% cumulative, $10 par value, with a liquidation value of $12 per share plus dividends in arrears. No stated value was given to the common shares.

On the date of organization, 7,000 preferred shares were issued at $13 per share, cash. 12,000 common shares were issued on the same day, also for cash.

600 preferred shares were acquired in 1959 for $14 per share; 400 of these shares were sold for $15 per share. 1,000 common shares were acquired during 1960; 200 of these shares were sold for $18 per share.

Subsequently during 1960, a stockholder donated 400 common shares, which were sold for $20 per share.

Earnings for the three years totaled $40,000.

Dividends were declared and paid in 1958, including $.50 per share on common.

State law requires that retained earnings be withheld from use for dividends to the extent of the cost of treasury stock.

Problem 7-12. Using the December 31, 1960 Stockholders' Equity section of the balance sheet, compute the book value per share for each class of stock. All outstanding shares were issued on the date of organization, January 2, 1945.

MARGINAL PRODUCT CORP.
Partial Balance Sheet
December 31, 1960

Stockholders' equity:
Capital stock:

First preferred stock—4% cumulative, fully participating; par value, $100; liquidation value, par plus unpaid dividends no longer than four years in arrears; authorized, 10,000 shares; issued and outstanding, 8,000 shares (Note 1)...............................	$800,000		
Second preferred stock—5% cumulative, non-participating; par value, $50; liquidation value, $60 plus unpaid dividends in arrears; authorized, 12,000 shares; issued and outstanding, 6,000 shares (Note 2)............	300,000		
Common stock—No par value; authorized and issued, 7,000 shares, of which 500 shares are in the treasury, at stated value of $50......	350,000		$1,450,000
Surplus:			
Paid-in:			
Premium on second preferred stock.........	$130,000		
Paid-in surplus—Common—Forfeited subscriptions............................	5,000		
Paid-in surplus—From treasury stock transactions...............................	10,000	$145,000	
Retained earnings:			
Appropriated:			
Reserve for contingencies................	$ 30,000		
Reserve for plant expansion.............	110,000		
Total..............................	$140,000		
Free (Note 3)...........................	50,000	190,000	335,000
Total..			$1,785,000
Less cost of treasury stock.......................................			25,000
Stockholders' equity			$1,760,000

Note 1.   Dividends have not been paid on this class of stock since 1956, when $24,000 was declared and paid.   Shares of this stock may be called at $102.

Note 2.   Dividends have not been paid on this class of stock since 1955, when $10,000 was declared and paid.   These shares are not callable.

Note 3.   State law provides that paid-in surplus may be charged to settle dividends in arrears at liquidation.   State law does not impose restrictions on retained earnings because of treasury stock holdings.

Problem 7-13.   Columbine Chemical Corporation was incorporated on July 1, 1957, with authorized capital consisting of 15,000 7% cumulative preferred shares, par $50, and 20,000 no-par common shares. The preferred stock was callable at $58 and was given a liquidation value of $55 plus dividends in arrears. The directors placed a $30 stated value on the common stock.

Subscriptions to 11,000 common shares, at $31 per share, were received on July 1, 1957. Subscription agreements provided that subscribers who had not defaulted were entitled to full voting and dividend privileges.

On July 5, 1957, 3,000 preferred shares were issued for cash at $67 per share.

All subscribers paid 40% of their obligations on September 1, 1957.

Subscribers to 10,800 shares paid the final 60% on December 1, 1957, and certificates were issued.

A. Marshall, subscriber to 200 shares, announced on December 27 his inability to fulfill his obligation. Accordingly, his shares were is ued to others at $30 per share, and the company paid selling expenses of $40. The balance of Marshall's account, after deducting therefrom (1) the difference between the subscription price and the issue price, and (2) the selling expenses, was refunded.

On December 31, 1957, the controller announced a net income of $45,000 for the year. On the same date, the directors declared a six-month dividend on preferred stock, payable January 10, 1958.

The directors declared a 6% common stock dividend on August 3, 1958; the shares were issued on August 28. Fair market value per share was $33; A. R. B. No. 43 was followed.

A net loss of $10,000 was reported for 1958.

On January 8, 1959, the company acquired 1,500 common shares, at $29 per share.

On January 25, 1959, the directors assessed common stockholders $2 per share. The full amount was received on February 20, 1959.

Improved land was acquired in exchange for 1,000 previously unissued common shares, 300 of which were immediately donated to the company. The donated shares were sold on the same day—June 1, 1959—for $34 per share.

700 treasury shares were sold for $25 per share, and 800 shares were retired, both on September 5, 1959. The retirement did not reduce the number of shares authorized; that is, they could be reissued.

Net income for the year, $100,000, was reported on December 31, 1959, and the directors declared a dividend for one year on the preferred stock.

(1) Prepare journal entries for the foregoing transactions, using the cost basis for treasury stock transactions; (2) construct the Stockholders' Equity section of the December 31, 1959 balance sheet; and (3) compute book value per share for each class of stock as of December 31, 1959.

Problem 7-14.   The transactions stated on the following page affecting stockholders' equity were completed by Baker's Dozen Shops, Inc., from the date of incorporation through December 31, 1959.

January 2, 1957—Received subscriptions to 40,000 shares of the 100,000 authorized preferred shares, at $12 per share. The 6% preferred stock had a par value of $10 and was cumulative and convertible. The subscription contract provided for payment in two equal installments. Issued 10,000 shares of $20 par common stock at $23 per share, cash. 60,000 shares were authorized.

March 18, 1957—All preferred subscribers paid the first installment.

April 3, 1957—Subscriber Patrick O'Fallon reported that he could not fulfill his agreement for 300 shares. Accordingly, the company sold his shares at $11 per share, cash, and paid $20 selling expenses. In harmony with state law, no refund was made.

June 19, 1957—Remaining subscribers paid the second installment and certificates were issued.

August 1, 1957—Under an employee stock option plan established by the directors on June 1, options for 5,000 common shares, to be purchased at $25 per share, were offered. Market price this date was $28 per share, and the options could not be exercised for 24 months from August 1. Expiration date was set as December 31, 1960.

October 8, 1957—Acquired 4,800 shares of common stock at a cash cost of $29 per share.

November 17, 1957—Issued stock rights to holders of $100,000 of bonds. Two rights were issued for every $1,000 bond. Each right entitled the holder to buy one share of common stock at $30 per share; rights were to expire on December 30, 1958.

December 31, 1957—Controller reported 1957 earnings of $50,000. The directors announced that when dividends are declared, present holders of preferred shares will be entitled to the full 1957 dividend—as though the shares were issued on January 2, 1957.

January 1, 1958—Stockholders donated 1,000 common shares to the company. Market price this date was $29.50 per share.

January 2, 1958—Issued 5,000 shares of common stock at $30 per share, cash. On the same date, issued 1,000 common shares for a tract of improved land, the market value of which could not be ascertained.

January 3, 1958—Directors announced a 5% common stock dividend on shares outstanding as of January 15, 1958. Issuance was effected on February 1, 1958. Fair value on January 3 was $30 per share; A.R.B. No. 43 was followed. Preferred stockholders, who had not yet received dividends for 1957, assented to the board action.

June 30, 1958—Sold 1,500 treasury shares at $35 per share, cash. (Assume first-in, first-out basis for sale of treasury shares.)

December 30, 1958—Holders of $95,000 of bonds exercised their rights. Cash was received. Remainder of rights expired.

December 31, 1958—Controller reported 1958 earnings of $250,000. Directors declared dividends of $64,000 to be paid to holders of outstanding shares on January 10, 1959. Dividends may be declared from paid-in surplus and retained earnings. Show how much goes to each class of stock.

January   12, 1959—Holders of $120,000 (par) of preferred stock exchanged
                          their holdings for common stock. One share of common was
                          given for every three shares of preferred. The converted
                          shares could not be reissued.

February   11, 1959—Directors authorized, with stockholders' consent, a change
                          in the common shares from $20 par to no par; stated value,
                          $25. The same number of shares were to be issued.

March   20, 1959—Directors instructed the controller to take proper account-
                          ing steps in order to withhold $100,000 from dividend use;
                          the related assets were intended to be used for expansion
                          of sales outlets.

August   1, 1959—Holders of stock options to 4,800 common shares made
                          purchases under the plan.

November   4, 1959—Sold 4,000 treasury shares at $26 per share, cash. (Assume
                          first-in, first-out basis.)

December 31, 1959—Controller reported 1959 earnings of $100,000.

(1) Prepare all necessary journal entries for the foregoing transactions. (Omit
entries for earnings.) Use the cost basis for treasury stock transactions.

(2) Prepare the Stockholders' Equity section of the December 31, 1959 balance
sheet.

Assignment Material for Chapter 8

Questions

Question 8-1. What is meant by the going concern assumption, and how does it affect the determination of net income?

Question 8-2. Why are accountants reluctant to abandon the stable dollar assumption?

Question 8-3. Do the income statement and the balance sheet show facts or opinions? Give reasons for your answer.

Question 8-4. Why do accountants subscribe to the cost principle?

Question 8-5. Why may balance sheet conservatism result in unconservative income statements?

Question 8-6. Distinguish between the gross concept and the net concept of revenue.

Question 8-7. The following have been suggested as possible bases for the recognition of profits:

(a) Upon signing of the contract of sale.
(b) Upon purchase of raw materials to fill the contract.
(c) In proportion to work completed.
(d) Upon completion of the manufacturing process.
(e) Upon segregation of the goods for the purchaser.
(f) Upon delivery to the purchaser.
(g) Upon collection of the account in full.
(h) In proportion to collections made.

When, if ever, could each of the above bases appropriately be used?

Question 8-8. A wholesale company which also manufactures most of the goods sold by it determines through its cost system in the factory the cost of manufacture and proposes to bill its wholesale department for all goods manufactured at cost plus 10%. The 10% is taken into income. What effect will such a procedure have on statements issued by this company?

Question 8-9. It is often stated that, in the computation of net income, all losses should be provided for and no profits should be anticipated. Does this mean that all possible future losses should be charged against current revenue?

Question 8-10. The text states that, if the current operating concept of income determination is applied, the reported net income is more affected by judgment decisions than is the case if the all-inclusive concept is applied. Why?

Question 8-11. During three-fourths of the month of August, a power shovel was used in constructing an improved new road on the property of a manufacturing company, giving direct access to its main plant, and for one-fourth of the month the shovel was used to clear the company's old road of material that had fallen onto it as a result of a storm and landslide. The old road must be used until the new one is completed in approximately a year. It is expected that the plant will be operated for not less than twenty years.

State how the costs of operating the shovel should be charged:

(a) while the shovel was used on the old road;
(b) for the remainder of August.

Give reasons for your answer.

Question 8-12.   On January 2, 1957, Doe paid $3,000 for a three-year fire insurance policy, effective January 1, 1957. As of December 31, 1958, a question has arisen as to the amount of prepaid insurance that should be shown on Doe's balance sheet.

One proposal is to show prepaid insurance at $600, which is the short-rate cancellation value of the policy on December 31, 1958.

A second proposal is to show prepaid insurance at $1,000, representing one-third of the original premium cost.

A third proposal is to show prepaid insurance at $1,200, which is the one-year premium cost for a policy for the same amount as the policy in force.

You are to discuss each of the proposals as to acceptability, as to the general principle underlying it, and as to its effect on reported income.

Problems

Problem 8-1.   Selected accounts from the ledger of Trim Company are presented below. In some instances the amounts represent aggregates for the year. If an account is presented, it may be assumed that the results of all transactions affecting the account are shown therein.

Using the information given, compute the revenue of Trim Company, distinguishing between earned and unearned amounts. Show the details of your computations.

Cash

	100,000		50,000
	120,000	Expenses	175,000
	12,000		
Cash sales	19,000		
	5,000		
	8,000		
	11,000		

Accounts Receivable

	198,000	120,000
Memo charge		10,000
for mdse out		15,000
on approval		
at year		
end.....	2,000	

Notes Receivable

15,000	5,000

Bank Loan

	12,000

Advances from Customers

Mdse de-	
livered... 4,000	8,000

Capital Stock

	100,000

Retained Earnings

Government Bonds		Gain on Sale of Bonds	
Received in settlement of account... 10,000	10,000		1,000

Equipment		Appreciation Resulting from Increase in Replacement Cost of Equipment	
50,000 7,000			7,000

Problem 8-2. The balance sheet of Eastman Products Company at the end of its fifth year in business, follows:

EASTMAN PRODUCTS COMPANY
Balance Sheet
December 31, 1958

Assets

Current assets:
Cash...		$ 18,156
Accounts receivable.............................	$39,423	
Less reserve for bad debts.......................	3,500	35,923
Finished goods...................................	$36,400	
Raw materials...................................	28,350	64,750
Total...		$118,829
Fixed assets:		
Land...		10,000
Building...	$48,000	
Less reserve for depreciation....................	12,000	36,000
Furniture and fixtures...........................	$ 9,000	
Less reserve for depreciation....................	8,000	1,000
		$165,829

Liabilities and Net Worth

Current liabilities:
Accounts payable...............................	$22,435	
Deferred gross profit............................	15,000	
Provision for dividends..........................	2,000	
Total...		$ 39,435
Long-term liability:		
Bonds payable—4%, due December 31, 1963................		20,000
Net worth:		
Common stock—$10 par value....................	$50,000	
Earned surplus.................................	56,394	
Total...		106,394
		$165,829

Investigation reveals that the company has followed ultraconservative accounting policies. It has taken depreciation at 5% on buildings and 20% on furniture and fixtures, whereas half of those rates would be ample. Since the company was organized it has consistently assigned no value to its prepaid expenses. The amounts thus ignored were: 1954, $800; 1955, $950; 1956, $1,000; 1957, $875; 1958, $1,096. It has also been the company's practice to state the raw materials inventory at liquidation value, which is 70% of cost. The finished goods have been priced at cost, which includes overhead amounting to 30% of the total cost.

Of this overhead, depreciation on the building amounts to 10%. The company defers the gross profit on goods sold until the return privilege period has expired. For the last three years the company has regularly declared 2% semiannual dividends payable June 15 and December 15. The company provides for such dividends in the year prior to their declaration.

(a) Restate the balance sheet on a more acceptable basis, but continue to use the company's account titles.

(b) Compute the average annual understatement of net income.

Problem 8-3.   The condensed income statement of Bell Company is presented below.

BELL COMPANY

Income Statement

For the Year Ended June 30, 1959

Sales..	$708,000	
Gross profit on firm orders........................	17,100	
Miscellaneous income.............................	19,244	$744,344
Deduct:		
Cost of goods sold...............................	$421,100	
Selling expenses.................................	121,400	
Administrative expenses..........................	81,560	
Provision for future price decline.................	15,000	639,060
Net income before income tax..............................		$105,284
Income tax—50%...		52,642
Net income...		$ 52,642

At the beginning of the current fiscal year the company made several changes in its accounting and business policies. The new policies are described below.

(1) When orders are received from customers, the gross profit thereon is credited to Gross Profit on Firm Orders. When the goods are delivered, such amounts are removed from the Gross Profit on Firm Orders account, and the Sales account is credited for the full selling price.

(2) Annual charges are to be made to cover future inventory price declines that might occur if a new invention should make the product sold by the company obsolete. The company plans to make such charges until the Reserve for Price Decline equals $60,000.

(3) As of July 1, 1958, the company discontinued the services of an advertising agency. According to the records, this change has resulted in a saving of $7,000 for the current year. In order to avoid distorting the operating results, $7,000 was charged to selling expenses at year end and credited to Reserve for Contingencies.

(4) As of July 1, 1958, the company adopted a policy of leasing all delivery trucks required by its volume of business. The lease period is three years and the company pays monthly rental charges. The company has the privilege of painting its name and colors on the leased trucks. However, if the trucks are so painted, the lease agreement states that the company must, at the end of the three-year period, repaint all of the leased trucks black. The company painted the trucks and charged the cost ($1,800) to selling expense. It is estimated that the same amount will be required to repaint the trucks at the end of the lease period.

(5) From time to time some of the floor space in the company's building is unused, owing to fluctuations in the volume of business. It was the company's practice to adjust the depreciation charges downward to allow for this condition.

This practice has been changed, with the result that the current year's depreciation charge to administrative expense is $800 higher than for the year ended June 30, 1958.

Prepare working papers to show the changes in the above income statement required by the application of generally accepted accounting principles. You may assume that a 50% income tax rate is applicable.

Problem 8-4. Following are the balance sheets of Devon Company on December 31, 1958 and June 30, 1959:

DEVON COMPANY
Balance Sheet
June 30, 1959

Cash....................	$ 17,341.22	Accounts payable.........	$ 10,968.12
Accounts receivable—net..	27,520.04	Bank loans..............	5,000.00
Inventories..............	163,150.13	Capital stock.............	200,000.00
Unexpired insurance.......	868.71	Retained earnings (includ-	
Stocks and bonds........	22,970.00	ing net income for the six	
Land....................	11,000.00	months, $53,256.66).....	208,298.23
Building—net.............	117,425.08		
Equipment—net..........	39,491.17		
Rental value of building in			
excess of cost...........	24,500.00		
	$424,266.35		$424,266.35

DEVON COMPANY
Balance Sheet
December 31, 1958

Cash....................	$ 13,762.41	Accounts payable.........	$ 9,341.71
Accounts receivable.......	21,346.01	Bank loans..............	10,000.00
Inventories..............	147,193.19	Capital stock.............	200,000.00
Unexpired insurance.......	1,317.22	Retained earnings.........	130,041.57
Stocks and bonds........	17,500.00		
Land....................	11,000.00		
Building—net.............	103,922.26		
Equipment—net..........	33,342.19		
	$349,383.28		$349,383.28

Public accountants were called in to make an audit as of June 30, 1959; the same auditors had made the audit as of December 31, 1958.

During the half-year ended June 30, the auditors found that:

(a) An expenditure of $1,500 had been capitalized, whereas it should have been charged to equipment repairs. No depreciation was taken on this amount.

(b) Salesmen's commissions of $725 had been paid on undelivered customers' orders.

(c) The company had changed its method of accounting for bad debts, and for the first time in its history had set up an Allowance for Doubtful Accounts. As of June 30, 1959, the allowance account was credited $650 by an adjusting entry and debited $250 for worthless accounts written off.

(d) The increase in stocks and bonds was the result of a trade with a customer for merchandise. Data with respect thereto appear on the following page.

Cost of merchandise exchanged......................... $5,470
Selling price of merchandise exchanged.................... 6,800
Market value of stocks and bonds received in the trade (based
    on last transaction price on security exchanges—although
    some of the securities are inactively traded).............. 6,500

(e) The company had made a comparative study of the cost of owning and operating its building as opposed to the annual rental charge for such facilities. The study revealed that the company was saving $1,000 a year by owning its building. As of January 1, 1959, when the building had a remaining use life of 25 years, the company set up this intangible value, which it intends to amortize over the remaining use life of the building.

The auditors also found that the adjustments they had recommended during their audit as of December 31, 1958, had neither been entered in the books nor reflected on the balance sheet as of that date. The auditors had recommended adjustments for the following items as of December 31, 1958:

(f) Inventory as of December 31, 1958, understated $1,100.
(g) Wages amounting to $2,530 for 1958 services, but not entered on the books until January, 1959.
(h) Ordinary building repairs, $3,417.02, charged to Accumulated Depreciation—Building.

From the above information, prepare working papers to obtain a corrected balance sheet on June 30, 1959, the corrected net income for the six months ended June 30, 1959, and the correct balance of Retained Earnings on December 31, 1958. You may ignore income taxes.

Do not prepare statements.

Problem 8-5. Real Estate Development Company was organized on July 1, 1958, to develop and sell building lots. The stockholders of the company paid $80,000 for their 8,000 shares of $10 par value stock. The following transactions occurred during the year ended June 30, 1959.

The company purchased 15 acres of undeveloped land, paying $30,000 in cash and signing a 6%, $20,000 mortgage for the balance of the purchase price. The mortgage was dated October 1, 1958. Interest thereon was payable each April 1 and October 1. On any interest date the company has the privilege of reducing the mortage indebtedness by $1,000.

The company spent $4,000 in grading and $12,000 for streets, including curbs and gutters. Payments totaling $18,000 were made to Local Sanitary District for water and sewer installations.

The property was divided into lots and offered for sale at prices as follows:

> 15 A lots at $3,200 per lot.
> 20 B lots at $2,400 per lot.
> 30 C lots at $1,800 per lot.

Six of the A lots, 8 of the B lots, and 12 of the C lots were sold for cash at the above prices. On April 1, 1959, the company paid $1,000 on the principal of the mortgage in addition to the semiannual interest.

Expenses for the year, paid in cash, consisted of: selling commissions amounting to $6,100; advertising and promotion, $2,900; office expense, $6,500; and the April 1 interest.

Prepare a balance sheet as of June 30, 1959.

Problem 8-6. From the following data, prepare a balance sheet and income statement for Cramer Magazine Company, which started business July 1, 1959, publishing a monthly magazine.

CRAMER MAGAZINE COMPANY
Trial Balance
December 31, 1959

Copyrights and goodwill............................	75,000	
Accounts receivable................................	95,000	
Advances to writers................................	20,000	
Accounts payable..................................		20,000
Common stock....................................		90,000
Cash..	50,000	
Furniture and fixtures............................	25,000	
Paper...	22,000	
Printing and binding..............................	50,000	
Editorial and art costs............................	50,000	
Advertising department expenses....................	43,500	
Advertising agency commissions.....................	31,500	
Subscription receipts..............................		280,200
Advertising revenue...............................		304,000
Mailing and delivery expenses......................	15,000	
Circulation department expenses....................	110,420	
Commissions for subscriptions......................	20,280	
Postage...	6,500	
Executive salaries................................	35,000	
Office salaries and expenses........................	45,000	
	694,200	694,200

The authorized common stock is 4,000 shares of $50 par value, of which 1,500 shares were issued for copyrights and goodwill and 300 shares were issued for cash.

The accounts receivable are all for advertising, which is billed monthly as the advertisements are published. All of the accounts are considered good. Agencies are entitled to a commission of 15% when advertising receivables are collected.

The inventory of paper on hand is $6,000.

Depreciation of furniture and fixtures is to be computed at the rate of 8% per annum.

Subscription receipts include single-copy sales and subscriptions. Each subscription became effective in the month following that in which it was received, and the first copy of the magazine sent to each subscriber was for the month following that in which the subscription was received.

An analysis of the account shows:

	Single-Copy Sales	Six-Months Subscriptions	One-Year Subscriptions
July.........................	$ 9,000	$4,200	$27,000
August.......................	9,500	4,500	30,000
September....................	10,000	5,400	30,000
October......................	9,900	6,600	33,000
November....................	10,700	6,000	36,000
December....................	11,500	6,900	30,000

The company pays a commission on all subscriptions received. The rate is 5% for six-months subscriptions and 10% for one-year subscriptions.

Problem 8-7. Prepare a balance sheet as of December 31, 1959, and an income statement for the year ended that date.

COMPANY A
Trial Balance
December 31, 1959

Cash..	60,000	
Accounts receivable—Customers..................	520,000	
Furniture and fixtures..........................	20,000	
Accumulated depreciation—Furniture and fixtures..		2,000
Trucks.......................................	60,000	
Accumulated depreciation—Trucks................		20,000
Accounts payable—Trade.......................		45,000
Accrued property taxes.........................		10,000
Capital stock (authorized and issued, 55,000 no-par shares)...................................		577,000
Sales..		720,000
Purchases—Lumber, steel, etc....................	430,000	
Wages.......................................	225,000	
Depreciation—Trucks..........................	20,000	
Depreciation—Furniture and fixtures..............	2,000	
Lease rentals.................................	25,000	
Selling and administrative expenses................	12,000	
	1,374,000	1,374,000

Company *A* rented display equipment on contract, and had obtained contracts for $720,000, covering a period of three years from January 1, 1959. The contracts provided that the company would bill for the earned portion of the contract price at the rate of $20,000 at the end of each month, beginning January 31, 1959.

The display equipment available for rental was constructed entirely by Company *A*, and during the month of January, 1959, such equipment was produced at a cost of $600,000, with an estimated average productive life of five years.

The locations on which the display equipment was erected had been leased to Company *A* for a period of five years from January 1, 1959, and the leases specified that rents for the full period were payable in advance on January 1, 1959.

All display equipment owned by Company *A* was in use under the contracts noted. Maintenance of this equipment in efficient operating condition cost the company $55,000 during 1959.

You may ignore income taxes.

Problem 8-8. You are retained by a small stockholder to make an examination of the records of High City Press. The company has been in business for one year and publishes a weekly newspaper. The company also does special-order printing. Since the company paid dividends of $15,000 during the first year of operations and reported a surplus balance of $33,986, your client is considering the merits of investing additional funds in the business.

You find the company's Surplus account to contain the following entries:

Surplus

1959			1959			
Dec. 15	Dividends............	15,000	Jan.	2	Premium on stock....	10,000
			Dec.	1	Value of circulation set up as intangible asset	25,000
				31	Net income...........	13,986

The income statement prepared by the company's bookkeeper is presented below.

HIGH CITY PRESS
Income Statement
For the Year Ended December 31, 1959

Revenue:

Newspaper subscriptions		$101,010
Advertising fees		182,960
Special-order printing		31,020
Rent		900
		$315,890

Expense:

Wages and salaries—Newspaper	$187,870	
Newsprint and related supplies	56,656	
Special-order direct costs	27,240	
Building rent	6,000	
Depreciation—Equipment	15,000	
Sundry	3,144	295,910
Net income before income tax		$ 19,980
Income tax—30%		5,994
Net income		$ 13,986

Your inquiries produce the following additional information:

(1) During the year the company collected $101,010 in cash for subscriptions to its newspaper. Forty per cent of the subscriptions were received when the company was organized and apply to the three-year period ending December 31, 1961. The balance of the subscriptions apply to the three-year period ending June 30, 1962.

(2) The advertising fees include $3,330 applicable to 1960 publication dates.

(3) Special printing orders are priced at 30% over estimated direct costs. When a special order is received, the customer is required to make a deposit equal to 25% of the estimated cost of the job. These amounts are credited to revenue when received. As of December 31, 1959, such deposits on unfinished jobs amount to $2,120. It is estimated that the jobs are 50% complete at year end.

(4) On July 1, 1959, the company sublet a small office to a news service on the following terms: $900 per year payable in advance.

Prepare computations to submit to your client showing the net income for the year and the year-end balance for retained earnings which you believe result from the application of generally accepted accounting principles.

Problem 8-9. The balance sheet of Continental Lumber Corporation is presented on page 740. The corporation produces lumber from its logging and sawmill operations.

Although the corporation owns some timber acreage, it secures a portion of its production from leased acreage. The lease agreements provide for an initial payment plus annual payments based on the volume of trees cut. The corporation spreads the initial payments over the life of the lease in proportion to the acreage cleared.

CONTINENTAL LUMBER CORPORATION
Balance Sheet
December 31, 1959

Assets

Current assets:

Cash...		$ 22,113	
Investments—at market value....................		28,000	
Accounts receivable—net........................		31,540	
Inventories:			
Lumber—at market value.............	$120,000		
Logs at mill........................	48,000		
Logs at acreage.....................	30,000	198,000	
Prepaid expenses...............................		1,967	$281,620
Fixed assets:			
Timber tracts—at cost less amortization...........		$375,000	
Sawmill...............................	$110,000		
Less accumulated depreciation.........	33,000	77,000	
Logging railroad......................	$240,000		
Less accumulated depreciation.........	120,000	120,000	
Equipment..........................	$180,000		
Less accumulated depreciation.........	105,000	75,000	
Leasehold payments....................	$ 80,000		
Less amortization....................	32,000	48,000	695,000
			$976,620

Liabilities and Stockholders' Equity

Current liabilities:

Accounts payable..............................		$ 21,112	
Accrued expenses..............................		18,127	$ 39,239
Long-term bank loan.......................................			150,000
Stockholders' equity:			
Common stock................................		$500,000	
Paid-in surplus................................		100,000	
Reserve for contingencies.......................		25,000	
Retained earnings..............................		162,381	787,381
			$976,620

The investments have been written down from their cost of $32,000.

In computing cost for purposes of pricing the inventory of logs at the sawmill, the cost of hauling the logs from the timber tracts to the sawmill is ignored. Such cost, if capitalized, would add 15% to the carrying value of this inventory category.

The lumber inventory is set up at selling price. You may assume that each $1 of lumber thus priced is composed of the following elements:

Cost of logs, with cost defined as used in pricing inventory of logs at the sawmill...	$ .55
Sawmill labor..	.10
Sawmill overhead..	.15
Gross profit...	.20
Total...	$1.00

The logging railroad is not complete. It is estimated that an additional $100,000 must be invested in the railroad before it can serve the remaining 40% of the acreage owned or controlled by the company. The trees have been cut and removed from half of the area presently served by the railroad.

During 1959, the corporation used $6,000 of its lumber, priced at selling price, in building some equipment for use in its logging activities. The cost of the equipment thus constructed was computed as $20,000. Since the cost exceeded the purchase price for such equipment by $500, $19,500 was charged to the Equipment account. However, no depreciation was taken on this equipment in 1959, as it was not completed until December 28.

The acreage leases provide that the corporation must clear the property of stumps by the lease termination date. The corporation plans to undertake this project after the cutting has been completed, which is now scheduled to occur in 1963. It estimates that the job will cost $30,000.

Revise the balance sheet of Continental Lumber Corporation in accordance with generally accepted principles of accounting.

Problem 8-10.   You are engaged by Iowa Supreme Company to examine its books, which have never been audited by outside accountants. The following unaudited statements are presented to you:

IOWA SUPREME COMPANY
Income Statement
For the Year Ended December 31, 1959

Net sales...	$836,000
Cost of goods sold...	602,000
Gross profit..	$234,000
Selling and administrative expenses.........................	220,115
	$ 13,885
Other income—from investments.............................	8,200
	$ 22,085
Interest on notes payable....................................	375
Net income before income tax...............................	$ 21,710
Income tax—30%...	6,513
Net income..	$ 15,197

IOWA SUPREME COMPANY
Statement of Retained Earnings
For the Year Ended December 31, 1959

Retained earnings—December 31, 1958.......................	$45,377
Net income..	15,197
	$60,574
Dividends—$4 per share declared and paid during December, 1959	24,000
Retained earnings—December 31, 1959.......................	$36,574

IOWA SUPREME COMPANY
Balance Sheet
December 31, 1959

Cash........................	$ 8,923	Accounts payable............	$ 11,227
Investments..................	62,000	Bank loan—6%..............	25,000
Accounts receivable..........	57,651	Accrued expenses............	950
Inventory....................	70,000	Reserve for income tax.......	6,513
Prepaid insurance............	10,000	Reserve for depreciation......	57,200
Property....................	230,000	Reserve for doubtful accounts.	1,110
		Common stock—$50 par value	300,000
		Surplus.....................	36,574
	$438,574		$438,574

As a result of your examination, the following information has become available. The investments consist of:

(1) A small parcel of land received in exchange for merchandise sold on February 20, 1959. As of February 20, 1959, the following information was available to the company:

Cost of land to customer	$12,000
Selling price of merchandise sold for land	15,000
Estimated market value of land	25,000

The company recorded the transaction at $25,000.

(2) 800 treasury shares adjusted to their December 31, 1959 market value, $37,000. This stock was purchased in December of 1958 for $32,000.

For convenience, the inventory is carried at 50% of selling price. Former inventories have always been carried at cost, and upon your advice it has been decided to continue this practice.

The prepaid insurance consists of:

Cash surrender value of life insurance	$8,100
Unexpired premiums on fire insurance	1,900

An analysis of the Property account shows the following composition:

Land	$ 20,00C
Building	120,000
Equipment	86,000
Penalty payment for cancellation of long-term lease in 1957	4,000
	$230,000

During 1959 the company used some of its inventory in constructing new equipment. The merchandise so used was charged to the Property account at selling price. The difference between cost and selling price, amounting to $6,000, was credited to the Sales account.

The Reserve for Depreciation has been analyzed for the year as follows:

	Building (2%)	Equipment (10%)
Balance—December 31, 1958	$19,200	$27,000
1959 provision for depreciation	2,400	8,600
Balance—December 31, 1959	$21,600	$35,600

The one-year bank loan was negotiated as of August 1, 1959. The quarterly interest payment of $375 was made as required on November 1.

Effective January 1, 1959, the company changed its policy regarding commission payments to salesmen. Under the new plan the company neither records nor pays the 20% salesmen's commission until 60 days after date of sale, which period coincides with the merchandise return privilege period. Sales for the last 60 days amounted to $130,000.

Prepare the financial statements in the form you would recommend for inclusion in the 1959 annual report to stockholders.

Assignment Material for Chapter 9

Questions

Question 9-1. In making the audit of a corporation's balance sheet, you find that all assets and liabilities are correctly stated, except for the situation disclosed by the following bank reconciliation. Show the extent to which you would insist on changes in the classification of items in the balance sheet.

Cash on hand as per balance sheet.........................		$249,932.19
Less:		
Advances to salesmen on account of salaries and commissions in excess of amounts earned....	$35,000.00	
Petty cash funds of branch offices............	7,500.00	
Cash placed in escrow with trust company pending consummation of real estate purchase.................................	50,000.00	92,500.00
Balance per cash book, December 31, 1958...........		$157,432.19
Add:		
Checks drawn and issued but not presented for payment at bank..................................		8,792.12
Checks drawn during last week of December, 1958, but not mailed to creditors until January, 1959..		17,240.50
Total..		$183,464.81
Less:		
Sight drafts on customers drawn December 29 and 31, 1958, collection of which was not reported by bank on December 31, 1958....	$47,925.00	
Discount on 6-month bank loan of $100,000 effected December 31, 1958...............	2,250.00	
Loans to corporation by individual officers, entered as cash receipts on December 26, 1958, but not received and deposited in bank prior to December 31, 1958................	75,000.00	
Checks and cash received from customers on December 30 and 31, 1958, not deposited in bank until January 2, 1959................	43,120.19	168,295.19
Balance per bank statement.......................		$ 15,169.62

Question 9-2. Postdated checks from customers totaling $12,500 appear as part of the cash on hand of a company you are auditing. These checks were ultimately deposited and collected in full. Would you object to their inclusion as cash?

Question 9-3. In an audit as of December 31, 1958, you find that the books show a $10,000 overdraft on the bank. Where should this item be shown in the balance sheet? Would you make any adjustment if you discovered that checks totaling $12,000 had been drawn and dated in December but that they were not mailed until January 5, 1959?

Question 9-4. Describe a procedure for safeguarding cash receipts and cash disbursements.

Question 9-5. Using your own figures, prepare an illustration of the operation of an imprest cash fund.

Question 9-6. Using your own figures, prepare an illustration of lapping of cash receipts.

Question 9-7. Why are outstanding certified checks ignored in preparing a reconciliation of the bank account?

Question 9-8. What internal control procedure should be applied to minimize the danger of covering a defalcation by making entries for noncash credits to accounts receivable?

Problems

Problem 9-1. The balance to the credit of O'Toole Novelties, Inc., at Cork County Bank was $3,500 on October 31, 1959. On November 30, 1959, you are asked to (1) determine the cash balance (including cash on hand and in bank) which should appear in the company books as of that date, and (2) prepare any necessary journal entries as of November 30, 1959.

The company had checks of $2,100 outstanding on October 31. The bank reports deposits of $17,000 since October 31 and charges amounting to $16,500, which include a charge of $10 for collections and a charge of $500 on the reduction of a loan, both unrecorded by the company. The company has undeposited collections of $1,500 on hand, and its check book shows that it has disbursed $17,500 since October 31.

The company prepares financial statements semiannually, on May 31 and November 30.

Problem 9-2. Journalize the following transactions and make any necessary adjusting entries in the books of Elton & Veamer, which closes its books annually on March 31.

An imprest petty cash fund was established at $120 on February 8, 1960. The composition of the fund on February 29 was as follows:

Currency and coin	$38.30
Vouchers showing expenditures for:	
Postage	24.60
Repairs	35.20
Office supplies	13.50
Sundry office expense	7.40

On this date a check was issued to replenish the fund and to increase its amount to $180.

An examination on March 31 disclosed the following composition of the fund:

Currency and coin	$27.90
Check of company treasurer, dated April 4, 1960	20.00
Vouchers showing expenditures for:	
Telephone and telegraph	27.30
Office supplies	15.20
Accounts payable	48.00
Postage	31.50
Sundry office expense	12.10

The fund was not replenished.

On April 4, 1960, the treasurer's check was cashed and the proceeds were added to the petty cash fund. The composition of the fund on April 30 was as follows:

Postage stamps	$ 2.50
Vouchers showing expenditures for:	
Postage	39.10
Telephone and telegraph	35.50
Office supplies	21.40
Accounts payable	48.00
Traveling expense	9.60
Entertainment expense	11.90
Sundry office expense	16.50

A check was drawn to replenish the fund on this date.

Problem 9-3. Fritz Food Stores, Inc., in order to present a more favorable current position in its balance sheet, held open its Cash account until it had collected $32,500. Of this amount, $22,000 was collected from customers who took cash discounts amounting to $400, and one deducted $50 for freight, which the company disputed and for which the customer was not given credit. The remainder of the cash came from cash sales, on which cash discounts of 2% were allowed. The company realized a 30% gross profit on the net selling price of these sales.

With the amounts so collected, accounts payable of $18,000 were paid, and discounts of $300 were taken on these. A note of $10,000 was paid, together with interest of $400, of which $10 accrued after the beginning of the year.

Subsequent to the preceding transactions, the current position in the balance sheet was set forth as follows:

Current assets:		Current liabilities:	
Cash	$10,000	Accounts payable	$1,000
Accounts receivable	8,000	Accrued taxes	7,000
Inventory	9,000		

(1) Prepare the current section of the balance sheet as it would have appeared prior to the above transactions.

(2) Compute the working capital and the working capital ratio for each balance sheet.

(3) Which statement should have been the one selected for publication? Why?

(4) Assume that the intent of management, in holding the Cash account open, was to present a *less* favorable current position. Assume also that subsequent transactions provided the desired results, that is, a lower working capital and working capital ratio. Under these circumstances, which statement should have been the one selected for publication? Why?

Problem 9-4. Adams-Masterson Construction Company maintains an imprest petty cash fund, which is carried on the books at $600. The company, as agent for Fast Express Company, issues and sells money orders to its employees, who may purchase them by applying to the petty cashier, who has a supply of blank forms. Settlement is made weekly with a representative of the express company. When the representative calls on the petty cashier at Adams-Masterson Construction Company, he collects for orders issued, accounts for unissued orders, and leaves additional blank money orders serially numbered.

On March 3, 1960, a surprise count of the petty cash fund was made by a company auditor. The count of the items presented by the cashier as composing the fund was as shown on the following page.

Currency (bills and silver)....................................... $150
Cashed checks...   30
Disbursement vouchers (signed by the recipients).................. 170
N.S.F. checks (dated October 11 and November 27, 1959)...........   40
Receipt vouchers:
  Refund of excess of petty cash disbursement over amount
    needed (expense advance).............................. $ 30
  Sale of money orders (#RN40136–40139)................... 100   130

Blank money orders—claimed to have been purchased for $25
  each from the express company (#RN40140–40141)...............   50

At the time of the count, 12 unissued money orders (#RN40142–40153) were also on hand.

The following day the cashier produced disbursement vouchers totaling $30 and explained that these vouchers had been temporarily misplaced the previous day.

(1) Compute the amount of the shortage as indicated by the surprise count.

(2) Why, in your opinion, did the cashier choose the amount $30 for "misplaced" vouchers?

Problem 9-5. The president of Lewisson Construction Company has asked you to determine whether there is a shortage of cash on January 31, 1960. Facts relevant to your investigation are as follows:

The January bank statement shows a final balance of $6,700. A balance of $9,000 appears in the company's Cash account, which includes cash on hand and in bank. A miscellaneous credit of $80 in the bank statement has not been entered in the company books. Deposits amounting to $25,000 were made during January. The bank statement shows deposits of $24,500 received during January. Deposits of $1,000 were in transit on December 31, 1959.

The following checks, issued during January, are not included among the cancelled checks returned with the January bank statement: #712, $140; #717, $295; #719, $175; #720, $110; #721, $80. Check #604, written for $60 in November and the only outstanding check on December 31, 1959, was returned as one of the January cancelled checks.

Before leaving for a two-week vacation, the cashier removed all of the cash on hand in excess of $1,325 and prepared the following reconciliation:

Balance per books, January 31, 1960............................ $9,000
Add outstanding checks:
  #712... $140
  #717... 295
  #720... 110
  #721...   80   525
                                                              ──────
                                                              $9,525
Deduct deposits in transit.................................... 1,500
                                                              ──────
                                                              $8,025
Deduct cash on hand... 1,325
Balance per bank, January 31, 1960......................... $6,700
Deduct unrecorded credit......................................   80
True cash, January 31, 1960................................. $6,620

(1) How much did the cashier remove, and how did he attempt to conceal his theft?

(2) Taking only the information given, name a specific feature of internal control which apparently was missing.

Problem 9-6. An examination of the cash journals, Cash account, cancelled checks, and the February, 1960 bank statement for Bjorklund Sporting Goods Company produced the following data:

(1) Balance per Cash account, 2/29/60, $100 (credit).
(2) Balance per bank statement, 2/29/60, $1,866.
(3) Outstanding checks, 2/29/60, $3,927.
(4) February service charge, $4.
(5) An N.S.F. check returned by the bank on February 9, was redeposited by mail on February 29 after the maker had assured Bjorklund Sporting Goods Company that the check would be honored. No entries were made on the books. Amount of the check was $638.
(6) Error in the cash journal when deposit of 2/7/60 was entered:

```
Entered as...........................................  $4,554
Correct amount.......................................   5,455
```

(7) During February, the bank certified a company check for $293. This check is included among the outstanding checks, above, as it was not among the cancelled checks.
(8) Cash sales proceeds of February 29 were mailed to the bank on that day, $1,817.
(9) On February 17, the bank charged the company's account for a $630 loan made to the company on December 19. Interest, at 6%, was deducted in advance, and charged to Interest Expense.
(10) A deposit of Bjorklund Feed Company, $131, was credited by the bank in error to the company's account.
(11) The company has neglected to record two reconciling items which appeared on the January bank statement:

(a) Collection by bank of a 6%, 30-day note and interest, less $1.00 collection fee. Date of note was December 7. Face of note was $400.
(b) January service charge, $3.

(12) Check #2017, for $386, made payable to a supplier, was reported as lost. The company thereupon ordered the bank to stop payment, and a new check was issued. Subsequently the old check was found and "voided." Accounts Payable was debited when the new check was journalized. Both checks are included among the outstanding checks above.
(13) The bank charged the company $2 as its "stop-payment" fee.
(14) Included among the cancelled checks was a $7 debit memo applicable to Berryland Plumbing Co. for checks printed. The bank, upon being notified of this error and the one described as (10), above, agreed to correct its records.

The books are closed annually on December 31, and proper adjusting entries made. Assume that reversing entries are not made.

No cash was kept on hand.

Required:

(1) Reconciliation of Bjorklund Sporting Goods Company's bank account as of February 29, 1960.
(2) Journal entries necessary to adjust the company's books to show the correct bank balance as of February 29, 1960.

Problem 9-7. J. R. Allen is contemplating going into business on January 1, 1960. He plans to sell product X on the installment plan. He will carry no inventory and will pay for the units of X and all associated expenses at the time of sale. Collections will be made in ten equal monthly installments, the first being made on the date of sale.

Mr. Allen prepared the following estimate of sales volume, which is not expected to vary from year to year.

Month	Units	Month	Units
January	40	July	350
February	80	August	300
March	110	September	310
April	175	October	240
May	270	November	190
June	390	December	120

You are given the following additional information:

Selling price of X	$150
Cost of X	100
Selling expense per unit	30
Net profit per unit	20

An important consideration is the amount of cash which Mr. Allen must tie up in the proposed business. During 1960, he intends to invest in a number of ventures. Therefore, it is necessary that Mr. Allen be informed of the extent to which his resources will be needed in this new business.

Assuming that the foregoing figures for sales volume are reliable, compute the minimum cash balance necessary to sustain operations for the first year.

Problem 9-8. The following information relates to King-Richards, Inc.:

	1959	
	August	September
Bank statement balance—at month end	$ 4,000	$ 4,860
Cash account balance—at month end		3,833
N.S.F. checks returned—at month end	80	160
Outstanding checks—at month end	1,200	1,930
Deposits in transit—at month end	500	850
Bank service charges	8	11
Check #411 was erroneously recorded in the company checkbook and journal as $286; the correct amount is (This check was not outstanding on September 30)		268
Drafts collected by bank (not recorded by the company until the month following collection)	400	300
Total credits to Cash account	29,705	34,605
Total deposits on bank statement		35,000

Of the outstanding checks on September 30, one check for $200 was certified on September 18.

All disbursements were made by check.

Prepare a reconciliation of receipts, disbursements, and bank account for the month of September.

Problem 9-9. On August 31, 1959, the bookkeeper for Balsam Specialties Company prepared the statement shown on the opposite page.

BALSAM SPECIALTIES COMPANY
Bank Reconciliation
August, 31, 1959

Balance per ledger—August 31.............................		$35,862.79
Add:		
Collections received on the last day of August and debited to Cash in Bank on books but not deposited...		4,859.83
Debit memo for customer's check returned unpaid (check is on hand but no entry has been made in the books)...		200.00
Debit memo for bank service charge for August............		11.26
		$41,033.88
Deduct:		
Checks drawn but not paid by bank (see detailed list below)................................	$4,471.09	
Credit memo for proceeds of a note receivable which had been left at the bank for collection but which has not been recorded as collected..	400.00	
Check for an account payable entered on the books as $468.13 but drawn and paid by bank as $706.11.................................	237.98	5,209.07
		$35,824.81
Unlocated difference......................................		200.00
Balance per bank statement—August 31...................		$35,624.81

Checks Drawn But Not Paid by Bank

No.	Amount	No.	Amount
8210.....................	$638.17	8513...................	$ 757.98
8407.....................	392.06	8514...................	316.79
8480.....................	475.00	8515...................	423.23
8493.....................	107.16	8516...................	542.55
8511.....................	600.28	8517...................	417.87
			$4,471.09

Required:

(1) A corrected bank reconciliation.
(2) Journal entries for items which should be adjusted prior to closing the books on August 31.

Problem 9-10. From the following information, construct a monthly cash budget for Jankowski Stores, Inc., for the three months ended September 30, 1959.

Jankowski Stores, Inc., purchases merchandise on terms of 1/10; n/60, and regularly takes discounts on the tenth day after the invoice date. For any month's purchases, assume that the tenth day after the invoice date on three-fourths of the purchases falls in the month of purchase, while the discount periods for the remaining purchases overlap into the next month.

The company's sales terms are 2/10; n/30, with the discount period beginning at the end of the month of sale. It has been the company's experience that discounts on 80% of billings have been allowed, and that, of the remainder, one-half have been collected during the month following sale and the balance during the second following month. Assume that no collections are made during a month on sales made in the same month.

The average rate of gross profit, based on sales price, is 30%. Total sales for the company's fiscal year ended December 31, 1959, have been estimated at 60,000 units, distributed monthly as follows:

January....... 7%   April........ 9%   July.......... 5%   October..... 8%
February..... 6   May........ 10   August....... 8   November... 11
March........ 7   June........ 12   September.... 9   December... 8

To insure prompt delivery of merchandise, inventories are maintained during July and August at 5% of the estimated annual unit sales, while during the rest of the year they are maintained at 10% of the estimated annual unit sales. Thus, the 5% level begins with the June 30 inventory, and is increased to 10% by the close of August.

Total budgeted selling, administrative, and general expenses for the fiscal year ended December 31, 1959, are $270,000, of which $60,000 are fixed expenses (inclusive of $12,000 annual depreciation). These fixed expenses are incurred uniformly throughout the year. The other selling, administrative, and general expenses vary with sales. Expenses are paid as incurred, without discounts.

It is assumed that on June 30, 1959, merchandise inventory, at the 5% level, will consist of 3,000 units, to cost $42,000, before discount, and the cash balance will be $105,000.

Problem 9-11. The December 31, 1959 audit of Balfour Hosiery Company was begun on January 6, 1960, at 9 a.m. The cash book contained the following entries for 1960:

	Cash Receipts	Checks Drawn
January 1, Balance............................	$4,731.46	
2.......................................	429.13	$1,613.91
3.......................................	673.14	422.33
4.......................................	931.64	310.14
5.......................................	510.22	525.33

The bank statement, dated at the close of business January 5, 1960, showed:

Balance, December 31, 1959............................... $4,445.77
Deposits... 2,784.85
Checks and vouchers (including a 60-day note for $2,000 due January 3, plus 6% interest, and all checks issued prior to January 4, except two checks for $100 and $150, dated January 2 and January 3, respectively)...................... 4,271.49

The daily cash receipts were deposited at noon of the following day and all disbursements were made by check, except that a postage bill of $3.92 was paid out of undeposited receipts on the afternoon of January 5.

Prepare the bank reconciliations as of December 31, 1959, and January 5, 1960. The company's bank account is not subject to bank service charges.

Assignment Material for Chapter 10

Questions

Question 10-1. The audit of a corporation on the instructions of its president reveals the fact that included in the accounts receivable balance of $275,000 is an item of $50,000 owed by the president of the company. The president requests you, in certifying to the balance sheet, not to show as a separate item the amount owed by him, but to include it in the accounts receivable, for the reason, you are informed, that your certificate is to be used for the purpose of selling $250,000 of bonds secured by a mortgage on the real estate, plant, and machinery, all valued at $500,000. The proceeds of the bonds will be used to liquidate the present notes payable of equal amount. The president of the company is reported to be worth $200,000 over and above the value of his stock in the company. What course of action would you take? State reasons therefor.

Question 10-2. Referring to the preceding question, assume that the president was also financially interested in Home Builders Company, that the $50,000 balance arose from sales to him of materials to be used by Home Builders Company in the construction of houses, and that the president has agreed to reimburse the company as soon as the houses are sold. In the past, Home Builders Company has found a ready market for their buildings. Under such circumstances, would you agree to include the $50,000 in accounts receivable?

Question 10-3. In the December 31, 1959 trial balance of a corporation, there is a debit of $55,000 against John Doe for a payment to him on account of material purchased from him to be delivered after said date. How should this item be classified in the balance sheet?

Question 10-4. You find the following items included among the accounts composing the Accounts Receivable controlling account balance of a concern you are auditing. State how you would show each item in the balance sheet.

Accounts receivable from employees.
Interest receivable on notes.
Rebates receivable on returned merchandise purchases.
Prepaid interest on notes payable.
Advances to salesmen.
Federal tax refunds receivable.

Question 10-5. Should amounts owed a holding company by a subsidiary be shown as accounts receivable in the holding company's balance sheet?

Question 10-6. If sales payable in installments are made, is it permissible to show under the Current Assets caption any installments not due within one year from the balance sheet date?

Question 10-7. When an account that has been charged off as uncollectible is eventually collected in whole or in part, why should the collection be passed through the customer's account? By what entries is this accomplished?

Question 10-8. In the trial balance prepared toward the close of a corporation's fiscal year, there is a debit balance in the account Allowance for Doubtful Accounts. Explain how the debit balance probably arose. Does the debit balance indicate that the allowance at the close of the prior fiscal year was inadequate?

Question 10-9. You found that, of the customers' accounts receivable, $200,000 was subject to a 5% discount if paid in ten days. What consideration would you give to this discount in the preparation of your balance sheet?

Question 10-10. If a customer pays an invoice less the cash discount and subsequently returns a portion of the goods, should he be credited with the pro rata amount of the gross list price of the goods returned or with the pro rata amount of the net price after deducting the cash discount?

Question 10-11. The Holden Company sells its accounts receivable to A and B Company without recourse. Is this an open accounts receivable financing transaction or a factoring transaction?

Question 10-12. Assume that Bailey Company obtains funds by open accounts receivable financing. Using figures of your own, compute the amount of the resulting contingent liability to be shown by Bailey Company as a balance sheet footnote.

Question 10-13. State two reasons why a bank may prefer to have a borrower discount its customers' trade acceptances rather than its own notes payable.

Problems

Problem 10-1. (a) Prepare a schedule as of October 31, 1959, for Matthews Sales Company aging the following accounts. Terms in all cases are thirty days.

Aaron			Beeson			Carlos		
Debits:			Debits:			Debits:		
5- 7	a	217.60	8- 2	a	89.93	9-3	a	716.01
7-30	b	124.41	8-17	b	110.00	10-7	b	334.52
10-10	c	191.20						
Credits:						Credit:		
8- 2	a	217.60				10-6	a	716.01
10-16	b	124.41						

Deming			Ealy			French		
Debits:			Debits:			Debits:		
6- 1	a	101.11	4-20	a	100.00	7-10	a	97.90
6-29	b	27.82	9-16	b	227.65	9-15	b	17.44
7-20	c	81.76	9-30	c	76.08	10-11	c	38.64
Credit:			Credits:			Credit:		
10- 2	b	27.82	7- 3	a	55.00	9- 2	a	97.90
			7-23	a	45.00			
			10-14	b	200.00			

(b) Matthews Sales Company provides an allowance for doubtful accounts equal to 10% of all balances which are 31 to 60 days past due, plus 20% of all balances which are more than 60 days past due. An account is regarded as due on the thirtieth day after the invoice date (debits to the above accounts were recorded on the invoice dates). There is a debit balance of $20 in the allowance account on October 31, 1959. Prepare a journal entry to record bad debts expense for the three months ended October 31, 1959.

Problem 10-2. The following transactions (in summary) affecting the accounts receivable of Lipstron Corporation occurred during the year ended January 31, 1960:

Sales (cash and credit)...................................	$243,610.24
Cash received from credit customers (Customers who paid $120,551.08 took advantage of the discount feature of the corporation's credit terms, 2/10; n/30.)..................	225,609.87
Cash received from cash customers.......................	86,116.79
Accounts receivable written off as worthless...............	2,001.14
Credit memoranda issued to credit customers for sales returns and allowances.......................................	23,402.69
Cash refunds given to cash customers for sales returns and allowances...	6,879.79
Recoveries on accounts receivable written off as uncollectible in prior periods (cash not included in amount stated above)	4,182.45

The following two balances were taken from the January 31, 1959 balance sheet:

Accounts receivable.....................................	$139,227.71
Allowance for doubtful accounts.........................	3,986.47

Required:

(1) Journal entries to record the transactions summarized for the year ended January 31, 1960.
(2) Adjusting journal entry for estimated bad debts on January 31, 1960. The corporation provides for its net bad debt losses by crediting its Allowance for Doubtful Accounts for 1½% of net credit sales for the fiscal period.

Problem 10-3. The November 30, 1959 balance sheet of Phalanx Corporation appeared as follows:

PHALANX CORPORATION
Balance Sheet
November 30, 1959

Assets

Cash...		$ 63,049
Receivables..		47,860
Inventories..		93,475
Investments, at cost.....................................		21,108
Equipment...	$78,100	
Less accumulated depreciation.....................	8,000	70,100
		$295,592

Liabilities and Stockholders' Equity

Accounts payable...	$ 40,918
Bonds payable—due June 1, 1980.........................	110,000
Capital stock, par $20...................................	80,000
Capital stock subscribed.................................	20,000
Retained earnings.......................................	44,674
	$295,592

An examination of the Receivables account revealed that it was composed of items shown on the following page.

Customers' accounts—debit balances............................ $21,018

Employees' accounts—current................................ 1,600

Advance to officer—noncurrent.......................... 850

Selling price of merchandise sent on consignment and not
    sold by consignees—at 120% of cost................ 6,480

Stockholders' subscriptions—considered collectible within nine
    months.. 15,875

Equity in $8,500 of uncollected accounts receivable assigned under
    guarantee.................................... 2,100

Notes receivable:

    On hand—not due............................. 3,564

    On hand—past due........................... 1,000

Discounted:

    Indorsed in blank.......................... $ (900

    Indorsed without recourse.................. (916)

    Total...................................... $52,487

Deduct:

    Customers' credit balances................. $2,721

    Allowance for doubtful accounts............ 1,906 4,627

                               $47,860

Prepare a revised balance sheet as of November 30, 1959.

Problem 10-4. Give necessary journal entries on the books of Malone Company for the following:

1959

February 14—Malone Company sold merchandise to Jackson Corporation for $16,800, f.o.b. destination point; terms, 2/10; n/30.

        22—Received a check and note from Jackson Corporation. The note, for 90 days at 4%, was written for $10,000. Its date was February 21. The remainder of the account was satisfied by the check. Jackson Corporation paid freight of $80, and the cash discount was allowed except for the portion of the account settled by the note.

March   5—Malone Company discounted the above note at Third National Bank. Discount rate was 5%.

April   11—Malone Company discounted its own $4,000 note at Third National Bank. The note was dated April 11, and was for 45 days. Proceeds of $3,975 were received on this date.

        30—Malone Company closed its books.

May   22—The note from Jackson Corporation was not honored. Upon proper notification from the bank, Malone Company paid the note plus a $3 protest fee.

        26—Malone Company paid its note to the bank.

July   21—Received a check from Jackson Corporation for its full obligation, including interest at 5% on the amount owed to Malone Company since May 22.

Problem 10-5. On the last day of 1959, its first year of operations, Coolidge Company had a balance of $14,434 in the Notes Receivable account.

Investigation revealed that $45,526 of notes, all at 6% for 60 days, were received from customers, and that one note, also at 6% for 60 days, for $1,800 was the result of a loan to Cervantes Chemical Company. Cervantes Chemical Company was not a customer of Coolidge Company. $18,763 of these notes had been collected at maturity, and $15,950 of the notes had been discounted at the bank. Of the discounted notes, $4,412 had been paid at maturity, and one note for $1,800 from Cervantes Chemical Company had been dishonored. Upon receiving due notice of this dishonor, Coolidge Company assumed the maker's obligation and paid the note, including a $3 protest fee. Notes Receivable was debited and Cash on Hand and in Bank was credited.

Partial payments of $2,316 were received on notes not yet due, and these collections—$48 of which represented interest—were credited to Partial Payments on Notes Receivable, which was classified by the company as a liability.

A customer's note for $1,761 was pledged as collateral for the payment of a bank loan.

A 90-day note for $375, given by an officer of the company, was treated as a cash item. Date of the note was September 3, 1959.

(1) Prepare journal entries necessary to correct the accounts of Coolidge Company. Assume that the books have not been closed and that adjusting entries have not been made. Year-end adjusting entries are not to be prepared for this problem.

(2) Show how the facts regarding all notes discussed above should be disclosed in a balance sheet to be used for credit purposes.

Problem 10-6. The Cambridge Corporation, on June 1, 1959, assigned the following trade accounts receivable to Flat Fee Finance Company: Alpha, $3,500; Beta, $5,000; Gamma, $6,500; Delta, $4,000; Epsilon, $1,000. After deducting $300 to apply against the payment of finance charges, the finance company remitted $14,700. The agreement with the finance company called for interest of $\frac{1}{30}$ of 1% per day on the uncollected balance of each assigned account for the period during which it was assigned and uncollected (including the day on which collection was received). The agreement also provided that The Cambridge Corporation was to pay all accounts which the finance company did not collect within 20 days of the due date. Sales terms of The Cambridge Corporation were 2/15; n/30.

On June 3, 1959, The Cambridge Corporation shipped merchandise on consignment to Melvin Stores, Inc., and sent the consignee a memorandum billing for $5,000.

On June 6, Beta's account was collected in full, less discount. The collection was transmitted to the finance company. The finance company acknowledged receipt of Beta's collection on June 7, and remitted 20% ($1,000) on this account.

On June 9, The Cambridge Corporation notified the finance company that Gamma had been permitted a $300 allowance for damaged merchandise.

Melvin Stores, Inc., remitted $3,150 on June 10 for sales of 70% of the merchandise, less a commission.

On June 12, Gamma paid his account, less discount. The finance company acknowledged receipt of this collection on June 13. Enclosed with the notice, the finance company remitted $1,200 to The Cambridge Corporation.

A check for $900 was received from Zeta on June 16 by The Cambridge Corporation. During 1958, the Zeta account had been written off against the allowance account, which was maintained by yearly adjustments in anticipation of net bad debt losses.

Alpha paid his account on June 20, without discount. According to a report from the finance company, it received the collection on June 21. A check for $875 was enclosed by the finance company.

On June 26, the finance company reported that the Epsilon account was 20 days overdue. Accordingly, The Cambridge Corporation mailed a check for $750 to the finance company. The check was received on the same day by the finance company.

On June 29, a check was received from Melvin Stores, Inc., as a result of the sale of the remaining merchandise, less its customary 10% commission.

The Cambridge Corporation closes its books annually on June 30.

(1) Prepare necessary entries for the foregoing transactions on the books of The Cambridge Corporation.

(2) Assuming that the aforementioned allowance transaction had not occurred, prepare an entry for the books of The Cambridge Corporation for the interest charges as of June 30. Show computations.

Problem 10-7.   Reaven Industries, Inc., entered into an agreement with Associated Credit Bureaus, Inc., whereby the latter was to purchase trade receivables from the former. The agreed commission was $1\frac{1}{8}\%$, and interest on advances (measured by the number of days through the date of settlement) was set at 6% per year. The holdback was established at 18%.

The agreement further provided that the commission, once computed on the "net," could not be raised or lowered due to (1) merchandise returns amounting to less than 30% of the invoice, and (2) sales discounts not taken.

Provide all necessary journal entries on the books of Reaven Industries, Inc., for the following unrelated transactions between the two companies.

(A) On January 26, 1960, five accounts were sold to Associated Credit Bureaus, Inc. Debtors' names and the gross amounts owed were: Abercrombie, $2,600; Buller, $4,110; Carr, $1,950; Dooley, $2,290; and Easter, $3,070. Terms of all Reaven Industries, Inc., sales were 1/10; n/30. The invoice dates applicable to the receivables were as follows: Abercrombie, January 25; Buller, January 26; Carr, January 23 ($820) and January 21 ($1,130); Dooley, January 19; and Easter, January 26.

In addition to the instructions above, compute the average "due date," using January 28 as the focal date.

(B) On April 23, 1960, an account receivable from Freeman, $880, was sold to the factoring company subject to the terms stated above. Invoice date was April 22, 1960, and terms of all sales of merchandise were 1/10; n/30. Reaven Industries, Inc., requested and received an advance of $600 from the factoring company on April 25. On April 28, Reaven Industries, Inc., notified the factoring company that Freeman had been allowed a credit of $30 for returned merchandise. Freeman paid the account directly to the factoring company on May 5, and the factoring company settled its affairs with Reaven Industries, Inc., on the due date.

Problem 10-8.   During December, 1959, the Accounts Receivable controlling account on the books of Timothy Textbook Corporation showed one debit posting and two credit postings. The debit represented receivables from December sales, $43,710.28. One credit was for $41,250.18, made as a result of cash collections on November and December receivables; the second credit was an adjustment for estimated uncollectibles, $700. The December 31 balance was $6,600.07.

During December, a check for $220.11 was received from Fisk Motors, whose account had been charged directly to Retained Earnings as a bad debt early in 1957. The collection was recorded by a credit to Miscellaneous Income.

Also during December, one customer tendered his 45-day, 6% note for $400 to apply on his outstanding account. No entry was made. The company discounted the note at 5% with First County Bank 32 days before its maturity. The proceeds were credited to Notes Receivable Discounted.

When receivables were collected, the bookkeeper credited Accounts Receivable for the cash collected. All customers who paid accounts during December took advantage of the 2% cash discount.

As of December 1, debit balances in customers' subsidiary accounts totaled $6,300.86. An adjustment for estimated doubtful accounts of $150 had been posted to the Accounts Receivable controlling account at the end of 1958, and no write-offs were recorded during 1959. In addition, a number of customers had overpaid their accounts, and as a result some of the customers' subsidiary accounts had credit balances on December 1. No overpayments were made during December, nor were any credit balances in customers' accounts reduced during December.

Required:

   (1) All entries as of December 31, 1959, the closing date, necessary to correct the Accounts Receivable account and any other entries suggested by the foregoing information.
   (2) The amount at which the accounts receivable should be shown in the December 31, 1959 balance sheet.

Problem 10-9.   The president of Empire Builders, Inc., on January 10, 1960, requested an auditor to make a special investigation of the bookkeeper-cashier's handling of trade accounts receivable. Two recent occurrences led to this decision: (1) When the president questioned two former debtors whose accounts had been written off as "bad," the customers objected, saying that they had mailed their checks several months ago. In each case, they produced cancelled checks endorsed by Empire Builders, Inc. (2) When asked by the president to explain why the balances of Sales Returns and Allowances and Bad Debts Expense were unusually large in the 1959 income statement, the sales manager responded that his (the sales manager's) informal records indicated much smaller figures.

In the course of his investigation, the auditor learned that the bookkeeper-cashier was in charge of all bookkeeping activities; the bookkeeper-cashier also prepared the semiannual financial statements. The auditor, upon communicating with debtors whose accounts had debit balances on December 31, further learned that, although the receivable balances agreed with the customers' records, the individual transactions did not so agree; he thus suspected that the bookkeeper-cashier had been taking cash.

The bookkeeper-cashier was hired on July 1, 1959, and was given a responsible job on the strength of several excellent out-of-town references. On that date, the accounts receivable balances were: A, $190; B, $85; C, $245; D, $415; and E, $320. During the final six months of 1959, sales were recorded as follows: B, $470; C, $685; D, $400; F, $700; G, $335; H, $550; I, $720; and J, $410. Collections during that period were recorded as follows: A, $100; B, $350; D, $415; F, $400; G, $200; and I, $300. Three accounts were written off as bad: A, $20; H, $550; and J, $390. Returns and allowances were credited to the following accounts: A, $70; C, $170; E, $40; G, $50; and J, $20.

An examination of copies of invoices in the sales manager's file revealed that sales of $6,485 had been made since July 1. Of these sales, invoices amounting to $405 were mailed after January 1, 1960, and pertained to sales consummated during 1960. These 1960 sales have not been recorded. The sales manager also produced evidence showing that sales returns of $85 and allowances of $175 were authorized during the last six months of 1959.

The company's president informed the auditor that *A* and *J* were the customers who proved they had paid $190 and $510, respectively. Both customers had produced invoices totaling these sums. As a result of an exchange of correspondence with the receiver for *H*, who had become a voluntary bankrupt, it was learned that all of *H*'s creditors were paid thirty cents on the dollar as the only payment on their claims. The checks had been mailed on November 10, 1959, and the receiver reported that they had all been returned by the bank, properly endorsed. The receiver reported that the check which was sent to Empire Builders, Inc., amounted to $180.

As a result of a surprise cash count and reconciliation, the auditor determined that there was a deficiency of cash.

(1) Determine the amount of the cash deficiency on December 31, 1959. Account for this discrepancy by showing the devices which the bookkeeper-cashier used to conceal his activities and the extent to which each device contributed to the total discrepancy.

(2) Prepare necessary correcting entries as of December 31, 1959. Assume that the books have not been closed, and that the company uses a controlling account.

In preparing the entries, use individual customer accounts wherever possible, as well as the controlling account. It is to be assumed that the company does not use an Allowance for Doubtful Accounts account.

Problem 10-10. Journalize the following transactions, together with necessary adjustments preliminary to the preparation of financial statements for August of 1959, on the books of Appleby Company. Debit Freight Charges for freight obligations of the seller which are paid by the buyers.

August   19—Sold merchandise to Danforth Sales Company on terms of 2/10; n/30, f.o.b. shipping point. Invoice price was $3,300, and invoice date was August 19.

24—Sold merchandise to Axiom Corp. for $2,180, f.o.b. shipping point. Invoice date was August 24 and terms were 2/10; n/30. This account was immediately assigned, in return for a 75% advance, to Old Main Finance Company. Interest was set at $\frac{1}{30}$ of 1% per day of the cash advanced.

26—The company authorized credits for sales returns of $110 to Danforth Sales Company and of $230 to Axiom Corp.

27—Sold merchandise to Aspen & Co. for $1,610, f.o.b. shipping point. Invoice date was August 27, and terms were 2/10; n/30. Freight charges of $110 were paid by the buyer.

28—Received a check from Danforth Sales Company in satisfaction of the sale of August 19. It was learned that freight charges, which were paid by Danforth Sales Company, amounted to $60.

30—Sold merchandise to Foothills, Inc., at terms of 2/10; n/30, f.o.b. destination. Invoice price was $2,710, and the invoice date was August 29. Foothills, Inc., paid freight of $75.

31—Adjustments include recognition of expected net bad debt losses, 1% of net charge sales. Data available:

Net sales	$300,000
Sales discounts on charge sales	4,000
Sales returns on cash sales	7,000
Sales returns on charge sales	11,000
Net cash sales	60,000

September 1—Sold merchandise to Derby Stores, Inc., for $6,550. Invoice date was September 1; terms were net 30, f.o.b. shipping point. Freight charges of $40 were paid by the buyer.

1—Received 30-day, 6% note from Derby Stores, Inc., for $6,550. Date of the note was September 1.

2—Received a check from Axiom Corp. in satisfaction of sale of August 24. It was learned that Axiom Corp. had paid freight charges of $38. The check was immediately forwarded to Old Main Finance Company, which received it on the same day. Therefore, the daily interest charge terminated on September 2.

4—Received a check from Old Main Finance Company in final settlement of the financing arrangement.

5—Sold merchandise to York Retailers, Inc., for $4,000; terms were 2/10; n/30, f.o.b. destination. Invoice date was September 5, and freight charges of $69 were paid by the buyer. The account was immediately sold, without guarantee, to Thompson Factoring Company. The agreed commission was 1⅛% of "net" after all deductions by the buyer, and the holdback was established at 20%. Interest of 6% per annum was agreed upon for advances. An advance of $2,000 was requested and received from the balance of $3,046.14 against which such advances could be drawn.

8—Received a $2,000 note from Foothills, Inc., and a check in satisfaction of the remainder of the sale of August 29. The note was dated September 7 and carried interest at 5%. Its life was 60 days. The cash discount was allowed on that part of the sales price which was paid by check.

11—Learned that Aspen & Co. had suffered several financial setbacks; hence wrote off its account.

12—Discounted the Derby Stores, Inc., note at The Last State Bank. Discount rate was 5%.

14—Learned that York Retailers, Inc., had paid its account in full to Thompson Factoring Company.

23—Received from Aspen & Co. a 90-day, 8% note for $1,200 and the balance of the account in cash.

25—Received a check from Thompson Factoring Company in settlement of the factoring arrangement.

October   1—Issued our check to The Last State Bank upon learning that the Derby Stores, Inc., note had been dishonored. A $4 protest fee was included in the check.

16—Received from Derby Stores, Inc., payment of the charge of October 1 plus interest thereon from that date at 7%.

Assignment Material for Chapter 11

Questions

Question 11-1. In preparing your worksheet at the close of the year, how would you treat the following invoices, dated December 28, for raw material shipped to your client but not received?

(a) Invoice for $25,000; terms, 30 days net; f.o.b. destination.
(b) Invoice for $10,000; terms, 2/10; 30 days net; f.o.b. point of origin.

Question 11-2. If purchases are received during the last part of the accounting period, why is it incorrect to omit the charge to Purchases and the credit to Accounts Payable, and also to omit the goods from the inventory?

Question 11-3. You are making an audit of a corporation engaged in the manufacture of clothing, and ascertain that cloth costing $100,000, received prior to the end of the period under audit, is for use in the manufacture of next season's goods. The client states that this cloth is not included in the inventory taken at the close of the audit period and requests that you do not include it in the inventory. Under what possible circumstances, if any, would you accede to his request?

Question 11-4. Under what circumstances should purchased goods in transit at the end of the period be included in the inventory?

Question 11-5. Before whiskey can be "bottled in bond" it must be at least four years old. Original cost includes materials, labor, overhead, and certain taxes. Additional costs for carrying the whiskey four years include insurance, taxes, depreciation (on warehouses), warehousing labor, light and heat, and recoopering costs. The distillery may have bank loans on which interest must be paid. It has a substantial investment in warehouses, on which it believes that it is entitled to a reasonable earning.

You are asked for an opinion about how to value the whiskey inventory at the end of the first full year after production.

Question 11-6. A manufacturer wishes to include as part of the cost of raw materials all of the cost of acquiring and handling incoming material. You are to:

(a) Name the principal items entering into the cost of material acquisition and handling.
(b) State the arguments for and against the inclusion of these items as a part of the cost of raw materials.

Question 11-7. What is direct costing? Give some arguments for and against its use.

Question 11-8. A standard cost system was installed by a company several years ago as a result of which the company has been distributing its factory overhead on a basis equivalent to approximately 200% of direct labor. For 1959, however, the actual ratio of factory overhead to direct labor was 400%, as compared

760

to 450% for 1958. Work in process and finished stock at the end of each of these years were valued as follows:

	December 31,	
	1958	1959
Material.......................................	$120,000	$150,000
Direct labor....................................	40,000	54,000
Factory overhead...............................	80,000	108,000
	$240,000	$312,000

Because of the poor showing in 1959, it has been suggested that the closing inventory be valued on the basis of the actual overhead rate for 1959, it having been determined that the closing inventory contained no items that were on hand January 1.

What position would you take regarding the above suggestion?

Question 11-9. Under what conditions might the valuation of an inventory on a cost basis be less than actual cost?

Question 11-10. The *ABC* Partnership is a general construction contractor engaged in constructing residences and small stores under firm price contracts. The partnership has under way, on December 31, 1958, ten contracts, each of which is 80% completed. The partnership follows the "completed contracts" basis of accounting, under which gains or losses on contracts are recognized only upon completion of the contract and acceptance by the customer. As of January 1, 1959, the partnership is to be converted into a corporation, with *A*, *B*, and *C* as the sole stockholders. It is proposed to continue the use of the "completed contracts" basis in the corporation and to transfer contracts in process from the partnership to the corporation at book value without recognition of gain or loss to December 31, 1958, subject only to normal year-end adjustments.

Discuss the propriety of this proposal from the accounting point of view, with special reference to its effect on a proper showing of profits in both the partnership and its corporate successor. Do not discuss income tax effects.

Problems

Problem 11-1. Information relative to commodity KK of The Cargo Company's inventory is presented below.

Inventories:

	Quantity	Amount
December 31, 1958...............................	12,000	$1,440
December 31, 1959...............................	18,000	

Purchases made during 1959:

		Quantity	Cost
January	28.......................................	8,000	$1,120
March	15.......................................	10,000	1,200
June	22.......................................	15,000	1,500
September	9.......................................	6,000	900
December	13.......................................	10,000	1,500

Required:

Invoice cost of the December 31, 1959 inventory by each of the following methods: (a) Simple average; (b) weighted average; (c) first-in, first-out.

Problem 11-2. The inventory records of Blasan Sales Company show that there were 10,000 units of commodity BB on hand on January 1, 1959, and 6,000 units of this commodity on hand on December 31, 1959. The opening inventory had a valuation of $3,000. Monthly purchases were made during 1959 as follows:

	Quantity	Cost
January	8,000	$2,560
February	5,000	1,500
March	7,000	2,380
April	4,000	1,400
May	10,000	2,800
June	8,000	2,320
July	6,000	2,040
August	9,000	2,880
September	3,000	990
October	12,000	3,600
November	7,000	2,100
December	8,000	2,320

Net sales of $31,600 were made in 1959, with the goods priced to yield a gross profit rate of 20%.

Purchases during January, 1960, amounted to 5,000 units at a cost of $1,710.

Required:

(a) Cost of the December 31, 1959 inventory using the gross profit method.
(b) The moving-average cost for January, 1960, using the widely-fluctuating cost modification.

Problem 11-3. A partial perpetual inventory record of Bloom and Company for the month of April, 1959, is presented below.

	Quantity			Cost		
Date	Into Stock	Out of Stock	Balance	Into Stock	Out of Stock	Balance
April 2	400		400	$480.00		$480.00
6	200		600	250.00		
8		100	500			
11	300		800	345.00		
15		200	600			
17		250	350			
21	500		850	600.00		
25		400	450			
28	300		750	390.00		
30		175	575			

Required:

A tabulation showing the computation of the moving-average unit costs.

Problem 11-4. Bolding Construction Company was engaged, on January 1, 1959, to erect a high school building under a contract which called for a total price of $850,000 to be paid to Bolding Construction Company in five payments. One-fifth of the price was to be paid upon the completion of each quarter of the work (as defined in detail by the terms of the contract), the final payment being due within 30 days after Bolding Construction Company had entirely executed its obligations under the contract.

On December 10, 1959, three-fourths of the building was completed, whereupon the third payment was made in accordance with the contract. On December 31,

1959, a total of $425,000 had been disbursed by Bolding Construction Company for costs incurred under this contract, and the outstanding accounts payable for materials purchased for this construction amounted to $125,000. It was estimated that an additional $150,000 would be required to complete the contract.

Prepare a statement showing the estimated income earned on the contract to December 31, 1959, if the company uses the percentage-of-completion method.

Problem 11-5. The Normandy Production Company began operations on January 1, 1959. During 1959 the following costs were incurred: materials, $220,000; direct labor, $377,400; and overhead, 120% of direct labor.

On December 31, 1959, 72,000 units of the company's only product had been completed and 8,000 units were still in the process of manufacture, one-fourth completed.

Assuming that all of the materials for each unit were put into process when work was started, compute the following:

(a) Unit cost of finished goods.
(b) Cost of the work in process on December 31, 1959.

Problem 11-6. The accounting year of Carbo Corporation ended on June 30, 1959. On this date, all revenue and expense accounts were closed to the Revenue and Expense account, but the closing of the latter account was delayed until the records could be examined and their accuracy determined.

An examination of the corporation's records for this year led to the discovery of the following facts:

(a) Merchandise costing $840.10 was excluded from the June 30, 1959 inventory because the goods had been transferred to the shipping department for crating on June 29, to fill an order which provided that the goods be shipped on July 2, 1959. The goods will be shipped f.o.b. shipping point.
(b) Merchandise costing $330.60 was ordered on June 28, 1959, and included in the June 30, 1959 inventory, although not received until July 3, 1959, and not recorded in the corporation's records until then. This merchandise was shipped by the seller on June 29, 1959, f.o.b. destination.
(c) Merchandise with an invoice price of $1,100.50 was received on June 26, 1959, and this amount was included in the June 30, 1959 inventory. As of July 2, 1959, $1,100.50 was credited to Purchase Returns and Allowances, and the merchandise was returned to the seller on this date.
(d) On June 29, 1959, merchandise costing $860.75 was shipped by the seller, f.o.b. destination, and was received by Carbo Corporation on June 30. This merchandise was not included in the June 30, 1959 inventory because no invoice had been received from the seller.
(e) Merchandise with an invoice price of $400.15 was received on June 30, 1959, with no entries being made until the condition of the merchandise could be determined, although these goods were included in the June 30, 1959 inventory. During the course of the examination, these goods were found to be undamaged and in accord with Carbo Corporation's order.

Prepare the journal entries that should be made as of June 30, 1959, in connection with the above transactions.

Problem 11-7. In the manufacture of the product of Bimco Corporation, all materials must be put into process at the start of production. At the beginning of 1959, there were 51,000 units in the work in process inventory, two-thirds complete. On December 31, 1959, there were 63,000 units which were only one-third complete. During 1959, 640,000 units were started in production, and the December 31, 1959 finished goods inventory contained 125,000 units.

The following balances were taken from the corporation's accounts on December 31, 1959:

Materials used... $420,000
Direct labor..   380,000
Overhead...   170,000

Required:

    (a) Computation of the cost of the work in process on December 31, 1959.
    (b) Computation of the cost of the finished goods inventory on December 31, 1959.

Compute unit costs to the nearest cent.

Problem 11-8. September 30, 1959, marked the end of Beagle Supply Company's accounting year. On this date the company was concluding arbitration proceedings with its employees to settle a strike which had begun one week before. As a consequence of the strike, the errors stated below were made in the computation of the ending inventory. The company does not use a perpetual inventory system.

    (a) Merchandise costing $4,200 was received on September 30, 1959, and was included in the inventory, although the invoice was not recorded until October 5, 1959.
    (b) Included in the inventory was merchandise with a cost of $280 which had been sold on September 25, 1959, for $340, the title passing to the purchaser at that time. However, the sale was not recorded until October 6, 1959, when the shipment was made.
    (c) Merchandise shipped to customers on September 30, 1959, f.o.b. destination, was not included in the inventory. This merchandise cost $960 and the sales were recorded at $1,240 on October 3, 1959.
    (d) One lot of merchandise, shipped to the company f.o.b. shipping point, was in transit on September 30, 1959. This merchandise was recorded at its purchase price of $1,630 on September 30 but was not included in the inventory.
    (e) Merchandise costing $415 was inadvertently overlooked when the inventory tabulation was made.

Required:

    (1) On the assumption that the company's books were closed September 30, 1959, without discovery of these errors, a computation of the amount of overstatement or understatement of cost of goods sold which would appear in the income statements for the years ended September 30, 1959 and 1960.
    (2) On the same assumption as in (1), a computation of the overstatement or understatement of retained earnings on September 30, 1959 and 1960.
    (3) On the assumption that the errors were discovered before the books were closed on September 30, 1960, the journal entry necessary to correct the books at that time. You may assume that the company follows the practice of charging or crediting Retained Earnings for the correction of prior years' earnings.

Problem 11-9.   Commodities X, Y, and Z are sold by Benton Sales, Incorporated. The merchandise inventory on December 31, 1958, was as follows:

Commodity X... $48,000
Commodity Y... 26,000
Commodity Z... 10,000

For a number of years the corporation has realized gross profit on the sales of commodities X, Y, and Z at the rates of 35%, 25%, and 20%, respectively. The gross profit rate on all sales for 1958 was 24%.

On December 1, 1959, a fire occurred in the corporation's building, resulting in the complete destruction of all inventories on hand. The only other available information concerning 1959 is that which follows:

	Commodities		
	X	Y	Z
Purchases to December 1....................	$280,000	$150,000	$90,000
Sales to December 1.......................	415,000	180,000	95,000

Required: •

(a) The approximate inventory of commodities X, Y, and Z on December 1, 1959.
(b) The approximate combined inventory on December 1, 1959, if the data had not been classified by commodity.

Problem 11-10.   The Gardner Cut-Sole Company bought 50 tons of leather, which was cut into men's outersoles. The leather cost 48 cents a pound, and cutting and sorting cost $1,620. It was considered that it was just as expensive to process one grade of soles as another. The grades obtained from sorting were as follows:

Grade	Number of Pairs	Market Value per Pair
X................................ ...	19,247	$.85
A................................ ...	28,410	.65
B................................	33,932	.45
C................................	10,624	.35
D................................	3,274	.25
M................................	1,408	.18

Scrap: 4 tons at $30 a ton.
Compute the unit cost per pair of each grade.

Problem 11-11.   Loft Manufacturing Company was organized on January 2, 1959. During its first year of operations it completed 45,000 units of the single product it manufactures. In the manufacturing operation, all production costs are incurred evenly as processing occurs.

Use what you need of the following data to determine the valuation of the year-end inventories, assuming that the company intends to adopt direct costing.

Materials purchased.. $398,000
Materials released to production............................ 376,000
Direct labor... 470,000
Freight in on materials.................................... 39,800
Indirect labor (60% of which is a fixed cost)............... 131,500
Heat, light, and power..................................... 21,000
Factory supplies used.... 16,800

Fixed charges:
Property taxes... $ 7,121
Depreciation... 36,218

Goods in process (⅔ complete)—7,500 units
Finished goods—10,000 units

The freight in on materials is the total paid for this element of cost; all materials are purchased from the same source and shipped in the same manner.

Problem 11-12. The information appearing below was taken from the records of The Hartley Company on December 31, 1959:

Work in process, at cost of materials and direct labor............ $18,000
Materials in transit (shipped f.o.b. destination)................. 1,750
Advances to suppliers for purchase commitments................ 800
Shipping supplies... 230
Finished goods in storeroom, at cost, which includes $10,485 of
overhead.. 52,425
Finished goods in transit (shipped out f.o.b. destination, to be billed
in 1960), including $280 freight charge....................... 2,120
Finished goods in hands of consignees (at 140% of cost).......... 8,400
Finished goods held by salesmen, at selling price (cost, $2,520)... 3,200
Unsalable finished goods, at cost............................. 4,910
Materials... 26,305
Defective materials returned to suppliers for replacement........ 8,192
Gasoline and oil for testing finished goods..................... 180
Prepaid machinery rentals.................................... 600
Machine lubricants.. 460

Prepare a partial balance sheet on December 31, 1959, giving proper disclosure of the above items.

Problem 11-13. City Company lost its entire inventory of merchandise by fire early in January, 1959, before completing the physical inventory which was being taken as of December 31, 1958. The following information was taken from the books of the company as of December 31, 1957 and 1958.

	December 31, 1957	December 31, 1958
Inventory—January 1.....................	$ 42,380	$ 45,755
Purchases...............................	159,045	174,433
Purchase returns and allowances............	8,021	10,015
Sales...................................	196,677	203,317
Sales returns and allowances................	2,402	2,167
Wages..................................	17,743	18,356
Salaries.................................	8,000	9,000
Taxes other than income...................	3,732	3,648
Rent....................................	5,400	5,400
Insurance...............................	967	982
Light, heat, and water.....................	1,134	1,271
Advertising..............................	4,250	2,680
Interest expense..........................	2,755	3,020
Depreciation expense......................	1,255	1,280
Furniture and fixtures, net of depreciation...	10,065	10,570
Miscellaneous expenses....................	6,634	6,897

From the above information, you are to estimate the book amount of the inventory destroyed by the fire, assuming that there were no transactions after December 31, 1958.

Problem 11-14. The Ready Manufacturing Corporation has followed the practice of inventorying its finished goods at selling prices and has applied the same per cent of mark-up to its goods in process; the company has prepared the following statement on this basis.

THE READY MANUFACTURING CORPORATION
Income Statement
For the Year Ended December 31, 1959

Sales...			$956,300
Cost of goods sold:			
Raw materials used (at cost).....................		$221,362	
Direct labor......................................		304,162	
Manufacturing overhead..........................		103,912	
Total manufacturing costs......................		$629,436	
Work in process (on selling price basis):			
December 31, 1958...................	$627,040		
December 31, 1959...................	427,350	199,690	
Goods manufactured............................		$829,126	
Finished goods (at selling prices):			
December 31, 1958..................	$165,760		
December 31, 1959..................	458,210	292,450	536,676
Gross profit..			$419,624
Selling and administrative expenses..........................			367,766
Net income..			$ 51,858

Prepare a corrected statement, assuming that the per cent of mark-up for the current year is normal. Show supporting computations.

Problem 11-15. Cement Construction Company was incorporated during the month of December, 1955, with authorized capital stock of 25,000 shares of $100 par value each, all of which were issued at that time for cash.

On January 1, 1956, the company entered into a contract for the construction of a flood-control dam. The contract price for the project was $15,000,000, with installment payments to be received on the basis of approved engineering estimates of percentage of completion. The contract called for the retention of 10% of each progress billing prior to final acceptance of the completed dam.

Funds have been received in connection with the contract as follows:

Advance for preparatory work.............................	$1,500,000
Payment for work completed as of November 30, 1958 (less 10% retained, and less repayment of a portion of amount advanced for preparatory work—equivalent to 10% of gross amount billed for completed work).......................	8,400,000
Total cash received.......................................	$9,900,000

As of December 31, 1958, approved engineering estimates showed that the work was considered to be 80% complete, and a progress billing for the work completed in December was made.

Direct costs to December 31, 1958, amounted to $6,090,210.

The cost of plant facilities acquired for this contract (buildings, cement mixers, rock crushers, trucks, cranes, and so forth), amounting to $2,430,000 less estimated salvage value of $486,000 (20% of cost), is depreciated on the basis of percentage of completion.

Other expenses are applicable to work completed. These costs are as shown on the following page.

Administrative and general expenses........................	$ 915,000
Maintenance of plant facilities...........................	762,300
Operation of plant facilities.............................	465,150
Total...	$2,142,450

In addition to these costs, annual provisions have been made for federal and state income taxes aggregating $1,000,000, which you may consider as being correct.

On December 30, 1958, a dividend of $20 per share of capital stock was paid in cash. This was the first dividend paid by the company.

Additional information as of December 31, 1958:

Cash on hand and in banks amounted to....................	$ 750,490

Inventories—not yet charged to construction costs—were as follows:

Work in progress.......................................	$ 111,625
Materials and supplies.................................	171,250
Total...	$ 282,875

The current liabilities consisted of:

Accounts payable to trade creditors.....................	$ 125,750
Accrued payroll..	27,200
Income taxes payable...................................	600,000
Social security taxes..................................	20,325
Income taxes withheld from compensation of employees....	22,750
Advance on construction contract.......................	300,000
	$1,096,025

You are to prepare a balance sheet as of December 31, 1958, in good form with necessary supporting schedules.

Problem 11-16. On January 2, 1959, a fire substantially destroyed the office and plant of Unlimited Company. You are to prepare an estimate of the inventory as of the date of the fire.

The merchandise handled by the company is divided into three lines or classes of goods, designated as X, Y, and Z. Classes X and Y each consists of a number of items which are bought and sold without change of form; Class Z consists of one item only, for which raw material is bought and put through a manufacturing process. It is established that there was no work in process when the fire occurred.

The following records and data are found to be available:

1. Duplicate sales invoices and credit memos, the totals of which are as follows:

	Sales	Credit Memos
Year 1956.................................	$122,785	$6,585
Year 1957.................................	110,942	7,542
Year 1958.................................	87,451	4,100

A check of the numbers discloses that approximately 9% of the duplicate sales invoices for 1958 are missing.

2. Duplicate bank deposit slips without any missing dates:

Year 1956...	$108,066
Year 1957...	96,008
Year 1958...	91,150

Duplicate bank deposit slips were found to represent receipts from accounts receivable and cash sales only. You learn on inquiry that the company has made a practice of paying some administrative expenses out of cash receipts not deposited. The amount of such payments cannot be determined.

3. Purchase invoice files, accompanied by adding machine tapes purporting to show the total purchases for each year, with totals as follows:

Year 1956...................................... $131,616
Year 1957...................................... 117,935
Year 1958......................................   76,158

4. Inventory sheets, as of January 1, 1956:

Class X.. $50,000
Class Y.. 24,000
Class Z—raw materials.......................... 15,000
Class Z—finished, ¾ of which is raw material... 14,000

The management stated that nothing was added to the cost of merchandise and raw materials in the 1956 inventory to cover freight and handling. A comparison of some of the inventory prices with purchase invoices at about the date of the inventory confirmed this statement. You find, however, that *2% of net purchases* is sufficient to cover freight and handling into the warehouse, and you allow this percentage in all cost computations. You find also that overhead is 50% of the direct labor.

5. Upon examination of the contents of the purchase invoice files, you find that credit memos representing allowances on purchases have been listed on the adding machine tapes as invoices and included in the totals, as follows:

Year 1956...................................... $7,548
Year 1957...................................... 7,225
Year 1958...................................... 6,120

All suppliers of merchandise and materials are circularized with a request for an itemized statement of account for the last three years, and these statements show additional credit memos in the following amounts:

Year 1956...................................... $1,741
Year 1957...................................... 3,122
Year 1958...................................... 5,610

6. Raw materials for Class Z are purchased in carload lots, and the invoices for the three years show total purchases of $33,000. You find that the shop foreman has kept a record showing that raw materials with an invoice cost of $34,000 have been put in process in the three years; and that the proportions of direct labor and overhead to material cost have been approximately maintained.

7. Analysis of a considerable number of sales invoices, selected in such a way as to give a fair sample of the entire file, and comparison with the computed cost of each item, give results which are summarized as follows:

	Per cent of Net Sales	Per cent of Gross Profit to Net Sales
Class X...........................	45%	10%
Class Y...........................	26	25
Class Z...........................	29	25

Assignment Material for Chapter 12

Questions

Question 12-1. The following data relate to an inventory item on hand at the year end: cost, $75; market value, $50; selling price less estimated cost to complete and sell, $68; selling price less estimated cost to complete and sell at a normal profit margin, $52. At what price should this item be inventoried at the year end in conformity with A.R.B. 43? What objection can you see to this inventory procedure?

Question 12-2. In taking its physical inventory, a concern used the following worksheet:

	Item		Total Value	
Quantity	Cost	Market	Cost	Market

Each item listed was extended into the total value columns at both cost and market price. These columns were then totaled. As the total of the market value column was the lower, this amount was used as the inventory value. Would you accept such a valuation?

Question 12-3. What are the general advantages of the reserve method of adjusting inventories to market value? Explain why this procedure is more desirable with the perpetual than with the periodical inventory procedure.

Question 12-4. Why is the propriety of the old cost-or-market rule now being subjected to some questioning?

Question 12-5. Explain how the application of the cost-or-market rule in the valuation of raw materials, goods in process, and finished goods may result in an incorrect statement of the cost of goods sold.

Question 12-6. On what basis should merchandise repossessed in a damaged condition be valued for inventory purposes?

Question 12-7. Mention two conditions under which it might be proper to value inventories on the basis of selling prices. Does "on the basis of selling prices" mean the same thing as "at selling prices"?

Question 12-8. The variety of methods of inventory pricing regarded as acceptable may affect the comparability of: (a) the income statements of a company for successive periods, and (b) the income statements of two or more companies for the same year. What accounting principle minimizes the hazards of noncomparability? Does the minimization apply equally to (a) and (b)?

Question 12-9. A trading concern valued its inventory on December 31, 1958 at market value, which was less than cost. The valuation on this basis was $60,000. Believing that there might be further declines in market value after the first of the year, the directors decided to set up a reserve of $5,000 to provide for possible losses resulting from such declines. During 1959 the market value did further decline, and it was estimated that the goods on hand on December 31, 1958, could have been purchased in 1959 for $57,000. At what value should the inventory on December 31, 1958 be shown in the income statements for the years

1958 and 1959? How should the $5,000 reserve have been set up on December 31, 1958? What disposition should finally be made of it?

Question 12-10. Under what conditions may it be unsatisfactory to allow a long period of time to elapse between inventory computations by the retail method?

Problems

Problem 12-1. State, for each of the items listed below, the unit value which would be employed for inventory-pricing purposes, using the lower of cost or market as defined by Bulletin 43 of the Committee on Accounting Procedure of the American Institute of Certified Public Accountants.

Item	Original Cost	Replacement Cost	Selling Price	Estimated Cost to Complete and Sell	Normal Profit Margin
a........	$ .67	$ .62	$ .72	$.04	$.03
b........	2.20	2.12	2.22	.12	.08
c........	1.48	1.52	1.72	.12	.06
d........	.22	.20	.24	.03	.01
e........	.93	.87	.97	.05	.04
f........	4.08	4.02	4.52	.33	.18
g........	3.18	3.24	3.52	.18	.06
h........	.44	.42	.46	.05	.02

Problem 12-2. The data presented below were taken from the June 30, 1959 inventory records of American Code Company.

Category	Merchandise Code Identification	Quantity	Unit Price Cost	Unit Price Market
A............	X.................	29	$ 16.50	$ 16.00
	Y.................	78	4.10	4.30
	Z.................	105	2.90	2.80
B............	XX................	24	162.10	157.00
	YY.......	18	203.00	209.00
	ZZ................	12	146.00	143.00
C............	I.................	294	1.18	1.16
	II................	197	1.37	1.40
	III................	130	1.68	1.70

Price the above inventory, using the lower of cost or market method, applied: (1) Item by item; (2) to categories of inventory; (3) to total inventory.

Problem 12-3. City Department Store opened a new department on January 1, 1959. In the table below are listed certain data, for the year ended December 31, 1959, taken from the bookkeeping records of the new department.

Purchases:
At cost... $40,016
At original selling prices.................................... 58,000
Mark-ups.. 3,000
Mark-downs... 2,110
Sales... 50,000
Inventory, December 31, 1959—at marked selling prices........ 8,890

Compute the inventory on December 31, 1959, by the retail method, as conventionally applied.

Problem 12-4. The inventory of Home Furnishing Company on December 31, 1959, was prepared as shown below:

	Classifi-cation	Count	Unit Cost	Unit market to replace on December 31, 1959	Unit sale price less costs of disposal	Unit sale price less costs of disposal and normal profit margin
Living room suites:	A-1....	5	$80	$85	$130	$82
	A-2....	2	70	68	115	69
	A-3....	4	50	46	72	50
Bedroom suites:	B-1....	6	60	58	84	61
	B-2....	1	55	56	82	56
	B-3....	3	30	35	50	32
	B-4....	2	35	33	57	34
Dining room suites:	C-1....	4	85	82	81	78
	C-2....	2	90	93	104	92
Dinette sets:	C-11....	6	40	37	64	42
	C-12....	7	30	26	25	22
Tables:	D-1....	11	30	35	48	34
	D-2....	14	22	24	24	21
	D-3....	6	10	9	13	8
	D-4....	5	14	15	20	16
Chairs.	E-1....	22	45	42	63	44
	E-2....	12	50	35	49	37
Lamps:	F-1....	17	9	11	14	10
	F-2....	6	10	9	15	11
	F-3....	14	7	8	10	8

Compute the December 31, 1959 inventory, using the lower of cost or market (by category) method as set forth in Accounting Research Bulletin 43 of the American Institute of Certified Public Accountants.

Problem 12-5. From the data presented below, for the sports department of Northern Department Store, compute the January 31, 1959 inventory, using the retail inventory method. Carry per cents to two decimal places.

```
Inventory—January 31, 1958:
    Cost.............................................. $ 26,250.00
    Selling price.....................................    43,510.00
Purchases:
    Cost..............................................   130,560.00
    Selling price.....................................   218,440.00
Freight in............................................     3,830.00
Returns:
    Purchases:
        Cost..........................................     1,310.00
        Selling price.................................     2,460.00
    Sales.............................................     4,140.00
Cash discounts:
    Purchases.........................................     2,410.00
    Sales.............................................     3,860.00
Mark-ups..............................................     5,310.00
Mark-downs............................................     8,120.00
Cancellations of:
    Mark-ups..........................................     1,860.00
    Mark-downs........................................     1,290.00
Sales.................................................   221,210.00
```

Problem 12-6. The following data regarding Drake Company are given.

Date	Inventory at Cost	Inventory at Cost or Market	Purchases	Sales
1- 1....................	$24,000	$23,000		
1-31....................	26,000	25,000	$38,000	$49,000
2-28....................	27,000	24,500	42,000	53,000
3-31....................	26,500	26,300	40,400	52,000

The company directs that the inventory be placed in the statements at cost, that the gain or loss from market fluctuations be shown separately, and that a reserve for the difference between cost and the lower of cost or market be set up.

Show, in columnar form, how the selling section of the income statement (for each of the three months) will look.

Problem 12-7. Jay-Bee Company uses a perpetual inventory method and values its inventory at the lower of cost or market. On December 31, 1958, the company used a reserve account for the $3,000 difference between cost and the lower of cost or market. On December 31, 1959, the market value of the inventory exceeded cost by $1,200. However, the company's accountant believed at that time that within one year the inventory could be replaced for $6,000 less money. On December 31, 1960, the company had an inventory of merchandise in the amount of $72,000, at cost, and $68,000 at the lower of cost or market. The company's accountant does not expect any price declines in the foreseeable future.

(a) By the use of general journal entries as of December 31, 1958, 1959, and 1960, show how the above might be treated in inventory reserve accounts.

(b) Describe the statement location of the reserve accounts used.

Problem 12-8. Woodside Corporation was organized and began operations on October 1, 1958, for the purpose of manufacturing and selling a single product. The manufacturing operations were organized into two departments. The first department manufactured parts which were assembled into the finished product in the second department. The condensed income statement for the year ended September 30, 1959, was as follows:

WOODSIDE CORPORATION
Income Statement
For the Year Ended September 30, 1959

Sales..		$222,400
Cost of goods sold:		
Materials used in the first department—Cost.......	$ 66,600	
Direct labor—Parts.............................	47,800	
Direct labor—Assembly.........................	41,200	
Overhead—Parts...............................	52,580	
Overhead—Assembly...........................	49,448	
Total......................................	$257,628	
Deduct work in process......................	16,698	
Cost of goods manufactured....................	$240,930	
Deduct finished goods.........................	55,000	185,930
Gross profit...		$ 36,470
Operating expenses....................................		44,200
Net operating loss.....................................		$ 7,730
Miscellaneous income—Scrap inventory.................		2,200
Net loss..		$ 5,530

An examination of the accounts of Woodside Corporation for the year ended September 30, 1959, disclosed the following:

(1) The inventory of work in process on September 30, 1959, consisted entirely of finished parts ready for assembly in the second department. Such parts equalled $\frac{1}{10}$ of the parts manufactured during the year.

(2) The September 30, 1959 balance sheet showed an inventory of scrap material of $2,200, representing the realizable value of material spoiled during the manufacture of parts.

(3) The finished goods on hand on September 30, 1959, are valued at the amount for which they could be purchased at wholesale from another company. 80% of the goods finished during the year have been sold.

Prepare a revised income statement for Woodside Corporation taking into account the information presented above. Show computations supporting any adjustments of the original figures.

Problem 12-9. From the following data compute:

(a) The cost of goods sold.
(b) The loss from inventory shortages.

Carry decimals to two places only.

	Cost	Retail
Opening inventory	$ 53,820	$ 86,640
Purchases (net)	244,390	376,230
Freight in	11,724	
Additional mark-ups		22,350
Cancellations of additional mark-ups		8,120
Mark-downs		13,330
Cancellations of mark-downs		4,170
Sales (net)		393,620
Physical inventory taken at retail		69,510

Problem 12-10. Accounting data relating to the operations of the shoe department of Campus Corner are presented below. Compute the ending inventory by the retail method.

Opening inventory—cost	$12,920
Opening inventory—sales price	19,105
Purchases—cost	33,771
Purchases—sales price	46,312
Purchase allowances	1,093
Freight in	845
Departmental transfers in—cost	100
Departmental transfers in—sales price	140
Additional mark-ups	1,207
Mark-up cancellations	274
Inventory shortage—sales price	704
Sales (including sales of $4,460 of items which were marked down from $5,920)	37,246

Problem 12-11. Quality Stores Corporation has employed a retail method in the computation of merchandise inventory for two years. The method was properly initiated by a certified public accountant. The corporation's procedures in applying the retail method are shown by the summary on the opposite page covering the two-year period ending January 31, 1960.

| | Data for the Year Ended January 31, | | | |
| | 1959 | | 1960 | |
	Cost	Retail	Cost	Retail
Beginning inventory..............	$ 52,100	$ 75,700	$ 58,212	$ 80,850
Purchases—net.................	274,610	382,800	334,167	439,150
Freight in.....................	3,410		2,801	
Totals.....................	$330,120	$458,500	$395,180	$520,000

Cost ratio:
      1959........ 72%
      1960........ 76%

Add net price changes on marked merchandise (Note)..........		6,550		9,545
Totals.....................		$465,050		$529,545
Sales.......................		384,200		415,845
Inventory at retail.............		$ 80,850		$113,700

Inventory computations:
    72% of $80,850, or $58,212
    76% of $113,700, or $86,412

Note. The records show that net mark-ups exceed net mark-downs by 100%.

During the month of December, 1959, the corporation made a purchase of special sale merchandise for $79,200, f.o.b. destination. The special sale merchandise was marked to sell for $90,000, and no changes have been made in such selling prices. As of January 31, 1960, two-thirds of this special-purchase merchandise has been sold.

The corporation did not take a physical inventory as of January 31, 1959. A physical inventory was taken as of January 31, 1960, at retail, but the corporation's accountant made no use of the information. The January 31, 1960 inventory sheets show the following totals:

Special sale merchandise.................................... $ 30,000
Regular merchandise....................................... 81,700
    Total inventory, at retail................................. $111,700

Compute the January 31, 1960 merchandise inventory as you would if you were the corporation's auditor. Show computations and carry per cents to two decimal places, for example, 45.85%.

Problem 12-12.   De Witt Corporation uses the lower of cost or market inventory method applied by comparing the total cost and market for the entire inventory and using the lower figure. It has been the company's experience that when changes in market value occur, such changes are likely to affect all categories of goods carried in stock. In other words, if the price of one type of merchandise declines, similar declines will occur in the prices of the other types of merchandise carried in stock.

Starting in 1959, the corporation adopted a modified perpetual inventory system, which was to operate as follows:

1. Purchases to be charged to the Inventory account at cost.
2. Cost of sales to be computed daily and credited to the Inventory account. The amount is based on the prices used in the beginning inventory; that is, the prices will be either exclusively cost or exclusively market, depending upon which were used in determining the preceding inventory.
3. A physical inventory to be taken semiannually and priced at the lower of cost or market, as described in the opening sentence.

4. The periodical inventory, as computed, to be entered in the accounts by adjusting the Inventory account to a balance equal to the ending inventory, with the Cost of Sales account debited or credited to balance the entry.

The following T-accounts show, in summary form in some instances, the entries made for the six months ended June 30, 1959, presumably in compliance with the above plan.

Inventory

12/31/58	Inventory, at market, which is below cost 11,500	1/1 to 6/30/59	Cost of goods sold, priced at 12/31/58 market prices...... 82,850
1/1 to 6/30/59	Purchases, at cost... 89,100	6/30/59	Adjustment of account balance to equal 6/30/59 physical inventory, priced at 12/31/58 market prices, which are below 1959 costs.... 6,600

Cost of Sales

1/1 to 6/30/59	Cost of goods sold.... 82,850	
6/30/59	Inventory adjustment. 6,600	

A portion of the June 30, 1959 physical inventory summary is reproduced below:

		Unit Price		Extended		Lower of
		1959	12/31/58	1959	12/31/58	Cost or
Item	Quantity	Cost	Market	Cost	Market	Market
A..................	20	$ 8	$7	$160	$ 140	
B..................	30	6	5	180	150	
C..................	10	10	9	100	90	

Total				$?	$11,150	$11,150

When quizzed, the bookkeeper said his reason for using December 31, 1958 market prices in computing the June 30, 1959 inventory was that the June 30, 1959 market values were uniformly above cost, while the December 31, 1958 market prices were uniformly below cost and thus more conservative.

Prepare a more acceptable estimate of the June 30, 1959 inventory. You may assume that the June 30, 1959 inventory was representative of the purchases made during the past six months (for instance, if January purchases were 10% of the goods purchased in the six months ended June 30, 1959, you may assume that 10% of the goods in the inventory were from January purchases); you may also assume that all of the items in the December 31, 1958 inventory have been disposed of by June 30, 1959.

Assignment Material for Chapter 13

Questions

Question 13-1. What are the major arguments advanced by the proponents of the *lifo* method of inventory valuation?

Question 13-2. What is the major argument advanced by the opponents of the *lifo* method?

Question 13-3. Under what circumstances might a strict application of the *lifo* method result in matching some old costs as well as some current costs against current revenues?

Question 13-4. In the statements prepared at the close of the period in which *lifo* is adopted, an accounting principle requires that a certain disclosure be made. What should be disclosed, and what principle requires the disclosure?

Question 13-5. Assume that the end-of-year inventory quantity of a certain article exceeded the beginning-of-year quantity. State three bases for determining the *lifo* cost of the incremental quantity. Which basis is consistent with *lifo* theory?

Question 13-6. The January 1, 1959 inventory in a department of a retail store was $30,000 at cost and $48,000 at retail on the *lifo* basis. The December 31, 1959 inventory in this department was $45,000 at retail. Retail prices at this time were 110% of retail prices on January 1, 1959. Mark-on for the year 1959 was 40%. Compute the December 31, 1959 inventory at cost on the *lifo* basis.

Question 13-7. Why may it be unwise to use the gross profit method of determining inventories when a company is on a last-in, first-out basis?

Question 13-8. Why is the opening inventory ignored in determining the cost ratio to apply in computing the inventory as of the date of change from conventional to *lifo* retail inventory procedure?

Question 13-9. A company uses the retail inventory procedure and prices inventories by the *lifo* method. In recent years, selling prices have increased considerably from year to year for the same inventory items. If these changes in selling price are ignored in the inventory computations, what will be the effect on the inventory figure? State how you would correct for the above situation in the computation of the inventory under the *lifo* retail method.

Problems

Problem 13-1. Specialized Product Company retails a single commodity. During 1959 its purchases were as follows:

Date		Quantity	Cost
February	6	8,000	$ 800
April	8	12,000	1,320
June	2	10,000	1,200
August	11	9,000	1,080
November	1	15,000	1,350
December	26	6,000	570

Compute the December 31, 1959 inventory following the last-in, first-out method under the conditions set forth below. In your solution, assume that any incremental quantity relates to the first acquisition made during the current year.

	Beginning Inventory	Ending Inventory
(a)	-0-	12,000 units
(b)	6,000 units at $.08	20,000 units
(c)	10,000 units:	20,000 units
	Base—7,000 units at $.08	
	Layer—3,000 units at $.085	
(d)	Same as (c)	8,000 units

Problem 13-2. Crusader Company decided to adopt the last-in, first-out inventory method as of December 31, 1959. The company also decided that in the application of the *lifo* method it would assume that incremental quantities related to the most recent acquisitions.

Using the following data, compute the December 31, 1959 inventory, following the *lifo* method. Also determine the effect of the change in inventory method on the 1959 net income before income taxes.

December 31, 1958 inventory (*fifo*):

Item	Quantity	Unit Cost	Total
X.................................	300	$5.00	$1,500.00
	200	5.09	1,018.00
	100	5.06	506.00
Total..........................			$3,024.00

1959 purchases of X:

Date	Quantity	Unit Cost	Total
January 20..........................	400	$5.08	$2,032.00
April 1..........................	420	5.09	2,137.80
June 5..........................	450	5.07	2,281.50
August 25..........................	310	5.08	1,574.80
October 10..........................	300	5.10	1,530.00
December 22..........................	100	5.12	512.00

December 31, 1959 inventory: 800 units of X

Problem 13-3. Sales Corporation adopted the last-in, first-out inventory procedure at the end of 1957.

Inventories on December 31, 1956 and 1957, for the single product sold by the corporation, were computed as follows:

	1956		1957	
12,000 units at $1.30.................	$15,600			
9,000 units at $1.40.................	12,600			
3,000 units at $1.50.................	4,500	$32,700		
24,000 units at $1.3625..............			$32,700	
2,000 units, assumed to relate to the				
last acquisition (3,500 units) of the				
current year, at $1.60..............			3,200	$35,900

Purchases for the years 1958, 1959, and 1960 are detailed on the opposite page.

1958:

January	27	3,000 units at $1.70
March	5	4,000 units at $1.80
May	30	20,000 units at $1.90
August	10	12,000 units at $2.10
October	1	5,000 units at $2.30
December	14	4,000 units at $2.20

1959:

January	10	2,000 units at $2.25
February	23	4,000 units at $2.30
May	3	7,000 units at $2.32
June	17	12,000 units at $2.40
September	30	8,000 units at $2.35
November	8	5,000 units at $2.40
December	26	12,000 units at $2.50

1960:

February	2	4,000 units at $2.52
April	8	3,000 units at $2.55
June	12	9,000 units at $2.56
August	15	15,000 units at $2.51
October	22	7,000 units at $2.50
December	5	2,000 units at $2.48

Inventories on December 31, 1958, 1959, and 1960, were 28,000, 25,000, and 30,000 units, respectively. Compute the cost of these inventories on the last-in, first-out basis, following the method established by the company.

Problem 13-4. The Northland Corporation has been using the first-in, first-out method of inventory valuation, but in 1959 the company decides to price its year-end inventories on the last-in, first-out basis. It plans to price any layers by reference to the first acquisitions of the current year.

The corporation gives you the following pertinent information and requests that you compute the cost of the December 31, 1959 inventory and also prepare an appropriate footnote, covering the above change, to accompany the financial statements in the corporation's published annual report for the year 1959.

	Quantity			Unit purchase price		
1958 purchases:	A	B	C	A	B	C
February 20	2,000	4,000		$6.20	$8.50	
April 29		9,000	1,000		8.50	$11.50
June 14	7,000		3,000	6.30		11.50
September 4		13,000	5,000		8.80	12.00
October 19	15,000	4,000	2,000	6.40	8.90	13.00
November 23	3,000			6.50		
December 15	2,000	3,000	1,000	6.60	9.00	13.40
1959 purchases:						
January 25			500			13.50
March 10	1,000	2,500	1,000	6.70	9.10	13.55
May 16	3,000	4,000		6.75	9.20	
August 8		8,000	2,000		9.25	13.60
October 21	8,000	10,000	6,000	6.76	9.27	13.64
December 12			3,000		9.30	
Inventory quantities:						
December 31:						
1958	2,500	2,500	2,000			
1959	3,700	2,400	2,200			

Problem 13-5. Small Corporation deals in one commodity. The following amounts were received and sold during 1959:

Period	Purchases Units	Unit Price	Units Sold
1st quarter	21,200	$2.10	
2nd quarter	34,000	2.20	
3rd quarter	26,800	2.30	
4th quarter	6,000	2.40	
Total sales for year			80,000

The company expects to pay $2.50 for purchases in the next year.

All purchases were made on the first day of the quarter; the inventory on January 1, 1959, consisted of 12,000 units priced at cost, $2.00 each.

The company is contemplating changing its inventory method and has requested its accountant to prepare a statement showing the results of several inventory methods on the income statement for 1959. The directors inform the accountant that an inventory of 8,000 units would be the minimum the company should have. The accountant prepared the following statement:

	Method			
	A	B	C	D
Sales	$287,000	$287,000	$287,000	$287,000
Cost of goods sold	178,560	174,560	177,600	176,360
Gross profit	$108,440	$112,440	$109,400	$110,640

Identify the inventory methods used, showing computations required to establish the identity of each method.

Problem 13-6. A portion of the income statement of Woods Company is presented below. It reveals a much improved gross profit rate compared to that earned by the company in recent years. You are asked to determine the most likely cause of this improvement and to compute the extent of its effect.

WOODS COMPANY
Partial Income Statement
For the Year Ended June 30, 1959

Sales			$811,350
Cost of goods sold:			
Inventory—June 30, 1958		$220,740	
Purchases (at an average cost of $22 per unit)		462,660	
Total		$683,400	
Inventory—June 30, 1959		142,500	540,900
Gross profit			$270,450

Additional data:

Inventory method—Last-in, first-out with perpetual inventory records.

Inventory—June 30, 1958:

Lifo base (1951)	10,000 units at $15.00	$150,000
1954 layer	3,000 units at $16.70	50,100
1957 layer	1,200 units at $17.20	20,640
Total		$220,740

Inventory—June 30, 1959:

Lifo base	9,500 units at $15.00	$142,500

Problem 13-7.   Given the following data, compute the inventory for December 31, 1957, 1958, 1959, and 1960, using the dollar-value *lifo* method. The company adopted *lifo* as of January 1, 1954. The inventory shown in the December 31, 1956 balance sheet amounted to $6,000, which was less than the inventory when *lifo* was adopted.

Inventory Data

	Inventory Computed by Using Average Costs of	
	Current Year	Base Year
December 31, 1957......................	$6,804	$6,480
December 31, 1958......................	7,128	6,480
December 31, 1959......................	7,392	6,600
December 31, 1960......................	7,475	6,500

Problem 13-8.   Homer Company has employed the retail method on a lower of cost or market basis for several years for the purpose of computing inventories. At the beginning of 1959, a decision was reached to adopt the last-in, first-out basis in connection with the use of the retail method.

The following information is made available to you covering the years ended December 31, 1958, 1959, and 1960:

	Year Ended December 31,					
	1958		1959		1960	
	Cost	Retail	Cost	Retail	Cost	Retail
Opening inventory....	$ 42,400	$ 60,800	?	$ 52,200	?	$ 60,200
Purchases....	367,474	500,100	$100,500	624,200	$400,824	601,500
Mark-downs..........		6,200		3,800		2,700
Mark-ups............		8,500		9,600		8,400
Sales...............		601,300		622,000		609,300

Compute the December 31, 1959 and 1960 inventories on the last-in, first-out basis. Assume no change in sales prices during the period of years covered.

Problem 13-9.   Bargain Retail Store had been using the retail inventory method. Early in 1955 a decision was reached to modify the retail method to last-in, first-out. Using the following data, compute the year-end inventories for the years 1955 through 1960. You may assume that prices remained stable during this period.

	Year Ended December 31,			
	1954		1955	
	Cost	Retail	Cost	Retail
Inventory—beginning of year....	$ 22,540	$ 32,200	?	$ 37,100
Purchases.....................	140,000	211,000	$153,318	217,440
Freight in.....................	8,674		9,132	
Mark-ups......................		2,100		2,220
Mark-downs...................		3,700		3,060
Sales.........................		204,500		212,500

Year Ended December 31,	Cost Ratio For Year	Inventory At Retail
1956..	77 %	$39,000
1957..	74	42,200
1958..	76	45,000
1959..	72	41,000
1960..	80	36,800

Problem 13-10. On December 31, 1954, *XYZ* Steel Company took a physical inventory of the Eureka-Bessemer grade iron ore at its East Works. The inventory represented a grade of ore which in the past had wide market fluctuations, but the company anticipated a steady rise in market prices in the succeeding years. This particular grade of ore had been stockpiled and not used by the company in the past, but with the installation of additional equipment it was planned to use large quantities of this ore in the future.

The December 31, 1954 physical inventory, valued at the lower of cost or market, consisted of 6,000 tons having a book value of $34,000. By reference to inventory records, it was established that the ore inventory of Eureka-Bessemer grade consisted of the following acquisitions:

Year	Tons	Unit Value	Amount
1952	2,000	$5.00*	$10,000*
1953	3,000	5.00*	15,000*
1954	1,000	9.00	9,000
	6,000		$34,000

* The 1952 and 1953 purchases were made at a cost of $6 and $7 per ton, respectively, but were written down to market price at December 31, 1953. The market price increased rapidly early in 1954.

On its federal income tax return for the year ended December 31, 1954, *XYZ* Steel Company elected to value its Eureka-Bessemer ore inventory at the East Works under the last-in, first-out method.

During the years 1955 through 1957, the following transactions were recorded in the East Works Eureka-Bessemer iron ore account:

Year	Purchases			Usage
	Tons	Unit Cost	Amount	(Tons)
1955	6,000	$ 9.00	$ 54,000	5,500
1956	12,000	10.00	120,000	8,000
1957	9,000	11.00	99,000	9,000

In 1955, the company started to accumulate an identical grade of Eureka-Bessemer iron ore at its South Works in anticipation of the introduction of new equipment which would use this grade of ore. In December of 1957, the company abandoned its plan for new equipment at the South Works and moved its inventory of Eureka-Bessemer iron ore that had accumulated at the South Works to the East Works. A physical inventory of this ore, as of December 31, 1957, showed 4,500 tons on hand with a cost of $52,000, composed of the following acquisitions:

Year	Tons	Unit Cost	Amount
1955	500	$10.00	$ 5,000
1956	1,000	11.00	11,000
1957	3,000	12.00	36,000
	4,500		$52,000

There was no usage of this ore at South Works during 1955, 1956, or 1957. Additional freight and handling costs account for the difference in costs between the South and East Works for comparable years.

In December of 1957, *XYZ* Steel Company obtained permission from the Treasury Department to merge, as of December 31, 1957, the above inventory, on a *lifo* basis, with the *lifo* inventory at the East Works.

During the years 1958 and 1959, the following transactions were recorded in the East Works Eureka-Bessemer iron ore account:

| Year | Purchases | | | Usage |
	Tons	Unit Cost	Amount	(Tons)
1958..............................	6,000	$12.00	$72,000	16,500
1959..............................	3,000	11.00*	33,000	2,000

* The market price of Eureka-Bessemer ore fell to $8.00 per ton by December 31, 1959.

Prepare a schedule showing the cost of Eureka-Bessemer grade iron ore used, by year, for the period 1955 through 1959, and the value and composition of the inventory as of December 31 of each year. (Limit all computations to the nearest cent.)

Problem 13-11. Duke Corporation adopted the dollar-value *lifo* method one year ago. Compute, to two decimal places, the inventories for years 1, 2, and 3. Last year's inventory (base) was $17,000.

Inventory Quantities

| Description | Year | | |
	1	2	3
X...	1,000	1,100	1,110
Y...	1,200	1,250	1,300
Z...	1,610	1,700	1,800

Inventory Prices

| Description | Year | | | |
	0	1	2	3
X....................................	$4.00	$4.04	$4.25	$4.40
Y....................................	4.60	4.65	4.85	5.05
Z....................................	5.00	5.16	5.30	5.49

Problem 13-12. Walker Company had used the retail inventory method for a number of years. In January of 1956, the company decided to change to the last-in, first-out modification of the retail inventory method. Using the following data, compute the year-end inventories for the years 1956 through 1960.

| | Year Ended December 31, | | | |
| | 1955 | | 1956 | |
	Cost	Retail	Cost	Retail
Inventory—beginning of year....	$ 20,160	$ 28,800	?	$ 31,500
Purchases......................	112,420	171,600	$114,822	170,200
Freight in.....................	3,588		3,772	
Mark-ups......................		1,870		1,780
Mark-downs...................		2,870		2,560
Sales.........................		167,900		167,260

Year Ended December 31,	Cost Ratio For Year	Inventory At Retail	Price Index*
1956.............................	—	—	102
1957.............................	72%	$35,700	105
1958.............................	71	36,850	110
1959.............................	74	32,400	108
1960.............................	75	36,960	112

* 1955 = 100.

Problem 13-13. Hosiery Specialty Shop sells nothing but ladies' stockings. As a matter of store policy, all merchandise is offered for sale at the same price per pair. This store-wide selling price is revised whenever the wholesale price of stockings changes, with the result that the percentage relationship between current wholesale prices and selling prices is constant. The business maintains perpetual inventory records and applies the last-in, first-out concept in the computation of the cost of goods sold and inventories. When the store adopted the *lifo* method, it carried an inventory of 18,500 pairs, whose average cost was 72 cents per pair.

On January 31, 1958, the inventory amounted to 18,200 pairs of stockings, whose *lifo* cost was 72 cents per pair. On January 31, 1959, the inventory was 21,800 pairs. The inventory records showed that 9,400 of these were carried at 72 cents per pair, with the remainder carried at an average cost of 88 cents per pair, which was also the average wholesale price of stockings during the year ended January 31, 1959.

The operating accounts for the year ended January 31, 1959, included:

Sales...	$101,300
Cost of goods sold.......................................	59,372

On April 5, 1959, the store was badly damaged by fire. The perpetual inventory records were destroyed, but the following data were obtained from other records:

Sales to April 5, 1959....................................	$21,000
Purchases to April 5, 1959	15,390

The wholesale price of stockings was 90 cents per pair for the period February 1, 1959 to April 5, 1959.

Compute the inventory loss, in terms of current purchase prices, caused by the fire. The inventory was completely destroyed and there was no salvage value.

Problem 13-14. Compute the inventories for Phoenix Company for the dates listed below:

December 31, 1958, 1959, and 1960.

You may assume that the company adopted the *lifo* retail method in 1958.

Year Ended December 31,	Cost	Retail
1957:		
Beginning inventory.........................	$ 23,920	$ 46,000
Purchases..................................	108,000	185,000
Freight in.................................	6,080	
Mark-ups—net...............................		2,000
Mark-downs—net.............................		3,000
Sales......................................		184,000
1958:		
Purchases..................................	124,000	230,000
Freight in.................................	9,110	
Mark-ups—net...............................		3,600
Mark-downs—net.............................		4,100
Sales......................................		224,500
1959:		
Purchases..................................	134,800	259,800
Freight in.................................	10,800	
Mark-ups—net...............................		4,100
Mark-downs—net.............................		3,900
Sales......................................		247,400

1960:
            Purchases.................................... $148,200 $270,400
            Freight in................................... 11,100
            Mark-ups—net...............................   4,200
            Mark-downs—net............................   4,600
            Sales......................................   270,900

Indexes of selling prices on December 31 were:

1957... 100
1958... 102
1959... 106
1960... 110

Assignment Material for Chapter 14

Questions

Question 14-1.   Explain the following terms:

Prior lien bonds.
Underlying bonds.
Junior bonds.

Question 14-2.   Describe a financial structure which includes an issue of collateral trust bonds.

Question 14-3.   How does a debenture bond differ from a mortgage bond?

Question 14-4.   Develop an illustration to show the entries to be made on an investor's books to record the conversion of preferred stock into common stock of the same company.

Question 14-5.   A Company invests its surplus cash, which will be needed in six months, in marketable bonds. Assume that the balance sheet date is one month before the bonds will be sold. Assume that the market quotation of the bonds at the balance sheet date is (a) 10 points below purchase price; (b) 10 points above purchase price. At what valuation should the bonds be stated in the balance sheet in each case?

Question 14-6.   Following is a transcript of all the items in the Investments account of Company A:

April 10, 1958—100 shares of Apex Foundries common stock purchased............ $4,826.25
June 25, 1958—1,180 shares of Southern Sugar preferred stock purchased........... 4,748.50
Nov. 26, 1958—100 shares of Apex Foundries common stock sold................ $2,960.00

The fair market value of Southern Sugar preferred stock on December 31, 1958, the date of your audit, as reflected by stock exchange quotations, was $6 per share; in view of this fact, the president of the company recommends that the book balance of the account be allowed to stand, since it is less than the market value of the stock remaining. The president explains that the account represented a temporary investment of cash, and that, in view of this single purpose, appreciation logically offset depreciation.

Explain what valuation should be placed on the account for balance sheet purposes.

Question 14-7.   If cost has been reduced to give recognition to a decline in the market value of securities, may cost be reinstated if the market value of the securities returns to cost?

Question 14-8.   During the course of an audit, you find the accounts shown on the following page.

Stock in A Company ($100 par per share)

1959			1959		
Jan. 2	Cost of 100 shares.....	18,000	July 1	25 shares of dividend stock sold............	3,125
Feb. 1	50 shares received as stock dividend.......	5,000			

Revenue and Expense

		1959		
		Feb. 1	Cash dividend on A Company stock...........	3,125
		1	Stock dividend on A Company stock, 50%......	5,000

What accounting errors were made?

Question 14-9.   Define a stock right.

The announcement of the granting of a stock right usually states the date on which the stock records will be closed to determine the stockholders of record to whom the rights will be issued, and also the later date when the subscriptions will be payable. For how long after the announcement will the stock be dealt in rights-on? What does this mean?

Between what two dates will the stock be dealt in ex-rights, and what does this mean?

Question 14-10.   In an audit of an investment company you find that bonds of another company are carried on the books at par although purchased at a discount, and that the discount has been credited to income as an earned commission.

What is your opinion of this matter? How would you have treated it?

Problems

Problem 14-1.   On February 26, 1959, Alvin Corporation purchased 700 shares of Thomas Corp. common stock at $20 per share plus brokerage fees of $80.

On April 16, 1959, Alvin Corporation converted 300 shares of Wilton, Inc., preferred stock into 75 shares of Wilton, Inc., common stock, par value, $10. It may be assumed that the preferred stock had a fair market value of $15 per share on this date.

Alvin Corporation, on August 3, 1959, paid an assessment of $2,000 to Thomas Corp.

Adhering to general practice, show the amount at which the above temporary investments in common stock should appear in the October 31, 1959 balance sheet, if the per-share market values on that date are as follows:

Thomas Corp. common stock....................................	$22
Wilton, Inc., preferred stock......................................	55
Wilton, Inc., common stock.......................................	75

Problem 14-2.   Between February 1, 1959 and January 31, 1960, Ravinia Corporation made the following cash expenditures for investments:

March   1—$604,000 for 5% bonds of Averrill Corporation; maturity date, June 1, 1968. Interest is payable June 1 and December 1, and accrued interest of $7,750 is included in the above payment. Bonds to be held as a long-term investment.

May   1—$54,100 for 3,000 shares of 4% preferred stock of Lupton, Inc. Brokerage fees of $300 are included in the above payment. Stock to be held as a temporary investment.

October 1—$68,000 for 6% second mortgage bonds and accrued interest of Atwood Companies. Interest is payable on February 1 and August 1. Maturity date is August 1, 1971. Par value of bonds purchased is $70,000, and they are to be held as a temporary investment.

December 1—$48,000 for shares of Mindell Corp. $5-par common stock. The purchase price includes a premium of $7 per share. Stock to be held as a long-term investment.

In addition, the directors decided on January 31, 1960, to treat $40,000 par value of Alcyon Corp. 3% bonds, due October 1, 1968, and purchased as a temporary investment on April 1, 1958, as a long-term investment. The bonds are presently carried at $40,660—the purchase price less a $1,000 write-down to market value made on January 31, 1959. Interest is payable April 1 and October 1.

(1) Show how the above investments should appear in the January 31, 1960 balance sheet. The company follows the practice of listing each long-term investment separately, while those shown as current assets are grouped and presented as one amount. The market prices on January 31, 1960, are as follows:

Averrill Corporation bonds............................ 95½% of par
Lupton, Inc., preferred stock........................... $18 per share
Atwood Companies second mortgage bonds............... 102% of par
Mindell Corp. common stock........................... $7 per share
Alcyon Corp. bonds................................... 101% of par

(2) Prepare all necessary adjusting entries as of January 31, 1960 for the Alcyon Corp. bonds.

Problem 14-3. Nederland Corporation acquired common stock of Madison Broadcasting Network as follows:

Date	Shares	Total Cost
November 9, 1958...................	150	$4,585.35
June 17, 1959.......................	80	2,538.80
September 28, 1960..................	160	4,057.60

On July 20, 1960, Madison Broadcasting Network issued a 10% stock dividend. On October 2, 1960, Nederland Corporation sold 210 shares of the stock at $27.75 per share.

The following cash dividends were declared during 1960:

April   1—40 cents per share to holders of record on April 15, payable on May 4.

September 15—50 cents per share to holders of record on September 30, payable on October 12.

December 2—70 cents per share to holders of record on December 23, payable on January 3, 1961.

No cash dividends were declared during 1959.

(1) Determine the gain or loss on the sale, computing the cost of shares sold on the basis of: (a) First-in, first-out; (b) average cost.
(2) Compute the amount of cash received during 1960 from dividends.
(3) Compute the amount of dividend income for 1960.

Problem 14-4. "Investment in Capitol Corp." appeared as follows on the books of Arcade Corporation at the end of 1958:

Investment in Capitol Corp.

1958				1958			
Jan.	2	300 shares..........	48,060	Mar. 24	1,250 shares at $36....	45,000
Mar. 13		1,200 shares.........	42,600	Apr.	1	400 shares at $36.....	14,400
Sept. 10		....	2,560				

Additional information:

(a) On January 26, 1958, 4 new shares were received in exchange for each old share.

(b) On March 22, 1958, a 10% stock dividend was issued to holders of record on March 5, 1958.

(c) On August 29, 1958, rights were issued entitling stockholders to subscribe to one share at $32 for each five shares held. On this date, rights were selling for $.75, and the stock ex-rights was selling for $35.25. During September, Arcade Corporation sold some of the rights at $1.00 (Retained Earnings was credited for the proceeds), and exercised the remainder.

(d) On October 26, 1958, a large paid-in surplus was created on the books of Capitol Corp. by a reduction of par value of the stock, and a cash dividend of $3 per share was paid on November 18, 1958, to holders of record on November 1, 1958, and charged to the newly created paid-in surplus.

Prepare all necessary adjusting entries as of December 31, 1958; assume that *fifo* procedures are applicable when securities are sold.

Problem 14-5. During 1959, Pine Point Corporation purchased common stock of Cleaver Corporation as follows:

January 23..............................	250 shares at $48 per share
April 4.................................	200 shares at $50 per share

Cleaver Corporation issued a 20% stock dividend on February 28, 1959.

Common stock rights were issued on September 18, 1959, entitling holders to purchase one new common share at $39 for each ten shares held. On September 18, 1959, the rights were being traded at $1 each, and the stock ex-rights was being traded at $49 per share.

On October 2, 1959, Pine Point Corporation sold 100 rights which pertained to the stock purchase of January 23, 1959. Sales price was $.90 per right. The corporation paid a brokerage fee of $5 on the sale of the rights. The remaining rights were exercised on October 5, 1959.

Required:

(a) Computation of gain or loss on the sale of the rights.

(b) Computation of the number of shares in each lot, and the cost basis of each lot as of January 1, 1960.

Problem 14-6. In the course of your examination of the accounts of Pearson-Wasley, Inc., for the year ended December 31, 1959, you find the following account:

Investment in bonds..	$130,560

Further investigation discloses that the balance of this account represents the total cost (including brokerage fees, $310, and accrued interest) of $130,000 par value of the 6% debenture bonds of Crucible Corporation acquired August 1, 1957. The maturity date of the bonds is March 1, 1982, and interest is paid on March 1 and September 1. The bonds are held as a long-term investment.

Since August 1, 1957, the only entries made by Pearson-Wasley, Inc., in connection with the bonds have been for the receipt of interest each six months.

Market price of the bonds as of December 31, 1959, was 98.

Prepare all necessary adjusting and correcting entries as of December 31, 1959.

Problem 14-7. "Investment in Convertible Bonds" was listed in the December 31, 1958 balance sheet of I. H. Lester Company at $25,936. Analysis of the account discloses that the securities are 20-year, 6% first convertible bonds of Ferris & Fortune, Inc. The bonds mature on January 1, 1975, and interest is payable on January 1 and July 1. The bonds were purchased two years after issue date for $25,553, including brokerage fees of $553. The bonds have been properly accounted for as long-term investments.

On June 1, 1959, I. H. Lester Company converted the bonds into $25-par common stock in the stipulated ratio of 10 shares of stock for each $1,000 bond. Accrued interest to date of conversion was paid by Ferris & Fortune, Inc. No fair market values were ascertainable on that date.

On November 1, 1959, Ferris & Fortune, Inc., issued a common stock dividend of one new share for every five shares outstanding.

As a part of a stockholder-approved reorganization on February 1, 1960, Ferris & Fortune, Inc., called in all $25-par common shares and replaced them with an equal number of new no-par shares and paid $5 per share to the stockholders as part of the exchange consideration.

I. H. Lester Company, on March 14, 1960, sold 60 shares of the new stock for $55 per share, cash.

Prepare all necessary journal entries relating to the above data for I. H. Lester Company from June 1, 1959, through March 14, 1960. Its books are closed on December 31.

Problem 14-8. Appleton Corporation, on February 1, 1958, purchased $8,000 par value of Broadway, Inc., 5% first mortgage bonds at 98 plus accrued interest. The bonds mature on June 1, 1970, and interest is payable June 1 and December 1.

$10,000 par value of Hallin Corporation 6% debenture bonds were purchased by Appleton Corporation on September 1, 1958, at 103 plus accrued interest. The bonds, dated February 1, 1958, have a 20-year life; interest is payable on February 1 and August 1.

Appleton Corporation sold $6,000 par value of Broadway, Inc., bonds at 101 plus accrued interest on July 1, 1959.

Appleton Corporation closes its books annually on October 31.

Prepare all necessary journal entries, including adjusting entries, for bond investments on the books of Appleton Corporation, from February 1, 1958 through July 1, 1959.

Problem 14-9. The Investment in Bonds account of Cary-Shaeffer, Inc., on December 31, 1959, is presented below:

Investment in Bonds, 6%, due 1/1/85

1955		1957	
Jan. 2 Cost of bonds purchased............. 189,250		Feb. 1	59,170
		1959	
		Oct. 31	53,760

These bonds, having a par value of $180,000, pay interest on January 1 and July 1.

Interest payments have been received regularly. The bonds sold on February 1, 1957 had a par value of $60,000; the bonds sold on October 31, 1959 had a par value of $50,000. The amounts credited to the Investment in Bonds account represent the proceeds from the sale of the bonds, including accrued interest.

Cary-Shaeffer, Inc., closes its books on December 31.

Prepare all necessary adjusting entries as of December 31, 1959, in connection with the bonds.

Problem 14-10.   T. T. Shine Corporation purchased $400,000 par value of Galenson Corp. 6% convertible debenture bonds, due April 1, 1968. The date of purchase was April 30, 1952, and the price was 96 plus brokerage fees of $120 and accrued interest. Interest was payable on April 1 and October 1. The bonds were held as a long-term investment.

On February 28, 1956, T. T. Shine Corporation sold $80,000 par value of the bonds for 96½ plus accrued interest. Brokerage fees of $25 were deducted from the above price.

T. T. Shine Corporation purchased, on December 1, 1956, also as a long-term investment, an additional $200,000 par value of Galenson Corp. 6% convertible debenture bonds, due April 1, 1968. The cash outlay was 102 plus brokerage fees of $65 and accrued interest.

$200,000 par value of the bonds purchased in 1952 and 60% of the bonds purchased during 1956 were converted into shares of common stock at the rate of 15 shares for each $1,000 bond. Accrued interest was paid on the conversion date, September 1, 1959. On this date, Galenson Corp. common stock had a fair market value of $66 per share.

T. T. Shine Corporation closes its books on December 31. Assume that amortization is recorded on interest and closing dates.

(a) Prepare all necessary journal entries for April 30, 1952, February 28, 1956, December 1, 1956, and September 1, 1959.

(b) At what amount should interest earned appear in the 1959 income statement? Show computations.

Problem 14-11.   The Investments account was listed at $501,540 in the November 30, 1959 trial balance of Newmark Canneries, Inc. An examination of the account revealed its composition as follows:

Fruitful Valley, Inc.:
> Common stock, 5,000 shares............................... $355,000
>> 6,000 shares were acquired during 1955 at a total cost of $80 per share. A stock dividend was issued in 1956. On June 4, 1959, 2,500 shares were sold at $50 per share. Fruitful Valley, Inc., declared a cash dividend of $3 per share on November 16, 1959, payable on December 5, 1959, to holders of record on November 27, 1959. No entries have been made for the cash dividend.

Taylor Co.:
> 6% convertible bonds ($80,000 par value) and common stock
> (506 shares)... 146,540
>> $140,000 par value of bonds were purchased as a temporary investment on August 1, 1957, for $147,850, including $2,100 accrued interest. Interest is payable semiannually, and the bonds mature in 1970. Some of the bonds were converted on June 1, 1958, into common stock in the ratio of

8 shares for each $1,000 bond. At June 1, 1958, the fair market value of the bonds was 102. Accrued interest on the bonds converted was received on that date and was credited to Interest Earned. On November 9, 1959, Taylor Co. issued stock rights to holders of common stock entitling the holders to purchase 1 additional common share at $55 for each 12 shares held. The rights expired on November 20, 1959. Some rights were exercised, some were still held by Newmark Canneries, Inc., on November 30, 1959, and the remaining rights were sold for $4 each. On the date of issuance of the rights, common shares ex-rights were selling for $115 and rights for $5. Investments was debited and Cash was credited when the rights were exercised. Cash was debited and Investments was credited when the rights were sold. Otherwise, no entries have been made for Taylor Co. securities since August 1, 1957, when the account was debited for cost less accrued interest.

$501,540

The company is desirous of having separate accounts for Fruitful Valley, Inc., common stock, Taylor Co. bonds, and Taylor Co. common stock.

Assume that no adjusting entries were made on November 30, 1957 or November 30, 1958, and that, as of November 30, 1959, the market values of the securities of Taylor Co. were in excess of aggregate cost. Prepare all necessary entries as of November 30, 1959.

Assignment Material for Chapter 15

Questions

Question 15-1. Booth Corporation organized a subsidiary, The Booth Company, investing $500,000 on January 2, 1958, for 5,000 shares of the subsidiary's stock with a par value of $100 per share. During 1958, the subsidiary's net income was $60,000 and it paid a dividend of $25,000 at the end of the year. During 1959, the subsidiary lost $15,000 and paid a dividend of $10,000. Give the entries to be made by the parent company by: (a) The legal-basis method; (b) the economic-basis method.

What was the stockholders' equity as shown by the books of the subsidiary at the end of 1959, and at what amount would the stock investment be shown on the parent's books at the end of that year by each of the accounting procedures mentioned above?

Question 15-2. What is meant by the term "minority interest"?

Question 15-3. Distinguish between funds and reserves.

Question 15-4. A company occupied a store under a ten-year lease effective January 1, 1954. Under the terms of the lease, the company was obligated to return the property to the owner at the termination of the lease in the condition existing on January 1, 1954, ordinary wear and tear excepted. The company was also required to establish a fund for such rehabilitation. How should the fund be classified in the company's balance sheet on December 31, 1954? On December 31, 1962?

Question 15-5. What is the distinction between a bond sinking fund (as strictly defined) and a bond redemption fund? Is this distinction generally made in practice?

Question 15-6. A company has established a fund for the retirement of a bond issue. Investments have been made in bonds of other companies; their present market value is somewhat below cost. Would you value them in the balance sheet at market?

Question 15-7. State four methods of stipulating the amount of the periodical contribution to be made to a sinking fund.

Why is the method of stipulating a certain number of cents per unit of output peculiarly suitable in connection with a company operating a wasting asset?

Question 15-8. What entries should be made to record the following sinking fund transactions? Reserve entries are not desired.

(a) Deposit of cash in the sinking fund.
(b) Purchase of sinking fund securities at an interest date.
(c) Purchase of sinking fund securities between interest dates.
(d) Collection of income on bonds in the fund purchased at par.
(e) Collection of income on bonds in the fund purchased at a discount.
(f) Collection of income on bonds in the fund purchased at a premium.

(g) Payment of expenses.

(h) Disposal of the sinking fund securities and cancellation of the liability at its maturity.

Question 15-9. A company operates a fund in connection with a bond issue, and purchases, from time to time, some of its own bonds. Under what conditions would it be desirable to hold the bonds alive in the fund?

Question 15-10. Discuss the legality of a provision in a preferred stock issue requiring the redemption of a stipulated amount of stock annually.

Question 15-11. List six purposes for which an industrial company might establish funds. Three of these should be current asset funds, and three noncurrent asset funds. What is the essential difference between the two types of funds mentioned above?

Problems

Problem 15-1. Present journal entries to record the selected transactions described below, relating to the sinking fund of Lakeview Apartments, Incorporated.

(1) The payment of $10,000 cash to the sinking fund.

(2) The purchase of securities for the sinking fund for $8,200, including $150 accrued interest.

(3) The payment of $75 from the sinking fund for sinking fund expenses.

(4) The sale for $28,000, including accrued interest of $60, of sinking fund securities having a book value of $26,400.

(5) The retirement, at par, of $30,000 par value of bonds payable before maturity. The bonds thus retired were issued at 103. Their carrying value at retirement was 101.

(6) The return to general cash of $920 remaining in the fund after the retirement of the bond issue.

Problem 15-2. Central Corporation organized The Center Sales Company on May 1, 1956, for the purpose of marketing the products of Central Corporation. The corporation paid $200,000 in cash to the company in exchange for the company's entire issue of authorized capital stock, consisting of 50,000 no-par shares.

The record of net income earned and dividends paid by The Center Sales Company during 1956, 1957, 1958, and 1959 appeared as follows:

Year Ended December 31,	Net Income	Cash Dividends Paid
1956	$14,000	$ —
1957	30,000	10,000
1958	36,000	24,000
1959	5,000*	10,000
* Loss.		

Required:

Tables showing the effect of the net income and dividends of The Center Sales Company on the accounts of Central Corporation, assuming that the corporation employs each of the following methods of accounting for its investment in the subsidiary: (1) Legal-basis method; (2) economic-basis method.

Problem 15-3. Action Company had been accumulating a sinking fund which was scheduled to amount to $200,000, the par value of the bond issue to be retired therewith, in 20 years. At the beginning of the twentieth year, the fund consisted of $182,400 in securities and $3,012 in cash. During the twentieth year, the securities in the fund earned 4% of their carrying value; and, at the end of the twentieth year, the regular contribution of $6,900 was made to the fund. This amount was not invested, as it was to be used to retire the maturing bond issue. The sinking fund investments were sold by the company and $179,560 was realized, after deduction of brokerage fees. The company contributed enough cash to the fund to cover the deficiency and retired the bond issue with the cash in the fund.

During the life of the bond issue the company had also been accumulating a sinking fund reserve by equal annual increments of $10,000, and the ledger shows a balance of $190,000 in the reserve as of the beginning of the twentieth year. The reserve is to be eliminated when the bonds are retired.

Prepare journal entries to record all sinking fund transactions during the twentieth year, including the retirement of the bonds and the elimination of the reserve.

Problem 15-4. Outdoor Company issued some sinking fund bonds as of January 1, 1959. The bond indenture calls for annual sinking fund deposits of $2,500 each July 1 with the City Trust Company, trustee. The trustee is required to submit annual reports as of December 31 on the sinking fund. The agreement with the trustee also provides that the trustee will credit the fund each December 31 for interest at 2% per annum on the average amount of uninvested cash in the fund during the year. Trustee's fees are to be billed separately and paid by Outdoor Company from its general cash.

The trustee's report as of December 31, 1959, included the following data:

August   1—Purchase of two $1,000 municipal bonds, 3%, February 1 and August 1, at par.
December 31—Interest on uninvested cash credited to fund, $5.
December 31—Fund balance, $2,505.

The trustee's report as of December 31, 1960, included the following data:

September 1—Purchase of three $1,000 utility bonds, 4%, March 1 and September 1, at par.
December 31—Interest collected on investments, $60.
December 31—Interest on uninvested cash credited to fund, $9.
December 31—Fund balance, $5,074.

Outdoor Company paid the trustee's fees as follows:

December 31, 1959—For 1959...................................... $ 7
December 31, 1960—For 1960......................................   22

Outdoor Company does not wish to maintain records showing the composition of the sinking fund, but it does desire to follow the principles of accrual accounting for the sinking fund.

Required:

All journal entries related to the sinking fund for 1959 and 1960.

Problem 15-5. The Rawhide Mining Company was required to create a sinking fund by the deposit of 20 cents for each ton mined; but it was also provided that the fund, at the end of any year, must be $10,000 times the number of years which have elapsed or the accumulated amounts of contributions on a tonnage basis, whichever is larger. Earnings of the fund were not to be considered in measuring this minimum. The fund earned 3% a year.

The following record of tons mined was presented:

1st year..	35,640 tons
2nd year...	44,720 tons
3rd year...	56,820 tons
4th year...	68,310 tons
5th year...	42,380 tons

Prepare a table showing (a) the annual contributions to the fund, (b) the annual amounts earned by the fund, and (c) the balance in the fund at the close of each year.

Give the journal entry to record the changes in the fund during the third year.

Problem 15-6.   On April 1, 1958, Morse Manufacturing Company acquired 17,000 of the 20,000 outstanding shares of stock of Cody Supply Corporation for $10 per share. On this date the stockholders' equity of Cody Supply Corporation included common stock of $100,000 and retained earnings of $64,500.

On April 25, 1958, Morse Manufacturing Company received a cash dividend of 50 cents per share which had been declared by Cody Supply Corporation on March 15, 1958, payable to stockholders of record on April 10, 1958.

Cody Supply Corporation reported net income of $36,000 for the year ended December 31, 1958, earned evenly during the year. No additional dividends were declared during the year 1958.

During 1959, net income of Cody Supply Corporation amounted to $34,000, and dividends declared were as follows:

April 30—5% stock dividend.
October 15—Cash dividend of 80 cents per share.

Required:

   (a) Journal entries to record the effect of the above transactions on the books of Morse Manufacturing Company, which employs the calendar year as its accounting period, using the economic-basis method.
   (b) Balance sheet presentation of the investment in Cody Supply Corporation on December 31, 1959.

Problem 15-7.   Toot Company purchased 8,000 of the 10,000 outstanding shares of $10 par value capital stock of Midwest Industries on July 1, 1957, for $11 per share. On January 2, 1959, Toot Company purchased an additional 1,000 shares for $12 per share. On January 2, 1960, Toot Company sold 500 shares from its last acquisition for $14 per share.

The earnings and dividend record of Midwest Industries subsequent to July 1, 1957, was as follows:

	Net Income* (Loss)	Cash Dividends	
		Date Paid	Amount Per Share
Year ended December 31:			
1957...................	$ 6,000	December 10	$ .50
1958...................	12,800	July 1	1.00
1959...................	26,400	September 10	1.20
1960...................	(1,000)	September 10	.50

* Assume that net income and loss accrue evenly throughout the year.

Give the journal entries on the books of Toot Company to record the data presented, except closing entries, using the economic-basis method of accounting for the investment in Midwest Industries.

Problem 15-8. City University suffered the loss of its plant department building as a result of a fire during December of 1956. As a temporary measure, Local Distribution Company agreed to co-operate with the University by leasing one of its storage buildings for the use of the plant department under the following terms:

Term of lease: Five years ending December 31, 1961.

Rental: $5,000 for the five-year term, payable in advance.

Restoration fund: $3,000 to be paid by the University at the end of the first and second years; $2,000 to be paid at the end of the third and fourth years. If the cost of restoring the building is less than $10,000, the difference is to be returned to the University. The lessor is required to establish a building restoration fund with such receipts.

Local Distribution Company received the following amounts from the University:

Date	Amount
January 2, 1957	$5,000
December 31, 1957	3,000
December 31, 1958	3,000
December 31, 1959	2,000
December 31, 1960	2,000

Local Distribution Company paid a contractor $9,940 on March 15, 1962, for work completed to restore the building to its condition as of January 1, 1957.

Give all of the entries on the books of Local Distribution Company associated with the above lease for the years 1957, 1960, and 1962. The company closes its books on December 31.

Problem 15-9. Nebraska Company issued $200,000 par value of 20-year bonds dated January 1, 1958, to be retired by means of a sinking fund accumulated by the deposit of 20 annual sinking fund installments. The company is to maintain a sinking fund reserve, the year-end balance of which is to equal the balance in the related fund. On December 31, 1958, the first installment of $10,000 is deposited with the designated trustee.

The report of the trustee received on December 31, 1959, showed the following transactions for the year 1959:

(1) The purchase of investments on April 1, as follows:

(a) $5,000 par value of 5% mortgage bonds, due July 1, 1970, (interest payable on January 1 and July 1), at 109 and accrued interest.

(b) $3,000 par value 4% debenture bonds, due March 1, 1968 (interest payable March 1 and September 1), at par and accrued interest.

(2) The regular collection of all interest.

On December 31, 1959, Nebraska Company remitted to the sinking fund trustee the second installment, $10,000 less earnings on the fund investments during 1959.

On December 31, 1960, the trustee reported the transactions for the year 1960 stated on the following page.

(1) The purchase of investments on February 1, as follows:

$10,000 par value of 3% bonds, due June 1, 1968 (interest payable on June 1 and December 1), at 97 and accrued interest.

(2) The sale of the 4% debenture bonds on April 1, at 102 and accrued interest.
(3) The regular collection of all interest.

On December 31, 1960, Nebraska Company remitted to the sinking fund trustee the third installment, $10,000 less earnings on the fund investments during 1960.

Prepare journal entries to record the transactions relating to the sinking fund, maintaining separate accounts for sinking fund cash and sinking fund investments.

Problem 15-10.   Bailey Corporation issued $300,000 of 5%, 20-year bonds on May 1, 1958, realizing $310,860, including accrued interest. The bonds were dated February 1, 1958, and interest was payable on February 1 and August 1. The indenture required the deposit of $15,000 with a trustee on January 31 of each year, beginning in 1959. The trustee had the power to purchase the corporation's bonds and hold them in the fund whenever they could be acquired below the call price of 105. The trustee agreed to credit Bailey Corporation on December 31 of each year with 2% of any funds from previous years on hand that date not used to purchase the corporation's bonds. The amount credited was to be applied as a reduction of the contribution to the trustee on the following January 31.

In the first year after the bonds were issued, the trustee was able to make the following purchase of the corporation's bonds: date, May 1, 1959; face value $12,000; price, 102¼ and accrued interest.

Give all journal entries, including closing entries, to account for the bonds and the sinking fund from the issue date of the bonds to January 1, 1960. The company operates on a calendar-year basis and desires to maintain detailed accounts showing the operation of the sinking fund.

Problem 15-11.   Use the data given in Problem 15-10 for Bailey Corporation, modified in only one respect; namely, that the fund is to operate as a redemption fund with the trustee being required to present for retirement immediately following the next interest date any bonds acquired by the fund.

Give all journal entries, including closing entries, to account for the bonds and the redemption fund from the issue date of the bonds to January 1, 1960. The company operates on a calendar-year basis and desires to maintain detailed accounts showing the operation of the redemption fund.

Assignment Material for Chapter 16

Questions

Question 16-1. What distinction, if any, should be made in the books and in the balance sheet between land held for speculation or plant enlargement and land used as a factory site?

Question 16-2. The Jordan Development Company purchases a plant which has been in use for 15 years for $75,000. This plant is in a run-down condition and it is necessary to spend $15,000 to put it into shape for use.

This expenditure is principally for repairs, painting, and similar work that would have been considered an operating charge had the plant been properly maintained by the previous owner. As auditor of The Jordan Development Company, what treatment of the $15,000 expenditure would you be prepared to approve?

Question 16-3. The Alpha Company purchased a store building for $100,000. Immediately thereafter $10,000 was spent to remodel the store front. In the opinion of competent real estate firms, the expenditure of this additional $10,000 did not add to the resale value of the building—that is, this building, which was purchased for $100,000, could not be resold for more than that amount even though the additional $10,000 was spent in improving the store front.

What is your advice regarding the accounting treatment of this $10,000 expenditure?

Question 16-4. Distinguish between ordinary and extraordinary repairs to fixed assets, and state how the two classes of repairs should be recorded.

Question 16-5. When machinery and other plant purchases are subject to cash discounts, how should the items be entered in the books? Give reasons for your answer.

Question 16-6. A contract for construction of a corporation's plant and machinery completely installed is executed. The cost in the aggregate is $200,000 and the payment is to be made in one sum within ten days after completion by the contractor and acceptance by the corporation. During the course of construction, the contractor finds that he will need funds at periodic intervals before the date set in the contract for the one and final payment. In consideration of the corporation's making such advance payments, it is mutually agreed that the total expenditure by the corporation shall be reduced to $190,000. Where should this unexpected saving of $10,000 be reflected in the books of account? Explain your reasoning.

Question 16-7. On January 2, 1958, *ABC* Company purchased display equipment for its store under the following terms: $2,000 to be paid upon installation, plus five annual payments of $1,000, the first installment note to be payable on December 31, 1958. Title to the display equipment was retained by the seller until the final payment was made. It is estimated that the display equipment will be used for ten years, with no residual value.

This same display equipment was available at a cash price of $6,600.

You are required to make all accounting entries relating to the display equipment as of January 2 and December 31, 1958, and as of December 31, 1959. For each entry, you are to give your supporting reasons. Do not consider income tax aspects of the transaction.

Question 16-8. A concern engaged in building locomotives wishes to equip its machine shop with some new machinery of standard types, and decides to have it made in its own plant by its own workmen from materials which are in stock. By this means the machinery will cost much less than if bought from outsiders. The company desires to charge its Machinery account with the current market prices of the machinery so produced, on the ground that the workmen, while making it, have been detached from other profitable employment.

Discuss this question pro and con, and state what you would advise.

Question 16-9. State clearly, but not at too great length, the proper manner of recording assets on the books of account in instances where payment has been made in stock, the face value of the stock being greatly in excess of the actual value of the assets acquired.

Question 16-10. The Chicago Manufacturing Company entered into a contract for the construction of a building. The contractor agreed to construct the building for $1,200,000 and to take as part payment the company's 4%, 20-year bonds in the amount of $1,000,000. These bonds were taken by the contractor at 90. In examining the company's accounts, you find that the discount has been charged to the property account. Discuss the propriety of this action.

Question 16-11. In 1958, Enterprise Electric Company built a new plant, chiefly with its own labor and under the direct supervision of its own engineers. Pursuant to instructions from the board of directors, a percentage of direct labor costs incident to this project was included in the cost of the new plant. Also, a portion of the salaries of the president, the general manager, and the controller were capitalized and included in the cost of the new plant.

(a) Discuss briefly the theoretical soundness of the procedure of including in the cost of construction any part of the salaries of such officials as are identified above.
(b) Indicate on what basis, if at all, any portion of such salaries should be charged to the cost of the new plant.

Question 16-12. The M Company buys the land, building, and machinery of L Company for a total price of $30,000. The building and machinery are in bad condition. It is expected that the building will be torn down and replaced and that before the machinery is used an expenditure of $10,000 will be necessary, after which it will be worth $25,000. The books of L Company show the land to have cost $2,000, the building to have cost $16,000 and to have an 80% depreciation credit, and the machinery to have cost $60,000, against which there was a $35,000 depreciation credit.

(a) How should the purchase price be recorded in the accounts of The M Company? Give reasons for your answer.
(b) How should the $10,000 cost of repairing the machinery be recorded in the accounts? Give the justification for your answer.

Question 16-13. A company, in manufacturing a machine for its own use, spends $2,000 for labor, uses material which cost $2,000, and charges the cost of construction with overhead of $1,000. The machine could not have been purchased for less than $6,000. At what price do you think the machine should be charged into the company's fixed asset account?

Question 16-14. Bonds amounting to $100,000 and bearing interest at 6% were issued to finance the purchase of a plant site and the construction of a suitable building. The land cost $20,000 and the building $180,000. Exactly a year elapsed from the date the bonds were issued until the building was ready for occupancy. How should the interest charge be journalized? Should any depreciation have been allowed during this period? If so, how should it have been journalized?

Question 16-15. *A* Company received a gift of several acres of land adjoining its present plant site. The assessed value of the property is $30,000. The day after the property had been transferred to it, *A* Company refused a firm offer of $100,000 for it. The donor had paid $150 for the land thirty years before.

Draft a journal entry to record the foregoing transaction in the accounts of *A* Company, indicating the reason for selecting whatever value, if any, you use for recording the gift.

Facts as to the valuation to be stated, other than those included in the question, may be assumed and stated, if necessary, to develop what you consider an appropriate accounting procedure and to provide adequate supporting reasons for that procedure.

Question 16-16. What items, in addition to the original purchase price, may properly be included in the cost of factory-site land?

Question 16-17. *A* acquired a building, subject to the rights of the tenants in the property, who could continue to occupy the building for six months. *A* intended to demolish the building as soon as he could obtain possession thereof, and to erect a building to be used in an entirely new enterprise. He proceeded to do this as soon as the tenants vacated the property. Is the rent collected from the tenants properly creditable to income, or should it be treated as a deduction from the cost of acquiring the old and erecting the new building?

Problems

Problem 16-1. Research Company made the following individual purchases:

From *XY* Realty Company:	
Land and buildings......................................	$ 60,000
From Acme Supply:	
Machinery and office equipment...........................	24,000
From Central Auto Agency:	
Delivery equipment.....................................	6,000

The question of apportioning the cost of the purchases among the assets arose, so an appraisal was made, shortly after the assets were purchased, which disclosed the following values:

Land..	$ 15,000
Buildings...	60,000
Machinery..	15,000
Office equipment...	10,000
Delivery equipment.......................................	5,200
Total..	$105,200

State the values properly assignable to each asset and your reasons therefor.

Problem 16-2.   Modern Company purchased some new machinery. From the following data prepare a schedule showing the proper amount to be capitalized as the cost of the new machinery.

List price of machinery......................................	$12,000
Cash discount available but not taken on purchase.............	240
Freight on new machinery.....................................	125
Cost of removing old machinery...............................	235
Installation costs of new machinery..........................	305
Testing costs before machinery was put into regular operation, including $80 wages of regular machine operator..............	165
Loss on premature retirement of old machinery.................	175
Estimated cost of manufacturing similar machinery in company's own plant, excluding overhead............................	7,500
Estimated cost of manufacturing similar machinery in company's own plant, including overhead............................	11,800

Problem 16-3.   Sooner Company was organized early in 1958. Soon thereafter it purchased a tract of land with an old building on it for $20,000 cash and assumed a liability of $900 for back taxes on the property. An appraisal revealed that the building was worth as much as the land alone. Nevertheless, the old building was torn down at a cost of $3,000. Materials salvaged from the building were sold for $860. Grading and leveling the tract of land cost $800. The company began construction of a new building during the summer of 1958. As of December 31, 1958, the company borrowed $20,000 through a one-year, 6% bank loan. The contractors estimated that the building would cost $80,000, but it was completed on December 31, 1959, at a cost of $82,000. In order to settle with the contractor, the company negotiated a 6%, ten-year mortgage for $50,000. The company occupied the building on January 2, 1960. Property taxes, based on an assessed valuation which did not include the new building, from the date of purchase to December 31, 1959, amounted to $400.

What amounts should be assigned to the land and the building, respectively, as of January 1, 1960?

Problem 16-4.   From the following information supplied by Local Printing Company, prepare a schedule showing the debits and credits that should appear in the Machinery account and the related Accumulated Depreciation account during the four years ended June 30, 1961, to account for a folding machine purchased on July 1, 1957.

The company closes its books as of June 30.

July 1, 1957—Folding machine purchased from Departure Machine Company. Invoice price, $6,700; terms, 2/10; n/30.
July 5, 1957—Paid freight on shipment of folding machine, $284.
July 8, 1957—Paid invoice dated July 1.

The machine was estimated to have a service life of 20 years, with no salvage value.

On December 31, 1958, an automatic counter was affixed to the folding machine. The counter cost $180. The company paid $23.50 to an electrician to wire the counter to the electric motor attached to the folding machine.

On July 1, 1959, the electric motor was replaced at a cost of $360. It was estimated that this was $30 above the cost of the motor purchased with the folding machine. The new motor did not alter the original estimate of service life of the folding machine. However, it did increase the speed of the machine.

During the first week of July, 1960, when the plant was closed for the vacation period, general maintenance was given to the folding machine. It was discovered that some of the rollers were showing excessive wear, and they were replaced by new-type rollers for $50. These are twice as expensive as the old-type rollers, but there is no assurance that they will improve the performance of the machine. Installation labor amounted to $15. The new rollers and other maintenance did not alter the original estimate of service life of the folding machine.

Problem 16-5. The Crandall Chamber of Commerce made a contract with Merrill Company whereby it agreed to give a vacant factory to Merrill Company provided that the company employed an average of 150 people a day for three years. If the company failed to meet this stipulation it could acquire the land and building for $50,000, the difference between this amount and the appraised value of the property being recognized as the valuation of the benefit derived by the community during the three-year period. At the time of the agreement the land was appraised for $8,000 and the building for $54,000. The estimated life of the building was 30 years.

(a) Journalize the following transactions:

    (1) Acceptance of the property at the beginning of the contract.
    (2) Payment of $1,200 in legal and other fees in connection with the contract.
    (3) Annual provision for depreciation, if any.
    (4) Transfer of title upon completion of contract.

(b) Give the journal entry made at the termination of the third year if the company failed to meet the average employment required by the contract and did not purchase the factory.

Problem 16-6. Prepare journal entries to record the following transactions involving the acquisition of fixed assets by Niles Company.

(1) Land and buildings were acquired on June 1, 1959, by the issuance of 5,200 shares of the corporation's $10 par value common stock. The seller had placed a value of $60,000 on the property, one-fourth of which was applicable to the land.
    The corporation's common stock was quoted at $11 on the stock exchange on June 1, 1959.

(2) On June 16, 1959, a tract of land, adjacent to the new plant, was acquired in exchange for an issue of 4% debenture bonds, dated June 1, 1959, with a face value of $60,000. An independent appraisal showed the value of the land to be $58,000.

(3) On July 1, 1959, an abandoned building was removed from the tract of land acquired in (2). The cost of removal, which was paid in cash, was $3,200, and $1,800 was received from the sale of salvaged materials.

(4) On July 22, 1959, a machine was purchased for cash. The invoice price thereof was $12,400 and a 2% discount was allowed for cash payment. Power and wages applicable to the breaking-in period and the testing period were estimated to be $10 and $90, respectively.

(5) On August 15, 1959, the company requested an allowance from the Machinery Manufacturing Company because the machine proved lacking in certain performance capabilities. The manufacturer granted a cash allowance of $1,000, which was received on August 31, 1959.

Problem 16-7. Midwest Flying Service expanded and improved its main hangar during 1959. The following information, related to this program, is given to you.

(1) On November 15, 1959, a 60-foot extension to the hangar was completed at a contract cost of $67,000.
(2) During construction, the following costs were incurred for the removal of the old hangar door and the installation of the new one:

   (a) Payroll costs arising from use of employees on this project, $1,243.
   (b) Payments to a salvage company for removing debris, $330.

(3) The old flooring was resurfaced with a new-type, long-lasting covering at a cost of $4,320.
(4) $1,576 was received from the construction company for assorted materials salvaged from those parts of the hangar that were torn down or remodeled during the construction of the extension.
(5) $140 of payroll costs were incurred in moving the inventory of repair parts to the new storage location in the hangar.
(6) Old heating pipes were replaced at a cost of $3,678, and new blowers were installed for $2,380.

   Cost of the old heating pipes removed was determined to be $2,800 with depreciation recorded to date of $1,830. The old blowers, which cost $1,200 and were 60% depreciated, can be sold for $200.

(7) $310 was spent on refreshments to celebrate the completion of the expansion program.

Prepare entries in general journal form to record the above facts.

Problem 16-8. (a) As of January 1, 1957, the city of Jackson made a conditional donation of land and factory buildings to Elmo Corporation. The gift was contingent upon the corporation's employing 225 men, on the average, each year for five years, at the end of which time title to the property would pass to the corporation. The land was appraised at $10,000 and the factory buildings at $60,000, with an estimated remaining life of 25 years. Expenses connected with formulating the contingent gift agreement amounted to $1,000.

Submit journal entries with explanations to record the contingent donation, the incidental expenses, the depreciation (if any) for 1957, and the passing of title at the end of the fifth year.

(b) Assume that the corporation failed to meet the employment conditions during the third year. Also assume that the corporation was able to negotiate a favorable purchase agreement with the city (the city being anxious to keep the corporation from moving to another location) and, as of January 1, 1960, took title to the land and factory buildings by the payment of $15,000 in cash and the signing of a ten-year mortgage note for $30,000.

Submit journal entries with explanations to record the lapse of the contingent gift and the purchase of the properties from the city.

Problem 16-9. Downward Company used its own facilities for the construction of certain fixed assets during 1959. The company normally apportions overhead on the basis of direct labor, but in the case of the fixed assets constructed during 1959 no overhead was assigned to the fixed assets in spite of the fact that $60,000 of direct labor was devoted to the construction work. The company used $80,000 of materials from its inventory for the construction and capitalized the completed fixed assets at $140,000.

The company's December 31, 1959 inventory of finished goods, representing 10% of the year's production, is set forth below. There is no work in process.

Direct labor...............................	$18,000
Materials...	12,000
Overhead...	16,000
Inventory of finished goods..................................	$46,000

It is estimated that the construction activities curtailed the production of finished goods during the year by 20%. The overhead for 1959, amounting to $160,000, approximately equaled the overhead incurred during 1958.

Compute two additional cost valuations for the assets constructed during 1959. Indicate which cost valuation is preferable.

Problem 16-10. Arizona Chemical Company purchases containers at $11 each. These are billed to customers at $15, but the customers are allowed to return them for credit. Customers who pay for the containers are allowed to keep them. The containers must be constantly repaired.

Give the journal entries for the following:

(1) 22,000 containers were purchased and paid for.
(2) $14,000 was spent reconditioning containers.
(3) During the year, billings of $6,420,000 were made, which included $147,000 of charges for containers.
(4) Credits were issued for 8,700 containers returned.
(5) 120 containers were scrapped as beyond repair, and salvage of $120 was obtained from them.
(6) 420 containers were paid for by customers.
(7) A physical inventory of the containers on hand and those with customers showed the following:

Quantity: 21,000
Depreciated value: 80% of cost

Problem 16-11. Spring Water Company delivers its product in large glass containers which are returnable. The containers cost $1.10 each, but are charged to customers at $1.50 each when delivered. A portion of the company's business is on a cash-and-carry basis. Cash customers are required to make a cash deposit of $1.50 for each container. It is the company's experience that cash customers return only 80% of their containers.

Data for the two years ended December 31, 1959, are as follows:

	Year Ended	
	December 31, 1958	December 31, 1959
Containers:		
Purchased............................	3,200	3,500
Delivered with charge sales.............	30,000	29,400
Used with cash sales....................	500	550
Returned by charge customers...........	26,000	26,200
Returned by cash customers.............	300	310
Destroyed during year by employees....	120	110
Collections from charge customers for unre-		
turned containers.....................	$3,600	$3,750
Charges for containers written off as uncol-		
lectible...............................		$ 30

Prepare journal entries summarizing all transactions related to containers in the two-year period, including adjusting entries and closing entries.

Problem 16-12. Rialto Theater bought some projection equipment on the installment basis. The contract price was $23,610, payable $5,610 down and $375 a month for four years. The price included interest, insurance, and service and repair charges. When the contract was completed, Rialto Theater had the equipment on its books at $23,610 and depreciation amounting to $6,744 had been set up, by charging to depreciation 10% of the balance in the projection equipment account at the end of each year.

In making the contract price, the selling company computed interest at 1% a month, not compounded, on deferred payments, 1% a year on the selling price for insurance, and a servicing and repair charge of $10 a month.

(a) What should have been the depreciated book value of the equipment at the time payments were completed?

(b) Give the journal entry to adjust the books, on the assumption that they have not been closed, at the end of the fourth year.

Problem 16-13. Chattanooga Auto Body Company operated two departments. Although it owned its own building, it charged the fair rental value of the space used to each department, in order to determine the profitableness of each department. The amount so charged was credited to the Building Expense and Income account, and the costs of ownership, such as taxes, insurance, repairs, and maintenance, were charged against this account. The balance represented what the company considered the net loss or gain from ownership of the building.

The 1959 income statement follows.

	Department A		Department B		Totals	
Sales.....................		$73,756		$84,650		$158,406
Less cost of sales:						
Materials used..........	$14,569		$18,758		$ 33,327	
Direct labor............	32,840		27,410		60,250	
Factory expense:						
Rent...............	12,000		8,000		20,000	
Other...............	14,162		14,038		28,200	
Totals.............	$73,571		$68,206		$141,777	
Less ending inventory of finished goods........	11,036	62,535	13,641	54,565	24,677	117,100
Gross profit..............		$11,221		$30,085		$ 41,306
Deduct:						
Selling expenses.........					$ 25,510	
Administrative expenses.					9,842	35,352
Net operating profit.......						$ 5,954
Building income..........						6,102
Net income..............						$ 12,056

Prepare a corrected income statement. Ignore income taxes.

Problem 16-14.   Young Corporation was organized as of January 1, 1958. In connection with the use and occupancy of its building, the corporation maintained the accounts shown below. As revealed by these accounts, the corporation rents a small portion of the building to outsiders; the space thus rented approximately doubled in 1959.

Costs Incurred in Lieu of Rent

1958			1958		
Dec. 31	Insurance............	900	Dec. 31	To Building Occupancy	8,400
31	Taxes..............	3,600			
31	Depreciation.........	3,900			
		8,400			8,400
1959			1959		
Dec. 31	Insurance............	900	Dec. 31	To Building Occupancy	8,450
31	Taxes..............	3,650			
31	Depreciation.........	3,900			
		8,450			8,450

Building Occupancy

1958			1958		
Dec. 31	Heat and light........	5,200	Dec. 31	To Rental Activities..	3,060
31	Maintenance.........	8,000	31	To Building Expense	
31	Housekeeping........	9,000		and Income........	27,540
31	Transfer.............	8,400			
		30,600			30,600
1959			1959		
Dec. 31	Heat and light........	5,310	Dec. 31	To Rental Activities..	6,930
31	Maintenance.........	8,780	31	To Building Expense	
31	Housekeeping........	12,110		and Income........	27,720
31	Transfer.............	8,450			
		34,650			34,650

Rental Activities

1958			1958			
Dec. 31	Transfer.............	3,060	Jan.	2	Rental income........	900
31	To Revenue and Ex-		April	1	Rental income........	900
	pense.............	540	July	1	Rental income........	900
			Oct.	1	Rental income........	900
		3,600				3,600
1959			1959			
Dec. 31	Transfer.............	6,930	Jan.	2	Rental income........	1,800
31	To Revenue and Ex-		April	1	Rental income........	1,800
	pense.............	270	July	1	Rental income........	1,800
			Oct.	1	Rental income........	1,800
		7,200				7,200

Building Expense and Income

1958			1958		
Dec. 31	Transfer.............	27,540	Dec. 31	Dept. A—Manufacturing................	18,000
31	To Revenue and Expense.............	12,460	31	Dept. B—Manufacturing................	12,000
			31	Selling and administrative..............	10,000
		40,000			40,000
1959			1959		
Dec. 31	Transfer.............	27,720	Dec. 31	Dept. A—Manufacturing................	18,000
31	To Revenue and Expense.............	8,280	31	Dept. B—Manufacturing................	12,000
			31	Selling and administrative..............	6,000
		36,000			36,000

The December 31, 1958 ending inventory of finished goods contained 8% of Department A's and 10% of Department B's total 1958 production. The December 31, 1959 ending inventory of finished goods contained 10% of Department A's and 15% of Department B's total 1959 production. There was no work in process at either year end.

What was the amount of error (if any) in the net income reported for 1958 and 1959?

Assignment Material for Chapter 17

Questions

Question 17-1. An electric lamp manufacturing company has charged to cost of manufacturing lamps as "depreciation" one-fourth of the value of the filament-filtering machinery acquired a little more than one year ago. The life of the machinery is estimated to be 10 years, but owing to discovery by a competitor of a new process of metal pulling which, while still imperfect, promises to revolutionize the lamp industry, the machinery in question will probably be obsolete within a period of three years. State what you would say concerning the propriety of making such a charge to cost of manufacturing.

Question 17-2. The chief engineer of a manufacturing firm suggested in a conference of the company's executives that the accountants should speed up depreciation on the machinery in Department 3 because improvements are making those machines obsolete very rapidly, and it is desirable to have a depreciation fund big enough to cover their replacement. Discuss the issues raised by the chief engineer.

Question 17-3. Should physical and recorded depreciation be equal in amount at all times?

Question 17-4. The management of a corporation suggests the reduction or elimination of depreciation charges on plant and machinery on these grounds:

(a) Nothing need be written off, since the plant is actually more valuable than it was when acquired, owing to a rise in the cost of similar machinery.
(b) Repairs have been fully maintained, and the plant is as good as ever.
(c) To charge depreciation to the same extent in a poor year as in a good year will prevent a dividend in the poor year, with a consequent objection from stockholders and a fall in the price of the shares.

Combat these arguments.

Question 17-5. What are the three principal factors to be considered in determining the amounts to be provided for depreciation?

Question 17-6. A vacant piece of land is purchased for use as a parking lot. In addition to the cost of the unimproved land, expenditures are made for grading, drainage, paving, curb and gutter, marking of parking spaces, and lighting installations. Which, if any, of these costs are subject to depreciation? Explain the general principle which is involved.

Question 17-7. The owner of a new office building estimates the life of the building to be 50 years if it is adequately maintained and repaired. The owner objects to the use of straight-line depreciation because, he says, his maintenance and repair costs are lowest in the early years and his rental income will be largest during this period, whereas in the late period of the building's life, the maintenance and repair costs will increase and rents decrease. Outline in detail the features of two depreciation methods which might possibly avoid his objections

809

to the usual depreciation method. State carefully how these methods might overcome the owner's objections, and also state any objections to the use of the depreciation procedures proposed.

Question 17-8. In determining the results of the operations of a company whose business requires the use of a large number of perishable tools, how would you treat depreciation on them?

Question 17-9. Is it good accounting to base the amount of the annual depreciation upon the amount of net income before depreciation, making large provisions in good years and small provisions in poor years?

Question 17-10. What do you understand by the retirement basis of accounting as applied to fixed assets, particularly of public utility companies? Do you approve of such basis? State your reasons.

Question 17-11. Because of its large volume of business, Hall Company is operating its plant 70 hours a week instead of the 35 hours a week which it usually operates. The company computes depreciation on a straight-line basis. Because of the increased rate of operation, the treasurer has suggested that depreciation rates should be doubled.

Discuss the suggestion of the treasurer, including a full discussion of the factors that should be considered by the company. Do not give consideration to income tax effects.

Question 17-12. A small manufacturing company owned one factory building in 1954 with a net depreciated cost of $90,000. Machinery and equipment was carried at $120,000. Because of expanding business in 1955 a new building was constructed at a cost of $150,000 and $210,000 of equipment was installed in it. In the period from 1955 to the end of 1958 some new equipment was put into the old building and the company continued to operate both plants. Depreciation has been computed on a straight-line basis.

In 1959, the company shut down the old plant because of lack of orders. They propose that they should quit taking depreciation on the old building and machinery. They suggest that, while the old plant is useful, it is not in use and is not wearing out. They also suggest that to take depreciation on it increases their cost, overvalues inventory, and places them in a poor competitive position to bid for business since their costs are high.

You are to give a full discussion of their proposal and of their arguments.

Question 17-13. Using simple assumed figures for life expectancy, cost, and salvage, show by a brief schedule the computation of composite life.

Problems

Problem 17-1. Pounce Company acquired a machine at a cost of $9,960. It was estimated that it would have a scrap value at the end of its life of $300. Prepare depreciation tables for 6 years and submit journal entries to record depreciation for the third year under each of the following methods:

(a) Sum of years' digits; estimated life—6 years.
(b) Working hours; estimated life in working hours—19,320 hours.
(c) Production; estimated life in units of product—77,280 units.

Additional data are given on the following page.

Year	Working Hours	Units of Product
1	2,900	11,600
2	3,250	13,000
3	3,100	12,400
4	3,000	12,000
5	3,410	13,640
6	3,660	14,640

Problem 17-2. Minnesota Corporation began business with the following fixed assets:

Asset	Cost	Estimated Scrap Value	Estimated Life In Years
Land.....................................	$25,000		
Building..............................	70,000	$1,000	25
Machinery...........................	41,930	2,000	10

The company has been in operation 5 years. Instead of recording depreciation on individual fixed assets on the straight-line basis, it adopted a policy of relating depreciation charges to net income by charging as depreciation each year an amount equal to 10% of that year's net income before depreciation. This was recorded by a debit to Depreciation and a credit to Accumulated Depreciation—Fixed Assets.

The net income before depreciation for each of the 5 years was as follows:

Year	Net Income Before Depreciation
1...	$20,000
2...	37,500
3...	52,000
4...	73,000
5...	68,000

You are to submit the journal entry to correct the books after the close of the fifth year, establishing a separate accumulated depreciation account for each asset, using the straight-line method for the building and the sum of years' digits method for the machinery.

Problem 17-3. The Milwaukee Tile Company bought a machine for $16,350. The freight in was $530 and the installation cost was $1,420. The estimated scrap value was $300 and the estimated life was 15 years. At the end of the second year, accessories costing $780 were added to the machine. They neither prolonged its life nor did they have any additional scrap value. State what the depreciation will be for the third year under each of the following methods of computing depreciation.

(a) Straight-line method.
(b) Working hours method. Total estimated hours, 36,000. Used the first year, 2,500; the second year, 2,200; the third year, 2,750.
(c) Production method. Total estimated units of production, 67,500. Produced the first year, 4,700; the second year, 4,400; the third year, 5,100.
(d) Constant rate on a diminishing value method.

$$r = 1 - \sqrt[15]{300 \div 18,300} = .2397$$
$$r = 1 - \sqrt[15]{300 \div 16,350} = .1657$$
$$r = 1 - \sqrt[13]{300 \div 11,358.43} = .2439$$
$$r = 1 - \sqrt[13]{1,080 \div 16,350} = .2648$$

(e) The sum of the years' digits method.

Problem 17-4. Using the following data, prepare a lapsing schedule covering the first 8 years of the business life of Georgia Corporation. The corporation was organized as of January 1, 1957.

	Asset					
	Acquisitions				Disposals	
Date	Description	Use Life	Cost	Scrap	Identity	Date
1/1/57	A	4 years	$3,600	—	A	12/31/60
7/1/57	B	5 years	4,000	—	B	12/31/61
4/1/58	C	6 years	5,000	$200	C	7/ 1/62
7/1/59	D	10 years	8,000	500		
1/1/61	E	4 years	4,200	—		
10/1/62	F	5 years	6,000	500		

Problem 17-5. A schedule of fixed assets owned by Stewart Manufacturing Corporation is presented below:

	Factory Building	Plant Equipment	Small Tools	Patterns
Total cost.....................	$260,000	$240,000	$78,000	$48,000
Estimated scrap value..........	20,000	16,000	6,000	—
Estimated life—in years........	40	20	8	4

(a) Determine the composite life of the assets listed above.
(b) Prepare journal entries for the depreciation of each class of asset for the third year of service life, using the following methods:

Factory building—Straight-line.
Plant equipment—Constant rate of 10% on declining balance.
Small tools—Sum of years' digits.
Patterns—Diminishing rates on cost: 40-30-20-10%.

Support the journal entries with appropriate computations.

Problem 17-6. Surface Mining Company purchased a tract of land containing veins of coal near the surface for $363,000. The tract is estimated to contain 990,000 tons of coal; it is expected that the quantity mined the first year of operations will be one-half of that mined in each succeeding year.

Fixed installations are set up at an additional cost of $77,000. The above transactions took place during the latter part of 1958. Equipment was purchased early in January of 1959 for $176,000, and operations were started as soon as employees were hired and trained.

It is estimated that the fixed installations could be used for 20 years. However, they will, of necessity, be abandoned when the coal deposit is exhausted. The equipment is estimated to have a useful life of 8 years and can be transferred conveniently to another location.

By the end of 1959, 90,000 tons had been mined and sold. The company has adopted the production method of depreciation.

Give the adjusting entries for depletion and depreciation as of December 31, 1959.

Problem 17-7. Border Company invests $60,000 in special-purpose machinery useful only in the manufacture of X, a new product. The management of the company is uncertain about the long-range consumer demand prospects for the product, and accordingly adopts the declining balance depreciation method with a 30% rate. It is expected that the machinery will have no resale or trade-in value and that its value as scrap will be only $200.

(a) Compute the carrying value of the special-purpose machinery at the end of the third year.

(b) Assume that there is no further demand for product X and that the company discontinues its manufacture at the end of the third year. Describe three accounting procedures that might be employed to give recognition to the obsolescence of the machinery at the end of the third year.

Problem 17-8. Submit the journal entry for depreciation for the year 1959 for the following asset, using the depreciation methods indicated below.

Date Acquired	Cost	Scrap Value	Estimated Useful Life
July 1, 1958	$110,000	$11,000	10 years

(a) Sum of years' digits method.
(b) Declining balance method, using a depreciation rate twice that of the straight-line rate.

Problem 17-9. Since Dodge Corporation was organized, as of January 1, 1953, it has purchased nine special-order delivery trucks. The following summary shows the facts relating to the acquisitions and disposals of the delivery trucks.

Truck Number	Date Acquired	Cost	Date Sold	Proceeds
1	January 2, 1953	$5,000	January 4, 1957	$510
2	January 2, 1954	5,000	January 10, 1958	505
3	January 2, 1955	5,000		
4	January 2, 1955	5,500	January 3, 1959	540
5	January 2, 1956	6,000	October 2, 1959	700
6	January 2, 1957	6,000		
7	July 1, 1958	6,400		
8	January 2, 1959	6,500		
9	October 1, 1959	6,800		

The management of the corporation has been operating with the expectation that the trucks could be sold at the end of four years, which is considered to be the average useful life of the trucks, for about 10% of cost.

Compute the depreciation charge for 1959 under the following methods:

(a) Straight-line.
(b) Declining balance, using a 40% rate.
(c) Retirement.
(d) Replacement.

Problem 17-10. The Canada Oil Corporation purchased a lease on potential oil property for $160,000, and spent $144,000 drilling producing wells on the property. It was estimated that the oil potential of the property was 1,800,000 barrels with a discovery value of $720,000.

During 1959, the first year of operations, 90,000 barrels of oil were produced, of which 81,000 were sold. Operating costs incurred during the year were $40,000.

Required:

(a) Set up the discovery value of the oil property and determine the cost of oil produced on this basis.

(b) Journal entries to record and amortize all costs and to adjust unrealized appreciation.

Problem 17-11. The Bishop Tungsten Company bought a mine estimated to have deposits totaling 3,500,000 tons for $315,000. The company spent $52,500 on developments and improvements at the mine. Of these, two-thirds were estimated to last until the mine was exhausted and the rest were estimated to last five years. During the first year of operations, costs, aside from depreciation and depletion, were $540,000. Of these costs, $80,000 were for general and selling expense. The company mined 125,000 tons, of which it sold 115,000 tons for $620,000.

They ask you to determine:

(a) The net income for the year.

(b) The amount legally available for dividends.

Problem 17-12. Everystate Trucking Company maintains an inventory of replacement truck tires. On the date of organization of the company, July 1, 1955, a working complement of replacement tires was acquired. Subsequent purchases were made to replace worn-out tires and to adjust the number of tires on hand to current operating needs. It is the company's policy to give all used tires one retreading, unless the casing has been damaged. Retreaded tires are placed in the inventory of replacement tires. They are used as outside tires on dual wheels.

The company's annual accounting period ends June 30.

A summary of transactions involving the inventory of replacement tires during the first four years of the company's operations appears below:

	Purchases		Retirements		Estimated Investment in Replacement Tires
Date	Units	Unit Cost	Units	Unit Salvage	on Hand at End of Year
July 1, 1955	300	$30.00			
Year ended:					
June 30, 1956	120	30.50	105	$1.80	$8,600.00
June 30, 1957	100	31.00	115	2.00	7,800.00
June 30, 1958	140	31.80	135	2.10	7,900.00
June 30, 1959	170	32.00	150	2.05	8,100.00

You may assume that purchases and retirements are cash transactions.

Prepare entries in general journal form to record all transactions indicated by the preceding summary, using the following methods of computing depreciation:

(a) Inventory method.

(b) Retirement method.

(c) Replacement method.

Problem 17-13. The Royal Company purchased a lumber tract in April of 1956 for $5,440,000. A cruise had shown that it held 1,460,000 M feet of lumber. It was estimated that the land, without trees, was worth $60,000. No lumbering operations were conducted on this property until 1958. During the intervening period, the company spent $73,100 protecting the property.

In January of 1958, another cruise was made which showed that the available timber had increased by 182,500 M feet. In recognition of this new information, the company added $722,700 to the carrying value of the tract.

Early in 1958, the company spent $98,550 on a railroad expected to last, with ordinary maintenance, until the tract was logged. The company took out 150,000 M feet during the year 1958, of which all but 7,500 M feet were sold at a price of $13 per M feet. The operating costs, exclusive of depletion and depreciation, were $937,000; selling and general expenses were $186,000.

Required:

(a) Income statement for 1958.
(b) The journal entry to record realized appreciation for 1958.
(c) The journal entry to record a dividend declaration of $400,000, as of December 31, 1958. Assume that the company had no retained earnings as of December 31, 1957.

Problem 17-14. General Insurance Agency maintains a separate account in its ledger for typewriters. New typewriters cost $200. As a general rule, the agency uses typewriters for four years and each year sells a number of its oldest typewriters when new ones are being purchased. It has been the agency's experience to realize about $44 from the sale of each such old machine.

Purchases and sales of typewriters for a five-year period are summarized below.

Year	Purchases of New Typewriters	Sales of Old Typewriters	Proceeds from Old Typewriters
1955	24	14	$560 — 100 Loss
1956	18	18	738
1957	20	20	880
1958	25	22	990
1959	22	24	960

You may assume that all purchases and sales of typewriters occur early in January.

As of December 31, 1954, the agency owned 80 typewriters; 15 were four years old, 18 were three years old, 22 were two years old, and 25 were one year old.

Prepare a schedule of the annual depreciation charges for the years 1955 through 1959, under the following depreciation plans:

(a) Straight-line method.
(b) Retirement method.
(c) Replacement method.

Problem 17-15. The Sulphur Company, organized January 1, 1954, was formed to mine, refine, and sell sulphur. To that end it secured a 20-year lease on 500 acres of known sulphur deposits, referred to as Section A, and 500 acres, referred to as Section B, of potential but undiscovered sulphur deposits. It was estimated after engineers' survey that there were 5,000,000 tons of sulphur under Section A at the time of acquisition. Mine reports showed the number of tons taken out by years as follows: 1954, 250,000; 1955, 300,000; 1956, 500,000; 1957, 800,000; 1958, 1,000,000. Year-end inventories in tons of crude sulphur were as follows: 1954, 50,000; 1955, 60,000; 1956, 75,000; 1957, 100,000; 1958, 200,000.

The statement on page 816 was prepared by the company's bookkeeper.

This statement is correct and all accounting requirements have been met, except that the company has never provided for amortization or depletion, since, in the words of the company's president, "it had discovered from prospecting more new deposits than it had mined." Nor has provision been made for depreciation or obsolescence of plant and equipment acquired January 1, 1954, which are

THE SULPHUR COMPANY
Balance Sheet
December 31, 1958

Cash..................... $	500,000	Current liabilities, including	
Receivables................	300,000	interest and taxes accrued $	150,000
Inventory of crude sulphur at		Bonds payable.............	300,000
cost of mining and extrac-		Capital stock.............	1,000,000
tion (Market value, $200,-		Earned surplus...........	610,000
000)...................	180,000	Revenue and expense, 1958.	230,000
Leaseholds—at cost........	600,000		
Section A—$500,000			
Section B—$100,000			
Plant and equipment.......	460,000		
Development—Section A...	200,000		
Prospecting—Section B.....	50,000		
	$2,290,000		$2,290,000

estimated to have a useful life greater than the 20-year period of the leases and a scrap value of $50,000.

The company had a survey made of Section B by competent engineers. This survey indicated sulphur deposits of 3,200,000 tons on January 1, 1958, which were estimated to have a fair value underground of eleven cents per ton. It was decided to increase the book value of the leasehold, now carried at $100,000, to that value. It was also decided that the company would charge the operations with depletion on the basis of the increased value.

Of the total 1958 production of 1,000,000 tons, 400,000 tons were mined from Section B, all of which were sold in 1958. Prior to December 31, 1958, the book-keeper had written down development costs by $50,000, charging this amount to Earned Surplus.

From the foregoing data prepare:

Journal entries setting up the proper allowances and reserves and making necessary adjustments to other accounts.

Columnar worksheet showing the changes caused by the adjustments.

Revised balance sheet.

Assignment Material for Chapter 18

Questions

Question 18-1. A manufacturing company purchased machinery five years ago at a cost of $15,000 and charged off 10% each year for depreciation. To meet requirements of the business, new and improved machinery was installed at a cost of $25,000, which was charged to the Machinery account, and the old machinery was sold for $10,000, which was credited to the Machinery account. Is this treatment of the matter correct? If you think otherwise, give your reasons.

Question 18-2. On July 15, 1959, Oldham Products Company sold its factory site and building for $1,000,000 cash, realizing a book gain of $400,000, and erected a more modern plant on the outskirts of the city at a cost of $1,300,000. In view of the fact that the capacity of the new plant is no greater than that of the old, the president of the company suggests that the gain be credited to the cost of the new plant; in this way, future depreciation charges will be reduced and income tax will be avoided.

Write a letter to the president, giving your views on the matter.

Question 18-3. List four depreciation policies that may be applied in connection with additions and disposals of fixed assets.

Question 18-4. The following information relates to the purchase of an asset which was paid for by a trade-in of an old asset and the balance in cash.

List price of new asset....................................	$10,000
Cash payment...	5,800
Cost of old asset..	8,000
Depreciation reserve—old asset...........................	5,000
Second-hand market value—old asset......................	3,600
Trade-in allowance......................................	4,000

You are to prepare journal entries to show three different methods of recording the transaction.

Question 18-5. What is an "involuntary conversion"? Develop an illustration to demonstrate how an involuntary conversion is handled in the accounts.

Question 18-6. A corporation has been engaged in business for three years, with an investment in machinery totaling $75,000 during that time. No depreciation has ever been provided. At the end of the third year, the directors decide that an annual charge of 5 per cent of the cost of the machinery should have been made for depreciation, and they now propose to set up such a reserve. State how the entry should be made.

Question 18-7. A new client has certain fully depreciated tangible fixed assets which are still used in his business.

(a) Discuss the possible reasons why this may have happened.
(b) Mention alternative accounting procedures that might be applied.

Question 18-8. How do you believe fully depreciated assets should be handled in the accounts?

Question 18-9. The *G* Corporation carries insurance considerably in excess of the book value of its fixed assets because of the increased cost of replacement. One of its buildings was destroyed by fire and the company collected an amount approximately three times the carrying value of the asset. It then used the entire proceeds from the insurance to construct a similar building. In your examination of the accounts you find that the company accountant, following instructions from the company president, has charged annual depreciation on the new building at the same amount as previously charged on the old building, although depreciation computed on the cost of the new building would be almost double the previous depreciation. The president's argument is that the company must be consistent. Discuss the propriety or impropriety of the procedure followed by the company. Do not consider income tax effects.

Question 18-10. A plant costing $1,000,000, against which depreciation of $400,000 has accumulated, has been appraised to be worth (sound value) $900,000. The appraisal shows reproduction value new of $1,500,000, with estimated depreciation of $600,000. The directors wish to show the appreciated value in the accounts. Draft necessary entries.

If the appraisal showed replacement cost new of $1,200,000, depreciation $300,000, and sound value $900,000, and the directors wished to record the appraisal and to adjust the accounts to reflect the depreciation percentage, how should the entries be made?

Question 18-11. It has been argued that if the replacement cost of fixed assets is greatly in excess of their cost, depreciation should be computed on the replacement values, so that the accumulated depreciation will be equal to the replacement value when the time arrives for abandoning the old property and acquiring new. It is contended that, if this procedure is followed, the company will have sufficient cash to make replacements without impairing the capital. State your opinion with regard to this matter.

Question 18-12. A corporation had its fixed assets valued by an expert, and the appraisal disclosed a valuation in excess of book value. The excess was credited to Retained Earnings, and as of the same date the directors declared a stock dividend, common on common, resulting in a charge to Retained Earnings in an amount equal to the excess credited thereto as a result of the appraisal. Do you see any objection to this procedure?

Question 18-13. State the arguments which have been advanced by proponents of the theory of basing depreciation on replacement costs and discuss objections which others have expressed to this theory.

Problems

Problem 18-1. The Delivery Trucks account in the ledger of Grand Corporation for the year 1958 contains the following entries:

Debits

January	1......Trucks 1, 2, 3, 4 at $3,000....................	12,000
May	1......Truck 5..................................	4,000
September	1......Truck 6..................................	5,000

Credits

September	1......Truck 2..................................	1,800
October	1......Truck 4..................................	1,600

The Accumulated Depreciation—Delivery Trucks account had a balance of $5,600 on January 1, 1958.

Upon analyzing the entries in the account, you find the following facts:

  (a) Truck 5 replaced Truck 1, which was junked. Depreciation accrued on January 1 for Truck 1 amounted to $1,400. Truck 5 was purchased for cash.
  (b) Truck 2 was traded in for $1,800 on the purchase of Truck 6, costing $5,000; the difference was paid in cash. Depreciation accrued on Truck 2 on January 1 amounted to $600.
  (c) Truck 4 was totally destroyed in an accident on October 1. Accumulated depreciation on this truck amounted to $1,000 on January 1; $1,600 was recovered from the insurance company.

The rate of depreciation is 25% per year. The company follows the practice of computing depreciation for fractional periods to the nearest full month.

Give journal entries to adjust the accounts in accordance with the above facts, and show balances of the asset and accumulated depreciation accounts as of December 31, 1958.

Problem 18-2. Precision Company owns three machines. The cost and accumulated depreciation data relating to the machines are shown below.

Machinery

1955		
Jan. 2	Machine A.........	3,000.00
1956		
Aug. 1	Machine B.........	4,000.00
1957		
April 1	Machine C.........	5,000.00

double-declining
20% rate

Accumulated Depreciation—Machinery

1955	
Dec. 31	600.00
1956	
Dec. 31	880.00
1957	
Dec. 31	1,604.00
1958	
Dec. 31	1,783.20

On different dates during 1959, the machines are traded in on new machines. The company pays cash, less the trade-in allowance, for each new machine. Data on the trade-ins are presented below.

Machine Traded In	Date of Trade-in	List Price of New Machine	Trade-In Allowance on Old Machine	2nd Hand Mkt Cash Value of Old Machine	Accounting Method to Be Followed
A....	Feb. 22, 1959	$3,200	$1,400	$1,200	Income tax rule
B....	May 1, 1959	4,300	1,825	1,700	Recognize cash value of old asset
C....	Oct. 10, 1959	5,500	2,850	2,400	Treat trade-in allowance as selling price of old asset

Give the entries required at the time of each trade-in.

Problem 18-3. Snow Corporation purchased a machine on July 1, 1956, for $51,000. It was estimated to have a life of 12 years with a $3,000 trade-in value. During 1959, it became apparent that this machine would be useless after January 1, 1965, and that it would have no trade-in or salvage value. The chief accountant was instructed to make the necessary corrections when making the annual adjustments for 1959. The corporation closed its books on December 31 of each year.

Required:

Relevant journal entries on December 31, 1956, 1957, 1959, and 1960, assuming the following:

(a) Past depreciation is to be corrected in 1959.
(b) Past depreciation is not to be corrected in 1959.

Problem 18-4. On January 2, 1954, Ripple Company purchased a machine for $17,550. It was estimated that this asset would have a scrap value of $500 after a service life of 10 years. The company closes its books on a calendar-year basis and records depreciation on its assets by the sum of years' digits method.

Early in 1958, it became apparent that the original use-life and scrap-value estimates were excessive. On the basis of the information available in 1958, it was evident that the original estimates should have been for an 8-year service life and a $90 scrap value.

The controller of the company has instructed the chief accountant to make any required corrections or revisions when preparing adjusting entries for 1958.

Submit all journal entries relating to the above information as of December 31, 1957, 1958, and 1959, assuming the following:

(a) Past depreciation is to be corrected in 1958.
(b) Past depreciation is not to be corrected in 1958.

Problem 18-5. Vermont Company acquired land and a building on October 1, 1952, at a cost of $88,000, of which $8,000 was allocated to land. The December 31, 1958 balance sheet showed that depreciation on the building had accumulated to $10,000. On April 1, 1959, the building was completely destroyed by fire.

Show all entries that would appear in the company's books as a result of the fire, the settlement by the insurance company, and the replacement of the building as of July 1, following income tax regulations relating to involuntary conversions,

(a) If $75,000 is received from the insurance company and $80,000 is invested in the new building.
(b) If $72,000 is received from the insurance company and $70,000 is invested in the new building.
(c) If $70,000 is received from the insurance company and $65,000 is invested in the new building.

Problem 18-6. On January 1, 1944, Layden Company purchased factory property for $110,000, of which $10,000 was assigned to the Land account. Straight-line depreciation was provided on the basis of an estimated life of 20 years with no scrap value.

On June 30, 1948, an independent appraisal indicated a replacement value new of $120,000 for the building and a remaining useful life of 20½ years.

Give the entries that should have been made as of June 30, 1948, assuming that the directors of the company ordered that the appraisal be given recognition in the accounts. Also give the December 31, 1948 and 1949 entries for depreciation and the piecemeal realization of the appraisal increment.

Problem 18-7. Jupiter Corporation purchased a building on January 2, 1940, for $81,000. The seller retained title to the land but granted Jupiter Corporation a 50-year lease of the premises for an annual rental. The expected useful life of the building was 30 years with no scrap value. As of January 1, 1958, an appraisal was made and recorded which indicated that the cost, new, of this building would be $121,500, and it was determined that the building would have a useful life of 18 years from that date. On March 31, 1960, the building was sold for $85,000, which was received in cash.

Required:

Journal entries to record the following:

   (1) The appraisal, as of January 1, 1958, assuming that the appraisal is to be recorded in separate accounts.
   (2) Depreciation of the building for 1958, assuming that the new estimate of remaining life is adopted, but that past depreciation is not to be corrected.
   (3) Amortization of appraisal increment as of December 31, 1958.
   (4) Depreciation for 1959 and 1960 and all other entries required at the time of the sale.

Problem 18-8. *XYZ* Corporation purchased a new machine in 1958, trading in an older machine of a similar type. The old machine, which was acquired in 1945, cost $77,250. However, it was written up $47,750 to $125,000 as of December 31, 1949, and Accumulated Depreciation—Appraisal Increase and Unrealized Increment per Appraisal accounts were credited. In subsequent years the unrealized increment account was partially amortized.

The old machine had an estimated useful life of 20 years, and reappraisal of the old machine did not affect its estimated life. *XYZ* Corporation takes one-half year of depreciation in years of acquisition and disposal.

The terms of the purchase provided for a trade-in allowance of $25,000 and called for a cash payment of $125,000 or 12 monthly payments of $11,000 each. *XYZ* Corporation chose to accept the latter alternative. Other expenses incurred in connection with the exchange were as follows:

Payroll charges:	
Removal of old machine...............................	$ 800.00
Repairs to factory floor................................	700.00
Installation of new machine...........................	900.00
Invoices received:	
Sales engineer who supervised installation, 40 hours at $10.00.	400.00
Hotel, meals, travel, etc., for sales engineer................	200.00
Freight in—new machine...............................	1,100.00

Prepare journal entries occasioned by the acquisition of the new asset on a basis acceptable for federal income tax purposes.

Problem 18-9. Holloway Company has used the sum of years' digits method in its depreciation of machinery since the company was organized as of January 1, 1953. At that time the company also adopted the following additional policies:

Scrap value, being insignificant in amount, was to be ignored.
A six-year estimated useful life was determined to be reasonable.

A full year's depreciation was to be taken during the year of acquisition and no depreciation was to be taken in the year of disposal.

Machinery was purchased by the company in 1953 at a cost of $378,000 and additional machinery was purchased in 1955 for $75,600.

Early in 1957, the company revised its estimate of useful life for machinery. Its experience indicated that eight years would be a more realistic estimate.

In 1958, machines costing $37,800 in 1955 were damaged in an accident and had to be discarded. The company realized $60 for their scrap value.

Required:

(a) A schedule showing the annual depreciation charges for the years 1953 through 1959, to the nearest dollar, (1) assuming that the revision is handled by a change in subsequent depreciation charges; and (2) assuming that accumulated depreciation is adjusted in 1957.

(b) The entry for the 1958 retirement of machinery under both assumptions.

Problem 18-10. The Trucks account of Tonawanda Metal Working Company had been poorly kept. Depreciation had been credited directly to the asset account and no entries were ever made for retirements or sales. Furthermore, the rates used were excessive. The December 31, 1958 balance of $27,314.56 was meaningless.

In order to straighten out this situation, the company has requested you to adjust the books to conform to the following policy: straight-line depreciation with a 5-year useful life and a scrap value equal to 10% of cost.

The costs of the trucks on hand January 1, 1958, and their expired lives were:

Truck #11	$8,240	5 years old
#12	6,140	3 years old
#13	3,520	4½ years old
#14	5,675	3 years old
#15	6,300	6 months old

On July 1, 1958, the company purchased truck #16, which had a list price of $7,200. Truck #12 was traded in on truck #16, and the company paid a cash difference of $4,300, which was the amount charged to the Trucks account.

The accounts have not been closed for 1958. The company had credited the Trucks account with 25% depreciation on the opening balance and had taken one-half the annual rate on truck #16.

Give the journal entries to correct the company's accounts.

Problem 18-11. The management of Company *A* has asked you to prepare analyses of the property and related accumulated depreciation accounts of that company and its subsidiary, Company *B*, for the year ended December 31, 1959, showing the following information:

Property accounts:
  Additions.
  Retirements.
  Sales.
  Intercompany transfers.

Accumulated depreciation accounts:
  Depreciation provisions.
  Charges for assets retired.
  Intercompany transfers.

The following facts are available:

	Company A	Company B
Property account balances:		
December 31, 1958	$180,921.37	$39,865.42
December 31, 1959	209,763.57	32,801.30
Accumulated depreciation:		
December 31, 1958	78,756.29	29,753.75
December 31, 1959	113,649.75	29,947.56
Depreciation expense for 1959	39,758.29	9,547.67

The following transfer took place during the year from Company B to Company A:

Property	$11,570.21
Accumulated depreciation	9,178.26

Company A sold a piece of land at cost to an outside interest for $10,000.

You may assume that the companies use the group basis in the application of their depreciation programs.

Problem 18-12.   You are making an examination of The Insulation Company as of December 31, 1958, which was the end of its first year of operation. All accounts except those for fixed assets and depreciation have been reviewed and necessary adjustments made. You find that the depreciation recorded for the year and the fixed asset accounts do not take into account the following facts:

1. Heavy flood damage to fixed assets was sustained during the period June 30–July 2, 1958. A written appraisal by competent appraisers as of July 5, 1958, contained the following information:

   a. The fixed assets were appraised at the following net sound values:

	Before Flood	After Flood
Land	$ 2,500	$ 2,500
Building	40,000	25,000
Equipment	13,000	10,000
Trucks and autos	21,000	21,000
	$76,500	$58,500

   b. The estimated lives on which depreciation charges had been based were considered appropriate. However, the appraisers reported that, in their opinion, contemplated rehabilitation of the building would not restore it to its original structural condition and that damage to equipment would shorten the equipment's useful life. Accordingly, they recommended that depreciation from July 1, 1958, be based on the following estimated remaining lives: building, 25 years; equipment, 8 years; trucks and autos, no change.

2. Balances in the fixed asset accounts represent original cost, and no additions or reductions had been made during the year.

3. Unallocated labor cost, cost of supplies used, and other variable overhead in the amount of $15,000 had been charged to Overhead Expenses. $12,000 of this amount is for time spent by employees and the variable overhead costs incurred in rehabilitating the building. The remainder is for clean-up expense for the building and equipment.

4. Upon receiving early warning of the flood, the company used its trucks and autos to transport the bulk of its materials on hand to higher ground.

Thereby, serious damage to materials and transportation equipment was avoided.

5. Regular operations were suspended during July. Rehabilitation and cleaning up of property were completed by August 1, 1958, at which time normal operations were resumed.

The following adjusted trial balance includes adjustments made during the audit work completed thus far. The flood loss already recorded represents losses of $2,450 on damaged materials and also fixed overhead of $4,000 for the month of July (exclusive of depreciation).

THE INSULATION COMPANY
Adjusted Trial Balance
December 31, 1958

	Debit	Credit
Cash..	21,000	
Accounts receivable..............................	52,000	
Inventory—Materials.............................	59,550	
Costs on jobs in progress........................	201,500	
Advances to officers.............................	9,900	
Prepaid expenses................................	2,200	
Investments....................................	14,000	
Land...	2,500	
Building.......................................	40,000	
Accumulated depreciation—Building...............		1,200
Equipment.....................................	13,500	
Accumulated depreciation—Equipment..............		1,350
Trucks and autos................................	22,500	
Accumulated depreciation—Trucks and autos..........		4,500
Accounts payable................................		72,000
Notes payable...................................		62,400
Accrued expenses................................		53,200
Estimates billed—Jobs incomplete..................		139,900
Capital stock...................................		88,000
Gross profit—Insulation contracts.................		144,000
Overhead expenses...............................	114,400	
Depreciation...................................	7,050	
Flood loss......................................	6,450	
	566,550	566,550

Required:

(a) Prepare analyses showing computation of the following: (Do not consider income tax treatment.)

    (1) Gross fixed asset values as of December 31, 1958.

    (2) Total flood loss for the year 1958.

    (3) Depreciation for the year 1958.

(b) Prepare journal entries reflecting the adjustments required by (a).

Problem 18-13. Washington Manufacturing Company started in business as of January 1, 1954, by acquiring three machines having a cost of $5,240, $4,000, and $4,400, respectively. Since that date the company has computed depreciation at 20% on the balance of the asset account at the end of each year, which amount has been credited directly to the asset account. All purchases since January 1, 1954, have been debited to the Machinery account and the cash received from sales has been credited to the account.

The transactions stated on the following page took place.

(a) On September 30, 1954, a machine was purchased on an installment basis. The list price was $6,000, but 12 monthly payments of $600 each were made by the company. Only the monthly payments were recorded in the Machinery account starting with September 30, 1954. Freight and installation charges of $200 were paid and entered in the Machinery account on October 10, 1954.

(b) On June 30, 1955, a machine was purchased for $8,000, 2/10; n/30, and recorded at $8,000 when paid for on July 7, 1955.

(c) On June 30, 1956, the machine acquired for $5,240 was traded for a larger one having a list price of $9,300. An allowance of $4,300 was received on the old machine, the balance of the list price being paid in cash and charged to the Machinery account.

(d) On January 2, 1957, the machine which cost $4,400 was sold for $2,500, but, because the cost of removal and crating was $125, the Machinery account was credited with only $2,375.

(e) On October 1, 1958, the machine purchased for $4,000 was sold for cash and the cash received was credited to the account.

(f) The balance of the account on January 1, 1958, was $14,505.50, and on December 31, 1958, after adjustment for depreciation, it was $10,644.40.

The company has decided that its method of handling its Machinery account has not been satisfactory. Accordingly, after the books were closed in 1958, the management decided to correct the account as of December 31, 1958, in accordance with usual accounting practices, and to provide depreciation on a straight-line basis with a separate accumulated depreciation account. Straight-line depreciation is estimated to be at the rate of 10% per annum computed on a monthly basis, over one-half of a month being considered a full month.

You are required to prepare in good form:

(a) A schedule showing the balance of the Machinery account and of the Accumulated Depreciation—Machinery account as of December 31, 1958, on the revised basis.

(b) A schedule showing the correct gain or loss on disposals of assets during the five-year period.

(c) A computation of the corrected depreciation expense for the year 1958 on the new basis.

You are not to consider income tax procedures in your solution.

Problem 18-14. You are engaged to make an audit of American Manufacturing Company for the year 1958. It has been the company's policy for a number of years to depreciate its machinery on a group basis, using a 20% rate applied to the net carrying value of the machinery. The management of the company wishes to continue with this depreciation policy. You are told, however, that during the year 1958 four different bookkeepers were employed by the company, three of whom were discharged for lack of experience, and that numerous errors had been discovered in their work.

In your examination of the Machinery account you find the following entries:

Machinery

1958			1958		
Jan. 1	Balance..............	11,600	July 15	Insurance Co. No. 6....	1,300
April 1	Cash No. 8...........	1,500			
July 1	Cash No. 9...........	650			
Sept. 1	Cash No. 10..........	3,000			

An analysis of the account discloses that the balance of $11,600 on January 1, 1958, is represented by the following: Machine 1, $1,500; machine 2, $2,000; machine 3, $1,500; machine 4, $1,500; machine 5, $1,200; machine 6, $2,400; machine 7, $1,500.

On January 1, 1958, the accumulated depreciation account for machinery showed a credit balance of $7,899. No entries were made in the account during 1958.

In connection with your audit you ascertain the following facts:

(a) Machines 1 and 4 were discarded on January 10, 1958. The machines were worthless.

(b) Machine 3 was purchased on January 2, 1952.

(c) Machine 2 was discarded on July 15, 1958. The machine was purchased on July 1, 1954. The $25 received from a junk dealer was credited to Miscellaneous Income.

(d) Machine 8 was purchased on April 1, 1958, at a cost of $3,000, payable one-half in cash and one-half with a 4% interest-bearing note maturing in one year.

(e) Machine 5 was traded in for $850 on the purchase of machine 9 costing $1,500. The difference was paid in cash. Machine 5 was purchased on January 2, 1955.

(f) Machine 6 was totally destroyed in a factory accident on July 1. The machine was acquired on July 1, 1956. Collection of the claim arising from the accident was received from the insurance company on July 15.

(g) Machine 10 was purchased for cash.

Prepare journal entries with suitable explanations to adjust the company's accounts on the basis of the above information. Set up T-accounts for Machinery and Accumulated Depreciation—Machinery, and show how these accounts would appear after your journal entries had been posted thereto. Rule and bring down the balance of the Machinery account.

Assignment Material for Chapter 19

Questions

Question 19-1. Are intangible assets subject to depreciation? Are they subject to depletion?

Question 19-2. What items can be included in the cost of a purchased patent? What items can properly be included in the cost of a patent developed by the business?

Question 19-3. A concern owning a patent brings a suit against a competitor for infringement. What entries should be made if the suit is successful? What entries should be made if the suit is lost?

Question 19-4. Assume that a concern buys a patent on an article that may prove to be a competing product. It does not manufacture this patented article. What should be done with the cost of the patent?

Question 19-5. Discuss the accounting problems involved in handling expenditures for experimental and research work.

Question 19-6. On July 1, 1953, Plaza Company bought for $15,000 a patent on a production process from the inventor. At that date the patent had a remaining life of 15 years. The company's policy is to amortize the cost of patents to production on a straight-line basis. The patented process proved successful, with the result that earnings were increased owing to reduced production costs and a larger volume of sales obtained by lowered sales prices. Because of these factors, the production manager in 1958 estimated that, if the inventor had retained the patent, it would have been more profitable to pay him royalties of $50,000 a year for an exclusive contract than to have continued with the former production methods.

On the basis of this estimate, the board of directors voted as of June 30, 1958, to write up the Patents account by $250,000. Out of the resulting credit, they declared a stock dividend of $200,000 consisting of 8,000 shares of their own $25 par value common stock.

Describe how the action taken June 30, 1958, will change the balance sheet in future years. Explain fully whether or not generally accepted accounting principles were applied.

Question 19-7. Is it ever permissible to write off a patent over a period in excess of 17 years? Over a period of less than 17 years?

Question 19-8. A manufacturing corporation occupying a factory under a long lease installs removable and nonremovable property on the premises of the lessor. State fully the basis on which the depreciation incident to such property should be determined.

Question 19-9. Your client, a small manufacturing concern, occupies rented land and has signed a 25-year lease, which does not contain a renewal clause. The

827

concern has erected on the land, at a cost of $15,000, a building having an estimated life of 40 years. A 4% depreciation rate has been employed, which will fully depreciate the building at the termination of the lease.

(a) Do you believe that the depreciation rate of 4% is correct?

(b) If, at the end of the fifteenth year, the lease is cancelled and a new one for 35 years is signed, would you at that time recommend any change in the depreciation rate?

(c) What depreciation rate would you have recommended at the outset, if the original lease had contained a clause giving your client the option of renewal for 25 years?

Question 19-10. Your client, a retailer, has recently taken occupancy of property under the terms of a ten-year renewable lease. In this connection, you note the following items of information:

(a) Annual rental under the lease is $12,000.

(b) At a cost of $60,000 your client has made leasehold improvements which have an estimated life of 30 years.

(c) The lease calls for removal of the improvements at the expiration of the lease. It is estimated that this will cost $15,000 net of salvage.

Describe fully the treatment of each of the above items in the financial statements. Justify the treatments you describe.

Question 19-11. (a) Where an intangible has no limited term of existence (such as limitation by law, regulation, or agreement), and where there is, at the time of acquisition, no indication that it will have a limited life, how should it be carried upon the books, and when, if ever, may it be written off?

(b) Name four such intangibles.

(c) When may a leasehold improvement be written off over a period less than the life of the lease?

(d) Under what circumstances may a leasehold be entered upon the books as an asset? Explain the accounting treatment covering the disposition of such charges.

Question 19-12. On January 1, 1958, B Company assigned to D Company, for a substantial consideration, its lease on a piece of vacant property which will run until January 1, 1989, with an option of renewal for an additional period of 20 years.

During the year 1958, D Company constructed on the property a building with an estimated life of 50 years. On January 1, 1959, the building was ready for occupancy and the company installed removable machinery with an estimated average service life of 20 years.

In view of the foregoing facts, state over what period each of the following on D Company's books should be written off:

(a) Bonus paid to B Company.

(b) Original cost of the building.

(c) Cost of building improvements.

(d) Machinery.

Give reasons for your answers.

Question 19-13. If expenses are incurred in obtaining a trademark, should they be immediately written off, should they be capitalized and carried indefinitely, or should they be capitalized and gradually written off?

Question 19-14. What is the test of the existence of goodwill in a business?

Question 19-15. R Company has agreed to sell its business to Q Company for a sum which represents the book value of its assets less its liabilities plus an amount for goodwill. The directors of R Company propose as the payment for goodwill the sum of the company's net income after income taxes for the years 1954, 1955, 1956, and 1957. You are asked to comment on the fairness of this proposal and to suggest a basis for determining the goodwill if you feel that the proposal of R Company is open to criticism.

Question 19-16. Is there any reason why goodwill carried as an asset on the books of a growing and prosperous manufacturing company should be depreciated, amortized, or otherwise written off?

Question 19-17. Two concerns have been in business for five years. They started with the same capital, the average earnings during the five years have been exactly the same, and the dividends have been the same. Does it necessarily follow that the goodwill of one company is the same as that of the other?

Problems

Problem 19-1. Hope Company was organized on March 1, 1953, on which date it issued 25,000 shares of $80 par value capital stock for cash at $74 per share.

On July 1, 1958, after several years of successful operations, the directors decided that formal recognition in the accounts should be given to the value of the excellent reputation which it had established among its customers and to the value of the franchise which it held to distribute the products of a particular automobile manufacturer. As a result, it was directed that Goodwill and Franchise accounts be established in the amounts of $350,000 and $200,000, respectively, the credits involved being employed to eliminate Discount on Capital Stock and to increase Retained Earnings.

The amounts of reported net income for the years 1958 and 1959 were $158,200 and $144,900, respectively, including amortization of the goodwill and franchise at an annual rate of 5%.

Required:

    (1) A schedule showing the correct net income for 1958 and 1959.

    (2) Adjusting journal entries on December 31, 1959, to correct the accounts for the intangibles mentioned above. The books have been closed for 1959.

Problem 19-2. The research staff of Spooner Manufacturing Company launched an intensive investigation early in 1956 in order to find a less costly process of manufacturing transistor radios. Research costs amounting to $82,600 were incurred in that year and $189,100 of research costs were incurred during 1957, until, in October, 1957, a successful process was developed. A patent was secured on January 3, 1958. Application fees amounted to $20. On that date, the board of directors decided to amortize the cost of the patent over ten years.

On August 8, 1958, Spooner Manufacturing Company named its chief competitor as defendant in a patent infringement suit. Legal fees amounting to $8,300 were incurred during 1958, and $2,600 of legal fees were incurred between January 1, 1959 and March 10, 1959, when arguments by opposing lawyers ended. The verdict, announced on June 1, 1959, was in favor of the plaintiff. The decision was appealed and legal costs of $2,300 were incurred during the last four months of 1959. The case was adjudicated on October 31, 1960, when the U. S. Supreme Court ruled against Spooner Manufacturing Company. A rehearing was denied.

Spooner Manufacturing Company closes its books annually on June 30.

Compute the amounts which should be charged to Amortization of Patents for the fiscal years ending June 30, 1958, 1959, and 1960. What journal entries, if any, should have been prepared when the case was finally decided?

Problem 19-3. "Unamortized Organization Costs" appears on the books of Melton, Incorporated, on December 31, 1959, before closing, at $162,000. Debits to the account, all recorded in 1956, were as follows:

Discount on issuance of common stock............................	$ 49,000
Attorney's fees for services in connection with organization of the corporation..	6,000
Advertising costs...	132,000
Charter fee paid to Secretary of State............................	1,000
Net loss for 1956..	28,000

Two credits, equal in amount, appear in the account and represent amortization adjustments for 1957 and 1958 at a per cent of the total debits which was specified by the board of directors on December 31, 1957.

The advertising costs resulted from an intensive "consumer education" campaign conducted early in 1956. The sales promotion director estimates that the campaign will benefit the five-year period ending December 31, 1960.

Prepare the necessary entries as of December 31, 1959, to correct the balance of the above account. The yearly rate of amortization which was established by the board of directors need not be changed.

Problem 19-4. Donna Dresses, Incorporated, is considering the purchase of all of the net tangible assets of Mastoon Corporation. The management of Donna Dresses, Incorporated, has decided that a proper offer for the goodwill amount to be added to net asset values is three times the current year's "normal" earnings.

The net income reported for 1958 was $330,000, after charges and credits for items listed below:

Loss on sale of land...	$30,000
Dividends received on securities..................................	9,000
Depreciation of fixed assets......................................	60,000
Gain from revaluation of securities...............................	7,000
Appropriation of net income for reserve for possible decline in value of inventories..	15,000
Plant rearrangement expense.....................................	13,000

The parties have agreed that the selling price of the tangible fixed assets is to be the book value of such assets plus 20%.

Compute the amount of goodwill to be included in the price to be offered to the directors of Mastoon Corporation.

Problem 19-5. The following data are taken from recent financial statements of *A-Z* Tractor Company:

Total assets, August 31, 1959...................................	$560,000
Recorded goodwill, August 31, 1959..............................	70,000
Total liabilities, August 31, 1959................................	60,000
Average earnings for past five years..............................	65,000
Expected increase in annual revenue due to addition of new plant facilities made just prior to August 31, 1959....................	46,000
Expected increase in annual expense due to addition of new plant facilities..	35,000
Normal rate of earnings for the industry..........................	10%

The total assets and total liabilities, as given above, are accepted by the parties as representative of the figures for recent years.

Compute the payment to be made for unrecorded goodwill if total goodwill is determined by each of the following methods:

(1) Purchase of average excess earnings for three years.
(2) Excess earnings capitalized at the normal rate.
(3) Purchase of average annual earnings for five years.
(4) Excess earnings up to $15,000 capitalized at the normal rate, and those above $15,000 capitalized at 20%.

Problem 19-6.   Porter and Quinby were partners sharing profits in the ratio of 25% and 75%, respectively. Quinby wanted to retire. To this end the partners agreed that partnership fixed assets were undervalued by $40,000, that goodwill was worth $60,000, and that only Quinby's share of these increases should be recorded and credited to his capital account. Since the working capital of the business was only $55,000, it was decided that Quinby should receive only one-fifth of his adjusted capital credit in cash. For the remainder he accepted, at book value, securities which were carried at $50,000 and short-term obligations of the business. The balance sheet which was prepared after (1) the above agreement was effected and (2) Porter had invested an additional $25,000 cash was as follows:

PORTER, PROPRIETORSHIP
Balance Sheet
December 31, 1959

Assets		Liabilities	
Current assets............	$125,000	Current liabilities........	$ 95,000
Investments.............	80,000	Long-term liabilities......	150,000
Fixed assets.............	100,000	**Owner's Equity**	
Goodwill...............	45,000	Porter, capital...........	105,000
	$350,000		$350,000

Reconstruct the partnership balance sheet before the adjustments were made for Quinby's withdrawal.

Problem 19-7.   On January 1, 1935, Sheridan Roads Corporation, as lessee, leased real estate, including a building which had been completed in December, 1890, with an expected useful life of 50 years. Under the terms of the lease agreement, the lessee was to make a down payment of $50,000 and annual rental payments of $12,000. The lease was to run for 25 years without renewal option. The agreement also specified that property taxes, insurance, maintenance and repairs, costs of remodeling, and new construction were to be borne by the lessee. Remodeling costs incurred before occupancy were $34,000.

At the end of the seventh year in the life of the lease, the building was torn down and a new one was erected at a cost of $346,000, including taxes and insurance during the period of construction. The new structure had an estimated life of 30 years, with no scrap value. Two years were required to remove the old and construct the new building.

Sheridan Roads Corporation subleased the buildings during the entire period, except during the construction period; rental income from the old building was $32,000, and from the new building $50,000, per annum. Taxes, insurance, and repairs aggregated $6,000 a year for the old and $9,100 a year for the new building.

(a) Show how the prepayment would appear in the balance sheet of Sheridan Roads Corporation as of January 1, 1935. (*Continued on page 832.*)

(b) Compute the aggregate net income, before income taxes, earned by Sheridan Roads Corporation during the life of the lease.

(c) Prepare income statements for the first and last years of the lease.

Problem 19-8. On the basis of the following information, prepare a schedule as of December 31, 1960, showing the estimated future annual net income which Algonquin Corporation may expect if it acquires the assets of Marchand, Incorporated. The estimated future annual net income will be used as a base from which goodwill is to be computed.

Average annual net income for the years 1955–1960, inclusive. . . . $65,800
Excess of agreed price for building acquired on January 1, 1939, over its book value (Marchand, Incorporated, has been using a depreciation rate of 2½% of cost). 26,100
Expected annual increase in executive salaries to take place upon change of ownership. 23,000

On the first business day of 1959, Marchand, Incorporated, replaced several of its old machines. The loss of $6,000 resulting from the disposal of the old machines was reported in the 1959 income statement. The loss was attributable to inadequate depreciation taken on the old machines during the eight years they were in use.

Certain patents are to be retained by Marchand, Incorporated. However, as a part of the agreement, full rights to these patents will be granted to Algonquin Corporation under a licensing arrangement, at an estimated annual royalty of $11,000. The company received annual royalties of $8,100 during 1957, 1958, 1959, and 1960. Half of these royalties were received from companies other than Algonquin Corporation, and the licensee of these patents may expect to continue to collect them.

Problem 19-9. Fantastic Creations, Incorporated, had the following debit items in its Patents account on January 1, 1959. All of the patents were developed by the corporation.

(a) Cost of developing a patent expiring December 31, 1968. . . . . $38,600
(b) Cost of developing a patent expiring June 30, 1971. 25,900
(c) Development costs of a patent granted to the corporation on April 1, 1957. 19,200
(d) Costs incurred in patent developments prior to 1958, with no resulting patents as of January 1, 1959. 22,000
(e) Cost incurred in patent development during 1958, with no resulting patents as of January 1, 1959. 8,600

On May 1, 1959, a patent is received on a process which, in effect, will prolong the life of the patent mentioned in (b) above, over the legal life of the new patent. The total cost assignable to this patent includes $13,100 of the costs incurred prior to 1958, $2,600 of the costs incurred during 1958, and $7,600 of the costs incurred in 1959.

During 1959, total patent development costs amounted to $20,800. One project was abandoned in 1959, and it was decided to write off past development costs amounting to $3,900. No entry has been made to give effect to this decision. The corporation does not charge development costs to expense when incurred; it charges these costs to the Patents account. Patent amortization has never been recorded.

Compute the correct balance of the Patents account on December 31, 1959, and journalize an entry to correct the account on that date. Assume that the books have not been closed.

Problem 19-10. The board of directors of Early Bird Producers, Incorporated, has entered into a contract with Arleigh Lambkin calling for the sale of the net assets (exclusive of cash) of the company, the consideration therefor to be computed as follows:

Net assets, less cash—at book values as adjusted by agreement of the parties. Goodwill—at an amount computed by capitalizing estimated future excess annual earnings at a rate of 20%. Excess annual earnings are defined as the excess of the estimated future net income over an amount equal to 10% of the book value, as adjusted for purposes of the sale, of net assets, including the cash.

You have been retained by the directors to compute the consideration to be received for the total net noncash assets of the company. The information presented below is made available to you for this purpose.

(1) The condensed balance sheet on December 31, 1959, the effective date of the sale, is as follows:

EARLY BIRD PRODUCERS, INCORPORATED
Balance Sheet
December 31, 1959

Assets		Liabilities	
Cash	$ 66,000	Accounts payable	$103,500
Accounts receivable—net of allowance of $3,000	47,700	**Stockholders' Equity**	
Inventory	113,000	Capital stock	290,000
Fixed assets—net	230,800	Retained earnings	64,000
	$457,500		$457,500

(2) Included in administrative expenses for the year 1958 were nonrecurring legal expenses of $9,000.

(3) It is anticipated that salesmen's salaries will increase in the amount of $13,000 per year.

(4) The average annual net income for the calendar years 1955–1959, inclusive, was $52,400.

(5) Through a clerical error, the December 31, 1959 inventory is understated. The correct valuation is $118,300.

(6) Fixed Assets account comprises land, building, equipment, and showroom facilities. The land is carried at cost, $40,000. The building and equipment, purchased for $268,000 on January 1, 1952, are to be valued at $198,000, which is replacement cost less depreciation.

(7) The showroom facilities were completed during December, 1959, at a cost of $30,000. It is expected that the utilization of the additional space will begin early in January, 1960, with a probable additional annual sales volume resulting therefrom of $16,000, on which a 25% gross margin is expected. The only additional expense arising from the use of these facilities will be depreciation on the facilities at the annual rate which the company has been using on the building and equipment.

(8) None of the depreciable fixed assets is expected to have salvage value.

(9) A 1956 expenditure of $36,000 for display advertising in trade publications was charged to that year's operations. It is estimated that this expenditure, which will continue to be made each sixth year, was of equal benefit to the operations of each year from 1956 to 1961, inclusive. There were no such advertising expenditures made prior to 1956.

Required:

   (a) An estimate of the future annual net income which the vendee may expect if he acquires the net noncash assets of Early Bird Producers, Incorporated.

   (b) A determination of the total consideration to be paid for the net noncash assets of Early Bird Producers, Incorporated, in accordance with the terms presented above.

   (c) Arleigh Lambkin's journal entries to record the acquisition of the net noncash assets of Early Bird Producers, Incorporated, as of December 31, 1959, assuming that he will operate the enterprise as a proprietorship and that he makes the cash payment for the net assets from personal funds. Lambkin has decided to debit one Fixed Assets account for the adjusted book values of the fixed assets.

Problem 19-11. On December 31, 1952, Jones Company acquired the net assets of Smith Corporation for $284,920. The parties agreed that this amount would include payment for five years' excess earnings, which were defined as those in excess of 10% of net assets. A Goodwill account was debited for this amount on the purchaser's books.

The earnings of Smith Corporation for several years prior to the sale had averaged $40,174. This included royalties earned on a patent expiring on December 31, 1957. The royalty agreement was dated January 2, 1945, and its term coincided with the life of the patent. However, the cost of developing the patent had never been capitalized by Smith Corporation and no value was ever assigned to the patent in the corporation's accounts. It was conceded by the parties that no excess earnings would exist without the royalty agreement.

During 1953, the controller of Jones Company decided to charge $1,000—an arbitrarily selected sum—of the goodwill to operations of that year. He charged all but one dollar of the remainder to Retained Earnings, viewing the write-off as a conservative step.

Also during 1953, Jones Company completed $173,520 of production research and, on December 31, 1953, was granted three patents for new manufacturing processes. The new patents were not related in any way to the patent acquired from Smith Corporation and were expected to have economic usefulness for 15 years. To be conservative, the controller decided to amortize the patents over 10 years.

On January 3, 1960, the Jones Company directors and principal stockholders entered into negotiations for a proposed sale of the company's net assets. The prospective purchaser agreed to pay a sum for goodwill equal to average annual excess earnings for the calendar years 1956–1959, inclusive, capitalized at the rate of 20%. Normal earnings were defined as earnings equal to 8% of net assets.

On January 3, 1960, the controller prepared a balance sheet which showed the stockholders' equity at $1,610,847. A supplementary statement listed average annual earnings for the calendar years 1956–1959, inclusive, as $148,074. The company uses the calendar year as its accounting year.

You have been retained by the parties to determine the amount of the goodwill.

Assignment Material for Chapter 20

Questions

Question 20-1. Among the assets of Soya Company, a going concern, are the following:

Trade debtors...	$48,250
U. S. Series H bonds......................................	25,000
Marketable securities (market value, $50,000) at cost............	42,800

The current liabilities include:

Notes payable to Bank A..................................	$40,000
Note payable to Bank B...................................	30,000
Accrued federal taxes......................................	35,000
Loan by company's president................................	50,000

The entire amount owing by trade debtors is pledged against the notes payable to Bank A; the marketable securities are held by the president of the company as security for his loan; and the president had pledged 600 shares (par value, $100 per share; book value, $110 per share; no listed market price) of Soya Company capital stock issued to him, as security for the loan from Bank B.

The treasurer of the company has prepared a balance sheet as of the close of its fiscal year in which the liabilities stated have been offset against the assets pledged against them, in such a way that the excess of a liability over the asset pledged as security for its payment appears as a liability and the excess of a pledged asset over the liability protected by it appears as an asset.

Comment on this procedure.

Question 20-2. A manufacturer of ice cream purchased, on the deferred payment plan, refrigerator units at a cost of $15,000. All these units were resold to customers at cost. Collections from the customers in payment of the units had been $3,126.18, while payments by the manufacturer to the distributor of the units totaled $6,180.31.

You are auditing the books of the manufacturer, who contends that he has no liability to the distributor because he purchased the refrigerator units for his customers, and that an asset should appear on his balance sheet as follows:

Advances to customers:	
Payment made for customers' account....................	$6,180.31
Less cash received from customers........................	3,126.18
Balance...	$3,054.13

Do you believe that your client is correct in his contentions? Why or why not?

Question 20-3. What entries should be made to record the deposit of cash with a fiscal agent for the payment of bond interest?

Question 20-4. A corporation was considering, in 1958, the issuance of bonds as of January 1, 1959, as stated on the following page.

835

Plan 1: $1,000,000 par value 5%, 1st mortgage, 20-year bonds at 94, due December 31, 1978, or

Plan 2: $1,000,000 par value 5%, 1st mortgage, 20-year bonds at par, due December 31, 1978, with provision for payment of a 6% premium upon maturity.

Give two separate sets of journal entries with appropriate explanations showing the accounting treatment which the foregoing bond issues would necessitate:

(a) At time of issue;
(b) Monthly thereafter;
(c) Upon payment at date of maturity.

Costs of issue, such as printing, lawyers' fees, and so forth, may be ignored for the purpose of answering this question. Discount and premium are to be allocated to accounting periods on a straight-line basis.

Question 20-5. What would be the proper treatment of unamortized bond discount and expense from time to time as holders of convertible bonds exercised their rights to convert them into capital stock?

Question 20-6. A company refunds a bond issue of $5,000,000 principal amount of 5% bonds, due five years hence, on which there is still an unamortized debt discount and expense of $250,000, by the issuance of $5,500,000 principal amount of 4% 20-year bonds at 90. The difference between the amount of cash necessary to retire the old bond issue and the amount produced by the refunding bonds is supplied from the general funds of the company. The expenses of the new issue are $50,000. Discuss briefly three procedures which may be followed by the company to dispose of the unamortized debt discount and expense applicable to the old issue, and list them in the order of your preference.

Question 20-7. When should liabilities for each of the following be recorded?

(1) Dividends
(2) Purchase commitments
(3) Acquisition of goods by purchase on credit
(4) Officers' salaries
(5) Special bonus to employees

Question 20-8. The December 31, 1958 balance sheet of a medium-sized manufacturing corporation did not include the following items among the current liabilities: (All are material in amount.)

(a) Notes payable to a group of twelve stockholders, the notes to become due and payable on demand of at least eight of the group.
(b) A note due March 31, 1959, in settlement of which the holder accepted preferred stock on January 6, 1959.
(c) Rent collected in advance.

For each of the items above you are to give arguments to justify the exclusion from current liabilities. If your answer involves assumptions as to facts not given in the question, state your assumptions.

Question 20-9. During the course of an audit as of December 31, 1959, you find that your client in 1953 purchased two acres of land adjacent to its present plant for future expansion, subject to a first mortgage, the maturity of which was May 10, 1957. The mortgage has not been refinanced but has been extended for one year at each May 10th since 1957, the date of the annual 5% interest payment. The bank which owns the mortgage informs you that, subject to the usual interest payment at May 10, 1960, it will grant the customary one-year extension of the mortgage to May 10, 1961. Your client is in a good financial position.

How will you show the mortgage liability on the balance sheet?

Question 20-10. In analyzing a deficit account having a balance of $50,000, you find a charge thereto of $10,000 which is credited to J. Jones, the president of the company. You are informed that this $10,000 represents dividends on common stock paid voluntarily and personally by the president. The directors of the company have voted thereupon as follows: "This company shall reimburse J. Jones for common stock dividends paid by him if, and when, its financial condition shall warrant the payment thereof."

Would you suggest any adjusting entries for this item? What entries? How would you show the credit of $10,000 to J. Jones in the balance sheet? Explain fully.

Question 20-11. An intercity bus company, wishing to equalize the expense caused by accidents, adopted the plan of depositing 2% of its gross receipts each month in a local savings bank, charging the funds so set aside to an account called Reserve for Accidents. The deposits in the fund during the year amounted to $4,869.26, and payments were made on account of accidents totaling $950.00. These payments were debited to Accidents and credited to Reserve for Accidents. The bookkeeper endeavored to close the books at the end of the year by debiting Accidents and crediting Reserve for Accidents with $3,919.26, thus making a total charge for accidents of $4,869.26. But the result was that the company was left with cash assets of $3,919.26 not represented on the books. Wherein did the bookkeeper err, and what entries should have been made to show the facts correctly?

Question 20-12. In making an audit of a corporation, you find certain liabilities, such as taxes, which appear to be overstated. Also, some semi-obsolete inventory items seem to be undervalued and the tendency is to expense rather than to capitalize as many items as possible.

In talking with management about the policies, you are told that "the company has always taken a very conservative view of the business and its future prospects." Management suggests that they do not wish to weaken the company by reporting any more earnings or paying any more dividends than are absolutely necessary, since they do not expect business to continue to be good. They point out that the undervaluation of assets, and so forth, does not lose anything for the company and creates reserves which can be called on in "hard times."

You are to discuss the policies followed by the company and comment on each of the arguments presented by management.

Question 20-13. *ABD* Company has just entered into a pension plan for the first time as a result of union contract negotiations. The plan became effective as of January 1, 1959. On December 31, 1959, you find that only two entries have been made on the books of *ABD* Company. The first entry (a debit to Retained Earnings and a credit to Cash, in the amount of $5,000) was the first of a series of five equal annual payments required to be made to an insurance company to cover the cost of pensions based on past services. The second entry was a debit to Factory Wages—Indirect and a credit to Cash in the amount of $3,000, to cover the current year's contribution to the insurance company for pension costs based on the current year's factory wages.

Did the two entries reflect properly the facts relative to the pension plan? Present your reasoning and describe any changes which you conclude are needed.

Problems

Problem 20-1. Smooth Sailing Corporation authorized the issuance of $1,000,000 of 4% bonds to be dated March 1, 1958. The bonds were due on March 1, 1978, with semiannual interest payments on March 1 and September 1. Bonds were issued as follows:

Date	Par Value	Issue Price
March 1, 1958	$600,000	102
February 1, 1959	200,000	100
October 31, 1959	200,000	97¼

Interest was paid on the due dates. The corporation operates on a calendar-year basis.

Submit the journal entries, except closing entries, for the years 1958 and 1959 that are required as a result of the above bond issuances.

Problem 20-2. Marks Company issued 5%, 30-year mortgage bonds in the principal amount of $6,000,000 on July 1, 1940, at a discount of $150,000 which it proceeded to amortize over the life of the issue. The indenture securing the issue provided that the bonds could be called for redemption in total but not in part at any time prior to maturity at 103% of the principal amount.

On July 1, 1960, the company issued its 4%, 25-year mortgage bonds in the principal amount of $6,000,000 at 101, and the proceeds were used in the refunding of the 5%, 30-year mortgage bonds on that date. The indenture securing the new issue did not provide for retirement before maturity.

Both bond issues provided for the payment of interest on January 1 and July 1. The company's fiscal year ends on September 30.

Submit all journal entries required during the calendar year 1960 in connection with the above bond issues.

Problem 20-3. Howes Company issued $200,000 of 20-year, 4% bonds, dated June 1, 1951, on September 1, 1951, at 98¾ plus accrued interest. These bonds were convertible into the company's common stock on a rising scale of prices for the stock. (Interest accrued to the date of conversion to be paid in cash.) The common stock had a par value of $25 per share. During 1958, the company's stock began to rise on the market, and conversions were made as follows:

Date		Par Value Converted	Conversion Price	Market Price
April 1, 1958		$21,000	$30	$40
October 1, 1958		64,000	32	44

Prepare the journal entries necessary to record the issuance of the bonds and the above conversions. Interest is paid semiannually. The company is on a calendar-year basis.

Problem 20-4. On July 1, 1955, Lyon Company realized $111,550 from a $100,000 issue of serial bonds dated July 1, 1955. Each bond has a par value of $1,000 and pays $30 interest semiannually. Starting in 1961, ten bonds mature each year on July 1. The last ten bonds mature on July 1, 1970.

(a) Set up an amortization schedule for the above serial bond issue.
(b) Assume that, on August 1, 1960, the company purchases six of the outstanding serial bonds maturing on July 1, 1968, for $6,400, including accrued interest. Give the journal entry for the purchase.

Problem 20-5. Dome Company issued $800,000 of 4% serial bonds on October 1, 1954. These bonds mature at the rate of $100,000 per year starting October 1, 1957. Interest is payable annually on October 1 and the bonds have a par value of $1,000. Discount and deferrible expense connected with this issue amounted to $34,580.

Compute the amortization of discount and expense for the year ended December 31, 1954, and for the year ended December 31, 1960. Also compute the gain or loss on retirement resulting from the April 1, 1961 purchase of $10,000 of the bonds, bearing a maturity date of October 1, 1962, at par plus accrued interest.

Problem 20-6. Byron-Ladd Company issued $200,000 20-year, 6% bonds on June 1, 1950, at 96, callable at 105. During the following eight years, whenever the market was favorable, the company bought in its bonds and cancelled them. At the beginning of 1959, bonds with a par value of $48,000 had been retired in this manner; but during the last two years it had become increasingly difficult to buy any bonds below the call price. The company was able to sell new bonds with an interest coupon of 5%, and it decided to call in the old issue, as of June 1, 1959, and issue $250,000 in new bonds. The excess was to be used to increase working capital. The new bonds were sold at 99 and ran for 15 years.

(1) Give the journal entries for the refunding operations.
(2) Compute the interest expense for the first year of the new issue.

Problem 20-7. Barron Manufacturing Corporation issued $500,000 of 4%, 20-year bonds at 102 on April 1, 1956. Under the terms of the indenture, the bonds were callable on any interest date (April 1 or October 1) at 104.

During 1957 and 1958, the corporation acquired bonds on the open market as follows:

Date	Par Value	Price
July 1, 1957	$12,000	98 plus interest
September 1, 1958	18,000	Par plus interest

Thereafter the corporation called bonds for redemption as follows:

Date	Par Value
April 1, 1959	$40,000
October 1, 1959	50,000

Required:

(1) A schedule showing all changes in the Bonds Payable and Premium on Bonds Payable accounts through December 31, 1959. The corporation uses a calendar-year accounting period.
(2) Journal entries for each retirement.

Problem 20-8. Nelson Company has worked out a plan with an insurance company for a pension program for its present staff of office workers, in recognition of the past and future services of the employees. In view of the retirement age set by the company and the age distribution of the office staff, the pension payments will not commence until 1963. Estimated pension payments in 1963 and thereafter to the covered employees are expected to be as follows:

1963	$ 5,000
1964	7,000
1965	10,000
1966	14,000
1967	16,000

1968..	$20,000
1969..	25,000
1970..	22,000
1971..	17,000
1972..	12,000
1973..	8,000
1974..	5,000
1975..	2,000
1976..	2,000

Under the plan the company is required to pay an initial premium of $15,667.34 as of January 1, 1958, and thereafter ten annual premiums of $10,000.

Determine the amount chargeable to expense for 1958, 1959, 1968, and 1969.

Problem 20-9. Reduction Corporation remits the semiannual interest payments on its $500,000 of outstanding 4½% bonds to The National Trust Company. The National Trust Company makes interest payments to the bondholders upon the presentation of interest coupons. Interest dates on the bonds are May 1 and November 1, and Reduction Corporation remits to The National Trust Company on April 20 and October 20. The trust company renders a report on the interest payments it has made, together with the paid interest coupons, as of June 30 and December 31.

The bonds were issued on May 1, 1959, and the trust company's reports for the years 1959 and 1960 showed the following interest payments to bondholders:

Date of Report	Coupons Paid
December 31, 1959..	$10,800
June 30, 1960..	11,295
December 31, 1960..	11,430

Required:

Journal entries to record the interest expense, the remittance to The National Trust Company of cash for the payment of interest, and the receipt of the reports from the trust company for the years 1959 and 1960. The corporation closes its books each December 31.

Problem 20-10. The board of directors of Gross Corporation authorized a $500,000 issue of 5% convertible 20-year bonds dated March 1, 1958. Interest is payable on March 1 and September 1 of each year. The conversion agreement provides that, until March 1, 1963, each $1,000 of bonds may be converted into 60 shares of $10 stated value common stock and that interest accrued to date of conversion will be paid in cash. After March 1, 1963, the bonds are convertible into 50 shares of common for each $1,000 of bonds.

The company sold the entire bond issue on June 30, 1958, at 98 and accrued interest. In addition, deferrible costs incurred in making the sale amounted to $8,320. The company adjusts its books at the end of each month and closes them on December 31 of each year. Interest is paid as due. On February 1, 1960, a holder of $20,000 of bonds converts them into common stock.

You are to prepare entries in journal form to reflect the transactions arising out of the existence of these bonds on each of the following dates:

(a) June 30, 1958.
(b) September 1, 1958.
(c) December 31, 1959 (including closing entries).
(d) February 1, 1960.
(e) December 31, 1960 (including closing entries).

Problem 20-11. Ohio Company regularly closes its plant for a two-week period in August for the purpose of changing dies and jigs and taking a physical inventory. The company's contract with the union provides that production workers shall receive two weeks of vacation with pay each year, and, to fulfill this requirement, the company has followed the practice of paying the workers for the weeks during which the plant is shut down.

During December of 1958, the executives estimate, on the basis of expected production and employment for 1959, that the required payment to vacationing workers during the shut-down period in 1959 will amount to $94,400. The actual payment made on August 14, 1959, for this purpose was $94,180.

The company prepares financial statements quarterly and has employed a budgetary reserve to account for vacation pay.

Required:

(1) The entry which would be made quarterly to record the estimated cost of vacation pay. The company uses the calendar year as its accounting period.
(2) The entry to record the payment of vacation pay.
(3) The amount and balance sheet location of the budgetary reserve on June 30, October 31, and December 31.

Problem 20-12. The right side of the December 31, 1959 balance sheet of Motel Appliance Corporation appears below.

Partial Balance Sheet
December 31, 1959

Current liabilities:

Accounts payable.................................... $	98,217	
Notes receivable discounted.........................	6,000	
Reserve for income taxes.............	114,500	
Accrued operating expenses..........................	17,211 $	235,928

Reserves:

Reserve for increased cost of replacement of machinery.. $	160,000	
Reserve for dealer warranties........................	78,610	
Reserve for self-insurance...........................	68,000	
Reserve for depreciation.............................	218,380	
Reserve for possible future decline in inventory value....	312,000	
Reserve for contingencies............................	80,000	
Reserve for additional income taxes..................	25,000	941,990

Net worth:

Common stock, $10 par value; authorized, 200,000 shares; issued and outstanding, 160,000 shares...............	$1,600,000	
Premium on common stock...........................	240,000	

Surplus:

Reserve for repairs and maintenance........ $	32,300		
Reserve for building fund.................	64,210		
Reserve for past-service pension cost........	314,206		
Unappropriated surplus...................	416,266	826,982	
Unrealized increment from revaluation of land..........		180,000	2,846,982
			$4,024,900

Prepare a revised presentation of the partial balance sheet eliminating the "Reserves" section and making any other changes in classification, terminology, or arrangement which you think are appropriate.

Problem 20-13. In order to reduce fluctuations in reported net income, Canning Corporation, as of January 1, 1956, adopted the following policies:

(1) Providing for advertising expense by annual credits to Allowance for Advertising for 2% of gross sales. All advertising costs are charged to the allowance account as incurred.
(2) Recording a debit or credit in the Revenue and Expense account equal to 80% of the difference between the net income after the above provision for advertising and $300,000. The entry to Revenue and Expense was to be offset by an addition to, or deduction from, Reserve for Profit Variation.

Net income reported by the corporation for the years 1956–1959, inclusive, was as follows:

1956...................	$340,000	1958.................	$270,000
1957...................	312,800	1959.................	297,400

The debits and credits to the Allowance for Advertising account, by years, are summarized below.

	Debits	Credits
1956..	$17,700	$21,000
1957..	19,940	20,850
1958..	23,800	20,270
1959..	22,650	21,110

The balance in the Reserve for Profit Variation account on December 31, 1959, after recording adjusting entries on that date, was $80,800—credit.

You may ignore income taxes.

Required:

(a) The correct net income for the years 1956–1959, inclusive.
(b) The necessary adjusting entry or entries, assuming that the books have been closed for 1959 and that the 1959 financial statements have been prepared and published.

Problem 20-14. Thumb Corporation, a client with a fiscal year ending on June 30, requests that you compute the appropriate balance for its Reserve for Product Warranty as of June 30, 1959.

Using the data below, draw up a suitable working paper, including the proposed adjusting entry. Assume that proper recognition of costs for financial accounting will be allowed for income tax purposes.

Thumb Corporation manufactures television tubes and sells them with a six-month guarantee under which defective tubes will be replaced without charge. Expenses and losses resulting from the return of tubes sold in the preceding fiscal year are charged to the Reserve for Product Warranty, while such charges incurred for tubes sold in the current year are debited to the Product Warranty Expense account. On June 30, 1958, the Reserve for Product Warranty had a balance of $51,000. By June 30, 1959, this reserve had been reduced to $1,250.

The company started the current fiscal year expecting 8% of the dollar volume of sales to be returned. However, owing to the introduction of new models during the year, this estimated percentage of returns was increased to 10% on May 1. It is assumed that no tubes sold during a given month are returned in that month. Each tube is stamped with a date at time of sale so that the warranty may be properly administered. The following table of percentages indicates the likely pattern of sales returns during the six-month period of the warranty, starting with the month following the sale of tubes.

Month following sale	Percentage of Total Returns Expected
First......	20
Second......	30
Third......	20
Fourth through sixth—10% each month......	30
Total......	100

Gross sales of tubes were as follows for the first six months of 1959:

Month	Amount
January......	$360,000
February......	330,000
March......	410,000
April......	285,000
May......	200,000
June......	180,000

The company's warranty also covers the payment of freight cost on defective tubes returned and on new tubes sent out as replacements. This two-way freight cost runs approximately 10% of the sales price of the tubes returned. The manufacturing cost of the tubes is roughly 80% of the sales price, and the salvage value of returned tubes averages 15% of their sales price.

Problem 20-15. The following accounts are found in the ledger of Howell Company on the dates indicated.

	December 31,	
	1958	1959
Reserve for patent amortization......	$137,580	$120,382
Reserve for bond sinking fund......	90,000	-0-
Reserve for plant expansion......	200,000	60,000
Reserve for income taxes......	45,000	40,000
Reserve for advertising......	200,000	120,000
Reserve for land appreciation......	-0-	200,000
Reserve for general contingencies......	60,000	100,000
Reserve for vacation pay......	-0-	-0-
Reserve for periodic payments under long-term lease..	-0-	200,000
Reserve for insurance......	100,000	50,000
Reserve for losses on treasury stock transactions......	10,000	15,000

Additional information:

  Early in 1959 it became apparent that the commercial life of the patent would be 12 years instead of 9 years.

  On November 1, 1959, a ten-year, $100,000 bond issue was retired.

  During 1959 the company spent $140,000 for architect's plans and site preparation, which was charged to the reserve account.

  During 1959 the company spent, and charged to Reserve for Advertising, $80,000 in an effort to halt an adverse sales trend. In 1958 the board of directors had appropriated $200,000 for such a purpose.

  During 1959 the company settled a customer's damage suit out of court by the payment of $10,000, which was charged to Reserve for General Contingencies.

During 1959 the company made monthly provisions for vacation pay in the amount of $10,000. The vacation pay disbursement amounted to $119,000.

On December 15, 1959, the company signed a long-term lease. One of the clauses in the lease provided that the company could purchase the property at the termination of the lease for $100.

During 1959 the company increased the amount of insurance carried with insurance companies and thereby reduced the potential loss it might suffer from inadequate insurance.

Dividends applicable to treasury stock are credited to a special reserve account. Only credits of this type are made to the account. There were no treasury stock transactions during 1959.

Required:

Journal entries made during 1959 in each of the above reserve accounts and any necessary correcting entries. The company uses a calendar-year accounting period.

Problem 20-16. In your audit of New Products Company as of June 30, 1959, you find that the company's prepared balance sheet shows a separate section after liabilities called Reserves and Miscellaneous Credits, $1,090,410. The following account balances are included in this total:

Reserve for vacation pay	$ 32,201
Premium on bonds payable (properly amortized to date)	26,080
Reserve for income tax	86,519
Reserve for restoration of leased building	55,200
Reserve for contingencies	136,000
Reserve for market fluctuation in merchandise on hand	46,750
Reserve for decline in value of short-term investments	26,030
Reserve for possible future decline in value of long-term investments	76,000
Reserve for employees' bonuses	86,200
Reserve for property damage insurance—Trucks	120,080
Reserve for bond purchase fund	76,860
Reserve for estimated loss on sale of nonoperating property	80,620
Reserve for retirement of preferred stock	50,000
Reserve for product warranties	191,870

Required:

(1) The probable journal entry (without amounts) to create each of the above accounts.

(2) The correct journal entry (without amounts) that would normally be made to reduce or dispose of each of the above accounts.

(3) The correct presentation of the above accounts in the year-end balance sheet.

Assignment Material for Chapter 21

Questions

Question 21-1. Why did the Institute's Committee on Accounting Procedure recommend the use of comparative statements?

Question 21-2. How would you distinguish between horizontal and vertical procedures for comparative statement analysis? What are the advantages of each procedure?

Question 21-3. Why may analytical per cents be deceptive?

Question 21-4. Statements are sometimes prepared for management purposes showing the results of operations for the current month and for the same month of the preceding year. Will such comparisons always be meaningful? Explain.

Question 21-5. If horizontal analysis per cents are included in a comparative income statement for three years, what base or bases should be used in the computation of the per cents to avoid misleading inferences? Why?

Question 21-6. In horizontal analysis, is it always possible to determine per cents of increase or decrease for each statement item? Explain.

Question 21-7. What advantages are alleged for the use of ratios expressed decimally in place of per cents?

Question 21-8. How are income taxes treated in computing the number of times bond interest has been earned?

Question 21-9. As a stockholder you are informed that the corporation's stockholders' equity per books has greatly increased. Why might you be pleased to hear this? Why might you not be pleased to hear this?

Question 21-10. What inference would you draw from the following data relating to a manufacturing corporation?

A low ratio of stockholders' equity to liabilities.
A high ratio of liabilities to assets.
A low ratio of stockholders' equity to assets.

Question 21-11. A stockholder who owns some stock in a listed corporation is concerned because she receives such small dividends. She has reviewed the last stockholders' report and has concluded there is ample cash available for much larger dividends. In addition to cash in banks, the corporation's balance sheet shows the following items which she believes represent cash funds:

(1) a large "paid-in surplus";
(2) plenty of "undivided profits";
(3) a large "reserve for general contingencies";
(4) a substantial "accumulated depreciation" balance.

The stockholder is further perturbed because the corporation's most recent balance sheet shows Goodwill at only $500,000, whereas a year before it had been shown at $1,000,000. She believes that a corporation which is losing goodwill so rapidly must be poorly managed.

In simple, nontechnical language, write a letter which should clear up the stockholder's misunderstanding.

Problems

Problem 21-1.   Refer to the following account balances taken from the ledger of The Dennis Company on the dates indicated and compute the amounts and per cents of the changes shown therein.

	December 31, 1959	December 31, 1958
Sales......................................	$305,200	$280,000
Officers' salaries...........................	30,000	30,000
Delivery expense..........................	10,110	12,270
Interest expense...........................	460	230
Commissions earned........................	3,000	2,225
Purchases.................................	188,368	195,200
Sales discounts............................	7,358	5,200
Purchase returns and allowances............	2,217	3,000
Gain (loss*) on disposal of machinery........	4,520	3,280*
Freight in.................................	2,268	2,400
Insurance expense.........................	600	450
Bad debts.................................	2,135	1,400

Problem 21-2.   Copy the following condensed comparative balance sheet and add columns showing:

(a) The per cent that each item in the December 31, 1959 balance sheet is of the balance sheet total.

(b) The amount and per cent of increase or decrease in each item. Note: Carry per cents to two decimal places.

THE HELENA CORPORATION
Comparative Balance Sheet
December 31, 1959 and 1958

	December 31,	
	1959	1958
Assets		
Current assets:		
Cash...	$ 14,200	$ 11,100
Accounts receivable—net.........................	46,400	52,300
Inventories......................................	41,800	36,600
Prepaid expenses................................	3,000	2,600
Total current assets.........................	$105,400	$102,600
Fixed assets:		
Machinery and equipment........................	$ 96,500	$ 80,200
Less accumulated depreciation....................	21,400	14,400
Net...	$ 75,100	$ 65,800
Deferred charge—unamortized bond discount.........	$ 1,500	$ 1,800
	$182,000	$170,200

	December 31,	
	1959	1958
Liabilities and Stockholders' Equity		
Current liabilities:		
Accounts payable.............................	$ 24,300	$ 18,400
Accrued expenses..............................	12,600	13,300
Total current liabilities.......................	$ 36,900	$ 31,700
Bonds payable....................................	50,000	50,000
Total liabilities..............................	$ 86,900	$ 81,700
Stockholders' equity:		
Capital stock (7,500 shares)......................	$ 75,000	$ 75,000
Retained earnings...............................	20,100	13,500
Total stockholders' equity......................	$ 95,100	$ 88,500
	$182,000	$170,200

Problem 21-3.

THE HELENA CORPORATION
Condensed Comparative Statement of Income and Expense
For the Years Ended December 31, 1959, 1958, and 1957

	Year Ended December 31,		
	1959	1958	1957
Gross sales..............................	$125,400	$82,800	$104,000
Sales allowances.........................	2,400	800	3,000
Net sales................................	$123,000	$82,000	$101,000
Cost of goods sold.......................	77,800	49,800	68,000
Gross profit on sales.....................	$ 45,200	$32,200	$ 33,000
Operating expenses:			
Selling expenses........................	$ 26,400	$16,800	$ 20,000
General expenses.......................	9,600	8,000	12,000
Total operating expenses..............	$ 36,000	$24,800	$ 32,000
Net operating income.....................	$ 9,200	$ 7,400	$ 1,000
Net financial expense.....................	2,400	2,400	4,000
Net income (loss*).......................	$ 6,800	$ 5,000	$ 3,000*

From the above data, prepare:

(a) A comparative statement of income and expense for the three years expressed in terms of per cents of net sales.

(b) A comparative statement of income and expense for the years ended December 31, 1959 and 1958, with columns for amounts and per cents of increase.

(c) A comparative statement of income and expense for the years ended December 31, 1959, 1958, and 1957, with columns showing differences between 1959 and 1958 amounts and between 1958 and 1957 amounts, and columns showing ratios of 1959 and 1958 amounts to 1957 amounts.

Problem 21-4. Use the data of Brewsters, Incorporated, on December 31, 1959 and 1958, on the following page to compute:

(a) Ratio of stockholders' equity to total assets.
(b) Ratio of security to long-term liabilities. (All of the fixed assets are pledged as security to the long-term liabilities.)
(c) Ratio of stockholders' equity to total liabilities.
(d) Ratio of net income to total assets.

	December 31,	
	1959	1958
Fixed assets.....................................	$380,000	$305,500
Total assets.....................................	510,000	445,000
Long-term liabilities.............................	75,000	100,000
Total liabilities.................................	150,000	170,000
Stockholders' equity.............................	360,000	275,000
Net income for the year ended on the stated date.....	38,000	29,500

Problem 21-5. The following information for 1959 and 1958 was gathered from the records of Power Company.

	1959	1958
Net sales.................................... ...	$106,000	$101,000
Purchases..................................... ..	72,100	65,400
Purchase returns.................................	1,200	800
Selling and administrative expenses..................	19,000	20,500
Bond interest....................................	600	450
Interest expense..................................	364	275
Net income......................................	6,000	5,000
Federal income tax...............................	4,000	3,500
Monthly average of notes payable..................	6,500	5,000

Compute the following ratios for these years:

(a) Purchase returns to purchases.
(b) Operating ratio.
(c) Income available for bond interest and number of times bond interest earned.
(d) Interest expense to monthly average of notes payable.

Problem 21-6. MacReynolds Company presented the following condensed income statements covering three calendar years.

	1959	1958	1957
Net sales..............................	$853,624	$652,424	$573,480
Cost of goods sold.......................	569,740	421,706	397,125
Gross profit on sales....................	$283,884	$230,718	$176,355
Operating expenses:			
Selling expenses.......................	$163,300	$142,240	$131,098
General expenses......................	72,290	47,265	37,120
Total operating expenses.............	$235,590	$189,505	$168,218
Net operating income.................. ..	$ 48,294	$ 41,213	$ 8,137
Net financial expense....................	18,365	21,485	12,652
Net income (loss*) before income tax	$ 29,929	$ 19,728	$ 4,515*
Federal income tax.......................	14,657	8,582	
Net income (loss*)......................	$ 15,272	$ 11,146	$ 4,515*

Prepare a comparative income statement, showing the increases and decreases from year to year, with ratios based on amounts for the preceding year.

Problem 21-7. Refer to Problem 21-6. Prepare a comparative income statement for the three-year period showing the increases and decreases in relation to 1957. Also compute ratios of the amounts based on the amounts for 1957.

Problem 21-8. Following are balances of selected asset accounts of The Oceanic Company on December 31, 1959.

Land (undeveloped real estate)...........................		$ 5,000
Land..		15,000
Buildings..	$60,000	
Less accumulated depreciation......................	25,000	35,000
Equipment...	$45,000	
Less accumulated depreciation......................	15,500	29,500

The undeveloped real estate has a market value of $8,000.

Compute the ratio of security to bonds outstanding for each of the following sets of facts:

(a) The Oceanic Company has outstanding 4% bonds amounting to $50,000 which are secured by the assets listed above. The sinking fund for the retirement of these bonds has a balance of $20,000; $15,000 of the fund is invested in the stock of Whipple Corporation, $3,000 is invested in the company's own bonds, and $2,000 remains in sinking fund cash.

(b) Assume the same facts as in (a) except that all of the sinking fund has been invested in the company's own bonds.

(c) Assume the same facts as in (a) but with no sinking fund.

Problem 21-9. Using the information presented below, compute:

(a) The ratio of total liabilities to total assets.

(b) The ratio of net income to stockholders' equity.

(c) The ratio of stockholders' equity to fixed assets.

(d) The ratio of net sales to fixed assets.

(e) The book value per share of common stock, assuming that the preferred stock is cumulative, but nonparticipating, and that dividends are in arrears on the preferred stock in the amount of $4,800.

(f) The earnings per share of common stock, assuming that 500 shares of the common stock outstanding were issued as a stock dividend on September 1, 1959, and that the preferred stock is fully participating.

(g) The earnings per share of common stock, assuming that the 500 shares of common stock issued on September 1, 1959, were issued for cash, and that the preferred stock is nonparticipating.

(h) The earnings per share of common stock, assuming that the preferred stock is nonparticipating and that all of the shares were issued before 1959.

TAPPAN ENTERPRISES, INCORPORATED
Condensed Balance Sheet
December 31, 1959

Assets

Current assets..		$162,000
Fixed assets—less accumulated depreciation..................		284,500
		$446,500

Liabilities and Stockholders' Equity

Liabilities..		$176,500
Stockholders' equity:		
Preferred stock—4% (600 shares).................	$ 60,000	
Common stock (1,500 shares).....................	150,000	
Retained earnings..............................	60,000	270,000
		$446,500

Net sales for 1959 were $160,500. Net income for 1959 was $20,000.

Problem 21-10. Refer to the financial statements of The Helena Corporation in Problem 21-2 and 21-3 and make the following computations for 1958 and 1959:

(a) The ratio of sales to stockholders' equity.
(b) The ratio of cost of goods manufactured to fixed assets. The finished goods inventories were: December 31, 1957, $18,400; December 31, 1958, $16,300; December 31, 1959, $20,200.
(c) The equity ratios.
(d) The ratio of net sales to fixed assets.
(e) The operating ratio.
(f) The book value per share of stock.
(g) The ratio of stockholders' equity to fixed assets.
(h) The earnings per share of stock.

Problem 21-11. Following are balance sheets of The Townsend Company.

		December 31, 1959		December 31, 1958
Assets				
Current assets:				
Cash..............................		$ 24,326		$ 27,865
Accounts receivable..................	$67,785		$56,384	
Less allowance for doubtful accounts..	3,486	64,299	2,755	53,629
Inventories..........................		39,742		31,465
Total current assets..............		$128,367		$112,959
Fixed assets:				
Land.............................		$ 12,000		$ 10,000
Buildings...........................	$35,000		$35,000	
Less accumulated depreciation........	7,700	27,300	7,000	28,000
Machinery..........................	$37,500		$40,000	
Less accumulated depreciation........	18,750	18,750	16,000	24,000
Total fixed assets................		$ 58,050		$ 62,000
		$186,417		$174,959
Liabilities and Stockholders' Equity				
Current liabilities:				
Accounts payable....................		$ 28,365		$ 19,320
Notes payable.......................		26,000		30,000
Total current liabilities...........		$ 54,365		$ 49,320
Stockholders' equity:				
Capital stock.......................		$ 75,000		$ 60,000
Retained earnings...................		47,052		65,639
Reserve for contingencies.............		10,000		
Total stockholders' equity.........		$132,052		$125,639
		$186,417		$174,959

An examination of the Retained Earnings account showed that a stock dividend of 25% and later a cash dividend of 5% were paid during the year 1959.

Prepare a statement accounting for the increase in stockholders' equity and the resulting increase in net assets during the year 1959, with supporting schedules.

Problem 21-12. Using the data presented in Problems 21-2 and 21-3, and the additional information below, prepare a statement accounting for the change in stockholders' equity for the year ended December 31, 1959, and the resulting change in net assets, with supporting schedules.

Dividends of $5,000 were declared and paid and a federal income tax refund of $4,800 applicable to 1955 was received.

Problem 21-13. From the following after-closing account balances of The Heathmire Corporation, on December 31, 1959, 1958, and 1957, prepare:

(a) A statement accounting for the changes in stockholders' equity and resulting changes in net assets for the years ended December 31, 1959 and 1958. Accompany your statement with schedules of working capital and fixed assets on December 31, 1959, 1958, and 1957.

(b) A comparative balance sheet for December 31, 1959 and 1958, showing per cents based on balance sheet totals and, in another column, per cents based on category totals.

(c) A comparative balance sheet for December 31, 1959, 1958, and 1957 with columns for the amount of change and the ratios of 1959 and 1958 amounts to 1957 amounts.

	December 31,		
	1959	1958	1957
Cash..	$143,500	$148,055	$137,760
Accounts receivable.............................	156,250	182,150	166,920
Allowance for doubtful accounts..................	9,220	8,235	7,500
Inventories.....................................	117,285	121,690	120,430
Land...	66,000	80,000	80,000
Buildings.......................................	259,165	180,005	186,040
Accumulated depreciation—Buildings..............	50,620	45,575	47,600
Furniture and fixtures...........................	13,460	16,630	14,350
Accumulated depreciation—Furniture and fixtures...	3,665	10,780	8,900
Deferred charges................................	9,130	8,315	7,450
Accounts payable................................	57,305	54,600	62,200
Notes payable...................................	38,000	45,000	16,000
Accrued expenses................................	10,700	12,545	9,240
Preferred stock.................................	200,000	200,000	185,000
Common stock...................................	350,000	300,000	325,000
Retained earnings...............................	45,280	60,110	51,510

The Retained Earnings account for 1959 appears below.

Retained Earnings

Loss on sale of land..........	2,000	Balance, January 1............	60,110
Stock dividend..............	50,000	Gain on sale of furniture and	
Cash dividends:		fixtures...................	500
Preferred.................	3,000	Net income..................	44,670
Common..................	5,000		
Balance, December 31........	45,280		
	105,280		105,280

The Retained Earnings account for 1958 follows:

Retained Earnings

Cash dividends:		Balance, January 1............	51,510
Preferred..................	6,000	Gain on sale of building........	1,500
Common..................	10,000	Net income..................	23,100
Balance, December 31.........	60,110		
	76,110		76,110

Problem 21-14. On December 31, 1958, The Pretzel Corporation issued 15-year, 4%, annual serial bonds in the amount of $75,000, secured by the stock held

in the Millvale Company and all of the fixed assets. The first of the 15 installments is due in 1960. The bond agreement calls for the following conditions to be maintained by The Pretzel Corporation: The bond security is to be maintained at not less than twice the bonds outstanding; the working capital ratio is never to fall below 2 to 1; and the ratio of stockholders' equity to total liabilities is never to be less than 1.50. An acceleration clause in the agreement provides that the bonds outstanding will become immediately due and payable at the bondholders' option if the corporation fails at any time to maintain the above requirements.

THE PRETZEL CORPORATION
Balance Sheet
December 31, 1958

Assets

Current assets:
Cash... $ 55,000
Accounts receivable—net......................... 26,400
Inventories.................................... 6,980
   Total current assets.................................... $ 88,380
Stock held in Millvale Company—at cost..................... 50,000
Fixed assets...................................... $117,500
Less accumulated depreciation.................... 12,000   105,500
$243,880

Liabilities and Stockholders' Equity

Current liabilities:
Accounts payable............................. $ 10,400
Notes payable................................. 4,000
   Total current liabilities............................... $ 14,400
Long-term liability:
Serial bonds payable..................................... 75,000
Stockholders' equity:
Preferred stock............................... $ 30,000
Common stock................................. 105,000
Retained earnings............................. 19,480
   Total stockholders' equity............................ 154,480
$243,880

On December 31, 1958, the market value of the Millvale stock was equal to its cost. But the market value of this stock declined to $40,000 on December 31, 1959. During 1959, The Pretzel Corporation acquired treasury stock at a cost of $35,000, and issued a stock dividend increasing the preferred stock by $5,000. The depreciation for 1959 was $6,000 and there was a net loss for the year of $9,000.

The December 31, 1959 balance sheet of the corporation is the same as the one prepared on December 31, 1958, except for the changes that the above information would effect.

Show, by means of ratios, the condition of The Pretzel Corporation's compliance with the bond agreement on December 31, 1959, and inform the bondholders as to whether or not they are entitled to declare the bonds outstanding on December 31, 1959, due and payable.

Problem 21-15. Selected information from the accounting records of Ackerman Company and Wharton Company is presented on page 853. Using the data presented (admittedly inadequate), compute ratios suitable for use in comparing the companies, briefly interpreting the results shown by the ratios.

	Ackerman Company	Wharton Company
Cost of goods manufactured	$ 71,000	$ 95,000
Fixed assets—less depreciation	310,000	355,000
Retained earnings	65,000	96,000
Total assets	400,000	525,000
Capital stock ($100 par value)	275,000	300,000
Total liabilities	60,000	129,000

Assignment Material for Chapter 22

Questions

Question 22-1. Tell how to estimate the average age of accounts receivable by using the total sales and the total accounts receivable.

Question 22-2. How is merchandise turnover computed?
What is the advantage of using monthly inventories in computing turnover?

Question 22-3. How is working capital turnover computed? Of what significance is this turnover?

Question 22-4. Define *working capital*.
What is meant by the "current ratio"?
Which is the more important factor in the analysis of the financial condition of a company: the working capital stated in dollars, or the working capital ratio?

Question 22-5. A statement analyst notes that the working capital and the working capital ratio for two companies being analyzed are identical. Is it safe for him to conclude that the working capital position of the two companies is identical? Explain.

Question 22-6. Give your reasons for the inclusion in or exclusion from current assets of the following items on December 31, 1958:

(a) Securities having a readily realizable market value at the balance sheet date. These identical securities have been owned for two years and the management states that the intention is to hold them until the funds represented therein are needed.
(b) Unexpired insurance premiums.
(c) A note receivable for $100,000 which falls due January 4, 1960.
(d) Inventories of obsolete parts whose sale is somewhat problematical. A supply of these parts is necessary in order to service old-style machines which are still in use throughout the country.
(e) Unamortized bond discount, all of which will be charged off during the coming year.
(f) Cash deposited in a special dividend account for the express purpose of paying a dividend already declared and due ten days following the balance sheet date.
(g) Cash in hands of sinking fund trustee, all of which is to be used to retire serial bonds and meet interest payments maturing within eight months after the balance sheet date.

Question 22-7. There is considerable agitation for the adoption of a natural business year. Are there any reasons why you as an auditor would recommend to some of your clients a change from the calendar-year to a fiscal-year closing? If so, give the reasons.

854

Question 22-8.   A corporation seeks to increase its working capital and its working capital ratio by discounting notes receivable, by giving a long-term bond and mortgage upon its plant, and by obtaining a short-term bank loan, by all of which methods it secures cash. To what extent is its objective accomplished in each instance? Explain fully.

Question 22-9.   A Company and B Company are engaged in the same type of merchandising business. For the year 1959, they report substantially the same amounts for sales, cost of goods sold, and gross profit. A Company reports a merchandise turnover of 10 while B Company reports one of 4.5. Explain, using an illustration if necessary, how such a difference might occur.

Question 22-10.   If merchandise is received during the last part of the accounting period, why is it incorrect to omit the charge to Purchases and the credit to Accounts Payable, and also to omit the goods from the inventory?

Question 22-11.   Prepare an estimate of the outstanding accounts receivable on December 31, 1959, on the basis of the following information:

Sales are made at an average gross profit of 40%.
The average inventory is $43,800 and the turnover is 8.
Terms of sale are 2/10; n/30, and customers take advantage of the discount
    on 55% of the sales, the remaining 45% being outstanding an average of
    45 days.

Question 22-12.   Does it follow that an improvement in the working capital ratio will be accompanied by an improvement in the equity ratios? State why or why not, giving your reasons.

Question 22-13.   A client submits for your evaluation a balance sheet of a prospective customer. State, in the order of importance, the points to which you would give consideration.

Question 22-14.   The Hunter Corporation manufactures a seasonal product, new models of which are brought out annually early in August. Sales of the old model are continued through August in outlying territories. Monthly sales to established outlets on net 20-day terms gradually increase until they are highest in the winter months and then taper off so that inventory quantities are lowest on June 30, before material and parts for the new model are purchased. Development of a new model is started in January and involves relatively large expenditures for design, engineering, dies, and tools, culminating in a plant shutdown the last ten days of July to prepare for volume production of the new model starting in August.

The company wishes to change from a calendar-year basis to some other closing date. What date would you suggest they use? Discuss the advantages and disadvantages of the date you suggest, including consideration of the problem of income determination and the presentation of other significant financial information. Do not consider income tax effects.

Problems

Problem 22-1.   Examine the partial balance sheets of Shrubbs, Incorporated, as of December 31, 1958 and December 31, 1959 on page 856 and determine whether the short-term borrowing power of the business improved during 1959. Present ratios and schedules, as you see fit, to support your conclusion.

SHRUBBS, INCORPORATED
Partial Balance Sheets

	December 31,	
	1959	1958
Current assets:		
Cash....................................	$210,750.40	$251,849.23
Accounts receivable—net..................	89,115.60	84,430.10
Notes receivable........................	32,649.37	30,600.82
Inventory..............................	281,829.36	157,235.80
Total current assets....................	$614,344.73	$524,115.95
Current liabilities:		
Accounts payable........................	$175,890.10	$160,520.20
Notes payable...........................	101,500.00	95,465.00
Bank loans..............................	24,896.60	19,865.30
Total current liabilities.................	$302,286.70	$275,850.50

Problem 22-2. By referring to Problem 22-1, and to the additional information given below, make a second determination as to whether Shrubbs, Incorporated, was a better credit risk on December 31, 1959 or on December 31, 1958. State any conclusions concerning the business which you may reach.

SHRUBBS, INCORPORATED
Inventory Balances by Month

	1959	1958
January 31............................	$ 194,680.40	$ 162,415.84
February 28............................	198,732.55	159,620.89
March 31..............................	210,460.10	158,994.62
April 30................................	225,890.66	156,145.20
May 31.................................	248,914.83	157,214.00
June 30................................	265,337.80	158,639.18
July 31................................	278,401.60	157,814.13
August 31..............................	285,892.30	158,722.17
September 30...........................	293,740.44	157,468.91
October 31.............................	295,830.50	156,892.25
November 30...........................	287,450.96	156,950.50
December 31...........................	281,829.36	157,235.80
	$3,067,161.50	$1,898,113.49

Cost of goods sold: During 1959, $2,536,464.00; during 1958, $471,707.40.

Problem 22-3. Use the data of Northern Company presented below to make the following computations for the years 1959 and 1958:

(a) Material turnovers and the number of days per turnover.
(b) Finished goods turnovers and the number of days per turnover.
(c) Average number of days' sales uncollected.
(d) Ratio of accounts payable to purchases.

	1959	1958	1957
Net sales...................................	$845,700	$832,900	
Finished goods inventory—December 31.....	67,000	60,000	$59,000
Materials inventory—December 31..........	70,000	65,000	67,000
Cost of goods manufactured................	531,600	525,400	
Net purchases—Materials..................	275,000	266,000	
Accounts receivable—December 31..........	189,000	188,700	
Accounts payable—December 31.............	51,500	53,400	
Freight in.................................	4,500	4,300	

Problem 22-4. Determine the relative liquidity of the following companies by means of a table showing the accumulation of the working capital ratios. Comment on the conclusions which may be drawn from this table.

	Steer Company	Pilot Company
Current assets:		
Cash.	$ 78,900	$ 52,900
Receivables.	135,620	89,800
Finished goods.	92,350	44,620
Goods in process.	107,450	35,090
Materials.	145,700	26,480
Unexpired insurance.	12,600	8,100
Current liabilities.	286,125	124,090

Problem 22-5. From the following data:

(a) Prepare a schedule of working capital, with a column showing the ratio of 1959 items to the corresponding 1958 items.
(b) Compute the working capital ratios.
(c) Compute the acid-test ratios.
(d) Prepare a table showing the percentage distribution of current assets.
(e) Prepare a table showing the accumulation of the working capital ratios.

	December 31,	
	1959	1958
Cash.	$145,000	$45,000
Accounts receivable—net.	108,500	70,000
Finished goods.	67,500	20,000
Goods in process. . . . . ?.	62,500	30,000
Materials.	45,000	20,000
Prepaid rent.	22,500	10,000
Accounts payable.	112,500	75,000
Notes payable.	43,500	19,000

Problem 22-6. Selected account balances of Faber Enterprises as of December 31, 1959, 1958, and 1957, are given below. Compute the working capital turnovers for 1959 and 1958.

	December 31,		
	1959	1958	1957
Accounts payable.	$104,000	$116,100	$112,800
Accounts receivable.	72,000	79,200	63,000
Accrued salaries and wages.	10,200	12,700	9,900
Allowance for doubtful accounts.	2,160	2,370	1,800
Cash.	58,600	69,400	47,300
Inventories.	99,900	106,000	94,700
Sales.	585,000	650,400	560,200
Sales discounts.	17,400	18,200	14,500
Sales returns and allowances.	12,800	15,100	9,600
Unexpired insurance.	3,000	4,500	2,000

Problem 22-7. The Warwick Corporation prepared the balance sheet appearing on the following page for presentation at the annual meeting of the stockholders of the corporation.

You have been engaged by a group of stockholders to examine the accounts and financial statements of The Warwick Corporation, and in the course of your examination you discover certain errors mentioned below the December 31, 1959 balance sheet and affecting it.

THE WARWICK CORPORATION
Balance Sheet
December 31, 1959

Assets

Current assets:

Cash..		$ 30,600	
Accounts receivable (net of allowance for			
doubtful accounts of $4,500)...................		37,600	
Notes receivable.............................		10,000	
Inventories...................................		86,300	
Prepaid insurance.............................		2,200	$166,700

Fixed assets:

Land......................................		$ 60,000	
Buildings.............................	$102,700		
Less accumulated depreciation.........	31,300	71,400	
Machinery and equipment...............	$232,800		
Less accumulated depreciation........	92,400	140,400	271,800
			$438,500

Liabilities and Stockholders' Equity

Current liabilities:

Accounts payable..............................		$ 43,700	
Accrued expenses................................		6,300	$ 50,000
Bonds payable...			142,500

Stockholders' equity:

Capital stock..................................		$200,000	
Retained earnings.............................		46,000	246,000
			$438,500

(a) The bank statement received on December 31, 1959, revealed that the corporation had checks outstanding amounting to $4,600. In an attempt to reconcile the accounts with the bank statement, an entry was made debiting Cash and crediting Accounts Payable for this amount.

(b) Materials amounting to $5,100 were ordered on account, f.o.b. destination. The purchase was recorded on December 31, 1959, and $5,100 was added to the December 31, 1959 inventory. The shipment is scheduled for delivery in January, 1960.

(c) On December 31, 1959, a $7,500 deposit was made in a fund for the retirement of bonds; the bookkeeper credited Cash and debited Bonds Payable.

(d) A three-year insurance policy costing $9,000 was purchased on July 1, 1959, with a charge to Insurance Expense. $1,500 of this amount was transferred to the Prepaid Insurance account by adjusting entry on December 31, 1959.

(e) A customer's non-interest-bearing note for $6,200, which had been discounted at the bank, was dishonored. The bookkeeper debited Notes Receivable Discounted and credited Cash, $6,200.

(1) Prepare a revised balance sheet as of December 31, 1959, giving effect to any corrections you think necessary.

(2) Prepare or compute the following tabulations or ratios (1) based on the original balance sheet, and (2) based upon your revised balance sheet: (a) Working capital ratio; (b) acid-test ratio; (c) percentage distribution of current assets; (d) accumulation of working capital ratio.

Problem 22-8.

THE CASCADE COMPANY
Schedule of Working Capital
December 31, 1959 and 1958

	December 31,	
	1959	1958
Current assets:		
Cash..	$ 29,000	$ 14,600
Receivables:		
Accounts....................................	$ 92,900	$ 99,000
Notes—From customers......................	8,500	9,600
Total receivables...........................	$101,400	$108,600
Less allowance for doubtful accounts............	2,200	3,100
Net receivables...........................	$ 99,200	$105,500
Inventories:		
Finished goods...............................	$ 38,500	$ 58,000
Goods in process............................	25,000	34,000
Materials...................................	29,000	40,000
Total inventories...........................	$ 92,500	$132,000
Prepaid expenses...............................	$ 4,600	$ 5,200
Total current assets.......................	$225,300	$257,300
Current liabilities:		
Bank loans...................................	$ 32,000	$ 83,000
Accounts payable.............................	39,200	43,000
Notes payable................................	8,000	10,500
Accrued expenses.............................	1,200	3,400
Total current liabilities...................	$ 80,400	$139,900
Net current assets—working capital................	$144,900	$117,400

THE CASCADE COMPANY
Income Statement
For the Years Ended December 31, 1959 and 1958

	1959	1958
Sales (net).....................................	$962,000	$816,000
Cost of sales:		
Materials:		
Inventory—January 1.........................	$ 40,000	$ 41,300
Purchases...................................	262,000	261,500
Total....................................	$302,000	$302,800
Inventory—December 31......................	29,000	40,000
Materials used.............................	$273,000	$262,800
Labor...	215,000	202,000
Factory expenses...............................	171,000	154,000
Total.......................................	$659,000	$618,800
Add decrease in inventory of goods in process.......	9,000	1,500
Cost of goods manufactured.....................	$668,000	$620,300
Add decrease in inventory of finished goods.........	19,500	6,300
Cost of sales...............................	$687,500	$626,600
Gross profit on sales.............................	$274,500	$189,400
Selling and general expenses........................	188,000	146,000
Net income.....................................	$ 86,500	$ 43,400

(1) As of December 31, 1959 and 1958, or for the respective years ended on those dates, compute:

   (a) Working capital ratio.
   (b) Acid-test ratio.
   (c) Per cent of each current asset to total current assets.
   (d) Accumulation of working capital ratio.
   (e) Number and profitability of current asset turnovers. (Total current assets on January 1, 1958—$240,000.)
   (f) Finished goods turnovers.
   (g) Material turnovers.
   (h) Trade receivables conversion periods.
   (i) Ratio of accounts payable to purchases.

(2) Comment briefly on the change in current position.

Problem 22-9.   The information presented below was taken from the records of Ashley Company and Southern Company on June 30, 1959, before closing entries were made.

Comment on the relative current financial position of the two companies at this date and show computations supporting your comments.

	Ashley Company	Southern Company
Cash...	$ 28,000	$ 64,000
Accounts receivable—net..........................	44,000	135,000
Notes receivable (Six-month loans to employees).....		26,000
Inventories—June 30, 1958.......................	164,000	189,000
Supplies...		12,000
Prepaid expenses................................	9,000	
Sinking fund cash...............................	10,000	20,000
Land..	30,000	40,000
Buildings—net...................................	80,000	115,000
Equipment—net..................................	116,000	225,000
Bank loans......................................	40,000	24,000
Accounts payable................................	65,000	114,000
Notes payable...................................		72,000
Accrued taxes and expenses......................	30,000	
Bonds payable...................................	75,000	100,000
Preferred stock..................................		150,000
Common stock...................................	225,000	300,000
Retained earnings—June 30, 1958.................	31,000	45,000
Net sales.......................................	560,000	820,000
Cost of sales....................................	425,000	690,000
Expenses.......................................	128,000	104,000
Current assets on June 30, 1958..................	225,000	458,000
Inventories on June 30, 1959.....................	156,000	194,000

Problem 22-10.   In January, 1960, Cressona Corporation applied to Arbor Thrift Savings and Loan Company for a five-year loan of $142,000. The corporation intends to use the proceeds for payment of the federal income taxes it owes and for retirement of its bonds.

Cressona Corporation submitted the following balance sheet and supplementary information to the savings and loan company.

CRESSONA CORPORATION
Balance Sheet
December 31, 1959

Assets

Current assets:

Cash	$ 31,500	
Accounts receivable—net	259,000	
Inventories	55,400	
Unexpired insurance	16,500	$362,400

Fixed assets:

Machinery and equipment	$239,200		
Less accumulated depreciation	30,300	$208,900	
Patents	$ 8,000		
Less accumulated amortization	2,000	6,000	214,900
			$577,300

Liabilities and Stockholders' Equity

Current liabilities:

Accounts payable	$ 69,700	
Notes payable	28,800	
Federal income taxes payable (assessment from prior years)	42,000	
Accrued expenses	6,100	$146,600
Bonds payable—due March 15, 1960		100,000

Stockholders' equity:

Capital stock	$225,000	
Paid-in surplus	12,700	
Retained earnings	93,000	330,700
		$577,300

Net sales in 1959................ $358,400

As consultant to the loan department of Arbor Thrift Savings and Loan Company, you are requested to analyze the above data and submit your advice and comments in a memorandum to the loan department.

Problem 22-11. The following information was taken from the records of Zan Company:

Acid-test ratio	.92
Average finished goods inventory	$52,000
Average number of days' sales uncollected	77
Expenses	$212,000
Finished goods turnovers	12.20
Ratio of net income to average total current assets	9.80%
Net sales	$900,000
Total current assets	$425,000
Working capital turnover	4.50

The records also revealed that the current assets and current liabilities both decreased by an equal amount during the last fiscal year.

Required:

(a) Working capital ratio.
(b) Total quick assets.
(c) Accounts receivable at end of year.
(d) Turnover of average total current assets.

Problem 22-12. Loretto Productions, Incorporated, is preparing a report for its stockholders as of December 31, 1959. The corporation wishes to include in its report a questionnaire grouping of ratios. Prepare such a questionnaire by using the comparative statements appearing below.

LORETTO PRODUCTIONS, INCORPORATED
Comparative Income Statement
For the Years Ended December 31, 1959 and 1958

	1959	1958
Sales—net	$985,000	$950,000
Cost of goods sold:		
Materials:		
Inventory—January 1	$ 50,000	$ 45,000
Purchases	300,000	375,000
Total	$350,000	$420,000
Inventory—December 31	37,000	50,000
Materials used	$313,000	$370,000
Labor	240,000	245,000
Factory expenses	170,000	150,000
Total manufacturing cost	$723,000	$765,000
Deduct increase (add decrease*) in inventory of goods in process	5,000*	3,200
Cost of goods manufactured	$728,000	$761,800
Add decrease in inventory of finished goods	14,000	3,600
Cost of goods sold	$742,000	$765,400
Gross profit on sales	$243,000	$184,600
Expenses	200,000	169,000
Net income for the year	$ 43,000	$ 15,600

LORETTO PRODUCTIONS, INCORPORATED
Comparative Balance Sheet
December 31, 1959 and 1958

	December 31,	
	1959	1958
Assets		
Current assets:		
Cash	$ 29,600	$ 15,000
Accounts receivable—net	$126,800	$115,200
Inventories:		
Finished goods	$ 20,000	$ 34,000
Goods in process	22,000	27,000
Materials	37,000	50,000
Total	$ 79,000	$111,000
Total current assets	$235,400	$241,200
Fixed assets:		
Equipment—net	250,500	263,000
	$485,900	$504,200
Liabilities and Stockholders' Equity		
Current liabilities:		
Bank loans	$ 38,000	$ 81,000
Accounts payable	31,000	50,000
Accrued expenses	2,100	6,200
Total current liabilities	$ 71,100	$137,200
Bonds payable	150,000	150,000
Total liabilities	$221,100	$287,200

	December 31,	
	1959	1958
Stockholders' equity:		
Preferred stock—$100 par value, 5%, nonparticipating	$ 50,000	$ 40,000
Common stock—$100 par value....................	175,000	150,000
Retained earnings.............................	39,800	27,000
Total stockholders' equity.................	$264,800	$217,000
	$485,900	$504,200

The bonds are secured by all of the fixed assets.
The current assets on December 31, 1957, totaled $236,700.

Assignment Material for Chapter 23

Questions

Question 23-1. Into what groups can you classify the causes of a change in the net income from one period to another?

Question 23-2. What two elements cause a change in the gross profit?

Question 23-3. How would you apportion the following expenses among the several departments of a retail store?

Advertising.   Salesmen's salaries.
Rent.   Fire insurance on merchandise.

Question 23-4. How much reliance can be placed on departmental net income figures?

Question 23-5. Assume that the sporting goods department of a department store shows a net loss. Should that fact be accepted as a conclusive reason for discontinuing the department? Explain.

Question 23-6. A company carries an average inventory of $50,000, which it turns three times per year at a gross profit of 40% and a net income of 10% of sales. If a 10% reduction in selling prices will result in four turnovers per year with a 10% increase in expenses, will the company make more or less net income, and how much?

Question 23-7. The inventory of a retail shoe store has been increasing each year over a three-year period, but gross profits have been declining. What probable reasons would you advance for that condition, and how would you proceed to determine the real cause?

Question 23-8. From the following data extracted from the audited statements of the CBC Company, determine the reason for the increase in gross profit and prepare a statement reflecting such changes.

	Year Ending June 30,	
	1958	1959
Sales.......	$329,729.40	$336,323.99
Cost of sales...............................	237,332.70	242,079.35
Gross profit.............	$ 92,396.70	$ 94,244.64

Units sold:
  1958—72,450.
  1959—73,899.

Question 23-9. Give a possible explanation of how a department store might, during a period of stable prices, show a 30% increase in gross profit over the preceding year, while sales increased only 10 per cent.

864

Question 23-10. During a period of business prosperity, a company's accountants make a very careful computation of the company's break-even point, using current accounting data. May this computation be used by the management without adjustment as an indication of the point where losses would develop during a period of business depression? Explain.

Question 23-11. Your client is offered an opportunity to purchase, at $45 per share, no-par stock of a company which will have 50,000 shares outstanding after reorganization and financing.

The following information is given to you:

Earnings for the past three years: $205,600, $785,400, and $297,500; average, $429,500.

Net tangible assets, after giving effect to new financing, $1,850,000.

You are informed that the present management will continue in charge of the company and that it has indicated its intention of paying dividends at the rate of $4 per share per annum. Your client asks your advice concerning the desirability of purchasing 1,000 shares of this offer. Submit a memorandum embodying your advice and giving your reasons therefor.

Question 23-12. A merchant regularly marked up his merchandise 50% on cost; at the end of the year he was surprised to find that, although his expenses were only 35% of his sales, he had suffered a loss instead of making a net profit of 15%.

What was his per cent of loss on sales?

What per cent should he add to cost to make a net profit of 15% on sales, assuming that the quantity of merchandise sold and the total expenses incurred will not be affected by the change in selling prices?

Problems

Problem 23-1.

THE MacFARLAND COMPANY
Comparative Income Statement
For the Years Ended December 31, 1959 and 1958

	1959	1958
Net sales..	$710,000	$622,000
Cost of goods sold................................	584,000	519,000
Gross profit on sales.............................	$126,000	$103,000
Operating expenses:		
Selling expenses................................	$ 58,000	$ 51,000
General expenses................................	24,000	26,000
Total.......................................	$ 82,000	$ 77,000
Net operating income.............................	$ 44,000	$ 26,000
Net financial income.............................	12,000	5,000
Net income.......................................	$ 56,000	$ 31,000

Prepare a statement accounting for the increase in net income.

Use columns for per cent of net sales, amounts, and ratio of 1959 to 1958.

Problem 23-2.

THE TONE COMPANY
Comparative Income Statement
For the Years Ended December 31, 1959 and 1958

	1959	1958
Net sales	$384,000	$438,000
Cost of goods sold	291,000	326,000
Gross profit on sales	$ 93,000	$112,000
Operating expenses:		
Selling expenses	$ 31,000	$ 46,000
General expenses	34,000	32,000
Total	$ 65,000	$ 78,000
Net operating income	$ 28,000	$ 34,000
Net financial expense	2,000	3,000
Net income	$ 26,000	$ 31,000

Prepare a statement accounting for the decrease in net income. Use columns for per cent of net sales, amounts, and ratio of 1959 to 1958.

Problem 23-3.

THE FOREST COMPANY
Condensed Comparative Statement of Gross Profit on Sales

	Year Ended December 31,	
	1959	1958
Net sales	$661,689	$583,500
Cost of goods sold	492,891	479,000
Gross profit on sales	$168,798	$104,500

During 1959:

(a) Volume increased 5%.
(b) Selling price increased 8%.
(c) Costs decreased 2%.

Account for the changes in sales, cost of goods sold, and gross profit.

Problem 23-4.   The following information was taken from the records of The Divers Company:

	1959	1958
Net sales	$88,825	$95,000
Cost of goods sold	46,852	52,000
Gross profit on sales	$41,973	$43,000

During 1959:

(a) Volume decreased 15%.
(b) Selling price increased 10%.
(c) Costs increased 6%.

Prepare a statement accounting for the changes in sales, cost of goods sold, and gross profit.

Problem 23-5. You are given the following information concerning The Morrell Company:

	1959	1958
Net sales	$342,608	$322,000
Cost of goods sold	233,016	219,000
Gross profit on sales	$109,592	$103,000

You learn that during 1959:

(a) Volume increased 12%.
(b) Selling price decreased 5%.
(c) Costs decreased 5%.

Account for the changes in sales, cost of goods sold, and gross profit.

Problem 23-6. Assume the following data:

	1959	1958
Sales	$423,696	$388,000
Cost of goods sold	307,632	290,000
Gross profit on sales	$116,064	$ 98,000

If selling prices increased 5% in 1959, what were the per cents of change in:

(a) Volume?
(b) Costs?

Problem 23-7. Assume the following data:

	1959	1958
Sales	$216,315	$237,500
Cost of goods sold	167,256	180,000
Gross profit on sales	$ 49,059	$ 57,500

If volume decreased 8% in 1959, what were the per cents of change in:

(a) Selling price?
(b) Costs?

Problem 23-8. Assume the following data:

	1959	1958
Sales	$133,518	$110,000
Cost of goods sold	116,739	90,000
Gross profit on sales	$ 16,779	$ 20,000

If costs increased 9% in 1959, what were the per cents of change in:

(a) Volume?
(b) Selling price?

Problem 23-9. Assume the following data:

	1959	1958
Sales	$159,936	$140,000
Cost of goods sold	140,448	110,000
Gross profit on sales	$ 19,488	$ 30,000

If volume increased 12% in 1959, what were the per cents of change in:

(a) Selling price?
(b) Costs?

Problem 23-10.   Assume the following data:

	1959	1958
Sales..	$250,792	$290,000
Cost of goods sold...............................	207,552	240,000
Gross profit on sales.............................	$ 43,240	$ 50,000

If selling prices decreased 6% in 1959, what were the per cents of change in:

(a) Volume?
(b) Costs?

Problem 23-11.   You are given the following information concerning the operations of The Hogan Company during the years 1958 and 1959. Prepare a comparative statement of cost of goods manufactured and sold, showing both total and per-unit costs.

	1959	1958
Materials used................................	$ 949,580	$ 979,920
Direct labor...................................	1,200,800	1,099,040
Manufacturing overhead........................	439,400	349,760

Analysis of Inventories

	Number of Units	Material	Labor	Manufacturing Expense	Total
January 1, 1958:					
Work in process..	2,000	$140,000	$170,000	$50,000	$360,000
Finished goods...	3,500				520,100
January 1, 1959:					
Work in process..	3,400	210,000	250,000	90,000	550,000
Finished goods...	4,500				
December 31, 1959:					
Work in process..	2,500	110,000	135,000	50,000	295,000
Finished goods...	4,000				

19,000 units were put into process in 1958 and 19,500 units were put into process in 1959. Inventories are valued on the first-in, first-out basis.

Problem 23-12.   You are given the following additional information relative to the operations of The Hogan Company during the years 1958 and 1959. Using this information plus the information contained in your answer to Problem 23-11, prepare a comparative income statement in total and per unit sold.

	1959	1958
Sales..	$3,421,330	$2,675,920
Selling expense................................	217,360	184,260
General expense...............................	144,210	121,180
Financial expense.............................	43,890	63,080

Problem 23-13.   From the following data prepare:

(a) A schedule showing annual gross profit rates by departments and for the business as a whole.

(b) A schedule showing the distribution of sales among departments in dollars and per cents.

(c) A schedule analyzing the departmental components of the annual gross profit rates.

	Total	Department X	Department Y	Department Z
1959:				
Sales.	$891,900	$488,500	$243,000	$160,400
Cost of goods sold. . .	637,961	375,168	160,137	102,656
Gross profit.	$253,939	$113,332	$ 82,863	$ 57,744
1958:				
Sales.	$829,200	$446,500	$267,000	$115,700
Cost of goods sold. . .	601,039	350,949	174,885	75,205
Gross profit.	$228,161	$ 95,551	$ 92,115	$ 40,495
1957:				
Sales.	$854,000	$425,600	$295,900	$132,500
Cost of goods sold. . .	599,294	319,200	195,294	84,800
Gross profit.	$254,706	$106,400	$100,606	$ 47,700

Problem 23-14.

THE CARSTENS CORPORATION
Income Statement
For the Year Ended December 31, 1959

	Department A	Department B	Total
Gross sales.	$115,000	$205,000	$320,000
Sales allowances.	2,000	4,000	6,000
Net sales.	$113,000	$201,000	$314,000
Cost of goods sold.	65,000	95,000	160,000
Gross profit on sales.	$ 48,000	$106,000	$154,000
Operating expenses:			
Selling expenses:			
Advertising.	$ 15,000	$ 9,000	$ 24,000
Delivery expense.	3,000	6,000	9,000
Salesmen's salaries.	20,000	15,000	35,000
Store rent.	2,000	2,000	4,000
Total selling expenses.	$ 40,000	$ 32,000	$ 72,000
General expenses:			
Office salaries.	$ 10,000	$ 12,000	$ 22,000
Officers' salaries.	15,000	20,000	35,000
Bad debts.	2,000	2,000	4,000
Depreciation—Office equipment. .	2,500	4,000	6,500
Total general expenses.	$ 29,500	$ 38,000	$ 67,500
Total operating expenses.	$ 69,500	$ 70,000	$139,500
Net income (loss*) before income tax. .	$ 21,500*	$ 36,000	$ 14,500

The president of The Carstens Corporation is considering closing Department A because it is operating at a loss. He asks you to give him your advice in the matter.

Your investigation discloses that the expenses stated on the following page, charged to Department A, would be eliminated by closing that department.

Completely eliminated:
Advertising; salesmen's salaries; bad debts.
Partially eliminated:
Delivery expense—$1,500 eliminated.
Depreciation—Office equipment—$1,000 eliminated.

Submit:

(a) A schedule showing the probable reduction in expenses which would result from closing Department A.
(b) A statement showing the probable net income before income tax which would result after closing Department A.
(c) Your opinion as to the advisability of closing Department A.

Problem 23-15.

THE BERFIELD COMPANY
Income Statement
For the Year Ended December 31, 1959

	Department A	Department B	Total
Net sales.................................	$580,000	$1,300,000	$1,880,000
Cost of goods sold........................	500,000	700,000	1,200,000
Gross profit on sales......................	$ 80,000	$ 600,000	$ 680,000
Operating expenses:			
Selling expenses:			
Salesmen's commissions...............	$116,000	$ 260,000	$ 376,000
Delivery truck drivers' salaries..........	3,000	5,000	8,000
Advertising............................	12,000	30,000	42,000
Depreciation—Delivery equipment......	1,000	2,000	3,000
Depreciation—Store building..........	5,000	7,500	12,500
Depreciation—Store fixtures............	4,000	6,000	10,000
Total selling expenses.................	$141,000	$ 310,500	$ 451,500
General expenses:			
Office salaries.........................	$ 20,000	$ 50,000	$ 70,000
Officers' salaries.......................	10,000	20,000	30,000
Insurance.............................	8,000	20,000	28,000
Bad debts............................	11,600	26,000	37,600
Total general expenses................	$ 49,600	$ 116,000	$ 165,600
Total operating expenses...........	$190,600	$ 426,500	$ 617,100
Net income (loss*) before income tax........	$110,600*	$ 173,500	$ 62,900

The management of The Berfield Company asks your advice as to whether or not to close Department A, which has been operating at a loss. Your investigation discloses the following additional information:

1. Salesmen are paid a straight commission equal to 20% of their sales.
2. The advertising for each of the departments is contracted for independently.
3. Depreciation is apportioned to each department on the basis of use or occupancy. Closing Department A will not reduce the total depreciation charge.
4. Three truck drivers operate the two delivery trucks in shifts. By eliminating Department A, one truck driver may be dispensed with.
5. Insurance is now carried on inventories in each department.
6. Bad debts are estimated at 2% of net sales.
7. Office and officers' salaries will not be reduced by the proposed change.

Submit:

(a) A schedule showing the probable reduction in expenses which would result from a discontinuance of Department A.

(b) A statement showing the probable net income before income tax which would result after discontinuance of Department A.

(c) Your opinion as to the advisability of closing Department A.

Problem 23-16.

THE EXPANDING COMPANY
Condensed Income Statement
For the Year Ended December 31, 1959

Net sales..		$320,000
Costs and expenses:		
Fixed..	$ 66,000	
Variable (62% of sales).........................	198,400	
Total...		264,400
Net income...		$ 55,600

The Expanding Company is considering making an investment in plant and equipment. This investment will increase the annual fixed costs by $32,000. The sales potential of the present plant is $340,000. With the new investment, the potential would be raised to $460,000.

Assuming that the variable costs will always be 62% of net sales:

(a) What is the break-even point under the conditions prevailing in 1959?

(b) What will the new break-even point be if the investment is made?

(c) What amount of sales would have to be made, after the investment, for the company to earn $55,600?

(d) What are the limits of net income under both the present and the proposed conditions?

Problem 23-17. The manager of The Quality Market received the following statements from the accounting department concerning the five departments of the store for 1959 and 1958.

1958:

		Net Income	
Department	Sales	Amount	Per Cent
A..............................	$ 69,100	$ 5,528	8%
B..............................	32,500	3,900	12
C..............................	118,600	17,790	15
D..............................	84,300	21,918	26
E..............................	12,400	2,232	18
Total......................	$316,900	$51,368	

1959:

		Net Income	
Department	Sales	Amount	Per Cent
A..............................	$120,800	$12,080	10%
B..............................	98,400	12,792	13
C..............................	102,700	18,486	18
D..............................	18,900	5,103	27
E..............................	4,600	874	19
Total......................	$345,400	$49,335	

The manager noted that the total sales and the rate of income of each department increased in 1959, and yet the 1959 net income decreased from the prior year.

You are asked to find a solution to this apparent inconsistency and to submit a report to the manager which will explain the reasons for this situation.

Problem 23-18. The departmental operating statement of The Dilworth Company for the year 1959 appears below.

	Department			
	A	B	C	Total
Sales........................	$122,000	$210,000	$188,000	$520,000
Cost of sales..................	96,000	110,000	120,000	326,000
Gross profit..................	$ 26,000	$100,000	$ 68,000	$194,000
Departmental expenses:				
Direct—salaries, advertising, bad debts, etc.............	$ 18,000	$ 55,900	$ 36,040	$109,940
Indirect—building and space costs (spread on basis of floor space)...................	12,000	16,000	14,000	42,000
Total..................	$ 30,000	$ 71,900	$ 50,040	$151,940
Operating income (loss*)........	$ 4,000*	$ 28,100	$ 17,960	$ 42,060
Financial expenses—divided equally....................	10,000	10,000	10,000	30,000
Net income (loss*).............	$ 14,000*	$ 18,100	$ 7,960	$ 12,060

Because of the continual losses incurred in Department A, the management has decided to eliminate this department and allocate its space to the other departments, assigning two-thirds of the space to Department B and one-third to Department C. It is the opinion of the management that under this arrangement Departments B and C (even without any sales increase) will remain profitable and that the annual income will increase.

Required:

(a) Proof or disproof of the management's opinion concerning the effects of eliminating Department A by preparing a departmental operating statement of The Dilworth Company for 1959 as if Department A had not been in operation.
(b) Sales volume that will be required after Department A is eliminated for the company to break even, assuming that Department B will account for 60% of the dollar volume.

Problem 23-19. Mr. Kula has been a stockholder of Regal Televisions, Incorporated, for a number of years, although never active in the corporation's management. He has received a dividend of $4.00 per share each year. The president of Regal Televisions, Incorporated, is attempting to increase his holdings in the corporation and has offered to purchase all of Mr. Kula's stock at book value.

Mr. Kula asks your opinion regarding the advisability of selling his stock. Prepare several pages of data and comment covering matters that should be brought to Mr. Kula's attention. The range of topics might include reference to the corporation's financial status, efficiency, management, policies, and prospects, to the extent permitted by an examination of the data presented. He informs you that his only purpose in holding the stock is a desire for a sound financial investment and that he is not interested in control or management of the corporation.

REGAL TELEVISIONS, INCORPORATED
Comparative Balance Sheet

	December 31,		Increase Decrease*
	1959	1958	
Assets			
Cash..	$ 90,000	$ 60,000	$ 30,000
Notes receivable—Black and white T.V............	15,000	4,000	11,000
Accounts receivable—Black and white T.V.........	100,000	85,000	15,000
Accounts receivable—Color T.V...................	110,000	60,000	50,000
Inventory—Black and white T.V.................	115,000	155,000	40,000*
Inventory—Color T.V..........................	245,000	190,000	55,000
Total current assets........................	$675,000	$554,000	$121,000
Land, buildings, and equipment—less depreciation..	280,000	250,000	30,000
	$955,000	$804,000	$151,000
Liabilities and Stockholders' Equity			
Notes payable—Bank...........................	$200,000	$ 75,000	$125,000
Accounts payable..............................	110,000	60,000	50,000
Total current liabilities......................	$310,000	$135,000	$175,000
Capital stock (Par value, $50)....................	400,000	400,000	-0-
Retained earnings..............................	245,000	269,000	24,000*
	$955,000	$804,000	$151,000

REGAL TELEVISIONS, INCORPORATED
Comparative Income Statement

	1959	1958	1957	1956
Net sales—Black and white T.V..	$365,000	$415,000	$435,000	$460,000
Net sales—Color T.V. (a)........	500,000	395,000	335,000	290,000
Total net sales.................	$865,000	$810,000	$770,000	$750,000
Cost of goods sold..............	612,000	536,000	457,000	425,000
Gross profit....................	$253,000	$274,000	$313,000	$325,000
Salesmen's commissions and expenses—Black and white T.V...	$ 60,000	$ 70,000	$ 75,000	$ 80,000
Salesmen's (two) salaries and expenses—Color T.V............	55,000	40,000	30,000	25,000
President's salary...............	30,000	30,000	30,000	30,000
Other expenses (including federal income taxes).................	100,000	100,000	100,000	100,000
Total expenses..............	$245,000	$240,000	$235,000	$235,000
Net income....................	$ 8,000	$ 34,000	$ 78,000	$ 90,000

(a) Sold entirely to one chain of stores and a mail-order house.

Problem 23-20. (a) Prepare a schedule showing sales, costs, and operating net income for each line of goods distributed by Argo Grocery Company. Furnish supporting schedules indicating clearly how the items of expense have been apportioned. Show results only to the nearest dollar.

(b) Also prepare a statement of income and expense showing each line's contribution to overhead. You may assume that it is impossible to predict the change that might occur in the office and clerical salaries, office supplies and equipment expense, and newspaper advertising if either of the lines were discontinued by the company.

Argo Grocery Company manufactures and distributes in a limited area two lines of grocery products. One line is distributed to hotels and restaurants, the other to retail grocers. Selling organizations for the two lines are separately set up and operated, and there is considerable rivalry between them. There is also a good deal of argument about which line nets the greater income to the company. Total dollar volumes of the two lines are roughly equal, but on account of competitive conditions, the margins in the restaurant line are relatively narrow, while wider margins are enjoyed by the retail line. From this fact the sales manager for the retail line argues that his line contributes more to the company's net income. The restaurant sales manager, however, insists that the distribution costs per dollar of sales for his line are sufficiently lower to make up for the difference in margin.

In an attempt to settle the argument the following facts about the company's 1959 business have been ascertained:

Schedule 1

Expense Data

Sales force salaries and expense:

Restaurant line..	$15,000
Retail line..	33,000
Warehouse depreciation, insurance, etc........................	4,000
Packing and shipping wages..................................	10,000
Shipping containers..	800
Other shipping supplies (proportionate to number of sales invoices)	600
Delivery wages, supplies, and expense.........................	5,000
Newspaper advertising......................................	9,000
Display material and dealers' helps...........................	1,500
Advertising salary...	4,650
Office and clerical salaries (see Schedule 2)....................	5,000
Office supplies and equipment expense.........................	1,600
Executive's salary and expense (apportion on basis of sales)......	8,000
Bad debts allowance..	1,590
Total...	$99,740

Schedule 2

Operating Data

	Restaurant	Retail
Sales..	$240,000	$270,000
Factory cost of sales..............................	$200,000	$180,000
Warehouse space occupied by $100 worth, at cost....	30 cu. ft.	60 cu. ft.
Average inventory, at cost........................	$ 20,000	$ 40,000
Number of sales invoices..........................	1,000	9,000
Average number of items per invoice..............	4	12
Number of customers.............................	28	224
Average customers' accounts outstanding...........	$ 20,000	$ 40,000

Analysis of Office and Clerical Time

Keeping warehouse stock records..............................	5%
Preparing order and sales invoice forms.........................	25
Posting sales invoices..	15
Receiving cash and posting cash receipts........................	5
Preparing customers' statements...............................	5
Credit and collection activities................................	10
General accounting and clerical (apportion on basis of sales)........	35
	100%

Both lines are stored in a single warehouse, and packing and shipping activities are carried on by the same crew. The restaurant line consists of 10 items and is sold in shipping containers supplied by the factory and included as part of factory cost. The retail line consists of 50 items. The goods must be assembled and packed in containers after orders are received. Time studies indicate that it takes about four times as long to prepare $100 worth (at selling price) of retail goods for shipment as in the case of restaurant goods. Restaurant goods are delivered at the warehouse dock to customers' trucks or to common carriers; in the latter case, the customers pay the freight. The company's own delivery equipment is used entirely for the retail line.

Advertising is directed entirely at the ultimate consumer, with the aim of persuading him to demand the company's products at stores and in public eating places. It consists of newspaper advertising and of display matter and leaflets supplied to dealers. About 10% as much newspaper space is devoted to the restaurant line as to the retail line. The company's advertising staff consists of one man, who spends two-thirds of his time on newspaper advertising and the balance on display and leaflet material.

Schedule 1 lists the operating expenses of the company other than those concerned with manufacturing. Schedule 2 lists important operating data ascertained in the course of your investigation. The apportionment of office and clerical time is the result of time studies and estimates. It is the opinion of the management that office supplies and equipment expense roughly parallels the office and clerical salaries. The management rejects as inadmissible the inclusion of interest on investment. Approximately one-half the time of credit and collection employees is spent in routine checking of orders for credit approval. The balance is spent on credit follow-ups and attempts to collect specific accounts. Experience indicates that the average retail account is about five times as likely to require such collection effort as the average restaurant account.

Historical records show that about $\frac{1}{2}$ of 1% of retail sales are never collected, while only $\frac{1}{10}$ of 1% of restaurant sales prove to be uncollectible.

90% of the job of keeping warehouse stock records is concerned with shipments and 10% with receipts from the factory. All items of the restaurant line are received at the warehouse every day, but items in the retail line are received, on the average, only every other day.

Make all computations to nearest dollar.

Assignment Material for Chapter 24

Questions

Question 24-1. Mention five charges or credits to operations which do not affect the working capital, and state how they should be shown in the statement of application of funds.

Question 24-2. If there has been a decrease in working capital, in what sequence should the funds provided and the funds applied appear in the statement of application of funds?

Question 24-3. The statement of application of funds is based on the increases and decreases in noncurrent account balances shown by a comparative balance sheet, but not all of these increases and decreases are shown in the statement. Give one illustration each of:

(a) Increases or decreases that are the result of mere book entries that did not record transactions either providing or applying funds.

(b) Increases or decreases that do not represent the true amount of funds provided or applied.

(c) Net increases or decreases that were caused by both a provision and an application of funds.

Question 24-4. How should a net loss (after adjustment for nonfund items) be shown in the statement of application of funds?

Question 24-5. The following accounts appear in a company's ledger. State how the data reflected by the accounts should be shown in the statement of application of funds.

Machinery

Jan.	1	Balance............	40,000	July 8	Sale................	5,000
June 15		Appraisal...........	10,000			
Sept. 9		Purchase...........	8,000			

Accumulated Depreciation—Machinery

July 8	Accumulated depreciation on machinery sold....	3,000	Jan. 1	Balance.............	6,000
Oct. 10	Extraordinary repairs..	600	June 15	Appraisal...........	3,000
			Dec. 31	Depreciation for year..	2,000

Appraisal Increment

	June 15	7,000

Retained Earnings

July 8	Loss on machinery sale...	300	Jan 1	Balance.............	12,000
			Dec. 31	Net operating income..	10,000

Question 24-6. During the year a portion of the Organization Expense account was written off. Under what circumstances would the amount thus written off be added back to net income in the preparation of a statement of application of funds? Under what circumstances would the amount thus written off not be added back to net income, and under such circumstances, how would it be handled in the working papers?

Question 24-7. A transaction occurred during the year that affected the accounts in the manner indicated below:

Land...	10,000	
Buildings.......................................	75,000	
Mortgage payable................................		60,000
Cash..		25,000

Show three ways in which the transaction may be reflected in the statement of application of funds.

Question 24-8. Company A owned all of the stock of Company B. At the end of the year it made the following entry:

Investment in stock of Company B......................	15,000	
Income from Company B....		15,000
To take up the increase in Company B's retained earnings during the year.		

How should this matter be dealt with in the preparation of a statement of application of funds?

Question 24-9. During the year a large short-term obligation was converted into a long-term obligation, no cash being transferred. How would this matter be dealt with in a statement of application of funds?

Question 24-10. In the preparation of an application of funds statement, what treatment would you accord the following items?

(a) Fully depreciated machinery scrapped.
(b) Periodic amortization of premium on bonds payable.
(c) Patents written off to Retained Earnings.
(d) Retirement of mortgage payable before maturity.
(e) Land acquired by issuance of capital stock.
(f) Sale of investments at a gain, which was credited to Retained Earnings.

Problems

Problem 24-1. The Osborne Company's balance sheets on December 31, 1958 and 1957 were:

	December 31,	
	1958	1957
Assets		
Cash..	$ 6,000	$ 9,000
Accounts receivable.............................	19,600	22,050
Allowance for doubtful accounts........	600*	700*
Merchandise.....................................	39,210	32,560
Investments in securities—Long-term...............	11,000	8,000
Furniture and fixtures...........................	8,200	6,500
Accumulated depreciation........................	1,200*	850*
	$82,210	$76,560

	December 31,	
	1958	1957
Liabilities and Stockholders' Equity		
Accounts payable................................	$29,000	$31,000
Notes payable....................................	7,500	10,000
Capital stock....................................	35,000	30,000
Retained earnings................................	10,710	5,560
	$82,210	$76,560

   * Deduction.

The increases in investments in securities and furniture and fixtures resulted from purchases. Capital stock of $5,000 par value was issued at par. A dividend of $5,000 was paid during the year.

Prepare:

   (a) A schedule of working capital.
   (b) Statement of application of funds working papers.
   (c) A statement of application of funds.

   Problem 24-2.   The following data were taken from the records of Oliver Corporation.

OLIVER CORPORATION
Comparative Balance Sheet
December 31, 1958 and 1957

	December 31,	
	1958	1957
Assets		
Cash..	$ 8,344	$ 4,652
Accounts receivable..............................	12,650	18,170
Allowance for doubtful accounts....................	1,750*	1,860*
Merchandise....................................	23,875	24,640
Furniture and fixtures...........................	17,500	12,000
Trucks...	19,000	11,500
Accumulated depreciation—Trucks.................	4,500*	3,000*
	$75,119	$66,102
Liabilities and Stockholders' Equity		
Accounts payable................................	$22,122	$19,280
Capital stock...................................	50,000	50,000
Retained earnings (Deficit).......................	2,997	3,178*
	$75,119	$66,102

   * Deduction.

The company paid a $5,000 dividend during 1958.
Depreciation of furniture and fixtures, in the amount of $1,200, was credited to the asset account.

Required:

   Schedule of working capital.
   Application of funds working papers.
   Statement of application of funds.
   Comments on any trends disclosed.

Problem 24-3. Dickson Company submitted the following comparative balance sheet.

DICKSON COMPANY
Comparative Balance Sheet
December 31, 1959 and 1958

	December 31,	
	1959	1958
Assets		
Cash...	$ 2,600	$ 3,000
Accounts receivable..............................	7,500	6,000
Allowance for doubtful accounts...................	1,200*	950*
Merchandise.....................................	23,600	22,000
Furniture and fixtures............................	20,000	15,000
Accumulated depreciation—Furniture and fixtures....	4,500*	3,000*
Delivery equipment..............................	15,000	10,000
Accumulated depreciation—Delivery equipment......	7,500*	5,000*
Goodwill..		5,000
	$55,500	$52,050
Liabilities and Stockholders' Equity		
Accounts payable................................	$ 5,750	$ 5,050
Notes payable...................................	6,000	7,000
Capital stock....................................	35,000	25,000
Premium on stock................................	1,000	
Retained earnings................................	7,750	15,000
	$55,500	$52,050

    * Deduction.

The decrease in retained earnings was caused by an operating loss of $2,250 and the write-off of the goodwill. The change in the balance of each of the other non-current accounts was caused by one entry only.

Prepare a schedule of working capital, working papers, and a statement of application of funds.

Problem 24-4. From the following information prepare a statement of application of funds and schedule of working capital. Submit working papers.

THE JACKSONIAN COMPANY
Balance Sheets
December 31, 1959 and 1958

	December 31,	
	1959	1958
Assets		
Cash...	$ 10,165	$ 24,815
Accounts receivable—net.........................	107,230	128,425
Notes receivable.................................	22,145	24,200
Accrued interest receivable.......................	725	1,435
Merchandise inventory...........................	156,010	115,300
Fixed assets.....................................	600,990	476,240
Accumulated depreciation.........................	112,625*	83,255*
Investment securities.............................		10,000
Organization expense.............................		25,000
	$784,640	$722,160

    * Deduction.

	December 31,	
	1959	1958
Liabilities and Stockholders' Equity		
Accounts payable.............................	$ 29,400	$ 20,945
Notes payable.................................	20,000	10,000
Accrued expenses..............................	1,300	1,450
Bonds payable—due December 31, 1962...........		50,000
Capital stock.................................	525,000	400,000
Unrealized increment per appraisal............	100,000	
Retained earnings.............................	108,940	239,765
	$784,640	$722,160

Summary of Retained Earnings

Balance, December 31, 1958................................		$239,765
Deduct:		
Net loss—1959—After crediting income with a gain		
of $500 on the sale of investment securities........	$25,825	
Dividends paid—Cash.............................	25,000	
Dividends paid—Stock.............................	50,000	
Discount on sale of stock.........................	5,000	
Write-off of organization expense..................	25,000	130,825
Balance, December 31, 1959.............................		$108,940

Extraordinary building repairs costing $1,800 were charged to Accumulated Depreciation.

The entry to record the appraisal included a $110,000 debit to Fixed Assets and a $10,000 credit to Accumulated Depreciation.

Problem 24-5. From the following data prepare a statement of application of funds (with supporting working papers) and a schedule of working capital.

HUDSON COMPANY
Comparative Balance Sheet
December 31, 1959 and 1958

	December 31,	
	1959	1958
Assets		
Cash...	$ 5,150	$ 4,500
Accounts receivable............................	31,600	29,700
Allowance for doubtful accounts.................	1,500*	1,200*
Finished goods................................	10,000	12,500
Goods in process...............................	18,320	15,800
Materials.....................................	9,700	10,000
Advances to salesmen...........................	1,000	750
Unexpired insurance............................	250	300
Land...	70,000	65,000
Buildings.....................................	155,000	110,000
Accumulated depreciation—Buildings..............	16,000*	10,000*
Machinery....................................	110,000	100,000
Accumulated depreciation—Machinery.............	13,500*	11,000*
Tools—less depreciation.........................	22,000	25,000
Patents—less amortization.......................	28,000	30,000
Investments in stocks...........................		25,000
Discount on bonds..............................	1,800	
	$431,820	$406,350

* Deduction.

		December 31,	
		1959	1958
Liabilities and Stockholders' Equity			
C	Accounts payable...............................	$ 12,000	$ 33,500
C	Notes payable..................................	5,000	27,000
C	Bank loans.....................................		20,000
L T	Bonds payable.................................	300,000	200,000
SE	Capital stock..................................	100,000	100,000
SE	Reserve for contingencies.........................		16,000
SE	Retained earnings...............................	14,820	9,850
		$431,820	$406,350

Analysis of Retained Earnings

I	Balance, December 31, 1958.................................		$ 9,850
	Add:		
	Net income—1959...		5,970
K	Return of Reserve for Contingencies........................		16,000
	Total...		$31,820
	Deduct:		
L	Dividends paid...................................	$15,000	
M	Loss on sale of investments.........................	2,000	17,000
	Balance, December 31, 1959.................................		$14,820

A — Bonds of $100,000 par value were issued at 98 at the beginning of 1959.
Depreciation and amortization were charged to operations during the year as follows:

By credit to accumulated depreciation accounts:

B	Buildings...	$6,000
C	Machinery...	6,500

By credit to fixed asset accounts:

D	Tools...	$5,000
E	Patents...	2,000

By credit to deferred charge account:

F	Discount on bonds...	$ 200

G - During the year, machinery which cost $10,000 was sold for $6,000. The accumulated depreciation account was debited $4,000 although depreciation of only $2,500 had been provided.

H - Land that cost $4,000 was sold for $4,300 and an additional parcel was purchased for $9,000.

Problem 24-6. From the following information prepare a statement of application of funds with supporting working papers and schedule of working capital.

THE LEWIS CORPORATION
Comparative Balance Sheet
December 31, 1958 and 1957

	December 31, 1958	December 31, 1957
Assets		
Cash...	$ 12,540	$ 8,420
Receivables—net..................................	45,623	46,195
Inventories..	38,653	29,378
Fixed assets—less depreciation.....................	82,420	84,620
Goodwill..		40,000
Patents...	16,000	17,000
	$195,236	$225,613
Liabilities and Stockholders' Equity		
Accounts payable..................................	$ 12,158	$ 21,462
Notes payable.....................................	15,000	10,000
Current installment of bonds payable...............	5,000	
Bonds payable.....................................	35,000	40,000
Capital stock—$100 par:		
Preferred.......................................	30,000	50,000
Common...	70,000	100,000
Paid-in surplus—Common stock donation............	10,000	
Paid-in surplus—Stock conversion..................	5,000	
Paid-in surplus—Common stock dividend...........	500	
Retained earnings.................................	12,578	4,151
	$195,236	$225,613

During the year the following transactions occurred:

A 5% stock dividend was distributed to the common stockholders. The stock had a fair value of $110 per share.

Common stock of $50,000 par value was donated to the corporation and canceled; out of the surplus so created, the goodwill was written off.

Preferred stock in the amount of $20,000 was converted into common stock in the amount of $15,000.

At the end of the year, a $3,500 cash dividend was paid on the common stock, and the regular 6% dividend was paid on the preferred stock.

All patents on hand were acquired at the close of 1957, and none have been sold.

Tangible fixed assets were depreciated $7,200.

Problem 24-7. The following comparative balance sheet is submitted to you. Prepare working papers, a statement of application of funds, and a schedule of working capital.

THORNDYKE COMPANY
Comparative Balance Sheet
December 31, 1959 and 1958

	December 31, 1959	December 31, 1958
Assets		
Cash..	$ 55,000	$ 21,080
Accounts receivable—net........................	25,000	22,700
Merchandise inventory..........................	65,000	51,000
Prepaid expenses...............................	3,500	4,640
Funds impounded for completion of building........	10,000	
Land..	15,000	
Buildings......................................	145,000	
Equipment.....................................	26,400	19,810
Accumulated depreciation—Buildings and equipment	17,600*	7,300*
	$327,300	$111,930
Liabilities and Stockholders' Equity		
Accounts payable..............................	$ 26,000	$ 23,500
Accrued taxes and expenses......................	18,900	17,200
Bonds payable.................................	100,000	
Unamortized premium on bonds payable...........	4,500	
Capital stock..................................	85,000	35,000
Premium on capital stock.......................	25,000	
Reserve for possible decline in inventory...........	10,000	8,000
Donated surplus...............................	15,000	
Retained earnings..............................	42,900	28,230
	$327,300	$111,930

* Deduction.

Thorndyke Company had operated for several years in leased premises in Springfield. Late in 1958 the city of York offered to donate land worth $15,000 to the company if it would build and operate a plant in that city. Title to the land was obtained early in 1959.

To finance the construction of the plant, Thorndyke Company issued $100,000 par value of bonds at 105, and $50,000 par value of capital stock at 150. The proceeds of the bond issue were impounded for construction purposes. The building was occupied during 1959, but a supplementary building remained to be constructed and $10,000 of cash continued to be impounded until the completion of this building.

A portion ($500) of the bond premium was amortized during 1959.

An $8,500 dividend was paid.

Problem 24-8. Following is a condensed comparative balance sheet of Henderson, Incorporated.

HENDERSON, INCORPORATED
Condensed Comparative Balance Sheet
December 31, 1959 and 1958

	December 31, 1959	December 31, 1958
Assets		
Working capital..............................	$ 93,200	$ 78,000
Land..	10,000	8,000
Buildings......................................	50,000	50,000
Accumulated depreciation—Buildings..............	8,000*	6,000*
Equipment.....................................	40,000	35,000
Accumulated depreciation—Equipment............	8,700*	6,300*
Stock of X Company............................	32,500	
Bonds of X Company...........................	25,000	
	$234,000	$158,700
Liabilities and Stockholders' Equity		
Mortgage payable..............................	$ 30,000	$ 30,000
Capital stock—Common.........................	110,000	100,000
Capital stock—Preferred........................	50,000	
Premium on preferred stock.....................	2,500	
Retained earnings..............................	41,500	28,700
	$234,000	$158,700

* Deduction.

During 1959 Henderson, Incorporated, acquired control of X Company in order to assure itself of a supply of raw materials. Details of the transaction are shown below:

Securities acquired:	
Capital stock of a par value of $30,000 acquired at a valuation of	$32,500
Bonds—at par...	25,000
Total X Company securities acquired......................	$57,500
Payment:	
Henderson, Incorporated, preferred stock:	
Par..	$50,000
Premium...	2,500
Total stock payment.................................	$52,500
Cash...	5,000
Total payment..	$57,500

Henderson, Incorporated, had a net income of $21,900 during 1959; it paid dividends of $6,600 on its common stock and $2,500 on its preferred stock.

Prepare working papers in accordance with Opinion 1. (See discussion starting on page 536.) From these working papers, prepare a statement of application of funds showing, with respect to the acquisition of the X Company securities, only the net funds applied. Also prepare a statement of application of funds in accordance with Opinion 1 but showing complete details of the transaction.

Also prepare working papers and a statement of application of funds in accordance with Opinion 2.

Problem 24-9.   Following is a summary of the noncurrent accounts of Burton Corporation for the year 1959. Prepare a statement of application of funds with working papers in the traditional form. Also satisfy the same requirements using the alternative form.

Land

Jan.	1	Balance............. 35,000	June 30........................	5,000

Buildings

Jan.	1	Balance............ 125,000
Mar.	1	 40,000

Accumulated Depreciation—Buildings

	Jan.	1	Balance............. 45,000
	Mar.	1	 15,000
	Dec. 31		 6,000

Equipment

Jan.	1	Balance............. 50,000	Nov. 30.....................	10,000
July	1	 10,000		

Accumulated Depreciation—Equipment

Nov. 30	 6,000	Jan. 1 Balance.............	20,000
		Dec. 31.....................	5,750

Investments

Jan.	1	Balance............. 45,000	April 1	10,000

Capital Stock

Jan. 1 Balance.............	100,000

Unrealized Increment per Appraisal of Real Estate

Mar. 1	25,000

Retained Earnings

Dec. 31	Dividend............. 6,000	Jan. 1 Balance.............	55,000
		Dec. 31 From Revenue and Expense.............	7,000

Revenue and Expense

Dec. 31	Cost of goods sold...	100,000	Dec. 31	Sales...............	185,000
31	Selling expense......	30,000	31	Gain on sale of investments.............	1,500
31	General expense.....	37,250			
31	Depreciation—Bldgs.	6,000			
31	Depreciation—Equip.	5,750			
31	Loss on sale of equipment.............	500			
31	To Retained Earnings	7,000			
		186,500			186,500

Problem 24-10.   From the following data you are to prepare working papers and a statement of application of funds.

ARUNDEL COMPANY

	December 31, 1959	December 31, 1958
Assets		
Cash.......................................	$ 63,000	$ 150,000
Accounts receivable........................	89,000	100,000
Allowance for doubtful accounts..............	3,600*	5,000*
Inventories................................	310,000	270,000
Prepaid expenses...........................	11,000	10,000
Cash surrender value of life insurance..........	21,200	17,500
Unamortized debt discount...................	12,800	14,600
Marketable securities held for plant expansion..	98,000	
Stock of subsidiary company.................	124,500	100,000
Machinery and equipment....................	823,200	743,800
Allowance for depreciation...................	378,700*	310,400*
Leasehold improvements (net)...............	96,500	104,600
	$1,266,900	$1,195,100
Liabilities and Stockholders' Equity		
Notes payable to banks......................	$ 100,000	$ 50,000
Accounts payable...........................	31,500	42,000
Accrued liabilities..........................	16,800	14,000
Federal taxes accrued.......................	58,400	63,200
Deferred income on sales....................	12,200	14,300
4% convertible debentures—due after one year.	250,000	310,000
Debenture installments due within one year....	60,000	65,000
Common stock—par, $5.....................	500,000	250,000
Retained earnings—January 1................	386,600	208,400
Net profit for year..........................	213,900	228,200
Dividend paid in stock......................	250,000*	
Dividend paid in cash.......................	62,500*	50,000*
Settlement of law suit......................	50,000*	
	$1,266,900	$1,195,100

* Deduction.

On June 10, 1959, the company's directors declared a cash dividend of $1.25 per share payable on July 1, 1959, to stockholders of record June 20, 1959, and also declared a 100% stock dividend payable at the same time. An analysis of the fixed asset accounts shows that machinery and equipment were purchased in 1959 at a cost of $197,900, and certain obsolete equipment having a net book value of $36,200 was sold for $25,000. No other entries were recorded in fixed asset and related accounts other than routine charges to operations for depreciation, and so forth. The company wrote off accounts receivable aggregating $2,400 during the year as uncollectible.

The subsidiary stock represents a 100% interest acquired at the end of 1958. No dividends have been received from the subsidiary, but Arundel Company took up its 100% interest in the $24,500 net income of the subsidiary for 1959 by a debit to the investment account and a credit to income.

Problem 24-11. From the following data prepare a statement of application of funds, working papers, and a schedule of working capital.

TEMPLETON MANUFACTURING COMPANY
Comparative Balance Sheet
December 31, 1959 and 1958

	December 31, 1959	December 31, 1958
Assets		
Cash..	$ 50,300	$ 40,750
Accounts receivable.........................	64,900	63,850
Allowance for doubtful accounts...............	3,100*	3,400*
Notes receivable—Trade......................	10,000	12,000
Accrued interest receivable....................	200	150
Finished goods..............................	31,000	29,950
Goods in process............................	5,100	4,975
Materials...................................	20,720	19,850
Unexpired insurance.........................	700	680
Factory supplies.............................	2,600	2,390
Fixed assets.................................	845,000	915,000
Accumulated depreciation.....................	160,000*	155,000*
Leasehold improvements......................	46,000	50,000
Sinking fund securities.......................	19,755	9,875
Sinking fund cash............................	11,805	10,645
	$944,980	$1,001,715
Liabilities and Stockholders' Equity		
Accounts payable............................	$ 39,540	$ 37,820
Bank loans..................................	30,000	40,000
Federal income tax payable....................	25,000	22,600
Service income collected in advance............	2,360	2,195
Sinking fund bonds payable....................	100,000	100,000
Unamortized bond premium....................	2,100	2,400
Capital stock...............................	400,000	400,000
Unearned increment per appraisal..............		75,000
Sinking fund reserve.........................	30,000	20,000
Retained earnings...........................	315,980	301,700
	$944,980	$1,001,715

* Deduction.

The bonds were issued at the beginning of 1957 at 103, and were to mature in ten years.

The bond indenture required the creation of a sinking fund by annual deposits of $10,000. Interest on sinking fund investments and amortizations of discounts or premiums on the investments were to be recorded in the sinking fund accounts; when the sinking fund thus accumulated amounted to $100,000, additional contributions were to cease. Sinking fund transactions during 1959 were:

Purchase of sinking fund securities from sinking fund cash........	$ 9,820
Collection of interest......................................	980
Amortization of discount...................................	60
Sinking fund deposit.......................................	10,000

The bond indenture also required the creation of a sinking fund reserve by annual credits of $10,000.

Fully depreciated fixed assets acquired at a cost of $8,000 were written off during the year.

At the end of 1957, an appraisal of the fixed assets was recorded by the following entry:

Fixed assets..	100,000	
Accumulated depreciation..........................		25,000
Unearned increment per appraisal..................		75,000

Depreciation for 1958 was computed on the basis of cost. New auditors, engaged at the end of 1959, insisted on basing the depreciation on the appraised value, and the directors thereupon decided to reverse the appraisal.

The net income for the year was $44,280 (including interest on sinking fund securities), and a $20,000 cash dividend was paid.

Land was sold at cost, $15,000. Other fixed assets were purchased for $53,000.

Problem 24-12. You are furnished the following statement and certain additional information.

THE ROSINANTE CORPORATION
Condensed Comparative Balance Sheet
December 31, 1959 and 1958

	December 31,	
	1959	1958
Assets		
Working capital...............................	$281,000	$ 190,000
Investment securities.........................	125,000	150,000
Fixed assets..................................	850,000	1,200,000
Accumulated depreciation—Fixed assets.........	365,000*	415,000*
	$891,000	$1,125,000
Liabilities and Stockholders' Equity		
Bonds payable.................................	$ —	$ 250,000
Capital stock.................................	750,000	1,000,000
Premium on stock.............................	25,000	
Paid-in surplus—From quasi-reorganization......	75,000	
Deficit.......................................		125,000*
Retained earnings—since January 1, 1959........	41,000	
	$891,000	$1,125,000

* Deduction.

Early in 1959, but as of December 31, 1958, the company effected a quasi-reorganization. The fixed asset accounts were reduced $400,000 and the accumulated depreciation was reduced $100,000. The capital stock was reduced from $1,000,000 to $500,000.

The bonds payable were retired at the end of 1959.

The $41,000 balance in the Retained Earnings account on December 31, 1959, resulted from the following:

Net income for 1959—including $1,000 gain on sale of investment securities (October 31, 1959) and $10,000 discount on retirement of bonds...	$86,000
Less dividend paid..	45,000
Net increase...	$41,000

Prepare a statement of application of funds with supporting working papers.

Problem 24-13. Using the following information, prepare working papers and a statement of application of funds.

AMSTERDAM COMPANY
Comparative Balance Sheet
December 31, 1959 and 1958

	December 31,	
	1959	1958
Assets		
Working capital...............................	$ 80,000	$ 95,000
Land..	20,000	20,000
Building.....................................	100,000	100,000
Accumulated depreciation—Building..............	20,000*	15,000*
Furniture and fixtures.........................	65,000	60,000
Accumulated depreciation—F. & F...............	16,000*	12,000*
Unamortized discount on second mortgage bonds...		1,000
	$229,000	$249,000
Liabilities and Stockholders' Equity		
First mortgage bonds payable...................	$ 25,000	$ 50,000
Unamortized premium on first mortgage bonds.....	1,125	2,500
Second mortgage bonds payable.................		20,000
Preferred stock...............................		50,000
Common stock................................	175,000	100,000
Premium on preferred stock....................		3,000
Premium on common stock......................	8,750	
Reserve for contingencies......................	10,000	
Retained earnings.............................	9,125	23,500
	$229,000	$249,000

* Deduction.

Following is a summary of the Retained Earnings account for 1959:

Balance, December 31, 1958.........................		$23,500
Net income for the year.............................		6,625
Loss on retirement of preferred stock.................	$ 2,000	
Transfer to Reserve for Contingencies.................	10,000	
Dividends:		
Preferred.......................................	3,000	
Common..	6,000	
Balance, December 31, 1959.........................	9,125	
	$30,125	$30,125

The following transactions took place at the end of 1959:

Common stock was issued at a premium.
The preferred stock was retired for $55,000.
Half of the first mortgage bonds were retired at 103. The gain was credited to income. (The premium amortization for 1959 was $250.)
All of the second mortgage bonds were retired at 98. The loss was charged to income. (The discount amortization for the year amounted to $200.)

Problem 24-14.   The following condensed comparative balance sheet is submitted to you.

THE HAWTHORNE COMPANY
Condensed Comparative Balance Sheet
December 31, 1959 and 1958

	December 31,	
	1959	1958
Assets		
Working capital....................................	$2,384,200	$1,207,000
Capital stock of subsidiary company..................	100,000	60,000
Advances to subsidiary.............................	125,000	100,000
Cash surrender value of life insurance................	25,000	20,000
First mortgage bond retirement fund.................	1,100	800
Investment securities..............................	65,000	100,000
Land..	600,000	500,000
Buildings..	1,100,000	1,600,000
Accumulated depreciation—Buildings.................	480,000*	725,000*
Equipment..	2,420,000	2,500,000
Accumulated depreciation—Equipment...............	840,000*	800,000*
Bond discount and expense—Second mortgage bonds....	54,000	60,000
	$5,554,300	$4,622,800
Liabilities and Stockholders' Equity		
First mortgage bonds..............................	$ 450,000	$ 500,000
Unamortized premium on first mortgage bonds.........	4,050	5,000
Second mortgage bonds............................	2,500,000	2,000,000
Preferred stock...................................	1,000,000	800,000
Common stock....................................	1,000,000	750,000
Reserve for possible future decline in inventory value....	50,000	
Reserve for contingencies..........................		75,000
Unearned increment from revaluation of assets.........		175,000
Retained earnings.................................	550,250	317,800
	$5,554,300	$4,622,800

* Deduction.

Subsidiary stock of $40,000 par value was purchased at a cost of $35,000; the discount was credited to Retained Earnings.

A $50,000 deposit was made in the fund for the retirement of first mortgage bonds.

Bonds of a par value of $50,000 were retired by payment of $49,700 from the fund. There was $450 of unamortized premium applicable to the bonds retired. The $750 gain on the retirement was credited to income.

Investment securities that cost $35,000 were sold for $32,000; the loss was charged to income.

Several years ago, in order to reflect an appraisal, the Buildings account was debited $500,000, with offsetting credits of $200,000 to the accumulated depreciation account and $300,000 to an unearned increment account. Thereafter, depreciation was computed on the gross appraised value. Depreciation of appreciation to December 31, 1958, amounted to $125,000, and annual entries to that date had been made transferring, in the aggregate, the entire $125,000 from the unrealized increment account to Retained Earnings. As of January 1, 1959, the directors ordered that all of the consequences of the appraisal should be eliminated from the accounts.

Equipment which cost $80,000, on which there was accumulated depreciation of $35,000, was sold for $36,000. The loss was charged to Retained Earnings.

Bond Discount and Expense was charged $16,000, the discount on $500,000 of second mortgage bonds sold during the year.

During 1958 the company, fearful that it might lose a suit in which it was defendant, created a reserve for contingencies in the amount of $75,000 by charge to Retained Earnings. The suit was settled in 1959 by the payment of $68,000.

A summary of the Retained Earnings account for 1959 appears below:

Balance, December 31, 1958		$317,800
Net income for the year		416,450
Discount on sale of $200,000 of preferred stock	$ 2,000	
Discount on stock of subsidiary purchased		5,000
Loss on sale of equipment	9,000	
Damages paid	68,000	
Return of reserve for contingencies		75,000
Provision of reserve for possible future decline in inventory value	50,000	
Dividends:		
Preferred	60,000	
Common	75,000	
Balance, December 31, 1959	550,250	
	$814,250	$814,250

Prepare working papers and a statement of application of funds.

Assignment Material for Chapter 25

Questions

Question 25-1. In general, why is the net income not offset by an equal increase in cash, and why is a net loss not offset by an equal decrease in cash?

Question 25-2. The accounts receivable of a business were $15,000 at the beginning of the year and $12,000 at the end of the year. Bad debts written off during the year amounted to $1,300, and cash discounts allowed customers amounted to $600. The sales for the year were $35,000. What were the cash receipts during the year from sales of the current and prior periods?

Question 25-3. The purchases of a business amounted to $50,000 during 1959. Accounts payable at the beginning and end of the year were $16,500 and $14,800; notes payable given to trade creditors in settlement of open accounts were $4,000 at the beginning of the year and $4,400 at the end of the year. Returns and allowances on purchases were $435. What were the cash payments during 1959 for purchases of 1959 and prior periods?

Question 25-4. The balance in the Small Tools account of a company increased $6,500 during 1959. Debits for purchases of tools amounted to $8,300, and credits for depreciation totalled $1,800. Discounts of $95 were taken on tool purchases and credited to Purchase Discounts. At the end of 1959 there was a $2,000 note outstanding, given in connection with a purchase of tools in 1959. What was the amount of the cash disbursement for tools during the year?

Question 25-5. The comparative balance sheet of John Henderson showed accrued interest payable at the beginning and end of the year in the amounts of $232 and $185, respectively; the income statement for the year showed interest expense of $757. What was the amount of the cash disbursement during the year for interest?

Question 25-6. The income statement of Hawthorne Corporation shows $115,000 as the cost of sales for 1959, without details. The inventory increased $4,500 during the year, and the accounts payable increased $5,200. Discounts on purchases amounted to $318. What was the amount of the cash disbursements during 1959 for purchases during that and prior years?

Question 25-7. Statements of Abernathy Company for 1958 and 1959 contained the following amounts:

	1958	1959
Common stock..............................	$100,000	$150,000
Discount on stock..................................	5,000	6,250
Stock subscriptions receivable	6,000	8,000
Stock dividend....................................		25,000

Stock certificates were issued and the Common Stock account was credited when subscriptions were received.

What was the amount of cash received during 1959 for stock issuances?

892

Problems

Problem 25-1. Following are selected account balances taken from the records of Jimsan Sales Company at the beginning and end of 1959.

	January 1, 1959	December 31, 1959
Accounts receivable............................	$ 2,300	$ 4,700
Accounts payable............................	1,800	1,650
Machinery..................................	36,000	37,500
Accumulated depreciation—Machinery.........	13,410	15,000
Sales......................................	-0-	62,000
Sales returns and allowances..................	-0-	1,210
Purchases..................................	-0-	58,100
Purchase returns and allowances..............	-0-	1,600
Loss on disposal of old machinery.............	-0-	400

Additional information:

(1) All sales and purchases were made on account.
(2) Accounts payable show transactions with merchandise creditors only.
(3) Machinery with a cost of $7,000 and accumulated depreciation of $4,500 was traded in during 1959 on new machinery. The newly purchased machinery was put into the asset account at its list price.

Required:

Computations to determine the following amounts for 1959:

(a) The amount of cash collected on accounts receivable.
(b) The amount of cash paid on accounts payable.
(c) The amount of the cash outlay for the machinery purchased during 1959.

Problem 25-2. The information below has been taken from the financial statements of Crystal Company. During the period covered, the company had no cash receipts or disbursements other than those related to revenues and expenses. Prepare cash-flow statement working papers.

	Year's Changes—Net	
	Debit	Credit
Balance sheet accounts:		
Cash..	5,520	
Accounts receivable..........................	310	
Allowance for doubtful accounts.................		100
Inventory...................................		3,000
Store supplies on hand.........................		600
Furniture and fixtures.........................		
Accumulated depreciation—Furniture and fixtures.		1,200
Accounts payable.............................	7,230	
Accrued rent payable.........................		50
Common stock...............................		
Retained earnings............................		8,110
	13,060	13,060

Details of changes in retained earnings during 1959 are on page 894.

	Debit	Credit
Sales......................................		180,000
Inventory—December 31, 1958................	30,000	
Purchases..................................	125,000	
Inventory—December 31, 1959................		27,000
Bad debts..................................	180	
Store rent.................................	2,700	
Store supplies expense......................	810	
Depreciation—Furniture and fixtures.........	1,200	
Salesmen's commissions......................	21,000	
Other expenses.............................	18,000	
Net increase in retained earnings...........	8,110	
	207,000	207,000

Problem 25-3. Using the information in the following financial statements, prepare working papers to show the cash flows related to operations.

WINTER CORPORATION
Comparative Balance Sheet
December 31, 1959 and 1958

| | December 31, ||
	1959	1958
Assets		
Cash...	$ 9,140	$ 8,200
Accounts receivable..................................	14,100	17,500
Allowance for doubtful accounts......................	195*	175*
Inventory..	43,000	40,000
Prepaid insurance....................................	220	330
Store fixtures.......................................	4,000	4,000
Accumulated depreciation—Store fixtures.............	1,800*	1,000*
	$68,465	$68.855
Liabilities and Stockholders' Equity		
Accounts payable—Merchandise suppliers.............	$ 3,680	$ 7,110
Accrued salaries.....................................	350	200
Common stock...	50,000	50,000
Retained earnings....................................	14,435	11,545
	$68,465	$68,855

* Deduction.

WINTER CORPORATION
Income Statement
For the Year Ended December 31, 1959

Sales...		$140,000
Deduct cost of goods sold:		
Inventory—December 31, 1958...................	$ 40,000	
Purchases.....................................	106,000	
Total...	$146,000	
Inventory—December 31, 1959...................	43,000	103,000
Gross profit on sales........................		$ 37,000
Deduct expenses:		
Bad debts.....................................	$ 200	
Depreciation—Store fixtures...................	800	
Insurance.....................................	110	
Salaries......................................	15,000	
Other expenses................................	18,000	34,110
Net income....................................		$ 2,890

Problem 25-4.   The Keller Company's comparative balance sheet for December 31, 1958 and 1957 was:

THE KELLER COMPANY
Comparative Balance Sheet
December 31, 1958 and 1957

	December 31,	
	1958	1957
Assets		
Cash...	$ 6,000	$ 9,000
Accounts receivable..............................	19,600	22,050
Allowance for doubtful accounts...................	600*	700*
Merchandise......................................	39,210	32,560
Investments in securities—Long-term...............	11,000	8,000
Furniture and fixtures............................	8,200	6,500
Accumulated depreciation.........................	1,200*	850*
	$82,210	$76,560
Liabilities and Stockholders' Equity		
Accounts payable.................................	$29,000	$31,000
Notes payable....................................	7,500	10,000
Capital stock....................................	35,000	30,000
Retained earnings................................	10,710	5,560
	$82,210	$76,560

* Deduction.

The company's income statement for 1958 was:

THE KELLER COMPANY
Income Statement
For the Year Ended December 31, 1958

Sales..	$192,300	
Less sales discounts.............................	2,150	$190,150
Cost of goods sold..............................		147,850
Gross profit on sales............................		$ 42,300
Deduct expenses:		
Bad debts expense...........................	$ 320	
Salesmen's commissions.......................	18,400	
Office expense..............................	6,730	
Depreciation—Furniture and fixtures..........	350	
Rent expense...............................	3,600	
Other expenses.............................	2,780	32,180
Net operating income............................		$ 10,120
Other revenue:		
Interest earned.............................	$ 550	
Other expense:		
Interest expense............................	520	30
Net income.....................................		$ 10,150

The increases in investments in securities and furniture and fixtures resulted from purchases. Capital stock of $5,000 par value was issued at par. A dividend of $5,000 was paid during the year.

Prepare:

   (a) Cash-flow statement working papers.
   (b) Cash-flow statement.

Problem 25-5.

SAVAGE COMPANY
Trial Balances
December 31, 1959 and 1958

	December 31,			
	1959 Before Closing		1958 After Closing	
	Debit	Credit	Debit	Credit
Cash...........................	10,000		8,000	
—Accounts receivable................	17,000		15,000	
—Reserve for bad debts..............		1,000		800
Merchandise inventory..............	30,000		25,000	
Prepaid expenses...................	3,000		2,000	
Land...........................	10,000		10,000	
Building........................	80,000		80,000	
Reserve for depreciation—Building....		10,000		7,500
Furniture and fixtures..............	15,000		12,000	
Reserve for depreciation—Furniture and fixtures.....................		4,000		4,000
Organization expense...............	9,000		10,000	
Accounts payable..................		21,000		27,200
Current installment due on bonds payable............................		5,000		
Bonds payable.....................		20,000		25,000
Capital stock.....................		100,000		90,000
Earned surplus....................		6,500		7,500
—Sales...........................		250,000		
Cost of goods sold.................	200,000			
Selling expense....................	20,000			
General expense...................	15,000			
Depreciation of building............	2,500			
Depreciation of furniture and fixtures..	1,000			
Dividends paid....................	5,000			
	417,500	417,500	162,000	162,000

Furniture which cost $1,500, and against which a reserve for depreciation amounting to $1,000 had been provided, was traded in on new furniture valued at $4,500. The difference of $4,000 was paid in cash.

Prepare:

(a) Cash-flow statement working papers.
(b) Cash-flow statement.
(c) Reconciliation of net income and cash increase from operations.

Problem 25-6. The accounts on the following pages were taken from the ledger of Nelson Company at the end of 1959. The company does a "cash-and-carry" business. The Cash account is not shown below; however, its December 31, 1959 balance was $46,750.

On the basis of this information, prepare cash-flow statement working papers.

Inventory

Jan.	1	Balance............ 60,000	Dec. 31	....	100,000
Various		 104,000			

Prepaid General Expense

Jan.	1	Balance........... 1,000	Dec. 31	....	100

Land

Jan.	1	Balance........... 35,000	June 30	....	5,000

Buildings

Jan.	1	Balance........... 125,000	
Mar.	1	 40,000	

Accumulated Depreciation—Buildings

			Jan.	1	Balance............ 45,000
			Mar.	1	 15,000
			Dec.	31	 6,000

Equipment

Jan.	1	Balance........... 50,000	Nov. 30	....	10,000
July	1	 10,000			

Accumulated Depreciation—Equipment

Nov. 30		 6,000	Jan.	1	Balance........... 20,000
			Dec.	31	 5,750

Investments

Jan.	1	Balance........... 45,000	April	1	 10,000

Accounts Payable

Various	 101,100	Jan.	1	Balance........... 21,300
		Various		 104,000

Accrued Selling Expense

Jan.	5	 900	Jan.	1	Balance........... 900
			Dec.	31	 700

Capital Stock

		Jan.	1	Balance............ 200,000

Unrealized Increment by Appraisal of Real Estate.			
	Mar. 1	....	25,000

Retained Earnings

Dec. 31	Dividend...........	6,000	Jan. 1	Balance.............	55,000
			Dec. 31	From Revenue and Expense..........	7,000

Revenue and Expense

Dec. 31	Cost of sales........	100,000	Dec. 31	Sales...............	185,000
31	Selling expense......	30,000	31	Gain on sale of invest-	
31	General expense.....	37,250		ments...........	1,500
31	Depreciation—Bldgs.	6,000			
31	Depreciation— Equipment.......	5,750			
31	Loss on sale of equip- ment............	500			
31	To Retained Earn- ings.............	7,000			
		186,500			186,500

Problem 25-7. Prepare a cash-flow statement for The A. B. C. Company. Also submit supporting working papers.

THE A. B. C. COMPANY
Comparative Balance Sheet
December 31, 1959 and 1958

	December 31,		Net Change	
	1959	1958	Debit	Credit
Assets				
Cash	$ 25,000	$ 9,000	$16,000	
Accounts receivable.....................	40,000	36,000	4,000	
Allowance for doubtful accounts..........	1,000*	900*		$ 100
Inventories:				
Finished goods........................	17,000	20,000		3,000
Goods in process......................	11,000	15,000		4,000
Materials.............................	9,000	12,000		3,000
Unexpired insurance....................	300	200	100	
Land.................................	10,000	8,000	2,000	
Buildings.............................	70,000	70,000		
Accumulated depreciation—Buildings......	15,500*	12,000*		3,500
Machinery and equipment................	60,000	58,000	2,000	
Accumulated depreciation—Machinery and equipment...........................	21,000*	15,000*		6,000
Furniture and fixtures...................	5,000	5,000		
Accumulated depreciation—Furniture and fixtures.............................	2,250*	1,500*		750
	$207,550	$203,800		
Liabilities and Stockholders' Equity				
Accounts payable—For materials.........	$ 22,800	$ 24,750	1,950	
Accrued direct labor....................	1,275	1,400	125	
Federal income tax payable..............	5,500	6,200	700	
Capital stock..........................	100,000	100,000		
Retained earnings......................	77,975	71,450		6,525
	$207,550	$203,800	$26,875	$26,875

DIV — 6,000

THE A. B. C. COMPANY
Income Statement
For the Year Ended December 31, 1959

Gross sales...		$300,000
Deduct:		
Sales returns and allowances.......................	$ 2,000	
Sales discounts...................................	2,500	4,500
Net sales..		$295,500
Deduct cost of goods sold:		
Finished goods inventory—December 31, 1958......	$ 20,000	
Cost of goods manufactured......................	209,525	
Total...	$229,525	
Deduct finished goods inventory—December 31, 1959	17,000	212,525
Gross profit on sales.....................................		$ 82,975
Deduct expenses:		
Selling...	$ 40,010	
General (including Bad Debts Expense of $800 and Depreciation Expense of $1,050, $300 of the depreciation relating to the buildings and the remainder to furniture and fixtures)......................	24,940	64,950
Net income before federal income tax........................		$ 18,025
Federal income tax.......................................		5,500
Net income..		$ 12,525

Handwritten annotation: —DL. MAT & OH

THE A. B. C. COMPANY
Statement of Cost of Goods Manufactured
For the Year Ended December 31, 1959

Materials:			
Inventory—December 31, 1958..........................			$ 12,000
Purchases......................................		$94,000	
Deduct:			
Purchase returns and allowances........	$1,500		
Purchase discounts....................	1,200	2,700	
Net purchases.............................		$91,300	
Transportation in................................		800	92,100
Total...			$104,100
Deduct inventory—December 31, 1959......................			9,000
Cost of materials used.................................			$ 95,100
Direct labor..			80,750
Manufacturing overhead (including depreciation on the buildings of $3,200 and depreciation on the machinery and equipment of $6,000)................			29,675
Total cost of manufacturing.................................			$205,525
Add goods in process—December 31, 1958.....................			15,000
Total...			$220,525
Deduct goods in process—December 31, 1959..................			11,000
Cost of goods manufactured................................			$209,525

Additional information:

(1) The company paid $6,000 in dividends during the year.

(2) The company paid insurance premiums amounting to $1,000 during 1959. Insurance expense is allocated 50% to manufacturing and 50% to general.

(3) No fixed assets were sold or retired during 1959.

Problem 25-8.   From the following information prepare a cash-flow statement and supporting working papers.

JEFFERSON COMPANY
Balance Sheets
December 31, 1959 and 1958

	December 31,	
	1959	1958
Assets		
Cash..	$ 10,165	$ 24,815
Accounts receivable—net.........................	107,230	128,425
Notes receivable—Officers........................	22,145	24,200
Accrued interest receivable.......................	725	1,435
Merchandise inventory...........................	156,010	115,300
Fixed assets......................................	600,990	476,240
Accumulated depreciation.........................	112,625*	83,255*
Investment securities.............................		10,000
Organization expense.............................		25,000
	$784,640	$722,160
Liabilities and Stockholders' Equity		
Accounts payable.................................	$ 29,400	$ 20,945
Notes payable....................................	20,000	10,000
Accrued salaries..................................	1,300	1,450
Bonds payable—due December 31, 1962...........		50,000
Capital stock.....................................	525,000	400,000
Unrealized increment per appraisal................	100,000	
Retained earnings................................	108,940	239,765
	$784,640	$722,160

/ 5 6 0 1 0
1 1 5 3 0 0
4 0 , 7 1 0

JEFFERSON COMPANY
Income Statement
For the Year Ended December 31, 1959

Sales...		$311,110
Deduct:		
Sales returns and allowances.......................	$ 2,010	
Sales discounts...................................	4,100	6,110
Net sales..		$305,000
Cost of sales..		245,000
Gross profit on sales................................		$ 60,000
Deduct expenses:		
Advertising.......................................	$ 3,100	
Sales salaries....................................	24,345	
Bad debts..	1,610	
Depreciation.....................................	21,170	
Office expense....................................	18,120	
Other expenses...................................	17,000	85,345
Net operating loss...................................		$ 25,345
Interest and miscellaneous nonoperating items:		
Interest expense..................................	$ 2,500	
Interest income...................................	1,520*	
Gain on sale of investment securities..............	500*	480
Net loss...		$ 25,825

* Deduction.

Summary of Retained Earnings

Balance, December 31, 1958.............................		$239,765
Deduct:		
Net loss—1959..............................	$25,825	
Dividends paid—Cash..........................	25,000	
Dividends paid—Stock.........................	50,000	
Discount on capital stock.	5,000	
Write-off of organization expense...............	25,000	130,825
Balance, December 31, 1959...........................		$108,940

Building repairs costing $1,800 were charged to Accumulated Depreciation.

The entry to record the appraisal included a $110,000 debit to Fixed Assets and a $10,000 credit to Accumulated Depreciation.

The company wrote off $1,000 of accounts receivable as uncollectible.

Problem 25-9. You have been contacted by the president of Area Sales Company. This company has never retained the services of a public accountant, all financial statements and tax returns having been prepared by the comptroller.

The president is disturbed that the cash balance as of December 31, 1959, is substantially lower than that of the previous year despite the fact that the net income for 1959, before taxes of $176,500, was $350,000.

You have been given the following financial statements and have satisfied yourself as to the correctness of the figures shown.

AREA SALES COMPANY
Balance Sheets
December 31, 1959 and 1958

	1959	1958	Increase or (Decrease)
Assets			
Cash in bank.................................	$ 42,000	$129,000	$ (87,000)
Accounts receivable (net of allowance for losses)..	133,000	85,500	47,500
Inventories.................................	192,000	152,500	39,500
Prepaid expenses.............................	21,000	14,000	7,000
Deposits—Utilities...........................	4,000	3,200	800
Fixed assets (net of allowance for depreciation)....	500,000	260,000	240,000
	$892,000	$644,200	$247,800
Liabilities and Stockholders' Equity			
Accounts payable and accrued charges...........	$263,000	$220,850	$ 42,150
Accrued income tax...........................	176,500	61,850	114,650
Mortgage payable............................	—	125,000	(125,000)
Capital stock................................	150,000	100,000	50,000
Retained earnings............................	302,500	136,500	166,000
	$892,000	$644,200	$247,800

AREA SALES COMPANY
Statement of Retained Earnings
For the Year Ending December 31, 1959

Balance—December 31, 1958.............................	$136,500
Net income for the year...............................	173,500
Total..	$310,000
Dividends paid.......................................	7,500
Balance—December 31, 1959.............................	$302,500

You have also obtained the following information:

(a) As of December 31, the allowance for depreciation on fixed assets was $180,000 in 1959 and $160,000 in 1958. Equipment costing $20,000, which was one-half depreciated, was abandoned and written off in 1959. Selling and administrative expense included $30,000 of depreciation.

(b) In 1959, sales were $3,300,000; cost of goods sold was $2,650,000, and selling and administrative expense (excluding taxes) was $290,000.

(c) On January 2, 1959, two insurance policies on inventory stored in a public warehouse were canceled. A premium refund of $2,000 was received from the insurance company. Insurance charged to Selling and Administrative Expense was $4,500 for the year. Other prepaid expense write-offs to Selling and Administrative Expense amounted to $12,000.

(d) The balance in the Allowance for Loss on Accounts at each year end was 5% of the gross amount of receivables. Write-offs of receivables amounted to $2,300 in 1959.

You have been asked to prepare a cash-flow statement and supporting working papers.

Problems 25-10.   Prepare a cash-flow statement and a reconciliation of net income and cash provided by operations.

Also submit working papers.

HYPERSONIC COMPANY
Comparative Balance Sheet
June 30, 1959 and 1958

	June 30, 1959	June 30, 1958	Net Changes Debit	Net Changes Credit
Assets				
Cash..........................	$ 28,000	$ 21,810	$ 6,190	
Accounts receivable.............	24,000	25,900		$ 1,900
Allowance for doubtful accounts..	350*	400*	50	
Merchandise inventory...........	31,450	31,150	300	
Prepaid rent....................	300		300	
Investments....................	12,000	15,000		3,000 — vou cash
Furniture and fixtures..........	18,000	20,000		2,000
Accumulated depreciation........	4,600*	5,600*	1,000	
	$108,800	$107,860		
Liabilities and Stockholders' Equity				
Accounts payable—Merchandise..	$ 8,400	$ 9,160	760	
Accrued salesmen's commissions..	600	800	200	
Dividends payable..............	2,750	2,500		250
Deposits from customers........	420			420
Federal income tax payable......	1,800	2,400	600	
Bonds payable—5%.............	10,000	10,000		
Bond premium..................	120	140	20	
Common stock..................	55,000	50,000		5,000
Paid-in surplus................	4,500	4,000		500
Reserve for contingencies........		5,000	5,000	
Retained earnings..............	25,210	23,860		1,350
	$108,800	$107,860	$14,420	$14,420

* Deduction.

HYPERSONIC COMPANY
Statement of Retained Earnings
For the Year Ended June 30, 1959

Balance—June 30, 1958....................................		$23,860
Add:		
Net income..	$4,600	
Release of Reserve for Contingencies.................	5,000	9,600
Total..		$33,460
Deduct:		
Dividends—Cash....................................	$2,750	
Dividends—Stock....................................	5,500	8,250
Balance—June 30, 1959....................................		$25,210

HYPERSONIC COMPANY
Income Statement
For the Year Ended June 30, 1959

Sales...	$210,000	
Cost of goods sold.................................	155,000	
Gross profit on sales...............................	$ 55,000	
Gain on sale of land...............................	1,500	
Interest earned....................................	400	$56,900
Deductions:		
Salesmen's commissions...........................	$ 12,400	
Rent expense.....................................	3,600	
Bad debts expense................................	800	
Depreciation.....................................	1,000	
Interest expense..................................	480	
Loss on sale of investments........................	300	
Other expenses...................................	31,920	50,500
Net income before income tax..........................		$ 6,400
Federal income tax..................................		1,800
Net income..		$ 4,600

Additional information:

During the year, the company retired fully depreciated fixtures which had cost $2,000.

On May 1, 1959, the company sold a parcel of land it had purchased on August 15, 1958, at a cost of $8,000.

On June 15, 1959, the company purchased additional investments at a cost of $1,200.

Problem 25-11. Burnside Corporation's condensed statements of income for the year 1959 and of financial position at the beginning and end of the year, together with other pertinent data, are reproduced below.

The board of directors of the corporation recognizes that the readers of the corporation's report to stockholders may be puzzled by the fact that, despite a substantial "net income after taxes," the cash balance decreased and the corporation resorted to some long-term borrowing.

Accordingly, the directors have requested that you prepare a statement which will reveal clearly the flow of cash into and out of the corporation during the year and which will indicate why operations alone did not provide sufficient cash for the corporation's needs. Support your work with suitable working papers.

BURNSIDE CORPORATION
Income Statement
Year Ended December 31, 1959

Income:
Gross operating income		$2,410,655
Nonoperating income, including dividends and interest		21,708
Total income		$2,432,363

Deductions:
Operating charges:
Materials and supplies used	$870,531	
Wages and salaries	906,387	
Provision for depreciation charged to operations	114,079	
Taxes, other than federal income	26,221	
Other operating charges	33,762	
Interest charges	1,297	
Loss on investments	6,016	
Estimated federal income tax	284,442	2,242,735
Net income		$ 189,628

BURNSIDE CORPORATION
Comparative Statement of Financial Position
December 31, 1959 and 1958

	1959	1958	Increase or Decrease*
Current assets:			
Cash	$ 215,221	$ 225,351	$ 10,130*
Marketable securities, at cost	180,767	251,388	70,621*
Receivables—Trade, less estimated uncollectibles	266,559	195,991	70,568
Inventories (at cost)	322,438	359,175	36,737*
Prepaid operating expenses	15,209	17,894	2,685*
Total current assets	$1,000,194	$1,049,799	
Less—Current liabilities:			
Accounts and notes payable—Trade	$ 108,623	$ 254,181	145,558*
Accrued wages and salaries	12,602	11,495	1,107
Accrued federal income tax	295,580	299,466	3,886*
Dividends payable	23,726	25,591	1,865*
Accrued interest payable	750	296	454
Other accrued operating expenses	12,622	14,942	2,320*
Total current liabilities	$ 453,903	$ 605,971	
Working capital	$ 546,291	$ 443,828	
Property, plant, and equipment—less amount of cost charged to operations to date	1,356,132	1,200,816	155,316
Total assets, less current liabilities	$1,902,423	$1,644,644	
Deduct—Long-term bank loans	50,000	—	50,000
Net assets	$1,852,423	$1,644,644	
Stockholders' equity:			
Preferred stock, 6% cumulative, par value $100 (2,602 shares)	$ 260,200	$ 265,200	5,000*
Common stock—Par value $100 (12,724 shares)	1,272,400	1,092,300	180,100
Amount paid in—in excess of par value	61,524	42,043	19,481
Retained earnings	258,299	245,101	13,198
Total	$1,852,423	$1,644,644	

Additional information:

1. During the year, marketable securities were purchased at a cost of $24,692.
2. The "estimated uncollectible receivables" increased $11,448, despite the write-off of $2,605 of bad accounts. During the year, an account of $2,000, written off in a prior year, was recovered; the credit was made to Recovery of Bad Debts, which was netted against "other operating charges" in the income statement.
3. During the year, 50 shares of preferred stock were reacquired by purchase at a 9% premium. These shares were canceled, at which time the excess of the purchase price over the average amount originally contributed for these shares ($105 per share) was debited to Retained Earnings.
4. The only entries in the Retained Earnings account for the year were for: Net income, dividend declaration, and the cancellation of preferred stock.
5. There were no sales or retirements of fixed assets during the year.

Assignment Material for Chapter 26

Questions

Question 26-1. For some time Mr. Friend has operated a small grocery. He has limited his accounts to single-entry records and has engaged outside assistance only for preparation of his tax return. He has never needed to obtain credit and does not expect to need to do so. Mr. Friend approaches you with the statement that he has heard of double-entry and would like to know what benefits, if any, he would derive from the use of such a system.

Prepare a brief statement of the advantages to Mr. Friend of using double-entry bookkeeping, and also indicate the disadvantages, if any.

Question 26-2. In each of the following cases, determine the net income or loss for the year 1959.

(a) Proprietorship equity—beginning of period..................... $23,000
   Additional investments during the period.................... 1,000
   Withdrawals during the period............................. 5,000
   Proprietorship equity—end of period....................... 25,000

(b) Proprietorship equity—beginning of period..................... $30,000
   Additional investments during the period.................... 5,000
   Withdrawals during the period............................. 3,000
   Proprietorship equity—end of period....................... 31,000

(c) Proprietorship equity—beginning of period..................... $20,000
   Additional investments during the period.................... 1,000
   Withdrawals during the period............................. 6,000
   Proprietorship equity—end of period....................... 18,000

(d) Proprietorship equity—beginning of period..................... $14,000
   Additional investments during the period.................... 5,000
   Withdrawals during the period............................. 2,000
   Proprietorship equity—end of period....................... 11,000

Question 26-3. The accounts receivable of a business at the beginning of a year were $15,000; the accounts receivable at the end of the year were $16,500; the cash collections from charge customers amounted to $95,000; and the cash sales were $15,000. What were the total sales for the year?

Question 26-4. Cash sales for the year were $23,000; the cash collections from charge customers were $63,200; the accounts receivable regarded as collectible decreased $2,470; one account, in the amount of $650, was determined during the year to be worthless. What were the total sales for the year?

Question 26-5. Accounts payable at the beginning of the year were $9,500, and at the end of the year were $10,600; payments to trade creditors during the year amounted to $83,000; and cash purchases of merchandise amounted to $55,900. Compute the total cost of purchases during the year.

Question 26-6. Prepare working papers showing the amounts of interest earned, wages expense, and interest expense for the year ended December 31, 1959.

	Beginning of Year	End of Year	During Year
Accruals:			
Interest receivable............	$280	$240	
Wages payable...............	475	100	
Interest payable..............	283	312	
Cash receipts and payments:			
Interest on notes receivable....			$ 620
Wages......................			32,000
Interest on notes payable......			465

Problems

Problem 26-1. The owner of Community Store has compiled the following comparative data.

	December 31,	
	1959	1958
Assets		
Cash in bank...................................	$ 4,000	$ 6,000
Accounts receivable.............................	30,000	20,000
Allowance for doubtful accounts..................	1,500*	1,000*
Inventory......................................	60,000	45,000
Investment securities............................	10,000	4,000
Store and delivery equipment.....................	25,000	20,000
Accumulated depreciation........................	6,000*	5,000*
	$121,500	$89,000
Liabilities		
Accounts payable..............................	$ 32,500	$15,000
Mortgage payable..............................		10,000
* Deduction.		

Upon inquiry you learn the following:

(1) The mortgage was on the owner's residence. It was paid by a store check, which included interest for 1959 in the amount of $100.
(2) The investment securities were paid for by the owner's wife with her funds, and the securities are held by the owner and his wife jointly.
(3) Cash receipts from customers during 1959 amounted to $185,000. Cash disbursements included drawings of $80 per week.
(4) The increase in fixed assets was accounted for by the acquisition of an additional delivery truck costing $5,000. Only $3,000 of the store's funds were spent for this purpose, since a $2,000 trade-in allowance was granted on a convertible previously used by the owner's son while in college.

Compute the net income or loss for 1959.

Problem 26-2. Y. A. Tuttle, a single proprietor, does not maintain an adequate set of accounting records for his business. However, an analysis of his records establishes that the following increases and decreases occurred during the twelve months ended December 31, 1959.

Increases:
Cash.. $4,200
Accounts receivable..................................... 2,430
Inventory... 3,000
Decreases:
Notes receivable.. 1,600
Accounts payable..   150
Notes payable... 2,000

Mr. Tuttle asks you to compute the net income (or loss) of his business during 1959. In connection with this request, he gives you the following additional information:

(1) No fixed assets were purchased during 1959. Those owned were acquired at the beginning of 1952 at a cost of $18,000 and, as of December 31, 1959, are believed to have remaining useful lives of four years.
(2) At the end of 1958, he had not paid the property taxes on his business assets. This tax bill, amounting to $185, and the current year's tax bill, amounting to $190, were both paid in 1959.
(3) During 1959 a $2,000 note payable matured and was paid, with interest of $120.
(4) During 1959 he cashed some of his personal savings bonds and used the $3,500 thus obtained to enlarge the store's inventory.
(5) He regularly withdrew $100 each week for personal living expenses.

Problem 26-3. Comparative balance sheet data for the business of R. A. Brown are presented below:

| | December 31, | |
	1959	1958
Balance sheet data:		
Cash..	$12,640	$ 3,940
Accounts receivable.........................	4,900	5,500
Notes receivable—Trade......................	2,900	2,400
Inventory...................................	16,100	15,560
Accounts payable............................	3,100	4,000
Taxes payable...............................	2,200	1,700
Owner's equity..............................	31,240	21,700

An analysis of the cash books for 1959 reveals the following data, presented in summary form:

Cash receipts:
Cash sales.. $30,000
Collections on accounts receivable...................... 94,000
Collections on notes receivable......................... 4,300
Bank loan... 3,000
Cash disbursements:
Cash purchases.. 2,400
Payments on accounts payable............................ 81,100
Repayment of bank loan—with interest.................... 3,090
Taxes... 1,700
Rent.. 2,400
Other expenses.. 27,110
Withdrawals... 4,800

Prepare the income statement for 1959. Submit working papers.

Problem 26-4. Valley Corporation, by analyzing its incomplete records, has been able to supply the following information.

List of Increases—June 30, 1959 Compared to June 30, 1958

Accounts receivable	$ 240
Inventory	1,800
Accounts payable	80
Accrued salesmen's commissions	160
Equipment	500

List of Decreases—June 30, 1959 Compared to June 30, 1958

Cash	$1,336
Notes receivable—Trade	700
Unexpired insurance	60

Summary of Cash Transactions—Year Ended June 30, 1959

Receipts:
Cash sales	$18,000
Collections from customers	52,000
Collections on notes receivable	1,400
Interest	90
Purchase returns	85

Disbursements:
Cash purchases	915
Sales returns	202
Payments on accounts payable	31,104
Insurance premium	300
Salesmen's commissions	9,106
New equipment	3,000
Rent	2,400
Office expense	5,711
Other operating expenses	20,173

The bookkeeper reported that a noninterest-bearing note in the amount of $300 proved to be uncollectible during the year just ended. No fixed assets were sold or retired from use. Prepare the income statement for the year ended June 30, 1959. Ignore income taxes. Submit working papers.

Problem 26-5.   The bookkeeper for Crossroads Store has analyzed the store's records and prepared the following data.

Summary of Cash Transactions for 1959

Receipts:
Cash sales	$32,000
Collections on account	14,125
Rent from upstairs apartment	720
Proceeds from 90-day bank loan	985

Disbursements:
Payments on account	25,108
Wages	8,844
Taxes	800
Advertising	190
Office expense	4,000
Bank loan	1,000
Sales returns	72
Insurance premium—Renewal of 3-year policy (no change in premium or coverage)	450
Equipment	2,000
Drawings of owner	6,000

Unpaid Bills

	12/31/59	12/31/58
For merchandise (amounting to 10% of the inventory).	$1,100	$980
For advertising...................................	35	50
For office expense................................	20	55

Uncollected Accounts

	12/31/59	12/31/58
A..		$ 85
B..		110
C..	$ 35	48
D..	200	190
F..	276	301
X..	42	
Z..	14	

A's account was written off as uncollectible during 1959.

Depreciation for the year is estimated as $2,800.

Prepare the 1959 income statement. You need not prepare working papers, but show all supporting computations.

Problem 26-6. The comparative statement of assets, liabilities, and stockholders' equity appearing below was prepared from the single-entry records and other data of State Company.

STATE COMPANY
Comparative Statement of Assets, Liabilities, and Stockholders' Equity
December 31, 1958 and December 31, 1959

	December 31, 1959		December 31, 1958	
Assets				
Current assets:				
Cash................................	$13,740		$12,825	
Accounts receivable..................	11,700		14,100	
Merchandise.........................	15,000	$40,440	12,720	$39,645
Fixed assets:				
Furniture and fixtures—less depreciation.		24,360		22,980
		$64,800		$62,625
Liabilities and Stockholders' Equity				
Current liabilities:				
Accounts payable.....................	$ 8,100		$ 3,300	
Notes payable:				
Bank..............................	3,000		750	
Trade.............................	—		4,500	
Total liabilities....................		$11,100		$ 8,550
Stockholders' equity:				
Capital stock........................	$49,500		$49,500	
Retained earnings....................	4,200	53,700	4,575	54,075
		$64,800		$62,625

A summary of cash receipts and payments for the year 1959 is as follows:

Receipts:	
Cash sales...	$ 5,850
From customers on account.................................	62,700
From notes payable—bank..................................	3,750
	$72,300

Payments:

For furniture and fixtures..................................	$ 3,000
To merchandise creditors on account........................	44,865
Retirement of notes payable (including interest of $350).......	6,350
For operating expenses.....................................	14,200
For dividends...	2,970
	$71,385

Bad debts were written off during 1959 in the amount of $735.

There were no disposals or retirements of fixed assets during 1959.

(a) Compute the net income or loss for the year 1959 by the single-entry method.

(b) Prepare an income statement using double-entry form.

Problem 26-7. Early in 1959, the records of Michigan Company were completely destroyed by fire. Since the company was a "family-owned" company, no published financial statements were available. However, in connection with a bank loan, the company had made it a practice to send to the local bank a copy of its year-end balance sheet.

The following comparative balance sheet has been taken from the balance sheets in the bank's possession.

MICHIGAN COMPANY
Comparative Balance Sheet
December 31, 1958 and 1957

	December 31,	
	1958	1957
Assets		
Cash...	$ 13,875	$ 5,000
Accounts receivable............................	41,000	45,000
Allowance for doubtful accounts.................	1,500*	1,000*
Notes receivable...............................	10,000	10,000
Accrued interest receivable......................	100	
Inventory.....................................	35,000	26,000
Interest paid in advance on bank loans............	50	
Unexpired insurance............................	200	300
Store equipment...............................	20,000	20,000
Accumulated depreciation—Store equipment.......	6,000*	5,000*
	$112,725	$100,300
Liabilities and Stockholders' Equity		
Accounts payable..............................	$ 30,000	$ 25,000
Bank loans....................................	10,000	10,000
Accrued salaries payable........................	750	1,000
Income tax payable............................	3,000	2,400
Service fees collected in advance..................	200	
Debentures payable............................	25,000	25,000
Premium on debentures.........................	1,125	1,250
Capital stock.................................	25,000	25,000
Retained earnings.............................	17,650	10,650
	$112,725	$100,300

* Deduction.

It is the practice of the local bank to maintain a Recordak file (a film record of all checks written by checking account customers), and from this file the following summary of disbursements for 1958 on the following page has been prepared.

To creditors for merchandise..................................	$104,000
To employees for salaries....................................	15,250
For operating expenses......................................	52,725
For interest on debentures...................................	1,500
For interest on bank loans...................................	550
To the District Director—Federal income tax..................	2,400

The deposit tickets on file at the bank have been analyzed to prepare the following summary of cash receipts for 1958.

Collections from customers..................................	$184,000
Collections for service fees..................................	900
Interest...	400

Required:

Income statement for 1958. Submit working papers.

Problem 26-8. Max Arthur, a merchant, kept only limited records. Purchases of merchandise were paid for by check, but most other disbursements were paid out of cash receipts. Any cash on hand at the end of the week was deposited in the bank. No record was kept of cash in bank nor was a record kept of sales. No record of accounts receivable was maintained other than by keeping a copy of the charge ticket, and this copy was given to the customer when he paid his account.

Arthur had started in business on January 1, 1959, with $20,000 cash and a building which had cost $15,000, of which one-third was the value of the building site. The building depreciated 4% a year. An analysis of the bank statements showed total deposits, including the original cash investment, of $120,500. The balance in the bank per bank statement on December 31, 1959, was $5,300, but there were checks amounting to $2,150 dated in December but not paid by the bank until January. During the year, Arthur wrote checks amounting to $1,000 for personal expenses. All other checks were for merchandise. Cash on hand December 31 was $334.

An inventory of merchandise taken on December 31, 1959, showed $21,710 of merchandise on a cost basis. Tickets for accounts receivable totaled $1,270, but $123 of that amount is probably not collectible. Customers may order special merchandise not carried in stock. A deposit equal to 50% of the selling price is required of the customer. Arthur has collected $150 of such deposits for merchandise still on order; the funds are included in the cash on hand. Unpaid suppliers' invoices for merchandise amounted to $3,780. Arthur has taken, from the collections, cash for personal expenses of $4,800. Expenses paid in cash were as follows:

Utilities...	$554
Advertising..	50
Sales help (part-time).......................................	590
Office expense..	100
Insurance (expires 12/31/59).................................	234
Real estate taxes...	350

Store fixtures with a list price of $7,200 were purchased on January 16 and Arthur signed a 6%, one-year note for the list price. The fixtures have an estimated useful life of ten years.

You are to prepare an income statement for 1959, supported by all necessary computations. Any fractional-period depreciation should be computed to the nearest half-month.

Problem 26-9. Small Corporation keeps its books by single entry. An inventory of assets and liabilities on December 31, 1959, is presented below:

Assets:

Cash on hand...	$ 1,622
Cash in bank...	9,732
Accounts receivable—Customers...........................	28,210
Merchandise inventory....................................	21,700
Prepaid expenses..	4,800
Land..	7,000
Buildings and machinery—net of depreciation..............	62,980
	$136,044

Liabilities:

Accounts payable—Merchandise............................	$ 18,610
Note payable—three-year loan due 2/15/60................	10,000
Mortgage payable..	26,000
	$ 54,610

The corporation has outstanding capital stock in the amount of $40,000, issued at par value.

From the asset and liability inventory prepared by an independent accountant at the beginning of the year, you find retained earnings at that time to have been $38,302. It also showed the following amounts: Cash on hand, $820; cash in bank, $2,152.

An analysis of cash payments for 1959 and accounts payable at the beginning of the year discloses the following:

(1) Payments for 1959 purchases—$458,080; for 1958 purchases—$17,200.

(2) Payments for expense items, other than interest and income tax—$123,015. The purchases, however, included $340 paid for personal items bought for the president of the corporation, for which he has not yet reimbursed the corporation. The president states that this is the first instance where corporation funds have been used for such a purpose. The expense payments included $250 advanced to a buyer for use as a working fund, which is in his possession on December 31, 1959.

(3) Income tax paid for 1958 amounted to $1,000; this is $200 more than the amount estimated to be payable during 1960 for 1959 taxable income.

Merchandise on hand at the beginning of the year amounted to $16,150; prepaid expenses on December 31, 1958, were $2,890.

During the year 1959, $3,090 of customers' accounts were written off.

Interest expense for the year amounted to $2,482. Of this amount, $200 was accrued and unpaid on December 31, 1959. There was no accrued interest as of December 31, 1958. There were no payments on the principal of the mortgage during 1959.

A 4% dividend was declared on December 10, 1959, payable January 10, 1960. This is the first dividend declaration in several years.

From an analysis of the inventory of assets and liabilities at the beginning and end of the year, it is found that the buildings and machinery have been decreased $10,400 during 1959. You are unable to find any record of purchases or sales of these items.

Required:

Working papers suitable for use in preparing income and retained earnings statements for Small Corporation for 1959.

Problem 26-10. Prepare income statements on the accrual basis for the fiscal year ended January 31, 1958, and for the seven months ended August 31, 1958.

Suburban Department Store was incorporated on February 1, 1957, and commenced business on that date. It filed federal income tax returns for the fiscal year ended January 31, 1958, from books kept on the cash basis. In August, 1958, after a field examination by the Internal Revenue Service, you are called in to convert the accounts from a cash to an accrual basis as of September 1, 1958.

1. The cash transactions and items thereof included in net income on the cash basis for the fiscal year ended January 31, 1958, follow:

	Amount	Net Income Items
Cash receipts:		
Capital stock, $100,000 par plus premium of $10,000......	$110,000	
Cash sales..	168,200	$168,200
Charge sales...	86,000	86,000
Notes payable—Banks (borrowed on two-month note dated January 2, 1958, face amount, $10,000; discount, $100)...	9,900	
Dividend income.....................................	2,840	2,840
Interest on bonds—4% on $10,000, collected 10/1/57......	200	200
Total..	$377,140	$257,240
Cash disbursements:		
Land and building (assessed values, $20,000 and $60,000, respectively; life of building, 15 years from date of purchase, 3/1/57)..	$ 60,000	
Furniture and fixtures (life, 10 years from date of purchase, 2/1/57)..	3,000	
Merchandise creditors—Purchases.......................	194,000	$194,000
Miscellaneous selling, administrative, and general expenses..	26,000	26,000
Officers' salaries—monthly salaries exclusive of January, 1958..	33,000	33,000
Fire insurance—3-year policy from 3/1/57................	640	640
Real estate taxes for 1957 (February 1—December 31, 1957)	2,200	2,200
Investment in 300 shares of X Co. stock..................	40,000	
Investment in bonds acquired at face value $10,000; interest 4%, April 1 and October 1; maturity date, 4/1/67......	10,000	
Dividends declared and paid...........................	1,800	
Total..	$370,640	$255,840

2. Inventory at January 31, 1958, is estimated at $10,000.

3. The cash transactions and items thereof included in net income on the cash basis for the seven months ended August 31, 1958, follow:

	Amount	Net Income Items
Cash receipts:		
Cash sales..	$112,000	$112,000
Charge sales (prior fiscal-year receivables, $12,000; current fiscal-year receivables, $40,000).......................	52,000	52,000
Notes receivable (principal, $20,000; interest, $1,500, including accrued interest to January 31, 1958, $600).........	21,500	1,500
Sale of 75 shares of X Co. stock........................	15,000	
Dividend income (dividend declared 1/23/58; paid 2/15/58)	1,200	1,200
Interest on bonds—collected 4/1/58.....................	200	200
Total..	$201,900	$166,900

	Amount	Net Income Items
Cash disbursements:		
Merchandise creditors—Purchases ($123,000, of which $10,000 was owing 1/31/58)	$123,000	$123,000
Other creditors—Selling, administrative, and general expenses (incurred subsequent to 1/31/58)	12,500	12,500
Notes payable to banks—paid 3/2/58	10,000	
Officers' salaries—monthly salaries, January through July	21,000	21,000
Real estate taxes for period 1/1/58–6/30/58, billed April 1, 1958 (identical billing to be made October 1, 1958 for the period 7/1/58–12/31/58)	1,200	1,200
Federal income tax	3,400	3,400
Total	$171,100	$161,100

4. Inventory as of August 31, 1958, is $18,000 at cost.
5. Inventory as of January 31, 1958, is to be stated at cost as may be determined by reference to the following tabulation which shows the gross profit of each merchandise line determined on a test basis.

	Test Data			Per Cent of Mdse. Line Sales to
Mdse. Line	Purchases	Sales	Gross Profit	Total Sales
1	$ 7,200	$ 12,000	$ 4,800	10%
2	10,500	15,000	4,500	15
3	7,500	10,000	2,500	20
4	13,000	20,000	7,000	20
5	18,750	25,000	6,250	25
6	10,800	18,000	7,200	10
Total	$67,750	$100,000	$32,250	100%

6. Memo records of receivables and payables show balances as of September 1, 1958, as follows: accounts receivable, $13,500; trade accounts payable (merchandise), $15,000; other accounts payable (selling, administrative, and general expenses), $3,800. These balances are the result of transactions occurring since April, 1, 1958. No notes receivable are held, nor are any notes payable outstanding.

7. Notes receivable collected during 1958 consisted of notes of $8,800 received in 1957 directly from customers for sales and notes of $11,200 received in 1957 in settlement of customers' open accounts.

8. For purposes of preparing income statements on the accrual basis, the effective rates of federal taxes on income may be considered as being: 30% on income not in excess of $25,000; 52% on income in excess of $25,000.

Assignment Material for Chapter 27

Questions

Question 27-1. Distinguish between a purchase and a pooling of interests.

Question 27-2. Give five reasons why the earnings data of two companies may not be comparable.

Question 27-3. Is it necessary to have par value stock to effect a quasi-reorganization? Give your reasons.

Question 27-4. By means of a reduction during the year in the stated value of its common no-par stock, a company has absorbed a large deficit existing at the beginning of the year. A net income is earned on the year's operations. How would you state these facts in your balance sheet at the close of the year?

Question 27-5. Is an accounting basis something that is identified with a particular asset or with a business entity? For example, if assets are transferred from the ownership of Company X to the ownership of Company Y, should the accounting basis ever be carried forward or transferred with the assets?

Question 27-6. Describe some of the tests used by accountants in differentiating a pooling of interests from a purchase.

Question 27-7. When a combination is being treated as a pooling of interests, the income statement issued by the surviving corporation for the year during which the combination occurred should normally include the combined operating results of the several entities for the entire year. What alternative is considered acceptable?

Question 27-8. Name some features of settlement plans in connection with a business combination that suggest a purchase rather than a pooling of interests.

Question 27-9. What is the nature of a divisive reorganization?

Question 27-10. Distinguish between the following: a spin-off, a split-off, and a split-up.

Question 27-11. When retained earnings are being transferred in conjunction with a pooling of interests, under what circumstances, if any, may the retained earnings of the new or surviving corporation be less than the sum of the retained earnings amounts of the combined corporations? Under what circumstances, if any, may such retained earnings be larger than the sum of the retained earnings amounts of the combined corporations?

Question 27-12. During the process of a quasi-reorganization, is it ever permissible to write up an asset?

Question 27-13. Is it acceptable to undertake a quasi-reorganization retroactively?

Problems

Problem 27-1.   South Belt Company had authorized and outstanding 40,000 shares of $25 par value common stock which had been issued at par. On December 31, 1959, the corporation had an operating deficit of $260,000.

The corporation was in need of additional cash, but the directors felt that borrowing or issuing additional stock was impractical because of the appearance of the balance sheet. For this reason, appropriate procedures were followed during January, 1960, to obtain authorization of the quasi-reorganization outlined below:

(1) Change the capitalization to 60,000 shares of no par value with a stated value of $15 per share.
(2) Exchange shares on a one-for-one basis.
(3) Write down the long-term investments by $25,000.
(4) Remove the deficit by a transfer from paid-in surplus.

The quasi-reorganization was completed and recorded in the corporation's accounts as of January 2, 1960.

On February 15, 1960, the company was able to issue 10,000 shares of stock for $17 per share.

Required:

(a) Journal entries to effect the quasi-reorganization as of January 2, 1960, and to record the issuance of the shares on February 15, 1960.
(b) The Stockholders' Equity section of the company's balance sheet as of December 31, 1960, assuming that the net income for 1960 was $35,000, and that no dividends were declared during the year.

Problem 27-2.   Companies *A*, *B*, *C*, and *D* are being combined. Just prior to combining, their stockholders' equity data were reported as follows:

	Company			
	A	*B*	*C*	*D*
Common stock..................	$100,000	$200,000	$150,000	$50,000
Premium on common stock........				5,000
Paid-in surplus..................		50,000	30,000	
Retained earnings...............	60,000	40,000	90,000	15,000
Total stockholders' equity........	$160,000	$290,000	$270,000	$70,000

Determine the amount of retained earnings that will be shown in the balance sheet as of the date when the combination becomes effective under each of the following plans.

(a) Company *A* is the surviving business entity with a stated capital of $600,000, and the plan is a pooling of interests.
(b) Company *B* is the surviving business entity with a stated capital of $350,000, and the plan is a purchase.
(c) Company *C* is the surviving business entity with a stated capital of $400,000, and the plan is a pooling of interests.
(d) Company *D* is the surviving business entity with a stated capital of $600,000, and the plan is a pooling of interests.

Problem 27-3. Corporations H, I, and J are to be combined by a pooling of interests. A new corporation, to be identified as FM Corporation, will be organized. Data on capital structures are presented below.

	Corporations		
	H	I	J
Preferred stock—5% cumulative and participating	$200,000	$300,000	—
Common stock	300,000	600,000	$400,000
Paid-in surplus	30,000	120,000	84,000
Premium on preferred stock	10,000	20,000	—
Retained earnings—Free	69,000	240,000	188,000
Reserve for expansion	45,000	—	60,000

Assuming that the stated capital of the new corporation is to be the amount indicated below, prepare a schedule showing the complete stockholders' equity structure of FM Corporation in each of the following cases:

	Stated Capital	Preferred Stock	Common Stock
Case a	$2,000,000	$500,000	$1,500,000
Case b	1,500,000	500,000	1,000,000
Case c	2,100,000	500,000	1,600,000
Case d	2,500,000	700,000	1,800,000

Problem 27-4. Round Company had an authorized issue of 10,000 shares of $50 par value stock, all of which was outstanding. Its condensed balance sheet on August 31, 1959, was as follows:

ROUND COMPANY
Balance Sheet
August 31, 1959

Assets		Liabilities and Stockholders' Equity		
Current assets	$142,800	Current liabilities		$126,400
Fixed assets (net)	523,600	5% bonds payable		200,000
		Capital stock	$500,000	
		Retained earnings— deficit	160,000	340,000
	$666,400			$666,400

In order to eliminate the deficit, the company obtained, during July and August, all the necessary authorizations to change its par value shares to a stated value of $10 and to increase the authorized number of shares to 50,000. Three shares of new stock are to be exchanged for each share of $50 par value stock.

Additional depreciation of $30,000 is to be recorded to bring the carrying value of the fixed assets into line with present replacement values.

Interest has not been paid on the bonds for two years preceding the balance sheet date, and the bondholders have agreed to accept 2,400 of the new shares of stock in payment of the accrued interest.

The deficit is to be eliminated.

Prepare journal entries, assuming that all of the above matters were effected as of September 1, 1959, and submit a balance sheet of the company after recording the above journal entries.

Problem 27-5. The balance sheet of Armstrong Company at the end of its fifth year in business is on the opposite page.

ARMSTRONG COMPANY
Balance Sheet
December 31, 1959

Assets

Current assets:

Cash		$ 18,156
Accounts receivable	$39,423	
Less allowance for doubtful accounts	3,500	35,923
Merchandise inventory		44,454
Total		$ 98,533

Fixed assets:

Land		10,000
Building	$48,000	
Less accumulated depreciation	11,000	37,000
Furniture and fixtures	$ 9,000	
Less accumulated depreciation	4,533	4,467
		$150,000

Liabilities and Stockholders' Equity

Current liabilities:

Accounts payable	$22,450	
Notes payable	15,000	
Total		$ 37,450

Long-term liability:

Bonds payable—4%, due December 31, 1973		20,000

Stockholders' equity:

Capital stock, $10 par	$50,000	
Retained earnings	42,550	
Total		92,550
		$150,000

The stockholders of Armstrong Company have decided on a split-up of the company in order to separate the ownership and management of the fixed assets from the merchandising operations. Two new corporations have been formed, and each has been authorized to issue 5,000 shares of $10 par value stock.

Armstrong Realty Company will take over the fixed assets and the bond indebtedness. (It plans to negotiate a short-term bank loan for the modest amount of cash it will need initially.) It will rent the properties thus taken over to Armstrong Retail Company.

Armstrong Retail Company will take over all of the other assets and liabilities of Armstrong Company. Armstrong Company will go out of existence.

You are asked to prepare the journal entries to effect the split-up on the books of the three corporations as of January 2, 1960. The stockholders have voted to transfer the retained earnings on a basis proportionate to the net assets transferred.

Problem 27-6. The stockholders of Cumulo Company and Nimbus Company are investigating the possibility of combining the two businesses and are considering the formation of a new corporation, The Cumulo-nimbus Corporation, to carry on the combined business.

The balance sheets of the separate companies, just prior to the combining, are presented in comparative form on page 920.

Balance Sheets
December 31, 1959

	Cumulo Company	Nimbus Company
Cash...	$ 80,000	$ 70,000
Accounts receivable:		
Nimbus Company...........................	15,000	
Other.....................................	35,000	60,000
Inventory....................................	65,000	80,000
Prepaid expenses.............................	3,000	4,000
Long-term investment—at cost.................	44,000	
Fixed assets—net.............................	90,000	130,000
	$332,000	$344,000
Accounts payable:		
Cumulo Company...........................		$ 15,000
Other.....................................	$ 95,000	62,000
Accrued expenses.............................		2,000
Common stock—authorized, issued, and outstanding	200,000	175,000
Paid-in surplus..............................	20,000	
Retained earnings............................	17,000	90,000
	$332,000	$344,000

The long-term investment consists of $40,000 face value of bonds, purchased 10 years ago when the 20-year bonds were issued.

Cumulo Company, as a matter of policy, does not record any accrued expenses. The company's accrued expenses as of December 31, 1958, and December 31, 1959, were $1,200 and $1,000, respectively.

You are asked to determine the amount of retained earnings, as of the combining date, under each of the following conditions:

(a) The Cumulo-nimbus Corporation is formed with a stated capital of $400,000. It takes over the assets and liabilities of the separate companies, and its shares are issued to the stockholders of Cumulo and Nimbus Companies.

(b) Nimbus Company carries on the combined businesses and doubles the number of its authorized shares, the newly authorized shares being issued to the stockholders of Cumulo Company.

(c) Nimbus Company doubles the number of its authorized shares and issues the newly authorized shares to its stockholders for $200,000, such proceeds being used to pay Cumulo Company for the purchase of its net assets.

Problem 27-7. (A) Welton Corporation had $105,000 of dividends in arrears on its preferred stock as of March 31, 1959. While retained earnings were adequate to meet the accumulated dividends, the company's management did not wish to weaken its working capital position. They also realized that a portion of the fixed assets were no longer used or useful in their operation. Therefore, they proposed the following reorganization, which was approved by stockholders to be effective as of April 1, 1959:

1. The preferred stock was to be exchanged for $300,000 of 5% debenture bonds. Dividends in arrears were to be settled by the issuance of $120,000 of $10 par value, 5% noncumulative preferred stock.
2. Common stock was to be assigned a stated value of $50 per share.
3. Goodwill was to be written off.
4. Property, plant, and equipment were to be written down, based on an appraisal, by a total of $103,200, consisting of $85,400 increase in accumulated depreciation and $17,800 decrease in certain assets.

5. Current assets were to be written down by $10,460 to reduce certain items to expected realizable values.

The condensed balance sheet as of March 31, 1959, was as follows:

WELTON CORPORATION
Balance Sheet
March 31, 1959

Assets

Cash..		$ 34,690
Other current assets.............................		252,890
Property, plant, and equipment.................	$1,458,731	
Accumulated depreciation......................	512,481	946,250
Goodwill..		50,000
		$1,283,830

Liabilities and Stockholders' Equity

Current liabilities................................		$ 136,860
Cumulative preferred stock (7%, $100 par)*.................		300,000
Common stock (9,000 shares, no-par)......................		648,430
Premium on preferred stock.............................		22,470
Retained earnings.....................................		176,070
		$1,283,830

* Dividends in arrears—$105,000.

Required:

(1) The journal entries to give effect to the reorganization as of April 1, 1959.
(2) A balance sheet as of April 30, 1959, assuming that net income for April was $10,320 after provision for taxes. The operations resulted in $5,290 increase in cash, $10,660 increase in other current assets, $2,010 increase in current liabilities, and $3,620 increase in the accumulated depreciation.

(B) In making an audit of Welton Corporation as of December 31, 1959, you find the following items had been charged or credited directly to Retained Earnings during the nine months since April 1, 1959:

(1) Debit of $14,496 arising from an income tax assessment applicable to prior years.
(2) Credit of $20,387 resulting from gain on sale on May 10, 1959, of equipment which was no longer used in the business. The carrying value of this equipment had been reduced by $10,000 at the time of the reorganization. The reduction had been accomplished by crediting Accumulated Depreciation—Equipment.
(3) Debit of $13,500 representing dividends declared on common and preferred stock.

Prepare any necessary correcting entries.

Problem 27-8. Fowler Company is a manufacturer of machine tools. Its business has shown wide fluctuations and there have been corresponding variations in earnings. For a number of years prior to 1958 there had not been any significant average earnings; however, for the year 1958 there was a net income of $942,100. As of December 31, 1958, the statement of stockholders' equity on the following page was prepared.

$3 cumulative preferred stock—$50 par value;
   outstanding, 96,200 shares (dividends in ar-
   rears since September 30, 1942)......................... $4,810,000
Common stock—No-par; outstanding, 120,000
   shares at stated value of.............................   3,365,473
Earned deficit, January 1, 1958............... ($1,174,280)
Net income for 1958........................   942,100   (232,180)
      Total... $7,943,293

   Parentheses ( ) denote red figure.

A plan of capital adjustment had been worked out during 1958, which was ratified by the stockholders and made effective as of January 1, 1959. This plan provided that the $3 preferred was to be reduced from $50 par value to $40 par value; that it would continue to be preferred for $3 per share dividends on a cumulative basis; and that it would be preferred in liquidation at $50 per share and redeemable at the option of the company at $55 per share. In settlement of dividends in arrears, the company paid $360,750 cash and issued 216,450 shares of "B" stock having a par value of $10 per share. The "B" shares are nonvoting and are not entitled to dividends. They are redeemable at $20 per share and entitled to $20 per share after preferred but prior to common in liquidation. The agreement under which they are issued provides that a cash redemption fund shall be set up equal to 50% of the yearly net earnings in excess of dividend requirements on preferred stock. The fund is to be used to purchase and retire "B" stock. "Tenders" are to be obtained from stockholders, the lowest being accepted. If no tenders are received within three months after January 1 of each year, the shares to be retired are to be determined by lot. The provisions of issue also state that as long as any "B" stock is outstanding, no dividends may be paid on common stock. The stated value of common was also reduced to $600,000.

The surplus created by this restatement of stock was treated in accordance with accepted accounting practice. All stockholders accepted the exchange offer.

The operations for the year 1959 resulted in a net income, after taxes, of $1,631,316. Dividends for the full year were paid on the preferred stock.

Show how the Stockholders' Equity section will appear in the December 31, 1959 balance sheet of Fowler Company.

Problem 27-9. Lately Company was organized in January, 1954, under the laws of the State of Delaware, with the following authorized capital:

20,000 shares of nonvoting, no-par, noncumulative preferred stock having an
   annual dividend rate of 80 cents per share, payable on February 1, and a
   stated value, as determined by the directors under the authority of the
   charter and by-laws, of $10 a share.
50,000 shares of no-par common having a stated value of $5 a share.

On February 1, 1954, 25,000 shares of common stock were issued for cash for $6.25 per share. The company acquired needed fixed assets and inventories and commenced operations during the spring of 1954.

As of December 31, 1955, the directors and officers of Lately Company arranged a pooling of interests with *RST* Company. Under the plan, Lately Company was the continuing company and issued additional shares as follows:

20,000 shares of preferred stock to the preferred stockholders of *RST* Company.
20,000 shares of common stock to the common stockholders of *RST* Company.

The December 31, 1955 balance sheet of *RST* Company showed the balances stated on the next page.

Goodwill	$100,000.00
Preferred stock	175,000.00
Premium on preferred stock	17,500.00
Common stock	90,000.00
Retained earnings	60,000.00

Net income of Lately Company was as follows:

1954 (February 1–December 31)	$ 26,423.26
1955	39,375.87
1956	6,391.22
1957	2,800.17
1958	112,647.90*
1959 (January 1–June 30)	134,520.71*
1959 (July 1–December 31)	6,118.16

* Loss.

No dividends were declared during this period, and no treasury stock was acquired.

On July 1, 1959, in connection with a quasi-reorganization authorized by the stockholders of Lately Company:

The stated value of the preferred stock was reduced to $6.00.
The stated value of the common stock was reduced to $1.00.
Goodwill was written off.
The carrying value of buildings and machinery was reduced by $32,968.23.
The Allowance for Doubtful Accounts was increased by $9,650.37.

Required:

The Stockholders' Equity section of Lately Company's balance sheet as of June 30, 1959 and December 31,1959.

Problem 27-10. Superior Equipment Corporation manufactures a diverse line of agricultural machines. These machines use several basic chemical compounds as operating supplies. The corporation's business has fluctuated considerably both by years and by seasons. As of December 31, 1959, the corporation had experienced several very profitable years; it had a large amount of liquid current assets, and was looking for some way to introduce more stability into its earnings picture.

After a careful search, the corporation made contact with Neutral Chemical Company, a growing company which needed additional funds for the expansion of facilities. A pooling of interests appeared ideal for the two companies, since the chemical compounds used in the machines of Superior Equipment Corporation formed an important part of the product line of Neutral Chemical Company. The following proposal was drawn up to be submitted to the respective stockholders for approval.

Superior Equipment Corporation would take over all of the assets and liabilities of Neutral Chemical Company, issuing shares of stock therefor to Neutral Chemical Company, which in turn would immediately distribute such shares to its stockholders. The number of shares of stock to be issued would be governed by the proportionate relationship between the estimated future average annual earnings of the separate companies, appropriately adjusted to achieve comparability. Thus, if the average earnings of Neutral Chemical Company equalled 40% of the average earnings of Superior Equipment Corporation, the shares to be issued to Neutral Chemical Company would equal 40% of the outstanding shares of Superior Equipment Corporation. The three years ending December 31, 1959, were to be used in estimating the future average annual earnings.

Relevant financial information, and the agreed adjustments worked out by the corporate officers, follow.

Balance Sheets, December 31, 1959

	Superior Equipment Corporation	Neutral Chemical Company
Assets		
Cash..	$ 833,430	$ 34,720
Receivables..................................	342,820	176,940
Inventory....................................	273,000	258,910
Chemical property lease.......................		150,000
Fixed assets.................................	944,550	256,300
Accumulated depreciation (Deduct*)...........	274,850*	125,400*
	$2,118,950	$751,470
Liabilities and Stockholders' Equity		
Accounts payable............................	$ 259,610	$ 96,470
Accrued expenses............................	175,340	31,800
Bonds payable—5%, J. and J..................		120,000
Common stock—$10 stated value..............	1,000,000	300,000
Paid-in surplus................................		45,000
Retained earnings............................	684,000	158,200
	$2,118,950	$751,470

Net Income

1957..	$ 232,100	$ 59,100
1958..	249,200	62,400
1959..	274,700	62,700
Total...	$ 756,000	$184,200

Superior Equipment Corporation has used first-in, first-out cost as a basis for pricing its inventory, and Neutral Chemical Company has used the last-in, first-out cost method. It is agreed that both companies should be placed on the last-in, first-out basis for greater comparability. Superior Equipment Corporation's inventories determined under the two methods were:

	Fifo	Lifo
December 31, 1956................................	$230,000	$210,000
December 31, 1957................................	246,000	218,000
December 31, 1958................................	258,000	224,000
December 31, 1959................................	273,000	229,000

Superior Equipment Corporation recorded a gain of $18,000 on the sale of unused land in 1957, and a $6,000 loss from disposal of obsolete fixed assets in 1959.

Superior Equipment Corporation has followed a policy of writing off as current expenses all minor equipment items costing less than $300. This was the practice of Neutral Chemical Company prior to 1957. In 1957, Neutral Chemical Company changed its policy and expensed only items costing less than $100. Both companies have charged a full year's depreciation in the year of acquisition, regardless of purchase date. Neutral Chemical Company is to make its accounts comparable to those of Superior Equipment Corporation in this regard. Items costing between $100 and $300 to be expensed, all having a ten-year life, by year of purchase by Neutral Chemical Company, are shown on the following page.

1957.. $3,000
1958.. 2,000
1959.. 5,000

No utilization has as yet been made of the resources available to Neutral Chemical Company through its lease agreement. However, partial development of the leased chemical property has disclosed that the actual chemical deposit is twice as large as originally estimated, and therefore it is agreed that the recorded lease valuation should be doubled.

It is agreed further that the Neutral Chemical Company's bonds will be redeemed at once by Superior Equipment Corporation, if the pooling is approved, and that the interest charge is not to be included in the computation of average earnings.

Development costs incurred in the past two years and charged to expense by Neutral Chemical Company are to be capitalized. The amounts were: 1958, $10,000; 1959, $14,400. It is estimated that, when utilization of the resources in the chemical tract begins, amortization of leasehold and development costs will average $5,000 per year. This amount is to be used in computing average earnings.

Superior Equipment Corporation is to change its corporate name to Super Machine and Supply Company and to double its stock authorization.

Submit the journal entry (or entries) on the books of the continuing corporation to effect the pooling of interests. Support the amounts with suitable schedules.

Assignment Material for Chapter 28

Questions

Question 28-1. Describe three causes for the existence of a difference between the net income per books, before taxes, and taxable net income. Cite an example under each cause.

Question 28-2. In essence, what is the objective of income tax allocation procedures?

Question 28-3. Describe the point of view adopted by the Securities and Exchange Commission in regard to income tax allocation when the question first became an important issue.

Question 28-4. Is it likely that the question of income tax allocation would continue to hold its present importance if (1) income tax rates applicable to corporations were cut in half, or if (2) accelerated depreciation methods were not permissible for income tax purposes?

Question 28-5. How is the subject of income tax allocation related to the current operating concept of net income?

Question 28-6. If income tax allocation procedures are applied, does it follow that the balance sheet will not show the estimated current tax liability?

Question 28-7. Devise an illustration of income tax allocation procedures involving the use of a Deferred Income Tax Liability account.

Question 28-8. Describe the nature of the Deferred Income Tax Liability and Deferred Income Tax Expense accounts.

Question 28-9. Describe what is meant by the phrase "net of tax."

Question 28-10. Assuming the general acceptability of income tax allocation procedures, are they applicable in all instances where there is a difference or divergence between book income and tax-return income?

Question 28-11. Does the matter of income tax allocation arise in connection with the correction of past depreciation?

Question 28-12. In your opinion, does the tax deductibility status of an asset affect its value?

Question 28-13. Present a brief argument against the use of income tax allocation procedures.

Problems

Problem 28-1. The accountant for Bright Company has prepared a tentative draft of the financial statements to be included in the company's annual report to stockholders. The income statement and statement of retained earnings thus prepared are on page 927. The president of the company is disturbed by the income statement because of the way the net income has been significantly reduced by the unusual loss.

Submit revised statements that avoid the distortion attributable to the unusual loss.

BRIGHT COMPANY
Income Statement
For the Year Ended June 30, 1959

Sales		$985,500
Cost of goods sold		515,500
Gross profit		$470,000
Deduct:		
Selling expenses	$205,000	
General expenses	125,000	
Loss from discontinuance of export branch	100,000	430,000
Net income before income tax		$ 40,000
Income tax—50%		20,000
Net income		$ 20,000

BRIGHT COMPANY
Statement of Retained Earnings
For the Year Ended June 30, 1959

Retained earnings—beginning of year	$175,450
Net income	20,000
Total	$195,450
Dividends	30,000
Retained earnings—end of year	$165,450

Problem 28-2. The adjusted trial balance of Cloud Company is presented below.

CLOUD COMPANY
Adjusted Trial Balance
June 30, 1959

Cash	11,700	
Inventory	27,000	
Prepaid expenses	1,400	
Equipment	80,000	
Accumulated depreciation—Equipment		22,500
Accounts payable		8,200
Income tax payable		8,100
Common stock		50,000
Retained earnings—June 30, 1958		8,700
Dividends	2,000	
Sales		120,000
Cost of goods sold	80,000	
Selling expenses	28,000	
Administrative expenses	9,000	
Gain on sale of land		30,000
Income tax	8,400	
	247,500	247,500

Prepare the income statement and statement of retained earnings for Cloud Company for the year ended June 30, 1959. The income tax attributable to the sale of land is $7,500. Assign the results of the sale of land to retained earnings.

Problem 28-3. Dakota Shipbuilding Company has contracts for four super tankers. Data relating to these contracts are presented below:

Tanker Identification	Year Started	Year Completed	Profit
I	1958	1960	$40,000
II	1959	1961	42,000
III	1959	1962	50,000
IV	1960	1962	30,000

Per cent of completion during year:	1958	1959	1960	1961	1962
I	20%	60%	20%		
II		30	60	10%	
III		10	30	50	10%
IV			10	40	50

The company uses the percentage-of-completion method of accounting in its books and the completed-contract method for income tax purposes.

Assuming that the applicable income tax rate is 50%, prepare journal entries for the income tax charges and payments relating to the years 1958 through 1962, following income tax allocation procedures.

Problem 28-4. Charter Flights, Inc., was organized on January 10, 1958. The corporation has made long-range plans for the purchase and use of airplanes and is interested in giving careful attention to the adoption of depreciation policies, for both book and tax purposes, that will be most suitable for its operating plans. One alternative being considered is the adoption of the straight-line depreciation method for book purposes and the years' digits method for income tax purposes.

Given the data presented below, you are asked to prepare a schedule showing prospective tax savings under such a plan for the decade ending December 31, 1967.

Develop your schedule under the following alternative assumptions:

(a) A tax rate of 50% for the first five years and 40% for the last five years.
(b) A tax rate of 50% for the first three years, 54% for the next three years, and 60% for the last four years.

Schedule of Proposed Purchases of Aircraft

Date of Delivery	Aircraft Number	Cost	Scrap Value	Use Life
September 1, 1958	1	$ 900,000	-0-	5 years
April 15, 1959	2	900,000	-0-	5 years
March 1, 1962	3	1,200,000	-0-	5 years
September 1, 1963	4	1,620,000	-0-	8 years
June 1, 1964	5	1,800,000	-0-	8 years

Note. For purposes of computing depreciation, it is assumed that new airplanes are acquired as of July 1 and are subject to depreciation for one-half of such initial year.

Problem 28-5. Equipment Hauling Company purchased five special trailers during the first five years of its business life. As shown by the schedule on the following page, it adopted different depreciation methods for books and tax return purposes. This is the only instance where the company's tax return differs from its books.

	Trailer Number								
	1		2		3		4		5	
	Depreciation Per		Depreciation Per		Depreciation Per		Depreciation Per		Depreciation Per	
	Tax		Tax		Tax		Tax		Tax	
Year	Return	Books	Return	Books	Return	Books	Return	Books	Return	Books
1957......	$25,000	$15,000	$20,000	$12,000						
1958......	20,000	15,000	16,000	12,000	$25,000	$15,000				
1959......	15,000	15,000	12,000	12,000	20,000	15,000	$20,000	$12,000		
1960......	10,000	15,000	8,000	12,000	15,000	15,000	16,000	12,000		
1961......	5,000	15,000	4,000	12,000	10,000	15,000	12,000	12,000	$30,000	$18,000

The net income before income tax, as shown in the company's books, for each of five years, is set forth below:

Year	Amount	Tax Rate
1957..	$200,000	50%
1958..	220,000	50
1959..	140,000	50
1960..	300,000	50
1961..	400,000	50

Prepare journal entries for the income tax charges and payments for the years covered by the above data following income tax allocation procedures.

Problem 28-6. The following accounts are among those in the ledger of Atlanta Company.

Bond Discount		Bonds Payable	
1955	1955	(5% bonds due	July 1, 1965)
July 1.....60,000	Dec. 31.....3,000		1955
	1956		July 1...500,000
	Dec. 31.....6,000		
	1957		
	Dec. 31.....6,000		
	1958		
	Dec. 31.....6,000		
	1959		
	Dec. 31.....6,000		
	1960		
	Dec. 31.....6,000		
	1961		
	Dec. 31.....6,000		

As of July 1, 1961, the company refunded the above bond issue and took as a deduction in its 1961 income tax return the balance of the Bond Discount account. However, the company continued its bond discount amortization program in its books.

The following data relating to 1961 are taken from the company's books and tax return.

	Books	Tax Return
Sales....................	$800,000	$800,000
Cost of sales and expenses, except the annual charge for amortization of bond discount...............	700,000	700,000
Amortization of bond discount....................	6,000	3,000
Write-off of unamortized discount.................		24,000

Assume that the income tax rate is 50% and that the income tax actually payable for the years indicated is as shown on the following page.

Year	Income Tax Liability
1961	$36,500
1962	40,000
1963	32,000
1964	28,500
1965	45,000

Prepare journal entries for the income tax charges and payments applicable to the years 1961 through 1965, following income tax allocation procedures.

Problem 28-7. Turboprop Company manufactures commercial airliners. During 1958 and 1959, it developed a prototype of a new airliner at a cost of twenty million dollars. It was successfully test-flown in 1960.

In 1960, the company received a ruling from the Treasury Department permitting it to write off for 1960 income tax purposes one-half of the cost of developing the new airliner. However, for book purposes, the company plans to amortize the development costs over the four-year period 1961–1964, which period covers the probable length of time during which the model will be manufactured for the airlines.

Assume that the income tax rate is 50% and that the income tax actually payable for the years indicated is as shown.

Year	Income Tax Payable
1960	$2,000,000
1961	6,000,000
1962	5,650,000
1963	1,125,000
1964	4.880,000

Prepare journal entries for the income tax charges and payments applicable to the years 1960 through 1964, following income tax allocation procedures.

Problem 28-8. A comparative adjusted trial balance of Waterford Company is presented below in condensed form.

WATERFORD COMPANY
Comparative Adjusted Trial Balance
December 31, 1958 and 1959

	1958		1959	
Cash	44,500		68,700	
Inventory	147,000		201,800	
Prepaid expense	3,000		2,400	
Land—held for future use	30,000		50,000	
Equipment	94,000		108,000	
Accumulated depreciation		32,500		41,300
Accounts payable		18,000		21,000
Income tax payable		55,000		42,500
Common stock		150,000		150,000
Retained earnings		58,000		83,600
Sales		900,000		940,000
Cost of goods sold	600,000		620,000	
Operating expenses	190,000		195,000	
Inventory write-down for obsolescence	50,000			
Gain on sale of obsolete inventory				10,000
Income tax	55,000		42,500	
	1,213,500	1,213,500	1,288,400	1,288,400

In 1958, the company wrote down a portion of its inventory to give recognition to its obsolescence. The write-down amounted to $50,000 and it was not considered to be deductible for income tax purposes. In 1959, the company found a buyer for its obsolete inventory and sold it for $10,000 more than anticipated. Thus, the loss on inventory obsolescence taken in the 1959 income tax return amounted to $40,000.

The company does not use income tax allocation procedures; however, it does follow the clean-surplus concept.

Required:

    (a) The 1958 income statement and December 31, 1958 balance sheet as they would have appeared if the company had followed income tax allocation procedures.

    (b) Journal entries as of December 31, 1958 and 1959 for the income tax, following tax allocation procedures.

Problem 28-9. The December 31, 1958 balance sheet of Shallow Mining Company included the following fixed assets:

Ore properties...............................	$6,000,000	
Less accumulated depletion..................	4,000,000	$2,000,000
Processing plant........................	$1,500,000	
Less accumulated depreciation...............	1,000,000	500,000

Since the use life of the plant exceeded that of the ore properties, the company was properly basing its depreciation charges on the life estimate of the ore reserves. Early in 1959, the company's engineers discovered that the ore reserves had been understated. Their new studies showed that only one-half of the ore properties had been exhausted. On the basis of this new information, it was reasonable to expect that mining operations could be continued for 5 years beyond the original estimate, or for a total of 15 remaining years. It was also reasonable to expect that the processing plant would continue to be useful for a total of 15 years.

The company desires to make a correction of prior years' earnings, as of January 2, 1959, on the basis of the above information. It realizes that such correction will not be given recognition for income tax purposes.

Required:

    (a) The journal entry for the correction of prior years' earnings, following income tax allocation procedures.

    (b) Journal entries for depletion and depreciation for 1959, assuming that one-fifteenth of the ore reserves available as of January 1, 1959, was mined, processed, and sold during 1959.

    (c) The journal entry required for the $400,000 of income taxes actually payable, resulting from 1959 operations.

You may assume an income tax rate of 50%.

Problem 28-10. Viscount Company purchased a large piece of equipment at the beginning of 1951 for $110,000. For this particular asset, the company adopted the sum of years' digits depreciation method for income tax purposes and the straight-line depreciation method for its books and financial statements. This was the only item of difference between the books and tax return. The equipment was depreciated on the basis of a ten-year useful life with the assumption that it would have no scrap value. A full year's depreciation was charged in 1951. The company followed income tax allocation procedures.

(a) Using the data presented below, prepare a schedule showing the net income amounts for each year for the ten-year period ending December 31, 1960, and the year-end balances in the Deferred Income Tax Liability account. You may assume that the company followed the clean-surplus concept of net income.

Year	Net Income Before Income Taxes	Income Tax Rate
1951	$ 50,000	40%
1952	80,000	70
1953	100,000	80
1954	40,000	60
1955	60,000	50
1956	70,000	50
1957	90,000	50
1958	50,000	50
1959	55,000	50
1960	10,000*	30

* Before correction of prior years' earnings.

(b) Give the adjusting journal entry for income taxes as of December 31, 1951, 1954, and 1958.

(c) Prepare a schedule comparing the aggregate net income for the ten-year period with and without income tax allocation procedures.

Assignment Material for Chapter 29

Questions

Question 29-1. Distinguish between the terms "economic" and "monetary" as they are used in describing income.

Question 29-2. Give one reason why accountants continue to rely on the assumption that the dollar is a unit of measurement having constant dimensions.

Question 29-3. What is meant by the phrase "dollar accounting"?

Question 29-4. Why might a profitable business need to borrow money merely to replace some of its fixed assets? Is the need for such borrowing more likely attributable to financial matters or to accounting matters?

Question 29-5. There has been a good deal of criticism of the traditional "historical" cost records and the data which they reflect, especially during times of inflation or deflation. In order to assist in the interpretation of accounting reports as normally prepared, many accountants have suggested that the recorded cost data be first utilized in the preparation of the conventional financial statements, and then, as a supplementary technique, that these statements be converted into dollars having a uniform purchasing power through the application of price indexes to the recorded dollar amounts. Evaluate this suggestion.

Question 29-6. Do you believe that improved interpretive techniques can be counted on to minimize the misunderstanding of financial statements attributable to changing price levels?

Question 29-7. List some of the criticisms of conventional accounting.

Question 29-8. Give some of the comments that are offered in support of conventional accounting.

Question 29-9. Present accounting theory is based on the assumption that the "value of money" is relatively stable. If there is a significant change in the price level, or in the purchasing power of the dollar, problems arise in interpreting income data as determined under conventional accounting procedures.

State and explain briefly the nature of such problems as related to inventories and fixed assets. You need not attempt to offer solutions to these problems.

Question 29-10. Some items in accounting statements are stated in current dollars, while other items are normally stated in less current dollars. Is this condition influenced in any way by the accounting procedures employed? Explain.

Question 29-11. What is the influence of rising prices over a period of time upon comparative financial statements? Of falling prices?

Question 29-12. When might an accountant advise a businessman to reduce the span of years covered by comparative statements? Explain.

Question 29-13. In considering the merits of using price indexes for the purpose of converting the accounting data as reflected in the conventional

933

historical cost accounts, some people have suggested that these price-level adjustments should be confined to the fixed assets and related depreciation. What can be said in favor of such a proposal? Against it?

Question 29-14. The price index rose from 125 to 175 during the previous year and from 175 to 225 during the current year. The dollar sales during the previous year were $240,000 and during the current year were $300,000.

(a) For comparative income statement purposes, you are to convert the sales figures for both years to the price level existing at the end of the current year. You are to assume that sales were made uniformly throughout both years, and that the change in price level was also uniform.

(b) What additional information is revealed by a comparison of the converted figures? How do you interpret them?

Question 29-15. Is the fact that the purchasing power of money varies of equal significance to the balance sheet and the income statement?

Question 29-16. Devise an example showing how index numbers may be used in computing depreciation charges.

Question 29-17. Summarize the position of the American Accounting Association in the matter of price level changes and financial statements.

Question 29-18. Why do some accountants resist any departure from the cost basis?

Index

c